New UK
GAAP 2015

Generally Accepted Accounting Practice
under UK and Irish GAAP

GW00702988

Mike Bonham

Rob Carrington

Tony Clifford

Larissa Connor

Matthew Curtis

Pieter Dekker

Julie Dempers

Alan Garry

Rabindra Jogarajan

Sharon Johal

Parbin Khatun

Dean Lockhart

Sharon MacIntyre

Amanda Marrion

Margaret Pankhurst

Michael Pratt

Hedy Richards

Timothy Rogerson

Claire Taylor

Michael Varila

EY
Building a better
working world

WILEY

A John Wiley and Sons, Ltd, Publication

This edition first published in 2015 by John Wiley & Sons Ltd.

Cover, cover design and content copyright © 2015 Ernst & Young LLP.

The United Kingdom firm of Ernst & Young LLP is a member of Ernst & Young Global Limited.

Registered office

John Wiley & Sons Ltd, The Atrium, Southern Gate, Chichester, West Sussex, PO19 8SQ, United Kingdom

For details of our global editorial offices, for customer services and for information about how to apply for permission to reuse the copyright material in this book please see our website at www.wiley.com

ISBN 978-1-119-03817-7 (paperback)

ISBN 978-1-119-03818-4 (ebk)
ISBN 978-1-119-03819-1 (ebk)

A catalogue record for this book is available from the British Library.

Printed and bound by TJ International Ltd, Padstow, Cornwall, UK.

This book is printed on acid-free paper responsibly manufactured from sustainable forestry.

About this book

This is the first edition of New UK GAAP 2015 which provides a comprehensive guide to interpreting and implementing the new UK accounting standards, particularly:

- FRS 100 – *Application of Financial Reporting Requirements*;

- FRS 101 – *Reduced Disclosure Framework – Disclosure exemptions from EU-adopted IFRS for qualifying entities*; and

- FRS 102 – *The Financial Reporting Standard applicable in the UK and Republic of Ireland.*

This book comprises 31 Chapters which cover the above standards. Some Chapters address more than one section of FRS 102 and those sections addressed are clearly marked at the beginning of each chapter.

Guidance on International Financial Reporting Standards can be found in EY's publication International GAAP 2015®.

Preface

Over the last few years the Financial Reporting Council (FRC) has fundamentally reformed its financial reporting standards in the UK and Ireland. Existing requirements have been replaced with new Financial Reporting Standards, including: FRS 100 – *Application of Financial Reporting Requirements*, FRS 101 – *Reduced Disclosure Framework* and FRS 102 – *The Financial Reporting Standard applicable in the UK and Republic of Ireland.* We refer to these standards, which are mandatory for accounting periods beginning on or after 1 January 2015, along with the associated accounting requirements of the Companies Act 2006, as new UK GAAP. The FRC is also updating the reporting regime for small and micro-entities, although these requirements and proposals are not covered in this publication.

Listed groups will continue to prepare their consolidated financial statements in accordance with IFRS. All other entities, including parent companies preparing their separate financial statements and subsidiaries of listed groups, should consider the options available to them under the new reporting framework. There can be significant business implications in changing the basis of financial reporting. In choosing which new reporting requirements to follow, entities should consider for example the implications on taxation, distributable reserves, banking covenants and remuneration schemes. Converting to a new basis of financial reporting can be an onerous experience, particularly for groups with a large number of subsidiaries. It is likely to require input from stakeholders outside of the finance function, staff training and changes to data gathering systems and processes.

This publication covers the requirements of FRS 100, FRS 101, FRS 102, and the associated accounting requirements of the Companies Act 2006. It explains the new reporting requirements in a way that is intended to help entities deal with everyday issues as well as more complex issues as they arise. It also highlights key differences between FRS 102, previous UK GAAP and IFRS, which should assist in the conversion process for those entities that choose to adopt FRS 102.

The new financial reporting requirements are much shorter than many of those they replace and, as a result, are less prescriptive on many issues. We expect the adoption of new UK GAAP to require the application of judgement when interpreting the standards. This publication includes our views on the judgemental areas we believe are likely to be most common in practice. Our views are based on our experience of similar issues under IFRS and previous UK GAAP. As experience of applying the new standards grows over time, we expect our views will continue to evolve.

It is not possible for this publication to cover every aspect of company reporting. For some of the more complicated or less common areas which are not covered by FRS

102 and for which IFRSs provide relevant guidance, further explanations can be found in our International GAAP 2015 publication.

FRS 102 is intended to provide a relatively stable platform for financial reporting. The FRC intends to carry out its first three year review of FRS 102 in 2016/17 with a view to a revised FRS 102 being effective in 2018. However, as companies prepare to apply FRS 102, the FRC has begun to consider queries arising from its implementation. As a result, since the initial issue of FRS 102 in March 2013, the FRC has issued several amendments to FRS 102, ranging from significant substantive changes to simple editorial improvements, as well as a number of clarification statements. Most of these amendments have been incorporated into the August 2014 edition of FRS 102 and are reflected in this publication. Clarification statements made up to September 2014 have also been reflected. However, it is possible that further amendments and clarifications will be issued prior to the first application of FRS 102. Companies are therefore advised to stay alert to further developments.

****

We are deeply indebted to many of our colleagues within the UK organisation of EY for their selfless assistance and support in the publication of this book.

Our thanks go particularly to those who reviewed, edited and assisted in the preparation of drafts, most notably: Justine Belton, Richard Crisp, Mike Davies, Tim Denton, Jane Hurworth, Bernd Kremp and Richard Moore.

Our thanks also go to everyone who directly or indirectly contributed to the book's creation, including the following members of the Financial Reporting Group in the UK: Denise Brand, Marianne Dudareva, Ted Jones and Emma Kavanagh.

We also thank Jeremy Gugenheim for his assistance with the production technology throughout the period of writing.

London,	*Mike Bonham*	*Alan Garry*	*Margaret Pankhurst*
December 2014	*Rob Carrington*	*Rabindra Jogarajan*	*Michael Pratt*
	Tony Clifford	*Sharon Johal*	*Hedy Richards*
	Larissa Connor	*Parbin Khatun*	*Timothy Rogerson*
	Matthew Curtis	*Dean Lockhart*	*Claire Taylor*
	Pieter Dekker	*Sharon MacIntyre*	*Michael Varila*
	Julie Dempers	*Amanda Marrion*	

Lists of chapters

References and abbreviations

The following references and abbreviations are used in this book:

References:

FRS 100.4	Paragraph 4 of FRS 100
FRS 100.AG7	Paragraph 7 of the Application Guidance to FRS 100
FRS 100 Appendix I	Appendix I of FRS 100
FRS 101.10	Paragraph 10 of FRS 101
FRS 101 Appendix I Table 1	Table 1 of Appendix I of FRS 101
FRS 102.23.9	Paragraph 9 of Section 23 of FRS 102
FRS 11.9	Paragraph 9 of FRS 11
SSAP 9.10	Paragraph 10 of SSAP 9
UITF 26.4	Paragraph 4 of UITF 26
S395(2)	Section 395 of the Companies Act 2006 subsection (2)
Regulations 6(2)	Paragraph 6(2) of the Large and Medium-sized Companies and Groups (Accounts and Reports) Regulations 2008
1 Sch 55	Paragraph 55 of Schedule 1 of the Large and Medium-sized Companies and Groups (Accounts and Reports) Regulations 2008
LLP Regulations 3	Paragraph 3 of the LLP Regulations
TECH 02/10	Technical Release 02/10 issued by the ICAEW and ICAS
FRED 56.3B	Paragraph 3B of Financial Reporting Exposure Draft 56
DTR 4.2.10	Paragraph 4.2.10 of the Disclosure and Transparency Rules
IFRS 1.D16	Paragraph D16 of IFRS 1
IAS 1.12	Paragraph 12 of IAS 1
IFRIC 18.BC22	Paragraph 22 of the Basis for Conclusions to IFRIC 18
Foreword to Accounting Standards.19	Paragraph 19 of the Foreword to Accounting Standards issued by the FRC

Professional and regulatory bodies:

ASB	Accounting Standards Board in the UK
BIS	Department for Business, Innovation and Skills
FRC	Financial Reporting Council
IASB	International Accounting Standards Board
ICAEW	Institute of Chartered Accountants in England and Wales
ICAS	Institute of Chartered Accountants of Scotland
IFRIC	International Financial Reporting Interpretations Committee

Accounting related terms:

AIM	Alternative Investment Market
CA 2006	Companies Act 2006
CGU	Cash-generating Unit
E&E	Exploration and Evaluation
EBIT	Earnings Before Interest and Taxes
EBITDA	Earnings Before Interest, Taxes, Depreciation and Amortisation
EBT	Employee Benefit Trust
EIR	Effective Interest Rate
EPS	Earnings per Share
FC	Foreign currency
FIFO	First-In, First-Out basis of valuation
FRED	Financial Reporting Exposure Draft
FRS	Financial Reporting Standard (issued by the ASB)
FRSSE	Financial Reporting Standard for smaller Entities
FTA	First-time Adoption
FVLCD	Fair value less costs of disposal
FVLCS	Fair value less costs to sell
GAAP	Generally Accepted Accounting Practice
IAS	International Accounting Standard (issued by the former board of the IASC)
IFRS	International Financial Reporting Standard (issued by the IASB)
IRR	Internal Rate of Return
JA	Joint Arrangement
JANE	Joint arrangement that is not an entity

JCA	Jointly Controlled Asset
JCE	Jointly Controlled Entity
JV	Joint Venture
LIBOR	London Inter Bank Offered Rate
LIFO	Last-In, First-Out basis of valuation
NCI	Non-controlling Interest
NBV	Net Book Value
NPV	Net Present Value
NRV	Net Realisable Value
OCI	Other Comprehensive Income
PP&E	Property, Plant and Equipment
R&D	Research and Development
Regulations	Large and Medium-sized Companies and Groups (Accounts and Reports) Regulations 2008
SCA	Service Concession Arrangement
SE	Structured Entity
Small Regulations	Small Companies and Groups (Accounts and Directors' Report) Regulations 2008
SME	Small or medium-sized entity
SORP	Statement of Recommended Practice
SPE	Special Purpose Entity
SSAP	Statement of Standard Accounting Practice
SV	Separate Vehicle
TSR	Total Shareholder Return
UITF	Urgent Issues Task Force
UK	United Kingdom
VIU	Value In Use
WACC	Weighted Average Cost of Capital

Authoritative literature

The content of this book takes into account all accounting standards and other relevant rules issued up to September 2014.

New UK and Ireland Reporting Standards

FRS 100	Application of Financial Reporting Requirements (November 2012)
FRS 101	Reduced Disclosure Framework – Disclosure exemptions from EU-adopted IFRS for qualifying entities (August 2014)
FRS 102	The Financial Reporting Standard applicable in the UK and Republic of Ireland (August 2014)
FRED 55	Draft Amendments to FRS 102 – Pension obligations (August 2014)

Financial Reporting Standard for Smaller Entities (effective January 2015)

Amendments to the FRSSE (effective January 2015)

FRSSE (effective January 2015) – Micro entities

Previous UK GAAP

FRS 1	Cash flow statements (revised 1996)
FRS 2	Accounting for subsidiary undertakings
FRS 3	Reporting financial performance
FRS 4	Capital instruments
FRS 5	Reporting the substance of transactions
FRS 6	Acquisitions and mergers
FRS 7	Fair values in acquisition accounting
FRS 8	Related party disclosures
FRS 9	Associates and joint ventures
FRS 10	Goodwill and intangible assets
FRS 11	Impairment of fixed assets and goodwill
FRS 12	Provisions, contingent liabilities and contingent assets
FRS 13	Derivatives and other financial instruments: Disclosures
FRS 14	Earnings per share
FRS 15	Tangible fixed assets
FRS 16	Current tax
FRS 17	Retirement benefits
FRS 18	Accounting policies
FRS 19	Deferred tax
FRS 20 (IFRS 2)	Share-based payment

FRS 21 (IAS 10)	Events after the balance sheet date
FRS 20 (IAS 33)	Earnings per share
FRS 23 (IAS 21)	The effects of changes in foreign exchange rates
FRS 25 (IAS 32)	Financial instruments: Presentation
FRS 26 (IAS 39)	Financial instruments: recognition and measurement
FRS 27	Life Assurance
FRS 28	Corresponding amounts
FRS 29	Financial instruments: disclosures
FRS 30	Heritage assets

Financial Reporting Standard for Smaller Entities (effective April 2008)

Amendments to the FRSSE (effective April 2008)

UITF Abstracts (under previous UK GAAP)

UITF 4	Presentation of long-term debtors in current assets
UITF 5	Transfers from current assets to fixed assets
UITF 9	Accounting for operations in hyper-inflationary economies
UITF 11	Capital instruments: issuer call options
UITF 15	(revised 1999) Disclosure of substantial acquisitions
UITF 19	Tax gains and losses on foreign currency borrowings that hedge an investment in a foreign operation
UITF 21	Accounting issues arising from the proposed introduction of the euro
UITF 22	The acquisition of a Lloyd's business
UITF 23	Application of the transitional rules in FRS 15
UITF 24	Accounting for start-up costs
UITF 25	National insurance contributions on share option gains
UITF 26	Barter transactions for advertising
UITF 27	Revision to estimates of the useful economic life of goodwill and intangible assets
UITF 28	Operating lease incentives
UITF 29	Website development costs
UITF 31	Exchanges of businesses or other non-monetary assets for an interest in a subsidiary, joint venture or associate
UITF 32	Employee benefit trusts and other intermediate payment arrangements
UITF 34	Pre-contract costs
UITF 35	Death-in-service and incapacity benefits
UITF 36	Contracts for sale of capacity
UITF 38	Accounting for ESOP trusts
UITF 39	(IFRIC Interpretation 2) Member's shares in co-operative entities and similar instruments
UITF 40	Revenue recognition and service contracts
UITF 41	Scope of FRS 20 (IFRS 2)
UITF 42	Reassessment of embedded derivatives
UITF 43	The interpretation of equivalence for the purposes of section 228A of the Companies Act 1985

UITF 44	(IFRIC Interpretation 11) FRS 20 (IFRS 2) Group and Treasury Share Transactions
UITF 45	(IFRIC Interpretation 6) Liabilities arising from participating in a specific market – Waste electrical and electronic equipment
UITF 46	(IFRIC Interpretation 16) Hedges of a net investment in a foreign operation
UITF 47	(IFRIC Interpretation 19) Extinguishing Financial Liabilities with Equity Instruments
UITF 48	Accounting implications of the replacement of the retail prices index with the consumer prices index for retirement benefits

Chapter 1   FRS 100

List of examples

Chapter 1

Chapter 1   FRS 100

1   INTRODUCTION

In 2012, 2013 and 2014 the Financial Reporting Council (FRC), following a lengthy period of consultation (between 2002 and 2012), changed financial reporting standards in the United Kingdom and the Republic of Ireland. Evidence from consultation supported a move towards an international-based framework for financial reporting that was proportionate to the needs of preparers and users. *[FRS 102 Summary (i), (ii), (v)].*

The new financial reporting framework, 'new UK and Irish GAAP' will replace almost all extant previous UK GAAP (see 4.3 below) with the following Financial Reporting Standards:

- FRS 100 – *Application of Financial Reporting Requirements*;

- FRS 101 – *Reduced Disclosure Framework: Disclosure exemptions from EU-adopted IFRS for qualifying entities*;

- FRS 102 – *The Financial Reporting Standard Applicable in the UK and Republic of Ireland*;

- FRS 103 – *Insurance Contracts – Consolidated accounting and reporting requirements for entities in the UK and Republic of Ireland issuing insurance contracts*; and

- *The Financial Reporting Standard for Smaller Entities* (FRSSE) (effective January 2015), with minor modifications to the existing FRSSE.

FRS 103, published in March 2014, applies to financial statements prepared in accordance with FRS 102.

During 2014, the FRC issued the following amendments to FRS 101, FRS 102 and the FRSSE:

- Amendments to FRS 101 – *Reduced Disclosure Framework (2013/14 Cycle)* (July 2014);

- Amendments to FRS 102 – *The Financial Reporting Standard Applicable in the UK and Republic of Ireland – Basic financial instruments and Hedge accounting* (July 2014);

- A*mendments to the Financial Reporting Standard for Smaller Entities (effective April 2008) and the Financial Reporting Standard for Smaller Entities (effective January 2015) – Micro entities* (April 2014) (see 6.2.1.D and 6.4 below).

FRS 100, which was issued in November 2012, sets out the new financial reporting framework and applies to entities preparing financial statements in accordance with legislation, regulation or accounting standards applicable in the UK and the Republic of Ireland. *[FRS 100.1]*. The new standards are mandatory for accounting periods beginning on or after 1 January 2015, but permit early application (subject to the requirements of the applicable standards). See 4.2 below.

Under the Companies Act 2006, UK companies with transferable securities admitted to trading on a regulated market (at the financial year end) are required under the IAS Regulation to prepare their consolidated financial statements using EU-adopted IFRS. A list of regulated markets is available online[1].

In addition, entities that are not required by UK company law to prepare financial statements using EU-adopted IFRS may be required to do so by other regulatory requirements, such as the AIM Rules (see 4.4.1 below) or by other agreements (e.g. shareholders' or partnership agreements).

However, other UK companies are permitted to prepare their consolidated and/or individual financial statements as IAS accounts (using EU-adopted IFRS) or Companies Act accounts (using 'applicable accounting standards' – see 4.6.1 below), subject to company law restrictions concerning the 'consistency of financial reporting framework' used in the individual accounts of group undertakings and over changes in financial reporting framework from IAS accounts to Companies Act accounts. See 6.1 below.

Prior to the implementation of FRS 100 to FRS 102, Companies Act accounts were prepared in accordance with 'previous UK GAAP'. In essence, under the new financial reporting framework, previous UK GAAP is replaced by FRS 100, FRS 101 and FRS 102 and the FRSSE. The requirements for preparation of financial statements under the Companies Act 2006 are addressed at 6 below. Except where otherwise stated, the rest of this chapter will refer to the requirements for UK companies, and therefore will refer to UK GAAP (prior to implementation of FRS 100 to FRS 103) as 'previous UK GAAP'. UK LLPs and other entities preparing financial statements in accordance with Part 15 of the Companies Act 2006 are subject to similar requirements, modified as necessary by the regulations that govern the content of their financial statements.

2   SUMMARY OF FRS 100

The following is a summary of FRS 100.

- FRS 100 sets out the application of the financial reporting framework for UK and Republic of Ireland entities (see 4 below). The detailed accounting requirements are included in EU-adopted IFRS, FRS 101 and FRS 102, depending on the choice of GAAP made by the entity. FRS 103 applies to financial statements prepared in accordance with FRS 102.

- FRS 100 sets out the effective date of the new standards. All are mandatory, effective for accounting periods beginning on or after 1 January 2015. Early adoption is permitted subject to the early application provisions in the applicable standards, FRS 101, FRS 102 or the FRSSE but must be stated (see 4.2 below).

- FRS 100 sets out the application of SORPs (see 4.7 below).

- FRS 100 sets out the transition arrangements to FRS 101, FRS 102 or the FRSSE (see 5 below).

- FRS 100 withdraws virtually all existing UK and Irish GAAP ('previous UK GAAP'), with effect from its application date. Some parts of previous UK GAAP have been retained by incorporation of their requirements into FRS 101 or FRS 102 (see 4.3 below).

- FRS 100 includes application guidance on the interpretation of 'equivalence' for the purposes of:

  (i)   the exemption from preparation of consolidated financial statements in section 401, Companies Act 2006 (based on a modified version of UITF 43 – *The interpretation of equivalence for the purposes of section 228A of the Companies Act 1985*[2] (see Chapter 6 at 3.1.1C);

  (ii)   the reduced disclosure framework included in FRS 101 and FRS 102 (see Chapter 31 and Chapter 2 at 3).

- FRS 100 sets out the definition of a 'financial institution' (which is replicated in FRS 101 and FRS 102). A financial institution:

  (i)   that applies FRS 102 needs to give the additional disclosures required by Section 34 – *Specialised Activities* – of FRS 102 in its individual financial statements; and

  (ii)   is not eligible for certain disclosure exemptions in its individual financial statements under the FRS 101 or FRS 102 reduced disclosure frameworks for qualifying entities.

The definition of a financial institution and the disclosure requirements for financial institutions are addressed in Chapter 31 at 6.4 (for FRS 101) and in Chapter 2 at 2.4.1 and 3.5 (for FRS 102).

3   DEFINITIONS

The following terms used in FRS 100 are as defined in the Glossary (included as Appendix I to FRS 100):

- *Act* – the Companies Act 2006;

- *Date of transition* – the beginning of the earliest period for which an entity presents full comparative information under a given standard in its first financial statements that comply with that standard;

- *EU-adopted IFRS* – IFRSs adopted in the European Union in accordance with EU Regulation 1606/2002 (IAS Regulation);

- *Financial institution* – see the definition included in Chapter 31 at 6.4 (for FRS 101) and Chapter 2 at 2.4.1 (for FRS 102). The definition is the same for both FRS 101 and FRS 102;

- *FRS 100, FRS 101 and FRS 102* – see 1 above;

- *FRSSE* – refers to the extant version of the Financial Reporting Standard for Smaller Entities;

- *IAS Regulation* – EU Regulation 1606/2002;

- *IFRS (or IFRSs)* – standards and interpretations issued or (adopted) by the International Accounting Standards Board (IASB). They comprise International Financial Reporting Standards, International Accounting Standards, Interpretations developed by the IFRS Interpretations Committee (the Interpretations Committee) or the former Standing Interpretations Committee (SIC);

- *Individual financial statements* – accounts that are required to be prepared by an entity in accordance with the Companies Act 2006 or relevant legislation.

  For example, this term includes 'individual accounts' as set out in section 394 of the Companies Act 2006, a 'statement of accounts' as set out in section 132 of the Charities Act 2011, or 'individual accounts' as set out in section 72A of the Building Societies Act 1986.

  Separate financial statements are included in the meaning of the term individual financial statements;

- *Public benefit entity* – an entity whose primary objective is to provide goods or services for the general public, community or social benefit and where any equity is provided with a view to supporting the entity's primary objectives rather than with a view to providing a financial return to equity providers, shareholders or members. Footnote 28 to FRS 102's Glossary includes further guidance on the definition of a public benefit entity;

- *Qualifying entity* – a member of a group where the parent of that group prepares publicly available consolidated financial statements, which are intended to give a true and fair view (of the assets, liabilities, financial position and profit or loss) and that member is included in the consolidation. For the purposes of FRS 101 only, a charity cannot be a qualifying entity. *[FRS 101.Glossary].* See Chapter 31 at 2.1 (for FRS 101) and Chapter 2 at 3.1 (for FRS 102);

- *Regulations – The Large and Medium-sized Companies and Groups (Accounts and Reports) Regulations 2008* (SI 2008/410); and

- *SORP* – an extant Statement of Recommended Practice (SORP) developed in accordance with the FRC's *SORPs: Policy and Code of Practice.* SORPs recommend accounting practices for specialised industries or sectors, and supplement accounting standards and other legal and regulatory requirements in light of the special factors prevailing or transactions undertaken in a particular industry or sector.

While this term is not defined in the Glossary, this chapter refers to *The Small Companies and Groups (Accounts and Directors' Report) Regulations 2008* (SI 2008/409) as the Small Companies Regulations.

4   FRS 100 – APPLICATION OF FINANCIAL REPORTING REQUIREMENTS

The publication of FRS 100 to FRS 102 followed a lengthy period of consultation from 2002 to 2012 on changes to financial reporting in the UK and Republic of Ireland (the 'Future of UK and Irish GAAP'). The consultations supported a move towards an international-based framework proportionate to the needs of preparers and users. Further background on these consultations and the evolution of the FRC's approach leading up to the development of the new standards is included in Appendix III to FRS 100. *[FRS 100.Summary (ii)].*

In developing the new standards, the FRC has set out an overriding objective to enable users of accounts to receive high-quality understandable financial reporting proportionate to the size and complexity of the entity and users' information needs. *[FRS 100.Summary (iii)].*

In meeting this objective, the FRC has stated that it aims to provide succinct financial reporting standards that:

- provide an IFRS-based solution (unless an alternative clearly better meets the overriding objective);

- are based on up-to-date thinking and developments in the way entities operate and the transactions they undertake;

- balance consistent principles for accounting by UK and Republic of Ireland entities with practical solutions based on size, complexity, public interest and users' information needs;

- promote efficiency in groups; and

- are cost effective to apply. *[FRS 100.Summary (iv)].*

The financial reporting framework set out in FRS 100 is summarised in the diagram below:

Figure 1.1 The UK Financial Reporting Framework

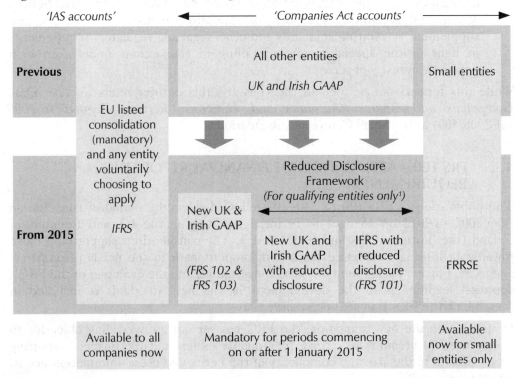

1: A qualifying entry (i.e. a parent or subsidiary undertaking) which is consolidated in publicly available consolidated financial statements that give a true and fair view can take advantage of the reduced disclosure framework. Applies to individual financial statements only and shareholders must be notified in writing about and not object to the disclosure exemptions. There are restrictions over IFRS 7, IFRS 13 and capital management disclosure exemptions (and in FRS 102, financial instruments-related disclosure exemptions) for financial institutions.

4.1   Scope of FRS 100

The objective of FRS 100 is to set out the applicable financial reporting framework for entities presenting financial statements in accordance with legislation, regulations or accounting standards applicable in the UK and Republic of Ireland. *[FRS 100.1].*

FRS 100 applies to financial statements intended to give a true and fair view of assets, liabilities, financial position and profit for a period. *[FRS 100.2].*

FRS 100 to FRS 102 can be applied by an entity that is not a UK or Irish company, preparing financial statements that are intended to give a true and fair view. However, Appendix II to FRS 100 states that the FRC sets accounting standards within the framework of the Companies Act 2006 and therefore it is the company law requirements that the FRC primarily considered when developing FRS 102. See 4.4 below.

4.2   Effective date

FRS 100 to FRS 103 are mandatory, effective for accounting periods beginning on or after 1 January 2015 but are available for early application as explained below. Early application must be disclosed in the notes to the financial statements. *[FRS 100.10, FRS 101.11, FRS 102.1.14, FRS 103.1.11].*

FRS 100 is mandatory for accounting periods beginning on or after 1 January 2015, with early application permitted subject to the early application requirements as set out in FRS 101, FRS 102 or the FRSSE (effective 1 January 2015). *[FRS 100.10].*

FRS 101 can be applied by a qualifying entity (see Chapter 31 at 3.1) in its individual financial statements. FRS 101 itself does not set out any restrictions on early application.

FRS 102 specifies that an entity may apply FRS 102 for accounting periods ending on or after 31 December 2012 but for entities within the scope of a SORP, this is providing it does not conflict with the requirements of a current SORP or legal requirements for the preparation of financial statements. *[FRS 102.1.14].* The FRC has clarified the meaning of 'providing it does not conflict with the requirements of a current SORP'. See Chapter 2 at 1.3.1.

FRS 103 applies to financial statements prepared in accordance with FRS 102 and so may similarly be applied for accounting periods ending on or after 31 December 2012 provided that FRS 102 is applied from the same date (and that the entity is not subject to the transitional arrangements in paragraph 1.14 of FRS 102 relating to entities within scope of a SORP). *[FRS 103.1.1, 1.11].*

4.3   Withdrawal of previous UK and Irish GAAP

FRS 100 withdraws all extant UK and Irish GAAP ('previous UK GAAP'), with the exception of FRS 27 – *Life assurance*, with effect from its application date. FRS 103 withdraws FRS 27 with effect from 1 January 2015 (or on early application of FRS 103). *[FRS 103.1.13].*

FRS 100 did not withdraw the non-mandatory Reporting Statements on Preliminary Announcements, Operating and Financial Review and Half-Yearly Reports. In June 2014, the FRC issued *Guidance on the Strategic Report* which superseded *Reporting Statement: Operating and Financial Review.* In November 2014, the FRC issued FRED 56 – *Draft FRS 104 Interim Financial Reporting* (see Chapter 2 at 1.2.3.D) which is based on IAS 34 – *Interim Financial Reporting*, with some modifications. This standard, once finalised, can be applied to the preparation of interim financial reports, provided that this is not prohibited by law or regulation. It is aimed primarily at FRS 102 reporters that prepare interim financial reports but can be applied by entities applying other accounting standards, such as FRS 101 reporters. *Reporting Statement – Half-Yearly Reports* and *Reporting Statement – Preliminary announcements* – will be withdrawn with immediate effect when the final standard is issued.

Some parts of previous UK GAAP are retained by direct incorporation of their requirements into FRS 100 or FRS 102.

4.4   Basis of preparation

FRS 100 does not address which entities must prepare financial statements, but sets out the applicable financial reporting framework for entities presenting financial statements in accordance with legislation, regulations or accounting standards applicable in the UK and Republic of Ireland. *[FRS 100.1]*.

The individual or consolidated financial statements of any entity within the scope of FRS 100 (that is not required by the IAS Regulation or other legislation or regulation to be prepared in accordance with EU-adopted IFRS) must be prepared in accordance with:

- EU-adopted IFRS (see 4.4.3 below);
- FRS 102 (see 4.4.4 below) and, where applicable, FRS 103 (see Chapter 2 at 1.2.4);
- FRS 101 (if the financial statements are individual financial statements of a qualifying entity) (see 4.4.5 below) *[FRS 100.4]*; or
- the FRSSE (if the entity is a small entity eligible to apply that standard and chooses to do so – see 4.4.6 below).

The above choices are also available for the individual financial statements of an entity that is required to prepare consolidated financial statements in accordance with EU-adopted IFRS. *[FRS 100.4, FRS 102.1.3]*.

Changes to the above financial reporting framework are expected, effective for financial years beginning on or after 1 January 2016, arising from implementation of the new Accounting Directive – see 4.4.2 below. In particular, the FRSSE is expected to be withdrawn, but the FRC propose a new standard for micro-entities and that small companies can apply FRS 102 (with presentation and disclosure requirements reflecting the new simpler statutory requirements).

An entity's choice of financial reporting framework must be permitted by the legal framework or other regulations or requirements that govern the preparation of the entity's financial statements. Other agreements or arrangements (such as shareholders' agreements, banking agreements) may restrict the choice of financial reporting framework.

4.4.1   *Company law and regulatory requirements governing financial reporting framework*

As required by Article 4 of the IAS Regulation, a UK parent company with transferable securities admitted to trading on a regulated market at its financial year end must prepare its consolidated financial statements as IAS group accounts. *[s403(1)]*. FRS 102 can be applied in its individual financial statements. *[s395(1)]*.

AIM is not a regulated market. An 'AIM company' (i.e. a company with a class of security admitted to AIM) incorporated in an EEA country (including, for this purpose, a company incorporated in the Channel Islands or the Isle of Man) must prepare and present its annual accounts in accordance with EU-adopted IFRS. However, an AIM company incorporated in an EEA country that is *not* a parent company at the end of the relevant financial period may prepare and present its annual accounts *either* in accordance with EU-adopted IFRS *or* in accordance with the accounting and company legislation and regulations that are applicable to that company due to its country of incorporation (which, under the new UK and Irish financial reporting framework, could include EU-adopted IFRS, FRS 101 – if a qualifying entity – and FRS 102). While the AIM Rules do not specifically differentiate between consolidated and individual financial statements, many AIM companies incorporated in the UK use EU-adopted IFRS in their consolidated financial statements but national GAAP in their individual financial statements. However, a parent company that only prepares individual financial statements, e.g. it is exempt from preparing consolidated financial statements, must prepare these in accordance with EU-adopted IFRS).[3]

For a UK company, the choice of framework is subject to the requirements in the Companies Act 2006 on change in financial reporting framework (from IAS accounts to Companies Act accounts) (see 6.1.2 below) and consistency of financial reporting framework in individual accounts of group undertakings (see 6.1.3 below). For the purposes of the Companies Act 2006, only statutory accounts prepared in accordance with full EU-adopted IFRS are IAS accounts, whereas statutory accounts prepared in accordance with FRS 102, FRS 101, or the FRSSE are Companies Act accounts. *[s395(1), s403(2)]*.

UK charitable companies are not permitted to prepare IAS accounts under the Companies Act 2006 *[s395(2), s403(3)]* and charities are not permitted to apply FRS 101 (as excluded from its definition of a qualifying entity) *[FRS 101.Glossary]*. UK charitable companies preparing financial statements under the Companies Act 2006 must, therefore, apply FRS 102 (or the FRSSE, but this is expected to be withdrawn for financial years beginning prior to 1 January 2016). Other charities in England and Wales and Scotland preparing financial statements under charities legislation must also apply FRS 102 (see Chapter 2 at 1.3.1.A).

There is further detail on the requirements of the Companies Act 2006 in relation to annual reports and accounts at 6 below.

In theory, FRS 100, FRS 101, FRS 102 and the FRSSE may also be used by entities preparing financial statements intended to give a true and fair view but that are not subject to the Companies Act 2006 (or Irish law). Entities preparing financial statements intended to give a true and fair view within other legal frameworks will need to satisfy themselves that FRS 102 does not conflict with any relevant legal obligations. *[FRS 100.A2.20, FRS 102.A4.41]*. Appendix II to FRS 100 and Appendix IV to FRS 102 include observations on the requirements of specific UK and Northern Ireland legislation. Where an entity is subject to a SORP, the relevant SORP will provide more details on the relevant legislation. *[FRS 100.A2.21, FRS 102.A4.2, A4.42]*.

4.4.2 New Accounting Directive

In July 2014, the new Accounting Directive was published in the EU's Official Journal. This consolidates the 4th and 7th Company Law Directives into a single document. It also repeals and incorporates the requirements of Directive 2012/6/EU (the Micros Directive) and amends Directive 2006/43/EC on statutory audits of individual and consolidated accounts.

The new Accounting Directive must be transposed into Member State law by 20 July 2015. However, the Directive allows Member States to permit that the changes apply to financial statements for financial years beginning on or after 1 January 2016.

In the UK, BIS propose that the new Accounting Directive (Chapters 1 to 9) is implemented for financial years beginning on or after 1 January 2016. It is not clear at this stage whether early adoption will be permitted. BIS's *Consultation on the UK Implementation of the EU Accounting Directive* (now closed) is available.[4]

Chapters 1 to 9 of the new Accounting Directive set out the minimum legal requirements for statutory accounts at EU level. Most of the EU's reporting framework remains unchanged, and most previously available Member State options have been retained. For most of these options, the UK has well-established positions and BIS has stated that generally, it is not intended these will change. The BIS consultation sets out the areas where a mandatory change is imposed and its proposals where a new Member State option is available or it is intended that an established position is changed.

The new Accounting Directive simplifies accounting requirements and reduces the associated administrative burden (particularly for small companies). The new Accounting Directive:

- requires increasing levels of disclosure dependent on the size of undertaking. The size thresholds for micro, small and medium-sized undertaking are raised. BIS is consulting on which companies are excluded from the small and medium-sized companies regimes (for accounting purposes). BIS will consult separately on the small companies audit exemptions;

- reduces the number of options available for preparers in respect of recognition and measurement and presentation;

- introduces a small number of mandatory accounting changes that will affect Companies Act accounts (such as FRS 101 and FRS 102 financial statements) and provides a Member State option for more flexibility over company law layouts which could facilitate use of IFRS layouts in Companies Act accounts, and

- creates a largely harmonised small company regime. The Directive limits the amount of information that Member States are permitted to require small undertakings to place in their annual statutory accounts (although financial statements prepared by small companies must still give a true and fair view). This restriction is considered to extend to the presentation and disclosure requirements in UK accounting standards.

In light of the new Accounting Directive, the FRC propose that the FRSSE will be withdrawn, effective for financial years beginning on or after 1 January 2016. In its place,

- micro-entities will be able to apply a new Financial Reporting Standard for Micro-Entities ('FRSME'); and

- small entities will be permitted to apply FRS 102, but with a new section covering the presentation and disclosure requirements applicable to small entities (based on the new legal provisions) replacing the presentation and disclosure requirements of FRS 102.

Otherwise the scope of FRS 102 remains the same, i.e. FRS 102 is applied by entities other than those applying the FRSME, EU-adopted IFRS, FRS 101 (or FRS 102, as applied by small entities). See Chapter 2 at 1.2.3.D for further discussion on the impact of the FRC's proposals for FRS 102.

Entities required by the IAS Regulation or other legislation or regulation to prepare financial statements in accordance with EU-adopted IFRS will continue to do so.

An entity will continue to have the option to apply a more comprehensive accounting standard, e.g. a micro-entity can choose the FRSME, the small companies regime within FRS 102, FRS 102 in full or EU-adopted IFRS. A qualifying entity will continue to have the option to apply FRS 101.

4.4.3   EU-adopted IFRS

EU-adopted IFRS means IFRSs as adopted by the EU pursuant to the IAS Regulation. *[s474]*.

4.4.4   FRS 102 – The Financial Reporting Standard applicable in the UK and Republic of Ireland

FRS 102 is a single, largely stand-alone, financial reporting standard based on a significantly modified version of the IFRS for SMEs issued by the IASB in 2009. The standard was originally issued in March 2013 and subsequently amended in July 2014. See Chapter 2 at 1.2.2 and 1.2.3 for a discussion of the July 2014 amendments and potential future changes to the standard.

FRS 102 is arranged into sections: Section 1 addresses scope, Sections 2 to 33 each address a separate accounting topic, Section 34 addresses specialised activities, and Section 35 addresses transition. There is a reduced disclosure framework available for qualifying entities (see 4.5 below) in their individual financial statements.

The IFRS for SMEs is in the main a simplified version of IFRSs (with fewer accounting options and disclosures) although in a number of areas, e.g. requiring amortisation of goodwill or the treatment of deferred tax, its requirements depart from IFRSs. Use of the IFRS for SMEs met many of the FRC's objectives (see 4 above). However, the FRC made further amendments to the IFRS for SMEs for application in the UK and Republic in order to meet its objectives (discussed further in Chapter 2 at 1.2).

While FRS 102 is a largely standalone standard, there are a number of references to IFRSs, as follows:

- the standard permits entities a policy choice to apply IFRS 9 – *Financial Instruments* – or IAS 39 – *Financial Instruments: Recognition and Measurement* – to the recognition and measurement of financial instruments, rather than Sections 11 and 12 of the standard); *[FRS 102.11.2, 12.2]*

- selection of accounting policies under the GAAP hierarchy (see Chapter 7 at 3.2); and

- certain types of entities are required to apply specific IFRSs (the IFRSs on earnings per share, exploration and evaluation activities and operating segments apply with the same scope as under the respective IFRSs (see Chapter 2 at 2.3).

4.4.5   FRS 101 – Reduced Disclosure Framework

FRS 101 was originally issued in November 2012 and subsequently amended in July 2014. The standard sets out a framework which addresses the financial reporting requirements and disclosure exemptions for the individual financial statements of qualifying entities (see 4.5 below and Chapter 31) that otherwise apply the recognition, measurement and disclosure requirements of standards and interpretations issued by the International Accounting Standards Board (IASB) that have been adopted in the European Union (EU-adopted IFRS).

An entity reporting under FRS 101 complies with EU-adopted IFRS except as modified by the standard. FRS 101 contains various recognition and measurement modifications to EU-adopted IFRS, primarily to ensure compliance with UK company law.

The Accounting Council advised the FRC to ensure that the disclosure framework remains consistent with EU-adopted IFRS. *[FRS 101.AC.20].* It is therefore expected that the standard will be reviewed regularly as EU-adopted IFRS changes.

Amendments to FRS 101 – *Reduced Disclosure Framework (2013/14 Cycle)*, issued in July 2014, include further disclosure exemptions in respect of impairment, a change to require investments in subsidiaries not providing investment-related services to be held at fair value through profit and loss in the separate financial statements of an investment entity, and a number of clarifications.

4.4.6   The Financial Reporting Statement for Smaller Entities ('FRSSE')

In November 2012, the FRC issued the FRSSE (effective January 2015) with minor modifications to the existing FRSSE (effective April 2008), which it supersedes. *[FRSSE.20.1].*

In April 2014, the FRC published *Amendments to the Financial Reporting Standard for Smaller Entities (effective April 2008) and the Financial Reporting Standard for Smaller Entities (effective January 2015) – Micro entities.* These enable entities applying the micro-entity provisions in the Companies Act 2006 to comply with the FRSSE. See 6.4 below.

The FRSSE is effective for accounting periods beginning on or after 1 January 2015 but earlier application is permitted. *[FRSSE.19.1].* There are no special transitional requirements – and therefore the FRSSE (effective January 2015) is retrospective.

The significant differences to its predecessor relate to implementation of the new UK and Irish GAAP framework and the withdrawal of extant FRSs and UITF Abstracts. The FRSSE (effective January 2015) also introduces a new requirement for a statement of compliance. See 4.4.6.A below.

The FRSSE may be applied to all financial statements intended to give a true and fair view of the financial position and profit or loss (or income and expenditure) of all entities that are:

(a)   companies incorporated under UK and Irish companies legislation and entitled to the exemptions available in the legislation for small companies when filing accounts with the Registrar of Companies.

In the UK, companies legislation refers to the Companies Act 2006. In the Republic of Ireland, companies legislation refers to the Companies Acts 1963-2003 and all other Regulations to be read as one with the Companies Acts. *[FRSSE.Glossary]*. The small companies regime in the UK is set out in sections 382 to 384 of the Companies Act 2006 (see 6.5 below). In the Republic of Ireland, the FRSSE can be applied to those companies meeting the criteria as set out in companies legislation that allow them to be treated as 'small' for the purpose of filing information with the Companies Registration Office;[5] or

(b) entities that would have come into category (a) above had they been companies incorporated under companies legislation, excluding building societies.

While not bound by the requirements of UK and Irish companies legislation reflected in the FRSSE (which are set out in small capitals in the standard), such entities must have regard to the accounting principles, presentation and disclosure requirements in UK and Irish companies legislation (or other equivalent legislation) that, taking into account the FRSSE, are necessary to present a true and fair view. *[FRSSE.1.1]*.

The FRSSE[6] also specifies which types of entities are not permitted to apply it. In most cases, these are examples of entities that would not meet the above two requirements. However, companies preparing individual or group accounts in accordance with the fair value accounting rules for certain assets and liabilities set out in Section D of Schedule 1 to the Small Companies Regulations are also not permitted to apply the FRSSE. This does not preclude companies accounting for fixed assets and investments at valuation from using the FRSSE.

It is beyond the scope of this publication to discuss the content of the FRSSE, which is expected to be withdrawn effective for financial years beginning on or after 1 January 2016 (see 4.4.2 above).

4.4.6.A   Statement of compliance with the FRSSE

Where the FRSSE is used, the statement of compliance should take the following form:

'*These financial statements have been prepared in accordance with the Financial Reporting Standard for Smaller Entities (effective January 2015)*'. *[FRSSE.2.6]*.

This statement may be included with the note of accounting policies or, for those entities taking advantage of the exemptions for small companies in companies legislation, combined with the statement required to be given on the balance sheet (in a prominent position above the directors' signature and printed name). *[s414(3)]*. See Example 1.1 below.

Example 1.1:   *Example of combined statement – use of small companies regime and compliance with the FRSSE*

These accounts have been prepared in accordance with the provisions applicable to companies subject to the small companies regime and with the *Financial Reporting Standard for Smaller Entities* (effective January 2015).

The above wording adapts that included in Companies House Guidance. The FRSSE, paragraph 2.6 (footnote 11) gives a slightly different wording for a combined statement.

If abbreviated accounts (see 6.5.5.A below) are also to be prepared, the statement of compliance with the FRSSE should be included with the note of accounting policies in the financial statements prepared for members so that it is reproduced in the abbreviated accounts.[7]

There are certain filing exemptions available for small companies – which are addressed at 6.5.5 below. Use of these filing exemptions requires further statements on the balance sheet (above the directors' signature and printed name) in the copy of the financial statements or abbreviated accounts delivered to the Registrar.

4.4.7   *Considerations on choice of financial reporting framework*

Entities will need to carefully consider their choice of financial reporting framework, based on their individual circumstances. In doing so, entities may need to consider the implications of a new financial reporting framework for other aspects of their business, such as covenants in loan agreements, employee remuneration (e.g. performance-related bonuses), the effect on key performance indicators, accounting systems, taxation and distributable profits.

Factors influencing the choice of financial reporting framework might include:

* whether the entity is a member of a group, and if so, what GAAP is used for group reporting. In particular, subsidiaries of groups reporting under IFRS or in multinational groups may prefer to apply IFRS or FRS 101 rather than FRS 102;

* the level of disclosures required in the financial statements.

    FRS 101 and FRS 102 financial statements prepared by a UK company are Companies Act accounts and therefore must comply with the requirements of the Companies Act 2006 and all applicable schedules of the Regulations (as well as accounting standards). Financial statements prepared under EU-adopted IFRS do not need to comply with Schedules 1 to 3 of the Regulations but must comply with the extensive disclosure requirements in IFRSs. See 6.7 below.

    The level of disclosure also depends on whether the entity is a qualifying entity and can make use of a reduced disclosure framework (under FRS 101 or FRS 102) in its individual financial statements (see 4.5 below). While FRS 102 has fewer disclosures than IFRS, the level of disclosure required may sometimes not be significantly different from FRS 101, but this will depend on the entity's individual circumstances.

* stability of the financial reporting framework (in general, there are more frequent changes to IFRSs than to FRS 102 – see Chapter 2 at 1.2.2 and 1.2.3 for information on the process of ongoing review of FRS 102 and anticipated changes before it becomes effective);

* the implications of new IFRSs (such as IFRS 9 or IFRS 15 – *Revenue from Contracts with Customers*) or expected changes to IFRSs (e.g. arising from the IASB's leases project) that will be implemented or expected to be finalised in future periods;

* IFRSs provide detailed and sometimes complex guidance, whereas the requirements in FRS 102 are much shorter (but lack the same level of

application guidance as in IFRSs, and are likely to involve increased application of management judgement in applying the standard); and

- the implications of different GAAPs for distributable profits (see 5.4 below) and taxation, in particular cash tax. This will also depend on the interaction with tax legislation, and whether tax elections are made.

4.5   Reduced disclosure framework

Both FRS 101 and FRS 102 provide for a reduced disclosure framework for qualifying entities in individual financial statements. The shareholders of the qualifying entity must be notified in writing and not object to use of the disclosure exemptions. While a charity cannot be a qualifying entity for FRS 101, there is no such restriction for use of the reduced disclosure framework in FRS 102. *[FRS 101.5, FRS 102.1.11]*.

A 'qualifying entity' is a member of a group (i.e. a parent or subsidiary) where the parent of that group prepares publicly available consolidated financial statements which are intended to give a true and fair view (of the assets, liabilities, financial position and profit or loss) and that member is included in the consolidation. *[FRS 100.Glossary, FRS 101.Glossary, FRS 102 Appendix I]*. The term 'included in the consolidation' has the meaning set out in section 474(1) of the Companies Act 2006, i.e. that the qualifying entity is consolidated in the financial statements by full (and not proportional) consolidation.

The disclosure exemptions available in FRS 102 are more limited than in FRS 101, which provides a reduced disclosure framework for qualifying entities under EU-adopted IFRS. However, this reflects the fact that FRS 102 (as a starting point) has much simpler disclosures than EU-adopted IFRS. Under the reduced disclosure framework in both standards, there are fewer disclosure exemptions available for the individual financial statements of financial institutions.

Certain disclosures require 'equivalent' disclosures to be included in the publicly available consolidated financial statements of the parent in which the qualifying entity is consolidated (i.e. of the parent referred to in the definition of qualifying entity). FRS 100 provides guidance on the concept of 'equivalence' for these purposes. *[FRS 100.AG8-10]*.

See Chapter 31 and Chapter 2 at 3 for discussion of the reduced disclosure framework under FRS 101 and FRS 102 respectively, including the detailed requirements for its use, the definitions of 'qualifying entity' and 'financial institution', the disclosure exemptions available, and guidance on 'equivalence' for the purpose of the reduced disclosure framework.

4.6   Statement of compliance

FRS 100 requires that an entity preparing its financial statements in accordance with FRS 101, FRS 102 (and where applicable, FRS 103) or the FRSSE includes a statement of compliance in the notes to the financial statements in accordance with the requirements of the relevant standard. *[FRS 100.9, FRS 103.1.12]*. See Chapter 31 at 1.3 (for FRS 101 financial statements), Chapter 4 at 3.8 (for FRS 102 financial statements) and 4.4.6.A above (for FRSSE financial statements) respectively.

This requirement is similar to that in IAS 1 – *Presentation of Financial Statements* – for an entity preparing its financial statements using EU-adopted IFRS to give an explicit and unreserved statement of compliance with IFRSs.

In the same way as required for IFRS financial statements, financial statements should not be described as complying with FRS 101, FRS 102 or the FRSSE, unless they comply with *all* of the requirements of the relevant standard. Indeed, FRS 102 includes an explicit requirement to this effect. *[FRS 102.3.3]*.

4.6.1   Related Companies Act 2006 requirements

Where the directors of a large or medium-sized company (i.e. a company not subject to the micro-entity provisions or the small companies regime – see 6.4 and 6.5 below) prepare Companies Act individual or group accounts (such as those prepared under FRS 101, FRS 102 and the FRSSE), the notes to the accounts must include a statement as to whether the accounts have been prepared in accordance with applicable accounting standards. Particulars of any material departure from those standards and the reasons for the departure must be given. This statement is not required in the individual accounts of medium-sized companies (see 6.6 below). *[Regulations 4(2) and 1 Sch 45]*.

'Applicable accounting standards' means statements of standard accounting practice issued by the FRC (and SSAPs, FRSs issued by the Accounting Standard Board and UITF Abstracts, until withdrawn).[8] Therefore, FRS 100 to FRS 103 are 'applicable accounting standards'.[9]

Where the directors of a company prepare IAS individual or IAS group accounts (see 6.1 below), the notes to the accounts must include a statement that the accounts have been prepared in accordance with international accounting standards (i.e. EU-adopted IFRS). *[s397, s406, s474]*.

4.7   SORPs

Statements of Recommended Practice ('SORPs') recommend accounting practices for specialised industries or sectors, and supplement accounting standards and other legal and regulatory requirements in light of the special factors prevailing or transactions undertaken in a particular industry or sector. *[FRS 102 Appendix I]*.

SORPs may only be developed and issued by 'SORP-making bodies', being bodies recognised by the FRC for the purpose of producing the SORP for a particular industry or sector. SORP-making bodies have a responsibility to act in the public interest when developing a SORP. The FRC's Codes & Standards Committee will recognise a body as a SORP-making body on the advice of the Accounting Council. To be recognised as a SORP-making body, the body must meet a set of criteria set by the FRC and agree to develop SORPs in accordance with the FRC's *Policy and Code of Practice on SORPs* (April 2014).

Only SORPs developed in accordance with the Policy and Code of Practice will be recognised by the FRC. An extant SORP must contain a statement by the FRC outlining the limited nature of the review undertaken by the FRC and confirming, as appropriate, that the SORP does not appear to contain any fundamental points of principle that are unacceptable in the context of current accounting practice or to conflict with an accounting standard. The FRC's limited review is undertaken on its behalf by the UK GAAP Technical Advisory Group (TAG) or the Committee for Accounting on Public Benefit Entities (CAPE), as appropriate. The FRC's Statement must be authorised by the FRC Board or the Codes & Standards Committee, on the advice of the Accounting Council. See 7.1 below.

SORPs recommend particular accounting treatments and disclosures with the aim of narrowing areas of difference and variety between comparable entities. Compliance with a SORP that has been generally accepted by an industry or sector leads to enhanced comparability between the financial statements of entities in that industry or sector. Comparability is further enhanced if users are made aware of the extent to which an entity complies with a SORP, and the reasons for any departures. *[FRS 100.7]*.

FRS 100 states that if an entity's financial statements are prepared in accordance with the FRSSE or FRS 102, SORPs apply in the circumstances set out in those standards. *[FRS 100.5]*.

The FRSSE states that SORPs and other equivalent guidance may specify the circumstances, if any, in which entities in the industry or sector covered by the SORP (or other equivalent guidance) may adopt the current version of the FRSSE. However, if the SORPs are drafted on the basis of the requirements of FRS 102, financial statements cannot be said to comply with those SORPs if prepared in accordance with the FRSSE. *[FRSSE.11-12]*. A Charities SORP (FRSSE), effective for financial years beginning on or after 1 January 2015 was published in July 2015.

The application of SORPs under FRS 102 is discussed at Chapter 2 at 2.2. There are certain constraints on early application of FRS 102 (see Chapter 2 at 1.3.1) where an entity is subject to a SORP and that standard also makes reference to extant SORPs as part of the hierarchy for management to consider when developing and applying accounting policies (see Chapter 7 at 3.2).

When a SORP applies, the entity should disclose in the financial statements the title of the SORP and whether the financial statements have been prepared in accordance with the SORP's provisions currently in effect. The provisions of a SORP cease to have effect, for example, to the extent they conflict with a more recent financial reporting standard. *[FRS 100.6]*.

Paragraph 6 of the FRC's Policy and Code of Practice explains that SORPs should be developed in line with current accounting standards and best practice. A SORP's provisions cannot override provisions of the law, regulatory requirements or accounting standards. Therefore, where at the time of issue, the SORP's provisions conflict with accounting standards or legal or regulatory requirements, these take precedence over the SORP and the FRC's Statement on the SORP will usually be varied to refer to this. When a more recently issued accounting standard or change in legislation leads to conflict with the provisions of an existing SORP, the relevant provisions of thc SORP cease to have effect. The SORP-making body is responsible for updating the relevant provisions of the SORP on a timely basis to bring them in line with new legislation or accounting standards, or to withdraw them, as appropriate.

Where an entity departs from the SORP's provisions, it must give a brief description of how the financial statements depart from the recommended practice set out in the SORP, which shall include:

- for any treatment that is not in accordance with the SORP, the reasons why the treatment adopted is judged more appropriate to the entity's particular circumstances; and

- brief details of any disclosures recommended by the SORP that have not been provided, together with the reasons why not. *[FRS 100.6]*.

The effects of a departure from a SORP need not be quantified, except in those rare cases where such quantification is necessary for the entity's financial statements to give a true and fair view. *[FRS 100.7]*.

Entities whose financial statements do not fall within the scope of a SORP may, if the SORP is otherwise relevant to them, nevertheless choose to comply with the SORP's recommendations when preparing financial statements, providing that the SORP does not conflict with the requirements of the framework adopted. Where this is the case, entities are encouraged to disclose this fact. *[FRS 100.8]*.

FRS 100, therefore, does not require an entity preparing its financial statements in accordance with FRS 101 or EU-adopted IFRS to disclose whether it has applied the relevant SORP. However, FRS 100 does not preclude such an entity from following a SORP (provided its requirements do not conflict with EU-adopted IFRS) but encourages the entity to disclose that it has done so.

4.7.1   Status of SORPs

Certain of the current SORPs are withdrawn on implementation of the new UK and Irish GAAP framework. Other SORPs have been updated to conform with FRS 102 (although two Charities SORPs have been issued, one for use with the FRSSE and one for use with FRS 102).

The following SORPs have been updated to conform with FRS 102: the SORPs on *Authorised Funds* (May 2014), *Charities* (July 2014), *Further and Higher Education* (March 2014), and *Limited Liability Partnerships* (July 2014), *Registered Social Housing Providers* (September 2014), *Investment Trust Companies and Venture Capital Trusts* (November 2014) and *Pension Schemes* (November 2014).

The *Banking Segments* and *Leasing* SORPs are to be withdrawn. The SORP on *Accounting for Insurance Business* (December 2005 and amended December 2006) is withdrawn on implementation of FRS 103. *[FRS 103.1.13]*.

The SORP on *Accounting for Oil and Gas Exploration, Development, Production and Decommissioning Activities* (updated June 2001) will not be updated. The OIAC website explains that the SORP remains applicable for non-listed UK entities until such time as those entities adopt FRS 100 to FRS 102 and therefore is not applicable to any entity for accounting periods beginning on or after 1 January 2015.

5 TRANSITION

FRS 100 sets out the requirements for transition to FRS 101, FRS 102 and the FRSSE. The requirements differ depending on the standard transitioned to and whether the entity previously reported under EU-adopted IFRS or other GAAP (such as previous UK GAAP).

The date of transition is the beginning of the earliest period for which an entity presents full comparative information under a given standard in its first financial statements which comply with that standard. *[FRS 100.Glossary]*. Therefore, 1 January 2014 is the date of transition for an entity with a 31 December year-end which prepares its first IFRS (or FRS 101 or FRS 102) financial statements for the financial year ended 31 December 2015.

Before deciding to transition to a particular standard in the new UK and Irish GAAP framework, entities should assess whether this is permitted by the statutory framework or other regulation that applies to them. See 6.1 and 6.2.1.D below for considerations applicable to the Companies Act 2006.

On first-time application of FRS 100 or when an entity changes its basis of preparation of its financial statements within the requirements of FRS 100, it shall apply the transitional arrangements relevant to its circumstances as explained at 5.1 to 5.3 below. There are no transitional requirements for the FRSSE so full retrospective application is required.

There is no requirement to change the GAAP applied by a UK parent and its UK subsidiaries at the same time. However, the Companies Act 2006 sets out restrictions over changes in financial reporting framework (in both individual and group accounts) and over consistency of financial reporting framework in individual accounts of group undertakings (see 6.1.2 and 6.1.3 below).

5.1 Transition to EU-adopted IFRS

An entity transitioning to EU-adopted IFRS must apply the transitional requirements of IFRS 1 – *First-time Adoption of International Financial Reporting Standards*, as adopted by the EU. *[FRS 100.11(a)]*.

An entity's first IFRS financial statements (to which IFRS 1 must be applied) are the first annual financial statements in which the entity adopts EU-adopted IFRS, by an explicit and unreserved statement in those financial statements of compliance with EU-adopted IFRS. *[IFRS 1.2-3]*.

An entity that has applied EU-adopted IFRS in a previous reporting period, but whose most recent previous annual financial statements did not contain an explicit and unreserved statement of compliance with EU-adopted IFRS must either apply IFRS 1 or else apply EU-adopted IFRS retrospectively in accordance with IAS 8 – *Accounting Policies, Changes in Accounting Estimates and Errors* – as if the entity had never stopped applying IFRSs. *[IFRS 1.4A]*.

The requirements of IFRS 1 are discussed in Chapter 5 of EY International GAAP 2015.

5.2   Transition to FRS 101

A qualifying entity can transition to FRS 101 from either EU-adopted IFRS or another form of UK GAAP. In this context, another form of UK GAAP means FRS 102, the FRSSE or previous UK GAAP. The transition requirements differ depending on whether the qualifying entity is applying EU-adopted IFRS or not prior to the date of transition. *[FRS 100.11(b)-13]*. The transition requirements to FRS 101 are explained in Chapter 31 at 3.

5.3   Transition to FRS 102

A first-time adopter of FRS 102 is an entity that presents its first annual financial statements that conform to FRS 102, regardless of whether its previous accounting framework was EU-adopted IFRS or another set of GAAP such as its national accounting standards, or another framework such as the local income tax basis. *[FRS 102.35.1, FRS 102 Appendix I]*. In practice, most first time adopters of FRS 102 will have applied previous UK GAAP. An entity transitioning to FRS 102 must apply the transitional arrangements set out in Section 35 – *Transition to this FRS* – of the standard. *[FRS 100.11(c), FRS 102.35.1]*.

FRS 102 also covers the situation where an entity has previously applied FRS 102, and then applies a different GAAP for a period before re-applying FRS 102. An entity that adopted FRS 102 in a previous reporting period but whose most recent annual financial statements did not contain an explicit and unreserved statement of compliance with FRS 102 must either apply Section 35 or else apply FRS 102 retrospectively in accordance with Section 10 – *Accounting Policies, Estimates and Errors*, as if the entity had never stopped applying the standard. *[FRS 102.35.2]*.

Chapter 30 addresses the transition arrangements to FRS 102.

An entity applying FRS 102 is required to apply FRS 103 to insurance contracts (including reinsurance contracts) that the entity issues and reinsurance contracts that the entity holds, and to financial instruments (other than insurance contracts) that the entity issues with a discretionary participation feature (see Chapter 2 at 1.2.4). *[FRS 103.1.2]*. An entity may, therefore, apply FRS 103 at the same time as it adopts FRS 102 or after it has adopted FRS 102, depending on whether it has transactions within scope of FRS 103 on adoption of FRS 102. It is not, however possible to apply FRS 103 without also applying FRS 102. *[FRS 103.1.11-12]*.

Section 6 – *Transition to this FRS* – of FRS 103 applies both when an entity applies FRS 103 for the first time (i.e. when it is already a FRS 102 reporter), and when an entity applies FRS 102 and FRS 103 together for the first time (in which case, Section 35 of FRS 102 also applies).

5.4   Impact of transition on distributable profits

There may be circumstances where a conversion to FRS 101, FRS 102 or EU-adopted IFRS eliminates an entity's realised profits or even turns those realised profits into a realised loss. TECH 02/10 – *Guidance on Realised and Distributable Profits under the Companies Act 2006*, issued by the ICAEW and ICAS, states that the change in the treatment of a retained profit or loss as realised (or unrealised) as a result of a change in the law or in accounting standards or interpretations would not render unlawful a distribution already made out of realised profits determined by reference to 'relevant accounts' which had been prepared in accordance with generally acceptable accounting principles applicable to those accounts (subject to the considerations below). This is because the Companies Act 2006 defines realised profits and realised losses for determining the lawfulness of a distribution as 'such profits or losses of the company as fall to be treated as realised in accordance with principles generally accepted at the time when the accounts are prepared, with respect to the determination for accounting purposes of realised profits or losses'.[10]

The effects of the introduction of a new accounting standard or of the adoption of IFRSs (or FRS 101 or FRS 102) become relevant to the application of the common law capital maintenance rule only in relation to distributions accounted for in periods in which the change will first be recognised in the accounts. This means that a change in accounting policy known to be adopted in a financial year needs to be taken into account in determining the dividend to be approved by shareholders in that year. Therefore, an entity converting to a new financial reporting framework (FRS 101, FRS 102 or EU-adopted IFRS) in 2015 must have regard to the effect of adoption of the new financial reporting framework in respect of all dividends payable in 2015 (including any final dividends in respect of 2014) even though the 'relevant accounts' may still be those for 2014 prepared under another GAAP. These considerations apply to all dividends whether in respect of shares classified as equity or as debt (or partly equity or debt).[11]

Statutory 'interim accounts' are required to be prepared under sections 836(2) and 838 of the Companies Act 2006 (and delivered to the Registrar, if the company is a public company) if a proposed distribution cannot be justified by reference to the relevant accounts. However, under common law, a company cannot lawfully make a distribution out of capital and the directors may therefore consider preparing non-statutory 'interim accounts' using the new financial framework to ascertain that there are sufficient distributable profits and, if the company is a public company, that the net asset restriction in section 831 of the Companies Act 2006 is not breached.[12] In some cases, however, the directors may be satisfied that no material adjustments arise from transition to the new financial framework (and therefore that there are sufficient distributable profits) without preparing such 'interim accounts'. Statutory 'interim accounts' would be required if transition to a new financial reporting framework increases distributable profits and the directors wish to make a distribution not justified by reference to the relevant accounts.[13] TECH 02/10 states that if the directors have not yet decided whether to adopt EU-adopted IFRS, say, for the current financial year, the company's accounting policies are those that it has previously applied until a decision is made to change them. Therefore, in applying the above, it is not necessary to have regard to possible changes of policy that are being considered but have not yet been agreed.[14] TECH 02/10, however, was written at a time where UK companies had a choice, subject to certain constraints in the Companies Act 2006 (see 6.1 below) of whether to change to EU-adopted IFRS or remain on previous UK GAAP; for financial years beginning on or after 1 January 2015, previous UK GAAP is withdrawn. It is possible for example that adoption of any of the financial reporting frameworks might have an adverse effect on the profits available for distribution.

6   COMPANIES ACT 2006

6.1   Basis of preparation of financial statements

The directors of every company (except certain dormant subsidiary undertakings that qualify for exemption from preparation of accounts – the criteria are set out in sections 394A to C) must prepare individual accounts for the company for each financial year (see 6.2 below). *[s394].* The directors of a parent company must prepare group accounts, unless there is an exemption available from preparation of group accounts (see 6.3 below).

Directors must not approve accounts unless they are satisfied that they give a true and fair view of the assets, liabilities, financial position and profit or loss of the company and in the case of group accounts, of the undertakings included in the consolidation as a whole, so far as concerns members of the company. *[s393].* See 7.2 below for a discussion of accounting standards and 'true and fair'.

6.1.1   Choice of IAS accounts and Companies Act accounts under the Companies Act 2006

The Companies Act 2006 distinguishes between IAS accounts and Companies Act accounts. Financial statements prepared in accordance with the Companies Act 2006 using EU-adopted IFRS are IAS accounts. Financial statements prepared in accordance with the Companies Act 2006 using FRS 101, FRS 102 or the FRSSE are Companies Act accounts.

See 6.2 below for the requirements for IAS accounts and Companies Act accounts.

A company's individual accounts may be prepared:

- in accordance with section 396 (Companies Act individual accounts); or
- in accordance with EU-adopted IFRS (IAS individual accounts). *[s395(1)].*

This is subject to the restrictions on changes of financial reporting framework and the requirements for consistency of financial reporting framework within the individual accounts of group undertakings (see 6.1.2 and 6.1.3 below).

The group accounts of certain parent companies are required by Article 4 of the IAS Regulation to be prepared in accordance with EU-adopted IFRS. *[s403(1)].* Article 4 of the IAS Regulation requires an EEA-incorporated company with securities admitted to trading on a regulated market (as at its financial year end) to prepare its consolidated financial statements in accordance with EU-adopted IFRS.

The group accounts of other companies may be prepared:

- in accordance with section 404 (Companies Act group accounts); or
- in accordance with EU-adopted IFRS (IAS group accounts). *[s403(2)].*

This is subject to the restrictions on changes of financial reporting framework (see 6.1.2 below).

The individual and any group accounts of a company that is a charity must be Companies Act accounts. *[s395(2), s403(3)]*

6.1.2   *Companies Act 2006 restrictions on changes of financial reporting framework*

Under the Companies Act 2006, a company which wishes to change from preparing IAS individual accounts to preparing Companies Act individual accounts (such as financial statements prepared under previous UK GAAP, the FRSSE, FRS 101 or FRS 102) may do so only:

- if there is a relevant change of circumstance (see below); or

- for financial years ending on or after 1 October 2012, for a reason other than a relevant change of circumstance, provided the company has not changed to Companies Act individual accounts in the period of five years preceding the first day of that financial year. In calculating the five year period, no account is taken of a change made due to a relevant change of circumstance. *[s395(3)-(5)]*.

The same requirements apply where a company wishes to change from preparing IAS group accounts to preparing Companies Act group accounts, except that the references to individual accounts above are to group accounts. *[s403(4)-(6)]*.

These requirements facilitate implementation of the new UK and Irish GAAP framework. They enable a group where the parent and subsidiary undertakings prepare IAS individual accounts to instead prepare FRS 101 financial statements or even FRS 102 financial statements (as these are both Companies Act individual accounts) where the above criteria are met.

A relevant change of circumstance in respect of individual accounts occurs if:

- the company becomes a subsidiary undertaking of another undertaking that does not prepare IAS individual accounts;

- the company ceases to be a subsidiary undertaking;

- the company ceases to be a company with securities admitted to trading on a regulated market in an EEA State; or

- a parent undertaking of the company ceases to be an undertaking with securities admitted to trading on a regulated market in an EEA State. *[s395(4)]*.

A relevant change of circumstance for the purposes of group accounts occurs where:

- the company becomes a subsidiary undertaking of another undertaking that does not prepare IAS group accounts;

- the company ceases to be a company with securities admitted to trading on a regulated market in an EEA State; or

- a parent undertaking of the company ceases to be an undertaking with securities admitted to trading on a regulated market in an EEA State. *[s403(5)]*.

Section 395's requirements in respect of individual accounts and section 403's requirements in respect of group accounts operate independently of each other. Therefore, an IFRS reporter would be permitted to move from IAS accounts to Companies Act accounts in its individual accounts, while continuing to prepare IAS group accounts.

Paragraph 9.18 of the June 2008 BERR document *Guidance for UK Companies on Accounting and Reporting: Requirements under the Companies Act 2006 and the application of the IAS regulation* notes that the first example of a relevant change in circumstance in the lists above is 'intended to deal with situations where a subsidiary undertaking is sold by a group generally using IAS, to another group or entity not generally using IAS. It is not intended that companies switch between accounting regimes on the basis of an internal group restructuring.'

The restriction is 'one-way' only from IAS accounts to Companies Act accounts. There is no restriction on the number of times a company can move from Companies Act accounts to IAS accounts or *vice versa* so theoretically a company could 'flip' from IAS accounts to Companies Act accounts and back again several times without a relevant change of circumstance provided it reverted back to Companies Act accounts no more than once every five years.

The Companies Act 2006 does not restrict changes made between previous UK GAAP, the FRSSE, FRS 102 or FRS 101 since these are all Companies Act accounts.

6.1.3   Consistency of financial reporting framework in individual accounts of group undertakings

The Companies Act 2006 requires that the directors of a UK parent company secure that the individual accounts of the parent company and of each of its subsidiary undertakings are prepared under the same financial reporting framework, be it IAS accounts or Companies Act accounts, except to the extent that in the directors' opinion there are 'good reasons' for not doing so. *[s407(1)]*. However, this rule does not apply:

- where the UK parent company does not prepare group accounts under the Companies Act 2006; *[s407(2)]*

- where the accounts of the subsidiary undertaking are not required to be prepared under Part 15 of the Companies Act 2006 (e.g. accounts of a foreign subsidiary undertaking); *[s407(3)]* or

- to the accounts of any subsidiary undertakings that are charities *[s407(4)]* (so charities and non-charities within a group are not required to use the same financial reporting framework in their accounts). Charities are not permitted to prepare either IAS group or IAS individual accounts. *[s395(2), s403(3)]*.

Additionally, a parent company that prepares both consolidated and separate financial statements under EU-adopted IFRS (i.e. as IAS group accounts and IAS individual accounts) is not required to ensure that its subsidiary undertakings all prepare IAS individual accounts. However, it must ensure that its subsidiary undertakings use the same financial reporting framework (i.e. all prepare IAS accounts or all prepare Companies Act accounts) in their individual accounts unless there are 'good reasons' for not doing so. *[s407(5)]*.

Although not explicitly stated by FRS 100, there appears to be no requirement that all subsidiary undertakings in a group must use, say, FRS 101 for their Companies Act individual accounts. Some could also use FRS 102, the FRSSE or previous UK GAAP (until withdrawn) since all are Companies Act individual accounts and therefore part of the same financial reporting framework. While this approach would comply with the statutory requirements of section 407, groups that use a 'mix' of GAAP in the individual financial statements may be challenged by HMRC, particularly if this results in tax arbitrage. Examples of 'good reasons' for not preparing all individual accounts within a group using the same financial reporting framework are contained in the June 2008 BERR document *Guidance for UK Companies On Accounting and Reporting: Requirements under the Companies Act 2006 and the application of the IAS regulation.* Paragraph 9.17 of the Guidance notes that this provision is intended to provide a degree of flexibility where there are genuine (including cost/benefit) grounds for using different accounting frameworks within a group of companies and identifies the following examples:

- 'A group using IAS acquired a subsidiary undertaking that had not been using IAS; in the first year of acquisition, it might not be practical for the newly acquired company to switch to IAS straight away.

- The group contains subsidiary undertakings that are themselves publicly traded, in which case market pressures or regulatory requirements to use IAS might come into play, without necessarily justifying a switch to IAS by the non-publicly traded subsidiaries.

- A subsidiary undertaking or the parent were planning to apply for a listing and so might wish to convert to IAS in advance, but the rest of the group was not planning to apply for a listing.

- The group contains minor or dormant subsidiaries where the costs of switching accounting framework would outweigh the benefits.

The key point is that the directors of the parent company must be able to justify any inconsistency to shareholders, regulators or other interested parties'.

6.2   Companies Act requirements for the annual report and accounts

Part 15 of the Companies Act 2006 sets out the requirements for the annual report and accounts for UK companies.

The company's 'annual accounts' are the company's individual accounts for that year and any group accounts prepared by the company for that year.

Section 408 permits a parent company preparing group accounts (whether as IAS group accounts or Companies Act group accounts) to omit the individual profit and loss account from the annual accounts, where the conditions for this exemption are met (see 6.3.2 below). *[s471(1)].*

References in Part 15 to the annual accounts (or to a balance sheet or profit and loss account) include notes to the accounts giving information required by any provision of the Companies Act 2006 or EU-adopted IFRS, and that is required or allowed by any such provision to be given in a note to the company's accounts. *[s472].*

The principal Companies Act requirements for annual accounts are set out at 6.2.1 below and for the annual report at 6.2.2 below. While this chapter focuses on the disclosure requirements for UK companies, LLPs and other types of entities other than companies are also subject to similar statutory requirements. Reference should be made to the legislation that applies to such entities.

The Listing Rules, Disclosure and Transparency Rules or rules of the relevant securities market may require additional information beyond that required by the

Companies Act 2006 (and related regulations) to be included in the annual reports. For example, premium listed companies must state how they apply the main principles of, and present a statement of compliance or otherwise with the provisions of the UK Corporate Governance Code.[15] It is beyond the scope of this chapter to cover such regulatory requirements.

6.2.1   Companies Act 2006 requirements for annual accounts

6.2.1.A   Companies Act accounts

Companies Act individual accounts and Companies Act group accounts are prepared in accordance with sections 396 and 403 of the Companies Act 2006 respectively. Companies Act accounts comprise:

- a balance sheet as at the last day of the financial year that gives a true and fair view of the state of affairs of the company (and in respect of group accounts, of the parent company and its subsidiary undertakings included in the consolidation) as at the end of the financial year; and

- a profit and loss account that gives a true and fair view of the profit or loss of the company (and in respect of group accounts, of the parent company and its subsidiary undertakings included in the consolidation) for the financial year. *[s396(1)-(2), s404(1)-(2)]*

The accounts must comply with regulations as to the form and content of the company balance sheet and profit and loss account (and in respect of group accounts, of the consolidated balance sheet and consolidated profit and loss account) and additional information provided by way of notes to the accounts. *[s396(3), s404(3)]*

These regulations are principally *The Large and Medium-sized Companies and Groups (Accounts and Reports) Regulations 2008* (Regulations). Companies subject to the small companies regime (see 6.5 below) are entitled to apply *The Small Companies and Groups (Accounts and Directors' Report) Regulations 2008* (Small Companies Regulations). Micro-entities (see 6.4 below) are entitled to apply *The Small Companies (Micro Entities' Accounts) Regulations 2013* (Micro-entity Regulations).

If compliance with the regulations and any other provisions made by or under the Companies Act 2006 as to the matters to be included in the accounts or notes to those accounts would not be sufficient to give a true and fair view, the necessary additional information must be given in the accounts or notes to the accounts. *[s396(4, s404(4)]*. If in special circumstances, compliance with any of those provisions is inconsistent with the requirement to give a true and fair view, the directors must depart from that provision to the extent necessary to give a true and fair view. *[s396(5), s404(5)]*. See Chapter 4 at 8.2 for further discussion of the 'true and fair override' provided for in the Companies Act 2006 and FRS 102's requirements on fair presentation (which overlaps with the statutory requirement for accounts to present a true and fair view).

A company's annual accounts must be approved by the board of directors and signed on behalf of the board by a director of the company, with the signature included on the company's balance sheet. *[s414(1)]*.

Financial statements prepared in accordance with FRS 101, FRS 102 or the FRSSE are Companies Act individual or group accounts, and are therefore required to comply with the applicable provisions of Parts 15 and 16 of the Companies Act 2006 and with the Regulations. *[FRS 102.A4.7]*.

6.2.1.B   IAS accounts

Where the directors prepare IAS individual and / or IAS group accounts, they must state in the notes to those accounts that they have been prepared in accordance with EU-adopted IFRS. *[s397, s406, 474]*.

Where the section 408 exemption to omit the individual profit and loss account is taken where group accounts are prepared, the notes to IAS individual accounts must state that they have been prepared in accordance with EU-adopted IFRS as applied in accordance with the provisions of the Companies Act 2006. See 6.3.2 below.

6.2.1.C   General – Companies Act accounts and IAS accounts

There are two types of Companies Act 2006 disclosures required for a UK company:

(a) those required by the Regulations (or other applicable regulations, as discussed below) for an entity preparing Companies Act accounts but not for an entity preparing IAS accounts (see 6.7.1 below); and

(b) those required for both IAS accounts (prepared under EU-adopted IFRS) and Companies Act accounts (see 6.7.2 below).

The Companies Act 2006 distinguishes between companies that are micro-entities (see 6.4 below), companies subject to the small companies regime (see 6.5 below), and medium-sized companies (see 6.6 below).

The above categories of company are all based on meeting certain size criteria and not being excluded from the applicable regime. These companies benefit from a lighter disclosure regime in the financial statements than for large companies, i.e. the default category of companies that are not medium-sized companies, subject to the small companies regime or micro-entities. Certain disclosure exemptions are available to companies preparing IAS accounts or Companies Act accounts, whereas others are only available to companies preparing Companies Act accounts. Companies subject to the small companies regime are entitled to follow the Small Companies Regulations and micro-entities are entitled to follow the Micro-entities (rather than the Regulations).

The Companies Act 2006 also distinguishes between quoted and unquoted companies. While there is no difference in the disclosures required in the financial statements by the Companies Act 2006 and the Regulations for quoted and unquoted companies, there are significant additional disclosures for quoted companies in the annual report (see 6.2.2 below).

6.2.1.D   Interaction with accounting standards

Companies applying the micro-entity provisions (see 6.4 below) are not able to apply FRS 102 (and would therefore apply the FRSSE, which was amended in April 2014 to enable micro-entities to comply with it – see 4.4.6 above). See Chapter 2 at 4.1.2.

Companies subject to the small companies regime are entitled to apply the FRSSE.

FRS 101 and FRS 102 (both forms of Companies Act accounts) do not permit use of the formats included in the Small Companies Regulations (see 6.5 below). *[FRS 101.5(b), AG1(h)-(i), FRS 102.4.2, 5.5, 5.7].* Our view is that companies subject to the small companies regime can still apply FRS 101 or FRS 102 and in doing so, are not precluded from taking advantage of other exemptions applicable to companies subject to the small companies regime. See Chapter 31 at 2 and Chapter 2 at 4.1.1

The FRC proposes withdrawal of the FRSSE, effective for financial years beginning on or after 1 January 2016. In its place, the FRC proposes a new standard to apply to micro-entities and for small entities to apply FRS 102, with presentation and disclosure modifications for small entities (see 4.4.2 above).

6.2.2   Companies Act requirements for annual reports

The content of the annual report depends principally on whether the company is an unquoted company or a quoted company.

A quoted company means a company whose equity share capital:

- has been included in the Official List (as defined in section 103(1) of the Financial Services and Markets Act 2000) in accordance with the provisions of Part 6 of the Financial Services and Markets Act 2000; or
- is officially listed in an EEA State; or
- is admitted to dealing on either the New York Stock Exchange or the exchange known as Nasdaq.

A company is a quoted company in relation to a financial year if it is a quoted company immediately before the end of the accounting reference period (defined in section 391 of the Companies Act 2006) by reference to which that financial year was determined. An unquoted company means a company that is not a quoted company. *[s385(1)-(3)].*

The content of the annual reports and accounts of an unquoted and a quoted company are as follows:

- an unquoted company's annual accounts and reports comprise its annual accounts, strategic report (if any), directors' report, any separate corporate governance statement and the auditor's report (unless the company is exempt from audit); and
- a quoted company's annual accounts and reports comprise its annual accounts, directors' remuneration report, strategic report, directors' report, any separate corporate governance statement, and the auditor's report.

Where the company is a parent company preparing group accounts, the directors' and strategic reports must be consolidated reports (i.e. a 'group directors' report' and 'group strategic report') relating to the undertakings included in the consolidation. These group reports may, when appropriate, give greater emphasis to the matters that are significant to the undertakings included in the consolidation. *[s414A-s414D, s415-s419, 7 Sch 10].*

Small and medium-sized companies are entitled to certain exemptions (see 6.2.2.A below). Companies with securities admitted to a regulated market must make statutory corporate governance disclosures in the annual report and quoted companies have extended disclosures (see 6.2.2.B below).

A company's strategic report (if any), directors' report, directors' remuneration report (if any), and separate corporate governance statement (if any) must be approved by the board of directors and signed on behalf of the board by a director or the secretary of the company. *[s414D(1), s419(1), s419A, s422(1)].*

It is beyond the scope of this chapter to set out the content of the directors' report, strategic report, directors' remuneration report or corporate governance statement. In June 2014, the FRC published best practice *Guidance on the Strategic Report.* This is intended to be persuasive rather than have mandatory force. In September 2013, the GC 100 and Investor Group published *Directors' Remuneration Report Guidance* which provides best practice guidance on the directors' remuneration report prepared by quoted companies.

6.2.2.A   Exemptions for micro, small and medium-sized companies

The directors of a company must prepare a strategic report for the financial year (unless the company is entitled to the *small companies exemption* – see 6.5.3 and 6.5.4 below. There are certain disclosure exemptions available in respect of the strategic report for a medium-sized company (see 6.6 below).

All companies must prepare a directors' report for the financial year, although BIS are consulting on removing this requirement for micro-entities as part of the implementation of the Accounting Directive (see 4.4.2 above). However, a company subject to the *small companies regime* (see 6.5.1 and 6.5.2 below) is entitled to prepare the directors' report in accordance with the Small Companies Regulations which has significantly fewer disclosures than a directors' report prepared in accordance with the Regulations. There are also certain disclosure exemptions available in respect of the directors' report for a company entitled to the *small companies exemption.*

6.2.2.B   Additional requirements for quoted companies and companies with transferable securities admitted to trading on a regulated market

The directors of a quoted company must prepare a directors' remuneration report for the financial year. *[s420-s422, 8 Sch 11].*

A quoted company must also include additional disclosures in the directors' report (greenhouse gas disclosures) and strategic report compared to those required for an unquoted company. Additional disclosures in the strategic report include:

*   the company's (or in group accounts, the group's) strategy and business model;
*   gender diversity disclosures; and
*   to the extent necessary for an understanding of the development, performance or position of the company's (or in group accounts, the group's) business,
    *   the main trends and factors likely to affect the future development, performance and position of the company's (or group's) business; and
    *   certain information about environmental matters (including the impact of the company's business on the environment), the company's employees and social, community and human rights issues). *[s414C(7)-(10)].*

UK companies with transferable securities admitted to trading on a regulated market are required to prepare a statutory corporate governance statement. *[s472A]*. The requirements for the statutory corporate governance statement are included in the FCA's Disclosure and Transparency Rules (DTR) for a UK company, although the DTR have extends the requirement to prepare a corporate governance statement to certain overseas listed companies *[DTR 1B.1.4-1.6, DTR 7.2]* and there may be corresponding requirements in other EEA states. UK and overseas premium listed companies are also required to state how they apply the main principles of, and present a statement of compliance or otherwise with the provisions of the UK Corporate Governance Code.[16] This UK Corporate Governance Code statement overlaps with certain of the content requirements in DTR 7.2 for the statutory corporate governance statement (and with the required statement on audit committees included in DTR 7.1 which applies to issuers with securities admitted to trading on a regulated market required to appoint a statutory auditor, unless exempted from the requirements). *[DTR 1B.1.1-1.3, DTR 7.1]*.

The statutory corporate governance statement can be included as part of the directors' report or as a separate corporate governance statement published together with and in the same manner as its annual report or on a website. *[DTR 7.2.9-11]*. A 'separate corporate governance statement' is defined as one not included in the directors' report, and therefore has its own approval and publication requirements. *[s472A(3)]*.

6.3   Preparation of consolidated financial statements

The Companies Act 2006 requires a UK company, that is a parent company at its financial year end, to prepare group accounts (i.e. consolidated financial statements) unless otherwise exempt (see below). *[s399]*. A company that is exempt from the requirement to prepare group accounts may still do so. *[s398, s399(4)]*.

A company that is subject to the small companies regime is not required to prepare group accounts, but may do so *[s398, s399(1)]* (see Chapter 8 at 3.1.1.D).

The other Companies Act 2006 exemptions from preparation of group accounts comprise:

- Section 400 (parent company is a majority or wholly owned subsidiary undertaking whose immediate parent undertaking is established under the law of an EEA State, and is consolidated in group accounts of a larger group drawn up by an EEA parent undertaking) (see Chapter 6 at 3.1.1.A);
- Section 401 (parent company is a majority or wholly owned subsidiary undertaking whose parent undertaking is not established under the law of an EEA State, and which is consolidated in group accounts of a larger group drawn up by a parent undertaking) (see Chapter 6 at 3.1.1.B and 3.1.1.C); and
- Section 402 (parent company, none of whose subsidiary undertakings need be included in the consolidation) (see Chapter 6 at 3.1.1.E).

FRS 102 has been developed to be consistent with the requirements for group accounts (and exemptions) included in Part 15 of the Companies Act 2006. Consequently, the detailed conditions for the above exemptions from preparing group accounts under the Companies Act 2006 are discussed further in Chapter 6 at 3.1.1

6.3.1   Requirements of accounting standards to prepare consolidated financial statements

FRS 100 does not address the requirements to prepare consolidated financial statements (nor does FRS 101, since it only addresses individual financial statements).

A UK parent company reporting under the FRSSE would be eligible for the small companies regime and is therefore not required to (but may choose to) prepare group accounts under the Companies Act 2006. *[s398, s399(1)]*. Where group accounts are prepared by a parent company subject to the small companies regime, the provisions of Schedule 6 to the Small Companies Regulations should be followed. The FRSSE sets out relevant legal provisions. *[FRSSE 16.3-16.8]*. An entity subject to the FRSSE should have regard to FRS 102, in developing its policies and practices for the preparation of consolidated financial statements (where it has no existing policy), not as a mandatory document but as a means of establishing current practice.[17]

EU-adopted IFRS and FRS 102 both include requirements on which entities should prepare consolidated financial statements and how these should be prepared. Their requirements need to be read in conjunction with the requirements of the relevant statutory framework for preparation of the entity's financial statements.

FRS 102 requires an entity, that is a parent at its year end, to present consolidated financial statements in which it consolidates all its investments in subsidiaries in accordance with the standard (except those permitted or required to be excluded from consolidation) unless it is exempt from the requirement to prepare consolidated financial statements provided in the standard. *[FRS 102.9.2-9.3]*. As noted above, FRS 102's requirements to prepare group accounts (and exemptions) are consistent with the requirements of the Companies Act 2006. See Chapter 6 at 3.1.

6.3.2   Exemption from publishing the individual profit and loss account where group accounts are prepared

Where a company prepares group accounts in accordance with the Companies Act 2006,

- the company's individual profit and loss account need not contain the information required in section 411 (i.e. staff costs and staff numbers must be given for the group, but are not also required to be given for the company) nor the information specified in paragraphs 65 to 69 of Schedule 1 to the Regulations (specified information supplementing the profit and loss account); and

- the company's individual profit and loss account must be approved by the directors in accordance with section 414(1) but may be omitted from the company's annual accounts.

This exemption is conditional on the notes to the company's individual balance sheet showing the company's profit or loss for the financial year (determined in accordance with the Companies Act 2006) and use of the exemption conferred by section 408 being disclosed in the annual accounts. *[s408, Regulations 3(2)]*.

Example 1.2:   Example of a section 408 statement

Basis of preparation
The group accounts consolidate the financial statements of ABC Limited (the company) and all its subsidiary undertakings drawn up to 31 December each year. No individual profit and loss account is presented for ABC Limited as permitted by section 408 of the Companies Act 2006.
.....

Notes to the parent company balance sheet
The profit for the financial year of the company is £130,000 (2014 £111,000).

The exemption is available for both Companies Act and IAS group accounts. Paragraph 9.24 of the June 2008 BERR document *Guidance for UK Companies on Accounting and Reporting: Requirements under the Companies Act 2006 and the application of the IAS regulation* clarifies that:

'The omission of the profit and loss account (referred to within IAS as the income statement) might be considered to be inconsistent with certain aspects of IAS, for example, the requirement in IAS 1 *Presentation of Financial Statements* in relation to a fair presentation. However, IAS does not in itself require the preparation of separate financial statements but permits the omission of certain elements. In other words, the separate financial statements required to be published under the 2006 Act are an extract of the full IAS separate financial statements. This exemption should not affect the ability of a parent company to be treated as a "first-time adopter" and hence to take advantage of exemptions for first time use under the provisions of IFRS 1. The company will need to provide the disclosure required by section 408(4) i.e. that advantage has been taken of the publication exemption in section 408(1). The auditor will also need to describe the accounting framework that has been used within its audit reports. In respect of individual accounts, the reference to the framework will need to make clear that its basis is IAS as adopted by the EU as applied in accordance with the provisions of the 2006 Act.'

Paragraph 9.25 of the BERR guidance further notes that:

'The exemption in the 2006 Act relates only to the profit and loss account. By virtue of section 472(2), the exemption also extends to the notes to the profit and loss account. The individual IAS accounts would, however, still need to include the other primary statements and note disclosures required by IAS, including a cash flow statement and a statement of changes in shareholders' equity.'

6.4   Micro-entity provisions

A new voluntary regime for companies that are micro-entities was introduced into UK companies legislation by *The Small Companies (Micro Entities' Accounts) Regulations 2013* (SI 2013/3008) (Micro-entities Regulations), and is effective for financial years ending on or after 30 September 2013 for companies filing their accounts on or after 1 December 2013. These regulations implement the provisions of the new EU Accounting Directive, which sets out certain minimum requirements for micro-entities into UK company law (see 4.4.2 above). There is no similar legislation currently applicable in the Republic of Ireland. *[FRSSE.Appendix I.18].*

6.4.1   Scope of the regime

A company can only use the micro-entity provisions if it meets the size criteria and is not excluded from being treated as a micro-entity. The size criteria operate in the same way as for the small companies regime (see 6.5 below).

The micro-entity provisions are not accessible to LLPs, qualifying partnerships, overseas companies and other entities. The Explanatory Note to the Micro-entities Regulations confirms that the regime is only available to companies formed and registered (or treated as formed and registered) under the Companies Act 2006.

The qualifying conditions are met in a year in which the company satisfies two or more of the following requirements:

- turnover must not exceed £632,000;

- balance sheet total (gross assets) must not exceed £316,000; and

- the number of employees must not exceed 10. *[s384A(4)-(7)]*.

In the case of a company which is a parent company, the company qualifies as a micro-entity in relation to a financial year only if the company qualifies as a micro-entity in relation to that year and the group headed by the company qualifies as a small group (see 6.5.1.B below). *[s384A(8)]*.

The micro-entity provisions do not apply to a company's accounts for a particular financial year if the company was at any time within that year:

- a company excluded from the small companies regime by section 384 (see 6.5.1.C below);

- an investment undertaking as defined in Article 2(14) of the EU Accounting Directive (Directive 2013/34/EU);

- a financial holding undertaking as defined in Article 2(15) of the EU Accounting Directive;

- a credit institution as defined in Article 4 of Directive 2006/48/EC (other than one referred to in Article 2 of that directive);

- an insurance undertaking as defined in Article 2(1) of Directive 91/674/EEC; or

- a charity. *[s384B(1)]*.

The micro-entity provisions also do not apply in relation to a company's accounts for a financial year if the company is a parent company which prepares group accounts for that year as permitted by section 398, or is not a parent company but its accounts are included in consolidated group accounts for that year. *[s384B(2)]*.

6.4.2   Micro-entity provisions

The regulations provide extensive presentation and disclosure exemptions for micro-entities (known as the micro-entity provisions). In summary, a micro-entity applies one of two abridged formats for the balance sheet and one abridged format for the profit and loss account, as set out in the Section C formats included in the Small Companies Regulations and presents limited prescribed notes which must be included at the foot of the balance sheet. The formats and related notes disclosures are known as the 'micro-entity minimum accounting items'. *[s472(1A)]*.

The prescribed notes comprise: information on directors' advances, credits and guarantees (required by section 413); and on financial guarantees and commitments (required by 1 Sch 57 to the Small Companies Regulations). The micro-entity is not required to give any of the other information required by way of notes to the accounts set out in Schedules 1 to 3 to the Small Companies Regulations. This means there is no requirement to give the information on related undertakings set out in Schedule 2 or the disclosures on directors' remuneration set out in Schedule 3. *[Small Regulations 4, 5, 5A]*.

If BIS proceeds with its proposal (as part of the implementation of the new Accounting Directive) not to require micro-entities to prepare a directors' report, the disclosure requirements on acquisition of own shares currently required in the directors' report will become a mandatory balance sheet note.

The alternative accounting rules and fair value accounting rules (explained further in Chapter 4 at 9) do not apply where the micro-entity provisions are applied; therefore a micro-entity applying the micro-entity provisions is not permitted to revalue tangible fixed assets, investment properties or financial instruments.

In considering whether the individual accounts give a true and fair view, the directors apply the following provisions:

- where the accounts comprise only micro-entity minimum accounting items, the directors must disregard any provision of an accounting standard which would require the accounts to contain information additional to those items;
- in relation to a micro-entity minimum accounting item contained in the accounts, the directors must disregard any provision of an accounting standard which would require the accounts to contain further information in relation to that item; and
- where the accounts contain an item of information additional to the micro-entity minimum accounting items, the directors must have regard to any provision of an accounting standard which relates to that item. *[s393(1A)]*.

Even though the presentation and disclosure requirements are minimal, 'the micro-entity minimum accounting items' included in the company's accounts for the year are presumed to give the true and fair view required (the usual requirements to give additional information where the matters required to be included in the accounts are not sufficient to give a true and fair view and the provisions on 'true and fair override' do not apply in relation to the micro-entity minimum accounting items included in the company's accounts for the year).

The auditor of a company which qualifies as a micro-entity in relation to a financial year applies the same provisions above in considering whether the individual accounts of the company for that year give a true and fair view. *[s495(3A)]*.

If the accounts are prepared in accordance with the micro-entity provisions, the balance sheet must contain a statement to this effect in a prominent place above the signature(s) of the director(s). *[s414(3)(a)]*.

Companies using the micro-entity provisions must file a copy of their accounts at Companies House (but are not permitted to file abbreviated accounts – see 6.5.5.A below). *[s444(3)-(3B)]*. However, micro-entities can use the other filing exemptions for companies subject to the small companies regime as set out in 6.5.5 below (subject to making the statement that the accounts (and reports) have been delivered in accordance with the provisions applicable to companies subject to the small companies regime). *[s444(1)-(2), (5)]*.

6.5   Small companies

There are two sets of exemptions available for small companies:

- the small companies regime – which applies to the preparation and / or filing of the financial statements; and

- the small companies exemption – which applies to the preparation and / or filing of the strategic report and directors' report.

A company subject to the small companies regime must meet certain small size criteria and not be excluded from the small companies regime, i.e. it must not be one of the types of ineligible company nor a member of an ineligible group (see 6.5.1 below).

A company entitled to the small companies exemption must meet the same small size criteria as for the small companies regime and must not be an ineligible company (although it may be a member of an ineligible group). (see 6.5.3 below). The criteria to be subject to the small companies regime are, therefore, more onerous than for the small companies exemption; companies subject to the small companies regime will also qualify for the small companies exemption.

A company that is subject to the small companies regime is entitled to apply the Small Companies Regulations, which requires fewer disclosures in the financial statements and the directors' report than the Regulations, and is also exempt from certain disclosures required in the notes to the financial statements by Part 15 of the Companies Act 2006. See 6.5.2 below. As noted at 6.3.1 above, a company that is subject to the small companies regime is not required to prepare group accounts, but may do so. *[s398, s399(1)]*.

A company that takes advantage of the small companies exemption is not required to prepare a strategic report and is entitled to certain disclosure exemptions in the directors' report. *[s414A, s415A]*. See 6.5.4 below.

Companies subject to the small companies regime or taking advantage of the small companies exemption are also entitled to certain (but different) filing exemptions. *[s444, s444A]*. See 6.5.5 below.

These exemptions operate independently from each other – a company entitled to both the small companies regime and the small companies exemption may choose to apply both, neither, the small companies regime only or the small companies exemption only.

If the accounts are prepared in accordance with the provisions applicable to companies subject to the small companies regime (unless applying the micro-entity provisions – see 6.4 above), the balance sheet must contain a statement to this effect in a prominent place above the signature(s) of the director(s). *[s414(3)(b)]*. See 4.4.6.A for an example of such a statement (combined with the statement of compliance with the FRSSE).

Where an entity has taken advantage of the small companies exemption in preparing the directors' report, a statement to this effect is required in the directors' report, in a prominent place above the signature(s) of the director(s) or secretary, as applicable. *[s419(2)]*. Note that the statement made in the directors' report refers to the small companies exemption *even if* the company is also subject to the small companies regime.

6.5.1   Criteria for use of the small companies regime

The small companies regime applies to a company for a financial year in relation to which the company qualifies as small *[s82-383(3)]* – see 6.5.1.A and 6.5.1.B below – and is not excluded from the regime *[s381]* – see 6.5.1.C below. *[s381]*.

6.5.1.A   *Companies qualifying as small – company is not a parent undertaking (size criteria)*

A company qualifies for the small companies regime in relation to its first financial year if the qualifying conditions (as set out below) are met in that year.

A company qualifies as small in relation to a subsequent financial year if the qualifying conditions are met in that year but, where on its balance sheet date a company meets or ceases to meet the qualifying conditions, that affects its qualification as a small company only if it occurs in two consecutive years. *[s382(1), (1A), (2)]*.

Therefore, there are provisions designed to assist companies which fluctuate in and out of the qualifying conditions. However, if a company fails to meet the criteria in two consecutive years, it will cease to qualify, and then would need to meet the criteria in two later consecutive years to re-qualify for the exemptions.

The qualifying conditions are met in a year in which the company satisfies two or more of the following requirements:

- turnover must not exceed £6.5 million;
- balance sheet total (gross assets) must not exceed £3.26 million; and
- the number of employees must not exceed 50.

If the company's financial year is not in fact a full year, the turnover figure should be adjusted proportionately. The 'balance sheet total' means the aggregate of the amounts shown as assets in the balance sheet, i.e. total assets. The number of employees means the average number of persons employed under contracts of service by the company in the year (determined on a monthly basis, with the monthly totals added together and then divided by the number of months in the financial year). *[s382(3)-(6)]*.

6.5.1.B   *Companies qualifying as small – company is a parent undertaking (size criteria)*

Where the company is itself a parent undertaking, then it only qualifies for the small companies regime if the group that it heads qualifies as a small group *[s382(7), 383(1)]*. This is the case whether or not group accounts are prepared.

A group qualifies as small in relation to the parent's first financial year if the qualifying conditions (as set out below) are met in that year.

A group qualifies as small in relation to a subsequent financial year if the qualifying conditions are met in that year but, where on its balance sheet date the group meets or ceases to meet the qualifying conditions, that affects the group's qualification as small only if it occurs in two consecutive years. *[s382(2), (2A), (3)]*.

The qualifying conditions for a small group are met in a year in which the group headed by the company satisfies two or more of the following requirements:

- turnover must not exceed £6.5 million net (or £7.8 million gross);
- balance sheet total (gross assets) must not exceed £3.26 million (or £3.9 million gross); and
- the number of employees must not exceed 50.

The aggregate figures for the above limits are ascertained by aggregating the relevant figures determined in accordance with section 382 for each member of the group. The figures used for each subsidiary undertaking are those included in its individual accounts for the relevant financial year, i.e. where its financial year is coterminous with that of the parent company, the financial year that ends at the same date as the parent company, or where its financial year is not coterminous, the financial year ending last before the end of the financial year of the parent company. If those figures are not obtainable without disproportionate expense or undue delay, the latest available figures are used. The turnover and balance sheet total criteria may be satisfied on either the gross or net of consolidation adjustments basis. It is permissible to satisfy one limit on the 'net' basis and the other on the 'gross' basis. *[s383(4)-(7)]*.

6.5.1.C   *Companies excluded from the small companies regime*

A company is excluded from the small companies regime if it is (or was at any time in the financial year to which the accounts relate):

- a public company;
- a company that is an authorised insurance company, a banking company, an e-money issuer, a MiFID investment firm or a UCITS management company;
- a company that carries on an insurance market activity; or
- a member of an ineligible group. *[s384(1)]*.

A group is ineligible if any of its members is:

- a public company;
- a body corporate (other than a company) whose shares are admitted to trading on a regulated market in an EEA State (as defined in Directive 2004/39/EC);

- a person (other than a small company) who has permission under Part 4 of the Financial Services and Markets Act 2000 to carry on a regulated activity;
- an e-money issuer;
- a small company that is an authorised insurance company, banking company, a MiFID investment firm or a UCITS management company; or
- a person who carries on an insurance market activity. *[s384(2)]*.

A company is a small company for the purposes of section 384(2) if it qualified as small in relation to its last financial year ending on or before the end of the financial year to which the accounts relate. *[s384(3)]*.

The reference to a 'company' above is to a company formed and registered (or treated as formed and registered) under the Companies Act 2006. This means a company formed and registered under the Companies Act 2006, or prior to 1 October 2009 under the Companies Act 1985, Companies (Northern Ireland) Order 1986 or former Companies Acts (i.e. an 'existing company' for the purposes of that Act and Order). *[s1]*.

A public company means a company limited by shares or limited by guarantee and having a share capital (a) whose certificate of incorporation states that it is a public company and (b) in relation to which the requirements of the Companies Act 2006 or former Companies Acts as to registration or re-registration as a public company have been complied with (on or after the relevant date, being 22 December 1980 in Great Britain and 1 July 1983 in Northern Ireland). *[s4]*. Therefore, a public company means a UK-incorporated company that is a 'plc' or 'PLC' rather than a publicly traded company.

An authorised insurance company is defined in section 1165(2), a banking company in section 1164(2)-(3) and insurance market activity in section 1165(7). See Chapter 4 at 4.1.2.

The terms e-money issuer, MiFID investment firm, regulated activity, and UCITS management company are defined in section 474 of the Companies Act 2006. The term 'e-money issuer' means an electronic money institution within the meaning of *The Electronic Money Regulations 2011* (SI 2011/99). *[s474]*.

A body corporate includes a body incorporated outside the UK but does not include (a) a corporation sole or (b) a partnership that, whether or not a legal person, is not regarded as a body corporate under the law by which it is governed. *[s1173(1)]*. Therefore, a body corporate would include an overseas company or a UK LLP.

6.5.2   Use of the small companies regime

A company preparing its accounts subject to the small companies regime must comply with the Small Companies Regulations, which contain the following schedules:

- Schedule 1 (Companies Act individual accounts);
- Schedule 2 (Information about related undertakings where company not preparing group accounts (Companies Act or IAS individual accounts));

- Schedule 3 (Information about directors' benefits: remuneration (Companies Act or IAS accounts));
- Schedule 4 (Companies Act abbreviated accounts for delivery to Registrar of Companies);
- Schedule 5 (Matters to be dealt with in directors' report);
- Schedule 6 (Group accounts);
- Schedule 7 (Definition of 'provision'); and
- Schedule 8 (General interpretation). *[Small Regulations 3-10].*

A company subject to the small companies regime preparing Companies Act accounts must comply with all applicable requirements of the Small Companies Regulations.

The schedules in the Small Companies Regulations provide simpler formats and reduced disclosures compared to the corresponding schedules in the Regulations applied by large and medium-sized companies and groups. However, companies are treated as complying with Schedule 1 and, in respect of group accounts, Part 1 of Schedule 6 to the Small Companies Regulations (which set out the formats for the profit and loss account and balance sheet, recognition and measurement principles, and disclosure requirements) if they comply with the corresponding provision of Schedule 1 and / or Part 1 of Schedule 6 to the Regulations. *[Small Regulations 3(3), 8(2)].* IAS accounts prepared by a company subject to the small companies regime do not apply Schedule 1 or Part 1 of Schedule 6 (Group accounts).

Companies subject to the small companies regime are entitled to apply the FRSSE (see 4.4.6 above)

FRS 101 and FRS 102 (both forms of Companies Act accounts) do not permit use of the formats included in the Small Companies Regulations. Therefore, these formats would only be used if the company is applying the FRSSE. As noted at 6.2.1.D above, our view is that companies subject to the small companies regime can still apply FRS 101 or FRS 102 and in doing so, are not precluded from taking advantage of other exemptions applicable to companies subject to the small companies regime.

The Small Companies Regulations include certain requirements that apply to companies subject to the small companies regime (whether or not preparing IAS accounts or Companies Act accounts). Therefore, both Companies Act accounts and IAS accounts must give the information required by the following schedules:

- information on related undertakings (Schedule 2 and, where group accounts are prepared, Part 2 of Schedule 6); and
- information on directors' benefits – remuneration (Schedule 3)

Companies subject to the small companies regime, whether preparing Companies Act accounts or IAS accounts, must provide the disclosures required by the Companies Act 2006 and other applicable regulations, but are exempt from certain disclosures required by companies not subject to the small companies regime. The main disclosure exemptions are listed at 6.5.2.A and 6.5.2.B below.

6.5.2.A   *Disclosure exemptions – financial statements*

Companies using the small companies regime and preparing Companies Act accounts are not required to disclose the following items in their financial statements (required under the Regulations for large and medium-sized companies preparing Companies Act accounts, but not included in Schedule 1 to the Small Companies Regulations):

- material differences between carrying value and replacement cost of stocks;
- whether the accounts have been prepared in accordance with applicable accounting standards and particulars of any material departures from those standards or from fundamental accounting principles set out in Regulations;
- details of shares held as treasury shares;
- details of contingent rights to the allotment of shares;
- details of debentures issued during the year (or held by a nominee of or trustee for the company);
- the split of land and buildings into freehold and leasehold or the leasehold land into short and long leases;
- the fair value (and extent and nature) of derivatives not held at fair value;
- deferred taxation, separately from the amount of provision for other taxation;
- interest and repayment terms of debt due after five years (but the aggregate of the amounts of debt repayable otherwise than by instalments and instalments of debt falling due for payment after more than five years are still required to be disclosed);
- the nature of any security given for creditors;
- any outstanding loans made for financial assistance for purchase of own shares;
- interest or similar charges separately in respect of bank loans and overdrafts, and other loans (excluding loans for group undertakings);
- an analysis of the tax charge, or details of special circumstances affecting the tax charge;
- details of turnover by class of business/geographical market – but the percentage of turnover that, in the directors opinion, is attributable to non-UK markets must be disclosed; and
- details of related party transactions.

Companies subject to the small companies regime (preparing IAS accounts or Companies Act accounts) are only required to show:

- the overall total (i.e. a single total rather than three separate totals) of:
    - the amount of remuneration paid to or receivable by directors in respect of qualifying services;
    - the amount of money paid to or receivable by directors and the net value of assets (other than money, share options or shares) received or receivable by directors, under long-term incentive schemes in respect of qualifying services; and

- the value of any company contributions paid or treated as paid to a pension scheme in respect of qualifying services and by reference to which the rate or amount of any money purchase benefits that may become payable will be calculated;

- the number of directors (if any) to whom retirement benefits are accruing in respect of qualifying services (a) under money purchase schemes and (b) under defined benefit schemes;

- the aggregate amount of any payments made to directors or past directors for loss of office; and

- the aggregate amount of any consideration paid to or receivable by third parties for making available the services of directors.

Companies subject to the small companies regime are, therefore, not required to disclose any gains made by directors on exercise of share options, the number of directors who exercised share options, the number of directors in respect of whose qualifying services shares were received or receivable under long-term incentive schemes, details of the highest paid director's remuneration or any excess retirement benefits of directors or past directors.

In addition, companies subject to the small companies regime (preparing IAS accounts or Companies Act accounts) are not required to disclose details of off-balance sheet arrangements *[s410A]* (see Chapter 4 at 7.7), or information about employee numbers and costs *[s411]* (see Chapter 4 at 7.6) or the date on which the last financial year of the subsidiary undertaking ended (i.e. the last financial year end of the subsidiary before the reporting company's financial year end), where not coterminous with that of the reporting company.

A company subject to the small companies regime is only required to disclose remuneration receivable by the company's auditor (but not the associates of the auditor) for the auditing of the annual accounts. *[s494]*.[18] Therefore, information on remuneration receivable for non-audit services is not required.

Companies subject to the small companies regime applying FRS 101 or FRS 102 must still give the disclosures required by accounting standards, e.g. small companies still need to give related party disclosures.

6.5.2.B   Disclosure exemptions – directors' report and strategic report

Where a company is subject to the small companies regime, it will also qualify for the small companies exemption. Therefore, the company is not required to prepare a strategic report and is entitled to disclosure exemptions in relation to the directors' report. See 6.5.4.A and 6.5.4.B below.

In addition, a company subject to the small companies regime is permitted to apply the (less onerous) requirements for the directors' report included in Schedule 5 to the Small Companies Regulations. *[Small Regulations 7 and 5 Sch].* Schedule 5 requires disclosure in respect of political donations and expenditure and the employment of disabled persons. However, companies subject to the small companies regime are not required to include the following disclosures in the directors' report (that are required to be given by large and medium-sized companies applying the Regulations):

- use of financial instruments – financial risk management objectives, policies and risk exposures;
- details of important post balance sheet events;
- an indication of likely future developments;
- an indication of research and development activities;
- an indication of branches outside the United Kingdom; and
- information about employee involvement.[19]

Where any of the above exemptions are taken, the required statement in the directors' report that the company has taken advantage of the small companies exemption in preparing the directors' report must be made. See 6.5.4 below.

6.5.3   *Criteria for use of the small companies exemption*

A company is entitled to the small companies exemption in relation to the directors' report (see 6.5.4.A below) and the strategic report (see 6.5.4.B below) for a financial year if it is entitled to prepare financial statements for the year in accordance with the small companies regime (see 6.5.1 above) or would be so entitled but for being or having been a member of an ineligible group. *[s415A(1), s414B]*.

The company must, therefore, meet the same small size criteria as for the small companies regime (including that if the company is a parent company, it does not head a small group) and not be an ineligible company itself.

The small companies exemption is available to both companies preparing Companies Act accounts and companies preparing IAS accounts (i.e. prepared using EU-adopted IFRS).

6.5.4   *Disclosure exemptions for the small companies exemption*

6.5.4.A   *Directors' report*

There are relatively few disclosure exemptions remaining for companies entitled to the small companies exemption.

Companies entitled to the small companies exemption are exempt from including the amount recommended by the directors to be paid by way of dividend (required by section 416(3)). *[s415A(2)]*.

If a company is entitled to the small companies exemption, the directors' report must still include:

- the names of persons who were, at any time during the financial year, directors of the company; *[s416(1)(a)]*
- the statement as to disclosure of relevant information to auditors (unless the company has taken advantage of an audit exemption). *[s418]*.

Where the company is entitled to the small companies exemption (but not subject to the small companies regime), the company must comply with the more extensive content requirements for the directors' report in Schedule 7 to the Regulations.

[para 10 and Sch 7, Regulations]. Where the company is entitled to the small companies regime, it may comply with Schedule 5 to the Small Companies Regulations which has fewer disclosures for the directors' report, as explained at 6.8.2.B above.

Where advantage of the small companies exemption is taken in preparing the directors' report, a statement to this effect is required in the directors' report, in a prominent position above the signature(s) of the director(s) or secretary. *[s419(2)]*.

6.5.4.B   *Strategic report*

A company entitled to the small companies exemption is not required to prepare a strategic report. *[s414A]*.

While there is no statutory requirement to do so, we would recommend that, where a company entitled to the small companies exemption takes advantage of the exemption not to prepare a strategic report, a statement is included in the directors' report, above the signature of the director or secretary to explain that it has done so.

6.5.5   *Filing exemptions – small companies*

Companies subject to the small companies regime have three choices:

- to deliver a copy of the full accounts and reports sent to members and a copy of the auditor's report (unless the company has taken advantage of an audit exemption) to the Registrar;

- to deliver a copy of the balance sheet and a copy of the auditor's report (unless the company has taken advantage of an audit exemption) on the accounts (and any directors' report) that are delivered. Companies may choose to omit a copy of the directors' report and / or a copy of the profit or loss account; or

- to deliver abbreviated accounts to the Registrar (unless the company is applying the micro-entity provisions) – see 6.5.5.A below. *[s444]*.

Companies subject to the small companies exemption (but not the small companies regime) need not deliver a copy of the directors' report. *[s444A]*.

References to the 'profit or loss account' above include its related notes. *[s472]*. TECH 14/13 FRF – *Disclosure of auditor remuneration* – clarifies that disclosure of auditor remuneration is not regarded as a related note to the profit and loss account and therefore must be given in the copy of the accounts and reports delivered to the Registrar. *[TECH 14/13 FRF.10.3]*

APB Bulletin 2008/04 – *The special auditor's report on abbreviated accounts in the United Kingdom* addresses the above filing exemptions (as well as abbreviated accounts) and the implications for the copy of the auditor's report delivered.

In all cases, the copies of the balance sheet and any directors' report delivered to the Registrar must be signed by and state the name of the person who signed it on behalf of the board. *[s444(6), s444A(3)]*.[20]

This exemption not to deliver a copy of the directors' report or profit and loss account is available both to IAS accounts and Companies Act accounts. Where these exemptions are taken, a separate statement is required in the copy of the accounts and reports delivered to the Registrar, given on the balance sheet (in a prominent position) that the company's annual accounts and reports have been delivered in accordance with the small companies regime. *[s444(5)]*. See Example 1.3 below.

Example 1.3:   Example statement where filing exemptions used by companies subject to the small companies regime

These accounts [and reports] have been delivered in accordance with the provisions applicable to companies subject to the small companies regime.

Companies House Guidance[21] notes that this statement should be included above the directors' signature and printed name. This statement is required *in addition* to any statements required where the accounts for members are prepared in accordance with the small companies regime (see 6.4 above) or the company has taken advantage of the small companies exemption in preparing the directors' report (see 6.5.4 above).

Companies entitled to the small companies exemption only (see 6.4.3 above) are not required to deliver a copy of the directors' report but must deliver a copy of the balance sheet, a copy of the profit or loss account and a copy of the auditor's report on the accounts (and any directors' report that it delivers), unless the company has taken advantage of an audit exemption. *[s444A(1)-(2)]*. While there is no statutory requirement to make a statement, it may be appropriate to explain that the company is taking advantage of the small companies exemption in not delivering the directors' report.

6.5.5.A   Companies subject to the small companies regime filing abbreviated accounts

Abbreviated accounts are a filing exemption only – full accounts and reports must still be prepared for the members. Abbreviated accounts are only available for Companies Act individual accounts and are not permitted for Companies Act group accounts or IAS accounts. Companies will not be able to prepare abbreviated accounts once the new Accounting Directive is implemented (see 4.4.2 above), although the formats and other presentation and disclosure requirements applicable for small companies will be simpler than at present.

The copies of accounts and reports delivered to the Registrar must be copies of the company's annual accounts and reports, except that companies subject to the small companies regime preparing Companies Act individual accounts are permitted to deliver a copy of the balance sheet prepared in accordance with Schedule 4 to the Small Companies Regulations to the Registrar. *[s444(3), Small Regulations 6(1)]*. Schedule 4 sets out an abbreviated balance sheet format and minimum required notes (including accounting policies and other specified disclosures). There is no requirement for companies subject to the small companies regime to file a copy of the profit and loss account. *[s444(1)(b), (3)]*. In addition, Companies Act individual accounts and Companies Act group accounts delivered to the Registrar need not give the information on shares of the company held by subsidiary undertakings (required by paragraph 4 of Schedule 2 and paragraph 25 of Schedule 6) or Schedule 3 (directors' benefits). *[Small Regulations 6(2) and 11]*. TECH 14/13 FRF notes that abbreviated accounts prepared by a small company need not include disclosure of auditors' remuneration. *[TECH 14/13 FRF.10.2]*. Since abbreviated accounts are not required to give a true and fair view,[22] the consensus is that these are not required to comply with the disclosure requirements in accounting standards.

Where abbreviated accounts are delivered, a copy of a special auditor's report (in place of the copy of the auditor's report on the full accounts and reports) is delivered to the Registrar, unless the company takes advantage of an audit exemption. *[s444(4)]*. This special auditor's report states that, in the auditor's opinion, the company is entitled to deliver abbreviated accounts in accordance with section 444(3) and that the abbreviated accounts have been properly prepared in accordance with the regulations made under that section. *[s449(3)]*. Section 449 and APB Bulletin 2008/04 give further guidance on this special auditor's report.

Abbreviated accounts delivered to the Registrar must be approved by the board of directors and signed on behalf of the board by a director, with the signature (and printed name) included on the balance sheet. In a prominent position, above the signature, the balance sheet must include the following statement *[s450(1)-(3)]*:

Example 1.4:   Example statement for abbreviated accounts of a small company

These accounts have been prepared in accordance with the special provisions applicable to companies subject to the small companies regime.

6.6   Medium-sized companies and groups

Medium-sized companies and groups must apply the Regulations in preparing their annual reports and accounts. A medium-sized company may take advantage of certain disclosure exemptions in its annual reports and accounts for a financial year in which the company qualifies as medium-sized (see sections 465 to 467) and is not an excluded company.

There is no requirement for the annual reports and accounts of a medium-sized company to state use of the disclosure exemptions.

6.6.1   Qualification as medium-sized company

The medium-sized company regime works in the same way as for the small companies regime (described in 6.5.1.A to 6.5.1.C above). The size criteria and excluded companies are detailed below.

6.6.1.A   Size criteria for medium-sized companies and groups

The qualifying conditions for a medium-sized company are met in a year in which the company satisfies two or more of the following requirements:

- turnover must not exceed £25.9 million;
- balance sheet total (gross assets) must not exceed £12.9 million; and
- the number of employees must not exceed 250. *[s465]*.

The qualifying conditions for a medium-sized group are met in a year in which the group headed by the company satisfies two or more of the following requirements:

- turnover must not exceed £25.9 million net (or £31.1 million gross);
- balance sheet total (gross assets) must not exceed £12.9 million (or £15.5 million gross); and
- the number of employees must not exceed 250. *[s466]*.

6.6.1.B   Companies excluded from medium-sized companies

A company is not entitled to take advantage of any of the provisions available for companies qualifying as medium-sized if it was at any time within the financial year to which the accounts relate:

- a public company;
- a company that has permission under Part 4 of the Financial Services and Markets Act 2000 to carry on a regulated activity;
- a company that carries on an insurance market activity;
- an e-money issuer; or
- a member of an ineligible group. *[s467(1)]*.

A group is ineligible if any of its members is:

- a public company;
- a body corporate (other than a company) whose shares are admitted to trading on a regulated market in an EEA State (as defined in Directive 2004/39/EC);
- a person (other than a small company) who has permission under Part 4 of the Financial Services and Markets Act 2000 to carry on a regulated activity;
- an e-money issuer;
- a small company that is an authorised insurance company, banking company, a MiFID investment firm or a UCITS management company; or
- a person who carries on an insurance market activity. *[s467(2)]*.

A company is a small company for the purposes of section 467(2) if it qualified as small in relation to its last financial year ending on or before the end of the financial years to which the accounts relate. *[s467(3)]*.

See 6.5.1.C above for relevant definitions.

6.6.2   Disclosure exemptions available for medium-sized companies

6.6.2.A   Disclosure exemptions available in the accounts and reports prepared for members

The disclosure exemptions for medium-sized companies include:

- no requirement to disclose non-financial key performance indicators, including information relating to environmental matters and employee matters, in the strategic report; *[s414C(6)]*
- no requirement to disclose the financial impact of material off-balance sheet arrangements on the company (or in group accounts, of the undertakings included in the consolidation as if a single company), although their nature and business purpose of the arrangements must still be disclosed. This disclosure exemption applies to Companies Act and IAS accounts (see Chapter 4 at 7.7); *[s410A(4)]*
- no requirement for Companies Act individual accounts to disclose the information required by paragraph 45 (the statement that the accounts have been prepared in accordance with applicable accounting standards, giving

particulars and reasons for any material departures from these standards) or paragraph 72 (related party disclosures) of Schedule 1 to the Regulations; *[s4]* (see 4.6.1 above) and

- no requirement to disclose auditor's remuneration in respect of non-audit services. Like companies subject to the small companies regime, only remuneration for the auditing of the annual accounts receivable by the company's auditor (but not the associates of the auditor) is required to be disclosed. *[s494]*.[23] TECH 14/13 FRF provides guidance on disclosure of auditor remuneration.

Medium-sized entities preparing financial statements in accordance with FRS 101 or FRS 102 must still give the disclosures required by accounting standards, e.g. medium-sized companies still need to give the related party disclosures required by accounting standards.

6.6.2.B   *Abbreviated accounts*

Abbreviated accounts are a filing exemption only – full accounts and reports must still be prepared for the members. Abbreviated accounts are only available for Companies Act individual accounts and may not be used for Companies Act group accounts or IAS accounts.

The directors of a medium-sized company preparing Companies Act individual accounts may deliver to the Registrar a copy of the accounts which:

- combines certain line items in the profit and loss account formats into one line (although turnover must be disclosed); and
- does not include the information required by paragraph 68 of Schedule 1 to the Regulations (particulars of turnover, analysed by class of business and geographical market by destination).

The line items that may be combined in the profit and loss account formats are:

- cost of sales, gross profit or loss (format 1 only), and other operating income (where formats 1 and 3 are used); and
- changes in stocks of finished goods and work in progress, own work capitalised, raw materials and consumables, other external charges and other operating income (where formats 2 and 4 are used). *[s445(3), s4]*.

The concessions available in medium-sized company abbreviated accounts are therefore somewhat limited. All other statutory disclosures required in the full accounts and reports must be given, including the disclosure of auditors' remuneration. *[TECH 14/13 FRF.10.2]*. Views are mixed as to whether the abbreviated accounts delivered to the Registrar must be the same as the full accounts for members, subject to the above concessions or whether disclosures required solely by accounting standards can be omitted.

Where abbreviated accounts are delivered, a copy of a special auditor's report (in place of the copy of the auditor's report on the full accounts and reports) is delivered to the Registrar, unless the company takes advantage of an audit exemption. *[s445(4)]*. This special auditor's report states that, in the auditor's opinion, the company is entitled to deliver abbreviated accounts in accordance with section 445(3) and that the abbreviated accounts have been properly prepared in accordance with the regulations made under that section. *[s449(3)]*. Section 449 and APB Bulletin 2008/04 gives further guidance on this special auditor's report.

Abbreviated accounts delivered to the Registrar must be approved by the board of directors and signed on behalf of the board by a director, with the signature and printed name included on the balance sheet. In a prominent position, above the signature, the balance sheet must include the following statement that:

'The accounts have been prepared in accordance with the special provisions of the Companies Act relating to medium-sized companies, as required by section 445(3) of the Companies Act 2006'. *[s450(1)-(3)]*.[24]

6.7   Disclosures

The Companies Act 2006 (particularly Part 15), the Regulations and other statutory instruments include disclosure requirements which apply to Companies Act accounts and IAS accounts. As discussed at 6.7.1 below, only some parts of the Regulations apply to IAS accounts. See 6.7.2 for a list of Companies Act disclosures applicable to both IAS accounts and Companies Act accounts.

The disclosure exemptions for companies subject to the small companies regime in the Companies Act 2006 and the Small Companies Regulations are addressed at 6.5.2 and 6.5.4 above.

6.7.1   *Disclosures required by the Regulations*

The Regulations contain the following schedules:

*   Schedule 1 (Companies Act individual accounts – companies other than banking and insurance companies);
*   Schedule 2 (Companies Act individual accounts: banking companies);
*   Schedule 3 (Companies Act individual accounts: insurance companies);
*   Schedule 4 (Information about related undertakings – Companies Act or IAS accounts);
*   Schedule 5 (Information about directors' benefits: remuneration – Companies Act or IAS accounts);
*   Schedule 6 (Companies Act group accounts);
*   Schedule 7 (Matters to be dealt with in directors' report);
*   Schedule 8 (Directors' remuneration report – quoted companies);
*   Schedule 9 (Definition of 'provision'); and
*   Schedule 10 (General interpretation).

A company preparing IAS individual accounts in accordance with section 397 (or IAS group accounts in accordance with section 406) does not apply Schedules 1 to 3, or Schedule 6 to the Regulations.

A company preparing Companies Act accounts must comply with all the requirements of the Regulations, including Schedules 1 to 3 (as applicable) and, where group accounts are prepared, Schedule 6. Schedules 1 to 3 include the formats for the profit and loss account and balance sheet, recognition and measurement principles, and disclosure requirements. Schedule 1 applies to all companies (other than banking companies and insurance companies), Schedule 2 to banking companies and groups, and Schedule 3 to insurance companies and groups. See Chapter 4 at 4.1.2.A for definitions of banking and insurance companies and groups.

The Regulations require various disclosures to be given in the financial statements. In particular, Parts 3 of Schedules 1 to 3 for Companies Act accounts require certain disclosures to be made in the notes to the financial statements if not given in the primary statements. The relevant paragraphs are as follows:

- Schedule 1 paragraphs 42 to 72; or
- Schedule 2 paragraphs 52 to 92; or
- Schedule 3 paragraphs 60 to 90; or
- Schedule 6, various.

Although some of these disclosure requirements are replicated in EU-adopted IFRS, others are not. Entities that move to FRS 101 or FRS 102 from previous UK GAAP will have been required to provide the statutory disclosures required for Companies Act accounts previously and therefore these requirements will not increase their reporting burden. Entities that move to FRS 101 or FRS 102 from EU-adopted IFRS are required to provide the additional statutory disclosures for Companies Act accounts and should consider carefully the impact of these new requirements against the benefits of the reduced disclosures under those standards.

6.7.2 Existing Companies Act disclosures in the accounts and reports applicable to IAS accounts and Companies Act accounts

Companies preparing IAS accounts or Companies Act accounts are subject to the following disclosures:

- section 409 (and Schedule 4 to the Regulations / Schedule 2 to the Small Companies Regulations) – information about related undertakings;
- section 410A – off-balance sheet arrangements (unless subject to the small companies regime). See Chapter 4 at 7.7;
- section 411 – employee numbers and costs (unless subject to the small companies regime). See Chapter 4 at 7.6;
- section 412 (and Schedule 5 to the Regulations / Schedule 3 to the Small Companies Regulations) – directors' benefits: remuneration;
- section 413 – directors' benefits: advances, credits and guarantees. See Chapter 4 at 7.8;
- sections 414A-D – strategic report (unless entitled to the small companies exemption). The FRC's *Guidance on the Strategic Report* (June 2014) provides best practice guidance. This is intended to be persuasive rather than have mandatory force;
- sections 236, 415 to 419 (and Schedule 7 to the Regulations / Schedule 5 to the Small Companies Regulations) – directors' report;
- sections 420 to 421 (and Schedule 8 to the Regulations) – directors' remuneration report (quoted companies only). The GC 100 and Investor

Group's *Directors' Remuneration Report Guidance* (September 2013) provides best practice guidance on the directors' remuneration report prepared by quoted companies; and

- section 494 (and *Companies (Disclosure of Auditor Remuneration and Liability Limitation Agreements) Regulations 2008*) – services provided by auditor and associates and related remuneration.

    Companies subject to the small companies regime or medium-sized companies are only required to disclose remuneration for the audit of the annual accounts receivable by the company's auditor (but not the associates of the auditor) and are not required to disclose remuneration for non-audit services. *[s494].*[25]

    TECH 14/13 FRF provides guidance on disclosure of auditor remuneration.

In addition, other Companies Act 2006 or related disclosures may apply depending on individual circumstances such as the disclosures required for a parent taking advantage of the exemption from preparing consolidated accounts under either sections 400 or 401 of the Companies Act 2006.

7   FINANCIAL REPORTING COUNCIL (FRC) AND ACCOUNTING STANDARD SETTING

The structure of the FRC was reformed with effect from 2 July 2012, and the FRC was given new statutory powers including assuming responsibility for accounting standards (see 7.1 below). The Accounting Standards Board, previously responsible for issuing accounting standards and the Urgent Issues Task Force have ceased to exist.

This section draws on information concerning the new FRC structure that is included on the FRC website.

The FRC Board is now supported by three business committees:

- the Codes & Standards Committee;
- the Conduct Committee; and
- the Executive Committee.

Of interest to this chapter, is the role of the FRC in accounting standard setting.

7.1   Accounting standards setting

Accounting standards are statements of standard accounting practice issued by such body or bodies prescribed by regulations.[26] *[s464(1)].* Prior to 2 July 2012, this body was the Accounting Standards Board and from 2 July 2012, the Financial Reporting Council. New accounting standards, or amendments to or withdrawal of existing accounting standards must be approved by the FRC Board, having received advice from the Accounting Council and/or the Codes and Standards Committee (see below).

The FRC's objective in setting accounting standards is to enable users of accounts to receive high quality, understandable financial reporting proportionate to the size and complexity of the entity and users' information needs. In developing future accounting standards, the FRC aims to provide accounting standards that have consistency with international accounting standards through application of an IFRS-based solution, unless an alternative clearly better meets its overriding objective. *[Foreword to Accounting Standards.6, 29]*. The FRC collaborates with accounting standard setters from other countries and the IASB to influence the development of international accounting standards and to ensure that its standards are developed with due regard for international developments. The FRC works closely with the European Financial Reporting Advisory Group (EFRAG), which advises the European Commission on IFRSs in Europe and with the International Forum of Accounting Standard Setters (IFASS).

The Codes & Standards Committee, which contains both FRC Board members and others with particular technical expertise (including practising professionals) is responsible, *inter alia*, for advising the FRC Board on maintaining an effective framework of UK codes and standards for Corporate Governance, Stewardship, Accounting, Auditing and Assurance, and Actuarial technical standards. In relation to accounting standard setting, the FRC Board and the Codes & Standards Committee are advised by the Accounting Council (which is appointed by the Codes & Standards Committee). Its advice is put fully to the FRC Board, with the Board member chairing the Council responsible for submitting the Council's advice to the Board. The Accounting Council, which is appointed by the Codes & Standards Committee:

- provides strategic input and thought leadership, in the fields of accounting and financial reporting and in the work-plan of the FRC as a whole;

- considers and advises the FRC Board upon draft codes and standards (or amendments thereto) to ensure that a high quality, effective and proportionate approach is taken;

- considers and comments on proposed developments in relation to international codes and standards and regulations; and

- considers and advises on research proposals and other initiatives undertaken to inform the FRC on matters material to its remit and any resultant publications.

In June 2013, the FRC established a UK GAAP Technical Advisory Group (TAG) to assist the Accounting Council. The TAG advises the Accounting Council on all issues relating to UK accounting standards, including areas where unsatisfactory or conflicting interpretations of accounting standards or Companies Act provisions have developed or seem likely to develop, as well as those relating to smaller entities.

The TAG and Committee for Accounting on Public Benefit Entities (CAPE) are advisory committees to assist the Accounting Council in relation to the development of SORPs by SORP-making bodies by carrying out a limited review of a SORP (see 4.7 above). An Academic Panel also meets regularly to discuss issues relating to the FRC's work. The Accounting Council may also establish short-term advisory groups to provide input to specific projects.

The FRC's procedure for issuing accounting standards is set out in *FRC Codes & Standards: Procedures.*[27]

7.2   Scope and authority of accounting standards

The *Foreword to Accounting Standards*, last updated in November 2012, explains the authority, scope and application of accounting standards, known as Financial Reporting Standards (FRSs) issued by the FRC. The Foreword addresses accounting standards applicable in Companies Act accounts. Some key points included in the Foreword are addressed below.

Statements of standard accounting practice issued prior to 2 July 2012, unless withdrawn, are treated as statements of standard accounting practice issued by the designated body.[28] Previous UK GAAP is withdrawn for financial years beginning on or after 1 January 2015 or on early application of FRS 100 and FRS 27 is withdrawn on implementation of FRS 103 (see 4.3 above). Therefore, extant SSAPs, FRSs, the FRSSE, UITF Abstracts and FRC Abstracts are 'accounting standards' for the purposes of the Companies Act 2006 and the Regulations or the Small Companies Regulations.

The Regulations require Companies Act accounts prepared by companies (other than those prepared by companies subject to the small companies regime, and the individual accounts of medium-sized companies) to state whether the accounts have been prepared in accordance with applicable accounting standards, giving particulars of any material departures from those standards and the reasons. *[Foreword to Accounting Standards.4, 7, Regulations 4].* See 4.6.1 above.

Accounting standards are applicable to the financial statements of a reporting entity that are intended to give a true and fair view of its state of affairs at the balance sheet date and of its profit or loss (or income or expenditure) for the financial period ending on that date. This includes entities incorporated under the Companies Act 2006 and preparing Companies Act accounts and also entities not constituted as companies but that are otherwise required to prepare financial statements that are intended to give a true and fair view. Accounting standards need not be applied to immaterial items. *[Foreword to Accounting Standard.13].*

Accounting standards should be applied to UK and Republic of Ireland group financial statements (including amounts relating to overseas entities included in those financial statements) but are not intended to apply to financial statements of overseas entities for local purposes. *[Foreword to Accounting Standards.14].*

Where accounting standards prescribe information to be contained in financial statements, such requirements do not override exemptions from disclosures given by law, and utilised by, certain types of entity. *[Foreword to Accounting Standards.15].*

Accounting standards are authoritative statements of how particular types of transactions and other events should be reflected in financial statements and accordingly, compliance with accounting standards will normally be necessary for financial statements to give a true and fair view. In applying accounting standards, it is important to be guided by the spirit and reasoning behind them (set out in the material accompanying FRSs or FRC Abstracts). *[Foreword to Accounting Standards.16-17].*

The FRC envisage that only in exceptional circumstances will departure from the requirements of an accounting standard be necessary in order to give a true and fair view. In such circumstances, the requirements of the accounting standard should be departed from to the extent necessary to give a true and fair view and informed and unbiased judgement used to devise an alternative appropriate accounting treatment, consistent with the economic and commercial characteristics of the circumstances concerned. Particulars of the departure, the reasons and the financial effects are required (the disclosures made should be consistent with that given for departures from specific accounting provisions of company law). *[Foreword to Accounting Standards.18-19].*

Where a FRED is issued, the requirements of any existing accounting standards that would be affected by the FRED proposals remain in force. Where reporting entities wish to provide additional information reflecting the FRED proposals, in the FRC's view this can be done by incorporating the information (providing it does not conflict with existing accounting standards) into the financial statements. However, the proposals may change and the consequences of this should be considered. Alternatively, the information could be presented in supplementary form. *[Foreword to Accounting Standards.27-28].*

7.2.1   Accounting standards and true and fair

Section 393 of the Companies Act 2006 requires that the directors of a company must not approve accounts unless they are satisfied that they give a true and fair view of the assets, liabilities, financial position and profit or loss. *[s393].*

Predecessor bodies to the FRC obtained legal opinions that have confirmed the centrality of the true and fair concept to the preparation and audit of financial statements, whether prepared in accordance with UK accounting standards or international accounting standards. The latest Opinion written by Martin Moore QC (2008) followed the enactment of the Companies Act 2006 and the introduction of international accounting standards and endorsed the analysis in the earlier Opinions of Leonard Hoffman QC (1983) and Mary Arden (1984) and Mary Arden QC (1993) as to the approach that Courts would take to accounting standards when considering whether accounts show a true and fair view.

In October 2013, the Department of Business, Skills and Innovation (BIS) published a ministerial statement:

'The Department of Business has given serious consideration to concerns raised by some stakeholders that accounts prepared over the past 30 years, in accordance with UK or international financial reporting standards, have not been properly prepared under UK and EU law.

'However, it is entirely satisfied that the concerns expressed are misconceived and that the existing legal framework, including international financial reporting standards, is binding under European Law.

'In preparing financial statements, achieving a true and fair view is and remains the overriding objective (and legal requirement). In the vast majority of cases, compliance with accounting standards will result in a true and fair view. However, where compliance with an accounting standard may not achieve that objective, accounting standards expressly provide that that standard may be overridden. ...'

The FRC published its independent legal advice, available on the FRC website. The Opinion written by Martin Moore QC (3 October 2013) – *International Accounting Standards and the true and fair view* – considered issues addressed in an Opinion written by George Bompas QC (8 April 2013), in particular the interaction of

International Accounting Standards and the legal requirement that directors must not approve accounts that do not show a true and fair view, and the place of prudence.

However, both the FRC (in its Press Notice of 3 October 2013) and the BIS ministerial statement noted scope for improvements in aspects of international financial reporting standards and the IASB's Conceptual Framework, for example:

- stewardship reporting (i.e. holding directors to account for their management of the company's property) should be regarded as a primary objective of financial reporting;

- prudence (i.e. the exercise of caution), should be explicitly acknowledged in the Conceptual Framework; and

- there should be clear principles to describe when specific measurement bases, such as fair value (which needs to be appropriately defined) should be used. Performance reporting should present movements in fair value clearly and appropriately.

The FRC noted that investors raised other concerns and that it looked forward to working with investors and other stakeholders to address the full range of issues.

In June 2014, the FRC issued updated guidance – *True and Fair*. This confirms the fundamental importance of the true and fair requirement in both IFRSs and UK GAAP, whether applying FRS 100 to FRS 103 or previous UK GAAP. This guidance emphasises the application of objective professional judgement, which applies at all stages of preparation of the financial statements, to ensure the financial statements give a true and fair view. The guidance specifically addresses the concept of prudence and reflecting the substance of transactions under both IFRSs and UK GAAP.

The FRC expects preparers, those charged with governance and auditors to stand back and ensure that the financial statements as a whole give a true and fair view, provide additional disclosures where compliance with an accounting standard is insufficient to present a true and fair view, to use the true and fair override where compliance with the standards does not result in the presentation of a true and fair view and to ensure that the consideration they give to these matters is evident in their deliberations and documentation. See Chapter 4 at 8.2.

7.3   UK GAAP

UK GAAP is a wider concept than accounting standards, as defined at 7.2 above. For example, UK GAAP can include:

- SORPs (where an entity is within the scope of a SORP – see 4.7 above);

- other pronouncements issued by the FRC or its predecessor bodies (such as FREDs or best practice Reporting Statements) – providing these do not conflict with an extant accounting standard;

- pronouncements by authoritative bodies, such as Technical Releases issued by the Institute of Chartered Accountants in England and Wales and/or the Institute of Chartered Accountants in Scotland (examples include TECH 02/10); and

- generally accepted accounting practice where areas are not covered by specific accounting standards. This could include reference to the requirements of other bodies of GAAP where it addresses an issue, but does not conflict with accounting standards. For example, FRS 102 permits but does not require management to refer to the requirements of EU-adopted IFRS dealing with similar and related issues in developing and applying a reliable and relevant accounting policy *[FRS 102.10.6]*. Generally accepted accounting practice can also include established industry practice in accounting for transactions.

In addition, an entity must comply with any legal or regulatory requirements applicable to its annual report and financial statements, including the overall requirement for directors of a company to prepare accounts that give a true and fair view.

References

1 http://ec.europa.eu/internal_market/securities/isd/mifid/index_en.htm

2 Now Section 401 of Companies Act 2006.

3 AIM Rules, para. 19, Glossary.

4 https://www.gov.uk/government/consultations/eu-accounting-directive-smaller-companies-reporting

5 FRSSE, footnote 9.

6 Status of the FRSSE, para. 9.

7 FRSSE, paragraph 2.6, footnote 11.

8 s464, *The Statutory Auditors (Amendment of Companies Act 2006 and Delegation of Functions etc.) Order 2012* (SI 2012/1741).

9 *The Accounting Standards (Prescribed Bodies) (United States of America and Japan) Regulations 2012* permits companies with securities registered with the SEC or publicly traded on specified Japanese exchanges (but that do not have securities admitted to trading on an (EEA) regulated market) to prepare consolidated financial statements (but not individual financial statements) using US GAAP or JGAAP. Such consolidated financial statements would also be Companies Act accounts. This dispensation applies for financial years ending on or prior to 31 December 2014.

10 *TECH 02/10 Guidance on the determination of realised profits and losses in the context of distributions under the Companies Act 2006*, ICAEW/ICAS, February 2010, paras. 3.28 and 3.29. Also section 853(4) of Companies Act 2006.

11 *TECH 02/10 Guidance on the determination of realised profits and losses in the context of distributions under the Companies Act 2006*, ICAEW/ICAS, February 2010, paras. 3.30 to 3.33.

12 *TECH 02/10 Guidance on the determination of realised profits and losses in the context of distributions under the Companies Act 2006*, ICAEW/ICAS, February 2010, paras. 3.35.

13 *TECH 02/10 Guidance on the determination of realised profits and losses in the context of distributions under the Companies Act 2006*, ICAEW/ICAS, February 2010, paras. 3.34 and 3.37.

14 *TECH 02/10 Guidance on the determination of realised profits and losses in the context of distributions under the Companies Act 2006*, ICAEW/ICAS, February 2010, para. 3.36.

15 Listing Rules, FCA, para. 9.8.6(5), (6).

Chapter 1

16 Listing Rules, FCA, para. 9.8.6(5), (6).
17 Status of the FRSSE 5 16.2.
18 Para 4, SI 2008/489.
19 This list omits the disclosures required in the directors' report by Schedule 7 to the Regulations for quoted companies, companies with securities carrying voting rights admitted to trading on a regulated market, or public companies acquiring their own shares. Most quoted companies and companies with securities carrying voting rights admitted to trading on a regulated market are likely to be public companies and, therefore, unlikely to qualify for the small companies regime.
20 Registrars' Rules.
21 Companies House Guidance is available at: http://www.companieshouse.gov.uk/ infoAndGuide/faq/exemptionStatements. shtml
22 APB Bulletin 2008/04 – *The special auditor's report on abbreviated accounts in the United Kingdom*, APB, para. 35.
23 Para 4, SI 2008/489.
24 Registrars' Rules.
25 Para 4, SI 2008/489.
26 See footnote 10 above. *The Accounting Standards (Prescribed Bodies) (United States of America and Japan) Regulations 2012* extended the prescribed bodies for issuing accounting standards to include the FASB and the Accounting Standards Board of Japan for group accounts of parent companies with securities registered with the Securities Exchange Commission of the United States of America and specified Japanese exchanges respectively, with the restrictions set out in the statutory instrument.
27 https://www.frc.org.uk/About-the-FRC/ Procedures/Regulatory-policies.aspx
28 s464, SI 2012/1741.

Chapter 2   Scope of FRS 102

Chapter 2 Scope of FRS 102

1 INTRODUCTION

FRS 100 – *Application of Financial Reporting Requirements*, which sets out the new financial reporting framework in the UK and Republic of Ireland, applies to entities preparing financial statements in accordance with legislation, regulation or accounting standards applicable in the UK and the Republic of Ireland (ROI). *[FRS 100.1]*. See Chapter 1.

Section 1 – *Scope* – sets out which entities can apply FRS 102 – *The Financial Reporting Standard Applicable in the UK and Republic of Ireland.* Its requirements, discussed further at 2.1 below, are consistent with the general financial reporting framework set out in FRS 100. The standard applies to financial statements intended to give a true and fair view. As its application is not restricted to UK and Irish companies, all entities should ensure that preparation of their financial statements in accordance with FRS 102 is permitted by the legal framework in which they operate. The legal framework for UK companies is discussed in more detail in Chapter 1 at 6.

FRS 103 – *Insurance Contracts – Consolidated accounting and reporting requirements for entities in the UK and Republic of Ireland issuing insurance contracts* (see 1.2.4 below) applies to financial statements prepared in accordance with FRS 102 by entities with insurance contracts and financial instruments with discretionary participation features. *[FRS 103.1.1]*.

Section 1 of this chapter sets out the development of FRS 102 and its ongoing review, its effective date, and structure of the standard. Section 2 of this chapter then addresses the scope of the standard, which is set out in Section 1 – *Scope* – of FRS 102. Section 3 of this chapter discusses the reduced disclosure framework available to qualifying entities in their individual financial statements. Section 4 discusses how exemptions available for small companies, companies that are micro-entities and medium-sized companies under UK companies legislation interact with the standard.

Except where otherwise stated, the rest of this chapter will refer to the requirements for UK companies, and therefore will refer to UK GAAP (prior to implementation of FRS 100 to FRS 103) as 'previous UK GAAP'. UK LLPs and other entities preparing financial statements in accordance with Part 15 of the Companies Act 2006 are subject to similar requirements, modified as necessary by the regulations that govern the content of their financial statements.

1.1   Summary

This summary covers a number of areas relevant to the scope of FRS 102 and to its structure which are addressed more fully in the chapter, as indicated.

- Adoption of FRS 102 is voluntary – the standard applies to the financial statements of entities preparing financial statements in accordance with legislation, regulation or accounting standards applicable in the UK and the Republic of Ireland that are *not* prepared in accordance with EU-adopted IFRS, FRS 101 – *Reduced Disclosure Framework* or the Financial Reporting Standard for Smaller Entities (FRSSE).

- The standard is effective for accounting periods beginning on or after 1 January 2015. It can be applied for accounting periods ending on or after 31 December 2012 except for entities within the scope of a SORP, this is providing it does not conflict with the requirements of a current SORP or legal requirements for the preparation of financial statements (see 1.3.1 below).

- FRS 102 applies to general purpose financial statements of entities, including public benefit entities (see 2.4.2 below) that are intended to give a true and fair view. FRS 102 can be applied in consolidated and/or individual financial statements.

- FRS 102 does not set out which entities must prepare financial statements; this is governed by the legal framework (or other regulation or requirements), if any, relating to the preparation of the entity's financial statements. Statutory accounts prepared in accordance with FRS 102 by a UK company are Companies Act accounts. See 2.1 below.

- FRS 102 is a single financial reporting standard based on the IFRS for SMEs, which itself generally includes simplified requirements and disclosures compared to full IFRSs. A number of modifications have been made to FRS 102 compared to the IFRS for SMEs (see 1.2 below). While largely based on IFRSs, FRS 102 is not just a simplified version of IFRSs. In certain cases, the standard includes direct references to IFRSs.

- Since FRS 102 includes less guidance than IFRSs, judgement is likely to be required in applying the standard. Section 10 – *Accounting Policies, Estimates and Errors* – of the standard sets out a 'GAAP hierarchy' that management should refer to in developing and applying relevant and reliable accounting policies where the standard does not specifically address the issue. This hierarchy includes references to applicable SORPs. Certain SORPs have been updated to comply with FRS 102 whereas others will be withdrawn on implementation of FRS 102. See 2.2 below. In addition, management may but is not required to refer to IFRSs addressing similar and related issues.

- FRS 102 requires certain types of entities to directly apply particular IFRSs, namely IAS 33 – *Earnings per Share*, IFRS 6 – *Exploration for and Evaluation of Mineral Resources* – and IFRS 8 – *Operating Segments*. These standards apply to FRS 102 reporters that would fall within the scope of these standards if applying IFRS. See 2.3 below.

- In addition, an entity applying FRS 102 has a choice of applying the recognition and measurement requirements for financial instruments in:

    - IAS 39 – *Financial Instruments: Recognition and Measurement*, or

    - IFRS 9 – *Financial Instruments* – and/or IAS 39 (as amended by IFRS 9), or

    - Section 11 – *Basic Financial Instruments* – and Section 12 – *Other Financial Instruments Issues* – of the standard.

  Whatever policy choice for the recognition and measurement of financial instruments is followed, FRS 102 reporters must give the disclosures included in Sections 11 and 12 and follow the presentation requirements (on offset of financial assets and financial liabilities – see 1.2.3.A below) in these sections, rather than those required by IFRSs. See Chapter 8 at 8.

- FRS 102 requires an entity to apply FRS 103 to insurance contracts (including reinsurance contracts) that it issues and reinsurance contracts that it holds, and financial instruments with a discretionary participation feature that it issues. FRS 103 is based on IFRS 4 – *Insurance Contracts*, with certain modifications, and includes relevant accounting requirements from FRS 27 – *Life assurance* – and the ABI SORP – *Accounting for Insurance Business* (which the standard supersedes). It permits entities, generally, to continue with existing accounting policies for insurance contracts, whilst permitting entities the same flexibility to make improvements (subject to legal and regulatory requirements) as for entities applying IFRS. The standard is likely to result in increased disclosures for many entities. See 1.2.4 below.

- Since statutory accounts prepared by UK companies in accordance with FRS 102 are Companies Act accounts, these must comply with the requirements of the Companies Act 2006 and of *The Large and Medium-Sized Companies and Groups (Accounts and Reports) Regulations 2008* (SI 2008/410) ('the Regulations') or *The Small Companies and Groups (Accounts and Directors' Report) Regulations 2008* (SI 2008/409) ('the Small Companies Regulations'), as applicable.[1] The Companies Act 2006 and the relevant regulations set out the formats for the balance sheet and profit and loss account (see below), recognition and measurement principles and further disclosure requirements. While FRS 102 (and Appendix IV to the standard) highlight certain issues relevant to Companies Act accounts, the discussion in the standard is not comprehensive. See 4 below, Chapter 1 at 6 and Chapter 4 at 8 and 9.

- FRS 102 reporters must prepare a balance sheet and profit and loss account (as a separate income statement or as a section of a single statement of comprehensive income) in accordance with the Regulations (or LLP Regulations), as applicable. This also applies even if an entity is not subject to the Regulations (or LLP Regulations), except to the extent that these requirements are not permitted by any statutory framework under which such entities report. See Chapter 4 at 4 and 5.

- Section 34 – *Specialised Activities* – sets out specific accounting and disclosure requirements for agriculture, extractive activities, service concession arrangements, financial institutions, retirement benefit funds, heritage assets, funding commitments, and certain issues specific to public benefit entities. Paragraphs marked PBE throughout the standard are specific to public benefit entities, and not for general application. See 2.4 below.

  Section 34, in particular, sets out additional disclosure requirements for the financial statements of a financial institution (or for the consolidated financial statements of a group containing a financial institution) and for the financial statements of a retirement benefit fund. The definition of a 'financial institution' is discussed at 2.4.1.A below.

- FRS 102 includes a reduced disclosure framework for qualifying entities, available in their individual financial statements only. A qualifying entity is a member of a group included in publicly available consolidated financial statements intended to give a true and fair view. Some of the disclosure exemptions available under the reduced disclosure framework are conditional on equivalent disclosures being included in the publicly available consolidated financial statements of a parent of the entity which are intended to give a true and fair view and in which the entity is consolidated. In addition, a financial institution has fewer exemptions than an entity that is not a financial institution. See 3 below.

- Section 35 – *Transition to this FRS* – addresses transition to FRS 102. Section 35 is based on a simplified version of IFRS 1 – *First-time Adoption of International Financial Reporting Standards*, but with significant modifications. See Chapter 30.

1.2   Development of FRS 102

FRED 44 – *Financial Reporting Standard for Medium-sized Entities*, published in 2010, proposed that the standard, based on the IFRS for SMEs, would apply to entities that did not have public accountability. Under the proposals, entities that did have public accountability would have been required to apply EU-adopted IFRS. However, respondents were not supportive of the extension of the application of EU-adopted IFRS, and the former ASB decided to amend the IFRS for SMEs so that it is relevant to a broader group of preparers and users. *[FRS 102 Summary (viii)]*. See 1.2.1 below.

In developing the new framework, the FRC has set out an overriding objective to enable users of accounts to receive high-quality understandable financial reporting proportionate to the size and complexity of the entity and users' information needs. See Chapter 1 at 4.

The Accounting Council noted that the IFRS for SMEs achieves a consistent accounting framework (as a simplification of IFRSs), reflects more up-to-date thinking and developments than current FRS, especially for financial instruments (where the Accounting Council did not consider the non-recognition of derivatives under current FRSs adequately reflected the risks arising from financial instruments), is a single book setting out clear accounting requirements, and is a cost effective way of updating current FRS. *[FRS 102.AC.22-23].*

The requirements in FRS 102 were principally consulted on in four exposure drafts:

- FRED 44 – *Financial Reporting Standard for Medium-sized Entities* (October 2010);
- FRED 45 – *Financial Reporting Standard for Public Benefit Entities* (March 2011);
- FRED 48 – *Financial Reporting Standard applicable in the UK and Republic of Ireland* (January 2012);
- Amendment to FRED 48 (October 2012).

FRS 102 was published in March 2013 (and FRS 103 in March 2014). Amendments to FRS 102 – *The Financial Reporting Standard applicable in the UK and Republic of Ireland – Basic financial instruments and Hedge Accounting –* were published in July 2014. See 1.2.3.B below.

1.2.1   Amendments made in FRS 102 compared to the IFRS for SMEs

The Accounting Council set out objectives and guidelines for amending the IFRS for SMEs, for application in the UK and Republic of Ireland (ROI).

The objective is that the FRC maintains its commitment to:

- ensuring high-quality financial reporting by UK and ROI entities applying FRS 102;
- operate under an international accounting framework; and
- acknowledge that users' preference for consistent financial reporting must be balanced with costs to preparers. *[FRS 102.AC.24].*

The guidelines followed in considering amendments to the IFRS for SMEs are:

- Changes should be made to permit accounting treatments that exist in FRSs at the transition date that align with EU-adopted IFRS.

    Examples include amendments to permit entities to adopt accounting policies of:

    (i)   capitalisation of borrowing costs (as an alternative to expensing borrowing costs required under the IFRS for SMEs);

    (ii) capitalisation of development costs (as an alternative to expensing development costs required under the IFRS for SMEs); and

    (iii) revaluation of property, plant and equipment (or where strict criteria are met, revaluation of intangible assets) (as an alternative to the cost model required under the IFRS for SMEs).

- Changes should be consistent with EU-adopted IFRS unless a non-IFRS based solution clearly better meets the objective of providing high-quality understandable financial reporting proportionate to the size and complexity of the entity and the users' information needs. In these cases, elements of an IFRS-based solution may nevertheless be retained.

Examples include:

(i)   alignment of the requirements for defined benefit pension accounting with IAS 19 (2011) – *Employee Benefits* (as the IFRS for SMEs was based on an earlier version of IAS 19);

(ii) amendment of the hedge accounting provisions, based on a simplified version of IFRS 9;

(iii) scoping out financial guarantee contracts from financial instruments accounting (a non-IFRS based solution);

(iv) Section 29 – *Income Tax* – was extensively re-written and sets out a 'timing differences plus' approach (which is neither previous UK GAAP nor IFRSs).

- Use should be made, where possible, of existing exemptions in company law to avoid gold-plating.

  Examples include:

  (i)   adding the related party disclosure exemption for intra-group transactions involving wholly-owned subsidiaries (previously in FRS 8 – *Related party disclosures*); and

  (ii) permitting merger accounting for group reconstructions (based on the requirements in FRS 6 – *Acquisitions and mergers*).

- Changes should be made to provide clarification, by reference to EU-adopted IFRS that will avoid unnecessary diversity in practice.

  Examples include requiring entities within the scope of these standards to apply IAS 33, IFRS 6 and IFRS 8.

- Changes necessary in order to comply with company law in the UK and ROI.

  Examples include:

  (i)   incorporation of the concept of the 'true and fair override';

  (ii) use of the profit or loss account and balance sheet formats in the Regulations;

  (iii) adding disclosures for certain financial instruments required by law;

  (iv) aligning the requirements for a UK (and Irish) company for preparation of consolidated accounts with UK (and Irish) company law; and

  (v)   ensuring consistency of the treatment of step-acquisitions (and disposals) with UK (and Irish) company law. [FRS 102.AC.24, 26].

The examples given above are not a complete list of the amendments. For instance, Section 34 addresses a broader range of topics than the same section in the IFRS for SMEs and includes significant modifications to the topics addressed by the latter.

Appendix II to FRS 102 summarises significant differences between FRS 102 and the IFRS for SMEs. The Accounting Council Advice includes a table of significant amendments made together with the reason for the amendment, by reference to the above guidelines and compliance with the law. [FRS 102.AC.26].

1.2.2 *Ongoing review of FRS 102*

It is expected that the FRC will consider whether to update FRS 102 (for changes to IFRSs or to the IFRS for SMEs) on a three-year cycle. *[FRS 102.AC.40]*.

The first periodic review of the standard will not be until 2016/2017, with a view to the revised FRS 102 being effective in 2018. Changes made to the IFRS for SMEs, following the IASB's recent review, will not impact FRS 102 (effective 1 January 2015) but would be reviewed in more detail as part of the three yearly review of FRS 102. This is in order to evaluate whether amendments to FRS 102 would be appropriate and/or desirable.[2]

However, the Accounting Council Advice noted that there may be circumstances where FRS 102 would require updating in an interim period between the three-year cycles, but where this occurred the amendments proposed should be limited. *[FRS 102.AC.40]*. Details of changes proposed or made to FRS 102 since its publication in March 2013 (aside from the publication of FRS 103) are at 1.2.3 below.

In June 2013, the FRC established a UK GAAP Technical Advisory Group (TAG) to assist the Accounting Council. The Accounting Council and the TAG will review any issues relating to the implementation of FRS 102, as they arise. Decisions will be taken on a case-by-case basis about the best way to address issues such as editorial points, areas where FRS 102 is silent, and areas where divergence in accounting practice seems to be emerging (see details on the FRC website).

1.2.3 *Changes made or anticipated prior to FRS 102 becoming effective 1 January 2015*

1.2.3.A *Editorial amendments and clarification statements made to FRS 102 (effective 1 January 2015)*

The FRC has made the following editorial amendments and clarification statements (which are published on the FRC website):

- Section 1 – early application of FRS 102 by entities within the scope of a SORP (August 2013) – see 1.3.1 below;
- Sections 11 and 12 – presentation requirements for financial instruments where IAS 39 or IFRS 9 (and/or IAS 39) is followed;
- Section 12 – Net investment hedges of foreign operations that are branches (November 2013);
- Section 29 – Deferred tax arising on a business combination (November 2013); and
- Section 35 – Transitional exemptions in relation to accounting for service concession arrangements (March 2014).

1.2.3.B *July 2014 Amendments to FRS 102 – Basic Financial Instruments and Hedge Accounting*

The Accounting Council originally intended to amend FRS 102 prior to its effective date should consultation determine that this is appropriate, although the exact timetable was dependent upon when IFRS 9's impairment and hedge accounting requirements are completed. *[FRS 102.AC.58]*. Given the delay in the timetable for finalising the impairment sections of IFRS 9 (the final standard was published in July 2014), the FRC has since announced it does not plan to make amendments concerning impairment of financial assets prior to 1 January 2015.[3] These amendments have the same effective date as the original standard (but there are some transitional reliefs set out in paragraphs 1.14A to 1.14B for those entities that authorised FRS 102 financial statements prior to 1 August 2014). See Chapter 8 for FRS 102's requirements (as amended) on financial instruments and hedge accounting and Chapter 30 at 5.16 and 5.17 for the transition requirements on hedge accounting and designation of financial instruments at fair value through profit and loss (including transitional reliefs available for entities that have already adopted the standard).

1.2.3.C   FRED 55 – Draft Amendments to FRS 102 – Pension Obligations

The FRC issued FRED 55 – *Draft Amendments to FRS 102 – Pension Obligations* – in August 2014. This clarifies, as a pragmatic solution, that, for entities already recognising assets or liabilities for defined benefit plans in accordance with FRS 102, no additional liabilities shall be recognised in respect of a 'schedule of contributions' even if such an agreement would otherwise be considered onerous. FRED 55 does not address the recognition of a plan surplus as an asset but clarifies that the effect of restricting the recognition of a surplus in a defined benefit plan (except for any amount included in net interest on the net defined benefit liability), where the surplus is not recoverable, shall be recognised in other comprehensive income (OCI) rather than in profit or loss.

1.2.3.D   FRED 56 – Draft FRS 104 – Interim Financial Reporting

The FRC issued FRED 56 – *Draft FRS 104 – Interim Financial Reporting* – in November 2014. FRS 104, once finalised, will apply to interim financial reports, providing applicable laws or regulations do not prohibit its application. It is intended for use by entities preparing annual financial statements in accordance with FRS 102 but can be applied by any entity (e.g. an FRS 101 reporter). An FRS 101 reporter should read any reference to a specific requirement in FRS 102 as a reference to the equivalent requirement in EU-adopted IFRS, as amended by AG1 of FRS 101 – *Reduced Disclosure Framework*.

Draft FRS 104 does not mandate which entities publish interim financial reports. If an entity makes a statement of compliance with the standard, then it must comply with all its provisions. The standard, once finalised, will be a pronouncement on interim reporting for the purposes of the directors' responsibility statement in relation to half-yearly reports in DTR 4.2.10(4)R, i.e. the responsibility statement can state that the interim financial report complies with FRS 104 rather than that it gives a true and fair view.

The draft standard is based on IAS 34 – *Interim Financial Reporting* – with some differences. These reflect differences between FRS 102 and IFRS, and also the fact that some requirements affecting interim financial reports are included in other IFRSs or IFRICs than IAS 34. Differences highlighted in the Accounting Council's Advice to draft FRS 104 include:

- fair value disclosure requirements apply only if the same disclosures are required in the FRS 102 annual financial statements;

- related party disclosures may be omitted for transactions between wholly owned members of a group;

- disclosure requirements when an entity adopts a new accounting framework, (e.g. converts to FRS 102) have been inserted. These are generally consistent with those required by Section 35 of FRS 102 and are less extensive than those required by IFRS 1;

- the omission of IAS 34's requirement to disclose, in the annual financial statements, significant changes of estimates reported in a previous interim period; and

- the principle that frequency of reporting should not affect the measurement of the annual results has been qualified where FRS 102 would prohibit a reversal of an impairment (this anticipates changes relating to reversal of impairment of goodwill pursuant to the new Accounting Directive – see 1.2.3.E below).

1.2.3.E   Amendments pursuant to the new EU Accounting Directive

The FRC issued *Consultation Document: Accounting standards for small entities – Implementation of the EU Accounting Directive* – in September 2014. See Chapter 1 at 4.4.2 for a discussion of the changes arising from the new Accounting Directive and the FRC's proposals on changes to the financial reporting framework arising from implementation of the new Accounting Directive.

The FRC propose that the FRSSE will be withdrawn, with effect for financial years beginning on or after 1 January 2016. In its place, micro-entities (see Chapter 1 at 4.4.2) will be able to apply the Financial Reporting Standard for Micro-Entities ('FRSME'). This new standard will be based on the recognition and measurement requirements in FRS 102 (but with significant simplifications) and its presentation and disclosure requirements will be in line with the statutory requirements for micro-entities. Small entities will be able to apply FRS 102's recognition and measurement requirements but a new section setting out the framework and presentation and disclosure requirements (limited to the statutory disclosures permitted by the Directive) for small entities will replace those in the standard. Small entities will not be required to present a cash flow statement or prepare group accounts. However, the financial statements of small companies will still be required to give a true and fair view. If the financial statements do not give a true and fair view, additional disclosures may be needed.

Otherwise, the scope of FRS 102 remains the same, i.e. FRS 102 is applied by entities other than those applying the FRSME, EU-adopted IFRS, FRS 101 (or FRS 102, as applied by small entities). An entity will continue to have the option to apply a more comprehensive accounting standard.

Amendments to FRS 102 will be necessary arising from implementation of the new Accounting Directive. These include amendments to:

- remove the concept of extraordinary items;

- change the useful life of goodwill and intangible assets to refer to 10 years where an entity is not able to reliably estimate the useful life;

- prohibit the reversal of goodwill impairment; and

- remove specific references to legal requirements that will have become out of date.

The FRC will also consider whether to amend FRS 102 if the legislation allows for alternative formats or the use of the equity method for investments in subsidiaries, associates and joint ventures in separate financial statements. Other amendments may be identified in the process of implementation of the new Accounting Directive.

1.2.4   FRS 103

FRS 103 provides consolidated accounting and reporting requirements for entities in the UK and Republic of Ireland issuing insurance contracts that apply FRS 102.

An entity applying FRS 102 is required to apply FRS 103 to insurance contracts (including reinsurance contracts) that the entity issues and reinsurance contracts that the entity holds, and to financial instruments (other than insurance contracts) that the entity issues with a discretionary participation feature. It is a transactional based standard and therefore applies to entities that are non-insurers as well as entities considered insurers for legal or supervisory purposes. *[FRS 103.1.2].*

The FRC states that FRS 103 (and its accompanying Implementation Guidance) consolidates existing financial reporting requirements for insurance contracts. FRS 103 is largely a copy of IFRS 4. In substance, FRS 103 allows entities, generally, to continue with their current accounting practices for insurance contracts, but permits entities the same flexibility to make improvements (subject to legal and regulatory requirements) as entities in the UK and Republic of Ireland that apply IFRSs. *[FRS 103.Summary (vii)].* Those current accounting practices will, in most cases, be based on the ABI SORP. For those entities which are insurance companies as defined by the Companies Act 2006, the financial statements will continue to be prepared under Schedule 3 to the Regulations. Entities are permitted to change their accounting policies for insurance contracts (on transition or subsequently) only if the change is either more reliable and no less relevant (to the economic decision-making needs of users) or more relevant and no less reliable. *[FRS 103.1.5, 2.3].*

FRS 103 replicates the definition of an insurance contract contained within IFRS 4. *[FRS 103.Glossary].* For those insurers previously applying FRS 26 – *Financial instruments: recognition and measurement*, which contains the same definition, we would not normally expect to see recognition or measurement differences in terms of what qualifies as an insurance contract upon transition from previous UK GAAP to FRS 103. For those insurers that have not previously applied FRS 26, there may be recognition and measurement differences and those insurers would be expected to perform a product classification exercise to determine the extent, if any, of such differences.

Although FRS 103 is largely a copy of IFRS 4, some changes have been made. The more important of these are that:

- equalisation reserves are permitted to be recognised as a liability where this is required by the regulatory framework that applies to the entity, e.g. Schedule 3 to the Regulations (IFRS 4 prohibits equalisation reserves to be recognised as a liability, although FRS 103 makes a consequential amendment to FRS 101 to permit recognition of equalisation reserves as a liability where this is required by the regulatory framework applying to the entity); *[FRS 103.1.14, 2.13(a), IG28]*

- a discretionary participation feature may only be recognised in equity where this is permitted by the Regulations (IFRS 4 does not have this restriction); *[FRS 103.2.30]*

- unearned premium reserves and deferred acquisition costs are considered to be monetary items for the purpose of Section 30 – *Foreign Currency Translation* – of FRS 102; *[FRS 103.2.26]*

- there is a requirement that entities setting accounting policies for the first time must first consider Section 3 – *Financial Statement Presentation* – of FRS 102, the Regulations and any relevant parts of FRS 102 as a means of establishing current practice as a benchmark before setting those policies (i.e. where the benchmark policies are not followed, the policies adopted should be more reliable and no less relevant, or more relevant and no less reliable than those benchmark policies). *[FRS 103.1.5]*.

- for long-term business, certain parts of the ABI SORP and FRS 27 have been embedded into FRS 103 (although an entity is permitted to change those policies). *[FRS 103.3.1-3.18]*.

- The non-mandatory Implementation Guidance and Illustrative Examples contained in IFRS 4 have been removed. Instead, FRS 103 contains its own non-mandatory Implementation Guidance, largely derived from the ABI SORP and FRS 27, explaining how to imply FRS 103, FRS 102 and the requirements of Schedule 3.

When FRS 103 is applied, both FRS 27 and the ABI SORP cease to have effect. *[FRS 103.1.13]*.

The main impact of FRS 103 will be an increase in disclosures. For those entities already adopting FRS 26 (i.e. many life insurers) the impact will be less significant. However, for those entities not already adopting FRS 26 (i.e. many general insurers) the impact of the new disclosures will be significant.

The FRC expects to review the standard once the IASB has issued its updated standard on insurance contracts, although the exact timing of this review has yet to be determined. The FRC may make interim amendments to the standard once changes in the regulatory regime for insurers have been finalised. *[FRS 103.Summary (viii)]*.

1.3   Effective date

FRS 100, which sets out the framework for financial reporting under 'New UK and Irish GAAP', is mandatory for accounting periods beginning on or after 1 January 2015, with early application permitted subject to the early application requirements as set out in FRS 101, FRS 102 or the FRSSE (effective January 2015). *[FRS 100.10]*.

FRS 102 and FRS 103 (which applies to financial statements prepared in accordance with FRS 102) are mandatory, effective for accounting periods beginning on or after 1 January 2015 but are available for early application as explained below. *[FRS 102.1.14, FRS 103.1.1, 1.11]*. The July 2014 amendments to FRS 102 (see 1.2.2.B above) have the same effective date.

Early application of FRS 102 is permitted for accounting periods ending on or after 31 December 2012 but for entities within the scope of a SORP, this is providing it does not conflict with the requirements of a current SORP or legal requirements for the preparation of financial statements. If an entity applies FRS 102 before 1 January 2015 it shall disclose that fact. *[FRS 102.1.14]*.

FRS 103 may similarly be applied for accounting periods ending on or after 31 December 2012, provided that FRS 102 is applied from the same date (and that the entity is not subject to the transitional arrangements in paragraph 1.14 of FRS 102 relating to entities within scope of a SORP – described above) and early application is disclosed. *[FRS 103.1.11]*.

1.3.1   Effective date – entity subject to SORP

Current SORPs were prepared for use by entities adopting previous UK GAAP (and for some charities (see A below), there are legal requirements relating to the application of the current SORP). The FRC anticipates that most SORPs will be updated for consistency with FRS 102 and therefore has imposed a restriction on early application of the standard. See Chapter 1 at 4.7.1 for further details of the plans for extant SORPs.

The FRC has clarified that 'current SORPs, despite being written in the context of accounting standards that will be superseded by FRS 102, may not necessarily conflict with FRS 102. In considering whether a current SORP conflicts with FRS 102 an entity should have regard to the overall effect in practice.

In particular an entity should consider whether or not the recognition and measurement requirements of FRS 102 are consistent with a current SORP. For example if a current SORP is silent on a topic, accounting policies determined in accordance with FRS 102 should not conflict with the current SORP. Similarly, if a current SORP uses different terminology to express the same recognition and measurement concepts as required by FRS 102, compliance with FRS 102 should not automatically lead to non-compliance with that SORP.

In relation to disclosure requirements, where a SORP requires specific disclosures that are not required by FRS 102, additional disclosure can be provided in addition to those required by FRS 102 in order to meet both requirements.

Nevertheless, entities within the scope of a SORP will need to consider whether a legal or regulatory requirement prohibits the early application of FRS 102.'[4]

1.3.1.A   Charities

The current SORP is *Accounting and Reporting by Charities: Statement of Recommended Practice* (revised 2005) (SORP 2005). SORP 2005 was updated in 2008 to add references rather than change its requirements. A new SORP, consistent with FRS 102, has been developed by the joint SORP-making body, the Charity Commission and the Office of the Scottish Charity Regulator and was published in July 2014. A second SORP, consistent with the FRSSE, was also published in July 2014.

In England and Wales, charities reporting under the Charities Act 2011 or, in Scotland under the Charities and Trustee Investment (Scotland) Act 2005, are required by legislation to prepare financial statements (other than receipts and payments accounts) in accordance with the methods and principles of SORP 2005. Now that the new SORP, consistent with FRS 102, has been issued new accounting regulations will be updated to enable the new SORP to be applied.

SORP 2005 also applies to charitable companies (in England and Wales) reporting solely in accordance with the Companies Act 2006, and to charities in Northern Ireland or the Republic of Ireland, although this is not a legislative requirement.

The Charity Commission and the Office of the Scottish Charity Regulator have published a statement in *SORP Information Sheet 4: the adoption of FRS 102 by charities reporting under the SORP* that early adoption of FRS 102 by charities required by charity law to follow the methods and principles of SORP 2005 would conflict with that legislation, and that early adoption of FRS 102 by charities not required by charity law to follow the methods and principles of SORP 2005 would be impracticable as a number of FRS 102 requirements would conflict with SORP 2005.[5]

1.4   Structure of FRS 102

FRS 102 includes Section 1 which addresses the scope of the standard, Section 2 – *Concepts and Pervasive Principles*, Sections 3 to 33 each addressing a separate accounting topic, Section 34 on specialised activities (see 2.4 below) and Section 35 on transition to the standard.

All paragraphs have equal authority. Some sections include appendices of implementation guidance or examples. Some of these are an integral part of FRS 102 whereas others provide guidance, but each specifies its status. *[FRS 102.Summary (xiiii)-(xv).]*.

There is a detailed Glossary included in Appendix AI. Terms defined in the Glossary are in bold type the first time they appear in each section of the standard and in each sub-section of Section 34. *[FRS 102.Summary (xv)]*.

Appendix A4 – *Note on Legal Requirements* – provides an overview of how the requirements in FRS 102 address the requirements of the Companies Act 2006 (Appendix A6 – *Republic of Ireland (RoI) Legal References* – addresses Irish law).

Section 1 is addressed in this chapter. Other chapters of this publication address the other sections of the standard.

2   SCOPE

FRS 102 applies to financial statements that are intended to give a true and fair view of a reporting entity's financial position and profit or loss (or income or expenditure) for a period. *[FRS 102.1.1]*.

FRS 102 is designed to apply to general purpose financial statements, i.e. financial statements which are intended to focus on the common information needs of a wide range of users (such as shareholders, lenders, other creditors, employees and members of the public). *[FRS 102.Summary (xii)]*.

The standard applies to public benefit entities (PBEs) and other entities not just to companies. *[FRS 102.1.2]*. Paragraph numbers prefixed with a 'PBE' are applicable to public benefit entities, and are not applied directly or by analogy to entities that are not public benefit entities (other than, where specifically directed, entities within a public benefit entity group). *[FRS 102.1.2]*. These paragraphs are generally found in Section 34 but are not restricted to that section. See 2.4.2 below.

An entity must apply FRS 103 to insurance contracts (including reinsurance contracts) that it issues and reinsurance contracts that it holds and financial instruments with a discretionary participation feature that it issues. This is the same scope as for IFRS 4. *[FRS 102.1.6]*. See 1.2.4 above for information on FRS 103.

2.1   Basis of preparation of financial statements

FRS 100, which sets out the new financial reporting framework, applies to entities preparing financial statements in accordance with legislation, regulation or accounting standards applicable in the UK and the Republic of Ireland. *[FRS 100.1]*.

The individual or consolidated financial statements of any entity within the scope of FRS 100 (that is not required by the IAS Regulation or other legislation or regulation to be prepared in accordance with EU-adopted IFRS) must be prepared in accordance with:

- FRS 102;
- EU-adopted IFRS;
- the FRSSE (if the entity is a small entity eligible to apply that standard and chooses to do so); or
- FRS 101 (if the financial statements are individual financial statements of a qualifying entity) (see Chapter 31). *[FRS 100.4, FRS 102.1.3]*.

In theory, FRS 102 can also be used by entities that are not subject to the Companies Act 2006 (or Irish law). An entity's choice of financial reporting framework must be permitted by the legal framework or other regulations or requirements that govern the preparation of the entity's financial statements. Other agreements or arrangements (such as shareholders' agreements, banking agreements) may restrict the choice of financial reporting framework.

The above requirements in Section 1 of the standard largely reinforce the general requirements on basis of preparation of financial statements in FRS 100. The basis of preparation of financial statements in the UK is addressed in more detail in Chapter 1 at 4.4. The requirements of the Companies Act 2006 (and certain other regulatory rules) governing preparation of financial statements by UK companies are discussed in Chapter 1 at 6. Section 4 below addresses how the scope of FRS 102 interacts with exemptions available in the Companies Act 2006 for small and medium-sized companies, and micro-entities that are companies.

2.2 Application of SORPs

SORPs recommend accounting practices for specialised industries or sectors, and supplement accounting standards and other legal and regulatory requirements in light of the special factors prevailing or transactions undertaken in a particular industry or sector. *[FRS 102 Appendix I]*.

A number of SORPs have been (or are in the process of being) updated or withdrawn prior to the mandatory effective date of the 'New UK and Irish GAAP' framework (see Chapter 1 at 4.7.1).

Early application of FRS 102 (and FRS 103) by an entity subject to a SORP is subject to not conflicting with the requirements of a current SORP or legal requirements for the preparation of financial statements. *[FRS 102.1.14, FRS 103.1.11]*. See 1.3.1 above.

FRS 102 also makes reference to current SORPs (to the extent the provisions are in effect) as part of the hierarchy for management to consider when developing and applying accounting policies. *[FRS 102.10.5]*. The provisions of a SORP cease to apply, for instance, where they conflict with a more recent financial reporting standard. *[FRS 100.6 and footnote 6]*. See Chapter 7 at 3.2.

FRS 100 sets out the requirements on application of SORPs and the related disclosures where a SORP is followed, or in respect of departures from a SORP. See Chapter 1 at 4.7.

2.3 Extension of specific IFRSs to certain types of entities

As FRS 102 is accessible to a wider scope of entities than the IFRS for SMEs, the FRC has extended its requirements (compared to the IFRS for SMEs) to address specific issues by way of direct references to IFRSs (as adopted by the EU). These IFRSs apply with the same scope as the related IFRSs, as follows:

- IAS 33 – this standard applies to an entity whose ordinary shares or potential ordinary shares are publicly traded or that files, or is in the process of filing, its financial statements with a securities commission or other regulatory organisation for the purpose of issuing ordinary shares in a public market, or an entity that chooses to disclose earnings per share; *[FRS 102.1.4]*

- IFRS 6 – this standard applies to an entity engaged in the exploration for/and or evaluation of mineral resources (extractive industries); *[FRS 102.34.11-11C]*

- IFRS 8 – this standard applies to an entity whose debt or equity instruments are publicly traded, or that files, or is in the process of filing, its financial statements with a securities commission or other regulatory organisation for the purpose of issuing any class of instruments in a public market, or an entity that chooses to provide information described as segment information. If an entity discloses disaggregated information but that information does not comply with IFRS 8's requirements, the information shall not be described as segment information. *[FRS 102.1.5]*.

References to other IFRSs made in IAS 33, IFRS 6 or IFRS 8 shall be taken to be references to the relevant section or paragraph made in FRS 102 (except that, in paragraph 21 of IFRS 6, a cash generating unit or group of cash generating units shall be no larger than an operating segment and the reference to IFRS 8 shall be ignored). *[FRS 102.1.7, FRS 102.34.11A-B].*

2.4   Specialised activities

FRS 102 has a section devoted to additional requirements specific to specialised activities. These include:

- financial institutions (disclosures) (see 2.4.1 below);
- agriculture;
- extractive industries;
- service concession arrangements;
- heritage assets;
- funding commitments;
- public benefit entities (see 2.4.2 below).

Accounting for retirement benefit plans (and disclosures for such plans) are not within the scope of this publication.

Importantly, Section 34 sets out requirements on certain areas not addressed directly by previous UK accounting standards or IFRSs. FRS 102's requirements on specialised activities are further addressed in Chapter 29.

2.4.1   *Financial institutions – disclosure requirements*

Section 34 includes additional disclosure requirements for financial institutions (see definition at 2.4.1.A below).

Financial institutions are not entitled to make use of the disclosure exemptions from Sections 11 and 12 when applying the reduced disclosure framework in their individual financial statements (see 3 below). *[FRS 102.1.9].* In addition, additional disclosures are specified in Section 34 in respect of:

- the individual financial statements of a financial institution (other than a retirement benefit plan), *[FRS 102.34.17]*, (see Chapter 8 at 8.3); and
- the consolidated financial statements of a group containing a financial institution (other than a retirement benefit plan) where the financial institution's financial instruments are material to the group, *[FRS 102.34.17]*, (see Chapter 8 at 8.3).

2.4.1.A   *Definition of a financial institution*

The FRC has opted not to provide a generic definition of a financial institution. Instead, it has provided a list of entities that are stated to be financial institutions. A 'financial institution' is stated to be any of the following: *[FRS 102 Appendix I]*

(a)   a bank which is:

    (i)   a firm with a Part IV permission (as defined in section 40(4) of the Financial Services and Markets Act 2000) which includes accepting deposits and:

(a) which is a credit institution; or

(b) whose Part IV permission includes a requirement that it complies with the rules in the General Prudential sourcebook and the Prudential sourcebook for Banks, Building Societies and Investment Firms relating to banks, but which is not a building society, a friendly society or a credit union;

(ii) an EEA bank which is a full credit institution;

(b) a building society which is defined in section 119(1) of the Building Societies Act 1986 as a building society incorporated (or deemed to be incorporated) under that Act;

(c) a credit union, being a body corporate registered under the Industrial and Provident Societies Act 1965 as a credit union in accordance with the Credit Unions Act 1979, which is an authorised person;

(d) custodian bank, broker-dealer or stockbroker;

(e) an entity that undertakes the business of effecting or carrying out insurance contracts, including general and life assurance entities;

(f) an incorporated friendly society incorporated under the Friendly Societies Act 1992 or a registered friendly society registered under section 7(1)(a) of the Friendly Societies Act 1974 or any enactment which it replaced, including any registered branches;

(g) an investment trust, Irish investment company, venture capital trust, mutual fund, exchange traded fund, unit trust, open-ended investment company (OEIC);

(h) a retirement benefit plan; or

(i) any other entity whose principal activity is to generate wealth or manage risk through financial instruments. This is intended to cover entities that have business activities similar to those listed above but are not specifically included in the list above. A parent entity whose sole activity is to hold investments in other group entities is not a financial institution.

Category (i) is potentially wide-ranging and, despite the reference to 'similar' business activities, appears to have a different emphasis from (a) to (h) which focus on entities that hold assets in a fiduciary capacity on behalf of others rather than wealth generation or risk management through the use of financial instruments.

The Accounting Council advised that 'a parent entity whose sole activity is to hold investments in other group entities is not a financial institution, but notes that a subsidiary entity engaged solely in treasury activities for the group as a whole is likely to meet the definition of a financial institution'. *[FRS 102.AC.37].*

In many groups, there will be entities falling between these two extremes and judgement will need to be applied in assessing whether the principal activities of the entity are to generate wealth or manage risk through financial instruments.

2.4.2   *Public benefit entities*

Paragraphs in FRS 102 that are prefixed by PBE are specific to public benefit entities (see definition in the Glossary to FRS 102, as discussed in Chapter 29 at 6).

These paragraphs must not be applied directly or by analogy to entities that are not public benefit entities (other than, where specifically directed, entities within a public benefit entity group, i.e. a public benefit entity parent and all its wholly-owned subsidiaries). *[FRS 102.1.2, Appendix I].*

Section 34 addresses incoming resources from non-exchange transactions, public benefit entity combinations, and public benefit entity concessionary loans. These sections include paragraphs prefixed by PBE and apply only to public benefit entities. In addition, other sections of FRS 102 also contain paragraphs prefixed by PBE. Section 34 also addresses other accounting topics such as heritage assets, funding commitments that may be of particular relevance to some public benefit entities. However, the paragraphs are not prefixed by PBE and apply to all entities. See Chapter 29.

Many public benefit entities may also be subject to the requirements of a SORP (see 2.2 above).

3   REDUCED DISCLOSURE FRAMEWORK

FRS 102 provides for a reduced disclosure framework available only in the individual financial statements of a 'qualifying entity' (see below). *[FRS 102.1.8-1.14].* A qualifying entity which is required to prepare consolidated financial statements (for example, it is a parent company required by section 399 of the Companies Act 2006 to prepare group accounts and is not entitled to any of the exemptions in sections 400 to 402 of the Companies Act 2006 or chooses not to take advantage of these exemptions) may not take advantage of the disclosure exemptions in its consolidated financial statements. *[FRS 102.1.10].* This does not preclude the reduced disclosure framework being applied in the individual financial statements of a parent preparing consolidated financial statements.

Individual financial statements to which FRS 102 applies are accounts that are required to be prepared by an entity in accordance with the Companies Act 2006 or relevant legislation. For example, this term includes 'individual accounts' as set out in section 394 of the Companies Act 2006, a 'statement of accounts' as set out in section 132 of the Charities Act 2011, or 'individual accounts' as set out in section 72A of the Building Societies Act 1986. Separate financial statements are included in the meaning of the term individual financial statements. *[FRS 102 Appendix I].*

It is worth noting that FRS 102 uses 'separate financial statements' to mean those presented by a parent in which the investments in subsidiaries, jointly controlled entities or associates are accounted for either at cost or fair value rather than on the basis of the reported results and net assets of the investees. *[FRS 102 Appendix I].* This differs to the definition of 'separate financial statements' in IFRS. *[IAS 27.4].*

This means that FRS 102's reduced disclosure framework can be used in:

- individual financial statements of subsidiary undertakings;
- separate financial statements of an intermediate parent undertaking which does not prepare consolidated financial statements; and

- separate financial statements of a parent undertaking which does prepare consolidated financial statements.

However, the entity applying FRS 102's reduced disclosure framework must be included in a set of publicly available consolidated financial statements intended to give a true and fair view (see 3.1.6 below).

A parent company that prepares consolidated financial statements but applies FRS 102 in its individual financial statements can also use the exemption in section 408 of the Companies Act 2006 from presenting a profit and loss account and related notes in the individual financial statements. This is the case whether or not it applies FRS 102's reduced disclosure framework.

3.1   Definition of a qualifying entity

FRS 102 defines a qualifying entity as 'a member of a group where the parent of that group prepares publicly available consolidated financial statements which are intended to give a true and fair view (of the assets, liabilities, financial position and profit or loss) and that member is included in the consolidation'. *[FRS 102 Appendix I]*. A charity can be a qualifying entity under FRS 102 (unlike under FRS 101).

The phrase 'included in the consolidation' is referenced to section 474(1) of the Companies Act 2006 which states that this means that 'the undertaking is included in the accounts by the method of full (and not proportional) consolidation and references to an undertaking excluded from consolidation shall be construed accordingly'. Therefore, entities that are not fully consolidated in the consolidated financial statements, such as subsidiaries of investment entities that are accounted for at fair value through profit and loss under IFRS 10 – *Consolidated Financial Statements*, cannot use FRS 102's reduced disclosure framework. Associates and jointly controlled entities are not qualifying entities since they are not members of a group (see 3.1.2 below).

3.1.1   *Reporting date of the consolidated financial statements of the parent*

The requirement for the qualifying entity to be included in the consolidation implies that the consolidated financial statements of the parent must be prepared before the FRS 102 individual financial statements of the qualifying entity, where the reduced disclosure framework is used. FRS 102 is silent on whether the reporting date and period of those consolidated financial statements has to be identical to that of the qualifying entity. In contrast, both sections 400 and 401 of the Companies Act 2006 require that the exemption from preparing group accounts for a parent that is also a subsidiary is conditional on the entity's financial statements being drawn up to the same date or an earlier date in the financial year as the parent undertaking. It would seem logical that the reporting date criteria in sections 400 and 401 can also be used for FRS 102.

Where the consolidated financial statements are prepared as at an earlier date than the date of the qualifying entity's financial statements, there will be a risk that some of the disclosure exemptions may not be available to the qualifying entity because the consolidated financial statements do not contain the 'equivalent' disclosures (see 3.6 below).

3.1.2   Definition of 'group' and 'subsidiary'

The definition of a qualifying entity contains a footnote that refers to section 474(1) of the Companies Act 2006 which defines a 'group' as a parent undertaking and its subsidiary undertakings. *[s474(1)].*

Section 1162 of the Companies Act 2006 states that an undertaking is a parent undertaking in relation to another undertaking, a subsidiary undertaking, if:

(a)   it holds a majority of the voting rights in the undertaking; or

(b)   it is a member of the undertaking and has the right to appoint or remove a majority of its board of directors; or

(c)   it has the right to exercise a dominant influence over the undertaking by virtue of provisions contained in the undertaking's articles or by virtue of a control contract; or

(d)   it is a member of the undertaking and controls alone, pursuant to an agreement with other shareholders or members, a majority of the voting rights in the undertaking.

An undertaking is treated as a member for the purposes above if any of its subsidiary undertakings is a member of that undertaking or if any shares in that other undertaking are held by a person acting on behalf of the undertaking or any of its subsidiary undertakings.

An undertaking is also a parent undertaking in relation to another undertaking if it has the power to exercise, or actually exercises, dominant influence or control over it, or it and the subsidiary undertaking are managed on a unified basis.

A parent undertaking shall be treated as the parent undertaking of undertakings in relation to which any of its subsidiary undertakings are, or are to be treated as, parent undertakings, and references to its subsidiary undertakings shall be construed accordingly.

Schedule 7 to the Companies Act 2006 provides interpretation and references to 'shares' in section 1162 and in Schedule 7 are to 'allotted shares'. *[s1162].*

The key issue for the application of FRS 102's reduced disclosure framework is whether the subsidiary is included in the consolidation of the parent's consolidated financial statements. A company which meets the definition of a subsidiary undertaking under the Companies Act 2006 but is not included in the consolidation of the consolidated financial statements of its parent cannot apply FRS 102's reduced disclosure framework.

3.1.3   Publicly available consolidated financial statements

By 'publicly available', the FRC appear to mean that the consolidated financial statements can be accessed by the public as the use of FRS 102's reduced disclosure framework is conditional on a disclosure by the qualifying entity indicating from where those consolidated financial statements can be obtained (see 3.2 below). This does not mandate that the consolidated financial statements must be filed with a regulator. However, it does mean that UK consolidated financial statements not yet filed with the Registrar of Companies, at the date that the subsidiary's financial statements prepared in accordance with FRS 102 are approved, must be publicly available via some other medium.

3.1.4   Non-UK qualifying entities

There is no requirement that a qualifying entity is a UK entity. Therefore, overseas entities can apply FRS 102's reduced disclosure framework in their individual or separate financial statements subject to meeting the criteria and subject to FRS 102 being allowed in their own jurisdiction.

There is also no requirement that the parent that prepares publicly available consolidated financial statements, in which the qualifying entity is included, is a UK parent (see 3.1.6 below).

3.1.5   Non-controlling interests

There is no ownership threshold for a subsidiary to apply FRS 102's reduced disclosure framework. Therefore, a qualifying entity can apply the reduced disclosure framework even if its parent (that consolidates the qualifying entity) holds less than a majority of the voting rights. However, other shareholders are permitted to object to the use of the reduced disclosure framework (see 3.2 below).

3.1.6   Intended to give a true and fair view

The consolidated financial statements in which the qualifying entity is consolidated are not required to give an explicit true and fair view of the assets, liabilities, financial position and profit or loss. Rather, they are 'intended to give a true and fair view'. This means that the consolidated financial statements in which the qualifying entity is consolidated need not contain an explicit opinion that they give a 'true and fair view' (for example, US GAAP financial statements do not have such an opinion) but, in substance, they should be intended to give such a view. The FRC obtained a QC's opinion in 2008 which stated that 'the requirement set out in international accounting standards to present fairly is not a different requirement to that of showing a true and fair view but is a different articulation of the same concept'.[6]

In our view, a set of consolidated financial statements drawn up in a manner equivalent to consolidated financial statements that are in accordance with the EU Seventh Directive (as modified, where relevant, by the provisions of the Bank Accounts Directive or the Insurance Accounts Directive) (i.e. a set of consolidated financial statements that meets the 'equivalence' test of section 401 of the Companies Act 2006) is intended to give a true and fair view. The concept of equivalence is discussed further at Chapter 6 at 3.1.1.C.

In theory, there is no reason why consolidated financial statements of a parent prepared under a GAAP that is not 'equivalent' to the Seventh Directive cannot be used provided those consolidated financial statements in which the entity is included are publicly available and are intended to give a true and fair view.

However, a parent company that wishes to claim an exemption from preparing group accounts under either section 400 or section 401 of the Companies Act 2006 must be a subsidiary of a parent that prepares consolidated accounts in accordance with the provisions of the EU Seventh Directive (as modified, where relevant, by the provisions of the Bank Accounts Directive or the Insurance Accounts Directive) or in a manner so equivalent. *[s400(2)(b), s401(2)(b)]*.

In addition, a number of the disclosure exemptions under FRS 102's reduced disclosure framework are conditional on 'equivalent' disclosures being made in those consolidated financial statements in which the qualifying entity is included. The meaning of 'equivalent disclosures' is discussed at 3.6 below. Where the equivalent disclosure is not made in the publicly available consolidated financial statements, the relevant disclosure exemptions cannot be applied in the qualifying entity's individual financial statements prepared under FRS 102. A GAAP that is not 'equivalent' to the Seventh Directive is less likely to have those 'equivalent' disclosures.

One issue not addressed by FRS 102 is the impact of a qualified audit opinion on the consolidated financial statements. The QC's opinion obtained by the FRC in 2008 stated that 'the scope for arguing that financial statements which do not comply with relevant accounting standards nevertheless give a true and fair view is very limited'.[7]

3.2   Use of the disclosure exemptions

The use of the disclosure exemptions in FRS 102's reduced disclosure framework (see 3.3 to 3.5 below) is conditional on all of the following criteria being met:

* the shareholders have been notified in writing about the use of the disclosure exemptions;

* the shareholders have not objected to the disclosure exemptions;

* the reporting entity applies the recognition, measurement and disclosure requirements of FRS 102;

* the reporting entity discloses in the notes to its financial statements:

  * a brief narrative summary of the disclosure exemptions adopted; and

  * the name of the parent of the group in whose consolidated financial statements its financial statements are consolidated (i.e. the parent identified in the definition of 'qualifying entity') and from where those financial statements may be obtained. *[FRS 102.1.11]*.

FRS 102 does not state whether the requirement of the reporting entity to notify its shareholders about the use of the disclosure exemptions is an annual requirement or whether a more open-ended notification can be provided. In addition, no timescale is mentioned. Therefore, there is no requirement that notification occurs in the period covered by the financial statements; it could be earlier or later. In the absence of clear guidance, we would recommend that entities obtain legal advice as to the form in which they should notify shareholders of their intention to use FRS 102's reduced disclosure framework.

Objections to the use of FRS 102's reduced disclosure framework may be served on the qualifying entity in accordance with reasonable timeframes and format requirements by a shareholder that is the immediate parent of the entity, or by a shareholder or shareholders holding in aggregate 5% or more of the allotted shares in the entity or more than half of the allotted shares in the entity that are not held by the immediate parent. *[FRS 102.1.11(a)]*.

FRS 102 does not explain what is meant by 'reasonable timeframes and format requirements' in respect of any shareholder objection.

An objection by a shareholder or shareholders holding in aggregate 5% or more of the total allotted shares or more than half of the allotted shares that are not held by the immediate parent (which could be less than 5% of the total allotted shares) automatically means that FRS 102's reduced disclosure framework cannot be applied by the entity. A shareholder is not required to supply a reason for any objection.

3.3   Entities that are not financial institutions

A qualifying entity that is not a financial institution may take advantage of the following disclosure exemptions in its individual financial statements:

- the requirements of Section 4 – *Statement of Financial Position*, paragraph 4.12(a)(iv) (see 3.3.1 below);

- the requirements of Section 7 – *Statement of Cash Flows* – and Section 3 – *Financial Statement Presentation*, paragraph 3.17(d) (see 3.3.2 below);

- the requirements of Section 11, paragraphs 11.39 to 11.48A and Section 12, paragraphs 12.26 to 12.29A providing the equivalent disclosures required by FRS 102 are included in the consolidated financial statements of the group in which the entity is consolidated.

    These disclosure exemptions are not available to a qualifying entity that is a financial institution. In addition, where a qualifying entity that is not a financial institution has financial instruments held at fair value subject to the requirements of paragraph 36(4) of Schedule 1 to the Regulations, there are additional disclosure requirements (see 3.3.3 and 3.4 below); *[FRS 102.1.8, 1.9]*

- the requirements of Section 26 – *Share-based Payment,* paragraphs 26.18(b), 26.19 to 26.21 and 26.23, provided that for a qualifying entity that is:

    (i)   a subsidiary, the share-based payment arrangement concerns equity instruments of another group entity;

    (ii)   an ultimate parent, the share-based payment arrangement concerns its own equity instruments and its separate financial statements are presented alongside the consolidated financial statements of the group;

    and, in both cases, provided that the equivalent disclosures required by FRS 102 are included in the consolidated financial statements of the group in which the entity is consolidated (see 3.3.4 below);

- the requirement of Section 33 – *Related Party Disclosures*, paragraph 33.7 (see 3.3.5 below). *[FRS 102.1.8, 1.12]*.

3.3.1   *Statement of financial position*

The exemption removes the requirement for a qualifying entity from disclosing a reconciliation of the number of shares outstanding at the beginning and at the end of the period. *[FRS 102.1.12(a)]*.

3.3.2   Statement of cash flows

The exemption removes the requirement for a cash flow statement for any qualifying entity in its individual financial statements.

Under previous UK GAAP, FRS 1 – *Cash flow statements* – provided an exemption from preparing a cash flow statement for only those subsidiary undertakings where 90% or more of the voting rights are controlled within the group, provided the consolidated financial statements in which the subsidiary undertakings are included are publicly available. *[FRS 102.1.12(b)].*

3.3.3   Financial instruments

The exemption removes all of the disclosure requirements of Sections 11 and 12. Financial institutions are not permitted to use this exemption (see 3.5 below). *[FRS 102.1.12(c)].*

The exemption depends on there being equivalent disclosures in the publicly available consolidated financial statements in which the qualifying entity is included. The standard is unclear as to whether the exemption can be taken where the qualifying entity holds financial instruments that are eliminated on consolidation in these consolidated financial statements. It is possible that the FRC may issue guidance in this area.

Notwithstanding this exemption, where a qualifying entity that is not a financial institution has financial instruments held at fair value subject to the requirements of paragraph 36(4) of Schedule 1 to the Regulations, it must apply the disclosure requirements of Section 11 to those financial instruments held at fair value, i.e. the disclosure requirements in Section 11 are given in respect of financial instruments held at fair value subject to paragraph 36(4) of Schedule 1 to the Regulations (see 3.4 below). *[FRS 102.1.8].*

FRS 102 financial statements prepared in accordance with Part 15 of the Companies Act 2006 are Companies Act accounts. Consequently, a UK company's statutory accounts prepared in accordance with FRS 102 should give all the disclosures in respect of financial instruments required in the financial statements by the Regulations or by the Small Companies Regulations, even if they qualify for the FRS 102 reduced disclosures.

In addition, the Regulations require that the Directors' Report of a UK company should contain an indication of the financial risk management objectives, policies (including the policy for hedging each major type of forecasted transaction for which hedge accounting is used) and the exposure of the company to price risk, credit risk, liquidity risk and cash flow risk, unless not material. In respect of a Group Directors' Report, this information is required for the company and its consolidated subsidiary undertakings. *[6 Sch 7].*

3.3.4   Share-based payment

This exemption removes all the disclosure requirements of Section 26 except for the following:

• a description of each type of share-based payment arrangements that existed at any time during the period, including the general terms and conditions of each arrangement, such as vesting requirements, the maximum term of options granted, and the method of settlement (e.g. whether in cash or equity). An entity with substantially similar types of share-based payment arrangement may aggregate this information; *[FRS 102.26.18(a)]* and

- if the entity is part of a group share-based payment plan, and it recognises and measures its share-based payment expense on the basis of a reasonable allocation of the expense recognised for the group, it shall disclose that fact and the basis for the allocation (addressed further in paragraph 26.16). *[FRS 102.26.22]*.

Where the qualifying entity is a subsidiary, the disclosure exemptions are available in respect of share-based payment arrangements concerning equity instruments of another group entity. Therefore, the Section 26 disclosures are required in full for share-based payment arrangements relating to its own equity instruments.

Where the qualifying entity is an ultimate parent and its separate financial statements are presented alongside the consolidated financial statements of the group, the disclosure exemptions are available in respect of share-based payments concerning its own equity instruments. However, the disclosure exemptions would appear not to be available in an ultimate parent's individual financial statements in the (albeit unusual situation) where the equity instruments related to another group entity.

3.3.5   *Related party transactions*

This exemption removes the requirement to disclose key management personnel compensation in total. *[FRS 102.1.12(e)]*.

3.4   Disclosures required by non-financial institutions for certain financial instruments held at fair value

Paragraph 36 of Schedule 1 to the Regulations (and its equivalents in Schedules 2 and 3 to the Regulations and other regulations)[8] allow financial instruments to be included in the financial statements at fair value, where this can be measured reliably, but exclude certain types of financial instruments. However, paragraph 36(4) of Schedule 1 to the Regulations (and its equivalents) allow a financial instrument that falls within the list of exclusions to be included at fair value *only* where it is permitted to be included in accounts at fair value, under IFRSs adopted by the EU before 5 September 2006, and 'provided that the disclosures required by such accounting standards are made'. *[1 Sch 36]*.

Financial instruments held at fair value subject to the requirements of paragraph 36(4) of Schedule 1 to the Regulations would include, *inter alia*:

- any financial liability unless it is held as part of a trading portfolio or is a derivative;
- loans and receivables originated by the reporting entity and not held for trading purposes;
- interests in subsidiary undertakings, associated undertakings and joint ventures;
- equity instruments issued by the company;
- contracts for contingent consideration in a business combination; or

- other financial instruments with such special characteristics that the instruments according to generally accepted accounting principles or practice, should be accounted for differently from other financial instruments. *[1 Sch 36].*

FRS 102 allows a choice of policy for the recognition and measurement of financial instruments. The situations in which financial instruments are carried at fair value differ depending on the standard applied.

Appendix IV to FRS 102 comments that an entity applying FRS 102 and holding financial instruments measured at fair value either in accordance with Section 11 or Section 12 may be required to provide the disclosures required by paragraph 36(4) of Schedule 1 to the Regulations. It notes that these disclosures have been incorporated into Section 11 and that some of the disclosure requirements of Section 11 apply to all financial instruments measured at fair value, whilst others (such as paragraph 11.48A) apply only to financial instruments that are not held as part of a trading portfolio and are not derivatives. The disclosure requirements of paragraph 11.48A will predominantly apply to certain financial liabilities, however, there may be instances where paragraph 36(3) of Schedule 1 to the Regulations requires that the disclosures must also be provided in relation to financial assets, e.g. investments in subsidiaries, associates or jointly controlled entities measured at fair value. *[FRS 102.A4.13].*

FRS 102 requires qualifying entities that are not financial institutions to apply the disclosure requirements of Section 11 *to those financial instruments held at fair value* [emphasis added] subject to the requirements of paragraph 36(4) of Schedule 1 to the Regulations. *[FRS 102.1.8].* FRS 102 clarifies that a qualifying entity can take advantage of the disclosure exemptions for financial liabilities that are held at fair value that are either part of a trading portfolio or are derivatives. *[FRS 102.1.8].*

These disclosures only apply to financial statements that are subject to the statutory requirements in paragraph 36(4) of Schedule 1 to the Regulations (or its equivalents). Amendments to FRS 101 – *Reduced Disclosure Framework (2013/14 Cycle)*, issued in July 2014, clarify the scope of the requirements for FRS 101 reporters to make the paragraph 36(4) disclosures; the same principles apply for FRS 102 reporters. FRS 101 now simply includes a footnote that states 'It should be noted that companies which are subject to the requirements of the Act and Regulations are legally required to provide disclosures related to financial instruments measured at fair value. Further guidance is included in Appendix II *Note on Legal Requirements.*' Paragraphs A2.7A to A2.7C of FRS 101 also clarify that the disclosures are required in relation to financial instruments measured at fair value, whether through profit or loss or through other comprehensive income.

3.5   Entities that are financial institutions

A qualifying entity that is a financial institution (see 2.4.1.A above) may take advantage in its individual financial statements of the disclosure exemptions set out in 3.3 above, except for the disclosure exemptions from Sections 11 and 12. *[FRS 102.1.9].*

Where a qualifying entity that is not a financial institution has financial instruments held at fair value subject to the requirements of paragraph 36(4) of Schedule 1 (or its equivalents in Schedules 2 and 3 to the Regulations or other regulations), it is required to give the disclosures required by IFRSs adopted by the EU on or before 5 September 2006. The FRC has identified these disclosures as being the disclosure requirements of Section 11 (see 3.4 above). Since financial institutions do not benefit from disclosure exemptions in respect of Section 11, under the reduced disclosure framework, they will already be giving the required disclosures.

An entity that is a financial institution must give the additional disclosures set out in Section 34, which sets out separate disclosures for financial institutions (see 2.4.1 above). An entity must also give the disclosures required by the Companies Act 2006 and the Regulations or the Small Companies Regulations, where subject to those statutory requirements.

3.6 Equivalent disclosures

The disclosure exemptions in respect of financial instruments and share-based payments set out in paragraphs 1.12(c) and (d) respectively of the standard are dependent on the provision of 'equivalent' disclosures in the publicly available consolidated financial statements of the parent in which the qualifying entity is consolidated.

FRS 102 refers users to the Application Guidance in FRS 100 in deciding whether the publicly available consolidated financial statements of the group in which the reporting entity is included provides disclosures that are 'equivalent' to the requirements of FRS 102 (i.e. the full requirements when not applying the disclosure exemptions) from which relief is provided. *[FRS 102.1.13]*.

The Application Guidance in FRS 100 states that:

- it is necessary to consider whether the consolidated financial statements of the parent provide disclosures that meet the basic disclosure requirements of the relevant standard or interpretation without regarding strict conformity with each and every disclosure. This assessment should be based on the particular facts, including the similarities to and differences from the requirements of the relevant standard from which relief is provided. 'Equivalence' is intended to be aligned to that described in section 401 of the Companies Act 2006 (see Chapter 6 at 3.1.1.C); *[FRS 100.AG8-9]* and

- disclosure exemptions for subsidiaries are permitted where the relevant disclosure requirements are met in the consolidated financial statements, even where the disclosures are made in aggregate or in an abbreviated form. If, however, no disclosure is made in the consolidated financial statements on the grounds of materiality, the relevant disclosures should be made at the subsidiary level if material in those financial statements. *[FRS 100.AG10]*.

This means that a qualifying entity must review the consolidated financial statements of its parent to ensure that 'equivalent' disclosures have been made for each of the above exemptions that it intends to use. Where a particular 'equivalent' disclosure has not been made then the qualifying subsidiary cannot use the exemption in respect of that disclosure.

4   COMPANIES ACT 2006 AND REGULATIONS

The requirements of the Companies Act 2006 (and certain other regulatory rules) governing preparation of financial statements by UK companies are addressed in Chapter 1 at 6. See also 2.1 above for the requirements on which entities can apply FRS 102.

Statutory accounts prepared by a UK company in accordance with FRS 102 are Companies Act individual or group accounts, and are therefore required to comply with the applicable provisions of Parts 15 and 16 of the Companies Act 2006 and with the Regulations. *[FRS 102.A4.7]*. These requirements include the rules on recognition and measurement, the Companies Act accounts formats and note disclosures. While Appendix IV to the standard refers to the 'Regulations', we do not consider that a small company applying FRS 102 in its statutory accounts is precluded from applying the Small Companies Regulations where it meets the criteria to be subject to the small companies regime (see 4.1 below and Chapter 1 at 6.8).

Appendix IV states that it does not list every legal requirement but instead focuses on those areas where greater judgement might be required in determining compliance with the law. *[FRS 102.A4.11]*. It notes that the standard 'is not intended to be a one-stop shop for all accounting and legal requirements, and although the FRC believes the FRS 102 is not inconsistent with company law, compliance with FRS 102 alone will often be insufficient to ensure compliance with all the disclosure requirements set out in the Companies Act 2006 and the Regulations. As a result preparers will continue to be required to have regard to the requirements of company law in addition to accounting standards.' *[FRS 102.A4.10]*.

4.1   Small and medium-sized companies

4.1.1   *Small companies regime and small companies exemption*

A UK company that is subject to the small companies regime can apply the Small Companies Regulations and is exempt from the requirement to prepare group accounts and from giving certain disclosures required in the notes to the financial statements by Part 15 of the Companies Act 2006.

A UK company that takes advantage of the small companies exemption is not required to prepare a Strategic Report (for financial years ended on or after 30 September 2013) *[s414A]* and is entitled to certain disclosure exemptions in the Directors' Report. *[s415A]*. Additionally, a UK company subject to the small companies regime or taking advantage of the small companies exemption is also entitled to certain filing exemptions.

The criteria for use of the small companies regime and the small companies exemption (which has a wider scope than the small companies regime), together with the exemptions available, are discussed in Chapter 1 at 6.5.

FRS 102 requires use of the profit and loss account and balance sheet formats included in Part 1 'General Rules and Formats' of Schedule 1 (or where applicable, Schedule 2 or Schedule 3) to the Regulations. Therefore, it does not permit the company law formats included in Part 1 'General Rules and Formats' of Schedule 1 to the Small Companies Regulations to be applied. Similarly, a small LLP would need to follow the formats included in Part 1 'General Rules and Formats' of Schedule 1 to the LLP Regulations.

However, our view is that companies subject to the small companies regime can still apply FRS 102, and in doing so, are not prevented from taking advantage of other exemptions applicable to companies subject to the small companies regime. This is because paragraph 3(3) of the Small Companies Regulations specifically states that 'Accounts are treated as having complied with any provision of Schedule 1 to these Regulations if they comply instead with the corresponding provision of Schedule 1 to the Large and Medium-sized Companies and Groups (Accounts and Reports) Regulations 2008.' Paragraph 8(2) of the Small Companies Regulations makes a similar statement in respect of the group accounts formats included in Schedule 6 to the Small Companies Regulations and Schedule 6 to the Regulations. The same conclusions apply for small LLPs. For LLPs, the corresponding statements are made in paragraphs 3(1) and 6(1) of the LLP Regulations.

4.1.2   Micro-entities

Companies that qualify as micro-entities and take advantage of the exemptions for micro-entities (for financial years ending on or after 30 September 2013) introduced by *The Small Companies (Micro-Entities' Accounts) Regulations 2013* (SI 2013/3008) would not be able to comply with FRS 102 (see Chapter 1 at 6.4). The FRC has published amendments to the FRSSE to enable such companies to comply with the FRSSE.

Effective for financial years beginning on or after 1 January 2016, the FRC is proposing withdrawal of the FRSSE and a new separate standard covering micro-entities. Small entities would apply FRS 102 (but with different sections on framework, presentation and disclosure applying to small entities). See 1.2.3.E above and Chapter 1 at 4.4.2.

4.1.3   Medium-sized companies

A medium-sized company may take advantage of certain disclosure exemptions for a financial year in which the company qualifies as medium-sized and is not an excluded company (see Chapter 1 at 6.6). *[s465-s467]*. Companies applying FRS 102 can make use of these exemptions to the extent they do not conflict with accounting standards, e.g. medium-sized companies would need to give related party disclosures in individual financial statements because this is required by FRS 102 notwithstanding the exemption in the Regulations. *[Regulations 4(2)(b)]*.

References

1 The equivalent references for LLPs are to *The Large and Medium-sized Limited Liability Partnerships (Accounts) Regulations 2008* (SI 2008/1911) and *The Small Limited Liability Partnerships (Accounts) Regulations 2008* (SI 2008/1912).

2 Accounting Council Minutes 12 December 2013.

3 PN009/14, 13.2.2014.

4 FRC Clarification – Section 1 (August 2013).

5 See SORP Information Sheet 4 at: http://www.charitycommission.gov.uk/ detailed-guidance/money-and-accounts/charity-reporting-and-accounting-the-essentials-2009-cc15b/sorp-documents/sorp-information-sheet-4-the-adoption-of-frs-102-by-charities-reporting-under-the-sorp/

6 The True and Fair Requirement Revised – Opinion, FRC, May 2008, para. 4(C).

7 The True and Fair Requirement Revised – Opinion, FRC, May 2008, para. 4(F).

8 The equivalent paragraphs are paragraph 44(4) of Schedule 2 to *The Large and Medium-sized Companies and Groups (Accounts and Reports) Regulations 2008,* paragraph 30(4) of Schedule 3 to *The Large and Medium-sized Companies and Groups (Accounts and Reports) Regulations 2008,* paragraph 36(4) of Schedule 1 to *The Small Companies and Groups (Accounts and Directors' Report) Regulations 2008,* paragraph 36(4) of Schedule 1 to *The Large and Medium-sized Limited Liability Partnerships (Accounts) Regulations 2008,* and paragraph 36(4) of Schedule 1 to *The Small Limited Liability Partnerships (Accounts) Regulations 2008.*

Chapter 3

Concepts and pervasive principles

Chapter 3   Concepts and pervasive principles

1   INTRODUCTION

Section 2 – *Concepts and Pervasive Principles* – describes the objectives of financial statements of entities within the scope of FRS 102 and the qualities that make those financial statements useful. It also sets out the concepts and basic principles underlying the financial statements of entities within the scope of FRS 102. *[FRS 102.2.1]*.

Section 2 is FRS 102's equivalent of the Statement of Principles for Financial Reporting under previous UK GAAP or the IFRS Conceptual Framework for Financial Reporting. However, it is not a statement or framework as such but a list of concepts and pervasive principles that underlie the Standard. The concepts and pervasive principles are largely derived from the equivalent concepts and pervasive principles section in the IFRS for SMEs. However, there are some differences in wording.

Section 2 affects recognition and measurement only when FRS 102, an FRC Abstract or a Statement of Recommended Practice (SORP) does not specifically address the accounting for a transaction, other event or condition. In the absence of such guidance, management has to refer to the definitions, recognition criteria and measurement concepts for assets, liabilities, income and expenses and the pervasive principles within Section 2 in using its judgment in developing and applying a relevant and reliable accounting policy for that transaction, other event or condition. *[FRS 102.10.4-5]*.

In recognition of this hierarchy of sources, it is reiterated that where there is an inconsistency between the concepts and principles in Section 2 and the specific requirements of another section of FRS 102, then the specific requirements of that other section take precedence. *[FRS 102.2.1A]*.

Section 2 introduces a number of definitions which are discussed separately below.

2   COMPARISON BETWEEN SECTION 2, PREVIOUS UK GAAP AND IFRS

There are some differences between the concepts and pervasive principles of FRS 102 and both the Statement of Principles for Financial Reporting under previous UK GAAP (FRC Statement of Principles) and the IFRS Conceptual Framework for Financial Reporting (the IFRS Conceptual Framework). However, these are unlikely to result in any recognition and measurement differences in practice since the definitions that actually affect amounts reported in the financial statements are virtually identical.

The two major conceptual differences are:

- Section 2 attributes a much broader objective to financial statements than the IFRS Conceptual Framework. In particular, like the FRC Statement of Principles,[1] it includes 'stewardship' as an objective of financial statements whereas stewardship was specifically removed from the revised version of the IFRS Conceptual Framework issued in 2010; and

- Section 2 does not identify any of its qualitative characteristics of information in financial statements as 'fundamental', 'key' or otherwise assign priority. The FRC Statement of Principles identified four key principles, relevance, reliability, comparability and understandability.[2] *[FRC Statement of Principles.3].* These are four of out the ten qualitative characteristics of FRS 102. The IFRS Conceptual Framework identifies two fundamental qualitative characteristics, relevance and faithful representation.[3] Faithful representation is not one of the qualitative characteristics of FRS 102. However, in terms of financial reporting, this difference of emphasis has little, if any, practical impact.

3   THE CONCEPTS AND PERVASIVE PRINCIPLES OF SECTION 2

Section 2 explains the objective of financial statements, the qualitative characteristics of information in financial statements, the financial position of an entity, performance, and the recognition and measurement principles of assets, liabilities, income and expenses. Each of these is discussed below.

3.1   Objective of financial statements

There are two overriding objectives of financial statements:

- to provide information about the financial position, performance and cash flows of an entity that is useful for economic decision-making by a broad range of users who are not in a position to demand reports tailored to meet their particular information needs; and

- to show the results of the stewardship of management – the accountability of management for the resources entrusted to it. *[FRS 102.2.2-3].*

These objectives are much broader than the IFRS Conceptual Framework which limits users to providers of capital.[4] In contrast, there is no limit put on the 'broad range of users' by Section 2.

The inclusion of stewardship as an objective of financial reporting in FRS 102 is unsurprising despite its omission from the IFRS Conceptual framework. In June 2007, the ASB (the predecessor body to the FRC) and others published a paper discussing the rationale for including stewardship, or directors' accountability to shareholders, as a separate objective of financial reporting.[5]

3.2   Qualitative characteristics of information in financial statements

Section 2 identifies ten qualitative characteristics of information in financial statements. It does not describe any of these qualitative characteristics as 'fundamental', 'key' or otherwise assign priority. However, the language that describes the qualitative characteristics places emphasis on how those qualitative characteristics make financial statements relevant and reliable.

Going concern is not one of the qualitative characteristics identified by Section 2. The subject of going concern is addressed separately in Section 3 – *Financial Statement Presentation* (see Chapter 4).

Each of FRS 102's ten qualitative characteristics are discussed in sections 3.2.1 to 3.2.10 below.

3.2.1   *Understandability*

Understandability is described as the presentation of information in a way that makes it comprehensible by users who have a reasonable knowledge of business and economic activities and accounting and a willingness to study the information with reasonable diligence. However, the need for understandability does not allow relevant information to be omitted on the grounds that it may be too difficult for some. *[FRS 102.2.4].*

3.2.2   *Relevance*

Relevance is described as the quality of information that allows it to influence the economic decisions of users by helping them evaluate past, present or future events or confirming, or correcting their past evaluations. Information provided in financial statements must be relevant to the decision-making needs of users. *[FRS 102.2.5].*

Where FRS 102 does not specifically address a transaction, other event or condition, Section 10 – *Accounting Policies, Estimates and Errors* – requires an entity's management to use its judgement in developing and applying an accounting policy that results in information that is both relevant to the economic decision-making needs of users and reliable. *[FRS 102.10.4].*

3.2.3   *Materiality*

Section 2 states that information is material – and therefore has relevance – if its omission or misstatement, individually or collectively, could influence the economic decisions of users taken on the basis of the financial statements. *Materiality* depends on the size and nature of the omission or misstatement judged in the surrounding circumstances. The size or nature of the item, or a combination of both, could be the determining factor. However, it is inappropriate to make, or leave uncorrected, immaterial departures from this FRS to achieve a particular presentation of an entity's financial position, financial performance or cash flows. *[FRS 102.2.6].*

Chapter 3

The ICAEW issued a technical release in June 2008, TECH 03/08 – *Guidance on Materiality in Financial Reporting by UK Entities*, which considers the issue of materiality in financial reporting and is intended to help with the practical application of the definition and explanations of materiality.

3.2.4   Reliability

Reliability is defined as the quality of information that makes it free from material error and bias and represents faithfully that which it either purports to represent or could reasonably be expected to represent. Information provided in financial statements must be reliable. Financial statements are not free from bias (i.e. not neutral) if, by the selection or presentation of information, they are intended to influence the making of a decision or judgement in order to achieve a predetermined result or outcome. *[FRS 102.2.7]*.

Where FRS 102 does not specifically address a transaction, other event or condition, Section 10 of FRS 102 requires an entity's management to use its judgement in developing and applying an accounting policy that results in information that is both relevant and reliable. *[FRS 102.10.4]*.

Section 10 of FRS 102 further states that for information to be reliable, financial statements should:

* represent faithfully the financial position, financial performance and cash flows of the entity;
* reflect the economic substance of transactions, other events and conditions and not merely their legal form;
* are neutral, i.e. free from bias;
* are prudent; and
* are complete in all material respects. *[FRS 102.10.4]*.

There may sometimes be a tension between 'neutrality' and 'prudence'. On the one hand, financial statements must be free from bias, i.e. neutral. On the other hand, they must also be prudent, i.e. prepared with a degree of caution such that assets or income are not overstated and liabilities or expenses are not understated. See 3.2.6 below.

'Completeness' is discussed at 3.2.7 below.

3.2.5   Substance over form

Transactions and other events and conditions should be accounted for and presented in accordance with their substance and not merely their legal form. This enhances the reliability of financial statements. *[FRS 102.2.8]*.

Substance over form is also a requirement of UK company law and is required by both *The Large and Medium-sized Companies and Groups (Accounts and reports) Regulations 2008 (SI 2008/410)* (the Regulations) and *The Small Companies and Groups (Accounts and Directors' Report) Regulations 2008 (SI 2008/409)* (the Small Companies' Regulations). *[1 Sch 9, 2 Sch 10, 3 Sch 8, 1 Sch 9 (SC)]*.

3.2.6   *Prudence*

Prudence is the inclusion of a degree of caution in the exercise of the judgements needed in making the estimates required under conditions of uncertainty, such that assets or income are not overstated and liabilities or expenses are not understated. The uncertainties that will inevitably surround many events and circumstances are acknowledged by the disclosure of their nature and extent and by the exercise of prudence in the preparation of the financial statements. However, the exercise of prudence does not allow the deliberate understatement of assets or income, or the deliberate overstatement of liabilities or expenses. In short, prudence does not permit bias. *[FRS 102.2.9]*.

For UK companies, the Regulations also require that the amount of any item must be determined on a prudent basis. In particular, only profits realised at the balance sheet date are to be included in the profit and loss account and all liabilities which have arisen in respect of the financial year in which the accounts relate or a previous financial year must be taken into account including those which only apply become apparent between the balance sheet date and the date on which it is signed on behalf of the board of directors in accordance with s414 of the Companies Act. *[1 Sch 13, 2 Sch 19, 3 Sch 18]*.

3.2.7   *Completeness*

To be reliable, the information in financial statements must be complete within the bounds of materiality and cost. An omission can cause information to be false or misleading and thus unreliable and deficient in terms of its relevance. *[FRS 102.2.10]*.

3.2.8   *Comparability*

Users must be able to compare the financial statements of an entity through time to identify trends in its financial position and performance. Users must also be able to compare the financial statements of different entities to evaluate their relative financial position, performance and cash flows. Hence, the measurement and display of the financial effects of like transactions and other events and conditions must be carried out in a consistent way throughout an entity and over time for that entity, and in a consistent way across entities. In addition, users must be informed of the accounting policies employed in the preparation of the financial statements, and of any changes in those policies and the effects of such changes. *[FRS 102.2.11]*.

There is more detailed guidance on comparability in Section 10 which requires an entity to select and apply its accounting policies consistently for similar transactions, other events or obligations unless an FRS or FRC Abstract specifically requires or permits categorisation of items for which different policies may be appropriate. *[FRS 102.10.7]*. Section 8 – *Notes to the Financial Statements* – requires an entity to disclose a summary of significant accounting policies *[FRS 102.8.4(b)]* and Section 10 requires disclosures where there are changes in accounting policies. *[FRS 102.10.13-14]*.

3.2.9   *Timeliness*

To be relevant, financial information must be able to influence the economic decisions of users. *Timeliness* means providing the information within the decision time frame. If there is undue delay in the reporting of information it may lose its relevance. Management may need to balance the relative merits of timely reporting and the provision of reliable information. In achieving a balance between relevance and reliability, the overriding consideration is how best to satisfy the needs of users in making economic decisions. *[FRS 102.2.12]*.

UK companies are required by law to file accounts within specified time limits. For a private company, the period allowed for filing is nine months after the end of the relevant accounting reference period and, for a public company, the period allowed for filing is six months after the end of the relevant accounting reference period. *[s442]*.

3.2.10   Balance between benefit and cost

Section 2 states that the benefits derived from information should exceed the cost of providing it. It is further stated that the evaluation of benefits and costs is substantially a judgemental process. Furthermore, the costs are not necessarily borne by those users who enjoy the benefits, and often the benefits of the information are enjoyed by a broad range of external users. *[FRS 102.2.13]*.

Section 2 also asserts that financial reporting information helps capital providers make better decisions, which results in more efficient functioning of capital markets and a lower cost of capital for the economy as a whole. In the FRC's view, individual entities also enjoy benefits, including improved access to capital markets, favourable effect on public relations, and perhaps lower costs of capital. The benefits may also include better management decisions because financial information used internally is often based at least partly on information prepared for general purpose financial reporting purposes. *[FRS 102.2.14]*.

3.3   Financial position

Section 2 defines the concepts behind the statement of financial position and the statement of comprehensive income. It does not define the concepts behind the other primary statements (the statement of changes in equity and the statement of cash flows).

The *statement of financial position* is a financial statement that presents the relationship of an entity's assets, liabilities and equity as of a specific date. The Companies Act 2006 refers to this financial statement as a balance sheet. *[FRS 102 Appendix I]*.

Assets, liabilities and equity are defined as follows:

- an asset is a resource controlled by the entity as a result of past events and from which future economic benefits are expected to flow to the entity – see 3.3.1 below;

- a liability is a present obligation of the entity arising from past events, the settlement of which is expected to result in an outflow from the entity of resources embodying economic benefits – see 3.3.2 below; and

- equity is the residual interest in the assets of the entity after deducting all its liabilities – see 3.3.3 below. *[FRS 102.2.15]*.

Some items that meet the definition of an asset or a liability may not be recognised as assets or liabilities in the statement of financial position because they do not satisfy the criteria for recognition – see 3.5 below. In particular, the expectation that future economic benefits will flow to or from an entity must be sufficiently certain to meet the probability criterion before an asset or liability is recognised. *[FRS 102.2.16]*.

In addition, FRS 102 does not generally allow the recognition of items in the statement of financial position that do not meet the definition of assets or liabilities regardless of whether they result from applying the notion commonly referred to as the 'matching concept' for measuring profit or loss – see 3.9.5 below.

3.3.1   Assets

The future economic benefit of an asset is its potential to contribute, directly or indirectly, to the flow of cash and cash equivalents to the entity. Those cash flows may come from using the asset or from disposing of it. *[FRS 102.2.17]*.

Many assets, for example property, plant and equipment, have a physical form. However, physical form is not essential to the existence of an asset. Some assets are intangible. *[FRS 102.2.18]*.

In determining the existence of an asset, the right of ownership is not essential. Thus, for example, property held on a lease is an asset if the entity controls the benefits that are expected to flow from the property. *[FRS 102.2.19]*.

3.3.2   Liabilities

An essential characteristic of a liability is that the entity has a present obligation to act or perform in a particular way. The obligation may be either a legal obligation or a constructive obligation. A legal obligation is legally enforceable as a consequence of a binding contract or statutory requirement. A constructive obligation is an obligation that derives from an entity's actions when:

- by an established pattern of past practice, published policies or a sufficiently specific current statement, the entity has indicated to other parties that it will accept certain responsibilities; and

- as a result, the entity has created a valid expectation on the part of those other parties that it will discharge those responsibilities. *[FRS 102.2.20]*.

The settlement of a present obligation usually involves the payment of cash, transfer of other assets, provision of services, the replacement of that obligation with another obligation, or conversion of the obligation to equity. An obligation may also be extinguished by other means, such as a creditor waiving or forfeiting its rights. *[FRS 102.2.21]*.

3.3.3   Equity

As equity is simply a residual figure, FRS 102 does not require that it be subdivided into any particular components although it is suggested that sub-classifications for a corporate entity may include funds contributed by shareholders, retained earnings and gains or losses recognised in other comprehensive income. *[FRS 102.2.22]*.

However, for a UK company, the balance sheet formats of the Regulations require separate disclosure of various elements of equity. These separate components are: called up share capital; share premium account; revaluation reserve; capital redemption reserve;

reserve for own shares; reserves provided by articles of association; other reserves and the profit and loss account (or retained earnings). *[1-3 Sch Balance sheet formats].*

Section 6 – *Statement of Changes in Equity and Statement of Income and Retained Earnings* – requires a reconciliation of each component of equity separately disclosing changes resulting from profit or loss, other comprehensive income and other transactions. An analysis of other comprehensive income by item for each component of equity is also required. *[FRS 102.6.3-3A].*

3.4　Performance

Performance is described as the relationship of the income and expenses of an entity during a reporting period. FRS 102 permits entities to present performance in a single financial statement (a statement of comprehensive income) or in two financial statements (an income statement and a statement of comprehensive income). *[FRS 102.2.23].* Section 2 states that total comprehensive income and profit or loss are frequently used as measures of performance or as the basis for other measures, such as return on investment or earnings per share.

Income and expenses are defined as follows:

- income is increases in economic benefits during the reporting period in the form of inflows or enhancements of assets or decreases of liabilities that result in increases in equity, other than those relating to contributions from equity investors.

- expenses are decreases in economic benefits during the reporting period in the form of outflows or depletions of assets or incurrences of liabilities that result in decreases in equity, other than those relating to distributions to equity investors. *[FRS 102.2.23].*

The recognition of income and expenses results directly from the recognition and measurement of assets and liabilities. *[FRS 102.2.24].* The definition means that any activity which does not increase or decrease an asset or liability cannot be regarded as income or expense unless specifically permitted by a section of FRS 102. Criteria for the recognition of income and expenses are discussed at 3.5 below.

3.4.1　Income

The definition of income (see 3.4 above) encompasses both revenue and gains.

Revenue is income that arises in the course of the ordinary activities of an entity and is referred to by a variety of names including sales, fees, interest, dividends, royalties and rent.

Gains are other items that meet the definition of income but are not revenue. When gains are recognised in the statement of comprehensive income, they are usually displayed separately because knowledge of them is useful for making economic decisions. *[FRS 102.2.25].*

This split of income between revenue and gains has little meaning for accounting purposes since Section 5 – *Statement of Comprehensive Income and Income Statement* – requires that the format of the income statement should comply with the Regulations (or, where applicable, the LLP Regulations) except to the extent that these requirements are not permitted by any statutory framework under which an entity is required to report. *[FRS 102.5.1]*.

3.4.2   Expenses

The definition of expenses encompasses losses as well as those expenses that arise in the course of the ordinary activities of the entity.

Expenses that arise in the course of the ordinary activities of the entity include, for example, cost of sales, wages and depreciation. They usually take the form of an outflow or depletion of assets such as cash and cash equivalents, inventory, or property, plant and equipment.

Losses are other items that meet the definition of expenses and may arise in the course of the ordinary activities of the entity. When losses are recognised in the statement of comprehensive income, they are usually presented separately because knowledge of them is useful for making economic decisions. *[FRS 102.2.26]*.

As discussed at 3.4.1 above, this split of expenses between expenses and losses has little meaning for accounting purposes since the format of the income statement is prescribed by the Regulations.

3.5   Recognition of assets, liabilities, income and expenses

Recognition is described as the process of incorporating in the statement of financial position or statement of comprehensive income an item that meets the definition of an asset, liability, equity, income or expense (discussed at 3.9.1 to 3.9.4 below) and satisfies the following criteria:

- it is probable that any future economic benefit associated with the item will flow to or from the entity (see 3.5.1 below); and
- the item has a cost or value that can be measured reliably (see 3.5.2 below). *[FRS 102.2.27]*.

The failure to recognise an item that satisfies those criteria is not rectified by disclosure of the accounting policies used or by notes or explanatory material. *[FRS 102.2.28]*.

3.5.1   The probability of future economic benefit

The concept of probability is used in the first recognition criterion to refer to the degree of uncertainty that the future economic benefits associated with the item will flow to or from the entity. Assessments of the degree of uncertainty attaching to the flow of future economic benefits are made on the basis of the evidence relating to conditions at the end of the reporting period available when the financial statements are prepared. Those assessments are made individually for individually significant items, and for a group for a large population of individually insignificant items. *[FRS 102.2.29]*.

Probability as applicable to recognition in the financial statements is discussed at Section 3.9 below.

3.5.2   Reliability of measurement

The second criterion for the recognition of an item is that it possesses a cost or value that can be measured with reliability. Reliability is discussed at 3.2.4 above.

In many cases, the cost or value of an item is known. In other cases it must be estimated. The use of reasonable estimates is an essential part of the preparation of financial statements and does not undermine their reliability. When a reasonable estimate cannot be made, the item is not recognised in the financial statements. *[FRS 102.2.30].*

An item that fails to meet these recognition criteria may qualify for recognition at a later date as a result of subsequent circumstances or events. *[FRS 102.2.31].*

Section 2 notes that an item that fails to meet the criteria for recognition may nonetheless warrant disclosure in the notes or explanatory material, or in supplementary schedules. This disclosure is considered appropriate when knowledge of the item is relevant to the evaluation of the financial position, performance and changes in financial position of an entity by the users of financial statements. *[FRS 102.2.32].* It is not clear what is meant by 'explanatory material or supplemental schedules' since a complete set of financial statements includes only the primary statements and the notes to the financial statements. *[FRS 102.3.17].*

3.6   Measurement of assets, liabilities, income and expenses

Measurement is the process of determining the monetary amounts at which an entity measures assets, liabilities, income and expenses in its financial statements. Measurement involves the selection of a basis of measurement. The various sections of FRS 102 specify (or, sometimes, allow a choice of) which measurement basis an entity shall use for many types of assets, liabilities, income and expenses. *[FRS 102.2.33].*

Two common measurement bases used by FRS 102 are historical cost and fair value. For assets, historical cost is the amount of cash or cash equivalents paid or the fair value of the consideration given to acquire the asset at the time of its acquisition. For liabilities, historical cost is the amount of proceeds of cash or cash equivalents received or the fair value of non-cash assets received in exchange for the obligation at the time the obligation is incurred, or in some circumstances (for example, income tax) the amounts of cash or cash equivalents expected to be paid to settle the liability in the normal course of business. Amortised historical cost is the historical cost of an asset or liability plus or minus that portion of its historical cost previously recognised as an expense or income.

Fair value is the amount for which an asset could be exchanged, a liability settled, or an equity instrument granted could be exchanged, between knowledgeable, willing parties in an arm's length transaction. In the absence of any specific guidance provided in a relevant section of FRS 102, where fair value measurement is permitted or required, the guidance in paragraphs 11.27 to 11.32 shall be applied. *[FRS 102.2.34].* Fair value guidance is discussed in Chapter 8 at 4.4.2.B.

Measurement at initial recognition is discussed at 3.10 below and subsequent measurement is discussed at 3.11 below. There is no overriding principle which determines whether historical cost or fair value is the more appropriate method of measurement.

3.7   Pervasive recognition and measurement principles

Section 2 refers to the hierarchy in Section 10 that applies for an entity to follow in deciding on the appropriate accounting policy in the absence of a requirement that applies specifically to a transaction or other event or condition. The second level of that hierarchy requires an entity to look to the definitions, recognition criteria and measurement concepts for assets, liabilities, income and expenses and the pervasive principles set out in Section 2. *[FRS 102.2.35]*. The hierarchy is discussed in Chapter 7 at 3.1.

This clarifies that guidance in Section 2 is subordinate to specific requirements in the other sections of FRS 102.

3.8 Accruals basis

Financial statements, except for cash flow information, should be prepared using the accrual basis of accounting. On the accrual basis, items are recognised as assets, liabilities, equity, income or expenses when they satisfy the definitions and recognition criteria for those items (see 3.9 below). *[FRS 102.2.36]*.

The definition of the accruals basis is somewhat circular as it means that an item is, for example, recognised as income when it meets the definition and recognition criteria of income. In contrast, FRS 18 – *Accounting policies* – stated that the accrual basis of accounting requires the non-cash effects of transactions and other events to be reflected, as far as possible, in the financial statements for the accounting period in which they occur and not, for example, in the period in which any cash involved is received or paid. *[FRS 18.27]*. Similarly, the Regulations require that all income and charges relating to the financial year to which the accounts relate must be taken into account, without regard to the date or receipt of payment. *[1 Sch 14, 2 Sch 20, 3 Sch 19]*.

In practice, we do not expect these wording differences to have a material effect as the impact, where applicable, is likely to be similar.

3.9 Recognition in the financial statements

3.9.1 Assets

Section 2 states that an entity shall recognise an asset in the statement of financial position when it is probable that the future economic benefits will flow to the entity and the asset has a cost or value that can be measured reliably. Conversely, an asset is not recognised in the statement of financial position when expenditure has been incurred for which it is considered not probable that economic benefits will flow to the entity beyond the current reporting period. Instead such a transaction results in the recognition of an expense in the statement of comprehensive income (or in the income statement, if presented). *[FRS 102.2.37]*.

Section 2 repeats the requirements of Section 21 – *Provisions and Contingencies* – that an entity shall not recognise a contingent asset as an asset but, when the flow of future economic benefits to the entity is virtually certain, then the related asset is not a contingent asset, and its recognition is appropriate. *[FRS 102.2.38]*.

It is clear from the scope of Section 21 that the 'virtually certain' criteria applies only to contingent assets within the scope of that section. Assets arising from financial instruments and executory contracts which are not onerous are not within the scope of Section 21 and the 'probable' criterion applies to the recognition of those assets.

Chapter 3

3.9.2   Liabilities

An entity shall recognise a liability in the statement of financial position when:

- the entity has an obligation at the end of the reporting period as a result of a past event;

- it is probable that the entity will be required to transfer resources embodying economic benefits in settlement; and

- the settlement amount can be measured reliably. *[FRS 102.2.39].*

A contingent liability is either a possible but uncertain obligation or a present obligation that is not recognised because it fails to meet one or both of the second or third conditions above. An entity should not generally recognise a contingent liability as a liability (see Chapter 17 at 3.4), except for contingent liabilities of an acquiree in a business combination (see Chapter 15 at 3.6.3.H). *[FRS 102.2.40].*

3.9.3   Income

The recognition of income results directly from the recognition and measurement of assets and liabilities. An entity shall recognise income in the statement of comprehensive income (or in the income statement, if presented) when an increase in future economic benefits related to an increase in an asset or a decrease of a liability has arisen that can be measured reliably. *[FRS 102.2.41].*

Although this states that the reduction of a liability is regarded as 'income', this does not mean that it should be presented as 'turnover' or 'revenue' in the statement of comprehensive income. The presentation of items in the statement of comprehensive income follows the required format of the Regulations or LLP Regulations (see Chapter 4).

3.9.4   Expenses

The recognition of expenses results directly from the recognition and measurement of assets and liabilities. An entity shall recognise expenses in the statement of comprehensive income (or in the income statement, if presented) when a decrease in future economic benefits related to a decrease in an asset or an increase of a liability has arisen that can be measured reliably. *[FRS 102.2.42].*

3.9.5   Total comprehensive income and profit or loss

Total comprehensive income is the arithmetical difference between income and expenses. It is not a separate element of financial statements, and a separate recognition principle is not needed for it. *[FRS 102.2.43].*

Profit or loss is the arithmetical difference between income and expenses other than those items of income and expense that FRS 102 classifies as items of other comprehensive income. It is not a separate element of financial statements, and a separate recognition principle is not needed for it. *[FRS 102.2.44].*

Generally, FRS 102 does not allow the recognition of items in the statement of financial position that do not meet the definition of assets or of liabilities regardless of whether they result from applying the notion commonly referred to as the 'matching concept' for measuring profit or loss. *[FRS 102.2.45].*

3.10 Measurement at initial recognition

At initial recognition, an entity shall measure assets and liabilities at historical cost unless FRS 102 requires initial measurement on another basis such as fair value. *[FRS 102.2.46]*.

3.11 Subsequent measurement

3.11.1 *Financial assets and financial liabilities*

As discussed in Chapter 8 at 4.1, an entity measures basic financial assets and basic financial liabilities at amortised cost less impairment except for:

- investments in non-convertible preference shares and non-puttable ordinary and preference shares that are publicly traded or whose fair value can otherwise be measured reliably, which are measured at fair value with changes in fair value recognised in profit or loss; and

- any financial instruments that upon their initial recognition were designated by the entity as at fair value through profit or loss. *[FRS 102.2.47]*.

An entity generally measures all other financial assets and financial liabilities at fair value, with changes in fair value recognised in profit or loss, unless FRS 102 requires or permits measurement on another basis such as cost or amortised cost. *[FRS 102.2.48]*.

3.11.2 *Non-financial assets*

Most non-financial assets that an entity initially recognised at historical cost are subsequently measured on other measurement bases. For example, as discussed in Chapter 13 at 3.5 and 3.6, an entity measures property, plant and equipment using either the cost model or the revaluation model and an entity measures inventories at the lower of cost and selling price less costs to complete and sell.

Measurement of assets at amounts lower than initial historical cost is intended to ensure that an asset is not measured at an amount greater than the entity expects to recover from the sale or use of that asset. *[FRS 102.2.49]*.

For certain types of non-financial assets, FRS 102 permits or requires measurement at fair value. For example:

- investments in associates and joint ventures that an entity measures at fair value (see Chapters 10 and 11);

- investment property that an entity measures at fair value (see Chapter 12);

- biological assets that an entity measures at fair value less estimated costs to sell in accordance with the fair value model and agricultural produce that an entity measures, at the point of harvest, at fair value less estimated costs to sell in accordance with either the fair value model or cost model (see Chapter 29);

- property, plant and equipment that an entity measures in accordance with the revaluation model (see Chapter 13);

- intangible assets that an entity measures in accordance with the revaluation model (see Chapter 14). *[FRS 102.2.50]*.

3.11.3   *Liabilities other than financial liabilities*

Most liabilities other than financial liabilities are measured at the best estimate of the amount that would be required to settle the obligation at the reporting date. *[FRS 102.2.51].*

This wording is identical to that required for provisions by Section 21 which provides additional explanatory guidance. *[FRS 102.21.7].* See Chapter 17.

3.12   Offsetting

An entity shall not offset assets and liabilities, or income and expenses, unless required or permitted by FRS 102. However, measuring assets net of valuation allowances (for example, allowances for inventory obsolescence and allowances for uncollectible receivables) is not offsetting. *[FRS 102.2.52].*

If an entity's normal operating activities do not include buying and selling fixed assets, including investments and operating assets, then the entity reports gains and losses on disposal of such assets by deducting from the proceeds on disposal the carrying amount of the asset and related selling expenses. *[FRS 102.2.52].*

This implies that no recycling of unrealised gains from a revaluation reserve within equity to profit and loss is generally permitted by FRS 102. However, such recycling is permitted for financial instruments held at available for sale under the provisions of IAS 39 – *Financial Instruments: Recognition and Measurement* – that can be applied under Section 12 – *Other Financial Instruments Issues* of FRS 102. *[FRS 102.12.2].*

References

1 *Statement of Principles for Financial Reporting (Statement of Principles)*, FRC, December 1999, Chapter 1.
2 *Statement of Principles*, FRC, para. 3.
3 *The Conceptual Framework for Financial Reporting (Conceptual Framework)*, IASB, September 2010, para. QC5.
4 *Conceptual Framework*, IASB, paras. OB2-OB11.
5 *Stewardship/Accountability As An Objective of Financial Reporting: A Comment on the IASB/FASB Conceptual Framework Project*, ASB, EFRAG and others, June 2007.

Chapter 4   Presentation of financial statements

Chapter 4

Chapter 4

Chapter 4

List of examples

Chapter 4   Presentation of financial statements

1   INTRODUCTION

The following sections of FRS 102 – *The Financial Reporting Standard Applicable in the UK and Republic of Ireland* – address the presentation, i.e. the form, content and structure, of financial statements:

*   Section 3 – *Financial Statement Presentation*;
*   Section 4 – *Statement of Financial Position*;
*   Section 5 – *Statement of Comprehensive Income and Income Statement*;
*   Section 6 – *Statement of Changes in Equity and Statement of Income and Retained Earnings*;
*   Section 7 – *Statement of Cash Flows*; and
*   Section 8 – *Notes to the Financial Statements*.

The above sections cover the content of a complete set of FRS 102 financial statements, i.e. the primary statements and notes required, as well as its concept of fair presentation, including general principles underlying preparation of financial statements.

This chapter deals only with Sections 3 to 6 (see 3 to 6 below), and Section 8 (see 7 below). Section 7 is addressed in Chapter 5. FRS 102's requirements on presentation overlap with Section 1 – *Scope* (which covers the reduced disclosure framework – see Chapter 2), Section 2 – *Concepts and Pervasive Principles* (see Chapter 3) and Section 10 – *Accounting Policies, Estimates and Errors* (see Chapter 7). These sections are referred to in places in this chapter.

Statutory accounts prepared in accordance with FRS 102 by UK companies are Companies Act accounts and must comply with:

*   the requirements of FRS 102, as well as
*   statutory requirements included in the Companies Act 2006 and the *Large and Medium-sized Companies and Groups (Accounts and Reports) Regulations 2008* ('Regulations') and / or other applicable regulations. See Chapter 1 at 6 for information on the Companies Act 2006 requirements for statutory accounts and reports.

In particular, Companies Act accounts are required to give a true and fair view, and to comply with the applicable regulations governing the form and content of the balance sheet and profit and loss account and additional notes. *[s396, s403].* Consequently, FRS 102 has been amended to mandate that UK companies and LLPs use the applicable company law formats. The standard has further extended this requirement to other entities except to the extent that this conflicts with the statutory frameworks that apply to their financial statements.

The Regulations and FRS 102 share basic principles underlying the preparation of financial statements such as going concern, prudence, accruals, materiality, aggregation, and consistency, although the Regulations restrict further when profits may be reported in the profit and loss account (see 8 below). The Regulations also set out certain requirements for recognition and measurement of assets and liabilities (see 9 below), namely the historical cost accounting rules, the alternative accounting rules and the fair value accounting rules.

Except where otherwise stated, the rest of this chapter will refer to the requirements for UK companies, and therefore will refer to UK GAAP (prior to implementation of FRS 100 to FRS 102) as 'previous UK GAAP'. UK LLPs and other entities preparing financial statements in accordance with Part 15 of the Companies Act 2006 are subject to similar requirements to those for UK companies preparing Companies Act accounts, modified as necessary by the regulations that govern the content of their financial statements.

2   SUMMARY OF PRESENTATION REQUIREMENTS OF FRS 102

The statutory accounts of a UK company prepared in accordance with FRS 102 are Companies Act accounts. Certain other entities are also required to prepare statutory accounts in accordance with Part 15 of the Companies Act 2006.

A complete set of FRS 102 financial statements contains: a statement of financial position, a statement of comprehensive income (either as a single statement or as a separate income statement and statement of comprehensive income), a statement of cash flows, a statement of changes in equity, together with accompanying notes to the financial statements. In certain circumstances, a statement of income and retained earnings can be presented instead of the statement of comprehensive income and statement of changes in equity. Comparatives must be presented. FRS 102 permits the use of other titles – such as balance sheet or profit and loss account for the primary statements – as long as they are not misleading. See 3.5 below. *[FRS 102.3.22].*

FRS 102 specifies the content of the primary financial statements and notes. The profit and loss account section of the statement of comprehensive income and the statement of financial position must follow the profit and loss account and balance sheet formats respectively set out in the Regulations or LLP Regulations, as applicable. An entity not subject to these requirements must also follow the same formats so long as these do not conflict with the statutory framework under which it reports. FRS 102 includes supplementary requirements, e.g. on presentation of discontinued operations (see 5.8 below). The requirements for the other primary financial statements are based on (but simpler than) the requirements in IAS 1 – *Presentation of Financial Statements.*

Financial statements must present fairly the financial position, financial performance and cash flows of the entity. Fair presentation usually requires compliance with FRS 102, with additional disclosure where needed but FRS 102 provides for a 'fair presentation override', consistent with the 'true and fair override' provided for in the Companies Act 2006. Like IAS 1 and the Regulations, FRS 102 sets out basic principles underlying the preparation of financial statements such as going concern, accruals, materiality and aggregation, and consistency. See 8 below.

A statement of compliance with FRS 102 (and, where applicable, FRS 103 – *Insurance Contracts – Consolidated and accounting reporting requirements for entities in the UK and Republic of Ireland issuing insurance contracts*) is required. FRS 102 contains certain requirements (marked PBE) to be applied only by public benefit entities. An entity that is a public benefit entity that applies these paragraphs must make an explicit and unreserved statement that it is a public benefit entity. See 3.8 below.

The notes to the financial statements should include: the basis of preparation; accounting policies (including judgements made and key sources of estimation uncertainty); disclosures required by FRS 102; and information relevant to understanding the financial statements that are not presented elsewhere in the financial statements. Entities applying FRS 102 may also be subject to other disclosure requirements deriving from statutory or other regulatory frameworks, e.g. a UK company's statutory accounts must be prepared in accordance with Part 15 of the Companies Act 2006 and the Regulations. See 7 below.

FRS 102 provides for a reduced disclosure framework in the individual financial statements of qualifying entities, i.e. members of a group included in publicly available consolidated financial statements intended to give a true and fair view. In particular, a qualifying entity need not present an individual cash flow statement. See Chapter 2 at 3.

FRS 102 does not address the requirements for preparation of interim reports but an entity must describe the basis of preparation and presentation of interim financial reports. *[FRS 102.3.25]*. The FRC has published FRED 56: Draft FRS 104 – *Interim Financial Reporting* – which, when finalised, is intended for use by FRS 102 reporters. See 3.3.1 below.

IFRS 8 – *Operating Segments* – is scoped in for publicly traded companies. If an entity discloses disaggregated information not complying with IFRS 8, this shall not be described as segment information. *[FRS 102.1.5]*. See 3.3.2 below.

A comparison of FRS 102 to previous UK GAAP and IFRS is presented in the Section 10.

3   COMPOSITION OF FINANCIAL STATEMENTS

Financial statements are a structured representation of the financial position, financial performance and cash flows of an entity. *[FRS 102 Appendix I]*. Section 2 of FRS 102 (see Chapter 3) explains the objective of financial statements and the conceptual and pervasive principles underlying financial statements.

Section 3 of the standard explains the concept of fair presentation of financial statements, what compliance with the standard requires and what a complete set of financial statements contains. *[FRS 102.3.1]*. Sections 4 to 9 of the standard set out the requirements in relation to the different components of financial statements. Each component of a complete set of financial statements is discussed in more detail at 4 to 7 below, with the exception of the Statement of Cash Flows which is discussed in Chapter 5. General principles underlying preparation of financial statements are discussed at 8 below.

UK companies preparing Companies Act accounts must also comply with the Companies Act 2006 and the Regulations. The Companies Act 2006 requirements are addressed, where appropriate, in the relevant sections below and the three accounting models in the Regulations for the recognition and measurement of assets and liabilities – historical cost accounting rules, alternative accounting rules (which provide an alternative measurement basis to the historical cost rules, usually at a valuation) and fair value accounting rules (which may be applied to living animals and plants, financial instruments and investment properties) are discussed at 9 below.

3.1   Key definitions

The following definitions, included in FRS 102's Glossary are relevant to presentation:

Term	*Definition*
Current assets	Assets of an entity which are not intended for use on a continuing basis in the entity's activities.
Equity	The residual interest in the assets of the entity after deducting all its liabilities.
Expenses	Decreases in economic benefits during the reporting period in the form of outflows or depletions of assets or incurrences of liabilities that result in decreases in equity, other than those relating to distributions to equity investors.
Fair presentation	Faithful representation of the effects of transactions, other events and conditions in accordance with the definitions and recognition criteria for assets, liabilities, income and expenses unless the override stated in paragraph 3.4 [of the standard] applies.
Fair value	The amount for which an asset could be exchanged, a liability settled, or an equity instrument granted could be exchanged, between knowledgeable, willing parties in an arm's length transaction. In the absence of any specific guidance provided in the relevant section of the FRS, the guidance in 11.27 to 11.32 [of the standard] shall be used in determining fair value.
Financial performance	The relationship of the income and expenses of an entity, as reported in the statement of comprehensive income.
Financial position	The relationship of the assets, liabilities, and equity of an entity as reported in the statement of financial position.

Financial statements	A structured representation of the financial position, financial performance and cash flows of an entity. General purpose financial statements (generally referred to simply as financial statements) are financial statements directed to the general financial information needs of a wide range of users who are not in a position to demand reports tailored to meet their particular information needs
Fixed assets	Assets of an entity which are intended for use on a continuing basis in the entity's activities.
Income	Increases in economic benefits during the reporting period in the form of inflows or enhancements of assets or decreases of liabilities that result in increases in equity, other than those relating to contributions from equity investors.
Income statement	Financial statement that presents all items of income and expense recognised in a reporting period, excluding the items of other comprehensive income (referred to as the profit and loss account in the Companies Act 2006).
LLP Regulations	The Large and Medium-sized Limited Liability Partnerships (Accounts) Regulations 2008 (SI 2008/1913)
Material	Omissions or misstatements of items are material if they could, individually or collectively, influence the economic decisions of users taken on the basis of the financial statements. Materiality depends on the size and nature of the omission or misstatement judged in the surrounding circumstances. The size or nature of the item, or a combination of both, could be the determining factor.
Other comprehensive income	items of income and expense (including reclassification adjustments) that are not recognised in profit or loss as required or permitted by FRS 102
Profit or loss	the total of income less expenses, excluding the components of other comprehensive income. In the not for profit sector, this may be known as income and expenditure (and the profit and loss account, as an income and expenditure account). *[s474(2)]*.
Regulations	The Large and Medium-sized Companies and Groups (Accounts and Reports) Regulations 2008 (SI 2008/410).
Statement of comprehensive income	A financial statement that presents all items of income and expense recognised in a period, including those items recognised in determining profit or loss (which is a subtotal in the statement of comprehensive income) and items of other comprehensive income. If an entity chooses to present both an income statement and a statement of comprehensive income, the statement of comprehensive income begins with profit or loss and then displays the items of other comprehensive income.
Total comprehensive income	The change in equity during a period resulting from transactions and other events, other than those changes resulting from transactions from equity participants (equal to the sum of profit or loss and other comprehensive income).

Chapter 4

While this term is not defined in the Glossary, this chapter refers to *The Small Companies and Groups (Accounts and Directors' Report) Regulations 2008* (SI 2008/409) as the Small Companies Regulations.

3.2   Objectives of sections in FRS 102 addressing presentation of financial statements

The objective of financial statements is to provide information about the financial position, performance and cash flows of an entity that is useful for economic decision-making by a broad range of users who are not in a position to demand reports tailored to meet their particular information needs. Financial statements also show the results of the stewardship of management – the accountability of management for the resources entrusted to it. *[FRS 102.2.2-2.3]*.

Sections 3 to 9 of the standard, which address presentation of financial statements, include the following objectives:

- to explain fair presentation of financial statements, what compliance with FRS 102 requires and what is a complete set of financial statements; *[FRS 102.3.1]*

- to set out the information required in the statement of financial position (referred to as the 'balance sheet' under the Companies Act 2006) and how to present it; *[FRS 102.4.1]*

- to require an entity to present total comprehensive income for a period, being its financial performance for the period – in one or two statements – and to set out the information required in these statements and how to present it; *[FRS 102.5.1]*

- to set out requirements for presenting changes in an entity's equity for the period in a statement of changes in equity, or if specified conditions are met and an entity chooses, in a statement of income and retained earnings; *[FRS 102.6.1]*

- to set out the information required in a statement of cash flows and how to present it. See Chapter 5 for further details; *[FRS 102.7.1]* and

- to set out the principles underlying information required in the notes to the financial statements and how to present it. In addition, nearly every section of FRS 102 requires disclosures that are normally presented in the notes. *[FRS 102.8.1]*.

3.3   Interim financial reports and segmental reporting

3.3.1   *Interim financial reporting*

FRS 102 does not address the presentation of interim financial reports. Entities preparing such reports must describe the basis for preparing and presenting such information. *[FRS 102.3.25]*. An interim financial report is a financial report containing either a complete set of financial statements or a set of condensed financial statements for an interim period, i.e. a financial reporting period shorter than a full financial year. *[FRS 102 Appendix I]*.

In November 2014, the FRC published FRED 56: Draft FRS 104 – *Interim Financial Reporting* – which, when finalised, is intended for use by FRS 102 reporters providing that applicable laws and regulations do not prohibit its application. *[FRED 56.2]*. Where an entity's interim financial statements are in compliance with the final standard, a statement of compliance must be given. *[FRED 56.3, 19]*. Like IAS 34 – *Interim Financial Reporting*, the final standard, therefore, will not be mandatory nor does it mandate which entities must publish interim financial reports, how frequently, or how soon after the end of the reporting period. *[FRED 56.2A]*.

The draft standard is based on IAS 34, with limited modifications, as explained further in Chapter 2 at 1.2.3.D. When the final standard is issued, the ASB's *Reporting Statement: Half-Yearly Reports* will be withdrawn.

A number of UK publicly traded companies that are not required to prepare group accounts currently apply previous UK GAAP in their financial statements, where this is permitted by the rules applying to the relevant market (see Chapter 1 at 6.1 to 6.3). Such companies may be required to prepare half-yearly financial reports and could apply FRS 102.

The Disclosure and Transparency Rules of the Financial Conduct Authority permit the 'persons responsible' (i.e. the directors) of UK issuers with transferable securities admitted to trading on a regulated markets that do not apply EU-adopted IFRS to make a responsibility statement in the half-yearly financial report that:

The condensed set of financial statements have been prepared in accordance with pronouncements on interim reporting issued by the Accounting Standards Board.

provided always that a person making such a statement has reasonable grounds that the condensed set of financial statements so prepared is not misleading. *[DTR 4.2.10]*.

FRS 104, when finalised, will be a pronouncement on interim reporting for the purposes of the above statement. *[FRED 56.3B]*.

3.3.2   *Segmental reporting*

IFRS 8 applies to an entity whose debt or equity instruments are publicly traded, or that files, or is in the process of filing, its financial statements with a securities commission or other regulatory organisation for the purpose of issuing any class of instruments in a public market, or an entity that chooses to provide information described as segment information.

If an entity discloses disaggregated information, but that information does not comply with IFRS 8's requirements, the information shall not be described as segment information. *[FRS 102.1.5]*.

3.3.2.A   *Segmental disclosures of turnover*

All UK companies preparing Companies Act accounts must also give the following disclosures required by the Regulations in the accounts or notes to the accounts:

- where the company has carried on business of two or more classes during the financial year that, in the opinion of the directors, differ substantially from each other, the amount of the turnover attributable to each class, and the description of the class; and

- where the company has supplied geographical markets during the financial year that, in the opinion of the directors, differ substantially from each other, the amount of the turnover attributable to each market.

The directors should have regard to the manner in which the company's activities are organised. Classes of business (or markets) which, in the opinion of the directors, do not differ substantially from each other must be treated as one class (or market). Amounts attributable to a class of business (or market) that are not material may be included in the amount stated in respect of another class of business (or market).

Where any of the above information required would, in the opinion of the directors, be seriously prejudicial to the interests of the company, that information need not be disclosed, but the fact that any such information has not been disclosed must be stated. [1 Sch 68].

For group accounts, the disclosures are given for the company and undertakings included (i.e. consolidated) in the consolidation. [6 Sch 1(1)].

See 5.6.1 below for discussion of turnover in the profit and loss account formats.

3.4   Frequency of reporting and period covered

An entity must present a complete set of financial statements (including comparative information) at least annually.

When the end of an entity's reporting period changes and annual financial statements are presented for a period longer or shorter than one year, the entity shall disclose that fact, the reason for using a longer or shorter period, and the fact that comparative amounts presented in the financial statements (including the related notes) are not entirely comparable. [FRS 102.3.10].

Normally, financial statements are consistently prepared covering a one year period. Some entities, particularly in the retail sector, present financial statements for a 52-week period. This practice is permitted by the Companies Act 2006 which allows companies to prepare financial statements to a financial year end, not more than 7 days before or after the accounting reference date notified to the Registrar. [s390(2)(b)]. While the standard does not explicitly address this issue, we consider that FRS 102 financial statements can be prepared to a financial year end, not more than 7 days from the accounting reference date (as defined in section 391 of the Companies Act 2006).

3.5   Components of a complete set of financial statements

A complete set of financial statements under FRS 102 includes all of the following, each of which should be presented with equal prominence: [FRS 102.3.17, 3.21]

- a statement of financial position as at the reporting date;
- a statement of comprehensive income for the reporting period to be presented either as:
  - a single statement of comprehensive income, displaying all items of income and expense recognised during the period including those items recognised in determining profit or loss (which is a subtotal in the statement of comprehensive income) and items of other comprehensive income; or
  - a separate income statement and a separate statement of comprehensive income. In this case, the statement of comprehensive income begins with profit or loss and then displays the items of other comprehensive income;

- a statement of changes in equity for the reporting period;

- a statement of cash flows for the reporting period (unless exempt – see Chapter 5 at 3.1);

- notes, comprising a summary of significant accounting policies and other explanatory information.

Other titles for the financial statements can be used, as long as they are not misleading. *[FRS 102.3.22]*. For instance, an entity may wish to refer to a balance sheet (for the statement of financial position) or the profit and loss account (instead of an income statement).

If an entity has no items of other comprehensive income in any of the periods presented, it may present only an income statement (or a statement of comprehensive income in which the 'bottom line' is labelled profit or loss). *[FRS 102.3.19]*.

If the only changes to equity during the periods presented in the financial statements arise from profit or loss, payments of dividends, corrections of prior period errors and changes in accounting policy, the entity may present a single statement of income and retained earnings in place of the statement of comprehensive income and statement of changes in equity. *[FRS 102.3.18]*.

FRS 102 explains that notes contain information in addition to that presented in the primary statements above, and provide narrative descriptions or disaggregations of items presented in those statements and information about items that do not qualify for recognition in those statements. *[FRS 102.8.1]*.

In addition to information about the reporting period, FRS 102 also requires comparative information about the preceding period, and therefore a complete set of financial statements includes, at a minimum, two of each of the required financial statements and related notes. *[FRS 102.3.20]*.

The Regulations also require only one comparative period to be presented for the balance sheet and profit and loss account formats. *[1 Sch 7]*. The Regulations do not specifically require comparative note disclosures but, as noted above, these are required by FRS 102. Other statutory or regulatory frameworks may require further periods to be presented. Comparative information is discussed at 3.6 below.

3.6   Comparative information

Except when FRS 102 permits or requires otherwise, an entity presents comparative information in respect of the preceding period for all amounts presented in the current period's financial statements. *[FRS 102.3.14]*. This means that the requirement to present comparative information applies both to mandatory and voluntary information presented for the current period.

In certain cases, FRS 102 provides specific exemptions from presenting comparatives. For example, there is no requirement to present comparatives for the reconciliations of movements in the number of shares outstanding, or of the movements in the carrying amounts of investment property, property, plant and equipment, intangible assets, goodwill, negative goodwill, provisions or biological assets. *[FRS 102.4.12(a)(iv), 16.10(e), 17.31(e), 18.27(e), 19.26, 19.26A, 21.14, 34.7, 34.10]*. These exemptions are addressed in the relevant chapters of this publication.

The Regulations require that for each item presented in the balance sheet and profit and loss account, the corresponding amount for the immediately preceding financial year (i.e. the comparative) must also be shown. *[1 Sch 5(1)]*.

3.6.1   Comparative information for narrative and descriptive information

An entity shall include comparative information for narrative and descriptive information when it is relevant to an understanding of the current period's financial statements. *[FRS 102.3.14]*. IAS 1, which has a similar requirement, illustrates the current year relevance of the previous year's narratives with a legal dispute, the outcome of which was uncertain at the end of the previous period and is yet to be resolved (the disclosure of contingent liabilities is addressed in Section 21 – *Provisions and Contingencies* (see Chapter 17 at 3.10.3). It observes that users benefit from information that the uncertainty existed at the end of the previous period, and about the steps that have been taken during the period to resolve the uncertainty. *[IAS 1.38B]*.

Another example would be the required disclosure of material items, which would include items commonly called exceptional items, although that expression is not used by FRS 102 (see 5.7.5 below). FRS 102 requires that the nature and amount of such items be disclosed separately in the statement of comprehensive income (or separate income statement) or in the notes. *[FRS 102.5.9A]*. Often a simple caption or line item heading will be sufficient to convey the 'nature' of material items. Sometimes, though, a more extensive description in the notes may be needed to do this. In that case, the same information is likely to be relevant the following year.

3.6.2   Consistency of, and reclassifications of comparative information

The objective of comparative information is comparability of an entity's financial statements through time to identify trends in its financial position and performance, and to enable users to compare the financial statements of different entities to evaluate their relative financial position, performance and cash flows. *[FRS 102.2.11]*.

Consequently, an entity must retain the presentation and classification of items in the financial statements from one period to the next unless: *[FRS 102.3.11]*

- it is apparent, following a significant change in the nature of the entity's operations or a review of its financial statements, that another presentation or classification would be more appropriate having regard to the criteria for selection and application of accounting policies in Section 10 (see Chapter 7 at 3.4); or

- where FRS 102 (or another applicable FRS or FRC Abstract) requires a change in presentation.

When entities change the presentation or classification of items in the financial statements, the comparatives must be reclassified, unless this is impracticable (in which case the reason should be disclosed). When comparative amounts are reclassified, the nature of the reclassification, the amounts of each item (or class of items) reclassified and the reasons for the reclassification must be disclosed.

Applying a requirement is impracticable when the entity cannot apply it after making every reasonable effort to do so. *[FRS 102.3.12-3.13, Appendix I]*.

This situation should be distinguished from a reclassification due to a change in use of an asset. An example would be a reclassification out of investment property because it ceases to meet the definition of investment property in the current period. This would be treated as a transfer arising in the current period and not lead to a reclassification of comparatives. *[FRS 102.16.9]*.

In addition, the initial application of a policy to revalue property, plant and equipment (or intangible assets, where the strict criteria are met) is treated as a revaluation in accordance with Section 17 – *Property, Plant and Equipment* – and Section 18 – *Intangible Assets other than Goodwill* – respectively. *[FRS 102.10.10A]*. This means that it is reflected as an adjustment in the period of application of the revaluation policy rather than retrospectively. This is consistent with IFRSs *[IAS 8.17]*, but differs to previous UK GAAP which required retrospective application. *[FRS 18.4, 48]*.

Restatements of comparatives may also arise from:

- changes in accounting policy (see Chapter 7 at 3.4);

- correction of material errors (see Chapter 7 at 3.6);

- presentation of discontinued operations (see 5.8 below); and

- hindsight adjustments in respect of provisional fair values of identifiable assets, liabilities and contingent liabilities arising on business combinations (see Chapter 15 at 2.1.6).

FRS 102 (unlike IAS 1) does not require presentation of a third balance sheet at the beginning of the preceding period when there is a retrospective restatement due to an accounting policy change, reclassification or correction of a material error. *[IAS 1.10(f), 40A-D]*.

Where the comparative shown in the balance sheet and profit and loss account formats (see 4.2 and 5.6 below which set out the balance sheet and profit and loss account formats respectively) is not comparable with the amount shown in the current period, the Regulations permit a UK company preparing Companies Act accounts to adjust the comparative to make these comparable with the current period amounts. Particulars of the non-comparability and of any adjustment must be disclosed in a note to the accounts. *[1 Sch 7]*. This statutory requirement would permit FRS 102's requirements on restatement of comparatives to be followed. Where amounts are not restated, e.g. due to transitional provisions in accounting policies or where it is impracticable to determine the effects of a change in accounting policies on earlier periods *[FRS 102.10.11-12]*, a note to the accounts will need to disclose the non-comparability.

3.7 Identification of financial statements

It is commonly the case that financial statements will form only part of a larger annual report, regulatory filing or other document, but FRS 102 only applies to the financial statements (including the notes). Chapter 1 at 6.2 addresses the content of the statutory annual report and accounts for a UK company.

Accordingly, FRS 102 requires that an entity clearly identifies the financial statements and the notes, and distinguishes them from other information in the same document. In addition, the entity must display the following information prominently, and repeat it when necessary, for an understanding of the information presented: *[FRS 102.3.23]*

- the name of the reporting entity and any change in its name from the end of the preceding reporting period;
- whether the financial statements cover the individual entity or a group of entities;
- the date of the end of the reporting period and the period covered by the financial statements;
- the presentation currency, as defined in Section 30 – *Foreign Currency Translation* (discussed in Chapter 25 at 3.7); and
- the level of rounding, if any, used in presenting amounts in the financial statements.

The above requirements are often met by the inclusion of a basis of preparation note within the accounting policies and through the use of appropriate titles for the primary financial statements (e.g. by distinguishing group and company primary statements) and headings in the columns in the primary financial statements and notes to the financial statements.

In practice, financial statements are presented to an appropriate level of rounding, such as thousands or millions of currency units. An appropriate level of rounding can avoid obscuring useful information (and hence cut clutter – see 8.4.1 below) but entities need to ensure that material information is not omitted. The level of rounding used must be clearly disclosed in the primary statements and notes to the financial statements. Entities are not precluded from using lower levels of rounding in certain notes to the financial statements. For example, where the financial statements are presented in millions of units of the presentation currency, it may be appropriate to include information on directors' remuneration at a lower level of rounding. In all cases, it is important that the units used are clearly stated.

3.8   Statement of compliance

A set of financial statements prepared in accordance with FRS 102 must contain an explicit and unreserved statement of compliance with FRS 102 in the notes to the financial statements. Financial statements must not be described as complying with FRS 102 unless they comply with *all* the requirements of the standard. *[FRS 102.3.3, FRS 100.9]*. This is similar to the requirement in IAS 1 for an entity preparing its financial statements to give an explicit and unreserved statement of compliance with IFRSs. *[IAS 1.16]*.

FRS 102 additionally requires a public benefit entity (see Chapter 29 at 6 for the definition of a public benefit entity) that applies the 'PBE' prefixed paragraphs to make an explicit and unreserved statement that it is a public benefit entity. *[FRS 102.PBE3.3A]*. This is because FRS 102 has specific requirements reserved for public benefit entities (prefixed with 'PBE'), which cannot be applied by analogy to other entities. *[FRS 102.1.2]*. See Chapter 2 at 2.4.2.

FRS 103 requires that an entity whose financial statements comply with FRS 103 shall, in addition to the statement of compliance made in accordance with FRS 102, make an explicit and unreserved statement of compliance with FRS 103 in the notes to the financial statements. *[FRS 103.1.12]*.

Example 4.1:   Statement of Compliance – illustrative wording

These financial statements were prepared in accordance with Financial Reporting Standard 102 'The Financial Reporting Standard applicable in the UK and Republic of Ireland' [and Financial Reporting Standard 103 'Insurance Contracts']*. [The [company/entity] is a public benefit entity as defined in Financial Reporting Standard 102 'The Financial Reporting Standard applicable in the UK and Republic of Ireland']*.

*delete as applicable.

In the extremely rare circumstances when management concludes that compliance with the standard would be so misleading that it would conflict with the objective of financial statements (see 3.2 above), an entity must depart from that requirement of the standard, giving the required disclosures set out in paragraph 3.5 of FRS 102. *[FRS 102.3.4-3.5]*. See 8.2 below for further discussion of the 'fair presentation override' under FRS 102 (and of the related 'true and fair override' under the Companies Act 2006) and the implications for the statement of compliance.

3.8.1   Statement that financial statements have been prepared in accordance with applicable accounting standards

The Regulations require a UK company (that is large) preparing Companies Act accounts to state in the notes to the accounts whether the accounts have been prepared in accordance with applicable accounting standards, giving particulars of any material departures from those standards and the reasons (see Chapter 1 at 4.6.1). This statement is also required in the group accounts of a medium-sized company (see Chapter 1 at 6.6) but not in its individual accounts. *[Regulations 4(2)(a), 1 Sch 45]*.

Where a 'fair presentation override' in accordance with paragraph 3.5 of the standard (see 8.2 below) is applied in the financial statements, the above statement will need to include or refer to the disclosures of the override.

Applicable accounting standards are defined in section 464 (see Chapter 1 at 4.6.1). Financial statements prepared in accordance with FRS 102 are prepared in accordance with applicable accounting standards.

4   STATEMENT OF FINANCIAL POSITION

The statement of financial position presents an entity's assets, liabilities and equity as of the end of the reporting period. *[FRS 102.4.1]*.

Under FRS 102, the format of the statement of financial position (known as the balance sheet under the Companies Act 2006) is determined by the balance sheet formats included in the applicable schedule to the Regulations or the LLP Regulations. *[FRS 102.4.1]*.

The statement of financial position in financial statements prepared in accordance with FRS 102 will, therefore, look similar to one prepared under previous UK GAAP, although there is potential for reclassifications of items due to differing accounting requirements in FRS 102.

Section 4 of the standard applies to *all* FRS 102 reporters, whether or not they report under the Companies Act 2006. Entities that do not report under the Companies Act 2006 are required to comply with the requirements set out in Section 4 and with the Regulations (or, where applicable, the LLP Regulations) where referred to in Section 4, except to the extent that these requirements are not permitted by any statutory framework under which such entities report. *[FRS 102.4.1]*.

4.1   Information to be presented in the statement of financial position

4.1.1   *Required formats for the balance sheet*

An entity must present its statement of financial position in accordance with one of the following balance sheet formats for individual financial statements: *[FRS 102.4.1]*

- Part 1 'General Rules and Formats' of Schedule 1 to the Regulations addresses the balance sheet formats applicable to companies other than banking companies (defined in section 1164) and insurance companies (defined in section 1165); *[Regulations 3]*

- Part 1 'General Rules and Formats' of Schedule 2 to the Regulations addresses the balance sheet formats applicable to banking companies; *[Regulations 5]*

- Part 1 'General Rules and Formats' of Schedule 3 to the Regulations addresses the balance sheet formats applicable to insurance companies; *[Regulations 6]* and

- Part 1 'General Rules and Formats' of Schedule 1 to the LLP Regulations addresses the balance sheet formats applicable to limited liability partnerships (LLPs). *[LLP Regulations 3]*.

Part 1 of Schedule 6 to the Regulations addresses the balance sheet formats applicable to group accounts of companies, modifying the formats included in the earlier schedules. The group accounts must comply, so far as practicable with the provisions of Schedule 1 to the Regulations (i.e. including the balance sheet formats) as if the undertakings included in the consolidation were a single company. *[6 Sch 1(1)]*.

The parent company of a banking group (defined in section 1164(4)-(5)) applies Part 1 of Schedule 6, as modified by Part 2 of Schedule 6 to the Regulations. The parent company of an insurance group (defined in section 1165(5)-(6)) applies Part 1 of Schedule 6, as modified by Part 3 of Schedule 6 to the Regulations. *[Regulations 9]*.

Part 1 of Schedule 3 to the LLP Regulations similarly addresses the balance sheet formats applicable to group accounts of LLPs. *[LLP Regulations 6]*. *[FRS 102.4.2]*.

The definitions of a banking company, insurance company, banking group and insurance group are at 4.1.2 below.

4.1.2 Which formats should be applied?

4.1.2.A UK companies

UK companies must apply the formats in the schedule that they are required to follow under the Regulations. As explained in Chapter 2 at 4.1, the formats in the Regulations are followed even if the company applies the small companies regime.

The Regulations require that the individual accounts of a banking or insurance company contain a statement that they are prepared in accordance with the provisions of the Regulations relating to banking or insurance companies, as the case may be. Similarly, the group accounts prepared by a parent of a banking or insurance group must make a statement that they are prepared in accordance with the provisions of the Regulations relating to banking groups or insurance groups, as the case may be. *[Regulations 5(3), 6(3), 9(4)]*.

4.1.2.B Definition of banking company and banking group

A 'banking company' means a person who has permission under Part 4 of the Financial Services and Markets Act 2000 to accept deposits, other than:

- a person who is not a company, and

- a person who has such permission only for the purpose of carrying on another regulated activity in accordance with permission under that Part.

This definition is to be read with section 22 of the Financial Services and Markets Act 2000, any relevant order under that section and Schedule 2 to the Financial Services and Markets Act 2000. *[s1164(2)-(3)]*

A 'banking group' means a group (i.e. a parent undertaking and its subsidiary undertakings) where the parent company is a banking company or where:

- the parent company's principal subsidiary undertakings are wholly or mainly credit institutions; and

- the parent company does not itself carry on any material business apart from the acquisition, management and disposal of interests in subsidiary undertakings. *[s1164(4), s1173(1)]*.

For the purposes of the definition of 'banking group', the 'principal subsidiary undertakings' are the subsidiary undertakings of the company whose results or financial position would principally affect the figures shown in the group accounts and the 'management of interests in subsidiary undertakings' includes the provision of services to such undertakings. *[s1164(5)]*.

A credit institution is defined in Article 4.1 of Directive 2006/46/EC (as last amended by Directive 2009/111/EC) as 'an undertaking the business of which is to receive deposits or other repayable funds from the public and to grant credits for its own account.'

4.1.2.C   Definition of insurance company and insurance group

An 'insurance company' means:

- an authorised insurance company (i.e. a person, whether incorporated or not, who has permission under Part 4 of the Financial Services and Markets Act 2000 to effect or carry out contracts of insurance); or

- any other person (whether incorporated or not) who:

  - carries on insurance market activity (as defined in section 316(3) of the Financial Services and Markets Act 2000); or

  - may effect or carry out contracts of insurance under which the benefits provided by that person are exclusively or primarily benefits in kind in the event of accident to or breakdown of a vehicle.

Neither expression includes a friendly society within the meaning of the Friendly Societies Act 1992. *[s1165(2)-(4)]*.

References to 'contracts of insurance' and 'to the effecting or carrying out of such contracts' must be read with section 22 of the Financial Services and Markets Act 2000, any relevant order under that section and Schedule 2 to the Financial Services and Markets Act 2000. *[s1165(8)]*.

An 'insurance group' means a group (i.e. parent undertaking and its subsidiary undertakings) where the parent company is an insurance company or where:

- the parent company's principal subsidiary undertakings are wholly or mainly insurance companies, and

- the parent company does not itself carry on any material business apart from the acquisition, management and disposal of interests in subsidiary undertakings. *[s1165(5)]*.

For the purposes of the definition of 'insurance group', the 'principal subsidiary undertakings' are the subsidiary undertakings of the company whose results or financial position would principally affect the figures shown in the group accounts and the 'management of interests in subsidiary undertakings' includes the provision of services to such undertakings. *[s1165(6)]*.

4.1.2.D   LLPs

LLPs must apply the formats in the LLP Regulations. As explained in Chapter 2 at 4.1, the formats in the Regulations are followed even if the company applies the small LLP regime.

4.1.2.E   Qualifying partnerships

A qualifying partnership (as defined in the *Partnerships (Accounts) Regulations 2008*) is required to prepare the like annual accounts and reports as would be required, if the partnership were a company under Part 15 and under the Small Companies Regulations or the Regulations, as the case may be. Part 1 of the Schedule to these regulations sets out certain modifications and adaptations to be made to the Regulations and Small Companies Regulations for these purposes.

The formats applied by a qualifying partnership are those in Parts 1 of Schedule 1 (and for group accounts, in Parts 1 of Schedule 6) to the Small Companies Regulations or the Regulations. As explained in Chapter 2 at 4.1, the formats in the Regulations (and not those in the Small Companies Regulations) must be applied, even where the qualifying partnership prepares its statutory accounts in accordance with the latter (as modified by the *Partnerships (Accounts) Regulations 2008*).

4.1.2.F Other entities required to prepare statutory accounts in accordance with Part 15 of the Companies Act 2006

Certain other entities are required by regulations to prepare annual accounts as if the entity is a company subject to Part 15 of the Companies Act 2006 and these regulations specify the formats to be applied for the balance sheet and profit and loss account. *The Bank Accounts Directive (Miscellaneous Banks) Regulations 2008* requires a 'qualifying bank' (as defined in those regulations) to prepare the like annual accounts and directors' report as if it were a banking company (or the parent company of a banking group) in accordance with Schedule 2 to the Regulations (with certain adaptations or modifications). Similarly, an insurance undertaking must prepare the like annual accounts and directors' report as if it were an insurance company (or the parent company of an insurance group) in accordance with Schedule 3 to the Regulations (with certain adaptations or modifications).

4.1.2.G Other entities

Other entities must also apply one of the balance sheet (or profit or loss account) formats included in the Regulations, except to the extent that these requirements are not permitted by any statutory framework under which such entities report. *[FRS 102.4.1].* The Accounting Council Advice states that 'this would have the consequence of all entities being required to comply with the company law formats, promoting consistency amongst all those preparing financial statements intended to give a true and fair view'. *[FRS 102.AC.42].*

As FRS 102 does not specify which format should be used, management of such entities must apply judgement in determining which is the most appropriate format to apply for the circumstances of the entity concerned.

4.1.3 Changes in formats

Schedule 1 to the Regulations and Schedule 1 to the LLP Regulations require that once a particular format for the balance sheet (or profit or loss account) has been adopted for any financial year, the company's directors must use the same format in preparing Companies Act individual accounts / group accounts for subsequent financial years, unless in their opinion there are special reasons for a change. Particulars of any such change must be given in a note to the accounts in which the new format is first used, and the reasons for the change must be explained. *[1 Sch 2, 6 Sch 1].*

Chapter 4

A change in the format applied would be regarded as a change in accounting policy for the purposes of FRS 102 and, therefore, would be retrospectively effected. Accounting policies are defined as 'the specific principles, bases, conventions, rules and practices applied by an entity in preparing and presenting financial statements'. *[FRS 102 Appendix I, 10.2]*. See Chapter 7 at 3.4 for the requirements on changes in accounting policy.

4.2   Format 1 Balance Sheet

Schedule 1 to the Regulations provides a choice of two formats for the balance sheet – Format 1 is a vertical format and is adopted by virtually all UK companies. Format 2 presents assets separately from liabilities (including capital and reserves) and is rarely used. This chapter only discusses the Format 1 balance sheet applicable to companies (other than banking or insurance companies) in Schedule 1 to the Regulations. It is beyond the scope of this chapter to discuss the formats in Schedule 2 applicable to banking companies and groups (defined in section 1165 of the Companies Act 2006) or the formats in Schedule 3 applicable to insurance companies and groups (defined in section 1173 of the Companies Act 2006). However, there is less flexibility to adapt the formats in Schedule 2 and Schedule 3 to the Regulations.

The standard requires an entity to present additional line items, headings and subtotals in the statement of financial position when such presentation is relevant to an understanding of the entity's financial position. *[FRS 102.4.3]*. It should be noted that any amendments would need to comply with the requirements governing modifications of the formats in the Regulations .

FRS 102, like IFRSs, has accounting requirements for various items that do not have separate line items in Format 1, but which would be presented separately on the face of the statement of financial position. Such items include investment property, financial assets, biological assets, cash and cash equivalents and deferred tax. FRS 102 generally requires separate disclosures of the amounts of these items in the notes to the financial statements (and sometimes requires reconciliations of the movements in the balances of such items).

As noted above, FRS 102 requires additional line items to be presented on the face of the statement of financial position where relevant to an understanding of the entity's financial position. So, for example, a property company may distinguish its investment property from other tangible fixed assets. The presentation of additional line items might require use of boxes and subtotals in order to comply with the balance sheet formats.

Format 1 sets out the following minimum line items that must be presented on the face of the balance sheet, as illustrated in Table 4.1 below:

Table 4.1   *Format 1 individual balance sheet (UK company other than a banking company or insurance company)*

A	**Called up share capital not paid***	
B	**Fixed assets**	
	I	Intangible assets
	II	Tangible assets
	III	Investments
C	**Current assets**	
	I	Stocks
	II	Debtors
	III	Investments
	IV	Cash at bank and in hand
D	**Prepayments and accrued income***	
E	**Creditors: amounts falling due within one year**	
F	**Net current assets (liabilities)**	
G	**Total assets less current liabilities**	
H	**Creditors: amounts falling due after more than one year**	
I	**Provisions for liabilities**	
J	**Accruals and deferred income***	
K	**Capital and reserves**	
	I	Called up share capital not paid*
	II	Share premium account
	III	Revaluation reserve
	IV	Other reserves
	V	Profit and loss account

*   The notes to Format 1 provide alternative positions for prepayments and accrued income, and accruals and deferred income, as sub-headings within C-II (for prepayments and accrued income) and within E and H (for accruals and deferred income). Called up share capital not paid may also be shown within C-II.

The following discussion relates to the balance sheet formats included in Schedule 1 to the Regulations only.

Each of the headings and sub-headings denoted with a capital letter or Roman numeral, as set out in Table 4.1, must be presented on the face of the balance sheet for the individual accounts of a company.

The Format 1 balance sheet includes sub-headings, denoted with an Arabic number, which have not been shown in Table 4.1 above. The individual line items in the balance sheet format are discussed at 4.6 below. The rest of this section addresses the general requirements on the formats set out in the Regulations.

The main modifications required for the group balance sheet format are the identification of minority interest / non-controlling interest (see 4.5 below) and the sub-heading 'Participating interests' (at B III in Table 4.1 above) is replaced by 'Interests in associated undertakings' and 'Other participating interests' (see 4.6.4 below).

The Regulations require that every balance sheet of a company must show the items listed in the balance sheet format adopted. The items must also be shown in the order and under the headings and sub-headings given in the particular format used, but the letters or numbers assigned to that item in the format do not need to be given (and are not in practice). The items listed in the formats need to be read together with the notes to the formats, which may also permit alternative positions for any particular items. *[1 Sch 1]*. The relevant notes to the balance sheet formats are discussed for each line item at 4.6 below.

Where the special nature of the company's business requires it, the company's directors *must* adapt the arrangement, headings and sub-headings otherwise required in respect of items given an Arabic number in the balance sheet (or profit or loss account) format used. The directors *may* combine items to which Arabic numbers are given in the formats if their individual amounts are not material to assessing the state of affairs (or profit or loss) of the company for the financial year in question or the combination facilitates that assessment. In the latter case, the individual amounts of any items combined must be disclosed in a note to the accounts. *[1 Sch 4]*. FRS 102's requirements on materiality and aggregation are discussed at 8.4 below.

The Regulations allow any item to be shown in the company's balance sheet in greater detail than required by the particular format used. The balance sheet may include an item representing or covering the amount of any asset or liability not otherwise covered by any of the items listed in the format used, but preliminary expenses, the expenses of, and commission on, any issue of shares or debentures, and the costs of research may not be treated as assets in the balance sheet. *[1 Sch 3]*. FRS 102 requires additional line items, headings and subtotals to be added where relevant to an understanding of the entity's financial position *[FRS 102.4.3]*. Where additional detail is provided on the face of the balance sheet, it is usual to provide a subtotal for the heading.

Where there is no amount in the current or immediately preceding financial year for a particular item in the balance sheet format, that line item should be omitted from the balance sheet. *[1 Sch 5]*.

The statutory requirements on comparatives are addressed at 3.6 above.

Amounts in respect of items representing assets may not be set off against amounts in respect of items representing liabilities and *vice versa*. *[1 Sch 8]*. FRS 102's requirements on offset are discussed at 8.1.1.C below.

The company's directors must, in determining how amounts are presented within items in the balance sheet, have regard to the substance of the reported transaction or arrangement, in accordance with generally accepted accounting principles or practice. *[1 Sch 9]*.

4.3   Fixed assets and current assets

The balance sheet formats set out in the Regulations distinguish between fixed assets and current assets. Under the Regulations, fixed assets are defined and current assets are the residual.

'Fixed assets' are assets of an entity which are intended for use on a continuing basis in the company's activities, and 'current assets' are assets not intended for such use. *[10 Sch 4 and FRS 102 Appendix I]*.

Current assets include debtors, even if due after more than one year. However, where the amount of debtors due after more than one year is so material in the context of net current assets that in the absence of disclosure of the debtors due after more than one year on the face of the statement of financial position readers may misinterpret the financial statements, the amount should be disclosed on the face of the statement of financial position within current assets. In most cases, it will be satisfactory to disclose the amount due after more than one year in the notes to the financial statements. *[FRS 102.4.4A]*.

The notes to the formats in the Regulations require that the amount falling due after more than one year is shown separately for each item included under debtors. *[1 Sch Note (5) on balance sheet formats,]*.

A UK company preparing Companies Act accounts must disclose the following, either in the accounts or notes to the accounts, for *each* category of fixed assets which would be shown in the balance sheet formats (or would be so shown, if line items were not combined as permitted by the Regulations):

- the gross cost (based on the historical cost – see 9.1 below) or valuation (using the alternative accounting rules – see 9.2 below) at the beginning and end of the financial year;

- the effects on gross cost / valuation of revaluations, acquisitions, disposals and transfers of assets;

- the cumulative amount of provisions for depreciation or diminution in value at the beginning and end of the financial year; and

- the provision for depreciation and diminution in respect of the financial year, and adjustments to such provisions in respect of disposal of assets and other adjustments. *[1 Sch 51]*.

The above requirement in the Regulations overlaps with FRS 102's requirements to provide reconciliations of changes in the carrying amounts for each class of property, plant and equipment *[FRS 102.17.31]* (see Chapter 13 at 3.8.1), each class of intangible asset *[FRS 102.18.27(e)]* (see Chapter 14 at 3.5.2), goodwill *[FRS 102.19.26]* (see Chapter 15 at 4.2), investment property at fair value through profit or loss *[FRS 102.16.10(e)]* (see Chapter 12 at 3.6), and biological assets (separately for each class carried under the cost model and each class carried under the fair value model) *[FRS 102.34.7(c), 34.10(e)]* (see Chapter 29 at 2).

The Regulations also require a UK company preparing Companies Act accounts to provide additional disclosures in the notes to the accounts where the alternative accounting rules are applied. See 9.2.4 below.

4.4 Creditors: amounts falling due within and after more than one year

The Regulations distinguish between:

- Creditors: amounts falling due within one year; and
- Creditors: amounts falling due after more than one year.

These two line items are shown on the face of the balance sheet in the Format 1 balance sheet. In the Format 2 balance sheet, more rarely used, the heading required on the face of the balance sheet is simply 'Creditors' which aggregates amounts falling due within one year with amounts falling due after more than one year. The analysis between amounts falling due within one year and amounts falling due after more than one year is given in total and for each line item within Creditors (either on the face of the balance sheet or in the notes). *[1 Sch Note 13 on Format 2 balance sheet]*.

In distinguishing amounts between the two categories of creditor, the deciding factor is the earliest date of payment. The Regulations state that a loan or advance (including a liability comprising a loan or advance) is treated as falling due for repayment, and an instalment of a loan or advance is treated as falling due for payment, on the earliest date on which the lender could require repayment or (as the case may be) payment, if he exercised all options and rights available to him. *[10 Sch 9]*.

FRS 102 specifies that an entity shall classify a creditor as due within one year when the entity does not have an unconditional right, at the end of the reporting period, to defer settlement of the creditor for at least twelve months after the reporting date. *[FRS 102.4.7]*. FRS 102 contains no further guidance over when an entity has an unconditional right to defer settlement of the creditor. However, IAS 1 includes detailed guidance on the impact of refinancing liabilities that an entity may refer to in accordance with the GAAP hierarchy in Section 10 *[FRS 102.10.3-10.6]* since part of IAS 1's definition of a current liability is that a liability is current if the entity 'does not have an unconditional right to defer settlement of the liability for at least twelve months after the reporting period', which is consistent with the definition of a creditor due within one year in FRS 102 (and the Regulations). *[IAS 1.69(d)]*. See EY International GAAP 2015, Chapter 3 at 3.14.

4.5   Non-controlling interests / minority interest in group accounts

Under FRS 102, non-controlling interest is defined as 'the equity in a subsidiary not attributable, directly or indirectly, to a parent'. *[FRS 102.22.19, Appendix I]*.

FRS 102 requires that non-controlling interest is presented in the consolidated balance sheet within equity, separately from the equity of the owners of the parent (meaning holders of instruments classified as equity). *[FRS 102.9.20, Appendix I]*.

The statement of changes in equity presents: *[FRS 102.6.3]*

- total comprehensive income, showing separately the total amounts attributable to owners of the parent and non-controlling interest; and

- since non-controlling interest is a component of equity, a reconciliation of the changes in the carrying amount of non-controlling interest.

In addition, the statement of comprehensive income (or separate income statement, where presented) shows as allocations of profit or loss and total comprehensive income: *[FRS 102.9.21, 5.6]*

- the profit or loss attributable to the owners of the parent separately from the profit or loss attributable to non-controlling interest; and

- the total comprehensive income attributable to the owners of the parent separately from the total comprehensive income attributable to non-controlling interest.

The definition of non-controlling interest (see Chapter 6 at 3.6) is wider than minority interest as used in previous UK GAAP and in the Regulations, although the Regulations do not use either term. Under previous UK GAAP, minority interest relates only to the amount of capital and reserves attributable to shares in subsidiary undertakings. *[FRS 2.35]*.

Paragraph 17 of Schedule 6 to the Regulations requires that: *[6 Sch 17, 25, 36]*

'(2)   In the balance sheet formats there must be shown, as a separate item and under an appropriate heading, the amount of capital and reserves attributable to shares in subsidiary undertakings included in the consolidation held by or on behalf of persons other than the parent company and its subsidiary undertakings.

(3)   In the profit and loss account formats there must be shown, as a separate item and under an appropriate heading –

(a)   the amount of any profit or loss on ordinary activities, and

(b)   the amount of any profit or loss on extraordinary activities,

attributable to shares in subsidiary undertakings included in the consolidation held by or on behalf of persons other than the parent company and its subsidiary undertakings.'

There are equivalent presentation requirements for minority interest in Schedule 3 to the LLP Regulations.

The reference to 'under an appropriate heading' would permit a presentation consistent with the requirements of FRS 102. Note that FRS 102's presentation requirements differ to a practice sometimes seen under previous UK GAAP (because it was specifically permitted as an alternative by the Companies Act 1985) where minority interest is shown after 'J Accruals and deferred income' in the balance sheet with a total for net assets after minority interests (rather than as a component of equity, as required by FRS 102), and as a line item after 'profit or loss on ordinary activities after taxation' but before arriving at profit or loss for the financial year (rather than as an appropriation of profit as required by FRS 102).

In most cases, the amounts shown as non-controlling interest under the standard and the amounts required by the Regulations will be the same. The Regulations do not require use of the term 'minority interest' and, therefore, in our view, the term 'non-controlling interest' could be used in providing the analysis of the profit and loss and balance sheet required by the Regulations. There is a theoretical possibility that the amounts required by the standard and the Regulations may differ. In such a case, two totals are strictly required to be presented to meet the requirements of both FRS 102 and the Regulations.

Schedule 1 to the Regulations requires the heading used in the balance sheet to be treated as if it has a letter assigned, meaning that it must be included on the face of the balance sheet. However, the heading used in the profit and loss account is treated as if it has an Arabic number assigned (allowing the adaptations permitted by 1 Sch 4, as described at 4.2 above). Note that the equivalent paragraph to paragraph 17(4) is modified where Schedule 2 or Schedule 3 to the Regulations are applied. *[1 Sch 17(4), 25(2), 36(b)].* FRS 102 requires, in any case, that non-controlling interest is presented on the face of the statement of financial position and as an allocation of profit (and total comprehensive income) on the face of the statement of comprehensive income (and separate income statement, if any).

Table 4.2 below illustrates the presentation of non-controlling interest in the statement of financial position. Table 4.3 illustrates the allocation of profit or loss to owners of the parent and to non-controlling interest where a separate income statement is presented. Where a separate income statement is presented, an allocation of total comprehensive income between owners of the parent and the non-controlling interest would also be presented at the end of the statement of total comprehensive income. Where a single statement of comprehensive income is presented (see 5.4 below), these allocations of profit or loss and of total comprehensive income would both be presented as two lines below the total comprehensive income for the period. An example of the presentation of non-controlling interest in the statement of changes in equity is shown at 6.1.1 below.

Table 4.2   *Presentation of non-controlling interest in statement of financial position*

	£'000
Capital and reserves	
Called up share capital	12,075
Share premium account:	493
Capital redemption reserve	500
Merger reserve	6,250
Profit and loss account	27,882
Equity attributable to owners of the parent company	47,200
Non-controlling interests	360
	47,560

Table 4.3   *Presentation of non-controlling interest in income statement (where presented separately)*

	£'000
Profit on ordinary activities before taxation	7,786
Tax on profit on ordinary activities:	(3,339)
Profit/(loss) for the financial year	4,447
Profit/(loss) for the financial year attributable to:	4,209
Owners of the parent company	238
Non-controlling interests	4,447

4.6   Implementation issues – balance sheet formats

In most cases, it will be straightforward to identify in which line items to present assets and liabilities in the balance sheet formats. All references to the balance sheet in this section are to the Format 1 balance sheet in Schedule 1 to the Regulations. The discussion in this section provides a commentary on each heading and subheading included in the Format 1 balance sheet and on the related notes to the formats.

Where disclosures in the Regulations are discussed in this section, these are not intended to be comprehensive but to highlight additional disclosures directly related to a specific line item. These do not cover all the related disclosures in Schedule 1 to the Regulations.

4.6.1   *Called up share capital not paid*

In the Format 1 balance sheet, this line item can be presented in the position of Called up share capital not paid (item A) on the face of the balance sheet. Alternatively, this line item can be presented either on the face of the balance sheet or in the notes to the accounts as item 5 within Current assets – Debtors (C II) (see 4.6.6 below).

Called up share capital (and paid up share capital) are explained at 4.6.12 below. Called up share capital not paid can arise because calls made on the shares have not been paid, or where the share capital is 'paid up' because the amounts are payable on a specified date under the articles or terms of allotment or other arrangement for payment of shares, but has not yet been settled (and therefore is called up share capital).

4.6.2   Intangible assets

Table 4.4 shows the analysis required in respect of intangible assets under format 1.

Table 4.4   *Analysis of intangible assets*

B	Fixed assets	
I	Intangible assets	
	1	Development costs
	2	Concessions, patents, licences, trade marks and similar rights and assets
	3	Goodwill
	4	Payments on account

Intangible assets are not defined in the Regulations, but include line items denoted with an Arabic number for development costs; concessions, patents, licences, trademarks and similar rights and assets; goodwill; and payments on account. Note (2) to the balance sheet formats states that amounts are only included in the balance sheet as concessions, patents, licences, trademarks and similar rights and assets if *either* the assets were acquired for valuable consideration and are not required to be shown under goodwill, *or* the assets in question were created by the company itself. However, entities preparing FRS 102 financial statements must apply the more restrictive requirements of the standard. See Chapter 14 for a discussion of FRS 102's requirements on intangible assets.

Note (3) to the balance sheet formats in the Regulations states that amounts representing goodwill are only included to the extent that the goodwill was acquired for valuable consideration. Therefore, consistent with FRS 102, internally generated goodwill cannot be capitalised. *[FRS 102.18.8C(f)].*

The following parts of this section address assets where there can be particular implementation issues, including potential changes in classifications of assets compared to those applied under previous UK GAAP.

4.6.2.A   Heritage assets

FRS 102 sets out separate requirements for heritage assets, being tangible and intangible assets with historic, artistic, scientific, technological, geophysical, or environmental qualities that are held and maintained principally for their contribution to knowledge and culture (see Chapter 29). *[FRS 102 Appendix I].* Therefore, heritage assets can in principle be tangible or intangible assets; whereas under previous UK GAAP, heritage assets were defined as tangible fixed assets. *[FRS 30.2, 18].*

Chapter 4

4.6.2.B   *Exploration and evaluation of mineral resources*

IFRS 6 – *Exploration for and Evaluation of Mineral Resources*, which is applied by FRS 102 reporters operating in the exploration for and / or evaluation of mineral resources, *[FRS 102.34.11]*, requires entities within its scope to classify exploration and evaluation assets as either intangible or tangible assets in accordance with the nature of the assets acquired and apply the classification consistently. *[IFRS 6.15]*.

For example, drilling rigs should be presented as intangible assets, whereas vehicles and drilling rigs are tangible assets. A tangible asset that is used in developing an intangible asset should still be presented as a tangible asset. However, 'to the extent that a tangible asset is consumed in developing an intangible asset, the amount reflecting that consumption is part of the cost of the intangible asset'. Therefore, the depreciation of a portable drilling rig would be capitalised as part of the intangible exploration and evaluation asset that represents the costs incurred on active exploration projects. *[IFRS 6.16, BC33]*.

4.6.2.C   *Service concession arrangements*

FRS 102 distinguishes two principal categories of service concession arrangements: a financial asset model and an intangible asset model. Sometimes a service concession arrangement may contain both types *[FRS 102.34.13-15]* (see Chapter 29 at [x]).

However, Section 35 – *Transition to this FRS* – permits first-time adopters (that are operators of service concession arrangements) to continue to use the same accounting policies as applied at the date of transition for service concession arrangements entered into before the date of transition (see Chapter 30 at 5.10). *[FRS 102.35.10(i)]*. FRS 5 Application Note F – *Private Finance Initiative and Similar Contracts* – distinguishes between arrangements where the property was the asset of the operator (and a tangible fixed asset was recognised) and where the property was the asset of the grantor / purchaser (and a financial asset / debtor was recognised by the operator). Where the transition exemption is taken, the previous UK GAAP classification would continue to be used.

4.6.2.D   *Software development costs*

Previous UK GAAP specifically addresses the classification of software development costs *[FRS 10.2]* and website development costs *[UITF 27]*. The definition of an intangible asset within Section 18 of FRS 102 requires that it lacks physical substance. However, intangible assets can be contained in or on a physical medium such as a compact disc (in the case of computer software), legal documentation (in the case of a licence or patent) or film, requiring an entity to exercise judgement in determining whether to apply Section 18 or Section 17 of the standard. FRS 102, unlike IAS 38 – *Intangible Assets*, which has the same definition of an intangible asset, provides no further guidance. See Chapter 14 at 3.2.2 and 4.1 for discussion of the classification of such costs. There is potential for reclassification of such costs under FRS 102.

4.6.2.E   Negative goodwill

The Regulations do not address the presentation of negative goodwill. However, FRS 102 requires that negative goodwill is disclosed immediately below positive goodwill, with a subtotal of the net amount of the positive goodwill and the negative goodwill. *[FRS 102.19.24(b)]*. This presentation is consistent with that required by FRS 10 – *Goodwill and intangible assets* – under previous UK GAAP. *[FRS 10.48]*. See Chapter 15 at 3.8.3.

4.6.2.F   Payments on account

The format 1 balance sheet includes a line item for payments on account, i.e. advance payments made for intangible fixed assets.

4.6.3   Tangible fixed assets.

Table 4.5 shows the analysis required in respect of tangible fixed assets under format 1.

Table 4.5   Analysis of tangible fixed assets

B	Fixed assets
II	Tangible assets
1	Land and buildings
2	Plant and machinery
3	Fixtures, fittings, tools and equipment
4	Payments on account and assets in course of construction

The Regulations define fixed assets (see 4.3 above) but not tangible fixed assets. While FRS 102 does not define the term 'tangible assets', these differ from intangible assets in that they are assets 'with physical substance'.

FRS 102 defines 'property, plant and equipment' as tangible assets that:

- are held for use in the production or supply of goods or services, for rental to others, or for administrative purposes; and

- are expected to be used during more than one period. *[FRS 102 Appendix I]*.

The distinction between fixed assets and current assets is usually clear and the statutory definition is not normally interpreted to mean that individual assets are transferred to current assets when a decision to dispose of them has been made. See 4.6.15 below.

In practice, most UK companies relegate the sub-headings within tangible assets denoted by an Arabic number to the notes to the accounts, showing only the net book value of tangible assets on the face of the balance sheet. UK companies preparing Companies Act accounts must also analyse 'land and buildings' between freehold land and leasehold land, providing a sub-analysis of land held on a long lease (i.e. the unexpired term at the end of the financial year is not less than 50 years) and leasehold land held on a short lease. *[1 Sch 53, 10 Sch 7]*.

Specific types of assets that may be recorded as tangible assets are discussed below.

4.6.3.A   Investment property

The Regulations do not require presentation of investment property on the face of the balance sheet but do permit items to be shown in greater detail. FRS 102 requires additional line items, headings and subtotals when relevant to an understanding of the entity's financial position (see 4.2 above). Therefore, some entities may consider it appropriate to present investment property as a separate line item on the face of the balance sheet.

There are a number of differences between the definition of investment property under previous UK GAAP and under FRS 102, and consequently, classification differences in respect of investment property may arise on transition to FRS 102.

4.6.3.B   Tangible fixed assets (other than property, plant and equipment)

Heritage assets (e.g. works of art), exploration and evaluation assets (e.g. drilling rigs) and biological assets (e.g. fruit orchards) and certain software development costs may fall to be classified as tangible fixed assets. See Chapter 29. In addition, service concession arrangements classified as tangible fixed assets under previous UK GAAP will continue to be so classified where the transition exemption is taken. See 4.6.2.A-D above and 4.6.17 below.

4.6.3.C   Lease premiums

It was common under previous UK GAAP for lease premiums paid upfront to be classified as a tangible fixed asset. Under IFRSs, premiums relating to an operating lease over land and/or buildings are classified as a prepayment (albeit there may be a non-current element). Such payments would not be classified as property, plant and equipment under IFRSs. The definitions of property, plant and equipment in FRS 102 (and IFRSs) are similar and, consequently, in our view, it would be appropriate to report an upfront operating lease premium as a prepayment under FRS 102, classified as appropriate between debtors: amounts falling due within one year and debtors: amounts falling due after more than one year.

4.6.3.D   Spare parts

Major spare parts and stand-by equipment are property, plant and equipment if expected to be used during more than one period. Similarly, if the spare parts can be used only in connection with an item of property, plant and equipment, they are considered property, plant and equipment. *[FRS 102.17.5]*.

4.6.3.E   Payments on account

The format 1 balance sheet includes a line item for payments on account, i.e. advance payments made for tangible fixed assets.

4.6.4   *Investments*

Table 4.6 shows the analysis required in respect of investments under format 1.

Table 4.6   Analysis of investments

B	**Fixed assets**	
III	Investments	
	1	Shares in group undertakings
	2	Loans to group undertakings
	3	Participating interests†
	4	Loans to undertakings in which the company has a participating interest
	5	Other investments other than loans
	6	Other loans
	7	Own shares
	†	In group accounts, this line item is replaced by two items: 'Interests in associated undertakings' and 'other participating interests'
C	**Current assets**	
III	Investments	
	1	Shares in group undertakings
	2	Own shares
	3	Other investments

4.6.4.A   *Current assets or fixed asset investments?*

The format 1 balance sheet distinguishes between fixed asset and current asset investments. It is necessary to apply the general rule that a fixed asset is one which is 'intended for use on a continuing basis in the entity's activities' and a current asset is one not intended for such use (see 4.3 above). However, this is an unhelpful distinction for investments which, by their nature, are not intended for use in an entity's activities at all, whether on a continuing basis or not.

Current asset investments may include cash equivalents, meaning: short-term, highly liquid investments that are readily convertible to cash (i.e. cash on hand and demand deposits) and that are subject to an insignificant risk of changes in value *[FRS 102 Appendix I]*. Examples of current asset investments that may qualify as cash equivalents, but do not fall within the statutory heading 'cash at bank and in hand', include investments in money market funds. Current asset investments may also include investments that do not qualify as cash equivalents but are still of a short-term nature, and investments held for trading purposes.

Investments in shares in subsidiaries or associates or trade investments will generally be fixed asset investments. Indeed, FRS 102 states that, unless otherwise required under the Regulations, investments in associates should be classified as fixed assets. *[FRS 102.14.11]*. However, entities frequently make loans to subsidiaries or associates which are often on terms that are repayable on demand or where the loan has a fixed term but the entity may rollover the loan if it reaches its maturity. Management will need to exercise judgement in determining whether such items are debtors or are a fixed asset investment in nature. Where the financing is provided for the long-term, with no intention of repayment in the foreseeable future, the balance may be more of a fixed asset investment in nature.

Discussion of the different sub-headings required to be shown for investments is included below. Care must be taken not to offset amounts owed by group undertakings with amounts owed to the same group undertaking or other group undertakings where the offset criteria in the standard are not met. The same principle applies to balances with undertakings in which the entity has a participating interest. Offset requires both a legally enforceable right of set off and an intention either to settle on a net basis or to realise the asset and settle the liability simultaneously. *[FRS 102.11.38A, 12.25A].*

Companies preparing Companies Act accounts are also required by the Regulations to present for each line item under current asset or fixed asset investments:

- the amount of listed investments included in that line item;
- the market value of the listed investments, if different from the carrying value, and also the stock exchange value if less than the market value so disclosed.

This disclosure can be given either in the accounts or notes to the accounts, and is also required for line items in the balance sheet format applied that have been combined on the balance sheet, as permitted by the Regulations (see 4.2 above).

A listed investment is an investment which has been granted a listing on a recognised investment exchange other than an overseas investment exchange (both as defined in Part 18 of the Financial Services and Markets Act 2000) or a stock exchange of repute outside the UK. *[1 Sch 54, 10 Sch 8].* A list of recognised investment exchanges (and recognised overseas investment exchanges) is available on the Financial Conduct Authority website. AIM is not a recognised investment exchange.

4.6.4.B   Group undertakings, participating interests and associated undertakings

Unlike previous UK GAAP (FRS 9 – *Associates and joint ventures*), FRS 102 does not require investments in associates and jointly controlled entities to be presented on the face of the statement of financial position in either the individual or consolidated financial statements. The gross equity presentation applied under previous UK GAAP for investments in joint ventures does not apply under FRS 102.

The standard requires disclosure of the carrying amount of investments in associates and of the carrying amount of investments in jointly controlled entities *[FRS 102.14.12(b), 15.19(b)].* This could be presented in the notes to the financial statements, although the standard requires additional line items, headings and subtotals when relevant to an understanding of the entity's financial position. *[FRS 102.4.3].*

The line items in the balance sheet formats in the Regulations refer to group undertakings, participating interests and associated undertakings. These terms are explained at 4.6.4.C to 4.6.4.E below.

UK companies preparing Companies Act accounts must also comply with the extensive requirements of paragraph 7 and Schedule 4 to the Regulations in relation to information about related undertakings (see Chapter 6 at 3.9.2).

4.6.4.C   Group undertakings

A 'group undertaking' is a parent undertaking or subsidiary undertaking of the reporting entity, or a subsidiary undertaking of any parent undertaking (i.e. a fellow subsidiary undertaking) of the reporting entity. *[s1161(5)]*. Parent and subsidiary undertakings are defined in section 1162 of the Companies Act 2006. See Chapter 2 at 3.1.2.

FRS 102 defines a subsidiary as an entity that is controlled by the parent. Control is the power to govern the financial and operating policies of an entity so as to obtain benefits from its activities. The standard goes on to explain in what circumstances control exists or can exist. *[FRS 102.9.4-9.6A]*. These circumstances are similar but not identical to those included in the definition of a subsidiary undertaking under section 1162.

Although there are slight differences in wording emphasis between this definition and the requirements in Section 9 – *Consolidated and Separate Financial Statements*, we would expect to see few conflicts arising in practice between Section 9 and the Companies Act 2006 (see Chapter 6 at 3.2).

4.6.4.D   Participating interest

A 'participating interest' means an interest held by, or on behalf of, an undertaking (or in group accounts, by the parent and its consolidated subsidiary undertakings) in the shares of another undertaking which it holds on a long-term basis for the purpose of securing a contribution to its activities (or in group accounts, the consolidated group's activities) by the exercise of control or influence arising from or related to that interest.

A holding of 20% or more of the shares of the undertaking is presumed to be a participating interest unless the contrary is shown. An interest in shares of another undertaking includes an interest which is convertible into an interest in shares and an option to acquire shares or any such interest, even if the shares are unissued until the conversion or exercise of the option.

In the context of the balance sheet formats, 'participating interest' does not include an interest in a group undertaking (see 4.6.4.C above). *[10 Sch 11]*.

4.6.4.E   Associated undertaking

An 'associated undertaking' is an undertaking in which an undertaking included in the consolidation:

- has a participating interest (as defined at 4.6.4.D above); and

- over whose operating and financial policy it exercises a significant influence; and

- which is not a subsidiary undertaking of the parent company or a joint venture dealt with in accordance with 6 Sch 18 to the Regulations (note that the accounting permitted by 6 Sch 18 is not consistent with the requirements of FRS 102) *[FRS 102.15.9A-9B]*).

A holding of 20% or more of the voting rights in another undertaking is presumed to exercise a significant influence over it unless the contrary is shown. Voting rights mean the rights conferred on shareholders in respect of their shares (or where the undertaking does not have a share capital, on members) to vote at general meetings of the undertaking on all, or substantially all matters – 7 Sch 5-11 applies in determining whether 20% or more of the voting rights are held. *[19 Sch 6, 7].*

The term 'associated undertaking' in the Regulations will generally include both an associate *[FRS 102.14.2]* (see Chapter 10 at 3.2) and a jointly controlled entity *[FRS 102 Appendix I]* (see Chapter 11 at 3.2), as defined under FRS 102. However, FRS 102's definition of an associate does not require the existence of a participating interest so it is theoretically possible that an associate under the standard may not be an associated undertaking under the Regulations.

4.6.4.F   Own shares

While 'own shares' have a sub-heading under investments in the balance sheet formats, FRS 102 requires investments in own shares to be treated as treasury shares and deducted from equity. *[FRS 102.22.16].* Consequently, this line item will not be used under FRS 102. The format 1 balance sheet has an alternative position 'reserve for own shares' within the capital and reserves section which will be used under FRS 102 (see 4.6.12 below).

4.6.5   Stocks

Table 4.7 shows the analysis required in respect of stocks under format 1.

Table 4.7   Analysis of stocks

C	Current assets	
I	Stocks	
	1	Raw materials and consumables
	2	Work in progress
	3	Finished goods and goods for resale
	4	Payments on account

The items reported under stocks in the balance sheet formats will generally correspond with inventories under FRS 102, which are assets: *[FRS 102 Appendix I, FRS 102.13.1]*

- held for sale in the ordinary course of business; or

- in the process of production for such sale; or

- in the form of materials or supplies to be consumed in the production process or in the rendering of services.

FRS 102 also introduces a concept of 'inventories held for distribution at no or nominal consideration' which could include advertising and promotional material (e.g. brochures not despatched) as well as items distributed to beneficiaries by public benefit entities (e.g. charities). *[FRS 102.13.4A, 18.8C(d), A4.36].*

Inventories also include agricultural produce harvested from biological assets and work in progress arising under construction contracts, including directly related service contracts. *[FRS 102.13.2].* Spare parts and servicing equipment are usually

4.6.6.D   Other debtors

This will cover debtors other than those identified in other line items, e.g. amounts receivable from a sale of property, plant and equipment.

4.6.6.E   Called up share capital not paid

The format 1 balance sheet permits called up share capital not paid to alternatively be shown in the position of line item A, i.e. on the face of the balance sheet (see 4.6.1 above).

4.6.6.F   Prepayments and accrued income

Prepayments and accrued income can alternatively be shown on the face of the balance sheet (line item D).

Prepayments and accrued income are not defined in the Regulations or in FRS 102. Prepayments arise where payments are made in advance of receiving the goods or services. They must meet the definition and recognition criteria of an asset, including recoverability, in the standard (see Chapter 3 at 3.3.1).

FRS 102 prohibits the recognition as an intangible asset of expenditure such as internally developed brand and similar intangible assets, start-up activities, training activities, advertising and promotional activities (except for inventories held for distribution at no or nominal consideration – see 4.6.5 above), relocation and reorganisation costs and internally generated goodwill. However, the standard does not preclude recognition of a prepayment where payment is made in advance of delivery of the goods or rendering of the services. *[FRS 102.18.8C-D].*

While the format 1 balance sheet combines prepayments and accrued income into one line item, these two items can have separate characteristics. The Financial Reporting Review Panel Annual Report 2012 indicated that a number of companies had been asked to show prepayments and accrued income separately in the notes to the financial statements as the assets differ in nature and liquidity. As noted at 4.2 above, the balance sheet formats allow any item to be shown in greater detail and FRS 102 requires additional line items, headings and subtotals when relevant to an understanding of the entity's financial position.

4.6.7   Cash at bank and in hand

The Regulations do not define cash at bank and in hand. This line item would include bank deposits with notice or maturity periods. Such bank deposits may or may not meet FRS 102's definition of 'cash' (i.e. cash on hand and demand deposits) or 'cash equivalents' (i.e. short-term, highly liquid investments that are readily convertible to known amounts of cash and that are subject to an insignificant risk of changes in value). *[FRS 102.7.2, Appendix I].* See Chapter 5 at 3.3 for the definition of cash and cash equivalents, and related disclosure requirements.

Care is needed with applying the requirements on offset of financial assets and financial liabilities, particularly in group arrangements with a bank where there are rights of offset. Offset requires both a legally enforceable right of set off and an intention either to settle on a net basis or to realise the asset and settle the liability simultaneously. *[FRS 102.11.38A, 12.25A].*

4.6.8 Creditors: amounts falling due within one year and after more than one year

Table 4.9 shows the analysis required in respect of creditors under format 1.

Table 4.9   Analysis of creditors: amounts falling due within one year

E	**Creditors: amounts falling due within one year**	
	1	Debenture loans
	2	Bank loans and overdrafts
	3	Payments received on account
	4	Trade creditors
	5	Bills of exchange payable
	6	Amounts owed to group undertakings
	7	Amounts owed to undertakings in which the company has a participating interest
	8	Other creditors including taxation and social security
	9	Accruals and deferred income*
H	**Creditors: amounts falling due within one year**	
	1	Debenture loans
	2	Bank loans and overdrafts
	3	Payments received on account
	4	Trade creditors
	5	Bills of exchange payable
	6	Amounts owed to group undertakings
	7	Amounts owed to undertakings in which the company has a participating interest
	8	Other creditors including taxation and social security
	9	Accruals and deferred income*

*   The notes to format 1 provide an alternative position for accruals and deferred income, at heading J.

The same line items are required for creditors: amounts falling due within one year, and creditors: amounts falling due after more than one year. See 4.4 above for discussion of these two categories of creditors.

In addition, in determining how amounts are presented within items in the balance sheet, the entity must have regard to the substance of the reported transaction or arrangement, in accordance with generally accepted accounting principles or practice. *[1 Sch 9]*. This provision facilitates the presentation of shares (such as certain preference shares) which are required to be classified as liabilities under accounting standards rather than as called up share capital under the balance sheet format. See Chapter 8.

As noted at 4.2 above, the balance sheet formats allow or, where the special nature of the company's business requires this, require certain adaptations to the balance sheet formats, as well as allowing line items to be shown in greater detail. The analysis of creditors is another area where entities may need to be mindful that FRS 102 requires additional line items, headings and subtotals when relevant to an understanding of the entity's financial position. For example, it may be appropriate to present preference shares classed as a liability, finance lease creditors and other items separately from other creditors.

The Regulations require UK companies preparing Companies Act accounts to state (in the accounts or notes to the accounts), for the aggregate of all items shown under creditors, the aggregate of:

(a)   the amount of any debts included in creditors which are payable or repayable otherwise than by instalments and fall due for payment or repayment after five years beginning with the day next following the end of the financial year; and

(b)   for debts payable or repayable by instalments, the amount of any instalments which fall due for payment after the end of that period.

In relation to each debt which is taken into account in (a) or (b) above, the terms of payment or repayment and rate of any interest payable must be stated. If the number of debts is such that, in the opinion of the directors, the statement would be of excessive length, a general indication of these terms and the interest rates payable can be given.

For each item shown under creditors, the aggregate amount of any debts included under that item in respect of which any security has been given, and an indication of the nature of the securities given must also be stated. *[1 Sch 61]*.

Where any outstanding loans made under the authority of section 682(2)(b), (c) or (d) (various cases of financial assistance by the company for the purchase of its own shares) are included under any item shown in the company's balance sheet, the aggregate amount of those items must be disclosed for each item in question. *[1 Sch 64(2)]*.

4.6.8.A   Debenture loans

The format 1 balance sheet has separate line items for debenture loans and bank loans and overdrafts. Therefore, bank loans and overdrafts need to be shown separately, even if they might also qualify as a debenture loan. The amount of any convertible loans must also be shown separately within debenture loans. *[1 Sch Note (7) on balance sheet formats]*.

A 'debenture' is not defined in the Companies Act 2006, except that it is stated to include 'debenture stock, bonds and other securities of a company, whether or not constituting a charge on the assets of the company.' *[s738]*. In general use, a 'debenture' is a term applying to any document evidencing a loan, and in the context of company law, it means a debt instrument issued by the company and usually giving some form of security or charge over its assets, although this is not an essential feature.

The Regulations require UK companies preparing Companies Act accounts to make the following disclosures in the accounts or notes to the accounts: *[1 Sch 50]*

* if the company has issued any debentures during the financial year, the classes of debentures issued during the financial year, and for each class of debentures, the amount issued and consideration received by the company for the issue; and

* where any of the company's debentures are held by a nominee of or trustee for the company, the nominal amount of the debentures and the amount at which they are stated in the accounting records.

4.6.8.B   Bank loans and overdrafts

In relation to bank loans and overdrafts, care is needed with applying the requirements on offset of financial assets and financial liabilities, particularly in group arrangements with a bank where there are rights of offset. Offset requires both a legally enforceable right of set off and an intention either to settle on a net basis or to realise the asset and settle the liability simultaneously. *[FRS 102.11.38A, 12.25A]*.

4.6.8.C   Payments on account

As noted at 4.6.5 above we would not expect payments on account to be deducted from stock (or inventory) as this would not meet the offset requirements of FRS 102. Also see 4.6.13 below for a discussion of how construction contract balances might be reflected in the balance sheet formats.

4.6.8.D   Trade creditors

Trade creditors are generally amounts payable to suppliers of goods and services, e.g. relating to amounts invoiced by suppliers.

Care must be taken not to offset any debit balances in trade debtors with trade creditors (and *vice versa*) where the offset criteria in the standard (see 4.6.8.B above) are not met. The separate line items for 'amounts owed to group undertakings' and 'amounts owed to undertakings in which the entity has a participating interest' will include trade creditors due to group undertakings and participating interests respectively (see 4.6.8.F below).

4.6.8.E   Bills of exchange

A bill of exchange is a written instrument used mainly in international trade, where one party agrees to pay an amount to another party on demand or on a specified date. The bill can often be transferred by the holder of the bill to a bank or finance house at a discount.

4.6.8.F   Amounts owed to group undertakings and to undertakings in which the company has a participating interest

The line items 'amounts owed to group undertakings' and 'amounts owed to undertakings in which the company has a participating interest' include all amounts owed by such undertakings which could include loans, dividend and interest payable, trading items such as current accounts and balances with group treasury companies. The meanings of 'group undertaking' and 'participating interest' are discussed at 4.6.4.D above.

Care must be taken not to offset debtors and creditors where the offset criteria in the standard (see 4.6.8.B above) are not met.

4.6.8.G   Other creditors, including taxation and social security

Other creditors are creditors that do not belong in other line items.

The amount for creditors in respect of taxation and social security must be shown separately from the amount for other creditors. *[1 Sch Note (9) on balance sheet formats]*. Taxation and social security creditors would include corporation tax, VAT, PAYE and

National Insurance, and other taxes, including overseas taxation. This analysis can be given in the notes to the accounts. In fact, FRS 102 does not explicitly require separate disclosure of the current tax creditor, although it requires disclosure of information that would enable users of the financial statements to evaluate the nature and financial effect of the current and deferred tax consequences of recognised transactions and other events. *[FRS 102.29.25].*

Deferred tax liabilities are not included in this heading but in 'Provisions for liabilities' (see 4.6.14 below).

4.6.8.H   Accruals and deferred income

Accruals and deferred income can alternatively be shown the face of the balance sheet (line item J). FRS 102 does not define accruals but under previous UK GAAP, the following distinction was drawn between accruals and provisions:

Accruals are liabilities to pay for goods or service that have been received or supplied but have not been paid, invoiced or formally agreed with the supplier including amounts due to employees (for example amounts relating to accrued holiday pay). Although it is sometimes necessary to estimate the amount or timing of accruals, the uncertainty is generally much less than for provisions. *[FRS 12.11(b)].*

Deferred income may arise where cash is received in advance of meeting the conditions for recognising the related revenue, e.g. rental income received in advance or where cash is received for goods not yet delivered or services not yet rendered. In addition, deferred income may arise in relation to government grants related to assets (which are recognised in income on a systematic basis over the expected useful life of the asset). *[FRS 102.24.5F-G].* See 4.6.19 below.

The Financial Reporting Review Panel Annual Report 2012 indicated that a number of companies had been asked to show accruals and deferred income separately in the notes to the financial statements as the liabilities differ in nature and timing. See the discussion on prepayments and accrued income at 4.6.6.F above.

4.6.9   Net current assets/ (liabilities)

The format 1 balance sheet requires a net current assets/(liabilities) subtotal.

The formats require that any amounts shown as prepayments and accrued income must be taken into account in determining net current assets/(liabilities), wherever shown (see 4.6.6.F above). *[1 Sch Note 11 on balance sheet formats].* Therefore, net current assets (liabilities) will represent the amounts reported at item C in the balance sheet formats plus prepayments and accrued income (at item D, if shown separately) less creditors: amounts falling due within one year (at item E).

4.6.10   Total assets less current liabilities

The format 1 balance sheet requires a subtotal for total assets less current liabilities. This subtotal would be the sum of fixed assets and net current assets/(liabilities).

While the format 1 balance sheet does not require a net assets subtotal (with a balancing subtotal for capital and reserves), most companies give this. Sometimes companies have presented a balancing subtotal for capital and reserves together with creditors: amounts falling due within one year, a practice not precluded by the Regulations.

4.6.11   Provisions for liabilities

Table 4.10 shows the analysis required in respect of provisions for liabilities under format 1.

Table 4.10   Analysis of provisions for liabilities

I		Provisions for liabilities
	1	Pensions and similar obligations
	2	Taxation, including deferred taxation
	3	Other provisions

References to 'Provisions for liabilities' in the Regulations are 'to any amount retained as reasonably necessary for the purpose of providing for any liability the nature of which is clearly defined and which is either likely to be incurred, or certain to be incurred but uncertain as to amount or as to the date on which it will arise.' *[9 Sch 2]*. FRS 102 defines a provision more succinctly as 'a liability of uncertain timing or amount.' *[FRS 102 Appendix I]*.

The Regulations provide specific line items for pensions and similar obligations, taxation (including deferred taxation) and other provisions.

As noted at 4.2 above, the balance sheet formats allow or, where the special nature of the company's business requires this, require certain adaptations to the balance sheet formats, as well as allowing line items to be shown in greater detail. The analysis of provisions is an area where entities may need to be mindful that FRS 102 requires additional line items, headings and subtotals when relevant to an understanding of the entity's financial position.

For UK companies preparing Companies Act accounts, the accounts or notes to the accounts must give particulars of each material provision included in the line item 'other provisions'. *[1 Sch 59(3)]*. Particulars must also be given of any pension commitments included under provisions, distinguishing commitments relating wholly or partly to pensions payable to past directors of the company. *[1 Sch 63(4)]*.

FRS 102 requires an entity to present a reconciliation of each class of provision, showing the carrying amounts at the beginning of the period, additions (including adjustments from changes in measuring the discounted amount), amounts charged against the provision in the period, unused amounts reversed, and the carrying amounts at the end of the period. *[FRS 102.21.14]*.

Where there have been transfers to provisions or from any provisions for a purpose different to that for which the provision was established (and the provisions are required to be shown as separate line items in the balance sheet, or would be if line items had not been combined in the balance sheet, as permitted by the Regulations), a UK company preparing Companies Act accounts must disclose the following information in respect of the aggregate of provisions included in the same item in the accounts or notes to the accounts:

- the amounts of the provisions at the beginning and end of the financial year;
- any amounts transferred to or from the provisions during that year; and
- the source and application respectively of any amounts transferred.

Comparatives are not required. *[1 Sch 59(1)-(2)]*. The above reconciliation required by the Regulations is similar to that required by FRS 102 (see Chapter 17 at 3.10.2).

4.6.12   Capital and reserves

Table 4.11 shows the analysis required in respect of capital and reserves under format 1.

Table 4.11   *Analysis of capital and reserves*

K	Capital and reserves
I	Called up share capital
II	Share premium account
III	Revaluation reserve
IV	Other reserves
1	Capital redemption reserve
2	Reserve for own shares
3	Reserves provided for by the articles of association
4	Other reserves
V	Profit and loss account

The capital and reserves section of the balance sheet includes a number of line items denoted by a Roman numeral which must be presented on the face of the balance sheet, with no adaptation of the wording permitted.

In addition, where there are transfers to or from any reserves required to be shown as a separate line item in the balance sheet (or would be, if not combined with other line items, as permitted by the Regulations), the Regulations require a UK company preparing Companies Act accounts to reconcile the movements in the aggregate of the reserves included in that item in the accounts or notes to the accounts (comparatives are not required). This requirement has some similarities to FRS 102's statement of changes in equity (with comparatives required) discussed further at 6 below.

4.6.12.A   Called up share capital

Called up share capital in relation to a company means so much of its share capital as equals the aggregate amounts of the calls made on its shares (whether or not those calls have been paid) together with:

- any share capital paid up without being called, and
- any share capital to be paid on a specified future date under the articles, the terms of allotment of the relevant shares or any other arrangements for payment of those shares.

Uncalled share capital is construed accordingly. *[s547]*.

Shares allotted by a company and any premium on them may be paid up in money or money's worth (including goodwill and know-how). This does not prevent a company allotting bonus shares to its members or from paying up, with sums available for the purpose, any amounts for the time being unpaid on any of its shares (whether on account of the nominal value of the shares or by way of premium). *[s582].* There are additional restrictions for payment of shares for public companies.

The Companies Act 2006 does not require that the shares issued are fully paid although a public company must not allot a share except where at least one quarter of the nominal value of the share and all of the premium is paid up (with certain limited exceptions). *[s586].*

A share in a company is deemed 'paid up' (as to its nominal value or any premium on it) in cash, or allotted for cash, if the consideration received for the allotment or payment up in cash is:

- cash received by the company;
- a cheque received by the company in good faith that the directors have no reason for suspecting will not be paid;
- a release of a liability of the company for a liquidated sum;
- an undertaking to pay cash to the company at a future date; or
- payment by any other means giving rise to a present or future entitlement (of the company or a person acting on the company's behalf) to a payment, or credit equivalent to payment. This can include payments made using the settlement system operated by Euroclear UK & Ireland (also known as the CREST system) – see *The Companies (Shares and Share Capital) Order 2009.*

Cash includes foreign currency. The payment of cash to a person other than the company or an undertaking to pay cash to a person other than the company is consideration other than cash. *[s583].*

Called up share capital not paid is explained at 4.6.1 above.

FRS 102's requirements on recording issuances of equity instruments are consistent with the presentation of called up share capital in the Regulations *[FRS 102.22.7-22.12]* (see Chapter 8 at 9.6).

4.6.12.B   *Share premium account*

Share premium account is a statutory reserve that arises on the issue of share capital. It is beyond the scope of this chapter to explain the rules governing share premium in detail – but the summary below explains how share premium arises and can be applied or reduced.

If a company issues shares at a premium, whether for cash or otherwise, a sum equal to the aggregate amount or value of the premiums on those shares must be transferred to an account called the share premium account, except to the extent that merger relief (as set out in sections 612 and 613) and group reconstruction relief (as set out in section 611) apply. This sum transferred to the share premium account can be used to write off the expenses of the issue of those shares and any commission paid on the issue of those shares. Share premium may be used to pay up new shares to be allotted to members as fully-paid bonus shares. *[s610(1)-(3), (5)]*.

Share premium also arises when treasury shares are sold for proceeds that exceed the purchase price paid by the company. *[s731(3)]*. This would include sales of treasury shares to an ESOP.

The share premium account may be reduced (by special resolution supported by a solvency statement or confirmed by the court). *[s610(4), s641-651]*.

Where a limited company purchases or redeems shares, normally the redemption or purchase must be made out of distributable profits or out of the proceeds of a fresh issue for the purposes of the purchase or redemption. However, any premium payable on redemption must be made out of distributable profits unless the shares were originally issued at a premium and the purchase or redemption is made in whole or in part out of proceeds of a fresh issue. In this case, the share premium account (rather than distributable profits) may be reduced up to an amount equal to the lower of the aggregate of the premiums received by the company on issue of the shares and the current level of the share premium account (including premiums on the issue of the new shares). Share premium may also be reduced, to the extent permitted by the Companies Act 2006, when a private limited company makes a payment out of capital under Chapter 5 of Part 18 of the Companies Act 2006. *[s687, s692, s734]*.

4.6.12.C   Revaluation reserve

The revaluation reserve arises where an asset is carried at valuation using the alternative accounting rules in the Regulations. *[1 Sch 35]*. See 9.2 below. Unlike the other reserves denoted with a Roman numeral, the amount of the revaluation reserve must be presented in the position denoted by K III (revaluation reserve) but need not be shown under that name. *[1 Sch 35(1)]*.

The uses of the revaluation reserve are explained further at 9.2.3 below.

4.6.12.D   Reserves provided for by the Articles of Association

Where the articles specifically provide for reserves to be established, this line item is used.

4.6.12.E   Other reserves

Other reserves may be combined on the face of the balance sheet, with the line items denoted by an Arabic number presented in the notes to the accounts where the individual amounts are not material or the combination facilitates the assessment of the state of affairs (in which case the individual line items are disclosed in the notes to the accounts). *[1 Sch 4(2)-(3)]*.

As noted at 4.2 above, the balance sheet formats allow or where the special nature of the company's business requires this, require certain adaptations to the balance sheet formats, as well as allowing line items to be shown in greater detail. The analysis of other reserves is an area where entities may need to be mindful that FRS 102 requires additional line items, headings and subtotals when relevant to an understanding of the entity's financial position. *[FRS 102.4.3]*.

4.6.12.F   Capital redemption reserve

The capital redemption reserve is a statutory reserve which is established when the shares of a limited company are redeemed or purchased wholly or partly out of the company's profits, or where treasury shares are cancelled. It is beyond the scope of this chapter to explain the rules governing redemptions/purchases of shares, treasury shares and the capital redemption reserve in detail. – but the summary below explains how capital redemption reserve arises and can be applied or reduced. *[s733]*.

As with the share premium account, the capital redemption reserve can be used to pay up new shares to be allotted to members as fully-paid bonus shares. *[s733(5)]*. The capital redemption reserve may also be reduced (by special resolution supported by a solvency statement or confirmed by the court) *[s733(6), s641-651]* and, to the extent permitted by the Companies Act 2006, when a private limited company makes a payment out of capital under Chapter 5 of Part 18 of the Companies Act 2006. *[s687, s692, s734]*.

4.6.12.G   Reserve for own shares

The reserve for own shares is used where the company purchases its own shares to be held by an ESOP (see Chapter 21 at 13.3) that is treated as an extension of the sponsoring entity or where shares are held as treasury shares. *[FRS 102.9.33-9.37, 22.16]*. The nominal value of the shares held must be shown separately in the notes to the accounts. *[1 Sch Note (4) on balance sheet formats]*.

4.6.12.H   Other reserves

Other reserves would include a reserve arising where merger relief (under sections 612 and 613) or group reconstruction relief (under section 611) is taken, but the company chooses to record a reserve equivalent to the share premium that would have been recorded but for the relief (as permitted by section 615).

Under FRS 102, certain items are recognised directly in other comprehensive income (and where required by the standard, later reclassified to profit or loss) – see 5.2 below.

Where a UK company prepares Companies Act accounts, the fair value accounting rules in the Regulations (see 9.3 below) have the effect that the changes in fair value:

- of the hedging instrument in respect of cash-flow hedges, and hedges of net investment in foreign operations (to the extent effective);
- relating to exchange differences on monetary items forming part of the company's net investment in a foreign entity; and
- of available for sale financial assets.

must or may be recognised in a separate statutory reserve (the fair value reserve). This would be an 'other reserve' in the statutory formats.

Note that while FRS 102 requires that exchange differences arising on translation of a foreign operation in the financial statements that include that foreign operation (including a monetary item that forms part of the net investment in that foreign operation) are recognised in other comprehensive income and accumulated in equity there is no requirement in the standard to accumulate these in a separate reserve. *[FRS 102.30.13, 30.22]*. See Chapter 25 at 3.7.4. Companies are not, however, precluded from doing so, and the fair value accounting rules imply that exchange differences on monetary items forming part of the company's net investment in a foreign entity are accumulated within the fair value reserve. See 9.3.2 below.

4.6.12.1   Profit and loss account

The profit and loss account (or retained earnings) arises from the accumulation of the results for the year, and other items taken to other comprehensive income or to equity, but not classified in another reserve.

Where profits are unrealised, companies may prefer to report these in a reserve other than retained earnings, so as to distinguish these from other profits that are realised.

4.6.13   Construction contracts

The percentage completion method is applied to construction contracts and revenue from rendering services. *[FRS 102.23.21]*.

FRS 102 requires that, for construction contracts, an entity shall present the gross amount due from customers for contract work as an asset, and the gross amount due to customers for contract work as a liability. *[FRS 102.23.32]*. However, the standard does not specifically address how assets and liabilities arising should be classified in the statement of financial position. IAS 11 – *Construction Contracts* – has a similar presentation requirement, which may provide clarification. IAS 11 requires presentation of:

- the gross amount due from customers for contract work as an asset – for all contracts in progress for which costs incurred plus recognised profits (less recognised losses) exceed progress billings; and

- the gross amount due to customers for contract work as a liability – for all contracts in progress for which progress billings exceed costs incurred plus recognised profits (less recognised losses). *[IAS 11.42-44]*.

FRS 102 implies that a single contract asset (being the aggregate of contracts in an asset position) and/or a single contract liability (being the aggregate of contracts in a liability position) should be reported in the statement of financial position. In our view, it would be appropriate to include the contract asset as a line item within debtors (see 4.6.6 above), and the contract liability within creditors – see 4.6.8 above. Where it is probable that the total contract costs will exceed total contract revenue, FRS 102 requires immediate recognition of the expected loss *and a corresponding provision for an onerous contract (and cross refers to Section 21)* [emphasis added]. *[FRS 102.23.26]*. The italicised words are not included in the IFRS for SMEs (or IAS 11). While these additional words could imply that the provision element of the overall contract liability is to be presented within Provisions for liabilities, we consider it more likely that the standard is intending a single contract asset and liability to be presented (as would be required by IAS 11). However, we would expect that full disclosures for provisions in accordance with Section 21 are provided, regardless of the presentation adopted.

Where the stage of completion is determined by reference to contract costs incurred for work performed to date as a proportion of estimated total costs, costs relating to future activity, such as for materials or prepayments, are excluded *[FRS 102.23.22(a)]*. Such costs are, however, recognised as an asset, where it is probable that the costs will be recovered. *[FRS 102.23.23]*. FRS 102 does not address the classification of such assets, e.g. whether part of the contract asset or liability, or as separate inventory or prepayments.

FRS 102 does not distinguish between the presentation of advances and progress billings (i.e. whether the contract asset or liability is determined after *all* payments on account – including advances – or only after progress billings) but under IAS 11, advances are not included in the determination of the contract asset or liability but are shown as a separate creditor (as in the Illustrative Examples). In our view, where advances are reported separately, these should be disclosed as 'payments received on account' within Creditors: amounts falling due within one year and Creditors: amounts falling due after more than one year, as appropriate.

Progress billings not yet received (including any contract retentions) would be included in trade debtors.

4.6.14   *Deferred tax*

FRS 102 requires deferred tax liabilities to be presented within Provisions for liabilities (see 4.6.11 above) and deferred tax assets to be presented within debtors. There is no requirement to present deferred tax separately on the face of the statement of financial position. *[FRS 102.29.23]*. This is consistent with the presentation required under previous UK GAAP, *[FRS 19.Appendix III.9-10]*, but differs from the presentation of deferred tax in IFRSs as a non-current asset and/or non-current liability on the face of the statement of financial position. *[IAS 1.54, 56]*.

Deferred tax debtors may include amounts due after more than one year. See 4.3 above for the disclosure requirements for Debtors: amounts due after more than one year in the standard and in the Regulations.

FRS 102 requires that the amount of deferred tax assets and liabilities at the end of the reporting period is disclosed for each type of timing difference and the amount of unused tax losses and tax credits (together with their expiry dates, if any). *[FRS 102.29.27(e)-(f)]*.

For UK companies preparing Companies Act accounts, the Regulations require that the provision for deferred tax is shown separately from any other tax provisions, *[1 Sch 60]*, in the accounts or notes to the accounts. Where there have been transfers to and from deferred tax, the amount of the provision at the beginning and end of the year, and the movements in that provision must also be disclosed in the accounts or notes to the accounts (see 4.6.11 above). *[1 Sch 59]*.

4.6.15   *Assets and disposal groups held for sale*

FRS 102 does not include a concept of assets and disposal groups held for sale, comparable to that in IFRS 5 – *Non-current Assets Held for Sale and Discontinued Operations*. The standard, therefore, does not require an entity to present a non-current asset classified as held for sale and the assets of a disposal group held for sale separately from other assets in the statement of financial position and the liabilities of a disposal group held for sale separately from other liabilities in the statement of financial position. *[IFRS 5.38, IAS 1.54]*. This presentation of disposal groups is not allowed by FRS 102 because the Regulations do not permit the aggregation of different line items into two lines, being assets and liabilities of the disposal group, in this way.

As noted at 4.6.3 above, the statutory definition of a fixed asset is not normally interpreted to mean that individual assets are transferred to current assets when a decision to dispose of them has been made (but see 4.6.5.A above which sets out some situations where we would expect a change in use of the asset to lead to reclassification as inventory). Nevertheless, some companies do make such transfers.

4.6.16   Post-employment benefit assets and liabilities

FRS 102 does not explicitly address the presentation of post-employment benefit assets and liabilities.

The format 1 balance sheet includes a line item 'Pensions and similar liabilities' within provisions for liabilities (see 4.6.11 above) and in our view, a pension asset could be presented as a separate line item within debtors.

Defined benefit assets may include amounts due after more than one year. See 4.3 above for the disclosure requirements for Debtors: amounts due after more than one year in the standard and in the Regulations.

However, under previous UK GAAP, FRS 17 – *Retirement benefits* – requires presentation of the pension asset or liability (net of deferred tax) separately on the face of the balance sheet following other net assets and before capital and reserves. Where an employer has more than one scheme, the total of any defined benefit assets and the total of any defined benefit liabilities are shown separately on the balance sheet. *[FRS 17.47, 49]*. An Appendix to FRS 17 includes: 'The Board has received legal advice that these requirements do not contravene the Companies Act 1985.' *[FRS 17.Appendix II.6]*. On that basis, we consider that a similar presentation remains possible under FRS 102 (although the related deferred tax asset or liability should be shown separately, as offset is not permitted under the standard).

The Regulations require a UK company preparing Companies Act accounts to disclose particulars of any pension commitments under any provision shown in the company's balance sheet, and any such commitments for which no provision has been made in the notes to the accounts. *[1 Sch 63(4)]*.

4.6.17   Biological assets

The format 1 balance sheet does not include a line item for biological assets, which should be reported within either tangible fixed assets (e.g. an apple orchard) or stock (e.g. farmed salmon), as appropriate.

4.6.18   Financial assets and financial liabilities

The format 1 balance sheet does not include specific line items for financial assets and financial liabilities.

Financial assets will generally be reported within cash at bank and in hand, debtors, current asset investments or fixed asset investments, as applicable. Financial liabilities will generally be reported within creditors: amounts falling due within one year and creditors: amounts falling due after more than one year or provisions for liabilities (e.g. contingent consideration on a business combination), as applicable.

FRS 102 requires the carrying amounts at the reporting date of the following categories of financial assets and financial liabilities, in total, to be disclosed either in the statement of financial position or in the notes to the financial statements:

- financial assets measured at fair value through profit or loss;
- financial assets that are debt instruments measured at amortised cost;
- financial assets that are equity instruments measured at cost less impairment;
- financial liabilities measured at fair value through profit or loss (showing financial liabilities that are not held as part of a trading portfolio and are not derivatives separately);
- financial liabilities measured at amortised cost; and
- loan commitments measured at cost less impairment. *[FRS 102.11.41]*.

The above disclosures are not required in individual financial statements of a qualifying entity that is not a financial institution, providing that the equivalent disclosures required by the standard are given in the publicly available consolidated financial statements of the group in which the qualifying entity is consolidated. *[FRS 102.1.8, 1.12(c)]*.

4.6.18.A   Compound instruments

FRS 102 requires that an entity issuing a convertible or compound instrument must allocate the proceeds between the liability component and the equity component. *[FRS 102.22.13]*. This classification is permitted by the Regulations which require that, in determining how amounts are presented within items in the balance sheet, the entity must have regard to the substance of the reported transaction or arrangement, in accordance with generally accepted accounting principles or practice. *[1 Sch 9]*.

Appendix 2 of TECH 02/10 *Guidance on the determination of realised profits and losses in the context of distributions under the Companies Act 2006* includes numerical illustrations of the treatment of compound instruments.

4.6.19   Government grants

FRS 102 sets out two models for recognising government grants – the accrual model (which is similar to that used under previous UK GAAP) and the performance model (see Chapter 19).

Where the performance model is used, FRS 102 states that grants received before the revenue recognition criteria are satisfied are recognised as a *liability* [emphasis added]. *[FRS 102.24.5B(c)]*. Since deferred income is not strictly a liability, it may be appropriate to include government grants not recognised within 'Other creditors including taxation and social security'.

Where the accrual model is used, FRS 102 requires that government grants related to assets are recognised in income on a systematic basis over the expected useful life of the asset. Where part of a grant relating to an asset is deferred, it is recognised as deferred income and not deducted from the carrying amount of the asset. *[FRS 102.24.5F-G]*. FRS 102 does not address the presentation where a grant has been received but does not meet the recognition criteria but it would be logical to present this as a liability rather than deferred income (consistent with the requirement for the performance model).

While there is no specific line item for government grants in the balance sheet formats, FRS 102 requires additional line items, headings and subtotals when relevant to an understanding of the entity's financial position. In any event, the standard specifically requires disclosure of the nature and amounts of grants recognised in the financial statements. *[FRS 102.24.6(b)]*.

4.7   Information to be presented either in the statement of financial position or in the notes

FRS 102 requires an entity with share capital to disclose the following information regarding equity and share capital either on the face of the statement of financial position or in the notes: *[FRS 102.4.12]*

(a)   for each class of share capital:

    (i)   the number of shares issued and fully paid, and issued but not fully paid;

    (ii)   par value per share, or that the shares have no par value;

    (iii) a reconciliation of the number of shares outstanding at the beginning and at the end of the period. This reconciliation need not be presented for prior periods;

    (v)   the rights, preferences and restrictions attaching to that class including restrictions on the distribution of dividends and the repayment of capital;

    (vi)   shares in the entity held by the entity or by its subsidiaries, associates or joint ventures;

    (vii) shares reserved for issue under options and contracts for the sale of shares, including the terms and amounts; and

(b)   a description of each reserve within equity.

An entity without share capital, such as a partnership or trust, must disclose information equivalent to that required by (a) above, showing changes during the period in each category of equity interest, and the rights, preferences and restrictions attaching to each category of equity interest. *[FRS 102.4.13]*.

4.7.1   *Information required by the Regulations*

Some of the FRS 102 disclosure requirements overlap with the disclosure requirements in relation to share capital included in the Regulations for UK companies preparing Companies Act accounts. The Regulations require the following disclosures in the accounts or in the notes to the accounts:

•   the amount of allotted share capital and, separately, the amount of called up share capital which has been paid up (on the face of the balance sheet or in the notes); *[1 Sch Note (12) on balance sheet formats]*.

- where shares of more than one class have been allotted, the number and aggregate nominal value of shares of each class allotted; *[1 Sch 47(1)(a)]*.

- where shares are held as treasury shares, the number and aggregate nominal value of the treasury shares and, where shares of more than one class have been allotted, the number and aggregate nominal value of the shares of each class held as treasury shares; *[1 Sch 47(1)(b)]*.

- where any part of the allotted share capital consists of redeemable shares:

  - the earliest and latest dates on which the company has power to redeem those shares;

  - whether those shares must be redeemed in any event or are liable to be redeemed at the option of the company or of the shareholder; and

  - whether any (and if so, what) premium is payable on redemption; *[1 Sch 47(2)]*.

- if the company has allotted any shares during the financial year:

  - the classes of shares allotted; and

  - for each class of shares, the number allotted, their aggregate nominal value, and the consideration received by the company for the allotment. *[1 Sch 48]*.

- with respect to any contingent right to the allotment of shares in the company (i.e. any option to subscribe for shares and any other right to require the allotment of shares to any person whether arising on the conversion into shares of securities of any other description or otherwise), particulars of:

  - the number, description and amount of the shares in relation to which the right is exercisable;

  - the period during which it is exercisable; and

  - the price to be paid for the shares allotted; *[1 Sch 49]*.

- if any fixed cumulative dividends on the company's shares are in arrears:

  - the amount of the arrear, and

  - the period for which the dividends or, if there is more than one class, each class of them are in arrear; and *[1 Sch 62]*.

- the number, description and amount of shares in the company held by, or on behalf of, its subsidiary undertakings (except where the subsidiary undertaking is concerned as personal representative, or, subject to certain exceptions, as trustee). *[4 Sch 3]*.

4.8   Information on disposal groups to be presented in the notes

FRS 102 requires only limited disclosures where there is, at the end of the reporting period, a disposal group. As discussed at 4.6.15 above, the Regulations do not permit the IFRS 5 presentation of separate line items for assets and liabilities of a disposal group held for sale in the statement of financial position.

If, at the reporting date, an entity has a binding sale agreement for a major disposal of assets, or a disposal group, the entity must disclose in the notes to the financial statements: *[FRS 102.4.14]*

- a description of the asset(s) or the disposal group;
- a description of the facts and circumstances of the sale; and
- the carrying amount of the assets or, for a disposal group, the carrying amounts of the underlying assets and liabilities.

FRS 102 defines a disposal group as 'a group of assets to be disposed of, by sale or otherwise, together as a group in a single transaction, and liabilities directly associated with those assets that will be transferred in the transaction. The group includes goodwill acquired in a business combination if the group is a cash-generating unit to which goodwill has been allocated in accordance with the requirements of paragraphs 27.24 to 27.27 of this FRS'. *[FRS 102 Appendix I].*

5   STATEMENT OF COMPREHENSIVE INCOME

FRS 102 requires an entity to present its total comprehensive income for a period, i.e. its financial performance for period, in one or two statements. Financial performance is the relationship of the income and expenses of an entity as reported in the statement of comprehensive income. Relevant definitions of terms applicable to the statement of comprehensive income are at 3.1 above.

Section 5 of the standard applies to all FRS 102 reporters whether or not they report under the Companies Act 2006. Other entities that do not report under the Companies Act 2006 are required to comply with the requirements set out in Section 5 and with the Regulations (or, where applicable, the LLP Regulations) where referred to in Section 5, except to the extent that these requirements are not permitted by any statutory framework under which such entities report. *[FRS 102.5.1].*

5.1   Format of the statement of comprehensive income

An entity must present its total comprehensive income for a period either: *[FRS 102.5.2, Appendix I]*

- in a single statement of comprehensive income which presents all items of income and expense (and includes a subtotal for profit or loss); or
- in two statements – an income statement (referred to as the profit and loss account in the Companies Act 2006) and a statement of comprehensive income, in which case the income statement presents all items of income and expense recognised in the period except those that are recognised in total comprehensive income outside of profit or loss as permitted or required by FRS 102.

A change from the single-statement approach to the two-statement approach, or *vice versa*, is a retrospective change in accounting policy to which Section 10 applies. *[FRS 102.5.3].* See Chapter 7 at 3.4.

These requirements apply both to consolidated and individual financial statements. However, entities preparing group accounts in accordance with the Companies Act 2006 can take advantage of the exemption not to present the individual profit and loss account and certain related notes. *[s408, s472(2), 1 Sch 65].* See Chapter 1 at 6.3.2. This exemption would not extend to individual financial statements prepared under other statutory frameworks, unless permitted by these frameworks.

5.2   Items presented in other comprehensive income

Other comprehensive income is items of income and expense (including reclassification adjustments), that are not recognised in profit or loss as required or permitted by FRS 102. Profit and loss is the default category – all comprehensive income is part of profit and loss unless FRS 102 permits or requires otherwise. *[FRS 102 Appendix I]*. See definitions at 3.1 above.

Tax expense / (income) is recognised in other comprehensive income where the transaction or other event that resulted in the tax is recognised in other comprehensive income. *[FRS 102.29.22]*. See Chapter 24 at 8.

FRS 102 requires the following items to be included in other comprehensive income:

(a)   changes in revaluation surplus relating to property, plant and equipment *[FRS 102.16.1, 17.15E-F]* (see Chapter 13 at 3.6.3) and intangible assets *[FRS 102.18.18G,H]* (see Chapter 14 at 3.4.2.C);

(b)   actuarial gains and losses, and the return on plan assets excluding amounts included in net interest on the net defined benefit liability (known collectively as 'remeasurements' of the net defined benefit liability) on defined benefit plans *[FRS 102.28.23(d), 25]* (see Chapter 23 at 3.6.8.B);

(c)   exchange gains and losses arising from translating the financial statements of a foreign operation (including in consolidated financial statements, exchange differences on a monetary item that forms part of the net investment in the foreign operation). However, under FRS 102 (unlike IAS 21 – *The Effects of Changes in Foreign Exchange Rates* – and FRS 23 – *The effects of changes in foreign exchange rates*), cumulative exchange differences accumulated in equity are not reclassified to profit and loss on disposal of a net investment in a foreign operation *[FRS 102.9.18A, 30.13]* (see Chapter 25 at 3.7.4);

(d)   the effective portion of fair value gains and losses on hedging instruments in a cash flow hedge or a hedge of the foreign exchange risk in a net investment in a foreign operation. The amounts taken to equity in respect of the hedge of the foreign exchange risk in a net investment in a foreign operation are not reclassified to profit or loss on disposal or partial disposal of the foreign operation. *[FRS 102.12.23]* (see Chapter 8 at 7.9);

(e)   fair value gains and losses through other comprehensive income for an investor that is not a parent measuring its interests in jointly controlled entities *[FRS 102.15.9(c), 15.14-15A]* and investments in associates in its individual financial statements *[FRS 102.14.4(c), 14.9-10A]* (see Chapter 10 at 2.1.2 and Chapter 11 at 3.6.2);

(f)   fair value gains and losses through other comprehensive income for investments in subsidiaries, associates and jointly controlled entities used by a parent in its separate financial statements *[FRS 102.9.26(b)]* (see Chapter 6 at 4.2); and

(g)   any unrealised gain arising on an exchange of business or non-monetary assets for an interest in a subsidiary, jointly controlled entity or associate *[FRS 102.9.31(c)]* (see Chapter 6 at 3.8).

Of the above items, only the amounts taken to other comprehensive income in relation to cash flow hedges (at (c) above) may be reclassified to profit or loss in a subsequent period under FRS 102.

Where the entity applies the recognition and measurement requirements of IAS 39 – *Financial Instruments: Recognition and Measurement* – or IFRS 9 – *Financial Instruments* to financial instruments, further items are reported in other comprehensive income (see 5.2.1 below).

Schedule 1 to the Regulations restricts when unrealised profits can be reported in the profit and loss account. Consequently, certain unrealised profits may be required to be reported in other comprehensive income (see 5.2.2 below).

5.2.1 Items reported in other comprehensive income where an entity chooses to apply the recognition and measurement provisions of IAS 39 or IFRS 9 (and/or IAS 39)

Where the recognition and measurement requirements of IFRS 9 (and/or IAS 39) are applied to financial instruments, as permitted by FRS 102, the following items would also be reported in other comprehensive income:

(a) gains and losses on remeasuring available-for-sale financial assets (if the entity chooses to apply IAS 39); *[IAS 39.55(b)]*

(b) gains and losses on remeasuring investments in equity instruments measured at fair value through other comprehensive income (if the entity chooses to apply IFRS 9); *[IFRS 9.5.7.5]*

(c) the effective portion of gains and losses on hedging instruments in a cash flow hedge or hedge of a net investment in a foreign operation (if the entity chooses to apply IAS 39 or IFRS 9); *[IAS 39.95-102, IFRS 9.6.5.11-6.5.14]*

(d) for liabilities designated as at fair value through profit or loss, fair value changes attributable to changes in the liability's credit risk, unless this would create or enlarge an accounting mismatch in profit and loss (if the entity chooses to apply IFRS 9); *[IFRS 9.5.7.7(a)]* and

(e) gains and losses on financial assets that are debt instruments (meeting the specified criteria) that are carried at fair value through other comprehensive income (if the entity chooses to apply IFRS 9). *[IFRS 9.5.7.10]*.

Only items (a), (e) and the effective portion of gains and losses on hedging instruments in a cash flow hedge at (c) above may be reclassified to profit or loss in a subsequent period. The requirements of IAS 39 and IFRS 9 are discussed in EY International GAAP 15 Chapters 50 and 51 respectively.

5.2.2 Impact of realised and unrealised profits on items reported in other comprehensive income

UK companies preparing Companies Act accounts need to be mindful of the requirements of paragraph 13(a) of Schedule 1 to the Regulations that 'only profits realised at the balance sheet are to be included in the profit and loss account'.

Notwithstanding this restriction, paragraph 40(2) of Schedule 1 to the Regulations requires that the changes in fair value of a financial instrument, living animal or plant, or investment property measured at fair value using the fair value accounting rules (where permitted by paragraphs 36 and 39 of Schedule 1) must be reflected in the profit and loss account. This is subject to the requirements of paragraphs 40(2) and (3) of Schedule 1 for available for sale financial assets, hedge accounting and for exchange differences on monetary items forming part of the net investment in a foreign entity, which permit or require certain movements on financial instruments to be reflected in a separate reserve, the fair value reserve. See 9.3 and 9.4 below for a discussion of the fair value accounting rules.

Interestingly, FRS 101 – *Reduced Disclosure Framework* – requires that 'an entity shall recognise all items of income and expense arising in a period in profit or loss unless an IFRS requires or permits otherwise or *unless prohibited by the Act*' [emphasis added]. *[FRS 101.AG1(k)]*. Whilst FRS 102 does not include the words italicised above, there are reasons to believe that the same treatment is intended. Appendix IV (Note on Legal Requirements) highlights the above requirements of paragraphs 13 and 40 of Schedule 1 to the Regulations. *[FRS 102.A4.25-A4.29]*. In addition, FRS 102's requirements for exchanges of businesses and non-monetary assets for an interest in a subsidiary, jointly controlled entity or an associate state that 'any unrealised gain arising on the exchange shall be recognised in other comprehensive income'. *[FRS 102.9.31(c)]*.

Where the standard is explicit that it requires that a particular gain must be reported in profit or loss but this would conflict with the Regulations or LLP Regulations, the entity should consider whether a 'true and fair override' of the requirements of the Companies Act 2006 is appropriate (see 8.2 below). Where the standard is not explicit, notwithstanding that profit and loss is the default location for gains and losses, in our view, entities should look to Appendix IV to FRS 102, which highlights the company law requirements on realised profits. However, such considerations are only relevant to entities subject to the Regulations or LLP Regulations (or corresponding requirements in another statutory or regulatory framework that applies to the entity).

Whether profits are available for distribution must be determined in accordance with applicable law. Entities should also refer to TECH 02/10 for guidance on the determination of the profits available for distribution (under the Companies Act 2006). *[FRS 102.A4.29]*.

5.3   Single-statement approach

In the single-statement approach, an entity must present the items to be included in a profit and loss account in accordance with Parts 1 of Schedules 1 to 3 (as applicable) to the Regulations, or where applicable, Part 1 of Schedule 1 to the LLP Regulations.

The consolidated statement of comprehensive income of a group must be presented in accordance with the requirements of Schedule 6 to the Regulations (or, where applicable, Part 1 of Schedule 3 to the LLP Regulations). *[FRS 102.5.5]*.

See 5.5 below for discussion as to which formats apply to which types of entity.

A subtotal for profit or loss is included in the statement of comprehensive income. *[FRS 102 Appendix I]*.

In addition, the statement of comprehensive income must include line items that present: *[FRS 102.5.5A]*

(a)   classified by nature (excluding amounts in (b)), each component of other comprehensive income, as permitted or required to be presented outside profit or loss by the standard. These must be either shown net of related tax, or gross of related tax (with a single amount shown for the aggregate amount of income tax relating to those components);

(b)   its share of the other comprehensive income of associates and jointly controlled entities accounted for by the equity method; and

(c)   total comprehensive income.

The statement of comprehensive income must also show the allocation of profit or loss for the period and of total comprehensive income for the period attributable to non-controlling interest and owners of the parent. *[FRS 102.5.6]*. See 4.5 above for a discussion of how this allocation should be presented under the formats for the group profit and loss account.

5.4   Two-statement approach

Under the two-statement approach, an entity must present in an income statement, the items to be included in a profit and loss account in accordance with Parts 1 of Schedules 1 to 3 (as applicable) to the Regulations, or where applicable, Part 1 of Schedule 1 to the LLP Regulations. The consolidated statement of comprehensive income of a group must be presented in accordance with the requirements of Schedule 6 to the Regulations (or, where applicable, Part 1 to Schedule 3 to the LLP Regulations). *[FRS 102.5.7]*.

See 5.5 below for discussion as to which formats apply to which types of entity.

The income statement must show the allocation of profit or loss for the period attributable to non-controlling interest and owners of the parent. *[FRS 102.5.7A]*.

The statement of comprehensive income begins with profit or loss as its first line and then includes, as a minimum, line items that present:

(a)   classified by nature (excluding amounts in (b)), each component of other comprehensive income. These must be shown either net of related tax, or gross of related tax (with a single amount shown for the aggregate amount of income tax relating to those components);

(b)   its share of the other comprehensive income of associates and jointly controlled entities accounted for by the equity method; and

(c)   total comprehensive income.

The statement of comprehensive income must also show the allocation of total comprehensive income for the period attributed to non-controlling interest and owners of the parent. *[FRS 102.5.7B]*.

See 4.5 above for a discussion of how the allocations of profit or loss and total comprehensive income should be presented under the formats for the group profit and loss account.

5.5   Statutory profit and loss account formats

An entity must present in the statement of comprehensive income, or in the separate income statement, the items to be presented in a profit and loss account in accordance with one of the following requirements for individual financial statements: *[FRS 102.5.5, 5.7]*

- Part 1 'General Rules and Formats' of Schedule 1 to the Regulations addresses the profit and loss account formats applicable to companies (other than banking and insurance companies); *[Regulations 3]*

- Part 1 'General Rules and Formats' of Schedule 2 to the Regulations addresses the profit and loss account formats applicable to banking companies; *[Regulations 5]*

- Part 1 'General Rules and Formats' of Schedule 3 to the Regulations addresses the profit and loss account formats applicable to insurance companies; *[Regulations 6]* and

- Part 1 'General Rules and Formats' of Schedule 1 to the LLP Regulations addresses the profit and loss account formats applicable to Limited Liability Partnerships. *[LLP Regulations 3]*.

Part 1 of Schedule 6 to the Regulations addresses the profit and loss account formats applicable to group accounts of companies, modifying the formats included in the earlier schedules. The group accounts must comply, so far as practicable with the provisions of Schedule 1 to the Regulations (i.e. including the profit and loss account formats) as if the undertakings included in the consolidation were a single company. *[6 Sch 1(1)]*.

The directors of a parent company of a banking company apply Part 1 of Schedule 6, as modified by Part 2 of Schedule 6 to the Regulations (and the directors of a parent company of an insurance company apply Part 1 of Schedule 6, as modified by Part 3 of Schedule 6 to the Regulations). *[Regulations 9]*. The definitions of a banking company, insurance company, banking group and insurance group are at 4.1.2.A below.

Part 1 of Schedule 3 to the LLP Regulations similarly addresses the profit and loss account formats applicable to group accounts of LLPs. *[Regulations 6]*. *[FRS 102.5.5, 5.7]*.

The discussions at 4.1.2 above as to which format should be applied and at 4.1.3 on changes in formats are equally relevant to the profit and loss account format. 5.6 below discusses the most commonly used formats in Schedule 1 to the Regulations.

FRS 102 includes additional requirements to supplement the statutory formats (see 5.7 below).

5.6   Format 1 and format 2 for the profit and loss account

The Regulations set out a choice of four formats for the profit and loss account, only two of which are used by the majority of companies and are discussed here, namely formats 1 and 2. Formats 3 and 4 are rarely used and are not discussed here.

The following discussion relates only to the profit and loss account formats included in Schedule 1 to the Regulations. It is beyond the scope of this publication to discuss the formats applicable to banking or insurance companies, but there is less flexibility to adapt the formats in Schedule 2 and Schedule 3 to the Regulations. Banking and insurance companies are defined at 4.1.2.A above.

Format 1 analyses expenses by function and is presented at Table 4.12 below.

Table 4.12   Format 1 profit and loss account (UK company other than a banking company or insurance company)

1	Turnover
2	Cost of sales
3	Gross profit or loss
4	Distribution costs
5	Administrative expenses
6	Other operating income
7	Income from shares in group undertakings
8	Income from participating interests†
9	Income from other fixed asset investments
10	Other interest receivable and similar income
11	Amounts written off investments
12	Interest payable and similar charges
	Profit or loss on ordinary activities before taxation*
13	Tax on profit or loss on ordinary activities
14	Profit or loss on ordinary activities after taxation
15	Extraordinary income
16	Extraordinary charges
17	Extraordinary profit or loss
18	Tax on extraordinary profit or loss
19	Other taxes not shown under the above items
20	Profit or loss for the financial year

*While not in format 1, every profit and loss account must show the amount of a company's profit or loss on ordinary activities before taxation (1 Sch 6, Regulations).
† See discussion below for modifications in group accounts.

Format 2 analyses expenses by nature and is presented at Table 4.13 below.

Table 4.13   *Format 2 for the profit and loss account (UK company other than a banking company or insurance company)*

1		Turnover
2		Change in stocks of finished goods and in work in progress
3		Own work capitalised
4		Other operating income
5	(a)	Raw materials and consumables
	(b)	Other external charges
6		Staff costs
	(a)	wages and salaries
	(b)	social security costs
	(c)	other pension costs
7	(a)	Depreciation and other amounts written off tangible and intangible fixed assets
	(b)	Exceptional amounts written off current assets
8		Other operating charges
9		Income from shares in group undertakings
10		Income from participating interests†
11		Income from other fixed asset investments
12		Other interest receivable and similar income
13		Amounts written off investments
14		Interest payable and similar charges
		Profit or loss on ordinary activities before taxation*
15		Tax on profit or loss on ordinary activities
16		Profit or loss on ordinary activities after taxation
17		Extraordinary income
18		Extraordinary charges
19		Extraordinary profit or loss
20		Tax on extraordinary profit or loss
21		Other taxes not shown under the above items
22		Profit or loss for the financial year

*While not in Format 2, every profit and loss account must show the amount of a company's profit or loss on ordinary activities before taxation (1 Sch 6, Regulations).
† See discussion below for modifications in group accounts.

Schedule 1 to the Regulations specifically requires the profit or loss on ordinary activities before taxation to be shown as a line item on the face of the profit and loss account (in both the format 1 and 2 profit and loss accounts). *[1 Sch 6]*.

The main modification required for group profit and loss account formats is the identification of minority interest/non-controlling interest (see 4.5 above) and replacing 'income from participating interests' with 'income from associated undertakings' and 'income from other participating interests' (see 5.6.5 below).

The individual line items in the profit and loss account formats are discussed at 5.6.1 to 5.6.15 below. The rest of this section addresses the general requirements on the formats set out in the Regulations.

The Regulations require that a company's profit or loss account shows the items listed in the profit and loss account format adopted. The items must also be shown in the order and under the headings and sub-headings given in the particular format used, but the letters or numbers assigned to that item in the format do not need to be given (and are not in practice). These items need to be read together with the notes to the formats, which may also permit alternative positions for any particular items. *[1 Sch 1]*. Therefore, the relevant notes to the formats have also been discussed at 5.6.1 to 5.6.15 below.

Where the special nature of the company's business requires it, the company's directors *must* adapt the arrangement, headings and sub-headings otherwise required in respect of items given an Arabic number in the balance sheet (or profit or loss account) format used. The directors *may* combine items to which Arabic numbers are given in the formats if their individual amounts are not material to assessing the state of affairs (or profit or loss) of the company for the financial year in question or the combination facilitates that assessment. In the latter case, the individual amounts of any items combined must be disclosed in a note to the accounts. *[1 Sch 4]*. FRS 102's requirements on materiality and aggregation are discussed at 8.4 below. FRS 102 requires an analysis of expenses by nature or function in the statement of comprehensive income (unless otherwise required by the Regulations). *[FRS 102.5.11]*. See 5.7.4 below.

The Regulations allow any item to be shown in the company's profit or loss account in greater detail than the particular format used. The profit and loss account may include an item representing or covering the amount of any income or expenditure not otherwise covered by any of the items listed in the format used. *[1 Sch 3]*. FRS 102 requires additional line items, headings and subtotals in the statement of comprehensive income (and in the income statement, where presented) where relevant to an understanding of the entity's financial performance *[FRS 102.5.9]*. Any amendments would need to comply with the requirements governing modifications of the formats in the Regulations. As all of the line items are denoted with Arabic numbers, the Regulations allow a degree of flexibility in the profit and loss account formats. See 5.7.2 below.

Where there is no amount in the current or immediately preceding financial year for a particular item in the profit and loss account format, that line item should be omitted from the balance sheet. *[1 Sch 5]*.

The statutory requirements on comparatives are addressed at 3.6 above.

Amounts in respect of items representing income may not be set off against amounts in respect of items representing expenditure and *vice versa*. *[1 Sch 8]*. FRS 102's requirements on offset are discussed at 8.1.1.C below.

The company's directors must, in determining how amounts are presented within items in the profit and loss account, have regard to the substance of the reported transaction or arrangement, in accordance with generally accepted accounting principles or practice. *[1 Sch 9]*.

5.6.1   Turnover (format 1 and format 2)

Turnover, in relation to a company, is defined as the 'amounts derived from the provision of goods and services falling within the company's ordinary activities, after deduction of:

(a)   trade discounts,

(b)   value added tax, and

(c)   any other taxes based on the amounts so derived.' *[s474(1)]*.

FRS 102 includes the same definition of turnover (but for an entity). *[FRS 102 Appendix I].* The standard further requires that turnover is presented on the face of the statement of comprehensive income (or separate income statement). *[FRS 102.5.7C].* See 5.7.1 below.

Not all income reported in the profit and loss account is turnover, nor is the concept of turnover synonymous with revenue. For example, a company may receive rental or interest income – while these would be types of revenue under FRS 102, these may or may not fall to be reported as turnover. Similarly, an entity whose business includes renting out properties to tenants would include rental income within turnover, but this may be 'other operating income' for another entity. An entity whose business is as a lessor and receives finance lease income would report that interest income in the position of the turnover line (although it may well be described as finance lease income), but a company that merely receives interest income on its bank deposits or other investments would report that interest income as 'Other interest receivable and similar income'. Where significant judgement is applied in determining which sources of revenue qualify as turnover, it may be appropriate to include an accounting policy for turnover and explain these judgements.

UK companies preparing Companies Act accounts must give segmental disclosures of turnover – see 3.3.2.A above.

5.6.2   Cost of sales, distribution costs and administrative expenses (format 1)

The format 1 profit and loss account requires a functional classification of expenses – between cost of sales, distribution costs and administrative expenses. These categories of cost are not defined in the Regulations. The allocation of costs will depend on the particular circumstances of an entity's business, and should be applied consistently. Judgement may be required in allocating costs to certain functions and, where this is the case, it may be appropriate to include an accounting policy for the allocation of expenses explaining significant judgements taken (see 7.3 below). The following discussion provides guidance for the types of items that often fall within these headings.

Cost of sales for a manufacturer would generally include production costs (including direct material, payroll and other costs and direct and indirect overheads attributable to the production function) and adjustments for opening and closing inventory. For a service provider, these would include the costs of providing the service.

Distribution costs would generally include transport and warehousing costs for the distribution of finished goods. UK companies also often include selling and marketing costs (such as advertising, payroll costs of the selling, marketing and distribution functions, sales commission and overheads attributable to the selling, marketing and distribution functions) in this heading.

Administrative expenses would generally include payroll costs of general management and administrative staff, general overheads, property costs not classified within cost of sales or distribution costs, bad debts, professional fees and often goodwill amortisation and impairment.

Cost of sales, distribution costs and administrative expenses are stated after taking into account any provisions for depreciation or diminution in value. *[1 Sch Note 11 to profit and loss account formats].*

UK companies sometimes show other line items (e.g. research and development costs) or amend or combine other line items, taking advantage of the flexibility available in the Regulations. FRS 102 requires additional line items, headings and subtotals when relevant to an understanding of the entity's financial performance. See 5.6 above.

5.6.3   Gross profit (format 1)

The format 1 profit and loss account requires gross profit or loss, i.e. turnover less cost of sales, to be shown as a separate line item.

5.6.4   Other operating income (format 1 and format 2)

Other operating income is not defined in the Regulations. In practice, this line item would often include government grant income, operating lease income, other rental income or negative goodwill amortisation.

This line item may include exchange gains arising from trading transactions, following previous GAAP practice. While this has not been included in FRS 102, the Legal Appendix to SSAP 20 – *Foreign currency translation* – states that 'Gains or losses arising from trading transactions should normally be included under "Other operating income or expense" while those arising from arrangements which may be considered as financing should be disclosed separately as part of "Other interest receivable/payable and similar income/expense". ...'. *[SSAP 20.68].*

5.6.5   Income from shares in group undertakings and income from participating interests (format 1 and format 2)

The formats for the individual profit and loss account include 'income from shares in group undertakings', and 'income from participating interests'. Dividend income from shares in group undertakings and from participating interests would be included within these line items.

For the group profit and loss account, the Regulations require 'income from participating interests' to be replaced by 'income from associated undertakings' and 'income from other participating interests'. Income from associated undertakings would usually include the share of the profit or loss of associates and jointly controlled entities. Income from shares in group undertakings will not arise in consolidated financial statements unless there are unconsolidated subsidiaries.

The meanings of group undertakings, participating interests and associated undertakings are explained at 4.6.4.B above.

Incoming dividends and similar income receivable are recognised at an amount that includes any withholding tax but excludes other taxes, such as attributable tax credits. Any withholding tax suffered is shown as part of the tax charge. *[FRS 102.29.19].* See 5.6.9 below.

FRS 102 requires separate disclosure of the entity's share of the profit or loss of associates accounted for using the equity method and the entity's share of any discontinued operations of such associates. *[FRS 102.14.14].* The same information is required for jointly controlled entities. *[FRS 102.15.20].* There is no requirement to present this information on the face of the statement of comprehensive income (or separate income statement). However, entities may consider adapting the heading 'income from associated undertakings' to show the share of the profit or loss of investments in associates and jointly controlled entities (even if the analysis of this between investments in associates and jointly controlled entities is relegated to the notes).

FRS 102 does not address where fair value movements are presented in the profit and loss account formats where investments in subsidiaries, associates and jointly controlled entities are carried at fair value through profit and loss in consolidated and/ or individual financial statements (see Chapter 6 at 3.4.2 for a discussion of the circumstances in which this is permitted or required). Entities may present fair value gains and fair value losses on such investments, where material, adjacent to income from shares in group undertakings and income from participating interests but disclosed separately, where relevant to an understanding of the entity's financial performance.

5.6.6   Income from other fixed asset investments and other interest receivable and similar income (format 1 and format 2)

The formats have two line items – 'income from other fixed asset investments', and 'other interest receivable and similar income'. Income and interest derived from group undertakings must be shown separately from income and interest derived from other sources. *[1 Sch Note (15) on profit and loss account formats].*

The presentation of gains on settlement of financial liabilities is not addressed by FRS 102. Entities may show the gains on settlement within other interest receivable and similar income, or where material, present the gains, adjacent to interest receivable and similar income but disclosed separately.

Incoming dividends and similar income receivable are recognised at an amount that includes any withholding tax but excludes other taxes, such as attributable tax credits. Any withholding tax suffered is shown as part of the tax charge. *[FRS 102.29.19].* See 5.6.9 below.

Section 28 – *Employee Benefits* – does not specify how the cost of a defined benefit plan should be presented in the profit and loss account. Therefore, entities may present the cost as a single item or disaggregate the cost into components presented separately – although it is likely many entities will want to continue with a presentation similar to that previously required by FRS 17. In our view, net interest income on defined benefit post-employment plans may be included as 'other finance income' adjacent to other interest receivable and similar income, i.e. consistent with the presentation required by FRS 17 for the net of the interest cost and the expected return on assets. *[FRS 17.56].* While this has not been included in FRS 102, Appendix II to FRS 17 states that 'The Board has received legal advice that these requirements do not contravene the Companies Act 1985 but that the interest cost and expected return should be presented in a new format heading separate from "interest and similar charges". Accordingly, the FRS requires these items to be included as other finance costs (or income) adjacent to interest'. *[FRS 17.Appendix II.6].*

This line item may include exchange gains arising from financing arrangements, e.g. loans, following previous UK GAAP practice. See 5.6.4 above.

Entities may present fair value gains and fair value losses on other fixed asset investments, where material, adjacent to income from shares in group undertakings and income from participating interests but disclosed separately, where relevant to an understanding of the entity's financial performance.

FRS 102 requires, *inter alia*, further analyses of income, expense and net gains or net losses (including fair value changes) by specified category of financial instrument. Interest expense and interest income (using the effective interest method) for financial assets and financial liabilities not at fair value, and impairment losses for each class of financial asset must also be disclosed. There are also extensive disclosures for financial instruments at fair value through profit or loss (that are not held for trading or derivatives). *[FRS 102.11.48-48A, 12.26]*. See Chapter 8 at 8.

5.6.7   Amounts written off investments (format 1 and format 2)

The line item 'amounts written off investments' would be used for impairments of fixed asset investments (including investments in subsidiaries, associates and jointly controlled entities) carried at cost less impairment in the individual financial statements. It would be usual to present a write-back of a previous provision under the same heading as where the provision was originally recognised (in the same way as an adjustment to reverse a bad debt provision would also be shown within administration expenses).

The positioning of this line item between 'other interest income receivable and similar income' and 'interest payable and similar charge' is below where many entities would position operating profit, where this subtotal is presented (see 5.7.3 below). Nevertheless, some companies may find it appropriate, based on the nature of their business, to report 'amounts written off investments' within operating profit. Previous UK GAAP requires impairment of investments in subsidiaries, joint ventures and associates in the individual financial statements to be included within operating profit. *[FRS 11.67]*. FRS 102, however, is silent on where impairments of investments should be presented so this potential for conflict between the accounting standards and the statutory formats has been removed.

FRS 102 requires disclosure of impairment losses for each class of financial asset, i.e. a grouping appropriate to the nature of the information disclosed that takes into account the characteristics of the financial assets. *[FRS 102.11.48(c)]*. In addition, disclosure of impairment losses and reversals (and the line items where recognised) is required separately for investments in associates and investments in jointly controlled entities. *[FRS 102.27.33(e)-(f)]*.

UK companies preparing Companies Act accounts must also disclose separately (1) provisions for diminution in value and (2) any write-back of such provisions in a note to the accounts (where not shown in the profit and loss account). This applies where the fixed asset investment is accounted for using the historical cost rules. *[1 Sch 19(2), (3)]*.

Chapter 4

5.6.8   *Interest payable and similar charges (format 1 and format 2)*

Interest payable and similar charges would include finance costs on financial liabilities (including shares classified as a financial liability or where a component of the share is classified as a financial liability). Interest payable to group undertakings is shown separately from income and interest derived from other sources. [1 Sch Note (16) on profit and loss account formats].

The presentation of losses on settlement of financial liabilities is not addressed by FRS 102. Entities may show the losses on settlement within other interest payable and similar charges, or where material, present the losses adjacent to other interest payable but disclosed separately.

Section 28 does not specify how the cost of a defined benefit plan should be presented in the profit and loss account. Therefore, entities may present the cost as a single item or disaggregate the cost into components presented separately. For the same reasons as discussed in 5.6.6 above, in our view, net interest costs on defined benefit post-employment plans may be included as 'other finance costs' adjacent to 'interest payable and similar charges'.

This line item may also include exchange losses arising from financing arrangements, such as loans, following previous UK GAAP practice. See 5.6.4 above.

FRS 102 does not address the presentation of the unwind of discounts on provisions. However, FRS 12 – *Provisions, contingent liabilities and contingent assets* – requires this to be disclosed as other finance costs adjacent to interest, following an amendment to the standard when FRS 17 was published. [FRS 12.48]. In our view, entities can continue to follow this previous UK GAAP presentation of the unwind of discounts under FRS 102.

FRS 102 requires, *inter alia*, further analyses of income, expense and net gains or net losses (including fair value changes) by specified category of financial instrument. Interest expense and interest income (using the effective interest method) for financial assets and financial liabilities not at fair value, and impairment losses for each class of financial asset must also be disclosed. There are also extensive disclosures for financial instruments at fair value through profit or loss (that are not held for trading or derivatives). [FRS 102.11.48-48A, 12.26]. See Chapter 8 at 8.

In addition, UK companies preparing Companies Act accounts must state in the notes to the accounts or on the face of the profit and loss account: the amount of interest on or any similar charges in respect of (1) bank loans and overdrafts, and (2) loans of any other kind made to the company. This analysis is not required in relation to interest or charges on loans to the company from group undertakings but applies to all other loans, whether made on security of debentures or not. [1 Sch 66].

5.6.9   *Tax on profit (or loss) on ordinary activities (format 1 and format 2)*

Tax includes current and deferred tax. FRS 102 states that income tax includes all income and domestic taxes that are based on taxable profit. Income taxes also include withholding tax on distributions payable by a subsidiary, associate or joint venture to the reporting entity. [FRS 102.29.1]. In some situations, entities may need to apply judgement in determining whether a particular tax or tax credit is an income tax and whether to classify interest and penalties as tax. See Chapter 24 at 3.2. FRS 102 requires disclosures of judgements in applying accounting policies with the most significant effect on the financial statements – see 7.3 below.

Incoming dividends and similar income receivable are recognised at an amount that includes any withholding tax but excludes other taxes, such as attributable tax credits. Any withholding tax suffered is shown as part of the tax charge. *[FRS 102.29.19].*

The Regulations require UK companies preparing Companies Act accounts to give further disclosures in respect of tax on profit or loss on ordinary activities in the accounts or notes to the accounts. *[1 Sch 67].*

5.6.10   *Extraordinary income, extraordinary charges, extraordinary profit or loss, and tax on extraordinary profit or loss (format 1 and format 2)*

Extraordinary items are expected to be extremely rare and are not expected to be encountered in practice. FRS 102's requirements on extraordinary items are discussed at 5.7.6 below.

The profit and loss account formats have separate line items for 'extraordinary income', 'extraordinary charges', 'extraordinary profit or loss' and 'tax on extraordinary profit or loss'. The group accounts must also disclose the amount of any profit or loss on extraordinary activities attributable to shares in subsidiary undertakings included in the consolidation held by or on behalf of persons other than the parent company and its subsidiary undertakings, *[6 Sch 17(3)(b)],* i.e. the minority interest / non-controlling interest in the profit or loss on extraordinary activities.

The Regulations require UK companies preparing Companies Act accounts to give particulars of any extraordinary income or charges arising in the financial year and further disclosures in respect of tax on extraordinary profit or loss, *[1 Sch 67(2), 69(2)],* in the accounts or notes to the accounts.

5.6.11   *Own work capitalised (format 2)*

The format 2 profit and loss account includes a line item for 'own work capitalised'.

Own work capitalised may arise, for example, where an entity capitalises the directly attributable costs of constructing its own property, plant and equipment. *[FRS 102.17.10].* The costs are reported in the relevant line items and a credit item is shown in own work capitalised.

5.6.12   *Staff costs (format 2)*

The format 2 profit and loss account has a line item for 'staff costs', to be analysed between wages and salaries, social security costs and pension costs (see 7.6 below for the definitions). The format 1 profit and loss account does not have a line item for staff costs.

UK companies (not subject to the small companies regime), whether preparing Companies Act or IAS accounts, must disclose information on staff numbers in the notes to the accounts and on staff costs in the notes to the accounts (insofar as not stated elsewhere in the accounts). *[s411].* See 7.6 below.

5.6.13   Depreciation (including amounts written off assets) and exceptional amounts written off current assets (format 2)

The format 2 profit and loss account has a line item for 'depreciation (including amounts written off assets)'.

The Regulations do not define 'exceptional amounts written off current assets'. In practice, entities may show provisions against current assets under different headings, e.g. changes in stocks /raw materials and consumables (for inventory – see 5.6.14 below) or other operating charges (for bad debts – see 5.6.15 below).

5.6.14   Changes in stocks of finished goods and work in progress/Raw materials and consumables (format 2)

The format 2 profit and loss account includes separate line items for the 'change in stocks of finished goods and work in progress' and for 'raw materials and consumables'. 'Raw materials and consumables' would include purchases of raw materials and consumables, adjusted for changes in stocks of raw materials and consumables.

5.6.15   Other external charges/Other operating charges (format 2)

The format 2 profit and loss account includes separate line items for: '(a) raw materials and consumables and (b) other external charges', and for 'other operating charges' but the Regulations do not define these terms. There is therefore likely to be diversity in practice in the allocation of costs between these headings, but a consistent policy should be followed.

Other operating charges may include exchange losses arising from trading transactions, following previous GAAP practice. See 5.6.4 above.

5.7   Requirements applicable to both approaches

FRS 102 includes supplementary requirements (beyond following the formats in the Regulations) relating to the statement of comprehensive income. The requirements for the presentation of discontinued operations are set out at 5.8 below, and for earnings per share, for those entities choosing or required to present this, at 5.9 below.

5.7.1   Disclosure of turnover on the face of the statement of comprehensive income (or separate income statement)

Turnover must always be presented on the face of the income statement (or statement of comprehensive income, if presented). *[FRS 102.5.7C]*. FRS 102's definition of turnover is the same as that used in the Regulations – see 5.6.1 above).

This requirement is likely included to ensure that disclosure of turnover is not relegated to the notes to the financial statements. Schedule 1 to the Regulations provides flexibility over whether line items in the profit and loss account (all of which are denoted with Arabic numbers in the formats) are combined or adapted. See 5.6 above.

5.7.2   Additional line items, headings and subtotals

An entity shall present additional line items, headings and subtotals in the statement of comprehensive income (and in the income statement, where presented) when such presentation is relevant to an understanding of the entity's financial performance. *[FRS 102.5.9]*. Examples might include fair value gains, and fair value losses on investment properties, where material.

While any amendments to the income statement (or profit and loss section of the statement of comprehensive income) would need to comply with the requirements governing modifications of the formats in the Regulations, these provide flexibility since the profit and loss account line items are denoted with Arabic numbers. See 5.6 above.

5.7.3   Disclosure of operating profit

FRS 102 does not require disclosure of 'operating profit'. If an entity elects to disclose the results of operating activities, it should ensure that the amount disclosed is representative of activities that would normally be regarded as 'operating', e.g. it would be inappropriate to exclude items clearly related to operations (such as inventory write-downs and restructuring and relocation expenses) because they occur irregularly or infrequently or are unusual in amount. Similarly, it would be inappropriate to exclude items on the grounds that they do not involve cash flows, such as depreciation and amortisation expenses. *[FRS 102.5.9B]*.

5.7.4   Analysis of expenses by nature or function

Unless otherwise required under the Regulations, an entity must present an analysis of expenses using a classification based on either the nature of expenses or the function of expenses within the entity, whichever provides information that is reliable and more relevant information. *[FRS 102.5.11]*.

Where classified by nature, expenses are aggregated in the statement of comprehensive income (or income statement, where presented) according to their nature (e.g. depreciation, raw materials and consumables and staff costs) and not reallocated among various functions within the entity. Where classified by function, expenses are aggregated according to their function as part of cost of sales or, for example, the costs of distribution or administrative activities. *[FRS 102.5.11]*. This means that cost of sales must always be presented separately.

Schedule 1 to the Regulations and Schedule 1 to the LLP Regulations both require an analysis of expenses by nature (where the format 2 profit and loss account is adopted) or function (where the format 1 profit and loss account is adopted). See 5.5 above.

The reference in paragraph 5.11 of FRS 102 to 'unless otherwise required under the Regulations' presumably reflects the fact that Schedules 2 and 3 to the Regulations do not offer a choice of profit and loss account format with an analysis of expenses based by nature or function, nor do the formats in these schedules include 'cost of sales' as a line item. There is limited flexibility to adapt the formats included in Schedules 2 and 3.

The Regulations require certain information about nature of expense to be provided as line items in format 2 and as notes disclosure where format 1 is applied:

Chapter 4

- the format 2 profit and loss account includes line items for staff costs (see 5.6.12 above) and depreciation and other amounts written off tangible and intangible fixed assets' (see 5.6.13 above);

- all UK companies, except companies subject to the small companies regime, preparing Companies Act accounts (or IAS accounts) must present the analysis of staff costs in the notes to the accounts, insofar as not stated elsewhere in the accounts (see 7.6 below); and

- Where the format 1 profit and loss account is applied, depreciation and other amounts written off tangible and intangible fixed assets is disclosed in a note to the financial statements. *[1 Sch Note (17) on profit and loss account formats].*

In addition, all UK companies preparing Companies Act accounts must disclose separately:

- provisions for diminution in value; and

- any writeback of such provisions in a note to the accounts (where not shown in the profit and loss account). *[1 Sch 19(2), (3)].*

These overlap with disclosures in FRS 102 of depreciation, amortisation and impairment charges (see Chapter 14 at 3.5.2 and Chapter 15 at 5.5) *[FRS 102.17.31(e), 18.27(e), 27.33]*, defined contribution expense *[FRS 102.28.40]*, and the cost of defined benefit plans (see Chapter 23 at 3.12.4) *[FRS 102.28.41(g)].*

5.7.5   *Presentation of 'exceptional items'*

FRS 102 does not use the phrase 'exceptional items', nor does it contain the prescriptive presentation requirements for exceptional items included in previous UK GAAP.

FRS 102 (like IAS 1) requires that when items included in total comprehensive income are material, their nature and amount should be disclosed separately in the statement of comprehensive income (and in the income statement, if presented) or in the notes. *[FRS 102.5.9A].* The level of prominence given to such items is left to the judgement of the entity concerned. Materiality is discussed at 8.4 below.

UK companies preparing Companies Act accounts, however, must state, in the accounts or notes to the accounts, the effects of any transactions that are exceptional by virtue of size or incidence, though they fall within the ordinary activities of the company. *[1 Sch 69(3)].*

Many UK companies preparing IFRS financial statements (to which 1 Sch 69 above does not apply) continue to refer to 'exceptional items' and this is likely to be the case under FRS 102 as well. Since the standard does not use the term 'exceptional items', it is important that the entity provides a definition of what items are considered to be 'exceptional items' (or other similar term used) in the accounting policies included in the financial statements. The FRC published a press release on exceptional items in December 2013 (see 5.7.5.B below).

The standard does not give examples of such items, but IAS 1 suggests that circumstances that would give rise to the separate disclosure of items of income and expense include: *[IAS 1.98]*

(a)   write-downs of inventories to net realisable value or of property, plant and equipment to recoverable amount, as well as reversals of such write-downs;

(b)   restructurings of the activities of an entity and reversals of any provisions for the costs of restructuring;

(c)   disposals of items of property, plant and equipment;

(d)   disposals of investments;

(e)   discontinued operations;

(f)   litigation settlements; and

(g)   other reversals of provisions.

FRS 102's requirements on disclosure of discontinued operations are discussed at 5.8 below.

5.7.5.A   Presentation in the statement of comprehensive income

As entities reporting under FRS 102 must follow the formats for the profit and loss account in the Regulations (or LLP Regulations), exceptional items will need to be included within the appropriate statutory format headings. In most cases, attributing exceptional items to the relevant format heading will be straightforward.

The Regulations allow the profit and loss account to include income or expenditure not otherwise covered by any of the items listed in the format, and permit or require certain adaptations to the line items given an Arabic number. See 5.6 above.

FRS 102 does not require disclosure of operating profit nor does it specify categories of exceptional items that must be reported below operating profit. However, the standard gives examples of items that should not be excluded from operating profit (see 5.7.3 above).

5.7.5.B   FRC Press release on exceptional items

In December 2013, the FRC issued Press Release PN 108 on the need to improve reporting of additional and exceptional items by companies and ensure consistency in their presentation. It notes that the Financial Reporting Review Panel has identified a significant number of companies that report exceptional items on the face of the income statement and include subtotals to show the profit before such items (sometimes referred to as 'underlying profit'). While the FRC stated that many companies present additional line items in the income statement to provide clear and useful information on the trends in the components of their profit in the income statement, as required by IAS 1, the FRC has identified a number where the disclosure fell short of the consistency and clarity required, with a consequential effect on the profit reported before such items.

The Financial Reporting Review Panel set out the following factors that companies should have regard to, in judging what to include in additional items and underlying profit:

- the approach taken in identifying additional items that qualify for separate presentation should be even handed between gains and losses, clearly disclosed and applied consistently from one year to the next. It should also be distinguished from alternative performance measures used by the company that are not intended to be consistent with IFRS principles;

- gains and losses should not be netted off in arriving at the amount disclosed unless otherwise permitted;

- where the same category of material items recurs each year and in similar amounts (for example, restructuring costs), companies should consider whether such amounts should be included as part of underlying profit;

- where significant items of expense are unlikely to be finalised for a number of years or may subsequently be reversed, the income statement effect of such changes should be similarly identified as additional items in subsequent periods and readers should be able to track movements in respect of these items between periods;

- the tax effect of additional items should be explained;

- material cash amounts related to additional items should be presented clearly in the cash flow statement;

- where underlying profit is used in determining executive remuneration or in the definition of loan covenants, companies should take care to disclose clearly the measures used; and

- management commentary on results should be clear on which measures of profit are being commented on and should discuss all significant items which make up the profit determined according to IFRSs.

While the press release refers to IFRSs, the same factors would apply to FRS 102 financial statements.

5.7.6   *Presentation of extraordinary items*

FRS 102 and the Regulations distinguish between ordinary activities and extraordinary items (whereas IAS 1 prohibits the presentation of extraordinary items). However, the standard is expected to be amended, to reflect implementation of the new Accounting Directive, to remove the concept of extraordinary items for financial years beginning on or after 1 January 2016 (see Chapter 2 at 1.2.3.E).

FRS 102 states that 'Extraordinary items are material items possessing a high degree of abnormality which arise from events or transactions that fall outside the ordinary activities of the reporting entity and which are not expected to recur.' The standard explains that the additional line items required to be disclosed by paragraph 5.9 (see 5.7.2 above) and material items required to be disclosed by paragraph 5.9A (see 5.7.5 above) are not extraordinary items when they arise from the entity's ordinary activities. In addition, extraordinary items do not include prior period items merely because they relate to a prior period. *[FRS 102.5.10A].*

Ordinary activities are defined as 'any activities which are undertaken by a reporting entity as part of its business and such related activities in which the reporting entity engages in furtherance of, incidental to, or arising from, these activities. Ordinary activities include any effects on the reporting entity of any event in the various environments in which it operates, including the political, regulatory, economic and geographical environments, irrespective of the frequency or unusual nature of the events'. *[FRS 102.5.10]*.

FRS 102 was modified compared to the IFRS for SMEs to comply with the profit and loss account formats of the Regulations which provide for 'extraordinary activities' (see 5.6.10 above). However, FRS 102's definition of 'ordinary activities' is the same as, and its definition of 'extraordinary items' is very similar to the respective definitions previously contained in FRS 3 – *Reporting financial performance.*

The explanatory guidance to FRS 3 states that 'Extraordinary items are extremely rare as they relate to highly abnormal events or transactions that fall outside the ordinary activities of a reporting entity and which are not expected to recur. In view of the extreme rarity of such items no examples are provided.' While this guidance has not been included in FRS 102, Appendix II to FRS 101 corroborates the view that there should be no change to previous GAAP practice (FRS 101 modifies IAS 1 to include the concept of extraordinary items). Appendix II states that 'Entities should note that extraordinary items are extremely rare as they relate to highly abnormal events or transactions'. *[FRS 101.A2.11]*. Consequently, we do not anticipate that entities will disclose extraordinary items under FRS 102.

5.8   Presentation of discontinued operations

FRS 102's definition of discontinued operations and presentation requirements differ from both IFRSs and previous UK GAAP.

FRS 102 requires an entity to disclose on the face of the income statement (or statement of comprehensive income) an amount comprising the total of:

(a)   the post-tax profit or loss of discontinued operations (see definition at 5.8.1 below); and

(b)   the post-tax gain or loss attributable to the impairment or on the disposal of the assets or disposal group(s) constituting discontinued operations (see 4.8 above for the definition of disposal group).

A line-by-line analysis must be presented in the income statement (or statement of comprehensive income), with columns for continuing operations, discontinued operations and for total operations. *[FRS 102.5.7D]*. This means more detailed disclosure than is commonly seen under IFRS 5, but this is to enable compliance with the profit and loss account formats in the Regulations (or, where applicable, the LLP Regulations). There is no requirement to analyse other comprehensive income between continuing and discontinued operations.

The disclosures for discontinued operations must relate to operations discontinued by the end of the reporting period for the latest period presented, with re-presentation of prior periods where applicable. *[FRS 102.5.7E]*.

An entity must also disclose its share of the profit or loss of associates accounted for using the equity method and its share of any discontinued operations of such associates *[FRS 102.14.14]* (and the same information for jointly controlled entities *[FRS 102.15.20]*).

5.8.1   Definition of discontinued operation

FRS 102 defines a discontinued operation as a component of an entity (i.e. operations and cash flows that can be clearly distinguished, operationally and for financial reporting purposes from the rest of the entity) that has been disposed of and: *[FRS 102 Appendix I]*

(a)   represented a separate major line of business or geographical area of operations;

(b)   was part of a single co-ordinated plan to dispose of a separate major line of business or geographical area of operations; or

(c)   was a subsidiary acquired exclusively with a view to resale.

The definition of discontinued operations in FRS 102 differs significantly from that included in FRS 3 and differs specifically to that included in IFRS 5 in that it refers to 'a component of an entity *that has been disposed of'* whereas IFRS 5 refers to a 'component of an entity that *either has been disposed of or is classified as held for sale'* [emphasis added]. As noted at 5.8 above, the presentation of discontinued operations relates to operations disposed of at the reporting date.

IFRS 5, which has the same definition of a component as in FRS 102, clarifies that 'a component of an entity will have been a cash-generating unit or a group of cash-generating units while being held for use'. *[IFRS 5.31]*. Under both IFRSs and FRS 102, a cash generating unit is 'the smallest identifiable group of assets that generates cash inflows that are largely independent of the cash inflows from other assets or groups of assets'. *[IFRS 5.Appendix A, FRS 102.27.8, Appendix I]*. See Chapter 22 at 4.2. An FRS 102 reporter may refer to IFRS 5's guidance on a component under the GAAP hierarchy in Section 10. *[FRS 102.10.3-6]*.

FRS 102 does not clarify the phrase 'has been disposed of'. In our view, the phrase 'has been disposed of' may be interpreted more widely than a sale. An entity's management must use judgement in developing and applying an accounting policy and may consider the requirements and guidance in IFRSs in this area. *[FRS 102.10.4-10.6]*. In our view, an entity could look to IFRS 5. IFRS 5's requirements would be consistent with a view that a component meeting any of the criteria (a) to (c) is discontinued if, at the end of the reporting period, the component is an abandoned operation, or the entity has partially disposed of (but lost control of) the operation or has distributed the operation. However, since the phrase 'has been disposed of' has not been explained further in FRS 102, different interpretations of what this means may be sustained.

5.8.2　Adjustments to amounts previously presented in discontinued operations in prior periods

FRS 102 does not address adjustments to amounts previously presented in discontinued operations. Given the absence of specific requirements in FRS 102, management may consider the requirements and guidance of IFRSs in this area. *[FRS 102.10.4-10.6].*

IFRS 5 requires that adjustments in the current period to amounts previously presented in discontinued operations that are directly related to the disposal of a discontinued operation in a prior period are classified separately in discontinued operations. The nature and amount of such adjustments must be disclosed. Examples given by the standard of circumstances in which these adjustments may arise include the following:

- the resolution of uncertainties that arise from the terms of the disposal transaction, such as the resolution of purchase price adjustments and indemnification issues with the purchaser;

- the resolution of uncertainties that arise from and are directly related to the operations of the component before its disposal, such as environmental and product warranty obligations retained by the seller; and

- the settlement of employee benefit plan obligations, provided that the settlement is directly related to the disposal transaction. *[IFRS 5.35].*

5.8.3　Trading between continuing and discontinued operations

Discontinued operations are incorporated in consolidated financial statements – and therefore, any transactions between discontinued and continuing operations are eliminated as usual in the consolidation. As a consequence, the amounts ascribed to the continuing and discontinued operations will be income and expense only from transactions with counterparties external to the group. Importantly, this means the results presented on the face of the income statement will not necessarily represent the activities of the operations as individual entities, particularly when there has been significant trading between the continuing and discontinued operations. Some might consider the results for the continuing and discontinued operations on this basis to be of little use to readers of accounts. One approach would be to fully eliminate transactions for the purpose of presenting the income statement then provide supplementary information.

5.8.4　First-time adoption

On first-time adoption of FRS 102, an entity shall not retrospectively change the accounting that it followed under its previous financial reporting framework for discontinued operations. *[FRS 102.35.9(d)].* Section 35 offers no further guidance on the meaning of this mandatory exception to the general transition requirements. See Chapter 30 at 4.3 for further discussion of the transition exception.

Chapter 4

5.8.5   *Example of presentation of discontinued operations*

Example 4.4:   Presentation of discontinued operations

Statement of comprehensive income

For the year ended 31 December 20X1

	20X1 Continuing operations	20X1 Discontinued operations	20X1 Total	20X0 Continuing operation (as restated)	20X0 Discontinued operations (as restated)	20X0 Total
	CU	CU	CU	CU	CU	CU
Turnover	4,200	1,232	5,432	3,201	1,500	4,701
Cost of sales	(2,591)	(1,104)	(3,695)	(2,281)	(1,430)	(3,711)
Gross profit	1,609	128	1,737	920	70	990
Administrative expenses	(452)	(110)	(562)	(418)	(120)	(538)
Other operating income	212	–	212	198	–	198
Profit in disposal of operations	–	301	301	–	–	–
Operating profit	1,369	319	1,688	700	(50)	650
Interest receivable and similar income	14	–	14	16	–	16
Interest payable and similar charges	(208)	–	(208)	(208)	–	(208)
Profit on ordinary activities before tax	1,175	319	1,494	508	(50)	458
Taxation	(390)	(4)	(394)	(261)	3	(258)
Profit on ordinary activities after taxation and profit for the financial year	785	315	1,100	247	(47)	200
Other comprehensive income						
Actuarial losses on defined benefit pension plans			(108)			(68)
Deferred tax movement relating to actuarial losses			28			18
Total comprehensive income for the year			1,020			150

The above example is taken from the Appendix to Section 5 (which accompanies but is not part of that section, and provides guidance on application of paragraph 5.7D for presenting discontinued operations).

5.9   Earnings per share

IAS 33 – *Earnings per Share* (as adopted by the EU) must be followed by an entity whose ordinary shares or potential ordinary shares are publicly traded or that files, or is in the process of filing its financial statements with a securities commission or other regulatory organisation for the purpose of issuing ordinary shares in a public market. IAS 33 also applies to an entity that chooses to disclose earnings per share (EPS). *[FRS 102.1.4].*

IAS 33 requires an entity to present the basic and diluted EPS attributable to ordinary equity holders of the parent entity for profit or loss from continuing operations and total profit or loss. This must be given for each class of ordinary share that has a different right to share in profit for the period. *[IAS 33.9, 33.12, 33.66]*. Basic and diluted EPS must be presented with equal prominence in the statement of comprehensive income (or on the face of the income statement, if presented) for every period for which a statement of comprehensive income is presented. *[IAS 33.66-67A]*.

An entity may disclose basic and diluted EPS for discontinued operations *either* in the statement of comprehensive income (or on the face of the income statement, if presented) *or* in the notes to the financial statements. *[IAS 33.68-68A]*. Basic and diluted EPS is presented even if the amounts are negative, i.e. a loss per share. *[IAS 33.69]*.

IAS 33 provides further requirements on the calculation of basic and diluted EPS and on the accompanying disclosures. See EY International GAAP 2015 at Chapter 34 for further details.

6   STATEMENT OF CHANGES IN EQUITY

An entity must present a statement of changes in equity, or if certain conditions are met and an entity chooses to, a statement of income and retained earnings (see 6.2 below). *[FRS 102.6.1]*.

Equity is the residual interest in the assets of the entity after deducting all its liabilities. It may be sub-classified in the statement of financial position. Sub-classifications may include funds contributed by shareholders, retained earnings, and gains or losses recognised directly in equity. *[FRS 102.2.22, Appendix I]*.

FRS 102's requirements for the statement of changes in equity are similar to those included in IFRSs. The Regulations and LLP Regulations do not require a statement of changes in equity to be presented. However, where there have been transfers to or from any reserves (and the reserves are required to be shown as separate line items in the balance sheet, or would be if line items had not been combined in the balance sheet, as permitted by the Regulations), a UK company preparing Companies Act accounts must disclose (in the accounts or notes to the accounts) the following information in respect of the aggregate of reserves included in the same item:

- the amount of the reserves at the beginning and end of the financial year;
- any amounts transferred to or from the reserve during that year; and
- the source and application respectively of any amounts transferred.

Comparatives are not required. *[1 Sch 59(1)-(2)]*. See 4.6.12 above.

In practice, the above analysis and reconciliation of reserves could be combined with the statement of changes in equity (for which comparatives are required).

6.1   Information to be presented in the statement of changes in equity

The statement of changes in equity presents an entity's profit or loss for a reporting period, other comprehensive income for the period, the effects of changes in accounting policies and corrections of material errors recognised in the period and the amounts of investments by, and dividends and other distributions to, equity investors during the period. *[FRS 102.6.2].*

The effects of corrections of material errors and changes in accounting policies are presented as retrospective adjustments of prior periods rather than as part of profit or loss in the period in which they arise. *[FRS 102.5.8].* This is why such errors and changes in accounting policies are reported as separate line items in the statement of changes in equity (or, if presented, the statement of income and retained earnings). *[FRS 102.6.3(b), 6.5(c), (d)].* The retrospective adjustments for material errors and changes in accounting policy are consistent with the requirements of IFRSs, but the treatment of errors differs significantly from previous UK GAAP which requires that only fundamental errors are retrospectively restated. A fundamental error is an error 'of such significance as to destroy the true and fair view and hence the validity of those financial statements'. *[FRS 3.60, 63].*

The statement of changes in equity shows:

(a)   total comprehensive income for the period (the sum of profit and loss and other comprehensive income – see 5 above) showing separately the total amounts attributable to owners of the parent and to non-controlling interests (see 4.5 above);

(b)   for each component of equity, the effects of retrospective application (of accounting policies) or retrospective restatement recognised in accordance with Section 10 of the standard; and

(c)   for each component of equity, a reconciliation between the carrying amount at the beginning and the end of the period, separately disclosing changes resulting from:

(i)   profit or loss;

(ii)   other comprehensive income (which must be analysed by item, either in the statement of changes in equity or in the notes to the financial statements); and

(iii)   the amounts of investments by, and dividends and other distributions to, owners, showing separately issues of shares, purchase of own share transactions, dividends and other distributions to owners, and changes in ownership interests in subsidiaries that do not result in a loss of control. *[FRS 102.6.3-6.3A, Appendix I].*

It can be seen that (a) above is effectively a sub-total of all the items required by (c)(i) and (c)(ii). Items required to be recognised in other comprehensive income are listed at 5.2 above.

FRS 102 does not define a 'component of equity'. However, IAS 1, which has a similar requirement to (c) above, states that 'components of equity' include each class of contributed equity, the accumulated balance of each class of other comprehensive income and retained earnings. *[IAS 1.108]*. Since FRS 102 requires all entities, except to the extent this is not permitted by the statutory framework under which the entity reports, to follow the balance sheet formats set out in the Regulations (or LLP Regulations), the components presented should (at a minimum) reflect the components of capital and reserves required to be disclosed as line items in the balance sheet format followed by the entity. *[FRS 102.4.1-4.2]*. See 4.6.12 above. However, this is likely to be supplemented by, for example, the cash flow hedge reserve or fair value movements accumulated in equity on available for sale financial assets (where IAS 39 is applied). For UK companies, these reserves would be included within the statutory fair value reserve required by the fair value accounting rules (see 9.3 below).

UK companies preparing Companies Act accounts are required to disclose in the accounts or notes to the accounts: *[1 Sch 43]*

- any amount set aside (or proposed to be set aside) to, or withdrawn from (or proposed to be withdrawn from) reserves;

- the aggregate amount of dividends paid in the financial year (other than those for which a liability existed at the immediately preceding balance sheet date);

- the aggregate amount of dividends that the company is liable to pay at the balance sheet date; and

- the aggregate amount of dividends proposed before the date of approval of the accounts, not otherwise disclosed above.

Where an entity declares dividends to holders of its equity instruments after the end of the reporting period, those dividends are not recognised as a liability because no obligation exists at that time, but FRS 102 permits an entity to show the dividend as a segregated component of retained earnings. *[FRS 102.32.8]*.

FRS 102 only requires an entity to *disclose* the fair value of non-cash assets distributed to owners in the reporting period (except where the non-cash assets are ultimately controlled by the same parties before and after the distribution). *[FRS 102.22.18]*.

6.1.1   Example of statement of changes in equity

FRS 102 does not include an illustrative statement of changes in equity. Example 4.5 illustrates the requirements below. The standard requires an analysis of other comprehensive income by item in the statement of changes in equity or in the notes to the accounts.

Example 4.5:   Combined statement of all changes in equity

XYZ Group – Statement of changes in equity for the year ended 31 December 201Y
(in thousands of currency units)

	Called up share capital	Share premium account	Revaluation reserve	Capital redemption reserve	Reserve for own shares	Merger reserve	Fair value reserve	Profit and loss account	Equity owners of parent	Non-controlling interest	Total equity
Balance at 1 January 201X	10,000	500	3,000	–	(774)	–	3,098	16,849	32,673	85	32,758
Changes in accounting policy	–	–	–	–	–	–	–	600	600	–	600
Restated balance	10,000	500	3,000	–	(774)	–	3,098	17,449	33,273	85	33,358
Profit for the year	–	–	–	–	–	–	–	4,872	4,872	35	4,907
Other comprehensive income	–	–	100	–	–	–	(574)	(541)	(1,015)	2	(1,013)
Total comprehensive income for the year [a]	–	–	100	–	–	–	(574)	4,331	3,857	37	3,894
Dividends paid	–	–	–	–	–	–	–	(1,170)	(1,170)	–	(1,170)
Share based payment expense	–	–	–	–	–	–	–	398	398	–	398
Balance at 31 December 201X	10,000	500	3,100	–	(774)	–	2,524	21,008	36,358	122	36,480

Profit for the year	–	–	–	–	–	–	–	4,674	4,674	235	4,909
Other comprehensive income	–	–	200	–	–	–	(665)	732	267	3	270
Total comprehensive income for the year (b)	–	–	200	–	–	–	(665)	5,406	4,941	238	5,179
Dividends paid	–	–	–	–	–	–	–	(1,400)	(1,400)	(31)	(1,431)
New shares issued	2,575	100	–	–	–	6,250	–	–	8,925	–	8,925
Share issue costs	–	(100)	–	–	–	–	–	–	(100)	–	(100)
Share buy back	(500)	–	–	500	–	–	–	(1,800)	(1,800)	–	(1,800)
Share based payment expense	–	–	–	–	–	–	–	307	307	–	307
Balance at 31 December 201Y	12,075	500	3,300	500	(774)	6,250	1,859	23,521	47,231	329	47,560

(a) The amount included in retained earnings for 201X of £4,331,000 represents profit attributable to owners of the parent of £4,872,000 less remeasurement losses (net of tax) on defined benefit pension plans of £541,000 (gross £676,000 less tax £135,000).

The amount included in the cash flow hedge reserve for 201X comprises a loss on cash flow hedges of £574,000 (£717,000 less tax £143,000) which represented losses (net of tax) transferred to cash flow hedge of £774,000 less reclassification of losses (net of tax) to profit and loss of £200,000. The amount included in non-controlling interest of £2,000 for 201X relates to exchange translation gains (no attributable tax). The amount included in the revaluation surplus of £100,000 for 201X represents the share of other comprehensive income of associates of £100,000 (gross £120,000 less tax £20,000). Other comprehensive income of associates relates solely to gains or losses on property revaluation.

(b) The amount included in retained earnings for 201Y of £5,406,000 represents profit attributable to owners of the parent of £4,674,000 plus remeasurement gains on defined benefit pension plans of £732,000 (£915,000 less tax £183,000).

The amount included in the cash flow hedge reserve for 201Y comprises a loss on cash flow hedges of £665,000 (£831,000 less tax £166,000) which represented losses (net of tax) transferred to cash flow hedge of £900,000 less reclassification of losses (net of tax) to profit and loss of £235,000. The amount included in non-controlling interest of £3,000 for 201Y relates to exchange translation gains (no attributable tax). The amount included in the revaluation surplus of £200,000 for 201Y represents the share of other comprehensive income of associates of £200,000 (gross £240,000 less tax £40,000). Other comprehensive income of associates relates solely to gains or losses on property revaluation.

6.2   Statement of income and retained earnings

The purpose of a statement of income and retained earnings is to present an entity's profit or loss and changes in retained earnings for the reporting period.

An entity is permitted (but is not required) to present a statement of income and retained earnings in place of a statement of comprehensive income and a statement of changes in equity if the only changes to its equity in the periods for which financial statements are presented arise from:

- profit or loss;
- payment of dividends;
- corrections of prior period errors; and
- changes in accounting policy. *[FRS 102.6.4].*

In essence, this means that the statement of income and retained earnings may be presented where the entity does not have items of other comprehensive income, investments by equity investors or non-dividend distributions to equity investors in the current or comparative periods presented.

The statement of income and retained earnings shows the following items in addition to the information required in the statement of comprehensive income by Section 5:

- retained earnings at the beginning of the reporting period;
- dividends declared and paid or payable during the period;
- restatements of retained earnings for corrections of prior period material errors;
- restatements of retained earnings for changes in accounting policy; and
- retained earnings at the end of the reporting period. *[FRS 102.6.5].*

Example 4.6:   Statement of income and retained earnings (extract)

	20x1	20x0 Restated
	CU	CU
Profit on ordinary activities before tax	1,494	458
Taxation	(394)	(258)
Profit on ordinary activities after taxation and profit for the financial year	1,100	200
Retained earnings brought forward at 1.1.x1 (1.1.x0) – as originally reported	12,285	13,500
Prior period adjustment – changes in accounting policy	(2,020)	(2,235)
Prior period adjustment – correction of error	(1,900)	(1,900)
Restated earnings at 1.1.x1 (1.1.x0) – as restated	9,465	9,565
Dividends paid [and payable]	(1,500)	(1,000)
Retained earnings carried forward at 31.12.x1 (31.12.x0)	7,965	8,565

7   NOTES TO THE FINANCIAL STATEMENTS

FRS 102 sets out the principles underlying information to be presented in the notes to the financial statements, and how to present the information. Notes contain information in addition to that presented in the primary statements. Notes provide narrative descriptions or disaggregations of items presented in those statements and information about items that do not qualify for recognition in those statements. Most sections of FRS 102 require disclosures that are normally presented in the notes. *[FRS 102.8.1].*

For UK companies preparing Companies Act accounts, the Companies Act 2006, principally Part 15, the Regulations and other statutory instruments require certain notes to be presented in the accounts. See, for example, Chapter 1 at 6.7. Certain of these disclosures have been commented on in the discussion of the formats (because they represent additional analyses for line items) at 4.6 and 5.6 above where the information may either be presented on the face of the primary statement or in the notes to the financial statements. This section looks at, in particular, the staff costs note, the disclosures on off-balance sheet arrangements and directors' advances, credits and guarantees. Companies Act accounts disclosures relevant to specific accounting topics are addressed in other Chapters of this publication. This publication is not intended to include a comprehensive discussion of all such disclosures.

In particular, this publication does not cover the statutory disclosures required in the notes to Companies Act and IAS accounts relating to directors' remuneration (in accordance with Schedule 5 to the Regulations) or auditors' remuneration for audit and non-audit services (in accordance with *Companies (Disclosure of Auditor Remuneration and Liability Limitation Agreements) Regulations 2008* (SI 2008/489, as amended by SI 2011/2198)). TECH 14/13FRF – *Disclosure of Auditor Remuneration,* published by the ICAEW in December 2013 provides guidance on the latter.

7.1   Structure of the notes

FRS 102 requires the presentation of notes to the financial statements that:

(a)   present information about the basis of preparation of the financial statements and the specific accounting policies used;

(b)   disclose the information required by FRS 102 that is not presented on the face of the primary statements; and

(c)   provide information that is not presented elsewhere in the financial statements, but is relevant to an understanding of any of them. *[FRS 102.8.2].*

The notes should, as far as practicable, be presented in a systematic manner. Each item in the financial statements should be cross-referenced to any related information in the notes. *[FRS 102.8.3].*

The notes are normally presented in the following order: *[FRS 102.8.4]*

(a)   a statement that the financial statements have been prepared in compliance with FRS 102 (see 3.8 above);

(b)   a summary of significant accounting policies applied (see 7.2 below);

(c)   supporting information for items presented in the financial statements, in the sequence in which each statement and each line item is presented; and

(d)   any other disclosures.

Traditionally, entities have presented financial statements starting with the primary statements, with line items cross referred to the relevant notes to the financial statements which present a more detailed analysis of the line items. The primary statements are followed by a summary of the accounting policies applied (including the statement of compliance) and then the supporting notes to the financial statements, which usually address the line items in the order that they appear in the primary statements. This traditional order is consistent with that proposed in FRS 102. However, this is not a 'hard and fast rule'.

In recent years, a number of entities have adopted a different placement of information with the aim of ensuring that the financial statements are understandable and avoid immaterial clutter that can obscure useful information. For example, some entities have grouped the notes to the financial statements so that these deal with related accounting topics and / or integrated the accounting policies for particular items within the relevant notes. Some entities have distinguished between the most significant accounting policies and other accounting policies, which may be relegated to an appendix to the financial statements.

The IASB have an ongoing Disclosure Initiative looking at materiality (see 8.4 below), principles for disclosure in the notes to the financial statements and other presentation and disclosure matters. As part of this initiative, in March 2014, the IASB published Exposure Draft ED/2014/1 – *Disclosure Initiative – Proposed amendments to IAS 1.* This clarifies, *inter alia*, that entities have flexibility over the systematic order of the notes (i.e. these do not need to be presented in the traditional order highlighted above) but emphasises that an entity should consider understandability and comparability when determining that order. It also allows entities to include the basis of preparation and specific accounting policies as notes in a separate section of the financial statements or as part of other notes.

In July 2014, the FRC Lab published a report – *Accounting policies and integration of related financial information*, following a project involving 16 companies and 19 institutional investors, analysts and representative organisations (supplemented by an online survey) which looked at:

- accounting policies: which are disclosed, the content of what is disclosed and their placement;
- notes to the financial statements: ordering, grouping and combining notes; and
- financial review: integration with the primary statements.

The FRC Lab report found that most investors viewed the combining of tax expense and tax balance sheet notes as logical but there was little support for combining other notes. The case for significant change in note order has not been made with some investors preferring the traditional order, some preferring company-specific ordering and some expressing no preference. Investors valued consistency of note order across companies and time; a table of contents was considered helpful, especially where notes are ordered differently. Most investors preferred the traditional approach of placing management commentary and financial statement information in separate sections of the annual report, while some saw merit in increased analysis of financial statement line items that an integrated commentary can provide.

7.2   Summary of significant accounting policies

The summary of significant accounting policies should disclose the measurement basis (or bases) used in preparing the financial statements and the accounting policies used that are relevant to an understanding of the financial statements. [FRS 102.8.5]. FRS 102 explains that measurement is the process of determining the monetary amounts at which assets, liabilities, income and expenses are measured in the financial statements and involves the selection of a basis of measurement. The standard specifies the measurement basis that an entity must use for many types of assets, liabilities, income or expense. Examples of common measurement bases are historical cost and fair value. *[FRS 102.2.33-2.34].*

It is clearly necessary to apply judgement when deciding which are the significant accounting policies and the level of detail required in a summary of accounting policies. In recent years, the FRC has commented particularly on the quality of revenue recognition policies and challenged companies where the information is: not company-specific: generic (including boilerplate text from accounting standards); or did not reflect revenue streams described in the business review or appeared inconsistent with changes in business model. The FRC does not expect immaterial or irrelevant policies to be disclosed.[1] The FRC Lab Report – *Accounting policies and integration of related financial information*, which is available on the FRC website, highlights the views of investors and sets out 'do's and don'ts' from the FRC's Corporate Reporting Review team.

Disclosure of particular accounting policies is especially useful to users when those policies are selected from alternatives allowed, e.g. the accrual or performance model for government grants in FRS 102 (see Chapter 19 at 3.4). Significant accounting policies not specifically required by the standard that have been selected by management in accordance with the GAAP hierarchy in Section 10 *[FRS 102.10.3-10.6]* should also be disclosed. In addition, FRS 102 specifically requires disclosure of certain accounting policies (where material), e.g. the accounting policy for recognising investments in associates and investments in jointly controlled entities in individual and consolidated financial statements must be disclosed. *[FRS 102.14.12(a), 15.19(a)].*

UK companies preparing Companies Act accounts are also required to disclose the accounting policies used in determining the amounts to be included in respect of items in the balance sheet and in determining the profit or loss of the company, in the notes to the accounts. The Regulations specifically require disclosure of policies with respect to the depreciation and diminution in value of assets, *[1 Sch 44, Regulations],* and the basis of translating sums denominated in foreign currencies into sterling (or the currency in which the financial statements are drawn up). *[1 Sch 70, Regulations].* Where the alternative accounting rules are used, e.g. property, plant and equipment is revalued (see 9.2 below), the items affected and the basis of valuation adopted must be disclosed in a note to the accounts. *[1 Sch 34(1)].*

It is common for financial statements to disclose the accounting convention used in their preparation. An example is given below, although the nature of the departures from the historic cost convention will depend on an entity's accounting policies.

Example 4.7:   Accounting convention

The financial statements are prepared in accordance with the historical cost convention, except for the revaluation of property, plant and equipment at market value under the alternative accounting rules and application of the fair value accounting rules to derivative financial assets and liabilities and hedging relationships.

7.3   Judgements in applying accounting policies

The summary of significant accounting policies or other notes should disclose the judgements, apart from those involving estimations, that management has made in the process of applying the entity's accounting policies and that have the most significant effect on the amounts recognised in the financial statements. *[FRS 102.8.6].*

This disclosure is not currently required by previous UK GAAP reporters, but IAS 1 has the same requirement. *[IAS 1.122]*. Examples of judgements in applying accounting policies include: whether a lease was classified as an operating or finance lease; whether a transaction was a business combination or an asset transaction; and whether the entity is acting as principal or agent in a revenue transaction.

FRS 102 specifically requires disclosure of certain judgements (although in general, there are fewer disclosures required than under IFRSs), e.g.:

- the basis for concluding that control exists where the entity does not own (directly or indirectly through its subsidiaries) more than half the voting power of an investee; *[FRS 102.9.23]*

- the reasons for a change in functional currency; *[FRS 102.30.27]* and

- the existence of material uncertainties over going concern, or the basis of preparation and the reasons when adopting the non-going concern basis. *[FRS 102.3.8-3.9]*.

7.4   Information about estimates

The notes to the financial statements should also disclose information about the key assumptions concerning the future, and other key sources of estimation uncertainty at the reporting date, that have a significant risk of causing a material adjustment to the carrying amounts of assets and liabilities within the next financial year. In respect of those assets and liabilities, the notes shall include details of their nature and their carrying amount as at the end of the reporting period. *[FRS 102.8.7]*.

FRS 102 specifically requires disclosure of certain key assumptions, e.g. the principal actuarial assumptions used (including discount rate, expected rates of salary increases, medical cost trend rates and any other material actuarial assumption used). *[FRS 102.28.41(k)]*.

IAS 1 has the same requirement, *[IAS 1.125]*, but with considerably more explanatory guidance that management may consider under the GAAP hierarchy in Section 10 of FRS 102 *[FRS 102.10.3-10.6]* in determining how to make the above disclosure. Determining the carrying amounts of some assets and liabilities requires estimation of the effects of uncertain future events on those assets and liabilities at the end of the reporting period. Examples given by IAS 1 are that, in the absence of recently observed market prices used to measure them, the following assets and liabilities require future-oriented estimates to measure them:

- the recoverable amount of classes of property, plant and equipment;

- the effect of technological obsolescence on inventories;

- provisions subject to the future outcome of litigation in progress; and

- long-term employee benefit liabilities such as pension obligations.

These estimates involve assumptions about such items as the risk adjustment to cash flows or discount rates used, future changes in salaries and future changes in prices affecting other costs. *[IAS 1.126]*.

IAS 1 goes on to observe that these assumptions and other sources of estimation uncertainty relate to the estimates that require management's most difficult, subjective or complex judgements. As the number of variables and assumptions affecting the possible future resolution of the uncertainties increases, those judgements become more subjective and complex, and the potential for a consequential material adjustment to the carrying amounts of assets and liabilities normally increases accordingly. *[IAS 1.127]*.

The disclosures should be presented in a manner that helps users of financial statements to understand the judgements management makes about the future and about other key sources of estimation uncertainty. The nature and extent of the information provided will vary according to the nature of the assumption and other circumstances. Examples given by IAS 1 of the types of disclosures to be made are: *[IAS 1.129]*

- the nature of the assumption or other estimation uncertainty;

- the sensitivity of carrying amounts to the methods, assumptions and estimates underlying their calculation, including the reasons for the sensitivity;

- the expected resolution of an uncertainty and the range of reasonably possible outcomes within the next financial year in respect of the carrying amounts of the assets and liabilities affected; and

- an explanation of changes made to past assumptions concerning those assets and liabilities, if the uncertainty remains unresolved.

IAS 1 also clarifies that these assumptions and other sources of estimation uncertainty are not required to be disclosed for assets and liabilities with a significant risk that their carrying amounts might change materially within the next financial year if, at the end of the reporting period, they are measured at fair value based on recently observed market prices. This is because, whilst their fair values might change materially within the next financial year those changes would not arise from assumptions or other sources of estimation uncertainty at the end of the reporting period. *[IAS 1.128]*. Also, it is not necessary to disclose budget information or forecasts in making the disclosures. *[IAS 1.130]*. While FRS 102 does not specifically exempt certain information from disclosure, it seems likely that the requirement is intended to be interpreted in the same way as under IFRSs. We consider that management may refer to the IAS 1 guidance under the GAAP hierarchy in Section 10.

When it is impracticable to disclose the extent of the possible effects of an assumption or another source of estimation uncertainty at the end of the reporting period, IAS 1 states that the entity should disclose that it is reasonably possible, on the basis of existing knowledge, that outcomes within the next financial year that are different from assumptions could require a material adjustment to the carrying amount of the asset or liability affected. In all cases, the entity should disclose the nature and carrying amount of the specific asset or liability (or class of assets or liabilities) affected by the assumption. *[IAS 1.131]*. This specific requirement has not been included in FRS 102, but may nevertheless be relevant information for users of the financial statements.

The extensive judgements required in deciding the level of detail to be given has resulted in a wide variety of disclosure in practice for the equivalent disclosure in IAS 1.

Chapter 4

7.5   Other notes disclosures in the presentation sections of FRS 102

An entity shall also disclose in the notes to the financial statements:

- the legal form of the entity, its country of incorporation and the address of its registered office (or principal place of business, if different from the registered office); and

- a description of the nature of the entity's operations and its principal activities unless this is disclosed in the business review (or similar statement) accompanying the financial statements. *[FRS 102.3.24].*

While the directors' report for a UK company no longer requires disclosure of the principal activities, these will often be explained in the strategic report as part of the business review.

The date the financial statements were authorised for issue and who gave that authorisation must be disclosed. If the entity's owners or others have the power to amend the financial statements after issue, the entity shall disclose that fact. *[FRS 102.32.9].* See Chapter 27 at 3.5.

IAS 10 – *Events after the Reporting Period* (which is similar to Section 32 – *Events after the End of the Reporting Period* – of FRS 102, and may be referred to under the GAAP hierarchy in Section 10 of the standard) clarifies that where an entity is required to submit its financial statements to its shareholders for approval after the financial statements have been issued, the financial statements are authorised for issue on the date of issue not the date the shareholders approve the financial statements. *[IAS 10.5].*

The above requirement overlaps with the requirements in the Companies Act 2006 for the directors to approve the annual accounts and for a director to sign the company balance sheet (with the printed name of the director stated in published and filed copies) *[s414, 433, 444-447].* The details on authorisation of the financial statements are also often included as a separate note to the financial statements.

7.6   Staff costs

A UK company preparing Companies Act accounts or IAS accounts, unless it is subject to the small companies regime (see Chapter 1 at 6.5), must disclose in the notes to the accounts:

- the average number of persons employed by the company in the financial year in total and analysed by category selected by the directors, having regard to how the company's activities are organised;

- in respect of the above persons, the aggregate amounts of:

  - wages and salaries paid or payable in respect of the year to those persons;

  - social security costs incurred by the company on their behalf; and

  - other pension costs so incurred.

The analysis of the staff costs is not required where the amounts are stated elsewhere in the company's accounts (as may be the case where the Format 2 profit and loss account is used). *[s411(1), (2), (5)].*

In group accounts, the requirements apply as if the undertakings included in the consolidation were a single company, i.e. the disclosures relate to the company and its consolidated subsidiary undertakings. *[s411(7)]*. Where group accounts are presented, the information on staff costs required in the individual profit and loss account need not be given where use of the section 408 exemption is disclosed (see Chapter 1 at 6.3.2). *[s408(2)]*.

The average number of persons employed is determined by dividing the 'relevant annual number' by the number of months in the financial year. The relevant annual number is the number of persons employed under contracts of service by the company for each month (whether throughout the month or not – so including both part- and full-time employees) in the financial year and then adding the monthly numbers. *[s411(3)-(4)]*.

Wages and salaries, and social security costs are determined by reference to payments made or costs incurred in respect of all persons employed by the company during the financial year under contracts of service. *[s411(5), 10 Sch 14]*.

Social security costs mean any contributions by the company to any state social security or pension scheme, fund or arrangement. *[s411(6), 10 Sch 14]*.

Pension costs include any costs incurred by the company in respect of any pension scheme established for the purpose of providing pensions for current or former employees, any sums set aside for the future payment of pensions directly by the company for current or former employees, and any pensions paid directly to such persons without having first been set aside. *[s411(6), 10 Sch 14]*. These exclude contributions to a state pension scheme which are disclosed as social security costs.

Since the disclosures relate to persons employed on 'contracts of service' with the company (meaning an employment contract), these exclude self-employed people such as contractors or consultants. Executive directors generally have a contract of service, but non-executive directors may not have contracts for services and would then be excluded from the above disclosure. All directors are within the scope of statutory directors' remuneration disclosures (as noted at 7 above, these are beyond the scope of this publication).

In groups, employees with contracts of service with one company (such as the holding company or service company) may be seconded to another group company or paid by another company, sometimes with costs recharged. In such cases, we would recommend that entities supplement the statutory disclosures for persons with contracts of service with additional information on staff costs and staff numbers, explaining the particular situation, including the impact on the company's/ group's profit and loss account.

7.7   Off balance sheet arrangements

A UK company preparing Companies Act accounts or IAS accounts, unless it is subject to the small companies regime (see Chapter 1 at 6.5), must disclose the following information in the notes to the accounts if, in any financial year, the company is or has been party to arrangements that are not reflected in its balance sheet and, at the balance sheet date, the risks or benefits arising from those arrangements are material:

- the nature and purpose of the arrangements; and

- the financial impact of the arrangements on the company (unless the company qualifies as medium-sized under sections 465 to 467 of the Companies Act 2006 (see Chapter 1 at 6.6)).

The information need only be given to the extent necessary for enabling the financial position to be assessed. In group accounts, the requirements apply as if the undertakings included in the consolidation were a single company, i.e. the disclosures relate to the company and its consolidated subsidiary undertakings. *[s410A]*. Consequently, UK companies preparing statutory group accounts must give the information for both the company and the consolidated group.

Section 410A implements the requirement for disclosure of 'off-balance sheet arrangements' included in Directive 2006/46/EC. Recital 9 to the EU Directive states:

'Such off-balance sheet arrangements could be any transactions or agreements which companies may have with entities, even unincorporated ones, that are not included in the balance sheet. Such off-balance sheet arrangements may be associated with the creation or use of one or more Special Purpose Entities (SPEs) and offshore activities designed to address, *inter alia*, economic, legal, tax or accounting objectives. Examples of such off-balance sheet arrangements include risk and benefit-sharing arrangements or obligations arising from a contract such as debt factoring, combined sale or repurchase agreements, consignment stock arrangements, take or pay arrangements, securitisation arranged through separate companies and unincorporated entities, pledged assets, operating leasing arrangements, outsourcing and the like. Appropriate disclosure of the material risks and benefits of such arrangements that are not included in the balance sheet should be set out in the notes to the accounts or the consolidated accounts.'

The examples listed in Recital 9 are not to be taken as exhaustive. FRS 102 and/or the Regulations already require disclosures about certain off-balance sheet arrangements, e.g. operating leases. As discussed at 7.3 above, FRS 102 requires significant judgements in applying accounting policies to be disclosed. Directors will, however, still need to consider whether the disclosures given are sufficient to meet the requirements of section 410A and whether the entity is party to material off-balance sheet arrangements not required to be disclosed by FRS 102 that should be disclosed in accordance with section 410A.

7.8   Directors' advances, credits and guarantees

A UK company preparing Companies Act accounts or IAS accounts must disclose the information concerning directors' advances, credits and guarantees required by section 413 of the Companies Act 2006.

A company that does not prepare group accounts must disclose in the notes to its individual accounts: *[s413]*

- advances and credits granted by the company to its directors; and

- guarantees of any kind entered into by the company on behalf of its directors.

A parent company that prepares group accounts must disclose in the notes to the group accounts: *[s413]*

- advances and credits granted to the directors of the parent company, by that company or by any of its subsidiary undertakings; and

- guarantees of any kind entered into on behalf of the directors of the parent company, by that company or by any of its subsidiary undertakings.

The details required for an advance or credit are: *[s413]*

- its amount (for each advance or credit and totals in aggregate);

- an indication of the interest rate;

- its main conditions; and

- any amounts repaid (for each advance or credit and totals in aggregate);

The details required for a guarantee are: *[s413]*

- its main terms;

- the amount (for each guarantee and totals in aggregate) of the maximum liability that may be incurred by the company (or its subsidiary); and

- any amount paid and any liability incurred by the company (or its subsidiary) for the purpose of fulfilling the guarantee (including any loss incurred by reason of enforcement of the guarantee). Details must be given for each guarantee and also totals in aggregate.

Disclosure is required: *[s413]*

- in respect of a person who was a director of the company at any time in the financial year to which the financial statements relate; and

- for every advance, credit or guarantee that subsisted at any time in the financial year:

  - whenever it was entered into;

  - whether or not the person concerned was a director of the company at the time it was entered into; and

  - in relation to an advance, credit or guarantee involving a subsidiary undertaking of the company, whether or not it was a subsidiary undertaking at the time the advance, credit or guarantee was entered into.

There are certain exemptions for banking companies (and the holding companies of credit institutions (see definitions at 4.1.2.A above), as explained at 7.8.1 below.

The terms advances, credits, and guarantees are not defined in the Companies Act 2006 itself. The rules governing the lawfulness of transactions in Part 10 of the Companies Act 2006 refer to loans, quasi-loans (including related guarantees or provision of security) and credit transactions. While these terms do not align with the terms used in the financial statements disclosure requirements, loans and quasi-loans and credit transactions would generally be considered as advances and credits; and guarantees or provision of security would be disclosed as guarantees (of any kind).

The requirements appear to require disclosure of each advance or credit, or guarantee made. This could be arduous in some contexts, as the definition of advances and credits could include directors' current accounts or personal purchases made using a company credit card (as well as loans and outstanding credit card balances provided by banks or finance subsidiaries of certain retailers).

7.8.1   Banking companies and holding companies of credit institutions

Such companies are required to disclose only the details in sections 413(5)(a) and 413(5)(c), i.e. the aggregate totals of:

- the amounts of advances or credits granted by the company (or in group accounts, by the company and its subsidiary undertakings); and

- the amounts of the maximum liability that may be incurred by the company (or its subsidiary) in respect of guarantees entered into by the company (or in group accounts, by the company and its subsidiary undertakings). *[s413(6)]*.

8   GENERAL PRINCIPLES FOR PREPARATION OF FINANCIAL STATEMENTS

The objective of financial statements is to provide information about the financial position, performance and cash flows of an entity that is useful for economic decision-making by a broad range of users who are not in a position to demand reports tailored to meet their particular information needs. Financial statements also show the results of the stewardship of management – the accountability of management for the resources entrusted to it. *[FRS 102.2.2-2.3]*.

FRS 102's general principles for preparation of financial statements are covered in Section 2 (see Chapter 3), Section 3 (covered in this chapter) and Section 10 (see Chapter 7) of FRS 102.

The selection of accounting policies is also critical in the preparation of financial statements. The requirements on selection of accounting policies and on accounting estimates are in Section 10. Disclosure of accounting policies, judgements and estimates are covered at 7.2 to 7.4 above.

This section concentrates on FRS 102's requirement for financial statements to give a fair presentation, adoption of the going concern basis, and materiality and aggregation, i.e. the issues which are addressed in Section 3 of the standard. There are similar requirements in the Regulations, as highlighted at 8.1 below.

8.1   Requirements of the Regulations

The Regulations (and where applicable, the LLP Regulations) include:

- the requirement for accounts to give a true and fair view, and the concept of a 'true and fair override' (see 8.2 below);

- general principles for the preparation of financial statements, similar to those included in FRS 102 (see 8.1.1 below);

- recognition and measurement principles, where assets and liabilities are measured under the historical cost convention, alternative accounting rules and fair value accounting rules (see 9 to 9.4 below);

- presentation requirements for the balance sheet and profit and loss formats (see 9.5 below); and

- disclosure requirements (see 9.6 below).

8.1.1 General principles for preparation of financial statements

The general principles set out in the Regulations for the preparation of financial statements are:

- the company is presumed to be carrying on business as a going concern (see 8.3 below);

- accounting policies must be applied consistently within the same accounts and from one financial year to the next (see 3.6.2 above and Chapter 3 at 3.2.8);

- the amount of any item must be determined on a prudent basis, and in particular –

  - only profits realised at the balance sheet date are to be included in the profit and loss account (except where fair value changes of financial instruments, investment property or living animals or plants are required to be included in the profit and loss account by the fair value accounting rules), and

  - all liabilities which have arisen in respect of the financial year to which the accounts relate or a previous financial year must be taken into account, including those which only became apparent between the balance sheet date and the date on which it is approved and signed by the Board;

- all income and charges relating to the financial year to which the accounts relate must be taken into account without regard to the date of receipt or payment (i.e. accrual concept – see Chapter 3 at 3.8); and

- in determining the aggregate amount of any item, the amount of each individual asset or liability that falls to be taken into account must be determined separately (i.e. no offsetting). *[1 Sch 10-15, Regulations 40(2)].*

FRS 102 has similar general principles. FRS 102's requirements on going concern, consistency and accruals are discussed in the sections indicated above. FRS 102 also addresses prudence (see 8.1.1.B below), albeit the standard's requirements are expressed somewhat differently from those in the Regulations. The standard also includes general principles on substance over form (see 8.1.1.A below), materiality and aggregation of items (see 8.4 below) and the criteria for offset of certain types of assets and liabilities (see 8.1.1.C below). These are highlighted briefly below (and in more detail in other chapters of this publication).

8.1.1.A Substance over form

FRS 102 does not have a separate section on 'substance over form' comparable to FRS 5 – *Reporting the substance of transactions*, but requires that 'Transactions and other events and conditions should be accounted for and presented in accordance with their substance and not merely their legal form. This enhances the reliability of financial statements.' *[FRS 102.2.8]* (see Chapter 3 at 3.2.5). In addition, where an FRS or FRC Abstract does not specifically address a transaction, management must use its judgement in developing and applying an accounting policy that results in relevant and reliable information. *[FRS 102.10.4]*. One of the characteristics of reliable information is that the financial statements 'reflect the economic substance of transactions, other events and conditions, and not merely the legal form' *[FRS 102.10.4(b)(ii)]*. In June 2014, the FRC issued updated guidance – *True and Fair* – which refers to the above requirement and makes the point that 'if material transactions are not accounted for in accordance with their substance it is doubtful whether the accounts present a true and fair view'.

The Regulations require that items in the balance sheet and profit and loss account formats are presented, having regard to the substance of the reported transaction or arrangement, in accordance with generally accepted accounting principles or practice. *[1 Sch 9]*. This requirement facilitates the presentation of certain shares as liabilities in accordance with FRS 102 (and previous UK GAAP). See 4.2, 4.6 and 5.6 above.

8.1.1.B   Prudence

FRS 102 identifies prudence as 'the inclusion of a degree of caution in the exercise of the judgements needed in making the estimates required under conditions of uncertainty, such that assets or income are not overstated and liabilities or expenses are not understated. However, the exercise of prudence does not allow the deliberate understatement of assets or income, or the deliberate overstatement of liabilities or expenses. In short, prudence does not permit bias'. *[FRS 102.2.9]*.

However, the standard does not specifically refer to realised profits. UK companies preparing Companies Act accounts are required to prepare the profit and loss account section of the statement of comprehensive income (or separate income statement) in accordance with the Regulations. As discussed in Appendix IV to FRS 102, the issue of realised profits is pertinent to whether a gain is reported in profit or loss in Companies Act accounts. *[FRS 102.A4.25-A4.27]*. This interaction with the Regulations may mean that UK companies preparing Companies Act accounts must present certain gains in other comprehensive income instead. Profit or loss and other comprehensive income, including the concept of realised profits, are discussed further at 5.2 above.

FRS 102 involves more use of fair values than previous UK GAAP. In particular, UK companies should be mindful that not all gains (even if recognised in profit or loss) may be distributable. Entities measuring investment properties, living animals or plants, or financial instruments at fair value should note that they may transfer such amounts to a separate non-distributable reserve, instead of a transfer to retained earnings, but are not required to do so. Presenting fair value movements that are not distributable profits in the separate reserve may assist with identification of profits available for that purpose. *[FRS 102.A4.28]*. Appendix IV to FRS 102 notes that the determination of profits available for distribution is a complex area where accounting and company law interface and that companies may need to refer to TECH 02/10 in determining profits available for distribution. *[FRS 102.A4.29]*. The impact of transition on distributable profits is discussed in Chapter 1 at 5.4.

8.1.1.C   Offset

FRS 102 prohibits offset of assets and liabilities, or income and expenses, unless required or permitted by the standard. *[FRS 102.2.52].* See Chapter 3 at 3.12 and the discussion of the balance sheet and profit and loss account formats at 4.2, 4.6 and 5.6 above.

The standard sets out when financial assets and liabilities *[FRS 102.11.38A* (refer to Chapter 8 at 6.7), employee benefits *[FRS 102.28.3(a), 28.14, 28.30]* (see Chapter 23 at 3.8.2), current tax and deferred tax (see Chapter 24 at 10.1) must be offset. In these cases, the standard is effectively saying that this is a single asset or liability.

In respect of the profit and loss account, gains and losses on disposal of fixed assets are shown net of costs, where not part of normal operating activities, *[FRS 102.2.52(b)],* and expenses for a provision are permitted to be shown net of the amount recognised for reimbursement of the provision *[FRS 102.21.9].* The standard also permits cash flows from operating, investing and financing activities to be presented on a net basis where specified criteria are met. *[FRS 102.7.10A-7.10D].*

Appendix IV to FRS 102 explains how the standard's requirements on government grants (no offsetting), reimbursement of provisions (offsetting permitted in profit and loss only) and financial assets (offsetting when the criteria in the standard are met) are consistent with the Regulations. *[FRS 102.A4.22-A4.23].*

8.2   Fair presentation and compliance with FRS 102

FRS 102 requires that financial statements present fairly the financial position, financial performance and cash flows of an entity. Fair presentation for these purposes requires the faithful representation of the effects of transactions, other events and conditions in accordance with the definitions and recognition criteria for assets, liabilities, income and expenses set out in Section 2 of the standard (see Chapter 3), unless the override set out in paragraph 3.4 of the standard applies. *[FRS 102.3.2, Appendix I].*

Application of FRS 102, with additional disclosure when necessary (see below), is presumed to result in financial statements that achieve a fair presentation of the financial position, financial performance and cash flows of entities within the scope of the standard. Additional disclosure is necessary when compliance with the specific requirements in the standard is insufficient to enable users to understand the effect of particular transactions, other events and conditions on the entity's financial position and performance. *[FRS 102.3.2].*

An important point here is that all paragraphs of FRS 102 have equal authority. Some sections of the standard include appendices containing implementation guidance or examples, some of which are an integral part of the standard and others provide application guidance (each specifies its status). *[FRS 102.Summary (xiv)].* We would generally expect that entities follow such guidance unless there is a valid reason. The presumption that application of the standard (with any necessary additional disclosure) results in a fair presentation is subject to a fair presentation override set out in paragraph 3.4 of the standard (and for entities preparing financial statements subject to the Companies Act 2006, the true and fair override). *[FRS 102.3.4, Appendix I].* See 8.2.1 and 8.2.2 respectively below.

Chapter 4

8.2.1   *The fair presentation override*

The FRC considers that accounting standards are authoritative statements of how particular types of transactions and other events should be reflected in financial statements and accordingly, compliance with accounting standards will normally be necessary for financial statements to give a true and fair view. In applying accounting standards, it is important to be guided by the spirit and reasoning behind them (set out in the material accompanying FRSs or FRC Abstracts). *[Foreword to Accounting Standards.16-17].*

The FRC envisage that only in exceptional circumstances will departure from the requirements of an accounting standard be necessary in order to give a true and fair view. In such circumstances, the requirements of the accounting standard should be departed from to the extent necessary to give a true and fair view and informed and unbiased judgement used to devise an alternative appropriate accounting treatment, consistent with the economic and commercial characteristics of the circumstances concerned. *[Foreword to Accounting Standards.18-19].*

IAS 1 provides the following additional requirements that management of an entity applying FRS 102 may consider. IAS 1 requires that when assessing whether complying with a specific requirement in [the standard] would be so misleading that it would conflict with the objective of financial statements, management considers:

(a)   why the objective of financial statements is not achieved in the particular circumstances; and

(b)   how the entity's circumstances differ from those of other entities that comply with the requirement. If other entities in similar circumstances comply with the requirement, there is a rebuttable presumption that the entity's compliance with the requirement would not be so misleading that it would conflict with the objective of financial statements. *[IAS 1.24].*

In the extremely rare circumstances when management concludes that compliance with FRS 102 would be so misleading that it would conflict with the objective of financial statements set out in the standard (see 8 above), the entity shall depart from that requirement. *[FRS 102.3.4].*

When an entity departs from a requirement of FRS 102 or from a requirement of applicable legislation, it shall disclose:

(a)   that management has concluded that the financial statements present fairly the entity's financial position, financial performance and cash flows;

(b)   that it has complied with FRS 102 or applicable legislation, except that it has departed from a particular requirement of the standard or applicable legislation set out in Section 2 to achieve a fair presentation; and

(c)   the nature of the departure, including the treatment that FRS 102 or applicable legislation would require, the reason why that treatment would be so misleading in the circumstances that it would conflict with the objective of financial statements and the treatment adopted. *[FRS 102.3.5].* FRS 102 includes a footnote linking this to the statutory disclosures required for a 'true and fair override' under the Companies Act 2006. See 8.2.2 below.

When an entity has departed from a requirement of FRS 102 or applicable legislation in a prior period and that departure affects the amounts recognised in the financial statements for the current period, it shall make the disclosures set out in (c) above. *[FRS 102.3.6].*

FRS 102, unlike IFRSs and previous UK GAAP, does not explicitly require the financial impact of the override to be disclosed, although the effect of the departure is explicitly required where the true and fair override is applied under the Companies Act 2006. See 8.2.2 below. However, the FRC's *Foreword to Accounting Standards* clearly envisages that particulars of the departure from an accounting standard, the reasons and the financial effects are required (the disclosures made should be consistent with that given for departures from specific accounting provisions of company law). *[Foreword to Accounting Standards.19].*

In the absence of guidance in FRS 102, management may consider the requirements of IFRSs. Where there is a departure from IFRSs in the current period (or a departure was made in a previous period which impacts the amounts recognised in the financial statements in the current period), IAS 1 requires disclosure for each period presented, of the financial impact of the departure on each item in the financial statements that would have been reported in complying with the requirement. *[IAS 1.20(d), 21].* Previous UK GAAP also normally required quantification of the financial effect on both the current financial year and corresponding amounts (i.e. the comparatives), except where quantification was evident from the financial statements themselves (e.g. where it was a matter of presentation rather than measurement) or where the effect cannot reasonably be quantified, in which case the directors should explain the circumstances. *[FRS 18.62-63].*

8.2.2   Companies Act 2006 requirements for 'true and fair override'

The Companies Act 2006 requires that directors of a company must not approve accounts unless satisfied that they give a true and fair view of the assets, liabilities, financial position and profit or loss of the company (and in respect of any group accounts, the undertakings included in the consolidation as a whole, so far as concerns the members of the company). *[s393].* The 'undertakings included in the consolidation' means the parent company and its consolidated subsidiary undertakings and is referred to as 'the group' below. See the discussion of 'true and fair' (and its relationship with accounting standards) at Chapter 1 at 7.2.

Companies Act accounts must include a balance sheet as at the financial year end and a profit and loss account for the financial year that give a true and fair view of the company's (and, where applicable, the group's) state of affairs as at the end of the financial year, and of the company's (and, where applicable, the group's) profit or loss for the financial year. The accounts must comply with regulations made by the Secretary of State as to the form and content of the balance sheet and profit and loss account, and additional information to be provided by way of notes to the accounts. *[s396(1)-(3), s404(1)-(3)].*

If compliance with the regulations, and any other provisions made by or under the Companies Act 2006, as to matters to be included in a company's individual (and/or group) accounts or in notes to those accounts, would not be sufficient to give a true and fair view, the necessary additional information must be given in the accounts or notes to them. *[s396(4), s404(4)]*.

If in special circumstances, compliance with any of those provisions is inconsistent with the requirement to give a true and fair view, the directors must depart from that provision to the extent necessary to give a true and fair view. Particulars of the departure, the reasons for it and its effect must be given in a note to the accounts. *[s396(5), s404(5)]*.

Where it appears to the directors that there are special reasons for departing from any of the general principles (see 8.1.1 above) in preparing the accounts for the financial year, the particulars of the departure, reasons and effect should be disclosed in a note to the accounts. *[1 Sch 10(2)]*.

Large- and medium-sized companies must make a statement in the notes to the accounts (see 3.8.1 above) as to whether the accounts have been prepared in accordance with applicable accounting standards, giving particulars of any material departures from those standards and the reasons. *[1 Sch 45]*. However, medium-sized companies are exempt from making this statement in individual accounts. *[Regulations 4(2)]*. Consistent with previous GAAP, in our view, this statement should either include or cross refer any disclosures of the true and fair override (which overlap with the 'fair presentation override' described by FRS 102 – see 8.2.1 above). *[FRS 18.62]*.

Appendix IV to FRS 102 highlights certain instances where the requirements of FRS 102 result in a departure from the requirements of the Regulations in order to give a 'true and fair view'. These examples, which are not exhaustive, are relevant to UK companies preparing Companies Act accounts (and similarly, LLPs preparing non-IAS accounts subject to the LLP Regulations).

8.3   Going concern

FRS 102 requires management, when preparing financial statements, to make an assessment of an entity's ability to continue as a going concern. An entity is a going concern unless management either intends to liquidate the entity or to cease trading, or has no realistic alternative but to do so. In assessing whether the going concern assumption is appropriate, management takes into account all available information about the future, which is at least, but is not limited to, twelve months from the date when the financial statements are authorised for issue. *[FRS 102.3.8, Appendix I]*. This review period is a longer minimum period than that specified in IAS 1 and is consistent with that specified for management's assessment of going concern in auditing standards by ISA (UK & Ireland) 570 – *Going Concern*.

When management is aware, in making its assessment, of material uncertainties related to events or conditions that cast significant doubt upon the entity's ability to continue as a going concern, those uncertainties should be disclosed in the financial statements. *[FRS 102.3.9]*.

When financial statements are not prepared on a going concern basis, that fact should be disclosed, together with the basis on which the financial statements are prepared and the reason why the entity is not regarded as a going concern.

[FRS 102.3.9]. FRS 102 states that an entity shall not prepare its financial statements on a going concern basis if management determines after the reporting period either that it intends to liquidate the entity or to cease trading or that it has no realistic alternative but to do so.

Deterioration in operating results and financial position after the reporting period may indicate a need to consider whether the going concern assumption is no longer appropriate. If the going concern assumption is no longer appropriate, a fundamental change in the basis of accounting rather than an adjustment to the amounts recognised within the original basis of accounting is required, and therefore the disclosures in paragraph 3.9 of the standard, as described above, apply. *[FRS 102.32.7A-7B].*

FRS 102 provides no further guidance concerning what impact there should be on the financial statements if it is determined that the going concern basis is not appropriate. Accordingly, entities will need to consider carefully their individual circumstances to arrive at an appropriate basis.

FRS 102's requirements are supplemented by FRC guidance. In September 2014, the FRC issued *Guidance on Risk Management, Internal Control: and Related Financial and Business Reporting.* This guidance integrates and replaces the previous *Internal Control: Revised Guidance for Directors on the Combined Code (2005)* and *Going Concern and Liquidity Risk: Guidance for Directors of UK companies 2009* ('the 2009 Going Concern Guidance') and reflects changes made to the UK Corporate Governance Code. This new guidance is aimed primarily at entities subject to the UK Corporate Governance Code (and applies for such entities for financial years beginning on or after 1 October 2014). The FRC hopes that other entities will find it helpful.

While many FRS 102 reporters will not be subject to or voluntarily applying the UK Corporate Governance Code, Section 6, Appendix A and Appendix D of *Guidance on Risk Management, Internal Control: and Related Financial and Business Reporting* include relevant information on adoption of the going concern basis of accounting (including disclosures on material uncertainties) in the financial statements, as well as reporting on principal risks and uncertainties (in the strategic report).

8.4   Materiality and aggregation

Financial statements result from processing large numbers of transactions or other events that are aggregated into classes according to their nature or function. The final stage in the process of aggregation and classification is the presentation of condensed and classified data, which form line items in the financial statements. *[FRS 102.3.16].*

As noted at 4.2, 4.6 and 5.6 above, FRS 102 reporters must comply with the balance sheet and profit and loss account formats set out in the Regulations (or LLP Regulations). FRS 102 requires an entity to present additional line items, headings and subtotals where relevant to an understanding of the financial position or financial performance. *[FRS 102.4.3, 5.9].*

The extent of aggregation versus detailed analysis is clearly a judgemental one, with either extreme eroding the usefulness of the information. FRS 102 resolves this issue with the concept of materiality (see Chapter 3 at 3.2.3). Materiality is defined as follows: 'Omissions or misstatements of items are material if they could, individually or collectively, influence the economic decisions of users taken on the basis of the financial statements. Materiality depends on the size and nature of the omission or misstatement judged in the surrounding circumstances. The size or nature of the item, or a combination of both, could be the determining factor.' However, it is inappropriate to make, or leave uncorrected, immaterial departures from the standard to achieve a particular presentation of an entity's financial position, financial performance or cash flows. *[FRS 102.2.6, Appendix I].*

FRS 102 requires each material class of similar items to be presented separately and items of a dissimilar nature or function to be presented separately unless they are immaterial. *[FRS 102.3.15].* If a line item is not individually material, it is aggregated with other items either in those statements or in the notes. An item that may not warrant separate presentation in those financial statements may warrant separate presentation in the notes. *[FRS 102.3.16].*

The Regulations (or, where applicable, the LLP Regulations) allow the directors to combine items denoted with Arabic numbers in the balance sheet and profit and loss account formats if their individual amounts are not material to assessing the state of affairs or profit or loss of the company for the financial year in question, or where the combination facilitates that assessment (in which case, the individual amounts of the line items combined must be disclosed in the notes). *[1 Sch 4(2)].*

FRS 102 states that an entity need not provide a specific disclosure required by the standard if the information is not material. *[FRS 102.3.16A].* UK companies preparing Companies Act accounts must also comply with the disclosure requirements of the Regulations (or, where applicable, the LLP Regulations). The Regulations permit that 'amounts which in the particular context of any provision of Schedules 1, 2 or 3 to these Regulations are not material may be disregarded for the purposes of that provision.' *[10 Sch 10].*

8.4.1   'Cutting Clutter'

In recent years, there has been increased recognition that the length and complexity of annual reports and financial statements can obscure key messages and make them less understandable. This has led to a regulatory focus on 'cutting clutter' with the aim of making financial statements more concise and relevant. The FRC have published a number of discussion papers including *Louder than Words: Principles and actions for making corporate reports less complex and more relevant* (June 2009), *Cutting Clutter: Combating clutter in annual reports* (April 2011), and *Thinking about Disclosures in a broader context: A road map for a disclosure framework* (October 2012). 'Cutting clutter' has been a recurrent message in the annual Corporate Reporting Review.

The IASB's recent Exposure Draft of amendments to IAS 1 (see 7.1 above), *inter alia*, clarifies the concept of materiality and aggregation and emphasises that:

- entities should not aggregate or disaggregate information in a manner that obscures useful information, e.g. by aggregating information with different characteristics or by overwhelming useful information with immaterial information;

- materiality requirements apply to the primary financial statements and the notes; and

- when a standard specifically requires a disclosure, the resulting information should be assessed to determine whether it is material and whether its presentation or disclosure is warranted. Conversely, an entity should consider whether information needs to be presented or disclosed to meet the needs of users of the financial statements, even if it is not a specific disclosure requirement.

While much of the regulatory focus has been on IFRS financial statements (and IFRS has more extensive disclosure requirements compared to FRS 102), the general messages above are also relevant for FRS 102 financial statements.

9   RECOGNITION AND MEASUREMENT, PRESENTATION AND DISCLOSURE – COMPANIES ACT ACCOUNTS

As previously discussed, FRS 102 financial statements are Companies Act accounts and, therefore, must comply with the recognition and measurement rules included in the applicable schedule of the Regulations or Small Companies Regulations.

FRS 102 has been modified compared to the IFRS for SMEs in order to ensure that it complies with these requirements. Appendix IV to the standard provides an overview of how FRS 102's requirements address UK company law requirements (written from the perspective of a company to which the Companies Act 2006 applies) but this is not comprehensive. Therefore, it is useful to have an understanding of the key recognition and measurement principles included in the Regulations and Small Companies Regulations.

Schedules 1 to 3 to the Regulations (and Schedule 1 to the Small Companies Regulations) set out fundamental accounting principles such as going concern, use of consistent accounting policies, prudence, and no offsetting of assets and liabilities (or income and expense). See 8.1.1 above.

The Regulations and Small Companies Regulations also set out the following three models for the recognition and measurement of assets and liabilities:

- historical cost accounting rules (see 9.1 below) *[1 Sch Section B]*.

- alternative accounting rules (see 9.2 below) *[1 Sch Section C]*.

- fair value accounting rules (see 9.3 and 9.4 below) *[1 Sch Section D]*.

The main requirements of the three models are set out below. However, entities preparing FRS 102 financial statements also need to comply with the requirements of FRS 102, which are sometimes more restrictive than the statutory requirements.

References given below are to Schedule 1 to the Regulations only, but there are equivalent paragraphs in Schedule 2 or Schedule 3 (albeit sometimes with modifications to those in Schedule 1) or in the Small Companies Regulations.

9.1   Historical cost accounting rules

FRS 102 makes use of the historical cost accounting rules for the following assets:

- basic financial instruments, except for:
    - investments in non-convertible preference shares and non-puttable ordinary shares or preference shares that are publicly traded or whose fair value can otherwise be measured reliably; or
    - debt instruments and commitments to receive a loan and to make a loan to another entity (meeting specified conditions) that are designated at fair value through profit or loss on initial recognition *[FRS 102.11.14]*;
- financial instruments that are not permitted by the Regulations or the LLP Regulations to be measured at fair value through profit or loss *[FRS 102.12.8(c)]*;
- inventories – except for inventories held for distribution at no or nominal consideration *[FRS 102.134-13.4A]*;
- property, plant and equipment – where the cost model is applied *[FRS 102.17.15-15A]*;
- intangible assets – where the cost model is applied *[FRS 102.18.18-18A]*;
- investments in subsidiaries, associates and joint ventures in separate or individual financial statements – where the cost model is applied *[FRS 102.9.26-9.26A, 14.4(a), 14.5-14.6, 15.9(a), 15.10-15.11]*; and
- investment property, where the cost model is applied since fair value cannot be measured reliably without undue cost or effort on an ongoing basis *[FRS 102.16.1]*.

Under the historical cost accounting rules,

- fixed assets are included at cost (i.e. purchase price or production cost – see 9.1.1 below) subject to any provisions for depreciation or diminution in value. *[1 Sch 17]*; and
- current assets are included at the lower of cost (i.e. purchase price or production cost) and net realisable value. Where the reasons for which any provision was made have ceased to apply to any extent, the provision must be written back to the extent that it is no longer necessary. *[1 Sch 23-24]*.

Fixed assets are assets intended for use on a continuing basis in the company's activities, and current assets are assets not intended for such use. *[10 Sch 4]*.

9.1.1   Definition of purchase price and production cost

The purchase price is the sum of the actual price paid (including cash and non-cash consideration) for the asset and any expenses incidental to its acquisition. *[1 Sch 27(1), 10 Sch 12]*.

The production cost is the sum of the purchase price of the raw materials and consumables, and directly attributable production costs. The Regulations permit the inclusion of: *[1 Sch 27(2)-(3)]*

- a reasonable proportion of costs incurred by the company which are indirectly attributable to the production of the asset (but only to the extent they relate to the period of production); and

- interest on capital borrowed to finance the production of the asset (to the extent it accrues in respect of the period of production), provided that a note to the accounts discloses that interest is capitalised in the cost of that asset and gives the amount of interest so capitalised.

Distribution costs may not be included in the production cost of a current asset. *[1 Sch 27(4)].*

The purchase price or production cost of stocks and any fungible assets (including investments) may be determined by one of the following methods, provided that the method chosen appears to the directors to be appropriate in the circumstances of the company: *[1 Sch 28(1)-(2)]*

- last in first out (LIFO) – this method is not permitted by FRS 102;

- first in first out (FIFO);

- weighted average price; and

- any other method similar to the methods above.

Fungible assets are assets that are substantially indistinguishable one from another. *[10 Sch 5].*

Where an item shown in the balance sheet includes assets whose purchase price or production cost has been determined using any of the above methods, the notes to the accounts should disclose the difference (where material) between: *[1 Sch 28(3)-(5)]*

- the carrying amount of that balance sheet item; and

- the amount that would have been shown if assets of any class included under that item at an amount determined using any of the above methods were included at their replacement cost as at the balance sheet date. This calculation can use the most recent actual purchase price or production cost before the balance sheet date instead of replacement cost if the former appears to the directors to be the more appropriate standard of comparison for assets of that class.

Where there is no record of the purchase price or production cost (or of any price, expenses or cost relevant for determining the purchase price or production cost) or any such record cannot be obtained without unreasonable expense or delay, the purchase price or production cost of the asset must be taken to be the value ascribed in the earliest available record of its value made on or after its acquisition or production by the company. *[1 Sch 29].*

The Regulations also permit tangible fixed assets and raw materials and consumables (within current assets) to be included at a fixed quantity and value, but only where the assets are constantly being replaced, their overall value is not material to assessing the company's state of affairs and their quantity, value and composition are not subject to material valuation. *[1 Sch 26].* Some companies capitalise minor items (such as tools, cutlery, small containers, sheets and towels) at a fixed amount when they are originally provided as a form of capital 'base stock' where the continual loss and replacement of stock does result in a base amount that does not materially vary.

This treatment is not compliant with FRS 102 and therefore would only be acceptable where the items in question are immaterial.

Where the amount repayable on a debt owed by a company exceeds the value of the consideration received in the transaction giving rise to the debt, the Regulations allow the difference to be treated as an asset, and written off by reasonable amounts each year (and must be completely written off before repayment of the debt). The current amount should be disclosed in a note to the accounts if it is not shown as a separate item in the balance sheet. *[1 Sch 25]*. This treatment would not comply with FRS 102's requirements on initial measurement of financial liabilities *[FRS 102.11.13]* (see Chapter 8 at 4.3).

9.1.1.A   *FRS 102 requirements*

FRS 102's requirements for measuring cost are consistent with but more prescriptive than the Regulations.

For example, only costs directly attributable to bringing the asset to the location and condition necessary for it to be capable of operating in the manner intended by management are permitted to be included in the cost of property, plant and equipment and intangible assets. Section 17 includes detailed requirements on which types of costs are capitalised. *[FRS 102.17.10-14]*. Section 25 – *Borrowing Costs* – permits an entity to either expense borrowing costs or to adopt a policy of capitalising borrowing costs directly attributable to the acquisition, construction or production of a qualifying asset (which must be applied consistently to a class of qualifying assets). Section 25's requirements are more detailed than the Regulations and specify the period for which borrowing costs can be capitalised, and how to determine the amounts capitalised. *[FRS 102.25.1-2D]*. See Chapter 20.

The cost of inventories includes all costs of purchase, costs of conversion (direct production costs and allocated variable and fixed production overheads) and other costs incurred in bringing the inventories to their present location and condition. *[FRS 102.13.5, 13.8]*. As noted above, the Regulations prohibit capitalisation of 'distribution costs' which are generally taken to mean costs of distribution to customers. Therefore, the costs of transporting goods to a warehouse or retail outlet for initial point of sale (which would be capitalised under FRS 102 as 'costs incurred in bringing the inventories to their present location and condition') would not fall within the meaning of this prohibition. FRS 102 permits use of the standard cost method, retail method or most recent purchase price provided the result approximates cost. The cost of inventories (other than those that are not ordinarily interchangeable or goods and services produced and segregated for specific projects – which are measured at their specifically identified individual costs) are measured using the FIFO or weighted average cost formula (LIFO is not permitted). The same cost formula must be used for all inventories having a similar nature and use to the entity. *[FRS 102.13.16-18]*.

9.1.2   *Depreciation and diminution of fixed assets*

Where a fixed asset has a limited useful economic life, its purchase price or production cost less its estimated residual value (if any) must be reduced by provisions for depreciation to write off that amount systematically over the period of the asset's useful economic life. *[1 Sch 18]*.

Where a fixed asset investment (item B.III in the balance sheet formats – see 4.6.4 above) has diminished in value, provisions for diminution in value *may* [emphasis added] be made and its carrying amount reduced accordingly. *[1 Sch 19(1)]*. Provisions for diminution in value *must* [emphasis added] be made in respect of any fixed asset which has diminished in value, if the reduction in value is expected to be permanent (whether or not the fixed asset has a limited useful life). *[1 Sch 19(2)]*.

Provisions for diminution not shown in the profit and loss account must be disclosed (either separately or in aggregate) in a note to the accounts. *[1 Sch 19(3)]*.

Where the reasons for which any provision (for diminution) was made have ceased to apply to any extent, the provision must be written back to the extent that it is no longer necessary. Any amounts written back which are not shown in the profit and loss account must be disclosed (either separately or in aggregate) in a note to the accounts. *[1 Sch 20]*.

9.1.2.A   FRS 102's requirements

The requirements for measuring cost in FRS 102 are consistent with the Regulations but more prescriptive. For example, Sections 17 and 18 contain detailed requirements on depreciation *[FRS 102.17.16-23]*. In addition, the Regulations only require a provision for diminution of a fixed asset where permanent, but Section 27 – *Impairment of Assets* – requires provisions for impairment of property, plant and equipment, investment property measured using the cost model, intangible assets and goodwill to be recognised when the carrying amount of the asset is not recoverable. *[FRS 102.27.5]*. Similarly, Sections 11 and 12 contain specific requirements for recognition of impairment of financial assets measured at cost or amortised cost, where there is objective evidence of impairment. *[FRS 102.11.21-11.26, 12.13]*.

9.1.3   Development costs

An amount may only be included as development costs in the balance sheet in 'special circumstances'. The reasons for capitalising the costs and the period over which the costs are being or will be written off must be disclosed in a note to the accounts. *[1 Sch 21]*.

Development costs shown as an asset are treated as a realised loss except where there are 'special circumstances' justifying the directors' decision not to treat these as a realised loss. TECH 02/10 clarifies that this would be the case where the costs are carried forward in accordance with applicable accounting standards. The note to the accounts referred to above states that the amount of the development costs shown as an asset is not to be treated as a realised loss, together with the circumstances relied upon to justify the directors' decision to that effect. *[s844, TECH 02/10, para. 2.38]*. See Chapter 14 at 3.5.2.

9.1.4   Goodwill

Goodwill capitalised as an asset must be reduced by provisions for depreciation so as to write off the goodwill systematically over a period chosen by the directors, which must not exceed its useful economic life. The period for write-off of the goodwill, together with the reasons for choosing that period must be disclosed in a note to the accounts. *[1 Sch 22]*.

FRS 102 requires amortisation of goodwill on a systematic basis over its finite useful life (which shall not exceed five years where the entity is unable to make a reliable estimate of the useful life). Section 27 is applied in recognising and measuring the impairment of goodwill. *[FRS 102.19.23(a)]*.

FRS 102's requirements to amortise goodwill are consistent with but more restrictive than the requirements of the Regulations. However, FRS 102's requirements on amortisation of goodwill are expected to be amended, effective for financial years beginning on or after 1 January 2016, to align with the Regulations following implementation of the new Accounting Directive (see Chapter 2 at 1.2.3.E).

9.2   Alternative accounting rules

Under the alternative accounting rules, assets are carried at a revalued amount (on one of the permitted bases set out in paragraph 32 of Schedule 1 to the Regulations – see 9.2.1 below).

FRS 102's requirements for revaluations of the following assets make use of the alternative accounting rules:

- property, plant and equipment carried at a revalued amount, being the fair value at the date of revaluation less any subsequent accumulated depreciation and subsequent accumulated impairment losses. The revaluation model must be applied to all items in the same class (i.e. having a similar nature, function or use in the business). *[FRS 102.17.15, 17.15B-F]*. See Chapter 13 at 3.6;

- intangible fixed assets carried at a revalued amount, being the fair value at the date of revaluation less any subsequent accumulated amortisation and subsequent accumulated impairment losses. The revaluation model must be applied to all items in the same class, and revaluations are only permitted provided that the fair value can be determined by reference to an active market. *[FRS 102.18.18, 18.18B-H]*. In practice, it is rare to meet the criteria for revaluation of an intangible fixed asset. See Chapter 14 at 3.4;

- investments in subsidiaries, associates and jointly controlled entities, where a policy of fair value through other comprehensive income is applied. *[FRS 102.9.26(b), 9.26A, 14.4(c), 15.9(c)]*. See Chapter 6 at 4.2, Chapter 10 and Chapter 11; and

- inventories held for distribution at no or nominal consideration are measured at cost adjusted, when applicable, for any loss of service potential. When distributed, the carrying mount of these inventories is recognised as an expense. *[FRS 102.13.4A, 13.20A]*. Such items might include items that might be distributed to beneficiaries by public benefit entities and items such as advertising and promotional material. As the items will be distributed at no or nominal cost, the net realisable value will usually be lower than the purchase price. Appendix IV to the standard notes that although the alternative accounting rules require measurement at current cost, for inventories held for distribution at no or nominal value, there is unlikely to be a significant difference between cost and current cost. *[FRS 102.A4.36-37]*.

Financial assets carried at fair value in accordance with Sections 11 and 12 or IAS 39 are measured using the fair value accounting rules rather than the alternative accounting rules. Where IFRS 9 is applied, and investments in equity instruments are carried at fair value through other comprehensive income *[IFRS 9.5.7.5]*, this would not appear to be permitted by the fair value accounting rules (since this differs from the accounting for available for sale financial assets under IAS 39, which is permitted under the fair value accounting rules). However, in our view, this accounting would be permitted under the alternative accounting rules for fixed asset investments.

9.2.1 Assets that may be revalued under the alternative accounting rules in the Regulations

Under the alternative accounting rules in the Regulations,

- tangible fixed assets may be included at market value determined as at the date of their last valuation or at current cost;

- fixed asset investments may be included either:

    - at a market value determined as at the date of their last valuation; or

    - at a value determined on a basis which appears to the directors to be appropriate to the company's circumstances (but in this latter case, particulars of the method of valuation adopted and of the reasons for adopting it must be disclosed in a note to the accounts); and

- intangible fixed assets (other than goodwill), current asset investments and stocks may be included at current cost. *[1 Sch 32]*.

9.2.1.A   FRS 102's requirements

FRS 102's requirements for the revaluation of property, plant and equipment and intangible assets at fair value are consistent with but more prescriptive than the alternative accounting rules.

Where investments in subsidiaries, associates and joint ventures are measured at fair value through other comprehensive income in separate or individual financial statements, a directors' valuation (that does not equate to fair value) may not be used. As noted at 9.2 above, other fixed asset or current asset investments included at fair value under FRS 102 make use of the fair value accounting rules.

Where investments in subsidiaries, associates and joint ventures are carried using the cost model in separate or individual financial statements under FRS 102, the previous GAAP carrying amount at the date of transition may be used as a deemed cost as at the date of transition. *[FRS 102.35.10(f)]*. Where this deemed cost contains a past revaluation subject to the alternative accounting rules, the requirements of the alternative accounting rules continue to apply.

FRS 102 does not permit use of the alternative accounting rules for inventory (with the minor exception for inventory held at distribution for nil or nominal value), which is carried at the lower of cost and estimated selling price less costs to complete and sell *[FRS 102.13.4]*. See 9.2 above.

9.2.2   Application of the depreciation and diminution rules under the alternative accounting rules

Where the alternative accounting rules are applied, the latest revalued amount (on any basis set out in paragraph 32 of Schedule 1 to the Regulations – see 9.2.1 above) is used in place of the purchase price or production cost or previous revaluation for the purposes of computing depreciation or provisions for diminution (or impairment) of the asset. *[1 Sch 33(1)]*. The Regulations refer to the provision for depreciation (or diminution) calculated using the latest revalued amount as the 'adjusted amount' and the provision for depreciation (and diminution) calculated using the historical cost accounting rules as the 'historical cost amount'. *[1 Sch 33(2)]*.

The Regulations allow a company to include under the relevant profit and loss account heading the amount of provision for depreciation for a revalued fixed asset based on historical cost, provided that the difference between the historical cost amount and the adjusted amount is shown separately in the profit and loss account or in a note to the accounts. *[1 Sch 33(3), FRS 15.Appendix 2.12]*. Appendix 4 to FRS 15 – *Tangible fixed assets* – notes, in respect of the equivalent paragraph 32(3) of Schedule 4 to the Companies Act 1985, that 'It is unclear whether the above-mentioned paragraph permits split depreciation. The Board therefore obtained a legal opinion on this issue. That opinion noted that the practical effect of the paragraph as drafted makes it arguable that the entirety of a given charge need not pass through the profit and loss account. However, the opinion went on to note the implications of the *Marleasing* decision. This case indicates that national courts of EU Member States are under a Community law obligation to interpret national law so that it conforms, so far as possible, with the underlying directive (in this case, the Fourth Directive). Articles 33.3 and 35.1(c)-(cc) of the Fourth Directive prohibit split depreciation'. *[FRS 15.Appendix 4.43-44]*. In any case, split depreciation is not permitted by FRS 102 and depreciation (based on the revalued amount) is charged to profit or loss (unless another section of the standard requires the depreciation to be recognised as part of the cost of an asset). *[FRS 102.17.17, 18.21]*.

The treatment of revaluations is discussed at 9.2.3 below, although the Regulations require permanent diminutions to be shown in the profit and loss account. *[1 Sch 19(2), 20(1)]*.

9.2.3   Revaluation reserve

When an asset is revalued under the alternative accounting rules, the Regulations require that the profit or loss arising from that determination (after allowing, where appropriate, for any provisions for depreciation or diminution in value made otherwise than by reference to the value so determined and any adjustments of any such provision made in light of that determination) must be credited or (as the case may be) debited to a separate revaluation reserve. *[1 Sch 35(1)]*. In effect, this means that the revaluation establishes a new 'base cost' for the asset and the revaluation gain or loss is based on the difference between the revalued amount and the previous carrying amount of the asset.

Under the alternative accounting rules, the initial recognition of the asset includes any expenses incidental to its acquisition. *[FRS 102.A4.34, 1 Sch 27, 35(1)]*.

The balance sheet formats include a line item for 'revaluation reserve' (see 4.6.12 above). The revaluation reserve must be reported in this position but there is no requirement that this name is used. *[1 Sch formats, 1 Sch 35(2)]*.

While the Regulations would permit temporary valuation deficits below historical cost to be charged to the revaluation reserve, even if this results in a negative reserve, FRS 102 is more prescriptive. The standard requires that a revaluation increase is recognised in other comprehensive income and accumulated in equity, except where a revaluation increase is recognised in profit or loss to the extent it reverses a revaluation decrease of the same asset previously recognised in profit or loss. A revaluation decrease is recognised in other comprehensive income to the extent of any previously recognised revaluation increase accumulated in equity in respect of that asset, with any excess recognised in profit or loss. *[FRS 102.17.15E-F, 18.18G-H]*. FRS 102's requirements, in effect, regards a downward revaluation that reverses previously recognised revaluation increases accumulated in equity as temporary in nature but where a downward revaluation exceeds the previously recognised revaluation increases accumulated in equity, the excess is recognised in profit or loss (as if permanent in nature).

The statutory revaluation reserve can be applied as follows:

- an amount may be transferred from the revaluation reserve to the profit and loss account, if the amount was previously charged to the profit and loss account or represents a realised profit. *[1 Sch 35(3)(a)]*

  - FRS 102's accounting for a revaluation increase that reverses a revaluation decrease of the same asset previously recognised in profit and loss is consistent with this.

  - Where depreciation or an impairment has been charged based on a revalued amount (exceeding historical cost), the excess depreciation (i.e. the depreciation based on the revalued amount less that which would have been charged based on historical cost) may be debited from the revaluation reserve to the profit and loss account reserve (as a reserves transfer in equity).

  - On sale of a revalued fixed asset was sold, the amount in the revaluation reserve, where realised on the sale, could be transferred to the profit and loss account reserve (as a reserves transfer in equity).

- an amount may be transferred from the revaluation reserve on capitalisation. *[1 Sch 35(3)(b)]*. Capitalisation means applying an amount to the credit of the revaluation reserve in wholly or partly paying up unissued shares in the company to be allotted to the members of the company as fully or partly paid share, i.e. a bonus issue of shares. *[1 Sch 35(4)]*; and

- an amount may be transferred to or from the revaluation reserve in respect of the taxation relating to any profit or loss credited or debited to the reserve. The treatment for taxation purposes of amounts credited or debited to the revaluation reserve must be disclosed in a note to the accounts. *[1 Sch 35(3)(c),35(6)]*.

The revaluation reserve must be reduced to the extent that the amounts transferred to it are no longer necessary for the purposes of the valuation method used and the revaluation reserve must not be reduced except as noted above. *[1 Sch 35(3), (5)]*. Although the word 'reduced' is ambiguous in the context of a reserve that may contain either debit or credit balances, the intention is to prevent companies from charging costs, e.g. valuation fees, directly to the reserve or from releasing credits to the profit and loss account, except in ways permitted by the Regulations. These provisions would also permit a company changing policy from revaluation to cost to write back the reduction in carrying value against any credit balance in the revaluation reserve.

The revaluation reserve may also be reduced, to the extent permitted by the Companies Act 2006, when a private limited company makes a payment out of capital under Chapter 5 of Part 18 of the Companies Act 2006. *[s734].*

Care needs to be taken on transition to identify whether a statutory revaluation reserve must be created or maintained. Where an asset is carried at a deemed cost (based on a previous GAAP revaluation which would include historic revaluations grandfathered as deemed cost on transition to FRS 15, or fair value at the date of transition), this makes use of the alternative accounting rules. This is discussed in Chapter 30 at 3.5.3 and 5.5.

9.2.4 *Disclosures*

Where the alternative accounting rules are used for any items shown in the accounts, the items affected and the basis of valuation adopted must be disclosed in a note to the accounts. For each balance sheet item affected (except stocks), either the comparable amounts determined using the historical cost accounting rules or the differences between those amounts and the amounts actually shown in the balance sheet for that item must be shown separately in the balance sheet or in a note to the accounts.

The comparable amounts required to be disclosed are: *[1 Sch 34]*

- the aggregate amount (i.e. aggregate cost) which would be required to be shown for that balance sheet item if the amounts to be included in respect of all the assets covered by that item were determined using the historical cost accounting rules; and

- the aggregate amount of the cumulative provisions for depreciation or diminution in value which would be permitted or required in determining those amounts according to the historical cost accounting rules.

Where any fixed assets (other than listed investments) are included at a valuation under the alternative accounting rules, the following information is required to be disclosed in the accounts or notes to the accounts: *[1 Sch 52]*

- the years (so far as they are known to the directors) in which the assets were severally valued and the several values; and

- where the assets have been valued during the financial year,

  - the names of the persons who valued them or particulars of their qualifications for doing so; and

  - the bases of valuations used by them.

9.3   Fair value accounting rules – financial instruments

Under FRS 102, where an entity carries financial assets or financial liabilities at fair value, or where a financial instrument is used in hedge accounting, this generally makes use of the fair value accounting rules. This is the case whatever the policy choice the entity applies to the recognition and measurement of financial instruments i.e. Sections 11 and 12, IAS 39 or IFRS 9 (and IAS 39, as amended by IFRS 9).

The fair value accounting rules also apply to certain commodity-based contracts which are required to be accounted for as financial instruments under accounting standards. References to 'derivatives' in the fair value accounting rules (in Schedule 1 to the Regulations) include commodity-based contracts that give either contracting party the right to settle in cash or in some other financial instrument, except where such contracts: *[10 Sch 2]*

- were entered into for the purpose of, and continue to meet the company's expected purchase, sale or usage requirements;

- were designated for such purpose at their inception; and

- are expected to be settled by delivery of the commodity.

Exceptions to this general rule (that instead make use of the alternative accounting rules – see 9.2 above) include:

- where investments in subsidiaries, associates and jointly controlled entities are carried at fair value through other comprehensive income in individual or separate financial statements; *[FRS 102.9.9B(a), 9.26(c), 14.4(d), 14.4B, 15.9(d), 15.9B]* and

- where IFRS 9 is applied, in relation to investments in equity instruments carried at fair value through other comprehensive income. *[IFRS 9.5.7.5]*.

Where a financial liability (other than a loan commitment or financial guarantee contract) is designated at fair value through profit and loss under IFRS 9, fair value changes attributable to changes in own credit risk are presented in other comprehensive income, unless that treatment would create or enlarge an accounting mismatch in profit or loss. *[IFRS 9.5.7.7-5.7.9]*. It is unclear how such accounting fits in with the accounting models included in the Regulations.

9.3.1   *Which financial instruments may be held at fair value under the Regulations?*

Where the fair value accounting rules are applied, financial instruments (including derivatives) may be included at fair value, only where this can be determined reliably. *[1 Sch 36(1), (5)]*.

The fair value of a financial instrument is determined as follows: *[1 Sch 37, Regulations]*

(a)   if a reliable market can readily be identified for the financial instrument, by reference to its market value;

(b)   if a reliable market cannot readily be identified for the financial instrument but can be identified for its components of a similar instrument, by reference to the market value of its components or of the similar instrument; or

(c)   if neither (a) nor (b) apply, a value resulting from generally accepted valuation models and techniques that must ensure a reasonable approximation of the market value.

Chapter 4

However, the following types of financial instrument are prohibited from being carried at fair value unless they meet the requirements of paragraph 36(4) of Schedule 1 to the Regulations (see below): *[1 Sch 36]*

- financial liabilities that are neither held as part of a trading portfolio nor are derivatives;
- financial instruments (other than derivatives) held to maturity;
- loans and receivables originated by the company and not held for trading purposes;
- interests in subsidiary undertakings (as defined in section 1162 of the Companies Act 2006 – see Chapter 2 at 3.1.2), associated undertakings (as defined in paragraph 19 of Schedule 6 to the Regulations) and joint ventures (as defined in paragraph 18 of Schedule 6 to the Regulations);
- equity instruments issued by the company;
- contracts for contingent consideration in a business combination; and
- other financial instruments with such special characteristics that the instruments, according to generally accepted accounting principles or practice should be accounted for differently from other financial instruments.

Paragraph 36(4) states that 'Financial instruments that, under international accounting standards adopted by the European Commission on or before 5th September 2006 in accordance with the IAS Regulation, may be included in accounts at fair value, may be so included, provided that the disclosures required by such accounting standards are made.' *[1 Sch 36(4)]*. These disclosures have been incorporated in Section 11 – *Basic Financial Instruments* – some apply to all financial instruments held at fair value and others to financial instruments that are not held as part of a trading portfolio and are not derivatives. FRS 102, therefore, requires the disclosures to be given *in respect of those financial instruments held at fair value in accordance with paragraph 36(4)* even where the reduced disclosure framework is applied in the individual financial statements of a qualifying entity. *[FRS 102.1.8, A4.13]*. In our view, this only applies where the entity is subject to the UK statutory requirements, not to all FRS 102 reporters.

It is important to ensure that the use of fair value accounting is indeed permitted by EU-adopted IFRS. This may become more of an issue where IFRS 9 is applied, since its accounting models diverge from those applying under IAS 39. For example, fair valuing investments in equity instruments through other comprehensive income would not have been permitted by EU-adopted IFRS on or before 5th September 2006. However, the new Accounting Directive includes a Member State option to allow the use of fair value for the instruments above where this treatment would be in conformity with EU-adopted IFRS (rather than EU-adopted IFRS on or before 5th September 2006). *[Directive 2013/34/EU, Article 8.6]*.

Situations in which a FRS 102 reporter would be permitted to carry financial instruments at fair value by paragraph 36(4), subject to making the Section 11 disclosures in respect of such financial instruments, are discussed at Chapter 2 at 3.4.

9.3.2   *Accounting for changes in fair value of financial instruments*

Notwithstanding the general requirement that only realised profits are included in the profit and loss account (from paragraph 13 of Schedule 1 to the Regulations), a change in the value of a financial instrument must be included in the profit and loss account except where:

(a)   the financial instrument accounted for is a hedging instrument under a hedge accounting system that allows some or all of the change in value not to be shown in the profit and loss account (see 9.3.3 below); or

(b)   the change in value relates to an exchange difference arising on a monetary item that forms part of a company's net investment in a foreign entity; or

(c)   the financial instrument is an available for sale financial asset (and is not a derivative). This treatment is permitted only where IAS 39 is applied by a FRS 102 reporter.

In respect of (a) and (b) above, the amount of the change in value must be credited (or as the case may be) debited from a separate reserve (the fair value reserve). In respect of (c) above, the amount of the change in value may be credited (or as the case may be) debited from a separate reserve (the fair value reserve). *[1 Sch 40]*

The fair value reserve must be adjusted to the extent that the amounts shown in it are no longer necessary. The treatment for taxation purposes of amounts credited to or debited to the fair value reserve must be disclosed in a note to the accounts. *[1 Sch 41]*.

FRS 102 requires that exchange differences arising on a monetary item that in substance forms part of a company's net investment in a foreign entity (which may include long-term receivables or loans, but not trade receivables or payables) are recognised in other comprehensive income (and accumulated in equity) in the financial statements that include the foreign operation and the reporting entity (e.g. consolidated financial statements). Such items are recognised in profit or loss in the separate financial statements of the reporting entity or the individual financial statements of the foreign operation, as appropriate. *[FRS 102.30.12-13]*. While not explicitly stated, it seems that (b) is intended to address accounts that include the foreign operation and the reporting entity.

9.3.3   *Hedge accounting*

9.3.3.A   *Fair value hedge accounting*

A company may include any assets and liabilities, or identified portions of such assets or liabilities, that qualify as hedged items under a fair value hedge accounting system at the amount required under that system. *[1 Sch 38]*.

The fair value accounting rules, therefore, permit the adjustments made to hedged items under fair value hedge accounting under IAS 39, IFRS 9 and Section 12 – *Other Financial Instruments Issues*. See Chapter 8 at 7 and EY International GAAP 2015 Chapters 50 and 51.

9.3.3.B   Cash flow hedge and net investment hedge accounting

Where the financial instrument accounted for is a hedging instrument under a hedge accounting system that allows some or all of the change in value not to be shown in the profit and loss account, the amount of the change in value must be credited to (or as the case may be) debited from a separate reserve ('the fair value reserve'). *[1 Sch 40(3)].*

The fair value reserve must be adjusted to the extent that the amounts shown in it are no longer necessary for the purposes of paragraph 40(3) (or 40(4)) of Schedule 1 to the Regulations. *[1 Sch 41].*

The fair value accounting rules, therefore, support hedge accounting of a net investment of a foreign operation and cash flow hedge accounting under IAS 39, IFRS 9 and Section 12. Under these forms of hedge accounting, the entity recognises in other comprehensive income only the effective portion of the hedge and amounts accumulated in equity are reclassified in profit or loss, where required by Section 12, IAS 39 or IFRS 9 for cash flow hedge accounting. FRS 102 does not permit reclassification of exchange differences accumulated in equity arising from hedges of a net investment of a foreign operation. See Chapter 8 at 7 and EY International GAAP 2015 Chapters 50 and 51.

9.3.4   Disclosures required by the Regulations in Companies Act accounts

The following disclosures are required in Companies Act accounts (as a note to the accounts, where not shown in the accounts) where financial instruments have been valued in accordance with paragraph 36 (i.e. at fair value) or paragraph 38 (i.e. adjustments to hedged items under a fair value hedge accounting system) of Schedule 1 to the Regulations: *[1 Sch 55]*

- the significant assumptions underlying the valuation models and techniques used where the fair value of the instruments has been determined in accordance with paragraph 37(4);

- for each category of financial instrument, the fair value of the instruments in that category and the changes in value –

  - included in the profit and loss account, or

  - credited to or (as the case may be) debited from the fair value reserve

  in respect of these instruments;

- for each class of derivatives, the extent and nature of the instruments, including significant terms and conditions that may affect the amount, timing and certainty of future cash flows; and

- where any amount is transferred to or from the fair value reserve during the financial year, there must be stated in tabular form –

  - the amount of the reserve as at the date of the beginning of the financial year and as at the balance sheet date respectively;

  - the amount transferred to or from the reserve during that year; and

  - the source and application respectively of the amounts so transferred.

Where the company has derivatives that it has not included at fair value, there must also be stated for each class of derivatives, the fair value of the derivatives in that class (if such a value can be determined in accordance with paragraph 37 – see 9.3.1 above) and the extent and nature of the derivatives. *[1 Sch 56]*. This situation should rarely arise under FRS 102 since the standard requires derivatives to be recorded at fair value.

If the company has financial fixed assets that could be included at fair value under paragraph 36 (see 9.3.1 above) and the amount at which those items are included in the accounts is in excess of their fair value, and the company has not made provision for diminution in value of those assets in accordance with paragraph 19(1) of Schedule 1 to the Regulations (see 9.1.2 above), there must also be stated:

- the amount at which either the individual assets or appropriate groupings of those individual assets are included in the company's accounts;

- the fair value of those assets or groupings; and

- the reasons for not making a provision for diminution in value of those assets, including the nature of the evidence that provides the basis for the belief that the amount at which they are stated in the accounts will be recovered. *[1 Sch 57]*.

9.4 Investment properties and living animals and plants

9.4.1 *Investment property and living animals and plants – use of fair value under the Regulations*

The fair value accounting rules allow investment property to be included at fair value, where this would be permitted under EU-adopted IFRS and provided that all such investment property is so included where its fair value can reliably be determined. Similarly, living animals and plants may be included at fair value, where this would be permitted under EU-adopted IFRS and provided that all such living animals and plants are so included where their fair value can reliably be determined. Fair value, for these purposes, is as determined in accordance with relevant EU-adopted IFRS. *[1 Sch 39]*.

Notwithstanding paragraph 13 of Schedule 1 to the Regulations (the general requirement that only realised profits are included in the profit and loss account), a change in the value of the investment property or living animal or plant must be included in the profit and loss account. *[1 Sch 40(1), (2)]*.

The requirements of FRS 102 for investment property (see 9.4.2 below) and biological assets (including agricultural produce) (see 9.4.3 below) make use of the fair value accounting rules described above. This differs from previous UK GAAP, where investment property was carried at open market value under SSAP 19 using the alternative accounting rules. *[SSAP 19.11]*. No accounting standard specifically addressed accounting for biological assets under previous UK GAAP but these would generally have been measured using the cost model.

Chapter 4

9.4.2   *Requirements of FRS 102 – investment property*

FRS 102 requires that investment property (and property subject to an operating lease, that would otherwise meet the definition of investment property, that an entity elects to treat as investment property) whose fair value can be measured reliably without undue cost or effort is measured at fair value at each reporting date with changes in fair value recognised in profit or loss. All other investment property is accounted for as property, plant and equipment using the cost model in Section 17. *[FRS 102.16.2-3, 7].*

While IAS 40 – *Investment Property* – permits a choice of the cost and fair value model (except that an entity must use the fair value model where it elects to treat a property subject to an operating lease as investment property), FRS 102's requirements do not conflict with the fair value accounting rules because in the situations where the fair value model is applied under FRS 102, this would also be permitted under IFRSs.

Fair value is defined in FRS 102 as 'the amount for which an asset could be exchanged, a liability settled, or an equity instrument granted could be exchanged, between knowledgeable, willing parties in an arm's length transaction. In the absence of any specific guidance provided in the relevant section of this FRS, the guidance in paragraphs 11.27 to 11.32 shall be used in determining fair value.' *[FRS 102 Appendix I, 16.7].* The Regulations could imply that fair value should be determined in accordance with EU-adopted IFRS (currently IFRS 13 – *Fair Value Measurement*). While FRS 102 has a slightly different definition of fair value, this has not been highlighted as a potential conflict by the FRC and in many circumstances, FRS 102's requirements are likely to give a fair value materially consistent with IFRS 13. We consider that the more specific guidance in FRS 102 should be referred to in determining fair value under the standard.

9.4.3   *Requirements of FRS 102 – biological assets and agricultural produce*

FRS 102's requirements for the fair value model and the interaction with the fair value accounting rules are discussed at Chapter 29 at 2.

IAS 41 – *Agriculture* – would require use of the fair value model (unless fair value could not be determined reliably) whereas FRS 102 offers a policy choice of the fair value and cost model. FRS 102's requirements do not conflict with the fair value accounting rules because where the fair value model is used under FRS 102, this would also be permitted under EU-adopted IFRS. There is, however, potential for fair value as determined under FRS 102 to differ from fair value as determined under IFRS 13 (see discussion at 9.4.2 above).

9.4.4   *Disclosures required by the Regulations in Companies Act accounts*

Where the amounts included in the accounts in respect of investment property or living animals and plants have been determined using the fair value accounting rules, the balance sheet items affected and the basis of valuation adopted in the case of each such item must be disclosed in the accounts or a note to the accounts. *[1 Sch 58(1), (2)].*

In the case of investment property, for each balance sheet item affected, the comparable amounts determined according to the historical cost accounting rules or the differences between those comparable amounts and the amounts actually shown in the balance sheet in respect of that item must be disclosed either separately in the balance sheet or in a note to the accounts. *[1 Sch 58(3)-(4)].* This is a similar disclosure to that required where an item is valued subject to the alternative accounting rules and is explained further at 9.2.4 above.

9.5   Presentation

While FRS 102 refers to a statement of financial position and a single statement of comprehensive income (or separate income statement and separate statement of comprehensive income), statement of changes in equity and statement of cash flows, it makes clear that an entity may use other titles for the financial statements so long as they are not misleading. *[FRS 102.3.17, 3.22].* Therefore, FRS 102 reporters may continue to refer to a balance sheet and profit and loss account, if they wish to.

FRS 102 financial statements prepared by a UK company are Companies Act accounts. Therefore, FRS 102 requires that the statement of financial position and the items to be included in a profit and loss account (whether or not a single statement of comprehensive income is presented, or an income statement ('profit and loss account' under the Companies Act 2006) and a statement of comprehensive income) are presented in accordance with the formats in the applicable schedule of the Regulations (or for an LLP, the LLP Regulations). *[FRS 102.4.2, 5.5].* The balance sheet and profit and loss account formats are discussed further at 4 and 5 above.

As noted at 5.1 above, a parent company that prepares consolidated financial statements but applies FRS 102 in its individual financial statements can also use the exemption in section 408 of the Companies Act 2006 from presenting a profit and loss account and related notes in the individual financial statements. *[FRS 102.A4.15].* This is the case whether or not it applies FRS 102's reduced disclosure framework.

Chapter 4

9.6   Disclosure

FRS 102 financial statements prepared by a UK company are Companies Act accounts and are subject to disclosures required by the Regulations as well as other disclosures required by the Companies Act 2006 or other related regulations. These disclosures are in addition to those required by FRS 102. See Chapter 1 at 6.7 for information on statutory disclosure requirements.

See 7.6 to 7.8 above for the notes required on staff costs, off balance sheet arrangements and directors' advances, credits and guarantees respectively. The disclosure requirements for financial instruments held at fair value subject to paragraph 36(4) of Schedule 1 to the Regulations are addressed at 9.3.1 above. These have the effect that the applicable disclosure requirements in Section 11 of the standard must be given in relation to those financial instruments (even if the reduced disclosure framework is applied in the individual accounts of a qualifying entity).

10   SUMMARY OF DIFFERENCES

This Appendix refers to the Regulations in the context of the columns addressing FRS 102 and previous UK GAAP. The Regulations apply only to statutory accounts prepared by UK companies (not applying the small companies regime or micro-entity provisions). For simplicity, the references to the Regulations below in these two columns assume that the entity is a UK company preparing its financial statements in accordance with Schedule 1 to the Regulations. Other UK companies and certain other entities are subject to similar statutory requirements.

All relevant schedules in the Regulations apply to Companies Act accounts (such as FRS 102 financial statements and financial statements prepared under previous UK GAAP). Only certain schedules in the Regulations apply to IAS accounts, i.e. statutory accounts prepared by UK companies in accordance with EU-adopted IFRS. Therefore, many of the requirements in the Regulations referred to in the FRS 102 and previous UK GAAP columns do not apply to IAS accounts. Except for the application of company law formats in the profit and loss account and balance sheet (explained in the table), the requirements of the Regulations only apply to entities subject to these statutory requirements.

	FRS 102	*Previous UK GAAP*	*IFRS*
Complete set of financial statements	A complete set of financial statements (see 3.5 above) includes a: • statement of financial position, • statement of comprehensive income (either as a single statement or as a separate income statement and statement of comprehensive income), • statement of cash flows (unless exempt), • statement of changes in equity, and • related notes. In certain circumstances, a statement of income and retained earnings can be presented as an alternative to a statement of changes in equity and a statement of comprehensive income. Comparatives must be presented. FRS 102 includes guidance on narrative as well as numerical information. FRS 102 permits the use of other titles – such as balance sheet or profit and loss account for the primary statements – as long as they are not misleading.	A complete set of financial statements includes a: • balance sheet, • profit and loss account • statement of recognised gains and losses, • cash flow statement (unless exempt), • reconciliation of movements in shareholders' funds (which may be presented as a primary statement or note); and • related notes. Entities with revalued assets give a statement of historical profits (where the historical cost profit is materially different to reported profit). Comparatives must be presented but there is no guidance on narrative information.	IFRS has the same content for a complete set of financial statements as FRS 102. There is more extensive guidance on comparatives. However, there are no exemptions from presenting a cash flow statement, and a statement of income and retained earnings is not available as an alternative primary statement.

Chapter 4

	FRS 102	*Previous UK GAAP*	*IFRS*
Application of company law formats for profit and loss account and balance sheet	The income statement (or profit and loss section of statement of comprehensive income) and statement of financial position of all entities must comply with the profit and loss account and balance sheet formats set out in the Regulations except to the extent that these requirements are not permitted by any statutory framework under which such entities report. See 4.1 and 5.5 above. Additional line items, headings and subtotals must be presented when relevant to an understanding of the financial position or financial performance (see 5.7.2 above).	The profit and loss account and balance sheet formats in the Regulations (or other applicable regulations) apply to UK companies (and other entities) subject to these statutory requirements. However, some entities (that are not subject to these requirements) preparing UK GAAP accounts also choose to apply these formats.	The company law formats in the Regulations are not applicable to financial statements prepared in accordance with IFRSs (or EU-adopted IFRSs). The statement of financial position and statement of comprehensive income follow the requirements of IAS 1 which sets out minimum line items. IAS 1 requires additional line items, headings and subtotals but provides more flexibility to amend its formats compared to those in FRS 102 (which follow the Regulations).
Definition of discontinued operations	Discontinued operations (see 5.8 above) are defined as a component of an entity that has been disposed of and: • represented a separate major line of business or geographical area of operations, or • was part of a single coordinated plan to dispose of a separate major line of business or geographical area of operations; or • was a subsidiary acquired exclusively with a view to resale. FRS 102 requires that the operations have been disposed of by the reporting date. There is no further guidance on the definition of discontinued operations.	FRS 3's definition of discontinued operation differs significantly to that in FRS 102. In particular, the sale or termination must be completed before the earlier of three months after the commencement of the subsequent period and the date of approval of the financial statements.	IFRS 5 has the same definition of discontinued operation as FRS 102, except that the definition refers to a component of an entity that either has been disposed of or is classified as held for sale. IFRS 5 includes extensive guidance on the definition. It is explicit that discontinued operations include sales of operations leading to loss of control, operations held for distribution (or distributed) and abandoned operations (in the period of abandonment).

Presentation of discontinued operations	FRS 102 requires a columnar line-by-line analysis of continuing, discontinued and total operations presented on the face of the statement of comprehensive income (or separate income statement) down to an amount that comprises the total of post-tax profit or loss of discontinued operations and the post-tax gain or loss attributed to the impairment or on the disposal of the assets or disposal group(s) comprising the discontinued operation. See 5.8.4 above.	FRS 3 requires the line items from turnover to operating profit and the non-operating exceptional items (see below) to be analysed between continuing (separately disclosing acquisitions) and discontinued operations. This is not required to be a columnar analysis. Only the analyses of turnover and operating profit (and of each of the non-operating exceptional items) are required on the face of the profit and loss account; the line items in between turnover and operating profit can be presented in the notes. An analysis of interest and tax is not required, but may be provided with the basis of allocation disclosed.	IFRS permits a one line presentation of discontinued operations comprising the total of post-tax profit or loss of discontinued operations and the post-tax gain or loss attributed to the impairment or on the disposal of the assets or disposal group(s). Additional analysis of this subtotal is required in the notes.
Operating profit subtotal	An operating profit subtotal is not required but FRS 102 includes guidance, where operating profit is presented. See 5.7.3 above.	FRS 3 requires an operating profit subtotal to be presented and specifies three categories of exceptional items reported outside operating profit. See 'Exceptional items' below.	Like FRS 102, IAS 1 does not require an operating subtotal to be presented and its basis of conclusions includes similar guidance to FRS 102 on operating profit, where this subtotal is presented.

Chapter 4

	FRS 102	*Previous UK GAAP*	*IFRS*
Exceptional items	FRS 102 requires separate disclosure of the nature and amount of material items included in total comprehensive income (and separate income statement, if presented). FRS 102 does not use the term 'exceptional items' (although the term is used in the Regulations). Like other profit and loss account items, exceptional items should be included in the applicable format heading. Additional line items, headings and subtotals must be presented when relevant to an understanding of the financial position or financial performance. FRS 102 does not require presentation of certain exceptional items below operating profit. See 5.7.5 above.	FRS 3 defines exceptional items, distinguishing between operating exceptional items (which must be presented in the appropriate format headings) and attributed to continuing and discontinued operations as appropriate and non-operating exceptional items. Exceptional items should be disclosed (and described) in a note or where such prominence is necessary to give a true and fair view, presented on the face of the profit and loss account. FRS 3 prescribes three categories of exceptional items to be reported below operating profit on the face of the profit and loss account.	IAS 1 has the same requirements as FRS 102 (although the requirements of the Regulations do not apply).
Extraordinary items	FRS 102 (and the Regulations) include the concept of an extraordinary item but such items are not expected to occur in practice. The concept of an extraordinary item will be withdrawn following implementation in the UK of the new Accounting Directive. See 5.7.6 above.	FRS 3 has the same requirements as FRS 102.	IAS 1 does not have a concept of an extraordinary item.

Current and fixed assets and creditors: amounts falling due within and after more than one year	The formats in Schedule 1 to the Regulations (followed under FRS 102) distinguish between current and fixed assets. Fixed assets are defined as assets of a company which are intended for use on a continuing basis in the company's activities, and current assets are assets not intended for such use. Current assets include debtors, even if these include items expected to be realised after more than one year. The distinction between current and fixed assets is not the same as that between current and non-current assets in IAS 1. FRS 102 requires disclosure of the amounts of debtors due after more than one year on the face of the statement of financial position where the amounts are so material in the context of net current assets, that the financial statements may otherwise be misinterpreted. The analysis of amounts due within and after more than one year must be presented for each line item in debtors in the notes (if not on the face of the balance sheet). See 4.3 above.	FRS 3 has the same requirements as FRS 102. UK companies preparing statutory accounts must follow the formats in the Regulations (and some entities not subject to these statutory requirements applying previous UK GAAP follow the same formats). UITF 4 has the same requirements on disclosure of debtors due after more than one year on the face of the balance sheet as FRS 102.	IAS 1 distinguishes between current assets (defined) and non-current assets (the residual), which are separate classifications on the statement of financial position. A presentation based on liquidity can be used where it provides reliable and more relevant information. Line items containing amounts falling due within and after more than one year must be separately analysed in the notes.

Chapter 4

	FRS 102	*Previous UK GAAP*	*IFRS*
Creditors: amounts falling due within and after more than one year	The formats in the Regulations distinguish between Creditors: amounts falling due within one year and Creditors: amounts falling due after more than one year. This differs from the distinction between current and non-current liabilities in IAS 1. For example, under IAS 1, an item which is not due for settlement within 12 months is reported as a current liability if the entity expects to settle it in its operating cycle. See 4.4 above.	UK companies preparing statutory accounts also follow the formats in the Regulations.	IAS 1 distinguishes between current liabilities (defined) and non-current liabilities (the residual), which are separate classifications on the statement of financial position. IAS 1 has detailed guidance on when a financial liability should be classified as current or non-current.
Provisions	The balance sheet formats in the Regulations have a single heading 'provisions for liabilities'. See 4.6.11 above.	UK companies preparing statutory accounts also follow the formats in the Regulations.	IAS 1 requires current and non-current provisions to be shown as separate line items.
Deferred tax	Deferred tax is shown as a debtor or a provision under the balance sheet formats in the Regulations. See 4.6.14 above.	UK companies preparing statutory accounts also follow the formats in the Regulations.	IAS 1 requires deferred tax to be shown as a non-current asset or non-current liability.
Retirement benefits	The presentation of assets and liabilities under defined benefit schemes is not addressed by FRS 102. However, these would generally be presented as a debtor or provision under the Regulations. An alternative is to apply the presentation used in FRS 17 (but not net of deferred tax). See 4.6.16 above.	FRS 17 specifies that assets and liabilities under defined benefit schemes (net of deferred tax) must be shown separately as a line item below all other net assets.	IFRS does not require assets and liabilities under defined benefit schemes to be analysed between current and non-current.

Assets and disposal groups held for sale	FRS 102 does not require separate presentation of assets and disposal groups held for sale. Presentation of the assets and liabilities of disposal groups as two line items (as required by IFRSs) would not comply with the balance sheet formats in the Regulations as it would aggregate various line items. See 4.6.15 above. FRS 102 requires disclosures where, at the reporting date, an entity has a binding sale agreement for a major disposal of assets or a disposal group (see 4.8 above).	Like FRS 102, previous UK GAAP includes no requirements to present assets and disposal groups held for sale separately. UK companies preparing statutory accounts also follow the formats in the Regulations. Previous UK GAAP does not include the same disclosure as FRS 102 on a binding sale agreement for a major disposal of assets or a disposal group.	IAS 1 requires separate presentation in the statement of financial position of: • non-current assets and assets of disposal groups classified as held for sale; and • liabilities of disposal groups classified as held for sale Additional information is required in the notes.
Items to be reported in other comprehensive income	Items reported in other comprehensive income include *inter alia*: • revaluations of property, plant and equipment, • revaluations of investments in subsidiaries, associates and jointly controlled entities (at fair value through other comprehensive income; • remeasurement gains and losses on defined benefit schemes, • exchange gains and losses on retranslation of foreign operations, • cash flow hedges and net investment hedges. There are further categories of other comprehensive income where IAS 39 or IFRS 9 is applied. The Regulations also require that only realised	Items reported in the statement of total recognised gains and losses differ to FRS 102 due principally to different accounting requirements for financial instruments.	Items reported in other comprehensive income may differ to FRS 102 (where sections 11 and 12 are applied) due principally to different accounting requirements in IFRSs for financial instruments. The items must be grouped between items that may be reclassified to profit and loss in a subsequent period, and items that may be reclassified subsequently to profit and loss. The requirements of the Regulations on realised profits do not apply.

Chapter 4

	FRS 102	Previous UK GAAP	IFRS
Items to be reported in other comprehensive income *(continued)*	profits are included in profit and loss (except for fair value movements in profit and loss, where the fair value accounting rules are applied). See 5.2 above.		
Statement of changes in equity (SOCIE) and Statement of Income and Retained Earnings	The SOCIE is a primary statement. Where the only movements in equity arise from profit or loss, dividends, corrections of errors or changes in accounting policy, a statement of income and retained earnings can be presented instead of the statement of changes in equity and a statement of comprehensive income. The statement of changes in equity can be combined with the analysis of movements in reserves required by the Regulations. See 6 above.	A reconciliation of shareholders' funds is presented as a primary statement or note. It can be presented in total (rather than for each component of equity). However, the Regulations require an analysis of movements in reserves (for the current period only).	IAS 1 has the same requirements as FRS 102 except that there is no alternative to present a statement of income and retained earnings. While the analysis of the reserves in the Regulations is not required, similar information is presented in the SOCIE.
Presentation of non-controlling interest in consolidated financial statements	FRS 102 requires presentation of non-controlling interest as a separate component of equity in the consolidated statement of financial position. The Regulations require presentation of the amount of capital and reserves attributable to shares in subsidiary undertakings but give flexibility over the heading used. This amount (which corresponds to minority interest under previous UK GAAP) will usually be the same as non-controlling interest under FRS 102. See 4.5 above.	FRS 2 – *Accounting for subsidiary undertakings* – and the Regulations require presentation of minority interest in the consolidated balance sheet. In practice, some UK GAAP financial statements present minority interest as a line item after consolidated profit and consolidated net assets, rather than as an appropriation of consolidated profit or as a component of equity. Others use a presentation where minority interest is a component of equity.	IAS 1 has the same presentational requirement for non-controlling interest as FRS 102. The requirements of the Regulations do not apply.

Presentation of associates and jointly controlled entities	The following items are shown as a single line (i.e. combined for associates and jointly controlled entities) in the respective financial statements: • Investments in associates and jointly controlled entities; • their share of profits or losses; and • their share of other comprehensive income are shown as a single line item However, the Regulations do not require presentation of investments in associates and jointly controlled entities on the face of the statement of financial position so this analysis can be relegated to the notes. FRS 102 requires separate disclosure for associates and jointly controlled entities in the notes. See 4.6.4.B and 5.6.5 above.	Previous UK GAAP requires • investments in associates (using the equity method) and joint ventures (using the gross equity method) to be presented separately on the face of the balance sheet; and • additional analysis of the group's share of profits (or losses) of associates and, separately, joint ventures on the face of the consolidated profit and loss account, i.e. not a one line presentation. The gross equity method requires disclosure of the group's share of joint ventures' turnover on the face of the profit and loss account, and its share of the gross assets and liabilities of joint ventures on the face of the consolidated balance sheet.	IAS 1's presentational requirements for investments in associates and joint ventures are similar to those for investments in associates and jointly controlled entities to FRS 102
Prior year adjustments	Prior year adjustments are required for retrospective correction for material errors, changes in accounting policies and reclassifications of items. The adjustment is shown as an item in the statement of changes in equity (or where presented, statement of income and retained earnings). See 3.6.2 and 6 above.	FRS 3's requirements on prior year adjustments are the same as FRS 102 except that these are required for retrospective correction of fundamental errors rather than material errors. The prior year adjustment is shown in the reconciliation of shareholders' funds and the cumulative adjustment is reported as a memorandum item at the foot of the statement of recognised gains and losses.	IAS 1's requirements are the same as FRS 102 (except there is no statement of income and retained earnings). IAS 1 additionally requires presentation of a third balance sheet at the beginning of the comparative period, where there is a restatement of comparatives.

Chapter 4

	FRS 102	*Previous UK GAAP*	*IFRS*
Reduced disclosure framework	The reduced disclosure framework (see Chapter 2 at 3) is available in individual financial statements of qualifying entities only, where the conditions for its use are met. Some of the disclosure exemptions require equivalent disclosures to be included in the publicly available consolidated financial statements in which the qualifying entity is consolidated. Cash flow exemptions are addressed in Chapter 5.	Previous UK GAAP provides reduced disclosures for subsidiaries and parents in respect of financial instruments, related parties and cash flow statements. The scope of and details of these exemptions differ to FRS 102. Cash flow exemptions are addressed in Chapter 5.	IFRSs provide no reduced disclosures for subsidiaries and parents.
Notes: judgements and estimation uncertainty	FRS 102 requires disclosure of • judgements, apart from those involving estimations, in applying accounting policies; and • key sources of estimation uncertainty at the reporting date that have a significant risk of causing a material adjustment to the carrying amounts of assets and liabilities within the next financial year. See 7.3 and 7.4 above.	Disclosures of judgements and key sources of estimation uncertainty are not required. However, FRS 18 – *Accounting policies* – requires details of significant estimation techniques.	Same requirement as FRS 102 but IAS 1 provides more guidance on disclosure of judgements and key sources of estimation uncertainty.

Notes: sources of disclosure requirements	FRS 102 and the Companies Act 2006, the Regulations (and other applicable regulations) include disclosure requirements for the notes. See 7 above and Chapter 1 at 6.7.	Previous UK GAAP has different (but generally more extensive) disclosure requirements to FRS 102. The same disclosures in the Companies Act 2006, Regulations (and other applicable regulations) apply as for FRS 102 financial statements.	IFRS's disclosures are more extensive than those required by FRS 102 or previous UK GAAP. The disclosures required by Schedule 1 to the Regulations do not apply to IAS accounts. However, IAS accounts must comply with disclosures in the Companies Act 2006, and other applicable schedules of the Regulations (and other applicable regulations)
Statement of compliance	A statement of compliance that the financial statements are prepared in accordance with FRS 102 (and where applicable, FRS 103) is required. Where an entity is a public benefit entity, a statement to this effect must also be included. The Regulations require large and medium-sized companies to state that the accounts have been prepared in accordance with applicable accounting standards, giving particulars of any departures. However, medium-sized companies do not need to give this statement in their individual accounts. See 3.8 above.	There is no requirement to give a statement of compliance, but UK companies make the statement that the accounts have been prepared in accordance with applicable accounting standards, required by the Regulations.	A statement of compliance that the financial statements are prepared in accordance with IFRSs (or EU-adopted IFRSs, where applicable) is required. The requirements of the Regulations do not apply.

Chapter 4

References

1 See, for example, the FRC's Corporate Reporting Review: Annual Report 2013 (October 2013), pages 15 to 17.

Chapter 5   Statement of cash flows

Chapter 5

Chapter 5   Statement of cash flows

1   INTRODUCTION

A Statement of Cash Flows provides useful information about an entity's activities in generating cash to repay debt, distribute dividends or reinvest to maintain or expand operating capacity; about its financing activities, both debt and equity; and about its investing and spending of cash. This information, when combined with information in the rest of the financial statements, is useful in assessing factors that may affect the entity's liquidity, financial flexibility, profitability, and risk.

Section 7 – *Statement of Cash Flows* – is based on the equivalent IFRS standard IAS 7 – *Statement of Cash Flows*. However a number of the explanatory paragraphs within IAS 7 have not been incorporated into Section 7 of FRS 102.

The statement of cash flows required by FRS 102 provides information about the changes in cash and cash equivalents for a reporting period, classifying these between operating activities, investing activities and financing activities. *[FRS 102.7.1].*

2   COMPARISON BETWEEN SECTION 7, PREVIOUS UK GAAP AND IFRS

As discussed at 1 above, the structure of the cash flow required by Section 7 is based on IFRS and not previous UK GAAP. Therefore, there are significant differences compared to previous UK GAAP but few differences compared to IFRS.

2.1   Key differences between Section 7 and previous UK GAAP

The key differences between Section 7 and FRS 1 – *Cash flow statements (Revised 1996)* are as follows:

- the Section 7 Statement of Cash Flows has three classifications instead of eight (see 2.1.1 below).

- the Section 7 Statement of Cash Flows reconciles to cash and cash equivalents rather than cash at bank and in hand (see 2.1.2 below);

- Section 7 does not require a net debt reconciliation (see 2.1.3 below); and

- FRS 102 does not require a qualifying entity to prepare a Statement of Cash Flows. Provided the criteria are met, any subsidiary can be a qualifying entity. Previous UK

GAAP did not have the concept of a qualifying entity but permitted an exemption from preparing a cash flow statement to subsidiary undertakings where 90% or more of the voting rights were controlled within the group. In addition, previous UK GAAP exempted small companies from the requirement to prepare a cash flow statement whereas FRS 102 has no equivalent exemption. See 2.1.4 below.

2.1.1   Classification differences

Section 7 has three classifications of cash flows (Operating, Finance and Investing), whereas FRS 1 had eight (Operating activities, Returns on investment and servicing of finance, Taxation, Capital Expenditure and financial investment, Acquisitions and disposals, Equity Dividends paid, Management of liquid resources and Financing). The table below maps the FRS 1 classifications into the expected FRS 102 Section 7 classifications.

Previous UK GAAP (FRS 1) classification	*Expected FRS 102 classification*
Operating activities	Operating activities
Returns on investment and servicing of finance – receipts resulting from the ownership of an investment and payments to providers of finance, non-equity shareholders and minority interests.	Investing activities or financing activities.
Taxation	Operating activities unless they can be specifically identified with financing or investing activities. *[FRS 102.7.17]*.
Capital expenditure and financial investment – cash flows related to the acquisition or disposal of any fixed asset other than those required to be classified under acquisitions and disposals.	Investing activities. *[FRS 102.7.5]*.
Acquisitions and disposals – those related to the acquisition or disposal of any trade or business, or of an investment in an entity that is or as a result of the transaction becomes or ceases to be either an associate, a joint venture or a subsidiary undertaking.	Investing activities. *[FRS 102.7.5]*.
Equity dividends paid	Can be included in operating, investing or financing activities, but classification must be consistent from period to period. *[FRS 102.7.16]*.
Management of liquid resources – withdrawals from or payments into short term deposits not qualifying as cash, inflows from the disposal or redemption of, or outflows to acquire any other investments held as liquid resources.	Amounts recorded in short term deposits are likely to meet the definition of cash and cash equivalents and therefore the cash flow will not require disclosure. Other cash flows are likely to meet the definition of an investing activity. *[FRS 102.7.5]*.
Financing – receipts and repayments of principal from or to external providers of finance.	Financing activities. *[FRS 102.7.6]*.

2.1.2　Cash and cash equivalents

Section 7 requires the Statement of Cash Flows to reconcile to cash and cash equivalents which are defined as short-term, highly liquid investments that are readily convertible into known amounts of cash and that are subject to an insignificant risk of changes in value. *[FRS 102.7.2]*.

FRS 1 required the cash flow statement to reconcile to cash which was defined as cash in hand and deposits repayable on demand with any qualifying financial institution, less overdrafts from any qualifying financial institution repayable on demand. *[FRS 1.2]*.

Therefore the Statement of Cash Flows under FRS 102 may reconcile to a different amount than the cash flow statement under previous UK GAAP.

2.1.3　Net debt reconciliation

FRS 1 required a note to be prepared reconciling the movement of cash in the period with the movement in net debt. *[FRS 1.33]*. This reconciliation is not a requirement under FRS 102.

2.1.4　Entities exempt from preparing a cash flow statement

FRS 102 permits a qualifying entity an exemption from preparing a Statement of Cash Flows in its individual financial statements. *[FRS 102.1.12]*. A qualifying entity can be any subsidiary provided that the entity has been included in the publicly available consolidated group accounts. The conditions required for a reporting entity to meet the criteria of a qualifying entity are discussed in Chapter 2. Small entities are not exempt from the requirement to prepare a statement of cash flows unless they are qualifying entities.

Previous UK GAAP did not have the concept of a qualifying entity. However, subsidiary undertakings where 90% or more of the voting rights are controlled within the group were not required to prepare a cash flow statement in either individual or group financial statements provided that the consolidated financial statements in which those subsidiary undertakings were included were publicly available. Small entities (based on the Companies Act exemption in companies legislation) were also exempt from the requirement to prepare a cash flow statement. *[FRS 1.5]*.

These scope differences mean that some reporting entities that prepared a cash flow statement under previous UK GAAP may not need to prepare one under FRS 102 and *vice versa*.

2.2　Key differences between Section 7 and IFRS

Apart from the scope exemptions discussed at 2.2.1 below, Section 7 of FRS 102 is essentially the same as IAS 7. However, a number of the explanatory paragraphs from IAS 7 have been excluded. The paragraphs that have been excluded generally provide further detail on presentation although applying Section 2 – *Concepts and pervasive principles* will probably lead a preparer of the financial statements to the same answer under FRS 102 in most situations.

Chapter 5

2.2.1   Entities exempt from preparing a statement of cash flows

There are no scope exemptions from preparing a statement of cash flows in IAS 7. In contrast, FRS 102 allows the following entities an exemption from preparing a Statement of cash flows: *[FRS 102.7.1A]*

- qualifying entities (see 2.1.4 above);
- mutual life assurance companies;
- retirement benefit plans; and
- investment funds meeting certain conditions.

Additionally, a financial institution that undertakes the business of effecting or carrying out insurance contracts should include the cash flows of their long-term business only to the extent of cash transferred and available to meet the obligations of the company or group as a whole. *[FRS 102.7.10E]*. IAS 7 has no equivalent concession.

2.2.2   Presentation using the indirect method

IAS 7 allows an alternative presentation for the indirect method whereby the net cash flow from operating activities may be presented by showing the revenues and expenses disclosed in the statement of comprehensive income and the changes during the period in inventories and operating receivables and payables. This option is not presented under FRS 102.

3   THE REQUIREMENTS OF SECTION 7 FOR A STATEMENT OF CASH FLOWS

Section 7 specifies how entities report information about the historical changes in cash and cash equivalents and has a relatively flexible approach, which allows them to be applied to all entities including financial institutions. This flexibility can be seen, for example, in the way entities can determine their own policy for the classification of interest and dividend cash flows, provided that they are separately disclosed and this is applied consistently from period to period. Additional disclosure is encouraged where this provides information on an entity's specific circumstances.

3.1   Scope

Section 7 is not mandatory for entities that are 'qualifying entities' (See Chapter 2). In substance, this means that most subsidiaries, regardless of the percentage of voting rights controlled within a group, and parents that also prepare publicly available consolidated financial statements, will not need to prepare a statement of cash flows in their individual financial statements. However, a qualifying entity that prepares consolidated financial statements will have to prepare a statement of cash flows in those consolidated financial statements.

Consistent with previous UK GAAP, the following entities are also not required to produce a statement of cash flows:

- mutual life assurance companies;
- retirement benefit plans; or
- Investment funds that meet all of the following conditions:
    - substantially all of the entity's investments are highly liquid;
    - substantially all of the entity's investments are carried at market value; and
    - the entity provides a statement of changes in net assets. *[FRS 102.7.1A]*

A financial institution that undertakes the business of effecting or carrying out insurance contracts (other than mutual life assurance companies scoped out above) should include the cash flows of their long-term business only to the extent of cash transferred and available to meet obligations of the company or group as a whole. *[FRS 102.7.10E].*

There is no exemption from preparing a statement of cash flows for small entities as defined by the Companies Act (unless they otherwise qualify via the exemptions described above).

3.2   Terms used by Section 7

The following terms are used in Section 7 with the meanings specified *[FRS 102 Appendix I]*:

Term	Definition
Cash	Cash on hand and demand deposits.
Cash equivalents	Short term, highly liquid investments that are readily convertible to known amounts of cash and that are subject to an insignificant risk of changes in value.
Cash flows	Inflows and outflows of cash and cash equivalents.
Financing activities	Activities that result in changes in the size and composition of contributed equity and borrowings of the entity
Investing activities	The acquisition and disposal of long-term assets and other investments not included in cash equivalents.
Operating activities	The principal revenue-producing activities of the entity and other activities that are not investing or financing activities.
Statement of cash flows	Financial statement that provides information about the changes in cash and cash equivalents of an entity for a period, showing separately changes during the period from operating, investing and financing activities.

3.3   Cash and cash equivalents

Since the purpose of the statement of cash flows is to provide information about changes in cash and cash equivalents, the definitions of cash and cash equivalents given in the Glossary of FRS 102 (see 3.2 above) are essential to its presentation. It is important to understand the reporting entity's cash management policies,

Chapter 5

especially when considering whether balances should be classified as cash equivalents. Section 7 states that cash equivalents (which may include some short-term investments) are short-term, highly liquid investments that are readily convertible into known amounts of cash and that are subject to an insignificant risk of changes in value. *[FRS 102.7.2]*.

Further guidance is provided on the components of cash equivalents by stating that an investment normally qualifies as a cash equivalent only when it has a short maturity of three months or less from the date of acquisition. Bank overdrafts are normally considered financing activities unless they are repayable on demand and form an integral part of an entity's cash management, in which case they are a component of cash and cash equivalents. *[FRS 102.7.2]*.

In practice, however, determining the components of cash equivalents can be difficult. This is discussed further at 3.3.1 to 3.3.4 below.

An entity must disclose the components of cash and cash equivalents and present a reconciliation of the amounts in the cash flow statement to the equivalent amounts in the balance sheet. *[FRS 102.7.20]*. This reconciliation is needed because the Large and Medium-sized Companies and Groups (Accounts and Reports) Regulations 2008 (SI 2008/410) (the Regulations) require the separate presentation of cash at bank and in hand on the face of the balance sheet. Banking Entities that apply Schedule 2 formats must include as cash only balances at central banks and loans and advances to banks repayable on demand within cash on the balance sheet. *[FRS 102.7.20A]*.

FRS 102 states that a complete set of financial statements should include in the notes a summary of significant accounting policies, which would include a policy on how the entity determines cash equivalents. *[FRS 102.3.17(e)]*. These cash equivalents would need to meet the three conditions to qualify as a cash equivalent described above. Changes in the accounting policy to determine cash and cash equivalents, such as a reclassification of financial instruments previously considered as being part of an entity's investment portfolio to cash and cash equivalents, should be accounted for retrospectively under Section 10 – *Accounting Policies, Estimates and Errors*. *[FRS 102.10.11(d)]*. This requires comparatives to be restated and additional disclosures to be given, including the reasons for the change in policy.

3.3.1   Short-term investments

As discussed at 3.3 above, for an investment to qualify as a cash equivalent it must be readily convertible to a known amount of cash and be subject to an insignificant risk of changes in value. Normally only an investment with a short maturity of, say, three months or less from the date of acquisition qualifies as a cash equivalent as it will meet these criteria. Whilst Section 7 does not address the matter, it would seem logical that equity instruments do not meet the definition of cash equivalents unless they are cash equivalents in substance, such as redeemable preference shares acquired within a short period to their maturity date, because equity instruments are usually exposed to a not insignificant risk of changes in value.

When the standard refers to a 'known amount of cash' it means that the amount should be known or determinable at the date on which the investment is acquired. Accordingly, traded commodities, such as gold bullion, would not normally be expected to be cash equivalents because the proceeds to be realised from such commodities is determined at the date of disposal rather than being known or determinable when the investment is made.

3.3.2 Money market funds

Entities commonly invest in money market funds (MMF) such as an open-ended mutual fund that invests in certificates of deposit, commercial paper, treasury bills, bankers' acceptances and repurchase agreements and other money market instruments. An investment in a MMF aims to provide investors with low-risk, low-return investment while preserving the value of the assets and maintaining a high level of liquidity. The question then arises as to whether investments in such funds can be classified as cash equivalents.

In most cases, a MMF investment is quoted in an active market and, as such, could be regarded as highly liquid. However, this is not enough to meet the definition of a cash equivalent. The short-term and highly liquid investment must be readily convertible into known amounts of cash which are subject to an insignificant risk of changes in value. *[FRS 102.7.2]*. Accordingly, investments in shares or units of money market funds cannot be considered as cash equivalents simply because they are convertible at any time at the then market price in an active market. An entity would have to satisfy itself that any investment was subject to an insignificant risk of change in value for it to be classified as a cash equivalent.[1]

Therefore in assessing whether the change in value of an investment in a money market fund can be regarded as insignificant, an entity has to conclude that the range of possible returns is very small. This evaluation is made at the time of acquiring the investment and will involve consideration of factors such as the maturity of the investment (which should not exceed 90 days); the credit rating of the fund (which should be AAA or an equivalent highest rating); the nature of the investments held by the fund (which should themselves not be subject to volatility); the extent of diversification in the portfolio (which should be very high); and any mechanisms by the fund to guarantee returns (for example by reference to short-term money market interest rates).

Investments are often held for purposes other than to act as a ready store of value that can be quickly converted into cash when needed to meet short-term cash commitments. It is therefore important to understand why the entity invested in a particular MMF when determining whether classification as a cash equivalent is appropriate.

3.3.3 Investments with maturities greater than three months

An investment qualifies as a cash equivalent only when it has a short maturity of, say, three months or less from the date of acquisition. *[FRS 102.7.2]*. Therefore, an investment with a term on acquisition of, say, nine months is not reclassified as a cash equivalent from the date on which there is less than three months remaining to its maturity. If such reclassifications were permitted, the statement of cash flows would have to reflect movements between investments and cash equivalents. This would be misleading because no actual cash flows would have occurred.

Chapter 5

An entity might justify including in cash equivalents a fixed deposit with an original term longer than three months if it effectively functions like a demand deposit. Typically, a fixed deposit will carry a penalty charge for withdrawal prior to maturity. A penalty will usually indicate that the investment is held for investment purposes rather than the purpose of meeting short-term cash needs. However, some fixed deposits carry a penalty whereby the entity will forego the higher interest that it would have received if held to maturity, but would still receive interest at a prevailing demand deposit rate. In this case, it may be arguable that there is effectively no significant penalty for early withdrawal, as the entity receives at least the same return that it otherwise would have in a demand deposit arrangement. Where an entity does assert that this type of investment is held for meeting short-term cash needs and classifies the investment as a cash equivalent, the accrual of interest receivable should be on a consistent basis. In this example, the entity should consider accruing interest receivable at the demand deposit rate.

3.3.4   *Restrictions on the use of cash and cash equivalents*

As discussed at 3.13 below, an entity must disclose, together with a commentary by management, the amount of significant cash and cash equivalent balances held by the entity that are not available for use by the entity. The nature of the restriction must be assessed to determine if the balance is ineligible for inclusion in cash equivalents because the restriction results in the investment ceasing to be highly liquid or readily convertible. For example, when an entity covenants to maintain a minimum level of cash or deposits as security for certain short term obligations, and provided that no amounts are required to be designated for that specific purpose, such balances could still be regarded as cash equivalents, albeit subject to restrictions, as part of a policy of managing resources to meet short-term commitments.

However, an entity may be required formally to set aside cash, for example by way of a deposit into an escrow account, as part of a specific project or transaction, such as the acquisition or construction of a property. In such circumstances, it is necessary to consider the terms and conditions relating to the account and the conditions relating to both the entity's and counterparty's access to the funds within it to determine whether it is appropriate for the deposit to be classified as cash equivalents.

3.3.5   *Reporting of differing cash flows arising from a single transaction*

Section 7 provides no guidance on how to report different types of cash flows arising from a single transaction. However, there is no prohibition on split presentation so, for example, when the cash repayment of a loan includes both interest and capital, the interest element may be classified as an operating activity and the capital element is classified as a financing activity.

3.4   Information to be presented in the statement of cash flows

The statement of cash flows reports inflows and outflows of cash and cash equivalents during the period classified under:

- Operating activities (see 3.5 below);
- Investing activities (see 3.6 below); and
- Financing activities (see 3.7 below). *[FRS 102.7.3].*

This classification is intended to allow users to assess the impact of these three types of activity on the financial position of the entity and the amount of its cash and cash equivalents. Although the presentation is not required to follow this layout, we would expect it to be followed in practice. Comparative figures are required for all items in the statement of cash flows and the related notes. *[FRS 102.3.14].*

3.5   Reporting cash flows from operating activities

Operating activities are the principal revenue-producing activities of the business and other activities that are not investing or financing activities. *[FRS 102.7.4, Appendix I].* This means that operating is the 'default' category, with all cash flows that do not fall within either the investing or financing classifications being automatically deemed to be operating.

Cash flows from operating activities generally result from transactions and other events that enter into the determination of profit or loss. Examples include:

- cash receipts from the sale of goods and the rendering of services;
- cash receipts from royalties, fees, commissions and other revenue;
- cash payments to suppliers for goods and services;
- cash payments to and on behalf of employees;
- cash payments or refunds of income tax, unless they are can be specifically identified with financing and investing activities;
- cash receipts and payments from investments, loans and other contracts held for dealing or trading purposes, which are similar to inventory acquired specifically for resale; and
- cash advances and loans made by financial institutions. *[FRS 102.7.4].*

An example of an item that enters into the determination of profit or loss that is not usually an operating cash flow is the proceeds from the sale of property, plant and equipment, which are usually included in cash flows from investing activities. *[FRS 102.7.4].*

Cash flows from operating activities may be presented using either:

- the indirect method; or
- the direct method. *[FRS 102.7.7].*

FRS 102 does not express a preference for the method to be used.

3.5.1   Indirect method

Under the indirect method the net cash flow from operating activities is determined by adjusting profit or loss for the effects of:

- changes during the period in inventories and operating receivables and payables;
- non-cash items such as depreciation, provisions, deferred tax, accrued income/(expenses) not yet received/(paid) in cash, unrealised foreign currency gains and losses, undistributed profits of associates, and non-controlling interests; and
- all other items for which the cash effects relate to investing or financing activities. *[FRS 102.7.8].*

Chapter 5

Section 7 does not define 'profit or loss'. However, we believe that this means profit or loss for the financial year either before or after tax per the Companies Act formats.

3.5.2   *Direct method*

The direct method arrives at the same value for net cash flow from operating activities, but does so by disclosing major classes of gross cash receipts and gross cash payments. Such information may be obtained either:

- from the accounting records of the entity (essentially based on an analysis of the cash book); or

- by adjusting sales, cost of sales and other items in the statement of comprehensive income (or income statement if presented) for:

  - changes during the period in inventories and operating receivables and payables;

  - other non-cash items; and

  - other items for which the cash effects are investing or financing cash flows. *[FRS 102.7.9].*

3.6   Reporting cash flows from investing activities

Unless a net presentation is permitted under FRS 102, an entity shall present separately major classes of gross cash receipts and gross cash payments arising from investing and financing activities.

Investing activities are defined as 'the acquisition and disposal of long-term assets and other investments not included in cash equivalents'. *[FRS 102.7.5].* This separate category of cash flows allows users of the financial statements to understand the extent to which expenditures have been made for resources intended to generate future income and cash flows. Cash flows arising from investing activities include:

- payments to acquire, and receipts from the sale of, property, plant and equipment, intangibles and other long-term assets (including payments and receipts relating to capitalised development costs and self-constructed property, plant and equipment);

- payments to acquire, and receipts from the sale of, equity or debt instruments of other entities and interests in joint ventures (other than payments and receipts for those instruments considered to be cash equivalents or those held for dealing or trading purposes);

- advances and loans made to, and repaid by, other parties (other than advances and loans made by a financial institution); and

- payments for, and receipts from, futures contracts, forward contracts, option contracts and swap contracts, except when the contracts are held for dealing or trading purposes, or the cash flows are classified as financing activities.

When a contract is accounted for as a hedge, an entity shall classify the cash flows of the contract in the same manner as the item being hedged. *[FRS 102.7.5].*

Major classes of gross receipts and gross payments arising from investing activities are reported separately, except for those items that are permitted to be reported on a net basis, as discussed at 3.8 below. *[FRS 102.7.10].*

Section 7 has no specific guidance on classification of cash flows arising from changes in ownership interests in subsidiaries or other businesses. See 4.6.1 below.

3.7 Reporting cash flows from financing activities

Financing activities are defined as those 'activities that result in changes in the size and composition of the contributed equity and borrowings of the entity'. *[FRS 102.7.6].*

Cash flows arising from financing activities include:

*   proceeds from issuing shares or other equity instruments;

*   payments to owners to acquire or redeem the entity's shares;

*   proceeds from issuing, and outflows to repay, debentures, loans, notes, bonds, mortgages and other short or long-term borrowings; and

*   payments by a lessee for the reduction of the outstanding liability relating to a finance lease. *[FRS 102.7.6].*

Major classes of gross receipts and gross payments arising from financing activities should be reported separately, except for those items that are permitted to be reported on a net basis, as discussed at 3.8 below. *[FRS102.7.10].*

3.8 Reporting cash flows on a net basis

In general, major classes of gross receipts and gross payments should be reported separately, except to the extent that net presentation is specifically permitted. *[FRS 102.7.10].* Operating, investing or financing cash flows may be reported on a net basis if they arise from:

*   cash flows that reflect the activities of customers rather than those of the entity and are thereby made on behalf of customers; or

*   cash flows that relate to items in which the turnover is quick, the amounts are large, and the maturities are short. *[FRS 102.7.10A].*

Examples of cash receipts and payments that reflect the activities of customers rather than those of the entity include:

*   the acceptance and repayment of demand deposits by a bank;

*   funds held for customers by an investment entity; and

*   rents collected on behalf of, and paid over to, the owners of properties. *[FRS 102.7.10B].*

Other transactions where the entity is acting as an agent or collector for another party would be included in the category of cash receipts and payments that reflect the activities of the customers rather than those of the entities, such as the treatment of cash receipts and payments relating to concession sales.

Chapter 5

Examples of cash receipts and payments in which turnover is quick, the amounts are large and the maturities are short include advances made for and the repayment of:

- principal amounts relating to credit card customers;
- the purchase and sale of investments; and
- other short-term borrowings, such as those with a maturity on draw down of three months or less. *[FRS 102.7.10C]*.

Financial institutions may report certain cash flows on a net basis. *[FRS 102.7.10D]*. These cash flows are:

- cash receipts and payments for the acceptance and repayment of deposits with a fixed maturity date;
- the placement of deposits with and withdrawal of deposits from other financial institutions; and
- cash advances and loans made to customers and the repayment of those advances and loans. *[FRS 102.34.33]*.

3.9   Foreign currency cash flows

Cash flows arising from transactions in a foreign currency should be reported in the entity's functional currency in the statement of cash flows by applying the exchange rate between the functional currency and the foreign currency at the date of the cash flow or an exchange rate that approximates the actual rate (for example, a weighted average exchange rate for the period). *[FRS 102.7.11]*. Similarly, the cash flows of a foreign subsidiary should be translated using the exchange rate between the entity's functional currency and the foreign currency prevailing at the dates of the cash flow or at an exchange rate that approximates the actual rate. *[FRS 102.7.12]*.

Unrealised gains and losses arising from exchange rate movements on foreign currency cash and cash equivalents are not cash flows. However, it is necessary to include these exchange differences in the statement of cash flows in order to reconcile the movement in cash and cash equivalents to the corresponding amounts shown in the balance sheet at the beginning and end of the period. The effect of exchange rate movements on cash and cash equivalents is presented as a single amount at the foot of the statement of cash flows, separately from operating, investing and financing cash flows and includes the differences, if any, had those cash flows been reported at period end exchange rates. *[FRS 102.7.13]*. This is illustrated in the example at 3.14 below.

3.10   Interest and dividends

An entity is required to disclose separately cash flows from interest and dividends received and paid, and their classification as either operating, investing or financing activities should be applied in a consistent manner from period to period. *[FRS 102.7.14]*. Section 7 states that:

- an entity may classify interest paid and interest and dividends received as operating cash flows because they are included in profit and loss; alternatively

- interest paid and interest and dividends received may be presented as financing cash flows or investing cash flows, because they are costs of obtaining financial resources or returns on investments respectively. *[FRS 10.7.15]*.

Dividends paid can either be classified as a financing cash flow (because they are a cost of obtaining financial resources) or as a component of cash flows from operating activities. *[FRS 102.7.16]*.

The flexibility in the above paragraphs of FRS 102 means that all of these treatments are equally acceptable. Nevertheless, it could be argued that entities which do not include interest or dividends received within revenue should not include interest or dividends in operating cash flows because cash flows from operating activities are primarily derived from the principal revenue-producing activities of the entity. *[FRS 102.7.4]*. On this basis, interest paid would be a financing cash flow and interest and dividends received classified as investing cash flows. *[FRS 102.7.15]*. Such entities would also treat dividends paid as a financing cash flow, because they are a cost of obtaining financial resources. *[FRS 102.7.16]*.

3.11   Income tax

Cash flows arising from taxes on income should be separately disclosed within operating cash flows unless they can be specifically identified with investing or financing activities. *[FRS 102.7.17]*. Where tax cash flows are allocated over more than one class of activity, FRS 102 requires that the total amount of taxes paid be disclosed. Whilst it is possible to match elements of tax expense to transactions for which cash flows are classified under investing or financing activities; taxes paid are usually classified as cash flows from operating activities because it is often impracticable to match tax cash flows with specific elements of tax expense. In addition, those tax cash flows may arise in a different period from the underlying transaction.

3.12   Non cash transactions

Non-cash transactions only ever appear in a statement of cash flows as adjustments to profit or loss for the period when using the indirect method of presenting cash flows from operating activities (as discussed at 3.5.1 above). Investing and financing transactions that do not involve cash or cash equivalents are always excluded from the statement of cash flows. Disclosure is required elsewhere in the financial statements in order to provide all relevant information about these investing and financing activities. *[FRS 102.7.18]*. Examples of such non-cash transactions include:

- acquiring assets by assuming directly related liabilities or by means of a finance lease;

- issuing equity as consideration for the acquisition of another entity; and

- the conversion of debt to equity. *[FRS 102.7.19]*.

Asset exchange transactions and the issue of bonus shares out of retained earnings are other examples of investing and financing transactions that do not involve cash or cash equivalents but require disclosure.

Chapter 5

3.13   Other disclosures

The amount of significant cash and cash equivalent balances held by the entity that are not available for use by the entity should be disclosed, together with a commentary by management. *[FRS 102.7.21]*. These restrictions may be due to foreign exchange controls or legal restrictions.

3.14   Example statement of cash flows using the indirect method

The following example is of a statement of cash flows and related notes prepared using the indirect method under FRS 102.

Group statement of cash flows

	Notes	2015 £000	2014 £000
Net cash (outflow)/inflow from operating activities	24(a)	(859)	3,964
Investing activities			
Dividends from joint venture		700	545
Interest received		993	345
Dividends received		200	160
Payments to acquire intangible fixed assets		(575)	(1,010)
Payments to acquire tangible fixed assets		(12,815)	(3,875)
Receipts from sales of tangible fixed assets		8,625	2,765
Payments to acquire investments		(465)	(230)
Receipts from sales of investments		125	–
Receipt of government grants		1,392	765
Sale of subsidiary undertaking	13	55	–
Net overdrafts disposed of with subsidiary undertaking	13	2,117	–
Purchase of subsidiary undertaking	13	(500)	–
Net cash acquired with subsidiary undertaking	13	230	–
Dividends from associate		135	105
Net cash flow from investing activities		217	(430)
Financing activities			
Dividends paid to non-controlling interests		(30)	(30)
Dividends paid to preference shareholders		(175)	(175)
Interest paid		(973)	(1,075)
Interest element of finance lease rental payments		(40)	(50)
Issue costs on new long-term loans		(50)	(56)
Issue of ordinary share capital		175	–
Share issue costs		(100)	–
Purchase of own shares		(1,700)	
Share purchase costs		(100)	
New long-term loans		4,660	4,500
Repayment of long-term loans		(500)	–
Repayments of capital element of finance leases and hire purchase contracts		(370)	(243)
Equity dividends paid	22	(1,431)	(1,170)
Net cash flow from financing activities		(634)	1,701
(Decrease)/Increase in cash and cash equivalents		(1,276)	5,235
Effect of exchange rates on cash and cash equivalents		(120)	(78)
Cash and cash equivalents at 1 January		7,560	2,403
Cash and cash equivalents at 31 December	24(b)	6,164	7,560

Notes to the statement of cash flows

Reconciliation of profit to net cash (outflow)/inflow from operating activities

	2015 £000	2014 £000
Group profit for the year before taxation	8,694	7,547
Adjustments to reconcile profit for the year to net cash flow from operating activities		
Loss on revaluation of investment properties	350	474
Depreciation and impairment of tangible fixed assets	5,590	2,610
Amortisation of development expenditure	125	40
Amortisation of patents	50	10
Amortisation of goodwill	160	25
Share-based payment	412	492
Difference between pension charge and cash contributions	(46)	(196)
Increase in provision for maintenance warranties	200	50
Increase in provision for National Insurance contributions on share options	4	4
Provision for maintenance warranties utilised	(219)	(25)
Deferred government grants released	(1,012)	(530)
Share of operating profit in joint venture	(2,435)	(1,007)
Share of operating profit in associate	(545)	(325)
(Profit)/loss on disposal of tangible fixed assets	(1,250)	850
Loss on disposal of fixed asset investments	350	–
Loss on sale of discontinued operations	2,037	–
Net finance costs	167	820
Amortisation of goodwill arising on acquisition of associate	70	70
Working capital movements		
Increase in debtors	(4,475)	(2,694)
Increase in stocks	(4,332)	(2,529)
Decrease in creditors	(1,917)	(389)
Taxation		
Corporation tax paid (including advance corporation tax)	(2,379)	(1,218)
Overseas tax paid	(458)	(115)
	(9,553)	(3,583)
Net cash (outflow)/inflow from operating activities	(859)	3,964

Cash and cash equivalents

Cash and cash equivalents comprise the following;

	Group		Parent company	
	At 31 December 2015 £000	*At 31 December 2014 £000*	*At 31 December 2015 £000*	*At 31 December 2014 £000*
Cash at bank and in hand	5,441	9,291	2,230	6,554
Short-term deposits	1,483	2,039	–	–
	6,924	11,330	2,230	6,554
Bank overdrafts	(760)	(3,770)	–	–
Cash and cash equivalents	6,164	7,560	2,230	6,554

Chapter 5

4   PRACTICAL IMPLEMENTATION ISSUES

4.1   VAT and other taxes

The presentation of VAT and other (non-income) taxes is not addressed in FRS 102 (or IAS 7).

In our view, consistent with the guidance that existed under previous UK GAAP, cash flows should be shown net of VAT and other sales taxes unless the tax is irrecoverable by the reporting entity. The net movement on the amount payable or receivable from, the taxing authority should be allocated to cash flows from operating activities unless a different treatment is more appropriate to the particular circumstances concerned. Where restrictions apply to the recoverability of such taxes, the irrecoverable amount should be allocated to the expenditures affected by the restrictions. If this is impracticable, the irrecoverable tax should be included under the most appropriate standard heading. *[FRS 1.39].*

4.2   Group relief

Section 7 does not address the presentation of cash flows relating to group relief in subsidiary entities. In our view, consistent with the guidance in previous UK GAAP, cash flows related to group relief can be included under 'taxation' even though they are not paid to a taxation authority. *[FRS 1.16].*

4.3   Cash flows from factoring of trade receivables

Section 7 does not address the classification of cash receipts arising from the factoring of trade receivables. In these circumstances, an entity uses a factoring structure to produce cash flow from trade receivables more quickly than would arise from normal collection from customers, generally by transferring rights over those receivables to a financial institution. In our view, the classification of the cash receipt from the financial institution depends on whether the transfer gives rise to the de-recognition of the trade receivable, or to the continued recognition of the trade receivable and the recognition of a financial liability for the funding received from the debt factor.

Only to the extent that the factoring arrangement results in the derecognition of the original trade receivable would it be appropriate to regard the cash receipt from factoring in the same way as any other receipt from the sale of goods and rendering of services and classify it in operating activities. *[FRS 102.7.4(a)].* In cases where the trade receivable is not derecognised and a liability is recorded, the nature of the arrangement is a borrowing secured against trade receivables and accordingly we believe that the cash receipt from factoring should be treated in the same way as any short-term borrowing and included in financing activities. *[FRS 102.7.6(c)].* The later cash inflow from the customer for settlement of the trade receivable would be included in operating cash flows and the reduction in the liability to the financial institution would be a financing outflow. Following the same principle in Section 11 – *Basic Financial Instruments* – for the disclosure of income and expenditure relating to a transferred asset that continues to be recognised, *[FRS 102.11.34],* these two amounts would not be netted off in the statement of cash flows. However, it would be acceptable for the entity to disclose the net borrowing receipts from, and repayments to, the financial institution, if it was determined that these relate to advances made for and the repayment of short-term borrowings such as those which have a maturity period of three months or less. *[FRS 102.7.10C]*.

In some cases, the factoring agreement requires customers to remit cash directly to the financial institution. When the transfer does not give rise to derecognition of the trade receivable, we believe that the later satisfaction of the debt by the customer can be depicted either;

- as a non-cash transaction. No cash flows would be reported at the time of the ultimate derecognition of the trade receivable and the related factoring liability; or

- as a transaction in which the debt factor collects the receivable as agent of the entity and then draws down amounts received in settlement of the entity's liability to the financial institution. In this case the entity would report an operating cash inflow from the customer and a financing cash outflow to the financial institution.

4.4   Acquisition of plant, property and equipment on deferred terms

The purchase of assets on deferred terms can be a complicated area because it may not be clear whether the associated cash flows should be classified under investing activities, as capital expenditure, or within financing activities, as the repayment of borrowings. FRS 102 includes the following requirements:

- when an entity acquires an asset under a finance lease, the acquisition of the asset is a non-cash transaction, *[FRS 102.7.19]*; and

- the payments to reduce the outstanding liability relating to a finance lease are financing cash flows. *[FRS 102.7.6]*.

In our view, this distinction should be applied in all cases where financing is provided by the seller of the asset, with the acquisition and financing being treated as a non-cash transaction and disclosed accordingly. Subsequent payments to the seller are then included in financing cash flows. Nevertheless, if the period between acquisition and payment is not significant, the existence of credit terms should not be interpreted as changing the nature of the cash payment from investing to financing. The period between acquisition and payment would be regarded as significant if it gave rise to the seller recognising imputed interest under Section 23 – *Revenue. [FRS 102.23.5]*. Therefore, the settlement of a short-term payable for the purchase of an asset is an investing cash flow, whereas payments to reduce the liability relating to a finance lease or other finance provided by the seller for the purchase of an asset should be included in financing cash flows.

4.5   Additional considerations for groups

Section 7 does not distinguish between single entities and groups, and there is no specific guidance as to how an entity should prepare a consolidated statement of cash flows. In the absence of specific requirements, cash inflows and outflows would be treated in the same way as income and expenses under Section 9 – *Consolidated and*

Separate Financial Statements. Applying these principles, the statement of cash flows presented in the consolidated financial statements should reflect only the flows of cash and cash equivalents into and out of the group, i.e. consolidated cash flows are presented as those of a single economic entity. *[FRS 102 Glossary Appendix I].* Cash flows that are internal to the group (such as payments and receipts for intra-group sales, management charges, dividends, interest and financing arrangements) should be eliminated. *[FRS 102.9.15].* However, dividends paid to non-controlling shareholders in subsidiaries represent an outflow of cash from the perspective of the shareholders in the parent entity. They should, accordingly, be included under cash flows from financing activities or operating activities, in accordance with the entity's determined policy for classification of dividend cash flows (see 3.10 above). Payments arising from other transactions with non-controlling interests are discussed at 4.5.1 below.

4.5.1   Acquisitions and disposals of subsidiaries

4.5.1.A   Acquisitions and disposals resulting in control or loss of control

The aggregate cash flows arising from obtaining or losing control of subsidiaries or other businesses are shown separately within investing activities. *[FRS 102.7.10].*

Section 7 does not address whether this amount should be shown net of cash acquired on acquisition of the subsidiary or disposed of with the subsidiary. In our view, the cash acquired of or disposed of with the subsidiary can be shown either as a separate line item within financing activities or netted against the cash received or paid on the acquisition or sale.

4.5.1.B   Disposals that do not result in loss of control

A disposal that does not result in a loss of control is a cash payment to an owner to acquire or redeem the entity's shares and should therefore be classified as a financing activity. *[FRS 102.7.6].*

4.5.2   Settlement of amounts owed by the acquired entity

A question that sometimes arises is how to treat a payment made by the acquirer to settle amounts owed by a new subsidiary, either to take over a loan that is owed to the vendor by that subsidiary or to extinguish an external borrowing.

Payments made to acquire debt instruments of other entities are normally included under investing activities. *[FRS 102.7.5].* Therefore, the payment to the vendor is classified under the same cash flow heading irrespective of whether it is regarded as being part of the purchase consideration or the acquisition of a debt. This presentation can be contrasted with the repayment of external debt by the new subsidiary, using funds provided by the parent, which is a cash outflow from financing activities. *[FRS 102.7.6].*

4.5.3   Settlement of intra-group balances on a demerger

A similarly fine distinction might apply on the demerger of subsidiaries. These sometimes involve the repayment of intra-group indebtedness out of the proceeds from external finance raised by the demerged subsidiary. If the external funding is raised immediately prior to the subsidiary leaving the group, it is strictly a financing inflow in the consolidated statement of cash flows, being cash proceeds from issuing short or long-term borrowings. *[FRS 102.7.6]*. If the subsidiary both raises the external funding and repays the intra-group debt after the demerger, the inflow is shown in the consolidated statement of cash flows under investing activities, being a cash receipt from the repayment of advances and loans made to other parties. *[FRS 102.7.5]*.

4.6   Cash flows in subsidiaries, associates and joint ventures

4.6.1   *Investments in subsidiaries, associates and joint ventures*

Section 9 requires that intragroup balances and transactions, including income, expenses and dividends, are eliminated in full. *[FRS 102.9.15]*.

FRS 102 requires a parent, in its consolidated financial statements, to account for investments in associates (which are not held as part of an investment portfolio) and joint ventures using the equity method. *[FRS 102.14.4A, 15.13]*. Therefore in order to be able to reconcile the movement in cash and cash equivalents the entity would need to record transactions with the associate or joint venture. The method for presenting cash dividends received from associates or joint ventures accounted for under the equity method will depend on the method of presentation of the statement of cash flow. Under the direct method, cash dividends received will be shown under operating or investing activities in accordance with the entity's determined policy for dividends received. Under the indirect method, the starting profit or loss would include the group's share of profits from equity-accounted investments. Unless profit is received from equity-accounted investments in the form of cash dividends, it does not give rise to any cash flow. Therefore the share of profits in equity-accounted investments has to be deducted as a non-cash adjustment in the reconciliation of profit or loss to operating cash flows, in order to show only the dividends received in the statement of cash flow.

4.6.2   *Transactions with non-controlling interests*

Dividends paid to non-controlling interest holders in subsidiaries are included under cash flows from financing activities or operating activities, in accordance with the entity's determined policy for dividends paid (see 3.10 above).

4.6.3   *Group treasury arrangements*

Some groups adopt treasury arrangements by which cash resources are held centrally, either by the parent entity or by a designated subsidiary. Any excess cash is transferred to the designated group entity. In some cases a subsidiary might not even have its own bank account, with all receipts and payments being made directly from centrally controlled funds. Subsidiaries record an intercompany receivable when otherwise they would have held cash and bank deposits at each period end. A question that arises is whether or not a statement of cash flows should be presented when preparing the separate financial statements of such a subsidiary given that there is no cash or cash equivalents balance held at each period end. In our view, the preparation of the statement of cash flows should be based upon the actual cash flows during the period regardless of cash and cash equivalents balance held at each period end. The cash and cash equivalents may fluctuate from being positive to overdrawn or nil as the subsidiary needs cash to conduct its operations, to pay its obligations and to provide returns to its investors, or sweeps up excess cash to the designated group entity. This approach is consistent with the requirements in Section 3 that all entities should prepare a statement of cash flows which forms an integral part of the financial statements. *[FRS 102.3.17].*

Where the subsidiary makes net deposits of funds to, or net withdrawals of funds from the designated group entity during the reporting period, a further question arises as to how movements should be presented in the subsidiary's statement of cash flows. Normally these transactions give rise to intercompany balances. Therefore, the net deposits or net withdrawals should be shown as investing activities or financing activities, respectively.

In extremely rare cases the intercompany balances may meet the definition of cash equivalents and be regarded as short-term highly liquid investments that are readily convertible into known amounts of cash and are subject to insignificant risk of changes in value. *[FRS 102.7.2].* However, in most cases such funds are transferred to the designated group entity for an indeterminate term and the fact that both the subsidiary and designated group entity are controlled by the parent company makes it difficult to conclude that the subsidiary could demand repayment of amounts deposited independently of the wishes of the parent company.

5   SUMMARY OF GAAP DIFFERENCES

The following table shows the differences between FRS 102, previous UK GAAP and IFRS.

	FRS 102	*Previous UK GAAP*	*IFRS*
Entities exempt from preparing a cash flow statement	• Qualifying entities; • mutual life assurance companies; • retirement benefit plans; and • investment funds that meet certain conditions. In addition, financial institutions that undertake insurance contracts should include cash flows in respect of their long-term business only to the extent of cash transferred and available to meet the obligations of the company or group as a whole.	• Subsidiary undertakings where 90% or more of the voting rights are controlled within the group can take advantage of the exemption from the preparation of a cash flow statement provided that consolidated financial statements in which the subsidiary is included is publicly available; • mutual life insurance companies; • pension funds; • open-ended investment funds that meet certain conditions; and	No exemptions available.

Entities exempt from preparing a cash flow statement *(continued)*		• companies entitled to the small companies exemption (and other entities that would be so entitled if they were companies). In addition, financial institutions that undertake insurance contracts should include cash flows in respect of their long-term business only to the extent of cash transferred and available to meet the obligations of the company or group as a whole.	
Cash/ Cash and cash equivalents	Statement of cash flows shows movements in cash and cash equivalents.	Cash flow statement shows only movements in cash.	Statement of cash flows shows movements in cash and cash equivalents.
Information to be presented in the statement of cash flows	Information is presented under the following classifications: • operating activities; • investing activities; and • financing activities.	Information is presented under the following classifications: • operating activities; • taxation; • capital expenditure and financial investment; • acquisitions and disposals; • equity dividends paid; • management of liquid resources; and • financing.	Information is presented under the following classifications: • operating activities; • investing activities; and • financing activities.
Disclosure	FRS 102 requires a reconciliation of cash and cash equivalents presented in the statement of cash flows to that presented in the statement of financial position. FRS 102 does not offer an alternative presentation for the indirect method.	FRS 1 requires a reconciliation of net debt. FRS 1 does not offer an alternative presentation for the indirect method.	Requires a reconciliation of cash and cash equivalents presented in the statement of cash flows to that presented in the statement of financial position. IAS 7 allows an alternative presentation for the indirect method.

Chapter 5

References

1 *IFRIC Update*, July 2009.

Chapter 6

Consolidated and separate financial statements

Chapter 6

List of examples

Chapter 6 — Consolidated and separate financial statements

1 INTRODUCTION

Section 9 – *Consolidated and Separate Financial Statements* – addresses the preparation and accounting for consolidated financial statements as well as accounting for investments in subsidiaries, associates and jointly controlled entities in individual and separate financial statements. It also contains guidance on consolidation of special purpose entities and the accounting for intermediate payment arrangements.

Although Section 9 is based on the IFRS for SMEs, it has been amended to comply with the requirements of UK Company Law, as well as being expanded to reflect guidance contained in several sources of previous UK GAAP and UK Company Law including FRS 2 – *Accounting for subsidiary undertakings,* FRS 5 – *Reporting the substance of transactions,* UITF 31 – *Exchanges of businesses or other non-monetary assets for an interest in a subsidiary, joint venture or associate,* UITF 32 – *Employee benefit trusts and other intermediate payment arrangements* – and UITF 38 – *Accounting for ESOP trusts.* By using the IFRS for SMEs as its basis, Section 9 therefore incorporates some requirements and guidance of IFRS that existed prior to the issuance of IFRS 10 – *Consolidated Financial Statements* – being IAS 27 – *Separate Financial Statements* (IAS 27 (2012)) and SIC 12 – *Consolidation – Special Purpose entities.*

Therefore, in contrast to most sections of FRS 102, the requirements of Section 9 are not based on current IFRS.

2   COMPARISON BETWEEN SECTION 9, PREVIOUS UK GAAP AND IFRS

As explained above, Section 9 is an amalgamation of requirements that existed in previous UK GAAP and IFRS extant before the issuance of IFRS 10.

2.1   Key differences between Section 9 and previous UK GAAP

2.1.1   *Definition of a subsidiary held exclusively with a view to subsequent resale*

Section 9 states that a subsidiary held exclusively with a view to subsequent resale (and is therefore excluded from consolidation) includes a subsidiary held as part of an investment portfolio which shall be measured at fair value through profit or loss (see 3.4.2 below). *[FRS 102.9.9B(a)]*.

FRS 2 did not include a subsidiary held as part of an investment portfolio within its definition of a subsidiary held exclusively with a view to subsequent resale for the purposes of excluding a subsidiary from consolidation. *[FRS 2.11]*.

This is likely to mean that more subsidiaries will be excluded from consolidation as a result of being classified as held exclusively with a view to subsequent resale under FRS 102 compared to previous UK GAAP.

2.1.2   *Special purpose entities*

Section 9 defines a special purpose entity and provides guidance explaining when such entities are likely to require consolidating in the financial statements of the reporting entity (see 3.3 below). *[FRS 102.9.10-12]*. This guidance is a summary of guidance contained previously in SIC 12.

Previous UK GAAP had no specific guidance in respect of special purpose entities. Entities with interests in special purposes entities would have had regard to the general control requirements of FRS 2 and the guidance on quasi-subsidiaries contained in FRS 5.

2.1.3   *Increasing a controlling interest in a subsidiary*

Section 9 states that when a parent increases its controlling interest in a subsidiary, the identifiable assets and liabilities and provision for contingent liabilities of the subsidiary shall not be revalued to fair value and no additional goodwill shall be recognised at the date the controlling interest is revalued (see 3.6.2 below). *[FRS 102.9.19C]*.

FRS 2 stated that when a group increased its interest in a subsidiary undertaking, the identifiable assets and liabilities of that subsidiary undertaking should be revalued to fair value and goodwill arising on the increase should be calculated by reference to those fair values (unless the difference between fair values and carrying amounts was not material). *[FRS 2.51]*.

This is a significant change in the accounting treatment.

2.1.4   Decreasing a controlling interest in a subsidiary

Section 9 states that when a parent reduces its holding in a subsidiary and control is retained it is accounted for as a transaction between equity holders and no profit or loss is recognised at the date of disposal (see 3.6.4 below). *[FRS 102.9.19A]*.

FRS 2 stated that when a group reduces its interest in a subsidiary undertaking, it should record any profit or loss arising as the difference between the carrying amount of the net assets of that subsidiary undertaking attributable to the group's interest before the reduction and carrying amount attributable to the group's interest after the reduction together with any proceeds received. *[FRS 2.52]*.

This is a significant change in the accounting treatment.

2.1.5   Accounting for exchange differences on the disposal of a foreign operation in consolidated financial statements

Section 9 states that the cumulative amount of any exchange differences that relate to a foreign subsidiary recognised in equity are not recycled to profit or loss on disposal of the subsidiary (see 3.6.3 below). *[FRS 102.9.18A]*.

SSAP 20 – *Foreign Currency Translation* – did not explicitly deal with the disposal of a foreign operation. However, the implication of the standard (when taken together with other UK standards) was that, when a foreign operation was sold, no adjustment should be made to the cumulative amount of the exchange differences previously recognised in the STRGL in respect of that foreign operation. However, FRS 23 – *The effects of changes in foreign exchange rates* – required the cumulative amount of those exchange differences to be reversed out of the STRGL and recycled in profit or loss. *[FRS 23.N30]*.

This means that there is an accounting difference between FRS 102 and FRS 23 but not between FRS 102 and SSAP 20.

2.1.6   Presentation of non-controlling interest

Section 9 requires that non-controlling interest is presented within equity (see 3.7.1 below). *[FRS 102.9.20]*.

Previous UK GAAP did not specify where non-controlling interest was presented. The Companies Act requires that minority (non-controlling) interest is presented separately but does not require it to be presented within equity.

2.1.7   Losses attributable to non-controlling interest

Section 9 has no explicit requirement to make a provision for any formal or implied legal obligation to provide finance that may not be recoverable in respect of the accumulated losses attributable to the non-controlling interest (see 3.7.1 below).

Previous UK GAAP stated that where losses in a subsidiary undertaking result in net liabilities rather than net assets then the group should make provision for any commercial or legal obligation (formal or implied) to provide finance that may not be recoverable in respect of the accumulated losses attributable to the non-controlling interest. *[FRS 2.37]*.

Chapter 6

2.1.8   *Investments in subsidiaries, associates and jointly controlled entities in separate financial statements*

Section 9 states that investments in subsidiaries, associates and jointly controlled entities in individual and separate financial statements can be measured only at cost, at fair value with changes recognised in other comprehensive income or at fair value with changes recognised in profit or loss. The same accounting policy must be applied to all investments in a single class (see 4.2 below). *[FRS 102.9.24-26]*.

Previous UK accounting standards were silent on accounting for investments in subsidiaries, associates and jointly controlled entities in individual and separate financial statements. However, entities reporting under UK Company Law looked to Schedules 1-3 of the Large and Medium-sized Companies and Groups (Accounts and Reports) Regulations 2008, (the Regulations) which permit investments in subsidiaries, associates and jointly controlled entities in individual Companies Act financial statements to be measured, depending on the applicable Schedule, at either historical cost, market value (at date of last valuation), directors' valuation, current cost, current value or fair value. Although the Regulations have not changed, the option to use a 'directors' valuation' (typically, net assets), an out-of-date market valuation or a current cost to measure an investment in a subsidiary, associate or jointly controlled entity (and such measurements are not the equivalent of fair value at the reporting date) is incompatible with Section 9 and entities using such measurement bases will have to change to either cost or fair value upon adoption of FRS 102. Schedule 3 of the Regulations continues to not permit insurers to use 'cost' for an investment in a subsidiary, associate or jointly controlled entity.

2.1.9   *Disclosure differences*

Disclosure differences between FRS 102 and previous UK GAAP are discussed at in the summary at 5 below.

2.2   Key differences between Section 9 and IFRS

As indicated at 1 above, Section 9 is not based on IFRS 10. This means that there are a number of significant differences compared with IFRS.

2.2.1   *Requirement to prepare consolidated financial statements*

Section 9 contains various exemptions from the basic requirement that a parent prepare consolidated financial statements. These exemptions are aligned with UK Company Law (see 3.1.1 below). In addition, a parent is required to prepare consolidated financial statements only if it is a parent at the end of the financial year. *[FRS 102.9.2]*.

IFRS 10 has different exemptions from consolidation compared to those exemptions permitted by Section 9. *[IFRS 10.4]*. In particular, IFRS does not have an exemption from consolidation for small groups and the financial statements in which an intermediate parent is consolidated must be prepared under IFRS rather than an equivalent GAAP for that intermediate parent to be exempt from preparing consolidated financial statements. In addition, consolidated financial statements must be prepared if an entity is a parent at any time during its financial year (unless otherwise exempt).

This means that more parents are likely to be exempt from preparing consolidated financial statements under FRS 102 than under IFRS.

2.2.2 *Investment entities*

Section 9 states that a subsidiary held as part of an investment portfolio is not consolidated but, instead, recognised at fair value through profit or loss (see 3.4.2 below). *[FRS 102.9.9B(a)]*.

IFRS 10 states that a parent must determine whether it is an investment entity *[IFRS 10.27]*. and that an investment entity should measure all subsidiaries (other than those that provide services that relate to investment management services) at fair value through profit or loss. *[IFRS 10.31]*. IFRS 10 also has more detailed conditions for the use of the exception to consolidation than Section 9. *[IFRS 10.B85A-J]*.

This means that there could be accounting differences between FRS 102 and IFRS in respect of investment entities since the Section 9 exception applies to a subsidiary whereas the IFRS exception applies to a parent. IFRS 10 also has more detailed conditions for the use of the exception than Section 9.

2.2.3 *Definition of control*

Section 9 defines control as the power to govern the financial and operating policies of an entity so as to obtain benefits from its activities. *[FRS 102.9.4]*.

IFRS 10 states that an investor controls an investee when it is exposed, or has rights, to variable returns from its involvement with the investee and has the ability to affect those returns though its power over the investee. *[IFRS 10.16]*.

The difference in the definition of control (and the related application guidance) means that there will be circumstances when an entity is controlled by a parent under FRS 102 and not controlled under IFRS 10 (and *vice versa*). Likely areas of difference include potential voting rights, where control is exercised through an agent, control of special purposes entities (see 2.2.4 below), interests held as trustee or fiduciary and *de facto* control.

2.2.4 *Special purpose entities and structured entities*

Section 9 provides guidance on circumstances that indicate that an entity may control a special purpose entity which is defined as an entity created to establish a narrow objective. A risks and rewards model applies for special purpose entities which is different from the single control model in IFRS 10 (see 3.3 below). No additional disclosures are required for special purpose entities.

IFRS 12 – *Disclosure of Interests in Other Entities* – defines a structured entity as an entity designed so that voting or similar rights are not the dominant factor in deciding who controls the entity. *[IFRS 12.A]*. No specific guidance is given on circumstances that indicate than an entity may control a structured entity as reporting entities are expected to apply the single control model in IFRS 10 in determining the entities they control. In addition, separate disclosures are required in respect of structured entities in which a reporting entity has an interest.

Chapter 6

This means that a special purpose entity under FRS 102 will not always be a structured entity under IFRS and *vice versa* and that the entity may be consolidated under FRS 102 but not consolidated under IFRS 10 (and *vice versa*).

2.2.5   Subsidiaries excluded from consolidation

Section 9 states that subsidiaries are excluded from consolidation if they operate under severe long term restrictions or are held exclusively with a view to subsequent resale (see 3.4 below). These exceptions are aligned with UK Company Law.

IFRS 10 does not have similar exceptions. However, a subsidiary which operates under severe long term restrictions may fail to meet the definition of a subsidiary in IFRS 10 (due to lack of control) and therefore the effect may be the same. Difference between IFRS 10 and Section 9 in respect of investment entities (included in Section 9's definition of subsidiaries held exclusively with a view to resale) are discussed at 2.2.2 above.

2.2.6   Accounting for a retained interest in a disposal where control is lost in consolidated financial statements

Section 9 states that when a parent loses control of a subsidiary but the former parent continues to hold an investment in that entity then the carrying amount of the net assets (and goodwill) at the date that the entity ceases to be a subsidiary shall be recognised as cost on initial measurement of the retained investment (see 3.6.3 below). *[FRS 102.9.19]*.

IFRS 10 states that when a parent loses control of a subsidiary any retained interest in the former subsidiary must be recognised at fair value on the date that control is lost. *[IFRS 10.25(b)]*.

2.2.7   Accounting for exchange differences on the disposal of a foreign operation in consolidated financial statements

Section 9 states that the cumulative amount of any exchange differences that relate to a foreign subsidiary recognised in equity are not recycled to profit or loss on disposal of the subsidiary (see 3.6.3 below). *[FRS 102.9.18A]*.

IAS 21 – *The Effects of Changes in Foreign Exchange Rates* – states that exchange differences that relate to a foreign subsidiary recognised in equity are reclassified to profit or loss on disposal. *[IAS 21.48]*.

2.2.8   Accounting for non-controlling interests in consolidated financial statements

Section 9 states that non-controlling interests are initially measured at the net amount of the identifiable assets recognised in accordance with the requirements for a business combination (see 3.7.1 below). *[FRS 102.9.13(d)]*.

IFRS 3 – *Business Combinations* – allows an accounting policy choice (for each business combination) for the acquirer to initially recognise non-controlling interests (that are present ownership interests and entitle their holders to a proportionate share of the entity's net assets in the event of liquidation) at either the net amount of the identifiable assets or at fair value. All other components of non-controlling interests are initially measured at their acquisition date fair values unless another measurement basis is required by IFRSs *[IFRS 3.19]*. FRS 102 is silent on the measurement of such other components of non-controlling interests.

2.2.9 Accounting for exchanges of business or other non-monetary assets for an interest in a subsidiary in consolidated financial statements

Section 9 requires that, to the extent that a reporting entity retains an ownership interest in the business, or other non-monetary asset exchanged, that retained interest should be treated as having been owned by the reporting entity throughout the transaction and included at its pre-transaction carrying amount. To the extent that the fair value of the consideration received exceeds the carrying value of what has been exchanged, together with any related goodwill and cash given up, a gain is recognised. Any unrealised gains arising are reported in other comprehensive income. To the extent that the fair value of the consideration received is less than the carrying value of what has been exchanged, together with any related goodwill and cash given up, a loss is recognised (see 3.8 below).

IFRS 10 does not distinguish between realised and unrealised gains for equivalent transactions and requires the gain or loss, realised or unrealised, to be recognised in profit or loss. *[IFRS 10.B98]*. Additionally, when the transferred assets remain controlled by the acquirer after the business combination the assets must be measured at their carrying amount immediately before the transfer and no gain or loss is recognised. *[IFRS 3.38]*.

2.2.10 Cost of investment in a subsidiary in separate financial statements

When an investment in subsidiary is measured using the cost model and merger relief or group reconstruction relief is available, in respect of shares issued as consideration, then these reliefs allow the initial carrying amount of the investment to be equal to the previous carrying amount of the investment in the transferor's books (if group reconstruction relief is available) or the nominal value of the shares issued (if merger relief is available). *[FRS 102.A4.24]*. See 4.2.1 below.

IAS 27 – *Separate Financial Statements* – permits a new parent the option to measure the cost of an investment in subsidiary at the carrying amount of its share of the equity items shown in the separate financial statements of the original parent only for certain types of group reorganisation when a new parent is established. *[IAS 27.13]*. There is no option to use the previous nominal value of the shares issued, or the previous carrying amount of the investment in the transferor's books, as cost.

This means that, in circumstances when an entity which uses the cost model for measuring investments in subsidiaries is entitled to use group reconstruction relief or merger relief, the 'cost' will be different under FRS 102 and IFRS.

2.2.11 Intermediate payment arrangements in separate financial statements

Section 9 defines an intermediate payment arrangement and states that when an entity has *de facto* control of such an arrangement the entity shall account for it as an extension of its own business in its separate financial statements (See 4.5 below). *[FRS 102.9.35]*.

Chapter 6

IFRS has no guidance on accounting for intermediate payment arrangements. In our view, as explained in Chapter 31 of EY International GAAP 2015 an intermediate payment arrangement under IFRS can be accounted for in the separate financial statements of the entity that has *de facto* control either as an extension of the entity or as an investment in a subsidiary.

2.2.12   *Disclosure differences*

Disclosure differences between FRS 102 and IFRS are discussed at 5 below.

3   CONSOLIDATED FINANCIAL STATEMENTS

Consolidated financial statements are designed to extend the reporting entity to embrace other entities which are subject to its control. They involve treating the net assets and activities of subsidiaries held by the parent entity as if they were part of the parent entity's own net assets and activities; the overall aim is to present the results and state of affairs of the group as if they were those of a single entity.

The following key terms in Section 9 are defined in the Glossary: *[FRS 102 Appendix I]*

Term	*Definition*
Consolidated financial statements	The financial statements of a parent and its subsidiaries presented as those of a single economic entity.
Control (of an entity)	The power to govern the financial and operating policies of an entity so as to obtain benefits from its activities.
An interest held exclusively with a view to subsequent resale	An interest: • for which a purchaser has been identified or is being sought, and which is reasonably expected to be disposed of within approximately one year of its date of acquisition; or • that was acquired as a result of the enforcement of a security, unless the interest has become part of the continuing activities of the group or the holder acts as if it intends the interest to become so; or • which is held as part of an investment portfolio.
held as part of an investment portfolio	An interest is held as part of an investment portfolio if its value to the investor is through fair value as part of a directly or indirectly held basket of investments rather than as media through which the investor carries out business. A basket of investments is indirectly held if an investment fund holds a single investment in a second investment fund which, in turn, holds a basket of investments.
Non-controlling interest	The equity in a subsidiary not attributable, directly or indirectly, to a parent.
Parent	An entity that has one or more subsidiaries.
Subsidiary	An entity, including an unincorporated entity such as a partnership, that is controlled by another entity (known as the parent).

3.1   Requirement to present consolidated financial statements

The basic legal framework for consolidated financial statements in the UK is found in the Companies Act 2006. This requires that a company which is a parent company at the end of a financial year must prepare group accounts for that year unless it is exempt from the requirement. *[s399(2)]*. The group accounts must be consolidated and must give a true and fair view of the state of affairs as at the end of the financial year, and the profit and loss for the financial year of the undertakings included in the consolidation as a whole, so far as concerns members of the company. *[s404(1)-(2)]*.

Section 9 replicates the requirements of the Companies Act by requiring that, unless exempt, an entity which is a parent at its year end shall present consolidated financial statements in which it consolidates all its investments in subsidiaries in accordance with FRS 102. *[FRS 102.9.2]*. An entity that was a parent at the beginning of a year but sold all of its subsidiaries during the year is not required to present consolidated financial statements for that year. The entity will therefore prepare individual financial statements for that year and the comparatives will be the separate financial statements prepared for the previous year, not the consolidated financial statements for the previous year.

Parents that do not report under the Companies Act (e.g. overseas entities) are required to comply with the requirements of Section 9, and the Companies Act when referred to in Section 9, unless these requirements are not permitted by any statutory framework under which such entities report. *[FRS 102.9.1]*.

Consolidated financial statements are the financial statements of parent and its subsidiaries presented as those of a single economic entity. A subsidiary is defined in terms of control as an entity that is controlled by the parent. *[FRS 102.9.4]*.

The Companies Act defines a subsidiary slightly differently to Section 9 although the clear intent of the FRC is that it is expected that the 'answer' will be the same except in very exceptional circumstances. This is discussed at 3.2 below.

When an entity is not controlled by an investor but that investor has an interest in the entity, the investment in that entity will be accounted for as follows:

- where the investing entity does not have significant influence or joint control the investment will be accounted for as a financial instrument under Sections 11 – *Basic Financial Instruments* – and Section 12 – *Other Financial Instruments Issues*;

- where the investing entity has significant influence but not joint control the investment will be accounted for as an associate under Section 14 – *Investments in Associates*; and

- where the investing entity has joint control the investment will be accounted for under Section 15 – *Investments in Joint Ventures*.

3.1.1   *Exemptions from preparing consolidated financial statements*

As well as various rules on exclusion of particular subsidiaries from consolidation (see 3.3 below), there are a number of provisions which exempt parent companies from having to prepare consolidated accounts at all.

Chapter 6

Most of these exemptions replicate those permitted under the Companies Act and specific reference is made by Section 9 to the legislation. The exemptions are as follows: *[FRS 102.9.3]*

- the parent is a wholly-owned subsidiary and its immediate parent is established under the law of an European Economic Area (EEA) state. Exemption is conditional on compliance with certain further conditions set out in s400(2) of the Companies Act (see 3.1.1.A below);

- the parent is a majority-owned subsidiary and meets all the conditions for exemption as a wholly-owned subsidiary set out in s400(2) of the Companies Act as well as the additional conditions set out in s400(1)(b) of the Companies Act (see 3.1.1.A below);

- the parent is a wholly-owned subsidiary of another entity and that parent is not established under the law of an EEA state. Exemption is conditional on compliance with certain further conditions set out in s401(2) of the Companies Act (see 3.1.1.B and 3.1.1.C below);

- the parent is a majority-owned subsidiary and meets all of the conditions for exemption as a wholly-owned subsidiary set out in s401(2) of the Companies Act as well as the additional conditions set out in s401(1)(b) of the Companies Act (see 3.1.1.B and 3.1.1.C below);

- the parent, and the group headed by it, qualify as small as set out in s383 of the Companies Act and the group is not ineligible as set out in s384 of the Companies Act (see 3.1.1.D below);

- all of the parent's subsidiaries are required to be excluded from consolidation by paragraph 9.9 of Section 9 (see 3.1.1.E below); or

- for parents not reporting under the Companies Act, if its statutory framework does not require the preparation of consolidated financial statements (see 3.1.1.F below).

The exemptions in respect of s400-401 of the Companies Act referred to above do not apply if any of the parent's securities are admitted to trading on a regulated market of any EEA State within the meaning of EC Directive 2004/39/EC. *[FRS 102.9.3]*. This requirement repeats a restriction already contained within both s400 and s401 although not within the paragraphs s400(2) and s401(2) referred to by Section 9 above. *[s400(4), s401(4)]*. 'Securities' in this context is defined widely and means virtually any type of equity or debt instrument being shares and stocks, debentures (including debenture stock, loan stock, bonds, certificates of deposit and other similar instruments), warrants and similar instruments, and specified certificates and other instruments that confer rights in respect of securities including contractual commitments. *[s400(6), s401(6)]*.

3.1.1.A   *Parents that are a subsidiary of an immediate EEA parent*

The exemption from preparing consolidated financial statements for intermediate parents that are wholly or majority owned subsidiaries of an immediate EEA parent is conditional on compliance with the following conditions set out in s400(2) of the Companies Act:

(a) the company must be included in consolidated accounts for a larger group drawn up to the same date, or to an earlier date in the same financial year, by a parent undertaking established under the law of an EEA State;

(b) those accounts must be drawn up and audited, and that parent undertaking's annual report must be drawn up according to that law:

   (i) in accordance with the provisions of the Seventh Directive (83/349/EEC) (as modified, where relevant, by the provisions of the Bank Accounts Directive (86/635/EEC) or the Insurance Accounts Directive (91/674/EEC), or

   (ii) in accordance with international accounting standards.

(c) the company must disclose in its individual accounts that it is exempt from the obligation to prepare and deliver group accounts;

(d) the company must state in its individual accounts the name of the parent undertaking that draws up the group accounts referred to above and:

   (i) if it incorporated outside the United Kingdom, the place in which it is incorporated, or

   (ii) if it is unincorporated, the address of its principal place of business.

(e) the company must deliver to the registrar, within the period for filing its accounts and reports for the financial year in question, copies of,

   (i) those group accounts, and

   (ii) the parent undertaking's annual report, together with the auditor's report on them.

(f) there must be a certified translation of any document delivered to the registrar under (e) above if they are not in English.

In addition to the conditions discussed above, a parent that is a majority-owned (rather than wholly-owned) subsidiary of an immediate EEA parent must comply with additional conditions set out in s400(1)(b) to be exempt from the requirement to prepare consolidated accounts. These additional conditions provide protection for minority shareholders and state that the use of the exemption applies only if notice requesting the preparation of group accounts has not been served on the company by shareholders holding in aggregate more than half of the remaining allotted shares in the company or 5% of the total allotted shares in the company. Such notice must be served not later than six months after the end of the financial year before that to which it relates. *[s400(1)(b)].*

The EEA states are the 28 member states of the European Union (EU) plus Iceland, Lichtenstein and Norway. The national GAAPs of the 28 member states of the EU should have implemented the Seventh Directive. In order for the exemption to be taken if the parent is established in the other three countries, it will need to be established whether that country GAAP is in accordance with the Seventh Directive or in accordance with international accounting standards.

UK company law states that 'included in the consolidation', in relation to group accounts, or 'included in consolidated group accounts', means that the undertaking

Chapter 6

is included in the accounts by the method of full (and not proportional) consolidation, and references to an undertaking excluded from consolidation shall be construed accordingly. *[s474(1)]*. Therefore, if a parent is included at fair value through profit or loss in the financial statements of an investment entity parent it would not be entitled to the exemption.

One situation where the exemption may not be available is in the accounting period when a parent company becomes a subsidiary of another EEA company. Under the legislation, the exemption is not available if the company has not been included in a set of consolidated accounts of the new parent made up to a date which is coterminous or earlier than its own year end. It should be noted that the requirement is not that the particular accounts of the company will be included in a set of consolidated accounts of the parent, but that the company is included in accounts made up to a date which is coterminous or earlier than its own year end. This is illustrated in Example 6.1 below.

Example 6.1:   Accounting period in which parent entity becomes a subsidiary

Entity A (a parent) is acquired by Entity B (a parent undertaking established in an EEA state) in October 2015. Entity A has an accounting period ending 31 December 2015. Entity B has an accounting period ending 31 March 2016.

Entity A is unable to use the s400 exemption from preparing consolidated financial statements for its accounting period ending 31 December 2015 because it has not been included in consolidated accounts drawn up to 31 December 2015 or earlier in that financial year.

Even where the year ends of the intermediate parent company and the parent company are the same, problems can arise. The directors of the intermediate parent company have to state in the company's accounts that they are exempt from the obligation to prepare consolidated financial statements. However, some of the conditions which have to be met may not have taken place by the time the directors approve the financial statements of the intermediate parent. For example, the consolidated accounts, in which the intermediate parent is to be included, may not have been prepared and audited; this will be the case if the intermediate parent company has a timetable which requires audited accounts to be submitted prior to the audit report on the consolidated accounts being signed.

3.1.1.B   Intermediate parents that are subsidiaries of non EEA parents

The exemption from preparing consolidated financial statements for intermediate parents that are wholly or majority owned subsidiaries of non EEA parents is conditional on compliance with the following conditions set out in s401(2) of the Companies Act:

(a)   the company and all of its subsidiary undertakings must be included in consolidated accounts for a larger group drawn up to the same date, or to an earlier date in the same financial year, by a parent undertaking;

(b) those accounts and, where appropriate, the group's annual report, must be drawn up:

  (i) in accordance with the provisions of the Seventh Directive (83/349/EEC) (as modified, where relevant, by the provisions of the Bank Accounts Directive (86/635/EEC) or the Insurance Accounts Directive (91/674/EEC), or

  (ii) in a manner equivalent to consolidated accounts and consolidated annual reports so drawn up;

(c) the group accounts must be audited by one or more persons authorised to audit accounts under the law under which the parent undertaking which draws them up is established;

(d) the company must disclose in its individual accounts that it is exempt from the obligation to prepare and deliver group accounts;

(e) the company must state in its individual accounts the name of the parent undertaking that draws up the group accounts referred to above and:

  (i) if it is incorporated outside the United Kingdom, the country in which it is incorporated, or

  (ii) if it is unincorporated, the address of its principal place of business.

(f) the company must deliver to the registrar, within the period for filing its accounts and reports for the financial year in question, copies of,

  (i) the group accounts, and

  (ii) where appropriate the consolidated annual report, together with the auditor's report on them.

(g) there must be a certified translation of any document delivered to the registrar under (f) above if they are not in English.

The condition described at (a) above is different to the equivalent condition for intermediate parents that are subsidiaries of an immediate EEA parent (see 3.1.1.A above) as it also requires all subsidiaries of the intermediate parent to be included in the larger consolidation. As discussed at 3.1.1.A above, UK company law states that 'included in the consolidation' means included by way of full consolidation.

In addition to the conditions discussed above, a parent that is a majority-owned subsidiary of a non EEA parent must comply with additional conditions set out in s401(1)(b) to be exempt from the requirement to prepare consolidated accounts. These additional conditions provide protection for minority shareholders and state that the use of the exemption applies only if notice requesting the preparation of group accounts has not been served on the company by shareholders holding in aggregate more than half of the remaining allotted shares in the company or 5% of the total allotted shares in the company. Such notice must be served not later than six months after the end of the financial year before that to which it relates. *[s401(1)(b)]*.

The comments at 3.1.1.A above, including Example 6.1, apply here also.

The concept of equivalence for the purposes of (b) above is discussed at 3.1.1.C below.

Chapter 6

3.1.1.C   *Equivalence for the purposes of the s401 exemption for intermediate parents that are subsidiaries of non EEA parents*

The exemption from preparing consolidated financial statements for intermediate parents that are subsidiaries of non EEA parents is conditional on the higher parent's consolidated financial statements being drawn up either in accordance with the provisions of the Seventh Directive or *in a manner equivalent* to consolidated accounts and consolidated annual reports so drawn up.

Use of the exemption in s401 requires an analysis of a particular set of consolidated financial statements to determine whether they are drawn up in a manner equivalent to consolidated financial statements that are in accordance with the Seventh Directive. *[FRS 100.AG4].*

The Application Guidance to FRS 100 states that it is generally accepted that the reference to equivalence in s401 of the Companies Act does not mean compliance with every detail of the Seventh Directive. When assessing whether consolidated financial statements of a higher non-EEA parent are drawn up in a manner equivalent to consolidated financial statements and in accordance with the Seventh Directive, it is necessary to consider whether they meet the basic requirements of the Fourth and Seventh Directives; in particular the requirement to give a true and fair view, without implying strict conformity with each and every provision. A qualitative approach is more in keeping with the deregulatory nature of the exemption than a requirement to consider the detailed requirements on a checklist basis. *[FRS 100.AG5].*

Consequently, consolidated financial statements of a higher parent will meet the test of equivalence in the Seventh Directive if they: *[FRS 100.AG6]*

- give a true and fair view and comply with FRS 102;
- are prepared in accordance with EU-adopted IFRS;
- are prepared in accordance with IFRS, subject to the consideration of the reasons for any failure by the European Commission to adopt a standard or interpretation; or
- are prepared using other GAAPs which are closely related to IFRS, subject to the consideration of the effect of any differences from EU-adopted IFRS.

The IFRS for SMEs shall be assessed for equivalence with the Seventh Directive considering a number of factors including the disclosure requirements for extraordinary items, additional disclosures for financial liabilities held at fair value, shortening the presumed life of goodwill from 10 to not exceeding 5 years, recognising 'negative goodwill' in the income statement only when it meets the definition of a realised profit, replacing the prohibition on reversal of impairment losses with a requirement to reverse the loss if, and only if, the reasons for the impairment cease to apply and removing the requirement for unpaid called up share capital to be recognised as an offset to equity. *[FRS 100.AG6(f)].*

Other GAAPs should be assessed for equivalence with the Seventh Directive based on the particular facts, including the similarities to and differences from the Seventh Directive. *[FRS 100.AG6(e)].*

The EU has a mechanism to determine the equivalence to IFRS of GAAP from other countries. As of April 2012, via a Commission Implementing Decision amending Decision 2008/961/EC, the EU had determined that the following standards were considered as equivalent to EU-adopted IFRS (for the purposes of the Transparency and Prospectus Directive):

- US GAAP;
- Japanese GAAP;
- GAAP of the People's Republic of China
- GAAP of Canada;
- GAAP of the Republic of Korea; and
- GAAP of the Republic of India (treated as equivalent for financial years starting before 1 January 2015). *[FRS 100.AG7]*.

3.1.1.D   *Exemption from preparing consolidated financial statements for small groups*

The Companies Act does not require that companies that are subject to the Small Companies Regime prepare group accounts. *[s399(1)]*. Consequently, Section 9 exempts a parent from preparing consolidated financial statements if the group headed by it is small as set out in s383 and the group is not ineligible as set out in s384.

A parent company qualifies as small only if the group headed by it qualifies as small. *[s383(1)]*.

A group qualifies as small in relation to the parent company's first financial year if the qualifying conditions are met in that year. *[s383(2)]*.

A group qualifies as small in relation to a subsequent financial year of the parent company: *[s383(3)]*

- if the qualifying conditions are met in that year and the preceding financial year;
- if the qualifying conditions are met in that year and the group qualified as small in relation to the preceding financial year; or
- if the qualifying conditions were met in the preceding financial year.

The qualifying conditions are that a group must satisfy two out of three size criteria as follows: *[s383(4)]*

- aggregate turnover of not more than £6,500,000 net (or £7,800,000 gross);
- aggregate balance sheet total of not more than £3,260,000 net (or £3,900,000 gross);
- not more than 50 average number of employees;

The aggregate figures are ascertained by aggregating the relevant figures determined in accordance with s382 for each member of the group. *[s383(5)]*.

'Net' means after any set-offs and other adjustments made to eliminate inter-group transactions. 'Gross' means without those set-offs and other adjustments. *[s383(6)]*. The use of a gross basis allows groups to claim exemption from preparing group accounts without having to perform a consolidation exercise to prove their entitlement. The basis can be mixed with one limit satisfied on a gross basis and another satisfied on a net basis.

The 'balance sheet total' means the aggregate of amounts shown as assets in the company's balance sheet. *[s382(5)].*

For a period that is a company's financial year but not in fact a year the maximum figures for turnover must be proportionately adjusted. *[s382(4)].*

'Average number of employees' means the total number of employees for each month divided by the number of the months in the financial year. *[s382(6)].*

Even if the small group size criteria is met, a parent will not be able to claim the exemption from preparing group accounts if it a member of an illegible group. A group is ineligible if any of its members is: *[s384]*

- a public company;
- a body corporate (other than a company) whose shares are admitted to trading on a regulated market in an EEA state;
- a person (other than a small company) who has permission under Part 4 of the Financial Services and Markets act 2000 (c.8) to carry on a regulated activity;
- an e-money issuer;
- a small company that is an authorised insurance company, a banking company, a MiFID investment firm or a UCITS management company; or
- a person who carries on insurance market activity.

3.1.1.E   Exemption due to all subsidiaries excluded from consolidation

This exemption is similar the exemption in the Companies Act which states that a parent is exempt from the requirement to produce group accounts if, under s405, all of its subsidiary undertakings could be excluded from consolidation in Companies Act group accounts. *[s402].*

The circumstances in which subsidiaries can be excluded from consolidation are discussed at 3.3 below.

3.1.1.F   Exemption under statutory framework

This exemption applies to those entities not required to report under the Companies Act. It applies only if preparation of consolidated accounts is not required by the applicable statutory framework.

3.2   The definition of a subsidiary

The question of the definition of a subsidiary is fundamental to any discussion of consolidated accounts. The question is also related to the subject of off-balance sheet financing, because frequently this hinges on whether the group balance sheet should embrace the accounts of an entity which holds certain assets and liabilities that management may not wish to include in the consolidated accounts.

A subsidiary is defined in terms of control as an entity that is controlled by the parent. *[FRS 102.9.4].*

Control (of an entity) is the power to govern the financial and operating policies of an entity so as to obtain benefits from its activities. *[FRS 102.9.4]*. In substance, this is the same definition as in previous UK GAAP which stated that control was the ability of an undertaking to direct the financial and operating policies of another undertaking with a view to gaining economic benefit from its activities. *[FRS 2.6]*.

The definition requires two criteria for control:

• power over the financial and operating policies; and

• benefits from the entities activities to be obtained from that power.

Although FRS 102 does not define what financial and operating policies are, these are generally understood to include such areas as budgeting, capital expenditures, treasury management, dividend policy, production, marketing, sales and human resources.

Although no guidance is given as to what benefits means, we believe that these are not restricted to gains resulting from the entity's activities such as dividends or increases in the value of the investment in the entity but could also include benefits such as cross-selling received by the investor as a result of its power over the entity.

There is no requirement to actually exercise control. The requirement is to have the power to do so. Hence, a passive investor that has the necessary power still controls a subsidiary.

There is a rebuttable presumption that control exists when the parent owns, directly or indirectly, more than half of the voting power of an entity. That presumption may be overcome in exceptional circumstances if it can be clearly demonstrated that such ownership does not constitute control. *[FRS 102.9.5]*. No examples of such exceptional circumstances are provided and it would seem that there is a high hurdle to overcome this presumption.

Control can also exist when the parent owns half or less of the voting power but it has: *[FRS 102.9.5]*

• power over more than half of the voting rights by virtue of an agreement with other investors;

• power to govern the financial and operating policies of the entity under a statute or an agreement;

• power to appoint or remove the majority of the members of the board of directors or equivalent governing body and control of the entity is by that board or body; or

• power to cast the majority of votes at meetings of the board of directors or equivalent governing body and control of the entity is by that board or body.

These points above are essentially anti-avoidance measures which extend the control concept from control of a company in a general meeting to control of the board, or control of an entity by a body that is not the board.

Control can also be achieved by having options or convertible instruments that are currently exercisable. *[FRS 102.9.6]*. See 3.2.1 below.

Control can also be exercised by having an agent with the ability to direct the activities for the benefit of the controlling entity. *[FRS 102.9.6]*. See 3.2.2 below.

Chapter 6

Control can also exist when the parent has the power to exercise, or actually exercises, dominant influence or control over the undertaking, or it and the undertaking are managed on a unified basis. *[FRS 102.9.6A]*. No further guidance is provided by FRS 102 in respect of dominant influence. However, the Companies Act states that an undertaking shall not be regarded as having the right to exercise dominant influence over another undertaking unless it has a right to give directions with respect to the operating and financial policies of that other undertaking which its directors are obliged to comply with whether or not they are for the benefit of that other undertaking. *[7 Sch 4(1)]*. FRS 2 defined dominant influence as influence that can be exercised to achieve the operating and financial policies desired by the holder of that influence notwithstanding the rights of any other party. The exercise of dominant influence was defined as being the exercise of an influence that achieves the result that the operating and financial policies of the undertaking influenced are set in accordance with the wishes of the holder of the influence and for the holder's benefit whether or not those wishes are explicit. The actual exercise of dominant influence is identified by its effect in practice rather than by the way in which it is exercised. *[FRS 2.7]*.

Entities that are not controlled by voting or similar rights or those that are created with legal arrangements that impose strict requirements over their operations pose special problems. As a result, Section 9 provides guidance on determining who controls these types of entity, described as 'special purpose entities'. See 3.3 below.

For UK companies, the Companies Act defines an entity as a parent undertaking in relation to a subsidiary undertaking if: *[s1162(2)]*

- it holds a majority of the voting rights in the undertaking; or
- it is a member of the undertaking and has the right to appoint or remove a majority of its board of directors; or
- it has the right to exercise dominant influence over the undertaking;
    - by virtue of provisions contained in the undertaking's articles; or
    - by virtue of a control contract; or
- it is a member of the undertaking and controls alone, pursuant to an agreement with other shareholders or members, a majority of the voting rights in the undertaking.

An undertaking is also a parent undertaking in relation to a subsidiary undertaking if: *[s1162(4)]*

- it has the power to exercise, or actually exercises, dominant influence or control over it; or
- it and the subsidiary undertaking are managed on a unified basis.

Although there are slight differences in wording emphasis between this definition and the requirements in Section 9, in our view, we would expect to see few conflicts arising in practice between Section 9 and the Companies Act that would require the use of a true and fair override.

3.2.1   Potential voting rights

Control can be achieved by having options or convertible instruments that are currently exercisable. *[FRS 102.9.6]*. These instruments may be shares, warrants, share call options, debt or equity instruments that are convertible into instruments that have the potential, if exercised or converted, to give the entity power or reduce another party's voting power over the financial and operating policies of another entity. Previous UK GAAP was silent on the matter of potential voting rights.

The existence and effect of potential voting rights must be considered when assessing whether an entity has the power to govern the financial and operating policies of another entity so as to obtain benefits from its activities. When an option to acquire a controlling interest in an entity has not yet been exercised, but can be freely exercised by its holder (that is, it could be exercised and, if exercised, would give the holder control) the holder in effect has the power of veto and has the power to govern the entity's financial and operating policies.

Potential voting rights are not currently exercisable or convertible when they cannot be exercised or converted until a future date or until the occurrence of a future event. Example 6.2 illustrates the meaning of currently exercisable.

Example 6.2:   Potential voting rights – meaning of currently exercisable

An entity (A) holds 40% of another entity (B). It also holds loan notes in B convertible, at A's option, into further shares in B, which if issued would give A a 60% interest in B. A can require conversion of its loan notes into shares at any time on or after the fifth anniversary of their issue.

Until that fifth anniversary occurs, A cannot exercise its conversion rights. Therefore, they are not currently exercisable and B is not (absent other circumstances) controlled by A and therefore not a subsidiary of A. Once the fifth anniversary has occurred, A's option to convert the loan into shares of B is currently exercisable. Therefore, at that date, A has control over the majority of the voting rights of B, such that B therefore becomes a subsidiary of A at that date.

An entity must exercise judgement when determining whether potential voting rights are currently exercisable. A literal reading might suggest that unless the potential voting right is exercisable immediately, the entity ignores the potential voting right when assessing control. In practice, however, many potential voting rights are not exercisable immediately but rather only exercisable after giving notice (e.g. options over the shares of unlisted entities often include a notice period of several days or a week). In practice, a short notice period is usually ignored when assessing whether the rights are currently exercisable.

Section 9 provides no guidance on whether the intention of management or the financial ability to exercise or convert a potential voting right are factors that must be considered in assessing whether those rights give control. However, the definition of a subsidiary (see 3.2 above) requires an entity to have the power to exercise dominant influence or control. In our view, this means that that the ability to exercise or convert a potential voting right should be considered in assessing whether those rights give control but not management intent (which can usually be changed on a whim). This is similar to the requirement in IFRS 10 that only substantive rights relating to an investee held by an investor are considered in assessing control and, for a right to be substantive, the holder must have the practical ability to exercise that right. *[IFRS 10.B22]*.

Chapter 6

3.2.2   Control exercised through an agent

Control can be achieved by having an agent with the ability to direct the activities for the benefit of the controlling entity. *[FRS 102.9.6]*.

The overall relationship between the investor and the agent must be assessed to determine whether the agent is acting as an agent for the controlling entity or as a principal in its own right.

3.2.3   Interests held as trustee or fiduciary

A reporting entity may hold, as a trustee or fiduciary on behalf of others, an interest in another entity that either on its own or when combined with any interest held on its own account, gives the reporting entity control of the majority of the voting rights in, or the ability to appoint or remove a majority of the members of the board of the other entity. This raises the question of whether that other entity is controlled by the reporting entity.

In our view, interests held in another entity on behalf of others generally do not give a reporting entity control over that other entity. Control is 'the power to govern the financial and operating policies of an entity *so as to obtain benefits from its activities*' (emphasis added). *[FRS 102.9.4]*. A trustee or other fiduciary exercises any decision-making powers relating to assets under its management so as to obtain benefits not for itself, but for those on whose behalf it exercises the powers.

As illustrated in Example 6.3, consolidation is still required if an entity legally owns and controls an investment, even if the risks and rewards have been passed on to a third party. Determining whether an entity controls an investment or merely holds an interest in a fiduciary capacity requires a careful assessment of the facts and circumstances.

Example 6.3:   Control over investment vehicle by an insurance entity

An insurance entity makes certain investments on behalf of unit-linked contract holders. One of those investments is an interest of more than 50% in an investment fund. The unit-linked contract holders are not the legal owner of the investment in the fund. In addition, the insurance entity is under no obligation to return the shares in the underlying investment to the unit-linked contract holders upon termination of the contract. The insurance entity is the legal owner and the unit-linked contract holders have no direct relationship with (and decision-making powers over) the investment fund.

The unit-linked contracts do not diminish the insurance entity's ability to control the investment fund. Therefore, the presumption is that the insurance entity consolidates the investment fund unless it can be demonstrated that it does not have control. While the insurance entity holds a matched position of units in the investment fund and unit-linked contracts, it is under no obligation to hold an investment in the units of the investment fund. Conversely, the unit-linked contract holders have no direct legal rights that entitle them to the units in the investment fund that are owned by the insurance entity. In other words, the insurance entity does not hold the units in the investment fund in a fiduciary capacity.

3.2.4   De facto control

De facto control over an entity by a minority shareholder may arise in a number of ways. A common example is when other shareholders are widely dispersed, and when a sufficient number of other shareholders regularly fail to exercise their rights as shareholders (e.g. to vote at general meetings), such that the minority shareholder wields the majority of votes actually cast.

However, we believe that Section 9 does not necessarily require consolidation of entities subject only to *de facto* control since the definition of control refers to the power to govern the financial and operating policies of an entity and power is explained as representing the ability to do or effect something, whether actively or passively.

The determination of whether *de facto* control exists is based on facts and circumstances. It is unlikely to be sufficiently certain that *de facto* control exists until actions taken provide evidence of control – i.e. control must be actively exercised. In general, the more that the legal or contractually-based powers that are held in relation to an entity fall short of 50% of the total powers, the greater is the need for evidence of actively exercised *de facto* control.

As noted at 3.2 above, control is defined as 'the power to govern the financial and operating policies of an entity so as to obtain benefits from its activities.' It follows from this definition that control involves the ability:

- to make decisions without the support or consent of other shareholders; and
- to give directions with respect to the operating and financial policies of the entity concerned, with which directions the entity's directors are obliged to comply.

Accordingly, control does not exist where an investor must obtain the consent of one or more other shareholders in order to govern the operating and financial policies of the investee.

To have the ability to govern the financial and operating policies of an entity, an investor must be able to hold the management of the entity accountable. It is therefore unlikely that *de facto* control over an entity can exist unless the investor has the power to appoint and remove a majority of its governing body (i.e. normally the board of directors in the case of a company). This power is normally exercisable by holders of the voting shares in general meeting.

In practice, *de facto* control is most likely to be evidenced where an investor with less than a 50% voting interest is able to have its chosen candidates (re)nominated for election to an entity's board of directors and its votes exceed 50% of the votes typically cast in the entity's election of directors. For example, if typically only 70% of the eligible votes are cast on resolutions for the appointment of directors, a minority holding of 40% might give *de facto* control if the remaining shares are widely held (for example, no party has an interest of sufficient size either of itself or with a small number of others, to block decisions).

The question also arises as to whether *de facto* control can exist where a minority voting interest represents less than 50% of votes typically cast in elections of directors, for example, a voting interest of 30% where, typically, 70% of the eligible votes are cast in elections. It is highly unlikely that *de facto* control exists in this case. As control is unilateral, when assessing whether *de facto* control exists, the entity does not consider the possibility that other shareholders will cast their votes in the same way as the entity.

Determining when an entity is subject to *de facto* control is not easy in practice. Consistency demands that the investment in an entity does not unnecessarily 'yo-yo' in and out of consolidation – resulting in a series of business combinations and disposals – where a more careful judgement would have avoided it.

Chapter 6

3.3   Special purpose entities (SPEs)

An SPE is described as an entity created to accomplish a narrow objective (e.g. to effect a lease, undertake research and development activities, securitise financial assets or facilitate employee shareholdings under remuneration schemes, such as Employee Share Ownership Plans (ESOPs)). An SPE may take the form of a corporation, trust, partnership or unincorporated entity. SPEs are often created with legal arrangements that impose strict requirements over the operations of the SPE. *[FRS 102.9.10].*

The requirements for SPEs do not apply to a post-employment benefit plan or other long-term employee benefit plan to which Section 28 – *Employee Benefits* – applies. *[FRS 102.9.12].*

Intermediate payment arrangements that are special purpose entities which are controlled by an entity are accounted in the separate financial statements of that entity using the parent extension method. See 4.5 above.

In our view, the description of an SPE is broader than a separate legal entity. For example, a parcel of 'ring fenced' assets and liabilities within a larger legal entity, such as a cell in a protected cell entity might be an SPE. A portfolio of securitised assets and the related borrowings might also be an SPE.

The sponsor (or entity on whose behalf the SPE was created) frequently transfers assets to the SPE, obtains the right to use assets held by the SPE or performs services for the SPE, while other parties ('capital providers') may provide funding to the SPE. An entity that engages in transactions with an SPE (frequently the creator or sponsor) may in substance control the SPE. For example, an entity might have a beneficial interest in an SPE, which may take the form of a debt instrument, an equity instrument, a participation right, a residual interest or a lease. Some beneficial interests provide the holder with a fixed or stated rate of return, while others give the holder rights or access to other future economic benefits of the SPE's activities. In most cases, the creator or sponsor (or the entity on whose behalf the SPE was created) retains a significant beneficial interest in the SPE's activities, even though it may own little or none of the SPE's equity.

Unless a parent is not required to prepare consolidated financial statements – see 3.1 above – a parent entity shall prepare consolidated financial statements that include the entity and any SPEs that controlled by that entity. In addition to the circumstances described at 3.2 above, the following circumstances may indicate that an entity controls an SPE (this is not an exhaustive list): *[FRS 102.9.11]*

- the activities of the SPE are being conducted on behalf of the entity according to its specific business needs;

- the entity has ultimate decision-making powers over the activities of the SPE even if the day-to-day decisions have been have been delegated;

- the entity has rights to obtain the majority of the benefits of the SPE and therefore may be exposed to risks incidental to the activities of the SPE; and

- the entity retains the majority of the residual or ownership risks related to the SPE or its assets.

Activities are likely to be conducted on behalf of the entity according to its specific business needs where the reporting entity created the SPE, directly or indirectly. Examples of decision-making powers over the activities of the SPE even where those decisions have been delegated, by for example setting up an auto pilot mechanism, would include the power to unilaterally dissolve the SPE or the power to change, or veto proposed changes to, the SPE's charter or byelaws. Rights to obtain benefits and exposure to risks incidental to the activities of the SPE may arise through statute, contract, agreement, trust deed or any other scheme, arrangement or device. Such rights to benefits in an SPE may be indicators of control when they are specified in favour of an entity that is engaged in transactions with an SPE and that entity stands to gain those benefits from the financial performance of the SPE. Residual or ownership risks may arise through the guarantee of a return or credit protection directly or indirectly through the SPE to outside investors who provide substantially all of the capital to the SPE. As a result of the guarantee, the entity could retain residual or ownership risks and the investors are, in substance, only lenders because their exposure to gains and losses is limited.

No relative weight is given to the various indicators when determining whether an SPE should be consolidated. However, control of an entity comprises the ability to govern the entity's financial and operating policies so as to obtain benefits from the activities of the entity. *[FRS 102.9.4]*. The ability to control decision-making alone is not sufficient to establish control, but must be accompanied by the objective of obtaining benefits from the entity's activities. This reminder counters arguments of those seeking to establish an off-balance sheet SPE, who tend to argue that a third party (such as a charitable trust) owns all the voting rights. However, if the trust does not obtain any real benefit from the SPE, (which is typically the case) this indicates that the trust does not control the SPE.

3.3.1 Benefits need not necessarily be financial

As discussed at 3.3 above, the first of the indicators of whether an entity is an SPE is that its activities are being conducted on behalf of the reporting entity according to its specific business needs.

In our view, this indicator does not necessarily require that the reporting entity has any direct financial benefit. The 'benefit' might be the avoidance of negative outcomes.

3.3.2 Majority of the benefits and risks

In our view, the reference to the majority of benefits and risks in the third and fourth indicators at 3.3 above refer to the majority of benefits and risks that are likely to arise in practice, rather than to the majority of all theoretically possible benefits and risks as illustrated by Example 6.4.

Example 6.4:   Assessment of majority of benefits and risks of an SPE

An SPE is established to undertake a securitisation of financial assets. The SPE has only nominal equity, but issues £1,000 of debt – £100 subordinated debt to the reporting entity and £900 senior debt to a financial institution. The SPE buys £1,000 of receivables from the reporting entity.

The terms of the two classes of debt have the effect that the reporting entity bears the first £100 of any credit losses and the financial institution the remainder. This could suggest that the financial institution is bearing the majority of the risks, since it has £900 of the possible £1,000 bad debt risk. However, if (as is likely to be the case) bad debt risk is in the range of 5% to 7%, all the losses that are likely to occur will be borne by the reporting entity as the holder of the subordinated debt. Therefore, the reporting entity should consolidate the SPE because it retains the majority of residual or ownership risks of the SPE.

3.3.3   Subsequent reassessment of control of an SPE

Section 9 is silent on whether an entity must reassess who controls an SPE after inception. In our view, the basic principles of consolidation must be considered. Section 9 requires consolidation when there is control. Ordinarily, for an SPE, one would not expect changes in control after inception. However, in our view, re-assessing whether a reporting entity continues to control an SPE is required when:

(a)   there is a change in the contractual arrangements between the parties to the SPE; or

(b)   any of the parties take steps to strengthen its position and, in doing so, acquires a greater level of control.

Reassessment of which party controls an SPE is a difficult issue; each situation must be assessed based on the facts and circumstances.

An example of the situation in (b) is that if in a period of financial difficulty, commercial paper cannot be reissued for longer than a certain period, the agreement governing the structure may require the assets to be liquidated. The liquidity provider, knowing that a sale of the assets in that difficult environment is likely to result in losses, might decide to extend the life of the structure by buying the new issue of commercial paper. This was not an action that was anticipated in the original agreement and may mean that the liquidity provider has changed the relative contractual positions of the parties to the SPE and taken effective control.

So long as the initial control assessment is not called into question (e.g. because it was based on incomplete or inaccurate information), subsequent changes in the relationship due to changes in the risk profile, or market events, do not necessarily mean that there has been any transfer of control between the parties. For example, the impairment of the assets owned by an SPE would not necessarily trigger reassessment. Similarly, if the losses incurred by an SPE exceed the capital provided to it, such that the residual risk now lies with another party, (for example the SPE sponsor), this event alone would not necessarily trigger reassessment. However, when events such as these occur, the party bearing the residual risk often takes steps to protect its position, which in turn might trigger a reassessment of whether that party controls the SPE and therefore consolidates the SPE.

3.3.4   Securitisation transactions

SPEs are most commonly found in, but are not unique to, the financial services sector, where they are used as vehicles for securitisation of financial assets such as mortgages or credit card receivables. The effect of these requirements combined with the derecognition provisions of Section 11 – *Basic Financial Instruments* – may be that:

- a securitisation transaction qualifies as a sale of the financial asset concerned (which is thus, in principle, derecognised, or removed from the financial statements); but

- the 'buyer' is an SPE, so that the asset is immediately re-recognised through consolidation of the SPE.

3.4   Subsidiaries excluded from consolidation

In general, a parent should consolidate all subsidiaries in its consolidated financial statements. However, there are various circumstances under which it is considered appropriate not to consolidate particular subsidiaries but instead either deal with them in some other manner or to exclude them from the consolidated financial statements altogether.

The Companies Act *permits* subsidiaries to be excluded from consolidation on certain grounds. *[s405]*. Within the constraints of the Companies Act, Section 9 *requires* exclusion from consolidation on certain grounds and interprets how the Companies Act is to be applied.

Section 9 requires a subsidiary to be excluded from consolidation where: *[FRS 102.9.9]*

- severe long-term restrictions substantially hinder the exercise of the rights of the parent over the assets or management of the subsidiary (see 3.3.1 below); or

- the interest in the subsidiary is held exclusively with a view to subsequent resale and the subsidiary has not previously been consolidated in the consolidated financial statements prepared in accordance with FRS 102 (see 3.3.2 below).

In addition to the circumstances of severe long-term restrictions and held exclusively with a view to subsequent resale, the Companies Act also permits subsidiaries to be excluded from consolidation if the information necessary for the preparation of group accounts cannot be obtained without disproportionate expense or undue delay. *[s405(3)(b)]*. However, Section 9 does not permit a subsidiary to be excluded from consolidation on these grounds unless its inclusion is not material (individually or collectively) for the purpose of giving a true and fair view in the context of the group. *[FRS 102.9.8A]*.

The Companies Act also permits subsidiaries to be excluded from consolidation on the grounds of immateriality (both individually and collectively). *[s405(2)]*. However, as discussed in the preceding paragraph, Section 9 has limited this materiality criterion so that it applies only to a subsidiary where information necessary for the preparation of consolidated accounts cannot be obtained without disproportionate expense or undue delay.

Section 9 states explicitly that a subsidiary is not excluded from consolidation because its business activities are dissimilar to those of other entities within the consolidation. In the opinion of the FRC, relevant information is provided by consolidating such subsidiaries and disclosing additional information in the consolidated financial statements about the different business activities of subsidiaries. *[FRS 102.9.8]*.

Chapter 6

3.4.1   *Subsidiaries excluded from consolidation due to severe long term restrictions*

A subsidiary excluded from consolidation because severe long-term restrictions substantially hinder the exercise of the rights of the parent over the assets or management of the subsidiary is accounted for in the consolidated financial statements as if it is an investment in a subsidiary in separate financial statements (i.e. either at cost less impairment, at fair value with changes in fair value recognised through other comprehensive income or at fair value with changes in fair value recognised in profit and loss). However, if the parent still exercises a significant influence over the subsidiary it should be treated as an associate using the equity method. *[FRS 102.9.9A]*. In our view, consistent with the requirements for disposal where control is lost (see 3.6.1 below), the initial cost of the investment in the subsidiary in these circumstances should be the carrying amount of the net assets (and goodwill) attributable to the investment on the date that the severe long term restrictions affected the parent's exercise of its rights over the subsidiary.

The Accounting Council's advice to the FRC which accompanies FRS 102 clarifies that a true and fair override is required for subsidiaries excluded from consolidation that are held at fair value through profit or loss as this accounting is not permitted by the Companies Act. *[FRS 102.AC.51]*.

Section 9 does not provide any examples of situations in which a subsidiary might be subject to severe long term restrictions that hinder the exercise of the parent's rights over the assets or management of the subsidiary. However, examples might include:

- insolvency or administration of the subsidiary; or
- veto powers held by a third party (e.g. a lender due to covenant breaches).

Section 9 provides no guidance as to the accounting if the severe long-term restrictions cease and the parent undertaking's rights are restored. In our view, since the parent has now obtained control, the appropriate accounting is to treat the restoration of control as a business combination under Section 19 – *Business Combinations and Goodwill* – with the difference between the fair value of the net assets of the subsidiary and the carrying value of the investment at the date control is restored recognised as goodwill.

3.4.2   *Subsidiaries held exclusively with a view to subsequent resale*

A subsidiary held exclusively with a view to subsequent resale is an interest:
[FRS 102 Appendix I]

- for which a purchaser has been identified or is being sought, and which is reasonably expected to be disposed of within approximately one year of its date of acquisition; or
- that was acquired as a result of the enforcement of a security, unless the interest has become part of the continuing activities of the group or the holder acts as if it intends the interest to become so; or
- which is held as part of an investment portfolio (see 3.4.2.A below).

For a subsidiary to be classified as held exclusively with a view to subsequent resale it must not have been consolidated previously in consolidated financial statements prepared under FRS 102. *[FRS 102.9.9(b)].*

A subsidiary excluded from consolidation on the grounds that is held exclusively for resale is accounted for in the consolidated financial statements as follows: *[FRS 102.9.9B]*

- a subsidiary held as part of an investment portfolio is measured at fair value with changes in fair value recognised in profit and loss; and

- a subsidiary not held as part of an investment portfolio is accounted for as if it was an investment in a subsidiary in separate financial statements either at cost less impairment, at fair value with changes in fair value recognised in other comprehensive income or at fair value with changes in fair value recognised in profit or loss.

The Accounting Council's advice to the FRC which accompanies FRS 102 clarifies that a true and fair override is required for subsidiaries excluded from consolidation that are held at fair value through profit or loss (whether or not these are subsidiaries held as part of an investment portfolio) as this is not permitted by the Companies Act. *[FRS 102.AC.51].*

Section 9 provides no guidance as to the accounting if a subsidiary is no longer considered to be held exclusively with a view to subsequent resale. In our view, the appropriate accounting is to consolidate the subsidiary at the date of the change in circumstances and to treat this consolidation as a business combination under Section 19. The difference between the fair value of the individual net assets of the subsidiary and the previous carrying value should be recognised as goodwill. This is consistent with the similar requirements of IFRS 10 for investment entities which cease to be investment entities.

3.4.2.A   Subsidiary held as part of an investment portfolio

A subsidiary is held as part of an investment portfolio if its value to the investor is through fair value as part of a directly or indirectly held basket of investments rather than as media through which the investor carries out business. A basket of investments is indirectly held if an investment fund holds a single investment fund in a second investment fund which, in turn, holds a basket of investments. *[FRS 102 Appendix I].*

The concept that an interest held as part of an investment portfolio meets the definition of an interest held exclusively with a view to subsequent resale is an interpretation of Company Law that did not exist in previous UK GAAP. The Accounting Council's advice to the FRC which accompanies FRS 102 states that this new interpretation takes into account the IASB's publication of *Investment Entities – Amendments to IFRS 10, IFRS 12 and IAS 27 –* in October 2012. *[FRS 102.AC.50].*

The entities most likely to be affected by this exception are:

- subsidiaries of private equity or venture capital funds; and

- investment fund subsidiaries of banks, insurers, asset managers and property managers.

The investment portfolio exception from consolidation is considerably different than that granted by the investment entity exception to IFRS 10. It applies to an individual subsidiary rather than to a parent, contains no requirement for the parent to have an exit strategy for its investment portfolio and the definition explicitly refers to indirectly held investments. It is therefore anticipated that this will have a wider application than the Investment Entity exception in IFRS 10 and that they may be considerable diversity in practice, especially in the financial services industry, as to what is considered to be an interest in an investment portfolio.

3.5   Consolidation procedures

Consolidated financial statements present financial information about a group as a single economic entity. Therefore, in preparing consolidated financial statements an entity shall: *[FRS 102.9.13]*

- combine the financial statements of the parent and its subsidiaries line by line by adding together like items of assets, liabilities, equity, income and expenses;

- eliminate the carrying amount of the parent's investment in each subsidiary and the parent's portion of equity of each subsidiary;

- measure and present non-controlling interest in the profit or loss of consolidated subsidiaries for the reporting period separately from the interest of the owners of the parent; and

- measure and present non-controlling interest in the net assets of consolidated subsidiaries separately from the parent shareholders' equity in them. Non-controlling interests in the net assets consist of:

  - the amount of the non-controlling interest's share in the net amount of the identifiable assets, liabilities and contingent liabilities recognised and measured in accordance with Section 19 at the date of the original combination; and

  - the non-controlling interest's share of changes in equity since the date of the combination.

The proportions of profit or loss and changes in equity allocated to owners of the parent and to the non-controlling interests are determined on the basis of existing ownership interests and do not reflect the possible exercise or conversion of options or convertible instruments. *[FRS 102.9.14]*. This means that, for example, although a parent may have control of an entity through the ability to exercise a currently exercisable option (see 3.2.1 above) the parent's and non-controlling interest's allocation of profit and loss and equity are not generally affected until the option is actually exercised. Example 6.5 illustrates this principle.

Example 6.5:   Potential voting rights

Entities A and B hold 40% and 60%, respectively, of the equity of Entity C. A also holds a currently exercisable option over one third of B's shares, which, if exercised, would give A a 60% interest in C. This would, absent exceptional circumstances, lead to the conclusion that C is a subsidiary of A. However, in preparing its consolidated financial statements, A attributes 60% of the results and net assets of C to non-controlling interests.

The following is discussed in more detail below:

- intragroup balances and transactions – see 3.5.1
- uniform reporting dates and reporting period – see 3.5.2
- uniform accounting policies – see 3.5.3
- consolidating foreign operations – see 3.5.4

The accounting for non-controlling interests is discussed further at 3.7 below.

3.5.1   Intragroup balances and transactions

Intragroup balances and transactions, including income, expenses and dividends must be eliminated in full. Profits and losses resulting from intragroup transactions that are recognised in assets, such as inventory and property, plant and equipment must also be eliminated in full. *[FRS 102.9.15].* Example 6.6 below illustrates this.

Example 6.6:   Eliminating intragroup transactions

Entity A holds a 75% interest in Entity B. A sold inventory to with a cost of £100 to B for £200 (i.e. a profit of £100). B still held the inventory at the end of the reporting period.

As well as the intragroup sale between A and B, the unrealised profit of £100 is eliminated from the group's point of view in consolidation (the consolidation adjustment is DR turnover in A £200, CR inventory in B £100, CR cost of sales in A £100). The profit from the sale of inventory of £100 is reversed against the group profit and loss. As the parent made the sale, no amount of the eliminated profit is attributed to the non-controlling interest.

If the fact pattern were reversed such that B sold inventory to A, and A still held the inventory at the end of the reporting period, the same consolidation journal entries above would still be reversed in the consolidated financial statements. However, in this instance, as the subsidiary made the sale, £25 of the eliminated profit (i.e. the non-controlling interest's 25% share of the £100 profit) would be allocated to the non-controlling interest.

If the inventory held by B had been sold to a third party for £300 before the end of the reporting period (resulting in a profit in A of £100 for the sale to B at £200 and a profit in B of £100 for the sale to a third party at £300) no intragroup elimination of profit is required. The group has sold an asset with a cost of £100 for £300 creating a profit to the group of £200. In this case, the intragroup elimination is limited to the sale between A and B (DR turnover in A £200, CR cost of sales in B £200).

Even though losses on intragroup transactions are eliminated in full, they may still indicate an impairment, under Section 27 – *Impairment of Assets,* that requires recognition in the consolidated financial statements. *[FRS 102.9.15].* For example, if a parent sells a property to a subsidiary at fair value and this is lower than the carrying amount of the asset, the transfer may indicate that the property (or the cash-generating unit to which that property belongs) is impaired in the consolidated financial statements. This will not always be the case as the asset's value-in-use may be sufficient to support the higher carrying value. See Chapter 22 at 4.1.

Intragroup transactions give rise to a tax expense or benefit in the consolidated financial statements under Section 29 – *Income Tax* – which applies to timing differences that arise from the elimination of profits and losses arising from intragroup transactions. *[FRS 102.9.15].* See Chapter 24 at 6.1.

Chapter 6

3.5.2   *Uniform reporting dates and reporting period*

The directors of a parent company have an obligation under the Companies Act to secure that, except where in their opinion there are good reasons against it, the financial year of each of its subsidiary undertakings coincides with the company's own financial year. *[s390(5)]*.

Therefore, Section 9 states that the financial statements of the parent and its subsidiaries used in the preparation of consolidated financial statements shall be prepared as of the same reporting date, and for the same reporting period, unless it is impracticable to do so. Impracticability is discussed in Chapter 7 at 3.3.2.

Paragraph 2 of Schedule 6 of the Regulations provides two options if the reporting date and reporting period of a subsidiary are not the same as the parent's reporting date and reporting period. These options are replicated by Section 9 which requires that the consolidated financial statements must be made up: *[FRS 102.9.16]*

- from the financial statements of the subsidiary as of its last reporting date before the parent's reporting date, adjusted for effects of significant transactions or evens that occur between the date of those financial statements and the date of the consolidated financial statements, provided that the reporting date is no more than three months before that of the parent; or

- from interim financial statements prepared by the subsidiary as at the parent's reporting date.

3.5.3   *Uniform accounting policies*

Consolidated financial statements must be prepared using uniform accounting policies for like transactions and other events and conditions in similar circumstances. Therefore, if a member of the group uses accounting policies other than those adopted in the consolidated financial statements for like transactions and events in similar circumstances, appropriate adjustments are to be made to its financial statements in preparing the consolidated financial statements. *[FRS 102.9.17]*.

However, as an exception to this rule, using non-uniform accounting policies for insurance contracts (and related deferred acquisition costs and related intangible assets, if any) is permitted if this is a continuation of an accounting policy used under previous GAAP. *[FRS 103.2.6(c)]*.

Other than for insurance contracts, non-uniform accounting policies are not permitted (unless the directors invoke a true and fair override) although the Regulations are more lenient and allow non-uniform accounting policies if it appears to the directors that there are special reasons for it and these reasons and their effect are disclosed. *[6 Sch 3(2)]*.

3.5.4   *Consolidating foreign operations*

Section 9 does not specifically address how to consolidate subsidiaries that are foreign operations. Section 30 – *Foreign Currency Translation* – states that when a group contains individual entities with different functional currencies, the items of income and expense and financial position of each entity are expressed in a common currency so that consolidated financial statements may be presented. *[FRS 102.30.17].* No preference is stated as to whether the financial statements of a foreign operation are translated directly into the presentation currency of the group (known as the direct method) or translated into the functional currency of any intermediate parent and then translated into the presentation currency of the group (known as the step-by-step method). Both methods produce exactly the same outcomes, with the exception of the currency translation differences that arise on consolidation. In our view, either method is acceptable provided it is applied consistently.

In incorporating the assets, liabilities, income and expenses of a foreign operation with those of the reporting entity, normal consolidation procedures are followed, such as the elimination of intragroup balances and intragroup transactions. However, an intragroup monetary asset, whether short-term or long-term, cannot be eliminated against the corresponding intragroup liability (or asset) without showing the results of the currency fluctuations in the consolidated financial statements which must be reflected in either profit or loss or other comprehensive income as appropriate. *[FRS 102.30.22].*

3.6 Acquisitions and disposals of subsidiaries

In consolidated financial statements, except where a business combination is accounted for by using the merger method under Section 19 or, for certain public benefit entity combinations accounted for under Section 34 – *Specialised Activities*, the income and expenses of a subsidiary are included from the acquisition date until the date on which the parent ceases to control the subsidiary. *[FRS 102.9.18].*

Section 9 observes that a parent may cease to control a subsidiary with or without a change in absolute or relative ownership levels, for example, when a subsidiary becomes subject to the control of a government, court, administrator or regulator. *[FRS 102.9.18].* Deemed disposals that may result in loss of control could also arise for other reasons including:

- a group does not take up its full allocation in a rights issue by a subsidiary in the group;

- a subsidiary declares scrip dividends that are not taken up by its parent, so that the parent's proportional interest is diminished;

- another party exercises its options or warrants issued by a subsidiary;

- a subsidiary issues shares to a third party; or

- a contractual arrangement by which a group obtained control over a subsidiary is terminated or changed.

Example 6.9 at 3.6.3 below illustrates a deemed disposal.

The requirements of Sections 9 and 19 dealing with acquisitions and disposals of subsidiaries in consolidated financial statements are based on the 2004 version of IFRS 3 – *Business Combinations*, and, in the view of the Accounting Council, are considered to provide a coherent model for increases and decreases in stakes held in another entity that is consistent with UK Company Law. *[FRS 102.AC.53].*

Chapter 6

3.6.1   *Accounting for an acquisition where control is achieved in stages*

When a parent acquires control of a subsidiary in stages, Section 9 refers to the requirements of paragraphs 11A and 14 of Section 19, applied at the date control is achieved. *[FRS 102.9.19B]*. This means that when control is achieved in stages, the cost of the business combination is the aggregate of the fair values of the assets given, liabilities assumed and the equity instruments issued by the acquirer at the date of each transaction in the series. *[FRS 102.19.11A]*. See Chapter 15.

3.6.2   *Accounting for an increase in a controlling interest in a subsidiary*

When a parent increases its controlling interest in a subsidiary, the identifiable assets and liabilities and a provision for contingent liabilities of the subsidiary are not revalued to fair value and no additional goodwill is recognised at the date the controlling interest is increased. *[FRS 102.9.19C]*.

The transaction is accounted for as a transaction between equity holders and accordingly the non-controlling interest shall be adjusted to reflect the change in the parent's interest in the subsidiary's net assets and any difference between the amount by which the non-controlling interest is so adjusted and the fair value of the consideration paid is recognised directly in equity and attributed to equity holders of the parent. No gain or loss is recognised on these changes in equity. *[FRS 102.9.19C, 22.19]*. Example 6.7 illustrates the accounting for increasing a controlling interest in a subsidiary.

Example 6.7:   Increase in controlling interest in subsidiary

A parent with a 70% controlling interest in a subsidiary purchases an additional 20% interest in that subsidiary for cash proceeds of £250. Following, the purchase, the Parent has a 90% controlling interest in the subsidiary. The carrying value of the subsidiary's net assets excluding goodwill is £450 and there is £50 of goodwill remaining from the subsidiary's acquisition.

The parent accounts for the acquisition of the additional 20% interest as follows:

	Dr	Cr
Cash		£250
Non-controlling interest (20% of £450)	£90	
Equity	£160	

The guidance on reattribution of items of other comprehensive income and accounting for transaction costs discussed at 3.6.4 below apply here also.

3.6.3   *Accounting for a disposal of a subsidiary when control is lost*

When a parent ceases to control a subsidiary, a gain or loss is recognised in the consolidated statement of comprehensive income (or in the income statement if presented) calculated as the difference between: *[FRS 102.9.18A]*

- the proceeds from the disposal (or the event that resulted in the loss of control); and

- the proportion of the carrying amount of the subsidiary's net assets, including any related goodwill, disposed of (or lost) as at the date of disposal (or date control is lost).

The gain or loss calculated above shall also include those amounts that have been recognised in other comprehensive income in relation to that subsidiary, where those amounts are required to be reclassified to profit or loss upon disposal in accordance with other sections of FRS 102. Amounts that are not required to be reclassified to profit or loss upon disposal of the related assets or liabilities in accordance with other sections of FRS 102 are transferred directly to retained earnings. *[FRS 102.9.18B]*.

Section 9 states that the cumulative amount of any exchange differences that relate to a foreign subsidiary recognised in equity in accordance with Section 30 is not recognised in profit or loss as part of the gain or loss on disposal of the subsidiary and is transferred directly to retained earnings. *[FRS 102.9.18A]*.

FRS 102 permits only the following unrealised gains and losses recognised in other comprehensive income to be recycled through profit or loss upon disposal of a subsidiary:

- unrealised gains and losses on available-for-sale (AFS) investments (if the entity has elected to use IAS 39 – *Financial Instruments: Recognition and Measurement* – for recognition and measurement of financial instruments as permitted by paragraph 11.2(b) of Section 11);

- unrealised gains and losses on cash flow hedges (except for the portion attributable to a hedge of a net investment in a foreign operation); *[FRS 102.12.23]* and

- unrealised gains and losses arising from the application of shadow accounting for insurance contracts. *[FRS 103.2.11]*.

No other unrealised gains and losses that have been recognised in other comprehensive income are recycled upon disposal of a subsidiary.

If an entity ceases to be a subsidiary but the former parent continues to hold:

- an investment that is not an associate or a jointly controlled entity that investment shall be accounted for as a financial asset in accordance with Section 11 or Section 12 (see Chapter 8) from the date the entity ceases to be the subsidiary;

- an associate, that associate shall be accounted for in accordance with Section 14 (see Chapter 10); or

- a jointly controlled entity, that jointly controlled entity shall be accounted for in accordance with Section 15 (see Chapter 11).

The carrying amount of the net assets (and goodwill) attributable to the investment at the date that the entity ceases to be a subsidiary shall be regarded as cost on initial measurement of the financial asset, investment in associate or jointly controlled entity, as appropriate. In applying the equity method to investments in associate or jointly controlled entities as required above, paragraph 14.8(c), which relates to the recognition of implicit goodwill, shall not be applied. *[FRS 102.9.19]*.

Chapter 6

Example 6.8 below illustrates the accounting for a disposal of a subsidiary:

Example 6.8:   Disposal of a subsidiary

A parent sells an 85% interest in a wholly owned subsidiary as follows:

- after the sale the parent accounts for its remaining 15% interest at fair value as an other financial instrument under Section 12;
- the subsidiary did not recognise any amounts in other comprehensive income;
- net assets of the subsidiary before the disposal including goodwill are £500;
- cash proceeds from the sale of the 85% interests are £750; and

The parent accounts for the disposal of an 85% interest as follows:

	Dr	Cr
Other financial instrument (15% of the net assets before disposal of £500)	£75	
Cash	£750	
Net assets of the subsidiary derecognised (summarised)		£500
Gain on loss of control of subsidiary		£325

The gain recognised on the loss of control of the subsidiary is calculated as follows:

Cash proceeds on disposal of 85% interest	£750
Carrying amount of 85% interest (85% × £500)	£(425)
	£325

In Example 6.8 above, the cost on initial measurement of the financial instrument is not its fair value. Therefore, when that financial instrument is subsequently measured at fair value, they will be a 'Day 2' gain or loss as the cost of the investment is adjusted to fair value.

A deemed disposal that results in loss of control of a subsidiary is accounted for as a regular disposal. This is illustrated in Example 6.9.

Example 6.9:   Deemed disposal through share issue by subsidiary

A parent entity P owns 600,000 of the 1,000,000 shares issued by its subsidiary S, giving it a 60% interest. The carrying value of S's net identifiable assets in the consolidated financial statements of P is £120 million. The non-controlling interest is £48 million (40% of £120 million). In addition, goodwill with a carrying value of £15 million remains from the acquisition.

Subsequently, S issues 500,000 shares to a new investor for £80 million. As a result, P's 600,000 shares now represent 40% of the 1,500,000 shares issued by S in total and S becomes an associate of P.

This results in a gain of £3 million on disposal, calculated as follows:

	Dr	Cr
Interest in S (40% of increased net assets of £200 million plus 40/60 of goodwill of £15 million)	£90m	
Non-controlling interest	£48m	
Gain on disposal		£3m
Net assets of S (previously consolidated)		£120m
Goodwill (previously shown separately)		$15m

As this is a deemed disposal resulting from the share issue of a subsidiary, P needs to consider whether the profit resulting is realised or unrealised. If unrealised, the profit would be taken to other comprehensive income and not to profit or loss.

3.6.4   Accounting for a part disposal of a subsidiary when control is retained

Where a parent reduces its holding in a subsidiary and control is retained, it shall be accounted for as a transaction between equity holders and the resulting change in non-controlling interest shall be accounted for in accordance with paragraph 22.19 of FRS 102. This means that the carrying amount of the non-controlling interest shall be adjusted to reflect the change in the parent's interest in the subsidiary's net assets. Any difference between the amount by which the non-controlling interest is so adjusted and the fair value of the consideration paid or received, if any, shall be recognised directly in equity and attributed to equity holders of the parent. No gain or loss shall be recognised at the date of disposal and the entity shall not adjust any change in the carrying amount of assets (including goodwill) or liabilities as a result of the transaction. *[FRS 102.9.19A, FRS 102.22.19].*

Example 6.10 illustrates the accounting for a disposal where control is retained.

Example 6.10:   *Disposal of a subsidiary where control is retained*

A parent sells a 20% interest in a wholly owned subsidiary for cash proceeds of £250. Parent still retains an 80% controlling interest in the subsidiary. The carrying value of the subsidiary's net assets excluding goodwill is £450 and there is £50 of goodwill remaining from the subsidiary's acquisition.

It is unclear whether a portion of goodwill should be regarded as now being attributable to the non-controlling interest in computing the difference to be taken to equity in these circumstances. This means that there are two alternatives for the accounting for the parent's disposal of the 20% interest as follows:

Alternative 1 – goodwill is not re-allocated to non-controlling interests:

	Dr	Cr
Cash	£250	
Non-controlling interest (20% of £450, i.e. excluding goodwill)		£90
Equity		£160

Alternative 2 – goodwill is re-allocated to non-controlling interests:

	Dr	Cr
Cash	£250	
Non-controlling interest (20% of £500, i.e. including goodwill)		£100
Equity		£150

Section 9 is silent as to whether amounts recognised in other comprehensive income and equity should be reattributed when a change in ownership in a subsidiary occurs that does not result in the loss of control. In our view, it is logical that such a reattribution should occur and this is consistent with Section 30 which requires that the accumulated exchange differences which relate to a foreign operation that is consolidated but not wholly-owned that are attributed to the non-controlling interest be recognised as part of non-controlling interest. *[FRS 102.30.20].*

Although Section 9 is clear that changes in a parent's ownership interest in a subsidiary that do not result in loss of control of the subsidiary are equity transactions, it does not specifically address how to account for related transaction costs. In our view, any directly attributable costs incurred to sell a non-controlling interest in a subsidiary without loss of control are deducted from equity (net of any related income tax benefit). A parent may choose where to allocate the costs (i.e. between the parent and the non-controlling interest) based on the facts and circumstances surrounding the change in ownership. These costs should not be reclassified to profit or loss in future periods as they do not represent components of other comprehensive income.

3.7   Non-controlling interest in subsidiaries

A non-controlling interest is the equity in a subsidiary not attributable, directly or indirectly, to a parent. *[FRS 102 Appendix I].* The reference to 'equity' in the definition of a non-controlling interest refers to those 'equity instruments' of a subsidiary that are not held, directly or indirectly, by its parent. This also means that financial instruments that are not classified within equity in accordance with Section 22 – *Liabilities and Equity* – are not included within the definition of a non-controlling interest.

The principle underlying accounting for non-controlling interests is that all residual economic interest holders of any part of the consolidated entity have an equity interest in that consolidated entity. This principle applies regardless of the decision-making ability of that interest holder and where in the group that interest is held. Therefore, any equity instruments issued by a subsidiary that are not owned by the parent (apart from those that are required to be classified as financial liabilities) are non-controlling interests, including:

- ordinary shares;
- convertible debt and other compound financial instruments;
- preference shares (including both those with, and without, an entitlement to a *pro rata* share of net assets on liquidation);
- warrants;
- options over own shares; and
- options under share-based payment transactions.

Options and warrants are non-controlling interests, regardless of whether they are vested and of the exercise price (e.g. whether they are 'in-the-money').

The definition of non-controlling interest is wider than minority interest as used in previous UK GAAP and in the Regulations. Where differences arise, it may be necessary to disclosure both the amounts for minority interest and non-controlling interest. See Chapter 4 at 4.5.

3.7.1   *Accounting and presentation of non-controlling interest*

A non-controlling interest in the net assets of a subsidiary is initially measured at non-controlling interest's share of the net amount of the identifiable assets, liabilities and contingent liabilities recognised in accordance with the requirements for a business combination (see Chapter 15) at the date of the original combination. *[FRS 102.9.13(d)]*. There is no option under FRS 102 to measure non-controlling interests at fair value.

FRS 102 does not distinguish between non-controlling interests that are present ownership interests and entitle their holders to a proportionate share of the entity's net assets in the event of liquidation and other components of non-controlling interests (e.g. perpetual debt classified as equity under Section 22). The implication is that all non-controlling interests are measured the same way based on present ownership interest. This means that any non-controlling interests, such as options, are valued at nil if they are not entitled to a present ownership interest.

Non-controlling interest shall be presented within equity, separately from equity of the owners of the parent in the consolidated financial statement of financial position. *[FRS 102.9.20]*.

Non-controlling interest in the profit or loss of the group is required to be disclosed separately in the statement of comprehensive income (or income statement, if presented). *[FRS 102.9.21]*.

Profit or loss and each component of other comprehensive income shall be attributed to the owners of the parent and to non-controlling interest. Total comprehensive income shall be attributed to the owners of the parent and to non-controlling interest even if this results in non-controlling interest having a deficit balance. *[FRS 102.9.22]*. This approach is consistent with the fact that the controlling and non-controlling interest participate proportionately in the risks and rewards of an investment in the subsidiary. When the non-controlling interest in a subsidiary is in deficit, there is no requirement to make a provision in the group financial statements to for any legal or commercial obligation (whether formal or implied) to provide for finance that may not be recoverable in respect of the accumulated losses attributable to the non-controlling interest.

The measurement of non-controlling interests in a business combination is illustrated in Example 6.11.

Example 6.11: Initial measurement of non-controlling interests in a business combination

Parent acquires 80% of the ordinary shares of Target for £950 in cash. The fair value of its identifiable net assets is £850. The impact of the business combination, and the measurement of non-controlling interests, are as follows:

	Dr	Cr
Fair value of identifiable net assets	£850	
Goodwill (£950 – (80% × £850))	£270	
Cash		£950
Non-controlling interest (20% × £850)		£170

The ordinary shares are present ownership interests and entitle their holders to a proportionate share of the Target's net assets in the event of liquidation. They are measured at the non-controlling interest's proportionate share of the identifiable net assets of Target.

Chapter 6

A proportion of profit or loss and changes in equity is only attributed to those ownership instruments included within non-controlling interest if they give rise to a present ownership interest. Non-controlling interests that include potential voting rights that require exercise or conversion (such as options, warrants, or share-based payment transactions) generally to not receive an allocation of profit or loss (see 3.4 above).

Where a subsidiary has granted options over its own shares under an equity-settled share-based payment transaction, the share-based payment expense recognised in profit or loss will be attributable to the parent and any other non-controlling interest that has a present legal ownership in the subsidiary.

Section 9 is silent on the accounting for shares of profit or loss on undeclared dividends in respect of outstanding cumulative preference shares classified as equity that are held by non-controlling interests.

3.7.2   *Call and put options over non-controlling interest*

Some business combinations involve options over some or all of the outstanding shares. For example, the acquirer might have a call option, i.e. the right to acquire the outstanding shares at a future date for a particular price. Alternatively, the acquirer might have granted a put option to other shareholders whereby they have the right to sell their shares to the acquirer at a future date for a particular price. In some cases, there may be a combination of put and call options, the terms of which may be equivalent or different.

FRS 102 gives no guidance on how to account for such options in a business combination. There is also no guidance where such contracts are entered into following a business combination. Therefore, when determining the appropriate accounting in such situations, Sections 9, 11, 12 and 22 must be considered.

3.7.2.A   *Call options only*

Call options are considered when determining whether an entity has obtained control as discussed at 3.2.1 above. Once it is determined whether an entity has control over another entity, the proportions of profit or loss and change in equity allocated to the parent and non-controlling interests are based on the present ownership interests and generally do not reflect the possible exercise or conversion of potential voting rights under call options. *[FRS 102.9.14].*

A call option is likely to give the acquiring entity present access to returns associated with the ownership interest in limited circumstances:

- when the option price is fixed with a low exercise price and it is agreed between the parties that either no dividends will be paid to the other shareholders or the dividend payments lead to an adjustment of the option exercise price; or

- the terms are set such that the other shareholders effectively receive only a lender's return.

This is because any accretion in the fair value of the underlying ownership interest under the option (for example, due to improved financial performance of the acquiree subsequent to the granting of the call option) is likely to be realised by the acquirer.

If a call option gives the acquiring entity present access to returns over all of the shares held by non-controlling shareholders, then there will be no non-controlling interest presented in equity. The acquirer accounts for the business combination as though it acquired a 100% interest. The acquirer also recognises a financial liability to the non-controlling shareholders under the call option. Changes in the carrying amount of the financial liability are recognised in profit or loss. If the call option expires unexercised, then the acquirer has effectively disposed of a partial interest in its subsidiary in return for the amount recognised as the 'liability' at the date of expiry and accounts for the transaction as a change in ownership interest without a loss of control, as discussed at 3.6.4 above.

A call option may not give present access to the returns associated with that ownership interest where the option's terms contain one or more of the following features:

- the option price has not yet been determined or will be the fair value of the shares at the date of exercise (or a surrogate for such a value);

- the option price is based on expected future results or net assets of the subsidiary at the date of exercise; or

- it has been agreed between the parties that, prior to the exercise of the option, all retained profits may be freely distributed to the existing shareholders according to their current shareholdings.

If a call option does not give present access to the returns associated with the ownership interest, the instruments containing the potential voting rights are accounted for as derivatives in accordance with Sections 11 and 12 unless the derivative meets the definition of an equity instrument of the entity in Section 22.

3.7.2.B   Put options only

A puttable instrument is a financial instrument that gives the holder the right to sell that instrument back to the issuer for cash or another financial asset or is automatically redeemed or repurchased by the issuer on the occurrence of an uncertain future event or the death or retirement of the instrument holder. *[FRS 102.22.4(a)]*.

A puttable instrument is classified as equity if, when the put option is exercised, the holder receives a pro-rata share of the net assets of the entity determined by:

- dividing the net assets on liquidation into units of equal amounts; and

- multiplying that amount by the number of units held by the financial instrument holder.

If the holder is entitled to an amount measured on some other basis the instrument is classified as a liability. *[FRS 102.22.5(b)]*.

In the context of the consolidated financial statements, an NCI put option is a form of puttable instrument in that it gives the holder the right to sell the shares in the subsidiary (presented as equity of the group) back to the group. Although it is clear that a put option that is not classified as equity itself must be recognised as a liability, there are a number of decisions that must be made in order to account for the arrangements, including:

- the measurement of the liability under the NCI put;

- whether the terms of the NCI put mean that it gives the parent a present ownership interest in the underlying securities; and

- whether or not a non-controlling interest continues to be recognised if the liability is measured based on its redemption amount, i.e. whether the parent recognises both the non-controlling interest and the financial liability for the NCI put.

In the latter case, there are a number of additional decisions that must be made, in particular the basis on which the non-controlling interest is recognised.

When the put option is a liability, Section 22 offers no guidance as to how that liability should be measured. Section 22 does not contain the requirement in FRS 25 – *Financial instruments: presentation* – and IAS 32 – *Financial Instruments: Presentation* – that an obligation for an entity to purchase its own equity instruments for cash or another financial asset gives rise to a financial liability for the present value of the redemption amount (for example, the present value of the forward purchase price, option price or other redemption amount). *[FRS 25.23, IAS 32.23].* In our view, as no guidance is contained in Section 22, unless the parent elects to consider the requirements and guidance in IAS 32 as permitted by paragraph 10.6 of FRS 102 (see Chapter 7), the financial liability for the put option is a derivative which should be measured at fair value according to Sections 11 and 12. When the put option is exercisable at fair value, this value will be zero. All subsequent changes to the liability are recognised in profit or loss.

In our view, in the same way as for call options, an entity has to consider whether the terms of the transaction give it present access to the returns associated with the shares subject to the put option.

If it is concluded that the acquirer has a present ownership interest in the shares concerned, it is accounted for as an acquisition of those underlying shares, and no non-controlling interest is recognised. Thus, if the acquirer has granted a put option over all of the remaining shares, the business combination is accounted for as if the acquirer has obtained a 100% interest in the acquiree. No non-controlling interest is recognised when the acquirer completes the purchase price allocation and determines the amount of goodwill to recognise. In this situation, in our view, the acquirer would recognise a liability for the present value of the amount required to be paid under the put option to obtain the interest (i.e. the redemption amount), rather than measuring it as a derivative. Changes in the carrying amount of the financial liability are recognised in profit or loss. If the put option is exercised, the financial liability is extinguished by the payment of the exercise price. If the put option is not exercised, then the entity has effectively disposed of a partial interest in its subsidiary, without loss of control, in return for the amount recognised as the financial liability at the date of expiry. The entity accounts for the transaction as discussed at 3.4 above, and measures the non-controlling interest as of the date that the put option expires.

When the terms of the transaction do not provide a present ownership interest, the entity will initially recognise both the non-controlling interest based on present ownership interest and the financial liability under the put at fair value as a derivative. If the put option is exercisable at fair value then the value of the derivative liability is zero. All subsequent changes in the liability are recognised in profit or loss.

Given the absence of guidance in Section 22 as to how a put option should be measured, an entity could, alternatively, under the FRS 102 hierarchy, look to IAS 32 for guidance. As stated above, IAS 32 states that an obligation for an entity to purchase its own equity instruments for cash or another financial asset gives rise to a financial liability for the present value of the redemption amount. If an entity chooses to do this (i.e. apply IAS 32) then different accounting policy choices are available which are discussed in Chapter 7 of EY International GAAP 2015.

3.7.2.C   Combination of put and call options

In some business combinations, there might be a combination of call and put options, the terms of which may be equivalent or may be different.

The appropriate accounting for such options is determined based on the discussions in 3.7.2.A and 3.7.2.B above. However, where there is a call and put option with equivalent terms, particularly at a fixed price, the combination of the options is more likely to mean that they give the acquirer a present ownership interest.

In such cases, where the options are over all of the shares not held by the parent, the acquirer has effectively acquired a 100% interest in the subsidiary at the date of the business combination. The entity may be in a similar position as if it had acquired a 100% interest in the subsidiary with either deferred consideration (where the exercise price is fixed) or contingent consideration (where the settlement amount is not fixed, but is dependent upon a future event).

The discussion in 3.7.2.A and 3.7.2.B above focused on call and put options entered into at the same time as control is gained of the subsidiary. However, an entity may enter into the options with non-controlling shareholders after gaining control. The appropriate accounting policy will still be based on the discussions in 3.7.2.A and 3.7.2.B above

Where the entity already has a controlling interest and as a result of the options now has a present ownership interest in the remaining shares concerned the non-controlling interest is no longer recognised within equity. The transaction is accounted for as an acquisition of the non-controlling interest, i.e. it is accounted for as an equity transaction (see 3.6.2 above), because such acquisitions are not business combinations under Section 19.

Chapter 6

3.8   Exchanges of businesses or other non-monetary assets for an interest in a subsidiary, jointly controlled entity or associate

A reporting entity may exchange a business, or other monetary asset, for an interest in another entity, and that other entity becomes a subsidiary, jointly controlled entity or associate of the reporting entity. The accounting issues that arise from these transactions are whether they should be accounted for at fair value or at previous book values and how the gain on the transaction should be reported.

The requirements in Section 9 for these transactions are the same as those contained in UITF 31 in previous UK GAAP. The principles behind the consensus reached by the UITF were that the only exception to the use of fair values should be in rare circumstances where the transaction is artificial and has no substance and that any unrealised gains should not be reported in profit or loss.

Accordingly, the following accounting treatment applies in the consolidated financial statements of the reporting entity: *[FRS 102.9.31]*

- to the extent that the reporting entity retains an ownership interest in the business, or other non-monetary assets, exchanged, even if that interest is then held through another entity, that retained interest, including any related goodwill, is treated as having been owned by the reporting entity throughout the transaction and should be included at its pre-transaction carrying amount
- goodwill is recognised as the difference between:
  - the fair value of the consideration given; and
  - the fair value of the reporting entity's share of the pre-transaction identifiable net assets of the other entity

  The consideration given for the interest acquired in the other entity will include that part of the business, or other non-monetary assets, exchanged and no longer owned by the reporting entity. The consideration may also include cash or monetary assets to achieve equalisation of values. Where it is difficult to value the consideration given, the best estimate of its value may be given by valuing what is acquired;
- to the extent that the fair value of the consideration received by the reporting entity exceeds the carrying value of the part of the business, or other non-monetary assets exchanged and no longer owned by the reporting entity, and any related goodwill together with any cash given up, the reporting entity should recognise a gain. Any unrealised gain arising on the exchange is recognised in other comprehensive income; and
- to the extent that the fair value of the consideration received by the reporting entity is less than the carrying value of the part of the business, or other non-monetary assets no longer owned by the reporting entity, and any related goodwill, together with any cash given up, the reporting entity should recognise a loss. The loss should be recognised as an impairment in accordance with Section 27 – *Impairment of Assets* – or, for any loss remaining after an impairment review of the relevant assets, in profit or loss.

The accounting treatment can be illustrated in Examples 6.12 and 6.13 below:

Example 6.12:   Creation of larger subsidiary by contribution of existing subsidiary (1)

A and B are two major pharmaceutical companies, which agree to form a new company (Newco) in respect of a particular part of each of their businesses. B will own 60% of Newco, and A 40%. The parties agree that the total value of the new business is £250m.

B's contribution to the venture is one of its subsidiaries, the net assets of which are included in B's consolidated balance sheet at £85m (including remained unamortised goodwill of £15m). The fair value of the separable net assets of the subsidiary contributed by B is considered to be £120m. The implicit fair value of the business contributed is £150m (60% of total fair value £250m).

The separable net assets of the business to be contributed by A have a carrying amount of £50m, but their fair value is considered to be £80m. A also has unamortised goodwill remaining of £10m. The implicit fair value of the business contributed is £100m (40% of total fair value £250m).

The book and fair values of the businesses contributed by A and B can therefore be summarised as follows:

(in £m)	A Book value	A Fair value	B Book value	B Fair value
Separable net assets	50	80	70	120
Goodwill	10	20	15	30
Total	60	100	85	150

How should B account for this transaction in its consolidated financial statements?

B accounts for the transaction on the basis that it has retained 60% of its existing business and has exchanged a 40% interest in that business for a 60% interest in the business contributed by A. It therefore continues to record the 60% retained at book value and recognise a gain or loss on disposal of the 40% calculated as the difference between the book value of the net assets and the consideration received (being the fair value of the 60% interest in A's business). The difference between the fair value of the 40% interest in the business given up and the new net assets acquired (i.e. the 60% of A's former assets) represents goodwill.

This gives rise to the following accounting entry.

	Dr	Cr
Net assets of Newco[1]	£150m	
Non-controlling interest in Newco[2]		£60m
Goodwill[3]	£21m	
Net assets contributed to Newco[4]		£85m
Other comprehensive income (gain on disposal) [5]		£26m

1   Book value of B's separable net assets + fair value of A's separable net assets) i.e. (£70m+£80m) = £150m. In reality there would be a number of entries to consolidate these on a line-by-line basis.

2   40% of (book value of B's separable net assets + fair value of A's separable net assets) i.e. 40% × (£70m+£80m) = £60m.

3   Fair value of business given up by B less fair value of separable net assets of A's business acquired, i.e. 40% of £150m less 60% of £80m = £12m, plus 60% of B's goodwill of £15m retained (£9m) = £21m.

4   Previous carrying amount of net assets contributed by B (including goodwill), now deconsolidated (although now deconsolidated in accounting for Newco). In reality there would be a number of entries to deconsolidate these on a line-by-line basis.

5   Fair value of business received, less book value of assets disposed of, 60% of £100m – 40% of £85m = £26m.

The accounting in Example 6.12 above is inconsistent with that for a partial disposal of an interest in a subsidiary with no loss of control (see 3.6.4 above), In that case, there would be no gain or loss but the difference of £26m (or £32m, if goodwill is not included) would be taken to equity.

The gain on the transaction in Example 6.12 is unrealised because qualifying consideration has not been received. Therefore, the gain is accounted for in other comprehensive income as only realised profits can be recognised in profit or loss. Where part of all of the gain is realised then that portion can be taken to profit and loss. This is illustrated in Example 6.13 below:

Example 6.13:   Creation of larger subsidiary by contribution of existing subsidiary (2)

Assume the same fact pattern as in Example 6.12 above, except that B was to receive a stake of only 50% in Newco (but still have control) and that A paid £25m direct to B in compensation for the reduction in the stake from 60% to 50%.

How should B account for this transaction in its consolidated financial statements?

B accounts for the transaction on the basis that it has retained 50% of its existing business and has exchanged a 50% interest in that business for a 50% interest in the business contributed by A plus cash of £25m. It therefore continues to record the 50% retained at book value and recognise a gain or loss on disposal of the 50% calculated as the difference between the book value of the net assets and the consideration received (being the fair value of the 50% interest in A's business plus cash of £25m). The difference between the fair value of the 50% interest in A's business given up and the new net assets acquired (i.e. the 50% of A's former assets) represents goodwill.

This gives rise to the following accounting entry.

	Dr	Cr
Net assets of Newco[1]	£150.0m	
Non-controlling interest in Newco[2]		£75.0m
Cash	£25.0m	
Goodwill[3]	£17.5m	
Net assets contributed to Newco[4]		£85.0m
Profit and loss (gain on disposal)[5]		£25.0m
Other comprehensive income (gain on disposal)[5]		£7.5m

1   Book value of B's separable net assets + fair value of A's separable net assets) i.e. (£70m+£80m) = £150m. In reality there would be a number of entries to consolidate these on a line-by-line basis.

2   50% of (book value of B's separable net assets + fair value of A's separable net assets) i.e. 50% × (£70m+£80m) = £75m.

3   Fair value of business given up by B (net of amount of cash of £25m received from A to achieve equalisation of values) less fair value of separable net assets of A's business acquired, i.e. 50% of £150m less £25m, less 50% of £80m = £10m, plus 50% of B's goodwill of £15m retained (£7.5m) = £17.5m.

4   Previous carrying amount of net assets (including goodwill) contributed by B, now deconsolidated (although now consolidated in accounting for Newco). In reality there would be a number of entries to deconsolidate these on a line-by-line basis.

5   Fair value of business received (50% of £100m) plus cash received of £25m less book value of assets disposed of i.e. (50% of £85m), The gain on disposal of £32.5m has been split based on an allocation between 'realised' and 'unrealised' as explained below.

Section 9 does not explain how a realised gain can be distinguished from an unrealised gain. In Example 6.13 above, we have used a 'top slicing' approach whereby as much as the total gain as is backed by cash is treated as realised (i.e. £25m). 'Top slicing' is the recommended approach to determining realised profits for exchanges of assets in paragraph 3.18 of the ICAEW/ICAS Technical Release 02/10 – *Guidance on the Determination of Realised and distributable Profits and Losses in the Context of Distributions under the Companies Act 2006.*

No gain or loss is recognised in those rare cases where the artificiality or lack of substance of the transaction is such that a gain or loss on the exchange could not be justified. When a gain or loss on the exchange is not taken into account because the transaction is artificial or has no substance, the circumstances should be explained. *[FRS 102.9.32].* There is no elaboration as to the circumstances where this might be applicable.

3.9   Disclosures in consolidated financial statements

3.9.1   *Disclosures required by Section 9*

A limited amount of disclosures in respect of consolidated financial statements are required by Section 9. This is because certain disclosures are already required by the Regulations.

The following disclosures are required by Section 9: *[FRS 102.9.23]*

- the fact that the statements are consolidated financial statements;

- the basis for concluding that control exists when the parent does not own, directly or indirectly through subsidiaries, more than half of the voting power;

- any difference in the reporting date of the financial statements of the parent and its subsidiaries used in the preparation of the consolidated financial statements;

- the nature and extent of any significant restrictions (e.g. resulting from borrowing arrangements or regulatory requirements) on the ability of subsidiaries to transfer funds to the parent in the form of cash dividends or to repay loans; and

- the name of any subsidiary excluded from consolidation and the reasons for its exclusion.

In addition, where a gain or loss on an exchange of a business or other non-monetary asset for an investment in a subsidiary, associate or jointly controlled entity has not been recognised because of the artificiality or lack of substance of the transaction, these circumstances should be explained (see 3.7 above).

3.9.2   *Additional disclosures required by the Regulations*

The following disclosures are required by the Regulations in respect of subsidiaries in the consolidated financial statements in addition to those required by Section 9 (except for business combinations which are provided in Chapter 15):

Chapter 6

- the name of each subsidiary undertaking and country of incorporation if outside the United Kingdom and, if unincorporated, the address of its principal place of business (this disclosure can be limited to the principal subsidiaries if it is otherwise of excessive length); [s409-410, 4 Sch 1].

- for each subsidiary not included in the consolidated accounts there must be disclosed the aggregated amount of its capital and reserves as at the end of its relevant financial year and its profit or loss for that year (unless the subsidiary is equity accounted, the subsidiary is not required to publish its balance sheet anywhere in the world and the holding is less than 50% of the nominal value of the shares, or if the information is not material); [4 Sch 2].

- the number, description and amount of shares in the parent company held by or on behalf of subsidiary undertakings must be disclosed; [4 Sch 3].

- it must be stated with respect of each subsidiary consolidated which of the conditions in s1162(2) or (4) result in it being a subsidiary (unless it is a subsidiary because the parent holds a majority of the voting rights); [4 Sch 16].

- for each subsidiary, there must be stated the identity of each class of shares held and the proportion of the nominal value of that class of shares held, with separate information on the interest held by the parent and by the group, if different; [4 Sch 17].

- when during the financial year, there has been a disposal of an undertaking or group which significantly affects the figures in the group accounts a note must disclose the name of the undertaking or the parent undertaking of the disposed group and the extent to which the profit or loss shown in the group accounts is attributable to profit of loss of that undertaking or group (although the disclosure need not be given for an undertaking either established outside the United Kingdom or carries on business outside the United Kingdom if seriously prejudicial to the business and the Secretary of State agrees). [6 Sch 15-16].

In addition, the Regulations also require that any differences of accounting rules as between a parent's individual accounts for a financial year and its group accounts must be disclosed in a note to the group accounts and the reason for the differences given. [6 Sch 4].

4   INDIVIDUAL AND SEPARATE FINANCIAL STATEMENTS

The Companies Act requires accounts to be prepared for each financial year. These are referred to as the company's individual accounts. [s394]. Other statutory frameworks will apply for those entities that are not required to produce Companies Act individual accounts. [FRS 102.9.23A].

The following key terms are defined in the FRS 102 Glossary: [FRS 102 Appendix I]

Individual financial statements are defined as the accounts that are required to be prepared by an entity in accordance with the Companies Act or relevant legislation, for example:

- 'individual accounts', as set out in s394 of the Companies Act;

- 'statement of accounts', as set out in s132 of the Charities Act 2011; or

- 'individual accounts' as set out in s72A of the Building Societies Act 1986.

Separate financial statements are included in the meaning of this term (i.e. both individual and separate financial statements as defined by FRS 102 are Companies Act individual accounts).

An entity that is not a parent (i.e. an entity that does not have subsidiaries) prepares individual financial statements and not separate financial statements.

Separate financial statements are defined as those financial statements presented by a parent in which the investments in subsidiaries, associates or jointly controlled entities are accounted for either at cost or fair value rather than on the basis of the reported results and net assets of the investees. Separate financial statements are included within the meaning of individual financial statements.

4.1   Accounting for associates and jointly controlled entities in individual financial statements of an entity that is not a parent

An entity that is not a parent accounts for investments in associates and jointly controlled entities using either:

- a cost model, i.e. at cost less impairment;

- a fair value model, i.e. at fair value with changes in fair value recognised in other comprehensive income; or

- at fair value with changes in fair value recognised in profit or loss. *[FRS 102.9.25, FRS 102.14.4, FRS 102.15.9].*

There is no option to use equity accounting in individual financial statements (although this option exists under IFRS) because equity accounting in individual financial statements is not permitted by the Regulations which permits only a cost or market value model. However, the individual financial statements of an investor that is not a parent shall disclose summarised financial information about investments in associates and jointly controlled entities, along with the effect of including those investments as if they had been accounted for using the equity method. Investing entities that are exempt from preparing consolidated financial statements, or would be exempt if they had subsidiaries, are exempt from this requirement. *[FRS 102.14.15A, FRS 102.15.21A].*

Although neither Section 14 nor Section 15 state so explicitly, it appears that, although associates and jointly controlled entities do not need to be measured the same way, all investments in a single class must be measured the same way. That is to say, all associates must be measured the same way (e.g. cost) and all jointly controlled entities must be measured the same way (e.g. at fair value through other comprehensive income). There is an explicit requirement in Section 9 for an entity that is a parent to apply the same accounting policy for all investments in a single class, the implications of which are discussed at 4.2 below.

The cost and fair value measurements for associates and jointly controlled entities are further discussed in Chapters 14 and 15.

Chapter 6

4.2   Accounting for subsidiaries, associates and jointly controlled entities in separate financial statements of an entity that is a parent

When an entity that is a parent prepares separate financial statements and describes them as conforming to FRS 102, those financial statements shall comply with all of the requirements of FRS 102. *[FRS 102.9.26].*

Separate financial statements are defined as those financial statements presented by a parent in which the investments in subsidiaries, associates or jointly controlled entities are accounted for at either cost, or fair value rather than on the basis of the reported results and net assets of the investees. Separate financial statements are included within the meaning of individual financial statements. *[FRS 102.9.24].*

A parent must select and adopt a policy of accounting for investments in subsidiaries, associates and jointly controlled entities either: *[FRS 102.9.26]*

- at cost less impairment;
- at fair value with changes in fair value recognised in other comprehensive income in accordance with paragraphs 15E and 15F of Section 17 – *Property, Plant and Equipment*; or
- at fair value with changes in fair value recognised in profit or loss (guidance on fair value is provided in Section 11).

A policy of measuring subsidiaries, associates and jointly controlled entities at fair value through profit or loss is permitted by paragraph 36(4) of Schedule 1 to Regulations (and its equivalents in Schedules 2 and 3) without the use of a true and fair override. However, additional disclosures are required – see 4.6.1 below.

A parent that is exempt from the requirement to prepare consolidated financial statements (see 3.1.1 above) and therefore presents separate financial statements as its only financial statements must also account for its investments in subsidiaries, associates and jointly controlled entities as above. *[FRS 102.9.26A].*

Section 9 states that a parent must apply the same accounting policy for all investments in a single class (subsidiaries, associates or jointly controlled entities) but it can elect different policies for different classes. *[FRS 102.9.26].*

This restriction means that a parent cannot use a different accounting policy for a class of investments even where individual investments within that class have different characteristics. Section 9 requires subsidiaries that are excluded from consolidation because they are held as part of an investment portfolio to be measured at fair value through profit or loss. *[FRS 102.9.9B].* This raises the issue that, if an entity has a number of subsidiaries where some are exempt from consolidation and some are not, would the requirement to measure any of those non-consolidated subsidiaries at fair value through profit or loss mean that the entity would have to measure all its subsidiaries (both exempt and not exempt from consolidation) at fair value through profit or loss or can different accounting policies be applied to those subsidiaries that are not consolidated and those that are not (i.e. can subsidiaries excluded from consolidation be a separate class of investments from subsidiaries that are consolidated)? In our view, it was not the intention of FRS 102 to limit an entity's choice of accounting policy (for its individual financial statements) in this way (i.e. to fair value through profit or loss) by virtue of the fact that the entity also happens to have investments in subsidiaries that are excluded from consolidation because they are held as part of an investment portfolio. Therefore, it is acceptable for an entity to select its accounting policy for its investments in subsidiaries, associates and jointly controlled entities independently of the requirement to measure certain exempted subsidiaries at fair value through profit or loss (i.e. subsidiaries that are excluded from consolidation can be considered a separate class of investment from subsidiaries that are consolidated).

There is no option under Section 9 to use a directors' valuation (typically, net assets), an out-of-date market value or current cost to value an investment in a subsidiary, associate or jointly controlled entity in individual or separate financial statements where such measurements are not the equivalent of fair value at the reporting date.

Section 9 does not distinguish between different types of entity (i.e. banking entities, insurance entities and other entities). The cost model is not permitted by Schedule 3 of the Regulations so an insurer that wished to use 'cost' to value investments in subsidiaries, associates and jointly controlled entities would need to invoke a true and fair override.

4.2.1   Cost of investment

Section 9 does not define 'cost'. The Regulations state that the purchase price of an asset is determined by adding to the actual price paid any expenses incidental to its acquisition. *[1 Sch 27(1)]*. This definition is consistent with Section 17 and 3.4 above, which state that cost is normally be either the purchase price paid (including directly attributable costs) or the fair value of non-monetary assets exchanged. *[FRS 102.17.10, FRS 102.9.31]*. The purchase price would generally represent the fair value of the consideration given to purchase the investment consistent with the guidance in respect of exchanges of businesses or other non-monetary items assets (see 3.8 above) and the requirements in respect of measuring the cost of a business combination (see Chapter 15 at 3.5).

However, where shares have been issued as consideration, the note on legal requirements which accompanies FRS 102 states that where the cost model is adopted, s611 to s615 of the Companies Act set out the treatment where 'merger relief' or 'group reconstruction relief' is available. These reliefs reduce the amount required to be included in share premium and also allow the initial carrying amount to be adjusted downwards so it is equal to either the previous carrying amount of the investment in the transferor's books or the nominal value of the shares issued, depending on which relief applies. The note on legal requirements goes on to state that this relief is not available where the fair value model is used although the provisions in the Companies Act in respect of amounts required to be recorded in share premium remain relevant. *[FRS 102.A4.24]*. In our view, the decision whether or not to use this relief to measure cost is an accounting policy choice that must be applied for all transactions of this type.

Group reconstruction relief applies when a wholly owned subsidiary issues shares to its parent or fellow wholly owned subsidiary in consideration for the transfer of non-cash assets of a company that is a member of the group of companies that comprises the holding company and all its wholly-owned subsidiaries. When the shares are issued at a premium the issuer (i.e. the subsidiary) is not required to transfer any amount to share premium in excess of net asset value of the non-cash assets held in the transferor's books. *[s611]*.

Merger relief applies when the issuing company (and subsidiaries) have secured at least an 90% equity holding in another company in pursuance of an arrangement where the issuing company allots equity shares in exchange for issue or transfer of equity shares in another company. No share premium is recorded. *[s612-613]*.

The amounts of the premiums which are not included in the share premium account by virtue of the above relief may also be disregarded in determining the amount at which any shares or other consideration provided for the shares issued is to be included in the company's balance sheet. *[s615]*.

Examples 6.14 and 6.15 illustrate the application of group reconstruction relief and merger relief on the cost of an investment in a subsidiary.

Example 6.14:   *Group reconstruction relief and cost of investment*

Company B (a wholly owned subsidiary of Company A) issues 100 £1 ordinary shares to its holding company, A, in return for an investment in Company C held by A. The investment in C was previously carried by A as its original cost of £400. The fair value of C (and the shares issued by A) is £1,000.

How should B account for this transaction in its separate financial statements?

The decision depends on B's accounting policy for its investments in subsidiaries. If B's accounting policy is to carry its investments in subsidiaries at cost less impairment then we believe that B has an accounting policy choice as follows:

	Dr	Cr
Investment in subsidiary	£400m	
Share capital		£100m
Share premium		£300m
OR		
Investment in subsidiary	£1,000m	
Share capital		£100m
Share premium		£300m
Merger reserve		£700m

As discussed above, the legal requirements appendix to FRS 102 states that where the cost model is applied s.615 allows the initial carrying amount to be adjusted downwards so that it is equal to the previous carrying amount of the investment in the transferor's books. Alternatively, an entity could ignore this option to reduce the carrying amount and use the fair value of C as its cost.

If B's accounting policy is to carry its investments at fair value (whether or not gains and losses on remeasurement are taken through profit and loss or through other comprehensive gains) then there is no choice and the investment in subsidiary must be measured at fair value.

Example 6.15: *Merger relief and cost of investment*

Company A issues 100 £1 ordinary shares to a third party for 100% of the ordinary shares of Company B, and pays cash of £200. The fair value of Company B (and the total consideration Paid by Company A) is £1,000.

How should A account for this transaction in its separate financial statements?

The decision depends on B's accounting policy for its investments in subsidiaries. If B's accounting policy is to carry its investments in subsidiaries at cost less impairment then we believe that B has an accounting policy choice as follows:

	Dr	Cr
Investment in subsidiary	£300m	
Share capital		£100m
Cash		£200m
OR		
Investment in subsidiary	£1,000m	
Share capital		£100m
Merger reserve		£700m
Cash		£200m

As discussed above, the legal requirements appendix to FRS 102 states that where the cost model is applied s615 allows the initial carrying amount to be adjusted downwards so that it reflects the nominal value of the shares issued depending on the relief applied. Alternatively, an entity could ignore this option to reduce the carrying amount and use the fair value of C as its cost.

If B's accounting policy is to carry its investments at fair value then there is no choice and the investment in subsidiary must be measured at fair value.

Section 9 is silent on accounting for contingent consideration on the acquisition of a subsidiary, associate or jointly controlled entity in individual or separate financial statements. However, we believe the guidance on contingent considerations in a business combination discussed at Chapter 15 should be applied. This means that the cost should include the estimated amount of the contingent consideration if it is probable and can be measured reliably and that future adjustments should be treated as an adjustment to the cost of the investment. *[FRS 102.19.12-13]*.

4.2.2   *Fair value of investment*

Fair value is the amount for which an asset could be exchanged, a liability settled, or an equity instrument granted could be exchanged, between knowledgeable willing parties in an arm's length transaction. In the absence of any specific guidance provided in the relevant section of FRS 102, the guidance in paragraphs 11.27 to 11.32 is used in determining fair value. *[FRS 102 Appendix I]*.

Having considered the guidance on fair value in paragraphs 11.27 to 11.32, investments in non-convertible preference shares and non-puttable ordinary shares or preference shares that do not have a quoted market price in an active market and whose fair value cannot be measured reliably must be measured at cost less impairment. *[FRS 102.11.14(d)]*. Section 9 does not explain what an entity should do in such circumstances (e.g. if it has elected to measure all subsidiaries at fair value but the fair values of one or more subsidiaries are not reliably measurable and therefore must be measured at cost less impairment). The practical answer is to address this matter by disclosure.

Chapter 6

4.3   Group reorganisations

Group reorganisations involve the restructuring of the relationships between companies in a group by, for example, changing setting up a new holding company, changing the direct ownership of a subsidiary with a group or transferring business form one company to another as part of divisionalisation. FRS 102 provides no explicit guidance on how to account for group reorganisations in separate financial statements. However, when the group reorganisation involves investments in subsidiaries, the requirements of Section 9 to account for investment in subsidiaries at either cost or fair value (see 4.2 above) will apply. When the cost model is applied, the discussion at 4.4.2 below should also be considered.

4.4   Common control transactions in individual and separate financial statements

Transactions often taken place between a parent entity and its subsidiaries or between subsidiaries within a group that may or may not be carried out at fair value. FRS 102 provides no accounting guidance on such transactions.

The Companies Act states that where a company makes a distribution consisting of, or including, or arising in consequence of the sale, transfer or other disposition of a non-cash asset such a distribution can be made at an undervalue only if the company has positive distributable reserves at the time of the distribution. [s845].

In addition, group reconstruction relief can be applied when a subsidiary issues shares in exchange for a non-cash asset (see at 4.2.1. above).

The following sections deal with common transactions between entities under common control.

4.4.1   Capital contributions

One form of transaction which is sometimes made within a group is a 'capital contribution', where one company injects funds in another (usually its subsidiary) in the form of a non-returnable gift. Whenever capital contributions are made, complex tax considerations can arise and should be addressed.

Capital contributions have no legal status in the UK – certainly the term is not used anywhere in the Companies Act or in FRS 102. This has led to uncertainty over the appropriate accounting treatment in the financial statements of both the giver and the receiver of the capital contribution.

4.4.1.A   Treatment in the financial statements of the paying company

In the most common situation, where the contribution is made by a company to one of its subsidiaries, the treatment is relatively straightforward; the amount of the contribution should be added to the cost of the investment in the subsidiary. As with any fixed asset, it will be necessary to write down the investment whenever it is recognised that its value has been impaired; this should be considered when subsequent dividends are received from the subsidiary which could be regarded as having been met out of the capital contribution and hence representing a return of it.

Where the contribution is made to a fellow-subsidiary, it will not be possible to regard it as an asset of any kind; it is neither an investment in the other company, nor can it be treated as a monetary receivable, since by definition there is no obligation on the part of the recipient to return it. Accordingly, the only available treatment to the paying company in these circumstances will be to write it off in the income statement of the period in which the payment is made.

There may be circumstances in which the nature of the transaction gives rise to a funding commitment and therefore the recognition of a liability and related expense prior to the actual transfer of resources. Funding commitments are discussed in Chapter 17 at 3.9.

4.4.1.B　Treatment in the financial statements of the receiving company

A subsidiary should include capital contributions received from its parent within equity, and in the year in which it is received, it should be reported in the statement of changes in equity. In terms of where it should be shown within equity, the most common treatment historically would appear to have been to credit the amount received to a separate reserve with a suitable title, such as 'capital contribution', or 'capital reserve'.

Notwithstanding this, the contribution could be regarded for distribution purposes as a realised profit, and accordingly be available to be paid out by way of dividend. However, where the contribution received is in the form of a non-monetary asset it is doubtful whether this should be the case. This is the position taken in Technical Release 02/10 which regards the contribution of assets from owners in their capacity as such as giving rise to a 'profit', but whether it is a realised profit will depend on the assets contributed meeting the definition of qualifying consideration. Where a contribution is regarded for distribution purposes as a realised profit, it may be appropriate to reclassify the reserve to which the contribution was originally taken as part of the profit and loss account balance.

Where the contribution is received from a fellow-subsidiary, and is to be regarded for distribution purposes as a realised profit, then it could be argued the contribution should be credited to the income statement in the year of receipt as it is not a transaction with the company's shareholder.

There is no compelling reason why there need be symmetry of treatment between the accounting used by the giving and receiving companies, although this will usually be the case; it would, for example, be theoretically possible for the giving company to charge the contribution made to the income statement, while the recipient credited the contribution directly to equity.

4.4.1.C　Contribution and distribution of non-monetary assets

These transactions involve transfers of inventory, property, plant and equipment, intangible assets, investment property and investment in associates and joint ventures from one entity to another for no consideration. These arrangements are not contractual but are equity transactions: either specie capital contributions (an asset is gifted by a parent to a subsidiary) or non-cash distributions (an asset is given by a subsidiary to its parent).

Chapter 6

The relevant Sections of FRS 102 (Sections 13, 16, 17 and 18) refer to assets being recognised at cost. Similarly, investments in subsidiaries, associates and jointly controlled entities may be recognised at cost as discussed at 4.1.1 and 4.1.2 above.

In our view, a choice exists as to how the cost is determined. The choice is:

- recognise the transaction at the consideration agreed between the parties (i.e. recognise it at zero); or

- recognise the transaction at fair value, regardless of the agreed consideration of zero, with the difference between that amount and fair value recognised as an equity transaction (capital contribution).

When fair value is used to determine cost, the difference between fair value and zero may reflect additional goods and services but, once they have been accounted for, any remaining difference will be a contribution or distribution of equity for a subsidiary or an increase in the investment held or the distribution received by the parent.

The entity that gives away the asset must reflect the transaction. A parent that makes a specie capital contribution to its subsidiary will recognise an increase investment in that subsidiary (in principle at fair value). If the transaction is recognised at fair value then any difference between that fair value and the existing carrying amount of the asset will be recognised in other comprehensive income as qualifying consideration has not been received.

A subsidiary that makes a distribution in specie to its parent shall account for the transaction by derecognising the distributed asset at its carrying value against retained earnings. The Accounting Council view is that a distribution to a shareholder does not generate a profit and therefore would not permit FRS 102 to include a requirement to recognise a liability to pay a dividend at fair value (as opposed to carrying value). However, disclosure of the fair value of dividends is required. *[FRS 102.AC.54]*. As the distribution received by the parent is a non-monetary asset, this is unlikely to represent 'qualifying consideration' under Technical Release 02/10 and therefore as an unrealised profit should not be reflected in the income statement, but in other comprehensive income.

4.4.1.D   Incurring expenses and settling liabilities without recharges

Entities frequently incur costs that provide a benefit to fellow group entities, e.g. audit, management or advertising fees, and do not recharge the costs. The beneficiary is not party to the transaction and does not directly incur an obligation to settle a liability. It may elect to recognise the cost, in which case it will charge profit or loss and credit retained earnings with equivalent amounts; there will be no change to its net assets. If the expense is incurred by the parent, it could elect to increase the investment in the subsidiary rather than expensing the amount. This could lead to a carrying value that might be impaired. Fellow subsidiaries would normally expense the cost as it would not be a transaction with the entity's shareholder.

Many groups recharge expenses indirectly, by making management charges, or recoup the funds through intra-group dividends, and in these circumstances it would be inappropriate to recognise the transaction in any entity other than the one that makes the payment.

A parent or other group entity may settle a liability on behalf of a subsidiary. If this is not recharged, the liability will have been extinguished in the entity's accounts. This raises the question of whether the gain should be taken to profit or loss or to equity. FRS 102 defines revenue as an inflow of benefits resulting in an increase in equity other than increases relating to contributions from equity participants. *[FRS 102 Appendix I]*. Except in unusual circumstances, the forgiveness of debt will usually be a contribution from owners and therefore ought to be taken to equity.

It will usually be appropriate for a parent to add the payment to the investment in the subsidiary as a capital contribution, subject always to impairment of the investment but a parent may conclude that it is more appropriate to expense the cost. If one subsidiary settles a liability of its fellow subsidiary then it will expense the payment made and, consistent with 4.4.1.B above, any settlement regarded as a realised profit by the fellow subsidiary could be argued to be a credit to profit and loss as it is not a transaction with the company's shareholder.

4.4.2   *Transactions involving non-monetary assets*

4.4.2.A   *The parent exchanges property, plant and equipment for a non-monetary asset of the subsidiary*

The exchange of an asset for another non-monetary asset is accounted for by recognising the received asset at fair value unless the transaction lacks commercial substance or the fair value of neither the asset received nor the asset given up is reliably measurable. *[FRS 102.17.14]*.

If the exchange is of assets with dissimilar values this indicates that, unless the difference means that other goods and services are being provided (e.g. a management fee) that the transaction includes an equity contribution. This means that the entity has the following accounting choice:

*   recognise the transaction as an exchange of assets at fair value with an equity transaction. Any difference between the fair value of the asset received and the fair value of the asset given up is an equity transaction (capital contribution) while the difference between the carrying value of the asset given up and its fair value is recognised in other comprehensive income as it is not a realised profit; or

*   recognise the transaction as an exchange of assets at fair value of the asset received. Any difference between the carrying value of the asset given up is recognised in other comprehensive income as it is not a realised profit.

4.4.2.B   *Acquisition and sale of assets for shares*

These transactions include the transfer of inventory, property, plant and equipment, intangible assets, investment property and investments in subsidiaries, jointly controlled entities and associates by one entity in return for the shares of the other entity. These transactions are usually between a parent and subsidiary where the subsidiary is the transferee that issues shares to the parent in exchange for the assets received.

For the subsidiary, transactions that involve the transfer of inventory, property, plant and equipment, intangible assets and investment property in exchange for shares are

Chapter 6

within the scope of Section 26 – *Share-based Payment*. Accordingly, the assets should be recognised at fair value unless that fair value cannot be estimated reliably. If the entity cannot estimate reliably the fair value of the goods or services received, the entity should measure their value, and the corresponding increase in equity, by reference to the fair value of the equity instruments granted. *[FRS 102.26.7]*.

However, for transactions in which a non-monetary asset is acquired from a parent company or another wholly-owned group company in exchange for the issue of shares by a wholly-owned subsidiary, the issuer (i.e. the wholly-owned subsidiary) has the option to apply group reconstruction relief and use the transferor's previous carrying value as cost. *[s611]*. The Accounting Council's Note on Legal Requirements refers only to using group reconstruction relief in terms of the 'cost' of investments in subsidiaries, *[FRS 102.A4.24]*, but there is no reason why it cannot be applied also to other asset purchases within the scope of the legislation.

For the parent, based on what is said at 4.2.1 above, the cost of the new investment should be recorded at the fair value of the consideration given (i.e. the fair value of the asset sold). Any gain recognised due to fair value being greater than the existing carrying amount of the asset will be recognised in other comprehensive income as it is not a realised profit.

4.4.3   *Financial instruments within the scope of Sections 11 and 12*

Section 11 requires the initial recognition of financial assets and financial liabilities to be transaction price unless the arrangement constitutes a financing arrangement when it should be measured at the present value of future payments discounted at a market interest rate. *[FRS 102.11.13]*.

When an entity has elected to apply IAS 39 and/or IFRS 9 – *Financial Instruments* – to recognise and measure financial instruments (as permitted by Sections 11 and 12) the initial recognition is fair value. Any difference between the fair value and the terms of the agreement are recognised as an equity transaction. So, for example, an interest-free or non-market interest rate loan from a parent to a subsidiary must be initially measured at fair value and the difference between fair value and the loan amount must be recorded as either an increase in the cost of investment (in the parent) or as a capital contribution (the subsidiary). Subsequently, the parent will recognise interest income and the subsidiary interest expense using the effective interest method so that the loan is stated at the amount receivable/payable at the redemption date. If the subsidiary makes the non-market loan to the parent, the difference between the loan amount and its fair value is treated as a distribution by the subsidiary to the parent, while the parent reflects the gain. Again, interest is recognised so that the loan is stated at the amount receivable and payable at the redemption date.

4.4.4   *Financial guarantee contracts – parent guarantee issued on behalf of subsidiary*

When an entity has elected to apply IAS 39 and/or IFRS 9 to its financial instruments financial guarantees must be initially recognised at fair value. Otherwise, they are recognised under Section 21 – *Provisions and Contingencies* – which means that a liability does not need to be recognised if it is not probable.

When a financial guarantee is initially recognised at fair value, it is normally appropriate for a parent that gives a guarantee to treat the debit that arises on recognising the guarantee at fair value as an additional investment in its subsidiary. The situation is different for the subsidiary or fellow subsidiary that is the beneficiary of the guarantee. There will be no separate recognition of the financial guarantee unless it is provided to the lender separate and apart from the original borrowing, does not form part of the overall terms of the loan and would not transfer with the loan if it were to be assigned by the lender to a third party. This means that few guarantees will be reflected separately in the financial statements of the entities that benefit from the guarantees. In any event the amounts are unlikely to be significant.

4.5 Intermediate payment arrangements

The requirements in respect of intermediate payment arrangements are, in substance, designed to 'consolidate' an employee benefit trust (EBT) or employee share option trust (ESOP) in individual or separate financial statements. These requirements are largely a replication of the previous UK GAAP guidance, UITF 32. The Accounting Council has explained that these requirements have been added to Section 9 to avoid an entity that has no entities that it controls other than an intermediate payment arrangement from having to prepare consolidated financial statements. *[FRS 102.AC.47].*

FRS 102 does not define intermediate payment arrangements. However, Section 9 states that intermediate payment arrangements may take a variety of forms and that: *[FRS 102.9.33]*

- the intermediary is usually established by the sponsoring entity and constituted as a trust, although other arrangements are possible;

- the relationship between the sponsoring entity and the intermediary may take different forms. For example, when the intermediary is constituted as a trust, the sponsoring entity will not have a right to direct the intermediary's activities. However, in these and other cases the sponsoring entity may give advice to the intermediary or may be relied upon by the intermediary to provide the information it needs to carry on its activities. Sometimes, the way the intermediary has been set up gives it little discretion in the broad nature of its activities;

- the arrangements are most commonly used to pay employees, although they are sometimes used to compensate supplies of goods and services other than employee services. Sometimes, the sponsoring entity's employees and other suppliers are not the only beneficiaries of the arrangement. Other beneficiaries may include past employees and their dependants, and the intermediary may be entitled to make charitable donations;

- the precise identity of the persons or entities that will receive payments from the intermediary, and the amounts that they will receive, are not usually agreed at the outset;

- the sponsoring entity often has the right to appoint or veto the appointment of the intermediary's trustees (or its directors or the equivalent); and

- the payments made to the intermediary and the payments made by the intermediary are often cash payments but may involve other transfers of value.

Chapter 6

Examples of intermediate payment arrangements are ESOPs and EBT's that are used to facilitate employee shareholders under remuneration schemes. Section 9 states that in a typical employee trust arrangement for share-based payments, an entity makes payments to a trust or guarantees borrowing by the trust and the trust uses its funds to accumulate assets to pay the entity's employees for services the employees have rendered to the entity.

Section 9 considers that although the trustees of an intermediary must act at all times in accordance with the interests of the beneficiaries of the intermediary, most intermediaries (particularly those established as a means of remunerating employees) are specifically designed so as to serve the purposes of the sponsoring entity, and to ensure that there will be minimal risk of any conflict arising between the duties of the trustees of the intermediary and the interest of the sponsoring entity, such that there is nothing to encumber implementation of the wishes of the sponsoring entity in practice. Where this is the case, the sponsoring entity has *de facto* control. *[FRS 102.9.33].*

4.5.1   *Accounting for intermediate payment arrangements*

When a sponsoring entity makes payments (or transfers assets) to an intermediary, there is a rebuttable presumption that the entity has exchanged one asset for another and that the payment itself does not represent an immediate expense. To rebut this presumption at the time the payment is made to the intermediary, the entity must demonstrate:

- it will not obtain future economic benefit from the amounts transferred; or
- it does not have control of the right or other access to future economic benefit it is expected to receive. *[FRS 102.9.34].*

When a payment to an intermediary is an exchange by the sponsoring entity of one asset for another, any asset the intermediary acquires in a subsequent exchange transaction will also be under the control of the entity. Accordingly, assets and liabilities of the intermediary will be accounted for by the sponsoring entity as an extension of its own business and recognised in its own individual financial statements. An asset will cease to be recognised as an asset of the sponsoring entity when, for example, the asset of the intermediary vests unconditionally with identified beneficiaries. *[FRS 102.9.35].*

A sponsoring entity may distribute its own equity instruments, or other equity instruments to an intermediary in order to facilitate employee shareholdings under a remuneration scheme. When this is the case and the sponsoring entity has control, or *de facto* control, of the assets and liabilities of the intermediary, the commercial effect is that the sponsoring entity is, for all practical purposes, in the same position as if it had purchased the shares directly. *[FRS 102.9.36].*

When an intermediary entity holds the sponsoring entity's equity instruments, the sponsoring entity shall account for the equity instruments as if it had purchased them directly. The sponsoring entity shall account for the assets and liabilities of the intermediary in its individual (or separate) financial statements as follows: *[FRS 102.9.37]*

- the consideration paid for the equity instruments of the sponsoring entity shall be deducted from equity until such time that the equity instruments vest unconditionally with employees;

- consideration paid or received for the purchase or sale of the sponsoring entity's own equity instruments shall be shown as separate amounts in the statement of changes in equity;

- other assets and liabilities of the intermediary shall be recognised as assets and liabilities of the sponsoring entity;

- no gain or loss shall be recognised in profit or loss or other comprehensive income on the purchase, sale, issue or cancellation of the entity's own equity instruments;

- finance costs and any administration expenses shall be recognised on an accruals basis rather than ad funding payments are made to the intermediary; and

- any dividend income rising on the sponsored entity's own equity instruments shall be excluded from profit or loss and deducted from the aggregate of dividends paid.

Example 6.16 illustrates the application of these requirements.

Example 6.16:   EBTs in individual or separate financial statements of sponsoring entity

A sponsoring entity lends its EBT £1 million which the EBT uses to make a market purchase of 200,000 shares in the entity. Employees of the entity are beneficiaries of the trust and, a short while after purchase, the shares vest unconditionally with the identified beneficiaries in exchange for a payment of £0.2m. During the period the EBT pays £0.1m of administration costs.

In the separate financial statements of the entity, on the basis that the sponsoring entity accounts for the EBT as an extension of its own business the following accounting entries result:

	£	£
Equity	1,000,000	
Cash (market purchase of shares)		1,000,000
Equity		800,000
Cash (Shares vest to employees)	200,000	
Profit or loss	100,000	
Cash (administration expenses)		100,000

No entries are made for the 'loan' between the sponsoring entity and the EBT as this is considered to be a transaction by the sponsoring entity with itself.

Any share-based payment charges incurred by the sponsoring employee in respect of the shares granted to the employees are accounted for separately under Section 26.

4.6   Disclosures in individual and separate financial statements

4.6.1   *Disclosures required by Section 9 in separate financial statements*

The following disclosures are required where a parent prepares separate financial statements:

- that the statements are separate financial statements;

- a description of the methods used to account for investments in subsidiaries, jointly controlled entities and associates; *[FRS 102.9.27]*

- a parent that uses one of the exemptions from presenting consolidated financial statements (described in 3.1 above) shall disclosure the grounds on which the parent is exempt; *[FRS 102.9.27A]* and

- when a parent adopts a policy of accounting for its subsidiaries, associates or jointly controlled entities at fair value with changes in fair value recognised in profit or loss, it must make the disclosures required by paragraph 11.48A of Section 11 (see Chapter 8 at 8.1) in order to comply with the requirements of paragraph 36(4) of Schedule 1 to the Regulations (and the equivalent paragraphs in Schedules 2 and 3). *[FRS 102.9.27B]*. These disclosures must be made even if the parent is a qualifying entity (see Chapter 1) since they are required by the Regulations.

4.6.2   *Disclosures required by Section 9 in individual and separate financial statements in respect of intermediate payment arrangements*

When a sponsoring entity recognises the assets and liabilities held by an intermediary, it should disclose sufficient information in the notes to its financial statements to enable users to understand the significance of the intermediary and the arrangement in the context of the sponsoring entity's financial statements. This should include: *[FRS 102.9.38]*

- a description of the main features of the intermediary including the arrangements for making payments and for distributing equity instruments;

- any restrictions relating to the assets and liabilities of the intermediary;

- the amount and nature of the assets and liabilities held by the intermediary which have not yet vested unconditionally with the beneficiaries of the arrangement;

- the amount that has been deducted from equity and the number of equity instruments held by the intermediary, which have not yet vested unconditionally with the beneficiaries of the arrangement;

- for entities that have their equity instruments listed or publicly traded on a stock exchange or market, the market value of the equity instruments held by the intermediary which have not yet vested unconditionally with employees;

- the extent to which the equity instruments are under options to employees, or have been conditionally gifted to them; and

- the amount that has been deducted from the aggregate dividends paid by the sponsoring entity.

4.6.3   *Additional disclosures required for separate financial statements by the Companies Act and the Regulations*

The following disclosures are required by the Companies Act and the Regulations in respect of subsidiaries and parent undertakings in separate financial statements in addition to those required by Section 9:

- the name of each subsidiary undertaking and country of incorporation if outside the United Kingdom and, if unincorporated, the address of its principal place of business (this disclosure can be limited to the principal subsidiaries if it is otherwise of excessive length); *[s409-410, 4 Sch 1]*

- for each subsidiary not included in the consolidated accounts there must be disclosed the aggregated amount of its capital and reserves as at the end of its relevant financial year and its profit or loss for that year (unless the company is exempt from preparing group accounts under s400 (see 3.1.1.A) or s401 (see 3.1.1.B), the subsidiary is not required to publish its balance sheet anywhere in the world and the holding is less than 50% of the nominal value of the shares, or if the information is not material); *[4 Sch 2]*

- if the company is not required to produce group financial statements, for each subsidiary, there must be stated the identity of each class of shares held and the proportion of the nominal value of that class of shares held, with shares held directly by the company itself distinguished from those attributed to the company held by subsidiaries; *[4 Sch 11]*

- if the company is not required to prepare group financial statements by virtue of s400 (see 3.1.1.A above), disclose that it is exempt from the obligation to prepare and deliver group accounts and, in respect of the undertaking in whose consolidated financial statements it is included, disclose the name, country of incorporation (if outside UK) and, if unincorporated, address of its principal place of business; *[s400(2)(c)-(d)]*

- if the company is not required to prepare group financial statements by virtue of s401 (see 3.1.1.B above), disclose that it is exempt from the obligation to prepare and deliver group accounts and, in respect of the undertaking in whose consolidated financial statements it is included, disclose the name, country of incorporation (if outside UK) and, if unincorporated, address of its principal place of business. *[s401(2)(d)-(e)]*.

Chapter 6

5   SUMMARY OF GAAP DIFFERENCES

	FRS 102	Previous UK GAAP	IFRS
Requirement to prepare consolidated financial statements	Required only if an entity is a parent at the reporting date.	Required only if an entity is a parent at the reporting date.	Required if an entity was a parent at any time during the reporting period.
Exemptions from consolidation for parents	Small groups are exempt. Intermediate parents are exempt (subject to conditions) if included in consolidated financial statements of parent prepared under an 'equivalent' GAAP.	Small groups are exempt. Intermediate parents are exempt (subject to conditions) if included in consolidated financial statements of parent prepared under an 'equivalent' GAAP.	No exemption for small groups. Intermediate parents are exempt (subject to conditions) but only if included in consolidated financial statements of parent prepared under IFRS.
Definition of control	Investor has the power to govern the financial and operating policies of an entity so as to obtain benefits from its activities. Limited application guidance.	Investor has the power to govern the financial and operating policies of an entity so as to obtain benefits from its activities. Limited application guidance.	Investor is exposed, or has rights to variable returns from involvement with the investee and has the ability to affect those returns through its power over the investee. More detailed application guidance.
Subsidiaries excluded from consolidation	Subsidiaries are excluded from consolidation if they operate under severe long term restrictions or are held exclusively with a view to subsequent resale.	Subsidiaries are excluded from consolidation if they operate under severe long term restrictions or are held exclusively with a view to subsequent resale.	No similar concepts. However, a subsidiary which operates under severe long-term restrictions may fail to meet the IFRS definition of a subsidiary due to lack of control.
Investment entities	Subsidiary held as part of an investment portfolio is not consolidated, but recognised at fair value through profit or loss.	No equivalent concept of investment subsidiary.	A parent that is an investment entity must measure all subsidiaries (other than those providing investment management services) at fair value through profit or loss.
Special purpose entity/Structured entity	A special purpose entity is an entity created to establish a narrow objective. Control of a special purpose entity is a risks/reward model. No separate disclosures are required for special purpose entities.	No concept of special purpose entities although guidance on circumstances in which 'quasi subsidiaries' should be consolidated.	A structured entity is an entity designed so that voting or similar rights are not the dominant factor in deciding who controls it. Same control criteria as for other entities. Separate disclosures required for structured entities.

	FRS 102	*Previous UK GAAP*	*IFRS*
Presentation of non-controlling interests	Within equity	Not required to be presented within equity.	Within equity.
Initial measurement of non-controlling interests in a business combination	Measured at share of the net amount of the identifiable assets recognised. Silent on measurement of other components of non-controlling interests.	Measured at share of the net amount of the identifiable assets recognised. Silent on measurement of other components of non-controlling interests	Accounting policy choice for acquirer to recognise non-controlling interests (that are present ownership interests and entitle the holder to a proportionate share of net assets in the event of a liquidation) at either their share of net amount of identifiable assets or at fair value. Other non-controlling interests must be recognised at fair value.
Losses attributable to non-controlling interests	No explicit requirement to make a provision for any formal or implied obligation to provide finance in the consolidated financial statements.	Provision required for any commercial or legal obligation to provide finance that may not be recoverable.	No explicit requirement to make a provision for any formal or implied obligation to provide finance in the consolidated financial statements.
Increasing a controlling interest in a subsidiary	Assets and liabilities are not revalued to fair value and no additional goodwill is recognised.	Assets and liabilities are revalued to fair value and goodwill arising on the increase is calculated by reference to those fair values.	Assets and liabilities are not revalued to fair value and no additional goodwill is recognised.
Decreasing a controlling interest in a subsidiary without loss of control	Accounted for as a transaction between equity holders and no profit/loss is recognised.	Profit/loss is the difference between the carrying amount of the net assets of the subsidiary attributable to the group's interest before the reduction and the attributable carrying amount after the reduction together with any proceeds received.	Accounted for as a transaction between equity holders and no profit/loss is recognised.
Accounting for retained interest on loss of control of a subsidiary	Carrying amount of net assets (and goodwill) is cost on initial measurement of retained investment.	Carrying amount of net assets (and goodwill) is cost on initial measurement of retained investment.	Retained investment must be recognised at fair value on date that control is lost.

Chapter 6

	FRS 102	Previous UK GAAP	IFRS
Cumulative exchange differences on disposal of a foreign operation when control of a subsidiary is lost	Not recycled to profit or loss.	Not recycled to profit or loss (SSAP 20). Recycled to profit or loss (FRS 23).	Recycled to profit or loss.
Cumulative exchange differences on partial disposal of a foreign operation without loss of control	Not recycled to profit and loss.	Not recycled to profit and loss (SSAP 20). Recycled to profit and loss on a proportionate basis (FRS 23).	Re-attributed to non-controlling interest on a proportionate basis .
Exchanges of business or other non-monetary assets for an interest in a subsidiary in consolidated financial statements	Gains that are not realised are reported in other comprehensive income.	Gains that are not realised are reported in other comprehensive income.	No distinction between realised and unrealised gains and all gains/losses reported in profit or loss.
Investments in subsidiaries, associates and jointly controlled entities in individual and separate financial statements	Accounting policy choice for each class (subsidiaries, associates and jointly controlled entities) to measure at either cost, fair value through other comprehensive income or fair value through profit and loss.	No guidance. The Regulations permit measurement, depending on the applicable Schedule, at either historical cost, or valuation through STRGL being either market value (at date of last valuation), directors' valuation current cost, current value or fair value.	Accounting policy choice for each category to measure at either cost, fair value through other comprehensive income or fair value through profit and loss.
Cost of investment in a subsidiary in separate financial statements	Merger relief and group reconstruction relief is available, in certain circumstances, that permits cost to be equal to the nominal value of shares issued (merger relief) or the previous carrying amount of the investment in the transferor's books (group reconstruction relief).	Merger relief and group reconstruction relief is available, in certain circumstances, that permits cost to be equal to the nominal value of shares issued (merger relief) or the previous carrying amount of the investment in the transferor's books (group reconstruction relief).	No option to use previous nominal value of the shares issued or the previous carrying amount of the investment in the transferor's books. A new parent has the option to measure cost at the carrying amount of its share of the equity items of the original parent for certain group reconstructions.
Intermediate payment arrangements	Accounted for as an extension of the parent's own business in its separate financial statements.	Accounted for as an extension of the parent's own business in its separate financial statements.	No guidance. In practice, an entity could use either the parent extension method or treat as an investment in subsidiary.

	FRS 102	Previous UK GAAP	IFRS
Disclosures in consolidated financial statements (key differences)			
Non-controlling interests that are material to the reporting entity	Summarised financial information is not required.	Summarised financial information is not required.	Summarised financial information is required for each subsidiary with material non-controlling interests.
Interests in consolidated special purpose or structured entities	No specific disclosures required for consolidated special purpose entities (would be included within the general disclosure requirements for subsidiaries).	No specific disclosures required for consolidated special purpose entities (would be included within the general disclosure requirements for subsidiaries).	Disclosures required in respect of contractual arrangements, obligations and intentions to provide financial support to consolidated structured entities.
Investments in unconsolidated special purpose/structured entities	No specific disclosures required (in addition to those required by other sections of FRS 102).	No specific disclosures required (in addition to those required by other FRSs).	Extensive disclosures required (in addition to disclosures required by other IFRSs).
Significant restrictions and financial support provided to subsidiaries	Disclosure of significant restrictions on ability to transfer funds to parent.	Disclosure of significant restrictions on ability to transfer funds to parent.	As well as disclosure of significant restrictions, disclosures required of guarantees, provisions of financial support (contractual and non-contractual) and current intentions to provide financial support.
Changes in ownership interest that do not result in loss of control	No separate schedule required.	No separate schedule required.	Separate schedule required showing the effects on equity.
Unconsolidated subsidiaries	The Regulations require disclosure of the capital and reserves and profit and loss for each material subsidiary not included in the consolidated accounts.	The Regulations require disclosure of the capital and reserves and profit and loss for each material subsidiary not included in the consolidated accounts.	Separate disclosure required of significant restrictions and financial support. No requirement to disclose the capital and reserves and profit and loss for each material subsidiary not included in the consolidated accounts.

Chapter 6

	FRS 102	Previous UK GAAP	IFRS
Differences of accounting rules as between a parent's group and individual accounts	Disclosure required by the Regulations.	Disclosure required by the Regulations.	No disclosure requirement.
Disclosures in individual and separate financial statements (key differences)			
Investments in unconsolidated special purpose/structured entities	No specific disclosures required (in addition to those required by other sections of FRS 102).	No specific disclosures required (in addition to those required by other FRSs).	Extensive disclosures required (in addition to disclosures required by other IFRSs).
Intermediate payment arrangements	Various disclosures required.	Various disclosures required.	No specific disclosures required for intermediate payment arrangements (although these may be structured entities – see above).

Chapter 7 Accounting policies, estimates and errors

List of examples

Chapter 7   Accounting policies, estimates and errors

1   INTRODUCTION

Section 10 – *Accounting Policies, Estimates and Errors* – provides guidance for selecting and applying the accounting policies used in preparing financial statements. It also covers changes in accounting estimates and corrections of errors in prior period financial statements. *[FRS 102.10.1].*

Overall, Section 10 is similar to IAS 8 – *Accounting Policies, Changes in Accounting Estimates and Errors.* The equivalent previous UK GAAP guidance on accounting policies and estimates was contained in FRS 18 – *Accounting policies* – and the guidance on correction of prior period errors was contained in FRS 3 – *Reporting financial performance.*

2   COMPARISON BETWEEN SECTION 10, PREVIOUS UK GAAP AND IFRS

Broadly, Section 10 is more comparable to IAS 8 than its equivalent sections in FRS 3 and FRS 18.

2.1   Key differences between Section 10 and previous UK GAAP

The key differences between Section 10 and FRS 3 and FRS 18 are as follows:

- Section 10 has a hierarchy that describes how to account for a transaction that is not specifically addressed within FRS 102. Old UK GAAP did not have such a hierarchy (see 2.1.1 below);

- Section 10 requires material prior period errors to be corrected retrospectively whereas previous UK GAAP required only fundamental prior period errors to be corrected retrospectively (see 2.1.2 below);

- Section 10 requires the effect of prior year restatements to be presented in the statement of changes in equity whereas previous UK GAAP required the effect of prior period restatements to be presented in the Statement of Recognised Gains and Losses (see 2.1.3 below);

- Section 10 provides more guidance than previous UK GAAP as to when prior period restatements are impracticable (see 2.1.4 below); and
- Section 10 requires more disclosures than previous UK GAAP when there are changes in accounting policies and estimates and prior period restatements (see 2.1.5 below).

2.1.1   Hierarchy for selecting accounting policies

Section 10 provides a hierarchy for how management must use its judgement in developing and applying an accounting policy when FRS 102 does not specifically address a transaction, other event or condition (see 3.2 below).

FRS 18 did not have a similar hierarchy. Instead, it stated that an accounting policy should be consistent with the requirements of accounting standards, Urgent Issues Task Force (UITF) Abstracts and companies legislation. *[FRS 18.14]*. When it was necessary to choose between accounting policies, an entity was required to select whichever of those policies was judged to be most appropriate to its particular circumstances for the purpose of giving a true and fair view. *[FRS 18.17]*.

2.1.2   Prior period errors

Section 10 requires entities to correct material prior period errors retrospectively. *[FRS 102.10.21]*.

FRS 3 required only fundamental prior period errors to be corrected retrospectively. A fundamental error was an error of such significance as to destroy the true and fair view and hence the validity of the financial statements. *[FRS 3.63]*.

This means that retrospective correction of prior period errors is likely to be more frequent under FRS 102 than under previous UK GAAP.

2.1.3   Presentation of prior year restatements

Section 6 – *Statement of Changes in Equity and Statement of Income and Retained Earnings* – requires the effect of each retrospective application or retrospective restatement required by Section 10 for each component of equity to be presented in the statement of changes in equity. *[FRS 102.6.3(b)]*.

FRS 3 required the cumulative effect of prior period adjustments to be noted at the foot of the statement of total recognised gains and losses. *[FRS 3.29]*.

2.1.4   Impracticability of prior year restatements

Section 10 states that when it is impracticable to apply a change in accounting policy fully retrospectively, the new accounting policy shall be applied as at the beginning of the earliest period for which retrospective application is possible. *[FRS 102.10.12]*. Similarly, if determining the period-specific impact of prior period errors is impracticable, the entity shall restate the opening balances for the earliest period for which retrospective restatement is practicable. *[FRS 102.10.22]*.

Previous UK GAAP contained no guidance on impracticability of retrospective prior year adjustments. Disclosure of prior period adjustments on the results for the preceding period and the effect of changes in accounting policies on the results for the current period were required only if practicable. *[FRS 18.55(c)(ii)-(iii)]*.

2.1.5 Key disclosure differences

Section 10 distinguishes disclosures in respect of changes in accounting policies between those required by a change to an FRS or FRC Abstract and those made voluntarily. It requires disclosure of the adjustment for each financial line item affected. *[FRS 102.10.13-14]*. FRS 18 did not distinguish disclosures between the two different types of change in accounting policy and did not require disclosure of the effect on each financial statement line item. *[FRS 18.55(c)]*.

Section 10 requires disclosure of the effect of a change in an accounting estimate on assets, liabilities, income and expense for the current period and on future periods if practicable. *[FRS 102.10.18]*. FRS 18 required disclosure of the effect of a change in accounting estimate only on the results for the current period. *[FRS 18.55(d)]*.

Section 10 requires disclosure of the nature and effect of material prior year errors including the amount of the correction for each financial line item affected. *[FRS 102.10.23]*. FRS 3 required only that the effect of a prior year adjustment on the results of the preceding period be disclosed without requiring disclosure of the impact on each line item or a description of the nature of the error. *[FRS 3.29]*.

2.2 Key differences between Section 10 and IFRS

The principal differences between Section 10 and IFRS are in respect of:

- the hierarchy established where the accounting for a transaction is not specifically addressed within the standard (see 2.2.1 below); and
- disclosures (see 2.2.2 below).

In summary, the disclosure requirements of Section 10 are less onerous to a reporting entity than those of IAS 8.

2.2.1 Hierarchy for selecting accounting policies

Section 10's hierarchy established to determine how management shall use its judgement in developing and applying an accounting policy where a section or standard does not specifically address a transaction, other event or condition permits but does not require an entity to refer to EU-adopted IFRS. *[FRS 102.10.6]*. IAS 8's equivalent wording refers to any other standard setting body that uses a similar conceptual framework (to IFRS). *[IAS 8.12]*. This may result in a different accounting answer in practice for similar transactions.

2.2.2 Key disclosure differences

Section 10 does not require disclosure of the impact on the financial statements of future periods of changes to FRS 102 that have been issued but are not yet effective. This would apply both to changes to individual sections of FRS 102 and changes to IFRSs which are being applied by a reporting entity under paragraphs 1.4 to 1.7 or 11.2(a) to 11.2(b) of FRS 102 (for example IAS 33 – *Earnings per Share*). IAS 8 requires disclosure of the impact of a new IFRS that is issued but not effective. *[IAS 8.30]*.

FRS 102 does not require a third statement of financial position as at the beginning of the preceding period to be presented whenever an accounting policy is applied retrospectively or a retrospective restatement or reclassification is made in the financial statements. IAS 1 – *Presentation of Financial Statements* – requires a third statement of financial position in such circumstances. *[IAS 1.40A].*

3   REQUIREMENTS OF SECTION 10 FOR ACCOUNTING POLICIES, ESTIMATES AND ERRORS

Section 10 provides guidance on selecting and applying accounting policies, as well as changes in accounting estimates and corrections of errors in prior period financial statements.

3.1   Terms used in Section 10

The following definitions are introduced: *[FRS 102 Appendix I]*

Accounting policies are the specific principles, bases, conventions, rules and practices applied by an entity in preparing and presenting financial statements.

A *change in accounting estimate* is an adjustment of the carrying amount of an asset or a liability, or the amount of the periodic consumption of an asset, that results from the reassessment of the present status of, and expected future benefits and obligations associated with, assets and liabilities. Changes in accounting estimates result from new information or new developments and, accordingly, are not corrections of errors.

Errors are omissions from, and misstatements in, the entity's financial statements for one or more prior periods arising from a failure to use, or misuse of, reliable information that: (a) was available when financial statements for those periods were authorised for issue; and (b) could reasonably be expected to have been obtained and taken into account in the preparation and presentation of those financial statements.

Applying a requirement is *impracticable* when the entity cannot apply it after making every reasonable effort to do so.

3.2   Selection and application of accounting policies

A reporting entity must select accounting policies to account for transactions, other events or conditions. The selection of accounting policies is obviously crucial in the preparation of financial statements. As a general premise, the whole purpose of accounting standards is to specify the accounting policies, presentation and disclosures that should be applied by an entity. Consistent with this premise, entities applying FRS 102 do not have a free hand in selecting accounting policies.

Accounting policies are defined as the specific principles, bases, conventions, rules and practices applied by an entity in preparing and presenting financial statements. *[FRS 102.10.2]*. This means that an accounting policy is not just a question of how to measure a transaction but also how items are classified and presented in the financial statements. For example, an entity makes an accounting policy choice as to whether to show a single statement of comprehensive income or show a two statement presentation. Similarly, an entity must make an accounting policy choice as to whether to present operating cash flows under the direct or indirect method.

The various sections of FRS 102 contain accounting policies that the FRC has concluded result in financial statements containing relevant and reliable information about the transactions, other events or conditions to which they apply. To this end, the starting point of Section 10 is that if an FRS or FRC Abstract specifically addresses a transaction, other event or condition, an entity shall apply that FRS or FRC Abstract. However, the requirement need not be followed if the effect of doing so would not be material. *[FRS 102.10.3]*.

There will be circumstances where a particular event, transaction or other condition is not specifically addressed by an FRS or FRC Abstract. When this is the case, Section 10 sets out a hierarchy of guidance to use. The primary requirement of the hierarchy is that management should use its judgement in developing and applying an accounting policy that results in information that is:

- relevant to the economic decision-making needs of users; and
- reliable in that the financial statements:
  - represent faithfully the financial position, financial performance and cash flows of the entity;
  - reflect the economic substance of transactions, other events and conditions, and not merely the legal form;
  - are neutral, i.e. free from bias;
  - are prudent; and
  - are complete in all material respects. *[FRS 102.10.4]*.

There may sometimes be a tension between 'neutrality' and 'prudence'. On the one hand, financial statements must be free from bias, i.e. neutral. *[FRS 102.2.7]*. On the other hand, they must be prudent, i.e. prepared with a degree of caution such that assets or income are not overstated and liabilities or expenses are not understated. *[FRS 102.2.9]*.

In support of the primary requirement that management should apply judgement in developing and applying appropriate accounting policies, Section 10 gives guidance on how management should apply this judgement. This guidance comes in two 'strengths' – certain things which management is *required* to consider and others which it *may* consider, as follows:

Chapter 7

Management is *required* to refer to and consider the applicability of the following sources in descending order of authority:

- the requirements and guidance in an FRS or FRC Abstract dealing with similar and related issues;

- where an entity's financial statements are within the scope of a Statement of Recommended Practice (SORP), the requirements and guidance in that SORP dealing with similar and related issues; and

- the definitions, recognition criteria and measurement concepts for assets, liabilities, income and expenses and the pervasive principles in Section 2 – *Concepts and Pervasive Principles*. *[FRS 102.10.5]*.

Management *may* also consider the requirements and guidance in EU-adopted IFRS dealing with similar and related issues. However, entities should exercise caution in considering the guidance in EU-adopted IFRS dealing with similar issues as not all of the sections in FRS 102 are based on EU-adopted IFRS. In addition, Section 1 – *Scope* – requires certain entities to apply IAS 33 – *Earnings per Share*, IFRS 8 – *Operating Segments* – or IFRS 6 – *Exploration for and Evaluation of Mineral Resources* – and therefore, where applicable, the accounting policies required by those standards must be followed. *[FRS 102.10.6]*.

Section 10 does not state that an entity may refer to any GAAP other than EU-adopted IFRS. However, in our opinion, an entity would not be prevented from continuing with an accounting policy for a transaction that was applied under previously extant UK GAAP, where FRS 102 does not specifically address the matter, provided the policy was consistent with the guidance, definitions, criteria and concepts contained in the sources referred to by the hierarchy above.

The hierarchy implies that it is not possible to apply an accounting policy for a transaction using the criteria in Section 2 where the accounting for that transaction is specifically addressed by FRS 102 (since Section 2 can only be consulted in the absence of specific guidance). However, Section 3 – *Financial Statement Presentation* – states that there may be extremely rare circumstances where management concludes that compliance with FRS 102 would be so misleading that it would conflict with the objective of financial statements of entities as set out with Section 2. In such circumstances, an entity can depart from the specific requirements of FRS 102 by use of a true and fair override. *[FRS 102.3.5]*. See Chapter 4 for a discussion of the use of the true and fair override. The hierarchy in Section 10 does not refer to Company Law. The implication from Section 10 is that, where choice is available, an accounting policy should be selected on its merits based on the criteria in FRS 102 (relevance and reliability) rather than to comply with the Regulations. Some accounting policy choices permitted or required by FRS 102, for example measuring certain financial liabilities at fair value through profit or loss, are not allowed by The Large and Medium-sized Companies and Groups (Accounts and reports) Regulations 2008 (SI 2008/410) (the Regulations). However, Section 3 requires an entity to make disclosures when it has departed from a requirement of applicable legislation. *[FRS 102.3.5-6]*.

3.3 Consistency of accounting policies

An entity shall select and apply its accounting policies consistently for similar transactions, other events or obligations unless an FRS or FRC Abstract specifically requires or permits categorisation of items for which different policies may be appropriate. If an FRS or FRC Abstract requires or permits such categorisation, an appropriate accounting policy shall be selected and applied consistently to each category. *[FRS 102.10.7]*.

There is no requirement for each entity within a group to have consistent accounting policies in their separate or individual financial statements. Indeed, FRS 102 anticipates that this will not be the case by requiring consolidated financial statements to be adjusted where a member of the group uses accounting policies other than those adopted in the consolidated financial statements for like transactions and events. *[FRS 102.9.17]*. The Regulations also do not require each entity within a group to have consistent accounting policies. However, Section 10 requires an entity to select accounting policies that are both relevant to the economic decision-making needs of its users and reliable. *[FRS 102.10.4]*. Therefore, factors that one group entity would take into accounting in setting accounting policies should normally also apply to other group entities.

3.4 Changes in accounting policies

An entity shall change an accounting policy only if the change:

* is required by an FRS or FRC Abstract; or

* results in the financial statements providing reliable and more relevant information about the effects of transactions, other events or conditions on the entity's financial position, financial performance or cash flows. *[FRS 102.10.8]*.

This means that a change in accounting policy cannot be made on an arbitrary basis. The change can be made only if required by a change in accounting literature or because the change results in reliable and more relevant financial information.

Reliability is defined as the quality of information that makes it free from material error and bias and represents faithfully that which it either purports to represent or could reasonably be expected to represent. *[FRS 102.2.7]*. Relevance is defined as the quality of information that allows it to influence the economic decisions of users by helping them evaluate past, present or future events or confirming, or correcting, their past evaluations. *[FRS 102.2.5]*.

If an FRS or FRC Abstract allows a choice of accounting treatment (including the measurement basis) for a specified transaction or other event or condition and an entity changes its previous choice, that is a change in accounting policy. *[FRS 102.10.10]*.

As noted at 3.2 above, an accounting policy is not restricted to measurement of a transaction but also includes how items are classified and presented in the financial statements. Therefore, changes in presentation, such as a decision to adopt a change from a single statement of comprehensive income approach to a two statement approach is a change in accounting policy. *[FRS 102.5.3]*.

Chapter 7

The following are stated specifically not to be changes in accounting policies:

- the application of an accounting policy for transactions, other events and conditions that differ in substance from those previously occurring;

- the application of a new accounting policy for transactions, other events or conditions that did not occur previously or were not material; and

- a change to the cost model when a reliable measure of fair value is no longer available (or *vice versa*) for an asset that an FRS or FRC Abstract would otherwise require or permit to be measured at fair value. *[FRS 102.10.9]*.

3.4.1   *Applying changes in accounting policies*

An entity shall account for changes in accounting policies as follows:

- a change in an accounting policy resulting from a change in the requirements of an FRS or FRC Abstract are accounted for in accordance with the transitional provisions, if any, specified in that amendment;

- where an entity has elected under paragraph 2 of Section 11 – *Basic Financial Instruments* – to follow IAS 39 – *Financial Instruments: Recognition and Measurement* – and/or IFRS 9 – *Financial Instruments* – and the requirements of IAS 39 and/or IFRS 9 change, then the entity must account for that change in accounting policy in accordance with the transition provisions, if any, specified in the revised IAS 39 and/or IFRS 9;

- where an entity is required or elected to follow IAS 33, IFRS 8 or IFRS 6 and the requirements of those standards change, the entity shall account for the change in accordance with the transitional provisions, if any, specified in those standards as amended; and

- all other changes in accounting policy are accounted for retrospectively. *[FRS 102.10.11]*.

As an exception to the above, the initial application of a policy to revalue assets in accordance with Section 17 – *Property, Plant and Equipment* – or Section 18 – *Intangible Assets other than Goodwill* – is a change in accounting policy to be dealt with as a revaluation in accordance with those sections. *[FRS 102.10.10A]*.

When an entity is applying an accounting policy based on an IFRS, other than the specific IFRSs referred to above (IFRS 6, IFRS 8, IFRS 9, IAS 33 and IAS 39), and that IFRS changes, an issue arising is whether the entity is obliged to also change its accounting policy to align to the amended IFRS. We believe that such a change is at the discretion of the entity. In our view, such a change is permitted only if it satisfies the relevance and reliability criteria and is not otherwise inconsistent with the FRS 102 hierarchy (see 3.2 above). All such accounting policy changes must be accounted for retrospectively regardless of the specific transitional rules that may apply in the IFRS (because the change does not meet any of the exceptions from retrospective application listed above).

3.4.2   *Retrospective application of accounting policy changes*

When a change in accounting policy is applied retrospectively in accordance with 3.4.1 above, the entity applies the new accounting policy to comparative information for prior periods to the earliest date for which it is practicable, as if the new accounting policy had always been applied. *[FRS 102.10.12].*

The following example illustrates how to apply retrospective accounting.

Example 7.1:   Retrospective application of change in accounting policy (ignoring tax)

Entity A makes a voluntary change in its accounting policy for measuring its investment in an associate in its separate financial statements to change the measurement basis from cost less impairment to fair value through profit or loss. Fair value through profit and loss is considered by Entity A to be more relevant than cost less impairment. The change is made in Entity's A annual reporting period ending 31 December 20X5. The fair value of the investment was £9,500 at 31 December 20X5, £10,000 at 31 December 20X4 and £9,000 at 31 December 20X3, respectively. The cost less impairment of the investment in associate was £5,000 at 31 December 20X5, 31 December 20X4 and 31 December 20X3, respectively.

Entity A restates its opening statement of changes in equity at 1 January 20X4 by £4,000 to account for the measurement difference between fair value and cost less impairment of the investment in associate at that date. This difference is credited to retained earnings. If the unrealised fair value gain is not a distributable profit, Entity A may wish, instead of crediting retained earnings, to create a separate non-distributable reserve within equity.

Entity A restates its profit and loss account for the year-ended 31 December 2004 by £1,000 to recognise the fair value gain on the investment in associate during the year. If the unrealised fair value gain is not a distributable profit, Entity A may wish to make a transfer of the unrealised gain in the statement of changes in equity from retained earnings to a separate non-distributable reserve within equity.

Entity A records a fair value loss of £500 in profit or loss for the year-ended 31 December 20X5.

As discussed above, applying a new accounting policy retrospectively means applying it as if that policy had always been applied. This implies that hindsight should not be used when applying a new accounting policy, either in making assumptions about what management's intentions would have been in a prior period or estimating the amounts recognised, measured or disclosed in a prior period. Hence, retrospectively applying a new accounting policy requires distinguishing information that provides evidence of circumstances that existed on the prior period date(s) from that information which would have been available when the financial statements for that prior period(s) were authorised for issue.

In certain circumstances, it might be impracticable to restate the financial statements of prior years for a change in accounting policy. Applying a requirement is impracticable when the entity cannot apply it after making every reasonable effort to do so. *[FRS 102 Appendix I].* Impracticability could arise when the relevant information for the prior years, for example fair value that is not based on an observable price or input, is not available and the entity is unable to calculate the amount after making every reasonable effort.

IAS 8 contains additional guidance on impracticability which is not included in Section 10 but which might be helpful to users and which could be applied via the hierarchy (see 3.2 above). This guidance states that it is impracticable to apply a change in accounting policy retrospectively or to correct an error retrospectively (see 3.6 below) if:

- the effects of the retrospective application or retrospective restatement are not determinable (because, say, data had not been collected in that way and it is impracticable to recreate the information);

- the retrospective application or retrospective restatement requires assumptions about what management's intent would have been in that period; or

- the retrospective application or retrospective restatement requires significant estimates of amounts and that it is impossible to distinguish objectively information about those estimates that:

  - provides evidence of circumstances that existed on the date(s) as at which those amounts are to be recognised, measured or disclosed; and

  - would have been available when the financial statements for that prior period were authorised for issue,from other information. *[IAS 8.5, 50]*.

When it is impracticable to determine the individual-period effects of a change in accounting policy on comparative information for one or more prior periods presented, the entity applies the new accounting policy to the carrying amounts of assets and liabilities as at the beginning of the earliest period for which retrospective application is practicable, which may be the current period, and shall make a corresponding adjustment to the opening balance of each affected component of equity for that period. *[FRS 102.10.12]*.

3.5   Changes in accounting estimates

Estimates are a fundamental feature of financial reporting, reflecting the uncertainties inherent in business activities. The use of reasonable estimates is an essential part of the presentation of financial statements and does not undermine their reliability. *[FRS 102.2.30]*. Unlike previous UK GAAP, FRS 102 does not define estimation techniques or accounting estimates. However, examples of estimates within FRS 102 include bad debt provisions, inventory obsolescence provisions, fair values of financial assets or liabilities and useful lives of depreciable assets.

Estimates will need revision as changes occur in the circumstances on which they are based or as a result of new information or more experience. Hence, a change in accounting estimate is an adjustment to the carrying amount of an asset or a liability, or the amount of the periodic consumption of an asset, that results from the present status of, and expected future benefits and obligations associated with, assets and liabilities. Changes in accounting estimates result from new information or new developments and, accordingly, are not corrections of errors. *[FRS 102.10.15]*. Errors do not result from changes in circumstances or the availability of new information. See 3.6 below.

The distinction between an accounting policy and an accounting estimate is particularly important because a very different accounting treatment is applied when there are changes in accounting policies or accounting estimates. When it is difficult to distinguish a change in accounting policy from a change in accounting estimate, the change is treated as a change in an accounting estimate. *[FRS 102.10.15]*.

By its nature, a change in an accounting estimate is not caused by a prior period event. Consequently, the effect of a change is required to be recognised prospectively in profit or loss by including it in:

- the period of the change, if the change affects that period only; or

- the period of the change and future periods, if the change affects both. *[FRS 102.10.16]*.

An example of a change in estimate which would affect the current period only is a change in an estimate of bad debts. An example of a change which would affect both current and future periods is a change in the estimated useful life of a depreciable asset.

Some changes in accounting estimates will give rise to changes in assets and liabilities, or relate to an item of equity. In those circumstances, the reporting entity adjusts the carrying amount of the related asset, liability or equity item in the period of the change. *[FRS 102.10.17]*.

3.6   Corrections of prior period errors

Errors can arise in respect of the recognition, measurement, presentation or disclosure of elements of financial statements. Such errors include the effects of mathematical mistakes, mistakes in applying accounting policies, oversights or misinterpretations of facts, and fraud. *[FRS 102.10.20]*.

FRS 102 states that information provided in financial statements must be reliable and in order to be reliable it must be free from material error. *[FRS 102.2.7]*.

Prior period errors are omissions from, and misstatements in, an entity's financial statements for one or more prior periods arising from a failure to use, or misuse of, reliable information that:

- was available when financial statements for those periods were authorised for issue; and

- could reasonably be expected to have been obtained and taken into account in the preparation and presentation of those financial statements. *[FRS 102.10.19]*.

When it is discovered that material prior period errors have occurred, Section 10 requires that they be corrected in the first set of financial statements prepared after the discovery. The correction should be excluded from the statement of comprehensive income for the period in which the error is discovered. Rather, it is corrected retrospectively by adjusting prior periods. This is done by:

- restating the comparative amounts for the prior period(s) presented in which the error occurred; or

- if the error occurred before the earliest period presented, restating the opening balances of assets, liabilities and equity for the earliest prior period presented. *[FRS 102.10.21]*.

This process corrects the recognition, measurement and disclosure of amounts of elements of financial statements as if a prior year error had never occurred.

The same caution on the use of hindsight in applying a new accounting policy (see 3.4.2 above) applies to correction of prior period errors. As is the case for the retrospective application of a change in accounting policy, retrospective restatement for the correction of prior period material errors is not required to the extent that it is impracticable to determine the period-specific effects on comparative information for one or more periods presented. In that case, the entity restates the opening balances of assets, liabilities and equity for the earliest period for which retrospective statement is practicable (which may be the current period). *[FRS 102.10.22]*. As discussed at 3.4.2 above, IAS 8 contains additional guidance on impracticability.

3.7   Disclosures of a change in accounting policy, changes in accounting estimates and corrections of prior period errors

3.7.1   *Disclosure of a change in accounting policy*

The disclosure requirements distinguish between a change in accounting policy that is compulsory (i.e. caused by a change to an FRS or FRC Abstract) and a change that is voluntarily.

For changes in an accounting policy caused by an amendment to an FRS or FRC Abstract that have an effect on the current period, any prior period or which might have an effect on future periods, an entity must disclose:

- the nature of the change in accounting policy;
- for the current period and each prior period presented, to the extent practicable, the amount of the adjustment for each financial statement line item presented;
- the amount of the adjustment relating to periods before those presented, to the extent practicable; and
- an explanation if it is impracticable to determine the amounts to be disclosed above.

This means that the nature of an accounting policy change that is expected to impact future periods should be disclosed but the financial impact of such a change need not be quantified.

Financial statements of subsequent periods need not repeat these disclosures. *[FRS 102.10.13]*.

When a voluntary change in accounting policy has an effect on the current period or any prior period, an entity shall disclose the following:

- the nature of the change in accounting policy;
- the reasons why applying the new accounting policy provides reliable and more relevant information;
- to the extent practicable, the amount of the adjustment for each financial statement line item affected, showing separately the amounts:
  - for the current period;
  - for each prior period presented; and
  - in the aggregate for periods before those presented; and
- an explanation if it is impracticable to determine the amounts to be disclosed for each financial statement line item above.

Financial statements of subsequent periods need not repeat these disclosures. *[FRS 102.10.14]*.

3.7.2 Disclosure of a change in accounting estimate

Disclosure is required of the nature of any change in an accounting estimate and the effect of the change on assets, liabilities, income and expense for the current period and, if practicable, the effect of the change on one or more future periods. *[FRS 102.10.18]*.

This means that where a change in accounting estimate affects future periods, such as a change in the estimated useful life of a depreciable asset, the reporting entity must provide users of the accounts information regarding the future impact of that change, if practicable. IAS 8 also requires this disclosure. *[IAS 8.39-40]*.

In contrast to a change in accounting policy, there is no requirement to disclose the impact of a change in accounting estimate on each financial statement line item.

3.7.3 Disclosure of prior period errors

The following is required to be disclosed in respect of material prior period errors:

- the nature of the prior period error;
- for each prior period presented, to the extent practicable, the amount of the correction for each financial statement line item affected;
- to the extent practicable, the amount of the correction at the beginning of the earliest prior period presented; and
- an explanation if it is not practicable to determine the amounts to be disclosed above.

Financial statements of subsequent periods need not repeat these disclosures. *[FRS 102.10.23]*.

These disclosures are similar to those required for a change in accounting policy.

There is no exemption from disclosure of a prior period error on the grounds that such information might prejudice seriously the position of the reporting entity.

The following example illustrates the disclosures required for a retrospective restatement of a prior period error.

Example 7.2:   Retrospective restatement of prior period error

During 20X5, Beta Co discovered that some products that had been sold during 20X4 were incorrectly included in inventory at 31 December 20X4 at £6,500.

Beta's accounting records for 20X5 show sales of £104,000, cost of goods sold of £86,500 (including £6,500 for the error in opening inventory), and income taxes of £5,250.

In 20X4, Beta reported:

	£
Sales	73,500
Cost of goods sold	(53,500)
Profit before income taxes	20,000
Income taxes	(6,000)
Profit	14,000

The 20X4 opening retained earnings were £20,000 and closing retained earnings were £34,000.

Beta's income tax rate was 30 per cent for 20X5 and 20X4. It had no other income or expenses.

Beta had £5,000 of share capital throughout, and no other components of equity except for retained earnings. Its shares are not publicly traded and it does not disclose earnings per share.

Beta Co
Extract from the statement of comprehensive income

	20X5	(restated) 20X4
	£	£
Sales	104,000	73,500
Cost of goods sold	(80,000)	(60,000)
Profit before income taxes	24,000	13,500
Income taxes	(7,200)	(4,050)
Profit	16,800	9,450

Beta Co
Statement of Changes in Equity

	Share capital £	Retained earnings £	Total £
Balance at 1 January 20X4	5,000	20,000	25,000
Profit for the year ended 31 December 20X4 as restated	–	9,450	9,450
Balance at 31 December 20X4	5,000	29,450	34,450
Profit for the year ended 31 December 20X5	–	16,800	16,800
Balance at 31 December 20X5	5,000	46,250	51,250

Extracts from the Notes

1. Some products that had been sold in 20X4 were incorrectly included in inventory at 31 December 20X4 at £6,500. The financial statements of 20X4 have been restated to correct this error. The effect of the restatement on each financial statement line item affected is shown below.

	Effect on 20X4 £
(Increase) in cost of goods sold	(6,500)
Decrease in income tax expense	1,950
(Decrease) in profit	(4,550)
(Decrease) in inventory	(6,500)
Decrease in income tax payable	1,950
(Decrease) in equity	(4,550)

4   COMPANY LAW MATTERS

4.1   Corrections of prior period errors and defective accounts

Restatement of the financial statements for prior years does not necessarily mean that a reporting entity has to withdraw its financial statements and reissue them under s454 of the Companies Act 2006 (i.e. the Defective Accounts regime). If an entity corrects errors by way of a prior year adjustment in its latest financial statements, it would not normally withdraw and amend any earlier years' financial statements.

5   SUMMARY OF GAAP DIFFERENCES

	FRS 102	*Previous UK GAAP*	*IFRS*
Hierarchy for selecting accounting policies when accounting not specifically not addressed	Yes	No – but must be consistent with standards, UITF Abstracts and legislation.	Yes
Hierarchy reference to other standard setters	May refer to EU-adopted IFRS.	No reference.	May refer to other standard setting bodies with similar conceptual framework.
Regular review of accounting policies required.	No	Yes (although in practice no GAAP difference expected)	No
Changes in accounting estimates	Only if new information or developments.	Not limited to new information or developments.	Only if new information or developments.
Prior period errors	Correct retrospectively if material.	Correct retrospectively only if fundamental.	Correct retrospectively if material.
Presentation of prior year restatements	Adjust through opening SOCIE.	Adjust at foot of current year STRGL.	Adjust through opening SOCIE.
Impracticability	Relief for prior year restatements if impracticable.	Prior year restatements required only if 'practicable'.	Relief for prior year restatements if impracticable (more guidance compared to FRS 102).

Chapter 7

	FRS 102	*Previous UK GAAP*	*IFRS*
Disclosures	Distinguishes between compulsory and voluntary changes in accounting policy.	Does not distinguish between different types of changes in accounting policy.	Distinguishes between compulsory and voluntary changes in accounting policy.
	Disclose amount of adjustment for each financial line item affected by retrospective changes.	Disclosure of effect of adjustment not required by financial line item.	Disclose amount of adjustment for each financial line item affected by retrospective changes.
	Disclose nature of accounting policy change affecting future periods.	No requirement to disclose accounting policy changes affecting future periods.	Disclose both nature and impact of IFRSs issued but not effective.
	Disclose impact of change in accounting estimates on future periods if practicable.	No requirement to disclose impact of change in accounting estimate effecting future periods.	Disclose impact of change in accounting estimate on future periods except when impracticable.
	Third balance sheet not required for prior period restatements.	Third balance sheet not required for prior period restatements.	Third balance sheet required for prior period restatements.

Chapter 8   Financial instruments

Chapter 8

List of examples

Chapter 8

Chapter 8   Financial instruments

1   INTRODUCTION

Sections 11 – *Basic Financial Instruments*, 12 – *Other Financial Instruments Issues* – and 22 – *Liabilities and Equity* – contain the accounting and disclosure requirements for financial instruments. Section 11 deals with what are termed 'basic' financial instruments, which are certain straightforward debt instruments and equity securities. It sets out the criteria for basic financial instruments and how they are measured, along with the impairment requirements. It also includes the derecognition requirements for financial instruments, and disclosure provisions for basic financial instruments. Section 11 has been structured to provide all the financial instrument accounting requirements for many entities, who do not enter into more complex transactions.

Section 12 applies to all other financial instruments, which need to be measured at fair value through profit or loss, and also addresses the hedge accounting requirements. It also contains disclosure provisions.

However, FRS 102 adopters also have the option of applying the recognition and measurement provisions of IAS 39 – *Financial Instruments: Recognition and Measurement* – or IFRS 9 – *Financial Instruments* (for which EU endorsement is not required), under an accounting policy choice afforded by FRS 102. This choice must be made for all financial instruments – entities cannot decide to elect to use IAS 39 (or IFRS 9) only for certain items.

It should be noted that Sections 11 and 12 have been amended since the initial publication of FRS 102 in March 2013. The first change was in respect of the hedge accounting requirements in Section 12. The original hedge accounting requirements were largely drawn from IAS 39. In November 2013, the IASB issued its new general hedge accounting requirements as part of the overall project to replace IAS 39 with IFRS 9. As a result, in July 2014, FRS 102 was amended to incorporate a more principles-based approach, similar to that in IFRS 9, without the detailed guidance of IFRS 9.

The second change was in respect of the criteria to permit the subsequent measurement of basic debt instruments at amortised cost. When applied in practice, the original Section 11 requirements were considered to be too restrictive and resulted in basic products such as certain standard variable rate ('SVR') mortgages and inflation-linked products failing the criteria and consequently being measured at fair value through profit or loss. As a result, the FRC decided to revisit the requirements and amended FRS 102 in July 2014. These amendments loosened the requirements, although they remain more rules-based than the IFRS 9 'contractual characteristics' test. Unlike IFRS 9, there is no 'business model' test.

The impairment requirements in Section 11 have been drawn from IAS 39's incurred loss model. Given that the IASB has finalised its IFRS 9 impairment requirements, which use an expected loss approach, it is likely that at some point in the future, the FRC will propose to incorporate the IFRS 9 principles into FRS 102. However, the timing of this remains uncertain and it is unlikely that the effective date will be any earlier than 1 January 2018.

Finally, the Section 22 requirements for classifying issued instruments as either liabilities or equity are closely modelled on those in FRS 25 – *Financial instruments: presentation* – and IAS 32 – *Financial Instruments: Presentation*, without the detailed guidance.

2   KEY DIFFERENCES BETWEEN SECTIONS 11 AND 12, PREVIOUS UK GAAP AND IFRS

2.1   Key differences from UK GAAP (not applying FRS 26)

The impact of Sections 11 and 12 for an entity using previous UK GAAP will depend largely on whether an entity has already adopted FRS 26 – *Financial instruments: recognition and measurement*. For entities that are currently applying FRS 26, there will be no impact from an accounting recognition and measurement perspective if they decide to apply IAS 39 under the accounting policy choice afforded by FRS 102. In this case, the only change will be moving from the FRS 29 – *Financial instruments: disclosures* – disclosure regime to the disclosures required by Sections 11 and 12. For those entities that are moving from FRS 26 to FRS 102, the differences will be the same as for entities transitioning from IFRS, and they are summarised together, in 2.2.

On the other hand, for those entities that are not applying FRS 26, either because they are not listed or they do not apply the fair value accounting rules set out in The Large and Medium-sized Companies and Groups (Accounts and Reports) Regulations 2008 or The Large and Medium-sized Limited Liability Partnerships (Accounts) Regulations 2008 ('the Regulations'), the scale of change may be significant. These entities will need either to apply the provisions of Sections 11 and 12 in full or apply a hybrid, consisting of the recognition and measurement provisions of IAS 39/IFRS 9 and the disclosure requirements of Sections 11 and 12.

Except for FRS 4 – *Capital instruments*, certain requirements in FRS 5 – *Reporting the substance of transactions* – and SSAP 20 – *Foreign Currency Translation*, the FRSs were essentially silent on the subject of financial instruments and their accounting was often dictated more by company law. As a result, most financial instruments held by non-financial institutions were held at cost less impairment.

Company law was silent on the recognition and measurement of derivatives and, as a result, there were various diverse practices. For example, under previous UK GAAP, an interest rate swap which is entered into to convert an entity's floating rate exposure on its borrowings to fixed rate will not necessarily have been recognised in the statement of financial position. Instead, it has been common for a swap used as a hedge to be accounted for on an accruals basis, with the net interest amount being recognised in profit or loss. Similarly, SSAP 20 permitted monetary assets and liabilities denominated in foreign currencies to be translated at the rate specified in related or matching forward contracts. *[SSAP 20.48].* Under FRS 102, all derivatives will need to be recorded in the statement of financial position at fair value. The default is for the revaluation to be recorded in the profit and loss account, although the impact on profit or loss may be reduced if hedge accounting is applied.

To achieve hedge accounting under FRS 102 will mean complying with some detailed requirements and recognising any actual hedge ineffectiveness.

More complex debt instruments will be required to be recorded at fair value through profit or loss under FRS 102. Another significant difference may be the accounting for investments in equity securities, which may currently be recognised at historical cost and only impaired if there has been a permanent diminution in value. Under FRS 102, equities are normally required to be measured at fair value through the profit and loss account and only at cost in limited circumstances.

For derecognition, entities would have applied FRS 5 in the past. Adoption of FRS 102 will often result in the same accounting outcomes, given FRS 5's focus on the underlying substance of arrangements or transactions and the transfer of risks and rewards. Perhaps the most significant difference is that FRS 102 does not share the FRS 5 concept of a 'linked presentation', for situations where the potential losses of a transferor are limited to a fixed amount.

Previously, the financial instrument disclosure requirements for those entities in scope were included in FRS 13 – *Derivatives and other financial instruments: disclosures.* There are similarities between the FRS 13 disclosures and those required by FRS 102, however, the scope of FRS 13 was limited, thus, most entities only had to make the disclosures required by the Companies Act, which were less onerous. Hence, the move to FRS 102 will result in the addition of new disclosures in the financial statements.

A more complete list of the differences can be found at 10 below.

FRS 25 has been mandatory for all UK entities since 1 January 2005 and the transition to Section 22 may not have any effect for most entities. Further discussion on Section 22 can be found at 9 below.

2.2   Key differences from IFRS/UK GAAP (applying FRS 26)

The comparable IFRSs are IAS 32, IAS 39 and IFRS 7 – *Financial Instruments: Disclosures* ('IFRS 7') while the comparable UK standards are FRS 25, FRS 26 and FRS 29. As these IFRSs and FRSs are almost identical, a comparison to FRS 102 will render the same differences.

Chapter 8

The main differences between FRS 102 and IFRS/UK GAAP (applying FRS 26) are as follows:

- FRS 102 has a two tiered measurement model: amortised cost/cost or fair value through profit or loss. That is, debt instruments may be measured at amortised cost if they meet the criteria or, if they do not, at fair value through profit or loss, while equities (and certain derivatives on equities) have to be measured at fair value through profit or loss and only at cost in limited circumstances. Hence, entities which prefer to recognise debt or equity securities at fair value through other comprehensive income may opt for IAS 39/IFRS 9;

- For basic debt securities, the criteria to recognise them at amortised cost under FRS 102 are less stringent than under FRS 26/IAS 39, as explained in 4.2;

- Unlike FRS 26 or IFRS, there is no concept in FRS 102 of 'held for trading'. Basic debt instruments that are held for trading purposes are not automatically required to be recorded at fair value, and entities will need to elect to use the 'fair value option' if they wish to record these instruments at fair value rather than at amortised cost;

- Unlike FRS 26/IAS 39, under FRS 102, assets which have been individually assessed for impairment and found not to be impaired do not subsequently need to be included in a collective assessment of impairment;

- The requirements for assessing hedge effectiveness for hedge accounting have changed significantly compared to FRS 26/IAS 39. Entities are no longer required to perform an onerous quantitative effectiveness assessment to demonstrate that the hedge relationship in any period was highly effective, using the 80%-125% bright line. Instead, the FRS 102 effectiveness test uses a new approach that focuses on the existence of an economic relationship between the hedged item and hedging instrument. However, there is still a need to measure any actual hedge ineffectiveness and record it in the same way as under FRS 26/IAS 39;

- A significant change from FRS 26/IAS 39 is that under the FRS 102 hedge accounting rules, it is possible to designate specific risk components of non-financial items where these are separately identifiable and reliably measurable;

- The complex embedded derivative separation rules in FRS 26/IAS 39 do not exist in FRS 102 and many instruments containing embedded derivatives, including financial liabilities, will need to be measured at fair value through profit or loss;

- A contractual obligation or even a potential obligation for an entity to purchase its own equity instruments for cash or another financial asset may be treated as a derivative within the scope of Section 12 and measured at fair value through profit or loss. In contrast, FRS 25/IAS 32 requires measurement at the present value of the financial liability's (gross) redemption amount. This point is further illustrated at 9.3 below; and

- The disclosure requirements in FRS 102 are less onerous than those in FRS 29/IFRS 7.

3   SCOPE OF SECTIONS 11, 12 AND 22

This section covers the scope of Sections 11, 12 and 22 and the key definitions used.

3.1   Definitions

Term	Definition
Active market	A market in which all the following conditions exist: (a) the items traded in the market are homogeneous; (b) willing buyers and sellers can normally be found at any time; and (c) prices are available to the public.
Amortised cost (of a financial asset or financial liability)	The amount at which the financial asset or financial liability is measured at initial recognition minus principal repayments, plus or minus the cumulative amortisation using the effective interest method of any difference between that initial amount and the maturity amount, and minus any reduction (directly or through the use of an allowance account) for impairment or uncollectability.
Compound financial instrument	A financial instrument that, from the issuer's perspective, contains both a liability and an equity element.
Derecognition	The removal of a previously recognised asset or liability from an entity's statement of financial position.
Derivative	A financial instrument or other contract with all three of the following characteristics: (a) its value changes in response to the change in a specified interest rate, financial instrument price, commodity price, foreign exchange rate, index of prices or rates, credit rating or credit index, or other variable (sometimes called the 'underlying'), provided in the case of a non-financial variable that the variable is not specific to a party to the contract; (b) it requires no initial net investment or an initial net investment that is smaller than would be required for other types of contracts that would be expected to have a similar response to changes in market factors; and (c) it is settled at a future date.
Effective interest method	A method of calculating the amortised cost of a financial asset or a financial liability (or a group of financial assets or financial liabilities) and of allocating the interest income or interest expense over the relevant period.
Effective interest rate	The rate that exactly discounts estimated future cash payments or receipts through the expected life of the financial instrument or, when appropriate, a shorter period to the carrying amount of the financial asset or financial liability.
Equity	The residual interest in the assets of the entity after deducting all its liabilities.

Chapter 8

Term	*Definition*
Fair value	The amount for which an asset could be exchanged, a liability settled, or an equity instrument granted could be exchanged, between knowledgeable, willing parties in an arm's length transaction. In the absence of any specific guidance provided in the relevant section of this FRS, the guidance in FRS 102.11.27 to FRS 102.11.32 shall be used in determining fair value.
Financial asset	Any asset that is: (a) cash; (b) an equity instrument of another entity; (c) a contractual right: (i) to receive cash or another financial asset from another entity, or (ii) to exchange financial assets or financial liabilities with another entity under conditions that are potentially favourable to the entity; or (d) a contract that will or may be settled in the entity's own equity instruments and: (i) under which the entity is or may be obliged to receive a variable number of the entity's own equity instruments; or (ii) that will or may be settled other than by the exchange of a fixed amount of cash or another financial asset for a fixed number of the entity's own equity instruments. For this purpose the entity's own equity instruments do not include instruments that are themselves contracts for the future receipt or delivery of the entity's own equity instruments.
Financial instrument	A contract that gives rise to a financial asset of one entity and a financial liability or equity instrument of another entity.
Financial liability	Any liability that is: (a) a contractual obligation: (i) to deliver cash or another financial asset to another entity; or (ii) to exchange financial assets or financial liabilities with another entity under conditions that are potentially unfavourable to the entity, or (b) a contract that will or may be settled in the entity's own equity instruments and: (i) under which the entity is or may be obliged to deliver a variable number of the entity's own equity instruments; or (ii) will or may be settled other than by the exchange of a fixed amount of cash or another financial asset for a fixed number of the entity's own equity instruments. For this purpose the entity's own equity instruments do not include instruments that are themselves contracts for the future receipt or delivery of the entity's own equity instruments.

Firm commitment	Binding agreement for the exchange of a specified quantity of resources at a specified price on a specified future date or dates.
Forecast transaction	Uncommitted but anticipated future transaction.
Hedging gain or loss	Change in fair value of a hedged item that is attributable to the hedged risk.
Highly probable	Significantly more likely than probable.
Liquidity risk	The risk that an entity will encounter difficulty in meeting obligations associated with financial liabilities that are settled by delivering cash or another financial asset.
Market risk	The risk that the fair value or future cash flows of a financial instrument will fluctuate because of changes in market prices. Market risk comprises three types of risk: currency risk, interest rate risk and other price risk.
	Interest rate risk – the risk that the fair value or future cash flows of a financial instrument will fluctuate because of changes in market interest rates.
	Currency risk – the risk that the fair value or future cash flows of a financial instrument will fluctuate because of changes in foreign exchange rates.
	Other price risk – the risk that the fair value or future cash flows of a financial instrument will fluctuate because of changes in market prices (other than those arising from interest rate risk or currency risk),whether those changes are caused by factors specific to the financial instrument or its issuer, or factors affecting all similar financial instruments traded in the market.
Non-controlling interest	The equity in a subsidiary not attributable, directly or indirectly, to a parent.
Probable	More likely than not.
Publicly traded (debt or equity instruments)	Traded, or in process of being issued for trading, in a public market (a domestic or foreign stock exchange or an over-the-counter market, including local and regional markets).
Transaction costs (financial instruments)	Incremental costs that are directly attributable to the acquisition, issue or disposal of a financial asset or financial liability, or the issue or reacquisition of an entity's own equity instrument. An incremental cost is one that would not have been incurred if the entity had not acquired, issued or disposed of the financial asset or financial liability, or had not issued or reacquired its own equity instrument.
Treasury shares	An entity's own equity instruments, held by that entity or other members of the consolidated group.

Chapter 8

3.2   Scope

Sections 11, 12 and 22 contain similar scope exceptions, which are largely consistent with those in FRSs 26 and 25 and IASs 39 and 32. The following are the exceptions:

- Investments in subsidiaries, associates and joint ventures, which should be accounted for in accordance with Sections 9, 14 and 15 respectively;

- Financial instruments, contracts and obligations to which Section 26 – *Share-based Payment* – applies except for contracts within the scope of FRS 102.12.5 (see below). However, the Section 22 requirements (see 9 below) in respect of the classification of an issued instrument as debt/equity applies to treasury shares issued, purchased, sold transferred or cancelled in connection with employee share option/purchase plans and other share based-payment arrangements;

- Insurance contracts (including reinsurance contracts) that the entity issues and reinsurance contracts that the entity holds, which are subject to FRS 103;

- Financial instruments issued by an entity with a discretionary participation feature (see FRS 103);

- Reimbursement assets accounted for in accordance with Section 21 – *Provisions and Contingencies*;

- Financial guarantee contracts (see Chapter 17);

- Employers' rights and obligations under employee benefit plans, to which Section 28 – *Employee Benefits* – applies, except for the determination of the fair value of plan assets;

- Leases to which Section 20 – *Leases* – applies, except for certain aspects such as derecognition and impairment of finance leases or if the lease could, as a result of non-typical contractual terms, result in a loss to the lessor or the lessee;

- Contracts for contingent consideration in a business combination (see Chapter 15). This exemption applies only to the acquirer;

- Any forward contract between an acquirer and a selling shareholder to buy or sell an acquiree that will result in a business combination at a future acquisition date. The terms of the forward contract should not exceed a reasonable period normally necessary to obtain the required approval and to complete the transaction. *[FRS 102.11.7, FRS 102.12.3, FRS 102.22.2]*.

In addition, contracts to buy or sell non-financial items such as commodities or inventory are excluded from the scope of Section 12 as they are not financial instruments. However, Section 12 would apply in instances where risks are imposed on the buyer/seller that are not typical of such contracts. For example, Section 12 may apply when the buyer/seller is required to absorb losses unrelated to price movements of the underlying non-financial items, except for default by one of the counterparties or fluctuations in foreign exchange rates. *[FRS 102.12.4]*.

Furthermore, Section 12 applies to contracts to buy or sell non-financial items if the contracts can be settled net in cash or another financial instrument with the exception of the 'own use' rules. That is, Section 12 does not apply to contracts that were entered into and continue to be held for the purpose of the receipt or delivery of a non-financial item in accordance with an entity's expected purchase, sale or usage requirements. *[FRS 102.12.5]*.

The one difference in the scope of FRS 102 compared to that of FRS 26/IAS 39 is that certain loan commitments are scoped out of FRS 26/IAS 39 and into FRS 12/IAS 37 – *Provisions, contingent liabilities and contingent assets* – while, under FRS 102, all loan commitments are within the scope of either Section 11 or 12. We do not expect this scope difference to have a significant impact in practice and it is more likely that any effect will only arise after the IFRS 9 impairment requirements are incorporated into FRS 102.

4   CLASSIFICATION AND MEASUREMENT

As discussed at 1 above, entities can choose for recognition and measurement to apply either:

- Sections 11 or 12; or
- IAS 39; or
- IFRS 9.

When an entity chooses to apply IAS 39 or IFRS 9, it applies the scope of the relevant standard to its financial statements. An entity's choice above is an accounting policy choice. Section 10 – *Accounting Policies, Estimates and Errors* contains requirements for determining when a change in accounting policy is appropriate, how such a change should be accounted for and what information should be disclosed. *[FRS 102.11.2, 12.2]*.

The accounting policy choice above applies only for recognition and measurement. For disclosure, an entity applies the disclosure requirements of Sections 11 and 12 (see 8 below).

The recognition and measurement requirements of IAS 39 and and IFRS 9 are discussed in EY International GAAP 2015.

The recognition and measurement requirements of Sections 11 and 12 are discussed below.

4.1   'Basic' financial instruments

Section 11 deals with the accounting for basic financial instruments. The introduction to the section provides a definition of a financial instrument, which is a contract that gives rise to a financial asset of one entity and a financial liability or equity instrument of another entity. *[FRS 102.11.3]*. This is identical to the definition in FRS 25 and IAS 32. This section then introduces the term 'basic financial instrument', without actually defining it. Instead, it lists those financial instruments that qualify as basic financial instruments. These are cash and those debt instruments that meet the criteria described in 4.2 below, such as demand and fixed term deposits, commercial paper, commercial bills held, loans receivable and payable and bonds. It also includes certain commitments to receive or make a loan and investments in non-convertible preference shares and non-puttable ordinary and preference shares. *[FRS 102.11.5, FRS 102.11.8]*.

Chapter 8

4.1.1   Basic debt instruments

The following six criteria all need to be satisfied so that debt instruments can be regarded as 'basic' and so may be accounted for in accordance with Section 11 at amortised cost:

Criterion 1

The contractual return to the holder, assessed in the currency in which the debt instrument is denominated is:

(i)   a fixed amount;

(ii)   a positive fixed rate or a positive variable rate; or

(iii)   a combination of a positive or a negative fixed rate and a positive variable rate (e.g. LIBOR plus 200 basis points or LIBOR less 50 basis points, but not 500 basis points less LIBOR). *[FRS 102.11.9(a)].*

This criterion will be satisfied by debt instruments that pay a fixed or variable coupon. In addition, as an example of (i), zero coupon loans will meet the criterion as their return represents a fixed amount, being the difference between the redemption value of a debt instrument and the amount lent at initial recognition. *[FRS 102.11.9.E1].* In respect of (iii), combinations of rates will meet the criteria provided they do not contain a negative variable rate. That is, any permutation that combines a positive fixed rate, a negative fixed rate or a positive variable rate is permitted. Examples will include LIBOR plus 1%, or LIBOR less 1%. In contrast, a security that pays, for instance, 500 basis points less LIBOR, contains a negative variable rate. It is known as an 'inverse floater'. Its return goes down as market interest rates rise and so, it is clearly not a basic financial instrument.

A variable rate is defined for this purpose as a rate which varies over time and is linked to a single observable interest rate, or to a single relevant observable index of general price inflation of the currency in which the instrument is denominated – see criterion 2, below, provided such links are not leveraged. *[FRS 102.11.9 footnote 11].* In our view, examples of such a rate would be LIBOR, a bank's SVR, Euribor and the Bank of England base rate. However, if the applied rate is a multiple of a variable rate such as two times SVR, the link to the observable interest rate would be considered leveraged and thus the rate is not a variable rate for the purposes of this requirement. *[FRS 102.11.9.E5].*

Criterion 2

The contract may provide for repayments of the principal or the return to the holder (but not both) to be linked to a single relevant observable index of general price inflation of the currency in which the debt instrument is denominated, provided such links are not leveraged. *[FRS 102.11.9(aA)].*

In respect of this requirement, the key point is that the inflation linked element must be based on an index that measures general price inflation such as the retail price index ('RPI') and the inflation linking can only be on either the return (e.g. interest or discount) or the principal amount, but not both. There is an example contained in the Standard that concludes that if the interest on a Sterling denominated mortgage is linked to the UK Land Registry House Price Index, it would not meet the criterion as that index is a measure of inflation for UK residential properties and not an index of 'general' price inflation. *[FRS 102.11.9.E7].*

Criterion 3

The contract may provide for a determinable variation of the return to the holder during the life of the instrument, provided that:

- the new rate satisfies criterion 1 and the variation is not contingent on future events other than:
    - a change of a contractual variable rate;
    - to protect the holder against credit deterioration of the issuer;
    - changes in levies applied by a central bank or arising from changes in relevant taxation or law; or
- the new rate is a market rate of interest and satisfies criterion 1. *[FRS 102.11.9(aB)].*

Contractual terms that give the lender the unilateral option to change the terms of the contract are not 'determinable' for this purpose. *[FRS 102.11.9(aB)(ii)].*

The crux of Criterion 3 is that variations in the rate after initial recognition are permitted provided that they are not contingent on future events, except in the limited scenarios mentioned above. That is, changing the contractual variable rate for example, from SVR to the Bank of England base rate, would be acceptable, as would increasing the interest rate due to a decline in the borrower's credit worthiness. For example, if a borrower breaches a debt covenant that was stipulated in the loan agreement, the bank would be entitled to increase the interest rate to ensure that its return from the loan mitigates its increased credit risk. Finally, if a rate change is required due to changes in levies or legislation or regulations, this would be permitted. However, if the lender has the unilateral option to change the terms of the contract, the instrument would fail the criterion and would need to be measured at fair value through profit or loss. We do not believe that the unilateral right of a bank to change its SVR was intended to be caught by this requirement.

Criterion 4

There is no contractual provision that could result in the holder losing the principal amount or any interest, whether for the current or prior periods (other than due to a failure to pay when due). The fact that an instrument may be subordinated to other debt instruments is not an example of such a provision. *[FRS 102.11.9(b)].*

Criterion 5

Contractual provisions that permit the borrower to prepay a debt instrument, or permit the holder to put it back to the issuer before maturity, must not be contingent on future events, other than to protect:

- the holder against the credit deterioration of the issuer (for instance, as a consequence of defaults, credit downgrades or loan covenant breaches), or a change in control of the issuer; or
- to protect the holder or the issuer against changes in levies applied by a central bank or arising from changes in relevant taxation or law.

Such contractual prepayment provisions may also include terms that require the issuer to compensate the holder for the early termination. *[FRS 102.11.9(c)].*

Chapter 8

In essence, prepayment of a debt instrument before maturity is permitted provided it is not contingent on future events other than the limited circumstances mentioned above. In such cases, compensation may be payable by either party that chooses to exercise the early termination option, however, no further guidance is provided as to what would be considered a reasonable amount of compensation. In this regard, we believe that entities will have a fair degree of discretion and judgement will need to be exercised. In our view, if the prepayment amount substantially represents the fair value of the instrument at that point, the compensation may be construed as reasonable. That is, the prepayment amount represents the present value of the remaining contractual interest and principal payments at the point of prepayment, discounted by the current market interest rate for the remaining tenure. For example, if a six year bond is prepaid at the end of the third year, the prepayment amount will be approximately the sum of the contractual interest and principal amounts due over the remaining three years, discounted using the current market interest rate for a bond with similar characteristics. Although different from FRS 26/IAS 39, this would be consistent with the approach taken in IFRS 9. *[IFRS 9.B4.1.12(b)].*

Criterion 6

Contractual provisions may permit the extension of the term of the debt instrument, provided that the return to the holder and any other contractual provisions applicable during the extended term satisfy the conditions of criteria 1 to 5. *[FRS 102.11.9(e)].*

Most 'plain vanilla' debt instruments will satisfy the six criteria and can therefore be accounted for at amortised cost. These include trade accounts and notes receivable/payable, and loans from banks or third parties. *[FRS 102.11.10(a)].* However, debt instruments whose return comprises, for example, both an interest rate element and a profit or revenue participation feature, would fail the requirements of paragraph 11.9 and would have to be recorded at fair value through profit or loss. Meanwhile, derivatives and investments in convertible debt would not satisfy the six criteria; hence, they would be within the scope of Section 12.

Commitments to receive or make a loan to another entity would also fall within the scope of Section 11 provided that the subsequent loan would meet the above criteria and the commitment cannot be settled net in cash. *[FRS 102.11.8(c)].*

Several examples of instruments that will meet the requirements of paragraph 11.9 are listed at the end of the paragraph. A loan with a fixed interest rate for an initial period which then reverts to the bank's SVR and a loan whose interest rate is the bank's SVR less 1% for the term but with a floor of 2.0%, are examples that would meet the criteria to be measured at amortised cost.

For those entities currently applying FRS 26, it will become easier in certain instances to measure a basic debt instrument at amortised cost. Under FRS 26, only financial assets that are classified as loans and receivables or held to maturity can be subsequently measured at amortised cost. For the former category, the financial asset must not be quoted in an active market and must contain fixed or determinable payments while for the latter category, in addition to the financial asset having fixed or determinable payments, the entity must have the positive intention and ability to hold it to maturity. *[FRS 26.9].* This means that, for example, most quoted debt securities, which could not be classified as a loan and receivable under FRS 26, will probably qualify for measurement at amortised cost under Section 11. Also, entities need not have to worry about the requirement to hold debt securities to maturity and the consequential 'tainting rules' if they failed to do so, if they were previously using the FRS 26 held to maturity category.

The six criteria are similar to the IFRS 9 'characteristics of the asset test', to determine whether a financial asset would qualify to be measured at amortised cost and, though they differ in detail will often give the same outcome. However, there is no equivalent of the IFRS 9 'business model test'. FRS 102 does not even have the concept of the 'trading book' contained in FRS 26/IAS 39/IFRS 9, so all basic debt instruments will be recorded at amortised cost, for whatever reason they were acquired or the purpose for which they are held, unless the entity makes use of the 'fair value option' (see 4.4.2 below).

4.1.2   Embedded derivatives

It is important to note that, unlike FRS 26/IAS 39, FRS 102 does not include the concept of embedded derivatives. An embedded derivative is a component of a hybrid (combined instrument) that also includes a non-derivative host contract with the effect that some of the cash flows of the combined instrument vary in a way similar to a standalone derivative. *[FRS 26.10]*. As the rules in respect of embedded derivatives have not been included in FRS 102, it is likely that many financial instruments that contain what would be treated under FRS 26 as embedded derivatives will have to be measured in their entirety at fair value through profit or loss as they would not be considered basic financial instruments. This is different from FRS 25 or FRS 26, where it was possible to separate the embedded derivative and measure it at fair value through profit or loss only while the host debt instrument could be measured at amortised cost.

4.1.3   Basic equity instruments

In addition to basic debt instruments, Section 11 includes as 'basic', those equity instruments that are investments in non-convertible preference shares and non-puttable ordinary shares or preference shares. *[FRS 102.11.8(d)]*. This refers to preference shares that are not convertible to other equity instruments and ordinary or preference shares that do not give the holder the right to sell those shares back to the issuer for cash or another financial asset at a future date. However, whereas the assessment of whether a debt instrument is basic also determines its accounting treatment, there is no consequence for whether an equity instrument is basic, as it will still need to be recorded at fair value through profit or loss, except as set out in 4.4.4 below.

4.2   Non-basic financial instruments

All financial instruments that are not 'basic' are dealt with in Section 12. They are mostly required to be measured at fair value through profit or loss.

4.2.1   Financial instruments not permitted to be measured at fair value through profit or loss by UK Company Law

Notwithstanding the definition of a basic financial instrument, financial instruments must be measured at amortised cost if they are not permitted by company law (paragraph 36 of Schedule 1 to The Large and Medium-sized Companies and Groups (Accounts and Reports) Regulations 2008 'the Regulations' or paragraph 36 of The

Large and Medium-sized Limited Liability Partnerships (Accounts) Regulations 2008) to be measured at fair value through profit or loss. *[FRS 102.12.8(c)]*.

The following financial instruments may be included in the financial statements at fair value only if fair value is permitted in accordance with IFRSs as adopted by the EU (on or before 5 September 2006). *[FRS 102.A4.12-12A]*.

- financial liabilities, unless they are held as part of a trading portfolio or are derivatives;

- financial instruments to be held to maturity, other than derivatives;

- loans and receivables originated by the company unless they are held for trading;

- interests in subsidiary undertakings, associated undertakings and joint ventures; and

- contracts for contingent consideration in a business combination;

In addition, the Regulations stipulate that a financial instrument can only be held at fair value where its fair value can be reliably measured.

EU-adopted IFRS requires financial instruments classified as held for trading or that are derivatives to be recognised at fair value through profit and loss. *[IAS 39.9]*. In addition, where an embedded derivative that is required by IAS 39 to be separated from its host contract cannot be measured separately either at acquisition or at the end of the reporting period, IAS 39 requires that the hybrid contract is designated at profit and loss. *[IAS 39.12]*.

EU-adopted IFRS also permits designation at fair value through profit or loss (the fair value option) on initial recognition in any of the following circumstances, set out in IAS 39 and reflected also in FRS 26:

- where doing so eliminates or reduces a measurement or recognition inconsistency, i.e. 'an accounting mismatch';

- a group of financial instruments is managed and their performance evaluated on a fair value basis; or

- for a hybrid financial instrument which contains an embedded derivative, unless the embedded derivative does not significantly modify the cash flows or it is clear, with little or no analysis, that separation of that derivative would be prohibited. *[IAS 39.9, 11A, FRS 102.A4.12A]*.

The effect of paragraph 12.8(c) of FRS 102 (together with paragraph 36 of Schedule 1 to the Regulations) is that a debt financial instrument that fails any of the FRS 102 criteria to be classified as a basic debt instrument would be recorded at fair value though profit or loss only if its fair value can be reliably measured and it is a derivative, is classified as held for trading, or would otherwise be required to be held at fair value in accordance with FRS 26/IAS 39 (as described above), or would be permitted to be recorded at fair value through profit or loss under the fair value option.

The Regulations were written with the application of IFRS in mind and terms such as 'loans and receivables', 'held to maturity' and 'held for trading' are not defined in FRS 102, although it would be logical to apply the same definitions as set out in

FRS 26 and IAS 39. FRS 102 does not repeat the guidance contained in FRS 26 and IAS 39 on when financial instruments are considered to be reliably measurable. In those standards, all financial instruments are deemed to be reliably measurable except for certain unquoted equity securities, or derivatives on such securities. *[FRS 26.46(c)]*. However, given that Sections 11 and 12 specifically preclude the use of fair value on the grounds of reliable measurement only for such equity instruments, it would make sense to assume that the reliable measurement constraint in FRS 102 is equivalent to that in FRS 26 and IAS 39.

'Derivatives' for this purpose will primarily be interpreted as set out in the Glossary to FRS 102, consistent with the definition in FRS 26 and IAS 39, as 'A financial instrument or other contract with all three of the following characteristics:

a)   its value changes in response to the changes in a specified interest rate, financial instrument price, commodity price, foreign exchange rate, index of prices, credit rating or credit index, or other variable (sometimes called the "underlying") provided in the case of a non-financial variable that the variable is not specific to a party to the contract;

b)   it requires no initial investment or an initial investment that is smaller than would be required for other types of contracts that would be expected to have a similar response to changes in market factors; and

c)   it is settled at a future date.' *[FRS 102 Appendix I]*.

The main issue relevant to entities reporting under FRS 102 is that financial instruments may contain features that would cause them to fail to be treated as basic debt instruments under FRS 102 even though they would not necessarily be required or permitted to be held at fair value through profit or loss under IAS 39. Such instruments would have to be recorded at amortised cost, irrespective of the requirements of FRS 102. This situation is likely to arise mainly where the instruments are not derivatives or classified as held for trading, the conditions for use of the fair value option are not met and the host contract includes an embedded derivative which IAS 39 does not permit to be separated.

IAS 39's requirements for the use of the fair value option are the same as those set out in FRS 102 – see 4.4.2.B below.

Under IAS 39, an embedded derivative must be separated from the host contract and accounted for as a derivative if, and only if:

(a)   the economic characteristics and risks of the embedded derivative are not closely related to the economic characteristics and risks of the host contract;

(b)   a separate instrument with the same terms as the embedded derivative would meet the definition of a derivative; and

(c)   the hybrid (combined) instrument is not measured at fair value with changes in fair value recognised in profit or loss (i.e. a derivative that is embedded in a financial asset or financial liability at fair value through profit or loss is not separated). *[IAS 39.11]*.

In most cases, the guidance in IAS 39 on whether a feature is 'closely related' to the host instrument is either similar to the FRS 102 basic debt criteria (in which case, the

Chapter 8

instrument would be classified at amortised cost under Section 11 as a basic financial instrument) or it would, arguably, require more than 'a little' analysis to determine if an embedded derivative would require separation (in which case IAS 39 would allow the fair value option to be used anyway and paragraph 12.8(c) would not require the financial instrument to be carried at amortised cost). Hence it should rarely be relevant.

More relevant for most FRS 102 reporters will be the second reason for not separating an embedded derivative under IAS 39: if the feature (in a separate instrument) would not itself meet the definition of a derivative, particularly on the grounds that the 'underlying' is a 'non-financial variable' specific to one of the parties to the contract. Hence, an embedded derivative is unlikely to be separated where, for example, the repayment of a loan depends on the borrower's performance of a service, or on a gain realised by the borrower on the sale of an asset whose construction has been financed by the financial instrument. The Accounting Council Advice to the FRC of 19 June 2014 ('the Advice') refers to financial instruments entered into by insurers where the amount that is to be repaid depends on the occurrence of an insured event specific to one of the parties to the instrument. Further, as recognised in the Advice, 'there are also divergent views on what constitutes a non-financial variable'. Examples of where there are differing views include measures of performance such as turnover, profits or EBITDA. *[FRS 102.AC.14-20].*

Given the wording in the Regulations and the lack of clarity as to what constitutes a non-financial variable specific to one of the parties to the contract, there will be cases when it may be concluded that non-basic debt instruments are required by FRS 102 to be recorded at amortised cost.

It should, however, be noted that the new Accounting Directive will allow Member States to permit or require the recognition, measurement and disclosure of financial instruments in conformity with EU-adopted IFRS (as opposed to EU-adopted IFRS on or before 5 September 2006). It seems likely that paragraph 36(4) of Schedule 1 to the Regulations will be amended, probably effective for financial years beginning on or after 1 January 2016, to accord with this. This would mean that entities applying Sections 11 and 12 would need to consider whether IAS 39 or IFRS 9 (once adopted by the EU) require or permit the financial instrument to be held at fair value. As IFRS 9 would, in most cases, require those instruments which would fail any of the FRS 102 basic debt instrument criteria to be recorded at fair value through profit or loss, this issue will largely fall away. Going forward, paragraph 12.8(c) of FRS 102 will lose most of its relevance and financial instruments that are otherwise required by the standard to be recorded at fair value through profit or loss will be accounted for on this basis.

4.3   Initial recognition and measurement

An entity shall recognise a financial asset or a financial liability only when the entity becomes a party to the contractual provisions of the instrument. *[FRS 102.11.12 and FRS 102.12.6].* The recognition criterion is consistent with that in FRS 26 *[FRS 26.14]* and we do not expect it to give rise to any differences in practice, even if an entity has not adopted FRS 26.

Financial instruments within the scope of Section 11 will be initially measured at transaction price, including transaction costs, unless they are subsequently measured at fair value though profit or loss. For these instruments and financial instruments within the scope of Section 12, initial measurement will be at fair value, which is normally the transaction price. Transaction costs are capitalised as part of the initial carrying value if they are subsequently measured at amortised cost or cost and expensed to the profit or loss account for those instruments that are subsequently measured at fair value through profit or loss. *[FRS 102.11.13, FRS 102.12.7].*

However, there is one exception to this general rule. That is, Sections 11 and 12 require 'financing transactions' to be measured at the present value of the future payments, discounted at a market rate of interest for a similar debt instrument. Financing transactions are not explicitly defined, however, two examples are given: if payment is deferred beyond normal business terms or if a loan is charged a rate of interest that is not a market rate. *[FRS 102.11.13, FRS 102.12.7].* In each case, by requiring the instrument to be recorded initially at its net present value, the future yield will be approximately the market rate.

Consider the following example, which illustrates the second scenario.

Example 8.1:   *Parent company provides a loan to its subsidiary at an off market interest rate*

A parent lends £100,000 to its subsidiary at 4% per annum for three years. Interest is payable annually in arrears, while the principal repayment is due at maturity. If the subsidiary were to borrow the same amount from a bank, it would be charged 5%. Hence, 5% would represent the market interest rate and this would constitute a financing transaction as the parent has lent to the subsidiary at an off market rate. The calculation of the present value would take into account the sum of the annual interest payments of £4,000 and the principal repayment at the end of three years, discounted by 5% as follows:

Present value = £4,000 / 1.04 + £4,000 / 1.04² + (£4,000 + £100,000) / 1.04³ = £97,277

In this example, the parent would record a loan receivable from its subsidiary of £97,277 in its separate financial statements, and the difference compared to the amount lent of £100,000 would probably be deemed a capital contribution, thus, increasing the parent's investment in the subsidiary.

As noted above, even though financial instruments within the scope of Section 12 are required to be initially measured at fair value, Section 12 acknowledges that fair value is 'normally' the transaction price. *[FRS 102.12.7].* A difference will only arise in rare circumstances where fair value does not equate to transaction price. One such example is the wholesale markets for dealers in financial instruments, where such dealers are able to recognise a profit, being the margin that has been 'locked in' as a result of the differential between the price charged to a customer and the prices available to the dealer in wholesale markets.

In addition, in some markets, dealers charge minimal or no explicit transaction costs but instcad quote differential prices for purchases and sales. Such prices are often referred to as 'bid' and 'asking' (or 'offer') prices. The term bid-ask spread is normally interpreted as the difference between the quoted bid and offer prices. The following example illustrates this point:

Chapter 8

Example 8.2:   Application of a bid-ask spread in the initial measurement of a financial instrument

A company acquires a quoted bond in an active market, where no explicit transaction costs are charged but separate bid and offer prices are quoted. On acquisition, the bond has an asking price of £102,000, which is the amount the purchaser is required to pay, and a bid price of £97,000, which is what the seller would receive were it to sell the bond. The fair value of a quoted asset is deemed to be its bid price (See 4.4.5 below for further fair value discussion) and this suggests that the entity should initially measure the bond at £97,000. This would result in an immediate loss of £5,000, the difference between the initial fair value and the cash paid. Section 12 does not address the accounting for the £5,000 loss, however, in our view; this should be treated as a transaction cost rather than a dealing loss, which would be consistent with the accounting under FRS 26 and IFRS.

4.4   Subsequent measurement

4.4.1   Amortised cost

For debt instruments within the scope of Section 11, subsequent measurement will be at amortised cost using the effective interest rate method *[FRS 102.11.14 (a)]* unless the fair value option is used (see 4.4.2 below). FRS 26 or IAS 39 adopters will be familiar with this measurement model and the transition to FRS 102 will have no impact on them as the effective interest rate requirements are identical to those in FRS 26. Those entities that did not apply FRS 26 under previous UK GAAP may be affected, depending on the nature of the instruments held.

When calculating the effective interest rate, an entity must estimate cash flows considering all contractual terms of the financial instrument (e.g. prepayment, call and similar options) and known credit losses that have been incurred. These cash flows must also include any related fees, finance charges paid or received, transaction costs and other premiums or discounts. It must not include possible future credit losses not yet incurred. *[FRS 102.11.17, FRS 102.11.18]*.

For variable rate financial assets and liabilities, periodic re-estimation of cash flows to reflect changes in market rates of interest alters the effective interest rate. If such instruments are recognised initially at an amount equal to the principal receivable or payable at maturity, re-estimating the future interest payments normally has no significant effect on the carrying amount of the asset or liability. *[FRS 102.11.19]*.

In contrast, in cases where estimates of payments or receipts are revised, the carrying amount of the financial asset or financial liability (or group of financial instruments) is adjusted to reflect actual and revised estimated cash flows. The entity must recalculate the carrying amount by computing the present value of the revised estimated future cash flows at the financial instrument's original effective interest rate (assuming it is a fixed rate instrument) or at the most recent effective interest rate if it is a variable rate instrument. The adjustment is recognised as income or expense in profit or loss at the date of the revision. *[FRS 102.11.20]*.

These requirements are identical to those in paragraphs AG7 and 8 of FRS 26 and IAS 39, hence, further information can be found in EY International GAAP 2015. The point to note is that changing cash flow assumptions such as, for instance, estimates of prepayments, has potentially a significant impact on profit or loss, as this involves booking 'catch up' adjustments to the financial instrument and to profit or loss.

Even though FRS 4 deals with the accounting for those instruments classified as liabilities, many entities that have not adopted FRS 26 will have used the principles in FRS 4 to account for their lending or investing activities as well. FRS 4 contains similar concepts to FRS 26 in respect of the effective interest rate method and requires a similar treatment of issue costs and finance costs, which would presumably be captured as part of the effective interest rate calculation provided they are integral to the yield on the instrument. Under FRS 4, finance costs are defined as the difference between the net proceeds of an instrument and the total amount of the payments (or other transfers of economic benefits) that the issuer may be required to make in respect of the instrument while issue costs are those that are incurred directly in connection with the issue of a capital instrument, that is, those costs that would not have been incurred had the specific instrument in question not been issued. *[FRS 4.8, FRS 4.10]*. Finance costs should be allocated to periods over the term of the debt at a constant rate on the carrying amount while issue costs are deducted from the proceeds received from the issue of an instrument. *[FRS 4.11, FRS 4.28, FRS 4.75]*. Consequently, it is unlikely that the implementation of the effective interest rate method will have a material impact where FRS 4 had been applied appropriately to those financial assets and liabilities within the scope of Section 11.

A simple example for determining the amortised cost for a five year bond is shown below. Further information and more complicated examples can be found in EY International GAAP 2015.

Example 8.3:   Determining the effective interest rate and its application to the measurement of amortised cost

A bond is acquired for £95,000 on 1 January 2014 and transaction costs amount to £1,000. The interest rate on the bond is 4%, paid annually in arrears, and the redemption value at maturity, which is in five years, is £100,000. The expected cash flows are the annual interest payments of £4,000 (i.e. 4% multiplied by the redemption value of £100,000) and a final bullet repayment of £100,000. The initial carrying amount is the acquisition price of £95,000 and £1,000 of transaction costs, equating to £96,000. The effective interest rate of 4.922% is the rate that discounts the expected cash flows to the initial carrying amount. The formula is as follows:

$$£4,000 \ / \ (1 + 4.922\%) + £4,000 \ / \ (1 + 4.922\%)^2 + £4,000 \ / \ (1 + 4.922\%)^3 + £4,000 \ / \ (1 + 4.922\%)^4 + (£100,000 + £4,000) \ / \ (1 + 4.922\%)^5 = £96,000$$

Year	Carrying amount at the beginning of the period (£)	Interest income @ 4.922% (£)	Cash inflow (£)	Carrying amount at the end of the period (£)
2014	96,000	4,725	(4,000)	96,725
2015	96,725	4,761	(4,000)	97,486
2016	97,486	4,798	(4,000)	98,284
2017	98,284	4,838	(4,000)	99,122
2018	99,122	4,878	(104,000)	–

4.4.2   Exceptions to amortised cost measurement

There are two exceptions to the general rule of amortised cost measurement for basic debt instruments.

Chapter 8

4.4.2.A   *Undiscounted cash flows*

Basic debt instruments that are payable or receivable within one year must be measured at their undiscounted amount expected to be paid or received, unless the arrangement is a financing transaction as explained at 4.3. *[FRS 102.11.14(a)].* We believe there to be an inadvertent wording error here, as it would make no sense for a debt instrument that pays interest, as illustrated by the following example.

Example 8.4:   Measurement of short-term debt instruments

Assume that an entity with a December year end borrows £100 for one year on 31 December 2014 at 3% per annum. If the entity were to measure the loan at the undiscounted amount expected to be paid, it would record a loan of £103 on 31 December 2014 even though the full amount of £103, consisting of the principal loan repayment of £100 and interest of £3 would only be due on 31 December 2015. Such measurement would contradict accrual accounting and we believe that this was not the FRC's intention. Hence, in our view, the loan should be recorded at £100 on 31 December 2014 and would only be recorded at £103 on 30 December 2015, assuming that the loan is repaid in full on 31 December 2015.

Even though this particular requirement refers to debt instruments, which are often interest bearing, in our opinion, the underlying objective here is to address the measurement basis for trade receivables, which are by their nature, short-term and interest free.

4.4.2.B   *The fair value option*

The second main exception to the use of amortised cost is that debt financial instruments and commitments to receive or make a loan that are within the scope of Section 11 may, upon initial recognition, be designated as at fair value through profit or loss, provided that doing so results in more relevant information. This will be because either:

- use of fair value eliminates or significantly reduces a measurement or recognition inconsistency (sometimes referred to as 'an accounting mismatch') that would otherwise arise; or

- a group of debt instruments or debt instruments and other financial assets is managed and its performance is evaluated on a fair value basis, in accordance with a documented risk management or investment strategy, and information is provided on that basis to the entity's key management personnel (as defined in Section 33 – *Related Party Disclosures*), for example, members of the entity's board of directors and its chief executive officer. *[FRS 102.11.14 (b)].*

This is similar to the fair value option under FRS 26 (or IAS 39), where designation is only possible at initial recognition of a financial instrument and not thereafter. However, unlike FRS 26/IAS 39, FRS 102 does not contain the further provision that the designation at initial recognition is irrevocable. *[FRS 26.50(b)].* Having said that, we do not believe that it was the FRC's intention for the designation to be revocable, and so capable of being switched on and off. Hedge accounting is more flexible in that sense but it is subject to the hedge accounting discontinuation rules, as set out in 7.10 below.

The fair value option has a greater relevance under FRS 102 than under FRS 26, IAS 39 or IFRS 9, as there is no concept in the measurement rules of 'held for trading'. Basic debt instruments that are held for trading purposes are not automatically measured at fair value through profit or loss. To do so requires the use of the fair value option, on the grounds that such instruments are managed and their performance is evaluated on a fair value basis. This means that entities have a choice of whether to apply amortised cost or fair value for such instruments.

One of the reasons for including the fair value option in FRS 102 was to mitigate some of the anomalies that would result from a mixed measurement model. It eliminates problems arising where financial assets are measured at fair value and related financial liabilities are measured at amortised cost, or *vice versa*, or even in some cases where both are measured at amortised cost. Its use can eliminate the burden of designating hedges, tracking and analysing hedge effectiveness, which is discussed at 7 below.

An example is the issuance of debt to fund the acquisition of trading assets such as bonds or equities. As the trading assets are bought and sold frequently to maximise/minimise their profits/losses, it may make sense to measure the assets, together with their underlying funding at fair value through profit or loss. This would avoid an accounting mismatch that would otherwise arise by measuring the assets at fair value through profit or loss and the underlying liabilities at amortised cost.

In respect of the second situation in which the fair value option may be applied, the requirement is that the group of instruments must be managed and its performance evaluated on a fair value basis and information is provided on that basis to key management personnel. As a result, the accounting would be consistent with the underlying business objective for the portfolio as that is how its performance is assessed. We would not expect an entity to prepare any incremental documentation to satisfy this requirement provided that existing documentation, as authorised by key management personnel, clearly shows that the use of the fair value option is consistent with the entity's risk management or investment strategy. The key requirement is that performance is actually managed and evaluated on a fair value basis. It is unlikely that outside the financial services or commodity trading sectors, there will be many entities that use the fair value option in this situation. Further information on the fair value option can be found in EY International GAAP 2015.

The wording of the second situation, 'a group of debt instruments or debt instruments and other financial assets' is a little odd, as it is unlikely that debt instruments would be managed together with other financial assets, such as equities. And it is unclear why other financial liabilities cannot form part of the portfolio. It is likely that most entities will not be troubled by this phrasing.

4.4.3   *Loan commitments*

Commitments to receive a loan and to make a loan that are within the scope of section 11 must be measured at cost (which may sometimes be nil) less impairment. *[FRS 102.11.14(c)].* Loan commitments are not defined in FRS 102 but they are essentially firm commitments to provide credit under pre-specified terms and conditions, as defined in FRS 26/IAS 39. *[FRS 26.BC15].* They can include arrangements such as offers to individuals in respect of mortgages as well as committed borrowing facilities granted to a company. For the holder of the commitment, the reference to cost is presumably in respect of any fees or premiums that have been paid. If an amount is paid upfront at the commencement of the loan commitment, this amount will be capitalised and subsequently amortised to the profit or loss account over the expected life of the commitment. If it is payable over the term of the commitment, it will be expensed as appropriate when incurred.

For the entity which has committed to advance a loan, the question arises as to what is the 'cost' to be measured, if any. Presumably, if the commitment is within the scope of Section 11, the cost would also be the amount of any fees or premium received, and so normally would be a liability.

The impairment requirements for loan commitments are discussed at 5 below.

4.4.4   Equity securities

Whether 'non-convertible preference shares and non-puttable ordinary shares or preference shares' dealt with in Section 11, or other forms of equity security instruments, addressed in Section 12, the rule is the same: if the shares are publicly traded or their fair value can be measured reliably, they must be measured at fair value through profit or loss (see 4.4.5 below); if they cannot be measured reliably, they must be measured at cost less impairment. This applies both to equity securities and to derivatives linked to such securities that, if exercised, will result in the delivery of such securities [FRS 102.11.14 (d), FRS 102.12.8-8(a)]

Fair value is considered reliably measurable when the range of reasonable fair value estimates is not significant or the probabilities of the various estimates within the range can be reasonably assessed and used in estimating fair value. [FRS 102.11.30]. No further guidance is provided to assess significance or probabilities in this context, hence, entities will need to exercise judgement. However, we believe that the bar for claiming that a fair value measurement is not reliably measurable is relatively high and it is limited to investments such as equity holdings in private companies, for which the investee has no comparable peers.

If subsequent to initial recognition, a reliable measure of fair value ceases to be available, an equity instrument's carrying amount at the last date it was reliably measurable becomes its new cost. Going forward, the instrument should be measured at its new cost less impairment until a reliable measure of fair value becomes available again. [FRS 102.11.32, FRS 102.12.9].

For entities that hold instruments that are required to be recorded at fair value though profit or loss, this could represent a potentially significant change from previous UK GAAP, irrespective of whether they were applying FRS 26. Under previous UK GAAP (excluding FRS 26) equities could be measured at cost less any impairment recognised in the event of a permanent diminution in value. Entities previously applying FRS 26 may have classified equities as available for sale ('AFS'), with fair value changes recorded in the Statement of Total Recognised Gains and Losses (STRGL).

The requirement to use cost less impairment for those equity investments that cannot be reliably measured is similar to that in FRS 26 (and IAS 39). The impairment requirements are discussed at 5.3 below.

4.4.5   Fair values

The guidance on how to calculate fair values is contained in Section 11 rather than Section 12. Figure 8.1 below shows the fair value hierarchy to be used.

Figure 8.1: Fair value hierarchy

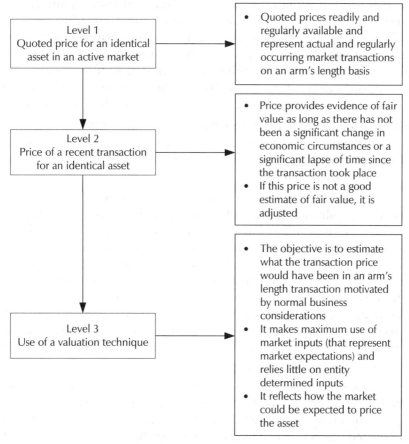

Level 1 Quoted price for an identical asset in an active market	• Quoted prices readily and regularly available and represent actual and regularly occurring market transactions on an arm's length basis
Level 2 Price of a recent transaction for an identical asset	• Price provides evidence of fair value as long as there has not been a significant change in economic circumstances or a significant lapse of time since the transaction took place • If this price is not a good estimate of fair value, it is adjusted
Level 3 Use of a valuation technique	• The objective is to estimate what the transaction price would have been in an arm's length transaction motivated by normal business considerations • It makes maximum use of market inputs (that represent market expectations) and relies little on entity determined inputs • It reflects how the market could be expected to price the asset

Section 11 is explicit that the best evidence of fair value is what we have referred to as a Level 1 fair value and it is only when quoted prices are unavailable, does an entity use a Level 2 fair value and failing that, a valuation technique. *[FRS 102.11.27].*

However, the above guidance is somewhat theoretical and no examples are provided to illustrate its application. 'Active market' is defined in the Glossary to FRS 102 as 'a market in which all the following conditions exist:

(a)   the items traded in the market are homogeneous;

(b)   willing buyers and sellers can normally be found at any time; and

(c)   prices are available to the public.'

Based on the above definition, most equities and bonds that are listed on an exchange for which there is a liquid secondary market in terms of regular trading will be considered to be traded in an active market. In addition, instruments that are frequently traded in over-the-counter markets (i.e. instruments that are not listed on an exchange) such as interest rate swaps and options, foreign exchange derivatives and credit default swaps, will also be captured.

The Section 11 requirement, that the best evidence of fair value is a quoted price for an identical asset in an active market, is similar to that in FRS 26 and IFRS 13.

Chapter 8

However, FRS 102 does not reproduce the additional guidance contained in those standards, that the fair value of a portfolio of financial instruments is the product of the number of units of the instrument and its quoted market price, known as "p times q". *[FRS26.AG72]*. This guidance means that an entity which has a very large holding of an actively traded financial instrument is unable to adjust the quoted price to reflect any discount or premium that might arise if the holding were to be unloaded onto the market. Given that this guidance is not contained in FRS 102, some might read it not to require the use of p times q in these circumstances.

The adjustment required for what we have termed Level 2 fair values, for when the last transaction is not a good estimate of fair value, refers to when they reflect an amount that an entity was forced to pay or receive in a forced transaction, involuntary liquidation or distressed sale. *[FRS 102.11.27(b)]*.

The fair value of a financial liability that is due on demand is deemed to be not less than the amount payable on demand, discounted from the first date that the amount could be required to be paid. *[FRS 102.12.11]*. The logic is that a rational lender would demand repayment if the fair value were ever less than the net present value of the amount repayable. Even though, in actual practice, many people do not withdraw their demand deposits in such circumstances, this should not be reflected in the fair value of the liability. No guidance is provided in this context as to the appropriate discount rate, although the guidance on financing transactions set out at 4.3 above would be appropriate. This requirement is identical to that in FRS 26 and IFRS 13 – *Fair Value Measurement*, hence, further information can be found in EY International GAAP 2015. *[FRS 26.49, IFRS 13.47]*.

Many entities adopting FRS 102 will not enter into instruments that are required to be recorded at fair value through profit or loss and do not have quoted prices in active markets. If they do invest in, or issue complex instruments that must be fair valued but do not have quoted prices in active markets, they may have to draw upon the larger body of guidance within IFRS 13 in making judgements regarding how to measure fair value, especially regarding the use of valuation techniques. Further information regarding IFRS 13 can be found in EY International GAAP 2015.

Having said that, IFRS 13 is clear that entities must include in the fair value of financial liabilities such as derivatives any changes in fair value attributable to their own credit risk. *[IFRS 13.42]*. This has the unintuitive consequence that such entities will record profits on revaluation when their credit risk increases. FRS 102 has no specific equivalent requirement, although entities are required to disclose the effect of own credit risk on liabilities recorded at fair value through profit or loss (see 8.1 below) for those financial liabilities that do not form part of trading book and are not derivatives. This implies that fair value for such liabilities should include the effects of changes in own credit risk.

Entities that have previously adopted FRS 29 will note that the fair value hierarchy in FRS 102 is different from that in FRS 29/IFRS 7 except for the top level (i.e. Level 1 in the FRS 29/IFRS 13 hierarchy). That is, some valuations that would fall into Level 2 under FRS 29/IFRS 13 (i.e. those based on observable data) will fall into Level 3 under FRS 102. Having said that, the impact of this difference in practice is not very significant because, unlike under FRS 29/IFRS 7, the only incremental disclosures arising from Level 3 fair valuations are those required by the Regulations (see 8.3 below).

5   IMPAIRMENT OF FINANCIAL ASSETS MEASURED AT COST OR AMORTISED COST

5.1   Introduction

The concept of impairment is relevant to financial assets that are measured at cost or amortised cost. FRS 102 uses the same principles and criteria as the incurred loss model under FRS 26 and IAS 39, but with one major difference. That is, unlike FRS 26, under FRS 102, assets that have been individually assessed for impairment and found not to be impaired do not subsequently need to be included in a collective assessment of impairment. *[FRS 26.64].* These requirements are set out at 5.2 below.

For those entities that have not previously adopted FRS 26, impairment is an area that could give rise to significant changes in accounting. Under previous UK GAAP, there was no specific standard that dealt with impairment of financial assets, although some entities may have applied FRS 26 by analogy in determining their impairment policies even though they were not required to adopt FRS 26.

Other entities may have drawn their guidance from the requirements of the Companies Act or the British Bankers' Association's Statement of Recommended Practice on Advances ('the BBA SORP'). Under the Companies Act, fixed asset investments (e.g. long-term loans) are generally accounted for on a historical cost basis (i.e. transaction price plus transaction costs incidental to acquisition) less a provision for permanent diminution in value, which if required is recognised in profit or loss. The Companies Act did not provide any further guidance as to what constituted a permanent diminution in value. Consequently, entities enjoyed a degree of latitude and discretion when establishing their internal impairment policies. For these entities, the adoption of the FRS 102 impairment requirements may represent a challenge and could give rise to differences in the amount of the impairment provision.

The BBA SORP was developed in accordance with the code of practice of the ASB, using 'incurred loss' principles which are broadly consistent with FRS 26/IAS 39 and thus (except as already mentioned) with FRS 102. Whilst not mandatory, banks and other lending institutions were encouraged to follow the BBA SORP and to state in their financial statements that they had done so.

The FRC had originally suggested that the impairment requirements of FRS 102 would be updated to reflect the IFRS 9 'expected loss' impairment model, once it was finalised. However, although it was completed in July 2014, the FRC is now intending only to revise FRS 102 after 1 January 2015 and it is likely that the effective date for any amendments will be no earlier than 1 January 2018. This means that entities may have to amend their impairment accounting twice, once on the move to FRS 102, and again when it is amended to include an expected loss model. Any entities who are concerned about this (and who would be capable of applying an expected loss model now) could in theory move immediately to the IFRS 9 model, but only by adopting IFRS 9 in its entirety.

The effect of moving from the current incurred loss model to the IFRS 9 expected loss approach will result in entities recognising impairment losses earlier. Entities will be required to recognise either 12-month or lifetime expected credit losses, depending on whether there has been a significant increase in credit risk since

Chapter 8

initial recognition. The measurement of expected credit losses will reflect a probability-weighted outcome, the time value of money and reasonable and supportable information. Further information regarding impairment under IFRS 9 can be found in EY International GAAP 2015.

5.2   Recognition of impairment

Under FRS 102, assessment should be made at the end of each reporting period as to whether there is any objective evidence of impairment. *[FRS 102.11.21]*. For the purpose of the impairment assessment, debt instruments that are individually significant must be assessed individually while other debt instruments should be assessed either individually, or grouped on the basis of similar credit risk characteristics. *[FRS 102.11.24]*. Grouping financial assets based on similar credit risk characteristics will be a matter of judgement for individual reporters. For example, a bank might split its loans to customers into several categories such as unsecured retail loans, secured retail loans, corporate loans and mortgages. Further stratification of these groupings may be appropriate; for example, mortgages might be split based on their loan-to-value ratios, or the location of the properties, while smaller corporate loans might be split based on the industry in which the borrower operates. A non-financial institution, might stratify their trade receivables based on their country of operation, lines of business or even brand names.

All equity instruments recorded at cost, regardless of their size, must be assessed individually for impairment. *[FRS 102.11.24(a)]*.

Objective evidence that a financial asset or group of assets is impaired includes observable data about loss events. Examples of loss events include:

(i)   significant financial difficulty of the issuer or obligor;

(ii)   a breach of contract such as a default or delinquency in interest or principal payments;

(iii)   the granting by the creditor of a concession for economic or legal reasons relating to the debtor's financial difficulty, that it would not otherwise consider;

(iv)   it is probable that the debtor will enter bankruptcy or other financial reorganisation;

(v)   significant changes which will adversely affect the borrower in the technological, market, economic or legal environment in which it operates; or

(vi)   for a group of financial assets, observable data indicating that there has been a measurable decrease in the estimated future cash flows from the group since the initial recognition of those assets, even though the decrease cannot yet be identified with the individual financial assets in the group, such as adverse national or local economic conditions or adverse changes in industry conditions. *[FRS 102.11.22-23]*.

If such evidence exists, an impairment loss should be recognised in profit or loss immediately. *[FRS 102.11.21]*.

5.3 Measurement and reversal of impairment

The impairment loss for amortised cost assets is measured as the difference between the asset's carrying amount and the present value of estimated cash flows, discounted at the asset's original effective interest rate. If it is a variable rate asset, the discount rate for measuring the impairment loss is the current effective interest rate. *[FRS 102.11.25(a)]*.

For equities measured at cost, the impairment loss will be the difference between its carrying amount and a best estimate of the amount that the entity would receive if it were sold at the reporting date. The best estimate will inevitably be an approximation and may be zero. *[FRS 102.11.25(b)]*.

The following example builds on Example 8.3, to illustrate the measurement of impairment.

Example 8.5:   *Calculating the impairment loss for amortised cost debt instruments*

For a bond measured at amortised cost, at the end of 2015, due to continuing deterioration in the borrower's financial performance, the lender assesses that 25% of all future cash flows (in 2016 to 2018) will not be recoverable. The future cash flows that were due were the 4% coupon per annum (i.e. £100,000 × 4%) and the principal repayment of £100,000 at the end of 2018, which works out to £4,000 in 2016 and 2017 respectively and £104,000 in 2018. If the 25% default rate were to be applied to these cash flows, the revised cash inflows would be £3,000 in 2016 and 2017 and £78,000 in 2018. As mentioned above, the impairment loss will be the difference between the present value of the revised future cash flows less the carrying amount before the impairment, which was £97,486. The present value of the revised future cash flows is £73,114 after discounting by the original effective interest rate of 4.922%. This is worked out as:

£3,000 / (1 + 4.922%) + £3,000 / (1 + 4.922%)^2 + £78,000 / (1 + 4.922%)^3 = £73,114. Hence, the impairment loss is £24,371, being the difference between £97,486 and £73,114.

Year	Carrying amount at the beginning of the period (£)	Interest income @ 4.922% (£)	Cash inflow (£)	Impairment loss (£)	Carrying amount at the end of the period (£)
2014	96,000	4,725	(4,000)	–	96,725
2015 (pre-impairment)	96,725	4,761	(4,000)	–	97,486
2015 (post-impairment)	97,486	–	–	(24,371)	73,114
2016	73,114	3,599	(3,000)	–	73,713
2017	73,713	3,628	(3,000)	–	74,341
2018	74,341	3,659	(78,000)	–	–

If, in a subsequent period, the amount of the impairment loss decreases and the decrease can be objectively related to an event occurring after the impairment was recognised (such as an improvement in the debtor's credit rating), the previously recognised impairment loss should be reversed and recognised in profit or loss, either directly or by adjusting an allowance account. However, the reversal should not result in a carrying amount of the asset that exceeds what its amortised cost would have been had the impairment not been recognised. *[FRS 102.11.26]*.

For further information about the FRS 26/IAS 39 impairment requirements, please refer to EY International GAAP 2015.

Chapter 8

6   DERECOGNITION

6.1   Introduction

Similar to impairment, derecognition is an area where the impact of transitioning to FRS 102 will very much depend on whether an entity currently applies FRS 26 or not. Those entities that are not using FRS 26 will have drawn their guidance from FRS 5. The FRS 102 derecognition requirements are located in Section 11, paragraphs 33 to 38, however, they are also applicable to financial assets and financial liabilities within the scope of Section 12. *[FRS 102.12.14].*

6.2   Derecognition of financial assets

The FRS 102 derecognition principles for financial assets are similar to those in FRS 26 but they have been simplified and do not contain the extensive body of guidance that can be found in FRS 26.

Under FRS 102, a financial asset is derecognised only when:

(a)   the contractual rights to the cash flows from the financial asset expire or are settled, or

(b)   the entity transfers to another party substantially all of the risks and rewards of ownership of the financial asset, or

(c)   the entity, despite having retained some significant risks and rewards of ownership, has transferred control of the asset to another party and the other party has the practical ability to sell the asset in its entirety to an unrelated third party and is able to exercise that ability unilaterally and without needing to impose additional restrictions on the transfer. In such situations, the asset shall be derecognised and any rights and obligations retained or created shall be recognised separately. *[FRS 102.11.33].*

The carrying amount of the transferred asset must be allocated between the rights or obligations retained and those transferred on the basis of their relative fair values at the transfer date. Newly created rights and obligations must be measured at their fair values at that date. Any difference between the consideration received and the amounts recognised and derecognised is recognised in profit or loss. *[FRS 102.11.33].*

These accounting requirements are illustrated by Example 8.6 at 6.3 below.

Section 11 provides no guidance on what is meant by a 'transfer'. FRS 26 (and IAS 39) address this in some detail and many more complex arrangements do not qualify for derecognition under those standards because they do not meet the transfer criteria. An example would be a securitization of short-term receivables, in which amounts collected are invested in further receivables. Further guidance is provided on this topic in EY International GAAP 2015. While it would be possible to draw on the guidance in those standards to interpret the requirements of FRS 102, we believe that the FRC deliberately intended the FRS 102 derecognition test to be simpler. Consequently, a wider range of transactions will perhaps qualify for derecognition, but are unlikely to be entered into by most adopters of FRS 102.

The standard, as it is written, is silent on those situations where the entity has transferred a financial asset in such a manner that it *retains* substantially all the risks and rewards. A reader might assume from reading paragraph 11.33 (c), that, as long as the transferor loses control, it should derecognise the asset. We do not believe that this is how the standard was intended to be read, and that it should be viewed as broadly equivalent to the model set out in FRS 26 (and hence IAS 39). That is, there are three situations:

- where the transferor has transferred substantially all the risks and rewards, as set out in (b) above, in which case it should derecognise the asset;

- where the transferor has neither transferred nor retained substantially all the risks and rewards, in which case the accounting treatment depends on whether control has been transferred, as set out in (c) above; or

- where the transferor has retained substantially all the risks and rewards, in which case the asset should not be derecognised.

This third situation will include transactions such as repurchase obligations (i.e. repos), stock lending agreements and factoring arrangements when the transferee has recourse to the transferor. This reading is consistent with the example in Section 11 of a transfer that does not qualify for derecognition, which deals with an arrangement in which an entity sells receivables to a bank, but continues to handle collections on the bank's behalf and has agreed to buy back from the bank any receivables for which the debtor is in arrears as to principal and interest for more than 120 days. The example states that as the entity has retained the risk of slow payment or non-payment, it should not derecognise the assets but must treat the proceeds from the bank as a loan secured by the receivables. Although this conclusion could also be arrived at using (c) above, as control of the assets has not been transferred, the example points to the retention of risk as the reason why derecognition is inappropriate.

6.3 Analysis of the derecognition requirements for financial assets

As noted at 6.2 above, the derecognition assessment needs to be undertaken by considering whether the entity is still exposed to the risk and rewards associated with the asset following the transfer as well as whether it still has control over the asset. In essence, the substance of the transaction needs to be evaluated in assessing derecognition and the mere transfer of legal ownership is not sufficient.

In most cases, we would expect the application of these requirements by FRS 102 adopters to be straightforward. That is, a financial asset such as a loan is settled on its scheduled maturity date or it is redeemed before maturity by the borrower in accordance with the stipulated terms of the loan. Another simple example would be the unconditional sale of a financial asset for a fixed price. It is only when an entity embarks on more complex transactions such as factoring or securitisations, does the application of the requirements become more challenging.

First, the standard does not provide any guidance as to what constitutes the transfer to another party of substantially all the risks and rewards of ownership. *[FRS 102.11.33(b)]*. The analysis needs to take into account all facts and circumstances and the most common risks to be evaluated will usually include credit risk, foreign exchange risk, late payment risk and price risk. In the case of

Chapter 8

trade receivables, which are usually short-term in nature, the main risks are normally late payment risk (e.g. the debtor does not settle within the stipulated credit period such as 30 days or 90 days but does eventually make payment in full for the amount due) or credit risk (i.e. the debtor is unable to make full payment for the amount owing and it results in a bad debt for the creditor). In most cases, we would expect the issue of whether substantially all risks and rewards have been transferred to be uncontroversial.

The analysis is more challenging when the asset is sold but either party or both have an option to buy/sell back the asset at some point in the future. In order to analyse the implications of the option on the risk and rewards assessment, the exercise price of the option relative to the current fair value of the asset would need to be considered, together with the term of the option. In the case of a call option that is deeply in the money (i.e. the exercise price of the option is so favourable when compared to the current market price of the asset and is expected to remain so), it is highly likely that the option will be exercised by the transferor before expiry. Consequently, derecognition would not be appropriate. However, if the circumstances were reversed, that is, the option is deeply out of the money and is highly unlikely to go into the money before maturity, derecognition would be appropriate as the transferor has transferred substantially all risks and rewards. In these situations, it is almost impossible to set bright lines as to when an option is considered deeply in or out of the money, hence, judgement is required by evaluating all relevant facts and circumstances on a case by case basis.

The same assessment will need to be made in respect of the sale of trade receivables, by analysing whether the seller has retained any risks and rewards following the sale. If the seller has not retained substantially any of the risks and rewards, derecognition would be appropriate. However, if the seller agrees to reimburse the buyer for all likely bad debts and late payments that will occur, the seller has retained substantially all risks and rewards, thus, derecognition would not be appropriate. The following example is included in the standard:

Example 8.6:   The sale of trade receivables with no retention of risk

A company sells a group of its accounts receivable to a bank at less than their face amount. The company continues to handle collections from the debtors on behalf of the bank, including sending monthly statements, and the bank pays the entity a market rate fee for servicing the receivables. The company is obliged to remit promptly to the bank any and all amounts collected, but it has no obligation to the bank for slow payment or non-payment by the debtors. In this case, the company has transferred to the bank substantially all of the risks and rewards of ownership of the receivables. Accordingly, the company removes the receivables from its statement of financial position (i.e. derecognises them), and it shows no liability in respect of the proceeds received from the bank. The company recognises a loss calculated as the difference between the carrying amount of the receivables at the time of sale and the proceeds received from the bank. The company recognises a liability to the extent that it has collected funds from the debtors but has not yet remitted them to the bank. *[FRS 102.11.35].*

Determination of whether the seller has transferred or retained substantially all the risks and rewards will often be more difficult in situations where the seller has retained, for example, the first £10m of future credit losses. In these circumstances, the answer will depend on an assessment of the quality of the receivables that were sold. If it is likely that the first £10m of future losses represent a substantial portion of the losses that are expected to occur, derecognition would not be appropriate as the seller has retained substantially all the risks and rewards. On the other hand, if the first £10m represents an immaterial portion of the expected future losses, derecognition may be appropriate.

In between the two extremes of transferring or retaining substantially all the risks and rewards, the transferor may have retained some risks and rewards. The derecognition assessment is then dependent on whether the transferor has retained control of the asset. This will depend on whether the transferee has the practical ability to sell the asset in its entirety to an unrelated third party and whether the transferee is able to exercise that ability unilaterally and without needing to impose additional restrictions on the transfer. *[FRS 102.11.33(c)]*.

This is where the second challenge arises, as no further guidance is given on what is meant by 'practical ability'. FRS 26.AG 42 contains the following guidance:

'An entity has not retained control of a transferred asset if the transferee has the practical ability to sell the transferred asset. An entity has retained control of a transferred asset if the transferee does not have the practical ability to sell the transferred asset. A transferee has the practical ability to sell the transferred asset if it is traded in an active market because the transferee could repurchase the transferred asset in the market if it needs to return the asset to the entity. For example, a transferee may have the practical ability to sell a transferred asset if the transferred asset is subject to an option that allows the entity to repurchase it, but the transferee can readily obtain the transferred asset in the market if the option is exercised. A transferee does not have the practical ability to sell the transferred asset if the entity retains such an option and the transferee cannot readily obtain the transferred asset in the market if the entity exercises its option.

In our view, most FRS 102 adopters will use this guidance when assessing the practical ability test. Consider the following example, which helps illustrate these requirements:

Example 8.7:   The sale of quoted bonds subject to a call option to buy them back

Company Y holds 200,000 corporate bonds issued by a listed company, Company X. Similar to company X's equity shares, the corporate bonds are listed on an exchange and are subject to regular trading in the market. The market price of the bonds at 31 December 2014 is £4.00, thus, the investment's fair value is £800,000. The bonds meet the criteria to be classified as basic financial instruments and are thus measured at amortised cost. However, there is no material difference between the amortised cost and the fair value of the bonds. On the same day, Company Y sells the bonds to a hedge fund for £750,000 but simultaneously obtains a call option to buy back the bonds on 31 December 2015 for £850,000. The sale agreement does not prevent the hedge fund from selling, exchanging or pledging the bonds to another party.

In these circumstances, due to the existence of the option, it is assessed that Company Y has retained some significant risk and rewards of ownership of the bonds because it will be able to benefit from fair value movements above the call option exercise price of £850,000 by exercising the option, however, is it not exposed to movements below the call option exercise price.

Chapter 8

In addition, because the bonds are listed and traded on an active market, (see 3.1 above for the definition of an active market), it is considered that the hedge fund has the practical ability to sell the bonds. Even if the hedge fund sells the bonds, if Company Y decides to exercise its call option, the hedge fund can repurchase the bonds in the market in order to sell them back to Company Y. Therefore, Company Y has transferred control of the bonds to the hedge fund. Consequently, Company Y derecognises the bonds and recognises an option asset, which is a new right that has arisen following the transfer. At 31 December 2014, the call option is 'out of the money' because the exercise price of £850,000 is greater than the fair value of £800,000. The premium paid on the option is £50,000, being the difference between the fair value of the bonds of £800,000 and the sale consideration of £750,000. The following accounting entries would be made by Company Y:

Dr Cash received from sale	£750,000	
Dr Fair value of call option	£50,000	
Cr Bond holding in Company X		£800,000

The call option is a derivative, which falls within the scope of Section 12 and thus would need to be measured at fair value through profit or loss until it expires. In this example, the practical ability test has been satisfied as the bonds are listed on an exchange and they are regularly traded, however, being exchange-listed is not necessarily itself a requirement, just that there is an active market.

6.4   Comparison with FRS 26 and FRS 5

Situations in which the transferor has neither transferred nor retained substantially all the risks and rewards as described in 6.3, give rise to the one difference from the FRS 26 derecognition requirements. This is the measurement of the transferor's ongoing involvement with the transferred asset. For example, if the bonds in Example 8.7 were not traded in an active market, the hedge fund would not have the practical ability to sell the bonds because it must be able to access the original bonds that were transferred by Company Y in case it exercises the call option. In these circumstances, as Company Y has not transferred control and has retained some risks and rewards, according to FRS 102, derecognition would not be appropriate. However, under FRS 26, in such circumstances, the bonds would only be recognised to the extent of the transferor's 'continuing involvement', that is, the extent to which Company Y is exposed to changes in the value of the transferred asset. [FRS 26.30]. In this case, where the transferor retains a call option, it would be the same as continuing to recognise the bonds in full, but if the asset was recorded at fair value though profit or loss, according to FRS 26, the associated liability should be measured such that the combination of the carrying values of the asset and the liability should equal the fair value of the retained option on a stand-alone basis. [FRS 26.AG48(c)]. This has the effect of not requiring the transferor to record a loss that it will never suffer when the fair value of the asset falls below the exercise price.

Meanwhile, if the transferor grants a put option to the buyer, whether the asset was previously recorded at amortised cost or fair value, FRS 26 requires the continuing involvement to be measured at the lower of the value of the transferred asset and the option exercise price. [FRS 26.30(b)]. This has the effect of requiring the transferor to recognise fair value losses on the put option while not allowing recognition of a gain above the exercise price.

For those entities still applying FRS 5, moving to FRS 102 may bring about changes in their accounting treatment for transfers of financial assets. The central premise of FRS 5 is that the substance and economic reality of an entity's transactions should be reported in its financial statements, and this substance should be identified by considering all the aspects and implications of a transaction, with the emphasis on those likely to have a commercial effect in practice. In practice, this will often give the same outcome, although there may be differences for individual transactions.

One definite difference will be 'linked presentation', which is not available under FRS 102. That is, FRS 5 permits non-recourse finance to be shown on the face of the statement of financial position as a deduction from the asset to which it relates (rather than in the liabilities section of the statement of financial position), provided that certain criteria are met. This form of presentation was common for transactions involving the securitisation of mortgages and consumer debt.

6.5   Accounting for collateral

FRS 102 also deals with the accounting consequences of transactions where a transferor provides non-cash collateral to the transferee. If the transferee has the right by contract to sell or re-pledge the collateral, the transferor should reclassify that asset in its statement of financial position separately from other assets. For example, it could be disclosed as a loaned asset or pledged asset. If the transferee sells collateral pledged to it, it shall recognise the proceeds from the sale and a liability measured at fair value for its obligation to return the collateral. If the transferor defaults under the terms of the contract and is no longer entitled to redeem the collateral, it shall derecognise the collateral, and the transferee shall recognise the collateral as its asset, initially measured at fair value or, if it has already sold the collateral, derecognise its obligation to return the collateral. In all circumstances, the transferor must continue to recognise the collateral as its asset while the transferee cannot, unless the transferor has defaulted and is no longer entitled to redeem the collateral. *[FRS 102.11.35]*.

6.6   Derecognition of financial liabilities

The FRS 102 derecognition requirements for financial liabilities are identical to those in FRS 26, hence, FRS 26 reporters will not be affected. In essence, a financial liability or a part of it is only extinguished when the obligations specified in the contract are discharged, cancelled or expire. If an existing borrower and lender exchange financial instruments with substantially different terms or substantially modify the terms of an existing financial liability, the transaction should be accounted for as an extinguishment of the original financial liability and the recognition of a new one. Any difference that may arise between the carrying amount of the financial liability that has been extinguished or transferred to another party and the consideration paid, including any non-cash assets transferred or liabilities assumed, is recognised in profit or loss. *[FRS 102.11.36-11.38]*. FRS 102 does not contain the additional guidance contained in FRS 26 on what constitutes 'substantially different'. While that guidance may be used by an entity reporting under FRS 102, it is, itself, not without issues of interpretation and we do not believe that it must be applied under FRS 102 or discuss it further here. As the FRS 26 guidance is identical to that in IAS 39, further details can be found in EY International GAAP 2015.

Chapter 8

For entities that are applying FRS 5, there is no equivalent guidance in respect of the derecognition of financial liabilities, as FRS 5 only addresses the derecognition of assets, not liabilities. In effect, FRS 5 approaches liability derecognition as an issue of derecognition of a related asset. For example, if a third party advances funds to an entity in connection with the transfer of an asset to the third party, FRS 5 requires the entity to assess whether or not it can derecognise the asset. If it can, the transaction is a sale; if it cannot, the transaction is a form of financing secured on the asset transferred.

6.7   Offsetting of financial instruments

The rules regarding the offsetting, sometimes called 'netting', of a financial asset and a financial liability are contained in both Sections 11 and 12. However, the guidance is identical, that is, a financial asset and a financial liability shall be offset and the net amount presented in the statement of financial position when and only when, an entity:

(a)   Currently has a legally enforceable right to set off the recognised amounts; and

(b)   Intends either to settle on a net basis, or to realise the asset and settle the liability simultaneously. *[FRS 102.11.38A, FRS 102.12.25A]*.

Similar to many other aspects of the accounting for financial instruments under FRS 102, the offsetting principle set out above is identical to that in FRS 25 and IAS 32 but minus the additional guidance contained in those standards. This is a topic on which the IASB has in recent years incorporated additional guidance into IAS 32 to deal with historical ambiguities as well as emerging practical application issues arising from the growth in the clearing of financial instruments. The additional guidance has helped to clarify aspects such as current legal enforceability and simultaneous settlement. We would expect FRS 102 reporters to default to the guidance within FRS 25 and IAS 32 where helpful, but this would not itself be a requirement. Further information on offsetting under IAS 32 can be found in EY International GAAP 2015.

7   HEDGE ACCOUNTING

7.1   Introduction

The hedge accounting model in FRS 102 is designed to allow entities to reflect their hedging activities in the financial statements in a manner that is consistent with the entity's risk management objectives. The hedge accounting approach in FRS 102 is based on a simplified version of that in IFRS 9. Hedge accounting is optional and an entity can choose not to designate exposures it is economically hedging. In that case the normal measurement rules in Sections 11 and 12 will apply.

Of course, if the entity has chosen to apply IAS 39 or IFRS 9 to its financial instruments, then it will apply the hedge accounting requirements of those standards.

The two main elements of a hedging relationship are the hedging instrument and the hedged item. Provided the qualifying conditions in FRS 102 Chapter 12 are met, hedge accounting can be applied prospectively from the date all of the conditions are met and documented. This section focuses on the definitions, components and criteria for hedge accounting under FRS 102.

7.1.1   *What is hedge accounting?*

Every entity is exposed to business risks from its daily operations. Many of those risks have an impact on the cash flows or the value of assets and liabilities, and therefore, ultimately affect profit or loss. In order to manage these risk exposures, companies often enter into derivative contracts (or, less commonly, other financial instruments) to hedge them. 'Hedging' can therefore be seen as a risk management activity in order to change an entity's risk profile.

Applying UK GAAP (FRS 102) to those risk management activities can result in accounting mismatches when the gains or losses on a hedging instrument are not recognised in the same period(s) and/or in the same place in the financial statements as gains or losses on the hedged exposure. The idea of hedge accounting is to reduce this mismatch by changing either the measurement or (in the case of certain firm commitments) recognition of the hedged exposure, or alternatively, the accounting for the hedging instrument.

Let us consider an example. A company may have entered into an interest rate swap to hedge its interest rate exposure on ten year borrowings. On application of previous UK GAAP, the swap contract would not necessarily be recognised on the balance sheet. Instead, it is common for a hedging swap to be accounted for on an accruals basis. Another example of accounting for a hedging swap under previous UK GAAP is where a company uses a forward currency contract to hedge the foreign currency exposure on a monetary asset. Previous UK GAAP permits the asset to be recorded using the contracted forward rate, effectively creating a 'synthetic' functional currency instrument *[SSAP 20.48]*, in which case the forward contract would not be separately recognised in the balance sheet or in the profit and loss account.

Under FRS 102, all derivatives are recorded on the balance sheet at fair value with subsequent fair value changes recorded in the profit and loss account. The impact on profit or loss from derivatives may be reduced if the hedge accounting criteria are met. FRS 102 describes three types of hedging relationships:

- fair value hedges (see 7.7 below);
- cash flow hedges (see 7.8 below); and
- hedges of net investments in foreign operations (see 7.9 below).

The resultant hedge accounting entries depend on the type of hedge accounting relationship.

For example, an entity may expect highly probable future revenue of FC200 in 3 months' time. As foreign currency exchange rates change, the revenue recognised by the entity in profit or loss will also change, as the entity's cash flows are exposed to foreign exchange risk. In order to reduce this potential profit or loss volatility, the entity may enter into a forward currency contract to pay FC200 and receive a fixed GBP equivalent. Under FRS 102, the forward currency contract will be recorded at fair value through profit or loss, and the forecast revenue will not be recognised until it occurs, resulting in a measurement and timing mismatch in profit or loss. If FRS 102 hedge accounting is applied, the forward currency contract would be accounted for differently, in order to reduce the mismatch. This is an example of a cash flow hedge, as the hedging instrument is reducing variability in the cash flows of the hedged item.

Chapter 8

The associated hedge accounting is to remove the effective portion of the change in fair value of the hedging derivative from profit or loss and recognise it in other comprehensive income, thereby reducing volatility in profit or loss (see 7.8.3 below).

Figure 8.2: Cash flow hedge accounting model

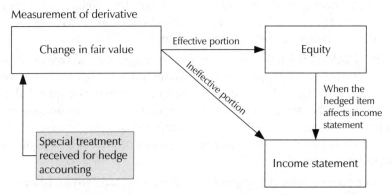

An entity could also transact a derivative that converts a fixed exposure into a variable one. This is described as a fair value hedge in FRS 102. An example of a fair value hedge would be an entity that has issued fixed rate debt and transacted an interest rate swap in which it receives a fixed rate and pays a variable rate of interest on an underlying notional value. The entity may economically transact this swap as they wish to convert the fixed interest flow into a variable interest flow, but the standard describes this as eliminating variability in fair value with respect to interest rate risk. Under previous UK GAAP, entities that do not apply FRS 26 could accrual account for both the fixed rate debt and the interest rate swap. However on application of FRS 102 (without hedge accounting) the interest rate swap would be accounted for at fair value through profit or loss, resulting in an accounting mismatch. If FRS 102 hedge accounting is applied to this fact pattern, an adjustment would be made to the carrying amount of the debt and to profit or loss, to reflect the revaluation of the debt with respect to interest rate risk. This hedge accounting adjustment would mitigate some of the volatility in profit or loss from fair value changes in the derivative (see 7.7.3 below).

Figure 8.3: Fair value hedge accounting model

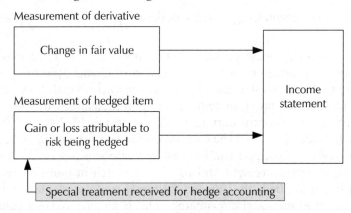

7.2 Hedged items

7.2.1 Introduction

A hedged item can be a recognised asset or liability, an unrecognised firm commitment, a highly probable forecast transaction, a net investment in a foreign operation, or a component of any such item, provided the item is reliably measurable. *[FRS 102.12.16].*

Recognised assets and liabilities can include financial items and non-financial items such as inventory.

Only assets, liabilities, firm commitments and forecast transactions with a party external to the reporting entity can qualify as hedged items. This means that hedge accounting can only be applied to transactions between entities in the same group in the individual financial statements of those entities, and not in the consolidated financial statements. Three exceptions to this rule are given in the standard:

- transactions with subsidiaries, where the subsidiaries are not consolidated in the consolidated financial statements;

- a hedge of the foreign currency risk of an intragroup monetary item if that foreign currency risk affects consolidated profit or loss; and

- foreign currency risk of a highly probable forecast intragroup transaction denominated in a currency other than the functional currency of the entity entering into the transactions, if the foreign currency risk affects consolidated profit or loss. *[FRS 102.12.16A].*

By way of example, foreign currency risk from intra group monetary items will usually affect consolidated profit or loss when the intra group monetary item is transacted between two group entities that have different functional currencies, as it will not eliminated on consolidation.

7.2.2 Components

FRS 102 permits components of an item to be hedged (including combinations of components). For example, an item may be hedged with respect to the risks associated with only a portion of its cash flow variability or fair value change as long as the risk component is separately identifiable and reliably measurable. *[FRS 102.12.16C].* For example, if an entity issued debt paying a coupon of LIBOR + 2%, it would be possible to only include the LIBOR component of the total interest rate exposure within the hedge accounting relationship. Similarly, for fixed rate debt, it would also be possible to identify, say, a 5% coupon component of debt paying a 6% fixed rate coupon.

If a risk component is contractually specified, as in the above LIBOR debt issued example, it would usually be considered separately identifiable. In this circumstance, the contractually specified risk component would usually be referenced to observable data, such as a published price index. Therefore, the risk component would usually also be considered reliably measurable.

Ordinary purchase or sales agreements sometimes contain clauses that determine the contract price via a specified formula linked into a benchmark commodity price.

Accordingly these contracts may also contain components that are separately identifiable and reliably measurable. Examples of contractually specified risk components in purchase and sale contracts are as follows:

- the price of wires contractually linked in part to a copper benchmark price and in part to a variable tolling charge reflecting energy costs; and

- the price of coffee contractually linked in part to a benchmark price of Arabica coffee and in part to transportation charges that include a diesel price indexation.

While it is certainly easier to determine that a risk component is separately identifiable and reliably measurable if it is specified in the contract, it is not a requirement that a component must be contractually specified in order for it to be eligible as a hedged item. In order to determine that the risk component is separately identifiable and reliably measurable and qualify for hedging, it must have a distinguishable effect on changes in the value or the cash flows that an entity is exposed to.

The fact that a commodity is a major physical input in a production process does not automatically translate into a separately identifiable effect on the price of the item as a whole, but it might. For example, crude oil price changes are unlikely to have a distinguishable effect on the retail price of plastic toys even though, in the longer term, changes in the crude oil price might influence the price of such toys to some degree. Similarly, the price for pasta at food retailers in the medium to long term also responds to changes in the price for wheat, but there is no distinguishable direct effect of wheat price changes on the retail price for pasta, which remains unchanged for longer periods even though the wheat price changes. If retail prices are periodically adjusted in a way that also directionally reflects the effect of wheat price changes, that is not sufficient to constitute a separately identifiable risk component. The evaluation would always have to be based on relevant facts and circumstances.

An example of a risk component that has a distinguishable effect on changes in the cash flows an entity is exposed to is provided in the application guidance to IFRS 9.

Example 8.8:   Hedge of a non-contractually specified risk component

An entity purchases a particular quality of coffee of a particular origin from its supplier under a contract that sets out a variable price linked to the benchmark price for coffee. The price is represented by the coffee futures price plus a fixed spread, reflecting the different quality of the coffee purchased compared to the benchmark plus a variable logistics services charge reflecting that the delivery is at a specific manufacturing site of the entity. The fixed spread is set for the current harvest period. For the deliveries that fall into the next harvest period this type of supply contract is not available.

The entity analyses the market structure for its coffee supplies, taking into account how the eventual deliveries of coffee that it receives are priced. The entity can enter into similar supply contracts for each harvest period once the crop relevant for its particular purchases is known and the spread can be set. In that sense, the knowledge about the pricing under the supply contracts also informs the entity's analysis of the market structure more widely, including forecast purchases which are not yet contractually specified. This allows the entity to conclude that its exposure to variability of cash flows resulting from changes in the benchmark coffee price is a risk component that is separately identifiable and reliably measurable for coffee purchases under the variable price supply contract for the current harvest period as well as for forecast purchases that fall into the next harvest period. *[IFRS 9.B6.3.10(b)].*

Other components that can be hedged include selected contractual cash flows and a specified part of the nominal amount of an item and combinations of these items. *[FRS 102.12.16].* FRS 102 does not provide detail on what is meant by a 'specified part of the nominal amount of an item'. The hedge accounting rules in FRS 102 are based on IFRS 9 and IFRS 9 states that such a component of a nominal amount could be a proportion of an entire item (such as, 60% of a fixed rate loan of £10 million) or a layer component (for example, the first £6 million of sales). *[IFRS 9.B6.3.16].*

In FRS 102, risk components also include a designation of changes in the cash flows or the fair value of a hedged item above or below a specified price or other variable (i.e. a one-sided risk). *[FRS 102.12.16C].* For example, an entity could hedge the cash flow losses resulting from an increase in the price of a forecast commodity purchase above a specified level. This would be useful when economically hedging with options, which only provide protection above or below a specified level.

An issue that entities have faced under FRS 26 (and also under IAS 39 and IFRS 9) is the prohibition on hedge accounting for changes in LIBOR when the hedged item attracts a 'sub-LIBOR' interest rate e.g. LIBOR–0.25%. Application of hedge accounting to the LIBOR component is not permitted under FRS 26 because the hedged component cannot be more than the total cash flows of the hedged item. Part of the rationale for this prohibition is that if LIBOR fell to 0.25% in this example, any changes in LIBOR below 0.25% would not ordinarily cause any further variability in cash flows on the hedged item, as an inherent floor usually exists. Whilst this restriction is not explicit in FRS 102, the logic would appear to be equally valid. However, an entity could still achieve hedge accounting by designating the cash flows of the hedged item in their entirety (e.g. LIBOR–0.25%) and for example, a LIBOR swap, although some ineffectiveness may arise.

7.2.3 Groups of items as hedged items

Hedging relationships typically include a single hedging instrument (e.g. an interest rate swap) hedging a single item (e.g. a loan). However, for operational reasons entities often economically hedge several items together on a group basis (e.g. a number of purchases in a foreign currency could be hedged with a single forward contract).

FRS 102 explains that a hedged item can either be a single item or a group of items, including components of items, provided that all of the following conditions for groups of items are met:

- the group consists of items that are individually eligible hedged items;
- the items in the group share the same risk;
- the items in the group are managed together on a group basis for risk management purposes; and
- the group does not include items with offsetting risk positions. *[FRS 102.12.16B].*

Whether the items in the group are managed together on a group basis is a matter of fact, i.e. it depends on an entity's behaviour and cannot be achieved by mere documentation. Examples of groups of items that could be eligible for hedging if all of the conditions are met are a portfolio of customer loans that pay interest based on LIBOR, or a portfolio of shares of Swiss companies that replicates the Swiss Market Index (SMI).

Hedge accounting for a net position (e.g. a group of assets and liabilities or income and expenses) is not permitted, as this would include offsetting risk positions. However, where an entity undertakes economic hedge accounting of a net position, the entity could still achieve hedge accounting under FRS 102 by designating a specified component of gross hedged items. For example, consider an entity that has forecast foreign currency sales of FC100 and purchases of FC80, both in 6 months. It hedges the net exposure using a single forward contract to sell FC20 in 6 months. Hedge accounting could be achieved by designating the forward contract as hedging FC20 of the FC100 forecast sales.

7.3   Hedging instruments

7.3.1   Introduction

FRS 102 defines a hedging instrument as a financial instrument measured at fair value through profit or loss that is a contract with a party external to the reporting entity and is not a written option unless:

- the written option is an offset to a purchased option in the hedged item and the combination is not a net written option; or

- the written option is combined with a purchased option and the combination is not a net written option. *[FRS 102.12.17C].*

Entities are therefore permitted to designate derivatives as hedging instruments, but also non-derivative financial assets or non-derivative financial liabilities that are accounted for at fair value through profit or loss are eligible hedging instruments. This can be helpful if an entity does not have access to derivatives markets or does not want to be subject to margining requirements and could also be operationally simpler than transacting derivatives.

Note that if a derivative is not measured at fair value (for example, if the fair value cannot be reliably measured *[FRS 102.11.32]*), then the derivative cannot be designated as a hedging instrument. With the exception of certain written options, the circumstances in which a derivative recorded at fair value through profit or loss may be designated as a hedging instrument are not restricted, provided the relevant conditions for hedge accounting are met. The reason written options cannot be designated as hedging instruments is because net options written by an entity do not reduce risk exposure or the potential effect on profit or loss. In practice many-called 'zero cost collars' (i.e. a combination of a put and call option, one of which is purchased and the other sold, priced so that the premiums offset to zero) are transacted as legally separate written and purchased options. However, paragraph 12.17C uses the example of a zero cost interest rate collar to illustrate circumstances under which a written option is combined with a purchased option such that the combination is not a net written option, and hence is eligible as a hedging instrument.

FRS 102 also permits the foreign currency risk component of a non-derivative financial instrument (for example, a basic foreign currency loan carried at amortised cost) to be designated as a hedging instrument in the hedge of foreign currency risk. *[FRS 102.12.17B].* This is illustrated in the following example.

Example 8.9:   *Hedging using a foreign currency component of a non-derivative instrument*

Company J has GBP functional currency. J issued fixed rate debt with principal of FC5 million due on maturity in two years. J had also entered into a fixed price sales commitment, accounted for as an executory contract, for FC5 million that will be paid in two years.

J could designate the foreign currency component of the fixed rate debt as a hedging instrument for the foreign currency exposure associated with the future receipt of FC5m on the fixed price sales commitment.

Similarly as for hedged items, a hedging instrument must be a contract with a party external to the reporting entity and there are no exceptions to this.

7.3.2   Combinations of hedging instruments

Paragraph 12.17A of the standard permits a combination of instruments that meet the criteria to be treated as hedging instruments to be designated in a hedge relationship. Hence a purchased bond measured at fair value through profit or loss and a derivative could be jointly designated as 'the hedging instrument'.

7.3.3   Proportions and components of instruments

FRS 102 specifies that a hedging instrument can only be designated in its entirety or a proportion (e.g. 50% of the nominal amount of the instrument). The requirement to designate an instrument in its entirety has been taken forward from IAS 39. The reason given for that original guidance is because there is normally a single fair value measure for a hedging instrument in its entirety and the factors that cause changes in its fair value are co-dependent.

This means, for instance, that the entity cannot designate a 'partial-term' component of a financial instrument as the hedging instrument (i.e. a part of the fair value change from a portion of the time period the instrument remains outstanding), but only the entire instrument for its remaining life. Nor can components of particular cash flows in the hedging instrument be designated in hedge relationships.

As noted at 7.3.1 above, for a hedge of foreign currency risk, the foreign currency risk component of a non-derivative financial instrument can be designated as a hedging instrument.

7.4   Criteria for hedge accounting

7.4.1   Introduction

In order to qualify for hedge accounting a hedging relationship has to consist of eligible hedging instruments and eligible hedged items as described at 7.2 and 7.3 above. In addition:

- the hedging relationship must be consistent with the entity's risk management objectives for undertaking hedges;
- there must be an economic relationship between the hedged item and hedging instrument;
- the entity must document the hedging relationship; and
- the entity must determine and document causes of hedge ineffectiveness. *[FRS 102.12.18]*.

Chapter 8

Each of these criteria is discussed below.

An entity is required to discontinue hedge accounting if the conditions for hedge accounting are no longer met. *[FRS 102.12.25(b)]*. This means that there is an ongoing requirement to assess whether the criteria are met. We would expect entities to undertake the assessment, at a minimum, at each reporting date. If it is determined that the criteria are no longer met, then hedge accounting should be discontinued prospectively from the last date that the hedge criteria were met (for example, at the last reporting date).

There is guidance in IFRS 9, to the effect that if the event or change in circumstances that caused the hedging relationship to no longer meet the hedge criteria can be identified and it can be demonstrated that the hedge accounting criteria were met before the event or change in circumstances occurred, hedge accounting should be discontinued prospectively from the date of the event or change in circumstances. Although this is not explicit in FRS 102 we would expect this same guidance to be applied.

7.4.2   *Risk management objectives*

Hedge accounting must reflect the entity's risk management objectives for undertaking a hedge. The risk management objective is set at the level of an individual hedging relationship and defines how a particular hedging instrument is designated to hedge a particular hedged item. For example, a risk management objective might be to designate a foreign exchange forward contract in a hedge of the foreign exchange risk of the first FC1m of sales in March 2015 or to designate a particular interest rate swap in a fair value hedge of £10m fixed rate debt. If this objective for the hedge relationship changed, then hedge accounting should cease.

7.4.3   *Economic relationship*

FRS 102 states that 'an economic relationship between a hedged item and hedging instrument exists when the entity expects that the values of the hedged item and hedging instrument will typically move in opposite directions in response to movements in the same risk, which is the hedged risk'. *[FRS102.12.18A]*.

This relationship should be based on an economic rationale rather than just by chance, as could be the case if the relationship is based only on a statistical correlation. However, a statistical correlation may provide corroboration of an economic rationale.

This requirement will quite obviously be fulfilled for many hedging relationships, for example if the underlying of the hedging instrument matches, or is closely aligned with the hedged risk in the hedged item. For example, an economic relationship clearly exists when hedging the 3 month LIBOR variable interest rate payable on a £100,000 loan with a 3 month LIBOR (pay fixed, receive floating) interest rate swap with a notional of £100,000 because the present value of the changes in the cash flows of the loan and the swap would move systematically in opposite directions in response to changes in the underlying interest rate. However, an economic relationship may not exist when an entity hedges a currency exposure using a different currency where the two currencies are not pegged, or otherwise, formally linked.

Even when there are differences between the hedged item and the hedging instrument, the economic relationship will often be capable of being demonstrated using a qualitative assessment. However, when the critical terms of the hedging instrument and hedged item are not closely aligned, it may be necessary to undertake a quantitative assessment.

7.4.4 Documentation

The documentation requirements are intended to be relatively informal and undemanding and should not pose a significant administrative burden on entities. The documentation supporting the hedge should include the identification of:

- the hedging instrument;
- the hedged item;
- the economic relationship between the hedging instrument and hedged item;
- the nature of the risk being hedged;
- how the hedge fits in with the entity's risk management objectives for undertaking hedges; and
- the possible causes of hedge ineffectiveness within the hedge relationship.

Designation of a hedge relationship takes effect prospectively from the date all of the criteria for hedging are met. In particular, hedge accounting can be applied only from the date all of the necessary documentation is completed (although there are different rules for transition – see Chapter 30 at 5.16). Therefore, hedge relationships cannot be designated retrospectively.

Hedge designation need not take place at the time a hedging instrument is entered into. For example, a derivative contract may be designated and formally documented as a hedging instrument any time after entering into the derivative contract. However, hedge accounting will only apply prospectively from documentation of the hedge designation, provided all other conditions are met.

7.5 Hedge ineffectiveness

Hedge ineffectiveness is the difference between the fair value change of a hedging instrument and the fair value change of the hedged item attributable to the hedged risk. It is required to be recorded in profit or loss. Hedge ineffectiveness can arise due to several reasons and the possible causes of hedge ineffectiveness in hedge relationships must be documented by an entity at the outset. *[FRS 102.12.18(e)].*

When considering possible sources of ineffectiveness in a hedge relationship, mismatches between the designated hedged item and the hedging instrument should be considered. For example, mismatches in the following terms are likely to be sources of ineffectiveness:

- maturity;
- volume or nominal amount;
- cash flow dates;
- interest rate or other market index basis, or quality and location basis differences;
- day count methods;
- credit risk, including the effect of collateral; and
- the extent that the hedging instrument is already 'in', or 'out of the money' when first designated.

Chapter 8

For example, if the interest rates on the hedging instrument and hedged item differ (e.g. 3 month LIBOR versus 6 month LIBOR), ineffectiveness will arise. Similarly, if an entity hedges a forecast commodity purchase using a forward contract, unless the forward contract is for the purchase of the same quantity of the same commodity at the same time and location as the hedged forecast purchase, there will be some ineffectiveness. Meanwhile, changes in the counterparty's credit risk and the value of collateral held, will be reflected in the fair value of the hedging instrument but not necessarily in the hedged item, resulting in ineffectiveness.

Unlike under FRS 26 or IAS 39, as there is not the explicit requirement to include changes in the entity's own credit risk in the valuation of derivatives (see 4.4.5), it is possible that these will not form part of hedge ineffectiveness. This is supported by the Illustrative Examples included in the standard that frequently say that, for simplicity, they have ignored counterparty credit risk but do not mention own credit risk.

As mentioned at 7.4.4 above, it is possible to designate a hedging instrument in a hedging relationship subsequent to its inception. For non-option derivatives, such as forwards or interest rate swaps, any fair value at inception of the hedge is likely to create 'noise' that may not be fully offset by changes in the hedged item, especially in the case of a cash flow hedge. This is because the derivative contains a 'financing' element (the initial fair value), gains and losses on which will not be replicated on the hedged item and therefore the hedge contains an inherent source of ineffectiveness.

Another source of ineffectiveness could be derivative valuation inputs that are not replicated when revaluing the hedged item (in addition to credit risk mentioned above). The hedged item is fair valued for the hedged risk only, whilst the hedging instrument is fair valued in its entirety. This means that ineffectiveness will arise as the hedging instrument will be fair valued for more than just the hedged risk. For example, the hedged item might be fair valued for interest rate risk only whilst the hedging instrument's fair value may be driven by interest rate risk but may also change due to counterparty and own credit risk and liquidity.

Ineffectiveness can also arise between interest rate reset dates when using hedging instruments such as interest rate swaps, in fair value hedges. This is often referred to as the 'most recently fixed floating leg' issue. The payments on the floating leg of an interest rate swap are typically 'fixed' at the beginning of a reset period and paid at the end of that period. Between these two dates the swap is no longer a pure pay-fixed receive-variable (or *vice versa*) instrument because not only is the next payment fixed, but the next receipt is also fixed. So although fair value changes in the fixed rate hedged item should provide some offset to fair value changes in the pay fixed leg of the swap, there is no offset from the hedged item for the fair value of the most recently fixed floating leg.

7.6   Hedging relationships

There are three types of hedging relationships in FRS 102, defined as follows:

A *fair value hedge*: a hedge of the exposure to changes in the fair value of a recognised asset or liability or an unrecognised firm commitment, or a component of any such item that are attributable to a particular risk and could affect profit or loss.

A *cash flow hedge*: a hedge of the exposure to variability in cash flows that is attributable to a particular risk associated with all, or a component of, a recognised asset or liability (such as all or some future interest payments on variable rate debt) or a highly probable forecast transaction, and could affect profit or loss.

A *net investment hedge*: a hedge of a net investment in a foreign operation. *[FRS 102.12.19]*.

These relationships are considered further in the remainder of this section.

7.7 Fair value hedges

7.7.1 Introduction

Typically a fair value hedge is undertaken where an entity wishes to convert a fixed rate exposure into a variable one. The fair value of an exposure that attracts a fixed or 'locked in' market index, is sensitive to changes in that market index. By converting the fixed index into a variable one, that fair value sensitivity is reduced. In many circumstances an entity may actually be more focused on creating variable rate cash flows, rather than eliminating fair value sensitivity. However the two economic perspectives are not dissimilar and both would fall within the FRS 102 description of a fair value hedge for accounting purposes.

An example of a fair value hedge is a hedge of the exposure to changes in the fair value of a fixed rate debt instrument (not measured at fair value through profit or loss) as a result of changes in interest rates – if interest rates increase, the fair value of the debt decreases and *vice versa*. If the debt instrument were to be sold before maturity, the fair value changes would affect profit or loss. Such a hedge could be entered into either by the issuer or by the holder.

Another example of a fair value hedge is where an entity wishes to eliminate the ongoing price risk from inventory. If an entity holds 100 tonnes of commodity A as inventory, for which they paid a price of 1 per tonne, the entity may wish to protect the value of that inventory against future changes in the market price that would affect profit or loss when the inventory is sold. In this case the entity would transact a derivative to sell that inventory forward at a locked in price.

7.7.2 Hedges of firm commitments

A hedge of a fixed price firm commitment (for instance, a hedge of the change in fuel price relating to an unrecognised contractual commitment by an electricity utility to purchase fuel at a fixed price) is considered a hedge of an exposure to a change in fair value. Accordingly, such a hedge is a fair value hedge.

However, a hedge of the foreign currency risk of a firm commitment may be accounted for as a fair value hedge or as a cash flow hedge. *[FRS 102.12.19A]*. This is because foreign currency risk affects both fair values and cash flows. This would mean that a foreign currency cash flow hedge of a forecast transaction need not be re-designated as a fair value hedge when the forecast transaction becomes a firm commitment.

Chapter 8

7.7.3   Accounting for fair value hedges

From the date the conditions for hedge accounting are met, a fair value hedge should be accounted for as follows:

- the gain or loss on the hedging instrument shall be recognised in profit or loss; and
- the hedging gain or loss on the hedged item shall adjust the carrying amount of the hedged item (if applicable). *[FRS 102.12.20].*

The gain or loss on the hedging instrument will be the change in its fair value. Accordingly, the application of FRS 102 hedge accounting does not change the usual measurement requirements for the hedging instrument. The hedging gain or loss on the hedged item is the change in its value attributable to the hedged risk, and this must be added to, or subtracted from, the carrying value of the hedged item. This has the effect that the carrying amount of the hedged item is a hybrid value. For example, in the case of hedged debt. the carrying amount is a combination of amortised cost plus the change in the valuation due to interest rates.

To the extent these amounts differ, a net amount will be recognised in profit or loss, commonly referred to as hedge 'ineffectiveness'. For fair value hedges all ineffectiveness is recognised in profit or loss.

The following example illustrates the basic mechanics of fair value hedge accounting.

Example 8.10:   Fair value hedge mechanics

On 1 January 2015 an investor purchases a fixed rate debt security for £100 and classified it as a basic financial instrument recorded at amortised cost. To protect the value of the investment, the investor entered into a hedge by transacting a derivative (e.g. an interest rate swap) with a nil fair value. The interest rate swap pays fixed rate and receives variable rate interest. During 2015 interest rates fell such that at the end of 2015, the change in value of the fixed rate debt attributable to the hedged risk (interest rate) since designation was £10. Other factors that might influence the full fair value of the debt are not included within the hedging gain or loss. The derivative fair value has fallen, resulting in a liability of £9.

The investor would record the following accounting entries:

1 January 2015	£	£
Dr Debt security	100	
Cr Cash		100

To reflect the acquisition of the security.

	£	£
Dr Derivative	nil	
Cr Cash		nil

To record the acquisition of the derivative at its fair value of nil.

31 December 2015		
Dr Profit or loss	9	
Cr Derivative		9

To recognise the decrease in the derivative's fair value.

Dr Debt security	10	
Cr Profit or loss		10

To recognise the change (increase) in value of the fixed rate debt attributable to the hedged risk

In this example, it can be seen that ineffectiveness of £1 has been recognised as a credit to profit or loss, reflecting some mismatches between the hedged debt security and hedging derivative.

Where the hedged item is a financial instrument for which the effective interest method of accounting is used, the adjustment to the hedged item referred to above, should be amortised to profit or loss. Amortisation may begin as soon as the adjustment exists and should begin no later than when the hedged item ceases to be adjusted for hedging gains and losses. The amortisation should be based on a recalculated effective interest rate at the date amortisation begins. *[FRS 102.12.22]*. For the fair value hedge of an exposure that is issued at par and redeems at par, any fair value adjustments to the hedged exposure during its life will automatically reverse through the natural unwind or pull to par of the revaluation adjustment, and hence amortisation is not necessary.

When the hedged item is an unrecognised firm commitment, the cumulative hedging gain or loss on the hedged item attributable to the hedged risk is recognised as an asset or liability with a corresponding gain or loss recognised in profit or loss. The initial carrying amount of the asset or liability that results from the entity meeting the firm commitment is adjusted to include the cumulative hedging gain or loss on the hedged item that was recognised in the statement of financial position. *[FRS 102.12.20-21]*.

The following example, based on Example 1 in the Appendix to Section 12 provides a more detailed illustration of the mechanics of a simple fair value hedge and in particular, a fair value hedge of a firm commitment.

Example 8.11:   *Fair value hedge accounting – Hedge of forward foreign currency risk of an unrecognised firm commitment*

In accordance with FRS 102.12.19A, a hedge of the foreign currency risk of an unrecognised firm commitment may be accounted for as a cash flow or fair value hedge. This example illustrates fair value hedge accounting.

On 9 June 2015 an entity enters into a purchase agreement with a third party over a non-financial asset in a foreign currency (FC) for FC515,000. On the same day, the entity enters into a forward currency contract to buy FC500,000 for CU1,000,000. Under the purchase agreement, the non-financial asset will be delivered and paid for on 30 March 2016, the same day the forward currency contract is required to be settled.

In this example the hedged item is the total of the commitment of FC515,000 and the hedging instrument is the forward contract to buy FC500,000. Since the nominal amounts of the two contracts do not match, hedge ineffectiveness arises. It should be noted that in practice an entity could avoid ineffectiveness arising for this reason by identifying an amount of FC500,000 of the total commitment as the hedged item in accordance with FRS 102.12.16C.

For simplification, this example disregards other sources of ineffectiveness, e.g. counter party credit risk associated with the forward currency contract.

The entity's financial year ends on 31 December.

This example assumes that the qualifying conditions for hedge accounting in FRS 102.12.18 are met from 9 June 2015.

Chapter 8

The table below sets out the applicable forward exchange rates, the fair value of the forward currency contract (the hedging instrument) and the hedging gains/losses on the purchase commitment (the hedged item) on the relevant dates. This example ignores the effects of discounting.

	9 June 2015	*31 Dec 2015*	*30 March 2016*
Forward exchange rate (CU:FC)	2:1	2.2:1	2.16:1
Forward currency contract (hedging instrument)			
Fair value	Nil	FC500,000 × CU0.2:FC = CU100,000	FC500,000 × CU0.16:FC = CU80,000[1]
Fair value change	Nil	CU100,000 – 0 = CU100,000	CU80,000 – CU100,000 = (CU20,000)
Purchase commitment (hedged item)			
Cumulative hedging (loss)[2]	nil	(FC515,000) × CU0.2:FC = (CU103,000)	(FC515,000) × CU0.16:FC = (CU82,400)
Hedging (loss)/gain	Nil	(CU103,000) – 0 = (CU103,000)	(CU82,400) – (CU103,000) = CU20,600

Key to table:

[1] This is the fair value of the contract prior to settlement.

[2] In accordance with FRS 102.12.20(b), the commitment is fair valued only for the hedged risk, which in this example is the forward exchange rate risk.

9 June 2015

Note that there are no hedge accounting entries on 9 June 20X5.

31 December 2015

(1) In accordance with FRS 102.12.20(a) the fair value gain of CU100,000 on the forward currency contract is recognised in profit or loss.

(2) In accordance with FRS 102.12.20(b) the cumulative hedging loss of CU103,000 on the commitment is recorded as a liability with a corresponding loss recognised in profit or loss.

Accounting entries:

Ref		Dr	Cr
(1)	Forward currency contract	CU100,000	
	Profit or loss		CU100,000
(2)	Profit or loss	CU103,000	
	Hedged item (commitment)		CU103,000

30 March 2016

(1) In accordance with FRS 102.12.20(a) the fair value loss of CU20,000 on the forward currency contract is recognised in profit or loss.

(2) In accordance with FRS 102.12.20(b) the hedging gain on the commitment of CU20,600 is recognised in profit or loss with a corresponding adjustment to the recognised liability from CU103,000 to CU82,400.

(3) In accordance with FRS 102.12.21 the non-financial asset's carrying amount is adjusted to include the cumulative hedging loss on the hedged item of CU82,400.

Note A: For illustrative purposes the accounting entry in respect of the settlement of the forward currency contract in cash for CU80,000 is shown below.

Note B: For illustrative purposes the accounting entry for the purchase of the non-financial asset at the applicable spot rate of FC2.16:CU for CU1,112,400 (settled in cash) is shown below.

Accounting entries:

Ref		Dr	Cr
(1)	Profit or loss	CU20,000	
	Forward currency contract		CU20,000
(2)	Hedged item (commitment)	CU20,600	
	Profit or loss		CU20,600
(3)	Hedged item (commitment)	CU82,400	
	Property, plant and equipment (PP&E)		CU82,400
(A)	Cash	CU80,000	
	Forward currency contract		CU80,000
(B)	Property, plant and equipment (PP&E)	CU1,112,400	
	Cash		CU1,112,400

7.8   Cash flow hedges

7.8.1   *Introduction*

Typically a cash flow hedge is undertaken where an entity wishes to convert a variable rate exposure into a fixed one. An example of a cash flow hedge is the use of an interest rate swap to change floating rate debt to fixed rate debt. The cash flows being hedged are the future interest payments.

An entity with GBP functional currency may have highly probable monthly forecast sales in a foreign currency over the next year. In order to eliminate variability from changes in foreign currency risk in the highly probable forecast revenue, the entity may transact a series of foreign currency forward contracts to lock in the GBP equivalent for that revenue. This scenario is an example of a cash flow hedge of foreign exchange risk.

Chapter 8

7.8.2   Highly probable forecast transactions

FRS 102 permits a cash flow hedge of a forecast transaction only where it is considered highly probable. The glossary to FRS 102 defines 'highly probable' and 'forecast transaction' (see 3.1). To meet the 'highly probable' criteria, entities are not required to predict and document the exact date a forecast transaction is expected to occur but should be able to identify and document the forecast transaction within a reasonably specific and generally narrow range of time from a most probable date, as a basis for determining fair values and assessing hedge effectiveness.

The high probability of a transaction should be supported by observable facts and attendant circumstances and should not be based solely on management intent, because intentions are not verifiable. In making this assessment, entities may find it helpful to consider the following (although this is not an exhaustive list):

- the frequency of similar past transactions;

- the financial and operational ability to carry out the transaction;

- whether there has already been a substantial commitments of resources to a particular activity, e.g. a manufacturing facility that can be used in the short run only to process a particular type of commodity;

- the extent of loss or disruption of operations that could result if the transaction does not occur;

- the likelihood that transactions with substantially different characteristics might be used to achieve the same business purpose, e.g. there may be several ways of raising cash ranging from a short-term bank loan to a public share offering; and

- the entity's business plan.

The length of time until a forecast transaction is projected to occur is also a consideration in determining probability. Other factors being equal, the more distant a forecast transaction is, the less likely it is to be considered highly probable and the stronger the evidence that would be needed to support an assertion that it is highly probable. For example, a transaction forecast to occur in five years may be less likely to occur than a transaction forecast to occur in only one year. However, forecast interest payments for the next 20 years on variable-rate debt would typically be highly probable if supported by an existing contractual obligation.

In addition, the greater the physical quantity or future value of a forecast transaction in proportion to transactions of the same nature, the less likely it is that the transaction would be considered highly probable and the stronger the evidence that would be required to support such an assertion. For example, less evidence would generally be needed to support forecast sales of 500,000 units in the next month than 950,000 units when recent sales have averaged 950,000 units for each of the past three months.

A history of having designated hedges of forecast transactions and then determining that the forecast transactions are no longer expected to occur, would call into question both the ability to accurately predict forecast transactions and the propriety of using hedge accounting in the future for similar forecast transactions. However the standard contains no prescriptive 'tainting' provisions in this area and entities are not automatically prohibited from using cash flow hedge accounting if a forecast transaction fails to occur. Instead, whenever such a situation arises, the particular facts, circumstances and evidence would normally need to be assessed to determine whether doubt has, in fact, been cast on an entity's ongoing hedging strategies.

If a hedged forecast transaction is no longer considered to be highly probable, the hedge must be discontinued prospectively (see 7.4.1 above and 7.10 below).

7.8.3 Accounting for cash flow hedges

From the date the conditions for hedge accounting are met, a cash flow hedge should be accounted for as follows:

'(a)   the separate component of equity associated with the hedged item (cash flow hedge reserve) is adjusted to the lower of the following (in absolute amounts):

(i)   the cumulative gain or loss on the hedging instrument from the date the conditions for hedging are met; and

(ii)   the cumulative change in fair value on the hedged item (i.e. the present value of the cumulative change of expected future cash flows) from the date the conditions for hedging are met.

(b)   the portion of the gain or loss on the hedging instrument that is determined to be an effective hedge (i.e. the portion that is offset by the change in the cash flow hedge reserve calculated in accordance with (a)) shall be recognised in OCI.

(c)   any remaining gain or loss on the hedging instrument (or any gain or loss required to balance the change in the cash flow hedge reserve calculated in accordance with (a)), is hedge ineffectiveness that shall be recognised in profit or loss. The reference to "balance" in here refers to the difference between the effective part of a hedge recorded in other comprehensive income and the fair value change on the derivative.

(d)   the amount that has been accumulated in the cash flow hedge reserve in accordance with (a) above shall be accounted for as follows:

(i)   if a hedged forecast transaction subsequently results in the recognition of a non-financial asset or non-financial liability, or a hedged forecast transaction for a non-financial asset or non-financial liability becomes a firm commitment for which fair value hedge accounting is applied, the entity shall remove that amount from the cash flow hedge reserve and include it directly in the initial cost or other carrying amount of the asset or liability (commonly referred to as a "basis adjustment").

(ii)   for cash flow hedges other than those covered by (i), that amount shall be reclassified from the cash flow hedge reserve to profit or loss in the same period or periods during which the hedged expected future cash flows affect profit or loss (for example, in the periods that interest income or interest expense is recognised or when a forecast sale occurs).

(iii)   if the amount accumulated in the cash flow hedge reserve is a loss, and all or part of that loss is not expected to be recovered, the amount of the loss not expected to be recovered shall be reclassified to profit or loss immediately.' *[FRS102.12.23]*.

Chapter 8

The cash flow hedge mechanics described in (a) to (c) above are often referred to as the 'lower of' calculation. This can be explained more easily by way of an example.

Example 8.12:   Cash flow hedge mechanics – 'lower of' calculation

	Scenario A			Scenario B		
Change in value of the hedged item (i.e. the present value of the cumulative change of expected future cash flows)	110			100		
Change in the fair value of the hedging instrument	(100)			(110)		
'Lower of' exposure	Hedging instrument			Hedged item		
Accounting entries		Dr	Cr		Dr	Cr
	Other comprehensive income	100		Other comprehensive income	100	
				Profit or loss	10	
	Derivative		100	Derivative		110
Ineffectiveness recognised	Nil			(10)		

So it can be seen from the above example, that for cash flow hedges, ineffectiveness is only recognised in profit or loss to the extent that the absolute change in fair value of the hedging instrument exceeds the absolute change in fair value of the hedged item. This comparison of value changes should be undertaken on a cumulative basis, i.e. the change in value over the life of the designated hedge relationship since inception.

If the hedging instrument's cumulative fair value changes are less than the cumulative fair value changes of the hedged item, no ineffectiveness is recorded in profit or loss (i.e. the full fair value change of the derivative would be recorded in other comprehensive income). If the hedging instrument's cumulative fair value changes are more than the cumulative fair value changes of the hedged item, the excess is recorded as ineffectiveness in profit or loss.

In practice entities often use what is called the 'hypothetical derivative' method to measure ineffectiveness in a cash flow hedge. As its name suggests, the hypothetical derivative method involves establishing a notional derivative that would be the ideal hedging instrument for the hedged exposure (normally an interest rate swap or forward contract with no unusual terms and a zero fair value at inception of the hedge relationship). The fair value of the hypothetical derivative is then used as a proxy for the net present value of the change in hedged future cash flows (requirement (a)(ii) above) against which changes in value of the actual hedging instrument are compared to measure ineffectiveness. The Appendix to Section 12 illustrates the use of the hypothetical derivative method to measure ineffectiveness (see Example 8.14 below).

In order to meet the requirements of (d) above, consideration must be given to the nature of the hedged item, let us consider some examples.

Example 8.13:   Cash flow hedge mechanics – recycling

	Hedge of purchase of fixed asset in foreign currency	*Monthly forecast sale of gas*	*Floating rate debt*
Hedged risk	Foreign currency	Gas price	Interest rates
Timing of recognition of hedged item	Purchase date	Throughout each month	Debt is already recognised, but interest is accrued over the remaining life of the debt
Timing of recycling of effective portion from other comprehensive income to profit or loss	Full amount recycled and included in cost of the fixed asset when purchased (a 'basis' adjustment)	The relevant component of the effective portion for each month of gas sales is to be recycled each month	The relevant component of the effective portion for each hedged interest accrual is to be recycled. This is often achieved by recycling the net interest accrual on the derivative from OCI into profit or loss

The purpose of the recycling is so that the impact of the cash flow hedge is reflected in profit or loss to match the timing of recognition of the hedged item. We believe the reclassification from accumulated other comprehensive income to profit or loss should be recognised in the same line item in profit or loss as the hedged transaction to reflect the offsetting effect of hedge accounting (see 7.11 below).

Chapter 8

The following example based on Example 2 in the Appendix to Section 12 illustrates in more detail how to account for a cash flow hedge.

Example 8.14:   Cash flow hedge accounting – Hedge of variability in cash flows in a floating rate loan due to interest rate risk

This example illustrates the accounting for a cash flow hedge of interest rate risk associated with a floating rate loan. The entity borrows money at a floating rate and enters into an interest rate swap with the effect of paying a fixed rate overall.

On 1 January 2015, an entity borrows CU10,000,000 from a bank at a floating rate of 3-month LIBOR plus 2.5%. The interest is payable annually in arrears on 31 December. The loan is repayable on 31 December 2017.

On 1 January 2015 the entity also enters into an interest rate swap with a third party, under which it receives 6-month LIBOR and pays a fixed rate of interest of 4.5%. The notional amount of the swap is CU10,000,000. The swap is settled annually in arrears on 31 December and expires on 31 December 2017.

The LIBOR rates on the loan and the interest rate swap are reset and fixed annually in advance on 31 December based on the expected LIBOR rates applicable at that time. Note that in practice the loan and swap interest rates would be reset more frequently than assumed for the purpose of simplification in this example.

The entity hedges the variability of the interest rate payments on the bank loan based on 3-month LIBOR. It should be noted that because the entity receives interest based on 6-month LIBOR under the interest rate swap, ineffectiveness will arise because the expected cash flows of the hedged item and the hedging instrument differ. The fair value of the interest rate swap may be affected by other factors that cause ineffectiveness, for example counter party credit risk, but these have been disregarded in this example. This example ignores the effect of discounting.

There are no transaction costs.

The entity's financial year ends on 31 December.

This example assumes that the qualifying conditions for hedge accounting in FRS 102.12.18 are met from 1 January 2015.

The table below sets out the applicable LIBOR rates, interest payments and swap settlements. The fair values of the interest rate swap and the hedged item shown in the table are shown for illustrative purposes only.

Note that in practice, when forecasted variable interest rate payments are the hedged item, the fair value of a hypothetical swap, that would be expected to perfectly offset the hedged cash flows, is used as a proxy of the fair value of the hedged item. The hypothetical derivative in this scenario is a fixed to floating interest rate swap with terms that match those of the loan and a fixed rate of 4.3%, which for the purpose of this example, is the interest rate where the fair value of the hypothetical swap is nil at the inception of the hedging relationship.

	1 Jan 2015	*31 Dec 2015*	*31 Dec 2016*	*31 Dec 2017*
Actual 3-month LIBOR	4.3%	5%	3%	n/a
Actual 6-month LIBOR	4.5%	4.9%	3.2%	n/a
Interest payments based on 3-month LIBOR	n/a	CU10 × (4.3% + 2.5%) = CU680,000	CU10 × (5% + 2.5%) = CU750,000	CU10 × (3% + 2.5%) = CU550,000

Interest rate swap (hedging instrument)

	1 Jan 2015	*31 Dec 2015*	*31 Dec 2016*	*31 Dec 2017*
Fair value	nil	CU78,000	(CU89,000)[1]	(CU130,000)[2]
Fair value change	nil	CU78,000 – 0 = CU78,000	(CU89,000) – CU78,000 = (CU167,000)	(CU130,000) – (CU40,000)[3] – (CU89,000) = (CU1,000)
Swap settlement receipts/(payments) based on 6-month LIBOR	n/a	CU10m × (4.5% – 4.5%) = nil	CU10m × (4.9% – 4.5%) = CU40,000	CU10m × (3.2% – 4.5%) = (CU130,000)

Hedged item

	1 Jan 2015	*31 Dec 2015*	*31 Dec 2016*	*31 Dec 2017*
Fair value	nil	(CU137,000)	CU59,000	CU130,000

Key to table:

1: This valuation is determined before the receipt of the cash settlement of CU40,000 due on 31 December 2016.

2: This valuation is determined before the payment of the cash settlement of CU130,000 due on 31 December 2017.

3: CU40,000 is the settlement of the interest rate swap as at 31 December 2016 which affects the fair value of the swap, but is not included in the fair value of the swap at 31 December 2016 of CU89,000.

31 December 2015

(1) In accordance with FRS 102.12.23(a), the cash flow hedge reserve is adjusted to the lower of (in absolute amounts) the cumulative gain on the hedging instrument (i.e. the interest rate swap), which equals its fair value, of CU78,000 and the cumulative change in fair value of the hedged item, which equals its fair value of (CU137,000).

In accordance with FRS 102.12.23(b), the gain of CU78,000 on the interest rate swap is recognised in other comprehensive income.

(2) The fixed interest element on the hypothetical swap is CU430,000, the same amount as the variable rate component. The variability of the 3-month LIBOR did therefore not affect profit or loss during the period. The reclassification adjustment in accordance with FRS 102.12.23(d)(ii) is nil. (Note that no accounting entry is shown below).

Note A: For illustrative purposes the accounting entry for interest payments is shown below. Note that in practice the accrual and payment of interest may be recorded in separate accounting entries.

Chapter 8

Accounting entries:

Note that the accounting entries shown are only those relevant to demonstrate the effects of hedge accounting. In practice other accounting entries would be required, e.g. an entry to recognise the loan liability.

Ref		Dr	Cr
(1)	Interest rate swap	CU78,000	
	Other comprehensive Income		CU78,000
(A)	Profit or loss	CU680,000	
	Cash		CU680,000

31 December 2016

(1) In accordance with FRS 102.12.23(a), the cash flow hedge reserve is adjusted to the lower of (in absolute amounts) the cumulative loss on the hedging instrument (i.e. the interest rate swap) which equals its fair value of (CU89,000) and the cumulative change in fair value of the hedged item, which equals its fair value of CU59,000. The cash flow hedge reserve moves from CU78,000 to (CU59,000), a change of (CU137,000).

In accordance with FRS 102.12.23(b), a loss of CU137,000 on the interest rate swap is recognised in other comprehensive income, as this part of the loss is fully off-set by the change in the cash flow hedge reserve. The remainder of the loss on the interest rate swap of CU30,000 is recognised in profit or loss, as required by FRS 102.12.23(c).

(2) The fixed interest element on the hypothetical swap is CU430,000, whilst the variable rate component is CU500,000. The variability of the 3-month LIBOR affects profit or loss during the period by CU70,000. Accordingly, the reclassification adjustment in accordance with FRS 102.12.23(d)(ii) is CU70,000.

Note A: For illustrative purposes the accounting entry for interest payments is shown below. Note that in practice the accrual and payment of interest may be recorded in separate accounting entries.

Note B: For illustrative purposes the accounting entry for the settlement of the swap is shown below.

Accounting entries:

Ref		Dr	Cr
(1)	Other comprehensive Income	CU137,000	
	Profit or loss	CU30,000	
	Interest rate swap		CU167,000
(2)	Other comprehensive Income	CU70,000	
	Profit or loss		CU70,000
(A)	Profit or loss	CU750,000	
	Cash		CU750,000
(B)	Cash	CU40,000	
	Interest rate swap		CU40,000

31 December 2017

(1) In accordance with FRS 102.12.23(a), the cash flow hedge reserve is adjusted to the lower of (in absolute amounts) the cumulative loss on the hedging instrument (i.e. the interest rate swap) which equals the fair value of (CU130,000) and the cumulative change in fair value of the hedged item, which equals its fair value of CU130,000.

The cash flow hedge reserve moves from (CU129,000) to (CU130,000), a change of (CU1,000). In accordance with FRS 102.12.23(b), the loss of CU1,000 on the interest rate swap is recognised in other comprehensive income.

(2) The fixed interest element on the hypothetical swap is CU430,000, whilst the variable rate component is CU300,000. The variability of the 3-month LIBOR affects profit or loss during the period by (CU130,000). Accordingly, the reclassification adjustment in accordance with FRS 102.12.23(d)(ii) is (CU130,000).

Note A: For illustrative purposes the accounting entry for interest payments is shown below. Note that in practice the accrual and payment of interest may be recorded in separate accounting entries.

Note B: For illustrative purposes the accounting entry for the settlement of the swap is shown below.

Accounting entries:

Ref		Dr	Cr
(1)	Other comprehensive Income	CU1,000	
	Interest rate swap		CU1,000
(2)	Profit or loss	CU130,000	
	Other comprehensive Income		CU130,000
(A)	Profit or loss	CU550,000	
	Cash		CU550,000
(B)	Interest rate swap	CU130,000	
	Cash		CU130,000

Chapter 8

The table below summarises the effects of the accounting entries shown above on the interest rate swap, profit or loss and other comprehensive income.

Description	Interest rate Swap	Other comprehensive income	Profit or loss
31 December 2015			
Opening balance	nil	nil[1]	–
Interest on the loan			CU680,000
Interest rate swap fair value movement	CU78,000	(CU78,000)	–
Closing balance	CU78,000	(CU78,000)[1]	–
31 December 2016			
Opening balance	CU78,000	(CU78,000)[1]	–
Interest on the loan			CU750,000
Interest rate swap fair value movement	(CU167,000)	CU137,000	CU30,000
Settlement receipt interest rate swap	(40,000)	–	–
Reclassification from cash flow hedge reserve	–	CU70,000	(CU70,000)
Closing balance	(CU129,000)	CU129,000[1]	–
31 December 20X7			
Opening balance	(CU129,000)	CU129,000[1]	–
Interest on the loan			CU550,000
Interest rate swap movement	(1,000)	1,000	–
Settlement receipt interest rate swap	CU130,000	–	–
Reclassification from cash flow hedge reserve	–	(CU130,000)	CU130,000
Closing balance	nil	nil[1]	–

Key to table:

[1] This is the balance of the cash flow hedge reserve.

7.9   Hedges of net investments in foreign operations

7.9.1   *Introduction*

Many reporting entities have investments in foreign operations which may be subsidiaries, associates, joint ventures or branches. Section 30 – *Foreign Currency Translation* requires an entity to determine the functional currency of each of its foreign operations as the currency of the primary economic environment of that operation. When translating the results and financial position of its foreign operation into a presentation currency, on consolidation foreign exchange differences should be recognised in other comprehensive income (with no reclassification to profit or loss in future periods).

From the perspective of an investor (e.g. a parent) it is clear that an investment in a foreign operation is likely to give rise to a degree of foreign currency exchange rate risk and an entity with many foreign operations may be exposed to a number of foreign currency risks.

FRS 102 defines a net investment in a foreign operation as 'The amount of the reporting entity's interest in the net assets of that operation'. *[FRS 102 Appendix I]*. A hedge of a net investment in a foreign operation is a hedge of the foreign currency exposure, not a hedge of the change in the value of the investment. The net investment hedge accounting rules can also be applied to a monetary item that is accounted for as part of the net investment (see Chapter 25 at 3.7.4). For example, if a parent grants a foreign currency loan to an overseas subsidiary and settlement is neither planned nor likely in the foreseeable future, the loan can be hedged as part of the net investment in the foreign subsidiary.

Net investment hedge accounting can be applied only when the net assets of the foreign operation (and not fair value or cost less impairment) are included in the financial statements. This will be the case for consolidated financial statements, financial statements in which investments such as associates or joint ventures are accounted for using the equity method or those that include a branch or a joint operation. Investments in foreign operations may be held directly by a parent entity or indirectly by its subsidiary or subsidiaries.

7.9.2   *Accounting for net investment hedges*

Hedges of a net investment in a foreign operation, including a hedge of a monetary item that is accounted for as part of the net investment are accounted for similarly to cash flow hedges from the date the conditions for hedging are met:

- the portion of the gain or loss on the hedging instrument that is determined to be an effective hedge is recognised in other comprehensive income; and
- the ineffective portion is recognised in profit or loss.

The effective portion is determined by applying the same cash flow hedge 'lower of' accounting, as explained at 7.8.3 above. However, the cumulative gain or loss on the hedging instrument relating to the effective portion of the hedge that has been accumulated in equity is not reclassified from equity to profit or loss in subsequent periods. *[FRS102.12.24]*. This ensures consistency with Section 30 which requires that foreign exchange gains and losses relating to the consolidation of a subsidiary are not recycled on disposal of the subsidiary. *[FRS 102.30.13]*.

Chapter 8

The following example based on the Appendix to FRS 102.12 illustrates how to account for a simple net investment hedge.

Example 8.15:   Hedge accounting: Net investment in a foreign operation

This example illustrates the accounting for a net investment hedge in the consolidated financial statements. The entity has a foreign operation and hedges its exposure to foreign currency risk in the foreign operation by the use of a foreign currency loan.

On 1 April 2015 an entity with functional currency CU acquires an investment in an overseas subsidiary (with functional currency FC) at a cost of FC1,200,000. On the same day the entity takes out a loan with a third party of FC1,200,000 to finance the investment. This example disregards the effects of interest or other transaction costs associated with the loan.

This example assumes that losses of FC200,000 are incurred in 2015, and profits of FC100,000 in 2016. The reduction in value below FC1,200,000 causes ineffectiveness.

The entity's financial year ends on 31 December.

This example assumes that the qualifying conditions for hedge accounting in FRS 102.12.18 are met from 1 April 2015.

The table below sets out the applicable exchange rates, the carrying amount of the loan and the foreign exchange gains and losses on the loan as determined in accordance with Section 30 – *Foreign Currency Translation*, as well as the retranslation differences on the foreign investment recognised in other comprehensive income in accordance with Section 30.

	1 April 2015	*31 December 2015*	*31 December 2016*
Spot exchange rate CU:FC	0.35:1	0.3:1	0.45:1
Loan (hedging instrument)			
Carrying amount under Section 30	(FC1,200,000) × CU0.35:FC= (CU420,000)	(FC1,200,000) × CU0.3:FC= (CU360,000)	(FC1,200,000) × CU0.45:FC= (CU540,000)
Cumulative gain/ (loss)	nil	(CU360,000) – (CU420,000)= CU60,000	(CU540,000) – (CU420,000)= (CU120,000)
Gain/(loss)	nil	(CU360,000) – (CU420,000)= CU60,000	(CU540,000) – (CU360,000)= (CU180,000)
Investment in foreign operation (hedged item)			
Retranslation difference in accordance with Section 30	nil	(CU55,000) [1]	CU157,500 [2]
Cumulative retranslation differences	nil	(CU55,000) – nil= (CU55,000)	CU157,500 + (CU55,000)= CU102,500

Key to table:

1   This is the exchange difference referred to in FRS 102.30.20 which is recognised in other comprehensive income. The amount under FRS 102.30.20(a) is CU5,000 and under FRS 102.30.20(b) (CU60,000). The calculation is based on the translation of the FC200,000 loss at the average rate of 0.325CU:FC.

2   This is the exchange difference referred to in FRS 102.30.20 which is recognised in other comprehensive income. The amount under FRS 102.30.20(a) is CU7,500 and under FRS 102.30.20(b) CU150,000. The calculation is based on the translation of the FC100,000 profit at the average rate of 0.375CU:FC.

31 December 2015

A component of equity is adjusted to the lower of (in absolute amounts) the cumulative exchange gain on the loan of CU60,000 and the cumulative retranslation difference on the net investment of (CU55,000).

In accordance with FRS 102.12.24(a), a gain of CU55,000 on the loan is recognised in other comprehensive income. The remainder of the gain of CU5,000 is recognised in profit or loss, as required by FRS 102.12.24(b).

Accounting entry:

Note that only the accounting entry in relation to hedge accounting as described in FRS 102.12.24 is shown. Other accounting entries in relation to the loan and the investment in the foreign operation would be required in practice.

	Dr	*Cr*
Loan	CU60,000	
Other comprehensive income		CU55,000
Profit or loss		CU5,000

31 December 2016

A component of equity is adjusted to the lower of (in absolute amounts) the cumulative exchange loss on the loan of CU120,000 and the cumulative exchange difference on the net investment of CU102,500.

The amount recorded in equity changes from CU55,000 to (CU102,500), a change of (CU157,500). In accordance with FRS 102.12.24(a) a loss of CU157,500 on the loan is recognised in other comprehensive income. The remainder of the loss of CU22,500 is recorded in profit or loss, as required by FRS 102.12.24(b).

Accounting entry:

	Dr	*Cr*
Other comprehensive income	CU157,500	
Profit or loss	CU22,500	
Loan		CU180,000

7.10   Discontinuing hedge accounting

Hedge accounting should be discontinued prospectively if any of the following occurs:

- the hedging instrument expires, is sold or terminated;
- the conditions for hedge accounting are no longer met; or
- the entity elects to discontinue the hedge. *[FRS102.12.25].*

Chapter 8

If the entity elects to voluntarily discontinue a hedge, it must document its decision and the discontinuation would be effective from that date.

Following discontinuation, in a fair value hedge, any adjustment to the hedged item arising as a result of fair value hedging, is amortised as discussed at 7.7.3 above.

In a cash flow hedge, if the hedged future cash flows are no longer expected to occur, the amount that has been accumulated in the cash flow hedge reserve is reclassified from the cash flow hedge reserve to profit or loss immediately.

If cash flow hedge accounting is discontinued and the hedged future cash flows are still expected to occur (for example a future cash flow that is no longer highly probable may still be expected to occur), the cumulative gain or loss in the cash flow hedge reserve should either:

- remain in equity and be recycled to profit or loss in line with 8.7.8.3 (d) above or

- be recorded in profit or loss immediately if the amount is a loss and is not expected to be recovered. *[FRS 102.12.25A, 23(d)]*

In a net investment hedge, the amount that has been accumulated in equity is not reclassified to profit or loss.

7.11   Presentation

FRS 102 does not address how hedges should be presented in profit or loss in the financial statements. Existing UK GAAP and IFRS reporters normally try to reflect the effect of the hedged item and hedging instrument in the financial statements so that they offset.

For derivatives designated in effective hedge relationships, the profit or loss related to the effective portion of the hedging instrument would normally be presented in the same line that the profit or loss arising on the hedged item is recorded. However, this is not mandated in the standard and it would also be acceptable to present the profit or loss from hedging derivatives similarly to non-hedging derivatives, if an entity so chooses as its accounting policy.

If a hedge does not qualify for hedge accounting, the profit or loss arising on the derivative would not necessarily be presented in the same income or expenditure line as the item that it was intended to hedge. The default is for the gain or loss to be recorded in trading income. However, gains or losses on interest rate derivatives are sometimes presented in interest income or expense. Also, gains and losses on currency derivatives may be presented in the foreign currency revaluation income or expense line. Presentation may be appropriate in cost of goods sold if the entity does not enter into derivatives for trading purposes and, hence, does not have a line item for trading instruments.

Presentation policies should be applied consistently to all similar instruments and should be clearly described in the accounting policies.

8   DISCLOSURES

As discussed at 4 above, the disclosure requirements of Sections 11 and 12 apply to all entities regardless of their accounting policy choice for recognition and measurement. However, a qualifying entity which is not a financial institution (i.e. most subsidiaries and parents in their separate financial statements) is not required to make any of the disclosures required by Sections 11 and 12 providing the equivalent disclosures are included in the consolidated financial statements of the group in which the entity is consolidated. *[FRS 102.1.12(d)]*. Qualifying entities are required only to make the disclosures required by the Regulations (see 8.3 below).

8.1   Disclosures for financial instruments (all entities)

The disclosure requirements for financial instruments can be found in paragraphs 39 to 48A of Section 11 and paragraphs 26 to 29A of Section 12, respectively. The disclosures contained in Section 11 are also applicable to financial instruments within the scope of Section 12, if relevant. *[FRS 102.12.26]*. The disclosure requirements are listed below:

- In the summary of significant accounting policies, the measurement basis (or bases) used for financial instruments and the other accounting policies used for financial instruments that are relevant to an understanding of the financial statements.

- The carrying amounts of each of the following categories of financial assets and financial liabilities at the reporting date, in total, either in the statement of financial position or in the notes:

  - financial assets measured at fair value through profit or loss;

  - financial assets that are debt instruments measured at amortised cost;

  - financial assets that are equity instruments measured at cost less impairment;

  - financial liabilities measured at fair value through profit or loss and those that are not held as part of a trading portfolio and are not derivatives shall be shown separately;

  - financial liabilities measured at amortised cost; and

  - loan commitments measured at cost less impairment.

- Information that enables users of an entity's financial statements to evaluate the significance of financial instruments for its financial position and performance. For example, for long-term debt, such information would normally include the terms and conditions of the debt instrument (such as interest rate, maturity, repayment schedule, and restrictions that the debt instrument imposes on the entity).

- For all financial assets and financial liabilities measured at fair value, the basis for determining fair value, (e.g. quoted market price in an active market or a valuation technique). When a valuation technique is used, the assumptions applied in determining fair value for each class of financial assets or financial liabilities. For example, if applicable, information about the assumptions relating to prepayment rates, rates of estimated credit losses, and interest rates or discount rates.

- The fact that a reliable measure of fair value is no longer available for ordinary or preference shares measured at fair value through profit or loss, if that is the case.
- If an entity has transferred financial assets to another party in a transaction that does not qualify for derecognition, for each class of such financial assets:
  - the nature of the assets;
  - the nature of the risks and rewards of ownership to which the entity remains exposed; and
  - the carrying amounts of the assets and of any associated liabilities that the entity continues to recognise.
- When an entity has pledged financial assets as collateral for liabilities or contingent liabilities, the carrying amount of the financial assets pledged as collateral and the terms and conditions relating to its pledge.
- For loans payable recognised at the reporting date for which there is a breach of terms or default of principal, interest, sinking fund, or redemption terms that has not been remedied by the reporting date:
  - details of that breach or default;
  - the carrying amount of the related loans payable at the reporting date; and
  - whether the breach or default was remedied, or the terms of the loans payable were renegotiated, before the financial statements were authorised for issue.
- An entity shall disclose the following items of income, expense, gains or losses:
  - income, expense, net gains or net losses, including changes in fair value, recognised on financial assets measured at fair value through profit or loss, financial liabilities measured at fair value through profit or loss (with separate disclosure of movements on those which are not held as part of a trading portfolio and are not derivatives), financial assets measured at amortised cost and financial liabilities measured at amortised cost.
  - total interest income and total interest expense (calculated using the effective interest method) for financial assets or financial liabilities that are not measured at fair value through profit or loss; and
  - the amount of any impairment loss for each class of financial asset. A class of financial asset is a grouping that is appropriate to the nature of the information disclosed and that takes into account the characteristics of the financial assets.
- For financial instruments at fair value through profit or loss that are not held as part of a trading portfolio and are not derivatives:
  - the amount of change, during the period and cumulatively, in the fair value of the financial instrument that is attributable to changes in the credit risk of that instrument, determined either:

- - as the amount of change in its fair value that is not attributable to changes in market conditions that give rise to market risk; or

  - using an alternative method the entity believes more faithfully represents the amount of change in its fair value that is attributable to changes in the credit risk of the instrument.

 - the method used to establish the amount of change attributable to changes in own credit risk, or, if the change cannot be measured reliably or is not material, that fact.

 - the difference between the financial liability's carrying amount and the amount the entity would be contractually required to pay at maturity to the holder of the obligation.

 - if an instrument contains both a liability and an equity feature, and the instrument has multiple features that substantially modify the cash flows and the values of those features are interdependent (such as a callable convertible debt instrument), the existence of those features.

 - any difference between the fair value at initial recognition and the amount that would be determined at that date using a valuation technique, and the amount recognised in profit or loss.

- Information that enables users of the entity's financial statements to evaluate the nature and extent of relevant risks arising from financial instruments to which the entity is exposed at the end of the reporting period. These risks typically include, but are not limited to, credit risk, liquidity risk and market risk. The disclosure should include both the entity's exposure to each type of risk and how it manages those risks. *[FRS 102.11.40-48A].*

- When hedge accounting is applied, entities are required to disclose the following, separately for three types of hedging relationships: *[FRS 102.12.27]*

 - a description of the hedge;

 - a description of the financial instruments designated as hedging instruments and their fair values at the reporting date;

 - a description of the hedged item; and

 - the nature of the risks being hedged.

- For fair value hedges, the following disclosures must be provided: *[FRS 102.12.28]*

 - the amount of the change in fair value of the hedging instrument recognised in profit or loss for the period, and

 - the amount of the change in fair value of the hedged item recognised in profit or loss for the period.

- For cash flow hedges, entities are required to disclose: *[FRS 102.12.29]*

 - the periods when the cash flows are expected to occur and when they are expected to affect profit or loss;

 - a description of any forecast transaction for which hedge accounting had previously been used, but which is no longer expected to occur;

Chapter 8

- the amount of the change in fair value of the hedging instrument that was recognised in other comprehensive income during the period;

- the amount, if any, that was reclassified from equity to profit or loss for the period; and

- the amount, if any, of any excess of the fair value of the hedging instrument over the change in the fair value of the expected cash flows that was recognised in profit or loss for the period (i.e. any ineffectiveness).

- For a hedge of net investment in a foreign operation entities must disclose separately: *[FRS 102.12.29A]*

  - the amounts recognised in other comprehensive income (i.e. fair value changes in the hedging instrument that were effective hedges); and

  - the amounts recognised in profit or loss (as ineffectiveness).

8.2   Additional disclosures required for financial institutions

For financial institutions (as defined in Chapter 1), additional disclosures are required, as follows:

- A disaggregation of the statement of financial position line item by class of financial instrument. A class is a grouping of financial instruments that is appropriate to the nature of the information disclosed and that takes into account the characteristics of those financial instruments.

- Where a separate allowance account is used to record impairments, a reconciliation of changes in that account during the period for each class of financial asset.

- For financial instruments held at fair value in the statement of financial position, for each class of financial instrument, an analysis of the level in the fair value hierarchy (as set out at 4.4.5 above) into which the fair value measurements are categorised.

- Information that enables users of the financial institution's financial statements to evaluate the nature and extent of credit risk, liquidity risk and market risk arising from financial instruments to which the institution is exposed at the end of the reporting period.

- For each type of risk arising from financial instruments:

  - the exposures to risk and how they arise;

  - the institution's objectives, policies and processes for managing the risk and the methods used to measure the risk; and

  - any changes from the previous period.

- By class of financial instrument:

  - The amount that best represents the institution's maximum exposure to credit risk at the end of the reporting period. This disclosure is not required for financial instruments whose carrying amount best represents the maximum exposure to credit risk.

- A description of collateral held as security and of other credit enhancements, and the extent to which these mitigate credit risk.

- The amount by which any related credit derivatives or similar instruments mitigate that maximum exposure to credit risk.

- Information about the credit quality of financial assets that are neither past due nor impaired.

- By class of financial asset, an analysis of:

  - the age of financial assets that are past due as at the end of the reporting period but not impaired; and

  - the financial assets that are individually determined to be impaired as at the end of the reporting period, including the factors the financial institution considered in determining that they are impaired.

- When financial or non-financial assets are obtained by taking possession of collateral it holds as security or calling on other credit enhancements (e.g. guarantees), and such assets meet the recognition criteria in other sections of FRS 102, a financial institution shall disclose:

  - the nature and carrying amount of the assets obtained; and

  - when the assets are not readily convertible into cash, its policies for disposing of such assets or for using them in its operations.

- A maturity analysis for financial liabilities that shows the remaining contractual maturities at undiscounted amounts separated between derivative and non-derivative financial liabilities.

- A sensitivity analysis for each type of market risk (e.g. interest rate risk, currency risk, other price risk) the institution is exposed to, showing the impact on profit or loss and equity. Details of the methods and assumptions used should be provided. If a sensitivity analysis, such as value-at-risk is prepared, that reflects interdependencies between risk variables (e.g. interest rates and exchange rates) and uses it to manage financial risks, it may use that sensitivity analysis instead.

- Information that enables users of the financial institution's financial statements to evaluate its objectives, policies and processes for managing capital.

- Qualitative information about its objectives, policies and processes for managing capital, including:

  - a description of what it manages as capital;

  - when the institution is subject to externally imposed capital requirements, the nature of those requirements and how those requirements are incorporated into the management of capital; and

  - how it is meeting its objectives for managing capital.

- Summary quantitative data about what the institution manages as capital. Some regard some financial liabilities (e.g. some forms of subordinated debt) as part of capital. Others regard capital as excluding some components of equity (e.g. components arising from cash flow hedges).

- Any changes in the above from the previous period.

Chapter 8

- Whether during the period the institution complied with any externally imposed capital requirements to which it is subject.

- When the institution has not complied with such externally imposed capital requirements, the consequences of such non-compliance.

A financial institution must base all these disclosures on the information provided internally to key management personnel.

- Where a statement of cash flows is presented, cash flows arising from each of the following activities may be reported on a net basis:

  - cash receipts and payments for the acceptance and repayment of deposits with a fixed maturity date;

  - the placement of deposits with and withdrawal of deposits from other financial institutions; and

  - cash advances and loans made to customers and the repayment of those advances and loans. *[FRS 102.34.20-33].*

8.3   Financial Instrument disclosures required by UK company law

The Regulations require various disclosures in respect of financial instruments. For a qualifying entity that is not a financial institution (see 8 above) these will be the only disclosures required in respect of financial instruments as those entities are exempt from the disclosure requirements of Sections 11 and 12.

The following must be disclosed:

- the amount of fixed asset or current asset investments ascribable to listed investments; *[1 Sch 54(1), 3 Sch 72]*

- the aggregate amount of listed investments where this is different from the amount recorded in the financial statements (and both market value and stock exchange value if market value is higher); *[1 Sch 54(2)]*

- the purchase price of listed investments (insurers only); *[3 Sch 73(3)]*

The following must be disclosed where financial instruments are recorded at fair value:

- significant assumptions underlying any valuation models and techniques used where the fair value has been determined using generally accepted valuation techniques and models; *[1 Sch 55(2)(a), 2 Sch 66(2)(a), 3 Sch 73(4)(a)]*

- the fair value of each category of financial instrument and the changes in value reported in profit and loss or credited/debited to the fair value reserve; *[1 Sch 55(2)(b), 2 Sch 66(2)(b), 3 Sch 73(4)(b)]*

- for each class of derivatives, the extent and nature of the instruments including significant terms and conditions that may affect the amount, timing and uncertainty of future cash flows; *[1 Sch 55(2)(c), 2 Sch 66(2)(c), 3 Sch 73(4)(c)]*

- where any amount is transferred to or from the fair value reserve, there must be stated in tabular form, the amount of the reserve at the beginning and end of the reporting period, the amount transferred to/from the reserve in the year and the source and application of the amounts so transferred; *[1 Sch 55(3), 2 Sch 56(3), 3 Sch 73(5)]*

In addition, entities shall disclose:

- the fair values of any derivatives not included at fair value together with the extent and nature of the derivatives; *[1 Sch 56, 2 Sch 67, 3 Sch 74]*

- the fair value of instruments that could be measured at fair value but are measured at a higher amount (i.e. amortised cost) and reasons for not making a provision for diminution in value, together with the evidence that provides a basis for recoverability of the amount in the financial statements. *[1 Sch 57, 2 Sch 68, 3 Sch 75]*.

8.4 Analysis of the FRS 102 disclosure requirements for financial instruments

As noted at 8 above, qualifying entities that are not financial institutions are not required to make the disclosures required by Sections 11 and 12. For those entities required to make these disclosures, with the exception of the financial institution specific disclosures (see 8.2 above), the disclosures are less onerous than the previous FRS 29 disclosures which applied only to a limited number of entities. *[FRS 29.2D]*.

Some previous UK GAAP reporters may have made the disclosures required by FRS 13. The FRS 13 disclosures are not as extensive as those required by FRS 29 and there are certain similarities with the requirements of FRS 102.

Those entities that did not apply FRS 13 or FRS 29 were only required to comply with the disclosure requirements of the Companies Act (see 8.3 above). In addition, the strategic report for all UK companies must include narrative disclosures on financial risk management objectives and policies, and the exposure to price, credit, liquidity and cash flow risk. The quantitative and narrative disclosures required by the Companies Act are less onerous than the FRS 102 disclosures. Hence, those entities that have not applied either FRS 13 or FRS 29 and are not qualifying entities will have to invest the time and effort required to ensure compliance with the new disclosures.

Financial institutions will have to provide the disclosures mentioned in 8.2 above in addition to the disclosures required by Sections 11 and 12. These disclosures would apply to the individual financial statements of a financial institution and the consolidated financial statements of a group containing a financial institution, when the financial instruments held by the financial institution are material to the group. This would apply regardless of whether the principal activity of the group is being a financial institution or not and is only required of financial instruments held by the financial institution entities within the group. *[FRS 102.34.17]*. These disclosures are similar to the disclosures required by FRS 29. Therefore, those financial institutions that have previously not applied either FRS 13 or FRS 29 will see a significant increase in disclosures.

Chapter 8

9   DEBT VERSUS EQUITY

9.1   Introduction

The classification of issued instruments as either debt or equity is one area where the impact of adopting FRS 102 will be the same, irrespective of whether an entity is currently applying FRS 26 or not. This is because the classification requirements are contained in FRS 25, which is mandatory for all UK entities, unlike FRS 26 and is equivalent to IAS 32.

9.2   Scope and definitions

The scope of Section 22 is similar to FRS 25 and that of section 11 of FRS 102, as set out at 3.2 above. Equity is defined within Section 22 as the residual interest in the assets of an entity after deducting all its liabilities. This is identical to the definition in FRS 25, but Section 22 elaborates on it by stating that equity includes investments by the owners plus retained profits, or minus losses. *[FRS 102.22.3]*.

A financial liability is:

(a)   a contractual obligation:

  (i)   to deliver cash or another financial asset to another entity; or

  (ii)   to exchange financial assets or financial liabilities with another entity under conditions that are potentially unfavourable to the entity; or

(b)   a contract that will or may be settled in the entity's own equity instruments and:

  (i)   under which the entity is or may be obliged to deliver a variable number of the entity's own equity instruments; or

  (ii)   which will or may be settled other than by the exchange of a fixed amount of cash or another financial asset for a fixed number of the entity's own equity instruments. For this purpose, the entity's own equity instruments do not include instruments that are themselves contracts for the future receipt or delivery of the entity's own equity instruments. *[FRS 102.22.3]*.

The basic premise of FRS 102 is similar to FRS 25 in the sense that an instrument can only be classified as equity under FRS 102 if the issuer has an unconditional right to avoid delivering cash or another financial instrument, or, if it is settled through own equity instruments, it is an exchange of a fixed amount of cash for a fixed number of the entity's own equity instruments. In all other cases, it would be classified as a financial liability.

9.3   Key differences with FRS 25/IAS 32

Under FRS 25, contracts that contain an obligation or even a potential obligation for an entity to pay cash or another financial asset to purchase its own equity instruments will give rise to a liability for the present value of the redemption amount (e.g. the present value of the forward repurchase price or option exercise price). *[FRS 25.23]*. Section 22 does not contain this requirement and in such cases, the obligation/potential obligation would presumably meet the definition of a derivative that must be measured at fair value through profit or loss. This could result in a potentially significant measurement difference.

For example, if a listed entity grants a written put option to a counterparty to sell the entity's own shares back to it for a fixed price at some point in the future, under FRS 25, the listed entity will need to measure that potential obligation at the present value of that fixed price. There would be a corresponding reduction in recorded equity. This is regardless of whether that option is likely to be exercised by the counterparty, In contrast, under FRS 102, the option would be treated as a derivative, measured at fair value through profit or loss, with no reduction in recorded equity.

A second difference is that FRS 25 clarifies that rights, options or warrants to acquire a fixed number of the entity's own equity instruments for a fixed amount of any currency are equity instruments if the entity offers those instruments *pro rata* to all of its existing owners of the same class of its own non-derivative equity instruments. *[FRS 25.11]*. FRS 102 does not explicitly address this point.

9.4   Contingent settlement provisions

Some financial instruments contain contingent settlement provisions whereby settlement is dependent on the occurrence or non-occurrence of uncertain future events beyond the control of the issuer and the holder and the issuer does not have the unconditional right to avoid settling in cash or by delivery of another financial asset when such an event happens. This could be the case where settlement is dependent on events such as amendments to tax legislation, regulatory requirements or changes in interest rates or price indices, or even changes in the credit rating of the issuer. These are events which the issuer and the holder cannot prevent from happening; consequently, such instruments shall be classified as financial liabilities unless:

- the part of the contingent settlement provision that could require settlement in cash or another financial asset is not *genuine*;

- the issuer can be required to settle the obligation in cash or another financial asset only in the event of liquidation of the issuer; or

- the instrument can be put by the holder back to the issuer, or else contains obligations arising only on liquidation and, in each case, meet certain criteria, described in 9.4.1 below. *[FRS 102.22.3A]*.

FRS 102 does not contain any guidance as to what constitutes a contingent settlement provision that is 'not genuine'. The limited guidance within FRS 25 states that 'not genuine' refers to the occurrence of an event that is extremely rare, highly abnormal or very unlikely to occur. *[FRS 25.AG 28]*. Terms that are contained within a contract are normally intended to have a commercial effect, thus, a high hurdle should apply to demonstrate that a specific term is not genuine. Nevertheless, individual facts and circumstances would need to be evaluated on a case by case basis.

In respect of the second bullet, a contingent settlement provision that is only effective on liquidation of the issuer may be ignored and the instrument would be treated as an equity instrument, as different rights and obligations apply in the event

Chapter 8

of liquidation. However, if the instrument provides for settlement on the occurrence of events that could lead to liquidation such as insolvency, the instrument would be a financial liability.

9.4.1   *Puttable instruments*

'Puttable instruments' are defined as financial instruments that give the holder the right to sell that instrument back to the issuer for cash or another financial asset, or is automatically redeemed or repurchased by the issuer on the occurrence of an uncertain future event or the death or retirement of the instrument holder. *[FRS 102.22.4(a)]*. In most cases, puttable instruments would meet the definition of a financial liability, such as a corporate bond that provides the holder with the option to require the issuer to redeem the instrument for cash or another financial asset at a future date. The option held by the holder means that the issuer does not have an unconditional right to avoid delivering cash, thus, the puttable instrument is a financial liability. However, if a puttable instrument meets *all* the five criteria stated below, it will, as an exception, be classified as an equity instrument:

- the instrument entitles the holder to a *pro rata* share of an entity's net assets on liquidation;

- the instrument is in the class of instrument that is most subordinate to all other classes of instruments. (i.e. it is the most junior class of instrument in the hierarchy to be applied if the entity were to be liquidated);

- all puttable instruments in the most subordinate class have identical features;

- apart from the put feature, the instrument does not contain any other liability features and is not a contract that will or may be settled in the entity's own equity instruments, as set out in 9.2 above; and

- the total expected cash flows attributable to the instrument over the instrument's life are based substantially on the profit or loss, the change in the recognised net assets or the change in the fair value of the recognised and unrecognised net assets of the entity over the instrument's life (excluding any effects of the instrument). *[FRS 102.22.4(a)]*. That is, the instrument's attributable cash flows should be based on the profit or loss or change in the entity's net assets in its entirety but should not include any cash flows directly attributable to the instrument itself.

If all the criteria mentioned above are met, a puttable instrument will be classified by exception as an equity instrument. These criteria are intended to prevent an inappropriate classification of such instruments in the financial statements of entities such as some open-ended mutual funds, unit trusts, limited life entities, partnerships and co-operative entities.

A puttable instrument is also classified as equity if, when the put option is exercised, the holder receives a pro rate share of the net assets of the entity. *[FRS 102.22.5(b)]*.

A puttable instrument classified as equity in a subsidiary's financial statements is classified as a liability in the consolidated financial statements of its parent, as they will not be the most subordinate instrument issued by the consolidated group. *[FRS 102.22.5(d)]*.

We would not expect many FRS 102 adopters to have issued puttable instruments. Thus, we shall not elaborate upon them any further in this book, but further information can be found in EY International GAAP 2015.

9.4.2 *Instruments that contain obligations only on liquidation*

Financial instruments, or components of instruments, that are subordinate to all other classes of instruments are classified as equity if they impose on the entity an obligation to deliver to another party a *pro rata* share of the net assets of the entity, only on liquidation. *[FRS 102.22.4(b)]*. This obligation arises because liquidation is either certain to occur and beyond the control of the entity (e.g. a limited life entity) or is not certain to occur but the holder of the instrument has the option to enforce liquidation. In these cases, the instrument is classified as equity. However, if the distribution of net assets on liquidation to the holder of such an instrument is subject to a maximum amount (a ceiling), the instrument would be classified as a financial liability. *[FRS 102.22.5(a)]*. Similar to the exception for certain puttable instruments, further information can be found in EY International GAAP 2015.

9.5 Other instruments

Section 22 also includes examples of other financial instruments that may be classified as liability or equity. Among the examples of financial liabilities are instruments that oblige the issuer to make payments to the holder before liquidation (e.g. a mandatory dividend) and preference shares that provide for mandatory redemption by the issuer for a fixed or determinable amount at a fixed or determinable future date, or the holder has the right to require the issuer to redeem the instrument at or after a particular date for a fixed or determinable amount. *[FRS 102.22.5(c), (e)]*. These are financial liabilities as there is a contractual obligation to make the said payments and the issuer has no discretion to avoid them.

On the other hand, members' shares in co-operative entities are classified as equity if the entity has an unconditional right to refuse redemption of the members' shares or the redemption is unconditionally prohibited by local law, regulation or the entity's governing charter. *[FRS 102.22.6]*.

9.6 Accounting recognition requirements for equity instruments

Unlike FRS 25, FRS 102 contains accounting recognition criteria for equity instruments, including options and warrants over equity instruments. Section 22 states that an entity shall recognise the issue of shares or other equity instruments as equity when it issues those instruments and another party is obliged to provide cash or other resources to the entity in exchange for those instruments. If the entity receives cash before the equity instruments are issued and it cannot be required to repay the cash, the entity should recognise an increase in equity for the consideration received. Conversely, if the equity instruments are subscribed for, but have not been issued or called up, and the entity has not yet received the cash or other resources, the entity cannot recognise an increase in equity. *[FRS 102.22.7]*.

Equity instruments must initially be measured at the fair value of the cash or other resources received or receivable, net of direct costs of issuing the equity instruments.

Chapter 8

If payment is deferred and the time value of money is material, the initial measurement shall be on a present value basis. No guidance is provided in this context as to the appropriate discount rate, although the guidance on financing transactions set out in 4.3 above would be appropriate. This would require the use of a market rate of interest for the amount receivable. Transaction costs shall be deducted from equity, net of any related income tax benefit. *[FRS 102.22.8-9]*.

Exactly how the increase in equity arising on the issue of shares or other equity instruments is presented is determined by applicable laws. For instance, the nominal value of the shares may need to be presented separately from any premium received. *[FRS 102.22.10]*.

With the exception of the requirement regarding the treatment of transaction costs, the other FRS 102 requirements mentioned here are not explicitly dealt with in FRS 25, however, these requirements are unlikely to cause any change in practice.

9.7   Other topics

Section 22 also includes provisions that deal with the accounting for bonus issues of shares and share splits, convertible debt instruments, treasury shares and distributions to owners.

9.7.1   *Bonus issues and share splits*

Capitalisation or bonus issues of shares entail the issue of new shares to shareholders in proportion to their existing holdings. For example, an entity might give its shareholders one bonus share for every four shares held. The entity may utilise one of its existing reserves such as the share premium account, retained earnings or capital redemption reserve to issue the bonus shares. The relevant reserve is debited with the nominal value of the shares issued while issued share capital is credited with an equivalent amount, if the bonus shares meet the criteria to be accounted for as equity. *[FRS 102.22.12]*.

Another common transaction is a share or stock split, which involves dividing an entity's existing shares into multiple shares. For example, in a share split, shareholders may receive five additional shares for each share held and, in certain cases, the previously outstanding shares may be cancelled and replaced by the new shares. *[FRS 102.22.12]*.

Bonus issues and stock splits do not change total equity but these transactions must be permitted by an entity's articles of association as well as comply with provisions of the Companies Act 2006.

9.7.2   *Compound instruments*

Some issued financial instruments cannot be classified in their entirety as either an equity instrument or a financial liability. These instruments, which are subject to a single contract, are known as compound instruments. A typical example is a convertible bond, whereby the issuer is obligated to pay principal and interest but the holder also has an option to convert their holding into a fixed number of equity shares of the issuer. Consequently, from the issuer's perspective, the bond contains two components, a financial liability and an equity element. A convertible bond that allows for conversion into a variable number of shares would contain no equity element. Consequently, the entire liability would be recorded at fair value through profit or loss, as it would not be a basic debt instrument (see 4.2 above).

The proceeds from issuing a compound instrument must be allocated between the two components. To perform that allocation, the issuer must first calculate the liability component by computing the fair value of a similar bond that does not have the conversion option. In essence, the entity would need to work out the fair value of the bond assuming it had issued it without the option to convert to its own equity. See 4.4.5 above for further information on how to calculate fair value. Once the fair value of the liability is determined, the residual amount (i.e. the difference between the proceeds received and the fair value of the liability) is the equity element. This allocation should not be revised subsequently. Transaction costs arising from the instrument's issue are allocated to the liability and equity components on the basis of their relative fair values. The subsequent measurement of the liability component will depend on whether it meets the criteria to be accounted for as a basic financial instrument (i.e. amortised cost), if not, it has to be subsequently measured at fair value through profit or loss. *[FRS 102.22.13-15]*.

9.7.3 Treasury shares and distributions to owners

Treasury shares are equity instruments of an entity that have been issued and subsequently reacquired by the entity. When acquiring treasury shares, the entity must deduct from equity the fair value of the consideration given. No gain or loss shall be recognised in profit or loss arising from the purchase, sale, transfer or cancellation of treasury shares. *[FRS 102.22.16]*. Distributions to owners (i.e. holders of an entity's equity instruments) are accounted for as a reduction in equity. *[FRS 102.22.17]*.

The accounting requirements in respect of compound instruments, treasury shares and distributions to owners are consistent with FRS 25 and IAS 32, thus, we do not address them further in this book, but further information on them can be found in EY International GAAP 2015.

9.7.4 Non-controlling interest and transactions in shares of a consolidated subsidiary

Chapter 15 deals with business combinations and goodwill while Chapter 6 addresses the measurement and presentation of non-controlling interest. In the parent's consolidated accounts, a non-controlling interest is measured as the share of the subsidiary's net assets at fair value at the date of acquisition, adjusted for any changes in the subsidiary's net assets subsequent to acquisition, which are attributable to the non-controlling interest. It is presented within equity.

Where there is a change in the equity interests of the respective parties (i.e. parent and non-controlling interest) in the subsidiary without the parent losing control, for example, the parent's equity interest in the subsidiary increases from 60% to 65%, the non-controlling interest balance is re-measured to the parent's revised attributable share of the subsidiary's net assets. If a difference arises between the re-

Chapter 8

measurement of the non-controlling interest and the fair value of the consideration paid by the parent, any difference is recognised in equity through retained earnings, with no gain or loss recognised in profit or loss. There is no re-measurement of the subsidiary's carrying amounts of assets (including goodwill) or liabilities as result of this transaction. *[FRS 102.22.19].*

This method of accounting is consistent with IFRS but is different to previous UK GAAP. Under previous UK GAAP, when a parent increases its interest in a non-wholly owned subsidiary, the identifiable assets and liabilities of the subsidiary are revalued to fair value and goodwill is calculated on the increase in interest. On the other hand, when a parent reduces its interest in a subsidiary without losing control, any gain or loss on disposal is recognised in the consolidated profit and loss account.

10   SUMMARY OF GAAP DIFFERENCES

	FRS 102	*Previous UK GAAP*	*IFRS*
Classification and Measurement	Option to adopt IAS 39 or IFRS 9 or FRS 102. FRS 102 is a simplified version of IAS 39/IFRS 9: • Cost less impairment. • Amortised cost. • Fair value (through profit or loss only). • No concept of held for trading, thus, such instruments could theoretically be measured at amortised cost unless the fair value option is elected. • No concept of fair value through other comprehensive income.	Adoption of FRS 26: • Same as IAS 39 Non adoption of FRS 26: • Not specified unless covered by SSAP 20, industry SORPs, FRS 4 or Companies Act.	IAS 39: According to the classification criteria, financial assets and liabilities are measured at: • Cost less impairment. • Amortised cost. • Fair value through profit or loss. • Available for sale, at fair value through other comprehensive income.
Derivatives	No concept of embedded derivatives. Derivatives recognised and measured at fair value.	Adoption of FRS 26: • Same as IFRS. Non adoption of FRS 26: • No requirement to measure derivatives at fair value (non-FRS 26 adopters).	Derivatives and some embedded derivatives are recognised and measured at fair value.

Impairment	Incurred loss model with assessment of objective evidence of impairment until IFRS 9's expected loss model is finalised and incorporated into FRS 102. Difference in the collective provision vs IAS 39.	Adoption of FRS 26: • Same as IFRS. Non adoption of FRS 26: • Provision for permanent diminution in value (less guidance).	IAS 39: Incurred loss model with assessment of objective evidence of impairment. IFRS 9 is an expected loss model.
Derecognition	Similar principles to IFRS but less guidance. No concept of 'continuing involvement' unlike IAS 39/FRS 26.	Adoption of FRS 26: • Same as IFRS. Non adoption of FRS 26: • FRS 5 is similar but not exactly the same. • FRS 5 has the concept of linked presentation.	Derecognition (IAS 39/IFRS 9) • Complex rules.
Disclosures	Disclosures as set out in Sections 11 and 12 and even more if considered a financial institution (Section 34).	Non adoption of FRS 29 • Very limited disclosures unless scoped into FRS 13. Adoption of FRS 29 • Same as IFRS.	Extensive disclosures (IFRS 7 and IFRS 13).
Liabilities and equity	Similar principle to IFRS but less guidance. • No requirement to measure a minority put at the present value of the forward repurchase price.	Same as IFRS (IAS 32).	Liabilities and equity (IAS 32).
Hedged items – risk components	All items.	Non adoption of FRS 26: • No rules. Adoption of FRS 26 : • Same as IAS 39.	IAS 39: only for financial items.
Hedging instruments – Non-derivative financial assets or liabilities at FVTPL	Hedging based on simplified version of IFRS 9.	Non adoption of FRS 26: • No rules. Adoption of FRS 26 : • Same as IAS 39.	IAS 39: may be hedging instruments only for FX risks.
Retrospective effectiveness test	None.	Non adoption of FRS 26: • No rules. Adoption of FRS 26 : • Same as IAS 39.	IAS 39: 80%-125% test.
Quantitative prospective effectiveness test	Depends	Non adoption of FRS 26: • No rules. Adoption of FRS 26 • Same as IAS 39.	IAS 39: yes.

Chapter 8

Chapter 9

Inventories

Chapter 9

List of examples

Chapter 9   Inventories

1   INTRODUCTION

Section 13 of FRS 102 – *Inventories* addresses the measurement and disclosure requirements of for inventories, referred to as stocks under previous UK GAAP.

The principles of Section 13 are broadly consistent with IFRS and previous UK GAAP.

2   COMPARISON BETWEEN SECTION 13, PREVIOUS UK GAAP AND IFRS

The accounting for inventories under IFRS is addressed by IAS 2 – *Inventories*. The requirements under previous UK GAAP are contained in SSAP 9 – *Stocks and long-term contracts.*

Section 13, IFRS and previous UK GAAP all use the principle that the primary basis of accounting for inventories is cost unless the amount that the inventories are expected to realise is lower than cost. Where this is the case, the inventories are written down to that amount.

Generally under Section 13, IFRS and previous UK GAAP, the cost of inventories comprises all costs of purchase and costs of conversion based on normal levels of activity and other costs incurred in bringing inventories to their present location and condition.

All three accounting frameworks allow the use of costing methods, such as standard costing, provided they approximate to cost.

There are, however, some areas of potential difference between the three frameworks in accounting for inventories. These differences mainly arise where more specific requirements are contained within IFRS or previous UK GAAP than is provided under Section 13. These areas are summarised at 4 below.

Chapter 9

3   REQUIREMENTS OF SECTION 13 FOR INVENTORIES

3.1   Terms used in Section 13

The following terms are used in Section 13 with the meanings specified. *[FRS 102 Appendix I].*

Term	Definition
Asset	A resource controlled by the entity as a result of past events and from which future economic benefits are expected to flow to the entity.
Fair value	The amount for which an asset could be exchanged, a liability settled, or an equity instrument granted could be exchanged, between knowledgeable, willing parties in an arm's length transaction.
Inventories	Assets: (a) held for sale in the ordinary course of business; (b) in the process of production for such sale; or (c) in the form of materials or supplies to be consumed in the production process or in the rendering of services.
Inventories held for distribution at no or nominal consideration	Assets that are: (a) held for distribution at no or nominal consideration in the ordinary course of operations; (b) in the process of production for distribution at no or nominal consideration in the ordinary course of operations; or (c) in the form of material or supplies to be consumed in the production process or in the rendering of services at no or nominal consideration.
Non-exchange transaction	A transaction whereby an entity receives value from another entity without directly giving approximately equal value in exchange, or gives value to another entity without directly receiving approximately equal value in exchange.
Public benefit entity	An entity whose primary objective is to provide goods or services for the general public, community or social benefit and where any equity is provided with a view to supporting the entity's primary objectives rather than with a view to providing a financial return to equity providers, shareholders or members.
Public benefit entity group	A public benefit entity parent and all of its wholly-owned subsidiaries.
Qualifying asset	An asset that necessarily takes a substantial period of time to get ready for its intended use or sale.
Service potential	The economic utility of an asset, based on the total benefit expected to be derived by the entity from use (and/or through sale) of the asset.

3.2 Scope

Inventories are assets:

(a) held for sale in the ordinary course of business;

(b) in the process of production or sale; or

(c) in the form of materials or supplies to be consumed in the production process or in the rendering of services. *[FRS 102.13.1].*

Inventories can include all types of goods purchased and held for resale including, for example, merchandise purchased by a retailer. The term also encompasses finished goods produced, or work in progress being produced by the entity, and includes materials and supplies awaiting use in the production process. If the entity is a service provider, its inventories may be intangible (e.g. the costs of the service for which the entity has not yet recognised the related revenue).

Section 13 applies to all inventories, except:

(a) work in progress arising under construction contracts, including directly related service contracts (addressed in Section 23 – *Revenue* – see Chapter 18);

(b) financial instruments (addressed in Section 11 – *Basic Financial Instruments* and Section 12 – *Other Financial Instruments Issues* – see Chapter 8); and

(c) biological assets related to agricultural activity and agricultural produce at the point of harvest (addressed in Section 34 – *Specialised Activities* – see Chapter 29). *[FRS 102.13.2].*

In addition, the measurement provisions of Section 13 do not apply to inventories measured at fair value less costs to sell through profit and loss at each reporting date. *[FRS 102.13.3].* Although these inventories are scoped out of the measurement requirements of Section 13, the other requirements of Section 13, such as disclosure, continue to apply.

3.2.1 Scope issues

For entities operating in some industries, it may not always be clear whether certain assets fall in scope of Section 13 or are covered by another section of FRS 102. Scope issues that entities may encounter include:

classification of core inventories as property, plant and equipment or inventory. Core inventories arise in industries where certain processes or storage arrangements require a core of inventory to be present in the system at all times. For example, in order for a crude oil refining process to take place, the plant must contain a certain minimum quantity of oil which can only be taken out once the plant is abandoned; and

classification of broadcast rights as intangible assets or inventory.

These scope issues are discussed in EY International GAAP 2015 at Chapter 22.

Chapter 9

3.2.1.A   *Spare parts*

Many entities carry spare parts for items of property, plant and equipment. Section 17 – *Property, Plant and Equipment* – requires that spare parts and servicing equipment are usually carried in inventory and recognised in profit and loss as consumed. However, they should be classified as property, plant and equipment if:

(a)   an entity expects to use them during more than one period; or

(b)   they can be used only in connection with an item of property, plant and equipment. *[FRS 102.17.5]*.

3.2.1.B   *Real estate inventory held for short term sale*

Many real estate businesses develop and construct residential properties for sale, often consisting of several units. The strategy is to make a profit from the development and construction of the property rather than to make a profit in the long term from general price increases in the property market. The intention is to sell the property units as soon as possible following their construction, and is therefore in the ordinary course of the entity's business. When construction is complete it is not uncommon for individual property units to be leased at market rates to earn revenues to partly cover expenses such as interest, management fees and real estate taxes. Large-scale buyers of property, such as insurance companies, are often reluctant to buy unless tenants are *in situ*, as this assures immediate cash flows from the investment.

It is our view that if it is in the entity's ordinary course of business (supported by its strategy) to hold property for short-term sale rather than for long-term capital appreciation or rental income, the entire property (including the leased units) should be accounted for and presented as inventory. This will continue to be the case as long as it remains the intention to sell the property in the short term. Rent received should be included in other income as it does not represent a reduction in the cost of inventory.

Investment property is defined in Section 16 – *Investment Property* ('Section 16') as 'property held to earn rentals or for capital appreciation or both, rather than for use in the production or supply of goods or services or for administrative purposes; or for sale in the ordinary course of business.' *[FRS 102.16.2]*. Therefore in the case outlined above, the property does not meet the definition of investment property. Properties intended for sale in the ordinary course of business – no matter whether leased out or not – are outside the scope of Section 16.

The accounting for real estate inventory is discussed at EY International GAAP 2015, Chapter 22.

3.3   Measurement

Inventories in scope of the measurement provisions of Section 13 should be measured at the lower of cost and estimated selling price less costs to complete and sell. *[FRS 102.13.4]*.

3.3.1   What is included in the cost of inventories?

The cost of inventories should include all costs of purchase, costs of conversion and other costs incurred in bringing inventories to their present location and condition. *[FRS 102.13.5]*.

Other costs should be included in the cost of inventories only to the extent that they are incurred in bringing them into their present location and condition. *[FRS 102.13.11]*. For example, design costs for a special order for a particular customer may be included in inventory.

3.3.2   Costs of purchase of inventories

The cost of purchase of inventories comprises the purchase price, transport, handling and other costs directly attributable to the acquisition of finished goods, materials and services. It also includes import duties and other unrecoverable taxes. Trade discounts, rebates and other similar items should be deducted in arriving at the cost of purchase. *[FRS 102.13.6]*.

Entities sometimes purchase inventories on deferred settlement terms. In some cases, the arrangement contains an unstated financing element, for example, a difference between the purchase price for normal credit terms and the deferred settlement amount. In these cases, the difference is usually recognised as an interest expense over the period of the financing. It is not added to the cost of inventories unless the inventory is a qualifying asset under Section 25 – *Borrowing Costs* – and the entity adopts a policy of capitalising finance costs. *[FRS 102.13.7]*. Inventories manufactured over a short period of time are not qualifying assets. Only inventories produced in small quantities over a long time period of time are likely to be qualifying assets under Section 25. Qualifying assets are discussed further at Chapter 20.

3.3.3   Costs of conversion

The cost of conversion of inventories includes costs directly related to the units of production, such as direct labour. It also includes a systematic allocation of the fixed and variable production overheads that are incurred in converting materials into finished goods. Fixed production overheads are those indirect costs of production that remain relatively constant regardless of the volume of production, such as depreciation and maintenance of factory buildings and equipment, and the cost of factory management and administration. Variable production overheads are those indirect costs of production that vary directly, or nearly directly, with the volume of production, such as indirect materials and indirect labour. *[FRS 102.13.8]*. It must be remembered that the inclusion of overheads is not optional.

The allocation of fixed production overheads should be based on the normal capacity of the production facilities. Normal capacity is defined as 'the production expected to be achieved on average over a number of periods or seasons under normal circumstances, taking into account the loss of capacity resulting from planned maintenance.' While actual capacity may be used if it approximates to normal capacity, increased overheads may not be allocated to production as a result of low production or idle plant. Unallocated overheads must be recognised as an expense in the period in which they are incurred. In periods of abnormally high production, the amount of fixed overhead allocated to each unit of production is decreased, as otherwise inventories would be recorded at an amount in excess of cost. *[FRS 102.13.9]*.

The allocation of variable production overheads should be based on the actual use of the production facilities in the period. *[FRS 102.13.9]*.

Some entities may have an obligation to dismantle, remove and restore a production site at some future date. For example, mining companies may have obligations to decommission mines and rehabilitate the impacted area on closure of the mine. Although provisions for such obligations are not specifically addressed by Section 21 – *Provisions and Contingencies* ('Section 21'), the recognition criteria within Section 21 may require entities to record a provision for these obligations. If the obligation arises as a result of production of inventory during the period, costs in respect of the obligation incurred during the period (measured in accordance with Section 21) should be included within production overheads to be allocated to the cost of inventories. *[FRS 102.13.8A]*. The estimated costs to dismantle, remove and restore a site which arise either when an item of property, plant or equipment is acquired or as a consequence of having used the property, plant or equipment for purposes other than to produce inventories during the period should be recognised as part of the cost of that item of property, plant and equipment. *[FRS 102.17.10]*.

Example 9.1:   Inclusion of costs for obligations within production overheads

An entity operates an offshore oilfield where its licensing agreement requires it to remove the oil rig at the end of production and restore the seabed. Ninety per cent of the eventual costs relate to the removal of the oil rig and restoration of damage caused by building it. Ten per cent of the eventual costs arise from the extraction of oil. The ten per cent of costs that arise through the extraction of oil are recognised as a liability when the oil is extracted. The amount of the additional provision recognised each year as a result of the extraction of oil should be part of the production overheads to be allocated to the cost of inventory. The ninety percent of costs that relate to the removal of the oil rig and restoration of damage caused by building it would be recognised as part of the cost of the oil rig.

3.3.4   *Costs excluded from inventories*

The following costs should not be included in the cost of inventories:

(a)   abnormal amounts of wasted materials, labour or other production costs;

(b)   storage costs, unless those costs are necessary during the production process before a further production stage;

(c)   administrative overheads that do not contribute to bringing inventories to their present location and condition; and

(d)   selling costs. *[FRS 102.13.13]*.

These costs should be recognised as expenses in the period in which they are incurred.

3.3.5   *Storage and distribution costs*

Storage costs are not permitted as part of the cost of inventories unless they are necessary in the production process. This appears to prohibit including the costs of the warehouse and the overheads of a retail outlet as part of inventory, as neither of these is a prelude to a further production stage.

When it is necessary to store raw materials or work in progress prior to a further processing or manufacturing stage, the cost of such storage should be included in production overheads. For example, it would appear reasonable to allow the costs of storing maturing stocks, such as cheese, wine or whisky, in the cost of production.

Although distribution costs in the general sense are obviously a cost of bringing an item to its present location, company law prohibits them from being added to the cost of stock. However, the Regulations do not define distribution costs. *[1 Sch 27(4)].* The question therefore arises as to whether costs of transporting inventory from one location to another are eligible.

Costs of distribution to the customer are not allowed; they are selling costs and FRS 102 prohibits their inclusion in the carrying value of inventory. It therefore seems probable that distribution costs of inventory whose production process is complete should not normally be included in its carrying value.

If the inventory is transferred from one of the entity's storage facilities to another and the condition of the inventory is not changed at either location, none of the warehousing costs should be included in inventory costs. The same argument appears to preclude transportation costs between the two storage facilities being included in inventory costs.

For large retailers, such as supermarkets, transport and logistics are essential to their ability to move goods from central distribution centres to initial points of sale at a particular location in an appropriate condition. It therefore seems reasonable to conclude that such costs are an essential part of the production process and can be included in the cost of inventory.

3.3.6 General and administrative overheads

FRS 102 specifically prohibits administrative overheads that do not contribute to bringing inventories to their present location and condition from being included in the cost of inventories. *[FRS 102.13.13(c)].* Costs and overheads that do contribute should be included in costs of conversion. There is a judgement to be made about such matters, as on a very wide interpretation, any department in an entity could be considered to make a contribution to inventories. For example, the accounts department will normally support the following functions:

(a) production – by paying direct and indirect production wages and salaries, by controlling purchases and related payments, and by preparing periodic financial statements for the production units;

(b) marketing and distribution – by analysing sales and by controlling the sales ledger; and

(c) general administration – by preparing management accounts and annual financial statements and budgets, by controlling cash resources and by planning investments.

Only those costs of the accounts department that can be reasonably allocated to the production function can be included in the cost of conversion. Part of the management and overhead costs of a large retailer's logistical department may be included in cost if it relates to bringing the inventory to its present location and condition. These types of cost are unlikely to be material in the context of the inventory total held by organisations. In our view, an entity wishing to include a material amount of overhead of a borderline nature must ensure it can sensibly justify its inclusion under the provisions of FRS 102 by presenting an analysis of the function and its contribution to the production process similar to the above.

3.3.7   Borrowing costs

In limited circumstances, borrowing costs may be included in the cost of inventories. Section 25 allows entities to adopt an accounting policy of capitalising borrowing costs that are directly attributable to the acquisition, construction or production of a qualifying asset as part of the cost of that asset. *[FRS 102.25.2]*. Qualifying assets are assets that necessarily take a substantial period of time to get ready for their intended use or sale, and may include inventories. *[FRS 102 Appendix I]*. Inventories that are manufactured in large quantities on a repetitive basis are unlikely to meet the definition of qualifying assets. However, any manufacturer that produces small quantities of inventories over a long period of time will have an accounting policy choice as to whether to include borrowing costs in the cost of these inventories. This is discussed further at Chapter 20.

3.3.8   Inventories acquired through a non-exchange transaction

Entities may sometimes enter into non-exchange transactions whereby the entity gives value to or receives value from another entity without directly receiving or giving approximately equal value in exchange. *[FRS 102 Appendix I]*.

Where inventories are acquired through a non-exchange transaction, their cost should be measured at their fair value as at the date of acquisition. *[FRS 102.13.5A]*. For entities other than public benefit entities, the fair value of inventories acquired through a non-exchange transaction should be determined by reference to the guidance in Section 11, which is discussed at Chapter 8.

For public benefit entities and entities within a public benefit entity group, Section 34 and the related Appendix B provide additional guidance on non-exchange transactions. As part of their normal business operations, public benefit entities may receive donations of cash, goods and services, and legacies which would meet the definition of non-exchange transactions. Public benefit entities and entities within a public benefit entity group should recognise inventories acquired through a non-exchange transaction at fair value only when required by Section 34. *[FRS 102.13.5A]*. Accounting for non-exchange transactions by public benefit entities and entities within a public benefit entity group is discussed further at Chapter 29.

3.3.9   Joint products and by-products

A production process may result in more than one product being produced simultaneously, for example when joint products are produced or where there is a main product and a by-product. If the costs of raw materials or converting each product are not separately identifiable, they should be allocated between the products on a rational and consistent basis. This may be, for example, based on the relative sales value of each of the products, either at the stage in the production process when the products become separately identifiable, or once production is complete. If the value of the by-product is immaterial, as is often the case, it should be measured at selling price less costs to complete and sell, with this amount then deducted from the cost of the main product. *[FRS 102.13.10]*.

3.3.10   Service providers

FRS 102 deals specifically with the inventories of service providers – effectively their work in progress. For this type of business, FRS 102 requires the labour and other costs of personnel directly engaged in providing the service, including supervisory personnel and attributable overheads, to be included in the costs of inventories. However, labour and other costs relating to sales and general administrative personnel must be expensed as incurred. Inventories should not include profit margins or non-attributable overheads. *[FRS 102.13.14]*.

As discussed at 3.3.3 above, FRS 102 requires attributable overheads to be allocated to the cost of inventories based on normal levels of capacity. Determining a normal level of activity may be difficult in the context of service industries where the 'inventory' is intangible and based on work performed for customers that has not yet been recognised as income. Entities must take care to establish an appropriate benchmark to avoid the distortions that could occur if overheads were attributed on the basis of actual 'output'.

3.3.11   Inventories held for distribution at no or nominal consideration

Inventories held for distribution at no or nominal consideration includes items such as advertising and promotional material, and also items that may be distributed to beneficiaries by public benefit entities. *[FRS 102.A4.36]*.

FRS 102 requires inventories held for distribution at no or nominal consideration to be measured at cost adjusted, when applicable, for any loss of service potential. *[FRS 102.13.4A]*.

IFRS requires advertising and promotional activities to be expensed as incurred, unless the entity has paid in advance for advertising goods or services that have not yet been made available to the entity, in which case a prepayment asset is recognised. *[IAS 38.69-90]*. In contrast, FRS 102 requires advertising and promotional material to be carried at inventory at cost adjusted, where applicable, for any loss of service potential. FRS 102 provides no further guidance on how, or at what unit of account, service potential should be measured. It does not specify whether this should be at the individual asset level (e.g. the extent to which an individual catalogue is expected to generate future revenue for the entity) or based on a class of promotional material (e.g. the extent to which all catalogues printed for a particular year / season are expected to generate future revenue for the entity). In our view, an entity wishing to recognise a material inventory balance for advertising and promotional expenditure must ensure that it can sensibly justify how the entity will derive future benefit from the use of the materials.

The carrying amount of inventories held for distribution at no or nominal consideration should be recognised as an expense when the inventories are distributed. *[FRS 102.13.20A]*.

Chapter 9

3.3.12   *Agricultural produce harvested from biological assets*

Inventories comprising agricultural produce that an entity has harvested from its biological assets should be measured on initial recognition, at the point of harvest, at either:

- their fair value less estimated costs to sell; or
- the lower of cost and estimated selling price less costs to complete and sell.

For the purposes of applying Section 13, this amount becomes the cost of the inventories at that date. *[FRS 102.13.15]*.

3.3.13   *Cost measurement methods*

FRS 102 allows the use of standard costing methods, the retail method or most recent purchase price for measuring the cost of inventories if the result approximates cost. *[FRS 102.13.16]*.

Standard costs should take into account normal levels of materials and supplies, labour, efficiency and capital utilisation. They must be reviewed regularly and revised where necessary.

The retail method measures cost by reducing the sales value of the inventory by the appropriate percentage gross margin. This method is typically used in businesses with high volumes of various line items of inventory, where similar marks-ups are applied to ranges of inventory items or groups of items. It may be unnecessarily time-consuming to determine the cost of the period-end inventory on a conventional basis. Consequently, the most practical method of determining period-end inventory may be to record inventory on hand at selling prices, and then convert it to cost by removing the normal mark-up.

A judgemental area in applying the retail method is in determining the margin to be removed from the selling price of inventory in order to convert it back to cost. The percentage has to take account of circumstances in which inventories have been marked down to below original selling price. Adjustments have to be made to eliminate the effect of these markdowns so as to prevent any item of inventory being valued at less than both its cost and its net realisable value. In practice, however, entities that use the retail method apply a gross profit margin computed on an average basis appropriate for departments and/or ranges, rather than applying specific mark-up percentages.

As noted above, FRS 102 also allows the use of the most recent purchase price as a cost measurement method. This method arrives at the cost of stock by applying the latest purchase price to the total number of units in stock. Whilst IAS 2 is silent on the use of this methodology, SSAP 9 under previous UK GAAP comments that this method is, in principal, unacceptable. This is because the most recent purchase price is not necessarily the same as actual cost and, in times of rising prices, will result in the taking of a profit which has not been realised. *[SSAP 9.Appendix 1.13]*. In practice, the use of the most recent purchase price is not a common method of measuring the cost of inventory. Where it is used, care should be taken to ensure that the result does approximate to the actual cost of inventories.

Items of inventory that are not interchangeable (i.e. where one item of inventory cannot easily be replaced with another item of inventory held by the entity) and goods or services produced and segregated for specific projects should have their costs specifically identified. *[FRS 102.13.17]*. These costs should be matched with the goods or services physically sold. Due to the clerical effort required, this is likely to be feasible only where there are relatively few high value items being bought or produced. Consequently, it would normally be used where inventory comprised items such as antiques, jewellery and vehicles in the hands of dealers.

When inventory comprises a large number of ordinarily interchangeable items, FRS 102 requires inventory to be measured using either a first-in, first-out (FIFO) or a weighted average cost formula. *[FRS 102.13.18]*. The FIFO method assumes that when inventories are sold or used in a production process, the oldest are sold or used first. Consequently, the balance of inventory on hand at any point represents the most recent purchases or production. The weighted average method involves the computation of an average unit cost by dividing the total cost of units by the total number of units. The average unit cost then has to be revised with every receipt of inventory, or at the end of predetermined periods. In practice, where it is not possible to value inventory on an actual costs basis, the FIFO method is generally used. However, the weighted average method is widely used in computerised inventory systems. In times of low inflation, or where inventory turnover is relatively quick, the FIFO and weighted average methods give similar results.

The last-in, first-out (LIFO) method of measuring the cost of inventory is not permitted by FRS 102. *[FRS 102.13.18]*. The LIFO method assumes that when inventories are sold or used in a production process, the most recent purchases are sold or used first. This method is an attempt to match current costs with current revenues so that the profit and loss account excludes the effects of holding gains. However, this results in inventories being stated on balance sheet at amounts which may bear little or no relationship to recent cost levels.

FRS 102 makes it clear that the same cost formula should be used for all inventories having a similar nature and use to the entity. However, different cost formulas may be justified for inventories with a different nature or use. *[FRS 102.13.18]*.

3.3.14 Additional company law considerations

As an alternative to the historical cost accounting rules set out above, the Regulations allow companies to record inventories at current cost. *[1 Sch 32(5)]*. This treatment is rarely seen in practice and is not generally permitted by FRS 102.

In addition, company law allows that where materials and consumables inventories are of a kind that are constantly being replaced they may be recorded at a fixed quantity and value if; *[1 Sch 26]*

- their overall value is not material to the company; and
- their quality, value and composition are not subject to material variation.

Chapter 9

3.4   Impairment of inventories

In accordance with the requirements of Section 27 – *Impairment of Assets*, entities should assess inventories for impairment at the end of each reporting period. Inventories are impaired if their carrying value exceeds their selling price less costs to complete and sell. Inventories may become impaired due to damage, obsolescence or declining selling prices. *[FRS 102.13.19]*. Where inventories are impaired, the carrying amount should be written down to selling price less costs to complete and sell. The reduction in carrying value is an impairment loss and should be recognised immediately in profit or loss. *[FRS 102.27.2]*.

Assessing inventories for impairment should normally be done on an item-by-item basis. However, in many circumstances it will be impracticable to determine the selling price less costs to complete and sell on this basis. Where this is the case, items of inventory may be grouped. This may be the case for items of inventory relating to the same product line that have similar purposes or end uses and are produced or marketed in the same geographical area, and cannot be practicably evaluated separately from other items in that product line. *[FRS 102.27.3]*.

3.4.1   *Selling price less costs to complete and sell*

Section 32 – *Events after the End of the Reporting Period* – states that 'the sale of inventories after the end of a reporting period may give evidence about their selling price at the end of the reporting period for the purpose of assessing impairment at that date.' *[FRS 102.32.5(b)(ii)]*. Events that have impacted selling prices after the end of the reporting period, such as damage to inventories as a result of a warehouse fire post year end, would not be relevant to the assessment of impairment at end of the reporting period. Other than this, FRS 102 gives no guidance on how to determine selling price or what costs should be included when assessing costs to complete and sell.

The requirement to measure inventories at the lower of cost and selling price less costs to complete and sell under FRS 102 is similar to the requirements under previous UK GAAP and IFRS to carry inventories at the lower of cost and net realisable value. Both IFRS and previous UK GAAP define net realisable value and provide guidance on determining net realisable value.

Previous UK GAAP defines net realisable value as the 'actual or estimated selling price (net of trade but before settlement discounts) less:

(a)   all further costs to completion; and

(b)   all costs to be incurred in marketing, selling and distribution'. *[SSAP 9.21]*.

IFRS defines net realisable value as 'the estimated selling price in the ordinary course of business less the estimated costs of completion and the estimated costs necessary to make the sale.' *[IAS 2.6]*.

Both previous UK GAAP and IFRS are explicit that materials and other supplies held for use in the production of inventories are not written down below cost if the final product in which they are to be used is expected to be sold at or above cost. Whilst this is not explicit in FRS 102, we consider that this is consistent with the measurement principle of FRS 102. As such, we would not expect a whisky distiller, for example, to write down an inventory of grain because of a fall in the grain price, so long as it expected to sell the whisky at a price sufficient to recover cost. Conversely, if a provision is required in respect of finished goods, then work in progress and raw materials should also be reviewed to see if any further provision is required. This is explicitly stated within previous UK GAAP, *[SSAP 9.17]*, and we consider this also appropriate under FRS 102.

In estimating net realisable value, IFRS requires that entities should take into consideration the purpose for which inventory is held. For example, the net realisable value of inventory held to satisfy firm sales contracts is based on that contract price. *[IAS 2.31]*. This reflects the fact that net realisable value, unlike fair value, is an entity specific value. In our view, selling price less costs to complete and sell is also an entity specific measure intended to reflect the amount that the entity actually expects to make from selling particular inventories.

In our view, costs to complete and sell should comprise only direct and incremental costs to complete and sell the inventory and should not include any profit margin on these activities. They should also not include overheads or the costs of the distribution channel, such as shops, since these costs will be incurred regardless of whether or not any sale of this inventory actually takes place. The only situation in which the cost of a shop might be considered to be included in these selling costs might be when one shop is entirely dedicated to selling impaired goods.

Given the consistent principles between previous UK GAAP, IFRS and FRS 102 with regards the impairment of inventories, we expect that many entities adopting FRS 102 from either previous UK GAAP or from IFRS may use existing accounting policies for determining net realisable value in order to estimate selling price less costs to complete and sell. In our view, whilst previous UK GAAP and IFRS provide more guidance then FRS 102 in this area, the guidance within both previous UK GAAP and IFRS is not inconsistent with the principle of FRS 102 that inventories be held at the lower of cost and estimated selling price less costs to complete and sell.

3.4.2   *Reversal of impairment of inventory*

As noted in 3.4 above, FRS 102 requires entities to assess inventories for impairment at the end of each reporting period. When the circumstances that previously caused inventories to be written down no longer exist, or when there is clear evidence of an increase in selling price less costs to complete and sell because of changed economic circumstances, the amount of the write down is reversed. The amount of the reversal cannot be greater than the amount of the original write down. This means that the new carrying amount of inventories following the reversal of an impairment will be the lower of its cost and the revised selling price less costs to complete and sell. *[FRS 102.27.4]*.

3.5   Recognition of inventory in profit or loss

When inventories are sold, the carrying amount of those inventories should be recognised as an expense in the period in which the related revenue is recognised. *[FRS 102.13.20]*.

However, some inventories go into the creation of another asset, such as self-constructed property, plant or equipment. In this case, the inventories form part of the cost of the other asset and are accounted for subsequently in accordance with the section of FRS 102 relevant to that asset type. *[FRS 102.13.21]*.

Chapter 9

Any impairment loss on inventory should be recognised immediately as an expense in profit or loss. *[FRS 102.27.2]*.

The carrying amount of inventories held for distribution at no or nominal consideration (as discussed at 3.3.11 above) is recognised as an expense when the inventories are distributed. *[FRS 102.13.20A]*.

3.6   Presentation and disclosure

3.6.1   *Presentation of inventories*

Entities are required by Schedule 1 of the Regulations to present inventories on the face of the balance sheet. Inventories should be further analysed, either on the face of the balance sheet or within the notes to the accounts, into:

- Raw materials and consumables;
- Work in progress;
- Finished goods and goods for resale; and
- Payments on account.

The classifications used in the disaggregation may be adapted dependent upon the nature of the company's business. *[1 Sch 4(1)]*. In practice, most companies present the disaggregation as a note to the financial statements.

3.6.2   *Disclosure of inventories*

FRS 102 requires an entity to disclose the following:

(a)   the accounting policies adopted in measuring inventories, including the cost formula used;

(b)   the total carrying amount of inventories and the carrying amount in classifications appropriate to the entity;

(c)   the amount of inventories recognised as an expense during the period;

(d)   impairment losses recognised or reversed in profit or loss; and

(e)   the total carrying amount of inventories pledged as security for liabilities. *[FRS 102.13.22]*.

These disclosures requirements are similar to those required by IFRS, although IAS 2 also contains additional disclosure requirements not replicated in Section 13. Disclosure (d) above requires entities to disclosure impairment losses on inventories recognised or reversed in profit or loss. This disclosure is not required under previous UK GAAP.

3.6.2.A   *Additional Company Law disclosures*

The Regulations includes the following additional disclosure requirements with respect to inventories:

- If finance costs are included in the cost of inventory, this fact, along with the amount included; *[1 Sch 27(3)]*
- For large and medium companies where a costing method (such as FIFO, LIFO, Weighted average price or similar) has been applied, the difference

between carrying value and replacement cost of inventories where this is material. This may be determined by reference to the most recent purchase or production cost before the balance sheet date if this is considered by the directors of the company to give a more appropriate comparison; *[1 Sch 28(3)]* and

- Where there has been a departure from the historical cost convention, the fact that this is the case, the balances affected and the basis of valuation adopted. *[1 Sch 34]*.

4 SUMMARY OF GAAP DIFFERENCES

	FRS 102	Previous UK GAAP	IFRS
Scope	Section 13 applies to inventories other than work in progress under construction contracts, financial instruments and biological assets related to agricultural activity and agricultural produce at the point of harvest. The measurement rules of Section 13 also exclude inventories measured at fair value less costs to sell through profit or loss. See 3.2 above.	SSAP 9 covers both stocks and long-term contracts. There are no specific scope exclusions.	Similar to FRS 102 although there is a specific exclusion for commodity broker-dealers who measure inventories at fair value through profit or loss rather than a general exclusion for inventories measured in this way.
Classification of spare parts and servicing equipment	Usually carried in inventory and recognised in profit or loss as consumed. Major spare parts and stand-by equipment may qualify as property, plant and equipment if certain conditions are met. See 3.2.1.A above.	No specific guidance. Practice varies, with some entities capitalising these assets as tangible fixed assets and others treating them as stock.	Treated as inventory unless meets the definition of property, plant and equipment.
Measurement of inventory	Inventories are measured at the lower of cost and estimated selling price less costs to complete and sell. Section 13 provides prescriptive guidance on what may be and what should not be included in the cost of inventory. See 3.3 above.	Similar to FRS 102.	Similar to FRS 102, although borrowing costs must be capitalised if inventories meet the definition of qualifying assets.

Chapter 9

	FRS 102	Previous UK GAAP	IFRS
Impairment of inventory	Provides limited guidance on assessing estimated selling price less costs to complete and sell. See 3.4 above.	Refers to 'net realisable value' rather than 'estimated selling price less costs to complete and sell' and provides more guidance than FRS 102 on the impairment of inventories. However, it is unlikely that a GAAP difference would arise in practice.	Refers to 'net realisable value' rather than 'estimates selling price less costs to complete and sell' and provides substantial guidance on the identification of net realisable value. However, it is unlikely that a GAAP difference would arise in practice.
Inventory purchased on deferred payment terms	If the inventory is a qualifying asset and the entity adopts a policy of capitalising borrowing costs, the interest expense should be added to the cost of inventory. See 3.3.2 above.	No specific guidance, therefore, practice varies. Differences may arise where the period of payment deferral and / or the amount of inventories purchased are significant.	If the inventory is a qualifying asset, the interest expense must be added to the cost of inventory.
Inventories of a service provider	Provides specific guidance on measuring inventories of a service provider. See 3.3.10 above.	No specific guidance on inventories of service providers.	Same as FRS 102.
Inventories held for distribution at no or nominal consideration	These inventories should be measured at cost adjusted, where applicable, for any loss of service potential. The carrying amount of those inventories should be recognised as an expense when they are distributed. See 3.3.11 above.	No general guidance on inventories held for distribution at no or nominal consideration.	No general guidance on inventories held for distribution at no or nominal consideration.
Advertising and promotional expenditure	May meet the definition of 'inventories held for distribution at no or nominal consideration'. Advertising and promotional material could therefore be recognised as inventory. See 3.3.11 above.	Practice varies.	IAS 38 – *Intangible Assets* – requires the cost of advertising and promotional material, such as mail order catalogues, to be recognised as an expense once the entity gains access to those materials. A GAAP difference may therefore arise.

	FRS 102	*Previous UK GAAP*	*IFRS*
Inventories acquired through non exchange transactions	Where an entity receives inventories without giving approximately equal value in exchange, the cost of the inventories should be measured as their fair value at the date of acquisition. See 3.3.8 above.	SSAP 9 provides no specific guidance on inventories that are acquired through a non-exchange transaction.	IFRS provides no specific guidance on inventories that are acquired through a non-exchange transaction.
Disclosures	See 2.6 above.	Similar requirements. FRS 102 requires some additional disclosures.	IAS 2 requires some additional disclosures beyond those required by FRS 102. Company law disclosures are not required by entities reporting under IFRS.

Chapter 9

Chapter 10

Investments in associates

Chapter 10

List of examples

Chapter 10   Investments in associates

1   INTRODUCTION

FRS 102 Section 14 – *Investments in Associates* – focuses on the accounting for associates in consolidated financial statements and for investments in associates in the individual financial statements of an investor that is not a parent.

2   COMPARISON BETWEEN SECTION 14, PREVIOUS UK GAAP AND IFRS

There are differences between the accounting and disclosure requirements in Section 14 compared to previous UK GAAP (FRS 9 – *Associates and joint ventures*) and IFRS (IAS 28 – *Investments in Associates and Joint Ventures*). The key ones are discussed at 2.1 and 2.2 below respectively and differences are summarised in section 6 of this chapter.

2.1   Key differences to previous UK GAAP

2.1.1   *Significant influence*

There is a subtle difference in the definition of significant influence and the exercising of this influence. Under FRS 102 significant influence is the power to participate in the financial and operating policies of an entity regardless of whether the power is actively exercised or not. *[FRS 102.14.3]*. FRS 9, however, requires the actual exercise of significant influence. *[FRS 9.4]*. This may result in more entities being accounted for as associates under FRS 102 than under previous UK GAAP.

2.1.2   *Measurement – entity that is not a parent*

FRS 102 permits entities that are not parents to account for their investment in associates using the cost model, fair value model or at fair value through profit or loss *[FRS 102.14.4]*. Under previous UK GAAP the option to account for associates at fair value through profit or loss did not exist.

2.1.3   *Investment portfolios*

Section 14 requires that investments in associates held by an investor that is a parent as part of an investment portfolio should be measured at fair value through profit or loss. *[FRS 102.14.4B]*. Under FRS 9 investments funds are given the option to recognise all investments held as part of their investment portfolio at either cost or market value (with changes in value reflected in the statement of recognised gains and losses) provided all investments are accounted for on the same basis. *[FRS 9.49]*.

2.1.4   *Implicit goodwill and fair value adjustments*

Section 14 refers to the requirements of Section 19 – *Business Combinations and Goodwill* – in the context of determining the implicit goodwill and fair value adjustments arising on the acquisition of an investment in an associate. As the requirements of Section 19 differ from previous UK GAAP (see Chapter 15) this may have consequential impact on accounting for associates, in particular on the accounting for the implicit goodwill. Previous UK GAAP has a rebuttable presumption that goodwill should not be amortised over a period exceeding 20 years. *[FRS 10.19]*. Section 19 states that unless a reliable estimate can be made goodwill should be amortised over a period not exceeding 5 years. *[FRS 102.19.23(a)]*.

2.1.5   *Losses in excess of investment*

Section 14 does not permit the recognition of the losses of associates in excess of the cost of investment unless the investor has legal or constructive obligations in respect of the excess losses. *[FRS 102.14.8(h)]*.

FRS 9 requires the continued recognition of losses for associates even if they exceed the cost of investment. *[FRS 9.44]*.

2.2   Key differences to IFRS

2.2.1   *Measurement – entity that is not a parent*

Section 14 permits entities that are not parents to account for their investment in associates using the cost model, fair value model or at fair value through profit or loss. *[FRS 102.14.4]*.

Under IFRS, an entity that is not a parent must prepare financial statements whereby its investments in associates are accounted for under the equity accounting method unless it meets the criteria for exemption. *[IAS 28.16 and 17]*.

2.2.2   *Investment portfolios / funds*

Under Section 14, an investor that is a parent and has investments in associates that are held as part of an investment portfolio is required to measure those investments at fair value with changes in fair value recognised in the profit or loss in the consolidated financial statements. *[FRS 102.14.4B]*. However, under IAS 28, the measurement of investments in associates at fair value through profit or loss is an option that is only available for certain investment funds. *[IAS 28.18]*.

2.2.3   *Acquisition accounting*

Section 14 requires the use of Section 19 to determine the implicit goodwill on the acquisition of an associate. This goodwill is then amortised. *[FRS 102.14.8(c), FRS 102.19.23]*. Under IAS 28, the implicit goodwill is not amortised, but tested annually for impairment.

2.2.4   *Loss of significant influence where the associate does not become a subsidiary or jointly controlled entity*

Section 14 requires that where there is a loss of significant influence is as a result of a partial disposal, a gain or loss is recognised based on the disposal proceeds and the carrying amount relating to the proportion disposed of. The carrying value of the equity interest retained at the date significant influence is lost becomes the cost of the retained investment.

If the loss of significant influence is for reasons other than a partial disposal, no gain or loss is recognised and the carrying value of the equity-accounted investment at the date significant influence is lost becomes the cost of the retained investment. *[FRS 102.14.8(i)]*.

Under IFRS, where there is loss of significant influence is as a result of a partial disposal, a gain or loss is recognised based on the disposal proceeds together with the fair value of any retained interest and the carrying amount of the total interest in the associate.

If the loss of significant influence is for reasons other than a partial disposal, a gain or loss is recognised based on the fair value of the retained interest and the carrying amount of the interest in the associate at that date. *[IAS 28.22]*.

3   REQUIREMENTS OF SECTION 14 FOR INVESTMENTS IN ASSOCIATES

3.1   Introduction

3.1.1   *Scope*

Section 14 applies to accounting for:

- associates in consolidated financial statements;
- investments in associates in the individual financial statements of an investor that is not a parent.

An entity that is a parent accounts for investments in associates in its separate financial statements in accordance with paragraphs 9.26 and 9.26A of FRS 102, as appropriate (see Chapter 6 at 4.2). *[FRS 102.14.1]*.

3.1.2   *Terms used in Section 14*

The following key terms are used in Section 14 with the meanings specified: *[FRS 102 Appendix I]*

Term	Definition
Associate	An entity, including an unincorporated entity such as a partnership, over which the investor has significant influence and that is neither a subsidiary nor an interest in a joint venture.
Consolidated financial statements	The financial statements of a parent and its subsidiaries presented as those of a single economic entity.
Held as part of an investment portfolio	An interest is held as part of an investment portfolio if its value to the investor is through fair value as part of a directly or indirectly held basket of investments rather than as a media through which the investor carries out business. A basket of investments is held indirectly if an investment fund holds a single investment in a second investment fund which in turn holds a basket of investments.
Individual financial statements	The accounts that are required to be prepared by an entity in accordance with the Companies Act 2006 or relevant legislation, for example 'individual accounts' as set out in section 394 of the Act.
Impracticable	Applying a requirement is impracticable when the entity cannot apply it after making every reasonable effort to do so.
Parent	An entity that has one or more subsidiaries.
Separate financial statements	The individual accounts prepared by a parent in which the investments in which the investments in subsidiaries, associates or jointly controlled entities are accounted for either at cost or fair value rather than on the basis of the reported results and net assets of the investees.
Significant influence	Significant influence is the power to participate in the financial and operating policy decisions of the associate but is not control or joint control over those policies.

3.2   Definitions of an associate, and related terms

3.2.1   *Associate*

Section 14 defines an associate as an entity, including an unincorporated entity such as a partnership, over which an investor has significant influence and that is neither a subsidiary nor an interest in a joint venture. *[FRS 102.14.2].*

3.2.2   *Significant influence*

Fundamental to the definition of an associate is a concept of significant influence. This is defined as 'the power to participate in the financial and operating policy decisions of the associate but is not control or joint control over those policies'. *[FRS 102.14.3]*.

Under Section 14, a holding of 20% or more of the voting power of the investee (held directly or indirectly, through subsidiaries) is presumed to give rise to significant influence, unless it can be clearly demonstrated that this is not the case. Conversely, a holding of less than 20% of the voting power is presumed not to give rise to significant influence, unless it can be clearly demonstrated that significant influence does exist. The existence of a substantial or majority interest of another investor does not necessarily preclude the investor from having significant influence. *[FRS 102.14.3]*.

An entity should consider both ordinary shares and other categories of shares in determining its voting rights.

Other factors need to be considered to determine whether significant influence exists or not and potentially rebut any presumptions above regarding voting power. There is no further guidance in Section 14 on how significant influence is demonstrated and it is appropriate to consider guidance in IAS 28 which notes that significant influence can be evidenced in one or more of the following ways: *[IAS 28.6]*

(a)   representation on the board of directors or equivalent governing body of the investee;

(b)   participation in policy-making processes, including participation in decisions about dividends and other distributions;

(c)   material transactions between the entity and the investee;

(d)   interchange of managerial personnel; or

(e)   provision of essential technical information.

Significant influence may also exist over another entity through potential voting rights (see 3.2.2.C below).

An entity loses significant influence over an investee when it loses the power to participate in the financial and operating policy decisions of that investee. The loss of significant influence can occur with or without a change in absolute or relative ownership levels. It could occur, for example, as a result of a contractual agreement or when an associate becomes subject to the control of a government, court, administrator or regulator.

An entity with an interest in an associate will need to evaluate the facts and circumstances to assess whether it is still able to exercise significant influence over the financial and operating policies of the investee.

The accounting for loss of significant influence over an associate is discussed at 3.3.2.J below.

3.2.2.A   Lack of significant influence

The presumption of significant influence due to the existence of 20% or more of the voting power can sometimes be rebutted, for example when:

- the investor has failed to obtain representation on the investee's board of directors;
- the investee or other shareholders are opposing the investor's attempts to exercise significant influence;
- the investor is unable to obtain timely financial information or cannot obtain more information – required to apply the equity method – than shareholders that do not have significant influence; or
- a group of shareholders that holds the majority ownership of the investee operates without regard to the views of the investor.

Determining whether the presumption of significant influence has been rebutted requires considerable judgement and sufficient evidence to justify rebutting the presumption.

3.2.2.B   Holdings of less than 20% of the voting power

Although there is a presumption that an investor that holds less than 20% of the voting power in an investee cannot exercise significant influence, *[FRS 102.14.3(b)]*, where investments give rise to only slightly less than 20% of the voting power careful judgement is needed to assess whether significant influence may still exist.

For example, an investor may still be able to exercise significant influence in the following circumstances:

- the investor's voting power is much larger than that of any other shareholder of the investee;
- the corporate governance arrangements may be such that the investor is able to appoint members to the board, supervisory board or significant committees of the investee. The investor will need to apply judgement to determine whether representation in the respective boards or committees is enough to provide significant influence; or
- the investor has the power to veto significant financial and operating decisions.

Determining which policies are significant requires considerable judgement.

3.2.2.C   Potential voting rights

An entity may own share warrants, share call options, debt or equity instruments that are convertible into ordinary shares, or other similar instruments that have the potential, if exercised or converted, to give the entity voting power or reduce another party's voting power over the financial and operating policies of another entity (potential voting rights).

Section 14 requires that an entity should consider the existence and effect of potential voting rights in deciding whether significant influence exists. *[FRS 102.14.8(b)]*. Whilst not explicitly stated in Section 14, by following the analogy in Section 9 Paragraph 6, such potential voting rights should be currently exercisable or convertible.

Potential voting rights are not currently exercisable or convertible when they cannot be exercised or converted until a future date or until the occurrence of a future event. The meaning of currently exercisable or convertible is discussed further in Chapter 6 at 3.2.1.

Consistent with that discussion, IAS 28 (on which the requirements of Section 14 are based) states that in assessing whether potential voting rights contribute to significant influence, an entity must examine all facts and circumstances (including the terms of exercise of the potential voting rights and any other contractual arrangements whether considered individually or in combination) that affect potential voting rights, except the intention of management and the financial ability to exercise or convert those potential voting rights. *[IAS 28.8].*

3.2.2.D   Voting rights held in a fiduciary capacity

Voting rights on shares held as security remain the rights of the provider of the security, and are generally not taken into account if the rights are only exercisable in accordance with instructions from the provider of the security or in his interest. Similarly, voting rights that are held in a fiduciary capacity may not be those of the entity itself. However, if voting rights are held by a nominee on behalf of the entity, they should be taken into account.

3.3   Measurement

3.3.1   Accounting policy options

3.3.1.A   Investor not a parent

An entity that is not a parent shall account for its investments in associates in its individual financial statements using either:

* the cost model (see 3.3.3 below);
* the fair value model (see 3.3.4 below); or
* fair value with changes in fair value recognised in profit or loss (see Chapter 11). *[FRS 102.14.4].*

3.3.1.B   Investor that is a parent

An investor that is a parent should, in its consolidated financial statements, account for all of its investments in associates using the equity method of accounting (see 3.3.2 below). *[FRS 102.14.4A].*

The exception to this is when the investment in an associate is held as part of an investment portfolio. These investments shall be measured at fair value with changes in fair value recognised in profit or loss in the consolidated financial statements. *[FRS 102.14.4B].*

An investment is held as part of an investment portfolio if its value to the investor is through fair value as part of a directly or indirectly held basket of investments rather than as a media through which the investor carries out business. A basket of investments is held indirectly if an investment fund holds a single investment in a second investment fund which in turn holds a basket of investments. *[FRS 102 Appendix I].*

An entity that is a parent should account for its investments in associates in its separate financial statements in accordance with paragraphs 9.26 and 9.26A of Section 9 – *Consolidated and Separate Financial Statements* (see Chapter 6). *[FRS 102.14.1].*

3.3.2   Equity method

Section 14 defines the equity method as a method of accounting whereby the investment is initially recognised at transaction price (including transaction costs) and is subsequently adjusted to reflect the investor's share of:

- profit or loss;
- other comprehensive income, and
- equity of the associate. *[FRS 102.14.8].*

The investor's share of the investee's profit or loss is recognised in the investor's profit or loss. *[FRS 102.5.5, 6 Sch 20(3)].* The investor's share of the investee's other comprehensive income is recognised in the investor's statement of comprehensive income. *[FRS 102.5.5, 6 Sch 20(3)].*

Transaction costs are defined in FRS 102 in the context of financial instruments as incremental costs that are directly attributable to the acquisition, issue or disposal of a financial asset or liability. *[FRS 102 Appendix I].*

In the context of Section 14, transaction costs will comprise any costs directly attributable to the acquisition of the interest in the associate.

The application of the equity method is illustrated in Example 10.1 below and the key features of the method are explained in the paragraphs that follow.

Example 10.1:   Application of the equity method

On 1 January 2015 entity A acquires a 35% interest in entity B, over which it is able to exercise significant influence. Entity A paid £475,000 for its interest in B. At that date the book value of B's net assets was £900,000, and their fair value £1,100,000, the difference of £200,000 relates to an item of property, plant and equipment with a remaining useful life of 10 years. During the year to 31 December 2015, B made a profit of £80,000 and paid a dividend of £120,000 on 31 December 2015. Entity B also had a gain in other comprehensive income of £20,000 during the year. Goodwill is assumed to have a 5 year useful life. For the purposes of the example, any deferred tax implications have been ignored.

Entity A accounts for its investment in B under the equity method as follows:

	£	£
Acquisition of investment in B		
Share in book value of B's net assets: 35% of £900,000	315,000	
Share in fair valuation of B's net assets: 35% of (£1,100,000 – £900,000) *	70,000	
Goodwill on investment in B: £475,000 – £315,000 – £70,000 *	90,000	
Cost of investment		475,000
Profit during the year		
Share in the profit reported by B: 35% of £80,000	28,000	
Adjustment to reflect effect of fair valuation *	(7,000)	
35% of ((£1,100,000 – £900,000) ÷ 10 years)		
Goodwill amortisation *(£90,000 ÷ 5 years)	(18,000)	
Share of profit in B recognised in income by A		3,000
Share of other comprehensive income recognised by A: 35% of £20,000		7,000

Dividend received by A during the year
35% of £120,000   (42,000)

At 31 December 2015
Share in book value of B's net assets:
   £315,000 + 35% (£80,000 − £120,000 + £20,000)   308,000
Share in fair valuation of B's net assets: £70,000 − £7,000 *   63,000
Goodwill on investment in B: £90,000 − £18,000*   72,000
Closing balance of A's investment in B   443,000

*   These line items are normally not presented separately, but are combined with the ones immediately above.

Through its significant influence over the associate the investor has an interest in the associate's performance and, as a result, a return on its investment. The investor accounts for this interest by extending the scope of its financial statements so as to include its share of profits or losses of the associate. As a result, application of the equity method provides more informative reporting of the net assets and profit or loss of the investor.

3.3.2.A   Date of commencement of equity accounting

An investor begins equity accounting for an associate from the date on which it gains significant influence over the associate (and is not otherwise exempt from equity accounting for it). In most situations, this will be when the investor purchases the investment in the associate. However, it may be that the investor only obtains significant influence over the investee at some date after having purchased its ownership interest. FRS 102 does not explicitly deal with this situation, but the investor should account for the associate by applying its selected accounting policy for such piecemeal acquisitions as discussed at 4.1.2 below.

3.3.2.B   Distributions and other adjustments to carrying amount

Distributions received from an associate will reduce the carrying amount of the investment. Adjustments to the carrying amount may also be necessary due to changes in the associate's equity from items of its other comprehensive income. *[FRS 102.14.8(a)].*

Such changes could include those arising from the revaluation of property, plant and equipment and from foreign exchange translation differences. The investor's share of the investee's other comprehensive income is recognised in the investor's statement of comprehensive income. *[FRS 102.5.5, 6 Sch 20(3)].*

3.3.2.C   Potential voting rights and share of the investee

In applying the equity method, the proportionate share of the associate to be accounted for, in many cases, will be based on the investor's ownership interest in the ordinary shares of the investee.

Although potential voting rights need to be considered in determining whether significant influence exists (see 3.2.2.C above) an investor should measure its share of profit or loss and other comprehensive income of the associate as well as its share of changes in the associate's equity based on present ownership interests. Those measurements should not reflect the possible exercise or conversion of potential voting rights. *[FRS 102.14.8(b)]*.

However, as an exception to this, in some rare cases potential voting rights may actually give rise to present access to the economic benefits inherent in those rights.

An example of such a circumstance might be a presently exercisable option over shares in the investee at a fixed price combined with the right to veto any distribution by the investee before the option is exercised or combined with features that adjust the exercise price with respect to dividends paid. In these rare cases, it might be appropriate to equity account for the share that would be held if the option were exercised.

If an associate has outstanding cumulative preference shares that are held by parties other than the investor and that are classified as equity, the investor should compute its share of profits or losses after adjusting for the dividends on such shares, whether or not the dividends have been declared.

Example 10.2:   Cumulative preference shares issued by an associate

An entity holds an investment of 30% in the ordinary shares of an associate that has net assets of £200,000 and net profit for the year of £24,500. The associate has issued 5,000 cumulative preference shares with a nominal value of £10 which entitle its holders to a 9% cumulative preference dividend. The cumulative preference shares are classified by the associate as equity in accordance with the requirements of Section 22 – *Liabilities and Equity*. The associate has not declared dividends on the cumulative preference shares in the past two years.

The investor calculates its share of the associate's net assets and net profit as follows:

	£
Net assets	200,000
9% Cumulative preference shares	(50,000)
Undeclared dividend on cumulative preference shares	
2 years × 9% × £50,000 =	(9,000)
Net assets value attributable to ordinary shareholders	141,000
Investor's 30% share of the net assets	42,300
Net profit for the year	24,500
Share of profit of holders of cumulative preference shares	
9% of £50,000 =	(4,500)
Net profit attributable to ordinary shareholders	20,000
Investor's 30% share of the net profit	6,000

If the investor also owned all of the cumulative preference shares then its share in the net assets of the associate would be £42,300 + £50,000 + £9,000 = £101,300. Its share in the net profit would be £6,000 + £4,500 = £10,500.

When an associate has a complicated equity structure with several classes of equity shares that have varying entitlements to net profits and equity, the investor needs to assess carefully the rights attaching to each class of equity share in determining the appropriate percentage of ownership interest.

Example 10.3: Preference shares with a liquidation preference

Entity A has issued 10,000 preference shares with a nominal value of £0.10. The preference shareholders are entitled to a cumulative dividend equal to 25% of the net profits, 35% of the equity upon liquidation and have a liquidation preference in respect of the nominal value of the shares. Entity A has also issued ordinary shares that are entitled to the remainder of the net profits and equity upon liquidation.

An investor that holds 40% of the ordinary shares of Entity A will need to assess carefully what its appropriate share in the profits and equity of Entity A is. The investor would take the liquidation preference into account in calculating its interest in the associate or joint venture to the extent that there is economic substance to that right.

Section 14 does not address the situation where in a group, shares in the associate are held by the parent and its subsidiaries. However, based on previous UK GAAP and the requirements of IAS 28, it is clear that a group's share in an associate is the aggregate of the holdings in that associate by the parent and its subsidiaries. Holdings of the group's other associates or joint ventures are ignored for this purpose.

Example 10.4: Share in an associate

Parent A holds a 100% investment in subsidiary B, which in turn holds a 25% investment in associate Z. In addition, parent A also holds a 30% investment in associate C and a 50% investment in joint venture D, each of which holds a 10% investment in associate Z.

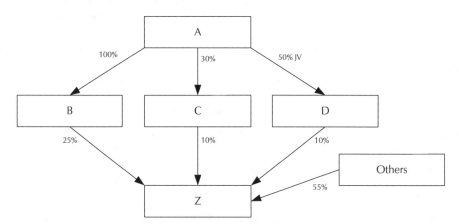

In its consolidated financial statements parent A accounts for a 25% investment in associate Z under the equity method because:

• the investments in associate Z held by associate C and joint venture D should not be taken into account; and

• the parent A fully consolidates the assets of subsidiary B, which include a 25% investment in associate Z.

Section 14 does not address the situation where an associate itself has subsidiaries, associates or jointly controlled entities. However, based on the Companies Act 2006, previous UK GAAP and the requirements of IAS 28, it is clear that profits or losses, other comprehensive income and net assets taken into account when the investor applies the equity method should be those recognised in the associate's consolidated financial statements, but after any adjustments necessary to give effect to uniform accounting policies (see 3.3.2.H below).

It may be that the associate does not own all the shares in some of its subsidiaries, in which case its consolidated financial statements will include non-controlling interests. Under the Companies Act 2006, any non-controlling interests are presented in the consolidated statement of financial position within equity, separately from the equity of the owners of the parent. Profit or loss and each component of other comprehensive income are attributed to the owners of the parent and to the non-controlling interests. *[FRS 102.6.3(a)].*

The profit or loss and other comprehensive income reported in the associate's consolidated financial statements will include 100% of the amounts relating to the subsidiaries, but the overall profit or loss and total comprehensive income will be split between the amounts attributable to the owners of the parent (i.e. the associate) and those attributable to the non-controlling interests. The net assets in the associate's consolidated statement of financial position will also include 100% of the amounts relating to the subsidiaries, with any non-controlling interests in the net assets presented in the consolidated statement of financial position within equity, separately from the equity of the owners of the parent.

Section 14 does not address whether the investor's share, for equity accounting purposes, of the associate's profits, other comprehensive income and net assets should be based on the amounts before or after any non-controlling interests in the associate's consolidated accounts. However, as the investor's interest in the associate is as an owner of the parent, it is appropriate that the share should be based on the profit or loss, comprehensive income and equity (net assets) that are reported as being attributable to the owners of the parent in the associate's consolidated financial statements, i.e. after any amounts attributable to the non-controlling interests.

3.3.2.D   Implicit goodwill and fair value adjustments

Section 14 states that on acquisition of an investment in an associate, any difference between the cost of the investment and the entity's share of the net fair values of the investee's identifiable assets and liabilities should be accounted for in accordance with Section 19, paragraphs 22 to 24 (see Chapter 15), as follows: *[FRS 102.14.8(c)]*

- any goodwill relating to an associate is included in the carrying amount of the investment. After initial recognition goodwill included in the carrying amount of the investment, should be recognised at cost less accumulated amortisation (but not impairment, see 3.3.2.E below), and any amortisation should be recognised against the investor's share of the associate's profit or loss; *[FRS 102.19.23]*

- any excess of the investor's share of the net fair value of the associate's identifiable assets and liabilities over the cost of the investment is included as income in the determination of the entity's share of the associate's profit or loss in the periods in which the non-monetary assets are recovered. *[FRS 102.19.24].*

Section 14 also states that an investor should adjust its share of the associate's profits or losses after acquisition in order to account, for example, for additional depreciation or amortisation of the depreciable assets or amortisable assets based on their fair values at the acquisition date. Similarly, appropriate adjustments to the entity's share of the associate's profits or losses after acquisition are made for impairment losses for such assets recognised in the associate's underlying accounts. *[FRS 102.14.8(c)]*.

However, an investor will not necessarily simply recognise impairment losses in respect of an associate equivalent to its share of the impairment losses recognised by the associate itself (even after fair value and other consolidation adjustments). Further impairment on the overall carrying value of the associate may be required and this is discussed further at 3.3.2.E below.

3.3.2.E   Impairment

An entity will have to test the carrying value of its investment in an associate for impairment only if an event has occurred that indicates that it will not recover the carrying value. *[FRS 102.27.7]*.

The most common of these events, trading losses in the associate, will automatically have been taken into account in determining the carrying value of the investment, leaving only the remaining net carrying amount (i.e. after deducting the share of trading losses) to be assessed for impairment.

Determining whether an investment in an associate is impaired may be more complicated than is apparent at first sight, as it involves carrying out several separate impairment assessments:

- *Underlying assets of the associate*

  It is generally not appropriate for the investor simply to multiply the amount of the impairment charge recognised in the investee's own books by the investor's percentage of ownership, because the investor should measure its interest in an associate's identifiable net assets at fair value at the date of acquisition of an associate (see 3.3.2.D above). Therefore, if the value that the investor attributes to the associate's net assets differs from the carrying amount of those net assets in the associate's own books, the investor should restate any impairment losses recognised by the associate and also needs to consider whether it needs to recognise any impairments that the associate itself did not recognise in its own books.

  Any goodwill recognised by an associate needs to be separated into two elements. Goodwill that existed at the date the investor acquired its interest in the associate is not an identifiable asset of the associate from the perspective of the investor. That goodwill should be combined with the investor's goodwill on the acquisition of its interest in the associate and any impairment losses of that goodwill recognised in the financial statements of the associate should be reversed when the investor applies the equity method. However, goodwill that arises on subsequent acquisitions by the associate should be accounted for as such in the books of the associate and tested for impairment in accordance with Section 27 – *Impairment of Assets* – by the associate. The investor should not make any adjustments to the associate's accounting for that goodwill.

- *Investment in the associate*

  As well as reflecting any impairment in the underlying assets of the associate using the equity method as discussed above, Section 14 requires an investor to test the overall investment in the associate for impairment as a single asset in accordance with Section 27. Any goodwill included as part of the carrying amount of the investment in the associate is not tested separately for impairment but is tested as part of the overall investment as a whole. *[FRS 102.14.8(d)].*

- *Other interests that are not part of the equity interest in the associate*

  The investor must also apply Section 11 – *Basic Financial Instruments* – in order to determine whether it is necessary to recognise any additional impairment loss with respect to that part of the investor's interest in the associate that does not comprise its net investment in the associate. This could include, for example, trade receivables and payables, and collateralised long-term receivables, but might also include preference shares or loans (see 3.3.2.I below). In this case, however, the impairment is calculated in accordance with Section 11, and not Section 27.

Where the carrying amount of an investment in an associate is tested for impairment in accordance with Section 27, an impairment loss recognised is not allocated to any individual asset, including goodwill, which forms part of the carrying amount of the associate. In addition, any reversal of that impairment loss is recognised in accordance with Section 27 to the extent that the recoverable amount of the investment subsequently increases. Previously recognised impairment losses of an investment in an associate are fully reversible under Section 27.

Example 10.5:   Impairment losses recognised by an associate

Entity A has a 40% interest in Entity B. Entity A has significant influence over Entity B and accounts for its investment under the equity method.

At 31 December 2015, Entity B, which prepares its financial statements under FRS 102, has carried out impairment tests under Section 27 and recognised an impairment loss of £140,000 calculated as follows:

	Carrying amount £'000	Recoverable amount £'000	Impairment loss £'000
CGU A	210	300	n/a
CGU B	250	450	n/a
CGU C	540	400	140
Total	1,000	1,150	140

In accounting for its associate, Entity B, in its consolidated financial statements for the year ended 31 December 2015, should Entity A reflect its 40% share of this impairment loss of £140,000?

As indicated above, it is generally not appropriate for the investor simply to multiply the amount of the impairment recognised in the investee's own books by the investor's percentage of ownership, because the investor should initially measure its interest in an associate's identifiable net assets at fair value at the date of acquisition of an associate. Accordingly, appropriate adjustments based on those fair values are made for impairment losses recognised by the associate (see 3.3.2.D above).

Prior to the recognition of the impairment loss by Entity B, the carrying amount of Entity A's 40% interest in the net assets of Entity B, after reflecting fair value adjustments made by Entity A at the date of acquisition, together with the goodwill arising on the acquisition is as follows:

	Carrying amount reflecting fair values made by Entity A £'000
CGU A	140
CGU B	100
CGU C	320
Net assets	560
Goodwill	40
Investment in associate	600

In applying the equity method, Entity A should compare its 40% share of the cash flows attributable to each of Entity B's CGUs to determine the impairment loss it should recognise in respect of Entity B. Accordingly, in equity accounting for its share of Entity B's profit or loss, Entity A should recognise an impairment loss of £180,000 calculated as follows:

	Carrying amount reflecting fair values made by Entity A £'000	**Recoverable amount (40%)** £'000	**Impairment loss** £'000
CGU A	140	120	20
CGU B	100	180	n/a
CGU C	320	160	160
Net assets	560	460	180

In addition, after applying the equity method, Entity A should calculate whether any further impairment loss is necessary in respect of its investment in its associate.

The carrying amount of Entity A's investment in Entity B under the equity method after reflecting the impairment loss of £180,000 would be as follows:

	£'000
CGU A	120
CGU B	100
CGU C	160
Net assets	380
Goodwill	40
Investment in associate	420

Based on Entity A's 40% interest in the total recoverable amount of Entity B of £460,000, Entity A would not recognise any further impairment loss in respect of its investment in the associate.

It should be noted that the impairment loss recognised by Entity A of £180,000 is not the same as if it had calculated an impairment loss on its associate as a whole i.e. by comparing its 40% share of the total recoverable amount of Entity B of £460,000 to its investment in the associate of £600,000 (prior to reflecting any impairment loss on its share of Entity B's net assets). Such an approach would only be appropriate if Entity B did not have more than one CGU. However, if in this example, the goodwill on the acquisition had been at least £80,000, the overall impairment loss recognised would have been the same, irrespective of whether the impairment loss had been calculated on an overall basis or as in the example.

3.3.2.F   Investor's transactions with associates

Section 14 requires unrealised profits and losses resulting from what it refers to as 'upstream' and 'downstream' transactions between an investor (including its consolidated subsidiaries) and an associate to be eliminated from the investor's financial statements to the extent of investor's interest in the associate. *[FRS 102.14.8(e)].*

'Upstream' transactions are, for example, sales of assets from an associate to the investor. 'Downstream' transactions are, for example, sales or contributions of assets from the investor to its associate.

Section 14 provides no further guidance as to how this broadly expressed requirement translates into accounting entries, but we suggest that an appropriate approach might be to proceed as follows:

- in the income statement, the adjustment should be taken against either the investor's profit or the share of the associate's profit, according to whether the investor or the associate recorded the profit on the transaction, respectively; and

- in the statement of financial position, the adjustment should be made against the asset which was the subject of the transaction if it is held by the investor or against the carrying amount for the associate if the asset is held by the associate.

This is consistent with the treatment where an investor exchanges a non-monetary asset for an interest in another entity that becomes an associate (see 3.3.2.K below).

Examples 10.6 and 10.7 below illustrate our suggested approach to this requirement of Section 14. Both examples deal with the reporting entity H and its 40% associate A. The journal entries are based on the premise that H's financial statements are initially prepared as a simple aggregation of H and the relevant share of its associate. The entries below would then be applied to the numbers at that stage of the process.

Example 10.6:   Elimination of profit on sale by investor to associate ('downstream transaction')

On 1 December 2015 H sells inventory costing £750,000 to A for £1 million. On 10 January 2016, A sells the inventory to a third party for £1.2 million. What adjustments are made in the group financial statements of H at 31 December 2015 and 31 December 2016?

In the year ended 31 December 2015, H has recorded revenue of £1 million and cost of sales of £750,000. However since, at the reporting date, the inventory is still held by A, only 60% of this transaction is regarded by FRS 102 as having taken place (in effect with the other shareholders of A). This is reflected by the consolidation entry:

	£	£
Revenue	400,000	
Cost of sales		300,000
Investment in A		100,000

This effectively defers recognition of 40% of the sale and offsets the deferred profit against the carrying amount of H's investment in A.

During 2016, when the inventory is sold on by A, this deferred profit can be released to group profit or loss, reflected by the following accounting entry.

	£	£
Opening reserves	100,000	
Cost of sales	300,000	
Revenue		400,000

Opening reserves are adjusted because the financial statement working papers (if prepared as assumed above) will already include this profit in opening reserves, since it forms part of H's opening reserves.

An alternative approach would be to eliminate the profit on 40% of the sale against the cost of sales, as follows:

	£	£
Cost of sales	100,000	
Investment in A		100,000

An argument in favour of this approach is that the revenue figures should not be adjusted because the sales to associates need to be disclosed as related party transactions. However, this may be outweighed by the drawback of the approach, namely that it causes volatility in H's reported gross margin as revenue and the related net margin are not necessarily recognised in the same accounting period.

Example 10.7:   *Elimination of profit on sale by associate to reporting entity ('upstream transaction')*

This is the mirror image of the transaction in Example 10.6 above. On 1 December 2015 A sells inventory costing £750,000 to H for £1,000,000. On 10 January 2016, H sells the inventory to a third party for £1.2 million. What adjustments are made in the group financial statements of H at 31 December 2015 and 31 December 2016?

H's share of the profit of A as included on the financial statement working papers at 31 December 2015 will include a profit of £250,000 (£1,000,000 – £750,000), 40% of which (£100,000) is regarded under FRS 102 as unrealised by H, and is therefore deferred and offset against closing inventory:

	£	£
Share of A's result (income statement)	100,000	
Inventory		100,000

In the following period when the inventory is sold H's separate financial statements will record a profit of £200,000, which must be increased on consolidation by the £100,000 deferred from the previous period. The entry is:

	£	£
Opening reserves	100,000	
Share of A's result (income statement)		100,000

Again, opening reserves are adjusted because the financial statement working papers (if prepared as assumed above) will already include this profit in opening reserves, this time, however, as part of H's share of the opening reserves of A.

A slightly counter-intuitive consequence of this treatment is that at the end of 2015 the investment in A in H's consolidated statement of financial position will have increased by £100,000 more than the share of profit of associates as reported in group profit or loss (and in 2016 by £100,000 less). This is because the statement of financial position adjustment at the end of 2015 is made against inventory rather than the carrying value of the investment in A, which could be seen as reflecting the fact that A has, indeed, made a profit. It might therefore be necessary to indicate in the notes to the financial statements that part of the profit made by A is regarded as unrealised by the group in 2015 and has therefore been deferred until 2016 by offsetting it against inventory.

Note that unrealised losses on upstream and downstream transactions may provide evidence of an impairment in the asset transferred. *[FRS 102.14.8(e)]*.

The effect of these requirements is illustrated in Examples 10.8 and 10.9 below.

Example 10.8:   Sale of asset from an investor to associate at a loss

Entity A holds 40% of entity B, giving it significant influence. B acquires a property from A for £8 million cash and the property was recorded in the financial statements of A at £10 million. £8 million is agreed to be the fair market value of the property. How should A account for these transactions?

The required accounting entry by A is as follows:

	£m	£m
Cash (1)	8	
Loss on sale (2)	2	
Property (3)		10

(1)   £8 million received from B.

(2)   Loss on sale of property £2 million (£8 million received from B less £10 million carrying value = £2 million) not adjusted since the transaction indicated an impairment of the property. In effect, it is the result that would have been obtained if A had recognised an impairment charge immediately prior to the sale and then recognised no gain or loss on the sale.

(3)   Derecognition of A's original property.

Example 10.9:   Sale of asset from associate to an investor at a loss

Entity A holds 40% of entity B giving it significant influence. B acquires a property for £8 million from an independent third party C. The property is then sold to A for £7 million, which is agreed to be its market value. How should A account for these transactions?

The required accounting entry by A is as follows:

	£m	£m
Property (1)	7.0	
Share of loss of B (2)	0.5	
Investment in B		0.5
Cash (3)		7.0

(1)   £7 million paid to B not adjusted since the transaction indicated an impairment of B's asset.

(2)   Loss in B's books is £1 million (£8 million cost of property less £7 million proceeds of sale). A recognises its 50% share because the transaction indicates an impairment of the asset. In effect, it is the result that would have been obtained if B had recognised an impairment charge immediately prior to the sale and then recognised no gain or loss on the sale.

(3)   £7 million consideration for the property.

Elimination of 'downstream' unrealised profits in excess of the investment

Occasionally an investor's share of the unrealised profit on the sale of an asset to an associate exceeds the carrying value of the investment held. In that case, to what extent is any profit in excess of the carrying value of the investment eliminated?

Section 14 provides no guidance on the elimination of 'downstream' unrealised gains in excess of the investment. Consequently, an investor needs to determine an appropriate policy for dealing with such a situation. We believe that the investor could either recognise the excess as 'deferred income' or restrict the elimination to the amount required to reduce the investment to zero.

Loans and borrowings between the reporting entity and its associates

The requirement in section 14 to eliminate partially unrealised profits or losses on transactions with associates is expressed in terms of transactions. In our view, the requirement for partial elimination of profits does not apply to items such as interest paid on loans and borrowings between the reporting entity and its associates, since such loans and borrowings do not involve the transfer of assets giving rise to gains or losses. Moreover, they are not normally regarded as part of the investor's share of the net assets of the associate, but as separate transactions, except in the case of loss-making associates, where interests in long-term loans and borrowings may be required to be accounted for as if they were part of the reporting entity's equity investment in determining the carrying value of the associate against which losses may be offset (see 3.3.2.I below). Likewise, loans and borrowings, and indeed other payables and receivables, between the reporting entity and its associates should not be eliminated in the reporting entity's consolidated accounts because associates are not part of the group.

However, if the associate has capitalised the borrowing costs then the investor would need to eliminate a relevant share of the profit, in the same way it would eliminate a share of the capitalised management or advisory fees charged to an associate.

In the statement of cash flows (whether in the consolidated or separate financial statements) no adjustment is made in respect of the cash flows relating to transactions with associates or joint ventures. This contrasts with the requirement, in any consolidated statement of cash flows, to eliminate the cash flows between members of the group in the same way that intragroup transactions are eliminated in the profit and loss account and statement of financial position.

3.3.2.G   Date of associate's financial statements

In applying the equity method, the investor should use the financial statements of the associate as of the same date as the financial statements of the investor unless it is impracticable to do so. *[FRS 102.14.8(f)].*

Applying a requirement is deemed to be impracticable when the entity cannot apply it after making every reasonable effort to do so. *[FRS 102 Appendix I].*

Otherwise an investor should use the most recent available financial statements of the associate. Adjustments must then be made for the effects of significant transactions or events, for example a sale of a significant asset or a major loss on a contract, that occurred between that date and the date of the investor's financial statements. There are no exemptions from this requirement despite the fact that it may be quite onerous in practice, for example, because the associate might need to produce non statutory or interim financial statements so that the investor can comply with this requirement.

3.3.2.H   Associate's accounting policies

If an associate uses accounting policies different from those of the investor for like transactions and events in similar circumstances, adjustments must be made to conform the associate's accounting policies to those of the investor when the associate's financial statements are used by the investor in applying the equity method unless it is impracticable to do so. *[FRS 102.14.8(g)]*.

In practice, this may be difficult, since an investor's influence over an associate, although significant, may still not be sufficient to ensure access to the relevant underlying information in sufficient detail to make such adjustments with certainty. Restating the financial statements of an overseas associate to UK GAAP may require extensive detailed information that may simply not be required under the associate's local GAAP (for example, in respect of business combinations, share-based payments, financial instruments and revenue recognition).

3.3.2.I   Losses in excess of investment

An investor in an associate should recognise its share of the losses of the associate until its share of losses equals or exceeds the carrying amount of its interest in the associate, at which point the investor discontinues recognising its share of further losses. *[FRS 102.14.8(h)]*.

Once the investor's interest is reduced to zero, additional losses are provided for, and a liability is recognised in accordance with Section 21 – *Provisions and Contingencies* (see Chapter 17), but only to the extent that the investor has incurred legal or constructive obligations or made payments on behalf of the associate. If the associate subsequently reports profits, the investor resumes recognising its share of those profits only after its share of the profits equals the share of losses not recognised. *[FRS 102 14.8(h)]*.

In addition to the recognition of losses arising from application of the equity method, an investor in an associate must consider the requirements of Section 27 – *Impairment of Assets* – in respect of impairment losses. An investor also needs to consider Section 11 in order to determine whether it is necessary to recognise any additional impairment loss with respect to that part of the investor's interest in the associate that does not comprise its net investment in the associate (see 3.3.2.E above).

Section 14 does not address any long-term interests that, in substance, form part of the investor's net investment in the associate. For example, an item for which settlement is neither planned nor likely to occur in the foreseeable future might be regarded as being, in substance, an extension of the entity's investment in that associate. An investor would need to consider whether these interests are recoverable in accordance with Section 27. IAS 28, on which Section 14 is based, considers that such items include:

- preference shares; or
- long-term receivables or loans (unless supported by adequate collateral),

but do not include:

- trade receivables;
- trade payables; or
- any long-term receivables for which adequate collateral exists, such as secured loans.

Example 10.10:   Accounting for a loss-making associate

At the beginning of the year entity H invests £5 million to acquire a 30% equity interest in an associate, entity A. In addition, H lends £9 million to the associate, but does not provide any guarantees or commit itself to provide further funding. How should H account for the £20 million loss that the associate made during the year?

H's share in A's loss is £20 million × 30% = £6 million. If H's loan to A is considered part of the net investment in the associate then the carrying amount of the associate is reduced by £6 million, from £14 million (= £5 million + £9 million) to £8 million. This would generally be done by reducing the equity interest to nil and reducing the loan to £8 million. However, if the loan is not part of the net investment in the associate then H accounts for the loss as follows:

– the equity interest in the associate is reduced from £5 million to zero;

– a loss of £1 million remains unrecognised because H did not provide any guarantees and has no commitments to provide further funding. If in the second year, however, A were to make a profit of £10 million then H would only recognise a profit of £2 million (= £10 million × 30% – £1 million). However, if in the second year H were to provide a £1.5 million guarantee to A and A's net profit were nil, then H would need to recognise an immediate loss of £1 million (i.e. the lower of the unrecognised loss of £1 million and the guarantee of £1.5 million) because it now has a legal obligation pay A's debts; and

– as there are a number of indicators of impairment, the loan from H to A should be tested for impairment in accordance with FRS 102 Section 11.

3.3.2.J   Discontinuing the equity method

An investor discontinues the use of the equity method from the date that significant influence ceases. The subsequent accounting depends upon the nature of the retained investment.

If the investment becomes a subsidiary (because control is obtained), it will be accounted for in accordance with Section 19 (i.e. a step-acquisition, see Chapter 15 at 3.10).

If an investment in an associate becomes an investment in a joint venture it will account for its investment in accordance with Section 15 – *Investments in Joint Ventures* (i.e. it will continue to be accounted for under the equity method, see Chapter 11).

Otherwise the retained investment should be accounted for as a financial asset in accordance with Sections 11 – *Basic Financial Instruments* – or Section 12 – *Other Financial Instruments Issues* – as discussed at below. *[FRS 102.14.8(i)]*.

If an investor disposes of some or all of its investment, such that it no longer has significant influence over the investee, it will discontinue the use of the equity method. In such situations, the entity derecognises the associate and recognises in profit or loss any difference between the:

(a)   the proceeds from the disposal, and

(b)   the carrying amount of the investment in the associate relating to the proportion disposed of or lost at the date significant influence is lost. *[FRS 102.14.8(i)(i)]*.

The investor shall account for the retained interest as a financial asset in accordance with Section 11 or Section 12 as appropriate. The carrying amount of the investment at the date that it ceases to be an associate shall be regarded as its cost on initial measurement as a financial asset.

Where an investor ceases to have significant influence due to a change in circumstances other than by partial disposal, for example, as a result of a changes to the board of directors or equivalent governing body of the associate results in a loss of significant influence, the investor will discontinue the use of the equity method. In that case, the investor does not recognise a profit or loss, but regards the carrying amount of the investment at that date as the new cost basis in accordance with Sections 11 or 12. *[FRS 102.14.8(i)(ii)]*.

If an investor loses significant influence as a result of a disposal the gain or loss arising on that disposal shall also include amounts recognised in other comprehensive income in relation to that associate where those amounts are required to be reclassified to profit or loss on disposal. *[FRS 102.14.8(i)]*. Under FRS 102 this includes fair value and cash flow hedges which have not yet been reclassified to profit or loss. Amounts that are not required to be reclassified to profit or loss upon disposal shall be transferred directly to retained earnings. *[FRS 102.14.8(i)]*.

3.3.2.K   *Transactions to create an associate*

An investor may exchange a business, or other non-monetary asset, for an interest in another entity, and that other entity becomes an associate of the investor. The accounting issues that arise from these transactions are whether they should be accounted for at fair value or at previous book values and how the gain on the transaction should be reported.

The requirements in respect of such transactions are set out in Section 9 (see also Chapter 6 at 3.8) and are the same as those contained in UITF 31 – *Exchanges of businesses or other non-monetary assets for an interest in a subsidiary, joint venture or associate* - in previous UK GAAP. The principles behind the consensus reached by the UITF were that the only exception to the use of fair values should be in rare circumstances where the transaction is artificial and has no substance and that any unrealised gains should not be reported in profit or loss.

Accordingly, the following accounting should be treatment applied in the consolidated financial statements of the reporting entity: *[FRS 102.9.31]*

- to the extent that the reporting entity retains an ownership interest in the business, or other non-monetary assets, exchanged, even if that interest is then held through the associate, that retained interest, including any related goodwill, is treated as having been owned by the reporting entity throughout the transaction and should be included at its pre-transaction carrying amount;
- goodwill is recognised as the difference between:
  - the fair value of the consideration given; and
  - the fair value of the reporting entity's share of the pre-transaction identifiable net assets of the other entity.

  The consideration given for the interest acquired in the associate will include that part of the business, or other non-monetary assets, exchanged and no longer owned by the reporting entity. The consideration may also include cash or monetary assets to achieve equalisation of values. Where it is difficult to value the consideration given, the best estimate of its value may be given by valuing what is acquired;

- to the extent that the fair value of the consideration received by the reporting entity exceeds the carrying value of the part of the business, or other non-monetary assets exchanged and no longer owned by the reporting entity, and any related goodwill together with any cash given up, the reporting entity should recognise a gain. Any unrealised gain arising on the exchange is recognised in other comprehensive income; and

- to the extent that the fair value of the consideration received by the reporting entity is less than the carrying value of the part of the business, or other non-monetary assets no longer owned by the reporting entity, and any related goodwill, together with any cash given up, the reporting entity should recognise a loss. The loss should be recognised as an impairment in accordance with Section 27 – *Impairment of Assets* – or, for any loss remaining after an impairment review of the relevant assets, in profit or loss.

The most common situation that fell within the scope of UITF 31 in practice had been the contribution of a business for equity in an associate (or joint venture).

Examples 11.7 and 11.8 in Chapter 11 illustrate the required accounting for such transactions.

Section 9 does not explain how a realised gain can be distinguished from an unrealised gain. In Example 11.7 in Chapter 11, we have used a 'top slicing' approach whereby as much of the total gain as is backed by cash is treated as realised (i.e. £10m). 'Top slicing' is the recommended approach in determining realised profits for exchanges of assets in paragraph 3.18 of the ICAEW/ICAS TECH 02/10 – *Guidance on the Determination of Realised Profits and Losses in the Context of Distributions under the Companies Act 2006.*

No gain or loss is recognised in those rare cases where the artificiality or lack of substance of the transaction is such that a gain or loss on the exchange could not be justified. When a gain or loss on the exchange is not taken into account because the transaction is artificial or has no substance, the circumstances should be explained. *[FRS 102.9.32].* There is no elaboration in the standard as to the circumstances where this might be applicable.

3.3.3   Cost model

An investor that is not a parent, and that chooses to adopt the cost model, should measure its investments in associates at cost less any accumulated impairment losses. Section 27 will apply to the recognition and measurement of impairment losses. *[FRS 102.14.5].*

Section 14 does not define 'cost'. The Regulations state that the purchase price of an asset is determined by adding to the actual price paid any expenses incidental to its acquisition. *[1 Sch 27(1)].* This definition is consistent with Section 17 – *Property, Plant and Equipment*, which states that cost is normally either the purchase price paid (including directly attributable costs) or the fair value of non-monetary assets exchanged. *[FRS 102.17.10].* The purchase price would generally represent the fair value of the consideration given to purchase the investment consistent with the guidance in respect of exchanges of businesses or other non-monetary items assets (see Chapter 6 at 3.8) and the requirements in respect of measuring the cost of a business combination (see Chapter 15 at 3.5).

An investor will recognise distributions received from its investments in associates as income irrespective of whether the distributions are from accumulated profits of the associate arising before or after the date of acquisition. *[FRS 102.14.6]*.

3.3.4   Fair value model

An investor that is not a parent, and that chooses to adopt the fair value model, should initially recognise its investment in an associate at the transaction price. *[FRS 102.14.9]*. 'Transaction price' is not defined, but it is presumably the same as its cost. Indeed, FRS 102 states that this paragraph requires 'transaction costs to be included as part of the transaction price on initial recognition'. *[FRS 102 Appendix II]*.

At each subsequent reporting date, the investor should measure its investments in associates at fair value using the fair value guidance in paragraphs 11.27 to 11.32 of FRS 102. Changes in fair value are recognised in accordance with paragraphs 17.15E and 17.15F. *[FRS 102.14.10]*. These are the paragraphs detailing the reporting of gains or losses on revaluation and are discussed further in Chapter 13 at 3.6.3.

An investor that uses the fair value model for accounting for its investments in associates should use the cost model for any investment in an associate for which it is impracticable to measure fair value reliably without undue cost or effort. *[FRS 102.14.10]*. Under FRS 102, applying a requirement is impracticable when the entity cannot apply it after making every reasonable effort to do so. *[FRS 102 Appendix I]*.

An investor will recognise distributions received from its investments in associates as income irrespective of whether the distributions are from accumulated profits of the associate arising before or after the date of acquisition. *[FRS 102 14.10A]*.

3.4   Presentation and disclosures

3.4.1   Presentation

An investor shall classify its investments in associates as fixed assets in the balance sheet. *[FRS 102.14.11]*.

Goodwill relating to an associate is included in the carrying amount of the investment, *[FRS 102.14.8(c)]*, whereas loans to associates due on demand are basic financial instruments and are therefore presented on the face of the balance sheet as a financial asset. *[FRS 102.11.10]*.

In the profit and loss account, the share of income from associates is presented as one line, after the effects of interest and tax (see Chapter 4).

3.4.2   Disclosures

3.4.2.A   General requirements

In both consolidated and individual financial statements where an entity holds an investment in an associate the following should be disclosed:

- the accounting policy for investments in associates;
- the carrying amount of investments in associates; and
- the fair value of investments in associates accounted for using the equity method for which there are published price quotations. *[FRS 102.14.12]*.

3.4.2.B   Consolidated financial statements

An investor shall disclose separately:

- its share of the profit or loss of associates accounted for in accordance with the equity method; and
- its share of any discontinued operations of such associates. *[FRS 102.14.14]*.

3.4.2.C   Individual financial statements of investors that are not parents

An investor should disclose:

- summarised financial information about the investments in associates; and
- the effect of including those investments as if they had been accounted for using the equity method.

Investors that are exempt, from preparing consolidated financial statements, or would be exempt if they had any subsidiaries are exempt from these requirements. *[FRS 102.14.14]*.

For investments accounted for in accordance with the cost model, an investor is required to disclose the amount of dividends and any other distributions recognised as income. *[FRS 102.14.13]*.

For investments in associates accounted for in accordance with and the fair value model an investor shall make the disclosure required by Section 11 paragraphs 11.43 and 11.44: *[FRS 102.14.15]*

- the basis for determining fair value; and
- if a reliable measure of fair value is no longer available for ordinary shares valued at fair value through profit or loss this fact shall be diclosed.

4.   PRACTICAL IMPLEMENTATION ISSUES

4.1   Changes in ownership interest

4.1.1   Initial carrying amount of an associate following loss of control of an entity

Under Section 9, if a parent entity loses control of an entity, then at the date that the entity ceases to be a subsidiary the retained interest is measured at the carrying amount of the net assets (and goodwill) attributable to the investment and shall be regarded as the cost on initial measurement of the financial asset or investment in the associate, as appropriate. In applying the equity method to a retained investment in an associate as required in Section 9, paragraph 9.19(b) states that the requirements of Section 14, paragraph 14.8(c) shall not be applied. *[FRS 102.9.19]*.

This means that in the case of a retained interest in an associate, there is no need to re-determine the implicit goodwill and fair values of the associate's assets and liabilities at the date it becomes an associate.

Example 10.11:   Accounting for retained interest in an associate following loss of control of an entity

Entity A owns 100% of the shares of Entity B. The interest was originally purchased for £500,000 and £40,000 of directly attributable costs relating to the acquisition were incurred. On 30 June 2015, Entity A sells 60% of the shares to Entity C for £1,300,000. As a result of the sale, Entity C obtains control over Entity B, but by retaining a 40% interest, Entity A determines that it still has significant influence over Entity B.

At the date of disposal, the carrying amount of the net assets of Entity B in Entity A's consolidated financial statements is £1,200,000 and there is also goodwill of £200,000 relating to the acquisition of Entity B. The fair value of the identifiable assets and liabilities of Entity B is £1,600,000. The fair value of Entity A's retained interest of 40% of the shares of Entity B is £800,000.

Upon Entity A's sale of 60% of the shares of Entity B, it deconsolidates Entity B and accounts for its investment in Entity B as an associate using the equity method of accounting.

Entity A's initial carrying amount of the associate must be based on the carrying value of the net assets (and goodwill) of the retained interest, i.e. £560,000 – 40% of the carrying amount of the net assets and goodwill totalling £1,400,000.

4.1.2   Piecemeal acquisition of an associate

There is no guidance in FRS 102 on how to account for the piecemeal acquisition of an associate and so different approaches could be applied in practice.

4.1.2.A   Financial instrument becoming an associate

An entity may gain significant influence over an existing investment upon acquisition of a further interest or due to a change in circumstances. Section 14 gives no guidance on how an investor should account for an existing investment that subsequently becomes an associate which should be accounted for under the equity method.

It is clear under Section 19 that in a business combination where control over an acquiree is achieved in stages following a series of transactions, the cost of the business combination is the aggregate of the fair values of the assets given, liabilities assumed and equity instruments issued by the acquirer at the date of each transaction in the series. *[FRS 102.19.11A]*. It might be argued that a similar approach should be adopted when an associate is acquired in stages.

4.1.3   Step increase in an existing associate

An entity may acquire an additional interest in an existing associate that continues to be an associate accounted for under the equity method. FRS 102 does not explicitly deal with such transactions.

In these situations, we believe that the purchase price paid for the additional interest is added to the existing carrying amount of the associate and the existing interest in the associate is not remeasured.

This increase in the investment must still be notionally split between goodwill and the additional interest in the fair value of the net assets of the associate. This split is based on the fair value of the net assets at the date of the increase in the associate. However, no remeasurement is made for previously unrecognised changes in the fair values of identifiable net assets.

Paragraph 14.8(c) of FRS 102 establishes the requirement that the cost of an investment in an associate is allocated to the purchase of a share of the fair value of net assets and the goodwill. This requirement is not limited to the initial application of equity accounting, but applies to each acquisition of an investment. However, this does not result in any revaluation of the existing share of net assets.

Rather, the existing ownership interests are accounted for under paragraph 14.8 of FRS 102, whereby the carrying value is adjusted only for the investor's share of the associate's profits or losses and other recognised equity transactions. No entry is recognised to reflect changes in the fair value of assets and liabilities that are not recognised under the accounting policies applied for the associate.

Example 10.12 below illustrates an increase in ownership of an associate that continues to be an associate.

Example 10.12: Accounting for an increase in the ownership of an associate

Entity A obtains significant influence over Entity B by acquiring an investment of 25% at a cost of £3,000 during 2014. At the date of the acquisition of the investment, the fair value of the associate's net identifiable assets is £10,000. The investment is accounted for under the equity method in the consolidated financial statements of Entity A.

In 2016, Entity A acquires an additional investment of 20% in Entity B at a cost of £4,000, increasing its total investment in Entity B to 45%. The investment is, however, still an associate and still accounted for using the equity method of accounting.

For the purposes of the example, directly attributable costs have been ignored and it is assumed that no profit or loss arose during the period since the acquisition of the first 25%. Therefore, the carrying amount of the investment immediately prior to the additional investment is £3,000. However, an asset held by the associate has increased in value by £5,000 so that the fair value of the associate's net identifiable assets is now £15,000.

To summarise, amounts are as follows:

	£
Fair value of net assets of Entity B in 2014	10,000
Increase in fair value	5,000
Fair value of net assets of Entity B in 2016	15,000

As a result of the additional investment, the equity-accounted amount for the associate increases by £4,000. The notional goodwill applicable to the second tranche of the acquisition is £1,000 [£4,000 − (20% × £15,000)].

The impact of the additional investment on Entity A's equity-accounted amount for Entity B is summarised as follows:

	% held	Carrying amount	Share of net assets	Goodwill included in investment
		£	£	£
Existing investment	25	3,000	2,500	500
Additional investment	20	4,000	3,000	1,000
Total investment	45	7,000	5,500	1,500

The accounting described above applies when the additional interest in an existing associate continues to be accounted for as an associate under the equity method.

The accounting for an increase in an associate that becomes a subsidiary is discussed in Chapter 15.

4.1.4   *Step increase in an existing associate that becomes a joint venture*

In the situation discussed at 4.1.3 above, the acquisition of the additional interest did not result in a change in status of the investee; i.e. the associate remained an associate. However, an entity may acquire an additional interest in an existing associate that becomes a joint venture. In this situation, although FRS 102 does refer to an associate that becomes a joint venture, it does not actually contain any specific guidance as to what should be done. *[FRS 102.14.8(i)]*. However, as a joint venture is also accounted under the equity method, the accounting described in Example 10.12 above would seem to apply.

4.2   Distributions received in excess of the carrying amount

When an associate makes dividend distributions to the investor in excess of the investor's carrying amount it is not immediately clear how the excess should be accounted for. A liability under Section 21 should only be recognised if the investor is obliged to refund the dividend, or has incurred a legal or constructive obligation or made payments on behalf of the associate. In the absence of such obligations, it would seem appropriate that the investor recognises the excess in net profit for the period. When the associate subsequently makes profits, the investor should only start recognising profits when they exceed the excess cash distributions recognised in net profit plus any previously unrecognised losses (see 3.3.2.I above).

4.3   Equity transactions in an associate's financial statements

The financial statements of an associate that are used for the purposes of equity accounting by the investor may include items within its statement of changes in equity that are not reflected in the profit or loss or components of other comprehensive income, for example, dividends or other forms of distributions, issues of equity instruments and equity-settled share-based payment transactions. Where the associate has subsidiaries and consolidated financial statements are prepared, those financial statements may include the effects of changes in the parent's (i.e. the associate's) ownership interest and non-controlling interest in a subsidiary that did not arise from a transaction that resulted in loss of control of that subsidiary.

Although the description of the equity method in Section 14 (together with the requirements in Section 5 – *Statement of Comprehensive Income and Income Statement*) requires that the investor's share of the profit or loss of the associate is recognised in the investor's profit or loss, and the investor's share of changes in items of other comprehensive income of the associate is recognised in other comprehensive income of the investor, *[FRS 102.14.8]*, no explicit reference is made to other items that the associate may have in its statement of changes in equity.

Investors will therefore need to determine an appropriate accounting treatment for these different types of transactions that may be accounted for by the associate in its statement of changes in equity.

5   COMPANY LAW MATTERS

5.1   Associated undertakings

An '*associated undertaking*' is defined in the Companies Act as an undertaking in which an undertaking included in the consolidation has a participating interest and over whose operating and financial policy it exercises a significant influence, and which is not:

- a subsidiary undertaking of the parent company, or
- a joint venture dealt with in accordance with the paragraph on joint ventures. *[6 Sch 19(1)]*.

Where an undertaking holds 20% or more of the voting rights in another undertaking, it is presumed to exercise such an influence over it unless the contrary is shown. *[6 Sch 19(2)]*.

A '*participating interest*' is an interest held by an undertaking in the shares of another undertaking which it holds on a long-term basis for the purpose of securing a contribution to its activities by the exercise of control or influence arising from or related to that interest. The interest in shares includes interests which are convertible into shares or options to acquire shares, regardless whether or not they are currently exercisable. Additionally, interests held on behalf of an undertaking are to be treated as held by it. *[10 Sch 11(1), 11(3), 11(4)]*.

5.2   Voting rights

The provisions of paragraphs 5 to 11 of Schedule 7 to the Companies Act (parent and subsidiary undertakings: rights to be taken into account and attribution of rights) apply in determining whether an undertaking holds 20% or more of the voting rights in another undertaking.

The '*voting rights*' in an undertaking are the rights conferred on shareholders in respect of their shares or, in the case of an undertaking not having a share capital, on members, to vote at general meetings of the undertaking on all, or substantially all, matters. *[6 Sch 19(3)]*.

Voting rights on shares held as security remain the rights of the provider of the security, and are not taken into account if the rights are only exercisable in accordance with instructions from the provider of the security or in his interest. *[8 Sch 7]*. Similarly, voting rights that are held in a fiduciary capacity may not be those of the entity itself *[6 Sch 7]*. Voting rights held by a nominee on behalf of the entity should not be treated as held by him and rights regarded as held as nominee for another if they are exercisable on his instruction. *[7 Sch 7]*.

The voting rights referred to above should be reduced by the rights held by the undertaking itself. *[10 Sch 7]*.

5.3   Presentation and disclosure

5.3.1   *Consolidated financial statements*

The Regulations require that investments in associates are presented in fixed assets in the balance sheet and that the equity accounted share of profit (after interest and tax) is reflected in the profit and loss account as a single line. *[4 Sch 20]*.

The format of the profit and loss account and balance sheet under FRS 102 are discussed further in Chapter 4.

The Regulations also require that the following information must be given where an undertaking included in the consolidation has an interest in an associate undertaking:

- the name of the associate;
- the country in which the associate is incorporated for those incorporated outside the United Kingdom;
- the address of the associate's principal place of business if unincorporated;
- The identity and proportion of the nominal value of each class of share held disclosing separately those held by the:
  - parent company; and
  - group. *[4 Sch 19]*.

5.3.2   *Individual financial statements*

In individual financial statements the Regulations require additional disclosures in respect of significant holdings in undertakings, other than subsidiary entities. A holding is deemed significant if:

- it amounts to 20% or more of the nominal value of any class of shares in the undertaking; or
- the amount of the holding as stated in the company's individual accounts exceeds 20% of the stated net assets of the company. *[4 Sch 4]*.

In practice, this definition will capture most investments in associates. The resulting disclosures in individual financial statements are:

- the name of each associate;
- the country in which each associate is incorporated for those incorporated outside the United Kingdom;
- the address of each associate's principal place of business if unincorporated;
- the identity and proportion of the nominal value of each class of share held. *[4 Sch 5]*.

For each associate detailed above there must also be disclosed the aggregate amount of the capital and reserves as at the end of its relevant financial year of each entity and its profit or loss for that year (unless the associate is not required to publish its balance sheet anywhere in the world and the holding is less than 50% of the nominal value of the shares, or the information is not material). *[4 Sch 6]*.

A parent that is exempt under sections 400 or 401 of the Act from the requirement to prepare group accounts is not required to give the additional disclosures in Schedule 4.6 of the Regulations in its separate financial statements if it discloses, in the notes to its accounts, the aggregate investment in all significant holdings in undertakings (including its associates) determined by way of the equity method of valuation. *[4 Sch 13]*.

A parent that prepares consolidated financial statements and discloses the information described at 5.3.1 above is not required to give the above disclosures in its separate financial statements.

6   SUMMARY OF GAAP DIFFERENCES

The key differences between FRS 102, previous UK GAAP and IFRS in accounting for associates are set out below.

	FRS 102	Previous UK GAAP	IFRS
Significant influence	Significant influence is the power to participate in the financial and operating policies of an entity regardless of whether the power is actively exercised or not.	Similar definition except that it requires the actual exercise of significant influence rather than just the power to exercise.	Significant influence is the power to participate in the financial and operating policies of an entity regardless of whether the power is actively exercised or not Additional guidance is given on indicators of significant influence.
Entity that is not a parent	An entity that is not a parent has the option to account for its investments in associates using either the cost model, fair value model or at fair value through profit or loss.	Under previous UK GAAP the option to account for associates at fair value through profit or loss did not exist.	An entity that is not a parent must prepare financial statements whereby its investments in associates are accounted for under the equity accounting method unless it meets criteria for exemption.
Investment portfolios / funds	Investments in associates held as part of an investment portfolio should be measured at fair value through profit or loss in the consolidated financial statements of an investor that is a parent.	Investments funds have the option to recognise all investments held as part of their investment portfolio at either cost or market value (with changes in value reflected in the statement of recognised gains and losses) provided all investments are accounted for on the same basis.	Venture capital organisations and similar entities can choose to measure investments in associates at fair value through profit or loss. Investment entities would elect to choose this option.
Implicit goodwill and fair value adjustments on acquisition of an associate	Follows the requirements of Section 19 of FRS 102 and in particular the requirement that unless a reliable estimate can be made implicit goodwill on the acquisition of an associate should be amortised over a period not exceeding 5 years.	Follows the requirements of previous UK GAAP regarding business combinations with consequential differences, in particular regarding implicit goodwill amortisation where there is a rebuttable presumption that goodwill should not be amortised over a period exceeding 20 years.	Follows the IFRS requirements regarding business combinations. Implicit goodwill is not amortised.

Chapter 10

	FRS 102	*Previous UK GAAP*	*IFRS*
Losses in excess of investment in an associate	Losses are recognised until the carrying value of the investment is reduced to nil and no further losses are recognised unless the entity has a legal or constructive obligation or has made payments on behalf of the associate	FRS 9 requires the continued recognition of losses even if they exceed the cost of investment.	Losses are recognised until the carrying value of the investment is reduced to nil and no further losses are recognised unless the entity has a legal or constructive obligation or has made payments on behalf of the associate
Loss of significant influence of an equity-accounted associate that does not become a subsidiary or an jointly controlled entity	If loss of significant influence is as a result of a partial disposal, a gain or loss is recognised based on the disposal proceeds and the carrying amount relating to the proportion disposed of. The carrying value of the equity interest retained at the date significant influence lost becomes the cost of the retained investment. If the loss of significant influence is for reasons other than a partial disposal, no gain or loss is recognised and the carrying value of the equity-accounted investment at the date significant influence is lost becomes the cost of the retained investment.	If loss of significant influence is as a result of a partial disposal, a gain or loss is recognised based on the disposal proceeds and the carrying amount relating to the proportion disposed of. The carrying value of the equity interest retained at the date significant influence lost becomes the cost of the retained investment. If the loss of significant influence is for reasons other than a partial disposal, no gain or loss is recognised and the carrying value of the equity-accounted investment at the date significant influence is lost becomes the cost of the retained investment.	If loss of significant influence is as a result of a partial disposal, a gain or loss is recognised based on the disposal proceeds together with the fair value of any retained interest and the carrying amount of the total interest in the associate.. If loss of significant influence is for reasons other than a partial disposal, a gain or loss is recognised based on the fair value of the retained interest and the carrying amount of the interest in the associate at that date.
Presentation of the equity accounted results of a jointly controlled entity	The share of income from jointly controlled entities is presented as one line, after the effects of interest and tax.	The share of operating profit of associates is presented after the group operating profit, with interest and tax related to associates being presented alongside the interest and tax line items in the group profit or loss account.	The share of income from joint ventures is presented as one line, after the effects of interest and tax.

Chapter 11   Investments in joint ventures

List of examples

Chapter 11

Chapter 11   Investments in joint ventures

1   INTRODUCTION

Section 15 – *Investments in Joint Ventures* – sets out the accounting and disclosure requirements for joint ventures in consolidated financial statements, separate financial statements of a venturer that is a parent and individual financial statements of a venturer that is not a parent. *[FRS 102.15.1]*.

The accounting requirements in Section 15 are based on the IASB's IFRS for SMEs, which in turn were derived from those in the then IAS on the topic, IAS 31 – *Interests in Joint Ventures*. It therefore does not reflect the requirements of IFRS 11 – *Joint Arrangements* – which is now the effective IFRS relevant to this topic. Although based on the IFRS for SMEs, Section 15 has also been amended, principally in relation to certain aspects of the accounting and disclosures for investments in a jointly controlled entity in the individual financial statements of a venturer that is not a parent. *[FRS 102 Appendix II]*.

A 'joint venture' is a strategic investment made by an entity where there is joint control of that investment with another party or parties. The exact form of the strategic investment can vary and Section 15 addresses that variation by classifying joint ventures into three categories: jointly controlled assets, jointly controlled operations and jointly controlled entities.

Joint ventures are commonplace in many industry sectors, often as a means of pooling resources or expertise, risk sharing or new product development. The term is sometimes used loosely to describe any commercial partnership type arrangement but it is important to emphasise that only those where there is contractually-based joint control will fall within the scope of Section 15.

2   COMPARISON BETWEEN SECTION 15, PREVIOUS UK GAAP AND IFRS

There are differences between the accounting and disclosure requirements in Section 15 compared with previous UK GAAP (FRS 9 – *Associates and joint ventures*) and IFRS (IFRS 11 – *Joint Arrangements*). The key ones are discussed at 2.1 and 2.2 below respectively and differences are summarised at 5 below.

2.1   Key differences between Section 15 and previous UK GAAP

2.1.1   *Scope and classification*

Section 15 classifies joint ventures as either jointly controlled operations, jointly controlled assets or jointly controlled entities with different accounting considerations for each. Classification as a jointly controlled entity is appropriate when the arrangement involves the creation of a separate entity, be it a corporation, partnership or other entity. *[FRS 102.15.8]*. A jointly controlled operation involves the venturers using their own assets to contribute to an activity, without the creation of a separate entity. *[FRS 102.15.4]*. A jointly controlled asset is an asset under joint control where each venturer obtains a share of the benefits from that asset. *[FRS 102.15.6]*.

FRS 9 covers joint ventures (the definition of which requires entities to be jointly controlled under a contractual arrangement) and also joint arrangements that are not entities (commonly referred to as 'JANEs'). Whilst joint ventures must be entities, they do not require the creation of a separate legal entity but require the joint venture to have, in substance, a trade or business of its own, separate from that of the venturers. JANEs are joint activities that in essence are an extension of the trades or businesses of their investors rather than a trade or business in their own right. *[FRS 9.4]*.

2.1.2   *Accounting for jointly controlled operations and assets*

Although the requirements are worded differently, the accounting for jointly controlled operations and assets will be broadly similar under Section 15 *[FRS 102.15.5, 15.7]* and FRS 9 (where they would fall under the requirements for JANEs *[FRS 9.18]* or a structure with the form but not the substance of a joint venture *[FRS 9.24]*).

2.1.3   *Measurement – entity that is not a parent*

FRS 102 permits entities that are not parents to account for their investment in jointly controlled entities using the cost model, fair value model or at fair value through profit or loss (see 3.6.2 below). *[FRS 102.15.9]*. Under previous UK GAAP the option to account for joint ventures at fair value through profit or loss did not exist.

2.1.4   *Investment portfolios / funds*

Section 15 requires that investments in jointly controlled entities held by a venturer that is a parent as part of an investment portfolio should be measured at fair value through profit or loss (see 3.6.3.B below). *[FRS 102.15.9B]*. Under FRS 9 investment funds are given the option to recognise all investments held as part of their investment portfolio at either cost or market value (with changes in value reflected in the statement of total recognised gains and losses) provided all investments are accounted for on the same basis. *[FRS 9.49]*.

2.1.5 Accounting for jointly controlled entities

Section 15 requires that (apart from those held as part of an investment portfolio described at 2.1.4 above) jointly controlled entities are equity accounted (using the procedures in Section 14 – *Investments in Associates*) in the consolidated financial statements of a venturer. *[FRS 102.15.13]*. The share of income is presented in the venturer's income statement as one line, after the effects of interest and tax, and the equity-accounted investment is presented as one line in the balance sheet. *[FRS 102.5.5, FRS 102.4.2]*. FRS 9 requires the use of 'gross equity accounting' for joint ventures which produces the same underlying effect on profit as equity accounting but also reflects the share of joint venture turnover. In the balance sheet, the investment is analysed into the share of total assets and share of total liabilities. *[FRS 9.20-21]*.

2.1.6 Implicit goodwill and fair value adjustments

Section 15 (via Section 14) refers to the requirements of FRS 102 Section 19 – *Business Combinations and Goodwill* – in the context of determining the implicit goodwill and fair value adjustments arising on the acquisition of an investment in a jointly controlled entity. As the requirements of Section 19 differ from previous UK GAAP (see Chapter 15) this may have consequential impact on accounting for joint ventures, in particular on the accounting for the implicit goodwill. Previous UK GAAP has a rebuttable presumption that goodwill should not be amortised over a period exceeding 20 years. *[FRS 10.19]*. Section 19 states that unless a reliable estimate can be made goodwill should be amortised over a period not exceeding 5 years. *[FRS 102.19.23(a)]*.

2.1.7 Losses in excess of investment

Section 15, in its application of equity accounting under Section 14, does not permit the recognition of losses of jointly controlled entities in excess of the cost of investment unless the venturer has legal or constructive obligations in respect of the excess losses. *[FRS 102.14.8(h)]*.

FRS 9 requires the continued recognition of losses for joint ventures even if they exceed the cost of investment. *[FRS 9.44]*.

2.2 Key differences between Section 15 and IFRS

2.2.1 Scope and classification

As noted above, Section 15 classifies joint ventures as either jointly controlled operations, jointly controlled assets or jointly controlled entities.

IFRS 11 addresses joint arrangements and only makes the distinction between joint operations and joint ventures. This distinction is based on the rights and obligations under the arrangement, rather than focussing on the legal form of the entity. *[IFRS 11.14]*. Where the parties with joint control have an interest in the net assets of the arrangement then the arrangement will be a joint venture, *[IFRS 11.15]*, which is the equivalent of a jointly controlled entity under Section 15. Otherwise, where the parties with joint control have rights to underlying assets and obligations for liabilities the arrangement will be a joint operation. *[IFRS 11.16]* Determining the appropriate classification under IFRS 11 involves an assessment of the venturer's rights and obligations under the arrangement, based on the detailed guidance within the standard.

Generally, arrangements that are jointly controlled operations or jointly controlled assets under Section 15 would be joint operations under IFRS 11. Although many arrangements that are jointly controlled entities under Section 15 would be classified as joint ventures under IFRS 11 some would have to be classified as joint operations due to the requirement to assess rights and obligations rather than focussing on the legal form of the entity.

2.2.2   Measurement – entity that is not a parent

FRS 102 permits entities that are not parents to account for their investment in jointly controlled entities using the cost model, fair value model or at fair value through profit or loss (see 3.6.2 below). *[FRS 102.15.9]*.

Under IFRS, an entity that is not a parent must prepare financial statements in which its investments in jointly controlled entities are accounted for under the equity accounting method unless it meets the criteria for exemption. *[IAS 28.16, 17]*.

2.2.3   Investment portfolios / funds

Section 15 requires that investments in jointly controlled entities held as part of an investment portfolio by a venturer that is a parent should be measured at fair value through profit or loss (see 3.6.3.B below). *[FRS 102.15.9B]*. Under IFRS, venture capital organisations and similar entities can choose to measure investments in joint ventures at fair value through profit or loss. *[IAS 28.18]*. Investment entities would elect this option. *[IFRS 10.B85L]*.

2.2.4   Accounting for the acquisition of a jointly controlled entity

Section 15 requires the use of Section 19 to determine the implicit goodwill on the acquisition of a jointly controlled operation. This is then amortised. *[FRS 102.14.8(c), FRS 102.19.23]*. Under IFRS, the implicit goodwill is not amortised.

2.2.5   Loss of joint control where the jointly controlled entity does not become a subsidiary or associate

Section 15 (via Section 14) requires that where loss of joint control is as a result of a partial disposal, a gain or loss is recognised based on the disposal proceeds and the carrying amount relating to the proportion disposed of. The carrying value of the equity interest retained at the date joint control is lost becomes the cost of the retained investment.

If the loss of joint control is for reasons other than a partial disposal, no gain or loss is recognised and the carrying value of the equity-accounted investment as at the date at which joint control is lost becomes the cost of the retained investment. *[FRS 102.14.8(i)]*.

Under IFRS, if loss of joint control is as a result of a partial disposal, a gain or loss is recognised based on the disposal proceeds together with the fair value of any retained interest and the carrying amount of the total interest in the joint venture.

If loss of joint control is for reasons other than a partial disposal, a gain or loss is recognised based on the fair value of the retained interest and the carrying amount of the interest in the joint venture at that date. *[IAS 28.22]*.

3 REQUIREMENTS OF SECTION 15 FOR INVESTMENTS IN JOINT VENTURES

3.1 Scope

Section 15 applies to accounting for:

- joint ventures in consolidated financial statements;
- investments in joint ventures in the individual financial statements of a venturer that is not a parent; and
- investments in jointly controlled operations and jointly controlled assets in the separate financial statements of a venturer that is a parent.

A venturer that is a parent accounts for interests in jointly controlled entities in its separate financial statements in accordance with paragraphs 9.26 and 9.26A of FRS 102, as appropriate (see Chapter 6 at 4.2). *[FRS 102.15.1].*

3.2 Terms used in Section 15

Terms defined within Section 15 are explained in this chapter. Those and other relevant terms used within Section 15 but defined elsewhere within FRS 102 have the meanings specified in the Glossary as shown in the following table: *[FRS 102 Appendix I]*

Term	*Definition*
Consolidated financial statements	The financial statements of a parent and its subsidiaries presented as those of a single economic entity.
Control (of an entity)	The power to govern the financial and operating policies of an entity so as to obtain benefits from its activities.
Held as part of an investment portfolio	An interest is held as part of an investment portfolio if its value to the investor is through fair value as part of a directly or indirectly held basket of investments rather than as a media through which the investor carries out business. A basket of investments is indirectly held if an investment fund holds a single investment in a second investment fund which, in turn, holds a basket of investments.
Individual financial statements	The accounts that are required to be prepared by an entity in accordance with the Act or relevant legislation, for example: (a) 'individual accounts', as set out in section 394 of the Act; (b) 'statement of accounts', as set out in section 132 of the Charities Act 2011; or (c) 'individual accounts', as set out in section 72A of the Building Societies Act 1986. Separate financial statements are included in the meaning of this term.
Joint control	The contractually agreed sharing of control over an economic activity. It exists only when the strategic financial and operating decisions relating to the activity require the unanimous consent of the parties sharing control (the venturers).

Term	Definition
Jointly controlled entity	A joint venture that involves the establishment of a corporation, partnership or other entity in which each venturer has an interest. The entity operates in the same way as other entities, except that a contractual arrangement between the venturers establishes joint control over the economic activity of the entity.
Joint venture	A contractual arrangement whereby two or more parties undertake an economic activity that is subject to joint control. Joint ventures can take the form of jointly controlled operations, jointly controlled assets or jointly controlled entities.
Parent	An entity that has one or more subsidiaries.
Separate financial statements	Those presented by a parent in which the investments in subsidiaries, associates or jointly controlled entities are accounted for either at cost or fair value rather than on the basis of the reported results and net assets of the investees. Separate financial statements are included within the meaning of individual financial statements.
Subsidiary	An entity, including an unincorporated entity such as a partnership, that is controlled by another entity (known as the parent).
Venturer	A party to a joint venture that has joint control over that joint venture.

3.3   Definition of a joint venture and related terms

Section 15 defines a joint venture as 'a contractual arrangement whereby two or more parties undertake an economic activity that is subject to joint control'. *[FRS 102.15.3]*.

An economic activity is not defined in FRS 102 but is intended to be broadly based given that joint ventures can take many forms (see 3.3.5 below).

Joint control is defined as 'the contractually agreed sharing of control over an economic activity, and exists only when the strategic financial and operating decisions relating to the activity require the unanimous consent of the parties sharing control (the venturers)'. *[FRS 102.15.2]*.

Although FRS 102 does not define what strategic, financial and operating decisions would cover, these are generally understood to include areas such as budgeting, capital expenditure, treasury management, dividend policy, production, marketing, sales and human resources.

FRS 102 defines control (of an entity) as 'the power to govern the financial and operating policies of an entity so as to obtain benefits from its activities'. *[FRS 102 Appendix I]*. The concept of control is discussed further in Chapter 6.

A venturer is defined as 'a party to a joint venture that has joint control over that joint venture'. *[FRS 102 Appendix I]*.

Section 15 offers no further guidance on the following: parties to a joint venture that are not venturers, the nature of the contractual arrangements or joint control (in particular the concept of unanimous consent) which are key to an understanding of a joint venture. These aspects are discussed in the following sections making reference to additional guidance in IAS 31 on which Section 15 is based.

3.3.1   'Venturer' versus 'investor'

In addition to 'venturers', there may well be other investors in the joint venture. In the absence of a definition in FRS 102, IAS 31 states that an investor in a joint venture is 'a party to a joint venture and does not have joint control over that joint venture'. *[IAS 31.3]*. The definitions of 'investor' and 'venturer' draw a distinction between participants in a joint venture who also participate in the joint control of that venture and more passive investors, as illustrated by Example 11.1.

Example 11.1:   'Venturer' versus 'investor'

A, B and C establish a fourth entity D, of which A owns 40%, B 11% and C 49%. A and B enter into a contractual arrangement whereby any financial and operating decisions taken by A and B relating to the activity of D require the unanimous consent of A and B. A simple majority of D's shareholders only is required for all major decisions. An analysis based on the relevant definitions would regard A and B as being 'venturers', and C as an 'investor', in D.

The interest of an 'investor' in a jointly controlled entity should be treated as either:

- an associate within the scope of Section 14 - *Investments in Associates* if the investor has significant influence over the entity (see Chapter 10); or

- otherwise as a financial asset within the scope of Section 11 – *Basic Financial Instruments* – or Section 12 – *Other Financial Instruments Issues* (see Chapter 8). *[FRS 102.15.18]*.

3.3.2   Contractual arrangement

Contractual arrangements can be evidenced in several ways. An enforceable contractual arrangement is often, but not always, in writing (although we expect unwritten agreements to be rare in practice). Statutory mechanisms can create enforceable arrangements, either on their own or in conjunction with contracts between the parties. A contractual arrangement may be incorporated into the articles or other formation documents of the entity.

The contractual arrangement sets out the terms upon which the parties agree to share control over the activity that is the subject of the arrangement. IAS 31 provides some relevant guidance on the aspects generally specified in the contractual arrangement for a joint venture:

(a)   the activity, duration and reporting obligations of the joint venture;

(b)   the appointment of the board of directors or equivalent governing body of the joint venture and the voting rights of the venturers;

(c)   capital contributions by the venturers; and

(d)   the sharing by the venturers of the output, income, expenses or results of the joint venture. *[IAS 31.10]*.

3.3.3   Joint control and unanimous consent

In order to establish whether joint control of an arrangement exists, it is necessary to establish whether the contractual arrangement gives all the parties to that arrangement (or a group of the parties) control of the arrangement in the collective sense. That means the parties (or a group thereof) must need to act together to direct the strategic, financial and operating policies of the arrangement. It follows that there must be at least two parties for there to be joint control.

Section 15 includes the specific requirement for 'unanimous consent' in the definition of joint control. Unanimous consent essentially means that any party to the arrangement can prevent any of the other parties, or group of the other parties, from making decisions of a strategic, financial or operating nature without its consent. This ensures that no single party can control the arrangement. This means, for example, that none of the parties to the contractual arrangement should have a casting vote that enables it to resolve a deadlock, as that would constitute a form of unilateral control.

IAS 31 provides guidance in a situation where a contractual arrangement may identify one venturer as the operator or manager of the joint venture. The operator does not control the joint venture but acts within the financial and operating policies agreed by the venturers in accordance with the contractual arrangement and delegated to the operator. If, however, the operator does have the power to govern (i.e. not merely to execute) the financial and operating policies of the economic activity, the operator controls the venture and the venture is a subsidiary of the operator and not a joint venture. *[IAS 31.12].*

3.3.4   Potential voting rights

An entity may own share warrants, share call options, debt or equity instruments that are convertible into ordinary shares, or other similar instruments that have the potential, if exercised or converted, to give the entity voting power or reduce another party's voting power over the financial and operating policies of another entity (potential voting rights).

Potential voting rights are not directly addressed in Section 15 (nor in IAS 31). Nevertheless, the existence of potential voting rights may be relevant to an assessment of joint control. However, the contractual arrangement giving rise to joint control will tend to over-ride relative ownership interests (voting and potential voting rights). This is an issue that will need to be addressed in the light of individual facts and circumstances.

3.3.5   Types of joint venture

Section 15 explains that joint ventures can take one of three forms, all sharing the common characteristics of an underlying contractual arrangement and joint control. The three forms are:

- jointly controlled operations (see 3.4 below);
- jointly controlled assets (see 3.5 below); and
- jointly controlled entities (see 3.6 below).

3.4   Jointly controlled operations

3.4.1   Definition

Jointly controlled operations arise when a joint venture is established that does not involve the formation of a separate corporation, partnership or other entity or financial structure that exists separately from the venturers. Instead the joint venture uses assets and other resources of the venturers. In such a case each venturer will use its own property, plant and equipment and carries its own inventories. It also incurs its own expenses and liabilities and raises its own finance, which represent its own obligations. The joint venture activities may be carried out by the venturer's employees alongside the venturer's similar activities. The joint venture agreement usually provides a means by which the revenue from the sale of the joint product and any expenses incurred in common are shared among the venturers. *[FRS 102.15.4].*

An example of a jointly controlled operation might be where two or more venturers combine their operations, resources and expertise in order to jointly manufacture, market and distribute a particular product. Each venturer undertakes a different part of the manufacturing process and bears its own costs. Revenue from the sale of the product is then shared on the basis of the contractual arrangement. There is no separate entity conducting the business of manufacturing and selling the product. It is merely an extension of the venturers' existing businesses.

3.4.2   Accounting requirements for jointly controlled operations

In respect of its interests in jointly controlled operations, a venturer recognises in its financial statements:

- the assets that it controls and the liabilities that it incurs; and

- the expenses that it incurs and its share of the income that is earns from the sale of goods or services by the joint venture. *[FRS 102.15.5].*

As the assets, liabilities, income and expenses will already be reflected in the individual financial statements of the venturer (including the separate financial statements of a venturer that is a parent) then no adjustments or other consolidation procedures are required in respect of these items if the venturer presents consolidated financial statements. Separate accounting records may not be required, nor financial statements prepared, for the joint venture itself, although the venturers may prepare management accounts in order to assess the performance of the joint venture.

When venturers are funding the operations of a jointly controlled operation they may need to account for a receivable or payable from other venturers, as illustrated in Example 11.2 below.

Example 11.2:   Loans to jointly controlled operations

Two entities – A and B – each own half of a jointly controlled operation. Entity A has lent £400 to the jointly controlled operation, while entity B has lent £300. How should entity A account for its loan?

The jointly controlled operation has total borrowings of £400 + £300 = £700. A's share in the borrowings of £350 (=50% of £700) should be offset against its receivable of £400. Entity A should, therefore, account for a net receivable from its joint venture partner of £50 (=£400 – £350).

The jointly controlled operation is not a separate legal entity and under the joint venture agreement A has a business relationship only with B. Gross presentation of a receivable of £200 (=£400 – 50% of £400) and a liability of £150 (=50% of £300) would therefore not be appropriate.

3.5   Jointly controlled assets

3.5.1   Definition

Jointly controlled assets arise in circumstances where one or more assets are contributed to or acquired for the purpose of the joint venture and those assets are jointly controlled and often jointly owned. *[FRS 102.15.6].*

The assets are used to obtain benefits for the venturers, who may each take a share of the output from the assets and bear an agreed share of the expenses incurred. Such ventures do not involve the establishment of an entity or financial structure separate from the venturers themselves, so that each venturer has control over its share of future economic benefits through its share in the jointly controlled assets.

Joint ventures of this type are particularly common in extractive industries. For example, a number of oil companies may jointly control and operate an oil pipeline. Each venturer uses the pipeline to transport its own product in return for which it bears an agreed proportion of the operating expenses of the pipeline. Another example of a jointly controlled asset could be that two entities jointly control a commercial property, each taking a share of the rents received and bearing a share of the expenses.

3.5.2   Accounting requirements for jointly controlled assets

In respect of its interest in a jointly controlled asset, a venturer recognises in its financial statements:

- its share of the jointly controlled assets, classified according to their nature (i.e. a share in a jointly controlled pipeline should be shown within property, plant and equipment rather than as an investment);

- any liabilities that it has incurred (e.g. those it has incurred in financing its share of the assets);

- its share of any liabilities incurred jointly with the other venturers in relation to the joint venture;

- any income from the sale or use of its share of the output of the joint venture, together with its share of any expenses incurred by the joint venture; and

- any expenses that it has incurred in respect of its interest in the joint venture (e.g. those relating to financing the venturer's interest in the assets and selling its share of the output). *[FRS 102.15.7].*

As with jointly controlled operations, the assets, liabilities, income and expenses will already be reflected in the individual financial statements of the venturer (including the separate financial statements of a venturer that is a parent), therefore no adjustments or other consolidation procedures are required in respect of these items if the venturer presents consolidated financial statements. Separate accounting records may be limited to a record of the expenses incurred in common, and ultimately borne by the venturers according to their agreed shares. Similarly, financial statements may not be prepared for the joint venture itself, although the venturers may prepare management accounts in order to assess the performance of the joint venture.

3.6 Jointly controlled entities

3.6.1 Definition

Section 15 defines a jointly controlled entity as 'a joint venture that involves the establishment of a corporation, partnership or other entity in which each venturer has an interest'. The entity would operate in the same way as other entities except that the venturers would have joint control over the entity and its economic activities by virtue of the existence of a contractual arrangement between them. *[FRS 102.15.8]*.

A jointly controlled entity controls the assets of the joint venture, incurs liabilities and expenses and earns income. It manages the joint venture and may enter into contracts in its own name and raise finance for the purposes of the joint venture activity. Each venturer is entitled to a share of the results of the jointly controlled entity based on the requirements in the joint venture agreement.

There are a number of different considerations for the accounting for interests in jointly controlled entities depending on whether the venturer is a parent or not, and if a parent, the financial statements being prepared. These are discussed in the sections that follow.

3.6.2 Venturer that is not a parent

Where a venturer is an entity that is not a parent and hence only prepares individual financial statements, then in those financial statements it has a choice in terms of how to recognise all of its interests in jointly controlled entities:

(a) apply the cost model (see 3.6.2.A below);

(b) apply the fair value model (see 3.6.2.B below); or

(c) carry them at fair value with changes in fair value recognised in profit or loss. *[FRS 102.15.9]*.

In terms of the option to carry interests in jointly controlled entities at fair value through profit or loss, fair value in that context should be determined by reference to the guidance in Section 11, paragraphs 11.27 to 11.32 (see Chapter 8 at 4.4.5). *[FRS 102.15.9(d)]*.

There is no option to use equity accounting in individual financial statements (although this option exists under IFRS) because equity accounting in individual financial statements is not permitted by the Regulations which permits only a cost or market value model. However, the individual financial statements of investor venturer that is not a parent have to disclose summarised financial information about its investments in jointly controlled entities, along with the effect of including those investments as if they had been accounted for using the equity method. Investing entities that are exempt from preparing consolidated financial statements, or would be exempt if they had subsidiaries, are exempt from this requirement. *[FRS 102.15.21A]*.

3.6.2.A   *Cost model*

A venturer that is not a parent, and that chooses to adopt the cost model, should measure its investments in jointly controlled entities at cost less any accumulated impairment losses. Section 27 – *Impairment of Assets* – will apply to the recognition and measurement of impairment losses. *[FRS 102.15.10]*.

Section 15 does not define 'cost'. The Regulations state that the purchase price of an asset is determined by adding to the actual price paid any expenses incidental to its acquisition. *[1 Sch.27(1)]*. This definition is consistent with Section 17 – *Property, Plant and Equipment*, which states that cost is normally either the purchase price paid (including directly attributable costs) or the fair value of non-monetary assets exchanged. *[FRS 102.17.10]*. The purchase price would generally represent the fair value of the consideration given to purchase the investment consistent with the guidance in respect of exchanges of businesses or other non-monetary assets (see Chapter 6 at 3.8) and the requirements in respect of measuring the cost of a business combination (see Chapter 15 at 3.5).

A venturer will recognise distributions received from its investments in jointly controlled entities as income irrespective of whether the distributions are from accumulated profits of the jointly controlled entity arising before or after the date of acquisition. *[FRS 102.15.11]*.

3.6.2.B   *Fair value model*

A venturer that is not a parent, and that chooses to adopt the fair value model, should initially recognise its investment in a jointly controlled entity at the transaction price. *[FRS 102.15.14]*. 'Transaction price' is not defined, but it is presumably the same as its cost (see 3.6.2.A above). Transaction costs should also be included as part of the transaction price on initial recognition. *[FRS 102 Appendix II]*.

At each subsequent reporting date, the venturer should measure its investments in jointly controlled entities at fair value using the fair value guidance in paragraphs 11.27 to 11.32 of FRS 102. Changes in fair value are recognised in accordance with paragraphs 17.15E and 17.15F of FRS 102. *[FRS 102.15.15]*. Those are the paragraphs detailing the reporting of gains or losses on revaluation and are discussed further in Chapter 13 at 3.6.

A venturer that uses the fair value model for its investments in jointly controlled entities should use the cost model for any investment in a jointly controlled entity for which it is impracticable to measure fair value reliably without undue cost or effort. *[FRS 102.15.15]*. Under FRS 102, applying a requirement is impracticable when the entity cannot apply it after making every reasonable effort to do so. *[FRS 102 Appendix I]*.

A venturer will recognise distributions received from its investments in jointly controlled entities as income irrespective of whether the distributions are from accumulated profits of the jointly controlled entity arising before or after the date of acquisition. *[FRS 102.15.15A]*.

3.6.3   Venturer that is a parent

3.6.3.A   Separate financial statements

A venture that is a parent accounts for interests in jointly controlled entities in its separate financial statements in accordance with the requirements of Section 9 – *Consolidated and Separate Financial Statements*, paragraphs 9.26 and 9.26A, as appropriate (see also Chapter 6 at 4.2). *[FRS 102.15.1].*

The parent is required to apply a policy of accounting for its investments in jointly controlled entities either:

- at cost less impairment (i.e. a cost model);

- at fair value with changes in fair value recognised in other comprehensive income in accordance with paragraphs 17.15E and 17.15F of Section 17 (i.e. a fair value model); or

- at fair value with changes in fair value recognised in profit or loss (guidance on fair value is provided in Section 11).

The discussion at 3.6.2.A and 3.6.2.B above with respect to the cost model and the fair value model will be relevant for a parent applying either of these models.

The same choices apply to a parent that is exempt in accordance with Section 9 paragraph 9.3 from the requirement to present consolidated financial statements and therefore presents separate financial statements as its only financial statements. *[FRS 102.9.26A].*

Section 9 states that a parent must apply the same accounting policy for all investments in a single class (subsidiaries, associates or jointly controlled entities) but it can elect different policies for different classes. *[FRS 102.9.26].*

This restriction appears to mean that a parent cannot use a different accounting policy for a class of investments (such as its jointly controlled entities) even where individual investments within that class have different characteristics. Section 15 requires investments in jointly controlled entities that are held as part of an investment portfolio to be measured at fair value through profit or loss in the parent's consolidated financial statements, rather than under the equity method (see 3.6.3.B below). *[FRS 102.15.9A-B].* This raises similar issues to that discussed in Chapter 6 at 4.2 with respect to subsidiaries that are required to be measured under different bases in the consolidated financial statements. In our view it is acceptable for an entity to select its accounting policy for its investments in its jointly controlled entities independently of the requirement to measure certain jointly controlled entities at fair value through profit or loss. Hence jointly controlled entities that are held as part of an investment portfolio can be considered a separate class of investment from jointly controlled entities that are equity accounted.

3.6.3.B   Consolidated financial statements

In its consolidated financial statements, a venturer that is a parent accounts for all of its investments in jointly controlled entities using the equity method, except where its investments in jointly controlled entities are held as part of an investment portfolio. In this case such investments in jointly controlled entities are required to be measured at fair value in its consolidated financial statements with the changes in fair value recognised in profit or loss. *[FRS 102.15.9A-B].*

Investments in jointly controlled entities are held as part of an investment portfolio if their value to the venturer is through fair value changes in a directly or indirectly held basket of investments rather than as a means through which the venturer carries out business. A basket of investments is held indirectly if a venturer holds a single investment in a second investment fund which, in turn, holds a basket of investments. *[FRS 102 Appendix I].*

3.7 Equity method

3.7.1 Overview

The equity method is explained in Section 14. It is described as a method of accounting whereby the investment is initially recognised at transaction price (including transaction costs) and is subsequently adjusted to reflect the investor's share of:

- profit or loss,
- other comprehensive income, and
- equity of the associate. *[FRS 102.14.8].*

The investor's share of the investee's profit or loss is recognised in the investor's profit or loss. *[FRS 102.5.5, 6 Sch 20(3)].* The investor's share of the investee's other comprehensive income is recognised in the investor's statement of comprehensive income. *[FRS 102.5.5, 6 Sch 20(3)].*

The requirements of Section 14.8 should be applied to jointly controlled entities, substituting 'joint control' for 'significant influence' and 'jointly controlled entity' for 'associate'. *[FRS 102.15.13].*

3.7.2 Summary of the equity method

The equity method is discussed in detail in Chapter 10. The key aspects of the equity method as applicable to an investment in a jointly controlled entity are therefore as follows: *[FRS 102.14.8]*

- A venturer should commence equity accounting for a jointly controlled entity from the date it begins to have joint control over the entity (see Chapter 10 at 3.3.2.A)

- Distributions received from the jointly controlled entity reduce the carrying amount of the investment. Adjustments to the carrying amount may also be required as a consequence of changes in the jointly controlled entity's equity arising from items of other comprehensive income (see Chapter 10 at 3.3.2.B).

- In applying the equity method, the proportionate share of the jointly controlled entity to be accounted for, in many cases, will be based on the venturer's ownership interest in the ordinary shares of the entity. A venturer should measure its share of profit or loss and other comprehensive income of the jointly controlled entity as well as its share of changes in the jointly controlled entities' equity based on present ownership interests. Those measurements should not reflect the possible exercise or conversion of potential voting rights (see Chapter 10 at 3.3.2.C).

- On acquisition of the investment in a jointly controlled entity a venturer accounts for any difference (whether positive or negative) between the cost of acquisition and the its share of the fair values of the net identifiable assets of the jointly controlled entity in accordance with Section 19, paragraphs 22 to 24 (see Chapter 15 at 3.8). A venturer adjusts its share of the jointly controlled entity's profits or losses after acquisition to account for additional depreciation or amortisation of the jointly controlled entity's depreciable or amortisable assets (including goodwill) on the basis of the excess of their fair values over their carrying amounts at the time the investment was acquired (see Chapter 10 at 3.3.2.D). If the interest in the jointly controlled entity is acquired on a piecemeal basis then the approach to such acquisitions is discussed, in the context of equity accounting, in Chapter 10 at 4.1.2 to 4.1.4.

- If there is an indication that an investment in a jointly controlled entity may be impaired a venturer shall test the entire carrying amount of the investment for impairment in accordance with Section 27 (see Chapter 22) as a single asset. Any goodwill included as part of the carrying amount of the investment in the jointly controlled entity is not tested separately for impairment but, rather, as part of the test for impairment of the investment as a whole (see Chapter 10 at 3.3.2.E).

- The venturer eliminates unrealised profits and losses resulting from upstream (jointly controlled entity to investor) and downstream (investor to jointly controlled entity) transactions to the extent of the venturer's interest in the jointly controlled entity. Unrealised losses on such transactions may provide evidence of an impairment of the asset transferred (see Chapter 10 at 3.3.2.F).

- In applying the equity method, the investor uses the financial statements of the jointly controlled entity as of the same date as the financial statements of the investor unless it is impracticable to do so. If it is impracticable, the investor uses the most recent available financial statements of the jointly controlled entity, with adjustments made for the effects of any significant transactions or events occurring between the accounting period ends (see Chapter 10 at 3.3.2.G).

- If the jointly controlled entity uses accounting policies that differ from those of the investor, the investor adjusts the jointly controlled entity's financial statements to reflect the investor's accounting policies for the purpose of applying the equity method unless it is impracticable to do so (see Chapter 10 at 3.3.2.H).

- If a venturer's share of losses of a jointly controlled entity equals or exceeds the carrying amount of its investment in the jointly controlled entity, the venturer discontinues recognising its share of further losses. After the venturer's interest is reduced to zero, the venturer recognises additional losses by a provision (see Section 21 – *Provisions and Contingencies*) only to the extent that the venturer has incurred legal or constructive obligations or has made payments on behalf of the jointly controlled entity. If the jointly controlled entity subsequently reports profits, the venturer resumes recognising its share of those profits only after its share of the profits equals the share of losses not recognised (see Chapter 10 at 3.3.2.I).

- A venturer discontinues the use of the equity method from the date that joint control ceases. The subsequent accounting depends on the nature of any retained investment. If the investment becomes a subsidiary (because control is obtained), it will be accounted for in accordance with Section 19 (i.e. a step-acquisition, see Chapter 15 at 3.10). If the investment becomes an associate, it will be accounted for in accordance with Section 14 (i.e. it will continue to be accounted for under the equity method, see Chapter 10). Otherwise, on a full or partial disposal, a profit or loss will be recognised based on the difference between the disposal proceeds and the carrying amount relating to the proportion of the jointly controlled entity disposed of. Any retained investment should be accounted for as a financial asset in accordance with Section 11 or Section 12 (see Chapter 10 at 3.3.2.J for further discussion).

3.8   Transactions between a venturer and joint venture

3.8.1   *Background*

It is common for venturers to transact with the joint venture, in particular on the formation of the venture. Typical transactions include:

*   the venturers contribute cash to the venture in proportion to their agreed relative shares. The venture then uses some or all of the cash to acquire assets from the venturers for use in the venture;

*   the venturers contribute other assets (or a mixture of cash and other assets) to the joint venture with fair values in proportion to the venturers' agreed relative shares in the venture;

*   the venturers contribute other assets to the joint venture with fair values not in proportion to the venturers' agreed relative shares. Cash 'equalisation' payments are then made between the venturers so that the overall financial position of the venturers corresponds to their agreed relative shares in the venture.

3.8.2   *Requirements*

When a venturer contributes or sells assets to a joint venture, Section 15 requires that the recognition of any portion of a gain or loss from the transaction should reflect the substance of the transaction. While the assets are retained by the joint venture, and provided the venturer has transferred the significant risks and rewards of ownership, the venturer should only recognise that portion of the gain or loss that is attributable to the interests of the other venturers. However, the venturer should recognise the full amount of any loss when the contribution or sale provides evidence of an impairment loss. *[FRS 102.15.16]*.

These requirements are illustrated in the following examples:

Example 11.3:   Sale of asset from venturer to joint venture at a profit

Two entities A and B establish a joint venture involving the creation of a jointly controlled entity C in which A and B each hold 50%. A and B each contribute £5 million in cash to the joint venture in exchange for equity shares. C then uses £8 million of its £10 million cash to acquire from A a property recorded in the financial statements of A at £6 million. It is agreed that £8 million is the fair market value of the property. How should A account for these transactions?

The accounting entry for A is as follows:

	£m	£m
Cash (1)	3	
Investment in joint venture C(2)	4	
Property (3)		6
Gain on sale (4)		1

(1)   £8 million received from C less £5 million contributed to C.

(2)   £5 million initial investment in C, less £1 million (share of profit eliminated – see (4) below. In effect, this treatment represents that A still holds 50% of the property at its original carrying value to A (50% of £6 million = £3 million) plus 50% of the cash held by the joint venture (50% of £2 million = £1m)

(3)   Derecognition of A's original property.

(4)   Gain on sale of property £2 million (£8 million received from C less £6 million carrying value = £2 million), less 50% eliminated (so as to reflect only profit attributable to interest of other venturer B) = £1 million.

In Example 11.3 above, the elimination of A's share of the profit has been made against the asset that was the subject of the transaction and now held by A. This is based on our suggested approach for the elimination of unrealised profits and losses resulting from downstream transactions (investor to jointly controlled entity) under Section 14, discussed in Chapter 10 at 3.3.2.F. It is also consistent with the treatment where a venture exchanges a non-monetary asset for an interest in another entity that becomes a jointly controlled entity of a venture (see 3.9 below).

Example 11.4:   Sale of asset from venturer to joint venture at a loss

Two entities A and B establish a joint venture involving the creation of a jointly controlled entity C in which A and B each hold 50%. A and B each contribute £5 million in cash to the joint venture in exchange for equity shares. C then uses £8 million of its £10 million cash to acquire from A a property recorded in the financial statements of A at £10 million. £8 million is agreed to be the fair market value of the property. How should A account for these transactions?

The accounting entry for A is as follows:

	£m	£m
Cash (1)	3	
Investment in joint venture C (2)	5	
Loss on sale (3)	2	
Property (4)		10

(1)   £8 million received from C less £5 million contributed to C.

(2)   £5 million initial investment in C. In effect, this treatment represents that A still holds 50% of the property at the current fair value (50% of £8 million = £4 million) plus 50% of the cash held by the joint venture (50% of £2 million = £1m).

(3)   Loss on sale of property £2 million (£8 million received from C less £10 million carrying value = £2 million) not adjusted since the transaction indicated an impairment of the property. In effect, it is the result that would have been obtained if A had recognised an impairment charge immediately prior to the sale and then recognised no gain or loss on the sale.

(4)   Derecognition of A's original property.

When a venturer purchases assets from a joint venture, the venturer should not recognise its share of the profits of the joint venture from the transaction until it resells the assets to an independent party. A venturer should recognise its share of the losses resulting from these transactions in the same way as profits except that losses shall be recognised immediately when they represent an impairment loss. *[FRS 102.15.17].*

These requirements are illustrated in the following examples:

Example 11.5:   Sale of asset from joint venture to venturer at a profit

Two entities A and B establish a joint venture involving the creation of a jointly controlled entity C in which A and B each hold 50%. A and B each contribute £5 million in cash to the joint venture in exchange for equity shares. C then uses £8 million of its £10 million cash to acquire a property from an independent third party D. The property is later sold to A for £12 million, which is agreed to be its market value. How should A account for these transactions?

The required accounting entry for A is:

	£m	£m
Property (1)	10	
Investment in joint venture C (2)	7	
Cash (3)		17

(1)   £12 million paid to C less elimination of A's share of the profit made by C £2 million (50% of [£12 million sales proceeds less £8 million cost to C]).

(2)   £5 million initial investment in C plus profit on sale of property by C that is attributable to B). In effect, this treatment represents A's 50% interest in the cash held by the joint venture (50% of £14 million).

(3)   £5 million cash contributed to C plus £12 million consideration paid for property.

In Example 11.5 above, the elimination of A's share of the profit made by C has been made against the asset that was the subject of the transaction and now held by A. This is based on our suggested approach for the elimination of unrealised profits and losses resulting from upstream transactions (jointly controlled entity to investor) under Section 14, discussed in Chapter 10 at 3.3.2.F.

Example 11.6:   Sale of asset from joint venture to venturer at a loss

Two entities A and B establish a joint venture involving the creation of a jointly controlled entity C in which A and B each hold 50%. A and B each contribute £5 million in cash to the joint venture in exchange for equity shares. C then uses £8 million of its £10 million cash to acquire a property from an independent third party D. The property is then sold to A for £7 million, which is agreed to be its market value. How should A account for these transactions?

The accounting entry for A is:

	£m	£m
Property (1)	7.0	
Investment in joint venture C (2)	4.5	
Share of loss of C (3)	0.5	
Cash (4)		12.0

(1)   £7 million paid to C not adjusted since the transaction indicated an impairment of C's asset.

(2)   £5 million initial investment in C less A's 50% share of loss in C's books of £1 million (£8 million cost of property less £7 million proceeds of sale). In effect, it is the result that would have been obtained if C had recognised an impairment charge immediately prior to the sale and then recognised no gain or loss on the sale.

(3)   Loss in C's books is £1 million (£8 million cost of property less £7 million proceeds of sale). A recognises its 50% share because the transaction indicates an impairment of the asset. In effect, it is the result that would have been obtained if C had recognised an impairment charge immediately prior to the sale and then recognised no gain or loss on the sale.

(4)   €5 million cash contributed to C plus €7 million consideration for property.

It may be that transactions occur between a venturer and a joint venture in assets, such as inventories, which are destined for onward sale in the normal course of business by the buying party. The accounting adjustments required are the same as for similar transactions between an investor and its associate – see Examples 10.6 and 10.7 in Chapter 10 at 3.3.2.F.

3.8.3   *Loans and borrowings between the venturer and joint ventures*

Section 15's requirement to eliminate partially unrealised profits or losses on transactions with joint ventures is expressed in terms of transactions involving the transfer of assets. This raises the question of whether this requirement is generally intended to apply to items such as interest paid on loans between joint ventures and the reporting entity.

In our view, the requirement for partial elimination of profits or losses does not apply to items such as interest paid on loans and borrowings between the reporting entity and its joint ventures, since such loans do not involve the transfer of assets giving rise to gains or losses. Moreover, the loans are not normally regarded as part of the venturer's share of the net assets of the joint venture, but as separate transactions, except in the case of loss-making joint ventures, where interests in long-term loans may be accounted for as if they were part of the reporting entity's equity investment in determining the carrying value of the joint venture against which losses may be offset.

3.9   Transactions to create a jointly controlled entity

A venturer may exchange a business, or other non-monetary asset, for an interest in another entity, and that other entity becomes a jointly controlled entity of the venturer. The accounting issues that arise from these transactions are whether they should be accounted for at fair value or at previous book values and how the gain on the transaction should be reported.

The requirements in respect of such transactions are set out in Section 9 (see also Chapter 6 at 3.8) and are the same as those contained in UITF 31 – *Exchanges of businesses or other non-monetary assets for an interest in a subsidiary, joint venture or associate* – in previous UK GAAP. The principles behind the consensus reached by the UITF were that the only exception to the use of fair values should be in rare circumstances where the transaction is artificial and has no substance and that any unrealised gains should not be reported in profit or loss.

Accordingly, the following accounting treatment applies in the consolidated financial statements of the reporting entity: *[FRS 102.9.31]*

* to the extent that the reporting entity retains an ownership interest in the business, or other non-monetary assets, exchanged, even if that interest is then held through the jointly controlled entity, that retained interest, including any related goodwill, is treated as having been owned by the reporting entity throughout the transaction and should be included at its pre-transaction carrying amount;

- goodwill is recognised as the difference between:
    - the fair value of the consideration given; and
    - the fair value of the reporting entity's share of the pre-transaction identifiable net assets of the other entity.

    The consideration given for the interest acquired in the jointly controlled entity will include that part of the business, or other non-monetary assets, exchanged and no longer owned by the reporting entity. The consideration may also include cash or monetary assets to achieve equalisation of values. Where it is difficult to value the consideration given, the best estimate of its value may be given by valuing what is acquired;

- to the extent that the fair value of the consideration received by the reporting entity exceeds the carrying value of the part of the business, or other non-monetary assets exchanged and no longer owned by the reporting entity, and any related goodwill together with any cash given up, the reporting entity should recognise a gain. Any unrealised gain arising on the exchange is recognised in other comprehensive income;

- to the extent that the fair value of the consideration received by the reporting entity is less than the carrying value of the part of the business, or other non-monetary assets no longer owned by the reporting entity, and any related goodwill, together with any cash given up, the reporting entity should recognise a loss. The loss should be recognised as an impairment in accordance with Section 27 or, for any loss remaining after an impairment review of the relevant assets, in profit or loss.

The most common situation that fell within the scope of UITF 31 in practice was the contribution of a business for equity in a joint venture (or associate), and such a transaction forms the basis of illustrating the above accounting requirements in Example 11.7 below.

Example 11.7:   Creation of a jointly controlled entity by the transfer of non – monetary assets (1)

A and B are two companies which agree to form a jointly controlled entity (JV Co) in respect of a particular part of each of their businesses. A will own 40% of the JV Co, and B 60%. The parties agree that the total value of the new business is £250m.

A's contribution to the venture is one of its subsidiaries, the net assets of which are included in A's consolidated balance sheet at £60m (including remaining unamortised goodwill of £10m). The fair value of the separable net assets of the subsidiary contributed by A is considered to be £80m. The implicit fair value of the business contributed is £100m (40% of total fair value £250m).

B also contributes a subsidiary, the net assets of which have a carrying amount of £85m (including remaining unamortised goodwill of £15m). The fair value of the separable net assets is considered to be £120m. The implicit fair value of the business contributed is £150m (60% of total fair value £250m).

The book and fair values of the businesses contributed by A and B are summarised as follows:

(in £m)	A Book value	A Fair value	B Book value	B Fair value
Separable net assets	50	80	70	120
Goodwill	10	20	15	30
Total	60	100	85	150

How should A account for the set-up of the jointly controlled entity?

The required entries in A would be:

	£m	£m
Share of net assets of JV Co (1)	68	
Goodwill (2)	16	
Net assets contributed to JV Co (3)		60
Other comprehensive income (gain on disposal) (4)		24

(1) 40% of (book value of A's separable net assets + fair value of B's separable net assets), i.e. 40% × (£50m+£120m) = £68m.

(2) Fair value of consideration given by A less fair value of separable net assets of B's business acquired, i.e. 60% of £100m less 40% of £120m = £12m (which can also be 'proved' as being 40% of B's inherent goodwill of £30m), plus 40% of A's original goodwill of £10m retained (£4m) = £16m. This goodwill will be included in the total carrying value of JV Co.

(3) Previous carrying amount of net assets contributed by A, now deconsolidated. In reality there would be a number of entries to deconsolidate these on a line-by-line basis.

(4) Fair value of consideration received, less book value of assets disposed of, i.e. 40% of £150m – 60% of £60m = £24m (which can also be 'proved' as being 60% of the £40m difference between the book value and fair value of A's business).

The gain on the transaction in Example 11.7 is unrealised because qualifying consideration has not been received. Therefore, the gain is accounted for in other comprehensive income as only realised profits can be recognised in profit or loss. Where part or all of the gain is realised then that portion can be taken to profit or loss. This is illustrated in Example 11.8 below:

Example 11.8:   Creation of a jointly controlled entity by the transfer of non – monetary assets (2)

Assume the same fact pattern as in Example 11.7 above, except that A was to receive a stake of only 36% in JV Co. In that case it would be expected that A, having contributed assets worth 40% of the combined entity, would receive a cash payment of £10m (4% of £250m) directly from B in compensation for the reduction in the stake from 40% to 36%.

How should A account for the set-up of the jointly controlled entity?

The required entries in A would be:

	£m	£m
Share of net assets of JV Co (1)	61.2	
Cash	10.0	
Goodwill (2)	14.4	
Net assets contributed to JV Co (3)		60.0
Profit and loss (gain on disposal)		10.0
Other comprehensive income (gain on disposal (4)		15.6

(1) 36% of (book value of A's separable net assets + fair value of B's separable net assets), i.e. 36% × (£50m+£120m) = £61.2m.

(2) Fair value of consideration given by A (net of £10m cash received from B) less fair value of separable net assets of B's business acquired, i.e. 64% of £100m (£64m) less £10m = £54m, less 36% of £120m = £10.8m (which can also be 'proved' as being 36% of B's goodwill of £30m, plus 36% of A's goodwill of £10m retained (£3.6m) = £14.4m). This goodwill will be included in the total carrying value of JV Co.

(3) Previous carrying amount of net assets contributed by A, now deconsolidated. In reality there would be a number of entries to deconsolidate these on a line-by-line basis.

(4) Fair value of consideration received (including £10m cash received from B), less book value of assets disposed of, i.e. 36% of £150m = £54m plus £10m cash = £64m − 64% of £60m = £25.6m (which can also be 'proved' as being 64% of the £40m difference between the book value and fair value of A's business). The gain on disposal of £25.6m has been split based on an allocation between 'realised' and 'unrealised' as explained below.

Section 9 does not explain how a realised gain can be distinguished from an unrealised gain. In Example 11.7 above, we have used a 'top slicing' approach whereby as much of the total gain as is backed by cash is treated as realised (i.e. £10m). 'Top slicing' is the recommended approach to determining realised profits for exchanges of assets in paragraph 3.18 of the ICAEW/ICAS Technical Release 02/10 – *Guidance on the Determination of Realised Profits and Losses in the Context of Distributions under the Companies Act 2006*.

No gain or loss is recognised in those rare cases where the artificiality or lack of substance of the transaction is such that a gain or loss on the exchange could not be justified. When a gain or loss on the exchange is not taken into account because the transaction is artificial or has no substance, the circumstances should be explained. *[FRS 102.9.32]*. There is no elaboration as to the circumstances where this might be applicable.

3.10   Variable profit share

Venturers may not always be entitled to a fixed proportion of the profit of a jointly controlled entity. Venturers that each have a 50% interest in a joint venture may, for example, agree that;

- in the initial three years of operation one of the venturers will be entitled to 75% of the profits in order to recover its investment quicker; or

- the venturers are entitled to a fixed proportion of cash flows 'as defined in the joint venture agreement'; or

- the profit of the joint venture will be distributed based on an alternative measure of profitability such as earnings before interest, tax, depreciation and amortisation (EBITDA).

It may not be appropriate in those cases for the venturers to account for 50% of the profit of the joint venture. Instead, they would need to take into account the substance of the profit sharing arrangements that apply in each reporting period, in determining their share of the profits and net assets of the joint venture. A venturer's profit share may therefore differ from its share in the net assets of the joint venture. This situation is not unlike the situation that arises in the case of an investment in an associate that has different classes of equity (see Chapter 10 at 3.3.2.C).

3.11   Disclosures

Section 15 requires the following disclosures in individual and consolidated financial statements:

(a)   the accounting policy for recognising investments in jointly controlled entities;

(b)   the carrying amount of investments in jointly controlled entities;

(c)   the fair value of investments in jointly controlled entities accounted for using the equity method for which there are published price quotations; and

(d)   the aggregate amount of commitments relating to joint ventures, including the venturers share in the capital commitments that have been incurred jointly with other venturers, as well as the share of the capital commitments of the joint ventures themselves. *[FRS 102.15.19].*

For jointly controlled entities accounted for in accordance with the equity method, a venturer should disclose separately its share of the profit or loss of such investments and its share of any discontinued operations of such jointly controlled entities. *[FRS 102.15.20].*

For jointly controlled entities accounted for in accordance with the fair value model, a venturer should make the disclosures required by paragraphs 11.43 and 11.44 (see Chapter 8). *[FRS 102.15.21].*

The individual financial statements of a venturer that is not a parent should disclose summarised financial information about its investments in the jointly controlled entities, along with the effect of including those investments as if they had been accounted for using the equity method. Investing entities that are exempt from preparing consolidated financial statements, or would be exempt if they had subsidiaries, are exempt from this requirement. *[FRS 102.15.21A].*

4   COMPANY LAW MATTERS

4.1   Jointly controlled entities

The Companies Act does not define a 'joint venture', but paragraph 18 of Schedule 6 of the Regulations refers to a 'joint venture' as an undertaking that is managed 'jointly with one or more undertakings not included in the consolidation' in its description of non-corporate joint ventures that are permitted to be dealt with in consolidated financial statements by way of proportional consolidation. *[6 Sch 18].* The disclosure requirements in the Act for 'joint ventures' are framed in the context of such joint ventures that are proportionally consolidated, *[3 Sch 18],* and hence under FRS 102, these requirements will not be relevant.

However, jointly controlled entities that are equity accounted will be captured by the accounting and disclosure requirements in paragraph 19 of Schedule 6 of the Regulations which refer to 'associated undertakings'.

Chapter 11

An '*associated undertaking*' is defined in the Regulations as an undertaking in which an undertaking included in the consolidation has a participating interest and over whose operating and financial policy it exercises a significant influence, and which is not:

- a subsidiary undertaking of the parent company, or

- a joint venture dealt with in accordance with the paragraph on joint ventures. *[6 Sch 19(1)].*

A '*participating interest*' is defined as an interest held by an undertaking in the shares of another undertaking which it holds on a long-term basis for the purpose of securing a contribution to its activities by the exercise of control or influence arising from or related to that interest. The interest in shares includes interests which are convertible into shares or options to acquire shares, regardless of whether or not they are currently exercisable. Additionally, interests held on behalf of an undertaking are to be treated as held by it. *[10 Sch 11(1), 11(3), 11(4)].*

Hence an equity interest in a jointly controlled entity, given the nature of the joint control, will meet the definition of an associated undertaking for the purposes of the Regulations.

4.2   Presentation and disclosure

4.2.1   *Consolidated financial statements*

For jointly controlled entities that are equity accounted, the Regulations require that investments in jointly controlled entities are presented in fixed assets in the balance sheet and that the equity accounted share of profit (after interest and tax) is reflected in the profit and loss account as a single line. *[SI 2008/410 Sch 4.20].*

The format of the profit and loss account and balance sheet under FRS 102 are discussed further in Chapter 4.

The Regulations also require that the following information must be given where an undertaking included in the consolidation has an interest in an 'associated undertaking' (which as discussed in 4.1 above will also be relevant for equity accounted jointly controlled entities):

- the name of the jointly controlled entity;

- the country in which the jointly controlled entity is incorporated for those incorporated outside the United Kingdom;

- the address of the jointly controlled entity's principal place of business if unincorporated;

- the identity and proportion of the nominal value of each class of share held, disclosing separately those held by the:

  - parent company; and

  - group. *[4 Sch 19].*

4.2.2   *Individual financial statements*

In individual financial statements the Regulations require additional disclosures in respect of significant holdings in undertakings, other than subsidiary entities. A holding is deemed significant if:

- it amounts to 20% or more of the nominal value of any class of shares in the undertaking, or

- the amount of the holding as stated in the company's individual accounts exceeds 20% of the stated net assets of the company. *[4 Sch 4]*.

In practice, this definition will capture most investments in jointly controlled entities. The resulting disclosures in individual accounts are:

- the name of each jointly controlled entity;

- the country in which each jointly controlled entity is incorporated for those incorporated outside the United Kingdom;

- the address of each jointly controlled entity's principal place of business if unincorporated;

- the identity and proportion of the nominal value of each class of share held. *[4 Sch 5]*.

Additional disclosure would also be required in respect of each jointly controlled entity detailed above of:

- the aggregate amount of the capital and reserves of each entity; and

- the profit or loss for the year of each entity. *[4 Sch 6]*.

An entity is not required to give the additional disclosures in Schedule 4.6 of the Regulations in its individual financial statements if it is exempt under sections 400 or 401 of the Act from the requirement to prepare group accounts and the company discloses, in the notes to its accounts, the aggregate investment in the relevant jointly controlled entities determined by way of the equity method of valuation. *[4 Sch 13]*.

5   SUMMARY OF GAAP DIFFERENCES

The key differences between FRS 102, previous UK GAAP and IFRS in accounting for joint ventures are set out below.

	FRS 102	*Previous UK GAAP*	*IFRS*
Classification	Classifies joint ventures as either jointly controlled operations, jointly controlled assets or jointly controlled entities with different accounting considerations for each. Classification as jointly controlled entity requires existence of a separate legal entity.	Differentiates between joint ventures (specifically defined as entities under joint control) and also joint arrangements that are not entities (commonly referred to as 'JANEs'). Classification as a joint venture depends on substance being a separate trade.	Makes the distinction between joint operations and joint ventures. Classification as a joint venture depends on assessment of the venturer's rights and obligations over the arrangement.

Chapter 11

	FRS 102	*Previous UK GAAP*	*IFRS*
Accounting for jointly controlled operations	A venturer recognises in its financial statements: • the assets that it controls and the liabilities that it incurs; and • the expenses that it incurs and its share of the income that it earns from the sale of goods or services by the joint venture.	Participants in a JANE (or in a structure with the form but not the substance of a joint venture) account for their own (or share of) assets, liabilities and cash flows.	A joint operator recognises: assets, including any share of assets held jointly; liabilities, including its share of any liabilities incurred jointly; revenue from the sale of its share of the output by the joint operation; share of the revenue from the sale of the output by the joint operation; and expenses, including its share of any expenses incurred jointly. The accounting and measurement for each of these items is in accordance with the applicable IFRS.
Accounting for jointly controlled assets	A venturer recognises in its financial statements: • its share of the jointly controlled assets, classified according to their nature; • any liabilities that it has incurred; • its share of any liabilities incurred jointly with the other venturers in relation to the joint venture; • any income from the sale or use of its share of the output of the joint venture together with its share of any expenses incurred by the joint venture; and • any expenses that it has incurred in respect of its interest in the joint venture.	Participants in a JANE (or in a structure with the form but not the substance of a joint venture) account for their own (or share of) assets, liabilities and cash flows.	N/A

Entity that is not a parent	An entity that is not a parent has the option to account for its investments in jointly controlled entities using either the cost model, fair value model or at fair value through profit or loss.	Under previous UK GAAP the option to account for jointly controlled entities at fair value through profit or loss did not exist.	An entity that is not a parent must prepare financial statements whereby its investments in jointly controlled entities are accounted for under the equity accounting method unless it meets criteria for exemption.
Investment portfolios / funds	Investments in jointly controlled entities held as part of an investment portfolio should be measured at fair value through profit or loss in the consolidated financial statements of a venturer that is a parent.	Investments funds have the option to recognise all investments held as part of their investment portfolio at either cost or market value (with changes in value reflected in the statement of total recognised gains and losses) provided all investments are accounted for on the same basis.	Venture capital organisations and similar entities can choose to measure investments in joint ventures at fair value through profit or loss. Investment entities would elect this option.
Accounting for jointly controlled entities	Apart from those held as above, jointly controlled entities are equity accounted in the consolidated financial statements of a venturer.	Apart from those held as above, FRS 9 requires the use of 'gross equity accounting' for joint ventures which produces the same underlying effect on profit as equity accounting but has a gross balance sheet presentation and also reflects share of joint venture turnover.	Apart from those held as above or are to be classified as held for sale under IFRS 5, joint ventures are equity accounted in the consolidated financial statements of a venturer.
Implicit goodwill and fair value adjustments on acquisition of an equity-accounted jointly controlled entity	Follows the requirements of Section 19 of FRS 102 and in particular the requirement that unless a reliable estimate can be made, implicit goodwill on the acquisition of a jointly controlled entity should be amortised over a period not exceeding 5 years.	Follows the requirements of previous UK GAAP regarding business combinations with consequential differences, in particular regarding implicit goodwill amortisation where there is a rebuttable presumption that goodwill should not be amortised over a period exceeding 20 years.	Follows the IFRS requirements regarding business combinations. Implicit goodwill is not amortised.

Chapter 11

	FRS 102	Previous UK GAAP	IFRS
Losses in excess of investment in an equity-accounted jointly controlled entity.	Losses of jointly controlled entities in excess of the cost of investment are not recognised unless the venturer has legal or constructive obligations in respect of the excess losses.	FRS 9 requires the continued recognition of losses for joint ventures even if they exceed the cost of investment.	Losses of joint ventures in excess of the cost of investment are not recognised unless the venturer has legal or constructive obligations in respect of the excess losses.
Loss of joint control of an equity-accounted jointly controlled entity that does not become a subsidiary or an associate	• If loss of joint control is as a result of a partial disposal, a gain or loss is recognised based on the disposal proceeds and the carrying amount relating to the proportion disposed of. The carrying value of the equity interest retained at the date joint control is lost becomes the cost of the retained investment. • If the loss of joint control is for reasons other than a partial disposal, no gain or loss is recognised and the carrying value of the equity-accounted investment at the date joint control is lost becomes the cost of the retained investment.	• If loss of joint control is as a result of a partial disposal, a gain or loss is recognised based on the disposal proceeds and the carrying amount relating to the proportion disposed of. The carrying value of the equity interest retained at the date joint control is lost becomes the cost of the retained investment. • If the loss of joint control is for reasons other than a partial disposal, no gain or loss is recognised and the carrying value of the equity-accounted investment at the date joint control is lost becomes the cost of the retained investment.	• If loss of joint control is as a result of a partial disposal, a gain or loss is recognised based on the disposal proceeds together with the fair value of any retained interest and the carrying amount of the total interest in the joint venture. • If loss of joint control is for reasons other than a partial disposal, a gain or loss is recognised based on the fair value of the retained interest and the carrying amount of the interest in the joint venture at that date.

Presentation of the equity accounted results of a jointly controlled entity	The share of income from jointly controlled entities is presented as one line, after the effects of interest and tax.	The share of operating profit of joint ventures is presented after the group operating profit, with interest and tax related to joint ventures being presented alongside the interest and tax line items in the group profit and loss account. FRS 9 requires the use of 'gross equity accounting' for joint ventures which produces the same underlying effect on profit as equity accounting but also reflects the share of joint venture turnover. In the balance sheet, the investment is analysed into the share of total assets and share of total liabilities.	The share of income from joint ventures is presented as one line, after the effects of interest and tax.

Chapter 11

Chapter 12   Investment property

Chapter 12   Investment property

1   INTRODUCTION

What primarily distinguishes investment property from other types of property interest is that its cash flows (from rental or sale) are largely independent of those from other assets held by the entity. By contrast, property used by an entity for administrative purposes or for the production or supply of goods or services do not generate cash flows themselves but do so only in conjunction with other assets. Therefore, FRS 102 proposes a different model for investment properties than for property, plant and equipment under Section 17 – *Property, Plant and Equipment*.

Section 16 – *Investment Property* – applies to accounting for investments in land or buildings that meet the definition of investment property and some property interests held by a lessee under an operating lease that are treated like investment property (see 3.1.5 below). However, only investment property 'whose fair value can be measured reliably without undue cost or effort on an on-going basis' shall be measured under Section 16 at fair value through profit or loss. If the investment property cannot be reliably measured, it is accounted for in accordance with Section 17 – *Property, Plant and Equipment* – unless a reliable measure of fair value later becomes available and is expected that it can be measured on an on-going basis.

2   COMPARISON BETWEEN SECTION 16, PREVIOUS UK GAAP AND IFRS

There are some differences between accounting for investment properties under Section 16 compared to previous UK GAAP (SSAP 19 – *Investment properties* – and UITF 28 – *Operating lease incentives*) and IFRS (IAS 40 – *Investment Property*). These are discussed at 2.1 and 2.2 below respectively.

2.1   Key differences between Section 16 and previous UK GAAP

2.1.1   *Accounting for changes in value*

Section 16 requires all changes in the fair value of all investment properties to be recognised in profit or loss.

SSAP 19 required changes in the open market value (OMV) of investment properties (except for those of insurance companies and pension funds) to be recognised in the statement of total recognised gains and losses (STRGL). These changes in value were accounted for as a movement on a revaluation reserve within equity, unless a deficit, or its reversal, was permanent in which case the movement was taken to profit or loss. Changes in the OMV of investment properties of insurance companies were recognised in profit or loss. Changes in the OMV of investment properties of pension funds were dealt with in the relevant fund account.

Although Section 16 requires investment property to be held at fair value and SSAP 19 required OMV, in practice, we do not foresee any significant valuation differences.

2.1.2   *Properties under construction*

Section 16 does not explicitly address assets under construction other than to define investment property as 'land or a building, or part of a building, or both...held...to earn rentals or for capital appreciation or both...'. *[FRS 102.16.2]*. It does, however, state how a self-constructed investment property shall be accounted for on initial recognition and therefore our view is that if an asset under construction meets the definition of an investment property, it shall be accounted for in accordance with Section 16.

Under SSAP 19, the definition of an investment property applied to land and buildings of which construction work and development has been *completed*. *[SSAP 19.7]*. Assets that are under construction would not therefore fall within the scope of SSAP 19 and were accounted for in accordance with FRS 15 – *Tangible fixed assets*. This means that they could be measured at either cost or at OMV.

2.1.3   *Property occupied by group companies*

Section 16 does not specifically address the situation when a property held by one group entity is leased to another group entity. The implication is that all such properties must be assessed as to whether they meet the definition of an investment property in the relevant financial statements of the reporting entity.

SSAP 19 specifically stated that 'a property let to and occupied by another group company is not an investment property' in either individual or group financial statements. *[SSAP 19.8(b)]*. This means that such property had to be accounted for in accordance with FRS 15.

2.1.4   *Mixed use property*

Section 16 states that property that has mixed use shall be separated between investment property and property, plant and equipment unless the fair value of the investment property element cannot be reliably measured without undue cost or effort, in which case the whole property is accounted for as property, plant and equipment. *[FRS 102.16.4]*.

SSAP 19 was silent on the subject of mixed use property and therefore diversity in practice was greater.

2.1.5 Property held for social benefits

Section 16 states that if a public benefit entity holds property primarily to provide social benefits e.g. social housing, the property shall be accounted for as property, plant and equipment rather than investment property. *[FRS 102.16.3A].*

SSAP 19 did not address public benefit entity accounting for investment properties and therefore there was diversity in practice.

2.1.6 Depreciation

Section 16 does not require investment properties to be depreciated.

Conversely, SSAP 19 required investment property held on a lease with an unexpired term of 20 years or less to be depreciated over the remaining term of the lease. *[SSAP 19.10].*

The absence of a requirement to depreciate investment properties in FRS 102 is not a departure from the requirements of UK company law because Schedule 1 of the Large and Medium-sized Companies and Groups (Accounts and Reports) Regulations 2008, (the Regulations), and its equivalents in Schedules 2 and 3, does not require depreciation of investment properties measured under the fair value accounting rules.

In contrast, depreciation of investment properties measured under SSAP 19 was required by the Regulations because investment properties are valued under the alternative accounting rules and not the fair value accounting rules. *[1 Sch 33].*

2.1.7 Inability to reliably measure fair value

Section 16 requires investment property to be transferred to or from property, plant and equipment if fair value could no longer be reliably measured without undue cost or effort. *[FRS 102.16.8-9].*

SSAP 19 was silent on what a reporting entity should do if it could no longer reliably measure the OMV of an investment property.

2.1.8 Properties held under operating leases

Section 16 allows properties held under operating leases to be classified as either investment property or property, plant and equipment on a property-by-property basis. See Section 3.1.5 below.

SSAP 19 implied that all investment property held on a lease with a relatively short term was investment property. *[SSAP 19.5].*

Therefore, investment properties held on operating leases may be treated as property, plant and equipment under FRS 102 but not under previous UK GAAP.

2.1.9 Disclosure differences

Disclosure differences between FRS 102 and previous UK GAAP at discussed in Section 4 below.

2.2   Key differences between Section 16 and IFRS

2.2.1   *Measurement basis after initial recognition*

Section 16 requires all property meeting the definition of investment property to be recorded at fair value. Only if fair value cannot be reliably measured is an investment property is classified as property, plant and equipment and recorded using the cost model. *[FRS 102.16.1].*

IAS 40 permits entities an accounting policy choice to use either cost or fair value for investment properties. Once an entity chooses a measurement basis, it must apply that basis to all of its investment properties. There are some exceptions for insurers and similar entities. *[IAS 40.30-32C].* IAS 40 does not identify a preferred method although the fair value model would appear to be the most widely adopted model amongst real estate entities.

Insurance companies and other entities that hold investment properties whose return is directly linked to the return paid on specific liabilities, can choose either the fair value or cost model for those specific investment properties without impacting the model adopted for the other investment properties. However all properties within a given fund must be valued on the same basis. *[IAS 40.32A-B].*

If an entity reporting under IFRS recognises operating leases as investment property, then it must apply the fair value model to all of its investment properties i.e. the option of cost is no longer available. *[IAS 40.34].* Not all property interests held under an operating lease need to be recognised as investment property and instead is assessed on a property-by-property basis. *[IAS 40.6].* However, an entity that chooses to apply the cost model must value all of its investment properties at cost and therefore is not permitted to recognise any property interests under operating leases.

2.2.2   *Valuation method*

The FRS 102 fair value definition is identical to the IAS 39 – *Financial Instruments: Recognition and Measurement* – definition of fair value prior to the adoption of IFRS 13 – *Fair Value Measurement.* Fair value as defined by FRS 102 is 'the amount for which an asset could be exchanged...between knowledgeable willing parties in an arm's length transaction'. *[FRS 102 Appendix I].* Hence the FRS 102 definition is a transaction (entry) price.

The IFRS 13 definition of fair value is 'the price that would be received to sell an asset...in an orderly transaction between market participants at the measurement date'. *[IFRS 13.9].* The IFRS measurement is an exit price from the perspective of a market participant that holds the asset rather than a transaction (entry) price and is a market based measurement rather than an entity specific measurement.

Therefore, differences may arise between FRS 102 and IAS 40 in respect of how fair value is measured.

2.2.3   *Mixed use property*

Section 16 states that property that has mixed use shall be separated between investment property and property, plant and equipment unless the fair value of the investment property element cannot be reliably measured without undue cost or effort, in which case the whole property is accounted for as property, plant and equipment. *[FRS 102.16.4]*. Section 16 requires consideration only of whether the separate investment property element can be fair valued. It does not require that the property could actually be physically and legally separated between investment property and property, plant and equipment.

IAS 40 requires that a property that has mixed use shall be separated between the owner-occupied element and the investment property element only if the two elements could be sold (or leased under a finance lease) separately. *[IAS 40.10]*. IAS 40 therefore has a higher hurdle to separate the two elements compared to Section 16.

2.2.4   Inability to reliably measure fair value

Section 16 requires investment property to be transferred to property, plant and equipment if fair value could no longer be reliably measured without undue cost or effort. *[FRS 102.16.8-9]*.

Although there is a choice under IAS 40 whether to apply either the fair value or cost model, where an entity adopts the fair value model, 'there is a rebuttable presumption that an entity can reliably measure the fair value of an investment property on a continuing basis' and only in exceptional circumstances may that presumption be rebutted *[IAS 40.53]*.

2.2.5   Disclosures

The disclosure requirements of Section 16 are less extensive than those of IFRS and are discussed in Section 4 below.

3   REQUIREMENTS OF SECTION 16 FOR INVESTMENT PROPERTY

3.1   Definition and initial recognition of investment property

Investment property is defined as property (land or a building, or part of a building, or both) held by the owner or by the lessee under a finance lease to earn rentals for capital appreciation or both. *[FRS 102.16.2]*.

Only investment property whose fair value can be measured reliably without undue cost or effort on an on-going basis can be accounted for at fair value through profit or loss. Otherwise, the investment property is accounted for at cost as property, plant and equipment. *[FRS 102.16.1]*.

Property used in the production or supply of goods or services or for administrative purposes (commonly referred to as 'owner-occupied') or sale in the ordinary course of business is not investment property. *[FRS 102.16.2]*. However, a property which has a mixed use shall be separated between property plant and equipment and investment property (see 3.1.7 below).

3.1.1   Investment property under construction

Section 16 does not explicitly address investment property under construction. However, it states that an entity shall determine the cost of a self-constructed investment property in accordance with paragraphs 17.10 to 17.14 of FRS 102. In summary, these paragraphs require cost to comprise of purchase price, costs directly attributable to bringing the asset to the location and condition necessary for it to be capable of operating in the manner intended by management, the initial estimate of costs of dismantling and removing the item and restoring the site and any capitalised borrowing costs in accordance with Section 25 – *Borrowing Costs*. See Chapter 13 for more detail on this.

The implication of this reference to Section 17 implies that that the FRC believes that an investment property under construction should normally be accounted for at cost under Section 17 on the grounds that the fair value cannot be reliably measurable without undue cost and effort until completion. However, if the fair value can be reliably measured without undue cost and effort during construction then FRS 102 would require that investment property under construction is held at fair value.

3.1.2   *Investment property leased to other group entities*

We believe that investment property leased to other group entities is within the scope of Section 16 as there is no specific exclusion.

In the consolidated financial statements transactions between group entities, including income and expenses in respect of inter-group leased property, would be eliminated on consolidation in accordance with Section 9 – *Consolidated and Separate Financial Statements*.

In the individual or separate financial statements, where a group entity (Entity A) leases a property to a fellow subsidiary (Entity B) on a finance lease, this property should be classified as an investment property by Entity A and classified as property, plant and equipment by Entity B.

3.1.3   *Property with the provision of ancillary services*

Section 16 provides no guidance on the impact (if any) of ancillary services on the classification of a property as an investment property where provided by the owner to the user.

However, the definition of an investment property requires that the property should be held for capital appreciation and/or rentals rather than for use in the production or supply of goods and services. Therefore, when an owner provides ancillary services to a leased property, judgement will be required to determine whether or not the property is being held for capital appreciation/rentals or for the income generated by the supply of those ancillary goods and services.

Guidance on the provision of ancillary services is provided by IAS 40 which states that where ancillary services provided to a property are 'significant' then the property cannot be classified as an investment property. An example of ancillary services which are insignificant to the arrangement as a whole provided by IAS 40 is where the owner of an office building provides security and maintenance services to the lessees who occupy the building. An example of a property subject to significant ancillary services provided by IAS 40 is a hotel which has been leased to a third party but where the owner retains significant exposure to variation in the cash flows generated by the operations of the hotel. *[IAS 40.11-13]*.

3.1.4   Land

The definition of an investment property refers to land as well as buildings. Therefore, land held to earn rentals or for capital appreciation or both is also investment property.

A situation may arise where an entity has land but has not yet decided what this land will be used for. Section 16 is silent on this matter but IAS 40 gives an example of such an asset specifically being an investment property on the grounds that if the entity has not determined what it will use the land for it must be being held for capital appreciation. *[IAS 40.8]*.

3.1.5   *Property interests held under operating leases*

A lessee of an operating lease may also classify its interest in the property as an investment property but only if: *[FRS 102.16.3]*

* the property would otherwise meet the definition of an investment property; and

* the lessee can measure the fair value of the property interest without undue cost or effort on an on-going basis.

This classification alternative is available on a property-by-property basis so that a lessee may decide to classify some property interests held under an operating lease as an investment property and classify others as property, plant and equipment in accordance with Section 17.

The accounting for investment properties held on operating leases is discussed at 3.2.3 below.

3.1.6   *Social benefit entities*

Section 16 specifically excludes properties whose main purpose is to provide social benefits from being accounted for as investment properties. For example, social housing held by an entity whose primary objective is to provide benefits to the general public or community rather than providing a financial return to its shareholders or members. Such properties are accounted for in accordance with Section 17. *[FRS 102.16.3A]*.

3.1.7   *Properties with mixed use*

A property may have mixed use and could be partly owner-occupied and partly held for rental. For example, an entity may own a building and occupy some floors for its own use but also sub-lease other floors to a tenant. Section 16 requires mixed use property to be separated and accounted for as investment property or property, plant and equipment, as applicable for the relevant components. However, if the entity cannot reliably measure the fair value of the investment property components without undue cost or effort, then it shall account for the entire property as property, plant and equipment in accordance with Section 17. *[FRS 102.16.4]*.

Section 16 requires consideration only of whether the separate investment property element can be fair valued. It does not require that the property could actually be physically and legally separated between investment property and property, plant and equipment.

3.2   Measurement at initial recognition

Section 16 requires investment property to be initially recognised at cost. The cost of purchased investment property comprises its purchase price and any directly attributable costs such as legal fees, brokerage fees, property transfer taxes and other transaction costs. *[FRS 102.16.5]*.

To determine the cost of a self-constructed investment property, Section 16 refers to the guidance in paragraphs 10-14 of Section 17. *[FRS 102.16.5]*. In addition to the purchase price and directly attributable costs, the cost of a self-constructed investment property also comprises the initial estimate of costs (if any) of dismantling and removing the property and restoring the site on which it is located and any borrowing costs capitalised in accordance with paragraph 2 of Section 25.

3.2.1   *Deferred payments*

In considering the purchase price, if payment for the property is deferred beyond normal credit terms, the present value of the future payments is calculated in order to arrive at the cost. *[FRS 102.16.5]*.

3.2.2   *Exchange for monetary and/or non-monetary assets*

Section 16 is silent on how to measure the cost of an investment property acquired in part or in whole in exchange for a non-monetary asset.

However, guidance is contained in Section 17 in respect of how to measure the cost of an item of property, plant and equipment in exchange for a non-monetary asset or combination of monetary and non-monetary assets. This states that the cost of acquired asset is measured at fair value unless:

- the exchange transaction lacks commercial substance; or
- the fair value of neither the asset received nor the asset given up is reliably measurable. In that case, the asset's cost is measured at the carrying amount of the asset given up. *[FRS 102.17.14]*.

This is further discussed in Chapter 13.

3.2.3   *Property interests held under a finance or operating lease*

The initial cost of a property interest held under a lease and classified as an investment property shall be as prescribed by paragraphs 9 and 10 of Section 20 – *Leases*. This applies even if the property interest would otherwise be classified as an operating lease if it was within the scope of Section 20 (see 3.1.5 above).

This means that initial cost of the asset is the lower of the fair value of the property and the present value of the minimum lease payments. An equivalent amount is recognised as a liability. Any premiums paid would be included in the minimum lease payments thus forming part of the asset but are clearly excluded from the liability. *[FRS 102.16.6]*.

3.3   Measurement after initial recognition

Investment property whose fair value can be measured reliably without undue cost or effort is measured at fair value through profit or loss at each reporting date.

If a property interest held under a lease is classified as investment property, the item accounted for at fair value is that interest only and not the underlying property.

All other investment property (i.e. investment property whose fair value cannot be reliably measured without undue cost or effort) is measured using the cost model in Section 17. *[FRS 102.16.7].*

The FRC's appendix on the legal requirements of FRS 102 clarifies that fair value movements on investment properties can be included in the profit and loss account under paragraph 40 of Schedule 1 of the Regulations despite the fact that unrealised gains on investment properties are not usually realised profits as defined by the Companies Act. *[FRS 102.A4.27].*

Although the default reserve within equity for fair value movements on investment property is retained earnings, the FRC observes that entities measuring investment properties at fair value may transfer such amounts to a separate non-distributable reserve, instead of a transfer to retained earnings, but are not required to do so. Presenting fair value movements that are not distributable profits in a separate reserve may assist with the identification of profits available for that purpose. *[FRS 102.A4.28].* Any such transfer from retained earnings to a non-distributable reserve should be made in the statement of changes in equity.

No depreciation is required on investment properties as the Regulations do not require depreciation of investment properties measured under the fair value accounting rules (see 2.1.6 above).

3.3.1   Determining fair value

Fair value is 'the amount for which an asset could be exchanged... between knowledgeable, willing parties in an arm's length transaction'. *[FRS 102 Appendix I].*

Section 16 refers users to the guidance on determining fair value in paragraphs 27 and 32 of Section 11 – *Basic Financial Instruments. [FRS 102.16.7].*

There is no requirement for an entity to use an independent valuer in determining the fair value of investment property. However, if there has been no such independent valuation, this must be disclosed (see 3.6.1 below)

3.3.2   Undue cost or effort

FRS 102 does not define 'undue cost or effort' and is also not defined in the IFRS for SME's which underlies much of FRS 102. However, in October 2013, the IASB issued an Exposure Draft (ED/2013/9), *IFRS for SMEs – Proposed Amendments to the International Financial Reporting Standard for Small and Medium-sized Entities.* EC/2013/9 sets out proposed amendments to IFRSs for SMEs, and includes 'undue cost or effort' as a concept. It clarifies the following: *[ED/2013/9 2.14A-C]*

- if obtaining or determining the information necessary to comply with the requirement would result in excessive incremental cost or an excessive additional effort for an SME, the SME would be exempt from that specific requirement;

- undue cost or effort depends on the entity's specific circumstances and on management's judgement when assessing the costs and benefits. Whether the cost or effort is excessive (undue) requires consideration of how the economic decisions of the expected users of the financial statements could be affected by the availability of the information; and

- assessing whether a requirement will result in undue cost or effort at the date of the transaction or event should be based on information about the costs and benefits of the requirement that is available at the time of the transaction or event. If the undue cost or effort exemption also applies to subsequent measurement of an item, for example, on the following reporting date, a new assessment of undue cost or effort should be made at that date, based on information available at that subsequent measurement date.

ED/2013/9 was open for comments until 3 March 2014 and provides useful guidance to assist users of FRS 102 to understand the concept of undue cost or effort.

3.3.3   *Double-counting of assets and liabilities*

Section 16 does not address the potential for double-counting assets and liabilities that are recorded separately in the balance sheet, but also included within a valuation of an investment property. Common examples include air-conditioning, lifts and fixtures and fittings, all of which may be recorded separately on the balance sheet as tangible fixed assets and also included within a valuation obtained for a furnished investment property.

An entity would need to consider the specific inputs included in the investment property valuation to assess whether it includes assets and liabilities which are also recognised separately on the balance sheet. If so, an adjustment is required to avoid double-counting these assets or liabilities.

When an entity recognises prepaid or accrued operating lease income in the balance sheet, the investment property valuation may also include such lease income. If so, an adjustment is required to avoid double-counting the asset or liability.

If a property valuation is obtained net of the valuer's estimate of the present value of the future lease obligations, (which is usually the case), an amount should be added back by adjusting for the finance lease obligation recognised in the financial statements, to arrive at the fair value of the investment property, since the lease obligation is already recognised in the balance sheet.

In our view, an adjustment will always be required to avoid double-counting assets or liabilities.

3.4   Transfers of investment property to/from property, plant and equipment

3.4.1   *Transfers of investment property to property, plant and equipment where a reliable measure of fair value is no longer available*

If a reliable measure of fair value of an investment property is no longer available without undue cost or effort, the investment property is accounted for as property, plant and equipment under Section 17 using the cost model until a reliable measure of fair value becomes available. The carrying amount of the investment property at the date of transfer becomes its cost under Section 17. *[FRS 102.16.8].* The cost model under Section 17 requires measurement at cost less accumulated depreciation and any accumulated impairment losses. *[FRS 102.17.15A].*

This transfer is caused by a change of circumstances and is therefore not a change of accounting policy. Disclosure is required of this change (see 3.6.1 below).

3.4.2   *Other transfers of investment property to/from property, plant and equipment*

An entity shall transfer a property to/from investment property only when the property first meets, or ceases to meet, the definition of an investment property. *[FRS 102.16.9].*

The same guidance on determining the cost of any investment property transferred to property, plant and equipment discussed at 3.4.1 applies here also. Investment property transferred to property, plant and equipment where the fair value of that property can still be measured reliably without undue cost or effort, for example a transfer caused because the property is not no longer held to earn rentals and/or capital appreciation, can be measured under either the cost or revaluation models of Section 17 (provided that where the revaluation model is selected, this shall be applied to all items of property, plant and equipment in the same class).

3.5   Derecognition

Accounting for disposals of investment property is not addressed specifically within Section 16. However Section 17 has requirements and guidance in respect of derecognition of property, plant and equipment which can be applied to investment properties. See Chapter 13 for further guidance.

Chapter 12

3.6   Disclosures

3.6.1   *Disclosures required by Section 16*

The following disclosures are required for all investment property accounted for at fair value through profit or loss: *[FRS 102.16.10]*

- the methods and significant assumptions applied in determining the fair value;

- the extent to which the fair value is based on a valuation by an independent valuer who holds a recognised and relevant professional qualification and has recent experience in the location and class of the investment property being valued. If there has been no such valuation, that fact shall be disclosed;

- the existence and amounts of any restrictions on the realisability of investment property or the remittance of income and proceeds of disposal;

- contractual obligations to purchase, construct or develop investment property or for repairs, maintenance or enhancements; and

- a reconciliation between the carrying amounts of investment property at the beginning and end of the period; showing separately:

  - additions, disclosing separately additions resulting from acquisitions through business combinations;

  - net gains and losses arising from fair value adjustments;

  - transfers to property, plant and equipment when fair value can no longer be measured reliably without undue cost or effort;

  - transfers to and from inventories and owner-occupied property; and

  - other changes.

  The reconciliation need not be presented for prior periods.

All relevant disclosures required for leases which a reporting entity has entered into must be disclosed in accordance with Section 20. *[FRS 102.16.11]*.

3.6.2   *Additional disclosures required by the Regulations*

The following disclosures are required by the Regulations for investment properties measured at fair value in addition to those required by Section 16:

- the comparable amounts determined under the historical accounting rules (aggregate cost and cumulative depreciation) or the differences between the fair value and historical cost, had the asset always been recorded at historical cost; *[1 Sch 58, 2 Sch 69, 3 Sch 76]* and

- an analysis of land and buildings between freehold tenure and leasehold tenure splitting the land held on leasehold tenure between land held on long lease (50 years or more) and short lease. *[1 Sch 53, 2 Sch 64, 3 Sch 71, 10 Sch 7]*.

4   SUMMARY OF GAAP DIFFERENCES

The key differences between FRS 102, previous UK GAAP and IFRS in accounting for investment properties (IP) are set out below.

	FRS 102	*Previous UK GAAP*	*IFRS*
Measurement basis after initial recognition	Fair value (FV)	Open Market Value	Choice between FV or cost model
Changes in FV	FV changes taken to profit or loss	Valuation changes taken to the statement of total recognised gains and losses except for insurers and pension schemes where valuation changes recognised in profit and loss or the relevant fund account respectively. Permanent deficits taken to profit or loss	FV changes taken to profit or loss
Inability to reliably measure FV	IP whose FV cannot be measured reliably without undue cost or effort on an on-going basis, shall be accounted for as property, plant and equipment (PPE) until FV can be reliably measured on an on-going basis	Silent on circumstances where OMV cannot be reliably measured.	Once FV model is selected, the only exemptions available is when the FV cannot be reliably measured on an on-going basis when an entity (i) initially acquires an IP or (ii) there is a change in use and an existing property meets the definition of an IP. That property is then accounted for using the cost model until disposal date
Properties under construction	Within scope	Excluded	Within scope
Properties occupied by group companies	Within scope	Excluded	Within scope
Mixed use properties	Separated unless FV for the IP component cannot be measured reliably	Silent. Practice is likely to have been mixed.	Separated if the IP and PPE components can be sold or leased separately
Ancillary services	No guidance	No guidance	Where ancillary services are significant, a property should be accounted for as owner-managed rather than as investment property

	FRS 102	Previous UK GAAP	IFRS
Property held for social benefits	Excluded	Silent	Silent
Investment properties held under operating leases	Classification choice of accounting for as IP or PPE on a property-by-property basis	Must be accounted for as investment property.	Classification choice of accounting for as IP or PPE on a property-by-property basis
Depreciation	IP properties are not depreciated	Assets under leases with 20 years or less remaining, are depreciated	Assets recognised using the cost model only are depreciated
Disclosures – FV model			
Method and significant assumptions in determining FV	Required to be disclosed	No requirement	Required to be disclosed
Valuer details	The extent to which the valuation is performed by an independent valuer with appropriate professional qualifications	Name or professional qualification of the valuer to be disclosed along with whether valuer is an employee or officer.	The extent to which the valuation is performed by an independent valuer with appropriate professional qualifications
FV hierarchy disclosures	No requirement	No requirement	Yes
Operating leases	No requirement	No requirement	Whether and under what circumstances property interests held under operating leases are classified and accounted for as IP
Classification of IP	No requirement	No requirement	Criteria used to distinguish IP from other assets, where classification is difficult
Reconciliation between carrying amounts at beginning and end of the period	Reconciliation of additions, acquisitions, net gains/losses from FV adjustments, transfers to/from PPE and inventory and other changes	No requirement	Reconciliation of additions, acquisitions including business combinations, assets classified as held for sale (or within a disposal group held for sale), net gains/losses from FV adjustments, net exchange differences, transfers to/from PPE and inventory, and other changes

Double-counting of assets or liabilities	No requirement	No requirement	Reconciliation between the valuation obtained and the adjusted valuation showing the aggregate add back of recognised lease obligations and any other significant adjustments
Inability to reliably measure FV without undue cost or effort	Transfers to PPE are included in the reconciliation above	Not applicable	Description of the IP and reasons for why an IP cannot be reliably measured, possible estimates of FV range and specific details on subsequent disposal of such IP
Amounts recognised in profit or loss	Net gains or losses included in reconciliation above.	No requirement	Amounts recognised in relation to rental income and operating expenses disclosed separately for let and vacant IP and cumulative change in FV recognised in P&L on a sale of IP from a pool of assets under the cost model into a pool of assets under the FV model
Restrictions	Disclosure of the existence and amount of restrictions on the realisability of IP or the remittance of income and proceeds of disposal	No requirement	Disclosure of the existence and amount of restrictions on the realisability of IP or the remittance of income and proceeds of disposal
Contractual obligations	Disclose contractual obligations to purchase, construct or develop IP or for repairs, maintenance or enhancements	No requirement	Disclose contractual obligations to purchase, construct or develop IP or for repairs, maintenance or enhancements

Chapter 12

Chapter 13 Property, plant and equipment

List of examples

Chapter 13

Chapter 13   Property, plant and equipment

1   INTRODUCTION

This chapter covers the accounting for property, plant and equipment and to investment property whose fair value cannot be measured reliably without undue cost or effort.

Overall, FRS 102 (Section 17 – *Property, Plant and Equipment*) is largely similar to both previous UK GAAP (FRS 15 – *Tangible fixed assets*) and IFRS (IAS 16 – *Property, Plant and Equipment*). All models have similar definitions of property, plant and equipment ('PP&E') (or tangible fixed assets under previous UK GAAP), and all require that such assets are initially recorded at cost and subsequently carried using either the cost model or the revaluation model. Revaluation gains and losses are recognised in the statement of other comprehensive income (or the statement of total recognised gains and losses under previous UK GAAP) except for losses below cost (which are recognised in profit and loss) and for gains to the extent that they reverse previously recognised losses in profit and loss.

2   COMPARISON BETWEEN SECTION 17, PREVIOUS UK GAAP AND IFRS

As discussed at 1 above, Section 17 is largely similar to previous UK GAAP and IFRS. However, there are also certain key differences which are discussed at 2.1 and 2.2 below, respectively. The summary at 4 below contains a three-way summary of the major GAAP differences.

2.1   Key differences between Section 17 and previous UK GAAP

2.1.1   *Measurement of residual values*

FRS 102 defines residual value as the estimated amount that an entity would currently obtain from disposal of the asset (residual values are based on prices at the balance sheet date), after deducting the estimated costs of disposal, if the asset were already of the age and in the condition expected at the end of its useful life. *[FRS 102 Appendix I].* This is further discussed at 3.5.2 below. FRS 15 describes residual value as the net realisable value of an asset at the end of its useful economic life, based on prices prevailing at the date of acquisition or revaluation of the asset (most recent valuation) and does not take account of future price changes. *[FRS 15.2].*

This means that where residual value rises over time, the depreciation charge on an asset under FRS 102 is likely to decline and may cease altogether when residual value exceeds the asset's carrying value. Under FRS 15, the depreciation charge would not change unless the asset was revalued.

2.1.2   *Revaluation model*

Under the revaluation model, FRS 102 requires assets to be measured at fair value. Fair value is usually determined from market-based evidence by appraisal for land and buildings or 'market value' determined by appraisal for plant and equipment. If there is no market-based evidence, due to the specialised nature of the asset and the item is rarely sold, fair value may need to be estimated using an income or depreciated replacement cost approach. *[FRS 102.17B-17D].* For further discussion, see 3.6 below.

The 'value to the business' model used under FRS 15 when assets are revalued, requires revaluations to 'current value' i.e. assets are measured at the lower of replacement cost and recoverable amount. FRS 15 may require revaluation to be based on existing use value which may be significantly lower than fair value in circumstances where the fair value reflects an alternative use.

2.1.3   *Initial adoption of revaluation model*

Under FRS 102, initial application of the revaluation policy is a period change and not a change in accounting policy to be treated retrospectively (see 3.6.5 below). *[FRS 102.10.10A].*

Under previous UK GAAP, a change to a revaluation model is a change in accounting policy and requires retrospective restatement. *[FRS 18.48].*

2.1.4   *Disclosure*

The reconciliation of opening and closing balances must be presented using gross amounts under FRS 102 – i.e. separately for cost (or revalued amount) and depreciation.

Previous UK GAAP allows the reconciliation to be presented using the net carrying amounts.

2.2   Key differences between Section 17 and IFRS

2.2.1   *Accounting for non-current assets held for sale*

FRS 102 does not have a 'held-for-sale' category for non-current assets. A plan to dispose of an asset before the previously expected date is an indicator of impairment that triggers the calculation of the asset's recoverable amount for the purpose of determining whether the asset is impaired. *[FRS 102.17.26].* Therefore, there is no reclassification of assets or suspension of depreciation – see 3.5.7.B below.

IFRS 5 – *Non-current Assets Held for Sale and Discontinued Operations* – requires that an item of PP&E should be classified as held for sale if its carrying amount will be recovered principally through a sale transaction rather than continuing use, though continuing use is not in itself precluded for assets classified as held for sale.

[IFRS 5.6]. Once this classification has been made, depreciation ceases, even if the asset is still being used, but the assets must be carried at the lower of their previous carrying amount and fair value less costs to sell. *[IFRS 5.15]*.

2.2.2 *Revenue-based depreciation method*

The use of 'revenue expected to be generated' as the basis to depreciate PP&E is not explicitly prohibited under FRS 102 (see 3.5.6 below).

Under IFRS, IAS 16 clarifies that effective from 1 January 2016, the use of revenue-based depreciation is inappropriate and therefore prohibited.

2.2.3 *Disclosures*

The disclosure requirements of Section 17 (see 3.8 below) are less extensive than those of IAS 16. In addition, unlike IAS 16, Section 17 does not require comparative information to be presented in the reconciliation of the carrying amount at the beginning and the end of the reporting period.

3 REQUIREMENTS OF SECTION 17 FOR PROPERTY, PLANT AND EQUIPMENT

3.1 Terms used in Section 17

The main terms used throughout Section 17 are as follows: *[FRS 102 Appendix I]*

Term	Definition
Borrowing costs	Interest and other costs incurred by an entity in connection with the borrowing of funds.
Depreciable amount	The cost of an asset, or other amount substituted for cost (in the financial statements), less its residual value.
Depreciated replacement cost	The most economic cost required for the entity to replace the service potential of an asset (including the amount that the entity will receive from its disposal at the end of its useful life) at the reporting date.
Depreciation	The systematic allocation of the depreciable amount of an asset over its useful life.
Property, plant and equipment	Tangible assets that: (a) are held for use in the production or supply of goods or services, for rental to others, or for administrative purposes; and (b) are expected to be used during more than one period.
Recoverable amount	The higher of an asset's (or cash-generating unit's) fair value less costs to sell and its value in use.

Chapter 13

Term	Definition
Residual value	The estimated amount that an entity would currently obtain from disposal of the asset, after deducting the estimated costs of disposal, if the asset were already of the age and in the condition expected at the end of its useful life.
Useful life	The period over which an asset is expected to be available for use by an entity, or the number of production or similar units expected to be obtained from the asset by an entity.

These definitions are discussed in the relevant sections below.

3.2   Scope of Section 17

Section 17 applies to the accounting for PP&E and to investment property whose fair value cannot be measured reliably without undue cost or effort.

All PP&E is within the scope of Section 17 except as follows:

* PP&E classified as investment property but whose fair value can be measured reliably without undue cost or effort (see Chapter 12);

* biological assets related to agricultural activity (see Chapter 29);

* heritage assets (see Chapter 29); and

* mineral rights and mineral reserves such as oil, gas, and similar 'non-regenerative' resources (see Chapter 29). [FRS 102.17.1-3].

Although Section 17 scopes out biological assets and mineral resources, any PP&E used in developing or maintaining such resources would be within scope.

Other sections of FRS 102 may require an item of PP&E to be recognised on a basis different from that required by Section 17. For example Section 20 – *Leases* – has its own rules regarding recognition and measurement. See Chapter 16 for a description of how an item of PP&E held under a finance lease is recognised and initially measured. However, once an item of PP&E has been recognised as a finance lease under Section 20, its treatment thereafter is in accordance with Section 17.

3.3   Recognition

An item of PP&E should be recognised (i.e. its cost included as an asset in the statement of financial position), only if it is probable that future economic benefits associated with the item will flow to the entity and if its cost can be measured reliably. [FRS 102.17.4].

3.3.1   *Aspects of recognition*

3.3.1.A   *Spare parts and minor items*

Spare parts and servicing equipment are usually carried as inventory and recognised in profit or loss as consumed. However, major spare parts and stand-by equipment are PP&E when an entity expects to use them during more than one period. If the spare parts and servicing equipment can be used only in connection with an item of PP&E, they are considered PP&E. [FRS 102.17.5].

The wording above is not without ambiguity and may result in spare parts and servicing equipment being classified as inventory where it is used during more than one period but not used only in connection with an item of PP&E. There was similar wording in IAS 16 but this perceived inconsistency in the classification requirements for servicing equipment was subsequently clarified by an amendment issued in 2012 that deleted the requirement that spare parts and equipment used 'in connection with an item of PP&E' must be classified as PP&E. Rather, items such as spare parts, stand-by equipment and servicing equipment are inventory unless they meet the definition of PP&E. *[IAS 16.8]*. In our view, it seems reasonable to consider the requirements of IAS 16 when applying FRS 102.

Some types of business may have a very large number of minor items of PP&E such as spare parts, tools, pallets and returnable containers, which nevertheless are used in more than one accounting period. There are practical problems in recording them on an asset-by-asset basis in an asset register; they are difficult to control and frequently lost. The main consequence is that it becomes very difficult to depreciate them. Section 17 does not prescribe what actually constitutes a single item of PP&E. Therefore, in our view, entities have to apply judgement in defining PP&E in their individual circumstances. Some parts such as tools, moulds and dies may appropriately be aggregated and the requirements of Section 17 be applied to the aggregate amount (presumably without having to identify the individual assets). As a practical matter, many companies have a minimum value for capitalising assets.

3.3.1.B   Environmental and safety equipment

There may be expenditures forced upon an entity by legislation that requires it to buy 'assets' that do not meet the recognition criteria because the expenditure does not directly increase the expected future benefits expected to flow from the asset. Examples would be safety or environmental protection equipment. While Section 17 has no specific guidance, it would be reasonable to consider the related guidance in IFRS.

IAS 16 explains that these expenditures qualify for recognition as they allow future benefits in excess of those that would flow if the expenditure had not been made; for example, a plant might have to be closed down if these environmental testing expenditures were not made. *[IAS 16.11]*.

An entity may voluntarily invest in environmental equipment even though it is not required by law to do so. The entity can capitalise those investments in environmental and safety equipment in the absence of a legal requirement as long as:

* the expenditure meets the definition of an asset; or

* there is a constructive obligation to invest in the equipment.

If the entity can demonstrate that the equipment is likely to increase the economic life of the related asset, the expenditure meets the definition of an asset. Otherwise, the expenditure can be capitalised when the entity can demonstrate all of the following:

- the entity can prove that a constructive obligation exists to invest in environmental and safety equipment (e.g. it is standard practice in the industry, environmental groups are likely to raise issues or employees demand certain equipment to be present);

- the expenditure is directly related to improvement of the asset's environmental and safety standards; and

- the expenditure is not related to repairs and maintenance or forms part of period costs or operational costs.

Consistent with IAS 16, whenever safety and environmental assets are capitalised, the resulting carrying amount of the asset, and any related asset, are required to be reviewed for impairment in accordance with Section 27 – *Impairment of Assets* (see 3.5.7 below).

3.3.1.C   Property economic benefits and property developments

Section 17 requires that PP&E only be recognised when it is probable that future economic benefits associated with the item will flow to the entity.

For example, in relation to property development, many jurisdictions require permissions prior to development whilst developers, including entities developing property for their own use, typically incur significant costs prior to such permissions being granted.

In assessing whether such pre-permission expenditures can be capitalised – assuming they otherwise meet the criteria – a judgement must be made at the date the expenditure is incurred of whether it is sufficiently probable that the relevant permission will be granted. Such expenditure does not become part of the cost of the land; to the extent that it can be recognised it will be as part of the cost of a separate building. Furthermore, if the granting of necessary permits is no longer expected, capitalisation of pre-permission expenditures should cease and the asset should be tested for impairment.

3.3.1.D   New technology costs – PP&E or intangible assets?

The restrictions in Section 18 – *Intangible Assets other than Goodwill* – in respect of capitalising certain internally-generated intangible assets focus attention on the treatment of many internal costs. In practice, items such as computer software purchased by entities are frequently capitalised as part of a tangible asset, for example as part of an accounting or communications infrastructure. Equally, internally written software may be capitalised as part of a tangible production facility, and so on. Judgement must be exercised in deciding whether such items are to be accounted for under Section 17 or Section 18, and this distinction becomes increasingly important if the two sections prescribe differing treatments in any particular case.

Both Section 17 and Section 18 do not refer to this type of asset, however, it is reasonable to consider guidance provided in IFRS. IAS 38 – *Intangible Assets* – states that an entity needs to exercise judgement in determining whether an asset that incorporates both intangible and tangible elements should be treated as PP&E or as an intangible asset, for example:

- computer software that is embedded in computer-controlled equipment that cannot operate without that specific software is an integral part of the related hardware and is treated as PP&E;

- application software that is being used on a computer is generally easily replaced and is not an integral part of the related hardware, whereas the operating system normally is integral to the computer and is included in PP&E; and

- a database that is stored on a compact disc is considered to be an intangible asset because the value of the physical medium is wholly insignificant compared to that of the data collection. *[IAS 38.4].*

It is worthwhile noting that as the 'parts approach' in Section 17 (see 3.3.2 below) requires an entity to account for significant parts of an asset separately, this raises 'boundary' problems between Section 17 and Section 18 when software and similar expenditure are involved. We believe that where Section 17 requires an entity to identify significant parts of an asset and account for them separately, the entity needs to evaluate whether any software-type intangible part is actually integral to the larger asset or whether it is really a separate asset in its own right. The intangible part is more likely to be an asset in its own right if it was developed separately or if it can be used independently of the item of PP&E.

3.3.1.E   *Classification of items as inventory or PP&E when minimum levels are maintained*

Entities may acquire items of inventory on a continuing basis, either for sale in the ordinary course of business or to be consumed in a production process or when rendering services. This means there will always be a core stock of inventory (i.e. a minimum level is maintained). This does not in itself turn inventory into an item of PP&E, since at an individual item level, each item will be consumed in one operating cycle. However, there may be cases where it is difficult to judge whether an item is part of inventory or is an item of PP&E. This may have implications on measurement because, for example, PP&E has a revaluation option (see 3.6 below) that is not available for inventory.

In our view, an item of inventory is accounted for as an item of PP&E if it:

- is not held for sale or consumed in a production process or during the process of rendering services;

- is necessary to operate or benefit from an asset during more than one operating cycle; and

- cannot be recouped through sale (or is significantly impaired after it has been used to operate the asset or benefit from that asset).

This applies even if the part of inventory that is an item of PP&E cannot physically be separated from the rest of inventories.

Chapter 13

Consider the following examples:

- An entity acquires the right to use an underground cave for gas storage purposes for a period of 50 years. The cave is filled with gas, but a substantial part of that gas will only be used to keep the cave under pressure in order to be able to get gas out of the cave. It is not possible to distinguish the gas that will be used to keep the cave under pressure and the rest of the gas.

- An entity operates an oil refining plant. In order for the refining process to take place, the plant must contain a certain minimum quantity of oil. This can only be taken out once the plant is abandoned and would then be polluted to such an extent that the oil's value is significantly reduced.

- An entity sells gas and has at any one time a certain quantity of gas in its gas distribution network.

In the first example, therefore, the total volume of gas must be virtually split into (i) gas held for sale and (ii) gas held to keep the cave under pressure. The former must be accounted for under Section 13 – *Inventories*. The latter must be accounted for as PP&E and depreciated over the period the cave is expected to be used.

In the second example the part of the crude that is necessary to operate (in technical terms) the plant and cannot be recouped (or can be recouped but would then be significantly impaired), even when the plant is abandoned, should be considered as an item of PP&E and amortised over the life of the plant.

In the third example the gas in the pipeline is not necessary to operate the pipeline. It is held for sale or to be consumed in the production process or process of rendering services. Therefore this gas is accounted for as inventory.

3.3.1.F   *Production stripping costs of surface mines*

Under FRS 102, there is no specific guidance on production stripping costs of surface mines. However, the approach in Section 17 in relation to accounting for parts (see 3.3.2 below) seems to be consistent with the specific guidance provided in IFRS.

IFRIC 20 – *Stripping Costs in the Production Phase of a Surface Mine* – states that costs associated with a 'stripping activity asset' (i.e. the costs associated with gaining access to a specific section of the ore body) are accounted for as an additional component of an existing asset. Other routine stripping costs are accounted for as current costs of production (i.e. inventory).

The Interpretations Committee's intention was to maintain the principle of IAS 16 by requiring identification of the *component* of the ore body for which access had been improved, as part of the criteria for recognising stripping costs as an asset. An entity will have to allocate the stripping costs between the amount capitalised (as it reflects the future access benefit) and the amount that relates to the current-period production of inventory. This allocation should be based on a relevant production measure.

This component approach follows the principle of separating out parts of an asset that have costs that are significant in relation to the entire asset and when the useful lives of those parts are different. *[IAS 16.45].*

3.3.2 Accounting for parts ('components') of assets

Section 17 has a single set of recognition criteria, which means that subsequent expenditure must also meet these criteria before it is recognised.

Parts of an asset are to be identified so that the cost of replacing a part may be recognised (i.e. capitalised as part of the asset) and the previous part derecognised. These parts are often referred to as 'components'. 'Parts' are distinguished from day-to-day servicing but they are not otherwise identified and defined; moreover, the unit of measurement to which Section 17 applies (i.e. what comprises an item of PP&E) is not itself defined.

Section 17 requires the initial cost of an item of PP&E to be allocated to its 'major components' and each component should be depreciated separately where there are different patterns of consumption of economic benefits. *[FRS 102.17.6, 16]*. 'Major components' is not defined and this will therefore require the exercise of judgement after considering the specific facts and circumstances. However, parts that have a cost that is significant in relation to the total cost of the asset will usually be a 'major component'.

An entity will have to identify the major components of the asset on initial recognition in order for it to depreciate the asset properly. There is no requirement to identify all components. Section 17 requires entities to derecognise an existing part or component when it is replaced, regardless of whether it has been depreciated separately. It might be acceptable to estimate, if necessary, the carrying value of the part that has been replaced if it is impossible to determine the carrying value of the replaced part. This is consistent with the treatment for 'major inspection' discussed in 3.3.3.A below.

As a consequence, an entity may not actually identify the parts or components of an asset until it incurs the replacement expenditure, as in the following example.

Example 13.1: Recognition and derecognition of parts

An entity buys a piece of machinery with an estimated useful life of ten years for £10 million. The asset contains two identical pumps, which are assumed to have the same useful life as the machine of which they are a part. After seven years one of the pumps fails and is replaced at a cost of £200,000. The entity had not identified the pumps as separate parts and does not know the original cost. It uses the cost of the replacement part to estimate the carrying value of the original pump. With the help of the supplier, it estimates that the cost would have been approximately £170,000 and that this would have a remaining carrying value after seven year's depreciation of £51,000. Accordingly it derecognises £51,000 and capitalises the cost of the replacement.

If the entity has no better information than the cost of the replacement part, it may be appropriate to use a depreciated replacement cost basis to calculate the amount derecognised in respect of the original asset.

3.3.2.A Land and buildings

Section 17 requires that the land and the building elements of property are treated as separate assets and accounted for separately, even when they are acquired together. *[FRS 102.17.8]*.

3.3.3   *Initial and subsequent expenditure*

Section 17 makes no distinction in principle between the initial costs of acquiring an asset and any subsequent expenditure upon it. In both cases any and all expenditure has to meet the recognition rules, and be expensed in profit or loss if it does not.

A distinction is drawn between servicing and more major expenditures. Day-to-day servicing (e.g. repairs and maintenance of PP&E, which largely comprises labour costs and minor parts) should be recognised in profit or loss as incurred. *[FRS 102.17.15]*. However, if the cost involves replacing a part of the asset, this replacement part should be recognised, i.e. capitalised as part of the PP&E, if the recognition criteria are met. The carrying amount of the part that has been replaced should be derecognised. *[FRS 102.17.6]*. Identification of replaced parts to be derecognised is discussed at 3.3.2 above.

Examples of parts which may require replacement at regular intervals during the life of the asset include the roofs of buildings, relining a furnace after a specified number of hours of use, or replacing the interiors of an aircraft several times during the life of the airframe. There could also be parts which may involve less frequently recurring replacements, such as replacing the interior walls of a building.

Section 17 does not state that these replacement expenditures necessarily qualify for recognition. For example, aircraft engines that require regular overhaul are clearly best treated as separate components as they have a useful life different from that of the asset of which they are part. With the other examples, such as interior walls, it is less clear why they meet the recognition criteria. However, replacing internal walls or similar expenditures may extend the useful life of a building while upgrading machinery may increase its capacity, improve the quality of its output or reduce operating costs. Hence, this type of expenditure may give rise to future economic benefits.

3.3.3.A   *Cost of major inspections*

A condition of continuing to operate an item of PP&E (e.g. a bus) may include a requirement to perform regular major inspections for faults regardless of whether parts of the item are replaced. Section 17 requires the cost of each major inspection performed to be recognised in the carrying amount of the item of PP&E as a replacement (and considered a separate part) if the recognition criteria are satisfied (see 3.3 above). Any remaining carrying amount of the cost of the previous major inspection (as distinct from physical parts) is derecognised. This is done regardless of whether the cost of the previous major inspection was identified in which the item was acquired or constructed. If necessary, the estimated cost of a future similar inspection may be used as an indication of what the cost of the existing inspection component was when the item was acquired or constructed. *[FRS 102.17.7]*. Accordingly, if the element relating to the inspection had previously been identified, it would have been depreciated between that time and the current overhaul. However, if it had not previously been identified, Section 17 appears to allow the entity to reconstruct the carrying amount of the previous inspection (i.e. to estimate the net depreciated carrying value of the previous inspection that will be derecognised) rather than simply using a depreciated replacement cost approach.

3.3.4   Properties with mixed use

There may be instances where a property has mixed use, for example, it could be partly owner-occupied and partly held for rental. Section 16 – *Investment Property* – provides guidance relating to the allocation of mixed use property between investment property and PP&E (see Chapter 12 at 3.17).

3.4   Measurement at initial recognition

Section 17 draws a distinction between measurement at initial recognition (i.e. the initial treatment of an item of PP&E on acquisition) and measurement after initial recognition (i.e. the subsequent treatment of the item). Measurement after initial recognition is discussed at 3.5 and 3.6 below.

Section 17 states that 'an entity shall measure an item of property, plant and equipment at initial recognition at its cost'. *[FRS 102.17.9]*. What may be included in the cost of an item is discussed below.

3.4.1   Elements of cost and cost measurement

The cost of an item of PP&E comprise all of the following:

(a)   Its purchase price, including import duties and non-refundable purchase taxes, after deducting trade discounts and rebates.

(b)   Any costs directly attributable to bringing the asset to the location and condition necessary for it to be capable of operating in the manner intended by management. These can include the costs of site preparation, initial delivery and handling, installation and assembly, and testing of functionality.

(c)   The initial estimate of the costs, recognised and measured in accordance with Section 21 – *Provisions and Contingencies* – of dismantling and removing the item and restoring the site on which it is located, the obligation for which an entity incurs either when the item is acquired or as a consequence of having used the item during a particular period for purposes other than to produce inventories during that period.

(d)   Any borrowing costs capitalised in accordance with paragraph 25.2 of Section 25 – *Borrowing Costs*. *[FRS 102.17.10]*.

The purchase price of an individual item of PP&E may be an allocation of the price paid for a group of assets. While FRS 102 does not provide specific guidance when an entity acquires a group of assets that do not comprise a business, it is reasonable that principles in Section 19 – *Business Combinations and Goodwill* – are applied to allocate the entire cost to individual items (see Chapter 15), except where such transaction or event does not give rise to goodwill. Accordingly, the entity would identify and recognise the individual identifiable assets acquired (including those assets that meet the definition of, and recognition criteria for intangible assets in Section 18) and liabilities assumed. The cost of the group of assets would be allocated to the individual identifiable assets and liabilities on the basis of their relative fair values at the date of purchase.

When there is no record of the purchase price or production cost of any asset of a company or of any price, expenses or costs relevant for determining its purchase price or production cost, or any such record cannot be obtained without unreasonable expense or delay, The Large and Medium-sized Companies and Groups (Accounts and Reports) Regulations 2008 (the Regulations or SI 2008/410) allow the purchase price or production cost of the asset to be the value ascribed to it in the earliest available record of its value made on or after its acquisition or production by the company. *[1 Sch 29]*.

The costs of obligations to dismantle, remove or restore the site on which an asset that is used to produce inventories has been located are dealt with in accordance with Section 13 – *Inventories* (discussed in Chapter 9).

Note that all site restoration costs and other environmental restoration and similar costs must be estimated and capitalised at initial recognition, in order that such costs can be recovered over the life of the item of PP&E, even if the expenditure will only be incurred at the end of the item's life. The obligations are calculated in accordance with Section 21.

A common instance of (c) above is dilapidation obligations in lease agreements, under which a lessee is obliged to return premises to the landlord in an agreed condition. Arguably, a provision is required whenever the 'damage' is incurred. Therefore, if a retailer rents two adjoining premises and knocks down the dividing wall to convert the premises into one and has an obligation to make good at the end of the lease term, the tenant should immediately provide for the costs of so doing. The 'other side' of the provision entry is an asset that will be amortised over the lease term – notwithstanding the fact that some of the costs of modifying the premises may also have been capitalised as leasehold improvement assets. This is discussed in more detail in Chapter 17.

3.4.1.A   'Directly attributable' costs

This is the key issue in the measurement of cost. Section 17 gives examples of types of expenditure that are, and are not, considered to be directly attributable. The following are examples of those types of expenditure that are considered to be directly attributable and hence may be included in cost at initial recognition:

- costs of site preparation;
- initial delivery and handling costs;
- installation and assembly costs; and
- cost of testing of functionality. *[FRS 102.17.10(b)]*.

While FRS 102 has no further guidance relating to costs of testing whether the asset is functioning properly, it is reasonable and common practice to recognise costs after deducting the net proceeds from selling any items produced while bringing the asset to its location and condition (such as samples produced when testing equipment). Income received during the period of construction of PP&E is considered further at 3.4.2 below.

In our view, amounts charged under operating leases during the construction period of an asset may also be a directly attributable cost that may be included as part of the cost of the PP&E if those lease costs are 'directly attributable to bringing the asset to the location and condition necessary for it to be capable of operating in the manner intended by management'. *[FRS 102.17.10(b)]*. This may be the case, for example, where a building is constructed on land that is leased under an operating lease. This approach must be applied consistently.

Other types of costs expected to be considered to be directly attributable costs are the following:

- costs of employee benefits (as defined in Section 28 – *Employee Benefits*) arising directly from the construction or acquisition of the item of property, plant and equipment. This means that the labour costs of an entity's own employees (e.g. site workers, in-house architects and surveyors) arising directly from the construction, or acquisition, of the specific item of PP&E may be recognised; and

- professional fees.

3.4.1.B   Borrowing costs

Entities are not required to capitalise borrowing costs. However, in line with item (d) at 3.4.1 above and Section 25, such costs may be capitalised in respect of certain qualifying assets to the extent that entities choose to capitalise borrowing costs in respect of such assets. The treatment of borrowing costs is discussed separately in Chapter 20.

3.4.1.C   Costs that are not PP&E costs

The following costs are not costs of PP&E and must be recognised as an expense when they are incurred:

- costs related to opening a new facility;

- costs of introducing a new product or service (including costs of advertising and promotional activities);

- costs of conducting business in a new territory or with a new class of customer (including costs of staff training); and

- administration and other general overhead costs. *[FRS 102.17.11]*.

These costs should be accounted for (in general, expensed as incurred) in the same way as similar costs incurred as part of the entity's on-going activities.

Administration and other general overhead costs are not costs of an item of PP&E. This means that employee costs not related to a specific asset, such as site selection activities and general management time, do not qualify for capitalisation.

3.4.1.D   Cessation of capitalisation

Only those costs directly attributable to bringing the asset to the location and condition for it to be capable of being operated in a manner intended by management can be capitalised. *[FRS 102.17.10(b)]*. Once that has occurred capitalisation should cease. This will usually be the date of practical completion of the physical asset. An entity is not precluded from continuing to capitalise costs during an initial commissioning period that is necessary for installation or assembly or testing equipment.

3.4.1.E   Self-built assets

Section 17 is silent on construction costs of an item of self-built PP&E. If an asset is self-built by the entity, the same general principles apply as for an acquired asset i.e. only those costs directly attributable to bringing the asset to the location and condition for it to be capable of being operated in a manner intended by management can be capitalised. This includes assembly costs. *[FRS 102.17.10(b)].* Consistent with IAS 16 and common practice, abnormal amounts of wasted resources, whether labour, materials or other resources, should not be included in the cost of self-built assets. *[IAS 16.22].* Section 25, discussed in Chapter 20, contains criteria relating to the recognition of any interest as a component of a self-built item of PP&E.

If the same type of asset is made for resale by the business, it should be recognised at cost of production, but including attributable overheads in accordance with Section 13 – *Inventories* (see Chapter 9 at 3.3.3). *[FRS 102.13.8-9].*

3.4.1.F   Deferred payment

The cost of an item of PP&E is its 'cash price equivalent' at the recognition date. This means that if payment is made in some other manner, the cost to be capitalised is the normal cash price. If the payment terms are extended beyond 'normal' credit terms, the cost to be recognised must be the present value of all future payments. *[FRS 102.17.13].* Accordingly, any difference between the present value and the total payments must be treated as an interest expense over the period of credit. Assets held under finance leases are discussed in Chapter 16.

3.4.1.G   Land and buildings to be redeveloped

It is common for property developers to acquire land with an existing building where the planned redevelopment necessitates the demolition of that building and its replacement with a new building that is to be held to earn rentals or will be owner occupied. Whilst Section 17 requires that the building and land be classified as two separate items, *[FRS 102.17.8],* in our view it is appropriate, if the existing building is unusable or likely to be demolished by any party acquiring it, that the entire, or a large part of, the purchase price be allocated to land. Similarly, subsequent demolition costs should be treated as being attributable to the cost of the land.

Owner-occupiers may also replace existing buildings with new facilities for their own use or to rent to others. Here the consequences are different and the carrying amount of the existing building cannot be rolled into the costs of the new development. The existing building must be depreciated over its remaining useful life to reduce the carrying amount of the asset to its residual value (presumably nil) at the point at which it is demolished. Consideration will have to be given as to whether the asset is impaired in accordance with Section 27. Many properties do not directly generate independent cash inflows (i.e. they are part of a cash-generating unit) and reducing the useful life will not necessarily lead to an impairment of the cash-generating unit, although by the time the asset has been designated for demolition it may no longer be part of a cash-generating unit (see Chapter 22).

Developers or owner-occupiers replacing an existing building with a building to be sold in the ordinary course of their business will deal with the land and buildings under Section 13 (see Chapter 9 at 3.2.1.B).

3.4.1.H   Transfers of assets from customers

Section 17 has no specific guidance on transfers of assets from customers other than for circumstances when the transfer involved an exchange of assets – see 3.4.4 below. Transfers that are government grants are within the scope of Section 24 – *Government Grants* (discussed in Chapter 19). Assets used in a service concession or resources from non-exchange transactions are within the scope of Section 34 – *Specialised Activities* (discussed in Chapter 29). Accordingly, an entity applying FRS 102 may use the principles set out in these sections of FRS 102 and at 3.4.4 below – i.e. recognition of the asset transferred at fair value. *[FRS 102.17.14, 24.5, 34.14].*

3.4.1.I   Variable consideration

The purchase price of an item of PP&E is not always known. It could vary based on future events, for example, amounts based on the performance of an asset. Generally in such a case, we believe a financial liability arises only when the item of PP&E has been delivered, and the measurement changes to that liability would flow through the statement of profit or loss as required by Section 11 – *Basic Financial Instruments*. However, in some instances contracts are more complex and it is argued that the subsequent changes of the payments are capitalised within the asset, similar to changes in a decommissioning liability (see 3.4.3 below). Further, many consider that these are executory payments that are not recognised until incurred.

In the absence of specific guidance, an entity would capitalise costs that meet the definition of an asset although it may choose to defer the recognition of these costs (i.e. as executory payments) until incurred. Accordingly in practice, there are two general approaches for variable payment and its subsequent changes – (i) not capitalise on initial recognition and expense variable payments or (ii) capitalise them at their fair value on initial recognition and recognise the changes in contingent consideration in profit or loss or as an asset if certain conditions are met. The accounting policy is applied consistently. For more discussion see 4.3 in Chapter 14.

3.4.2   Incidental and non-incidental income

The cost of an item of PP&E includes any costs directly attributable to bringing the asset to the location and condition necessary for it to be capable of operating in the manner intended by management. *[FRS 102.17.10(b)].* However, during the construction of an asset, an entity may enter into incidental operations that are not, in themselves, necessary to bring the asset itself to the location and condition necessary for it to be capable of operating in the manner intended by management. Using a building site as a car park prior to starting construction is an example of an incidental operation.

Income and expenses related to incidental operations are recognised in profit or loss because incidental operations during construction or development of PP&E are not necessary to bring an item to the location and operating condition intended by management. *[FRS 102.17.12].* These income and expenses would be included in their respective classifications of income and expense in profit and loss and not included in determining the cost of the asset.

However, if some income is generated wholly and necessarily as a result of the process of bringing the asset into the location and condition for its intended use, for example from the sale of samples produced when testing the equipment concerned to determine whether the asset is functioning properly, then the income should be credited to the cost of the asset. It is reasonable that the cost of such testing is reduced by the net proceeds from selling any items produced while bringing the asset to that location and condition. It will be a matter of judgement as to when the asset is in the location and condition intended by management, but capitalisation (including the recording of income as a credit to the cost of the asset) ceases when the asset is fully operational, regardless of whether or not it is yet achieving its targeted levels of production or profitability.

If the asset is *already in* the location and condition necessary for it to be capable of being used in the manner intended by management then capitalisation should cease and depreciation should start. In these circumstances all income earned from using the asset must be recognised as revenue in profit or loss and the related costs should include an element of depreciation of the asset.

3.4.2.A   Income received during the construction of property

One issue that commonly arises is whether rental and similar income generated by existing tenants in a property development may be capitalised and offset against the cost of developing that property.

The relevant question is whether the leasing arrangements with the existing tenants are a necessary activity to bring the development property to the location and condition necessary for it to be capable of operating in the manner intended by management. Whilst the existence of the tenant may be a fact, it is not a necessary condition for the building to be developed to the condition intended by management; the building could have been developed in the absence of any existing tenants.

Therefore, rental and similar income from existing tenants are incidental to the development and should not be capitalised. Rather rental and similar income should be recognised in profit or loss in accordance with the requirements of Section 20 together with related expenses.

3.4.2.B   Liquidated damages

Income may arise in other ways, for example, liquidated damages received as a result of delays by a contractor constructing an asset. Normally such damages received should be set off against the asset cost – the purchase price of the asset is reduced to compensate for delays in delivery.

3.4.3   Accounting for changes in decommissioning and restoration costs

Section 17 is unclear about the extent to which an item's carrying amount should be affected by changes in the estimated amount of dismantling and site restoration costs that occur *after* the estimate made upon initial measurement. Accordingly, an entity may consider the approach applied by IFRIC 1 – *Changes in Existing Decommissioning, Restoration and Similar Liabilities* (see Chapter 17 at 4.1).

IFRIC 1 applies to any decommissioning or similar liability that has both been included as part of an asset measured in accordance with IAS 16 (or Section 17) and measured as a liability in accordance with IAS 37 – *Provisions, Contingent Liabilities and Contingent Assets* (or Section 21). *[IFRIC 1.2]*. It deals with the impact of events that change the measurement of an existing liability. Events include a change in the estimated cash flows, the discount rate and the unwinding of the discount. *[IFRIC 1.3]*.

IFRIC 1 differentiates between the treatment required depending upon whether the items of PP&E concerned are valued under the cost or under the revaluation model (see also 3.6 below). If the asset is carried at cost, changes in the liability are added to, or deducted from, the cost of the asset. *[IFRIC 1.4-5]*. This deduction may not exceed the carrying amount of the asset and any excess over the carrying value is taken immediately to profit or loss. If the change in estimate results in an addition to the carrying value, the entity is required to consider whether this is an indication of impairment of the asset as a whole and test for impairment, *[IFRIC 1.5(c)]*, in accordance with Section 27.

If the related asset is measured using the revaluation model, changes in the estimated liability alter the revaluation surplus (i.e. the re-estimation takes place independently of the valuation of the asset) and a decrease in the liability is credited directly to the revaluation surplus, unless it reverses a revaluation deficit on the asset that was previously recognised in profit or loss, in which case it should be taken to profit or loss. Similarly, an increase in the liability is taken straight to profit or loss, unless there is a revaluation surplus existing in respect of that asset. *[IFRIC 1.6]*. This is consistent with the accounting for valuation surpluses and deficits discussed at 3.6.3 below.

Consistent with the principles applied for reversals of downward valuations discussed in 3.6.4 below, if the liability decreases and the deduction exceeds the amount that the asset would have been carried at under the cost model (e.g. its depreciated cost), the amount by which the asset is reduced is capped at this amount. Any excess is taken immediately to profit or loss. *[IFRIC 1.6(b)]*. This means that the maximum amount by which an asset can be reduced is the same whether it is carried at cost or revaluation.

This change in the revalued amount must be assessed against the requirements in Section 17 regarding revalued assets, particularly the requirement that they must be carried at an amount that does not differ materially from fair value (see also 3.6 below for the rules regarding revaluations of assets). Such an adjustment is an indication that the carrying amount may differ from fair value and the asset may have to be revalued. Any such revaluation must, of course, take into account the adjustment of the estimated liability. If a revaluation is necessary, all assets of the same class must be revalued.

Any changes in estimate taken to other comprehensive income (OCI) must be disclosed on the face of the statement of changes in equity or in the notes in accordance with Section 6 – *Statement of Changes in Equity and Statement of Income and Retained Earnings* (see Chapter 4). Depreciation of the 'decommissioning asset' and any changes thereto are covered by 3.5.2 and 3.5.3 below. The unwinding of the discount must be recognised in profit or loss as a finance cost as it occurs. Capitalisation of such costs would not be permitted under Section 25.

Chapter 13

A first-time adopter of FRS 102 is not required to restate the carrying amount included in an asset in respect of decommissioning that occurred before the date of transition to FRS 102, e.g. those changes in respect of estimated cash outflows, discount rate and unwinding discount. Instead, the exemption allows the entity to estimate the liability by calculating it at the transition date in accordance with Section 21. *[FRS 102.35.10(l)]*. This could be done by discounting the estimated liability at the transition date at its best estimate of the historical risk-adjusted discount rate(s) that would have applied over the intervening period. Accumulated depreciation as at the transition date is then based on the current estimate of the useful life of the asset, using the depreciation policy adopted by the entity under Section 17. See also Chapter 30.

3.4.4   *Exchanges of assets*

An entity might swap an asset it does not require in a particular area, for one it does from another area – the opposite being the case for the counterparty. Such exchanges are common in the telecommunications, media and leisure businesses, particularly after an acquisition. Governmental competition rules sometimes require such exchanges. The question arises whether such transactions give rise to a gain in circumstances where the carrying value of the outgoing facility is less than the fair value of the incoming one. This can occur when carrying values are less than market values, although it is possible that a transaction with no real commercial substance could be arranged solely to boost apparent profits.

Section 17 requires all acquisitions of PP&E in exchange for non-monetary assets, or a combination of monetary and non-monetary assets, to be measured at fair value, unless:

(a)   the exchange transaction lacks commercial substance; or

(b)   the fair value of neither the asset received nor the asset given up is reliably measurable.

In that case, the asset's cost is measured at the carrying amount of the asset given up. *[FRS 102.17.14]*.

The recognition of income from an exchange of assets does not depend on whether the assets exchanged are dissimilar. If at least one of the two fair values can be measured reliably, that value is used for measuring the exchange transaction; if not, then the exchange is measured at the carrying value of the asset the entity no longer owns. For example, if the new asset's fair value is higher than the carrying amount of the old asset, a gain may be recognised. This relatively understandable requirement is qualified by a 'commercial substance' test.

If it is not possible to demonstrate that the transaction has commercial substance, assets received in exchange transactions will be recorded at the carrying value of the asset given up. Accordingly, there is no gain on such a transaction.

If the transaction passes the 'commercial substance' test, then the exchanged asset is to be recorded at its fair value. As discussed in 3.7 below, Section 17 requires gains or losses on items that have been derecognised to be included in profit or loss in the period of derecognition (except for certain assets previously held for rental) but does not allow gains on derecognition to be classified as revenue. *[FRS 102.17.28]*. However, under current UK law, this gain is likely to be an unrealised profit and therefore should be included in other comprehensive income (OCI) i.e. only profits realised at the balance sheet date are to be included in the profit and loss account. *[1 Sch 13(a) SI2008/410].* For consolidated financial statements, the gain is also recognised in OCI if the new asset acquired is an interest in another entity (see Chapter 6). *[FRS 102.9.31(c)].*

3.4.4.A   Commercial substance

Section 17 does not provide further guidance on 'commercial substance' therefore the application of this term will involve judgement and careful consideration of facts and circumstances. In addition, an entity may also consider the guidance provided under IFRS – the commercial substance test was put in place as an anti-abuse provision to prevent gains in income being recognised when the transaction had no discernible effect on the entity's economics. *[IAS 16.BC21].* The commercial substance of an exchange is to be determined by forecasting and comparing the future cash flows budgeted to be generated by the incoming and outgoing assets. For there to be commercial substance, there must be a significant difference between the two forecasts. IAS 16 sets out this requirement as follows:

'An entity determines whether an exchange transaction has commercial substance by considering the extent to which its future cash flows are expected to change as a result of the transaction. An exchange transaction has commercial substance if:

(a)   the configuration (risk, timing and amount) of the cash flows of the asset received differs from the configuration of the cash flows of the asset transferred; or

(b)   the entity-specific value of the portion of the entity's operations affected by the transaction changes as a result of the exchange; and

(c)   the difference in (a) or (b) is significant relative to the fair value of the assets exchanged.' *[IAS 16.25].*

As set out in the definitions of IAS 16, entity-specific value is the net present value of the future predicted cash flows from continuing use and disposal of the asset. Post-tax cash flows should be used for this calculation. IAS 16 contains no guidance on the discount rate to be used for this exercise, nor on any of the other parameters involved, but it does suggest that the result of these analyses might be clear without having to perform detailed calculations. *[IAS 16.25].* Care will have to be taken to ensure that the transaction has commercial substance as defined in IAS 16 if an entity receives a similar item of PP&E in exchange for a similar asset of its own. Commercial substance may be difficult to demonstrate if the entity is exchanging an asset for a similar one in a similar location. However, in the latter case, the risk, timing and amount of cash flows could differ if one asset were available for sale and the entity intended to sell it whereas the previous asset could not be realised by sale or only sold over a much longer timescale. It is feasible that such a transaction could meet the conditions (a) and (c) above. Similarly, it would be unusual if the entity-specific values of similar assets differed enough in any arm's length exchange transaction to meet condition (c).

Chapter 13

Other types of exchange are more likely to pass the 'commercial substance' test, for example exchanging an interest in an investment property for one that the entity uses for its own purposes. The entity has exchanged a rental stream and instead has an asset that contributes to the cash flows of the cash-generating unit of which it is a part. In this case it is probable that the risk, timing and amount of the cash flows of the asset received would differ from the configuration of the cash flows of the asset transferred.

3.4.5   Assets held under finance leases

The cost at initial recognition of assets held under finance leases is determined in accordance with Section 20, *[FRS 102.20.9, 10]*, as described in Chapter 16.

3.5   Measurement after initial recognition: Cost Model

Section 17 allows one of two alternatives to be chosen as the accounting policy for measurement of PP&E after initial recognition. The choice made must be applied to an entire class of PP&E, which means that not all classes are required to have the same policy. *[FRS 102.17.15]*.

The first alternative is the 'cost model' whereby the item is carried at cost less any accumulated depreciation and less any accumulated impairment losses. *[FRS 102.17.15A]*. The other alternative, the revaluation model, is discussed below at 3.6.

Whichever model is used after initial recognition, the provisions discussed in 3.5.1 to 3.5.7 below are applicable:

3.5.1   Depreciation by component of an item of PP&E

Section 17 links its recognition concept of a component of an asset, discussed at 3.3.2 above, with the analysis of assets for the purpose of depreciation. Each major component of an item of PP&E with significantly different patterns of consumption of economic benefits must be depreciated separately over its useful life, which means that the initial cost must be allocated between the major components by the entity. Other assets are depreciated over their useful lives as a single asset. *[FRS 102.17.16]*. Components are identified by their patterns of consumption of economic benefits and they may have the same useful lives and depreciation method. Practically, they could be grouped for the purposes of calculating depreciation charge.

Section 17 does not provide guidance for depreciating the remainder of an asset that has not separately been identified into components. These may consist of other components that are individually not significant. An entity may consider the approach in IAS 16 and thus, the entity may use estimation techniques to calculate an appropriate depreciation method for all of these parts. *[IAS 16.46]*. An entity may also depreciate separately components that are not significant in relation to the whole.

The depreciation charge for each period is recognised in profit or loss unless it forms part of the cost of another asset, for example, the depreciation of manufacturing PP&E is included in the costs of inventories (see Section 13 – *Inventories*). *[FRS 102.17.17]*.

3.5.2 *Depreciable amount and residual values*

The *depreciable amount* of an item of PP&E is its cost or valuation less its estimated residual value. The *residual value* of an asset is the estimated amount that an entity would currently obtain from disposal of the asset, after deducting the estimated costs of disposal, if the asset were already of the age and in the condition expected at the end of its useful life. *[FRS 102 Appendix I]*.

Factors such as a change in how an asset is used, significant unexpected wear and tear, technological advancement, and changes in market prices may indicate that the residual value or useful life of an asset has changed since the most recent annual reporting date. Entities should assess if such indicators exist. If such indicators are present, an entity shall review its previous estimates and, if current expectations differ, amend the residual value, depreciation method or useful life. The entity shall account for the change in residual value, depreciation method or useful life as a change in an accounting estimate in accordance with paragraphs 15 to 18 of Section 10 – *Accounting Policies, Estimates and Errors* (see Chapter 7). *[FRS 102.17.19]*. This requirement applies to all items of PP&E, and therefore applicable to all components of them.

A change in the estimated residual value is generally recognised prospectively from the date of the change.

As the definition implies, the residual value of an item of PP&E today is to be calculated by taking the price such an asset would fetch today, but assuming that it was already in the condition it will be in at the end of its useful life. This would mean that price changes (e.g. due to inflation) would be taken into account only up to the reporting date and expectations as to future increases or decreases of asset's disposal value after the reporting date are not taken into account. Accordingly, Section 17 contains an element of continuous updating of an asset's carrying value.

As any change in the residual value directly affects the depreciable amount, it may also affect the depreciation charge. This is because the depreciable amount (i.e. the amount actually charged to profit or loss over the life of the asset) is calculated by deducting the residual value from the cost or valuation of the asset, although for these purposes the residual value would be capped at the asset's carrying amount (see 3.1 above). In periods of rising prices, the residual value for assets will typically appreciate in value (e.g. buildings). Accordingly, where residual value rises over time the depreciation charge on an asset is likely to decline and may cease altogether when the residual value exceeds the asset's carrying value. Although many items of PP&E have a negligible residual value because they are kept for significantly all of their useful lives, there are a number of types of asset where this requirement could have a significant effect, and conceivably cause noticeable volatility in the depreciation charge. The residual values, and hence depreciation charges, of ships, aircraft, hotels and other assets of this nature, could potentially be significantly affected by this requirement.

Chapter 13

This means that it is important that residual values are considered and reviewed in conjunction with the review of useful lives. The useful life is the period over which the entity expects to use the asset, not the asset's economic life.

Residual values are of no relevance if the entity intends to keep the asset for significantly all of its useful life. In such circumstances, if an entity points to the prices fetched in the market by a type of asset that it holds, it must also demonstrate an intention to dispose of it before the end of its economic life.

3.5.3   *Depreciation charge*

Section 17 requires the depreciable amount of an asset to be allocated on a systematic basis over its useful life. *[FRS 102.17.18]*.

As described above, depreciation must be charged on all items of PP&E. This requirement applies even to PP&E measured under the revaluation model, even if the fair value of the asset at the year-end is higher than the carrying amount, as long as the residual value of the item is lower than the carrying amount. If the residual value exceeds the carrying amount, no depreciation is charged until the residual value once again decreases to less than the carrying amount. Repair and maintenance of an asset would not of itself negate the need to depreciate it.

3.5.4   *Useful lives*

One of the critical assumptions on which the depreciation charge depends is the useful life of the asset. Useful life is defined as either:

•   the period over which an asset is expected to be available for use by an entity; or

•   the number of production or similar units expected to be obtained from the asset by an entity. *[FRS 102 Appendix I]*.

As discussed at 3.5.2 above, asset's useful life shall be estimated on a realistic basis and reviewed at the end of each reporting period for indicators that would suggest it has changed. The effects of changes in useful life are recognised prospectively, over the remaining life of the asset. *[FRS 102.17.19]*.

The useful life is the period over which the present owner will benefit and not the total potential life of the asset; the two will often not be the same.

It is quite possible for an asset's useful life to be shorter than its economic life. Many entities have a policy of disposing of assets when they still have a residual value, which means that another user will benefit from the asset. This is particularly common with property and motor vehicles, where there are effective second-hand markets, but less usual for plant and machinery. For example, an entity may have a policy of replacing all of its motor vehicles after three years, so this will be their estimated useful life for depreciation purposes. The entity will depreciate them over this period down to the estimated residual value. The residual values of motor vehicles are often easy to obtain and the entity will be able to reassess these residuals in line with the requirements of the standard.

Judgement is necessary in determining the useful life of an asset. Section 17 provides the following guidance about the factors to be considered when determining the useful life of an asset:

(a)   The expected usage of the asset. Usage is assessed by reference to the asset's expected capacity or physical output.

(b)   Expected physical wear and tear, which depends on operational factors such as the number of shifts for which the asset is to be used and the repair and maintenance programme, and the care and maintenance of the asset while idle (see 3.5.4.A below).

(c)   Technical or commercial obsolescence arising from changes or improvements in production, or from a change in the market demand for the product or service output of the asset (see 3.5.4.C below).

(d)   Legal or similar limits on the use of the asset, such as the expiry dates of related leases. *[FRS 102.17.21].*

Factor (d) above states that the 'expiry dates of related leases' is considered when determining the asset's useful life. Generally, the useful life of the leasehold improvement is the same or less than the lease term, as defined by Section 20 (see Chapter 16). However, a lessee may be able to depreciate an asset whose useful life exceeds the lease term over a longer period if the lease includes an option to extend that the lessee expects to exercise, even if the option is not considered 'reasonably certain' at inception (a higher threshold than the estimate of useful life in Section 17). In such a case, the asset may be depreciated either over the lease term or over the shorter of the asset's useful life and the period for which the entity expects to extend the lease.

3.5.4.A   Repairs and maintenance

The initial assessment of the useful life of the asset will take into account the expected routine spending on repairs and expenditure necessary for it to achieve that life. Although Section 17 implies that this refers to an item of plant and machinery, care and maintenance programmes are relevant to assessing the useful lives of many other types of asset. For example, an entity may assess the useful life of a railway engine at thirty-five years on the assumption that it has a major overhaul every seven years. Without this expenditure, the life of the engine would be much less certain and could be much shorter. Maintenance necessary to support the fabric of a building and its service potential is also taken into account in assessing its useful life. Eventually, it will always become uneconomic for the entity to continue to maintain the asset so, while the expenditure may lengthen the useful life, it is unlikely to make it indefinite.

Note that this applies whether the expenditure is capitalised because it meets the definition of a 'major inspection' (see 3.3.3.A above) or if it is repairs and maintenance that is expensed as incurred.

3.5.4.B   Land

As discussed in 3.3.2.A above, land and buildings are separable assets and must be accounted for separately, even when they are acquired together. *[FRS 102.17.8]*. Land, which generally has an unlimited life, is not usually depreciated. *[FRS 102.17.16]*. A building is a depreciable asset and its useful life is not affected by an increase in the value of the land on which it stands.

Although land generally has an unlimited useful life, there may be circumstances in which depreciation could be applied to land. In those instances in which land has a finite life it will be either used for extractive purposes (a quarry or mine) or for some purpose such as landfill; it will be depreciated in an appropriate manner but it is highly unlikely that there will be any issue regarding separating the interest in land from any building element. However, the cost of such land may include an element for site dismantlement or restoration (see 3.4.3 above), in which case this element will have to be separated from the land element and depreciated over an appropriate period (i.e. the period of benefits obtained by incurring these costs) which will often be the estimated useful life of the site for its purpose and function. An entity engaged in landfill on a new site may make a provision for restoring it as soon as it starts preparation by removing the overburden. It will separate the land from the 'restoration asset' and depreciate the restoration asset over the landfill site's estimated useful life. If the land has an infinite useful life, an appropriate depreciation basis will have to be chosen that reflects the period of benefits obtained from the restoration asset.

While FRS 102 provides no specific guidance related to revision of estimated costs, an entity may consider the approach applied by IFRIC 1 – *Changes in Existing Decommissioning, Restoration and Similar Liabilities* (see 3.4.3 above and Chapter 17 at 4.1). Accordingly, if the estimated costs are revised, in accordance with IFRIC 1, the adjusted depreciable amount of the asset is depreciated over its useful life. Therefore, once the related asset has reached the end of its useful life, all subsequent changes in the liability shall be recognised in profit or loss as they occur, irrespective of whether the entity applies the cost or revaluation model. *[IFRIC 1.7]*.

3.5.4.C   Technological change

The effects of technological change are often underestimated. It affects many assets, not only high technology plant and equipment such as computer systems. For example, many offices that have been purpose-built can become obsolete long before their fabric has physically deteriorated, for reasons such as the difficulty of introducing computer network infrastructures or air conditioning, poor environmental performance or an inability to meet new legislative requirements such as access for people with disabilities. Expected future reductions in the selling price of an item that was produced using an asset could also indicate the expectation of technical or commercial obsolescence of the asset, which, in turn, might reflect a reduction of the future economic benefits embodied in the asset. Therefore, the estimation of an asset's useful life is a matter of judgement and the possibility of technological change must be taken into account.

3.5.5   *When depreciation starts and ceases*

Section 17 is clear on when depreciation should start and finish, and sets out the requirements as follows:

- Depreciation of an asset begins when it is available for use, which is defined further as occurring when the asset is in the location and condition necessary for it to be capable of operating in the manner intended by management. This is the point at which capitalisation of costs relating to the asset cease.

- Depreciation of an asset ceases when the asset is derecognised. *[FRS 102.17.20].*

Therefore, an entity does not stop depreciating an asset merely because it has become idle or has been retired from active use, unless the asset is fully depreciated. However, if the entity is using a usage method of depreciation (e.g. the units of production method) the depreciation charge can be zero while there is no production. *[FRS 102.17.20].* Of course, a prolonged period in which there is no production may raise questions as to whether the asset is impaired: an asset becoming idle is a specific example of an indication of impairment in Section 27 (see Chapter 22). *[FRS 102.27.9(f)].*

3.5.6   *Depreciation methods*

Section 17 does not prescribe a particular method of depreciation. It simply states that 'an entity shall select the depreciation method that reflects the pattern in which it expects to consume the asset's future economic benefits', mentioning straight-line, diminishing balance and units of production methods as possibilities. *[FRS 102.17.22].* The overriding requirement is that the depreciation charge reflects the pattern of consumption of the benefits the asset brings over its useful life, and is applied consistently from period to period unless there is a change in the expected pattern of consumption of those future economic benefits. *[FRS 102.17.22, 23].*

Section 17 contains an explicit requirement that the depreciation method be reviewed to determine if there is an indication that there has been a significant change since the last annual reporting date in the pattern by which an entity expects to consume an asset's future economic benefits. This would mean, for example, concluding that the unit of production method was no longer appropriate and changing to a straight line or diminishing balance method. Nevertheless, if there has been such a change, the depreciation method should be changed to reflect it. However, under paragraphs 15 to 18 of Section 10 (see Chapter 7), this change is a change in accounting estimate and not a change in accounting policy. *[FRS 102.17.23].* This means that the consequent depreciation adjustment should be made prospectively, i.e. the asset's depreciable amount should be written off over current and future periods. *[FRS 102.10.16].*

Some industries use revenue as a practical basis to depreciate PP&E. These industries argue that there is a linear relationship between revenue and the units of production method (discussed below at 3.5.6.C). Unlike IFRS, FRS 102 does not explicitly prohibit the use of revenue as the basis to depreciate assets.

3.5.6.A   *Straight-line method*

The straight-line method of depreciation is well known and understood. Its simplicity makes it the most commonly used method in practice. The method is time-based and involves the use of a fixed percentage of the original cost of the asset

Chapter 13

in spreading the depreciable amount evenly over the useful life of the asset resulting in a constant depreciation charge over such period. It is considered the most appropriate method to use when the pattern of consumption of future economic benefits of an asset is expected to be constant year-on-year or when such pattern cannot be readily determined.

3.5.6.B   *Diminishing balance method*

The diminishing balance method involves determining a percentage depreciation that will write off the asset's depreciable amount over its useful life. This involves calculating a rate that will reduce the asset's net book value to its residual value at the end of the useful life.

Example 13.2:   Diminishing balance depreciation

An asset costs £6,000 and has a life of four years and a residual value of £1,500. It calculates that the appropriate depreciation rate on the declining balance is 29% and that the depreciation charge in years 1-4 will be as follows:

		£
Year 1	Cost	6,000
	Depreciation at 29% of £6,000	1,757
	Net book value	4,243
Year 2	Depreciation at 29% of £4,243	1,243
	Net book value	3,000
Year 3	Depreciation at 29% of £3,000	879
	Net book value	2,121
Year 4	Depreciation at 29% of £2,121	621
	Net book value	1,500

The sum of digits method is another form of the diminishing balance method, but one that is based on the estimated life of the asset and which can easily be applied if the asset has a residual value. If an asset has an estimated useful life of four years then the digits 1, 2, 3, and 4 are added together, giving a total of 10. Depreciation of four-tenths, three-tenths and so on, of the cost of the asset, less any residual value, will be charged in the respective years. The method is sometimes called the 'rule of 78', 78 being the sum of the digits 1 to 12.

Example 13.3:   Sum of the digits depreciation

An asset costs £10,000 and is expected to be sold for £2,000 after four years. The depreciable amount is £8,000 (£10,000 – £2,000). Depreciation is to be provided over four years using the sum of the digits method.

		£
Year 1	Cost	10,000
	Depreciation at 4/10 of £8,000	3,200
	Net book value	6,800
Year 2	Depreciation at 3/10 of £8,000	2,400
	Net book value	4,400
Year 3	Depreciation at 2/10 of £8,000	1,600
	Net book value	2,800
Year 4	Depreciation at 1/10 of £8,000	800
	Net book value	2,000

3.5.6.C   Units of production method

Under this method, the asset is written off in line with its estimated total output. By relating depreciation to the proportion of productive capacity utilised to date, it reflects the fact that the useful economic life of certain assets, principally machinery, is more closely linked to its usage and output than to time. This method is normally used in extractive industries, for example, to amortise the costs of development of productive oil and gas facilities.

The essence of choosing a fair depreciation method is to reflect the consumption of economic benefits provided by the asset concerned. In most cases the straight-line basis will give perfectly acceptable results, and the vast majority of entities use this method. Where there are instances, such as the extraction of a known proportion of a mineral resource, or the use of a certain amount of the total available number of working hours of a machine, it may be that units of production method will give fairer results.

3.5.7   Impairment

All items of PP&E accounted for under Section 17 are subject to the impairment requirements of Section 27 – *Impairment of Assets*. That section explains when and how an entity reviews the carrying amount of its assets, how it determines the recoverable amount of an asset, and when it recognises or reverses an impairment loss. *[FRS 102.17.24]*. Impairment is discussed in Chapter 22.

There is no requirement in Section 17 for an automatic impairment review if no depreciation is charged.

3.5.7.A   Compensation for impairment

The question has arisen about the treatment of any compensation an entity may be due to receive as a result of an asset being impaired. For example an asset that is insured might be destroyed in a fire, so repayment from an insurance company might be expected. These two events – the impairment and any compensation – are separate economic events and should be accounted for separately as follows:

- impairments of PP&E are recognised in accordance with Section 27 (see Chapter 22);

- derecognition of items retired or disposed of should be recognised in accordance with Section 17 (derecognition is discussed at 3.7 below); and

- compensation from third parties for PP&E that is impaired, lost or given up is included in profit and loss only when the compensation is virtually certain. *[FRS 102.17.25]*.

Therefore any compensation is accounted for separately from any impairment. Although the question as to when compensation is 'virtually certain' is not discussed further in Section 17, a similar concept is discussed in Section 21 which requires that reimbursements from third parties should be recognised as a separate asset when it is 'virtually certain' that the reimbursement will be received. *[FRS 102.21.9]*. See Chapter 17.

Chapter 13

3.5.7.B   PP&E held for sale

An entity's plan to dispose of an asset before the previously expected date is an indicator of impairment that triggers the calculation of the asset's recoverable amount for the purpose of determining whether the asset is impaired. *[FRS 102.17.26, 27.9(f)]*. If the asset is impaired, then the carrying amount of the asset should be written down to its recoverable amount.

Although the entity plans to dispose of the asset, depreciation should continue until the asset is disposed. In addition, the plan to dispose an asset might indicate that the residual value or the remaining life of the asset needs adjustment even if there is no impairment.

3.6   Measurement after initial recognition: Revaluation Model

If the revaluation model is adopted, PP&E is initially recognised at cost and subsequently measured at fair value less subsequent accumulated depreciation and impairment losses. *[FRS 102.17.15B]*. In practice, 'fair value' will usually be the market value of the asset. There is no requirement for a professional external valuation or even for a professionally qualified valuer to perform the appraisal, although in practice professional advice is often sought.

Section 17 does not prescribe the frequency of revaluations and simply states that revaluations are to be made with sufficient regularity to ensure that the carrying amount does not differ materially from the fair value at the end of the reporting period. *[FRS 102.17.15B]*. When the fair value of a revalued asset differs materially from its carrying amount, a further revaluation is necessary. As some items of PP&E have frequent and volatile changes in fair value, these would need to be revalued more frequently (e.g. annually).

If the revaluation model is adopted, all items within a class of assets are to be revalued simultaneously. This prevents selective revaluations particularly choosing to revalue only those assets that significantly increased in value. A class of PP&E is a grouping of assets of a similar nature, function or use in an entity's business. *[FRS 102.17.15]*. This is not a precise definition. The following could be examples of separate classes of asset:

- land;
- land and buildings;
- machinery;
- ships;
- aircraft;
- motor vehicles;
- furniture and fixtures; and
- office equipment.

These are very broad categories of asset and it is possible for them to be classified further into groupings of assets of a similar nature and use. Office buildings and factories or hotels and fitness centres, could be separate classes of asset. If the entity used the same type of asset in two different geographical locations, e.g. clothing

Property, plant and equipment

manufacturing facilities for similar products or products with similar markets, say in the United Kingdom and the Republic of Ireland, it is likely that these would be seen as part of the same class of asset. However, if the entity manufactured pharmaceuticals and clothing, both in European facilities, then few would argue that these could be assets with a sufficiently different nature and use to be a separate class. Ultimately, it must be a matter of judgement in the context of the specific operations of individual entities.

A rolling valuation of a class of assets could be made provided that the class is revalued over a short period of time and that the valuations are kept up to date. In practice, a rolling valuation is usually performed if the value of the assets changes very insignificantly (in which case the valuations may only be performed less frequently) because if a significant change is revealed, then presumably a new revaluation for the entire class is required to keep the valuation up to date.

3.6.1   The meaning of fair value

Fair value is defined as the amount for which an asset could be exchanged, a liability settled, or an equity instrument granted could be exchanged, between knowledgeable, willing parties in an arm's length transaction. In the absence of any specific guidance provided in the relevant section of FRS 102, the guidance in Section 11 – *Basic Financial Instruments* – paragraphs 27 to 32 shall be used in determining fair value (see Chapter 8). *[FRS 102 Appendix I].*

Section 17 describes the process of determining fair value for assets within its scope. For land and buildings, fair value is usually determined from market-based evidence by appraisal that is normally undertaken by professionally qualified valuers (although income or depreciated replacement cost approaches are permitted if no such evidence is available because of the specialised nature of the item of PP&E – see 3.6.2 below). For other items of PP&E, the fair value is usually their market value determined by appraisal. *[FRS 102.17.15C, 15D].* Section 17 does not imply that fair value and market value are synonymous, although it states that the fair value of items of PP&E is usually their market value determined by appraisal. *[FRS 102.17.15C].*

3.6.2   Fair value in the absence of market-based evidence

Section 17 allows other methods of estimating fair value of assets in the absence of market-based evidence because of the specialised nature of the asset and it is rarely sold except as part of a continuing business. In such cases, an entity may need to estimate fair value using an income or a depreciated replacement cost (DRC) approach (see 3.6.2.A and 3.6.2.B below). *[FRS 102.17.15D].*

The basis underlying the income or DRC approach is that the asset is so specialised that there is no market value for it. There are three main subsets of such assets: (a) those that are only ever sold as part of a business; (b) assets primarily used to provide services to the public (whether on a paying or non-paying basis); and (c) assets that are so specialised by nature of their size or location or similar features that there is no market for them.

Examples of specialised properties include:

- oil refineries and chemical works where, usually, the buildings are no more than housings or cladding for highly specialised plant;

- power stations and dock installations where the building and site engineering works are related directly to the business of the owner, it being highly unlikely that they would have a value to anyone other than a company acquiring the undertaking;

- schools, colleges, universities and research establishments where there is no competing market demand from other organisations using these types of property in the locality;

- hospitals, other specialised health care premises and leisure centres where there is no competing market demand from other organisations wishing to use these types of property in the locality; and

- museums, libraries, and other similar premises provided by the public sector.

In addition, there may be no market-based evidence for properties of such specialised construction, arrangement, size or specification that it is unlikely that there would be a single purchaser. The same may be the case even for standard properties in geographical areas remote from main business centres, perhaps originally located there for operational or business reasons that no longer exist. This could occur if the buildings were of such an abnormal size for the district that no market for them would exist.

3.6.2.A   Income approach to fair value

Section 17 does not define what it means by an income approach. However, a definition is provided in IFRS 13 – *Fair Value Measurement* – which states that the *income approach* converts future amounts (e.g. cash flows or income and expenses) to a single discounted amount. The fair value reflects current market expectations about those future amounts. In the case of PP&E, this will usually mean using a discounted cash flow technique. *[IFRS 13.B10, B11].*

Further discussion of this valuation technique can be found in Chapter 14 of EY International GAAP 2015.[1]

3.6.2.B   Depreciated replacement cost

Depreciated replacement cost is defined as the most economic cost required for the entity to replace the service potential of an asset (including the amount that the entity will receive from its disposal at the end of its useful life) at the reporting date. *[FRS 102 Appendix I].* The objective of DRC is to make a realistic estimate of the current cost of constructing an asset that has the same service potential as the existing asset.

As a DRC valuation is based on replacement cost, it is likely to give a higher valuation than one using market-based evidence that reflects the actual current condition of the asset. For this reason, it is necessary to ensure that the asset really is so specialised that such evidence cannot be obtained. It is also necessary to be satisfied that the potential profitability of the business is adequate to support the value derived on a DRC basis.

DRC approaches are often applied to the valuation of plant and machinery, as distinct from property assets, where there is rarely a market from which to derive a fair value.

3.6.3   Accounting for revaluation surpluses and deficits

With respect to any determination of the value of an asset of a company on any basis of the alternative accounting rules, the amount of any profit or loss arising from that determination must be credited or (as the case may be) debited to a separate reserve ('the revaluation reserve') as required by the Companies Act. *[1 Sch 35(1)]*.

Accordingly, increases as a result of revaluation are recognised in OCI and accumulated in equity i.e. revaluation reserve. If a revaluation increase reverses a revaluation decrease of the same asset that was previously recognised as an expense, it may be recognised in profit or loss. *[FRS 102.17.15E]*. Decreases as a result of revaluation are recognised in OCI to the extent of any previously recognised revaluation increase accumulated in revaluation reserve in respect of the same asset. If a revaluation decrease exceeds the revaluation gains accumulated in revaluation reserve in respect of that asset, the excess is recognised in profit or loss. *[FRS 102.17.15F]*. This means that it is not permissible under Section 17 to carry a negative revaluation reserve in respect of any item of PP&E.

The same rules apply to impairment losses. Any impairment loss of a revalued asset shall be treated as a revaluation decrease in accordance Section 17. *[FRS 102.27.6]*.

3.6.3.A   Depreciation of revalued assets

The fundamental objective of depreciation is to reflect in operating profit the cost of use of an item of PP&E (i.e. the amount of economic benefits consumed) in the period. This requires a charge to operating profit even if the asset has changed in value or has been revalued.

Section 17 is not specific as to the base amount of an item of PP&E to be used when computing the depreciation charge for the period. It might be best to use the average carrying value during the year, or else, the opening or closing balance may be used provided that it is used consistently in each period. In practice, the depreciation charge is generally based on the opening value and the written down asset is revalued as at the end of accounting period. The depreciation charge should be recognised as an expense, unless it qualifies to be capitalised as part of another asset (see discussion at 3.5.1 above).

While not explicitly addressed in Section 17, the revaluation surplus included in OCI may be transferred directly to retained earnings as the surplus is realised. *[1 Sch 35(3)]*. Accordingly, the difference between depreciation based on the revalued carrying amount of the asset and depreciation based on its original cost may be transferred from the revaluation reserve to retained earnings as the asset is used by the entity. Any depreciation of the revalued part of an asset's carrying value is considered realised by being charged to profit or loss. Thus a transfer may be made of an equivalent amount from the revaluation surplus to retained earnings. However any transfer is made directly from revaluation surplus to retained earnings and not through profit or loss. This is illustrated in Example 13.4 below. Any remaining balance may be transferred from revaluation reserve to retained earnings when the asset is derecognised (see 3.7 below). Revaluation gains or losses arising from the disposal of PP&E are not recycled to profit or loss.

Example 13.4:   Effect of depreciation on the revaluation reserve

On 1 January 2012 an entity acquired an asset for £1,000. The asset has an economic life of ten years and is depreciated on a straight-line basis. The residual value is assumed to be £nil. At 31 December 2015 (when the cost net of accumulated depreciation is £600) the asset is valued at £900. The entity accounts for the revaluation by debiting the carrying value of the asset (using either of the methods discussed below) £300 and crediting £300 to the revaluation reserve. At 31 December 2015 the useful life of the asset is considered to be the remainder of its original life (i.e. six years) and its residual value is still considered to be £nil. In the year ended 31 December 2016 and in later years, the depreciation charged to profit or loss is £150 (£900/6 years remaining).

Accordingly, the treatment thereafter for each of the remaining 6 years of the asset's life, is to transfer £50 (£300/6 years) each year from the revaluation reserve to retained earnings (not through profit or loss). This avoids the revaluation reserve being maintained indefinitely even after the asset ceases to exist, which does not seem sensible. This treatment is also permitted by Companies Act which allows amounts to be transferred to the profit and loss account reserve if the amount has previously been charged in that account or is a realised profit. A transfer is possible because the amount of £50 is a realised profit in terms of the Companies Act. *[s841(5), 1 Sch 35(3)].*

The effect on taxation, both current and deferred, of a policy of revaluing assets is recognised and disclosed in accordance with Section 29 – *Income Tax*. This is dealt with in Chapter 24.

FRS 102 does not provide specific guidance on accounting for accumulated depreciation when an item of PP&E is revalued. There are two usual methods of adjusting the carrying amount when an item of PP&E is revalued. At the date of revaluation, the asset is treated in one of the following ways:

- The accumulated depreciation is eliminated against gross carrying amount of the asset and the carrying amount is then restated to the revalued amount of the asset.

- The gross carrying amount is adjusted in a manner that is consistent with the revaluation of the carrying amount of the asset. For example, the gross carrying amount may be restated by reference to observable market data or it may be restated proportionately to the change in the carrying amount of the asset. The accumulated depreciation at the date of the revaluation is adjusted to equal the difference between the gross carrying amount and the carrying amount of the asset after taking into account accumulated impairment losses.

The first method available eliminates the amount of accumulated depreciation to the extent of the difference between the revalued amount and the carrying amount of the asset immediately before revaluation. This is illustrated in Example 13.5.

Example 13.5: *Revaluation by eliminating accumulated depreciation*

On 31 December, a building has a carrying amount of £40,000, being the original cost of £70,000 less accumulated depreciation of £30,000. A revaluation is performed and the fair value of the asset is £50,000. The entity would record the following journal entries:

	Dr £	Cr £
Accumulated depreciation	30,000	
Building		20,000
Asset revaluation reserve		10,000

	Before £	After £
Building at cost	70,000	
Building at valuation		50,000
Accumulated depreciation	30,000	–
Net book value	40,000	50,000

Under the observable market data approach, the gross carrying amount will be restated and its difference compared to the revalued amount of the asset will be absorbed by the accumulated depreciation. Using the example above, assume the gross carrying amount is restated to £75,000 by reference to the observable market data and the accumulated depreciation will be adjusted to £25,000 (i.e. the gross carrying amount of £75,000 less the carrying amount adjusted to its revalued amount of £50,000).

Alternatively, the gross carrying amount is restated proportionately to the change in carrying amount (i.e. a 25% uplift) resulting in the same revaluation movement as the methods above but the cost and accumulated depreciation carried forward reflect a gross cost of the asset of £87,500 and accumulated depreciation of £37,500. This method may be used if an asset is revalued using an index to determine its depreciated replacement cost (DRC) (see 3.6.2.B above).

3.6.4 Reversals of downward valuations

Section 17 requires that, if an asset's carrying amount is increased as a result of a revaluation, the increase should be credited directly to OCI and accumulated in equity. However, the increase should be recognised in profit or loss to the extent that it reverses a revaluation decrease of the same asset previously recognised in profit or loss. *[FRS 102.17.15E]*.

If the revalued asset is being depreciated, the full amount of any reversal is not taken to profit or loss. Rather, the reversal should take account of the depreciation that would have been charged on the previously higher book value. The text of Section 17 does not specify this treatment but such treatment is consistent with Section 27, which states:

> 'The reversal of an impairment loss shall not exceed the carrying amount of the asset above the carrying amount that would have been determined (net of amortisation or depreciation) had no impairment loss been recognised for the asset in prior years'. *[FRS 102.27.30(c)]*.

The following example demonstrates a way in which this could be applied:

Example 13.6:   Reversal of a downward valuation

An asset has a cost of £1,000,000, a life of 10 years and a residual value of £nil. At the end of year 3, when the asset's depreciated cost is £700,000, it is revalued to £350,000. This write down below cost of £350,000 is taken through profit or loss.

The entity then depreciates the asset by £50,000 per annum, so as to depreciate the revalued carrying amount of £350,000 over the remaining 7 years.

At the end of year 6, the asset's NBV is £200,000 but it is now revalued to £500,000. The effect on the entity's asset is as follows:

	£000
Valuation	
At the beginning of year 6	350
Surplus on revaluation	150
At the end of the year	500
Accumulated depreciation	
At beginning of year 6 *	100
Charge for the year	50
Accumulated depreciation written back on revaluation	(150)
At the end of the year	–
Net book value at the end of year 6	500
Net book value at the beginning of year 6	250

* Two years' depreciation (years 4 and 5) at £50,000 per annum.

Upon the revaluation in year 6 the total uplift in the asset's carrying amount is £300,000 (i.e. £500,000 less £200,000). However, only £200,000 is taken through profit or loss. £100,000 represents depreciation that would otherwise have been charged to profit or loss in years 4 and 5. This is taken directly to the revaluation surplus in OCI.

From the beginning of year 7 the £500,000 asset value will be written off over the remaining four years at £125,000 per annum.

In Example 13.6 above, the amount of the revaluation that is credited to the revaluation surplus in OCI represents the difference between the net book value that would have resulted had the asset always been held on a cost basis since initial recognition (£400,000) and the net book value on a revalued amount (£500,000).

This might be considered as an extreme example. Most assets that are subject to a policy of revaluation would not show such marked changes in value and it would be expected that there would be valuation movements in the intervening years rather than dramatic losses and gains in years 3 and 6. However, we consider that in principle this is the way in which downward valuations should be recognised.

There may be major practical difficulties for any entity that finds itself in the position of reversing revaluation deficits on depreciating assets, although whether in practice this eventuality often occurs is open to doubt. If there is any chance that it is likely to occur, the business would need to continue to maintain asset registers on the original, pre-write down, basis.

3.6.5   *Adopting a policy of revaluation*

Although the adoption of a policy of revaluation by an entity that has previously used the cost model is a change in accounting policy, it is not dealt with as a prior year adjustment in accordance with Section 10. Instead, the change is treated as a revaluation during the year. *[FRS 102.10.10A]*. This means that the entity is not required to obtain valuation information about comparative periods.

3.6.6   *Assets held under finance leases*

Once assets held under finance leases have been capitalised as items of PP&E, their subsequent accounting is the same as for any other asset so they do not constitute a separate class of assets. Therefore such assets may also be revalued using the revaluation model but, if the revaluation model is used, then the entire class of assets (both owned and those held under finance lease) must be revalued. *[FRS 102.17.15]*.

Whilst it is not explicit in Section 17, in our view, to obtain the fair value of an asset held under a finance lease for financial reporting purposes, the assessed value must be adjusted to take account of any recognised finance lease liability. Accordingly, if the entity obtains an asset valuation net of the valuer's estimate of the present value of future lease obligations, which is usual practice, to the extent that the lease obligations have already been accounted for in the balance sheet as a lease obligation, an amount must be added back to arrive at the fair value of the asset for the purposes of the financial statements. Such a valuation adjustment is achieved by adjusting for the finance lease obligation recognised in the financial statements. This is consistent with the mechanism discussed at 3.3.3 of Chapter 12.

For disclosure purposes PP&E acquired under a finance lease should be considered to be the same class of asset as those with a similar nature that are owned. Consequently, there is no need to provide separate reconciliations of movements in owned assets from assets held under finance leases (see 3.8 below).

3.7   Derecognition

Derecognition (i.e. removal of the carrying amount of the item from the financial statements of the entity) occurs when an item of PP&E is either disposed of, or when no further economic benefits are expected to flow from its use or disposal. *[FRS 102.17.27]*. The actual date of disposal is determined in accordance with the criteria in Section 23 – *Revenue* – for the recognition of revenue from the sale of goods *[FRS 102.17.29]* (revenue recognition is discussed in Chapter 18). All gains and losses on derecognition must be included in profit and loss for the period (although, except as discussed in 3.7.1 below, gains should not be classified as revenue) when the item is derecognised, unless another standard applies – for example under Section 20, a sale and leaseback transaction might not give rise to a gain. *[FRS 102.17.28]*. See Chapter 16 for more detail.

Gains and losses are to be calculated as the difference between any net disposal proceeds and the carrying value of the item of PP&E *[FRS 102.17.30]* – this means that any revaluation surplus relating to the asset disposed of is transferred directly to retained earnings when the asset is derecognised and not reflected in profit or loss.

Replacement of 'parts' of an asset requires derecognition of the carrying value of the original part, even if that part was not being depreciated separately. In these circumstances, it might be acceptable to estimate using the cost of a replacement part to be a guide to the original cost of the replaced part, if that cannot be determined. See discussion at 3.3.2 above.

Any consideration received on the disposal of an item should be recognised at its fair value. If deferred credit terms are given, the consideration for the sale is the cash price equivalent, and any surplus is treated as interest revenue using the effective yield method as required by Section 23 (see Chapter 18).

There could be a few fully depreciated assets still in use. For those fully depreciated assets that are no longer in use, it may be practical to derecognise them, rather than continue rather than continue to carry them at their gross cost and accumulated depreciation.

3.7.1   *Sale of assets held for rental*

If an entity, in the course of its ordinary activities, routinely sells PP&E that it has held for rental to others, it should transfer such assets to inventories at their carrying amount when they cease to be rented and are now held for sale. Accordingly, the proceeds from the sale of such assets should be recognised as revenue. While this is not specified in Section 17, this treatment appears reasonable and is consistent with the specific provisions in IAS 16 paragraph 68A. In contrast, the sale of investment property is generally not recognised as revenue.

A number of entities sell assets that have previously been held for rental, for example, car rental companies that may acquire vehicles with the intention of holding them as rental cars for a limited period and then selling them. One issue is whether the sale of such assets (which arguably have a dual purpose of being rented out and then sold) should be presented gross (revenue and cost of sales) or net (gain or loss) in profit or loss.

It would be reasonable to consider the IFRS conclusion in this scenario. The IASB concluded that the presentation of gross revenue, rather than a net gain or loss, would better reflect the ordinary activities of some such entities. Accordingly, when preparing statement of cash flows, both (i) the cash payments to manufacture or acquire assets held for rental and subsequently held for sale; and (ii) the cash receipts from rentals and sales of such assets would be presented as from operating activities. *[IAS 7.14]*. This is intended to avoid initial expenditure on purchases of assets being classified as investing activities while inflows from sales are recorded within operating activities.

3.7.2   *Partial disposals and undivided interests*

Section 17 requires an entity to derecognise 'an item' of PP&E on disposal or when it expects no future economic benefits from its use or disposal. *[FRS 102.17.27]*.

Items of PP&E are recognised when their costs can be measured reliably and it is probable that future benefits associated with the asset will flow to the entity. *[FRS 102.17.4]*. Section 17 does not prescribe the unit of measure for recognition, i.e. what constitutes an item of PP&E.

However, items that are derecognised were not necessarily items on initial recognition. The item that is being disposed of may be part of a larger 'item' bought in a single transaction that can be subdivided into parts (i.e. separate items) for separate disposal; an obvious example is land or many types of property. The principle is the same as for the replacement of parts, which may only be identified and derecognised so that the cost of the replacement part may be recognised (see 3.3.2 above). The entity needs to identify the cost of the part disposed of by allocating the carrying value on a systematic and appropriate basis.

Section 17 assumes that disposal will be of a physical part (except in the specific case of major inspections and overhauls – see 3.3.3.A above). However, some entities enter into arrangements in which they dispose of part of the benefits that will be derived from the assets.

Although Section 17 defines an asset by reference to the future economic benefits that will be controlled by the entity as a result of the acquisition, it does not address disposals of a proportion of these benefits. An entity may dispose of an undivided interest in the whole asset (sometimes called an ownership 'in common' of the asset). This means that all owners have a proportionate share of the entire asset (e.g. the purchaser of a 25% undivided interest in 100 acres of land owns 25% of the whole 100 acres). These arrangements are common in, but are not restricted to, the extractive and property sectors. Vendors have to determine how to account for the consideration they have received from the purchaser. This will depend on the details of the arrangement and, in particular, whether the entity continues to control the asset or there is joint control.

(a)   Joint control

In some cases there may be joint control over the asset (e.g. sale of an asset to a joint venture), in which case the arrangement will be within scope of Section 15 – *Investments in Joint Ventures* – which will determine how to account for the disposal and the subsequent accounting. Joint control is discussed in Chapter 11.

The retained interest will be analysed as a jointly controlled operation (JCO), a jointly controlled assets (JCA) or a jointly controlled entity (JCE). Undivided interests cannot be accounted for as joint ventures in the absence of joint control.

(b)   Vendor retains control

If the asset is not jointly controlled in the subsequent arrangement, the vendor might retain control over the asset. The vendor will recognise revenue or it will be a financing arrangement. If it is the former, then the issue is the period and pattern over which revenue is recognised.

If the vendor retains control then it will not meet the criteria in Section 23 for treating the transaction as a sale, i.e. recognising revenue on entering into the arrangement. As discussed in Chapter 18, the entity must retain neither continuing managerial involvement to the degree usually associated with ownership nor effective control over the goods sold in order to recognise revenue from the sale of goods. *[FRS 102.23.10].*

The arrangement could be akin to a lease, especially if the disposal is for a period of time. However, arrangements are only within the scope of Section 20 if they relate to a specified asset. Generally, a portion of a larger asset that is not physically distinct is not considered to be a specified asset. See Chapter 16.

If it is not a lease and the vendor continues to control the asset, the arrangement might be best characterised as a performance obligation for services to be spread over the term of the arrangement. That is, the initial receipt would be a liability and recognised in profit and loss over time.

Alternatively, it could be a financing-type arrangement, in which case the proceeds would be classified as a financial liability. In effect, the vendor is trading a share of any revenue to which it is entitled in exchange for funding by the purchaser of one or more activities relating to the asset. The purchaser receives a return that is comparable to a lender's rate of return out of the proceeds of production. This could be by receiving a disproportionate share of output until it has recovered its costs (the financing it has provided) as well as the agreed rate of return for the funding. These arrangements are found in the extractive sector, e.g. carried interests and farm-outs (Chapter 29). In the development stage of a project, the asset in question will be classified as PP&E or as an intangible asset under Section 18. Under a carried interest arrangement the carried party transfers a *portion* of the risks and rewards of a property, in exchange for a funding commitment from the carrying party.

(c)   Partial sale of a single-asset entity

Certain assets, particularly properties, may be bought and sold by transferring ownership of a separate legal entity formed to hold the asset (a 'single-asset' entity) rather than the asset itself. The asset could be realised through either an outright sale or partial disposal. If the asset is sold in its entirety the gain or loss on disposal is the difference between the net disposal proceeds and the carrying amount of the asset (which, in this example, is assumed to be equal to the carrying amount of the investment in a single-asset entity). *[FRS 102.17.30].* This scenario may be straight-forward but in instances where there is a partial disposal of an investment in a single-asset entity (including a partial disposal of an asset) that results in a loss of control, the type of investment that is retained should be considered in determining the gain or loss on disposal.

If the retained interest is not a joint venture within the scope of Section 15, the structure should be assessed to determine whether the retained interest represents an undivided interest in the asset or an investment in an entity. This assessment is important if the structure would result in a different amount of gain or loss on disposal. Therefore, if the retained interest represents an undivided interest in the asset, the accounting result is the same as that for an investment in a jointly controlled asset i.e. a gain or loss is recognised only to the extent of the portion sold, because the sale of a portion of the shares in the entity that holds the asset is regarded as a partial sale of the asset. However, if the retained interest represents an investment in an entity, a gain or loss is recognised as if 100% of the investment in the single-asset entity had been sold because control has been lost. This is consistent with principles when an entity lost control of a subsidiary or lost joint control of a jointly controlled entity – see Chapter 6 and Chapter 11, respectively. A financial asset or an interest in an associate is recognised, as appropriate, for the ownership interest retained. *[FRS 102.9.19, 15.18].*

3.8   Disclosures

The main disclosure requirements of Section 17 are set out at 3.8.1 below. Other disclosures required by other sections of FRS 102 and Companies Act in respect of PP&E are included in 3.8.2 and 3.8.3 below, respectively.

3.8.1 *Disclosures required by Section 17*

For each class of PP&E the following should be disclosed in the financial statements:

- the measurement bases used for determining the gross carrying amount (e.g. cost or revaluation);
- the depreciation methods used;
- the useful lives or the depreciation rates used;
- the gross carrying amount and the accumulated depreciation (aggregated with accumulated impairment losses) at the beginning and end of the reporting period;
- a reconciliation of the carrying amount at the beginning and end of the reporting period, which need not be presented for prior periods, showing separately the following:
  - additions;
  - disposals;
  - acquisitions through business combinations;
  - revaluations;
  - transfers to or from investment property if a reliable measure of fair value becomes available or unavailable; *[FRS 102.16.8]*
  - impairment losses recognised or reversed in profit or loss during the period under Section 27;
  - depreciation for the period; and
  - other changes. *[FRS 102.17.31]*.

The entity should also disclose the following:

- the existence and carrying amounts of PP&E to which the entity has restricted title or that is pledged as security for liabilities; and
- the amount of contractual commitments for the acquisition of PP&E. *[FRS 102.17.32]*.

In addition to above disclosures, if items of PP&E are stated at revalued amounts, the following should be disclosed:

- the effective date of the revaluation;
- whether an independent valuer was involved;
- the methods and significant assumptions applied in estimating the items' fair values; and
- for each revalued class of PP&E, the carrying amount that would have been recognised had the assets been carried under the cost model. *[FRS 102.17.32A]*.

The requirement under the last bullet point above can be quite onerous for entities, as it involves maintaining asset register information in some detail in order to meet it.

When both the cost model and the revaluation model have been used, the gross carrying amount for that basis in each category will have to be disclosed (however the standard requires that if revaluation is adopted the entire class of PP&E must be revalued – see 3.6 above). The selection of the depreciation method, useful lives or depreciation rates used is a matter of judgement and the disclosure should provide information to allow users to review the policies selected by management and to compare with other entities.

3.8.2   Disclosures required by other sections of FRS 102 in respect of PP&E

In addition to the above disclosures, other sections of FRS 102 require disclosures of specific information relating to PP&E.

*   If, at the reporting date, an entity has a binding sale agreement for a major disposal of assets (i.e. PP&E held for sale), a description of the facts and circumstances of the planned sale, and the carrying amount of the assets, is required to be disclosed. *[FRS 102.4.14].* See Chapter 4 for further details.

*   In accordance with Section 10, the nature and effect of any changes in accounting estimate (e.g. depreciation methods, useful lives, residual values, estimated cost of dismantling, removing or restoring items of PP&E) that have a material effect on the current or future periods must be disclosed. *[FRS 102.10.18].* See Chapter 7 for further details.

*   Disclosures required for a lessee under finance lease agreement or a lessor under operating lease agreement (i.e. the party that recognises the PP&E in its statement of financial position) are covered by Section 20. See Chapter 16 for details.

*   In the case of PP&E that is impaired, disclosures are required by Section 27. See Chapter 22 for further details.

*   Disclosures in relation to borrowing costs that are capitalised as part of the cost of an item of PP&E are required by Section 25. See Chapter 20 for details.

3.8.3   Additional disclosures required by the Companies Act and the Regulations

The following disclosures are required by the Companies Act and the Regulations in respect of PP&E in addition to those disclosures required by FRS 102:

*   On the face of statement of financial position, the main heading should be 'Tangible assets'. The following required subheadings may be shown either on the face of the statement of financial position or in the notes:

    *   land and buildings;
    *   plant and machinery;
    *   fixtures, fittings, tools and equipment; and
    *   payments on account and assets in course of construction. *[1 Sch Balance sheet formats].*

    Subheadings may not be limited to those above. Presentation rules are further discussed in Chapter 4.

*   An analysis of freehold, long leasehold and short leasehold in respect of disclosures of land and buildings. *[1 Sch 53].* For this purpose, a 'lease' is defined to include an agreement for a lease and a 'long lease' as a lease which has 50 years or more to run at the end of the financial year in question, otherwise, it would be a 'short lease'. *[10 Sch 7].*

- In addition to the disclosures described at 3.8.1 above, the following information should be given for any PP&E that are measured using the revaluation model (i.e. alternative accounting rules) and that have been valued during the financial year:

  - the year of valuation and the amounts of the revaluation;

  - in the year of valuation, the names of the persons who valued them or particulars of their qualifications for doing so; and

  - the bases of valuation used by them. *[1 Sch 52].*

- The treatment for taxation purposes of amounts credited or debited to the revaluation reserve must be disclosed in a note to the accounts. *[1 Sch 35(6)].*

- Where an entity has determined the purchase price or production cost of any asset for the first time using the value ascribed to it in the earliest available record of its value made on or after its acquisition or production by the company, this fact should be disclosed in the notes to its financial statements (see 3.4.1 above). *[1 Sch 64(1)].*

4   SUMMARY OF GAAP DIFFERENCES

The key differences between FRS 102, previous UK GAAP and IFRS in accounting for PP&E are set out below.

	FRS 102	*Previous UK GAAP*	*IFRS*
Scope	Applies to all items of PP&E except for biological assets related to agricultural activity, heritage assets, mineral rights and reserves and PP&E classified as held for sale. Investment properties (including investment properties under construction) whose fair value cannot be measured reliably without undue cost or effort are within the scope of Section 17. A plan to dispose of an asset (i.e. held-for-sale asset) before the previously expected date is an indicator of impairment (i.e. no reclassification or suspension of depreciation).	Applies to all tangible fixed assets except investment properties (but applies to investment properties in the course of construction) and PP&E classified as held for sale. Heritage assets are in scope for measurement but not for disclosure. There is no concept of non-current assets held for sale thus, depreciation continues until the asset is actually disposed of.	Applies to all items of PP&E except PP&E classified as held for sale, biological assets related to agricultural activity, mineral rights and reserves and investment properties held at fair value. Recognition and measurement of exploration and evaluation assets are also excluded from its scope. Entities using the cost model for investment properties (including investment properties under construction) use the cost method as prescribed in IAS 16. PP&E classified as held for sale is accounted for under IFRS 5.

(Chapter 13)

	FRS 102	Previous UK GAAP	IFRS
Classification of computer software	No specific guidance on classification of computer software. We expect entities will follow the guidance under IFRS (see 3.3.1.D above).	Computer software is included in tangible assets.	Most computer software is an intangible asset whereas computer software which is integral to a tangible asset remains in tangible assets.
Cost	If payment for the asset is deferred beyond normal credit terms, the cost is the present value of all future payments (although expected to be materially similar, it is not the cash price equivalent at the recognition date like in IAS 16).	There is no specific guidance for the treatment where payment is deferred but in practice, where the payment is material, it may be discounted.	If payment for the asset is deferred beyond normal credit terms, interest is recognised over the period of credit (unless capitalised per IAS 23) i.e. the measurement of cost of a PP&E is the cash price equivalent at the recognition date.
	Capitalisation of directly attributable borrowing costs in respect of a qualifying asset is permitted but not required.	Capitalisation of directly attributable finance costs is permitted, but not required.	Borrowing costs related to a qualifying asset must be capitalised.
	Subject to conditions (e.g. transaction has economic substance and fair value is reliably measurable), FRS 102 requires all acquisitions of PP&E in exchange for non-monetary assets, or a combination of monetary and non-monetary assets, to be measured at fair value. Any resulting gain or loss is likely to be an unrealised profit or loss and would be reported in OCI.	FRS 15 does not provide guidance on the measurement of exchanged assets.	Subject to conditions (e.g. transaction has economic substance and fair value is reliably measurable), IAS 16 requires all acquisitions of PP&E in exchange for non-monetary assets, or a combination of monetary and non-monetary assets, to be measured at fair value. Any resulting gain or loss is reported in the income statement.

Capitalisation of subsequent costs	Subsequent costs should meet the same recognition criteria for capitalisation as the initial expenditure on the asset, i.e. when it is probable that future economic benefits associated with the item will flow to the entity and the cost of the item can be measured reliably.	Subsequent expenditure is capitalised only when it improves the condition of the asset beyond its previously assessed standard of performance. Expenditure to maintain the asset's previously assessed performance standard is expensed.	Subsequent costs should meet the same recognition criteria for capitalisation as the initial expenditure on the asset, i.e. when it is probable that future economic benefits associated with the item will flow to the entity and the cost of the item can be measured reliably.
Accounting for replaced parts	If part of an asset is replaced, the old part is derecognised (even if not previously depreciated separately), and the new part is capitalised provided the recognition criteria are met.	The cost of replacing or restoring a component is expensed as incurred if the component has not been treated separately for depreciation purposes.	If part of an asset is replaced, the old part is derecognised (even if not previously depreciated separately), and the new part is capitalised provided the recognition criteria are met.
Cost of major inspection and overhaul	The cost of a major inspection is capitalised and depreciated provided that the PP&E recognition criteria are met.	Costs of a major overhaul or inspection should only be capitalised where the subsequent expenditure restores the economic benefits of the assets that have been consumed by the entity and already reflected in depreciation.	The cost of a major inspection is capitalised and depreciated provided that the PP&E recognition criteria are met.
	The costs of parts replaced in an overhaul would be accounted for in the manner discussed under 'Accounting for replaced parts' above.	The cost capitalised should be depreciated over the period to the next overhaul or inspection.	The costs of parts replaced in an overhaul would be accounted for in the manner discussed under 'Accounting for replaced parts' above.
	Any remaining carrying amount of any previous major inspection is derecognised at the same time even if it had not been depreciated separately.	The remaining carrying amount of previous overhaul or inspections is derecognised.	Any remaining carrying amount of any previous major inspection is derecognised at the same time even if it had not been depreciated separately.

Chapter 13

	FRS 102	*Previous UK GAAP*	*IFRS*
Revaluation model	Assets are revalued to 'fair value', determined from market-based evidence by appraisal for land and buildings or 'market value' determined by appraisal for other items of PP&E. Where there is no market-based evidence, due to the specialised nature of the asset and it is rarely sold, an estimation using an income or depreciated replacement cost approach may be used.	The 'value to the business' model used requires revaluations to 'current value' i.e. assets are measured at the lower of replacement cost and recoverable amount. FRS 15 may require revaluation based on existing use value which may be significantly lower than fair value in circumstances where the latter reflects an alternative use. FRS 15 is more prescriptive in the basis of valuation of both specialised and non-specialised properties and other assets and the processes required for valuation e.g. use of independent valuers. These bases may differ from fair value under IFRS.	Assets are revalued to 'fair value', which is defined by IFRS for non-financial assets as being the value attributable to the 'highest and best use' of that asset by a market participant even if the entity intends a different use.
	Initial application of the revaluation policy is a period change and not a change in policy to be treated retrospectively.	A change to a revaluation model is a change in accounting policy and requires retrospective restatements.	Initial application of the revaluation policy is a period change and not a change in policy to be treated retrospectively.
	Section 17 does not have detailed guidance on accumulated depreciation when assets are revalued. However, we expect that FRS 102 adopters will follow the approach similar to IFRS (see 3.6.3.A above).	No detailed guidance on accumulated depreciation when assets are revalued. In practice, guidance on IFRS is followed.	IAS 16 provides detailed guidance on accumulated depreciation when assets are revalued.
	Section 17 is silent on transfers of a revaluation surplus to retained earnings. However, the Regulations permit such transfers of amounts if the amount represents realised profit (see 3.6.3.A above).	No specific guidance on transfers of revaluation surplus to retained earnings in FRS 15. However, the Regulations permit such transfers of amounts if the amount represents a realised profit.	IAS 16 provides detailed guidance on transfers of revaluation surplus to retained earnings – i.e. as the asset is used by an entity or when the related asset is derecognised.

Revaluation model (continued)	Frequency of valuation is not prescribed but must be made with sufficient regularity to ensure that the carrying amount does not differ materially from the fair value at the end of the reporting period.	FRS 15 requires 5-yearly full valuations, with interim updates (interim valuation in year three).	Frequency of valuation is not prescribed but must be made with sufficient regularity to ensure that the carrying amount does not differ materially from the fair value at the end of the reporting period.
	There is no requirement for a professional external valuation or even for a professionally qualified valuer to perform the appraisal. Thus, it permits an internal valuer to perform the valuations.	FRS 15 requires the 5-yearly full valuations to be performed by a qualified external valuer or a qualified internal valuer provided it was reviewed by a qualified external valuer.	There is no requirement for a professional external valuation or even for a professionally qualified valuer to perform the appraisal.
Revaluation losses	A revaluation loss is recognised in profit or loss, except to the extent that it reverses an increase previously recognised in OCI. Thus, it is not permissible to carry a negative revaluation reserve in respect of any asset.	Revaluation losses are recognised in the profit and loss account if they result from a clear consumption of economic benefits. All other losses are recognised in the STRGL until revaluation gains are exceeded. Excess losses are recognised in the STRGL to the extent that the asset's recoverable amount is greater than its revalued amount. It is possible to have debit balances in the revaluation reserves.	A revaluation loss is recognised in profit or loss, except to the extent that it reverses an increase previously recognised in OCI. Thus, it is not permissible to carry a negative revaluation reserve in respect of any asset.

Chapter 13

	FRS 102	*Previous UK GAAP*	*IFRS*
Depreciation of assets / impairment	Each part of an item of PP&E that has a cost that is significant in relation to the cost of the item must be depreciated separately. Parts may be grouped if they have a similar useful life and depreciation method or if insignificant.	Assets should be analysed into major components with substantially different useful economic lives, but there is no requirement to separately depreciate parts of an asset.	Each part of an item of PP&E that has a cost that is significant in relation to the cost of the item must be depreciated separately. Parts may be grouped if they have a similar useful life and depreciation method or if insignificant.
	Renewals accounting is not permitted.	In some industries (e.g. water industries) renewals accounting is applied in accounting for tangible fixed assets within a system or network.	Renewals accounting is not permitted.
	Depreciation ceases at the end of the useful life or on disposal of the asset.	Depreciation ceases at the end of the useful life or on disposal of the asset.	Depreciation of an asset ceases when the asset is either classified as held for sale or derecognised.
	No equivalent guidance in respect of non-depreciation if an asset's residual value is equal to or exceeds its carrying amount. However, we expect that FRS 102 adopters will follow an approach similar to IFRS (see 3.5.2 above).	FRS 15 permits non-depreciation if an asset's residual value is equal to or exceeds its carrying amount. The only grounds for not charging depreciation are that the depreciation charge and accumulated depreciation are immaterial.	If an asset's residual value is equal to or exceeds its carrying amount the asset is not depreciated until its residual value subsequently decreases to an amount below the assets' carrying amount.
	There is no specific requirement to perform a mandatory annual impairment review for assets with no depreciation (as immaterial) or for assets where the remaining useful life exceeds 50 years.	If no depreciation is charged (as immaterial) or the remaining useful life of asset exceeds 50 years, a mandatory annual impairment review is required.	There is no specific requirement to perform a mandatory annual impairment review for assets with no depreciation (as immaterial) or for assets where the remaining useful life exceeds 50 years.
	There is no explicit prohibition of the use of 'revenue expected to be generated' as the basis to depreciate PP&E.	There is no explicit prohibition of the use of 'revenue expected to be generated' as the basis to depreciate PP&E.	IAS 16 clarified that, effective 1 January 2016, the use of revenue-based depreciation is inappropriate and thus, prohibited.

Reassessment of depreciation methods and residual values	Reassessment of depreciation methods and residual values are only required if there is an indication that it has changed since the most recent annual reporting date.	Reassessment of residual values is only required for material residual values and should take account of the effects of technological changes. A change in depreciation method is permitted only if it gives a fairer presentation, and there is no requirement for annual review.	Depreciation methods and residual value should be reassessed at least annually. Depreciation methods are changed if there is a significant change in the expected pattern of consumption.
Measurement of residual values	Residual value is the amount that an entity would currently obtain from disposal of the asset (residual values are based on prices at the balance sheet date), after deducting the estimated costs of disposal, if the asset were already of the age and in the condition expected at the end of its useful life.	Residual value is the net realisable value of an asset at the end of its useful economic life, based on prices prevailing at the date of acquisition or revaluation of the asset (most recent valuation) and does not take account of future price changes.	Residual value is the amount that an entity would currently obtain from disposal of the asset (residual values are based on prices at the balance sheet date), after deducting the estimated costs of disposal, if the asset were already of the age and in the condition expected at the end of its useful life.
Disclosures	Reconciliation disclosure (i.e. opening balances to ending balances) requires only the current period. The reconciliation must be presented using gross amounts – separately for cost (or revalued amount) and depreciation – similar to IFRS.	Reconciliation disclosure (i.e. opening balances to ending balances) requires only the current period. The reconciliation of opening and closing balances may be presented using the net carrying amounts, rather than separately for cost (or revalued amount) and depreciation.	Reconciliation disclosure (i.e. opening balances to ending balances) requires comparative period. The reconciliation of opening and closing balances must be presented using gross amounts – separately for cost (or revalued amount) and depreciation.

Chapter 13

References

1 *International GAAP 2015* ('IGAAP 2015') *Generally Accepted Accounting Practice under International Financial Reporting Standards*, written by the International Financial Reporting Group of Ernst & Young, January 2015.

Chapter 14   Intangible assets other than goodwill

Chapter 14

Chapter 14   Intangible assets other than goodwill

1   INTRODUCTION

Intangible assets represent a significant class of assets for a wide range of entities. The existence of a corporate identity or brand; intellectual property rights protecting an entity's knowledge, products and processes; or contractual and other rights to exploit both physical and intellectual resources can be as important to an entity's success as its physical asset base and infrastructure. The cost and uncertainty of outcome associated with developing these types of assets from scratch contribute in part to the premiums paid by acquirers of businesses that already have these attributes. Accordingly, there has for some time been a strong link between accounting for intangible assets and accounting for business combinations.

Section 18 – *Intangible Assets other than Goodwill* – addresses the nature, recognition and measurement of intangible assets other than goodwill. It also sets out the disclosures requirements. The accounting for goodwill is addressed in Section 19 – *Business Combinations and Goodwill* (See Chapter 15). Section 18 does not address the impairment of intangible assets, which is dealt with in Section 27 – *Impairment of Assets* (See Chapter 22).

There are some differences between the accounting for intangible assets under Section 18 compared to previous UK GAAP and IFRS. The key differences are discussed at 2 below.

2   COMPARISON BETWEEN SECTION 18, PREVIOUS UK GAAP AND IFRS

2.1   Key differences to previous UK GAAP

The accounting for intangible assets under previous UK GAAP was addressed by FRS 10 – *Goodwill and intangible assets* – and SSAP 13 – *Accounting for research and development*.

2.1.1   Definition of an intangible asset

Under Section 18, an intangible asset must be separable *or* arise from contractual or other legal rights. *[FRS 102.18.2]*. It is not necessary under FRS 102 for an intangible asset to meet both of these criteria.

FRS 10 required an intangible asset to be identifiable *and* controlled by the entity through custody or legal rights, *[FRS 10.2]*, i.e. both were necessary to meet the definition of an intangible asset. An identifiable asset was one that could be disposed of without disposing of a business of the entity. *[FRS 10.2]*. More assets may therefore meet the definition of an intangible asset under FRS 102.

2.1.2   Intangible assets acquired in a business combination

We expect that more intangible assets acquired in a business combination will be recognised separately from goodwill under FRS 102.

FRS 10 required intangible assets acquired as part of the acquisition of a business to be recognised separately from goodwill if their value could be measured reliably on initial recognition. Unless the intangible assets had a readily ascertainable market value, the fair value attributed to intangible assets acquired as part of a business was limited to an amount that neither created nor increased negative goodwill arising on the acquisition. *[FRS 10.10]*. FRS 102 does not place a cap on the value attributed to intangible assets acquired in a business combination. Given the absence of such a cap, together with the broader definition of intangible assets under FRS 102 (see 2.1.1 above), it is likely that more intangible assets will be recognised on the acquisition of a business under FRS 102 than under previous UK GAAP. However, intangible assets that are acquired in a business combination and arise from legal or other contractual rights may be recognised under FRS 102 only where there is a history or evidence of exchange transactions for the same or similar assets, or otherwise estimating fair value would not be dependent on immeasurable variables. *[FRS 102.18.8]*.

2.1.3   Indefinite life intangible assets

Under FRS 102 all intangible assets are considered to have a finite life. *[FRS 102.18.19]*. Under FRS 10 the useful life of intangible assets was limited to 20 years unless the durability of the asset could be demonstrated and justified a useful life in excess of 20 years, or even indefinite, and the intangible asset was capable of continued measurement.*[FRS 10.19]*. If an entity cannot make a reliable estimate of the useful life of an intangible asset under FRS 102, the life should not exceed five years. *[FRS 102.18.20]*. However, it is unlikely that such a short useful life would be appropriate for an intangible asset that had been assessed as having an indefinite life under previous UK GAAP.

2.1.4   Amortisation of capitalised development expenditure

Section 18 requires amortisation to commence when an intangible asset is available for use. For entities who adopted an accounting policy of capitalising development expenditure, SSAP 13 required amortisation to commence with the commercial production or application of the product, service, process or system. *[SSAP 13.28]*. The point at which an intangible asset is available for use may be earlier than the point at which commercial production commences and therefore amortisation may commence earlier under FRS 102.

2.1.5 First year impairment reviews

Under FRS 102, intangible assets are reviewed for impairment only if there are indicators that the asset may be impaired. *[FRS 102.27.7]*. There is no requirement for a first year impairment review of intangible assets. This differs from FRS 10 which required entities to review an intangible asset for impairment at the end of the first full financial year following its acquisition. *[FRS 10.34]*.

2.1.6 Exchanges of assets

Unlike FRS 102, FRS 10 was silent on the subject of intangible assets acquired in exchange for non-monetary assets or a combination of monetary and non-monetary assets.

2.1.7 Classification of computer software

FRS 102 is silent on the treatment of software that is directly attributable to bringing hardware or machinery to its working condition. Under previous UK GAAP, software development costs that were directly attributable to bringing a computer system or other computer operated machinery into working condition were treated as part of the cost of the related hardware rather than a separate intangible asset. *[FRS 10.2]*.

In addition, UITF 29 required website development costs meeting certain criteria to be capitalised as tangible fixed assets. These website development costs may meet the definition of an intangible asset under FRS 102. *[UITF 29.11-12]*.

2.1.8 Disclosures

There are some differences between the disclosure requirements of Section 18 and previous UK GAAP. These are addressed at 5 below.

2.2 Key differences to IFRS

2.2.1 Intangible assets acquired in a business combination

Under FRS 102, intangible assets that are acquired in a business combination and arise from legal or other contractual rights may be recognised only where there is a history or evidence of exchange transactions for the same or similar assets, or otherwise estimating fair value would not be dependent on immeasurable variables. *[FRS 102.18.8]*. This is more restrictive than IAS 38 – *Intangible Assets* ('IAS 38'), which considers that intangible assets acquired in a business combination can always be measured reliably. *[IAS 38.33]*. We would therefore expect less intangible assets to be recognised on the acquisition of a business under FRS 102 than under IFRS.

2.2.2 Indefinite lived intangible assets

Under FRS 102 all intangible assets are considered to have a finite life. *[FRS 102.18.19]*. If an entity cannot make a reliable estimate of the useful life of an intangible asset, the life should not exceed five years. *[FRS 102.18.20]*. This differs from IAS 38 which

Chapter 14

requires an intangible asset to be regarded as having an indefinite life when there is no foreseeable limit to the period over which the asset is expected to generate net cash inflows for the entity. *[IAS 38.88*]. Intangible assets with indefinite useful lives are not amortised. *[IAS 38.107]*.

2.2.3   Development costs

Section 18 allows an entity to capitalise expenditure incurred in developing an intangible asset, provided certain criteria are met. *[FRS 102.18.8H]*. Alternatively, entities may choose to expense development expenditure as incurred. The policy adopted must be applied consistently to all development projects. *[FRS 102.18.8K]*. IAS 38 does not allow an accounting policy choice. An intangible asset arising from the development phase of a project must be capitalised if certain criteria (the same as those in Section 18) are met. *[IAS 38.57]*.

2.2.4   Advertising and promotional activities

Under FRS 102, promotional stocks, such as catalogues and other promotional material may be recognised as inventory (see chapter 9 at 3.3.11). IAS 38 does not allow entities to capitalise expenditure on advertising and promotional activities, including mail order catalogues. *[IAS 38.69(c)]*.

2.2.5   Intangible assets acquired by way of government grant

Section 18 requires intangible assets acquired by way of a grant to be recorded at fair value at the date the grant is received or receivable. *[FRS 102.18.12]*. In contrast, IAS 38, allows an accounting policy choice between recognising the intangible asset at fair value or at a nominal amount. *[IAS 38.44]*.

2.2.6   Disclosures

There are some differences between the disclosure requirements of Section 18 and IFRS. These are addressed at 5 below.

3   REQUIREMENTS OF SECTION 18 FOR INTANGIBLE ASSETS OTHER THAN GOODWILL

3.1   Terms used in Section 18

The following terms are used in Section 18 with the meanings specified *[FRS 102 Appendix I]*:

Term	Definition
Active market	A market in which all the following conditions exist: (a) the items traded in the market are homogeneous; (b) willing buyers and sellers can normally be found at any time; and (c) prices are available to the public.
Amortisation	The systematic allocation of the depreciable amount of an asset over its useful life.

Asset	A resource controlled by an entity as a result of past events and from which future economic benefits are expected to flow to the entity.
Class of assets	A grouping of assets of a similar nature and use in an entity's operations.
Depreciable amount	The cost of an asset, or other amount substituted for cost (in the financial statements), less its residual value.
Development	The application of research findings or other knowledge to a plan or design for the production of new or substantially improved materials, devices, products, processes, systems or services before the start of commercial production or use.
Fair value	The amount for which an asset could be exchanged, a liability settled, or an equity instrument granted could be exchanged, between knowledgeable, willing parties in an arm's length transaction.
Identifiable	An asset is identifiable when: (a) it is separable, i.e. capable of being separated or divided from the entity and sold, transferred, licensed, rented or exchanged, either individually or together with a related contract, asset or liability; or (b) it arises from contractual or other legal rights, regardless of whether those rights are transferable or separable from the entity or from other rights and obligations.
Impairment loss	For assets other than inventories, the amount by which the carrying amount of an asset exceeds its recoverable amount.
Intangible asset	An identifiable non-monetary asset without physical substance.
Inventories held for distribution at no or nominal consideration	Assets that are: (a) held for distribution at no or nominal consideration in the ordinary course of operations; (b) in the process of production for distribution at no or nominal consideration in the ordinary course of operations; or (c) in the form of material or supplies to be consumed in the production process or in the rendering of services at no or nominal consideration.
Monetary items	Units of currency held and assets and liabilities to be received or paid in a fixed or determinable number of units of currency.
Research	Original and planned investigation undertaken with the prospect of gaining new scientific or technical knowledge and understanding.
Residual value	The estimated amount that an entity would currently obtain from disposal of an asset, after deducting the estimated costs of disposal, if the asset were already of the age and in the condition expected at the end of its useful life.
Useful life	The period over which an asset is expected to be available for use by an entity or the number of production or similar units expected to be obtained from the asset by an entity.

Chapter 14

3.2   Scope and definition

Section 18 applies to the accounting for all intangible assets, other than the following:

- Goodwill (dealt with by Section 19 of FRS 102) (see Chapter 15); *[FRS 102.18.1]*.

- Intangible assets held for sale in the ordinary course of business (dealt with by FRS 102 Section 13 – *Inventories* – and FRS 102 Section 23 – *Revenue*). *[FRS 102.18.1]*. (See Chapter 9 and Chapter 19);

- Deferred acquisition costs and intangible assets arising from contracts in the scope of FRS 103 – *Insurance Contracts* ('FRS 103'). However, the disclosure requirements of Section 18 apply to intangible assets arising from contracts in the scope of FRS 103; *[FRS 102.18.1A]*.

- Financial assets (dealt with by FRS 102 Section 11 – *Basic Financial Instruments* – and Section 12 – *Other Financial Instruments Issues*). *[FRS 102.18.3(a)]*. (See Chapter 8);

- Heritage assets (dealt with by FRS 102 Section 34 – *Specialised Activities*). *[FRS 102.18.3(b)]*. (See Chapter 29); and

- Mineral rights and mineral reserves, such as oil, natural gas and similar non-regenerative resources (dealt with by FRS 102 Section 34 – *Specialised Activities*). *[FRS 102.18.3(c)]*. (See Chapter 29).

FRS 102 defines an intangible asset as 'an identifiable non-monetary asset without physical substance'. *[FRS 102.18.2]*. The essential characteristics of intangible assets are therefore that they:

- are identifiable (see 3.2.1 below);

- lack physical substance (see 3.2.2 below);

- are controlled by the entity (see 3.2.3 below); and

- will give rise to future economic benefits for the entity (see 3.2.4 below).

However, in order to determine whether an intangible asset that meets all of these criteria should be recognised, an entity must also consider whether it satisfies the applicable recognition criteria set out within Section 18. The principles for the recognition of intangible assets are discussed at 3.3 below.

3.2.1   *Identifiability*

An asset is identifiable when it:

(a)   is separable, i.e. capable of being separated or divided from the entity and sold, transferred, licensed, rented or exchanged, either individually or together with a related contract, asset or liability; or

(b)   arises from contractual or other legal rights, regardless of whether those rights are transferable or separable from the entity or from other rights and obligations. *[FRS 102.18.2]*.

Applying this definition means that assets arising from contractual rights alone may meet the definition of an intangible asset under FRS 102. For example, a licence that, legally, is not transferable except by sale of the entity as a whole. However, preparers should not restrict their search for intangible assets to those embodied in contractual or other legal rights. Non-contractual rights may also meet the definition of an intangible asset if the right *could be* sold, transferred, licensed, rented or exchanged.

3.2.2 Lack of physical substance

The definition of an intangible asset within Section 18 requires that it lacks physical substance. However, intangible assets can be contained in or on a physical medium such as a compact disc (in the case of computer software), legal documentation (in the case of a licence or patent) or film, requiring an entity to exercise judgement in determining whether to apply Section 18 or Section 17 *Property, Plant and Equipment* – of FRS 102. FRS 102 provides no further guidance on this issue. Where there is no specific guidance within FRS 102, Section 10 *Accounting Policies, Estimates and Errors* of FRS 102 allows entities to consider the requirements in IFRS in developing an accounting policy. *[FRS 102.10.4-6].* Entities may therefore choose to look to IFRS for further guidance. IAS 38 provides the following relevant examples *[IAS 38.4,5]*:

- Software that is embedded in computer-controlled equipment that cannot operate without it is an integral part of the related hardware and is treated as property, plant and equipment.

- The operating system of a computer is normally integral to the computer and is included in property, plant and equipment.

- Software which is not an integral part of the related hardware is treated as an intangible asset.

- Research and development expenditure may result in an asset with physical substance (e.g. a prototype), but as the physical element is secondary to its intangible component, the related knowledge, it is treated as an intangible asset.

It is worthwhile noting that the 'parts approach' in Section 17 requires an entity to account for significant components of an asset separately if they have significantly different patterns of consumption of economic benefits *[FRS 102.17.6].* This raises 'boundary' problems between Section 17 and Section 18 when software and similar expenditure is involved. We believe that where Section 17 requires an entity to identify parts of an asset and account for them separately, the entity needs to evaluate whether any intangible-type part is actually integral to the larger asset or whether it is really a separate asset in its own right. The intangible part is more likely to be an asset in its own right if it was developed separately or if it can be used independently of the item of property, plant and equipment of which it apparently forms part.

3.2.3 Control

In the context of intangible assets, control normally results from legal rights, in the way that copyright, a restraint of trade agreement or a legal duty on employees to maintain confidentiality would protect the economic benefits arising from market and technical knowledge. While it will be more difficult to demonstrate control in the absence of legal rights, legal enforceability of a right is not a necessary condition for

Chapter 14

control. An entity may be able to control the future economic benefits in some other way, for example, through custody. However, determining that this is the case in the absence of observable contractual or other legal rights requires the exercise of judgement based on an understanding of the specific facts and circumstances involved.

For example, an entity usually has insufficient control over the future economic benefits arising from an assembled workforce (i.e. a team of skilled workers, or specific management or technical talent) or from training for these items to meet the definition of an intangible asset. There would have to be other legal rights before control could be demonstrated.

Similarly, an entity would not usually be able to recognise an asset for an assembled portfolio of customers or a market share. In the absence of legal rights to protect or other ways to control the relationships with customers or the loyalty of its customers, the entity usually has insufficient control over the expected economic benefits from these items to meet the definition of an intangible asset. However, exchange transactions (other than as part of a business combination) involving the same or similar non-contractual customer relationships may provide evidence of control over the expected future economic benefits, in the absence of legal rights. In that case, those customer relationships could meet the definition of an intangible asset.

3.2.4   *Future economic benefits*

The future economic benefit of an asset is its potential to contribute, directly or indirectly, to the flow of cash and cash equivalents to the entity. Those cash flows may come from using the asset or from disposing of it. *[FRS 102.2.17].*

Future economic benefits include not only future revenues from the sale of products or services but also cost savings or other benefits resulting from the use of the asset by the entity. For example, the use of intellectual property in a production process may create future economic benefits by reducing future production costs rather than increasing future revenues.

3.3   Recognition and initial measurement of an intangible asset

An item that meets the definition of an intangible asset (see 3.2 above) should be recognised if and only if, at the time of initial recognition of the expenditure: *[FRS 102.18.4]*

(a)   it is probable that the expected future economic benefits that are attributable to the asset will flow to the entity; and

(b)   the cost or value of the asset can be measured reliably.

'Probable' is defined as 'more likely than not'. *[FRS 102 Appendix I].* In assessing whether expected future economic benefits are probable, the entity should use reasonable and supportable assumptions representing management's best estimate of the set of economic conditions that will exist over the useful life of the asset. *[FRS 102.18.5].* In making the judgement over the degree of certainty attached to the flow of future economic benefits attributable to the use of the asset, the entity considers the evidence available at the time of initial recognition, giving greater weight to external evidence. *[FRS 102.18.6].*

The test that the item meets both the definition of an intangible asset and the criteria for recognition is performed at the time of initial recognition of the expenditure. On initial recognition, any intangible asset meeting these criteria should be measured at cost. *[FRS 102.18.9]*. If these criteria are not met at the time the expenditure is incurred, an expense is recognised and it is never reinstated as an asset. *[FRS 102.18.17]*.

The guidance in Section 18 on the recognition and initial measurement of intangible assets takes account of the way in which an entity obtained the asset. Separate rules for recognition and initial measurement apply for intangible assets depending on whether they were:

- acquired separately (see 3.3.1 below);

- acquired as part of a business combination (see 3.3.2 below);

- generated internally (see 3.3.3 below);

- acquired by way of government grant (see 3.3.5 below); or

- obtained in an exchange of assets (see 3.3.6 below).

3.3.1   Separately acquired intangible assets

3.3.1.A   Recognition of separately acquired intangible assets

Separately acquired intangible rights will normally be recognised as assets.

The criteria for recognising an intangible asset are set out at 3.3 above. The probability recognition criterion in (a) at 3.3 above is always considered satisfied for intangible assets that are separately acquired. *[FRS 102.18.7]*. The Standard assumes that the price paid to acquire an intangible asset separately usually reflects expectations about the probability that the future economic benefits embodied in it will flow to the entity. In other words, the entity always expects there to be a flow of economic benefits, even if it is uncertain about the timing or amount. In addition, the cost of a separately acquired intangible asset can usually be measured reliably, especially in the case of a monetary purchase consideration.

However, not all external costs incurred to secure intangible rights automatically qualify for capitalisation as separately acquired assets, because they do not meet the definition of an intangible asset in the first place. An entity that subcontracts the development of intangible assets (e.g. development-and-supply contracts or R&D contracts) to other parties (its suppliers) must exercise judgement in determining whether it is acquiring an intangible asset or whether it is obtaining goods and services that are being used in the development of an intangible asset by the entity itself. For example, if the entity pays a supplier upfront or by milestone payments during the course of a project, it will not necessarily recognise an intangible asset on the basis of those payments. Only those costs that are incurred after it becomes probable that economic benefits are expected to flow to the entity will be part of the cost of an intangible asset. If a supplier is working on an internal project for the entity, costs can only be capitalised after the criteria have been met for recognising an internally developed intangible asset (see 3.3.3 below).

In determining whether a supplier is providing services to develop an internally generated intangible asset, it can be useful to consider the terms of the supply agreement, in particular whether the supplier is bearing a significant proportion of the risks associated with a failure of the project. For example, if the supplier is always compensated under a development-and-supply contract for development services and tool costs irrespective of the project's outcome, the entity on whose behalf the development is undertaken should account for those activities as its own.

3.3.1.B   Initial measurement of separately acquired intangible assets

The cost of a separately acquired intangible asset comprises:

(a)   its purchase price, including import duties and non-refundable purchase taxes, after deducting trade discounts and rebates; and

(b)   any directly attributable cost of preparing the asset for its intended use. *[FRS 102.18.10]*.

Section 18 does not elaborate on what costs may be directly attributable to preparing a separately acquired intangible asset for its intended use. Examples may include:

- costs of employee benefits arising directly from bringing the asset to its working condition;

- professional fees arising directly from bringing the asset to its working condition; and

- costs of testing whether the asset is functioning properly.

Capitalisation of expenditure should cease when the asset is in the condition necessary for it to be capable of operating in the manner intended by management. This may well be before the date on which it is brought into use.

3.3.2   Intangible assets acquired as part of a business combination

3.3.2.A   Recognition of intangible assets acquired as part of a business combination

The general criteria for recognising an intangible asset are set out at 3.3 above.

If an intangible asset is acquired in a business combination, the cost of that intangible asset is its fair value at the acquisition date. *[FRS 102.18.11]*. As the fair value of an intangible asset should reflect expectations about the probability that the future economic benefits embodied in it will flow to the entity, the probability criterion is always assumed to be satisfied for intangible assets acquired as part of a business combination. In other words, the existence of a fair value means that an inflow of economic benefits is considered to be probable, in spite of any uncertainties about timing or amount.

An intangible asset acquired in a business combination is therefore normally recognised as an asset because its fair value can be measured with sufficient reliability. *[FRS 102.18.8]*. However, an intangible asset acquired in a business combination that arises from contractual or legal rights should not be recognised when there is no history or evidence of exchange transactions for the same or similar assets, and otherwise estimating fair value would be dependent upon immeasurable variables. *[FRS 102.18.8]*. The measurement of intangible assets acquired in a business combination is considered at 3.3.2.B below.

An intangible asset in a business combination needs to be identifiable to distinguish it from goodwill and, as explained in 3.2.1, the two elements of identifiability are the existence of contractual or other legal rights or separability. The requirement for an intangible asset to be identifiable is consistent with IFRS 3 – *Business Combinations* ('IFRS 3') which provides examples of identifiable intangible assets that may be acquired in a business combination. These include: trademarks, trade names, internet domain names, order or production backlog, customer lists, non-contractual customer relationships, films, music videos, television programmes, franchise agreements, unpatented technology and databases. *[IFRS 3.IE16-IE44]*.

However, FRS 102 may not require the recognition of as many intangible assets acquired in a business combination and arising from contractual or other legal rights as we typically see under IFRS. This is because, under FRS 102, these intangible assets should not be recognised when there is no history or evidence of exchange transactions or otherwise measuring fair value would be dependent upon immeasurable variables. IAS 38, on the other hand, includes a presumption of reliable measurement for all intangible assets acquired in a business combination *[IAS 38.35]*.

The separability criterion of Section 18 requires an acquired intangible asset to be *capable* of being separated or divided from the acquiree. *[FRS 102.18.2(a)]*. This is regardless of the intentions of the acquirer. An acquired intangible asset should be recognised separately from goodwill if there is evidence of exchange transactions for that type of asset or an asset of a similar type, even if those transactions are infrequent and regardless of whether the acquirer is involved in them. For example, customer and subscriber lists are frequently licensed and thus merit recognition as an intangible asset. An acquiree might try to distinguish its customer lists from those that are frequently licensed generally, in order to justify no recognition. However, in the absence of a truly distinguishing feature, such as the existence of confidentiality or other agreements that prohibit an entity from selling, leasing or otherwise exchanging information about its customers, these non-contractual rights should be recognised separately from goodwill.

An intangible asset that is not individually separable from the acquiree or combined entity should still be recognised separately from goodwill if it could be separable in combination with a related contract, identifiable asset or liability. *[FRS 102.18.2(a)]*. For example an acquiree owns a registered trademark and documented but unpatented technical expertise used to manufacture the trademarked product. The entity could not transfer ownership of the trademark without everything else necessary for the new owner to produce an identical product or service. Because the unpatented technical expertise must be transferred if the related trademark is sold, it is separable and not included in the carrying value of goodwill.

The process of identifying intangible assets in a business combination might involve, for example:

- reviewing the list of items that meet the definition of an intangible asset in IFRS 3 referred to above (subject to assessing whether there is a history or evidence of exchange transactions for intangible assets that arise from contractual or legal rights, or whether fair value can be otherwise estimated without being dependent upon immeasurable variables);

- reviewing documents such as those related to the acquisition, other internal documents produced by the entity, public filings, press releases, analysts' reports, and other externally available documents; and

- comparing the acquired business to similar businesses and their intangible assets.

Intangible assets that are used differ considerably between industries and between individual entities. Therefore, considerable expertise and careful judgement is required in determining whether there are intangible assets that need to be recognised and valued separately.

3.3.2.B   Initial measurement of intangible assets acquired as part of a business combination

The cost of an intangible asset acquired in a business combination is its fair value at the acquisition date. *[FRS 102.18.11]*. Section 18 provides no specific guidance on how to determine the fair value of intangible assets acquired in a business combination. Therefore the guidance in Section 11 should be used. *[FRS 102 Appendix I]*. Section 11 requires fair value to be determined using the following hierarchy:

(a)   The best evidence of fair value is a quoted price for an identical asset in an active market.

(b)   Where quoted prices are unavailable, the price of a recent transaction for an identical asset provides evidence of fair value as long as there has not been a significant change in economic circumstances or a significant lapse of time since the transaction took place.

(c)   If the market for the asset is not active and recent transactions of an identical asset on their own are not a good estimate of fair value, an entity estimates the fair value by using a valuation technique. *[FRS 102.11.27]*.

Some intangible assets may be traded in an active market, for example certain licenses, such as taxi licenses. However, the unique nature of many intangible assets means that they are unlikely to have a quoted market price. Similarly, there are unlikely to be recent transactions in identical assets. Therefore fair value will most frequently be determined using valuation techniques. The objective of using a valuation technique is to estimate what the transaction price would have been on the measurement date in an arm's length exchange motivated by normal business considerations. The valuation technique used should make maximum use of market inputs and rely as little as possible on entity-determined inputs. *[FRS 102.11.29]*. If there is a valuation technique commonly used by market participants to price the asset and that has been demonstrated to provide reliable estimates of prices obtained in actual market transactions, the entity should use that technique. *[FRS 102.11.28]*.

In practice there are three broad approaches to valuing intangible assets:

(a) The market approach, which determines fair value based on observable market prices and comparable market transactions;

(b) The cost approach, the premise of which is that an investor would pay no more for an intangible asset than the cost to recreate it; and

(c) The income approach, which involves identifying the expected cash flows or economic benefits to be derived from the ownership of the particular intangible asset.

3.3.3   *Internally generated intangible assets*

It may be difficult to decide whether an internally generated intangible asset qualifies for recognition because of problems in:

(a) confirming whether and when there is an identifiable asset that will generate expected future economic benefits; and

(b) determining the cost of the asset reliably, especially in cases where the cost of generating an intangible asset internally cannot be distinguished from the cost of maintaining or enhancing the entity's internally generated goodwill or of running day-to-day operations.

To avoid the inappropriate recognition of an asset, Section 18 requires that internally generated intangible assets are not only tested against the general requirements for recognition and initial measurement (discussed at 3.2 above), but also meet criteria which confirm that the related activity or project is at a sufficiently advanced stage of development, is both technically and commercially viable and includes only directly attributable costs. Those criteria comprise guidance on accounting for intangible assets in the research phase (see 3.3.3.A below), the development phase (see 3.3.3.B below) and on components of cost of an internally generated intangible asset (see 3.3.3.C below).

To assess whether an internally generated asset meets the criteria for recognition, an entity classifies the generation process for the asset into a research phase and a development phase. *[FRS 102.18.8A]*. If it is too difficult to distinguish an activity between a research phase and a development phase, all expenditure is treated as research. *[FRS 102.18.8B]*.

3.3.3.A   *Research*

The standard gives the following examples of research activities: *[FRS 102.18.8G]*

(a) activities aimed at obtaining new knowledge;

(b) the search for, evaluation and final selection of, applications of research findings and other knowledge;

(c) the search for alternatives for materials, devices, products, processes, systems or services; and

(d) the formulation, design, evaluation and final selection of possible alternatives for new or improved material, devices, projects, processes, systems or services.

An entity cannot recognise an intangible asset arising from research or from the research phase of an internal project. Instead, any expenditure on research or the research phase of an internal project should be expensed as incurred. *[FRS 102.8E]*. In the research phase of an internal project the entity cannot demonstrate that there is an intangible asset that will generate probable future economic benefits. *[FRS 102.8F]*.

If an entity cannot distinguish the research phase from the development phase, it should treat the expenditure on that project as if it were incurred in the research phase only and recognise an expense accordingly. *[FRS 102.18.8B]*.

3.3.3.B   Development

The standard gives the following examples of development activities: *[FRS 102.18.8J]*

(a)   the design, construction and testing of pre-production or pre-use prototypes and models;

(b)   the design of tools, jigs, moulds and dies involving new technology;

(c)   the design, construction and operation of a pilot plant that is not of a scale economically feasible for commercial production; and

(d)   the design, construction and testing of a chosen alternative for new or improved materials, devices, products, processes, systems or services.

In the development phase of an internal project, an entity can, in some instances, identify an intangible asset and demonstrate that the asset will generate probable future economic benefits. This is because the development phase of a project is further advanced than the research phase. *[FRS 102.18.8I]*.

FRS 102 allows entities to make an accounting policy choice of whether to capitalise qualifying development expenditure. Entities may either recognise an internally generated intangible asset arising from the development phase of a project (provided that specific recognition criteria are met, see below) or recognise the expenditure in profit or loss as incurred. Where an entity adopts a policy of capitalising expenditure in the development phase, the policy should be applied consistently to all expenditure that meets the recognition criteria set out in Section 18. Expenditure that does not meet the conditions for capitalisation must be expensed as incurred. *[FRS 102.18.8K]*.

An intangible asset arising from development may be recognised if, and only if, the entity can demonstrate all of the following: *[FRS 102.18.8H]*

(a)   the technical feasibility of completing the intangible asset so that it will be available for use or sale;

(b)   its intention to complete the intangible asset and use or sell it;

(c)   its ability to use or sell the intangible asset;

(d)   how the intangible asset will generate probable future economic benefits. Among other things, the entity can demonstrate the existence of a market for the output of the intangible asset or the intangible asset itself or, if it is to be used internally, the usefulness of the intangible asset;

(e)   the availability of adequate technical, financial and other resources to complete the development and to use or sell the intangible asset; and

(f)   its ability to measure reliably the expenditure attributable to the intangible asset during its development.

It may be challenging to demonstrate each of the above conditions because:

- condition (b) relies on management intent; and

- conditions (c), (e) and (f) are entity-specific, i.e. whether development expenditure meets any of these conditions depends both on the nature of the development activity itself and the financial position of the entity.

Evidence may be available in the form of:

- a business plan showing the technical, financial and other resources needed and the entity's ability to secure those resources;

- a lender's indication of its willingness to fund the plan confirming the availability of external finance; and

- detailed project information demonstrating that an entity's costing systems can measure reliably the cost of generating an intangible asset internally, such as salary and other expenditure incurred in securing copyrights or licences or developing computer software.

In any case, an entity should maintain books and records in sufficient detail that allow it to prove whether it meets the conditions set out in (a) to (f) above. Certain types of product (e.g. pharmaceuticals, aircraft and electrical equipment) require regulatory approval before they can be sold. Regulatory approval is not one of the criteria for recognition and therefore entities are not prohibited from capitalising development costs in advance of approval. However, in some industries regulatory approval is vital to commercial success and its absence indicates significant uncertainty around the possible future economic benefits. This is the case in the pharmaceuticals industry, where it is rarely possible to determine whether a new drug will secure regulatory approval until it is actually granted. Accordingly it is common practice in this industry for costs to be expensed until such approval is obtained.

3.3.3.C   *Measurement of internally generated intangible assets*

The cost of an internally generated intangible asset is the sum of the expenditure incurred from the date when the intangible asset first meets the recognition criteria in paragraph 18.4 of the Standard (see 3.3 above) and meets the conditions for capitalising development costs set out in paragraph 18.8H (see 3.3.3.B above). *[FRS 102.18.10A].*

Costs incurred before these criteria are met are expensed and cannot be reinstated retrospectively. *[FRS 102.18.17].*

Chapter 14

The cost of an internally generated intangible asset comprises all directly attributable costs necessary to create, produce, and prepare the asset to be capable of operating in the manner intended by management. Examples of directly attributable costs are: *[FRS 102.18.10B]*

(a)   costs of materials and services used or consumed in generating the intangible asset;

(b)   costs of employee benefits arising from the generation of the intangible asset;

(c)   fees to register a legal right;

(d)   amortisation of patents and licences that are used to generate the intangible asset; and

(e)   borrowing costs eligible for capitalisation under Section 25 – *Borrowing Costs*, provided the entity adopts an accounting policy of capitalising eligible borrowing costs. (See Chapter 20)

Indirect costs and general overheads, even if they can be allocated on a reasonable and consistent basis to the development project, should not be recognised as part of the cost of any intangible asset.

3.3.3.D   *Expenditure that does not qualify for recognition as an internally generated intangible asset*

Expenditure on the following items must be recognised as an expense and should not be recognised as intangible assets: *[FRS 102.18.8C]*

(a)   Internally generated brands, logos, publishing titles, customer lists and items similar in substance;

(b)   Start-up activities (i.e. start-up costs), which include establishment costs such as legal and secretarial costs incurred in establishing a legal entity, expenditure to open a new facility or business (i.e. pre-opening costs) and expenditure for starting new operations or launching new products or processes (i.e. pre-operating costs);

(c)   Training activities;

(d)   Advertising and promotional activities (unless it meets the definition of inventories held for distribution at no or nominal consideration. See 3.3.4 below);

(e)   Relocating or reorganising part or all of an entity; and

(f)   Internally generated goodwill.

For these purposes no distinction is made between costs that are incurred directly by the entity and those that relate to services provided by third parties. However, the standard does not prevent an entity from recording a prepayment if it pays for the delivery of goods before obtaining a right to access those goods. Similarly, a prepayment can be recognised when payment is made before services are received. *[FRS 102.18.8D]*.

3.3.4   *Advertising and promotional expenditure*

As set out at 3.3.3.D above, FRS 102 generally requires expenditure on advertising and promotional activities to be recognised as an expense as incurred. However, the standard gives an exception for advertising and promotional activities that meet the definition of inventories held for distribution at no or nominal consideration. *[FRS 102.18.8C(d)]*.

Items covered by this definition may include stocks of brochures and other marketing material. Advertising and promotional expenditure that meets the definition of inventories held for distribution at no or nominal consideration should be included within inventories. This is discussed further in Chapter 9 at 3.3.11.

3.3.5 Intangible assets acquired by way of a grant

An intangible asset may sometimes be acquired free of charge, or for nominal consideration, by way of a government grant. Governments frequently allocate airport-landing rights, licences to operate radio or television stations, emission rights, import licences or quotas, or rights to access other restricted resources.

Section 18 does not set out any separate recognition criteria for intangible assets acquired by way of a grant. The recognition criteria for government grants are set out in Section 24 – *Government Grants* (See Chapter 19).

The cost of an intangible asset acquired by way of a grant is its fair value at the date the grant is received or receivable, determined in accordance with Section 24. *[FRS 102.18.12]*. Some permits allocated by government, such as milk quotas, are freely traded and therefore have a readily ascertainable fair value. However, it may be difficult to reliably measure the fair value of all of the permits allocated by governments because they may have been allocated for nil consideration, may not be transferable and may only be bought and sold as part of a business. Despite this, FRS 102 does not permit entities to recognise intangible assets acquired by way of government grant at nominal value.

3.3.6 Exchanges of assets

An entity might swap certain intangible assets that it does not require or is no longer allowed to use for those of a counterparty that has other surplus assets. For example, it is not uncommon for airlines and media groups to exchange landing slots and newspaper titles, respectively, to meet demands of competition authorities.

Section 18 requires intangible assets acquired in exchange for non-monetary assets, or a combination of monetary and non-monetary assets, to be measured at fair value unless: *[FRS 102.18.13]*

(a) the exchange transaction lacks commercial substance; or

(b) the fair value of neither the asset received nor the asset given up is reliably measurable.

If the fair value of neither the asset received, nor the asset given up, can be measured reliably the acquired intangible asset is measured at the carrying amount of the asset given up. *[FRS 102.18.13(b)]*.

The acquired intangible asset should also be measured at the carrying amount of the asset given up if the exchange transaction lacks commercial substance. This is because it would not be appropriate to recognise a gain or loss on a transaction that lacks commercial substance. FRS 102 provides no guidance to assist entities in assessing whether a transaction has commercial substance. Under IFRS, IAS 38 requires that an entity determines whether an exchange transaction has commercial substance by considering the extent to which its future cash flows are expected to

Chapter 14

change as a result of the transaction. *[IAS 38.46]*. A similar assessment may need to be made under Section 18. In some cases, the assessment may be clear without an entity having to perform detailed calculations.

3.4   Measurement after initial recognition

Section 18 permits an entity to choose between two alternative treatments for the subsequent measurement of intangible assets: *[FRS 102.18.18]*

- the *cost model*; or
- the *revaluation model*.

When the revaluation model is selected, it must be applied to all intangible assets in the same class, unless an intangible asset in that class cannot be revalued because there is no active market for certain assets within that class in which case these assets are carried at cost less any accumulated amortisation and impairment. *[FRS 102.18.18]*. A class of intangible assets is a grouping of assets of a similar nature and use in an entity's operations. *[FRS 102 Appendix I]*. Examples of separate classes of intangible asset may include:

(a)   brand names;

(b)   mastheads and publishing titles;

(c)   computer software;

(d)   licences and franchises;

(e)   copyrights, patents and other industrial property rights, service and operating rights;

(f)   recipes, formulae, models, designs and prototypes; and

(g)   intangible assets under development.

3.4.1   *Cost model for measurement of intangible assets*

Under the cost model, an entity should measure its intangible assets at cost less accumulated amortisation and any accumulated impairment losses. *[FRS 102.18.18A]*. The rules on amortisation of intangible assets are discussed at 3.4.3 below; and impairment is discussed at 3.4.5 below.

3.4.2   *Revaluation model for measurement of intangible assets*

The revaluation model is only available if there is an active market for the intangible asset. *[FRS 102.18.18B]*. This will only rarely be the case (see 3.4.2.A below). There are no provisions in Section 18 that allow fair value to be determined indirectly, for example by using the valuation techniques applied to estimate the fair value of intangible assets acquired in a business combination.

After initial recognition an intangible asset should be carried at a revalued amount, which is its fair value at the date of the revaluation less any subsequent accumulated amortisation and subsequent accumulated impairment losses. *[FRS 102.18.18B]*. To prevent an entity from circumventing the recognition rules of the standard, the revaluation model does not allow: *[FRS 102.18.18C]*

- the revaluation of intangible assets that have not previously been recognised as assets; or

- the initial recognition of intangible assets at amounts other than cost.

These rules are designed to prevent an entity from recognising at a 'revalued' amount an intangible asset that was never recorded because its costs were expensed as they did not at the time meet the recognition rules. Section 18 does not permit recognition of past expenses as an intangible asset at a later date. *[FRS 102.18.17]*.

However, it is permitted to apply the revaluation model to the whole of an intangible asset even if only part of its cost was originally recognised as an asset because it did not meet the criteria for recognition until part of the way through the development process. *[FRS 102.18.18F]*.

3.4.2.A   Revaluation is allowed only if there is an active market

An entity can only elect to apply the revaluation model if the fair value can be determined by reference to an active market for the intangible asset. *[FRS 102.18.18B]*. An active market is a market in which all the following conditions exist: *[FRS 102 Appendix I]*

(a)   the items traded in the market are homogeneous;

(b)   willing buyers and sellers can normally be found at any time; and

(c)   prices are available to the public.

Few intangible assets will be eligible for revaluation as such an active market would be uncommon. By their very nature most intangible assets are unique or entity-specific. Intangible assets such as brands, newspaper mastheads, music and film publishing rights, patents or trademarks are ineligible for revaluation because each such asset is unique. The existence of a previous sale and purchase transaction is not sufficient evidence for the market to be regarded as active because of the requirement in the definition for a sufficient frequency and volume of transactions to allow the provision of ongoing pricing information. In addition, if prices are not available to the public, this is evidence that an active market does not exist.

If an intangible asset in a class of revalued intangible assets cannot be revalued because there is no active market for that particular asset, the asset should be carried at its cost less any accumulated amortisation and impairment losses. *[FRS 102.18.18]*.

If the fair value of a previously revalued intangible asset can no longer be determined by reference to an active market, the valuation is 'frozen' at the date of the last revaluation by reference to the active market. The carrying amount of the asset is reduced thereafter by subsequent accumulated amortisation and any subsequent accumulated impairment losses. *[FRS 102.18.18E]*.

3.4.2.B   Frequency of revaluations

If there is an active market, Section 18 requires revaluation to be performed 'with sufficient regularity to ensure that the carrying amount does not differ materially from that which would be determined using fair value at the end of the reporting period'. *[FRS 102.18.18D]*. The standard lets entities judge for themselves the frequency of revaluations depending on the volatility of the fair values of the underlying intangible assets. Significant and volatile movements in quoted prices may necessitate annual

Chapter 14

revaluation, whereas a less frequent update would be required for intangibles whose price is subject only to insignificant movements. Nevertheless, since an entity can only revalue assets for which a price is quoted in an active market, there should be no impediment to updating that valuation at each reporting date.

Where the revaluation model is applied, assets in the same class should be revalued at the same time. To do otherwise would allow selective revaluation of assets and the reporting of a mixture of costs and values as at different dates within the same asset class.

3.4.2.C   Accounting for gains and losses on revaluations

Increases in an intangible asset's carrying amount as a result of a revaluation should be recognised in other comprehensive income and accumulated in equity, except to the extent that the revaluation reverses previous revaluation decreases of the same asset that were recognised in profit or loss. In this case, the increases should be recognised in profit or loss. *[FRS 102.18.18G]*. Conversely, decreases in an intangible asset's carrying amount as a result of a revaluation should be recognised in OCI to the extent of any previous revaluation increases of the same asset that are accumulated in equity. Any excess revaluation loss should be recognised in profit or loss. *[FRS 102.18.18H]*.

For UK entities, the Regulations require that revaluation surpluses, net of provisions for amortisation or impairment, must be shown in the balance sheet within a separate reserve (the revaluation reserve) and not within retained earnings. *[1 Sch 35]*.

3.4.3   Amortisation of intangible assets

After initial recognition, Section 18 requires an entity to allocate the depreciable amount of an intangible asset on a systematic basis over its useful life. *[FRS 102.18.21]*. Depreciable amount is the cost, or other amount substituted for cost, of the intangible asset, less its residual value. *[FRS 102 Appendix I]*. The amortisation charge each period is dependent upon the useful life of the intangible asset, the amortisation method applied and the residual value of the intangible asset. These factors are discussed at 3.4.3.A, B and C below.

The amortisation charge for each period should be recognised in profit or loss, unless another section of FRS 102 requires the cost to be recognised as part of the cost of an asset. For example, the amortisation of an intangible asset may be included in the costs of inventories or property, plant and equipment. *[FRS 102.18.21]*.

Amortisation must be charged on all intangible assets. This requirement applies even to intangible assets measured under the revaluation model. For guidance on depreciation of revalued assets see chapter 13 at 3.6.3.A.

3.4.3.A   Assessing the useful life of an intangible asset

The useful life of an intangible asset is: *[FRS 102 Appendix I]*

(a)   the period over which an asset is expected to be available for use by an entity; or

(b)   the number of production or similar units expected to be obtained from the asset by an entity.

Thus, if appropriate, the useful life of an intangible asset should be expressed as a number of production or similar units rather than a period of time.

For the purposes of FRS 102, all intangible assets including those under the revaluation model, should be considered to have a finite useful life. *[FRS 102.18.19].*

Where an intangible asset arises from contractual or other legal rights, its useful life is the shorter of: *[FRS 102.18.19]*

- the period of the contractual or other legal rights; and

- the period over which the entity expects to use the asset.

If the contractual or other legal rights can be renewed, the useful life of the intangible asset should include the renewal period only if there is evidence to support renewal by the entity without significant cost. *[FRS 102.18.19].* An entity needs to exercise judgement in assessing what it regards as a significant cost. The following factors may indicate that an entity is able to renew the contractual or other legal rights without significant cost:

(a)   there is evidence, possibly based on experience, that the contractual or other legal rights will be renewed. If renewal is contingent upon the consent of a third party, this includes evidence that the third party will give its consent;

(b)   there is evidence that any conditions necessary to obtain renewal will be satisfied; and

(c)   the cost to the entity of renewal is not significant when compared with the future economic benefits expected to flow to the entity from renewal.

If there is no evidence to support renewal of the contractual or legal rights by the entity without significant cost, then the useful life of the intangible asset must not include the renewal period. In this case, the original asset's useful life ends at the contractual renewal date. If the rights are then renewed at the renewal date, we would expect the renewal cost to be treated as the cost to acquire a new intangible asset.

In our view, a number of factors may be considered in estimating the useful life of an intangible asset, including:

(a)   the expected usage of the asset by the entity and whether the asset could be managed efficiently by another management team;

(b)   typical product life cycles for the asset and public information on estimates of useful lives of similar assets that are used in a similar way;

(c)   technical, technological, commercial or other types of obsolescence;

(d)   the stability of the industry in which the asset operates and changes in the market demand for the products or services output from the asset;

(e)   expected actions by competitors or potential competitors;

(f)   the level of maintenance expenditure required to obtain the expected future economic benefits from the asset and the entity's ability and intention to reach such a level;

(g)   the period of control over the asset and legal or similar limits on the use of the asset, such as the expiry dates of related leases; and

(h)   whether the useful life of the asset is dependent on the useful life of other assets of the entity.

Chapter 14

If an entity is unable to make a reliable estimate of the useful life of an intangible asset, the life should not exceed five years. *[FRS 102.18.20]*. However, this should not be considered an automatic default. Entities should not underestimate the useful life of an intangible asset on the basis of this requirement. Similarly, it should not be used to justify a useful life of five years for an intangible asset for which a shorter useful life may be appropriate.

Under previous UK GAAP, FRS 10 limited the useful life of intangible assets to 20 years unless: *[FRS 10.19]*

(a)   the durability of the intangible asset could be demonstrated and justified estimating the useful economic life to exceed 20 years; and

(a)   the intangible asset was capable of continued measurement.

If these conditions were met, the useful life of the intangible asset could be regarded as longer than 20 years, or even indefinite. In this case, an annual impairment review of the intangible asset was required. As a result of the rebuttable presumption within FRS 10 and the requirement for annual impairment testing if a longer life was applied, it was common practice under previous UK GAAP for many entities to amortise intangible assets over 20 years. This implies that such entities were able to justify a 20 year life under previous UK GAAP. It is unlikely to be appropriate in such circumstances for these entities to default to a five year useful life on transition to FRS 102.

Entities with indefinite lived intangible assets capitalised under previous UK GAAP must also have previously demonstrated the durability of the intangible asset for a period beyond 20 years. It is therefore unlikely that a change from an indefinite life to a five year life on transition to FRS 102 could be justified.

3.4.3.B   Amortisation method

An entity should choose an amortisation method that reflects the pattern in which it expects to consume the asset's future economic benefits. If the entity cannot determine that pattern reliably, it should use the straight-line method. *[FRS 102.18.22]*. A variety of amortisation methods may be used to depreciate an intangible asset on a systematic basis over its useful life. The straight-line method is most commonly seen in practice. The unit of production method or reducing balance method are also sometimes seen. Whilst an amortisation method based on estimated total output (a unit of production method) may be appropriate, an amortisation method based on the pattern of expected revenues is not. This is because a revenue-based method reflects a pattern of generation of economic benefits from operating the business (of which the asset is a part), rather than the consumption of the economic benefits embodied in the asset itself. The difference is more obvious when unit prices are expected to increase over time.

Amortisation should begin when the intangible asset is available for use, i.e. when it is in the location and condition necessary for it to be useable in the manner intended by management. *[FRS 102.18.22]*. Therefore, even if an entity is not using the asset, it should still be amortised if it is available for use. Amortisation should cease when the asset is derecognised. (See 3.4.6 below). *[FRS 102.18.22]*.

3.4.3.C   Residual value

Section 18 requires entities to assume a residual value of zero for an intangible asset, unless there is a commitment by a third party to purchase the asset at the end of its useful life or there is an active market for the asset from which to determine its residual value and it is probable that such a market will exist at the end of the asset's useful life. *[FRS 102.18.23].*

Given the definition of 'active market' (see 3.4.2.A above) it seems highly unlikely that – in the absence of a commitment by a third party to buy the asset – an entity will ever be able to prove that the residual value of an intangible asset is other than zero.

3.4.3.D   Review of amortisation period and amortisation method

Factors such as a change in how an intangible asset is used, technological advancement, or changes in market prices may indicate that the residual value or useful life of an intangible asset has changed since the most recent annual reporting date. If such indicators are present, management should review previous estimates and, if current expectations differ, amend the residual value, amortisation method or useful life to reflect current expectations. *[FRS 102.18.24].*

Changes in residual value, amortisation method or useful life should be accounted for prospectively as a change in accounting estimate in accordance with Section 10 of FRS 102. *[FRS 102.18.24].*

If the residual value of an intangible asset increases to an amount greater than the asset's carrying amount, the asset's amortisation charge would be zero until its residual value decreases to an amount below the asset's carrying amount.

3.4.4   Subsequent expenditure

Entities may sometimes incur expenditure on an acquired intangible asset after its initial recognition or on an internally generated intangible asset after its completion.

Section 18 provides no separate rules on the recognition of subsequent expenditure on intangible assets. Instead, subsequent expenditure that meets the general recognition criteria for intangible assets, discussed at 3.3 above, may be recognised as an addition to an intangible asset. In practice, it is expected that most subsequent expenditure on intangible assets will maintain the expected future economic benefits embodied in the existing intangible asset and will not satisfy the recognition criteria in Section 18. Therefore only rarely would we expect subsequent expenditure to be recognised in the carrying amount of an asset.

3.4.5   Impairment losses

Entities should refer to the requirements of Section 27 to determine whether an intangible asset is impaired. *[FRS 102.18.25].* (See Chapter 22).

Section 27 requires entities to assess at each reporting date whether these is any indication that an intangible asset may be impaired. If there are indicators of impairment, the entity must estimate the recoverable amount of the intangible asset. *[FRS 102.27.7].* Section 27 explains how the entity should do this and when it should recognise or reverse an impairment loss. *[FRS 102.18.25].*

If there are indicators that an intangible asset is impaired, this could indicate that the entity should review the remaining useful life, amortisation method or residual value of the intangible asset, even if no impairment loss is recognised for the asset. *[FRS 102.27.10].*

3.4.6   Retirements and disposals

An intangible asset should be derecognised on disposal or when no future economic benefits are expected from its use or disposal. *[FRS 102.18.26].*

The gain or loss on derecognition, being the difference between the net disposal proceeds and the carrying amount of the asset *[FRS 102.2.52(b)])* should be accounted for in profit or loss. *[FRS 102.18.26].* This means that any revaluation surplus relating to the asset disposed of is transferred directly to retained earnings and not reflected in profit or loss.

3.5   Presentation and disclosure

The main requirements of Section 18 are set out below, but it may be necessary to refer also to the disclosure requirements of Section 27 in the event of an impairment of an intangible asset (see Chapter 22).

3.5.1   Presentation of intangible assets

Entities are required by Schedule 1 of the Regulations to present a separate heading for intangible assets on the face of the balance sheet. Intangible assets should be analysed into the following sub-headings, either on the face of the balance sheet, or within the notes to the accounts:

- Development costs;
- Concessions, patents, licenses, trade-marks and similar rights and assets;
- Goodwill; and
- Payments on account.

However, company law permits all entities to adapt the subheadings set out above to suit the nature of the entity's business. *[1 Sch 4(1), 1 Sch 4(1)].*

3.5.2   General disclosures

Section 18 requires certain disclosures to be presented by class of intangible assets.

The following must be disclosed for each class of intangible assets: *[FRS 102.18.27]*

(a)   the useful lives or the amortisation rates used and the reasons for choosing those periods;

(b)   the amortisation methods used;

(c)   the gross carrying amount and any accumulated amortisation (aggregated with accumulated impairment losses) at the beginning and end of the period;

(d)   the line item(s) of the statement of comprehensive income (or the income statement, if presented) in which any amortisation of intangible assets is included; and

(e)   a reconciliation of the carrying amount at the beginning and end of the reporting period showing separately:

   (i)   additions, indicating separately those from internal development and those acquired separately;

   (ii)   disposals;

   (iii)   acquisitions through business combinations;

   (iv)   revaluations;

   (v)   amortisation;

   (vi)   impairment losses; and

   (vii)   other changes.

The reconciliation in (e) above does not need to be presented for prior periods.

In addition to the disclosures required above, any impairment of intangible assets is to be disclosed in accordance with Section 27. *[FRS 102.27.33(d)].* The nature and effect of any change in useful life, amortisation method or residual value estimates should be disclosed in accordance with the provisions of Section 10 of FRS 102. *[FRS 102.10.18].*

There are a number of additional disclosure requirements, some of which only apply in certain circumstances: *[FRS 102.18.28]*

(a)   a description, the carrying amount and remaining amortisation period of any individual intangible asset that is material to the entity's financial statements;

(b)   for intangible assets acquired by way of a government grant and initially recognised at fair value:

   (i)   the fair value initially recognised for these assets; and

   (ii)   their carrying amounts.

(c)   the existence and carrying amounts of intangible assets to which the entity has restricted title or that are pledged as security for liabilities; and

(d)   the amount of contractual commitments for the acquisition of intangible assets.

3.5.3   Disclosure of research and development expenditure

Entities should disclose the aggregate amount of research and development expenditure recognised as an expense during the period (that is, the amount of expenditure incurred internally on research and development that has not been capitalised as an intangible asset or as part of the cost of another asset that meets the recognition criteria of FRS 102). *[FRS 102.18.29].*

Where an entity has elected to capitalise development costs, company law requires disclosure of:

(a)   the period over which the amount of the costs that were originally capitalised is being written off; and

(b)   the reasons for capitalising the development costs. *[1 Sch 21(2)].*

Unamortised development costs included as an asset in a company's accounts should be treated as a realised loss for the purpose of calculating a company's distributable profits. However, in special circumstances directors may be able to justify a decision that unamortised development costs included as an asset in a company's accounts should not be treated as a realised loss. In such cases, the circumstances relied upon by the directors in reaching this justification must be disclosed. *[s844]*.

The Companies Act also requires that the directors' report of large and medium-sized companies and groups should contain an indication of the activities of the company (and its subsidiary undertakings) in the field of research and development. *[7 Sch 7(c)]*.

3.5.4   *Additional disclosures when the revaluation model is applied*

If intangible assets are accounted for at revalued amounts, an entity should disclose the following: *[FRS 102.18.29A]*

(a)   the effective date of the revaluation;

(b)   whether an independent valuer was involved;

(c)   the methods and significant assumptions applied in estimating the assets' fair values; and

(d)   for each revalued class of intangible assets, the carrying amount that would have been recognised had the assets been carried under the cost model.

Company law requires the following additional disclosures:

(a)   the years in which the intangible assets were separately valued (so far as known to the directors) and the separate values; and

(b)   for intangible assets that have been revalued in the financial year, the names of the persons who valued them or particulars of their qualifications for doing so, and the basis of valuation used by them. *[1 Sch 52, 1 Sch 49]*. However, as FRS 102 allows the use of the revaluation model only where fair value can be determined by reference to an active market, this company law requirement is likely to be of limited relevance to FRS 102 reporters.

(c)   Separate disclosures of the revaluation reserve on the company balance sheet. *[1 Sch 35(2)]*.

4   PRACTICAL IMPLEMENTATION ISSUES

4.1   Website costs

There is no specific guidance on the accounting for website development costs under FRS 102. Given their lack of physical substance, it is likely that they would be classified as intangible assets under FRS 102 (see 3.2.3 above). However, certain elements related to developing a website, such as web servers, do have physical substance. Entities may therefore have to exercise judgement in determining whether to apply Section 18 or Section 17 of FRS 102 to the elements of a website with physical substance.

Website costs classified as intangible assets would be subject to the specific recognition requirements for internally generated intangible assets within Section 18. These criteria are similar to those within UITF 29 – *Website development costs* under previous UK GAAP. UITF 29 required website planning costs to be charged to the profit and loss account as incurred. Other website development costs, including design and content costs meeting certain criteria, were required to be capitalised as tangible fixed assets. We would expect costs capitalised under UITF 29 to meet the capitalisation criteria of Section 18. However, many website costs would likely be classified as intangible assets rather than property, plant and equipment under FRS 102. Costs not meeting the recognition criteria of UITF 29 would be unlikely to meet the criteria for recognition of an internally generated intangible asset in Section 18.

4.2   Measurement of intangible assets: Income from incidental operations while an asset is being developed

When an entity generates income while it is developing or constructing an asset, the question arises as to whether this income should reduce the initial carrying value of the asset being developed or be recognised in profit or loss. Section 18 is silent on this issue, as were FRS 10 and SSAP 13. For IFRS reporters, IAS 38 requires the entity to consider whether the activity giving rise to income is necessary to bring the asset to the condition necessary for it to be capable of operating in the manner intended by management, or not. Entities reporting under FRS 102 may consider applying a similar assessment. IAS 38 requires the income and related expenses of incidental operations (being those not necessary to develop the asset for its intended use) to be recognised immediately in profit or loss and included in their respective classifications of income and expense. *[IAS 38.31].*

Whilst IAS 38 is not explicit on the matter, it follows that when the activity is determined to be necessary to bring the intangible asset into its intended use, any income should be deducted from the cost of the asset. An example would be where income is generated from the sale of samples produced during the testing of a new process or from the sale of a production prototype. However, care must be taken to confirm whether the incidence of income indicates that the intangible asset is ready for its intended use, in which case capitalisation of costs would cease, revenue would be recognised in profit or loss and the related costs of the activity would include a measure of amortisation of the asset.

4.3   Measurement of intangible assets: Intangible assets acquired for contingent consideration

The consideration payable on acquisition of an intangible asset may sometimes be contingent upon a specified future event or condition. For example, an entity may acquire an intangible asset for consideration comprising a combination of up-front payment, guaranteed instalments for a number of years and additional amounts that vary according to future activity (revenue, profit or number of units output).

Transactions involving contingent consideration are often very complex and payment can be dependent on a number of factors. In the absence of specific guidance in Section 18, entities will be required to determine an appropriate accounting treatment based on the commercial circumstances of the transaction. In practice there are two general approaches. One includes the fair value of all contingent payments in the initial measurement of the asset. The other excludes executory payments from initial measurement. Under both approaches, contingent payments are either capitalised when incurred if they meet the definition of an asset, or expensed as incurred.

4.4   Industry specific practical implementation issues

Entities in certain industries may encounter issues in accounting for intangible assets that are common across the industry. Industry specific issues are not explicitly addressed by Section 18. Entities encountering the following industry specific issues may wish to consider guidance in EY International GAAP 2015 in formulating appropriate accounting policies under FRS 102:

- Research and development in the pharmaceutical industry;
- Rate-regulated activities;
- Emission trading schemes;
- Accounting for green certificates or renewable energy certificates;
- Accounting for REACH costs; and
- Television and telecommunications programme and broadcast rights.

5   SUMMARY OF GAAP DIFFERENCES

The following table shows the differences between FRS 102, previous UK GAAP and IFRS.

	FRS 102	*Previous UK GAAP*	*IFRS*
Definition	Must be separable or arise from contractual or other legal rights. See 3.2.1 above.	Must be identifiable and controlled by the entity through custody or legal rights.	Same as FRS 102.
Software development costs	No specific guidance. We would expect entities to look to the guidance in IFRS. See 3.2.2 above.	Treated as part of the cost of related hardware if directly attributable to bringing computer system / computer operated machinery into working condition. Certain website development costs capitalised as tangible fixed assets.	Required to use judgement to assess which element is more significant when an asset incorporates both tangible and intangible elements. Software that is not integral to related hardware is treated as an intangible asset.

Cost of separately acquired intangible assets	Comprises purchase price, import duties and non-refundable taxes, trade discounts and rebates; and directly attributable costs of preparing the asset for its intended use. See 3.3.1.B	No specific guidance	Similar to FRS 102, with additional guidance provided.
Intangible assets acquired in a business combination	Not recognised separately from goodwill if fair value cannot be measured reliably. Otherwise, recognised at fair value at the date of acquisition See 3.3.2 above.	Recognised separately from goodwill if fair value can be measured reliably on initial recognition, subject to the constraint that, unless the asset had a readily ascertainable market value, the fair value was limited to an amount that did not create or increase any negative goodwill arising on the acquisition. This, in addition to the wider definition of an intangible asset under FRS 102 means we expect more intangible assets acquired in a business combination to be recognised separately from goodwill under FRS 102.	Presumes that intangible assets acquired in a business combination can always be measured reliably. We therefore expect less intangible assets to be recognised on the acquisition of a business under FRS 102 than under IFRS.
Intangible assets acquired by government grant	Cost of the asset is its fair value at the date the grant is received or receivable. See 3.3.5 above.	SSAP 4 – *Accounting for Government Grants* requires recognition at fair value. However, this requirement is not always followed in practice.	Accounting policy choice – measure at fair value or a nominal amount.
Advertising and promotional expenditure	Certain advertising and promotional expenditure should be carried as an asset within inventories. See 3.3.4 above.	No guidance. Practice varies.	Expenditure on advertising and promotional activities is recognised as an expense when it is incurred.

Chapter 14

	FRS 102	Previous UK GAAP	IFRS
Development expenditure	Accounting policy choice – an entity may recognise an intangible asset arising from development or from the development phase of an internal project if certain criteria are met.	Accounting policy choice – an entity may recognise an intangible asset arising from development if certain criteria (which are similar, but not identical, to FRS 102) are met. Does not cover the development phase of an internal project, therefore possibly a narrower definition than FRS 102.	An entity must recognise an intangible asset arising from development or from the development phase of an internal project if certain criteria (which are consistent with FRS 102) are met.
	Where the development project is likely to lead to a loss, an asset may be recognised although it may need to be written down to reflect impairment.	Where the development project is likely to lead to a loss, no asset may be recognised.	Same as FRS 102
	Amortisation begins when the intangible asset is available for use. See 3.3.3 above.	Amortisation commences with the commercial production or application of the product, service, process or system.	Same as FRS 102.
Start-up costs	Should not be recognised as an intangible asset. See 3.3.3.D above.	Start-up costs may be included in the cost of an intangible asset if that treatment is consistent with similar costs incurred as part of the entity's on-going activities. In practice, such costs are rare.	Similar to FRS 102.

Revaluation model	Where selected, the revaluation model must be applied to all intangible assets in the same class unless no active market for those assets.	If one intangible asset is revalued, all other intangible assets of the same class should be revalued.	Same as FRS 102.
	If only part of the cost of an intangible asset is recognised as an asset because the asset did not meet the recognition criteria until part way through the process (e.g. for research and development projects), the revaluation model may be applied to the whole of that asset. See 3.4.2 above.	No guidance	Same as FRS 102
Revaluation model – no longer an active market	Where fair value can no longer be measured by reference to an active market, the carrying amount of the asset should be its revalued amount at the date of the last revaluation, less any subsequent accumulated amortisation and impairment losses. See 3.4.2 above.	No guidance.	Same as FRS 102
Revaluation losses	Decreases in carrying amount as a result of a revaluation should be recognised in OCI to the extent of any previous revaluation increases of the same asset that are accumulated in equity. Any excess revaluation loss should be recognised in profit or loss. See 3.4.2 above. Revaluation surpluses must be maintained in a statutory revaluation reserve.	Negative revaluation reserve is possible, although unlikely to see this in practice.	Same as FRS 102.

	FRS 102	*Previous UK GAAP*	*IFRS*
Amortisation	Intangible assets are amortised over a finite useful life. If an entity is unable to make a reliable estimate, the useful life should not exceed five years.	Intangible assets with finite useful lives amortised over their useful life. Intangible assets presumed to have a useful life of no longer than 20 years unless certain conditions met. Intangible assets with indefinite lives not amortised	Intangible assets with finite useful lives are amortised over their useful lives. An intangible asset with an indefinite useful life is not amortised.
	Renewal periods included in the useful life of intangible assets that arise from contractual or legal right conveyed for a finite term only if there is evidence to support renewal by the entity without significant cost.	Renewal periods included in the useful life of intangible assets arising from contractual or legal rights conveyed for a finite term only if renewal assured. FRS 10 sets out conditions (similar, but not identical, to IFRS) that should be met in order for renewal to be regarded as assured.	Same as FRS 102. Additionally, IAS 38 provides examples of indicators that an entity could renew the contractual or legal rights without significant cost.
	Review the amortisation method, useful life and residual value of intangible assets if there are indicators that any of these have changed. See 3.4.3 above.	Useful economic lives reviewed at the end of each reporting period.	Review the amortisation method, useful life and residual value of intangible assets at least at each financial year end.
Residual value	The residual value of an intangible asset is zero except in certain circumstances.	Similar to FRS 102.	Same as FRS 102.
	Residual value is based on the amount an entity would currently obtain from disposal of an intangible asset if it were already of the age and in the condition expected at the end of its useful life. See 3.4.3.C above.	Residual value based on prices prevailing at the date of acquisition (or revaluation) of the asset.	Same as FRS 102

Impairment reviews	Required if there are indicators of impairment. See 3.4.5 above.	Required at the end of the first full year after acquisition for intangibles with an amortisation period of 20 years or less Thereafter, required if indicators of impairment. Required annually for intangible assets amortised over a period exceeding 20 years.	Same as FRS 102 except impairment reviews required annually and whenever indicators of impairment for indefinite lived intangibles.
Intangible assets acquired in exchange for non-monetary assets	Measured at fair value unless the exchange transaction lacks commercial substance; or the fair value of neither the asset received nor the asset given up is reliably measurable. In that case, the asset's cost is measured at the carrying amount of the asset given up. See 3.3.6 above.	No guidance.	Similar to FRS 102. IAS 38 additionally provides guidance on determining whether a transaction has commercial substance.
Disclosures	The disclosures required by FRS 102 are set out at 3.5 above.	Similar to FRS 102. However, FRS 102 requires some additional disclosures and does not require certain disclosures required by previous UK GAAP. FRS 10 required a reconciliation of the carrying amount of intangible assets at the beginning and end of the reporting period for both the current and comparative period.	Similar to FRS 102. IFRS requires a reconciliation of the carrying amount of intangible assets at the beginning and end of the reporting period for both the current and comparative period. In addition, there are some differences in the items to be included in the reconciliation table

Chapter 14

Chapter 15   Business combinations and goodwill

Chapter 15

List of examples

Chapter 15   Business combinations and goodwill

1   INTRODUCTION

Section 9 – *Consolidated and Separate Financial Statements* – of FRS 102, which is dealt with in Chapter 6 of this publication, *inter alia*, addresses the preparation of consolidated financial statements by parents. Its focus is on matters such as when consolidated financial statements should be prepared, what entities should be considered to be part of the group for the purposes of inclusion therein, and the mechanics of how such entities should be dealt with in the consolidated financial statements. It also deals with the accounting for disposals of, and increased interests in, existing subsidiaries of the group. This chapter focuses on those situations where the group structure changes through subsidiaries joining the group as a result of the parent obtaining control of its new subsidiary.

Section 19 – *Business Combinations and Goodwill* – of FRS 102 applies to the accounting for business combinations. A business combination is defined as 'the bringing together of separate entities or businesses into one reporting entity'. *[FRS 102.19.3, FRS 102 Appendix I].* While this chapter is written primarily in the context of an entity becoming a subsidiary of another, the guidance also applies to individual financial statements in situations where an entity purchases (or combines with) an unincorporated business, for example, through the acquisition of the trade and net assets, including goodwill, of another entity.

Section 19 provides guidance on the most common issues facing preparers in relation to the accounting for business combinations – namely, detecting a business combination, identifying the acquirer, determining the acquisition date, measuring the cost of the business combination, and then allocating that cost to the acquirer's interest in the identifiable assets and liabilities of the acquiree. It also addresses the initial and subsequent accounting treatment of goodwill or any excess over cost of the acquirer's interest in the identifiable assets and liabilities of the acquiree.

This chapter also looks at some issues relating to group reorganisations. These involve the restructuring of the relationships between companies in a group by, for example, setting up a new holding company, changing the direct ownership of a subsidiary within a group, or transferring businesses from one company to another because of a process of divisionalisation. Most of such changes should have no impact on the consolidated financial statements (provided there are no non-controlling interests affected), because they are purely internal and cannot affect the group when it is being portrayed as a single entity. However, all such transactions can have a significant impact on the financial statements of the individual companies in the group.

1.1   Background

There were traditionally two distinctly different forms of reporting the effects of a business combination; acquisition accounting (or the purchase method) and merger accounting (or the pooling of interests method). These two methods look at business combinations from quite different perspectives. An acquisition is seen as the absorption by the acquirer of the target; there is continuity only of the acquirer, with only the post-acquisition results of the target reported in earnings of the acquirer, and the comparatives remaining those of the acquirer. In contrast, a merger is seen as the uniting of the interests of two formerly distinct shareholder groups, and in order to present continuity of both entities there is retrospective restatement to show the enlarged entity as if the two entities had always been together, by combining the results of both entities pre- and post-combination and restating the comparatives. Over the years, the accounting landscape has changed in attempts to distinguish between the circumstances when each of these methods is appropriate.

Another area of historical debate when it comes to accounting for business combinations has been how to treat any difference between the cost of the acquisition and the cost of the identifiable assets and liabilities of the target. Where the amounts allocated to the assets and liabilities are less than the overall cost, the difference is accounted for as goodwill. Over the years, there have been different views on how goodwill should be accounted for, but the general method has been to deal with it as an asset. The question has been: should it be amortised over its economic life or should it not be amortised at all, but subjected to some form of impairment test? Where the cost has been less than the value allocated to the identifiable assets and liabilities, then this has traditionally been treated as negative goodwill. The issue has then been how such a credit should be released to the income statement.

1.2   The FRS 102 approach to business combinations and goodwill

The business combinations section of FRS 102 is broadly based on the equivalent section of the IFRS for SMEs. Consequently, Section 19 is – subject to some amendments by the Accounting Council – ultimately derived from the version of IFRS 3 – *Business Combinations* – prior to the amendments made by the IASB in 2008.

As it relates to the two matters discussed at 1.1 above:

- under previous UK GAAP, FRS 6 – *Acquisitions and mergers* ('FRS 6') provided that merger accounting should only be applied to those rare business combinations that could properly be regarded as mergers in substance, and that, otherwise, business combinations were more appropriately accounted for as acquisitions. FRS 6 set out five criteria that a business combination had to meet for it to be accounted for as a merger, in addition to being permitted by company law. Therefore, and while rare, FRS 6 did provide for the possibility of merger accounting on the occurrence of a 'true merger'. FRS 102 closes this possibility, by prohibiting merger accounting in all but two instances:

  - merger accounting permitted by FRS 6 for group reconstructions has been carried forward into FRS 102. The Accounting Council's advice to the FRC, which accompanies FRS 102, asserted that the accounting provided by FRS 6 is well understood and provides useful requirements. In practice, the Accounting Council does not expect the introduction of FRS 102 to change the accounting for group reconstructions. *[FRS 102.AC.64]*.

  - a type of merger accounting is also permitted, in certain circumstances, for combinations between public benefit entities. In its advice to the FRC, the Accounting Council noted concern as to whether acquisition accounting appropriately caters for such combinations, particularly if there is a gift of one entity to another in a combination at nil or nominal consideration, or where two or more organisations genuinely merge to form a new entity. *[FRS 102.AC.135]*. In the latter situation, the Accounting Council considered acquisition accounting does not reflect the true substance of such transactions, *[FRS 102.AC.137]*, and so advised that merger accounting should be retained for such instances; and further, that while the criteria to apply merger accounting set out in FRS 6 provided a starting point, they were framed in the context of the commercial sector, and therefore the criteria had to be adapted to make them more appropriate for public benefit entities. *[FRS 102.AC.138]*.

- to the treatment of goodwill, FRS 102 is largely consistent with the principles of previous UK GAAP – positive goodwill is to be recognised as an asset and amortised over its useful life. There is, however, no longer provision for a determination of indefinite lived goodwill as was possible under FRS 10 – *Goodwill and intangible assets* ('FRS 10'). Also, where an entity is otherwise unable to make a reliable estimate of the useful life, the presumed life for goodwill is restricted to five years to be consistent with company law. *[FRS 102.AC.117(e)]*. The requirements of FRS 10 as to negative goodwill have largely been continued in FRS 102.

Section 2 of this chapter discusses what are likely to be the most notable differences in accounting for business combinations for preparers transitioning from previous UK GAAP, as well as alluding to some of the more significant differences to extant IFRS.

Chapter 15

2   COMPARISON BETWEEN SECTION 19, PREVIOUS UK GAAP AND IFRS

The main changes from previous UK GAAP, and the significant differences to the requirements of IFRS 3 (Revised) – *Business Combinations* [being the version issued by the IASB in January 2008] ('IFRS 3'), are set out below.

2.1   Key differences between Section 19 and previous UK GAAP

2.1.1   *Method of accounting*

As discussed at 1.2 above, FRS 102 requires all business combinations (other than those that meet the definition of a group reconstruction, and certain combinations of public benefit entities) to be accounted for using the purchase method (acquisition accounting).

Under previous UK GAAP, FRS 6 permitted merger accounting for those rare mergers that constituted 'true mergers', as well as for certain group reconstructions.

As discussed above, with the exception of combinations involving public benefit entities, there are unlikely to be practical differences on application of the requirements of FRS 102 given: (1) 'true mergers' under FRS 6 were extremely rare; and (2) the Accounting Council has indicated that, in practice, it does not expect the introduction of FRS 102 to change the accounting for group reconstructions. *[FRS 102.AC.64].*

2.1.2   *Definition of a business combination*

The definition of a business combination in FRS 102 is 'the bringing together of separate entities or businesses into one reporting entity'. *[FRS 102.19.3].*

This definition is not notably different to that in previous UK GAAP ('the bringing together of separate entities into one economic entity as a result of one entity uniting with, or obtaining control over the net assets and operations of, another'). *[FRS 6.2].*

While there is unlikely to be any new accounting consequences driven by the definition of a 'business combination', there may be potential for differences in the scope of application due to the first time definition of a 'business' in UK GAAP, as discussed below.

2.1.3   *Definition of a business*

FRS 102 includes an explicit definition of what constitutes a business in Appendix I: Glossary to FRS 102 (see 3.2.1 below). The standard thereby requires that, regardless of the structure of a transaction, if its substance is that of a 'business combination' then the requirements of Section 19 apply.

Previous UK GAAP did not define a 'business'. It is possible the default treatment of an acquisition of a subsidiary may have been a business combination, while a purchase of a group of assets and liabilities may have been as an asset purchase.

FRS 102 should oblige preparers to closely consider, notwithstanding the structure of the transaction, whether the arrangement constitutes a business combination or an asset purchase.

2.1.4   *Identifying an acquirer*

FRS 102 includes, as an explicit step in applying the purchase method, 'identifying an acquirer'. *[FRS 102.19.7(a)]*.

Previous UK GAAP did not include such a step, with FRS 6, consistent with company law, framed in terms of an entity becoming a subsidiary of a parent company.

Through the inclusion of this as a mandatory step in applying FRS 102's purchase method of accounting to business combinations, the standard requires preparers to consider all pertinent facts and circumstances in order to determine which of the combining entities is, from an accounting perspective, the acquirer, i.e. the combining entity that obtains control of the other combining entities or businesses. *[FRS 102.19.8]*.

Whilst unlikely to become a common occurrence, this change may result in a greater incidence of 'reverse acquisition' accounting in the UK GAAP landscape.

A 'reverse acquisition' occurs when the owners of a company being 'acquired' (say, Company B) receive as consideration sufficient voting shares of the 'acquiring company' (say, Company A) so as to obtain control over the new combined entity. The acquisition is 'reverse' because, from an economic perspective, the acquirer (Company A) is being taken over by the acquiree (Company B).

Notwithstanding the economic substance, company law regards the party transferring consideration (be it cash or shares) in return for ownership of another as being the parent undertaking, and requires that company to prepare consolidated financial statements and apply acquisition accounting for the acquisition of its subsidiary.

FRS 6 was likewise framed in terms of an entity becoming a subsidiary of a parent company. Nevertheless, it was considered that there were some instances where it would be right and proper to invoke the true and fair override and apply reverse acquisition accounting, although the incidence of doing so has historically been rare.

FRS 102 does not provide guidance on the application of reverse acquisition accounting. See 3.4 and 3.9 below for more on reverse acquisition accounting.

2.1.5   *Cost of a business combination*

2.1.5.A   *Acquisition expenses*

FRS 102 requires the 'costs directly attributable to the business combination' *[FRS 102.19.11(b)]* to be included in the cost of the business combination – effectively reflecting them within goodwill.

This requirement is broadly consistent with previous UK GAAP, whereby FRS 7 – *Fair values in acquisition accounting* ('FRS 7') required fees and similar incremental costs (but excluding the issue costs of shares or other securities required to be accounted for as a reduction in the proceeds of a capital instrument) incurred directly in making an acquisition be included in the cost of acquisition. Internal costs, and other expenses that cannot be directly attributed to the acquisition, were to be charged to the profit and loss account. *[FRS 7.28]*. FRS 7 further expanded on incremental costs as including 'professional fees paid to merchant banks, accountants, legal advisers, valuers and other consultants', whilst excluding 'any allocation of costs that would still have been incurred had the acquisition not been entered into – for example, the cost of maintaining an acquisitions department or management remuneration'. *[FRS 7.85].*

2.1.5.B   Contingent consideration

FRS 102 requires recognition of any contingent consideration to be made at the acquisition date if the adjustment is 'probable and can be measured reliably'. *[FRS 102.19.12].* If the potential adjustment is not recognised at the acquisition date, but subsequently becomes probable and can be measured reliably, the additional consideration is treated as an adjustment to the cost of the combination. *[FRS 102.19.13].*

FRS 7 required the cost of acquisition to include a reasonable estimate of the fair value of the amounts expected to be payable in the future. *[FRS 7.27].* Where it was not possible to estimate the total amounts payable with any degree of certainty, at least those amounts that are reasonably expected to be payable would be recognised. *[FRS 7.81].* Subsequent adjustments to the cost (and therefore goodwill) were recognised when revised estimates were made – effectively leaving the determination of goodwill open for several periods after the acquisition.

As can be seen, while not identical, the requirements of FRS 102 are similar to previous UK GAAP. In practice, the same treatment as under FRS 7 is likely under FRS 102, with subsequent changes made to the cost being reflected as adjustments to goodwill.

2.1.5.C   Contingent payments to employees or selling shareholders

Other than noting that the cost of a business combination are those assets given, liabilities incurred or assumed, and equity instruments issued 'in exchange for control of the acquiree', *[FRS 102.19.11],* FRS 102 provides no further guidance in determining whether any of those assets given, liabilities incurred or assumed, or equity instruments issued are in connection with such exchange, or are payments pertaining to other arrangements, such as future services.

A common example of a situation where vendors may have a continuing relationship with the acquirer is where they become, or continue to be, key employees of the acquiree subsequent to the acquisition.

FRS 102 provides no guidance on the accounting to be applied in such situations, and does not distinguish between contingent consideration that, in substance, is additional purchase price, and contingent consideration that, in substance, represents compensation for future services.

Whilst previous UK GAAP discussed situations where acquisition agreements may require further payments to vendors who continue to work for the acquired company and identified the need to determine whether the substance of the agreement is payment for the business acquired, or an expense such as compensation for services or profit sharing, *[FRS 7.84],* little guidance on how to make this distinction was offered.

Under FRS 102, we believe that an acquirer must make such a distinction and therefore identify contingent consideration that is, in substance, compensation for future services, and account for this separately from the cost of the combination. This is because FRS 102's *Concepts and Pervasive Principles*, as outlined in Section 2, includes as one of the qualitative characteristics of information in financial statements 'substance over form', requiring that 'transactions and other events and conditions should be accounted for and presented in accordance with their substance and not merely their legal form'. *[FRS 102.2.8]*. Therefore, where a vendor is also a continuing employee it is necessary to determine whether payments are made to them in their capacity as vendor or as employee.

2.1.6 Measurement period

FRS 102 acknowledges that an acquirer requires a period of time to identify and determine appropriate fair values for the acquiree's identifiable assets, liabilities and contingent liabilities. Under FRS 102, provisional amounts in the first post-acquisition financial statements are to be finalised within twelve months after the acquisition date – and, where amendments are required to the provisional amounts recognised in the previous financial statements, they are to be made retrospectively by restating comparatives, i.e. by accounting for them as if they were made at the acquisition date. *[FRS 102.19.19]*.

FRS 7 required the determination of the fair value of the identifiable assets and liabilities acquired to be completed by the date on which the first post-acquisition financial statements of the acquirer were approved by the directors; or failing that, any provisional valuations used in those financial statements were to be amended, if necessary, in the next financial statements with a corresponding adjustment to goodwill *[FRS 7.23-25]* – i.e. such adjustments were dealt with in the period in which they were identified.

2.1.7 Initial measurement of acquiree's assets, liabilities and contingent liabilities

FRS 102 requires the acquiree's identifiable assets and liabilities and a provision for those contingent liabilities (that satisfy the recognition criteria in paragraph 19.20) to be measured at their acquisition-date fair values (except for deferred tax, employee benefit arrangements and share-based payments, which are to be recognised and measured in accordance with the respective section of FRS 102). *[FRS 102.19.4]*.

Other than in respect of deferred tax, employee benefit arrangements and share-based payments, Section 19 offers no guidance on how to derive this acquisition date fair value. Section 2 – *Concepts and Pervasive Principles* – states that 'fair value is the amount for which an asset could be exchanged, a liability settled, or an equity instrument granted could be exchanged, between knowledgeable, willing parties in an arm's length transaction', and guides that 'In the absence of any specific guidance provided in the relevant section of this FRS, where fair value measurement is permitted or required the guidance in paragraphs 11.27 to 11.32 shall be applied'. *[FRS 102.2.34(b)]*.

While the general position under previous UK GAAP is likewise initial measurement at fair value, FRS 7 contained detailed application guidance for attributing fair values to particular categories of assets and liabilities. *[FRS 7.9-22]*. No such guidance is provided in FRS 102.

2.1.8   Recognition of intangible assets separate from goodwill

Under FRS 102, an intangible asset acquired in a business combination shall be separately recognised so long as: (i) it is 'identifiable'; and (ii) its fair value can be measured reliably.

An intangible asset is 'identifiable' under FRS 102 when it is either: (a) 'separable' (capable of being separated or divided from the entity and sold, transferred, licensed, rented or exchanged, either individually or together with a related contract, asset or liability); or (b) it arises from contractual or other legal rights, regardless of whether those rights are transferable or separable from the entity or from other rights and obligations. *[FRS 102.18.2]*. FRS 102 states that an intangible asset acquired in a business combination is normally recognised as an asset because its fair value can be measured with sufficient reliability. However, an intangible asset is not recognised when it arises from legal or other contractual rights and there is no history or evidence of exchange transactions for the same or similar assets, and otherwise estimating fair value would be dependent on immeasurable variables. *[FRS 102.18.8]*.

Other than requiring that where an intangible asset acquired as part of the acquisition of a business is recognised, its fair value should be based on its replacement cost, *[FRS 7.10]*, FRS 7 included no specific guidance on the recognition of intangible assets. As such, separate recognition was required where the requirements of FRS 10 were met.

FRS 10 required an intangible asset to be both identifiable (capable of being disposed of separately without disposing of a business of the entity) and controlled by the entity through legal rights (for example, a franchise or licence granting the entity access to benefits; or a patent or trademark restricting the access of others to those benefits), or in the absence of legal rights, through custody (for example, technical or intellectual knowledge arising from development activity is maintained secretly). FRS 10 provided an example of an entity having a portfolio of clients or a team of skilled staff where, notwithstanding the expectation that future benefits will flow to the entity, as the entity does not have legal rights to retain those clients or employees, the entity does not have sufficient control over the benefits to recognise an intangible asset. *[FRS 10.2]*.

Further, and in addition to requiring an asset to be both identifiable and controlled through custody or legal requirements, previous UK GAAP required that an intangible asset acquired as part of the acquisition of a business should only be capitalised separately from goodwill if its value can be measured reliably on initial recognition. *[FRS 10.10]*. Otherwise, it should be subsumed within the amount of the purchase price attributed to goodwill. *[FRS 10.13]*.

As a result of the foregoing changes, on application of FRS 102 there may be more intangible assets identified and recognised, and a consequent reduction in goodwill.

2.1.9   Deferred tax

FRS 102 provides that when the amount that can be deducted for tax for an asset (other than goodwill) that is recognised in a business combination is less (more) than the value at which it is recognised, a deferred tax liability (asset) shall be recognised for the additional tax that will be paid (avoided) in respect of that difference. Similarly, a deferred tax asset (liability) shall be recognised for the additional tax that will be avoided (paid) because of a difference between the value at which a liability is recognised and the amount that will be assessed for tax. The amount attributed to goodwill shall be adjusted by the amount of deferred tax recognised. *[FRS 102.29.11].*

Such treatment differs from that under previous UK GAAP due to the requirement under FRS 7, as it related to deferred tax, that adjustments to record assets and liabilities of the acquiree at their fair values were treated in the same way as they would be if they were timing differences arising in the entity's own accounts – in other words, any tax that would become payable if the asset were sold at that value would be provided only where the acquiree had entered into a binding agreement to sell the asset before the acquisition and rollover relief was not available. *[FRS 7.74].*

As a consequence, more deferred tax on attributed fair values are likely to be recognised in business combinations under FRS 102 than was the case under previous UK GAAP due to the requirement that deferred tax be recognised for the difference between the tax base and accounting base of assets and liabilities recognised in a business combination. *[FRS 102.29.11].* This matter is discussed further in Chapter 24 which addresses Section 29 – *Income Tax.*

2.1.10   Step acquisitions

FRS 102 provides that where a parent acquires control of a subsidiary in stages, the cost of the business combination is the aggregate of the fair values of the assets given, liabilities assumed, and equity instruments issued by the acquirer at the date of each transaction in the series *[FRS 102.19.11A]* whereas the 'normal' rules on allocating the cost of the business combination to the acquisition date fair value of the identifiable assets, liabilities and contingent liabilities apply. *[FRS 102.19.14].*

This approach is consistent with previous UK GAAP and the requirements of the Companies Act 2006. See 3.10 below.

2.1.11   Non-controlling interests in a business combination

Section 9 identifies the initial measurement of any non-controlling interest as the non-controlling interest's share in the net amount of the identifiable assets, liabilities and contingent liabilities recognised and measured in accordance with Section 19 at the date of the original combination. *[FRS 102.9.13(d)].*

This approach is consistent with previous UK GAAP. See 3.7 below.

2.1.12   Subsequent accounting for goodwill

FRS 102 requires goodwill acquired in a business combination to be recognised as an asset and amortised over its useful life. As to that useful life, FRS 102 mandates that goodwill shall have a finite useful life, and further, where the entity is unable to make a reliable estimate of the useful life of goodwill, the life shall not exceed five years. *[FRS 19.23].*

In contrast, FRS 10 provided a rebuttable presumption that the useful economic life was limited to periods of 20 years or less such that the useful life could be longer or indefinite. *[FRS 10.19]*. There was therefore the possibility of invoking a true and fair view override of the company law requirement that goodwill be amortised systematically over a finite period, where a preparer determined goodwill had an indefinite useful life. *[FRS 10.18]*. Where goodwill was amortised over a period exceeding 20 years or was not amortised at all, it was required to be reviewed for impairment on an annual basis. *[FRS 10.37]*.

The requirements of FRS 10 *[FRS 10.48-51]* as to negative goodwill have largely been continued by FRS 102.

2.1.13 Disclosures

The FRS 102 disclosure requirements are to be found in paragraphs 19.25 and 19.25A, and are discussed at 4 below. It sets out disclosures which are required individually for material business combinations in the period, and for those combinations not individually material, aggregate disclosures, if material.

Most disclosures relating to business combinations under previous UK GAAP arose from the requirements of FRS 6. FRS 6 set out an approach whereby disclosures were required for (1) individually material acquisitions; (2) acquisitions not individually material, but material in the aggregate; and (3) additional disclosures required for 'substantial acquisitions'. *[FRS 6.23]*.

Disclosures required for material acquisitions under FRS 6, but not carried into FRS 102, include *inter alia*:

- a table setting out, for each class of asset and liability of the acquired entity, the book values, as recorded in the acquired entity's books immediately before the acquisition and before any fair value adjustments; the fair value adjustments, analysed into revaluations, adjustments to achieve consistency of accounting policies and any other significant adjustments; and the fair values at the date of acquisition. *[FRS 6.25]*. (While this disclosure requirement is not included in FRS 102, Schedule 6 of the Regulations (which is applicable only to group accounts) continues to require such disclosure).

- provisions for reorganisation and restructuring costs that are included in the liabilities of the acquired entity, and related asset write-downs, made in the twelve months up to the date of acquisition were to be identified separately in the above table. *[FRS 6.26]*.

- where the fair values of the identifiable assets or liabilities, or the purchase consideration, could be determined only on a provisional basis at the end of the accounting period in which the acquisition took place, this was to be stated and the reasons given. Any subsequent material adjustments to such provisional fair values, with corresponding adjustments to goodwill, were to be disclosed and explained. *[FRS 6.27]*.

- for an individually material acquisition, the profit after taxation and minority interests of the acquired entity was to be given for the period from the beginning of the acquired entity's financial year to the date of acquisition giving the date on which the period began; and its previous financial year. *[FRS 6.35]*.

Additionally, for 'substantial acquisitions', FRS 6 required the following information to be disclosed in the financial statements of the combined entity for the period in which the acquisition took place:

- summarised profit and loss account and statement of total recognised gains and losses of the acquired entity for the period from the beginning of its financial year to the effective date of acquisition, giving the date on which this period began; this summarised profit and loss account should show as a minimum the turnover, operating profit and those exceptional items falling within paragraph 20 of FRS 3 – *Reporting financial performance*; profit before taxation; taxation and minority interests; and extraordinary items;

- the profit after tax and minority interests for the acquired entity's previous financial year. *[FRS 6.36]*.

This concept, and these disclosures, are not carried forward into FRS 102.

One other notable difference to previous UK GAAP is the explicit removal *[FRS 102.19.25]* of the standard disclosures where the combination effected during the period is a group reconstruction, instead replacing them by the requirement only to disclose the names of the combining entities, the method of accounting, and the date of the combination. *[FRS 102.19.33]*.

2.2 Key differences between Section 19 and IFRS

As discussed at 1 above, Section 19 is not based on the current version of IFRS 3. This means that there are a number of significant differences to the requirements of IFRS 3.

2.2.1 Method of accounting

IFRS 3 requires all business combinations within its scope to be accounted for using the purchase method – one difference to FRS 102 being that IFRS 3 excludes business combinations under common control from its scope, whereas FRS 102 specifically caters for group reconstructions. What constitutes a 'business combination under common control' under IFRS 3 however is wider than what meets the definition of a 'group reconstruction' under FRS 102 (see 5.1 below). Additionally, IFRS 3 makes no special proviso for business combinations involving public benefit entities.

Another difference is that the 'purchase method' required by FRS 102 is conceptually different from that in IFRS 3. FRS 102 is a 'cost-based' approach, whereby the cost of the business combination is allocated to the assets and liabilities acquired. In contrast, IFRS 3 adopts an approach whereby the various components of a business combination are measured at their acquisition-date fair values (albeit with a number of exceptions). This results in a number of the differences, which are identified below.

2.2.2 Definition of a business combination

The definition of a business combination in FRS 102 is 'the bringing together of separate entities or businesses into one reporting entity'. *[FRS 102.19.3]*.

IFRS 3 defines a business combination as 'a transaction or other event in which an acquirer obtains control of one or more businesses'. *[IFRS 3.Appendix A Defined Terms]*. It is notable that the Basis of Conclusions accompanying the revised IFRS 3 identifies that the definition is intended to include all transactions and events initially included in the scope of IFRS 3 (2004). *[IFRS 3.BC11]*.

As FRS 102's definition is identical to that in IFRS 3 (2004), it follows that there is not likely to be differences in practice as a result of the differing definitions of a 'business combination'. However, differences could arise as a result of the definition of a 'business'.

2.2.3   Definition of a business

Like FRS 102, IFRS 3 includes an explicit definition of what constitutes a business. However, by inclusion of the additional underlined words in the definition of a business – 'an integrated set of activities and assets that is capable of being conducted and managed ...' (emphasis added) *[IFRS 3.Appendix A Defined Terms]* – IFRS 3's definition of a business is wider than that in FRS 102. Additionally, while FRS 102 indicates that a business generally consists of three different elements – (1) inputs, (2) processes that are applied to those inputs, and (3) resulting outputs that are, or will be, used to generate revenues *[FRS 102 Appendix I]*; IFRS 3 further defines these elements, and clarifies that a business would only be required to have the first two of these three elements (i.e. inputs and processes), which together have the ability to create outputs. As such, although businesses usually have outputs, under IFRS 3 they would not need to be present for an integrated set of assets and activities to be a business. As such, it is possible certain acquisitions that would constitute a business under IFRS 3 would not do so under FRS 102.

2.2.4   Identifying an acquirer

FRS 102 includes as an explicit step in applying the purchase method 'identifying an acquirer', *[FRS 102.19.7(a)]*, and identifies that the acquirer is the combining entity that obtains control of the other combining entities or businesses. *[FRS 102.19.8]*. It further includes three indicators in assisting the identification of the acquirer:

- If the fair value of one of the combining entities is significantly greater than that of the other combining entity, the entity with the greater fair value is likely to be the acquirer.

- If the business combination is effected through an exchange of voting ordinary equity instruments for cash or other assets, the entity giving up cash or other assets is likely to be the acquirer.

- If the business combination results in the management of one of the combining entities being able to dominate the selection of the management team of the resulting combined entity, the entity whose management is able so to dominate is likely to be the acquirer. *[FRS 102.19.10]*.

IFRS 3 likewise explicitly requires that for each business combination, one of the combining entities be identified as the acquirer. *[IFRS 3.6]*. As for guidance on identifying that acquirer, IFRS 3 in the first instance refers to the guidance in IFRS 10 – *Consolidated Financial Statements* ('IFRS 10'); and failing a clear indication from IFRS 10, sets out specific factors in paragraphs B14-B18 of Appendix B *Application Guidance to IFRS 3*. *[IFRS 3.6]*.

While there is some level of consistency between the indicators contained in FRS 102.19.10 and IFRS 3.B14-B18 (for example, consideration of the relative fair value of the combining entities discussed at FRS 102.19.10(a) is similar, although not identical to, IFRS 3.B16 ('The acquirer is usually the combining entity whose relative size (measured in, for example, assets, revenues or profit) is significantly greater than that of the other combining entity or entities'. *[IFRS 3.B16]*, the guidance included in IFRS 3 is more extensive to that in FRS 102.19.10.

While FRS 102 gives rise to the possibility of a reverse acquisition by requiring identification of the acquirer, the accounting treatment for reverse acquisitions is not explicitly mentioned in FRS 102. In contrast, IFRS 3 defines a reverse acquisition, as well as containing specific requirements about reverse acquisition accounting and providing an example illustrating the accounting for a reverse acquisition. Refer to paragraphs B19-B27 of Appendix B *Application guidance* to IFRS 3 and paragraphs IE1-IE15 in the Illustrative Examples accompanying IFRS 3.

2.2.5   Cost of a business combination

2.2.5.A   Acquisition expenses

The inclusion of directly attributable costs within the cost of a business combination (effectively reflecting them within goodwill) under FRS 102 differs significantly from IFRS 3, whereby acquisition-related transaction costs are expensed.

2.2.5.B   Contingent consideration

FRS 102 requires recognition of any contingent consideration to be made at the acquisition date if the adjustment is 'probable and can be measured reliably'. *[FRS 102.19.12]*. If the potential adjustment is not recognised at the acquisition date, but subsequently becomes probable and can be measured reliably, the additional consideration is treated as an adjustment to the cost of the combination. *[FRS 102.19.13]*.

In contrast, under IFRS 3, the acquisition-date fair value of any contingent consideration is recognised as part of the consideration transferred in acquiring the business – regardless of whether payment is probable or can be measured reliably. Subsequent changes in the fair value of the liability for such contingent consideration are not accounted for as adjustments to the consideration transferred, but are reflected in profit or loss – they therefore do not result in changes to goodwill.

2.2.5.C   Contingent payments to employees or selling shareholders

FRS 102 provides no guidance on the accounting to be applied where further contingent amounts may be payable to vendors who become, or continue to be, key employees of the acquiree subsequent to the acquisition.

In contrast, IFRS 3 specifically identifies a transaction that remunerates employees or former owners of the acquiree for future services as not part of the cost of the business combination *[IFRS 3.52(b)]* and contains specific guidance to assist in the determination of whether arrangements for contingent payments to employees or selling shareholders are contingent consideration in the business combination or are separate transactions in paragraphs B54 and B55 of Appendix B *Application*

Guidance to IFRS 3. That guidance specifically states that 'a contingent consideration arrangement in which the payments are automatically forfeited if employment terminates is remuneration for post-combination services'. *[IFRS 3.B55(a)].*

Under FRS 102, we believe that an acquirer must make such a distinction and therefore identify contingent consideration that is, in substance, compensation for future services, and account for this separately from the cost of the combination. This is because FRS 102's *Concepts and Pervasive Principles*, as outlined in Section 2, includes as one of the qualitative characteristics of information in financial statements 'substance over form', requiring that 'transactions and other events and conditions should be accounted for and presented in accordance with their substance and not merely their legal form'. *[FRS 102.2.8].* Therefore, where a vendor is also a continuing employee, it is necessary to determine whether payments are made to them in their capacity as vendor or as employee.

2.2.6   *Measurement period*

Under FRS 102, provisional amounts in the first post-acquisition financial statements are to be finalised within twelve months after the acquisition date – and, where amendments are required to the provisional amounts recognised in the previous financial statements, they are to be made retrospectively by restating comparatives, i.e. by accounting for them as if they were made at the acquisition date. *[FRS 102.19.19].*

These FRS 102 provisions are broadly consistent with IFRS 3; one nuance being the measurement period afforded by IFRS 3 ends the sooner of: (i) one year from the acquisition date; and (ii) when the acquirer receives the information it was seeking about the facts and circumstances that existed as of the acquisition date or learns that it cannot obtain more information. *[IFRS 3.45].* This distinction may have little practical difference.

2.2.7   *Initial measurement of acquiree's assets, liabilities and contingent liabilities*

FRS 102 requires the acquiree's identifiable assets and liabilities and a provision for those contingent liabilities (that satisfy the recognition criteria in paragraph 19.20) to be measured at their fair values at the acquisition date (except for deferred tax, employee benefit arrangements and share-based payments, which are to be recognised and measured in accordance with the respective section of FRS 102). *[FRS 102.19.4].*

Other than in respect of deferred tax, employee benefit arrangements and share-based payments, Section 19 offers no guidance on how to derive this acquisition date fair value. Section 2 – *Concepts and Pervasive Principles* – states that 'fair value is the amount for which an asset could be exchanged, a liability settled, or an equity instrument granted could be exchanged, between knowledgeable, willing parties in an arm's length transaction. In the absence of any specific guidance provided in the relevant section of this FRS, where fair value measurement is permitted or required the guidance in paragraphs 11.27 to 11.32 shall be applied'. *[FRS 102.2.34(b)].*

IFRS 3 includes a similar requirement to measure the identifiable assets acquired and liabilities assumed at their acquisition-date fair values. *[IFRS 3.18].* Consistent with FRS 102, the standard provides specific recognition and measurement guidance for deferred tax, employee benefits and share-based payments. However, unlike FRS 102, IFRS 3 includes specific guidance on the recognition/measurement of indemnification assets, *[IFRS 3.27-28],* re-acquired rights, *[IFRS 3.29],* assets held for sale, *[IFRS 3.31],* operating leases and intangible assets. *[IFRS 3.B28-B40].* For the purpose of IFRS 3, the definition of 'fair value' is that in IFRS 13 – *Fair Value Measurement,* being 'the price that would be received to sell an asset or paid to transfer a liability in an orderly transaction between market participants at the measurement date under current market conditions'. *[IFRS 13.2].* It is explicitly an exit price. Where IFRS 3 requires assets and liabilities to be measured at fair value, the guidance in IFRS 13 would be applied.

2.2.8 *Recognition of intangible assets separate from goodwill*

Under FRS 102, an intangible asset acquired in a business combination shall be separately recognised so long as: (i) it is identifiable; and (ii) its fair value can be measured reliably.

As such, FRS 102 does not extend as far as IFRS 3, as a result of FRS 102's requirement for fair value to be capable of reliable measurement, and that intangible assets that arise from legal or contractual rights are not recognised if there is no history or evidence of exchange transactions for the same or similar assets, and otherwise estimating fair value would be dependent on immeasurable variables. Under IFRS 3, it is not necessary that the intangible asset be capable of reliable measurement in order for it to be recognised. Under IFRS, so long as an intangible asset meets either the separability or contractual-legal criterion in IFRS 3, a measure is assigned to it. *[IFRS 3.B31-B34].* Paragraphs IE16-IE44 in the Illustrative Examples accompanying IFRS 3 provides a large number of examples of identifiable intangible assets acquired in a business combination.

2.2.9 *Deferred tax*

FRS 102 provides that when the amount that can be deducted for tax for an asset (other than goodwill) that is recognised in a business combination is less (more) than the value at which it is recognised, a deferred tax liability (asset) shall be recognised for the additional tax that will be paid (avoided) in respect of that difference. Similarly, a deferred tax asset (liability) shall be recognised for the additional tax that will be avoided (paid) because of a difference between the value at which a liability is recognised and the amount that will be assessed for tax. The amount attributed to goodwill shall be adjusted by the amount of deferred tax recognised. *[FRS 102.29.11].*

The treatment under FRS 102 will be largely consistent with the requirements of IFRS.

2.2.10 *Step acquisitions*

FRS 102 provides that where a parent acquires control of a subsidiary in stages, the cost of the business combination is the aggregate of the fair values of the assets given, liabilities assumed, and equity instruments issued by the acquirer at the date

Chapter 15

of each transaction in the series, *[FRS 102.19.11A]*, whereas the 'normal' rules on allocating the cost of the business combination to the acquisition date fair value of the identifiable assets, liabilities and contingent liabilities apply. *[FRS 102.19.14]*.

This approach differs to the requirements under IFRS 3, whereby the acquirer remeasures any previously held equity investment in the acquiree immediately before obtaining control at its acquisition-date fair value and recognises any resulting gain or loss in profit or loss. *[IFRS 3.42]*. The acquisition-date fair value of the previously held equity investment is included in the computation of goodwill or gain on bargain purchase recognised under IFRS 3. *[IFRS 3.32, 34]*.

2.2.11   *Non-controlling interests in a business combination*

Section 9 identifies the initial measurement of any non-controlling interest as the non-controlling interest's share in the net amount of the identifiable assets, liabilities and contingent liabilities recognised and measured in accordance with Section 19 at the date of the original combination. *[FRS 102.9.13(d)]*.

This conflicts with IFRS 3 where, for those non-controlling interests that are present ownership interests and entitle their holders to a proportionate share of the entity's net assets in the event of liquidation, there is a choice to two methods in measuring non-controlling interests arising in a business combination:

- Option 1, to measure the non-controlling interest at its acquisition-date fair value; or
- Option 2, to measure the non-controlling interest at the proportionate share of the value of net identifiable assets acquired.

All other non-controlling interests (for example, preference shares not entitled to a *pro rata* share of net assets upon liquidation, equity component of convertible debt and other compound financial instruments, share warrants, etc.) are measured at their acquisition date fair value under IFRS 3. *[IFRS 3.19]*. FRS 102 is silent on the measurement of such components of non-controlling interests.

2.2.12   *Subsequent accounting for goodwill*

FRS 102 requires goodwill acquired in a business combination to be recognised as an asset and amortised over its useful life. As to that useful life, FRS 102 mandates that goodwill shall have a finite useful life, and further, where the entity is unable to make a reliable estimate of the useful life of goodwill, the life shall not exceed five years. *[FRS 102.19.23]*.

This treatment is in contrast to the IFRS 3 requirement that goodwill is not amortised, but instead subjected to (at least) annual impairment tests under IAS 36 – *Impairment of Assets*. FRS 102 requires, instead, a review for impairment indicators at each reporting date, with impairment tests performed only where indications of such impairment exist.

Where negative goodwill arises, FRS 102 requires the acquirer to reassess the identification and measurement of the acquiree's identifiable assets, liabilities and contingent liabilities and the measurement of the cost of the combination. *[FRS 102.24(a)]*. Having undertaken that reassessment, the standard then requires that any excess remaining after that reassessment be recognised and separately disclosed on the face of the statement of financial position on the acquisition date, immediately below goodwill, and followed by a subtotal of the net amount of goodwill and the excess.

This treatment remains in contrast to IFRS 3 whereby any excess of the acquirer's interest in the net fair value of the acquiree's identifiable assets, liabilities and contingent liabilities over cost is recognised by the acquirer immediately in profit or loss. *[IFRS 3.34].*

2.2.13 Disclosures

The FRS 102 disclosure requirements are considerably less extensive that those under IFRS 3; for example, IFRS 3 requires specific disclosures in respect of the following areas that are not included in FRS 102: *[IFRS 3.B64]*

- the primary reasons for the business combination and a description of how the acquirer obtained control of the acquiree;
- a qualitative description of the factors that make up the goodwill recognised;
- contingent consideration and indemnification assets;
- acquired receivables;
- the total amount of goodwill that is expected to be deductible for tax purposes;
- transactions recognised separately from the business combination;
- acquisition-related costs;
- bargain purchases;
- non-controlling interests;
- business combinations in stages;
- revenue and profit of the combined entity as though the acquisition date of all business combinations had been at the beginning of the year;
- provisional amounts and measurement period adjustments. *[IFRS 3.B67].*

3 REQUIREMENTS OF SECTION 19 FOR BUSINESS COMBINATIONS AND GOODWILL

A business combination is defined by FRS 102 as 'the bringing together of separate entities or businesses into one reporting entity' *[FRS 102.19.3, FRS 102 Appendix I].* This applies not only when an entity becomes a subsidiary of another, but also when an entity purchases (or combines with) an unincorporated business, for example, through the acquisition of the trade and net assets, including any goodwill, of another entity.

3.1 Objective and scope of Section 19

Section 19 of FRS 102 has as its objective the provision of 'guidance on identifying the acquirer, measuring the cost of the business combination, and allocating that cost to the assets acquired and liabilities and provisions for contingent liabilities assumed. It also addresses accounting for goodwill both at the time of a business combination and subsequently'. *[FRS 102.19.1].*

Chapter 15

3.1.1   Scope

Section 19 deals with all business combinations except:

- the formation of a joint venture; and
- the acquisition of a group of assets that does not constitute a business. *[FRS 102.19.2].*

The first exception scopes out the requirements of Section 19 for the accounting for the formation of a joint venture. In such circumstances, in the financial statements of the newly formed joint venture, the entity would need to determine an appropriate accounting policy to account for the transaction.

While worded similarly to an original exception in IFRS 3, *[IFRS 3.2(a)]*, that exception under IFRS was clarified as part of the *Annual Improvements to IFRSs 2011-2013 Cycle* to make it clear that the exception applies only to the accounting for the formation of a joint venture in the financial statements of the joint arrangement itself. While FRS 102 contains no such clarification, we consider the exception does not apply to the accounting for the formation of the joint venture in the consolidated financial statements of the venturers. That said, Section 19 does not apply directly as the venturers have not obtained control of the joint venture. However, on acquisition of an investment in a jointly-controlled entity in such circumstances, the initial recognition requirements of the equity method, as described in FRS 102.14.8, applies in terms of accounting for any difference between the cost of acquisition and the investor's share of the fair values of the net identifiable assets of the jointly-controlled entity in accordance with FRS 102.19.22 to 24.

The second exception is a truism in that Section 19 only applies to business combinations – so if the group of assets is not a business, Section 19 does not apply, nor does it specify how to account for a group of assets. The initial recognition and measurement of the assets acquired will depend on the nature of the particular assets and the requirements of FRS 102 for such assets. For many assets such as property, plant and equipment, intangible assets or inventories these are required to be measured initially at cost. Therefore it will be necessary to make some apportionment of the overall cost of the group of assets to the individual assets.

One possible approach to making such an allocation would be to apply the guidance in IFRS 3 for the acquisition of a group of assets that is not a business, which is to allocate the cost to the individual identifiable assets and liabilities on the basis of their relative fair values at the date of purchase, *[IFRS 3.2(b)]*, but other approaches may be appropriate. Whatever approach is used to allocate the overall cost to the individual assets or liabilities, no goodwill arises as goodwill is only recognised in a business combination.

It may be difficult to determine whether or not an acquired group of assets constitutes a business (see 3.2.1 below for the definition of a business and a business combination), yet this decision can have a considerable impact on an entity's reported results and the presentation of its financial statements; accounting for a business combination differs considerably from accounting for an asset acquisition in a number of important respects:

- goodwill (positive or negative) only arises on business combinations;

- assets acquired and liabilities assumed are generally accounted for at fair value in a business combination, while they are assigned a carrying amount based on an allocation of the overall cost in an asset acquisition;

- while deferred tax assets and liabilities must be recognised if the transaction is a business combination, they are not recognised if it is an asset acquisition; and

- disclosures are more onerous for business combinations than for asset acquisitions.

3.1.2   Application of the purchase method

FRS 102 requires all business combinations to be accounted for using the purchase method, except for:

- group reconstructions which may be accounted for by using the merger accounting method; and

- public benefit entity combinations that are in substance a gift or that are a merger which shall be accounted for in accordance with Section 34 – *Specialised Activities*. *[FRS 102.19.6(b)]*.

The accounting for group reconstructions under FRS 102 is discussed at 5 below.

Public benefit entity combinations are discussed in Chapter 29 at 6.

3.2   Identifying a business combination

3.2.1   Business combination defined

FRS 102 defines a business combination as 'the bringing together of separate entities or businesses into one reporting entity'. *[FRS 102.19.3]*. The standard then goes on to say that 'the result of nearly all business combinations is that one entity, the acquirer, obtains control of one or more other businesses, the acquiree'. *[FRS 102.19.3]*.

For this purpose, FRS 102 defines a 'business' as 'an integrated set of activities and assets conducted and managed for the purpose of providing:

- a return to investors; or

- lower costs or other economic benefits directly and proportionately to policyholders or participants'. *[FRS 102 Appendix I]*.

It goes on to say that 'a business generally consists of inputs, processes applied to those inputs, and resulting outputs that are, or will be, used to generate revenues. If goodwill is present in a transferred set of activities and assets, the transferred set shall be presumed to be a business.' *[FRS 102 Appendix I]*.

Chapter 15

3.2.2   *Inputs, processes and outputs*

FRS 102 does not discuss further the meaning or interaction of inputs, processes or outputs. However, the application guidance to IFRS 3 expands upon them as follows:

- Input: Any economic resource that creates, or has the ability to create, outputs when one or more processes are applied to it. Examples include non-current assets (including intangible assets or rights to use non-current assets), intellectual property, the ability to obtain access to necessary materials or rights and employees.

- Process: Any system, standard, protocol, convention or rule is a process if, when applied to an input or inputs, it either creates or has the ability to create outputs. Examples include strategic management processes, operational processes and resource management processes. These processes typically are documented, but an organised workforce having the necessary skills and experience following rules and conventions may provide the necessary processes that are capable of being applied to inputs to create outputs. Accounting, billing, payroll and other administrative systems typically are not processes used to create outputs so their presence or exclusion generally will not affect whether an acquired set of activities and assets is considered a business.

- Output: The result of inputs and processes applied to those inputs that provide or have the ability to provide a return in the form of dividends, lower costs or other economic benefits directly to investors or other owners, members or participants. *[IFRS 3.B.7].*

As discussed at 3.1.1 above, the acquisition of a group of assets – notwithstanding that they may be held within a separate entity or entities – which do not constitute a business, is excluded from the scope of Section 19. In some situations, there may be difficulties in determining whether or not an acquisition of a group of assets constitutes a business, and judgement will need to be exercised based on the particular circumstances.

The following are examples from extractive and real estate industries that illustrate the issues.

Example 15.1:   Extractive industries – definition of a business (1)

E&P Co A (an oil and gas exploration and production company) acquires a mineral interest from E&P Co B, on which it intends to perform exploration activities to determine if reserves exist. The mineral interest is an unproven property and there have been no exploration activities performed on the property.

Inputs – mineral interest

Processes – none

Output – none

Conclusion

In this scenario, we do not believe E&P Co A acquired a business. While E&P Co A acquired an input (mineral interest), it did not acquire any processes and there were no outputs.

Example 15.2:   Extractive industries – definition of a business (2)

E&P Co A acquires a property similar to that in Example 15.1 above, except that oil and gas production activities are in place. The target's employees are not part of the transferred set. E&P Co A will take over the operations by using its own employees.

Inputs – oil and gas reserves

Processes – operational processes associated with oil and gas production

Output – revenues from oil and gas production

Conclusion

In this scenario, we generally consider that E&P Co A acquired a business. The acquired set has all three components of a business (inputs, processes and outputs) and is providing a return to its owners. Although the employees are not being transferred to the acquirer, E&P Co A is able to produce outputs by:

- supplying the employees necessary to continue production; and
- integrating the business with its own operations while continuing to produce outputs.

Example 15.3:   Real estate – definition of a business (1)

Company A acquires land and a vacant building from Company B. No processes, other assets or employees (for example, leases and other contracts, maintenance or security personnel, or a leasing office) are acquired in the transaction.

Inputs – land and vacant building

Processes – none

Output – none

Conclusion

In this scenario, we do not believe Company A acquired a business. While Company A acquired inputs (land and a vacant building), it did not acquire any processes and there were no outputs.

Example 15.4:   Real estate – definition of a business (2)

Company A acquires an operating hotel, the hotel's employees, the franchise agreement, inventory, reservations system and all 'back office' operations.

Inputs – non-current assets, franchise agreement and employees

Processes – operational and resource management processes associated with operating the hotel

Output – revenues from operating the hotel

Conclusion

In this scenario, we generally believe Company A acquired a business. The acquired set has all three components of a business (inputs, processes and outputs) and is providing a return to its owners.

There is a rebuttable presumption that if goodwill arises on the acquisition, the acquisition is a business. *[FRS 102 Appendix I].* If, for example, the total fair value of an acquired set of activities and assets is £15 million and the fair value of the net identifiable assets is only £10 million, the existence of value in excess of the fair value of identifiable assets (i.e. goodwill) creates a presumption that the acquired set is a business. However, care should be exercised to ensure that all of the identifiable net assets have been identified and measured appropriately. While the absence of goodwill may be an indicator that the acquired activities and assets do not represent a business, it is not presumptive.

3.2.3   *Differing combination structures*

FRS 102 indicates that a business combination may be structured in a variety of ways for legal, taxation or other reasons. It may involve:

- the purchase by an entity of the equity of another entity;
- the purchase of all the net assets of another entity;
- the assumption of the liabilities of another entity; or
- the purchase of some of the net assets of another entity that together form one or more businesses. *[FRS 102.19.4].*

It may be effected by the issue of equity instruments, the transfer of cash, cash equivalents or other assets, or a mixture of these. The transaction may be between the shareholders of the combining entities or between one entity and the shareholders of another entity. It may involve the establishment of a new entity to control the combining entities or net assets transferred, or the restructuring of one or more of the combining entities. *[FRS 102.19.5].* Whatever the legal structure, if it is a 'business combination' then the requirements of Section 19 of FRS 102 apply (unless it is specifically excluded by the section).

As indicated above, a business combination may involve the purchase of the net assets, including any goodwill, of another entity rather than the purchase of the equity of the other entity. Such a combination does not result in a parent-subsidiary relationship. Nevertheless, the acquirer (even if it is a single entity), will account for such a business combination in its individual or separate financial statements and consequently in any consolidated financial statements.

3.3   The purchase method

All business combinations (apart from those excluded from the scope of Section 19 of FRS 102, and group reconstructions which may be accounted for by using the merger accounting method, and certain public benefit entity combinations) are accounted for by applying the purchase method. *[FRS 102.19.6].*

As discussed at 1.1 above, the purchase method views a business combination from the perspective of the combining entity that is identified as the acquirer. The acquirer recognises the assets acquired and liabilities and contingent liabilities assumed, including those not previously recognised by the acquiree.

Applying the purchase method involves the following steps: *[FRS 102.19.7]*

- identifying an acquirer (3.4 below);
- measuring the cost of the business combination (3.5 below); and
- allocating, at the acquisition date, the cost of the business combination to the assets acquired and liabilities and provisions for contingent liabilities assumed (3.6 below).

While not identified by FRS 102 as an explicit step, the determination of the acquisition date is critical to accounting for a business combination, as it is both the date from which the results of the acquiree are incorporated into the financial statements of the acquirer, and the date on which the cost of the business combination is allocated to the fair values of the assets acquired and liabilities and provisions for contingent liabilities assumed. The acquisition date is the date on which the acquirer obtains control of the acquiree. *[FRS 102.19.3]*.

The acquirer's statement of comprehensive income incorporates the acquiree's profits or losses after the acquisition date by including the acquiree's income and expenses based on the cost of the business combination to the acquirer. For example, depreciation expense included after the acquisition date in the acquirer's statement of comprehensive income that relates to the acquiree's depreciable assets shall be based on the fair values of those depreciable assets at the acquisition date, i.e. their cost to the acquirer. *[FRS 102.19.16]*.

Application of the purchase method starts from the acquisition date, which is the date on which the acquirer obtains control of the acquiree. Because control is the power to govern the financial and operating policies of an entity or business so as to obtain benefits from its activities, it is not necessary for a transaction to be closed or finalised at law before the acquirer obtains control. All pertinent facts and circumstances surrounding a business combination shall be considered in assessing when the acquirer has obtained control. *[FRS 102.19.17]*.

No further guidance is given in FRS 102 as to how to determine the acquisition date, but it is clearly a matter of fact. It cannot be artificially backdated or otherwise altered, for example, by the inclusion of terms in the agreement indicating that acquisition is to be effective as of an earlier date, with the acquirer being entitled to profits arising after that date, even if the purchase price is based on the net asset position of the acquiree at that date.

The date control is obtained will be dependent on a number of factors, including whether the acquisition arises from a public offer or a private deal, is subject to approval by other parties, or is effected by the issue of shares.

For an acquisition by way of a public offer, the date of acquisition could be when the offer has become unconditional as a result of a sufficient number of acceptances being received or at the date that the offer closes. In a private deal, the date would generally be when an unconditional offer has been accepted by the vendors.

It can be seen from the above that one of the key factors is that the offer is 'unconditional'. Thus, where an offer is conditional on the approval of the acquiring entity's shareholders then until that approval has been received, it is unlikely that control will have been obtained. Where the offer is conditional upon receiving some form of regulatory approval, then it will depend on the nature of that approval. Where it is a substantive hurdle, such as obtaining the approval of a competition authority, it is unlikely that control could have been obtained prior to that approval. However, where the approval is merely a formality, or 'rubber-stamping' exercise, then this would not preclude control having been obtained at an earlier date.

Where the acquisition is effected by the issue of shares, then the date of control will generally be when the exchange of shares takes place.

However, as indicated above, whether control has been obtained by a certain date is a matter of fact, and all pertinent facts and circumstances surrounding a business combination need to be considered in assessing when the acquirer has obtained control.

The purchase method as outlined in Section 19 of FRS 102 corresponds with the description of the acquisition method in UK company law:

- the identifiable assets and liabilities of the undertaking acquired must be included in the consolidated balance sheet at their fair values as at the date of acquisition;

- the income and expenditure of the undertaking acquired must be brought into the group accounts only as from the date of the acquisition;

- there must be set off against the acquisition cost of the interest in the shares of the undertaking held by the parent company and its subsidiary undertakings the interest of the parent company and its subsidiary undertakings in the adjusted capital and reserves of the undertaking acquired; and

- the resulting amount if positive must be treated as goodwill, and if negative as a negative consolidation difference. *[6 Sch 9].*

3.4   Identifying an acquirer

Section 19 of FRS 102 requires that an acquirer shall be identified for all business combinations accounted for by applying the purchase method. The acquirer is the combining entity that obtains control of the other combining entities or businesses. *[FRS 102.19.8].*

Control is defined as 'the power to govern the financial and operating policies of an entity or business so as to obtain benefits from its activities'. *[FRS 102.19.9].* Section 19 cross-references to Section 9 for a description of control of one entity by another in the context of identification of subsidiaries for the purposes of consolidation:

'Control is presumed to exist when the parent owns, directly or indirectly through subsidiaries, more than half of the voting power of an entity. That presumption may be overcome in exceptional circumstances if it can be clearly demonstrated that such ownership does not constitute control. Control also exists when the parent owns half or less of the voting power of an entity but it has:

(a)   power over more than half of the voting rights by virtue of an agreement with other investors; or

(b)   power to govern the financial and operating policies of the entity under a statute or an agreement; or

(c)   power to appoint or remove the majority of the members of the board of directors or equivalent governing body and control of the entity is by that board or body; or

(d)   power to cast the majority of votes at meetings of the board of directors or equivalent governing body and control of the entity is by that board or body'. *[FRS 102.9.5].*

Additionally, Section 9 identifies that control 'can also be achieved by having options or convertible instruments that are currently exercisable or by having an agent with the ability to direct the activities for the benefit of the controlling entity' *[FRS 102.9.6],* and 'can also exist when the parent has the power to exercise, or actually exercises, dominant influence or control over the undertaking or it and the undertaking are managed on a unified basis'. *[FRS 102.9.6A]*.

The requirements of Section 9 relating to 'control' are discussed in Chapter 6 at 3.2.

Section 19 of FRS 102 notes that although it may sometimes be difficult to identify an acquirer, there are usually indicators that one exists. For example:

- If the fair value of one of the combining entities is significantly greater than that of the other combining entity, the entity with the greater fair value is likely to be the acquirer.

- If the business combination is effected through an exchange of voting ordinary equity instruments for cash or other assets, the entity giving up cash or other assets is likely to be the acquirer.

- If the business combination results in the management of one of the combining entities being able to dominate the selection of the management team of the resulting combined entity, the entity whose management is able so to dominate is likely to be the acquirer. *[FRS 102.19.10]*.

Determination of the acquirer may require significant judgement and consideration of the pertinent facts and circumstances must be considered.

While not explicitly mentioned in FRS 102, the standard implicitly recognises that in some business combinations, commonly referred to as reverse acquisitions, the acquirer is the entity whose equity interests have been acquired and the issuing entity is the acquiree. This might be the case when, for example, a private entity arranges to have itself 'acquired' by a small public entity as a means of obtaining a stock exchange listing and, as part of the agreement, the directors of the public entity resign and are replaced with directors appointed by the private entity and its former owners. Although legally the issuing public entity is regarded as the parent and the private entity is regarded as the subsidiary, the legal subsidiary is the acquirer if it has the power to govern the financial and operating policies of the legal parent so as to obtain benefits from its activities. See 3.9 below for further discussion on reverse acquisitions.

Occasionally, a new entity is formed to issue equity instruments to effect a business combination between, for example, two other entities. FRS 102 does not explicitly deal with such a situation, but it is one that is dealt with in IFRS 3 and under previous UK GAAP in FRS 6. In such a situation, IFRS 3 requires that one of the combining entities that existed before the combination be identified as the acquirer. *[IFRS 3.B18]*. Similarly, FRS 6 required that where the combination of the entities other than the new parent would have been an acquisition, one of the combining entities would be identified as having the role of the acquirer. This acquirer and the new parent company would be first combined by using merger accounting, and the other entities would be treated as having been acquired by this combined company. *[FRS 6.14]*. While FRS 102 contains no such explicit stipulation, we believe that such an approach should be adopted in such a situation; the substance of the transaction is that one of the two other entities has acquired the other, but they have been brought together legally under the new entity rather than one of these entities acquiring the other. The new entity, itself, has little substance other than as a vehicle to hold the shares in the combining entities, and may have been structured in this way for legal, taxation or other reasons. Therefore, in such a transaction, the combination between the new entity and the identified acquirer is effectively the same as if a new entity had been inserted above an existing entity. Such a 'group reconstruction' would be accounted for under merger accounting (see 5.3 below).

However, that is not to say that a new entity that is established to effect a business combination cannot be identified as the acquirer. For example, there may be situations where a new entity is established and used on behalf of a group of investors or another entity to acquire a controlling interest in a 'target entity' in an arm's length transaction.

Example 15.5:   Business combination effected by a Newco for cash consideration

Entity A intends to acquire the voting shares (and therefore obtain control) of Target Entity. Entity A incorporates Newco and uses this entity to effect the business combination. Entity A provides a loan at commercial interest rates to Newco. The loan funds are used by Newco to acquire 100% of the voting shares of Target Entity in an arm's length transaction. The group structure post-transaction is as follows:

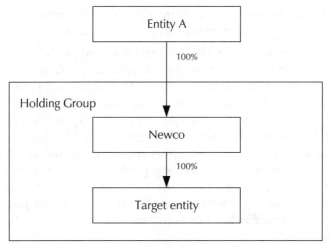

Newco is required to prepare consolidated financial statements for the Holding Group (the reporting entity). (In most situations like this, Newco would be exempt from preparing consolidated financial statements – see Chapter 6).

The acquirer is the entity that obtains control of the acquiree. Whenever a new entity is formed to effect a business combination other than through the issue of shares, it is appropriate to consider whether Newco is an extension of one of the transacting parties. If it is an extension of the transacting party (or parties) that ultimately gain control of the other combining entities, Newco is the acquirer.

In this situation, Entity A has obtained control of Target Entity in an arm's length transaction, using Newco to effect the acquisition. The transaction has resulted in a change in control of Target Entity and Newco is in effect an extension of Entity A acting at its direction to obtain control for Entity A. Accordingly, Newco would be identified as the acquirer at the Holding Group level.

If, rather than Entity A establishing Newco, a group of investors had established it as the acquiring vehicle through which they obtained control of Target Entity then, we believe, Newco would be regarded as the acquirer since it is an extension of the group of investors.

3.5   Measuring the cost of the business combination

Having identified the acquirer, the next step is for the acquirer to measure the cost of the business combination. Section 19 of FRS 102 requires this to be the aggregate of:

- the fair values, at the acquisition date, of assets given, liabilities incurred or assumed, and equity instruments issued by the acquirer, in exchange for control of the acquiree; plus

- any costs directly attributable to the business combination. *[FRS 102.19.11].*

In a step acquisition, i.e. where control is achieved in a series of transactions, the cost of the business combination is the aggregate of the fair values of the assets given, liabilities assumed, and equity instruments issued by the acquirer at the date of each transaction in the series. *[FRS 102.19.11A].* The accounting treatment for step acquisitions is discussed further at 3.10 below.

Assets given and liabilities incurred or assumed by the acquirer in exchange for control of the acquirer are required to be measured at their fair values at the acquisition date.

Fair value is defined as 'the amount for which an asset could be exchanged, a liability settled, between knowledgeable, willing parties in an arm's length transaction'. *[FRS 102 Appendix I].* Section 19 gives no guidance as to how such fair values might be arrived at. However, where the assets given as consideration or the liabilities incurred or assumed by the acquirer are financial assets or financial liabilities, paragraphs 11.27 to 11.32 of FRS 102 should be used in determining fair value (see Chapter 8 at 4.4.5).

Where equity instruments issued by the acquirer are given as consideration, again Section 19 of FRS 102 provides no further guidance to determine the fair value of such equity instruments. In such circumstances, the acquirer should have reference to paragraphs 11.27 to 11.32 as it relates to the measurement of investments in equity instruments. (Note, while 'merger relief' under the Companies Act 2006 includes relief from recognising share premium where certain conditions are met, this impacts the accounting considerations for capital and reserves of the issuing entity only, and is not relevant for the purposes of measuring the cost of the combination in connection with application of the purchase method – see 5.3 below for discussion on merger relief and group reconstruction relief).

3.5.1   Costs directly attributable to the combination

The cost of a business combination includes any costs directly attributable to the combination, such as professional fees paid to accountants, legal advisers, valuers and other consultants to effect the combination. General administrative costs, including the costs of maintaining an acquisitions department, and other costs that cannot be directly attributed to the particular combination being accounted for are not included in the cost of the combination: they are recognised as an expense when incurred. While not explicitly stated, it would appear that it is only incremental costs that should be included.

It may be that an entity engages another party to investigate or assist in identifying a potential target. Whether any fee payable to such party can be included as part of the cost of the business combination will depend on whether the work performed can be regarded as directly attributable to that particular business combination. Where the fee is payable only if the combination takes place then it should be included as part of the cost.

Chapter 15

Transaction costs, i.e. incremental costs that are directly attributable to the issue of equity instruments or financial liabilities, are not included as costs of the business combination, but are included as issue costs of those instruments. They therefore do not affect the measurement of goodwill in the business combination.

Where professional advisors provide advice on all aspects of the business combination, including the arranging and issuing of financial liabilities and/or issuing equity instruments, it will be necessary for some allocation of the fees payable to be made, possibly by obtaining a breakdown from the relevant advisor.

It may be that an entity at its balance sheet date is in the process of acquiring another business and has incurred costs that are considered to be directly attributable to that expected business combination. At the balance sheet date, the entity has not yet obtained control over the business. In this situation how should the costs be accounted for? One view would be that the costs have to be expensed since at the balance sheet date there has been no business combination. However, we believe that since directly attributable costs are to be included in the cost of a business combination, then the costs should be carried forward as an asset from the date that is considered probable that the business combination will be completed. Any costs incurred prior to the date that it is considered probable that the business combination will be completed should be expensed, and remain written off regardless of whether the acquisition takes place; they cannot be reinstated and capitalised at a later date. In the subsequent period, when the business combination is completed, the costs carried forward will be reclassified as part of the cost of the business combination (and therefore into goodwill). If in the subsequent period it is no longer considered probable that the business combination will be completed, then the costs initially recognised as an asset will be expensed to the income statement.

3.5.2   Adjustments to the cost of a business combination contingent on future events ('Contingent consideration')

FRS 102 recognises that the terms of a business combination agreement may provide for an adjustment to the cost of the combination contingent on future events, and requires that, in such cases, the acquirer includes an estimate of that adjustment in the cost of the combination at the acquisition date if the adjustment is probable (more likely than not) and can be measured reliably. *[FRS 102.19.12]*.

Such future events might relate to a specified level of profit being maintained or achieved in future periods. A provision for an adjustment is more likely to be made in those situations where the contingent consideration is based on the acquiree maintaining a level of profits which it is currently earning (either for a particular period or as an average over a set period) or achieving profits which it is currently budgeting.

If the potential adjustment is not recognised at the acquisition date but subsequently becomes probable and can be measured reliably, the additional consideration shall be treated as an adjustment to the cost of the combination. *[FRS 102.19.13]*. Any subsequent adjustments in respect of such contingent consideration will consequently be reflected in the carrying amount of goodwill. However, if an impairment loss has already been recognised in respect of the goodwill (see Chapter 22 at 5), this is likely to require a further impairment loss to be recognised.

The standard does not explicitly address what amount should be recognised as an adjustment to the cost of a business combination where it has become probable after the date of acquisition, nor what to do in situations where the potential adjustment was recognised at the acquisition date, but subsequently, that estimate is revised. The previous version of IFRS 3 (on which the requirements of FRS 102 are based) specified that if the future events do not occur or the estimate needs to be revised, the cost of the business combination shall be adjusted accordingly. *[IFRS 3(2004).33].* This treatment would appear appropriate under FRS 102 also.

The following example illustrates how we believe such adjustments for contingent consideration should be subsequently recognised.

Example 15.6:   Contingent consideration subsequently recognised

Entity A acquires Entity B on 31 December 2015 where consideration of £8 million is contingent on meeting a profit target by 31 December 2018.

At the date of acquisition it is not considered probable that the acquiree will meet the profit target. Accordingly, no amount is recognised as part of the cost of the business combination in the financial statements for 31 December 2015. However, at 31 December 2016 it is considered probable that Entity B will meet the profit target.

Assuming a discount rate of 8% as at the date of acquisition (31 December 2015) and a discount rate of 7% as at the date of probability of meeting conditions (31 December 2016) the relevant present values are as follows:

	PV at 8% £	PV at 7% £
31 December 2015	6,350,658	6,530,383
Interest for 2016	508,053	457,127
31 December 2016	6,858,711	6,987,510
Interest for 2017	548,696	489,126
31 December 2017	7,407,407	7,476,636
Interest for 2018	592,593	523,364
31 December 2018	8,000,000	8,000,000

What amount should be recognised as an adjustment to the cost of the combination at 31 December 2016 and how should it be reflected in the financial statements?

One view is that the adjustment should be calculated retrospectively, as if it had occurred as at the date of acquisition. Accordingly, the cost of the investment and goodwill would be adjusted by £6,350,658 (being the present value at the date of acquisition), with interest charged since the date of acquisition of £508,053.

However, we do not consider this view appropriate. The adjustment is due to a change in probability which is generally considered to be a change in estimate. Changes in estimates are recognised prospectively from the date of change. Therefore at the date that the contingent event becomes probable it should be recognised as a change in estimate and measured at that date, taking into account the period in which the expected payment will be made. It is, therefore, discounted at the rate determined at the date that the contingent consideration is recognised to reflect the fair value of the consideration expected to be given. Accordingly, an adjustment of £6,987,510 to the purchase price and therefore goodwill is recognised at 31 December 2016. The unwinding of the discount will be reflected in the income statement in 2017 and 2018. However, the resulting liability should continue to be reassessed at each reporting date thereafter for changes in estimated cash flows, including changes in discount rates, and any necessary adjustment made to the cost of the combination (and therefore goodwill).

Chapter 15

3.5.3   *Distinguishing 'contingent consideration' from other arrangements*

Other than noting that the cost of a business combination are those assets given, liabilities incurred or assumed, and equity instruments issued 'in exchange for control of the acquiree', *[FRS 102.19.11]*, FRS 102 provides no further guidance in determining whether adjustments to those assets given, liabilities incurred or assumed, and equity instruments issued are adjustments in connection with such exchange, or payments pertaining to other arrangements.

It is important to be able to identify those arrangements that represent contingent consideration and those that do not, as contingent consideration generally results in some form of adjustment to the accounting for a business combination. Notwithstanding the structuring of a purchase agreement, which may be for legal, tax, or other reasons, transactions and other events and conditions should be accounted for and presented in accordance with their substance and not merely their legal form. *[FRS 102.2.8].*

In our view, an arrangement that provides for additional payments to be made to the vendors of an acquiree should be accounted for as contingent consideration if the payment:

(a)   is made as consideration for the acquisition of a controlling interest in the acquiree (based on the substance of the arrangement); *and*

(b)   is contingent on future events that relate to the value of the acquiree (for example, an acquirer makes an additional cash payment if the acquiree achieves a profit target).

As above, it is necessary to consider the substance of the arrangement to determine whether additional payments are made as consideration of the acquisition of a controlling interest in the acquiree (criterion (a) above). Where a vendor has a continuing relationship with the acquirer (for example, an on-going customer or supplier relationship) it is necessary to determine in what capacity payments are made to the vendor. As there is no specific guidance, the following factors may be considered in evaluating the substance of the arrangement:

•   whether the additional payments are linked to the on-going relationship;

•   what are the reasons for the contingent payments; and

•   the nature of the formula for determining the contingent payments.

Criterion (b) above involves a consideration of whether the contingency relates to the value of the acquiree. If it is not clear what the contingency relates to, it will be necessary to consider its nature carefully in order to determine whether it should be accounted for as contingent consideration or separately from the business combination.

3.5.3.A   *Examples of 'contingent consideration' relating to the value of the acquiree*

Arrangements that provide for additional payments to be made to the vendors of an acquiree that are contingent on future events relating to the value of the acquiree, and thus will result in adjustments to the cost of the business combination, can take a number of forms. Examples would include:

- an additional payment of £1 million if the acquiree's profit in the year after acquisition exceeds £2 million;

- an additional payment of £1 million if a drug currently under development receives regulatory approval at a later date; and

- an additional payment of x% of actual EBITDA of the acquiree in the year after acquisition.

The first example of an 'earn-out' clause – whereby the acquirer agrees to pay additional amounts if the future earnings of the acquiree exceed specified amounts – is a typical example of contingent consideration relating to the value of the acquiree. The second example is where the contingency relates to a key business-related milestone that will have an impact on the value of the acquiree.

In both of these examples, there is uncertainty linked to a specific event as to whether an additional payment will be made (profit exceeding X or drug approval). In the third case, which also relates to the value of the acquiree, there will be an additional payment (on the assumption that a negative EBITDA is highly unlikely for that business) but there is uncertainty as to how much the payment will be.

In our view, FRS 102 requires an adjustment to the cost of the business combination in all of these situations. 'Future events' should include events that affect the amount of the payment and not just those that affect whether a specified payment is required or not. Thus, any consideration for a business combination where the amount or the timing is unknown with certainty is contingent consideration.

3.5.3.B   Example of an arrangement that is not 'contingent consideration'

The following example illustrates an arrangement where the additional payments that may be made to the vendors under the business combination agreement should not be accounted for as 'contingent consideration' under FRS 102.

Example 15.7:   Vendor retains a customer relationship with acquiree and is entitled to volume rebates on purchases it makes

Target is a subsidiary of Vendor Entity. Target provides goods and services to Vendor Entity that represent a significant portion of Target's business. Acquirer acquires 100% of the issued shares of Target. The purchase price is considered to represent the fair value of Target.

As part of the business combination agreement, Acquirer agrees to pay Vendor Entity a volume rebate for the next 5 years if Vendor Entity's purchases from Target exceed a specified amount in each of those years. The volume rebate offered is consistent with terms offered to other customers.

The volume rebate agreement with the vendor should not be accounted for as contingent consideration as it is not consideration for the acquisition of control in Target. The purchase price paid for the issued shares of Target is considered to represent fair value of Target; and Acquirer will only be required to pay the volume rebates in the event that Vendor Entity's purchases exceed a specified amount. The volume rebate arrangement is merely a means of securing Vendor Entity's custom for the next 5 years. Therefore, whilst the volume rebate arrangement arises by virtue of Acquirer having acquired Target, it does not represent additional consideration for the acquisition of a controlling interest in Target. Additionally, the contingency does not relate to the value of the business acquired because payment is contingent on Vendor Entity's future purchases exceeding a specified amount.

3.5.4   Contingent consideration relating to future services

A particular example of a situation where vendors may have a continuing relationship with the acquirer is where they become, or continue to be, key employees of the acquiree subsequent to the acquisition.

While IFRS 3 specifically identifies a transaction that remunerates employees or former owners of the acquiree for future services as not part of the cost of the business combination, *[IFRS 3.52(b)]*, FRS 102 does not distinguish between contingent consideration that, in substance, is additional purchase price and contingent consideration that, in substance, represents compensation for future services. However, consistent with the discussion above, we believe that an acquirer must make such a distinction and therefore identify contingent consideration that is, in substance, compensation for future services, and account for this separately from the cost of the combination. This is because FRS 102's *Concepts and Pervasive Principles*, as outlined in Section 2, includes as one of the qualitative characteristics of information in financial statements 'substance over form', requiring that 'transactions and other events and conditions should be accounted for and presented in accordance with their substance and not merely their legal form'. *[FRS 102.2.8]*. Therefore, where a vendor is also a continuing employee it is necessary to determine whether payments are made to them in their capacity as vendor or as employee.

If, for example, the consideration takes the form of share-based payments, it is necessary to determine how much of the share-based payment relates to the acquisition of control (which forms part of the cost of combination, accounted for under Section 19) and how much relates to the provision of future services (which is a post-combination operating expense accounted for under Section 26 of FRS 102). This would be the case if, for example, the vendor of an acquired entity receives a share-based payment for transferring control of the entity and for remaining in continuing employment.

In the absence of specific guidance, entities will need to apply judgment for evaluating the substance of the contingent consideration or determining an appropriate split. In making such a judgement, entities may consider the requirements and guidance in EU-adopted IFRS. *[FRS 102.10.6]*. IFRS 3 contains specific guidance to assist in the determination of whether arrangements for contingent payments to employees or selling shareholders are contingent consideration in the business combination or are separate transactions. This includes consideration of a number of indicators relating to continuing employment, duration of continuing employment, level of remuneration, incremental payments to employees, number of shares owned, linkage to valuation, formula for determining consideration, and other agreements and issues. *[IFRS 3.B54 and B55]*.

In making such an evaluation, all terms of the agreement have a critical role in this assessment, and the reasons for structuring the terms of the transaction in a particular way, and the identity of the initiator, should be understood. Nevertheless, in general, when the agreement includes employment conditions such that the payments are forfeited upon termination of employment, all or a portion of, the additional payments will generally be classified as employment compensation.

3.5.5   *Contingent transaction costs*

As indicated above, one of the examples of contingent consideration is where an additional payment is made if the acquiree's profits exceed a certain amount. In some business combinations an entity may agree to pay an adviser a fee for services relating to a business combination. If that fee is contingent on the acquiree achieving a specified profit hurdle can this be accounted for as contingent consideration arising on the business combination?

Example 15.8:   Contingent transaction costs

Entity A engages Entity X, which has specific technical knowledge, to assist in identifying an investment target. Entity X recommends that Entity A purchase Entity B. Entity A has agreed to pay Entity X a performance fee in the event that the return from its investment in Entity B exceeds a specified target. Can such a fee be regarded as 'contingent consideration' and therefore any reassessment of the fee payable accounted for as an adjustment to the cost of the business combination, and therefore adjusted against goodwill?

The contingent consideration requirements of FRS 102 only apply 'when a business combination agreement provides for an adjustment to the cost of the combination'. *[FRS 102.19.12]*. By its nature, a business combination agreement is an agreement between the vendor and the purchaser – it does not include agreements between the purchaser and third parties unconnected with the vendor. Thus, in our view, the payment to Entity X is not contingent consideration as it is not part of the agreement between the vendor and the purchaser. It arises from a separate agreement with the third party adviser.

Accordingly, whilst the payment to Entity X is part of the cost of the combination it must be measured as at the date of acquisition. Any subsequent remeasurement cannot be adjusted against the cost of the combination except where it is an adjustment upon completion of the initial accounting. However, an adjustment to the initial accounting must reflect conditions as they existed at the date of the combination and does not take into account subsequent events.

3.5.6   *Contingent consideration to be settled by equity instruments*

In some business combination agreements involving contingent consideration, it may be that additional consideration will not be settled by cash, but by shares.

Section 19 makes no explicit reference to such a situation. Section 11 – *Basic Financial Instruments* scopes out from its provisions 'Financial instruments that meet the definition of an entity's own equity', *[FRS 102.11.7(b)]*, while Section 12 – *Other Financial Instruments Issues* – and Section 22 – *Liabilities and Equity* – both scope out from their respective provisions 'Contracts for contingent consideration in a business combination' as it relates to the acquirer *[FRS 102.12.3(g), FRS 102.22.2(c)]*.

Section 26 – *Share-based Payment* applies its provisions to 'share-based payment transactions' *[FRS 102.26.1]*. Section 26 does not explicitly scope out from its provisions transactions in which an entity acquires goods as part of the net assets acquired in a business combination to which Section 19 applies nor equity instruments issued in a business combination in exchange for control of an acquiree. On this matter, IFRS 2 – *Share-based Payment* – explicitly scopes these out from its requirements. *[IFRS 2.5]*.

In our view, while not explicitly excluded, as the nature of a business combination is fundamentally different from a transaction to acquire goods or services, we do not consider the provisions of Section 26 should extend to equity instruments issued in a business combination.

Chapter 15

In practice, there is a wide variety of share-settled contingent consideration arrangements, but they are generally based on one of two models:

- Arrangements whereby shares are issued to a particular value based on certain conditions being met, e.g. if profits are £A then additional consideration of £M will be given, to be satisfied by shares based on the share price at date of issue;

- Arrangements whereby a particular number of shares are issued if certain conditions are met, e.g. if profits are £A then X shares will be issued, but if profits are £B then Y shares will be issued.

The issues that need to be considered in accounting for such arrangements are:

- If the consideration is recognised, should it be classified as a liability or as equity?

- How should the consideration be valued, both on initial recognition and if reassessed at a later date?

Example 15.9:   Share-settled contingent consideration (1)

Entity P acquires a 100% interest in Entity S on 31 December 2015. As part of the consideration arrangements, additional consideration will be payable on 1 January 2019, based on Entity S meeting certain profit targets over the 3 years ended 31 December 2018, as follows:

Profit target (average profits over 3 year period)	Additional consideration
£1m but less than £1.25m	£5m
£1.25m but less than £1.5m	£6m
£1.5m+	£7.5m

Any additional consideration will be satisfied by issuing the appropriate number of shares with a value equivalent to the additional consideration payable based on Entity P's share price at 1 January 2019.

At the date of acquisition, Entity P considers that it is probable that Entity S will meet the first profit target, but not the others.

How should Entity P classify the additional consideration in its financial statements for the year ended 31 December 2015, and what amount should be recognised in respect of it?

As discussed above, contracts for contingent consideration are specifically scoped out of Section 22, and we consider the provisions of Section 26 should not apply. Section 26 requires equity-settled share-based payment transactions to be reflected in equity. However, in our view the principles of Section 22 appear more relevant than those of Section 26 in determining the appropriate classification of such arrangements. On that basis, the contingent consideration in this situation is 'a contract that will or may be settled in the entity's own equity instruments and ... under which the entity is or may be obliged to deliver a variable number of the entity's own equity instruments', [FRS 102.22.3(b)], and therefore classification as a liability seems appropriate.

On the basis that the consideration is reflected as a liability then, as with contingent consideration payable in cash, the amount to be recognised at 31 December 2015 should be the present value of the £5m consideration expected to be payable on 1 January 2019.

If at 31 December 2016, Entity P considers that is it is probable that Entity S will now meet the second target, it should remeasure the liability at that date to the present value of the £6m that is now expected to be payable on 1 January 2019 with a corresponding adjustment to goodwill, having reflected the unwinding of the discount on the original £5m in the income statement.

In the above example, the arrangement was of the type where the shares issued to settle the consideration were equivalent to a particular value. However, what if the arrangement was of the type where a particular number of shares are to be issued to satisfy the consideration?

Example 15.10:   *Share-settled contingent consideration (2)*

Assume the same facts as in Example 15.9 above, except that the additional consideration will be payable as follows:

Profit target (average profits over 3 year period)	*Additional consideration*
£1m but less than £1.25m	100,000 shares
£1.25m but less than £1.5m	150,000 shares
£1.5m+	200,000 shares

How should Entity P classify the additional consideration in its financial statements for the year ended 31 December 2015, and what amount should be recognised in respect of it?

Although in our view the principles of Section 22 generally appear more relevant than those of Section 26 it is less clear whether the contingent consideration in this situation is the type of arrangement that ought to be classified as a liability.

Section 22 does not consider a contract to be equity where it 'will or may be settled in the entity's own equity instruments and ... under which the entity is or may be obliged to deliver a variable number of the entity's own equity instruments'. *[FRS 102.22.3(b)].* One view would be that on the basis that the number of shares to be issued does vary (depending on profit), such an arrangement constitutes a liability. However this analysis does not seem entirely satisfactory when applied to contingent consideration.

In determining the contingent consideration to be recorded, Entity P has to estimate what level of profit it anticipates Entity S will achieve and the relevant number of shares to be issued as a result. At 31 December 2015, Entity P has determined that it is probable that Entity S will meet the first target level, and as a result Entity P will issue 100,000 shares on 1 January 2019. Thereafter, if that level of profit is achieved there will no variation in the number of shares issued. Clearly Entity P may reassess the level of profit it expects to be achieved and revise the number of shares it expects to issue, but again once that determination is made if the revised estimate is achieved there is no variation in the number of shares to be issued.

Fundamentally, paragraph 3(b) of Section 22 appears to be addressing situations where shares to be issued vary such that they are equal in value to a fixed or variable, but determinable, monetary amount. Unlike Example 15.9 above, that is not the case in this situation once the expected outcome of the contingency has been determined. Accordingly, we believe that it is appropriate that the consideration is classified as an equity instrument.

On the basis that the consideration is reflected as equity, we believe that the amount recognised for the consideration should be based on the requirements of Section 19 in respect of equity instruments issued as consideration, i.e. at the fair value at the date of exchange (31 December 2015). However, in this situation the fair value of the 'equity instrument' at the date of exchange would need to take into account, for example, an allowance for any estimated dividends on the shares that will not be payable during the period until they are issued on 1 January 2019.

One other issue that arises in this situation is whether adjustments should be made to the consideration, and thus goodwill, to reflect subsequent changes in the fair value of the shares such that the consideration is ultimately measured at Entity P's share price at the date the shares are finally issued. Although the requirements for contingent consideration would generally require subsequent changes in the estimate of the consideration that will ultimately be given to be recognised, we do not believe that this should reflect such changes in fair value. Since the consideration is regarded as equity, changes in the fair value of an equity instrument are not recognised in the financial statements.

If at 31 December 2016, Entity P considers that is it is probable that Entity S will now meet the second target, then the financial statements at that date need to reflect that Entity P now expects to issue 150,000 shares. As discussed above, we do not believe that any change should be made to reflect changes in the value of Entity P's shares since the date of exchange (31 December 2015), and so the additional consideration of 50,000 shares should be valued using the same value per share as the original estimated consideration of 100,000 shares.

3.6   Allocating the cost of the business combination to the assets acquired and liabilities and contingent liabilities assumed

Having determined the cost of the business combination, the next stage is to allocate that cost to the assets acquired and liabilities and contingent liabilities assumed.

FRS 102 requires that the acquirer shall, at the acquisition date, allocate the cost of a business combination by recognising the acquiree's identifiable assets, liabilities and contingent liabilities that satisfy the recognition criteria in paragraph 19.20 of the standard at their fair values at that date, except for deferred tax assets and liabilities, employee benefit assets and liabilities and share-based payment arrangements. Any difference between the cost of the business combination and the acquirer's interest in the net amount of the identifiable assets, liabilities and provisions for contingent liabilities so recognised is accounted for as goodwill or negative goodwill (see 3.8 below). *[FRS 102.19.14]*.

The standard goes on to state that the acquirer shall recognise separately the acquiree's identifiable assets, liabilities and contingent liabilities at the acquisition date only if they satisfy the following criteria at that date:

*   in the case of an asset other than an intangible asset, it is probable that any associated future economic benefits will flow to the acquirer, and its fair value can be measured reliably.

*   in the case of a liability other than a contingent liability, it is probable that an outflow of resources will be required to settle the obligation, and its fair value can be measured reliably.

*   in the case of an intangible asset or a contingent liability, its fair value can be measured reliably. *[FRS 102.19.15]*.

The identifiable assets acquired and liabilities assumed must meet the definition of assets ('a resource controlled by the entity as a result of past events and from which future economic benefits are expected to flow to the entity') and liabilities ('a present obligation of the entity arising from past events, the settlement of which is expected to result in an outflow from the entity of resources embodying economic benefits') in FRS 102. *[FRS 102 Appendix I]*.

It can be seen that the recognition criteria for intangible assets and contingent liabilities are different from those of other assets and liabilities. In the case of intangible assets, FRS 102 reflects the view taken by the IASB in developing the version of IFRS 3 (on which FRS 102 is based) that the probability recognition criteria is always considered to be satisfied for such assets acquired in a business combination. Instead, the fair value of the intangible asset would factor in market expectations about the probability that the future economic benefits associated with the intangible asset will flow to the acquirer.

Similarly, in the case of contingent liabilities, FRS 102 reflects the view taken by the IASB in developing the version of IFRS 3 (on which FRS 102 is based) that, whilst not meeting the recognition criteria under the standard in the financial statements of the acquiree, the contingent liability has a fair value, which reflects market expectations about any uncertainty surrounding the possibility that an outflow of resources will be required to settle the possible or present obligation. As such, the standard provides that the allocation of the cost of the business combination includes the separate recognition of the acquiree's contingent liabilities, if its fair value can be reliably measured.

Since the recognition of this liability is not what would be required by Section 21 – *Provisions and Contingencies* – of FRS 102, Section 19 therefore includes requirements for the subsequent measurement of such liabilities. Accordingly, after their initial recognition, the acquirer measures contingent liabilities that are recognised separately in accordance with paragraph 19.15(c) at the higher of:

(a)   the amount that would be recognised in accordance with Section 21; and

(b)   the amount initially recognised less amounts previously recognised as revenue in accordance with Section 23 – *Revenue. [FRS 102.19.21].*

The implications of part (a) of this requirement are clear. Part (b) implies that if the provision turns out to be lower than the amount initially recognised on acquisition, it is not reduced until the contingency no longer exists; the reference to Section 23 presumably applies where the contingent liability related to a revenue-earning activity.

If the fair value of a contingent liability cannot be measured reliably, the acquirer discloses the information about that contingent liability as required by Section 21. *[FRS 102.19.20].*

It is notable that, notwithstanding the recognition of contingent liabilities in allocating the cost of the business combination, the recognition criteria make no reference to contingent assets of the acquiree.

3.6.1   *Acquiree's identifiable assets and liabilities*

3.6.1.A   *Acquiree's intangible assets*

As indicated at 3.6 above, the allocation of the cost of the business combination includes the separate recognition of the acquiree's intangible assets. This is irrespective of whether the asset had been recognised by the acquiree before the business combination.

Under FRS 102, an intangible asset acquired in a business combination shall be separately recognised so long as: (i) it is 'identifiable'; and (ii) its fair value can be measured reliably.

An intangible asset is 'identifiable' under FRS 102 when it is either: (a) 'separable' (capable of being separated or divided from the entity and sold, transferred, licensed, rented or exchanged, either individually or together with a related contract, asset or liability); or (b) it arises from contractual or other legal rights, regardless of whether those rights are transferable or separable from the entity or from other rights and obligations'. *[FRS 102.18.2].* FRS 102 states that an intangible asset acquired in a business combination is normally recognised as an asset because its fair value can be measured with sufficient reliability. However, an intangible asset is not recognised when it arises from legal or other contractual rights and there is no history or evidence of exchange transactions for the same or similar assets, and otherwise estimating fair value would be dependent on immeasurable variables. *[FRS 102.18.8].*

FRS 102 does not identify examples of intangible assets that may be recognised on accounting for business combinations. Other guidance that might be relevant to the identification of specific items includes that included in the version of IFRS 3 on which FRS 102 is based. These are considered below.

IFRS 3 (2004) gives guidance in an Illustrative Example that provides a large list of examples of items acquired in a business combination that meet the definition of an

Chapter 15

intangible asset and are therefore to be recognised separately from goodwill, provided that their fair values can be measured reliably, whilst noting that they are not intended to be an exhaustive list of items acquired in a business combination that meet the definition of an intangible asset.[1] A non-monetary asset without physical substance acquired in a business combination might meet the identifiability criterion for identification as an intangible asset but not be included in the guidance. The guidance designates the assets listed with symbols to identify those that meet part (a) of the definition and those that meet part (b) of the definition, whilst noting that those designated as meeting part (b) might also be separable. However, it emphasises that separability is not a necessary condition for an asset to meet the contractual-legal criterion.

The table below summarises the items included in the Illustrative Example that the IASB regard as meeting the definition of an intangible asset and are therefore to be recognised separately from goodwill, provided that their fair values can be measured reliably. Reference should be made to the Illustrative Example for any further explanation about some of these items.

Intangible assets arising from contractual or other legal rights (regardless of being separable)	*Other intangible assets that are separable*
Marketing-related • Trademarks, trade names, service marks, collective marks and certification marks • Internet domain names • Trade dress (unique colour, shape or package design) • Newspaper mastheads • Non-competition agreements	
Customer-related • Order or production backlogs • Customer contracts and the related customer relationships	• Customer lists • Non-contractual customer relationships
Artistic-related • Plays, operas and ballets • Books, magazines, newspapers and other literary works • Musical works such as compositions, song lyrics and advertising jingles • Pictures and photographs • Video and audio-visual material, including films, music videos and television programmes	

Contract-based • Licensing, royalty and standstill agreements • Advertising, construction, management, service or supply contracts • Lease agreements • Construction permits • Franchise agreements • Operating and broadcasting rights • Use rights such as drilling, water, air, mineral, timber-cutting and route authorities • Servicing contracts such as mortgage servicing contracts • Employment contracts that are beneficial contracts from the perspective of the employer because the pricing of those contracts is below their current market value	
Technology-based • Patented technology • Computer software and mask works • Trade secrets such as secret formulas, processes or recipes	• Unpatented technology • Databases

It can be seen from the table that customer relationships can potentially fall under either category. Where relationships are established with customers through contracts, those customer relationships arise from contractual rights, regardless of whether a contract exists, or there is any backlog of orders, at the date of acquisition. In such cases, it does not matter that the relationship is separable. It would only be if the relationship did not arise from a contract that the recognition depends on the separability criterion.

It is clear from the table above that the IASB envisages a wide range of items meeting the definition of an intangible asset, and therefore potentially being recognised separately from goodwill.

Whether any such intangible assets are recognised separately or not under FRS 102 will depend on whether their fair values can be measured reliably. As indicated above, when an intangible asset arises from legal or other contractual rights, it will not recognised if there is no history or evidence of exchange transactions for the same or similar assets, and otherwise estimating fair value would be dependent on immeasurable variables. *[FRS 102.18.8]*.

3.6.1.B   Reorganisation provisions

FRS 102 makes it clear that in accordance with paragraph 19.14, the acquirer recognises separately only the identifiable assets, liabilities and contingent liabilities of the acquiree that existed at the acquisition date and satisfy the recognition criteria in paragraph 15 discussed above. It therefore states that 'the acquirer shall recognise liabilities for terminating or reducing the activities of the acquiree as part of allocating the cost of the combination only to the extent that the acquiree has, at

Chapter 15

the acquisition date, an existing liability for restructuring recognised in accordance with Section 21 – *Provisions and Contingencies*'. *[FRS 102.19.18(a)].*

3.6.1.C   Future operating losses

The standard also makes it clear that the acquirer, when allocating the cost of the combination, shall not recognise liabilities for future losses or other costs expected to be incurred as a result of the business combination. *[FRS 102.19.18(b)].*

3.6.2   Exceptions to the general recognition and measurement rules

Section 19 makes three exceptions from the general requirements of recognising and measuring the acquiree's assets and liabilities at their acquisition-date fair values.

3.6.2.A   Deferred tax assets and liabilities

Section 19 defers to Section 29 – *Income Tax* – for guidance on the recognition and measurement of deferred tax assets and liabilities arising from the assets acquired and liabilities assumed. *[FRS 102.19.15A].* This is a necessary exception in that requiring the normal fair value treatment on acquisition would have resulted in immediate gains or losses being recognised when the deferred tax assets and liabilities were subsequently measured in accordance with Section 29, for example where fair values reflected the effects of discounting, but measurement under Section 29 would be on an undiscounted basis.

As discussed at 2.1.9 above, more deferred tax is likely to be recognised on attributed fair values in business combinations under FRS 102 than was the case under previous UK GAAP due to the requirement that deferred tax be recognised for the difference between the tax base and accounting base of assets and liabilities recognised in a business combination. *[FRS 102.29.11].*

Refer to Chapter 24 of this publication which addresses Section 29.

3.6.2.B   Employee benefit assets and liabilities

Similarly, an acquiree's employee benefit arrangements are exempted from the usual rules of Section 19, and instead recognition and measurement is to be in accordance with Section 28 – *Employee Benefits*. *[FRS 102.19.15B].*

Refer to Chapter 23 of this publication which addresses Section 28.

3.6.2.C   Share-based payment transactions

The acquirer recognises and measures a share-based payment in accordance with Section 26 – *Share-based Payment*. *[FRS 102.19.15C].*

Refer to Chapter 21 of this publication which addresses Section 26.

3.6.3   Determining the acquisition-date fair values

There is no specific guidance in Section 19 on the determination of the fair value of particular assets and liabilities, nor does it make explicit reference to the fair value guidance in paragraphs 11.27 to 11.32 of FRS 102. Nevertheless, in the Glossary to the standard, fair value is defined as 'the amount for which an asset could be exchanged, a liability settled, between knowledgeable, willing parties in an arm's length transaction. In the absence of any specific guidance provided in the relevant section of this FRS, the guidance in paragraphs 11.27 to 11.32 shall be used in determining fair value'. *[FRS 102 Appendix I].*

Refer to Chapter 8 at 4.4.5 of this publication which addresses the guidance in paragraphs 11.27 to 11.32.

Other guidance that might be relevant to the determination of the fair values of specific items includes that in other sections of FRS 102 and also guidance included in the version of IFRS 3 on which FRS 102 is based. *[IFRS 3(2004).B16].* These are considered below.

3.6.3.A   Property, plant and equipment

In approaching the recognition and measurement of, for example, property, plant and equipment of the acquiree, the acquirer might look to the revaluation guidance included within Section 17 – *Property, Plant and Equipment,* particularly paragraphs 17.15C and 17.15D which, in addition to cross-referencing to the guidance on fair value in paragraphs 11.27 to 11.32 notes that 'the fair value of land and buildings is usually determined from market-based evidence by appraisal that is normally undertaken by professionally qualified valuers. The fair value of items of plant and equipment is usually their market value determined by appraisal' *[FRS 102.17.15C]* as well as providing that where there is no market-based evidence of fair value because of the specialised nature of the item of property, plant and equipment and the item is rarely sold, except as part of a continuing business, an entity may need to estimate fair value using an income or a depreciated replacement cost approach. *[FRS 102.17.15D].* This guidance in Section 17 is similar to that included in the version of IFRS 3 on which FRS 102 is based. *[IFRS 3(2004).B16].*

As, under FRS 102, assets are recognised at fair value, it follows that the acquirer may not recognise a separate provision or valuation allowance for assets – such as accumulated depreciation.

3.6.3.B   Intangible assets

Section 18 – *Intangible Assets other than Goodwill,* provides no guidance on the determination of fair value given that its revaluation model is limited for intangible assets where the fair value can be determined by reference to an active market.

The version of IFRS 3 on which FRS 102 is based contained some guidance for determining the fair value of intangible assets arising on a business combination, supplemented by specific guidance in IAS 38 – *Intangible Assets* ('IAS 38'). Under this guidance, intangible assets were to be valued by reference to an active market. *[IFRS 3(2004).B16].* IAS 38 considered that 'the appropriate market price is usually the current bid price. If current bid prices are unavailable, the price of the most recent similar transaction may provide a basis from which to estimate fair value, provided that there has not been a significant change in economic circumstances between the transaction date and the date at which the asset's fair value is estimated.' *[IAS 38.39].*

However, it was noted that it is uncommon for an active market to exist for intangible assets and that such a market cannot exist for brands, newspaper mastheads, music and publishing rights, patents or trademarks, i.e. many of the intangible assets that IFRS 3 (and FRS 102) require an acquirer to recognise as part

Chapter 15

of the allocation process. Accordingly, if no active market exists, the intangible assets were to be valued on a basis that reflects the amounts the acquirer would have paid for the assets in arm's length transactions between knowledgeable willing parties, based on the best information available. *[IFRS 3(2004).B16].* In determining this amount, an entity would consider the outcome of recent transactions for similar assets. For example, an entity may apply multiples reflecting current market transactions to factors that drive the profitability of the asset (such as revenue, operating profit or earnings before interest, tax, depreciation and amortisation). *[IAS 38.40].*

IAS 38 acknowledged that entities that are regularly involved in the purchase and sale of unique intangible assets may have developed techniques for estimating their fair values indirectly. Accordingly, it allows these techniques to be used for initial measurement of an intangible asset acquired in a business combination if their objective is to estimate fair value and if they reflect current transactions and practices in the industry to which the asset belongs. These techniques include, for example: *[IAS 38.41]*

(a)   discounting estimated future net cash flows from the asset; or

(b)   estimating the costs the entity avoids by owning the intangible asset and not needing:

    (i)   to license it from another party in an arm's length transaction (as in the 'relief from royalty' approach, using discounted net cash flows); or

    (ii)   to recreate or replace it (as in the cost approach).

Accordingly, under IFRS, it is generally considered that there are three broad approaches to valuing intangible assets as shown in the diagram below.

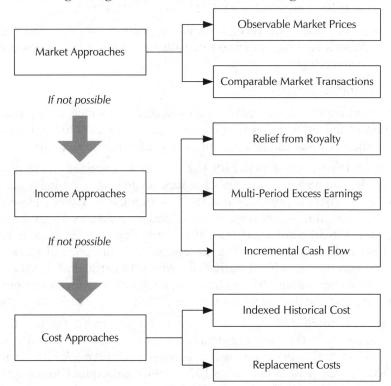

Under a market-based approach, if no actual market prices are available for the respective asset, the fair value of the intangible is derived by analysing similar intangible assets that have recently been sold or licensed, and then comparing these transactions to the intangible asset that needs to be valued. This approach is regarded as preferable where an active market for the assets exist. However, in practice, the ability to use such an approach is very limited. Intangible assets are generally unique, and there is rarely an active market to examine.

A cost-based approach is generally regarded as having limited application and difficult to use in many cases. The premise of the cost approach is that an investor would pay no more for an intangible asset than the cost to recreate it. However, for most intangibles, cost approaches are rarely consistent with the definition of 'fair value'.

Income-based approaches are much more commonly used. These involve identifying the expected economic benefits to be derived from the ownership of the particular intangible asset, and calculating the fair value of an intangible asset at the present value of those benefits. These are discussed further below.

For each asset, there are often several methodologies which can be applied. The choice will depend on the circumstances, in particular the nature of the value brought by the asset to the company (i.e. additional revenue, cost savings, replacement time, etc.). In some cases, two methods may be used for the same asset – one as the primary approach to valuing the asset and the other as a check for reasonableness.

The two main income-based approaches that are used are:

- the Multi Period Excess Earnings Method ('MEEM'); and
- the Relief from Royalty method.

A discounted cash flow method may be used, for example, in determining the value of cost-savings that will be achieved as a result of having a supply contract with advantageous terms in relation to current market rates.

The MEEM approach will generally be used in valuing the most important intangible asset. This is because it is effectively a residual cash flow approach. The key issue in using this approach is how to determine the income/cash flow that is related to the intangible asset being valued, and the fact that it is not the full cash flow of the business that is used. As its name suggests, the value of an intangible asset determined under the MEEM approach is estimated through the sum of the discounted future excess earnings attributable to the intangible asset. The excess earnings is the difference between the after-tax operating cash flow attributable to the intangible asset and the required cost of invested capital on all other assets used in order to generate those cash flows. These contributory assets include property, plant and equipment, other identifiable intangible assets and net working capital. The allowance made for the cost of such capital is based on the value of such assets and a required rate of return reflecting the risks of the particular assets.

The Relief from Royalty method is used in many cases to calculate the value of a trademark or trade name. This approach is based on the concept that if an entity owns a trademark, it does not have to pay for the use of it and therefore is relieved from paying a royalty. The amount of that theoretical payment is used as a surrogate for income attributable to the trademark. The valuation is arrived at by computing the present value of the after-tax royalty savings using an appropriate discount rate. The after-tax royalty savings are calculated by applying an appropriate royalty rate to the projected revenue, deducting the legal protection expenses relating to the trademark, and an allowance for tax at the appropriate rate.

3.6.3.C   Inventories

Section 13 – *Inventories*, provides no guidance on revaluation given FRS 102 mandates a cost model for these assets.

The version of IFRS 3 on which FRS 102 is based contained the following guidance for determining the fair value of inventories arising on a business combination. Finished goods were to be valued using selling prices less the costs of disposal and a reasonable profit allowance for the selling effort of the acquirer based on profit for similar finished goods. Work in progress was to be valued using selling prices of finished goods less the sum of the costs to complete, the costs of disposal and a reasonable profit allowance for the completing and selling effort based on profit for similar finished goods. Raw materials were to be valued using current replacement costs. *[IFRS 3(2004).B16].*

Example 15.11:   Fair value of work in progress

Entity A acquires Entity B on 30 June 2015. Entity B operates a dairy business and included in its inventory at the date of acquisition was work in progress being inventory of cheddar cheese in cellars of the dairy left to mature for a year. The carrying amount of this inventory, being the costs incurred to the date of acquisition, is £400,000.

The intention is to sell the cheese once it has matured. The sales price of fully-matured cheese of the same quality at 30 June 2015 is £900,000. Future storage, marketing and selling expenses required to complete the process and market the product to retailers are estimated at £185,000.

How should the fair value of the work in progress be determined?

Based on the guidance in IFRS 3 (2004), the work in progress would be valued using selling prices of finished goods less the sum of the costs to complete, the costs of disposal and a reasonable profit allowance for the completing and selling effort based on profit for similar finished goods. Judgement is required by entities in calculating a reasonable profit allowance relating to the completing and selling efforts.

One approach would be to use the cost structure of Entity B to determine the reasonable profit allowance for subsequent costs to be incurred. Accordingly, it may be that if Entity B had not been acquired by Entity A, it would have incurred total costs of £585,000. Based on the estimated selling price of £900,000, this would result in an overall profit of £315,000. Consequently, the profit allowance to be made for the completing and selling effort would be £100,000 (being £315,000 × £185,000 ÷ £585,000). On this basis, the fair value of the work in progress would be £615,000 (being £900,000 – £185,000 – £100,000).

3.6.3.D   Financial instruments

The guidance in paragraphs 11.27 to 11.32 of FRS 102 will clearly be of relevance in determining the fair value of financial instruments. Financial instruments traded in an active market should be valued at their quoted price, which is usually the current bid price. When quoted prices are unavailable, the price of a recent transaction for an identical asset provides evidence of fair value as long as there has not been a significant change in economic circumstances or a significant lapse of time since the transaction took place. If the market for the asset is not active and recent transactions of an identical asset on their own are not a good estimate of fair value, the acquirer estimates fair value by using a valuation technique. *[FRS 102.11.27].* This guidance is similar to that included in the version of IFRS 3 on which FRS 102 is based. *[IFRS 3(2004).B16].* Further guidance on these concepts is provided in Chapter 8 of this publication which addresses Section 11 – *Basic Financial Instruments.*

Under the above guidance, receivables would likely be valued based on the present values of the amounts to be received, determined at appropriate current interest rates, less allowances for uncollectibility and collection costs, if necessary. Again, as receivables are recognised and measured at fair value at the acquisition date, any uncertainty about collections and future cash flows are included in the fair value measure – and therefore, the acquirer should not recognise a separate provision or valuation allowance. In other words, an acquirer cannot 'carry over' any provision or valuation allowance already recognised by the acquiree. This guidance is similar to that included in version of IFRS 3 on which FRS 102 is based. That guidance also stated that discounting is not required for short-term receivables, beneficial contracts and other identifiable assets when the difference between the nominal and discounted amounts is not material. *[IFRS 3(2004).B16].*

Similarly, under the above guidance in Section 11, accounts and notes payable, long-term debt, liabilities, accruals and other claims payable should be valued using the present values of amounts to be disbursed in settling the liabilities determined at appropriate current interest rates. Again, this guidance is similar to that included in version of IFRS 3 on which FRS 102 is based. That guidance also stated that discounting is not required for short-term liabilities when the difference between the nominal and discounted amounts is not material. *[IFRS 3(2004).B16].*

3.6.3.E   Investments in an associate or jointly controlled entity

Where as part of a business combination one of the identified assets is an investment in an associate or a jointly controlled entity, the fair value should be determined in accordance with the above guidance for financial instruments, rather than calculating a fair value based on the appropriate share of the fair values of the identifiable assets, liabilities and contingent liabilities of the associate or jointly controlled entity. By doing so, any goodwill relating to the associate or jointly controlled entity is subsumed within the carrying amount for the associate or jointly controlled entity rather than within the goodwill arising on the overall business combination. Nevertheless, although this fair value is effectively the 'cost' to the group to which equity accounting is applied, the underlying fair values of the identifiable assets, liabilities and contingent liabilities also need to be determined to apply equity accounting (see Chapter 10 at 3.3.2).

If the fair value exercise results in an excess of assets over the fair value of the consideration (commonly referred to as 'negative goodwill'), in accordance with the requirements of FRS 102 discussed at 3.8.3 below, the acquirer should challenge the fair value placed on the associate or jointly controlled entity as it re-challenges the values placed on all of the assets, liabilities and contingent liabilities of the acquiree to ensure that the value has not been overstated.

Chapter 15

3.6.3.F   *Onerous contracts and operating leases*

Clearly a provision for an onerous contract that would be recognised under Section 21 by the acquiree at the acquisition date, should be recognised and measured at its fair value on allocation of the cost of the business combination.

An onerous contract is one in which the 'unavoidable costs of meeting the obligations under the contract exceed the economic benefits expected to be received under it. The unavoidable costs under a contract reflect the least net cost of exiting from the contract, which is the lower of the cost of fulfilling it and any compensation or penalties arising from failure to fulfil it. For example, an entity may be contractually required under an operating lease to make payments to lease an asset for which it no longer has any use', *[FRS 102.21A.2]*, i.e. a contract that is directly loss-making, not simply uneconomic by reference to current prices.

Consistent with the measurement requirements for provisions in Section 21, the fair value should be the present value of the amounts expected to be required to settle the obligation. *[FRS 102.21.7]*. The is similar to the guidance included in the version of IFRS 3 on which FRS 102 is based which stated that 'onerous contracts and other identifiable liabilities of the acquiree should be valued using the present values of amounts to be disbursed in settling the obligations determined at appropriate current interest rates.' *[IFRS 3(2004).B16]*. However, in allocating the cost of a business combination, the acquirer should go further than considering just onerous contracts that are directly loss-making. We believe that contracts that are 'onerous' by reference to market conditions at the date of acquisition should be recognised as liabilities. This is consistent with the requirements for intangible assets.

In addition to contracts which are onerous, in allocating the cost of a business combination to the assets acquired, liabilities and contingent liabilities assumed, we consider that favourable contracts should be recognised as intangibles assets and unfavourable contracts recognised as liabilities.

3.6.3.G   *Contingent liabilities*

No specific guidance is included in FRS 102 in determining the fair value of a contingent liability. The version of IFRS 3 on which FRS 102 is based contained the following guidance – contingent liabilities of the acquiree should be valued using the amounts that a third party would charge to assume those contingent liabilities. Such an amount shall reflect all expectations about possible cash flows and not the single most likely or the expected maximum or minimum cash flow. *[IFRS 3(2004).B16]*. This is especially relevant given that many contingent liabilities are so defined because it is not probable that an outflow of resources embodying economic benefits will be required to settle the obligation – even though the minimum cash flow may be zero, a third party would still charge a sum to assume the contingent liability.

3.6.3.H   Deferred revenue

An acquiree may have recorded deferred revenue at the date of acquisition for a number of reasons. For example, it might represent upfront payments for services or products that have yet to be delivered, or payments for delivered goods or services sold as a part of a multiple-element arrangement that could not be accounted for separately from undelivered items included in the same arrangement.

In accounting for a business combination, an acquirer should only recognise a liability for deferred revenue of the acquiree if it relates to an outstanding performance obligation assumed by the acquirer. Such performance obligations would include obligations to provide goods or services or the right to use an asset.

The measurement of the deferred revenue liability should be based on the fair value of the obligation at the date of acquisition, which will not necessarily be the same as the amount of deferred revenue recognised by the acquiree. In general, the fair value would be less than the amount recognised by the acquiree, as the amount of revenue that another party would expect to receive for meeting that obligation would not include any profit element relating to the selling or other efforts already completed by the acquiree.

Example 15.12:   Deferred revenue of an acquiree

Target is an electronics company that sells contracts to service all types of electronics equipment for an upfront annual fee of £120,000. Acquirer purchases Target in a business combination. At the acquisition date, Target has one service contract outstanding with 6 months remaining and for which £60,000 of deferred revenue is recorded in Target's pre-acquisition financial statements.

To fulfill the contract over its remaining 6-month term, Acquirer estimates that another party would expect to receive £54,000 for fulfilling that obligation. It has estimated that the other party would incur direct and incremental costs of £45,000, and expect a profit margin for that fulfillment effort of 20%, i.e. £9,000, and would, thus, expect to receive £54,000.

Accordingly, Acquirer should recognise a liability of £54,000 in respect of the deferred revenue obligation.

However, if the acquiree's deferred revenue does not relate to an outstanding performance obligation but to goods or services that have already been delivered, no liability should be recognised by the acquirer.

3.6.4   Subsequent adjustments to fair values

If the initial accounting for a business combination is incomplete by the end of the reporting period in which the combination occurs, the acquirer recognises in its financial statements provisional amounts for the items for which the accounting is incomplete. Within twelve months after the acquisition date, the acquirer retrospectively adjusts the provisional amounts recognised as assets and liabilities at the acquisition date (i.e. account for them as if they were made at the acquisition date) to reflect new information obtained. *[FRS 102.19.19].*

As a result, FRS 102 effectively requires that the allocation of the cost of the business combination be completed within twelve months of the acquisition date, so an acquirer ought to be able to demonstrate that any such adjustments were made by such a date, rather than up to the subsequent period end date or subsequent date of approval of the financial statements for that date.

Chapter 15

Where as a result of completing the initial accounting within twelve months from the acquisition date adjustments to the provisional values have been found to be necessary, FRS 102 requires them to be recognised from the acquisition date. Although not explicitly stated in FRS 102, this means, therefore, that:

(a)   the carrying amount of the identifiable asset, liability or contingent liability that is recognised or adjusted as a result of completing the initial accounting is calculated as if its fair value at the acquisition date had been recognised from that date;

(b)   goodwill is adjusted from the acquisition date by an amount equal to the adjustment to the fair value at the acquisition date of the identifiable asset, liability or contingent liability being recognised or adjusted; and

(c)   comparative information presented for the periods before the initial accounting for the combination is complete is presented as if the initial accounting had been completed from the acquisition date. This includes any additional depreciation, amortisation or other profit or loss effect recognised as a result of completing the initial accounting.

These requirements are illustrated in the following example; the deferred tax implications have been ignored.

Example 15.13:   Finalisation of provisional values upon completion of initial accounting

Entity A prepares financial statements for annual periods ending on 31 December and does not prepare interim financial statements. The entity acquired another entity on 30 September 2015. Entity A sought an independent appraisal for an item of property, plant and equipment acquired in the combination. However, the appraisal was not finalised by the time the entity completed its 2015 annual financial statements. Entity A recognised in its 2015 annual financial statements a provisional fair value for the asset of £30,000, and a provisional value for acquired goodwill of £100,000. The item of property, plant and equipment had a remaining useful life at the acquisition date of five years.

Six months after the acquisition date, the entity received the independent appraisal, which estimated the asset's fair value at the acquisition date at £40,000.

In preparing its 2016 financial statements, Entity A is required to recognise any adjustments to provisional values as a result of completing the initial accounting from the acquisition date.

Part (a) above means that an adjustment is made to the carrying amount of the item of property, plant and equipment. That adjustment is measured as the fair value adjustment at the acquisition date of £10,000, less the additional depreciation that would have been recognised had the asset's fair value at the acquisition date been recognised from that date (£500 for three months' depreciation to 31 December 2015), i.e. an increase of £9,500. Part (b) means that the carrying amount of goodwill to be adjusted for the increase in value of the asset at the acquisition date of £10,000. Part (c) means the 2015 comparative information to be restated to reflect these adjustments. Accordingly, the 2015 balance sheet is restated by increasing the carrying amount of property, plant and equipment by £9,500, reducing goodwill by £10,000 and retained earnings by £500. The 2015 income statement is restated to include additional depreciation of £500.

While FRS 102 does not mandate disclosures on these matters, we consider it appropriate that Entity A would disclose in its 2015 financial statements that the initial accounting for the business combination has been determined only provisionally, and explain why this is the case. In its 2016 financial statements it would disclose the amounts and explanations of the adjustments to the provisional values recognised during the current reporting period. Therefore, Entity A would disclose that:

- the fair value of the item of property, plant and equipment at the acquisition date has been increased by £10,000 with a corresponding decrease in goodwill; and

- the 2015 comparative information is restated to reflect this adjustment, including additional depreciation of £500 relating to the year ended 31 December 2015.

The above example illustrates a situation where a provisional value of an asset was finalised at a different amount as part of the completion of the initial accounting.

Example 15.14: Identification of an asset upon completion of initial accounting

Entity C prepares financial statements for annual periods ending on 31 December and does not prepare interim financial statements. The entity acquired another entity on 30 November 2015. Entity C engaged an independent appraiser to assist with the identification and determination of fair values to be assigned to the acquiree's assets, liabilities and contingent liabilities and the cost of the business combination. However, the appraisal was not finalised by the time the entity completed its 2015 annual financial statements, and therefore the amounts recognised in its 2015 annual financial statements were on a provisional basis.

As part of the work carried out in finalising the initial accounting, it was identified by the independent appraiser that the acquiree had an intangible asset (meeting all of the Section 18 recognition and identification criteria) with a fair value at the date of acquisition of £20,000. However, this had not been identified at the time when Entity C was preparing its 2015 annual financial statements. Thus, no value had been included for this intangible asset.

In preparing its 2016 financial statements, Entity C is required to recognise any adjustments to provisional values as a result of completing the initial accounting from the acquisition date. In this case, no value had been recognised, and indeed, the intangible asset had not even been identified at the time of preparing its 2015 financial statements. So, can an adjustment be made under the provisions of paragraph 19.19?

In our view, an adjustment is appropriate. The requirements are not limited to measurement adjustments. Adjustments to recognise subsequently identified assets or liabilities are permitted as a result of completing the initial accounting. The initial accounting involves the identification as well as the measurement of the acquiree's assets, liabilities and contingent liabilities, and it is clear from (a) above that adjustments are to be made for items that are recognised as a result of completing the exercise.

It is important that any adjustments to the provisional allocation reflect conditions as they existed at the date of the acquisition, rather than being affected by subsequent events; the objective is to determine the fair values of the items at the date of acquisition. There is a parallel to be drawn here with the accounting treatment of events subsequent to the balance sheet date. Only those events which provide further evidence of conditions as they existed at the acquisition date should be taken into account.

Beyond twelve months after the acquisition date, adjustments to the initial accounting for a business combination are to be recognised only to correct a material error in accordance with Section 10 – *Accounting Policies, Estimates and Errors.* *[FRS 102.19.19].* This would probably be the case only if the original allocation was based on a complete misinterpretation of the facts which were available at the time; it would not apply simply because new information had come to light which changed the acquiring management's view of the value of the item in question.

Adjustments to the initial accounting for a business combination after it is complete are not made for the effect of changes in estimates. In accordance with Section 10, the effect of a change in estimates is recognised in the current and future periods (see Chapter 7 at 3.5). *[FRS 102.10.15-17].*

Chapter 15

Where it is determined that an error has been made, Section 10 requires an entity to account for an error correction retrospectively, and to present financial statements as if the error had never occurred by restating the comparative information for the prior period(s) in which the error occurred. *[FRS 102.10.21]*. The accounting is similar to that outlined above for adjustments upon completion of initial accounting. The only difference being there is no time limit as to when such adjustments may be required.

3.7   Non-controlling interests

Non-controlling interests, which may be referred to as 'minority interests', is the equity in a subsidiary not attributable, directly or indirectly, to a parent. *[FRS 102 Appendix I]*.

Section 19 provides no guidance at to the recognition and measurement of any non-controlling interests in explaining the purchase method, other than – in setting out the goodwill calculation – alluding to the possibility of the acquirer having less than a one hundred percent interest in the acquiree's identifiable assets, liabilities and provisions for contingent liabilities: 'Any difference between the cost of the business combination and the acquirer's interest in the net amount of the identifiable assets, liabilities and provisions for contingent liabilities so recognised shall be accounted for in accordance with paragraphs 19.22 to 19.24.' *[FRS 102.19.14]*.

It is left to Section 9 to address the initial recognition and measurement of any non-controlling interests arising on a business combination, being the non-controlling interest's share in the net amount of the identifiable assets, liabilities and contingent liabilities recognised and measured in accordance with Section 19 at the date of the original combination. *[FRS 102.9.13(d)]*.

As such, under FRS 102, where the acquirer obtains less than a 100% interest in the acquiree, a non-controlling interest in the acquiree is recognised reflecting the non-controlling interest's proportion of the net identifiable assets, liabilities and contingent liabilities of the acquiree at their attributed fair values at the date of acquisition; no amount is included for any goodwill relating to the non-controlling interests. There is no option under FRS 102 to measure non-controlling interests at fair value.

FRS 102 does not distinguish between non-controlling interests that are present ownership interests and entitle their holders to a proportionate share of the entity's net assets in the event of liquidation and other components of non-controlling interests (e.g. perpetual debt classified as equity under Section 22). The implication is that all non-controlling interests are measured the same way based on present ownership interest. This means that any non-controlling interests, such as options, are valued at nil if they are not entitled to a present ownership interest.

The measurement of non-controlling interests in a business combination is illustrated in Example 6.11 in Chapter 6 at 3.7.1.

3.8   Goodwill

FRS 102 defines 'goodwill' in terms of its nature, rather than in terms of its measurement. It is defined as 'future economic benefits arising from assets that are not capable of being individually identified and separately recognised'. *[FRS 102 Appendix I]*.

Section 19 addresses accounting for goodwill both at the time of a business combination and subsequently. *[FRS 102.19.1]*.

3.8.1   *Initial recognition*

Section 19 requires that an acquirer, at the acquisition date, recognises goodwill acquired in a business combination as an asset. However, rather than attributing a fair value to the goodwill directly, the standard requires that the initial measurement of goodwill is its cost, being the excess of the cost of the business combination over the acquirer's interest in the net amount of the identifiable assets, liabilities and contingent liabilities recognised and measured in accordance with the standard. *[FRS 102.19.22]*. Thus, and as we have seen at 3.7 above, no amount is included for any goodwill relating to the non-controlling interests.

FRS 102 considers goodwill acquired in a business combination to represent a payment made by the acquirer in anticipation of future economic benefits from assets that are not capable of being individually identified and separately recognised.

Since goodwill is measured as the residual cost of the business combination after recognising the acquiree's identifiable assets, liabilities and contingent liabilities, then, to the extent that the acquiree's identifiable assets, liabilities and contingent liabilities do not satisfy the criteria for separate recognition at the acquisition date, there is a resulting effect on the amount recognised as goodwill. Indeed, Section 19 makes an explicit statement that this will be the case if the fair value of a contingent liability cannot be measured reliably. *[FRS 102.19.20(a)]*.

3.8.2   *Subsequent measurement*

Following its initial recognition and measurement, the main issue relating to goodwill is then how it should be subsequently accounted for.

FRS 102 requires that after initial recognition, an acquirer measures goodwill acquired in a business combination at cost less accumulated amortisation and accumulated impairment losses. *[FRS 102.19.23]*. Section 19 requires that goodwill is considered to have a finite useful life, and is to be amortised on a systematic basis over its life, and that Section 27 – *Impairment of Assets* – is to be followed for recognising and measuring any impairment of goodwill. *[FRS 102.19.23]*. This differs both to the IFRS 3 requirement that goodwill is not amortised, but instead subject to annual impairment tests; as well as to the provisions of FRS 10 whereby, notwithstanding a rebuttable presumption of a maximum life of 20 years, it was possible goodwill could be regarded as having an indefinite useful life if the durability of the acquired business could be demonstrated and justifies estimating the useful economic life to exceed 20 years and if the goodwill was capable of continued measurement. *[FRS 10.19]*. UK accounting standards, therefore, now correspond with UK company law with regards to the requirement under law for goodwill to be 'reduced by provisions for depreciation calculated to write off that amount systematically over a period chosen by the directors of the company', *[1 Sch 22(2)]*, thus practically removing the possibility of a invoking a 'true and fair override' under UK company law *[1 Sch 10(2)]* so as to depart from that specific principle.

Chapter 15

Section 19 defers to Section 18 and Section 27 for the detailed requirements in relation to amortisation and impairment, respectively – however, critically, states that 'if an entity is unable to make a reliable estimate of the useful life of goodwill, the life shall not exceed five years'. *[FRS 102.19.23(a)]*. Therefore, while FRS 102 is not setting out a 'default life' or a rebuttable presumption that the useful life of goodwill should be five years or less, it appears to be setting a higher hurdle for an acquirer to evidence a useful life in excess of five years, than may have been the case under FRS 10. Such reasons supporting a useful life in excess of five years are required to be disclosed. *[FRS 102.19.25(g)]*.

See Chapters 14 and 22 for further discussion of the requirements of Sections 18 and 27 regarding estimating the useful life, and impairment, respectively.

3.8.3   *Excess over cost of acquirer's interest in the net fair value of acquiree's identifiable assets, liabilities and contingent liabilities*

In some business combinations, the acquirer's interest in the net fair value of the acquiree's identifiable assets, liabilities and contingent liabilities exceeds the cost of the combination. Traditionally, that excess has been commonly referred to as 'negative goodwill'.

Where such an excess arises, Section 19 requires the acquirer to reassess the identification and measurement of the acquiree's identifiable assets, liabilities and contingent liabilities and the measurement of the cost of the combination. *[FRS 102.24(a)]*. While not further discussed in FRS 102, we note the discussion in the Basis for Conclusions of IFRS 3 (2004) noted that the existence of this excess might indicate that:

- the values attributed to the acquiree's identifiable assets have been overstated;
- identifiable liabilities and/or contingent liabilities of the acquiree have been omitted or the values attributed to those items have been understated; or
- the values assigned to the items comprising the cost of the business combination have been understated. *[IFRS 3(2004).BC146]*.

Having undertaken that reassessment, the standard then requires that any excess remaining after that reassessment be recognised and separately disclosed on the face of the statement of financial position, immediately below goodwill, and followed by a subtotal of the net amount of goodwill and the excess. *[FRS 102.19.24(b)]*. This treatment is a continuation of the requirements for negative goodwill under paragraph 48 of FRS 10, but is at odds with the IFRS 3 requirement for any excess remaining after reassessment to be recognised immediately in profit or loss.

Following initial recognition on the statement of financial position, FRS 102 requires the negative goodwill up to the fair value of the non-monetary assets acquired be recognised in profit or loss in the periods in which the non-monetary assets are recovered. *[FRS 102.19.24(c)]*. The reference to 'non-monetary assets', which includes items such as inventories, may not actually postpone recognition of negative goodwill for very long. Since inventories are usually turned over relatively quickly, any negative goodwill up to the fair value of the inventories may be released to the profit and loss account over a short period following the acquisition.

The secondary basis on which negative goodwill should be released to profit or loss involves that element, if any, of negative goodwill in excess of the fair values of non-monetary assets acquired. This element should be released in the periods expected to benefit. *[FRS 102.19.24(c)].* The exact meaning of this wording is not completely clear, but any reasonable interpretation is likely to be acceptable. It is unusual for negative goodwill to exceed the non-monetary assets acquired.

3.9   Reverse acquisitions

As discussed at 2.1.4 and 3.4 above, a reverse acquisition occurs when the owners of a company being 'acquired' (Company B) receive as consideration sufficient voting shares of the 'acquiring company' (Company A) so as to obtain control over the new combined entity. The acquisition is 'reverse' because, from an economic point of view, the acquirer (Company A) is being taken over by the acquiree (Company B).

As the Companies Act regards Company A as being the parent undertaking of Company B it requires Company A to prepare consolidated accounts. In preparing those accounts, Company A is required by the Companies Act 2006 to acquisition account for the acquisition of its subsidiary undertaking, Company B. *[6 Sch 9].*

In these circumstances, as Company B obtains control (power to govern the financial and operating policies of an entity or business so as to obtain benefits from its activities) of Company A, and is therefore the acquirer under FRS 102, Company A should be deemed to have been acquired by Company B and reverse acquisition accounting should be applied.

To adopt reverse acquisition accounting represents a departure from company law which does not envisage such occurrence. Such departure is required where it is necessary to give a true and fair view. In such circumstances, there should be disclosure of a true and fair view override departure from the Companies Act 2006, and disclosure of the particulars, reasons and effect.

In the absence of guidance within FRS 102, the discussion that follows is based on the guidance in IFRS 3. *[IFRS 3.B19-27].*

3.9.1   *Measuring the cost of the business combination*

In a reverse acquisition, the cost of the business combination is deemed to have been incurred by the legal subsidiary (i.e. the acquirer for accounting purposes) in the form of equity instruments issued to the owners of the legal parent (i.e. the acquiree for accounting purposes). If the published price of the equity instruments of the legal subsidiary is used to determine the cost of the combination, a calculation is made to determine the number of equity instruments the legal subsidiary would have had to issue to provide the same percentage ownership interest of the combined entity to the owners of the legal parent as they have in the combined entity as a result of the reverse acquisition. The fair value of the number of equity instruments so calculated is used as the cost of the combination.

On the other hand, if the fair value of the equity instruments of the legal subsidiary is not otherwise clearly evident, the total fair value of all the issued equity instruments of the legal parent before the business combination is used as the basis for determining the cost of the combination.

Example 15.15:   Reverse acquisition – calculating the cost of the business combination using the fair value of the equity shares of the legal subsidiary

Entity A, the entity issuing equity instruments and therefore the legal parent, is acquired in a reverse acquisition by Entity B, the legal subsidiary, on 30 September 2015.

Balance sheets of Entity A and Entity B immediately before the business combination follow:

	Entity A £	Entity B £
Tangible fixed assets	1,300	3,000
Debtors	500	700
	1,800	3,700
Creditors: amounts falling due within one year	300	600
Creditors: amounts falling due after more than one year	400	1,100
	700	1,700
Net assets	1,100	2,000
Capital and reserves		
Called up share capital		
100 ordinary shares	100	
60 ordinary shares		60
Share premium account	200	540
Profit and loss account	800	1,400
	1,100	2,000

On 30 September 2015, Entity A issues 2½ shares in exchange for each ordinary share of Entity B. All of Entity B's shareholders exchange their shares in Entity B. Therefore, Entity A issues 150 ordinary shares in exchange for all 60 ordinary shares of Entity B.

The fair value of each ordinary share of Entity B at 30 September 2015 is £40. The quoted market price of Entity A's ordinary shares at that date is £12.

The fair values of Entity A's identifiable assets and liabilities at 30 September 2015 are the same as their carrying amounts, with the exception of tangible fixed assets. The fair value of Entity A's tangible fixed assets at 30 September 2015 is £1,500. (For the purposes of illustration, deferred tax implications have been ignored.)

As a result of the issue of 150 ordinary shares by Entity A, Entity B's shareholders own 60 per cent of the issued shares of the combined entity (i.e. 150 shares out of 250 issued shares). The remaining 40 per cent are owned by Entity A's shareholders. If the business combination had taken place in the form of Entity B issuing additional ordinary shares to Entity A's shareholders in exchange for their ordinary shares in Entity A, Entity B would have had to issue 40 shares for the ratio of ownership interest in the combined entity to be the same. Entity B's shareholders would then own 60 out of the 100 issued shares of Entity B and therefore 60 per cent of the combined entity.

As a result, the cost of the business combination is £1,600 (i.e. 40 shares each with a fair value of £40).

In the above example, a reliable estimate of the fair value of the ordinary shares of Entity B was available. However, in those situations where a private entity arranges to have itself 'acquired' by a smaller public entity as a means of obtaining a stock exchange listing, it may be that this will not be the case. In which case, the fair value of the shares of the legal parent should be used. If in the above example, a reliable estimate of the fair value of the ordinary shares of Entity B was not available, the total fair value of all the issued equity instruments of the Entity A before the business combination would be used as the basis for determining the cost of the combination. The total fair value of all of Entity A's shares before the business combination was £1,200 (i.e. 100 shares each with a fair value of £12). Since Entity B is treated as having acquired a 100% interest in Entity A, then the cost of the business combination would be £1,200.

3.9.2 Preparation and presentation of consolidated financial statements

Since the legal parent is the acquiree for accounting purposes, the consolidated financial statements prepared following a reverse acquisition reflect the fair values of the assets, liabilities and contingent liabilities of the legal parent, not those of the legal subsidiary. Therefore, the cost of the business combination is allocated by measuring the identifiable assets, liabilities and contingent liabilities of the legal parent that satisfy the recognition criteria at their fair values at the acquisition date. Any excess of the cost of the combination over the acquirer's interest in the net fair value of those items is then accounted for as goodwill.

In Example 15.15 above, goodwill of £300 would be calculated as the difference between the cost of the combination of £1,600 and the fair value of the assets acquired of £1,300. If the cost of the business combination had been determined based on the value of Entity A's shares, i.e. £1,200, then negative goodwill of £100 would have arisen.

Although the accounting for a reverse acquisition reflects the legal subsidiary as being the acquirer, the consolidated financial statements prepared following a reverse acquisition are issued under the name of the legal parent. Consequently we believe that they should be described in the notes as a continuation of the financial statements of the legal subsidiary, with one adjustment, which is to adjust retrospectively the accounting acquirer's legal capital to reflect the legal capital of the accounting acquiree. Comparative information presented in those consolidated financial statements is therefore that of the legal subsidiary (accounting acquirer), not that originally presented in the financial statements of the legal parent (accounting acquiree), as adjusted to reflect the legal capital of the legal parent (accounting acquiree).

Because the consolidated financial statements represent the continuation of the financial statements of the legal subsidiary except for its capital structure, the consolidated financial statements reflect:

- the assets and liabilities of the legal subsidiary (accounting acquirer) recognised and measured at their pre-combination carrying amounts, i.e. not at their acquisition-date fair values.

- the assets and liabilities of the legal parent (accounting acquiree) recognised and measured in accordance with Section 19, i.e. generally at their acquisition-date fair values.

- the retained earnings and other equity balances of the legal subsidiary (accounting acquirer) *before* the business combination, i.e. not those of the legal parent (accounting acquiree).

- the amount recognised as issued equity interests in the consolidated financial statements determined by adding the issued equity interest of the legal subsidiary (accounting acquirer) outstanding immediately before the business combination to the fair value of the legal parent (accounting acquiree). However, the equity structure (i.e. the number and type of equity interests issued) reflects the equity structure of the legal parent (accounting acquiree), including the equity interests the legal parent issued to effect the combination. Accordingly, the equity structure of the legal subsidiary (accounting acquirer) is restated using the exchange ratio established in the acquisition agreement to reflect the number of shares of the legal parent (accounting acquiree) issued in the reverse acquisition.

- any non-controlling interest's proportionate share of the legal subsidiary's (accounting acquirer's) pre-combination carrying amounts of retained earnings and other equity interests (as discussed in 3.9.3 below).

- the income statement for the current period reflects that of the legal subsidiary (accounting acquirer) for the full period together with the post-acquisition results of the legal parent (accounting acquiree) based on the attributed fair values.

Example 15.16: Reverse acquisition – consolidated balance sheet at date of the business combination

If we consider the transaction in Example 15.15 above and assume that the cost of consideration is calculated using the fair value of the shares of the legal subsidiary, the consolidation at the date of the business combination would be as follows:

	Entity A	Entity B	Consolidation adjustments	Consolidated
	£	£	£	£
Tangible fixed assets	1,300	3,000	200 [1]	4,500
Goodwill			300 [2]	300
Debtors	500	700		1,200
	1,800	3,700		6,000
Creditors: amounts falling due within one year	300	600		900
Creditors: amounts falling due after one year	400	1,100		1,500
	700	1,700		2,400
Net assets	1,100	2,000		3,600
Capital and reserves				
Called up share capital				
100 ordinary shares	100		(100) [3]	–
60 ordinary shares		60	1,600 [3]	1,660
Share premium account	200	540	(200) [3]	540
Profit and loss account	800	1,400	(800) [3]	1,400
	1,100	2,000		3,600

[1] To recognise Entity A's tangible fixed assets at their fair value at the acquisition date.

[2] To recognise goodwill on consolidation, representing the difference between the cost of the combination, £1,600, and the fair value of Entity A's net assets acquired, £1,300.

[3] To recognise the cost of the acquisition and to eliminate Entity A's share capital and reserves as at the date of the acquisition.

It can be seen from the above example that the amount of share capital in the consolidated balance sheet does not equal the nominal value of either Entity B's share capital (£60) or that of Entity A following the acquisition (£250). Although the total share capital and share premium in the consolidated balance sheet of £2,200 is equivalent to what the total would have been if Entity B had been the legal acquirer, some view this as a bizarre outcome. In a UK GAAP context, it is advocated that since the equity structure (i.e. the number and type of equity instruments issued) should reflect that of the legal parent, the amounts for share capital and related reserves, such as share premium, in the consolidated financial statements should also reflect the legal position. On this basis, a 'reverse acquisition reserve' would need to be reflected as illustrated below.

Example 15.17: Reverse acquisition – recognition of a reverse acquisition reserve

	Entity A	Entity B	Consolidation adjustments	Consolidated
	£	£	£	£
Tangible fixed assets	1,300	3,000	200[1]	4,500
Goodwill			300[2]	300
Debtors	500	700		1,200
	1,800	3,700		6,000
Creditors: amounts falling due within one year	300	600		900
Creditors: amounts falling due after one year	400	1,100		1,500
	700	1,700		2,400
Net assets	1,100	2,000		3,600
Capital and reserves				
Called up share capital				
100 ordinary shares	100		150[3]	250
60 ordinary shares		60	(60)[4]	
Share premium account	200	540	(540)[4]	200
Merger reserve			1,650[5]	1,650
Reverse acquisition reserve			100	100
Profit and loss account	800	1,400	(800)[6]	1,400
	1,100	2,000		3,600

[1] To recognise Entity A's tangible fixed assets at their fair value at the acquisition date.

[2] To recognise goodwill on consolidation, representing the difference between the cost of the combination, £1,600, and the fair value of Entity A's net assets acquired, £1,300.

[3] To recognise the nominal value of the shares issued by Entity A on the acquisition.

[4] To eliminate the share capital and share premium of Entity B (as the capital reserves on this basis reflect those of the legal acquirer).

[5] Entity A's shares were effectively issued for their fair value of £12 each, representing a premium of £1,650 over their nominal value. In this example, the entity has been able to take advantage of merger relief under section 612 of the Companies Act 2006 and has recorded this amount in a merger reserve.

[6] To eliminate the profit and loss reserves of Entity A.

The amount recognised as a reverse acquisition reserve, £100 in the example above, can be thought of as a combination of two amounts:

- the difference between the cost of the acquisition recognised under reverse acquisition accounting and the amount which would have been recorded under acquisition accounting if Entity A was the acquirer i.e. £1,600 less £1,800 in this case; and

- the difference between the capital reserves of Entity B and Entity A at the date of acquisition i.e. £600 less £300 in this case.

Chapter 15

3.9.3   *Non-controlling interests*

In some reverse acquisitions, it may be that some of the owners of the legal subsidiary (accounting acquirer) might not exchange their equity interests for equity interests of the legal parent (accounting acquiree), but retain their interest in the equity instruments of the legal subsidiary. Those owners are treated as a non-controlling interest in the consolidated financial statements after the reverse acquisition. That is because the owners of the legal subsidiary that do not exchange their equity interests for equity interests of the legal acquirer have an interest in only the results and net assets of the legal subsidiary – not in the results and net assets of the combined entity. Conversely, even though the legal parent is the acquiree for accounting purposes, the owners of the legal parent have an interest in the results and net assets of the combined entity.

The assets and liabilities of the legal subsidiary are measured and recognised in the consolidated financial statements at their pre-combination carrying amounts. Therefore, in a reverse acquisition, the non-controlling interest reflects the non-controlling shareholders' proportionate interest in the pre-combination carrying amounts of the legal subsidiary's net assets. These requirements are illustrated in the following example.

Example 15.18:   Reverse acquisition – non-controlling interests

This example uses the same facts in Example 15.15 above, except that in this case only 56 of Entity B's ordinary shares are tendered for exchange rather than all 60. Because Entity A issues 2½ shares in exchange for each ordinary share of Entity B, Entity A issues only 140 (rather than 150) shares. As a result, Entity B's shareholders own 58.3 per cent of the issued shares of the combined entity (i.e. 140 shares out of 240 issued shares).

As in Example 15.15 above, the cost of the business combination is calculated by assuming that the combination had taken place in the form of Entity B issuing additional ordinary shares to the shareholders of Entity A in exchange for their ordinary shares in Entity A. In calculating the number of shares that would have to be issued by Entity B, the non-controlling interest is ignored. The majority shareholders own 56 shares of Entity B. For this to represent a 58.3 per cent ownership interest, Entity B would have had to issue an additional 40 shares. The majority shareholders would then own 56 out of the 96 issued shares of Entity B and therefore 58.3 per cent of the combined entity.

As a result, the cost of the business combination is £1,600 (i.e. 40 shares each with a fair value of £40). This is the same amount as when all 60 of Entity B's ordinary shares are tendered for exchange (see Example 15.15 above). The cost of the combination does not change simply because some of Entity B's shareholders do not participate in the exchange.

The non-controlling interest is represented by the 4 shares of the total 60 shares of Entity B that are not exchanged for shares of Entity A. Therefore, the non-controlling interest is 6.7 per cent. The non-controlling interest reflects the non-controlling shareholders' proportionate interest in the pre-combination carrying amounts of the net assets of the legal subsidiary. Therefore, the consolidated balance sheet is adjusted to show a non-controlling interest of 6.7 per cent of the pre-combination carrying amounts of Entity B's net assets (i.e. £134 or 6.7 per cent of £2,000).

The consolidated balance sheet at 30 September 2015 (the date of the business combination) reflecting the non-controlling interest is as follows (the intermediate columns for Entity B, non-controlling interest and Entity A are included to show the workings):

	Entity B Book values £	Non-controlling interest £	Entity A Fair values £	Consolidated £
Tangible fixed assets	3,000		1,500	4,500
Debtors	700		500	1,200
Goodwill			300	300
	3,700		2,300	6,000
Creditors: amounts falling due within one year	600		300	900
Creditors: amounts falling due after one year	1,100		400	1,500
	1,700		700	2,400
Capital and reserves				
Called up share capital				
240 ordinary shares	60	(4)	1,600	1,656
Share premium account	540	(36)	–	504
Profit and loss account	1,400	(94)	–	1,306
Minority interest	–	134	–	134
	2,000	–	1,600	3,600

3.10 Business combinations achieved in stages (Step acquisitions)

So far, this chapter has discussed business combinations which result from a single purchase transaction. However, in practice, some subsidiaries are acquired in a series of steps which take place over an extended period, during which the underlying value of the subsidiary is likely to change, both because of the trading profits (or losses) which it retains and because of other movements in the fair value of its assets and liabilities. The accounting problems which this creates are therefore how to determine the cost of the business combination, allocating that cost to the assets acquired and liabilities and provisions for contingent liabilities assumed, and the resulting goodwill where a business combination is achieved in stages.

FRS 102 provides that where a parent acquires control of a subsidiary in stages, the transaction is to be accounted for in accordance with paragraphs 19.11A and 19.14 applied at the date control is achieved. *[FRS 102.9.19B]*.

Paragraph 19.11A states that, where control is achieved following a series of transactions, the cost of the business combination is the aggregate of the fair values of the assets given, liabilities assumed, and equity instruments issued by the acquirer at the date of each transaction in the series. *[FRS 102.19.11A]*.

Paragraph 19.14 is the normal rules on allocation of the cost of the business combination in applying the purchase method whereby 'the acquirer shall, *at the acquisition date* [emphasis added], allocate the cost of a business combination by recognising the acquiree's identifiable assets, liabilities and contingent liabilities ... *at their fair values at that date* [emphasis added]'. *[FRS 102.19.14]*.

This approach is consistent with the requirements of the Companies Act 2006, whereby goodwill must be recognised as the difference between the fair value at the acquisition date of the identifiable assets and liabilities of the undertaking acquired and the acquisition cost of the interest in the shares of the undertaking. *[6 Sch 9]*.

The following example illustrates the application of these principles.

Example 15.19:   Business combination achieved in stages (step acquisition) (1)

Company A acquires a 10% ownership interest in Company B on 1 January 2013 for £5,000,000 cash. Company A acquired a further 20% ownership interest in Company B for £10,000,000 cash on 1 January 2015 and obtained significant influence. At 1 January 2017, Company A's equity interest in Company B was £18,000,000. Company A acquired a further 30% of Company B for £30,000,000 cash on 1 January 2017, and obtained control. The fair value of Company B's identifiable net assets at 1 January 2017 was £60,000,000.

In accordance with paragraph 19.11A, the cost of the business combination is £45,000,000, being the aggregate of the cash paid at each stage in exchange for control. Company A's share of the identifiable net assets of Company B is £36,000,000 (being 60% of £60,000,000), resulting in goodwill of £9,000,000.

Company A will record the following entries in its consolidated financial statements at the date of the business combination:

	Dr	Cr
	£m	£m
Identifiable net assets of Company B	60	
Goodwill (£45m – (60% of £60m))	9	
Non-controlling interest (40% of £60m)		24
Cash		30
Equity investment in Company B		18
Other comprehensive income*	3	

* This 'dangling entry' represents the different between previous cash paid (£15m) and the share of the net assets at date control is obtained (£18m). As this not a profit or loss it should be taken to other comprehensive income.

However, in certain circumstances, this approach to the measurement of goodwill, as prescribed by both FRS 102 and the Companies Act 2006, may give rise to an unexpected answer, as illustrated in the below example:

Example 15.20:   Business combination achieved in stages (step acquisition) (2)

Company A acquires a 100% holding in Company B as a result of two separate transactions, several years apart, as set out in the table below.

Transaction number	Holding acquired	Fair value of net assets	Total value of investee	Price paid	Cumulative price paid
1	49%	£8m	£10m	£4.9m	£4.9m
2	51%	£30m	£40m	£20.4m	£25.3m

At the time of the first investment, Company A determined that it had significant influence of Company B and that it was neither a subsidiary nor an interest in a jointly controlled entity. In its consolidated financial statements, Company A accordingly accounted for its investment in Company B using the equity method, in accordance with Section 14 – *Investments in Associates,* with the investment initially recognised at £4.9m.

Company A subsequently obtained control of Company B through a transaction with Company B's other shareholder, paying £20.4m in return for acquiring its 51% interest in Company B. At that date, the carrying value of Company A's 49% investment in Company B, accounted for under the equity method, was £10.8m, having reflected £5.9m for share of profits of £12m.

Applying the purchase method as stipulated by FRS 102 results in Company A determining the cost of the business combination at £25.3m, and recognising identifiable net assets of Company B at the acquisition date of £30m – resulting in the recognition of negative goodwill of £4.7m. This is despite the fact that Company A had paid more than its proportionate share of the fair value of the net assets at each transaction. There will also be a debit of £5.9m taken to other comprehensive income, being the difference between the original price paid (£4.9m) and the investment under the equity method (£10.8m). This is effectively the reversal of the previously recognised equity-accounted share of profits. As discussed at 3.8.3 above, Company A will recognise this negative goodwill to profit or loss in the periods in which the non-monetary assets are recovered.

While FRS 102's approach to step acquisitions is a practical (or convenient) means of applying the purchase method because it does not require retrospective assessments of the fair value of the identifiable assets and liabilities of the subsidiary, the FRC notes that in certain circumstances not using the fair values at the dates of earlier purchases may result in accounting that is inconsistent with the way the investment has been treated previously and, for that reason, may fail to give a true and fair view. *[FRS 102.A4.19].*

In addition to the example above where the group's share of profits or losses of its associate effectively become reclassified as goodwill (or negative goodwill), a similar problem may arise where an investment was impaired to nil, but subsequently, application of the purchase method would increase reserves and create an asset. *[FRS 102.A4.20].*

As such, the FRC acknowledges that, in such rare cases where the method for calculating goodwill set out in company law and paragraph 9.19B of FRS 102 would be misleading, the goodwill should be calculated as the sum of the goodwill arising from each purchase of an interest in the relevant undertaking, adjusted as necessary for any subsequent impairment. In such circumstances, goodwill arising on each purchase should be calculated as the difference between the cost of that purchase and the fair value at the date of that purchase of the identifiable assets and liabilities attributable to the interest purchased. The difference between the goodwill calculated using this method and that calculated using the method provided by company law and FRS 102 is shown in reserves. Section 404(5) of the Companies Act 2006 sets out the disclosures required in cases where the statutory requirement is not applied. Paragraph 3.5 of FRS 102 sets out the disclosures when an entity departs from a requirement of FRS 102 or from a requirement of applicable legislation. *[FRS 102.A4.21].*

Assuming that the accounting for goodwill in Example 15.20 above was considered misleading, goodwill would be calculated as £6.1m, being £1.0m for the first transaction (£4.9m – £3.9m (49% × £8.0m)) and £5.1m for the second transaction (£20.4m – £15.3m (51% × £30.0m)). The difference between this goodwill of £6.1m and the negative goodwill of £4.7m (calculated using the method provided by company law and FRS 102), i.e. £10.8m, is to be taken to reserves (presumably through other comprehensive income). This difference of £10.8m, together with the previously calculated debit to other comprehensive income of £5.9m, means that a credit of £4.9m is taken to other comprehensive income. This effectively represents

49% of the fair value increase of £10m in the assets of Company B at the date of the business combination (i.e. £30m – £20m, being £8m + £12m (Company B profits recognised between transaction 1 and 2)).

4   DISCLOSURES

The disclosure requirements of FRS 102 in relation to business combinations and goodwill are considerably less onerous than those required by both previous UK GAAP and IFRS, and are to be found mostly in paragraphs 19.25 – 19.26A. The Companies Act contains a number of detailed disclosure requirements. Some of these duplicate those contained in FRS 102 but there are a few additional matters in the legislation, and these are considered at 4.3.3 below.

4.1   Business combinations during the reporting period

For each business combination, excluding any group reconstruction (see 5.5 for disclosure requirements in respect of group reconstructions), that was effected during the period, the acquirer shall disclose the following:

- the names and descriptions of the combining entities or businesses;
- the acquisition date;
- the percentage of voting equity instruments acquired;
- the cost of the combination and a description of the components of that cost (such as cash, equity instruments and debt instruments);
- the amounts recognised at the acquisition date for each class of the acquiree's assets, liabilities and contingent liabilities, including goodwill;
- the useful life of goodwill, and if this exceeds five years, supporting reasons for this; and
- the periods in which any negative goodwill (see 3.8.3 above) will be recognised in profit or loss. *[FRS 102.19.25].*

Disclosure is required of the amounts of revenue and profit or loss of the acquiree since the acquisition date included in the consolidated statement of comprehensive income. Such disclosure should be provided for individual business combinations that are material; or in aggregate for business combinations that are not individually material. *[FRS 102.19.25A].*

Whilst FRS 6 required disclosure of reasons for fair values having been determined on a provisional basis, along with disclosure and explanation of subsequent material adjustments to those provisional fair values, *[FRS 6.27],* FRS 102 is silent on such requirements. Nonetheless, we believe good practice would be to disclose where provisional fair values have been used; as any subsequent adjustments will be accounted for retrospectively by restating comparatives, we would expect disclosure that such adjustments have been made, and the reasons therefore.

4.2   All business combinations

In addition to disclosures for business combinations effected during the period, an acquirer should disclose a reconciliation of the carrying amount of goodwill at the beginning and end of the reporting period, showing separately:

- changes arising from new business combinations;
- amortisation;
- impairment losses;
- disposals of previously acquired businesses; and
- other changes. *[FRS 102.19.26]*.

A similar reconciliation is also required in respect of any negative goodwill – albeit with no impairment, and with 'amortisation' replaced by 'amounts recognised in profit or loss in accordance with paragraph 19.24(c)'. *[FRS 102.19.26A]*.

Reconciliations need not be presented for prior periods. *[FRS 102.19.26 and 26A]*.

Where impairment losses arise on goodwill, Section 27 of the standard dictates further disclosures be made in respect of the amount of the impairment losses on goodwill, a description of the events and circumstances leading to the recognition of impairment losses, as well as disclosure of any reversals of impairment losses (see Chapter 22 at 7).

4.3   Other disclosures

4.3.1   Contingent liabilities

Where contingent liabilities of the acquiree cannot be reliably measured, the acquirer discloses the information about that contingent liability as required by Section 21 (see Chapter 17 at 3.10.3). *[FRS 102.19.20(b)]*.

4.3.2   Step acquisitions

As discussed at 3.10 above, in rare cases where the method for calculating goodwill set out in company law and paragraph 9.19B of FRS 102 would be misleading, the goodwill should be calculated as the sum of goodwill arising from each purchase of an interest in the relevant undertaking adjusted as necessary for any subsequent impairment. Where the FRS 102 or statutory requirement is not applied, paragraph 3.5 of FRS 102 sets out the necessary disclosures.

4.3.3   Company law disclosures

The Companies Act contains a number of detailed disclosure requirements that are relevant for business combinations. Some of these duplicate those contained in FRS 102 but there are a few additional matters in the legislation that need to be considered.

The Companies Act requires disclosure of the names of subsidiaries acquired, and whether they have been accounted for by the acquisition or the merger method of accounting, even if they do not significantly affect the figures shown in the consolidated financial statements. *[1 Sch 13(2)]*.

Chapter 15

In relation to acquisitions which significantly affects the figures shown in the consolidated financial statements, the Companies Act requires disclosures of:

- the composition and the fair value of the consideration for the acquisition given by the parent company and its subsidiary undertakings;
- where the acquisition method of accounting has been adopted:
  - the book values immediately prior to the acquisition of each class of assets and liabilities of the undertaking or group acquired in tabular form;
  - the fair values at the date of acquisition, of each class of assets and liabilities of the undertaking or group acquired in tabular form;
  - a statement of the amount of any goodwill or negative consolidation difference arising on the acquisition;
  - an explanation of any significant adjustments made. *[6 sch 3(3), (4)]*.

There must also be stated the cumulative amount of goodwill resulting from acquisitions in that and earlier years which has been written off otherwise than in the consolidated profit and loss account. *[CA2006, Sch 6, para. 14(1)]*.

UK company law does provide that the above information need not be disclosed with respect to an undertaking which:

- is established under the law of a country outside the United Kingdom, or
- carries on business outside the United Kingdom,

if in the opinion of the directors of the parent company the disclosure would be seriously prejudicial to the business of that undertaking or to the business of the parent company or any of its subsidiary undertakings and the Secretary of State agrees that the information should not be disclosed. *[6 Sch 16]*.

5   GROUP RECONSTRUCTIONS

As we have seen, unlike IFRS 3 which explicitly scopes out combinations of entities or businesses under common control *[IFRS 3.2(c)]*, Section 19 is applicable to business combinations which constitute group reconstructions – albeit the 'normal' rules are tailored for those situations.

FRS 102 requires that all business combinations shall be accounted for by applying the purchase method except for group reconstructions which *may* be accounted for using the merger accounting method [emphasis added]. *[FRS 102.19.6]*.

The Accounting Council advised the FRC that FRS 102 should retain the current accounting permitted by FRS 6 for group reconstructions. The Accounting Council noted that whilst EU-adopted IFRS does not provide accounting requirements for the accounting for business combinations under common control the accounting provided by FRS 6 is well understood and provides useful requirements. It therefore decided to carry forward these requirements into FRS 102. *[FRS 102.AC.64]*.

As such, and consistent with the wording of FRS 6, it can be seen that under FRS 102 the use of merger accounting for group reconstructions is to be optional. In most cases where the criteria to apply merger accounting are met, the 'acquirer' will wish to use merger accounting, thereby avoiding the need to determine fair values of the identifiable assets, liabilities and contingent liabilities of the 'acquiree' as well as the fair value of the consideration given.

Where the option of using the merger accounting method is not taken, or, technically, cannot be taken because cash is involved, it would seem that the purchase method (acquisition accounting) needs to be used. Historically, FRS 6 stated 'acquisition accounting would require the restatement at fair value of the assets and liabilities of the company transferred, and the recognising of goodwill, which is likely to be inappropriate in the case of a transaction that does not alter the relative rights of the ultimate shareholders' *[FRS 6.78]*, and this sentence in FRS 6 was used as support for the argument that application of acquisition accounting was unlikely to give a true and fair view. While FRS 102 contains no such health warning, the position is likely to remain the same that, in certain circumstances, notwithstanding that it is permitted (or required, where the strict criteria of merger accounting are not met) by company law and FRS 102, the application of the purchase method and all that entails would not be appropriate, and that a 'true and fair override' to apply the merger accounting method may be necessary.

5.1 Scope and applicability to various structures

FRS 102 defines a group reconstruction as any of the following arrangements:

- the transfer of an equity holding in a subsidiary from one group entity to another;

- the addition of a new parent entity to a group;

- the transfer of equity holdings in one or more subsidiaries of a group to a new entity that is not a group entity but whose equity holders are the same as those of the group's parent; or

- the combination into a group of two or more entities that before the combination had the same equity holders. *[FRS 102 Appendix I].*

Additionally, the standard identifies that while the wording explaining the merger accounting method (see 5.3 below) is drafted in terms of an acquirer or issuing entity issuing shares as consideration for the transfer of shares in the other parties to the combination, the provisions also apply to other arrangements that achieve similar results. *[FRS 102.19.28].* As such, it would seem that – subject to meeting the criteria for applying the merger method (see 5.2 below) – arrangements such as acquisition by an individual entity of the trade and net assets of another entity within the same group would appear to be within the scope of the provisions around group reconstructions.

5.2 Qualifying conditions

Under FRS 102, group reconstructions may be accounted for by using the merger accounting method provided:

- the use of the merger accounting method is not prohibited by company law or other relevant legislation;

- the ultimate equity holders remain the same, and the rights of each equity holding, relative to the others, are unchanged; and

- no non-controlling interest in the net assets of the group is altered by the transfer. *[FRS 102.19.27].*

Chapter 15

5.2.1   *Company law considerations*

The Companies Act requirements result from the implementation of the EC Seventh Directive on Company Law, and hence apply only to consolidated financial statements. The conditions laid down in UK company law which have to be met before merger accounting can be applied are as follows:

(a)   that at least 90% of the nominal value of the relevant shares in the undertaking acquired (excluding any shares held as treasury shares) is held by or on behalf of the parent company and its subsidiary undertakings,

(b)   that the proportion referred to in paragraph (a) was attained pursuant to an arrangement providing for the issue of equity shares by the parent company or one or more of its subsidiary undertakings,

(c)   the fair value of any consideration other than the issue of equity shares given pursuant to the arrangement by the parent company and its subsidiary undertakings did not exceed 10% of the nominal value of the equity shares issued, and

(d)   that adoption of the merger method of accounting accords with generally accepted accounting principles or practice. *[6 Sch 10(1)].*

'Relevant shares' for the purposes of condition (a) are defined as being those carrying unrestricted rights to participate both in distributions and in the assets upon liquidation. *[6 Sch 10(2)].*

In satisfying condition (c), it should be noted that it refers to the *nominal* value of the shares issued, rather than their *fair* value in setting the 10% limit, and therefore could be quite restrictive. It should also be noted that as the limit applies to any consideration other than the issue of equity shares, it does not just apply to cash consideration, but also to other forms such as loan stock or the assumption of debt. (This differs from Article 20 of the Seventh Directive which disqualifies transactions where the consideration includes a cash payment exceeding 10% of the nominal value of the shares issued to effect the business combination. However, in transposing into UK law, the restriction on cash was extended to cover any form of consideration other than equity).

In addition to these conditions in the Act applying only to consolidated financial statements, it should also be noted that the conditions only apply where an undertaking becomes a subsidiary undertaking of the parent company. *[6 Sch 7(1)].* They do not apply to group reconstructions involving a business which is not a subsidiary undertaking.

5.3   Merger accounting method

The standard explains that where the merger accounting method is applied:

(a)   the carrying values of the assets and liabilities of the parties to the combination are not required to be adjusted to fair value, although appropriate adjustments should be made to achieve uniformity of accounting policies in the combining entities. *[FRS 102.19.29].*

(b)   the results and cash flows of all the combining entities should be brought into the financial statements of the combined entity from the beginning of the financial year in which the combination occurred, adjusted so as to achieve uniformity of accounting policies.

(c)   the comparative information should be restated by including the total comprehensive income for all the combining entities for the previous reporting period and their statement of financial position for the previous reporting date, adjusted as necessary to achieve uniformity of accounting policies. *[FRS 102.19.30]*.

(d)   the difference, if any, between the nominal value of the shares issued plus the fair value of any other consideration given, and the nominal value of the shares received in exchange should be shown as a movement on other reserves in the consolidated financial statements. Any existing balances on the share premium account or capital redemption reserve of the new subsidiary should be brought in by being shown as a movement on other reserves. These movements should be shown in the statement of changes in equity. *[FRS 102.19.31]*.

(e)   merger expenses are not to be included as part of this adjustment, but should be charged to the statement of comprehensive income as part of profit or loss of the combined entity at the effective date of the group reconstruction. *[FRS 102.19.32]*.

We note that this description of the merger accounting method explicitly requires the results of all combining entities to be included from the beginning of the financial year and for comparatives to be restated. *[FRS 102.19.29 and 30]*. While these paragraphs are framed in the context of a parent combining with a new subsidiary, and will apply to consolidated financial statements prepared by the parent, paragraph 19.28 extends group reconstruction to other arrangements that achieve similar results, for example, the acquisition by an individual entity of the trade and net assets of a fellow subsidiary within the same group. In such circumstances, it has been common for UK companies to 'merger account' only from the date of transfer of the unincorporated businesses meeting the criteria for merger accounting, rather than reflecting it from the beginning of the financial year and for comparative periods. We note the Accounting Council does not expect the introduction of FRS 102 to change the accounting for group reconstructions. *[FRS 102.AC.64]*. Since there are no changes to the requirements of FRS 6, it would appear that this practice might continue.

5.3.1   Equity eliminations

As well as combining the assets and liabilities of the companies concerned, it will be necessary to eliminate the share capital of the subsidiary against the cost of the investment as stated in the balance sheet of the holding company. This is in principle a straightforward exercise, but when the two amounts do not equate to each other, the question arises of what to do with the difference, positive or negative.

The description of the merger accounting method above appears to presume that the cost of the investment will normally be carried at the nominal value of the shares of the holding company which have been issued to effect the combination, together with the fair value of any other consideration given. (The ability to record these shares at nominal rather than fair values on issue depends on qualifying for merger relief under section 612 of the Companies Act 2006, which is discussed under 5.4.1 below.) This will not be the case in a group reconstruction falling within the ambit of group reconstruction relief under section 611 of the Companies Act 2006 (see 5.4.2 below) where as a result of recognising a minimum premium value in share premium, the cost reflects an amount in excess of the nominal value of the shares issued. However, we believe such cost should be used in determining the difference to be accounted for under FRS 102.

FRS 102 requires the difference to be shown as a movement on other reserves in the consolidated financial statements and also to be shown in the statement of changes in equity. *[FRS 102.19.31]*. The Companies Act 2006 also requires such difference to be shown as a movement in consolidated reserves. *[6 Sch 11(6)]*. However, neither the standard nor the legislation specifies any particular reserve.

Where the cost of the investment is less than the nominal value of the share capital of the subsidiary, the elimination of these two amounts will leave a residual credit in shareholders' funds in the consolidated balance sheet; this is generally classified as some form of capital reserve.

Where the reverse situation applies, the net debit has to be eliminated against consolidated reserves in some way and choices have to be made as to the order in which the group's reserves should be applied for this purpose. There are no particular rules on the matter in any authoritative document, but the normal practice under previous UK GAAP (and the requirements in this respect are unchanged in FRS 102) is to apply these first against the most restricted categories of reserves, and subsequently if any excess remains, against the group's retained earnings. Where the reserves are in the subsidiary concerned then, in effect, this is equivalent to the partial capitalisation of the reserves of the subsidiary; if they had had a bonus issue out of their own reserves prior to the group reconstruction, to make their share capital equal to the consideration shares offered by the new holding company, no consolidation difference would have emerged.

Apart from the effects of dealing with any imbalance as discussed above, there is no other elimination of the reserves of the subsidiary, which are combined with those of the holding company, in contrast to the treatment under the purchase method. However, some of the subsidiary's reserves may need to be reclassified in order to make sense in the context of the group financial statements.

FRS 102 requires that any existing balance on the share premium account or capital redemption reserve of the new subsidiary undertaking should be brought in by being shown as a movement on other reserves. *[FRS 102.19.31]*. This is because they do not relate to the share capital of the reporting entity. Again, this difference should be shown in the statement of changes in equity. *[FRS 102.19.31]*. Such a difference should probably be taken to the same reserve as that on the elimination of the share capital of the subsidiary, because in reality the distinction between share capital and share premium can be seen to be arbitrary in this context.

5.3.2 Expenses of the merger

One other question which sometimes arises in this context is how to account for the expenses of the merger. FRS 102 requires that all merger expenses should be charged to the statement of comprehensive income as part of profit or loss of the combined entity at the effective date of the group reconstruction. *[FRS 102.19.32]*.

However, some of these costs may be regarded as share issue expenses and therefore qualify to be written off against any share premium account recognised by the holding company in respect of the shares issued to effect the group reconstruction. FRS 102 does not prohibit the subsequent charging of such costs to the share premium account by means of a transfer between reserves.

5.4 Implications on the share premium account

Under the Companies Act 2006, a company issuing shares at a premium must transfer a sum equal to the aggregate amount or value of premiums on those shares to an account called 'the share premium account'. *[s.610(1)]*.

UK company law includes certain relief – 'merger relief' and 'group reconstruction relief' – from recognising share premium at all, or in full, where certain conditions are met. These reliefs, which are discussed further below, impact the accounting considerations for capital and reserves of the issuing entity only, but are not relevant for the purposes of measuring the cost of the combination in connection with application of the purchase method.

The implications of these reliefs in measuring the cost of investments in subsidiaries in separate financial statements are discussed further in Chapter 6 at 4.2.1.

5.4.1 Merger relief

The rules on merger relief and those on merger accounting are frequently confused with each other. However, not only are they based on the satisfaction of different criteria, they in fact have quite distinct purposes. As discussed at 5.3 above, merger accounting is a form of financial reporting which applies to a group reconstruction which meet certain qualifying conditions, but although the merger relief provisions were originally brought in to facilitate merger accounting, merger relief is purely a legal matter to do with the maintenance of capital for the protection of creditors and has very little to do with accounting *per se*. Moreover, merger relief may be available under transactions which are accounted for as acquisitions, rather than mergers, and the two are not interdependent in that sense.

Section 612 of the Companies Act 2006 broadly relieves companies from the basic requirement of section 610 to set up a share premium account in respect of equity shares issued in exchange for shares in another company in the course of a transaction which results in the issuing company securing at least a 90% holding in the equity shares of the other company. The precise wording of section 612 (and related sections) should be considered carefully in order to ensure that any particular transaction falls within its terms.

There are some differences of legal opinion as to whether merger relief is in fact *compulsory* when the conditions of section 612 are met, or whether it is optional. The Act says that where the conditions are met, then section 610 'does not apply to the premiums on those shares' issued. Therefore some people argue that the effect of this relief is simply to make section 610 optional rather than mandatory, but others take the view that it makes it illegal to set up a share premium account.

Where merger relief is taken, and the purchase method is applied, as the cost of the business combination is based on the fair value, any amount that would have been taken to share premium account needs to be reflected in another reserve, generally a 'merger reserve' in the consolidated financial statements. Where merger accounting is applied, such an amount is not reflected in any 'merger reserve' as the mechanics of merger accounting uses the nominal value of shares issued. Whether such a reserve arises in the separate financial statements is discussed in Chapter 6 at 4.2.1.

It should be noted, however, that merger relief is not applicable in a case falling within the ambit of 'group reconstruction relief'. *[s612(4)].*

5.4.2   *Group reconstruction relief*

Section 611 of the Companies Act 2006 provides a partial relief from the basic requirement to Section 610 as regards transfers to the share premium account where the issuing company is a wholly-owned subsidiary of another company and allots shares to that other company or another wholly-owned subsidiary of that other company in consideration for the transfer to the issuing company of non-cash assets of a company that is a member of the group of companies that comprises the holding company and all its wholly-owned subsidiaries. *[s611(1)].*

Application of the relief in this instance means that just a 'minimum premium value' is required to be transferred to the share premium account – that amount being the amount (if any) by which the base value of the consideration for the shares allotted (being the base value of the assets transferred less the base value of any liabilities of the transferor company assumed by the issuing company) exceeds the aggregate nominal value of the shares. *[s611].*

Where group reconstruction relief is taken, and the purchase method is applied, as the cost of the business combination is based on the fair value, any amount that would otherwise have been taken to share premium account needs to be reflected in another reserve, generally a 'merger reserve' in the consolidated financial statements. Where merger accounting is applied, such an amount is not reflected in any 'merger reserve' as the mechanics of merger accounting uses the nominal value of shares issued (or the base value of the consideration). Whether such a reserve arises in separate financial statements is discussed in Chapter 6 at 4.2.1.

5.5   Disclosure requirements

As discussed at 4 above, group reconstructions are scoped out of the 'normal' business combination disclosures required by FRS 102. Instead, FRS 102 provides that, for each group reconstruction that was effected during the period, the combined entity shall disclose:

- the names of the combining entities (other than the reporting entity);

- whether the combination has been accounted for as an acquisition or a merger; and

- the date of combination. *[FRS 102.19.33].*

Additional disclosures required to be given for a group reconstruction accounted for as a merger by virtue of the Companies Act are:

- The composition and fair value of the consideration given by the parent company and its subsidiary undertakings must be stated. *[6 Sch 13(3)].*

- Any adjustment to consolidated reserves as a result of setting off the amount in respect of qualifying shares issued by the parent or its subsidiary undertakings in consideration for the acquisition and the fair value of any other consideration for the acquisition of shares against the nominal value of the issued share capital of the undertaking acquired held by the parent company and its subsidiary undertakings. *[6 Sch 11(6)].*

Additional disclosures required to be given for a group reconstruction accounted for as an acquisition by virtue of the Companies Act are discussed at 4.3.3 above.

6   SUMMARY OF GAAP DIFFERENCES

The key differences between FRS 102, previous UK GAAP and IFRS in accounting for business combinations are set out below.

	FRS 102	*Previous UK GAAP*	*IFRS*
Method of accounting for business combinations	Purchase method used for all business combinations except certain group reconstructions and public benefit entity combinations.	Purchase method used for all business combinations except those meeting specific criteria for merger accounting.	Purchase method used for all business combinations (apart from common control transactions that may be accounted for by merger accounting if applying the GAAP hierarchy).
Common control transactions	Merger accounting permitted for certain group reconstructions. Merger method of accounting explained.	Merger accounting permitted for certain group reconstructions. Merger method of accounting explained.	Out of scope.

Chapter 15

	FRS 102	*Previous UK GAAP*	*IFRS*
Definition of a business	Integrated set of activities and assets conducted and managed for providing a return to investors or lower costs or other economic benefits to policyholders or participants.	Not defined.	Integrated set of activities and assets capable of being conducted and managed for providing return in form of dividends, or lower costs or other economic benefits to investors or other owners, members or participants.
Identifying the acquirer	There must be an acquirer for all business combinations using purchase method.	Not explicitly addressed.	There must be an acquirer for all business combinations within scope of IFRS 3.
Acquisition expenses	Capitalise as part of cost/goodwill.	Capitalise as part of cost/goodwill.	Expense.
Contingent consideration	Recognise if probable and can be reliably measured. Subsequent adjustments to goodwill.	Reasonable estimate of fair value of amounts payable. Subsequent adjustments to goodwill.	Fair value. Subsequent adjustments to profit or loss.
Contingent payments to employees or selling shareholders	No specific guidance.	Limited guidance.	Contingent consideration forfeit if employment terminates is post employment remuneration.
Initial measurement of acquiree's assets, liabilities and contingent liabilities	Fair value (except deferred tax, employee benefits, share-based payments).	Fair value (but then provides application guidance for determining fair value for different assets/liabilities).	Fair values (except deferred tax, employee benefits, share-based payments, assets held for sale, reacquired rights, indemnification assets).
Measurement period – adjustments to provisional fair values in subsequent periods	Retrospective (12 month period after acquisition to make adjustments).	Prospective (up until end of first full financial year following acquisition).	Retrospective (12 month period after acquisition to make adjustments).
Recognition of intangible assets separate from goodwill	Recognise if fair value can be measured reliably. However, not recognised if it arises from legal or other contractual rights *and* no history or evidence of exchange transactions for same/similar assets and fair value dependent on immeasurable variables.	Recognised if fair value can be measured reliably. However, not recognised if not controlled through legal rights or custody or can be disposed of only as part of a business.	Recognise at fair value if meets either separability or contractual – legal criterion (regardless of being separable).

Deferred tax	Recognised on differences between acquisition fair value and tax base (including revaluations and intangibles 'created' as a result of the combination but excluding goodwill).	Not usually recognised on differences between acquisition fair value and tax base.	Recognised on differences between acquisition fair value and tax base (including revaluations and intangibles 'created' as a result of the combination but excluding goodwill)
Step acquisitions	Cost of business combination is aggregate of fair values of assets given, liabilities assumed and equity instruments issued at each stage of transaction plus any directly attributable costs.	Cost of business combination is aggregate of fair values of assets given, liabilities assumed and equity instruments issued at each stage of transaction plus any directly attributable costs.	Existing interest held immediately before control is achieved is remeasured at fair value with gain or loss recognised in profit or loss. Fair value is used in computing goodwill. Changes in value in other comprehensive income reclassified to profit or loss.
Non-controlling interests	Measure at share of net assets.	Measure at share of net assets.	Policy choice for each business combination to use fair value or share of net assets for interests entitled to proportionate net assets share. Otherwise, fair value.
Positive goodwill	Amortise on systematic basis over useful life (cannot be indefinite). If no reliable estimate of useful life default is 5 years. Test for impairment if impairment indicators.	Amortise on systematic basis over useful life (can be indefinite with T&F override). Rebuttable presumption that maximum useful live is 20 years. Test for impairment if impairment indicators. Annual impairment test if life considered indefinite or in excess of 20 years.	Not amortised. Measured at cost less impairment. Mandatory annual impairment test.
Negative goodwill	Amount up to fair value of non-monetary assets recognised n periods in which non-monetary assets are recovered. Excess amortised over periods expected to benefit.	Amount up to fair value of non-monetary assets recognised in periods in which non-monetary assets are recovered. Excess amortised over periods expected to benefit.	Immediate gain in profit or loss.
Disclosures	Less onerous disclosure requirements.	Extensive disclosures for material acquisitions, and additional disclosures for 'substantial acquisitions'.	Extensive disclosure requirements.

Chapter 15

References

1 IFRS 3 (2004), Illustrative Examples, *Examples of items acquired in a business combination that meet the definition of an intangible asset.*

Chapter 16   Leases

List of examples

Chapter 16

Chapter 16   Leases

1   INTRODUCTION

Section 20 – *Leases* – of FRS 102 follows the precedent of earlier UK and international accounting standards such as SSAP 21 – *Leases and Hire Purchase Contracts* – and IAS 17 – *Leases.* Although a lease is an agreement whereby the lessor conveys to the lessee the right to use an asset for an agreed period of time in return for a payment or series of payments, companies are required in certain circumstances to capitalise these assets in their statements of financial position, together with the corresponding obligations, irrespective of the fact that legal title to those assets is vested in another party.

A finance lease is essentially regarded as an entitlement to receive, and an obligation to make, a stream of payments that are substantially the same as blended payments of principal and interest under a loan agreement. Consequently, the lessee accounts for an asset and the obligation to pay the amount due under the lease contract; the lessor accounts for its investment in the amount receivable under the lease contract rather than for the leased asset itself. An operating lease, on the other hand, is regarded primarily as an uncompleted contract committing the lessor to provide the use of an asset in future periods in exchange for consideration similar to a fee for a service payable by the lessee. The lessor continues to account for the leased asset itself rather than any amount receivable in the future under the contract.

The term 'lease' also applies to arrangements that do not take the form of leases. Instead, they essentially combine rights to use assets and the provision of services or outputs, for agreed periods of time in return for a payment or series of payments, e.g. outsourcing arrangements that include the provision of assets and services. Entities have to consider the substance of these arrangements to see if they are, or contain, leases. If so, then the elements identified as a lease will be subject to the requirements of Section 20.

FRS 102 has been derived from IFRS for SMEs, so its underlying principles and the language used more closely resemble IAS 17 than SSAP 21. It also incorporates some treatments from previous UK GAAP that are not present in IAS 17. However, although there are differences between FRS 102 and previous UK GAAP, these may well have minor or no effects on the majority of leases. The most important differences are described at 2 below.

2   COMPARISON BETWEEN SECTION 20, PREVIOUS UK GAAP AND IFRS

FRS 102 has been derived from IFRS for SMEs, so Section 20 more closely resembles IAS 17 than SSAP 21 and it includes some matters covered in IAS 17 but not in SSAP 21. However, in certain important respects, FRS 102 includes measurement rules that more closely resemble those in SSAP 21.

The following sections discuss the main differences between FRS 102 and SSAP 21 (2.1 below) and IAS 17 (2.2 below), although the practical application of SSAP 21 discussed in 2.1 below also takes account of interpretations that had become accepted as part of previous UK GAAP, relevant UITF pronouncements and the effects of FRS 5 – *Reporting the substance of transactions* – as appropriate.

2.1   Key differences between FRS 102 and previous UK GAAP

2.1.1   Scope

2.1.1.A   Leases classified as financial instruments

FRS 102 excludes from scope leases that could lead to a loss to the lessor or the lessee as a result of non-typical contractual terms, e.g. embedded derivatives that are not closely related to the host contract. This scope exclusion is discussed at 3.1.3 below. There is no such scope exclusion under SSAP 21, although entities that have adopted FRS 26 – *Financial Instruments: recognition and measurement* – are required to identify embedded derivatives that are not closely related to the host (lease) contract and account separately for these derivatives in accordance with FRS 26.[1]

2.1.1.B   Arrangements that do not take the legal form of a lease ('embedded leases')

FRS 102 includes within its scope rights to use assets in return for payments contained within arrangements that do not take the legal form of a lease. This is derived from IFRIC 4 – *Determining whether an Arrangement contains a Lease* – and these are often referred to as embedded leases. This is described at 3.2 below.

There is no equivalent formal guidance in SSAP 21 but the absence of an equivalent to IFRIC 4 in previous UK GAAP does not mean that leases embedded within an arrangement are ignored.

The term 'lease' as used in SSAP 21 'also applies to other arrangements in which one party retains ownership of an asset but conveys the right to the use of the asset to another party for an agreed period of time in return for specified payments'. This statement is ambiguous as it is not clear whether the 'specified payments' are those that convey the right to use the asset or the payments made under the arrangement. Therefore, entities have looked to FRS 5 to see if more complex arrangements contain 'in substance' or 'embedded' leases. Although FRS 5 does not override SSAP 21, it provides additional guidance where arrangement terms are more complex, or the lease is only one element in a larger series of transactions. An analogy can also be drawn from FRS 5's Application Note F, addressing the Private Finance Initiative, which requires private and public sector bodies to analyse these transactions into their components and, if required by the analysis, to account for the asset-related part as if it were a finance lease.

This means that it is not uncommon under SSAP 21 for arrangements to be examined to see if they contain payments for the right to use assets that should be accounted for as leases.

2.1.2 Lease classification

FRS 102 bases lease classification on the extent to which the risks and rewards incidental to ownership of a leased asset lie with the lessor or the lessee. The standard lists a number of examples of situations that individually or in combination would be expected to lead to a lease being classified as a finance lease; these are described at 3.4.1 below.

Whilst not formally part of SSAP 21, similar lists of indicators (developed by the ICAEW) are taken into account in classifying leases under previous UK GAAP.[2]

SSAP 21 includes a rebuttable presumption that transfer of risks and rewards occurs if the present value of the minimum lease payments discounted at the interest rate implicit in the lease, amounts to substantially all (normally 90% or more) of the fair value of the leased asset. There is no such rebuttable presumption in FRS 102.

One must not overestimate the importance of the '90% test' as a difference between FRS 102 and SSAP 21. The 90% test does not provide a strict mathematical definition of a finance lease and other factors must be considered, including those in the lists of indicators developed by the ICAEW. By comparison, one of FRS 102's indicators refers to the present value of the minimum lease payments being at least 'substantially all of the fair value of the asset' but the standard does not put a percentage to 'substantially all'. FRS 102 is the same as IAS 17 in this respect. This is discussed further at 3.4.1 below.

In practice, therefore, there will be little difference in classification between the two standards.

2.1.2.A Inception of the lease

Both FRS 102 and previous UK GAAP require lease classification to be made at the inception of the lease but this term is defined differently.

Under FRS 102, as defined in the Glossary, the inception of the lease is the earlier of the date of the lease agreement and the date of commitment by the parties to the principal provisions of the lease.

SSAP 21 defines 'inception' as the earlier of the time the asset is brought into use and the date from which rentals first accrue.[3] In other words, the date of inception is the date on which there are accounting entries are required to be made. The term is therefore more akin to the date of commencement under FRS 102, which is the date from which the lessee is entitled to exercise its right to use the leased asset and the date of initial recognition of the lease. *[FRS 102 Appendix I].*

Inception and commencement of the lease under FRS 102 are discussed further at 3.4.2 below.

Chapter 16

This means that the inception of the lease could be at an earlier date under FRS 102 than under previous UK GAAP, usually in the case of assets constructed for the purpose of the lease. For example, an airline may enter into a contract to lease aircraft with a manufacturer for which the aircraft have not yet been constructed. Under FRS 102, classification of the arrangement as a finance or operating lease takes place at the inception of the lease which is before construction. Accounting entries are made at the commencement of the lease, which will usually be on delivery of an asset such as an aircraft or on completion of construction of a property. Under previous UK GAAP, the lease would not be classified as a finance or operating lease until this point.

Because a lease is classified at inception, FRS 102's requirements regarding changes to classification apply from this date, even though no accounting entries are made prior to lease commencement. Briefly, this means that changes to lease terms but not changes to estimates can affect lease classification; see 3.4.3 below. In addition, the final cost of the asset, and its fair value, may not be known until after the date of inception, e.g. if the asset is in the course of construction. Changes to the lease payments as a result of such events should be taken into account in establishing, at inception, whether it is a finance or operating lease; see 3.4.2 below.

2.1.3   Measurement: operating leases

2.1.3.A   Straight-line basis for lease payments

SSAP 21 states that operating lease rentals should be charged to the income statement on a straight-line basis. *[SSAP 21.37]*. FRS 102 contains this same requirement with one exception: if lease payments increase annually by fixed increments intended to compensate for expected annual inflation over the lease period, the fixed minimum increment that reflects expected general inflation will be recognised as an expense as incurred. See 3.8.1.A below.

However, previous UK GAAP practice is often based on the substance of such arrangements and many entities do not account for fixed increments in operating lease payments on a straight-line basis if they are intended to compensate for expected annual inflation. This has the effect that there is no difference between SSAP 21 as applied and FRS 102.

2.1.3.B   Lease incentives

UITF 28 – *Operating lease incentives* – requires lease incentives to be recognised over the shorter of the lease term and a period ending on a date from which it is expected the prevailing market rental will be payable.[4]

FRS 102 requires the incentives to be recognised over the lease term (see 3.8.1.A and 3.8.1.C below).

2.1.4   Measurement: finance leases

2.1.4.A   Initial direct costs

Under FRS 102, initial direct costs incurred in arranging a lease are included in the initial measurement of a finance lease receivable and factored into the calculation of the interest rate implicit in the lease. Under SSAP 21, initial direct costs may be deferred and apportioned over the period of the lease or, as deferral is not mandatory, they may be expensed immediately, in which case the earnings under SSAP 21 will be greater by this amount. If initial direct costs are deferred, SSAP 21 does not require them to be included in the initial measurement of a finance lease receivable but requires them to be apportioned over the period of the lease on a systematic and rational basis. *[SSAP 21.44]*. Unless they are included in the initial measurement of the finance lease receivable, they will be excluded from the calculation of the interest rate implicit in the lease.

Initial direct costs are discussed below at 3.7.1.A (lessees) and 3.7.2 (lessors).

2.1.4.B   Recognition of finance income/gross earnings by lessors

FRS 102 requires finance income, which is the difference between the net and gross investment in the lease, to be recognised on a pattern reflecting a constant periodic rate of return on the net investment in the finance lease. This is discussed at 3.7.2.A below.

SSAP 21 requires the difference, called gross earnings, to be allocated to accounting periods to give a constant periodic rate of return on the lessor's net *cash* investment. *[SSAP 21.39]*. The lessor's net cash investment includes other cash flows, mainly those relating to tax in the lease. In principle this might defer income recognition if the entity receives up-front tax allowances for the asset.

2.1.5   Disclosure: operating leases

FRS 102 requires a lessee to disclose the total of future minimum lease payments under non-cancellable operating leases, analysed by the amount that will fall due in not more than one year, in one to five years and in more than five years from the date of the statement of financial position. *[FRS 102.20.16]*.

By contrast, SSAP 21 requires an analysis of the following year's commitment analysed into the same bands as those required by FRS 102. *[SSAP 21.56]*. It does not require disclosure of amounts falling due after more than one year.

2.2   Key differences between FRS 102 and IFRS

2.2.1   Scope

2.2.1.A   Transactions that are not, in substance, leases

SIC-27 – *Evaluating the Substance of Transactions in the Legal Form of a Lease* – includes guidance regarding 'lease agreements' that are not, in substance, leases.

An entity may enter into a transaction or a series of structured transactions with an unrelated party or parties that involves the legal form of a lease. Although the details may vary considerably, a typical example involves an entity leasing or selling assets to an investor and leasing the same assets back. The sale and leaseback transactions are often entered into so that the investor may achieve a tax advantage. *[SIC-27.5]*. In recent years these arrangements have become less common as taxation authorities in various jurisdictions have restricted the potential tax benefits.

If the transaction does not meet the definition of a lease under IAS 17, SIC-27 deals with the extent to which the arrangement gives rise to other assets and liabilities of the reporting entity, the reporting of any other obligations and the recognition of fee income. *[SIC-27.2].*

FRS 102 does not include specific guidance regarding arrangements that are not in substance leases. There is a general 'substance over form' requirement, which states that transactions and other events and conditions should be accounted for and presented in accordance with their substance and not merely their legal form, as this enhances the reliability of financial statements. *[FRS 102.2.28].* SIC-27 may provide relevant guidance in the absence of specific requirements in FRS 102.

2.2.2   Measurement: operating leases

2.2.2.A   Straight-line basis for lease payments

IAS 17 requires all operating lease payments to be recognised as an expense on a straight-line basis, unless another systematic basis is more appropriate.

FRS 102 contains this same requirement with one exception: if lease payments increase annually by fixed increments intended to compensate for expected annual inflation over the lease period, the fixed minimum increment that reflects expected general inflation will be recognised as an expense as incurred. *[FRS 102.20.15(b)].* See the discussion at 3.8.1.A below.

2.2.2.B   Leases of land and buildings

IAS 17 requires leases of land to be assessed separately from building leases and classified as finance or operating leases in accordance with the general rules. The minimum lease payments are allocated between land and buildings in proportion to the relative fair values of the interests in each element, i.e. the leasehold interest in the land and buildings at the inception of the lease.

FRS 102 is silent about separating the land and buildings elements of leases. Generally, in the context of the UK property market, the minimum lease payments are attributed to a single leased asset and land and buildings are not separately accounted for. Only those leases of land and buildings that are of such length that they allow the lessee to redevelop the site are likely to include a significant value for the land element. In such cases, it may be necessary to account separately for the building and the land.

3   REQUIREMENTS OF SECTION 20 FOR LEASES

3.1   Scope

The standard applies in accounting for all leases other than: *[FRS 102.20.1]*

- leases to explore for or use minerals, oil, natural gas and similar non-regenerative resources;
- licensing agreements for such items as motion picture films, video recordings, plays, manuscripts, patents and copyrights (see 3.1.1 below);

- the measurement of property held by lessees that is accounted for as investment property and measurement of investment property provided by lessors under operating leases. Investment properties are accounted for in accordance with Section 16 – *Investment Property* (see Chapter 12);

- measurement of biological assets held by lessees under finance leases and biological assets provided by lessors under operating leases. Biological assets are addressed in Section 34 – *Specialised Activities* (see Chapter 29); and

- leases that could lead to a loss to the lessor or the lessee as a result of non-typical contractual terms (see 3.1.3 below).

3.1.1   Licensing agreements

FRS 102 does not define a licensing agreement so the distinction between 'leases' and 'licensing agreements' is not clear.

A conventional licence over an intangible asset such as a film or video commonly gives a non-exclusive 'right of access' to show or view the video simultaneously with many others but not a 'right of use' of the original film or video itself because the licensee does not control that asset. Arguably, this puts such a conventional licence outside the scope of Section 20. The relationship between rights of access to and rights of use over the underlying asset is explored further at 3.2 below.

Intangible assets themselves may be the subject of leases, as discussed below.

3.1.2   Arrangements over intangible assets

Section 20 applies to leases over intangible assets although there are additional issues when the right is not tangible.

First, the 'right' in question must be an asset that meets the definition of an intangible asset in Section 18 – *Intangible Assets other than Goodwill* (see Chapter 14). Second, because many of these rights are either acquired for an up-front sum or for a series of periodic payments and by definition the period covered by the payments equals the life of the right, there is divergence in practice in how to account for them, i.e. whether they are leases (and if so, whether finance or operating leases) or whether they are acquisitions of assets on deferred payment terms.

Many intangible assets are capable of being subdivided with the part subject to the lease itself meeting the definition of an intangible asset. If the rights are exclusive, the part will meet the definition of an intangible asset because it is embodied in legal rights that allow the acquirer to control the benefits arising from the asset. For example, an entity might sell to another entity rights to distribute its product in a particular geographical market. If the right is not on an exclusive basis then it may not be within scope of Section 20, e.g. it may be a licensing agreement as discussed at 3.1.1 above. Other arrangements may, on analysis, prove to be for services and not for a right of use of an intangible asset; see 3.1.4 below.

Note that it is irrelevant to the analysis whether the original right is recognised in the financial statements of the lessor prior to the inception of the arrangement.

Rights that do meet the definition of an intangible asset often have a finite life, e.g. a radio station may acquire a licence that gives it a right to broadcast over specified frequencies for a period of seven years. Yet the underlying asset on which the right depends exists both before and after the 'right' has been purchased and may have an indefinite life, as is the case with the broadcast spectrum. Many intangible rights can be purchased for an upfront sum, which will be accounted for as the acquisition of an intangible asset that is capitalised at cost. As an alternative to up-front purchase, an entity may pay for the same right in a series of instalments over a period of time. Does it become an operating lease because it is only a short period out of the life of the underlying asset? Usually the answer is no: these rights will not be accounted for as operating leases by comparison to the total life of the underlying asset as the arrangement is over the *right* in question.

If the arrangement is considered to be a lease, then it will be accounted for in accordance with Section 20, whatever the pattern of payment. If it is a finance lease then the asset will be measured using the methodology prescribed by FRS 102 described in 4 below.

If, rather than as a lease, the arrangement is seen as the acquisition of an asset on deferred payment terms, the effective interest rate method is mandated. The effective interest rate is the rate that exactly discounts estimated future cash payments or receipts through the expected life of the financial instrument or, when appropriate, a shorter period, to the carrying amount of the financial asset or financial liability. The effective interest rate is determined on the basis of the carrying amount of the financial asset or liability at initial recognition. *[FRS 102.11.16]*. This will take account of estimated future cash payments or receipts through the expected life of the financial instrument that may include some of the 'contingent' payments that are excluded from the measurement of finance leases (see 3.4.5 below).

Therefore, there are arguments as to whether there are assets and liabilities to be recognised and, even if recognition is accepted, measurement depends on the view that is taken of the applicable Section. In the absence of a clear principle, there is likely to be diversity in practice.

3.1.3   Leases with non-typical contractual terms classified as financial instruments

Certain leases are not accounted for as leases in accordance with Section 20 but instead classified as financial instruments within scope of Section 12 – *Other Financial Instruments Issues* – if the lease could, as a result of non-typical contractual terms, result in a loss to the lessor or the lessee. The Accounting Council's Advice to the FRC to issue FRS 102 states in paragraph 65 that this could include contractual terms that are unrelated to changes in the price of the leased asset, changes in foreign exchange rates, or a default by one of the counterparties. In paragraph 66 of its advice, the Accounting Council notes that 'the reference to "changes in the price of the leased asset" is framed widely and in practice it does not expect many leases to fall within the scope of Section 12.' (Section 12 is addressed in Chapter 8.)

Although it is not clear precisely what contractual terms are referred to, it is likely that this does *not* refer to rents that vary according to:

- non-financial variables specific to the parties to the contract, e.g. rents that vary with future sales or amount of future use; or

- future price indices and future market rates of interest that are relevant to the parties to the contract.

Accounting for these contingent rents is addressed by Section 20 (see 3.4.5 below). Briefly, they are excluded from the minimum lease payments so do not affect the measurement of assets and liabilities in finance leases; instead, whatever the classification of the lease, they are treated as income or an expense as incurred.

3.1.4 Arrangements that include services

Agreements that transfer the right to use assets contain leases even if the lessor is obliged to provide substantial services in connection with the operation or maintenance of the assets. *[FRS 102.20.2]*. Costs for services are excluded from the minimum lease payments in assessing or measuring leases; see the definition in 3.3 and the discussion at 3.8.1.B and 3.8.2 below.

A contract for services that does not transfer the right to use assets from one contracting party to the other will not be accounted for under Section 20. *[FRS 102.20.2]*. Instead, the provider of services will recognise revenue by applying the principles in Section 23 – *Revenue* – while the purchaser will recognise costs as incurred (see Chapter 18). However, these contracts have to be examined carefully to see if they do, in fact, contain an embedded lease arrangement; see 3.2 below.

Service concession arrangements also contain services as well as the provision of assets. There are separate accounting requirements for these arrangements, which are characterised by control of the asset and services by the 'grantor', a public sector body, a public benefit entity or other entity operating to fulfil a public service obligation. The contractual terms of certain contracts or arrangements may meet both the scope requirements of Section 20 and those of Section 34 that pertain to service concessions. *[FRS 102.34.12, 12A]*. Where this is the case, the arrangement must be accounted for as a service concession in accordance with the requirements of Section 34 (see Chapter 29). *[FRS 102.34.12C]*.

3.2 Determining whether an arrangement contains a lease

Some arrangements do not take the legal form of leases. Instead, they essentially combine rights to use assets and the provision of services or outputs, for agreed periods of time in return for a payment or series of payments. Examples include outsourcing arrangements, telecommunication contracts that provide rights to capacity and take-or-pay contracts. *[FRS 102.20.3]*. Entities have to consider the substance of these arrangements to see if they are, or contain, leases.

This will depend on whether: *[FRS 102.20.3A]*

(a) a specific asset or assets must be used in order to fulfil the arrangement (see 3.2.1 below); and

(b) the arrangement conveys a right to use the asset. This will be the case where the arrangement conveys to the purchaser the right to control the use of the underlying asset (see 3.2.2 below).

3.2.1   *A specified asset*

Section 20 does not include much additional explanation. It notes that an asset may be explicitly or implicitly identified; in neither case does this automatically mean that the arrangement contains a lease. Although a specific asset may be explicitly identified in an arrangement, it is not the subject of a lease if fulfilment of the arrangement is not dependent on the use of the specified asset. An asset is implicitly specified if, for example, the supplier owns or leases only one asset with which to fulfil the obligation and it is not economically feasible or practicable for the supplier to perform its obligation through the use of alternative assets. *[FRS 102.20.3A].*

For example, an arrangement in which an entity (the purchaser) outsources its product delivery department to another organisation (the supplier) will not contain a lease if the supplier is obliged to make available a certain number of delivery vehicles of a certain standard specification and the supplier is a delivery organisation with many suitable vehicles available.

The arrangement is more likely to contain a lease if the supplier identifies specific vehicles out of its fleet and those vehicles must be used to provide the service. If the supplier has to supply and maintain a specified number of specialist vehicles in the purchaser's livery, then this arrangement is likely to contain a lease. These arrangements may be commercially more akin to outsourcing the purchaser's acquisitions of delivery vehicles rather than its delivery functions.

Similar issues would have to be taken into account if data processing functions are outsourced as these may require substantial investment by the supplier in computer hardware dedicated to the use of a single customer.

Some arrangements may allow the supplier to replace the specified asset with a similar asset if the original asset is unavailable (e.g. because one of the delivery vehicles has broken down). As this is in effect a warranty obligation it does not preclude lease treatment.

The supplier may have a substantive right to substitute other vehicles at will for the vehicles it has identified. This is common in transport arrangements where a contract may identify the original asset (e.g. a particular truck, aircraft or ship) used for the service but the supplier is not obliged to use the asset identified by the contract. Fulfilment of the arrangement would not then be dependent on the use of the specified asset and the identification of the asset does not indicate that the arrangement contains a lease.

Where arrangements are likely to contain leases (e.g. delivery vehicles in livery, dedicated hardware), the purchaser cannot be unaware that there are specific assets underlying the service. There would have been negotiations between supplier and purchaser that would probably be reflected in the contract documentation. By contrast, if the purchaser does not know what assets are used to provide the service (beyond the fact that they are trucks and computers, of course), and in the circumstances it is reasonable not to know, it is plausible that there is no underlying lease in the arrangement. This remains true even if the supplier has dedicated specific assets to the service being provided and expects their cost to be recouped during the course of the contractual relationship.

3.2.1.A   *Parts of assets and the unit of account*

Some issues relating to units of account in relation to intangible rights are discussed at 3.1.2 above; this section deals more directly with parts (or 'components') of physical assets.

Some arrangements transfer the right to use an asset that is a part of a larger asset which raises the issue of whether and when such rights should be accounted for as leases.

Generally, a portion of a larger asset that is not physically distinct is not considered to be a specified asset. Therefore an arrangement that allows an entity to use a quarter of the capacity of a whole pipeline will not usually be considered to contain a lease.

However, some arrangements refer to physical 'parts' of larger assets. For example, a plant may contain more than one production unit or line that might be regarded as a single 'part' (because each makes the same product) or alternatively each of its units or lines might be regarded as separate 'parts'. Depending on other aspects of the arrangement, a particular production line may be the asset that is the subject of a lease, if the supplier cannot transfer production to a different line to supply the goods.

Similar examples from the telecommunications industry include fibre optical cable, satellite and wireless tower arrangements. Fibre agreements vary from those that allow use of the whole cable, through those that specify the wavelength or spectrum within a fibre to the most common arrangements which are essentially for transmission capacity within the vendor's fibre cable or network. As a result, arrangements have to be examined carefully to determine if they do specify an asset.

3.2.2   A right to use the asset

The arrangement will not contain a lease unless it conveys a right to use the asset. This will be the case where the arrangement conveys to the purchaser the right to control the use of the underlying asset. *[FRS 102.20.3A].* Section 20 does not give any further explanation. FRS 102 defines control solely in the context of control of an entity.

There is no equivalent to IFRIC 4 which provides further guidance about control in the context of leases and which may help identify whether an arrangement contains a lease. Entities may use this guidance in the absence of further explanation in Section 20.

IFRIC 4 suggests that certain features may indicate that the purchaser (lessee) controls the asset:[5]

(a)   the purchaser takes all, or all but an insignificant amount, of the output, unless the purchaser pays:

    (i)   the current market price per unit of output as of the time of delivery of the output; or

    (ii)   a contractually fixed price per unit of output.

    If an entity pays amounts that vary according to the specific terms of the arrangement between it and the supplier, this suggests that there may be a lease.

(b)   the asset may be on the purchaser's premises or in another location where the purchaser has the ability or right to control physical access and also obtains or controls more than an insignificant amount of the output.

If an entity physically controls the asset as well as benefiting from its output, this is *prima facie* evidence that the arrangement contains a lease.

(c)   the purchaser has the ability or right to operate the asset or direct others to operate the asset in a manner it determines while obtaining or controlling more than an insignificant amount of the output of the asset.

This is similar to the previous point but based on controlling how the asset is operated, rather than controlling access to that asset.

3.2.2.A   *Market price or fixed price per unit*

An entity might take all, or almost all, of the output yet the arrangement will not contain a lease if an entity pays market price for the output or a fixed amount per unit. The payment for the output is not related to the use of the underlying asset. This is illustrated in Example 16.1 (a) and (b) below.

If the arrangements are neither for a fixed amount nor at market price, this will suggest a more direct relationship with the underlying asset. The price per unit of output may vary with volume, or may be calculated based on a variety of market inputs. There is a link between the output and the underlying asset and the arrangement may contain a lease. These arrangements will always be more complex and are illustrated in Example 16.1 (c) and (d) below.

Example 16.1:   *Control of assets*

(a)   Entity A, a privately owned shipping company that runs ferries between a port and an offshore island pays Entity B, the company that constructed and operates the port terminal, £3.50 for each passenger that uses the terminal.

(b)   Entity C enters into a take-or-pay contract to buy electricity from Entity D, a private sector supplier. The amount of electricity that Entity C is committed to buy is equivalent to the total output of one of the supplier's plants, which is located close to the purchaser's factory and is specified in the lease agreement. In the jurisdiction, there is a market price for electricity and Entity C pays that market price. An efficient distribution network means that Entity D would be able to sell any power not taken by Entity C and would also be able to use other power plants to supply electricity to Entity C. Entity C does not control the power supply plant so the arrangement does not contain a lease.

Examples (a) and (b) illustrate arrangements that depend on the use of an asset, although in the case of (b) it may not even be a specified asset if the supplier D could use other plants. There is no evidence from the contractual arrangements that Entity A or Entity C controls the asset that underlies the output that they are purchasing, so the arrangements do not contain leases. Instead these are arrangements for services.

(c)   Purchaser E and supplier F enter into a parts supply agreement for the lifetime of the finished product concerned. F uses tooling equipment that is specific to the needs of E. The tooling is explicitly identified in the agreement and F could not use an alternative asset. The estimated capacity of the tooling equipment is 500,000 units which corresponds to the total production of the finished product units over its life cycle. E takes substantially all of the output produced by F using the specific tooling.

Purchaser E and supplier F agree on the following unit price reductions in the parts supply agreement to reflect F's increasing efficiencies and economies of scale:

from 0 to 100,000 units, price per unit £150;

from 100,001 to 200,000, price per unit £140;

from 200,001 to 300,000, price per unit £135;

from 300,001 to 400,000, price per unit £132;

above 400,000, price per unit £130.

Stepped pricing does not mean price 'fixed per unit of output' and, particularly as the stepped pricing is agreed in advance, it is not equal to the current market price per unit as of the time of delivery of the output. The arrangement contains a lease.

The purchaser will have to determine whether it is a finance or operating lease.

(d) Entity G purchases power from a specified plant that has been newly built by Supplier H to ensure sufficient capacity to meet all of G's needs. G will pay charges that contain the following elements:

(i) a fixed charge that is based on the plant's depreciation, ongoing maintenance and estimated costs of power generation; and

(ii) a cost per unit of power produced that is indexed by the current market price.

Although the power supply varies with the market price, it is not the market price per unit. Therefore, unlike (b) above, the arrangement will contain a lease and the entity will have to assess whether it is a finance or operating lease.

3.2.2.B   *Control of physical access and ability or right to operate the asset*

These are less often encountered in practice. IFRIC 4 suggests that an arrangement might contain a lease if an entity physically controls the asset as well as benefiting from its output, i.e. even though the supplier might be able to use those assets to provide output for others. Clearly, if the asset is on the purchaser's premises this will suggest that it might control the asset.

The ability of the purchaser to operate the asset may be evidenced by its ability to hire, fire or replace the operator of the asset or its ability to specify significant operating policies and procedures in the arrangement. In substance, the effect of these powers must be to reduce the role of the supplier to that of an agent, working to the instructions of the purchaser. If the purchaser only has the right to monitor the supplier's activities (e.g. for quality) and no ability to direct the detailed operating policies and procedures of the supplier, then the purchaser would not control the asset.

3.3   Terms used in Section 20

The following terms in Section 20 are defined in the Glossary to FRS 102:

Term	Definition
Asset	A resource controlled by the entity as a result of past events and from which future economic benefits are expected to flow to the entity.
Commencement of lease term	The date from which the lessee is entitled to exercise its right to use the leased asset. It is the date of initial recognition of the lease (i.e. the recognition of the assets, liabilities, income or expenses resulting from the lease, as appropriate).
Contingent rent	That portion of the lease payments that is not fixed in amount but is based on the future amount of a factor that changes other than with the passage of time (e.g. percentage of future sales, amount of future use, future price indices, and future market rates of interest).

Chapter 16

Fair value	The amount for which an asset could be exchanged, a liability settled, or an equity instrument granted could be exchanged, between knowledgeable, willing parties in an arm's length transaction. In the absence of any specific guidance provided in the relevant section of ... [FRS 102], the guidance in paragraphs 11.27 to 11.32 shall be used in determining fair value.
Finance lease	A lease that transfers substantially all the risks and rewards incidental to ownership of an asset. Title may or may not eventually be transferred. A lease that is not a finance lease is an operating lease.
Fixed assets	Assets of an entity which are intended for use on a continuing basis in the entity's activities.
Gross investment in a lease	The aggregate of: (a) the minimum lease payments receivable by the lessor under a finance lease; and (b) any unguaranteed residual value accruing to the lessor.
Inception of the lease	The earlier of the date of the lease agreement and the date of commitment by the parties to the principal provisions of the lease.
Interest rate implicit in the lease	The discount rate that, at the inception of the lease, causes the aggregate present value of: (a) the minimum lease payments; and (b) the unguaranteed residual value to be equal to the sum of: (i) the fair value of the leased asset; and (ii) any initial direct costs of the lessor.
Lease	An agreement whereby the lessor conveys to the lessee in return for a payment or series of payments the right to use an asset for an agreed period of time.
Lease incentives	Incentives provided by the lessor to the lessee to enter into a new or renew an operating lease. Examples of such incentives include up-front cash payments to the lessee, the reimbursement or assumption by the lessor of costs of the lessee (such as relocation costs, leasehold improvements and costs associated with pre-existing lease commitments of the lessee), or initial periods of the lease provided by the lessor rent-free or at a reduced rent.
Lease term	The non-cancellable period for which the lessee has contracted to lease the asset together with any further terms for which the lessee has the option to continue to lease the asset, with or without further payment, when at the inception of the lease it is reasonably certain that the lessee will exercise the option.
Lessee's incremental borrowing rate (of interest)	The rate of interest the lessee would have to pay on a similar lease or, if that is not determinable, the rate that, at the inception of the lease, the lessee would incur to borrow over a similar term, and with a similar security, the funds necessary to purchase the asset.

Minimum lease payments	The payments over the lease term that the lessee is or can be required to make, excluding contingent rent, costs for services and taxes to be paid by and reimbursed to the lessor, together with:
	(a) for a lessee, any amounts guaranteed by the lessee or by a party related to the lessee; or
	(b) for a lessor, any residual value guaranteed to the lessor by:
	(i) the lessee;
	(ii) a party related to the lessee; or
	(iii) a third party unrelated to the lessor that is financially capable of discharging the obligations under the guarantee.
	However, if the lessee has an option to purchase the asset at a price that is expected to be sufficiently lower than fair value at the date the option becomes exercisable for it to be reasonably certain, at the inception of the lease, that the option will be exercised, the minimum lease payments comprise the minimum payments payable over the lease term to the expected date of exercise of this purchase option and the payment required to exercise it.
Net investment in a lease	The gross investment in a lease discounted at the interest rate implicit in the lease.
Onerous contract	A contract in which the unavoidable costs of meeting the obligations under the contract exceed the economic benefits expected to be received under it.
Operating lease	A lease that does not transfer substantially all the risks and rewards incidental to ownership. A lease that is not an operating lease is a finance lease.

3.4 Lease classification

A lease is classified as a finance lease if it transfers substantially all the risks and rewards incidental to ownership. A lease is classified as an operating lease if it does not transfer substantially all the risks and rewards incidental to ownership. *[FRS 102.20.4]*.

The individual circumstances of a lessor and lessee may differ in respect of a single lease contract. As a result, the application of the definitions to the circumstances of the lessor and lessee may result in the same lease being classified differently by them. For example, a lease may be classified as an operating lease by the lessee and as a finance lease receivable by the lessor if it includes a residual value guarantee provided by a third party. Residual value guarantors are discussed further at 3.4.6.A below.

Lease classification is made at the inception of the lease, which is the earlier of the date of the lease agreement or of a commitment by the parties to the principal provisions of the lease. Classification is not changed during the term of the lease unless the lessee and the lessor agree to change the provisions of the lease (other than simply by renewing the lease), in which case the lease classification must be re-evaluated (see 3.4.3 below). *[FRS 102.20.8]*.

Chapter 16

3.4.1   *Classification as finance or operating leases*

The classification of leases adopted in the standard is based on the extent to which the risks and rewards incidental to ownership of a leased asset lie with the lessor or the lessee. Risks include the possibilities of losses from idle capacity or technological obsolescence and of variations in return due to changing economic conditions. Rewards may be represented by the expectation of profitable operation over the asset's economic life and of gain from appreciation in value or realisation of a residual value.

SSAP 21 includes the rebuttable presumption that the transfer of substantially all of the risks and rewards occurs if, at the inception of the lease, the present value of the minimum lease payments amounts to substantially all (normally 90% or more) of the fair value of the leased asset. *[SSAP 21.15]*. Section 20 provides no numerical guidelines to be applied in classifying a lease as either finance or operating. Lease classification should not be reduced to a single pass or fail test.

Instead, the section takes a more principles-based substance over form approach. It makes the statement that the classification of a lease depends on the substance of the transaction rather than the form of the contract, and lists a number of examples of situations that individually or in combination would normally lead to a lease being classified as a finance lease: *[FRS 102.20.5]*

(a)   the lease transfers ownership of the asset to the lessee by the end of the lease term;

(b)   the lessee has the option to purchase the asset at a price which is expected to be sufficiently lower than the fair value at the date the option becomes exercisable such that, at the inception of the lease, it is reasonably certain that the option will be exercised (frequently called a 'bargain purchase' option);

(c)   the lease term is for the major part of the economic life of the asset even if title is not transferred;

(d)   at the inception of the lease the present value of the minimum lease payments amounts to at least substantially all of the fair value of the leased asset; and

(e)   the leased assets are of a specialised nature such that only the lessee can use them without major modifications being made.

All of these are indicators that the lessor will only look to the lessee to obtain a return from the leasing transaction, so it can be presumed that the lessee will, in fact, pay for the asset.

Title does not have to be transferred to the lessee for a lease to be classified as a finance lease. The point is that the lease will almost certainly be classified as a finance lease if title does transfer.

Options such as those referred to under (b) are common in lease agreements. The bargain purchase option is designed to give the lessor its expected lender's return (comprising interest on its investment perhaps together with a relatively small fee), but no more, over the life of the agreement.

Lease term (criterion(c)) must be measured by reference to economic life, which is the period for which the asset is expected to be usable by one or more users, not the physical life. The economic life will usually be shorter than the physical life if the asset is subject to technological obsolescence. A computer may be capable of use for six or seven years but would rarely be used beyond three years. It is not so well appreciated that buildings suffer from technological obsolescence which means that an office building with a fabric life of sixty years may have an economic life of half of that. It becomes increasingly hard to adapt buildings to rapidly-changing IT or energy efficiency requirements. The residual value of these assets at the end of the economic life is minimal.

The economic life would therefore include additional lease terms with the same or different lessees. It is not the same as the useful life which is specific to the lessee and is the estimated remaining period, from the commencement of the lease term but without the limitation of the lease term, over which the entity expects to consume the economic benefits embodied in the asset (see 3.7.1.D below).

Criteria (c) and (d) above also include the unquantified expressions 'major part of' and 'substantially all', which means that judgement must be used in determining their effect on the risks and rewards of ownership. By contrast, in US GAAP the equivalent to (c) above that was in SFAS 13 – *Accounting for leases* (now in Accounting Standards Codification [ASC] 840 – *Leases*) does quantify when a lease will be a capital lease (the equivalent of a finance lease). In ASC 840, if the lease term is equal to 75% or more of the estimated economic life of the leased asset, the lease will normally be a capital lease (there is an exception if the beginning of the lease term falls within the last 25% of the total estimated economic life of the leased asset, including earlier years of use, where this criterion is not used for purposes of classifying the lease).[6] In practice, if the lease is for the major part of the economic life of the asset, it is unlikely that the lessor will rely on any party other than the lessee to obtain its return from the lease. This would still not be conclusive evidence that the lease should be classified as a finance lease. There could be other terms that indicate that the significant risks and rewards of ownership rest with the lessor, e.g. lease payments might be reset periodically to market rates or there might be significant technological, obsolescence or damage risks borne by the lessor.

Similarly, whilst (d) above refers to the present value of the minimum lease payments being at least 'substantially all of the fair value of the asset', it does so without putting a percentage to it; FRS 102, like IAS 17, has no '90% test'. However, we see no harm in practice in at least applying the '90% test' as a rule of thumb benchmark as part of the overall process in reaching a judgement as to the classification of a lease. Clearly, though, it cannot be applied as a hard and fast rule.

For an example of the 90% test, see Example 16.3 at 3.5 below. In that example, the present value of the minimum lease payments is calculated to be 92.74% of the asset's fair value; as this exceeds 90%, this would normally indicate that the lease is a finance lease. Nevertheless, the other criteria discussed above would need to be considered as well.

Consequently, we would stress that the 90% test is not an explicit requirement of the standard and should not be applied as a rule or in isolation, but it may be a useful tool to use in practice in attempting to determine the economic substance of a lease arrangement.

Chapter 16

The standard then goes on to list the following indicators of situations that, individually or in combination, could also lead to a lease being classified as a finance lease: *[FRS 102.20.6]*

(a)   if the lessee can cancel the lease, the lessor's losses associated with the cancellation are borne by the lessee;

(b)   gains or losses from the fluctuation in the residual value of the leased asset accrue to the lessee (for example, in the form of a rent rebate equalling most of the sales proceeds at the end of the lease); and

(c)   the lessee has the ability to continue the lease for a secondary period at a rent which is substantially lower than market rent.

If it is clear from other features that the lease does not transfer substantially all risks and rewards incidental to ownership, the lease is classified as an operating lease. *[FRS 102.20.7]*.

Other considerations that could be made in determining the economic substance of the lease arrangement include the following:

●   are there contingent rents, as a result of which the lessee does not have substantially all risks and rewards incidental to ownership? For example are the lease rentals based on a market rate for use of the asset (which would indicate an operating lease) or a financing rate for use of the funds, which would be indicative of a finance lease? and

●   is the existence of put and call options a feature of the lease? If so, are they exercisable at a predetermined price or formula (indicating a finance lease) or are they exercisable at the market price at the time the option is exercised (indicating an operating lease)?

Note that these two considerations mean that an arrangement for the whole of an asset's useful life may be an operating lease, as may an agreement in which the lessee has a right to obtain title to the asset at market value.

3.4.2   *Inception and commencement of the lease*

The standard distinguishes between the inception of the lease (when leases are classified) and the commencement of the lease term (when recognition takes place).

The *inception* of the lease is the earlier of the date of the lease agreement and the date of commitment of the parties to the principal terms of the lease. *[FRS 102 Appendix I]*. This is the date on which a lease is classified as a finance or operating lease.

The *commencement* of the lease term is the date on which the lessee is entitled to exercise its right to use the leased asset and is the date of initial recognition of the assets, liabilities, income and expenses of the lease in the financial statements. *[FRS 102 Appendix I]*.

This means that the entity makes an initial calculation of the assets and liabilities under a finance lease at inception of the lease but does not recognise these in the financial statements until the commencement date, if this is later. The amounts in the initial calculation may in some circumstances be revised. It is not uncommon for the two dates to be different, especially if the asset is under construction. Section 20 requires the lessee under a finance lease to recognise the asset at its fair value or, if lower, at the present value of the minimum lease payments, determined at the inception of the lease. *[FRS 102.20.9].* This means that, if the final cost of the asset, and hence its fair value, is not known until after the date of inception, hindsight should be used to establish that fair value.

IAS 17 explicitly notes that lease payments may be adjusted for changes in the lessor's costs during the period between inception and commencement. The lease may allow for changes in respect of costs of construction, acquisition costs, changes in the lessor's financing costs and any other factor, such as changes in general price levels, during the construction period. *[IAS 17.5].* Such changes are also relevant in establishing the fair value and minimum lease payments for the purposes of Section 20. Changes to the lease payments as a result of such events should be deemed to take place at inception of the lease and be taken into account in establishing whether it is a finance or operating lease at inception and, if it is a finance lease, the amount at which the asset and liability should be recorded (see 3.7 below). A contract might estimate the cost of construction to be £1 million but allow for additional specific increased costs of up to 5% to be reflected in increased payments made by the lessee. If those increased costs are incurred, then the fair value and minimum lease payments at inception will take account of the increased cost of the asset (£1.05 million) and the increased lease payments.

The fair value may be known at inception but payment delayed until commencement, which may happen with large but routinely constructed assets such as aircraft or railway locomotives. The lease liability will increase between the date of inception and the date of commencement, taking account of payments made and the interest rate implicit in the lease. Again, this is not addressed by Section 20 but the lessee ought to add the increase in the liability until the commencement date to the asset. It is not a finance cost on the liability (no liability is recognised prior to commencement) and nor need it be an expense. It is not appropriate to recognise at commencement the liability that was calculated at inception as that would change the interest rate implicit in the lease.

Circumstances in which lease classification might be changed are discussed below.

3.4.3 Changes to the classification of leases

Classification is not changed during the term of the lease unless the lessee and the lessor agree to change the provisions of the lease (other than simply by renewing the lease), in which case the lease classification must be re-evaluated. *[FRS 102.20.8].*

Changes in estimates (for example, changes in estimates of the economic life or of the residual value of the leased item) or changes in circumstances (for example, default by the lessee) do not result in the lease being reclassified for accounting purposes.

The distinction between changes to the provisions of the lease and changes in estimate is that the former, unlike the latter, are always the result of agreements between the lessee and lessor.

This section does not address the measurement of these changes. References to the sections in which the changes are dealt with are given below.

(a)   Changes to the provisions or terms of an existing lease ('modifications')

Changes to the provisions or terms of an existing lease (referred to here as 'modifications') are changes to the contractual terms and conditions that are not part of the original lease. Modifications that affect a lease's classification are those that affect the risks and rewards incidental to ownership of the asset by changing the terms and cash flows of the existing lease. Examples of modifications that could affect classification include those that change the duration of the lease and the number, amount and timing of lease payments or the inclusion or an option to acquire not previously part of the lease terms.

The revised agreement resulting from the modification is considered as if it were a new agreement which should be accounted for appropriately, as a finance or operating lease, prospectively over the remaining term of the lease.

FRS 102 does not give any specific guidance on how to assess whether modified lease terms give rise to a new classification so the general classification rules described in 3.4.1 above must be applied. Nor does it explain how to measure modifications of leases if changes affect the value of the assets and liabilities for both lessor and lessee. These issues are discussed at 3.9 below. See section 3.9.1 below for discussion on how to assess whether the classification has changed, based on the revised cash flows, and how to account for the reclassification is in 3.9.2.

If lease terms are modified but the classification does not change, the entity will still have to account for the modified cash flows. How to account for the changes if a finance lease remains a finance lease is discussed at 3.9.3.A below. Accounting for changes to the terms of operating leases, where those changes do not result in reclassification, is considered at 3.9.3.B below.

Some changes to lease terms will not affect the cash flows at all, e.g. those that change terms such as the names of the contracting parties. Other changes could affect only the lessor, e.g. a transfer from one lessor to another that requires no consent or other action by the lessee and where there is no change to the lease cash flows.

(b)   the lessor and lessee renew the lease

If the lessee and lessor renew the lease, this could mean one of the following:

- exercising an option to extend the lease or purchase the underlying asset, when these options were included in the original lease but exercise of the options was not considered probable at its inception. Changes in circumstances or intentions do not give rise to a new classification of the original lease, unless they indicate that the initial classification was made in error because it was not based on the substance of the arrangement at the time it was entered into. This means that the intention to exercise a renewal option in a lease originally classified as an operating lease will not change that classification.

- entering into a new lease with the lessor. For example, an entity may have a right to 'renew' a lease of business premises for a further term after expiry of the initial term at the market rent at the date the new agreement is entered into. This is not a change to the terms of the original lease. It may be under the terms of a statutory right to extend commercial leases found in many jurisdictions, whose purpose is to ensure that businesses are not forced to relocate. This is similar in effect to an option to extend at market value so under a risks and rewards model the secondary term would not pass the significant risks and rewards to the lessee.

The lessor and lessee could revoke the original lease and enter into a new one in its place, which would also be considered a renewal. It is necessary to ensure that the new lease terms are at fair value at the time it is entered into so it does not reflect, for example, underpayments made by the lessee under the terms of the original lease.

• extending the existing lease without changing any other term, e.g. with the consent of the lessor, continuing to use the asset for a period of time after the original expiry at the original rental. This has to be distinguished on the facts from a negotiation between the lessee and lessor that changes the terms of the original lease before its expiry, although this will probably also include other changes such as a different rental.

A new, renewed or extended lease will be classified on its own terms without any consideration of the terms and provisions of the original lease.

Example 16.2: Lease classification

Consider the following scenarios:

(a) Entity A leases a motor vehicle from Entity B for a non-cancellable three-year period. At the inception of the lease, the lease was assessed as an operating lease. The lease did not contain any explicit option in the lease contract to extend the term of the lease. A short period of time before the end of the lease term, Entity A applies to Entity B to extend the lease for a further two years. This extension is granted by the leasing company at fair value.

Entity A's negotiations result in a renewed (i.e. new) lease, not a change in the provisions of the original lease, which will be accounted for on its own terms. This does not affect the classification of the original lease.

(b) Entity C leases a machine tool from Entity D for 5 years, expecting to purchase a new asset after the lease expires. After 3 years, Entity C concludes that it is more economically viable for it to lease the asset from Entity D for a total of 8 years. The lessor agrees to revised lease terms and the lease is extended by 3 years, giving a total term of 8 years. At the same time the lease payments for years 4 and 5 are revised so that Entity C will pay a new rental for each of the years 4 to 8.

This is a lease modification as it has resulted in a change to the terms of the original lease. The entity will have to assess whether the revised lease is an operating or finance lease.

(c) Entity E leases an asset from Entity F for 10 years. The lease includes a purchase option under which Entity E may purchase the asset from Entity F at the end of the lease. The exercise price is fair value. Entity E is required to give notice of its intention to purchase no later than the end of the eighth year of the lease (since this arrangement allows Entity F time to market the leased asset for sale). On inception, Entity E classifies the lease as an operating lease, believing it was not reasonably certain that it would exercise the option. Near the end of the eighth year of the lease, Entity E serves notice that it will purchase the asset, thereby creating a binding purchase commitment.

Entity E exercises an option that was not considered reasonably certain at inception; this is a change in estimate and does not affect lease classification. Many entities would consider the arrangement to be executory at the time that the notice is given even though there is a legal obligation to make the option payment and therefore would account for the purchase option only when it is exercised.

Chapter 16

3.4.4   Lease term

The lease term is the non-cancellable period for which the lessee has contracted to lease the asset together with any further terms for which the lessee has the option to continue to lease the asset, with or without further payment, when at the inception of the lease it is reasonably certain that the lessee will exercise the option. *[FRS 102 Appendix I].*

A lease may contain terms that effectively force the lessee to continue to use the asset for the period of the agreement. Arguably, the substance of the transaction should be taken into account. Therefore, a lease may be non-cancellable if it can be cancelled only:

(a)   on the occurrence of a remote contingency;

(b)   with the permission of the lessor;

(c)   if the lessee enters into a new lease with the same lessor for the same or an equivalent asset; or

(d)   if the lessee is required to pay additional amounts that make it reasonably certain at inception that the lessee will continue the lease.

An example of (d) is a requirement that the lessee pays a termination payment equivalent to the present value of the remaining lease payments.

3.4.5   Contingent rent and minimum lease payments

Contingent rent is that portion of the lease payments that is not fixed in amount but is based on the future amount of a factor that changes other than with the passage of time (e.g. percentage of future sales, amount of future use, future price indices, and future market rates of interest). *[FRS 102 Appendix I].*

In the case of finance leases, contingent rents are excluded from minimum lease payments. Lessees charge contingent rents as expenses in the periods in which they are incurred. *[FRS 102.20.11].*

Contingent payments will be taken into account in assessing whether substantially all of the risks and rewards of ownership have been transferred; for example, property rentals that are periodically reset to market rates would tend to indicate that risks and rewards rest with the lessor – see the discussion at 3.4.1 above. This still leaves open to debate whether a particular 'contingency' is in fact contingent or is so certain that it ought to be reflected in the minimum lease payments for the purposes of classifying the lease. In practice this will always be based on an assessment of the individual circumstances.

For operating leases, FRS 102 is not explicit on the treatment of contingent rent. Practice under previous UK GAAP and current practice under IAS 17 is to exclude such amounts and we would expect this to be the general practice under FRS 102 as well. Accordingly, lease payments or receipts under operating leases may exclude contingent amounts. However, the area remains contentious and practice undoubtedly varies. Views are divided on whether minimum lease payments determined at the inception of the lease are revised on the occurrence of the contingency, e.g. whether minimum lease payments change when there are rent revisions that are stipulated in the original lease agreement, either for straight-line recognition or disclosure purposes.

Section 20 excludes from its scope 'leases that could lead to a loss to the lessor or the lessee as a result of non-typical contractual terms'. *[FRS 102.20.1(e), FRS 102.12.3(f)].* These contractual terms would be unrelated to changes in the price of the leased asset, changes in foreign exchange rates, or a default by one of the counterparties. Generally we would expect this to exclude contingent rents relating to the factors described above as they are not included in the measurement of assets and liabilities. Leases excluded from scope on this basis are discussed at 3.1.3 above and 3.6 below.

3.4.6 Residual values

The guaranteed residual value is:

(a) for a lessee, the part of the residual value that is guaranteed by itself or by one of its related parties. The amount of the guarantee is the maximum amount that could, in any event, become payable; and

(b) for a lessor, the part of the residual value that is guaranteed by the lessee or by a third party unrelated to the lessor who is financially capable of discharging the obligations under the guarantee.

This means that the lessor's unguaranteed residual value is any part of the residual value of the leased asset, whose realisation is not assured or is guaranteed solely by a related party of the lessor. If the net present value of the residual value of an asset is significant and is not guaranteed by the lessee or a party related to it, then the lease is likely to be classified as an operating lease. The risks of recovering the significant residual value will be the lessor's; consequently it is unlikely that 'substantially all' of the risks and rewards of ownership will have passed to the lessee.

There are frequently problems of interpretation regarding the significance of residual values in lease classification. Lessees may find it difficult to obtain information in order to calculate the unguaranteed residual values.

If lessees guarantee all or part of the residual value of the asset, this has to be taken into account in the lease classification.

If a related party, e.g. a member of the same group as the lessee, guarantees the residual, this can result in recognition of a finance lease in the consolidated financial statements and an operating lease in the individual entity. This assumes that there are no intra-group arrangements that transfer the guarantee back to the lessee.

3.4.6.A Residual value guarantors

A lessee and lessor may legitimately classify the same lease differently if the lessor has received a residual value guarantee provided by a third party. Residual value guarantors undertake to acquire the assets from the lessor at an agreed amount at the end of the lease term because they can dispose of the assets in a ready and reliable market. As a result, the lease is an operating lease for the lessee and a finance lease for the lessor. Residual value guarantors may be prepared to take the residual risk with many types of assets as long as there is a second-hand market. This is

Chapter 16

particularly common with vehicle leases where there is an efficient second-hand market, including price guides, many car dealers and car auctions.

3.5   Calculating the net present value of the minimum lease payments

An entity will frequently have to calculate the net present value of the minimum lease payments in order to classify a lease as a finance or operating lease as well as in accounting for finance leases. In order to do so, it must consider the residual value of the asset and whether there are any residual value guarantors. Once it has this information then it can calculate the implicit interest rate and present value of minimum lease payments, as in the following example:

Example 16.3:   Calculation of the implicit interest rate and present value of minimum lease payments

Details of a non-cancellable lease are as follows:

(i)   Fair value = £10,000

(ii)   Five annual rentals payable in advance of £2,100

(iii)   Lessor's unguaranteed estimated residual value at end of five years = £1,000

The implicit interest rate in the lease is that which gives a present value of £10,000 for the five rentals plus the total estimated residual value at the end of year 5. This rate can be calculated as 6.62%, as follows:

Year	Capital sum at start of period £	Rental paid £	Capital sum during period £	Finance charge (6.62% per annum) £	Capital sum at end of period £
1	10,000	2,100	7,900	523	8,423
2	8,423	2,100	6,323	419	6,742
3	6,742	2,100	4,642	307	4,949
4	4,949	2,100	2,849	189	3,038
5	3,038	2,100	938	62	1,000
		10,500		1,500	

In other words, 6.62% is the implicit interest rate that, at the inception of the lease, causes the aggregate present value of the minimum lease payments (£10,500) and the unguaranteed residual value (£1,000) to be equal to the fair value of the leased asset. Lessor's initial direct costs have been excluded for simplicity.

This implicit interest rate is then used to calculate the present value of the minimum lease payments, i.e. £10,500 discounted at 6.62%. This can be calculated at £9,274, which is 92.74% of the asset's fair value, indicating that the present value of the minimum lease payments is substantially all of the fair value of the leased asset and a finance lease is therefore indicated.

It would be appropriate for the lessee to record the asset at £9,274 as the present value of the minimum lease payments is lower than the fair value and this would take account of the lessor's residual interest in the asset.

The lessor will know all of the information in the above example, as it will have been used in the pricing decision for the lease. However, the lessee may not know either the fair value or the unguaranteed residual value and, therefore, not know the implicit interest rate. In such circumstances the lessee will substitute a rate from a similar lease or its incremental borrowing rate. The lessee is also unlikely to know the lessor's initial direct costs even if the other information is known, but this is unlikely to have more than a marginal effect on the implicit interest rate.

3.5.1 Fair value

Fair value is defined in Section 2 – *Concepts and Pervasive Principles* – as the amount for which an asset could be exchanged, a liability settled, or an equity instrument granted could be exchanged, between knowledgeable, willing parties in an arm's length transaction (see Chapter 3). *[FRS 102.2.34(b)].* Additional guidance is given in Section 11 – *Basic Financial Instruments* (see Chapter 8). *[FRS 102.11.27-11.32].* Although this does not refer to Section 20, it is used as guidance in establishing the fair value of property, plant and equipment and will therefore be relevant in establishing the fair value of assets held under leases. *[FRS 102.17.15(c)].*

In practice, the transaction price, i.e. the purchase price of the asset that is the subject of the lease, will be its fair value, unless there is evidence to the contrary.

3.6 Leases as financial instruments

Leases 'that could lead to a loss to the lessor or the lessee as a result of non-typical contractual terms' are out of scope of Section 20. *[FRS 102.20.1(e), FRS 102.12.3(f)].* This could include contractual terms that are unrelated to any of the following:

- changes in the price of the leased asset;
- changes in foreign exchange rates; or
- a default by one of the counterparties.

These leases with non-typical contractual terms are, in effect, financial instruments that are carried at fair value in accordance with Section 12 (see Chapter 8).

In general the lease rights and obligations that come about as a result of FRS 102 are recognised and measured in accordance with the rules in Section 20 and are not included within the scope of Section 11 or Section 12. The exceptions are:

- derecognition and impairment of receivables recognised by a lessor; and
- derecognition of payables recognised by a lessee arising under a finance lease.

In these cases the derecognition requirements (in paragraphs 11.33 to 11.35 and paragraphs 11.36 to 11.38, addressing respectively derecognition of financial assets and financial liabilities) and impairment accounting requirements (in paragraphs 11.21 to 11.26) apply. These are discussed at 3.7.4.B below.

Finance lease assets and liabilities are not necessarily stated at the same amount as they would be if they were measured as financial instruments. The most obvious differences are those between the interest rate implicit in the lease (IIR) and the effective interest rate, both of which are defined in the Glossary. *[FRS 102 Appendix 1].* The IIR (as described in 3.5 above) is the discount rate that, at the inception of the lease, causes the aggregate present value of the minimum lease payments (receivable during the non-cancellable lease term and any option periods that it is reasonably certain at inception the lessee will exercise) and the unguaranteed residual value to be equal to the sum of the fair value of the leased asset and any initial direct costs of the lessor. The effective interest rate, by contrast, is the rate that exactly discounts estimated future cash payments or receipts through the expected life of the financial instrument. The latter may include payments that would be considered contingent rentals, and hence excluded from the calculation of the IIR, and may take account of cash flows over a different period.

3.7   Accounting for finance leases

Lessees recognise finance leases as assets and liabilities in their statements of financial position at the commencement of the lease term at amounts equal at the inception of the lease to the fair value of the leased item or, if lower, at the present value of the minimum lease payments. In calculating the present value of the minimum lease payments the discount factor is the interest rate implicit in the lease, if this is practicable to determine; if not, the lessee's incremental borrowing rate should be used. Any initial direct costs of the lessee are added to the asset. 'Fair value' and 'minimum lease payments' are defined in 3.5.1 and 3.4.5 above.

The fair value and the present value of the minimum lease payments are both determined as at the inception of the lease. *[FRS 102.20.5(d)]*. At commencement, the asset and liability for the future lease payments are recognised in the statement of financial position at the same amount, calculated as at inception (see 3.4.2 above). The terms and calculations of initial recognition by lessees are discussed further in 3.7.1 below.

Lease payments made by the lessee are apportioned between the finance charge and the reduction of the outstanding liability. The finance charge should be allocated to periods during the lease term using the effective interest method so as to produce a constant periodic rate of interest on the remaining balance of the liability for each period. This is covered in 3.7.1.B below.

Lessors recognise assets held under a finance lease as receivables in their statements of financial position and present them as a receivable at an amount equal to the net investment in the lease. Lessors who are not manufacturers or dealers include costs that they have incurred in connection with arranging and negotiating a lease as part of the initial measurement of the finance lease receivable. Initial recognition by lessors, which is in many respects a mirror image of lessee recognition, follows at 3.7.2 below. The recognition of finance income and other issues in connection with subsequent measurement of the lessor's assets arising from finance leases is dealt with in 3.7.2.A below.

Residual values, to which finance leases are very sensitive, are discussed in 3.7.3 below.

The consequences of terminating a finance lease are described in 3.7.4 below. Subleases and back-to-back leases are discussed at 3.7.4.B below, as the principal accounting issue is the whether or not the conditions for derecognition are met by the intermediate party.

Manufacturer or dealer lessors have specific issues with regard to recognition of selling profit and finance income. These are dealt with at 3.7.5 below.

3.7.1   Accounting by lessees

3.7.1.A   Initial recognition

At commencement of the lease, the right of use and obligations for the future lease payments are recorded in the statement of financial position at the same amount. This is equal to the fair value of the leased asset or, if lower, the present value of the minimum lease payments, determined at the inception of the lease. *[FRS 102.20.9]*. The present value of the minimum lease payments is to be calculated using the interest rate implicit in the lease or, if this cannot be determined, at the lessee's incremental borrowing rate. *[FRS 102.20.10]*. An example of the calculation is given in Example 16.3 at 3.5 above.

Initial direct costs of the lessee, which are incremental costs directly attributable to negotiating and arranging the lease, are added to the asset. *[FRS 102.20.9]*.

3.7.1.B   Allocation of finance costs

Lease payments must be apportioned between the finance charge and the reduction of the outstanding liability using the effective interest method. The finance charge is allocated to periods during the lease term so as to produce a constant periodic rate of interest on the remaining balance of the liability. *[FRS 102.11.15-20, FRS 102.20.11]*.

A lessee must charge contingent rents as expenses in the periods in which they are incurred. *[FRS 102.20.11]*.

Example 16.4:   Allocation of finance costs

In Example 16.3 above, the present value of the lessee's minimum lease payments was calculated at £9,274 by using the implicit interest rate of 6.62%. The total finance charges of £1,226 (total rentals paid of £10,500 less their present value of £9,274) are allocated over the lease term as follows:

Year	Liability at start of period £	Rental paid £	Liability during period £	Finance charge (6.62% per annum) £	Liability at end of period £
1	9,274	2,100	7,174	475	7,649
2	7,649	2,100	5,549	368	5,917
3	5,917	2,100	3,817	253	4,070
4	4,070	2,100	1,970	130	2,100
5	2,100	2,100	–	–	–
		10,500		1,226	

SSAP 21 specifically refers in Part B of its guidance notes to the use of methods such as the sum of digits, or even the straight-line method, if they provide a reasonable approximation to the 'actuarial method', i.e. allocating the finance charge to periods during the lease term so as to produce a constant periodic rate of interest on the remaining balance of the liability. While Section 20 makes no mention of simplified methods, there is of course no prohibition on using an approximation if differences between that method and that mandated by the standard are not material. However, by contrast with the 1970s when SSAP 21 was originally issued, computer

Chapter 16

applications that make it much easier to calculate the IIR and allocate finance costs are now widely available.

3.7.1.C   Recording the liability

The carrying amount of the liability will always be calculated in the same way, by adding the finance charge to the outstanding balance and deducting cash paid. The liability in each of the years, as apportioned between the current and non-current liability, is as follows:

Example 16.5:   Lessee's liabilities and interest expense

The entity entering into the lease in Example 16.3 will record the following liabilities and interest expense in its statement of financial position:

Year	Liability at end of period £	Current liability at end of period £	Non-current liability at end of period £	Interest expense (at 6.62%) for the period £
1	7,649	1,732	5,917	475
2	5,917	1,847	4,070	368
3	4,070	1,970	2,100	253
4	2,100	2,100	–	130
5	–	–	–	–
				1,226

3.7.1.D   Accounting for the leased asset

At commencement of the lease, the asset and liability for the future lease payments are recorded in the statement of financial position at the same amount, with initial direct costs of the lessee then being added to the asset. *[FRS 102.20.9]*. These are costs that are directly attributable to the lease in question and are added to the carrying value in an analogous way to the treatment of the acquisition costs of property, plant and equipment.

Accounting for the leased asset follows the general rules for accounting for property, plant and equipment or intangible assets. A finance lease gives rise to a depreciation expense for depreciable assets as well as a finance expense for each accounting period. The depreciation policy for depreciable leased assets should be consistent with that for depreciable assets that are owned, and the depreciation recognised should be calculated in accordance with Section 17 – *Property, Plant and Equipment* (see Chapter 13). If there is no reasonable certainty that the lessee will obtain ownership by the end of the lease term, the asset should be depreciated over the shorter of the lease term and its useful life. *[FRS 102.20.12]*.

Section 20 does not address the situation in which an entity expects to extend a lease but it is not reasonably certain at inception that it will do so. In our view, the entity is not precluded from depreciating assets either over the lease term or over the shorter of the asset's useful life and the period for which the entity expects to extend the lease.

Because the interest expense and depreciation must be calculated separately and are unlikely to be the same it is not appropriate simply to treat the lease payments as an expense for the period. This is demonstrated in the following example.

Example 16.6:   Lessee's depreciation and interest expense

The entity that has entered into the lease agreement described in Example 16.3 will depreciate the asset (whose initial carrying value, disregarding initial direct costs, is £9,274) on a straight-line basis over five years in accordance with its depreciation policy for owned assets, i.e. an amount of £1,855 per annum. The balances for asset and liability in the financial statements in each of the years 1-5 will be as follows:

Year	Carrying value of asset at end of period £	Total liability at end of period £	Total charged to income statement* £	Lease payments £
1	7,419	7,649	2,330	2,100
2	5,564	5,917	2,222	2,100
3	3,709	4,070	2,108	2,100
4	1,855	2,100	1,985	2,100
5	–	–	1,855	2,100
			10,500	10,500

*   The total charge combines the annual depreciation of £1,855 and the interest calculated according to the IIR method in Example 16.3, which is in aggregate the initial carrying value of the asset of £9,274 and the total finance charge of £1,226, i.e. the total rent paid of £10,500. Note that this example assumes that the asset is being depreciated to a residual value of zero over the lease term, which is shorter than its useful life.

A lessee must also assess at each reporting date whether an asset leased under a finance lease is impaired. *[FRS 102.20.12].*

Assets held under finance leases may also be revalued using the revaluation model but the entire class of assets (both owned and those held under finance lease) must be revalued. *[FRS 102.17.15].*

Whilst it is not explicit in Section 20, in our view, to obtain the fair value of an asset held under a finance lease for financial reporting purposes, the assessed value should be adjusted to avoid double counting of any recognised finance lease liability.

3.7.2   Accounting by lessors

Under a finance lease, a lessor retains legal title to an asset but passes substantially all the risks and rewards of ownership to the lessee in return for a stream of rentals. In substance, therefore, the lessor provides finance and expects a return thereon.

The standard requires lessors to recognise assets held under a finance lease in their statement of financial position as a receivable at an amount equal to the net investment in the lease. The net investment in a lease is the lessor's gross investment discounted at the interest rate implicit in the lease. The gross investment in the lease is the aggregate of:

(a)   the minimum lease payments receivable by the lessor under a finance lease; and

(b)   any unguaranteed residual value accruing to the lessor. *[FRS 102.20.17].*

Initial direct costs (costs that are incremental and directly attributable to negotiating and arranging a lease) may include commissions, legal fees and internal costs. They are included in the measurement of the net investment in the lease at inception, except in the case of finance leases involving manufacturer or dealer lessors. *[FRS 102.20.18].*

Chapter 16

As they are included in the initial measurement of the finance lease receivable, they reduce the amount of income recognised over the lease term.

At any point in time the net investment comprises the gross investment after deducting gross earnings allocated to future periods. The lessor's gross investment is, therefore, the same as the aggregate figures used to calculate the implicit interest rate and the net investment is the present value of those same figures – see Example 16.3 above. Therefore, at inception, the lessor's net investment in the lease is the cost of the asset as increased by its initial direct costs. The difference between the net and gross investments is the gross finance income to be allocated over the lease term. Example 16.7 below illustrates this point.

3.7.2.A   Allocation of finance income

The lease payments received from the lessee, excluding costs for services, are treated as repayments of principal and finance income; in other words, they reduce both the principal and the unearned finance income. Finance income should be recognised at a constant periodic rate of return on the lessor's net investment in the finance lease. *[FRS 102.20.19]*.

If there is an indication that the estimated unguaranteed residual value used in computing the gross investment in the lease has changed significantly, the income allocation over the lease term should be revised. Any reduction in amounts accrued is recognised immediately in profit or loss (see 3.7.3.A below). *[FRS 102.20.19]*.

Example 16.3 in 3.5 above can be examined from the lessor's perspective:

Example 16.7:   The lessor's gross and net investment in the lease

The lease has the same facts as described in Example 16.3, i.e. the asset has a fair value of £10,000, the lessee is making five annual rentals payable in advance of £2,100 and the total unguaranteed estimated residual value at the end of five years is estimated to be £1,000. The lessor's direct costs have been excluded for simplicity.

The lessor's gross investment in the lease is the total rents receivable of £10,500 and the unguaranteed residual value of £1,000. The gross earnings are therefore £1,500. The initial carrying value of the receivable is its fair value of £10,000, which is also the present value of the gross investment discounted at the interest rate implicit in the lease of 6.62%.

Year	Receivable at start of period £	Rental received £	Finance income (6.62% per annum) £	Gross investment at end of period £	Gross earnings allocated to future periods £	Receivable at end of period £
1	10,000	2,100	523	9,400	977	8,423
2	8,423	2,100	419	7,300	558	6,742
3	6,742	2,100	307	5,200	251	4,949
4	4,949	2,100	189	3,100	62	3,038
5	3,038	2,100	62	1,000	–	1,000
		10,500	1,500			

The gross investment in the lease at any point in time comprises the aggregate of the rentals receivable in future periods and the unguaranteed residual value, e.g. at the end of year 2, the gross investment of £7,300 is three years' rental of £2,100 plus the unguaranteed residual of £1,000. The net investment, which is the amount at which the debtor will be recorded in the statement of financial position, is £7,300 less the earnings allocated to future periods of £558 = £6,742.

If the lessor's initial direct costs of £500 are included, then it is likely that these will be recouped by the lessor through higher rental charges, as in the following example.

Year	Receivable at start of period £	Rental received £	Finance income (6.62% per annum) £	Gross investment at end of period £	Gross earnings allocated to future periods £	Receivable at end of period £
1	10,500	2,213	549	8,835	1,017	7,818
2	8,835	2,213	438	7,061	558	6,503
3	7,061	2,213	321	5,169	251	4,918
4	5,169	2,213	196	3,151	62	3,089
5	3,151	2,213	62	1,000	–	1,000
		11,066	1,566			

The lessor has recovered an additional 566 from the lessee (11,066 – 10,500); this is the additional debtor of 500 for the initial direct costs, together with interest at 6.62%.

3.7.3 Residual values

Residual values have to be taken into account in assessing whether a lease is a finance or operating lease as well as affecting the calculation of the IIR and finance income.

- Unguaranteed residual values have to be estimated in order to calculate the IIR and finance income receivable under a finance lease. If there is an indication that the estimated unguaranteed residual value has changed significantly, the income allocation over the lease term is revised, and any reduction in respect of amounts accrued is recognised immediately in profit or loss. Any impairment in the residual must be taken into account. *[FRS 102.20.19]*. This is illustrated in 3.7.3.A below.

- Residual values can be guaranteed by the lessee or by a third party. The effects of third party guarantees on risks and rewards are described in 3.4.6.A above.

- The terms of a lease guarantee can affect the assessment of the risks and rewards in the arrangement as in Example 16.9 in 3.7.3.B below.

- A common form of lease requires the asset to be sold at the end of the lease term. The disposition of the proceeds has to be taken into account in assessing who bears residual risk, as described in 3.7.3.C below.

3.7.3.A Unguaranteed residual values

Income recognition by lessors can be extremely sensitive to the amount recognised as the asset's residual value. This is because the amount of the residual directly affects the computation of the amount of finance income earned over the lease term – this is illustrated in Example 16.8 below. If there has been a reduction in the estimated value, the income allocation over the lease term is revised and any reduction in respect of amounts accrued is recognised immediately. *[FRS 102.20.19]*. Section 20, like SSAP 21 and IAS 17, gives no guidance regarding the estimation of unguaranteed residual values.

Chapter 16

Example 16.8:   Reduction in residual value

Taking the same facts as used in Example 16.3 above, the lessor concludes at the end of year 2 that the residual value of the asset is only £500 and revises the income allocation over the lease term accordingly. It continues to apply the same implicit interest rate, 6.62%, as before.

Year	Receivable at start of period £	Rental received £	Finance income (6.62% per annum) £	Gross investment at end of period* £	Gross earnings allocated to future periods £	Receivable at end of period £
2	8,423	2,100	419	6,800	471	6,329
3	6,329	2,100	280	4,700	191	4,509
4	4,509	2,100	160	2,600	31	2,569
5	2,569	2,100	31	500	–	500

*   The gross investment in the lease now takes account of the revised unguaranteed residual of £500, rather than the original £1,000.

The lessor will have to write off £413, being the difference between the carrying amount of the receivable as previously calculated in Example 16.7 and the revised balance above (£6,742 – £6,329). This is the present value as at the end of year 2 of £500 and represents the part of the unguaranteed residual written off.

This is the same method as is used for impairment of lease receivables, which is within the scope of Section 11. *[FRS 102.11.7(c)].* Impairment of leases is described in 3.7.4.B below.

3.7.3.B   Residual values guaranteed by the lessee

Although a lessee may give a residual value guarantee in a lease, the lease itself may be structured so that the most likely outcome of events relating to the residual value indicates that no significant risk will attach to the lessee.

Example 16.9:   A lease structured such that the most likely outcome is that the lessee has no significant residual risk

Brief details of a motor vehicle lease are:

Fair value   –   £10,000
Rentals   –   20 monthly payments of £300, followed by a final rental of £2,000

At the end of the lease, the lessee sells the vehicle as agent for the lessor and if it is sold for:

(i)   more than £3,000, 99% of the excess is repaid to the lessee; or

(ii)   less than £3,000, the lessee pays the deficit to the lessor up to a maximum of 0.4 pence per mile above 25,000 miles p.a. on average that the leased vehicle has done.

The net present value of the minimum lease payments excluding the guarantee amounts to £7,365.

This lease involves a guarantee by the lessee of the residual value of the leased vehicle of £3,000, as a result of (ii) above. However, the guarantee will only be called on if both:

(a)   the vehicle's actual residual value is less than £3,000; and

(b)   the vehicle has travelled more than 25,000 miles per year on average over the lease term.

Further, the lessee is only liable to pay a certain level of the residual; namely, £100 for each 2,500 miles above 25,000 miles that the vehicle has done.

There are several ways in which the residual value might be taken into account.

One could argue that the guarantee should be assumed to apply only to the extent that experience or expectations of the sales price and/or the mileage that vehicles have done (and the inter-relationship between these) indicate that a residual payment by the lessee will be made and if this best estimate is that a zero or minimal payment will be made, this should be used for the purposes of lease classification. This would be applying the principles in Section 21 – *Provisions and Contingencies* – to the calculation of the liability (see Chapter 17).

The maximum guarantee might be taken into account, in which case the present value of the minimum lease payments might equal or exceed the fair value of the asset. This does not mean that the lease will automatically fall to be treated as a finance lease. This depends on the substance of the arrangement and the entity may well take account of the residual it estimates will actually be paid in making this assessment.

Another interpretation is given in Example 16.11 below, in which the entity capitalises the full residual guarantee and factors the amount that it expects to recover into the residual value of the asset.

3.7.3.C   Rental rebates

FRS 102 suggests that it is an indicator that the lease is a finance lease if the gains or losses from the fluctuation in the fair value of the residual accrue to the lessee, e.g. in the form of a rent rebate equalling most of the sales proceeds at the end of the lease. *[FRS 102.20.6].* This is because a lessee that obtains most of the sales proceeds has received most of the risks and rewards of the residual value in the asset. This would indicate that the lessor has already been compensated for the transaction and hence that it is a finance lease.

Other leases require the asset to be sold at the end of the lease but the lessor receives the first tranche of proceeds and only those proceeds above a certain level are remitted to the lessee. These arrangements may have a different significance as the lessor may be taking the proceeds to meet its unguaranteed residual value. Lessors are prepared to take risks on residual values of such assets if there is an established and reliable market in which to sell them. This could mean that the gains or losses from the fluctuation in the fair value of the residual do not fall predominantly to the lessee and, in the absence of other factors, could indicate that it is an operating lease.

Example 16.10:   Rental rebates

The lease arrangements are as in Example 16.9 except that at the end of the lease, the lessee sells the vehicle as agent for the lessor, and if it is sold for

(i)   up to £3,000, the guaranteed residual value, all of the proceeds are received by the lessor; or

(ii) more than £3,000, 99% of excess is repaid to the lessee. The lessee does not have to make good any deficit, should one arise.

In this example, it appears that the lessor is using the sale proceeds to meet its unguaranteed residual value but it is also taking the first loss provision. Only thereafter does the lessee gain or lose from the fluctuations in the fair value. The lessee's minimum lease payments have a net present value of £7,365, it has not guaranteed the residual value at all and is not exposed to any risk of any fall in value, although it may benefit from increases in the fair value in excess of £3,000. On balance this indicates that the arrangement is an operating lease.

3.7.4   Termination of finance leases

The expectations of lessors and lessees regarding the timing of termination of a lease may affect the classification of a lease as either operating or finance. This is because it will affect the expected lease term, level of payments under the lease and expected residual value of the lease assets.

Termination during the primary lease term will generally not be anticipated at the lease inception because the lessee can be assumed to be using the asset for at least that period. In addition, early termination is made less likely because most leases are non-cancellable. A termination payment is usually required which will give the lessor an amount equivalent to most or all of the rental receipts which would have been received if no termination had taken place, which means that it is reasonably certain at inception that the lease will continue to expiry.

However, there are consequences if the lease is terminated. The issues for finance lessees and lessors are discussed in the following sections.

3.7.4.A   Termination of finance leases by lessees

Finance lease payables recognised by a lessee are subject to the derecognition provisions of Section 11. *[FRS 102.11.7(c)]*.

Section 11 requires an entity to derecognise (i.e. remove from its statement of financial position) a financial liability (or a part of a financial liability) when, and only when, it is 'extinguished', that is, when the obligation specified in the contract is discharged, cancelled, or expires. *[FRS 102.11.36]*. (This is discussed in Chapter 8.)

The difference between the carrying amount of all or part of a financial liability extinguished or transferred to another party and the consideration paid, including any non-cash assets transferred or liabilities assumed, is to be recognised in profit or loss. *[FRS 102.11.38]*.

In order to identify the part of a liability derecognised, an entity allocates the previous carrying amount of the financial liability between the part that continues to be recognised and the part that is derecognised based on the relative fair values of those parts on the date of the partial derecognition.

Unless it is part of a renegotiation or business combination or similar larger arrangement, the lessee will derecognise the capitalised asset on early termination of a finance lease, with any remaining balance of the capitalised asset being written off as a loss on disposal. Any payment made by the lessee will reduce the lease obligation that is being carried in the statement of financial position. If either a part of this obligation is not eliminated or the termination payment exceeds the previously existing obligation, then the remainder or excess will be included as a gain or loss respectively on derecognition of a financial liability.

A similar accounting treatment is required where the lease terminates at the expected date and there is a residual at least partly guaranteed by the lessee. For the lessee, a payment made under such a guarantee will reduce the obligation to the lessor as the guaranteed residual would obviously be included in the lessee's finance lease obligation. If any part of the guaranteed residual is not called on, then the lessee would treat this as a profit on derecognition of a financial liability.

The effect on the derecognition of the capitalised asset will depend on the extent to which the lessee expected to make the residual payment as this will have affected the level to which the capitalised asset has been depreciated. For example, if the total guaranteed residual was not expected to become payable by the lessee, then the depreciation charge may have been calculated to give a net book value at the end of the lease term equal to the residual element not expected to become payable. If this estimate was correct then the remaining obligation will equal the net book value of the relevant asset, so that the gain on derecognition of the liability will be equal to the loss on derecognition of the asset.

Example 16.11:   Early termination of finance leases by lessees

In Example 16.10 in 3.7.3.C above there is effectively a guarantee of a residual of £3,000 dependent on the mileage done by the leased vehicle. Assuming that the lease is capitalised as a finance lease, if the lessee considers at the lease inception that the guarantee will not be called on, then he will depreciate the vehicle to an estimated residual value of £3,000 over the lease term. In the event that his estimate is found to be correct, then the loss on disposal of the asset at its written down value will be equal and opposite to the gain on derecognition of the lease obligation of £3,000. However, if, for example, £1,000 of the guarantee was called on, whereas the lessee had estimated that it would not be, then the net book value of £3,000 and the unused guarantee of £2,000 will both be derecognised and a loss of £1,000 will be shown on disposal of the vehicle.

3.7.4.B   Termination and impairment of finance leases by lessors

Although lease receivables are not financial instruments, the carrying amounts recognised by a lessor are subject to the derecognition and impairment provisions of Section 11 (see Chapter 8). Generally, a financial asset is derecognised when the contractual rights to the cash flows from that asset have expired. *[FRS 102.11.33(a)]*. This will apply to most leases at the end of the term when the lessor has no more right to cash flows from the lessee.

If the cash flows from the financial asset have not expired, it is derecognised when, and only when, the entity 'transfers' the asset within the specified meaning of the term in FRS 102, and the transfer has the effect that the entity has either: *[FRS 102.11.33(b), (c)]*

- transferred substantially all the risks and rewards of the asset; or
- the entity retains some significant risks and rewards of ownership but has transferred control of the asset to another party. The other party has the practical ability to sell the asset in its entirety to an unrelated third party and is able to exercise that ability unilaterally and without needing to impose additional restrictions on the transfer. In this case, the entity must:
  - (i) derecognise the asset, and
  - (ii) recognise separately any rights and obligations retained or created in the transfer.

These requirements are relevant to lease situations such as sub-leases and back-to-back leases.

If a lease receivable is impaired, for example, because the lessee is in default of lease payments, the amount of the impairment is measured as the difference between the carrying value of the receivable and the present value of the estimated future cash flows, discounted at the implicit interest rate used on initial recognition. Therefore, if the lessor makes an arrangement with the lessee and reschedules and/or reduces amounts due under the lease, the loss is by reference to the new carrying amount of the receivable, calculated by discounting the estimated future cash flows at the original implicit interest rate. *[FRS 102.11.25]*. This is the same methodology that was used in Example 16.8 at 3.7.3.A above to reflect a reduction in the estimated residual value.

Chapter 16

Any termination payment received by a lessor on an early termination will reduce the lessor's net investment in the lease shown as a receivable. If the termination payment is greater than the carrying amount of the net investment, the lessor will account for a gain on derecognition of the lease; conversely, if the termination payment is smaller than the net investment, a loss will be shown.

Losses on termination in the ordinary course of business are less likely to arise because a finance lease usually has termination terms so that the lessor is compensated fully for early termination and the lessor has legal title to the asset. The lessor can continue to include the asset in current assets as a receivable to the extent that sales proceeds or new finance lease receivables are expected to arise. If the asset is then re-leased under an operating lease, the asset may be transferred to property, plant and equipment and depreciated over its remaining useful life. There is no guidance about the amount at which the asset is recognised in PP&E. Although the net investment (i.e. the lease receivable recognised by the lessor) is not a financial instrument (see 3.6 above) and there is no specific guidance, the most straightforward method is for entities to use the carrying amount of the net investment as the cost of the reacquired item of PP&E.

It is common for entities whose business is the leasing of assets to third parties to finance these assets themselves through leasing arrangements. There are also arrangements in which a party on-leases assets as an intermediary between a lessor and a lessee while taking a variable degree of risk in the transaction. The appropriate accounting treatment by the intermediate party depends on the substance of the series of transactions. Either the intermediate party will act as lessee to the original lessor and lessor to the ultimate lessee or, if in substance it has transferred the risks and rewards of ownership, it may be able to derecognise the assets and liabilities under its two lease arrangements and recognise only its own commission or fee income. Therefore, in practice, this only creates accounting issues if the lease between the original lessor and the intermediate party is a finance lease.

These are known as sub-leases or back-to-back leases. The difference between the two arrangements is that, for a back-to-back lease, the terms of the two lease agreements match to a greater extent than would be the case for a sub-lease arrangement. This difference is really only one of degree.

The accounting treatment adopted by the lessor and ultimate lessee will not be affected by the existence of sub-leases or back-to-back leases. The original lessor has an agreement with the intermediate party, which is not affected by any further leasing of the assets by the intermediate party unless the original lease agreement is thereby replaced.

Similarly, the ultimate lessee has a lease agreement with the intermediate party. The lessee will have use of the asset under that agreement and must make a decision, in the usual way, as to whether the lease is of a finance or operating type under the requirements of Section 20.

The important decision to be made concerns whether the intermediate party is acting as both lessee and lessor in two related but independent transactions or whether the nature of the interest is such that it need not recognise the rights and obligations under the leases in its financial statements.

In order to analyse the issues that may arise, the various combinations of leases between lessor/intermediate and intermediate/lessee are summarised in the following table:

| | Lessor | Intermediate party | | Lessee |
	Lease to Intermediate	*Lease from Lessor*	*Lease to Lessee*	*Lease from Intermediate*
(1)	Operating lease	Operating lease	Operating lease	Operating lease
(2)	Finance lease	Finance lease	Operating lease	Operating lease
(3)	Finance lease	Finance lease	Finance lease	Finance lease

Only in unusual circumstances could there be an operating lease from the lessor to the intermediate and a finance lease from the intermediate to the lessee. The intermediate would have to acquire an additional interest in the asset from a party other than the lessor in order to be in a position to transfer substantially all of the risks and rewards incidental to ownership of that asset to the lessee.

There are no significant accounting difficulties for the intermediate party regarding (1), an operating lease from the lessor to the intermediate and from the intermediate to the lessee. The intermediate may be liable to the lessor if the lessee defaults, e.g. in some forms of property lease assignment, in which case it would have to make an appropriate provision, but otherwise both contracts are executory and will be accounted for in the usual way.

In situation (2), the intermediate will record at commencement of the lease term an asset acquired under a finance lease and an obligation to the lessor of an equal and opposite amount. As it has granted an operating lease to the lessee, its risks and rewards incidental to ownership of the asset exceed those assumed by the lessee under the lease. It is appropriate for the intermediate party to record an item of PP&E, which it will have to depreciate as set out in 3.7.4.B above.

However, under scenario (3), the intermediate is the lessee under a finance lease with the lessor and lessor under a finance lease with the lessee. Its statement of financial position, *prima facie*, records a finance lease receivable from the lessee and a finance lease obligation to the lessor. Both of these are treated as if they are financial instruments for derecognition purposes (see 3.6 above).

The intermediate may be in a position to derecognise its financial asset and liability if it 'transfers' the asset within the specified meaning of the term in FRS 102. 'Transfer' can mean one of two things.

- the entity has transferred substantially all the risks and rewards of the asset to another party. *[FRS 102.11.33(b)]*.

- the entity has transferred control of the asset to another party while retaining some significant risks and rewards of ownership. The other party must have the practical ability to sell the asset in its entirety to an unrelated third party and must be able to exercise that ability unilaterally and without needing to impose additional restrictions on the transfer. In this case, the entity must derecognise the asset, and recognise separately any rights and obligations retained or created in the transfer. *[FRS 102.11.33(c)]*.

Agents do not retain significant risks and rewards of ownership. An intermediate party that is acting as an agent for the original lessor must be able to demonstrate

Chapter 16

that it has transferred substantially all the risks and rewards of the asset to another party. If so, then it can derecognise its interest in the two leases. It should not include any asset or obligation relating to the leased asset in its statement of financial position. The income received by the intermediary should be taken to profit or loss on a systematic and rational basis – the discussion of the recognition of fee income in SIC-27, as discussed in 2.2.1.A above, may be helpful.

If, on the other hand, the intermediate party is taken to be acting as both lessee and lessor in two independent although related transactions, the assets and obligations under finance leases should be recognised in the normal way.

It should not be inferred that all situations encountered can be relatively easily analysed. In practice this is unlikely to be the case, as the risks and rewards will probably be spread between the parties involved. Further discussion is beyond the scope of this publication.

3.7.5   *Manufacturer or dealer lessors*

Manufacturers or dealers often offer customers the choice of either buying or leasing an asset. While there is no selling profit on entering into an operating lease because it is not the equivalent of a sale, a finance lease of an asset by a manufacturer or dealer lessor gives rise to two types of income:

(a)   the profit or loss equivalent to the profit or loss resulting from an outright sale of the asset being leased, at normal selling prices, reflecting any applicable volume or trade discounts; and

(b)   the finance income over the lease term. *[FRS 102.20.20]*.

If the customer is offered the choice of paying the cash price for the asset immediately or paying for it on deferred credit terms then, as long as the credit terms are the manufacturer or dealer's normal terms, the cash price (after taking account of applicable volume or trade discounts) can be used to determine the selling profit. However, in many cases such an approach should not be followed as the manufacturer or dealer's marketing considerations often influence the terms of the lease. For example, a car dealer may offer 0% finance deals instead of reducing the normal selling price of his cars. It would be wrong in this instance for the dealer to record a profit on the sale of the car and no finance income under the lease.

The standard, therefore, requires sales revenue to be based on the fair value of the asset (i.e. usually the cash price) or, if lower, the present value of the minimum lease payments computed at a market rate of interest. As a result, selling profit is restricted to that which would apply if a commercial rate of interest were charged. The cost of sale is reduced to the extent that the lessor retains an unguaranteed residual interest in the asset. Selling profit is recognised in accordance with the entity's policy for outright sales. *[FRS 102.20.21]*. This also means that the entity will ignore artificially low rates of interest quoted by the lessor; profit will be restricted by substituting a market rate of interest. *[FRS 102.20.22]*.

Initial direct costs should be recognised as an expense in the income statement at the inception of the lease when the selling profit is recognised. This is not the same as the treatment when a lessor arranges a finance lease where the costs are added to the finance lease receivable; this is because the costs are related mainly to earning the selling profit. *[FRS 102.20.22]*.

If the manufacturer or dealer is in the relatively unlikely position of incurring an overall loss because the total rentals receivable under the finance lease are less than the cost to it of the asset then this loss should be taken to the income statement at the inception of the lease. This emphasises the importance of calculating an appropriate market interest rate.

If the manufacturer or dealer does not conduct other leasing business, an estimate will have to be made of the implicit rate for the leasing activity.

3.8   Accounting for operating leases

3.8.1   *Operating leases in the financial statements of lessees*

Lease payments under an operating lease, excluding costs for services such as insurance and maintenance, are to be recognised as an expense on a straight-line basis over the lease term unless:

(a)   another systematic basis is representative of the time pattern of the user's benefit, even if the payments are not on that basis; or

(b)   the payments to the lessor are structured to increase in line with expected general inflation (based on published indexes or statistics) to compensate for the lessor's expected inflationary cost increases. *[FRS 102.20.15]*.

Payments that vary because of factors other than general inflation will not meet condition (b).

Generally, the only bases that are considered acceptable under (a) apart from the straight-line basis are those where rentals are based on a unit of use or unit of production.

Section 20 requires straight-line recognition of the lease expenses that do not fall within (b) even when amounts are not payable on this basis. This does not require the entity to anticipate contingent rental increases, such as those that will result from a periodic re-pricing to market rates or those that are based on some other index. Although FRS 102, like SSAP 21 and IAS 17, is not explicit on this point, we expect that entities will expense these contingent rents as incurred, which is the usual treatment under these standards.

However, lease payments may vary over time for other reasons that will have to be taken into account in calculating the annual charge. Described in more detail below are some examples: leases that are inclusive of services and leases with increments intended to substitute for inflation.

Lease incentives are another feature that may affect the cash flows under a lease; they are dealt with in more detail in 3.8.1.C (for lessees) and 3.8.2.A (for lessors).

3.8.1.A   *Lease payments intended to compensate for inflation*

There are some lease payments that increase annually by fixed increments intended to compensate for expected annual inflation over the lease period. Others allow for an annual increase in line with an index but with a fixed minimum increment. As long as the fixed minimum increment reflects expected general inflation, this element of the rental payment will be recognised as an expense as incurred. *[FRS 102.20.15]*. The amount in excess of the fixed minimum increment is a contingent rent and, as discussed above, contingent rents are usually excluded from the lease payments and expensed as incurred.

Chapter 16

Escalating payments may be structured to compensate for factors other than expected inflation, e.g. a lessee may arrange a lease that increases in line with expected sales or utilisation of the asset. These annual rent expenses will be recognised on a straight-line basis.

Example 16.12:   Lease payments containing fixed increments

(a)   Entity A operates in a country in which the consensus forecast by local banks is that the general price level index, as published by the government, will increase by an average of 10% annually over the next five years. Entity A leases some office space for five years under an operating lease. The lease payments are structured to reflect the expected 10% annual general inflation (cost and prices index (CPI)) over the five-year term of the lease as follows:

Year	Annual rental £
1	100,000
2	110,000
3	121,000
4	133,000
5	146,000

Entity A recognises annual rent expense equal to the amounts owed to the lessor as shown above.

(b)   Entity B has negotiated a lease under which the payments increase by 10% per annum, in order to correspond to the expected growth in its retail activity. The lease payments are the same as above. The increases in rental are not compensation for expected annual inflation. Entity B will recognise an annual rent expense on a straight-line basis of £122,000 each year (the sum of the amounts payable under the lease divided by five years).

(c)   Entity C leases a property at an initial rent of £1,000,000 per annum. The lease has a non-cancellable term of 20 years and rent increases annually in line with the CPI of the country in which the property is situated but with a minimum increase of 2% and a maximum of 5% per annum. The estimated long-term rate of inflation in the country in question is 2.5%.

The rental payment charged by the lessor, which will include a minimum increase of 2% per annum whatever the actual rate of inflation, will be recognised as an expense as incurred. The entity will not be obliged to make a straight-line adjustment for the 2% minimum increase. The fixed minimum increment is considered to be a proxy for expected general inflation. It is reasonable to have a range rather than a single figure.

This analysis would be the same if the estimated long-term rate of inflation were some other figure within the range, e.g. 2% or 3%, as long as both the long-term rate and minimum and maximum increases were reasonable estimates in the circumstances of the country in question.

3.8.1.B   Leases that include payments for services

There is a wide range of services that can be subsumed into a single 'lease' payment. For a vehicle, the payment may include maintenance and servicing. Property leases could include cleaning, security, reception services, gardening, utilities and local and property taxes. Single payments for operating facilities may include lease payments for the plant and the costs of operating them. The costs of services should be excluded to arrive at the lease payments. This is straightforward enough if the payments are made by the lessor and quantified in the payments made by the lessee. It will be somewhat less so if, for example, the lessor makes all maintenance payments but does not specify the amounts; instead, payments are increased periodically to take account of changes in such costs. In such a case the lessee will have to estimate the amount paid for services and deduct them from the total. The remaining payments, which relate solely to the right to use the asset, will then be spread on a straight-line basis over the non-cancellable term of the lease.

3.8.1.C   Lease incentives – accounting by lessees

Incentives that may be given by a lessor to a lessee as an incentive to enter into a new or renewed operating lease agreement include an up-front cash payment to the lessee or the reimbursement or assumption by the lessor of costs of the lessee, such as relocation costs, leasehold improvements and costs associated with a pre-existing lease commitment of the lessee. Alternatively, the lessor may grant the lessee rent-free or reduced rent initial lease periods.

The lessee should recognise the aggregate benefit of incentives as a reduction of rental expense over the lease term, on a straight-line basis unless another systematic basis is representative of the time pattern of the lessee's benefit from the use of the leased asset. *[FRS 102.20.15A].*

Costs incurred by the lessee, including costs in connection with a pre-existing lease (for example, costs for termination, relocation or leasehold improvements), are to be accounted for by the lessee in accordance with the relevant section of FRS 102. *[FRS 102.20.15A].*

The following two examples illustrate how to apply the requirements:

Example 16.13:   Accounting for lease incentives

Example 1

An entity agrees to enter into a new lease arrangement with a new lessor. As an incentive for entering into the new lease, the lessor agrees to pay the lessee's relocation costs. The lessee's moving costs are £1,000. The new lease has a term of 10 years, at a fixed rate of £2,000 per year.

The lessee recognises relocation costs of £1,000 as an expense in Year 1. Both the lessor and lessee would recognise the net rental consideration of £19,000 (£2,000 for each of the 10 years in the lease term, less the £1,000 incentive) over the 10 year lease term using a single amortisation method.

Example 2

An entity agrees to enter into a new lease arrangement with a new lessor. The lessor agrees to a rent-free period for the first three years. The new lease has a term of 20 years, at a fixed rate of £5,000 per annum for years 4 to 20.

Net consideration of £85,000 consists of £5,000 for each of 17 years in the lease term. Both the lessor and lessee would recognise the net consideration of £85,000 over the 20-year lease term using a single amortisation method.

Incentives must be spread over the lease term. Incentives are seen in the context of the total cash flows under the lease and, except where the benefit of the lease is not directly related to the time during which the entity has the right to use the asset, cash flows are taken on a straight-line basis.

There is a similar argument when lessees contend (as they often do) that they should not be obliged to spread rentals over a void period as they are not actually benefiting from the property during this time – it is a fit-out period or a start-up so activities are yet to increase to anticipated levels. However, the argument against this is really no different to the above: the lessee's period of benefit from the use of the asset is the lease term, so the incentive cannot be taken over the initial period.

Chapter 16

3.8.1.D   *Onerous contracts*

If an operating lease becomes onerous, the entity must also apply Section 21 (see Chapter 17). *[FRS 102.20.15B]*.

An onerous contract as defined is one in which the unavoidable costs of meeting the obligations under the contract exceed the economic benefits expected to be received under it (see 3.3 above).

The appendix to Section 21 expands on onerous contracts. 'The unavoidable costs under a contract reflect the least net cost of exiting from the contract, which is the lower of the cost of fulfilling it and any compensation or penalties arising from failure to fulfil it. For example, an entity may be contractually required under an operating lease to make payments to lease an asset for which it no longer has any use.' *[FRS 102.21A.2]*.

In an onerous lease, there is a present obligation as a result of a past obligating event. The obligating event is the signing of the lease contract, which gives rise to a legal obligation and the entity is contractually required to pay out resources for which it will not receive commensurate benefits. The entity has to recognise the present obligation under the contract as a provision. *[FRS 102.21A.2]*. This is measured at the best estimate of the amount required to settle the obligation at the reporting date.

Care must be taken to ensure that the lease itself is onerous. If an entity has a number of retail outlets and one of these is loss-making, this is not sufficient to make the lease onerous. However, if the entity vacates the premises and sub-lets them at an amount less than the rent it is paying, then the lease becomes onerous and the entity should provide for its best estimate of the unavoidable lease payments. This will include the difference between the lease and sub-lease payments, together with provision as appropriate for any period where there is no sub-tenant.

3.8.2   *Operating leases in the financial statements of lessors*

Lessors should present assets subject to operating leases in their statements of financial position according to the nature of the asset, i.e. usually as PP&E or as an intangible asset. *[FRS 102.20.24]*.

Lease income from operating leases should be recognised in income on a straight-line basis over the lease term, unless another systematic basis is representative of the time pattern of the lessee's benefit from the leased asset. *[FRS 102.20.25]*. Generally, the only other basis that is encountered is based on unit-of-production or service.

In the same way as for lessees, payments to the lessor that are structured to increase in line with expected general inflation (based on published indexes or statistics) to compensate for the lessor's expected inflationary cost increases are exempt from the requirement to be accounted for on a straight-line basis. This is the mirror image of accounting by lessees, so the guidance described in detail at 3.8.1.A above is also relevant for lessors. *[FRS 102.20.25]*.

Lease income excludes receipts for services provided such as insurance and maintenance. Section 23 provides guidance on how to recognise service revenue (see Chapter 18). Costs, including depreciation, incurred in earning the lease income are recognised as an expense. *[FRS 102.20.26]*. Initial direct costs incurred specifically to earn revenues from an operating lease are added to the carrying amount of the leased asset and allocated to profit or loss as an expense over the lease term on the same basis as the lease income. *[FRS 102.20.27]*. This means that the costs will be depreciated on a straight-line basis if this is the method of recognising the lease income, regardless of the depreciation basis of the asset.

As there are no specific requirements about depreciation in Section 20, the entity will depreciate leased assets in a manner that is consistent with the entity's policy for similar assets under Section 17 (see Chapter 13). This also means that the lessor is obliged to consider the residual value, useful life and depreciation method of the assets if there is any indication that these have changed since the last financial statements were prepared. *[FRS 102.17.19, 23]*. There are similar requirements in the case of intangible assets in Section 18 (see Chapter 14) although they rarely have a residual value because of the conditions that must apply before recognition. *[FRS 102.18.23, 24]*. These assets are also tested for impairment in a manner consistent with other tangible and intangible fixed assets applying the requirements of Section 27 – *Impairment of Assets* (see Chapter 22). *[FRS 102.20.28]*.

Manufacturer or dealer lessors do not recognise any selling profits on entering into operating leases because they are not the equivalent of a sale. *[FRS 102.20.29]*.

3.8.2.A   Lease incentives – accounting by lessors

In negotiating a new or renewed operating lease, a lessor may provide incentives for the lessee to enter into the arrangement. In the case of a property lease, the tenant may be given a rent-free period but other types of incentive may include up-front cash payments to the lessee or the reimbursement or assumption by the lessor of lessee costs such as relocation costs, leasehold improvements and costs associated with a pre-existing lease commitment of the lessee. FRS 102 requires the lessor to recognise the aggregate cost of incentives as a reduction of rental income over the lease term, on a straight-line basis unless another systematic basis is representative of the time pattern over which the benefit of the leased asset is diminished. *[FRS 102.20.25A]*. Lessor accounting is, therefore, the mirror image of lessee accounting for the incentives, as described in 3.8.1.C above.

3.8.3   Payments made in connection with the termination of operating leases

Payments for terminating operating leases are extremely common. FRS 102 states that any such costs incurred by the lessee, such as costs for termination of a pre-existing lease, relocation or leasehold improvements are to be accounted for in accordance with the applicable section of the FRS. *[FRS 102.20.15A]*. The following table addresses a variety of payments that might arise in connection with terminating an operating lease over a property and suggests ways in which they might be accounted for. As well as payments in connection with the lessee, i.e. the new tenant, it also describes certain payments in connection with previous tenants.

Chapter 16

Example 16.14:   Payments made in connection with terminating an operating lease

	Treatment in the financial statements of		
Transaction	*Lessor*	*Old tenant*	*New tenant*
Lessor pays			
Old tenant – lessor intends to renovate the building	Expense immediately, or Capitalise as part of the carrying amount of the leased asset if the payment meets the definition of construction costs in Section 17 (note 1)	Recognise income immediately (note 1)	
Old tenant – new lease with higher quality tenant	Expense immediately	Recognise income immediately (note 1)	
New tenant – an incentive to occupy	Prepayment amortised over the lease term on a straight-line basis (see 3.8.3.A above)		Deferred lease incentive amortised over the lease term on a straight-line basis (see 3.8.1.C above)
Building alterations specific to the tenant with no further value to the lessor after completion of the lease period	Prepayment amortised over the lease term on a straight-line basis (see 3.8.3.A above)		Leasehold improvements capitalised and depreciated. Deferred lease incentive amortised over the lease term on a straight-line basis (see 3.8.1.C above)
Old tenant pays			
Lessor, to vacate the leased premises early	Recognised as income immediately to the extent not already recognised (note 2)	Recognised as expense immediately to the extent not already recognised (note 2)	
New tenant to take over the lease		Recognise as an expense immediately (note 3)	Recognise as income immediately, unless compensation for above market rentals, in which case amortise over expected lease term (note 3)

Transaction	Lessor	Old tenant	New tenant
New tenant pays			
Lessor to secure the right to obtain a lease agreement	Recognise as deferred revenue and amortise over the lease term on a straight-line basis (see 3.8.3.A above)		Recognise as a prepayment and amortise over the lease term on a straight-line basis (see 3.8.1.C above)
Old tenant to buy out the lease agreement		Recognise as a gain immediately (note 4)	Recognise as an intangible asset with a finite economic life (note 4)

Note 1   A payment by a lessor to a lessee to terminate the lease is not dealt with under FRS 102. If the lessor's payment meets the definition of a cost of an item of PP&E, which might be the case if the lessor intends to renovate, it must be capitalised. *[FRS 102.17.4]*. If not, the payment will be expensed, as it does not meet the definition of an intangible asset in Section 18 (see Chapter 14). *[FRS 102.18.2]*. As the lessee has no further performance obligation the receipt should be income.

Note 2   A payment made by the lessee to the lessor to get out of a lease agreement does not meet the appropriate definitions of an asset in Section 17 (see Chapter 13) or Section 18 (as above) and does not fall within Section 20 as there is no longer a lease – the payments are not for the use of the asset. Therefore it should be expensed. Similarly, from the lessor's perspective, income should be recorded.

Note 3   A payment made by an existing tenant to a new tenant to take over the lease would also not meet the definition of an asset under Section 17 or Section 18 (see notes above) and falls outside Section 20 as the lease no longer exists. The old tenant must expense the cost. The new tenant will recognise the payment as income except to the extent that it is compensation for an above-market rental, in which case the treatment for a lease incentive must be applied and it will be amortised over the lease term (see 3.8.1.C above).

Note 4   The new tenant has made a payment to an old tenant, and while it is in connection with the lease arrangements, it is not directly related to the actual lease as it was made to a party outside the lease contract. Therefore it cannot be accounted for under Section 20. The old tenant will treat the receipt as a gain immediately. Any remaining balances of the lease will be removed and a net gain (or loss) recorded. The payment by the lessee will generally meet the definition of an intangible asset and therefore will be amortised over the useful life, being the term of the lease. However, if other conditions and circumstances in the arrangement mean that this definition is not met, the payment will be expensed in the period in which it is incurred.

3.8.3.A   *Compensation for loss of profits*

Compensation amounts paid by lessors to lessees are sometimes described as 'compensation for loss of profits' or some similar term. This is a method of calculating the amount to be paid and the receipt is not a substitute for the revenue or profits that the lessee would otherwise have earned. The description will not affect the treatment described above.

Chapter 16

3.9   Accounting for modifications to leases

Lessees may renegotiate lease terms for a variety of reasons. They may wish to extend the term over which they have a right to use the asset or to alter the number of assets that they have a right to use. They may consider that the lease is too expensive by comparison with current market terms. The renegotiations may deal with several such issues simultaneously.

Lessors may also renegotiate leases, for example one lessor may sell the lease to another that offers to provide the lease service more cheaply to the lessee, usually because the new lessor's transactions have different tax consequences.

Lease contracts may allow for changes in payments if specified contingencies occur, for example a change in taxation or interest rates.

As described at 3.4.3 above, classification is not changed during the term of the lease, i.e. after its inception, unless the lessee and the lessor agree to change the provisions of the lease (other than simply by renewing the lease), in which case the lease classification must be re-evaluated. *[FRS 102.20.8].* This means that an agreement that is reclassified (e.g. an operating lease is reassessed as a finance lease or *vice versa*) will be accounted for prospectively in accordance with the revised terms. However, FRS 102 provides no practical guidance on what to take into account to determine whether there would have been a different classification. It does not explain how to account for the consequences of modifications, whether or not they would lead to a different classification. These matters are described below.

Other changes to lease terms that do not lead to reclassification but that nevertheless need to be accounted for, for example variations due to changes in rates of taxation or interest rates, are discussed in 3.9.3 below.

Changes in estimates, for example changes in estimates of the economic life or of the residual value of the leased item, or changes in circumstances, for example default by the lessee, do not result in a different classification. Changes in estimates also include the renewal of a lease or the execution of a purchase option, if these were not considered probable at the inception of the lease (see 3.4.3 above).

3.9.1   *Determining whether there is a different classification*

This section addresses ways of assessing whether the lease classification has changed. Accounting for reclassified leases is addressed at 3.9.2 below while changes that do not result in reclassification but that must nevertheless be addressed are considered at 3.9.3 below.

While the focus of the section is on ways of quantifying differences between the original and modified lease, all features of any arrangement must be considered as part of an assessment of whether or not the modified lease transfers substantially all of the risks and rewards of ownership. However, in order for a change to the provisions of a lease to result in a change of classification, it must be one that affects the risks and rewards incidental to ownership of the asset by changing the terms and cash flows of the existing lease. An example of such a change is a renegotiation that changes the lease's duration and/or the payments due under the lease.

One of the indicators used in practice is an assessment of the net present value of the minimum lease payments and whether or not these amount to substantially all of the fair value of the leased asset. An entity might use this test to help assess whether the revised lease is a finance or operating lease, in conjunction with a reassessment of the other factors described at 3.4.1 above. Therefore, the entity might use one of the following methods to calculate the net present value:

(a)   recalculate the net present value of the lease from inception based on the revised lease term and cash flows (and revised residual value, if relevant), which will result in a different implicit interest rate to that used in the original calculation;

(b)   take into consideration the changes in the agreement but calculate the present value of the asset and liability using the interest rate implicit in the original lease. This approach is consistent with the remeasurement of the carrying value of financial instruments applying the effective interest rate method. This will result in a 'catch up' adjustment as at the date of the reassessment; or

(c)   consider the revised agreement to be a new lease and assess the classification based on the terms of the new agreement and the fair value and useful life of the asset at the date of the revision. The inference of this method, unlike (a) and (b), is that the entity already considers that there is likely to be a new classification to the lease, based on an assessment of other factors.

The methodology is straightforward in the case of (a) and (c) above as it involves using updated cash flows, either from inception (method (a)) or from the date of the revised agreement (method(c)) to calculate the net present value, using the methodology described at 3.5 above and illustrated in Example 16.15 below. A lessee under a lease originally classified as an operating lease will be able to apply both of these methods but method (b) will not be available to it unless it has sufficient information to be able to calculate the IIR at the inception of the original lease. Lessees that are party to more complex leases or sale and leaseback arrangements are more likely to have the necessary information available to them.

Each of these three approaches is likely to lead to a different net present value for the minimum lease payments.

Example 16.15:   Modifying the terms of leases

Details of a non-cancellable lease taken out on the first day of the year are as follows:

(i)   Fair value = £25,000

(ii)   Estimated useful life of asset = 8 years

(iii) Five annual rentals payable in advance of £4,200

(iv) At the end of year 5, the asset must be sold and all proceeds up to £8,292 taken by the lessor. If any amount in excess of £8,292 is received, 99% of the excess is repaid to the lessee.

The lease does not contain any renewal options.

The lessee assesses this as an operating lease because the terms suggest that substantially all of the risks and rewards of ownership have not been transferred to it – the lease term is only 62.5% of the useful life of the asset and there is clearly significant residual value.

At the end of year 2, the parties renegotiate the lease, with the changes coming into effect on the first day of year 3. The lease term is to be extended for a further two years, making the term seven years in total. Payments for the four years 3-6 have been reduced to £4,000 and £1,850 is payable for year 7. At the time of the renegotiation the estimated fair value of the asset is £17,500 and its residual value at the end of year 7 is £1,850.

The implicit interest rate in the original lease can be calculated because the maximum amount receivable by the lessor on the sale of the asset at the end of the lease term is the residual value (on the assumption that the lessor disregards any potential upside in its contingent 1%); the IIR is 5.92%, as follows:

Year	Capital sum at start of period £	Rental paid £	Capital sum during period £	Finance charge (5.92% per annum) £	Capital sum at end of period £
1	25,000	4,200	20,800	1,231	22,031
2	22,031	4,200	17,831	1,056	18,887
3	18,887	4,200	14,687	869	15,556
4	15,556	4,200	11,356	672	12,028
5	12,028	4,200	7,828	464	8,292
		21,000		4,292	

This supports the lessee's assessment that this is an operating lease as the present value of the minimum lease payments is £18,780, which is 75% of the fair value of the asset at the commencement of the lease.

If these revised terms had been in existence at inception then the implicit interest rate and NPV calculation would have been as follows. This corresponds to (a) above.

Year	Capital sum at start of period £	Rental paid £	Capital sum during period £	Finance charge (4.10% per annum) £	Capital sum at end of period £
1	25,000	4,200	20,800	853	21,653
2	21,653	4,200	17,453	715	18,168
3	18,168	4,000	14,168	581	14,749
4	14,749	4,000	10,749	441	11,190
5	11,190	4,000	7,190	294	7,484
6	7,484	4,000	3,484	143	3,627
7	3,627	1,850	1,777	73	1,850
		26,250		3,100	

The NPV of the lessee's minimum lease payments is £23,603 which is 94% of the fair value of the asset at the commencement of the lease. The lease would be classified as a finance lease.

Method (b) results in the following calculation:

Year	Capital sum at start of period £	Rental paid £	Capital sum during period £	Finance charge (5.92% per annum) £	Capital sum at end of period £
1	25,000	4,200	20,800	1,231	22,031
2	22,031	4,200	17,831	1,056	**18,887**
3	**17,566**	4,000	13,566	803	14,369
4	14,369	4,000	10,369	613	10,982
5	10,982	4,000	6,982	414	7,396
6	7,396	4,000	3,396	201	3,597
7	3,597	1,850	1,747	103	1,850
		26,250		4,421	

The present value of the total payments over the revised lease term at the original discount rate is £22,585, which is 90.3% of the fair value of the asset at commencement of the lease. In addition, the residual value of £1,850 would have had a present value of only £1,237; it is a feature of the methodology that the present value of the lease payments and the present value of the residual do not add up to the fair value of the asset at inception. In order to make the computation, an adjustment is made to the capital amount as at the date that the lease is renegotiated. The outstanding amount is recomputed from £18,887 (the balance at the end of year 2 calculated using the original assumptions) to £17,566, the amount that corresponds to the new assumptions. Note that it is not relevant that the method results in a change to the 'capital sum' of only 7% ((18,887 − 17,566) ÷ 18,887). The assessment is based on the net present value of the minimum lease payments over the lease term and other features of the revised agreement.

If method (c) is applied, the modified lease is considered as if it were a new five year lease. The IIR calculated prospectively over the remaining term is now 6.13%:

Year	Capital sum at start of period £	Rental paid £	Capital sum during period £	Finance charge (6.13% per annum) £	Capital sum at end of period £
3	17,500	4,000	13,500	827	14,327
4	14,327	4,000	10,327	633	10,960
5	10,960	4,000	6,960	426	7,386
6	7,386	4,000	3,386	207	3,593
7	3,593	1,850	1,743	107	1,850
		17,850		2,200	

The present value of the remaining payments is £16,126, which is 92.15% of the fair value of the asset (£17,500) at the date of entering into the new lease.

In this example, all three methods result in a present value of the minimum lease payments that exceeds 90% but this would not, of course, always be the case.

3.9.2   Accounting for reclassified leases

If the original lease was a finance lease and the revised lease is an operating lease, then the balances relating to the finance lease must be derecognised. For the lessee, this involves derecognising both the asset (which will have been depreciated up to the point of derecognition over the shorter of the useful life or the lease term) and the finance lease liability. Finance lease derecognition is discussed further at 3.7.4 above.

If the original lease was an operating lease and the revised lease is a finance lease, then any balances resulting from recognising the lease cost on a straight-line basis will be expensed and the balances relating to the finance lease must be recognised for the first time.

The most obvious way in which to account for the revised finance lease is as a new lease as from the date on which the terms were changed, based on the fair value of the assets as at the date of revision. The assets and liabilities under the finance lease would be recognised initially as in method (c) in 3.9.1 above, which calculates the assets and liabilities as if the revised agreement were a new lease as from the date of reassessment.

This is consistent with using either method (a) or method (c) in 3.9.1 above to help determine the revised classification. However, it is also acceptable to recognise the new lease using method (b) above, by taking into consideration the changes in the agreement but calculating the present value of the asset and liability by using the interest rate implicit in the original lease. This uses an accepted methodology and is

Chapter 16

consistent with the fact that there has, in fact, only been a change to the original terms and not a completely new lease; it also has the advantage that the revised fair value of the asset does not have to be known.

If the original lease agreement and the revised lease agreement are both finance leases, then the modification will have accounting consequences that are discussed in the following section.

3.9.3   *Changes to leases terms that do not result in reclassification*

3.9.3.A   *Accounting for changes to the terms of finance leases*

If the rights under a finance lease have changed without a change in the classification, these changes to lease term and cash flows must be accounted for.

The two most obvious methods of calculating the impact of the changes are as follows:

(a)   even though the classification has not changed, the revised agreement is accounted for as if it were a new lease. The calculation will be based on the fair value and useful life of the asset at the date of the revision.

(b)   use the original IIR to discount the revised minimum lease payments and (for a lessee) adjust any change in lease liability to the carrying amount of the asset. Lessors will adjust the carrying value of the asset, taking gains or losses to income.

These are described in 3.9.1 above (method (c) and method (b)). For lessees, both of these methods will affect the carrying value of the asset and hence its future amortisation.

Another method that might be considered is to reflect changes prospectively over the remaining term of the lease; this is only likely to be appropriate if the cash flows are modified but all other rights remain unchanged, e.g. the effects of a tax or interest variation clause.

3.9.3.B   *Accounting for changes to the terms of operating leases*

Lessees may renegotiate terms with lessors, e.g. in circumstances in which the lessee has financial difficulties or where there is evidence that the lease terms are at higher than market rates.

Operating leases may include explicit or implicit options to extend the lease and the extension may have different payment terms. If there is a formal option, the lessee might be required to give notice to the lessor of its intention to extend at a set date before the lease expires. There may be similar arrangements with purchase options.

The revised terms should be taken into account prospectively from the date of the agreement. A catch-up adjustment as if the new terms had always existed is not consistent with the fact that the modification is a change in estimate and these are normally accounted for prospectively.

If the lessee renews a lease or exercises a purchase option, it does not have to re-assess the classification of a lease if the renewal and exercise were not considered probable at the inception of the lease (see 3.4.3 above). There may still be accounting consequences in connection with spreading the lease costs because of FRS 102's requirement to expense lease costs on a straight-line basis over the lease term, save in unusual circumstances (see 3.8.1 and 3.8.1.A above).

3.10 Sale and leaseback transactions

These transactions involve the original owner of an asset selling it and immediately leasing it back. The lease payment and the sale price are usually interdependent because they are negotiated as a package. The accounting treatment of a sale and leaseback transaction depends on the type of lease. *[FRS 102.20.32]*.

Sometimes, instead of selling the asset outright, the original owner will lease the asset to the other party under a finance lease and then lease it back. Such a transaction is known as a 'lease and leaseback' and has similar effects so for these purposes is included within the term 'sale and leaseback'.

Sale and leaseback transactions are a fairly common feature in sectors that own many properties, such as the retail and hotel industries. Many parties are involved as buyer/lessors, not only finance houses and banks but also pension funds and property groups. From a commercial point of view, the important point of difference lies between an entity that decides that it is cheaper to rent than to own – and is willing to pass on the property risk to the landlord – and an entity which decides to use the property as a means of raising finance – and will therefore retain the property risk. However from the accounting point of view, a major consideration is whether a profit can be reported on such transactions.

These parties will be termed the seller/lessee and buyer/lessor respectively.

The buyer/lessor will treat the lease in the same way as it would any other lease that was not part of a sale and leaseback transaction. The accounting treatment of the transaction by the seller/lessee depends on the type of lease involved, i.e. whether the leaseback is under a finance or an operating lease.

3.10.1 Sale and finance leaseback

In order to assess whether the leaseback is under a finance lease, the seller/lessee will apply the qualitative tests that are described at 3.4.1 above. If a sale and leaseback transaction results in a finance lease, any excess of sales proceeds over the carrying amount should not be recognised immediately as income by a seller/lessee. Instead, the excess is deferred and amortised over the lease term. *[FRS 102.20.33]*.

It is inappropriate to show a profit on disposal of an asset which has then, in substance, been reacquired by the entity under a finance lease as the lessor is providing finance to the lessee with the asset as security.

The implication of Section 20 is that the previous carrying value is left unchanged, with the sales proceeds being shown as a liability, usually accounted for under Section 11 (see Chapter 8). The creditor balance represents the finance lease liability under the leaseback. This treatment is consistent with Section 23 (see Chapter 18) as the seller/lessee has by definition not transferred to the buyer the significant risks and rewards of ownership of the goods. *[FRS 102.23.10]*. Therefore it would not be recorded as a sale. It is also consistent with the treatment under previous UK GAAP.

However, another way of accounting for the transaction is for the asset to be restated to its fair value (or the present value of the minimum lease payments, if lower) in exactly the same way as any other asset acquired under a finance lease.

Chapter 16

Both treatments have the same net effect on the income statement.

Example 16.16:   Sale and finance leaseback – accounting for the excess sale proceeds

An asset that has a carrying value of £700 and a remaining useful life of 7 years is sold for £1,200 and leased back on a finance lease. If this is accounted for as a financing transaction with the property used as security for a loan, the asset will remain at £700 and will be amortised over the remaining 7 years at £100 per year.

If it is accounted for as a disposal of the original asset and the acquisition of an asset under a finance lease for £1,200, the excess of sales proceeds of £500 over the original carrying value should be deferred and amortised (i.e. credited to profit or loss) over the lease term.

The net impact on income of the charge for depreciation based on the carrying value of the asset held under the finance lease of £171 and the amortisation of the deferred income of £71 is the same as the annual depreciation of £100 based on the original carrying amount.

If the sales value is less than the carrying amount, does the apparent 'loss' need to be taken to profit or loss? IAS 17 explicitly states that no impairment need be taken unless there has been an impairment under IAS 36 – *Impairment of Assets*. *[IAS 17.64]*. Although this requirement is not replicated in Section 20, the underlying principles suggest that the same accounting can be applied under FRS 102. There may be an obvious reason why the sales proceeds are less than the carrying value; for example, the fair value of a second-hand vehicle or item of plant and machinery is frequently lower than its carrying amount, especially soon after the asset has been acquired by the entity. This fall in fair value after sale has no effect on the asset's value-in-use. What this means is that in the absence of impairment, a deficit (sales proceeds lower than carrying value) may be deferred in the same manner as a profit and spread over the lease term.

3.10.2   *Sale and operating leaseback*

If a sale and leaseback transaction results in an operating lease, and it is clear that the transaction is established at fair value, any profit or loss should be recognised immediately by the seller/lessee. If the sale price is below fair value, any profit or loss should be recognised immediately unless the loss is compensated for by future lease payments at below market price, in which case it should be deferred and amortised in proportion to the lease payments over the period for which the asset is expected to be used. If the sale price is above fair value, the excess over fair value should be deferred and amortised over the period for which the asset is expected to be used. *[FRS 102.20.34]*.

The rationale behind these treatments is that if the sales value is not based on fair values then it is likely that the normal market rents will have been adjusted to compensate. For example, a sale at above fair value followed by above-market rentals is similar to a loan of the excess proceeds by the lessor that is being repaid out of the rentals. Accordingly, the transaction should be recorded as if it had been based on fair value.

Where the sales value is less than fair value there may be legitimate reasons for this to be so, for example where the seller has had to raise cash quickly. In such situations, as the rentals under the lease have not been reduced to compensate, the profit or loss should be based on the sales value.

The following table reproduces part of the *Guidance on Implementing* IAS 17 to assist in interpreting the various permutations of facts and circumstances.

Sale price established at fair value	Carrying amount equal to fair value	Carrying amount less than fair value
Profit	no profit	recognise profit immediately
Loss	no loss	not applicable
Sale price below fair value		
Profit	no profit	recognise profit immediately
Loss *not* compensated for by future lease payments at below market price	recognise loss immediately	recognise loss immediately
Loss compensated for by future lease payments at below market price	defer and amortise loss	defer and amortise loss
Sale price above fair value		
Profit	defer and amortise profit	defer and amortise excess profit
Loss	no loss	no loss

IAS 17 also includes a requirement to write down the carrying amount of an asset if the fair value is lower at the time the operating lease is entered into. *[IAS 17.63]*. This has no overall effect on the transaction unless the sale price is above fair value, in which case the entity will recognise a loss on writing down the asset but defer and amortise the profit above fair value. Section 20 contains no such mandatory requirement.

3.10.3 *Sale and leaseback arrangements with put and call options*

Sale and leaseback arrangements may also include features such as repurchase options. These are not directly addressed by FRS 102 but affect the disposition of risks and rewards in the overall arrangement.

If a lease arrangement includes an option that can only be exercised by the seller/lessee at the then fair value of the asset in question, the risks and rewards inherent in the residual value of the asset have passed to the buyer/lessor. The option amounts to a right of first refusal to the seller/lessee.

Where there is both a put and a call option in force on equivalent terms at a determinable amount other than the fair value, it is clear that the asset will revert to the seller/lessee. It must be in the interests of one or other of the parties to exercise the option so as to secure a profit or avoid a loss, and therefore the likelihood of the asset remaining the property of the buyer/lessor rather than reverting to the seller

Chapter 16

must be remote. In such a case, this is a bargain purchase option and the seller/lessee has entered into a finance leaseback.

However, the position is less clear where there is only a put option or only a call option in force, rather than a combination of the two. The overall commercial effect will have to be evaluated and one-sided options may be an indication that the arrangement contains non-typical contractual terms which will put it out of scope of lease accounting altogether (see 3.1.3 above).

These arrangements are not common in practice and further discussion is beyond the scope of this publication.

3.11   Disclosures

The disclosure requirements of Section 20 are derived from IAS 17. For lessees, disclosures are broadly similar to previous UK GAAP, taking into account the requirements of both Section 20 and other relevant sections. Lessors will have to make additional disclosures not required by SSAP 21 that mirror the lessee disclosure requirements as well as other disclosures relating to both the statement of financial position and the effect of finance leases on the income statement (see 3.11.2 below).

3.11.1   *Disclosures by lessees*

There is a requirement for lessees to give a general description of significant finance leasing arrangements which is not explicitly present under previous UK GAAP. Section 3 – *Financial Statement Presentation* – contains the requirement to disclose accounting policies (see Chapter 4).

3.11.1.A   *Disclosure of finance leases*

Lessees must make the following disclosures for finance leases: *[FRS 102.20.13]*

(a)   the net carrying amount at the end of the reporting period by class of asset;

(b)   the total of future minimum lease payments at the end of the reporting period, for each of the following periods:

    (i)   not later than one year;

    (ii)   later than one year and not later than five years; and

    (iii)   later than five years; and

(c)   a general description of the lessee's significant leasing arrangements including, for example, information about contingent rent, renewal or purchase options and escalation clauses, subleases, and restrictions imposed by lease arrangements.

In addition, the requirements for disclosure about assets in accordance with Sections 17, 18 and 27 apply to lessees for assets leased under finance leases (see Chapters 13, 14 and 22). *[FRS 102.20.14].*

There is no requirement to disclose separately depreciation, amortisation or impairment of assets held under finance leases from owned assets or to disclose separately lease obligations in the statement of financial position.

3.11.1.B   Disclosure of operating leases

A lessee must make the following disclosures for operating leases: *[FRS 102.20.16]*

(a)   the total of future minimum lease payments under non-cancellable operating leases for each of the following periods:

    (i)   not later than one year;

    (ii)   later than one year and not later than five years; and

    (iii) later than five years; and

(b)   lease payments recognised as an expense.

3.11.2   Disclosures by lessors

SSAP 21 does not require the maturity analysis of the financial asset required by Section 20, described below.

3.11.2.A   Disclosure of finance leases

A lessor must make the following disclosures for finance leases: *[FRS 102.20.23]*

(a)   a reconciliation between the gross investment in the lease at the end of the reporting period, and the present value of minimum lease payments receivable at the end of the reporting period.

    In addition, a lessor must disclose the gross investment in the lease and the present value of minimum lease payments receivable at the end of the reporting period, for each of the following periods:

    (i)   not later than one year;

    (ii)   later than one year and not later than five years; and

    (iii) later than five years;

(b)   unearned finance income;

(c)   the unguaranteed residual values accruing to the benefit of the lessor;

(d)   the accumulated allowance for uncollectible minimum lease payments receivable;

(e)   contingent rents recognised as income in the period; and

(f)   a general description of the lessor's significant leasing arrangements, including, for example, information about contingent rent, renewal or purchase options and escalation clauses, subleases, and restrictions imposed by lease arrangements.

Chapter 16

3.11.2.B   Disclosure of operating leases

Lessors must disclose the following for operating leases: *[FRS 102.20.30]*

(a)   the future minimum lease payments under non-cancellable operating leases for each of the following periods:

   (i)   not later than one year;

   (ii)   later than one year and not later than five years; and

   (iii)   later than five years;

(b)   total contingent rents recognised as income; and

(c)   a general description of the lessor's significant leasing arrangements, including, for example, information about contingent rent, renewal or purchase options and escalation clauses, and restrictions imposed by lease arrangements.

The requirements for disclosure about assets in accordance with Sections 17 and 27 apply to lessors for assets provided under operating leases (see Chapters 13 and 22). *[FRS 102.20.31]*.

3.11.3   Disclosures of sale and leaseback transactions

Disclosure requirements for lessees and lessors apply equally to sale and leaseback transactions. The required description of significant leasing arrangements includes description of unique or unusual provisions of the agreement or terms of the sale and leaseback transactions. *[FRS 102.20.35]*.

3.12   Transition

3.12.1   Applying the general transition rules

Lease arrangements should be assessed under FRS 102 as finance or operating leases as at the date these arrangements were entered into. Entities will then apply FRS 102's measurement rules appropriately as at the date of transition. Key differences between FRS 102 and previous UK GAAP or IFRS are described in 2 above.

Similarly, disclosures must be made in accordance with FRS 102. Transition is discussed in Section 35 – *Transition to this FRS* (see Chapter 30).

3.12.2   Exemptions

FRS 102 includes the following exemptions that first-time adopters may apply as at the date of transition.

3.12.2.A   Arrangements containing a lease

A first-time adopter is permitted to determine whether an arrangement existing at the date of transition contains a lease (see 3.2 above) on the basis of facts and circumstances existing at that date, rather than when the arrangement was entered into. *[FRS 102.35.10(k)]*.

3.12.2.B   Lease incentives

Unlike previous UK GAAP, FRS 102 requires lease incentives to be spread over the lease term (see 3.8.1.C and 3.8.2.A above). First-time adopters do not have to apply this treatment to lease incentives if the term of the lease commenced before the date of transition. Instead, they may continue to recognise any residual benefit or cost associated with these lease incentives on the same basis as before. *[FRS 102.35.10(p)].*

4   SUMMARY OF GAAP DIFFERENCES

	FRS 102	*Previous UK GAAP*	*IFRS*
Leases classified as financial instruments	Leases that could lead to a loss to the lessor or the lessee as a result of non-typical contractual terms are excluded from scope.	There is no such scope exclusion under SSAP 21. Entities that have adopted FRS 26 are required to identify embedded derivatives that are not closely related to the host (lease) contract and account separately for these derivatives in accordance with FRS 26	
Arrangements that do not take the legal form of a lease	In scope are rights to use assets in return for payments contained within arrangements that do not take the legal form of a lease (so-called embedded leases).	No equivalent guidance in SSAP 21 but entities look to FRS 5 to see if more complex arrangements contain 'in substance' or 'embedded' leases.	
Lease classification	FRS 102 includes a number of situations that individually or in combination would be expected to lead to a lease being classified as a finance lease. There is no 90% test rule.	Previous UK GAAP considers a similar list of indicators (not formally part of SSAP 21), but has a rebuttable presumption that transfer of risks and rewards occurs if the present value of the minimum lease payments discounted at the interest rate implicit in the lease, amounts to substantially all (normally 90% or more) of the fair value of the leased asset.	
Inception of the lease	The inception of the lease is the earlier of the date of the lease agreement and the date of commitment by the parties to the principal provisions of the lease.	Inception is the earlier of the time the asset is brought into use and the date from which rentals first accrue.	

Chapter 16

	FRS 102	*Previous UK GAAP*	*IFRS*
Straight-line basis for lease payments	Operating lease rentals should be charged to the income statement on a straight-line basis with one exception: if lease payments increase annually by fixed increments intended to compensate for expected annual inflation over the lease period, the fixed minimum increment that reflects expected general inflation will be recognised as an expense as incurred.	Operating lease rentals should be charged to the income statement account on a straight-line basis (SSAP 21).	All operating lease payments are to be recognised as an expense on a straight-line basis, unless another systematic basis is more appropriate.
Lease incentives	FRS 102 requires lease incentives to be recognised over the lease term.	Lease incentives are recognised over the shorter of the lease term and a period ending on a date from which it is expected the prevailing market rental will be payable (UITF 28).	
Initial direct costs	Initial direct costs incurred in arranging a lease are included in the initial measurement of a finance lease receivable and factored into the calculation of the interest rate implicit in the lease.	Entities do not have to include initial direct costs in the initial measurement of a finance lease receivable. Initial direct costs may be deferred and apportioned over the period of the lease or, as deferral is not mandatory, they may be expensed immediately (SSAP 21).	
Recognition of finance income/gross earnings by lessors	Finance income, which is the difference between the net and gross investment in the lease, is to be recognised on a pattern reflecting a constant periodic rate of return on the net investment in the finance lease.	The difference between the net and gross investment in the lease, called gross earnings, is allocated to accounting periods to give a constant periodic rate of return on the lessor's net cash investment. The lessor's net cash investment includes other cash flows, mainly those relating to tax in the lease (SSAP 21).	

Leases of land and buildings		FRS 102 is silent about separating the land and buildings elements of leases.	Leases of land are to be assessed separately from building leases and the leases over land classified as finance or operating leases in accordance with the general rules.
Disclosure: operating leases	A lessee must disclose the total of future minimum lease payments under non-cancellable operating leases, analysed into the amounts that will fall due in not more than one year, in one to five years and more than five years from the date of the statement of financial position. [FRS 102.20.16].	SSAP 21 requires an analysis of the next year's commitment analysed into the amounts that will fall due in not more than one year, in one to five years and more than five years from the date of the statement of financial position.	

References

1 FRS 26, *Financial Instruments: Recognition and Measurement*, ASB, December 2004, para. 2(b)(iii).
2 ICAEW, Technical Release 664, *Implementation of SSAP 21 'Accounting for leases and hire purchase contracts'*, July 1987 and ICAEW, *Financial Reporting & Auditing Group, Technical Release FRAG 9/92*, March 1992.

3 SSAP 21, *Accounting for leases and hire purchase contracts*, ASB, February 1997, para. 29.
4 UITF 28 – *Operating lease incentives*, ASB, February 2001, para. 13.
5 IFRIC 4, para. 9.
6 ASC 840–10–25–1.

Chapter 16

Chapter 17

Provisions and contingencies

List of examples

Chapter 17

Chapter 17

Provisions and contingencies

1   INTRODUCTION

Section 21 of FRS 102 – *Provisions and Contingencies* – addresses the recognition, measurement and disclosure of provisions and the disclosure of contingent liabilities and contingent assets.

The principle of Section 21 for the recognition and measurement of provisions is consistent with that applied by FRS 12 – *Provisions, contingent liabilities and contingent assets* – and IAS 37 – *Provisions, Contingent Liabilities and Contingent Assets*. A provision should be recognised by an entity if the entity has a present obligation (legal or constructive) as a result of a past event, payment is probable and the amount expected to settle the obligation can be measured reliably. *[FRS 102.21.4]*.

The approach to contingent liabilities and contingent assets under Section 21 is also consistent with that taken by FRS 12 and IAS 37. These items should not be recognised on balance sheet but may require disclosure. *[FRS 102.21.12]*. The only exception to this is for contingent liabilities of an acquiree in a business combination, which should be recognised on the balance sheet of the acquirer. *[FRS 102.19.14]*.

However, FRS 12 and IAS 37 provide more guidance than Section 21 in certain areas. In addition, there are some minor differences between Section 21 and the equivalent guidance under UK GAAP and IFRS. These are addressed at 2 below.

2   KEY DIFFERENCES TO IFRS AND PREVIOUS UK GAAP

As stated at 1 above, Section 21, FRS 12 and IAS 37 apply the same principle to the recognition and measurement of provisions. The approach to the disclosure of contingent liabilities and contingent assets is also consistent between Section 21, FRS 12 and IAS 37.

2.1   Key differences to previous UK GAAP

2.1.1   *Scope – Provisions, contingent liabilities and contingent assets covered by another section*

Section 21 does not apply to provisions, contingent liabilities and contingent assets covered by another section of FRS 102. However, where those other sections contain no specific requirements to deal with contracts that have become onerous, Section 21 applies to those contracts. *[FRS 102.21.1]*.

Under FRS 12, where a provision, contingent liability or contingent asset was covered by another Standard and that Standard contained no specific requirements to deal with onerous contracts, there was no requirement that FRS 12 be applied to those contracts. However, operating leases that became onerous were explicitly in scope of FRS 12. *[FRS 12.8]*.

2.1.2   *Scope – Financial guarantee contracts*

Entities should account for financial guarantee contracts in accordance with Section 21 unless certain elections are made (see 3.2 below).

For those companies applying the measurement requirements of FRS 26 – *Financial instruments: recognition and measurement*, financial guarantee contracts were outside the scope of FRS 12. They were instead accounted for in accordance with FRS 26 and were generally measured at fair value on initial recognition (subject to certain exemptions), regardless of whether or not it was considered probable that the guarantee would be called.

2.1.3   *Recognition of provisions for future operating losses*

Section 21 requires that provisions should not be recognised for future operating losses *[FRS 102.21.11B]* (see 3.3.4.A below). This is consistent with FRS 12. *[FRS 12.68]*. However, FRS 3 – *Reporting financial performance* – included an exception to this rule where a decision had been made to sell or terminate an operation, and the entity was demonstrably committed to the sale or termination. In this case, a provision would be recognised to cover the direct costs of the sale or termination and any operating losses of the operation up to the date of sale or termination to the extent that both were expected to be covered by the future profits of the operation. *[FRS 3.18]*.

2.1.4   *Disclosures*

The disclosures required by Section 21 are discussed at 3.10 below.

Section 21 does not require two specific disclosures required by FRS 12. These are:

- the disclosure of major assumptions concerning future events that may affect the amount required to settle an obligation where this is necessary to provide adequate information; *[FRS 12.90(b)]* and

- a separate line item in the reconciliation of opening and closing provision balances showing the increase during the period in the discounted amount arising from the passage of time and the effect of any change in discount rate. *[FRS 12.89(e)]*. Section 21 allows the line showing additions to provisions in the period to include adjustments that arise from changes in measuring the discounted amount. *[FRS 102.21.14(a)(ii)]*.

Section 21 does, however, require an entity to disclose the expected amount and timing of any payments resulting from an obligation. *[FRS 102.21.14(b)]*. FRS 12 required disclosure only of the expected timing of payments resulting from an obligation. *[FRS 12.90(a)]*.

Section 21 requires an entity to disclose the nature and business purpose of any financial guarantee contracts it has issued, regardless of whether a provision is required or contingent liability disclosed *[FRS 102.21.17A]*. This was not specifically required under previous UK GAAP (regardless of whether or not FRS 26 was applied).

2.2   Key differences compared to IFRS

2.2.1   *Scope – Provisions, contingent liabilities and contingent assets covered by another section*

Section 21 does not apply to provisions, contingent liabilities and contingent assets covered by another section of FRS 102. However, where those other sections contain no specific requirements to deal with contracts that have become onerous, Section 21 applies to those contracts. *[FRS 102.21.1]*.

Under IAS 37, where a provision, contingent liability or contingent asset is covered by another Standard and that Standard contains no specific requirements to deal with onerous contracts, there is no requirement that IAS 37 be applied to those contracts. However, operating leases that become onerous are explicitly in scope of IAS 37. *[IAS 37.5(c)]*.

2.2.2   *Scope – Financial guarantee contracts*

Entities should account for financial guarantee contracts in accordance with Section 21 unless certain elections are made (see 3.2 below).

Under IFRS, financial guarantee contracts are outside the scope of IAS 37. They are instead accounted for in accordance with IAS 39 – *Financial Instruments: Recognition and Measurement* – and are generally measured at fair value on initial recognition (subject to certain exemptions), regardless of whether or not it is considered probable that the guarantee will be called, unless the entity has elected under IFRS 4 – *Insurance Contracts* – to continue the application of insurance contract accounting.

2.2.3   *Disclosures*

The disclosures required by Section 21 are discussed at 3.10 below.

Section 21 does not refer specifically to the following two specific disclosures required by IAS 37. These are:

- the disclosure of major assumptions concerning future events that may affect the amount required to settle an obligation where this is necessary to provide adequate information; *[IAS 37.85(b)]* and

- a separate line item in the reconciliation of opening and closing provision balances showing the increase during the period in the discounted amount arising from the passage of time and the effect of any change in discount rate. *[IAS 37.84(e)]*. Section 21 allows the line showing additions to provisions in the period to include adjustments that arise from changes in measuring the discounted amount. *[FRS 102.21.14(a)(ii)]*.

Chapter 17

Section 21 does, however require, an entity to disclose the expected amount and timing of any payments resulting from an obligation. *[FRS 102.21.14(b)]*. IAS 37 requires disclosure only of the expected timing of payments resulting from an obligation.

Section 21 requires an entity to disclose the nature and business purpose of any financial guarantee contracts it has issued, regardless of whether a provision is required or contingent liability disclosed *[FRS 102.21.17A]*. This is not specifically required under IFRS. In addition, to the extent a provision is recognised, or contingent liability disclosed, for financial guarantee contracts, the general provisions or contingent liabilities disclosures set out at 3.10 below are also required. This is not required under IFRS as financial guarantee contracts are excluded from the scope of IAS 37.

3   REQUIREMENTS OF SECTION 21 FOR PROVISIONS AND CONTINGENCIES

3.1   Terms used in Section 21 of FRS 102

The following terms are used in Section 21 with the meanings specified. *[FRS 102 Appendix I]*.

Term	*Definition*
Provision	A liability of uncertain timing or amount
Liability	A present obligation of the entity arising from past events, the settlement of which is expected to result in an outflow from the entity of resources embodying economic benefits.
Contingent liability	(a) a possible obligation that arises from past events and whose existence will be confirmed only by the occurrence or non-occurrence of one or more uncertain future events not wholly within the control of the entity; or (b) a present obligation that arises from past events but is not recognised because: (i) it is not probable that an outflow of resources embodying economic benefits will be required to settle the obligation; or (ii) the amount of the obligation cannot be measured with sufficient reliability.
Contingent asset	A possible asset that arises from past events and whose existence will be confirmed only by the occurrence or non-occurrence of one or more uncertain future events not wholly within the control of the entity.
Onerous contract	A contract in which the unavoidable costs of meeting the obligations under the contract exceed the economic benefits expected to be received under it.

Probable	More likely than not.
Constructive obligation	An obligation that derives from an entity's actions where: (a) by an established pattern of past practice, published policies or a sufficiently specific current statement, the entity has indicated to other parties that it will accept certain responsibilities; and (b) as a result, the entity has created a valid expectation on the part of those other parties that it will discharge those responsibilities.
Financial guarantee contract	A contract that requires the issuer to make specified payments to reimburse the holder for a loss it incurs because a specified debtor fails to make payments when due in accordance with the original or modified terms of a debt instrument.
Executory contract	A contract under which neither party has performed any of its obligations; or both parties have partially performed their obligations to an equal extent. *[FRS 102.21.2].*
Present value	A current estimate of the present discounted value of the future net cash flows in the normal course of business.
Restructuring	A programme that is planned and controlled by management and materially changes either: (a) the scope of the business undertaken by the entity; or (b) the manner in which that business is conducted.
Impracticable	Applying the requirement is impracticable when the entity cannot apply it after making every reasonable effort to do so.

3.2 Scope

Section 21 applies to all provisions, contingent liabilities and contingent assets other than those covered by other sections of FRS 102. Where those other sections contain no specific requirements to deal with contracts that become onerous, Section 21 applies to those contracts. *[FRS 102.21.1].*

Financial guarantee contracts are included in the scope of Section 21 unless:

* the entity has chosen to apply IAS 39 and / or IFRS 9 – *Financial Instruments* ('IFRS 9') to its financial instruments (see Chapter 8); or

* the entity has elected under FRS 103 – *Insurance Contracts* ('FRS 103') to continue the application of insurance contract accounting. *[FRS 102.21.1A].*

The requirements of Section 21 relating to financial guarantee contracts are discussed at 3.3.5.F below.

The following table lists the specific types of transaction or circumstances referred to in Section 21 that might give rise to a provision, contingent liability or contingent asset. In some cases, the transaction is identified in Section 21 only to prohibit recognition of any liability, such as for future operating losses (see 3.3.4.A below). This chapter does not address those items identified below as falling outside the scope of Section 21.

Chapter 17

Types of transactions or circumstances referred to	In scope	Out of scope	Another section
Restructuring costs	•		
Product warranties / refunds	•		
Legal claims	•		
Reimbursement rights	•		
Future operating costs (e.g. training)	•		
Future operating losses	•		
Onerous contracts	•		
Financial guarantee contracts	•		
Provisions for depreciation, impairment or doubtful debts		•	
Executory contracts (unless onerous)		•	
Financial Instruments in the scope of Section 11		•	Section 11
Financial Instruments in the scope of Section 12		•	Section 12
Contingent liabilities acquired in a business combination		•	Section 19
Leases (unless onerous operating leases)		•	Section 20
Construction contracts		•	Section 23
Employee benefits		•	Section 28
Income taxes		•	Section 29
Insurance contracts		•	FRS 103

3.2.1   Items outside the scope of Section 21

3.2.1.A   Executory contracts, except where the contract is onerous

Section 21 does not apply to executory contracts unless they are onerous. Executory contracts are contracts under which neither party to the contract has performed any of their obligations or where both parties have performed their obligations to an equal extent. *[FRS 102.21.2].* This means that contracts such as supplier purchase contracts and capital commitments, which would otherwise fall within the scope of the Standard, are exempt unless the contract becomes onerous. Onerous contracts are addressed at 3.3.5.A below.

3.2.1.B   Financial instruments

Section 21 does not apply to financial instruments (including loan commitments) that are within the scope of Section 11 – *Basic Financial Instruments* – or Section 12 – *Other Financial Instruments Issues. [FRS 102.21.1B].*

As noted at 3.2 above, an entity must apply Section 21 to financial guarantee contracts unless it has chosen to apply IAS 39 or IFRS 9 to its financial instruments or FRS 103 to continue to account for these guarantees as insurance contracts. *[FRS 102.21.1A]*.

3.2.1.C   Insurance contracts

Insurance contracts (including reinsurance contracts) that an entity issues and reinsurance contracts that the entity holds fall within the scope of FRS 103 and not FRS 102. *[FRS 102.21.1B]*. An insurance contract is defined as 'a contract under which one party (the insurer) accepts significant insurance risk from another party (the policyholder) by agreeing to compensate the policyholder if a specified uncertain future event (the insured event) adversely affects the policyholder'. *[FRS 102 Appendix I]*. A reinsurance contract is 'an insurance contract issued by one insurer (the reinsurer) to compensate another insurer (the cedant) for losses on one or more contracts issued by the cedant'. *[FRS 102 Appendix I]*.

Section 21 also excludes from its scope financial instruments issued by an entity with a discretionary participation feature that are within the scope of FRS 103. *[FRS 102.21.1B]*. These features are most commonly found in life insurance policies and are essentially contractual rights of the holder to receive, as a supplement to guaranteed benefits, significant additional benefits whose amount or timing are contractually at the discretion of the issuer and based on the performance of the insurer, a fund or a specified pool of investments. *[FRS 102 Appendix I]*.

3.2.1.D   Areas covered by other sections of FRS 102

Section 21 does not apply to those provisions covered by other sections of FRS 102. *[FRS 102.21.1]*. However, other than financial instruments and insurance contracts which are explicitly excluded from its scope, Section 21 does not fully elaborate on what transactions or circumstances this exclusion is intended to cover. However, where those other sections of the FRS do not contain specific requirements on accounting for onerous contracts, Section 21 should be applied. *[FRS 102.21.1]*.

Section 21 notes that the word 'provision' is sometimes used in the context of items such as depreciation, impairment of assets and doubtful debts and that such 'provisions' are not covered by Section 21 because they are adjustments to the carrying amounts of assets rather than the recognition of liabilities. *[FRS 102.21.3]*. Examples of other transactions and circumstances which are covered elsewhere in the FRS and that we would therefore expect to fall outside the scope of Section 21 are included in the table at 3.2 above.

3.3   Determining when a provision should be recognised

Section 21 requires that a provision should be recognised only when:

(a)   an entity has an obligation at the reporting date as a result as a result of a past event;

(b)   it is probable (i.e. more likely than not) that the entity will be required to transfer economic benefit in settlement; and

(c)   the amount of the obligation can be measured reliably. *[FRS 102.21.4]*.

No provision should be recognised unless all of these conditions are met. Each of these conditions is discussed separately below.

Where all of these three conditions are met, a provision should be recognised as a liability in the statement of financial position. In most cases, the recognition of a provision results in an immediate expense in profit or loss. However, in some cases, it may be appropriate to recognise the amount of the provision as part of the cost of an asset such as inventories or property plant and equipment. *[FRS 102.21.5]*. A common case when a provision is recognised as part of the cost of an asset is in relation to decommissioning costs (see 4.1 below).

3.3.1   The entity has an obligation at the reporting date as a result of a past event

An obligation at the reporting date can be either a legal obligation that can be enforced by law, or a constructive obligation. A constructive obligation arises when an entity has created a valid expectation in other parties that it will discharge the obligation. *[FRS 102.21.6]*. This may be as a result of past practice, published policies or a sufficiently specific current statement. *[FRS 102 Appendix I]*. The entity must have no realistic alternative to settling the obligation, whether legal or constructive, in order to meet condition (a) of the recognition criteria for provisions set out at 3.3 above. *[FRS 102.21.6]*.

The following example from Section 21 illustrates how a constructive obligation may be created.

Example 17.1:   Recognising a provision because of a constructive obligation

Refunds policy *[FRS 102.21A.5]*

A retail store has a policy of refunding purchases by dissatisfied customers, even though it is under no legal obligation to do so. Its policy of making refunds is generally known.

In this scenario, the sale of the product gives rise to a constructive obligation because the store, through its policy and past conduct, has created a valid expectation on the part of its customers that a refund will be given if they are dissatisfied with their purchase.

The assessment of whether an entity has a constructive obligation may not always be straightforward, but in our opinion will have to be accompanied by evidence of communication between the entity and the affected parties in order to be able to conclude that they have a valid expectation that the entity will honour its obligations. In this context, an internal memo or board decision is not sufficient. It is not necessary for the entity to know the identity of the other party. In Example 17.1 above, the other party comprises all the retail store customers and they were aware of the entity's returns policy. Restructuring provisions give rise to another case where judgment is needed to determine whether a valid expectation exists, as discussed at 3.3.5.B below.

In addition to an entity having an obligation at the reporting date, the obligation must arise as a result of a past event. Obligations that will arise from an entity's future actions do not satisfy condition (a) of the recognition criteria set out at 3.3 above, regardless of how likely the future actions are to occur, and even if they are contractual. *[FRS 102.21.6]*. This is illustrated in the following scenarios.

Example 17.2:   No provision within a past obligating event

Scenario 1: Requirement to fit smoke filters [FRS 102.21.6]

An entity may intend or need to carry out expenditure to fit smoke filters in a particular type of factory in the future, as a result of either legal requirements or commercial pressures.

In this scenario, the entity can avoid the expenditure required to fit smoke filters by its future actions, for example by changing its method of operation or selling the factory. It therefore has no obligation at the reporting date arising as a result of a past event and no provision is recognised.

Scenario 2: Staff retraining as a result of changes to the income tax system [FRS 102.21A.8]

The government introduces changes to the income tax system. As a result of those changes, an entity in the financial services sector will need to retrain a large proportion of its administrative and sales workforce in order to ensure continued compliance with tax regulations. At the end of the reporting period, no retraining of staff has taken place.

In this scenario, no event has taken place at the reporting date to create an obligation. Only once the training has taken place will there be a present obligation as a result of a past event.

Sometimes it is not always clear whether a present obligation exists as a result of a past event, in which case judgement is required. A common example is a lawsuit, in which the responsibility of the defendant has not yet been established. IAS 37 and FRS 12 suggests that entities would recognise an obligation if, taking account of all available evidence it is 'more likely than not' that a present obligation exists at the end of the reporting period. *[IAS 37.15, FRS 12.15]*. In this context, 'all available evidence' would include the opinion of experts together with any additional evidence provided by events after the reporting period. *[IAS 37.16, FRS 12.16]*. Indeed, Section 32 - *Events after the End of the Reporting Period* cites the settlement of a court case as such an example of facts that might indicate the existence of an obligation at the reporting date. *[FRS 102.32.5(a)]*.

3.3.2   A transfer of economic benefits is probable

A transfer of economic benefits is considered probable by Section 21 if it is more likely than not to occur. *[FRS 102.21.4]*. In practice this is taken as meaning a probability of greater than 50%.

Where an entity has a number of similar obligations, the probability that a transfer of economic benefits will occur should be based on the class of obligations as a whole. Whilst this is not explicitly stated in Section 21, it is implied in an example in the Appendix to the section, where a manufacturer recognises a provision for warranties given at the time of sale to purchasers of its product. The obligating event is the sale of a product with a warranty and an outflow of resources in settlement is determined to be probable for the warranties as a whole (i.e. it is more likely than not that the entity will have to honour some warranties claims). *[FRS 102.21A.4]*. Warranty provisions are discussed further at 3.3.5.C below.

3.3.3   The amount of the obligation can be measured reliably

Section 21 provides no guidance on how this condition should be applied. The general concept of reliability Section 2 – *Concepts and Pervasive Principles* (see Chapter 3) requires only that information is free from material error and bias. *[FRS 102.2.7]*. Combined with the requirement that a provision is measured at the 'best estimate' of the amount required to settled the obligation at the reporting date, *[FRS 102.21.7]*, it could be argued that only in rare cases would a lack of a reliable measure prohibit recognition of an obligation. Both IAS 37 and FRS 12 take the view that a sufficiently reliable estimate can almost always be made for a provision where an entity can determine a range of possible outcomes. Hence IAS 37 and FRS 12 contend that it will only be in extremely rare cases that a range of outcomes cannot be determined. *[IAS 37.25, FRS 12.25]*. Whether such a situation is as rare as IAS 37 and FRS 12 assert may be open to question, especially for entities trying to determine estimates relating to potential obligations that arise from litigation and other legal claims. However, given the consistent principles applied by Section 21, IAS 37 and FRS 12 to the recognition of provisions, we would expect entities applying FRS 102 to apply a similarly thorough approach in assessing whether a reliable estimate can be made of the amount of an obligation.

In the event that an obligation cannot be measured reliably, it is regarded as a contingent liability *[FRS 102 Appendix I]* (see 3.4 below).

3.3.4   *Cases where recognition of a provision is prohibited*

3.3.4.A   *Future operating losses*

Section 21 prohibits the recognition of provisions for future operating losses. *[FRS 102.21.11B]*. This is illustrated by Example 1 in the Appendix to Section 21, which is reproduced below.

Example 17.3:   Future operating losses *[FRS 102.21A.1]*

An entity determines that it is probable that a segment of its operations will incur future operating losses for several years.

In this situation, no provision is recognised. There is no past event that obliges the entity to pay out and expected future losses do not meet the definition of a liability. However, the expectation of future losses may be an indicator that one or more assets are impaired.

As alluded to in Example 17.3, it would be wrong to assume that the prohibition of provisions for future operating losses in Section 21 has effectively prevented the effect of future operating losses from being anticipated. They may sometimes be recognised as a result of requirements in another section of FRS 102. For example:

- Under Section 27 of FRS 102 – *Impairment of Assets* – impairment is assessed on the basis of the present value of future operating cash flows, meaning that the effect of not only future operating losses but also sub-standard operating profits will be recognised;

- Under Section 27, inventories are written down to the extent that they will not be recovered from future revenues, rather than leaving the non-recovery to show up as future operating losses; and

- Under Section 23 of FRS 102 – *Revenue* – provision is made for losses expected on construction contracts.

This is therefore a rather more complex issue than Section 21 acknowledges. Indeed, Section 21 itself has to navigate closely the dividing line between the general prohibition of the recognition of future losses and the recognition of contractual or constructive obligations that are expected to give rise to losses in future periods.

3.3.4.B   Staff training costs

Example 17.2 at 3.3.1 above reproduces an example from the Standard where the government introduces changes to the income tax system. An entity needs to retrain a large proportion of its administrative and sales workforce in order to ensure continued compliance with tax regulations. Section 21 argues that there is no present obligation until the actual training has taken place and so no provision should be recognised. In many cases the need to incur training costs could also be avoided by the entity by its future actions. For example, the cost could be avoided by hiring new staff who were already appropriately qualified.

3.3.5   Examples of provisions in Section 21

3.3.5.A   Onerous contracts

Although future operating losses in general cannot be provided for, Section 21 requires that 'if an entity has an onerous contract, the present obligation under the contract shall be recognised and measured as a provision'. *[FRS 102.21.11A]*.

FRS 102 defines an onerous contract as a 'contract in which the unavoidable costs of meeting the obligations under the contract exceed the economic benefits expected to be received under it.' *[FRS 102 Appendix I]*. This seems to require that the contract is onerous to the point of being directly loss-making, not simply uneconomic by reference to current prices.

The unavoidable costs under a contract reflect the least net cost of exiting from the contract. This is the lower of the cost of fulfilling it and any compensation or penalties arising from failure to fulfil it. *[FRS 102.21A.2]*. This evaluation does not require an intention by the entity to fulfil or to exit the contract. It does not even require there to be specific terms in the contract that apply in the event of its termination or breach. Its purpose is to recognise only the unavoidable costs to the entity. In the absence of specific clauses in the contract relating to termination or breach could include an estimation of the cost of walking away from the contract and having the other party go to court for compensation for the resultant breach.

There is a subtle yet important distinction between making a provision in respect of the unavoidable costs under a contract (reflecting the least net cost of what the entity has to do) compared to making an estimate of the cost of what the entity *intends* to do. The first is an obligation, which merits the recognition as a provision. The second is a choice of the entity, which fails the recognition criteria because it does not exist independently of the entity's future actions *[FRS 102.21.6]*, and is therefore akin to a future operating loss.

Example 17.4:   Onerous supply contract

Entity P negotiated a contract in 2012 for the supply of components when availability in the market was scarce. It agreed to purchase 100,000 units per annum for 5 years commencing 1 January 2013 at a price of £20 per unit. Since then, new suppliers have entered the market and the typical price of a component is now £5 per unit. Whilst its activities are still profitable (Entity P makes a margin of £6 per unit of finished product sold) changes to the entity's own business means that it will not use all of the components it is contracted to purchase. As at 31 December 2015, Entity P expects to use 150,000 units in future and has 55,000 units in inventory. The contract requires 200,000 units to be purchased before the agreement expires in 2017. If the entity terminates the contract before 2017, compensation of £1 million per year is payable to the supplier. Each finished product contains one unit of the component.

Therefore, the entity expects to achieve a margin of £900,000 (150,000 × £6) on the units it will produce and sell; but will make a loss of £15 (£20 − £5) per unit on each of the 105,000 components (55,000 + 200,000 − 150,000) it is left with at the end of 2017 and now expects to sell in the components market.

In considering the extent to which the contract is onerous, Entity P in the example above must compare the net cost of the excess units purchased of £1,575,000 (105,000 × £15) with the related benefits, which includes the profits earned as a result of having a secure source of supply. Therefore the supply contract is onerous (directly loss making) only to the extent of the costs not covered by related revenues, justifying a provision of £675,000 (£1,575,000 − £900,000).

Section 21 gives the example of a contractual requirement to make payments under an operating lease for an asset which is no longer used by a business as an example of an onerous contract. However, it provides no specific guidance on the recognition or measurement of provisions for onerous leases. The most common examples of onerous contracts in practice relate to leasehold property. The recognition and measurement of provisions for vacant and occupied leasehold property is discussed in detail in EY International GAAP 2015, Chapter 27, section 6.2.

3.3.5.B   *Restructuring provisions*

An entity should recognise a provision for restructuring costs only when it has a legal or constructive obligation at the reporting date to carry out the restructuring. *[FRS 102.21.11D].*

The specific requirements within Section 21 for the recognition of a restructuring provision seek to define the circumstances that give rise to a constructive obligation to restructure. Section 21 restricts the recognition of a restructuring provision to cases when an entity:

- has a detailed formal plan for the restructuring identifying at least:
  - the business or part of a business concerned;
  - the principal locations affected;
  - the location, function, and approximate number of employees who will be compensated for terminating their services;
  - the expenditures that will be undertaken; and
  - when the plan will be implemented; and
- has raised a valid expectation in those affected that it will carry out the restructuring by starting to implement that plan or announcing the main features to those affected by it. *[FRS 102.21.11C].*

A restructuring is defined as 'a programme that is planned and controlled by management, and materially changes either:

- the scope of a business undertaken by an entity; or
- the manner in which that business is conducted.' *[FRS 102 Appendix I].*

In practice a restructuring may include changes such as the sale or termination of a line of business, the closure of business locations in a country or region, changes in management structure or fundamental reorganisations that have a material effect on the nature and focus of the entity's operations. Whilst the definition of a restructuring may be widely interpreted, there must be a material change to either the scope of the business or the way in which it is conducted, which goes beyond normal changes arising as a result of operating in a dynamic business environment. This may be a subjective judgement. However, it is important in order to prevent entities from classifying all kinds of operating costs as restructuring costs, thereby inviting the user of the accounts to perceive them differently from the 'normal' costs of operating in a dynamic business environment.

The following examples taken from the Appendix to Section 21 illustrate how a constructive obligation for a restructuring may or may not be created.

Example 17.5:   The effect of timing of the creation of a constructive obligation on the recognition of a restructuring provision

Scenario 1: Closure of a division – no implementation before the end of the reporting period [FRS 102.21A.6]

On 12 December 2015 the board of an entity decided to close down a division. Before the end of the reporting period (31 December 2015) the decision was not communicated to any of those affected and no other steps had been taken to implement the decision.

In these circumstances, no provision is recognised at 31 December 2015 because the actions of management prior to this date are insufficient to create a constructive obligation.

Scenario 2: Closure of a division – Communication and implementation before the end of the reporting period [FRS 102.21A.7]

On 12 December 2015, the board of an entity decided to close a division making a particular product. On 20 December 2015 a detailed plan for closing the division was agreed by the board, letters were sent to customers warning them to seek an alternative source of supply, and redundancy notices were sent to the staff of the division.

The communication of management's decision to customers and employees on 20 December 2015 creates a valid expectation that the division will be closed, thereby giving rise to a constructive obligation from that date. Accordingly a provision is recognised at 31 December 2015 for the best estimate of the costs of closing the division.

In practice it can be very difficult to determine whether it is appropriate to recognise a provision for the future costs of a restructuring programme. The determination of whether an organisational change is a material change or just part of a process of continuous improvement is a subjective judgement. Once it has been established that the activities in question constitute a restructuring rather than an ongoing operating cost, it can be difficult to determine whether management's actions before the reporting date have been sufficient to have 'raised a valid expectation in those affected'. *[FRS 102.21.11C(b)]*. Even if a trigger point is easily identifiable, such as the date of an appropriately detailed public announcement, it might not necessarily commit management to the whole restructuring, but only to specific items of expenditure such as redundancy costs. When the announcement is less clear, referring for example to consultations, negotiations or voluntary arrangements, particularly with employees, judgement is required. Furthermore, taken on its own, the 'valid expectation' test is at least as open to manipulation as one based on the timing of a board decision. Entities anxious to accelerate or postpone recognition of a liability could do so by advancing or deferring an event that signals such a commitment, such as a public announcement, without any change to the substance of their position.

Chapter 17

In these situations it is important to consider all the related facts and circumstances and not to focus on a single recognition criterion. The objective of the analysis is to determine whether there is a past obligating event at the reporting date. The guidance in Section 21 about restructuring, referring as it does to constructive obligations and valid expectations is ultimately aimed at properly applying the principle in Section 21 that only those obligations arising from past events and existing independently of an entity's future actions are recognised as provisions. *[FRS 102.21.6]*. In essence, a restructuring provision qualifies for recognition if, as at the reporting date, it relates to a detailed plan of action from which management cannot realistically withdraw.

Section 21 does not address which costs may or may not be included within a restructuring provision. Both IAS 37 and FRS 12 impose criteria to restrict the types of cost that can be provided for. They specify that a restructuring provision should include only the direct expenditures arising from the restructuring, which are those that are both:

- necessarily entailed by the restructuring; and
- not associated with the ongoing activities of the entity. *[IAS 37.80, FRS 12.85]*.

Both standards give specific examples of costs that may not be included within the provision, because they relate to the future conduct of the business. Such costs include:

- retraining or relocating continuing staff;
- marketing; and
- investing in new systems and distribution networks. *[IAS 37.81, FRS 12.86]*.

Given the consistent principles of Section 21 with IAS 37 and FRS 12 in respect of the recognition of provisions, including restructuring provisions, entities may consider it appropriate to apply the criteria above in quantifying a restructuring provision under Section 21. The application of these criteria would ensure that entities do not contravene the general prohibition in Section 21 against provisions for operating losses. *[FRS 102.21.11B]*.

Costs that should and should not be included in a restructuring provision under IAS 37 are discussed further in Chapter 27 of EY International GAAP 2015 at 6.1.4.

3.3.5.C   *Warranty provisions*

Warranty provisions are specifically addressed by Example 4 in the Appendix to Section 21, which is reproduced in Examples 17.7 and 17.8 at 3.7 below.

In Examples 17.7 and 17.8 the assessment of the probability of an outflow of economic resources is made across the population of warranties as a whole, and not using each potential claim as the unit of account. This makes it more likely that a provision will be recognised, because the probability criterion is considered in terms of whether at least one item in the population will give rise to a payment. Recognition then becomes a matter of reliable measurement and entities calculate an expected value of the estimated warranty costs.

3.3.5.D   Refunds policy

Example 5 from the Appendix of Section 21 (reproduced in Example 17.1 above) addresses a retail store that has a policy of refunding goods returned by dissatisfied customers. There is no legal obligation to do so, but the company's policy of making refunds is generally known. The example argues that the conduct of the store has created a valid expectation on the part of its customers that it will refund purchases. The obligating event is the original sale of the item, and the probability of some economic outflow is greater than 50%, as there will nearly always be some customers demanding refunds. Hence, a provision should be made for the best estimate of the amount required to settle the refunds. *[FRS 102.21A.5]*.

The assessment of whether a provision is required may be straightforward when the store has a very specific and highly publicised policy on refunds. However, some stores' policies on refunds might not be so clear cut. A store may offer refunds under certain conditions, but not widely publicise its policy. In these circumstances, there might be doubt as to whether the store has created a valid expectation on the part of its customers that it will honour all requests for a refund.

3.3.5.E   Litigation and other legal costs

The Appendix to Section 21 includes an example of a court case to illustrate how the principles of Section 21 distinguish between a contingent liability and a provision in such situations. This example is reproduced in Example 17.6 at 3.4 below. However, the assessment of the particular case in the example is clear-cut. In most situations, assessing the need to provide for legal claims is one of the most difficult tasks in the field of provisioning. This is due mainly to the inherent uncertainty in the judicial process itself, which may be very long and drawn out. Furthermore, this is an area where either provision or disclosure might risk prejudicing the outcome of the case, because they give an insight into the entity's own view on the strength of its defence that can assist the claimant. Similar considerations apply in other related areas, such as tax disputes.

Whether an entity should make provision for the costs of settling a case or to meet any award given by a court will depend on a reasoned assessment of the particular circumstances, based on appropriate legal advice. The evidence to be considered should also include any additional evidence occurring after the end of the reporting period that confirms whether the entity had a present obligation at the reporting date. This is relevant if, for example, the court case is settled in the period between the reporting date and the date on which the financial statements are authorised for issue. *[FRS 102.32.5(a)]*.

3.3.5.F   Financial guarantee contracts

A financial guarantee contract is a 'contract that requires the issuer to make specified payments to reimburse the holder for a loss it incurs because a specified debtor fails to make payments when due in accordance with the original or modified terms of a debt instrument'. *[FRS 102 Appendix I]*.

As discussed at 3.2 above, in some cases, financial guarantee contracts may be excluded from the scope of Section 21. For financial guarantee contracts in the scope

Chapter 17

of Section 21, a provision should be recognised if the general recognition criteria for provisions are met. This would include it being probable that the issuer would be required to make a payment under the guarantee.

3.4   Contingent liabilities

A contingent liability is defined as:

- a possible obligation that arises from past events and whose existence will be confirmed only by the occurrence or non-occurrence of one or more uncertain future events not wholly within the control of the entity; or

- a present obligation that arises from past events but is not recognised because:

  - it is not probable that an outflow of resources embodying economic benefits will be required to settle the obligation; or

  - the amount of the obligation cannot be measured with sufficient reliability. *[FRS 102 Appendix I].*

The term 'possible' is not defined in FRS 102. Literally, it could mean any probability greater than 0% and less than 100%. However, with the Standard defining 'probable' to mean 'more likely than not', *[FRS 102 Appendix I]*, it would be reasonable to use the term 'possible' in the context of contingent liabilities as meaning a probability of 50% or less. Accordingly, the above definition restricts contingent liabilities to those where either the existence of an obligation or an outflow of economic resources is less than 50% probable, or in those rare cases when a probable obligation cannot be measured with sufficient reliability.

Section 21 requires that contingent liabilities should not be recognised as liabilities on the balance sheet. The only exception to this is contingent liabilities of an acquiree in a business combination. *[FRS 102.21.12]*. Such contingent liabilities are covered by the requirements of Section 19 – *Business Combinations and Goodwill* (see Chapter 15).

Information about contingent liabilities should be disclosed unless the probability of an outflow of resources is remote (see 3.10 below). *[FRS 102.21.12]*. When an entity is jointly and severally liable for an obligation (see 3.7.6 below), the part of the obligation that is expected to be met by other parties is treated as a contingent liability and disclosed. *[FRS 102.21.12]*.

Although it is not explicitly required by Section 21, we would expect contingent liabilities to be assessed continually to determine whether an outflow of resources embodying economic benefits has become probable. Where this becomes the case, then the provision should be recognised in the period in which the change in probability occurs, except in the circumstances where no reliable estimate can be made. This is illustrated by Example 9 to Section 21, which is reproduced below.

Example 17.6:   When the likelihood of an outflow of economic benefits becomes probable [FRS 102.21A.9]

A customer has sued Entity X, seeking damages for injury the customer allegedly sustained from using a product sold by Entity X. Entity X disputes liability on grounds that the customer did not follow directions in using the product. Up to the date the board authorised the financial statements for the year to 31 December 2015 for issue, the entity's lawyers advise that it is probable that the entity will not be found liable. However, when the entity prepares the financial statements for the year to 31 December 2015, its lawyers advise that, owing to developments in the case, it is now probable that the entity will be found liable.

At 31 December 2015, no provision is recognised and the matter is disclosed as a contingent liability unless the probability of any outflow is regarded as remote. On the basis of evidence available when the financial statements were approved, there is no obligation as a result of a past event.

At 31 December 2016, a provision is recognised for the best estimate of the amount required to settle the obligation as at that date. The fact that an outflow of economic benefits is now believed to be probable means that there is a present obligation. The expense is recognised in profit or loss. It is not a correction of an error in 2015 because, on the basis of the evidence available when the 2015 financial statements were approved, a provision should not have been recognised at that time.

3.5   Contingent assets

A contingent asset is defined as 'a possible asset that arises from past events and whose existence will be confirmed only by the occurrence or non-occurrence of one or more uncertain future events not wholly within the control of the entity'. *[FRS 102 Appendix I].* In contrast to the case of contingent liabilities (see 3.4 above), the word 'possible' in the context of contingent assets is not confined to a probability level of 50% or less because Section 21 states that a contingent asset should never be recognised. *[FRS 102.21.13].*

Only when the flow of economic benefits to the entity is virtually certain is the related asset not contingent and capable of recognition. *[FRS 102.21.13].* 'Virtually certain' is not defined in FRS 102. However, in addressing the same requirements in IAS 37 and FRS 12, this has been interpreted as being as close to 100% as to make the remaining uncertainty insignificant. We would expect a similar interpretation under FRS 102.

Contingent assets should be disclosed when an inflow of economic benefits is probable, *[FRS 102.21.13],* with 'probable' meaning 'more likely than not'. *[FRS 102 Appendix I].* The disclosure requirements for contingent assets are discussed at 3.10.4 below.

As with contingent liabilities, we would expect contingent assets to be assessed continually to ensure that developments are appropriately reflected in the financial statements. If it has become virtually certain that an inflow of economic benefits will arise, the asset and the related income should be recognised in the period in which the change occurs.

Chapter 17

3.6   How probability determines whether to recognise or disclose

The following matrix summarises the treatment of contingencies under Section 21:

Likelihood of outcome	*Accounting treatment: contingent liability*	*Accounting treatment: contingent asset*
Virtually certain	Recognise	Recognise
Probable	Recognise	Disclose
Possible, but not probable	Disclose	No disclosure permitted
Remote	No disclosure required	No disclosure permitted

FRS 102 does not put a numerical measure of probability on either 'virtually certain' or 'remote'. In our view, the use of such measures would downgrade a process requiring the exercise of judgement into a mechanical exercise. It is difficult to imagine circumstances when an entity could reliably determine an obligation to be, for example, 92%, 95% or 99% likely, let alone be able to compare those probabilities objectively. Accordingly, we think it reasonable to regard 'virtually certain' as describing a likelihood that is as close to 100% as to make any remaining uncertainty insignificant; to see 'remote' as meaning a likelihood of an outflow of resources that is not significant; and for significance to be a matter for judgement and determined according to the merits of each case.

3.7   Initial measurement

3.7.1   Best estimate of provision

Section 21 requires the amount recognised as a provision to be the best estimate of the amount required to settle the obligation at the reporting date. This is the amount an entity would rationally pay to settle the obligation at the end of the reporting period or to transfer it to a third party at that time. *[FRS 102.21.7]*.

It is implicit in the definition of a provision that there are often uncertainties around the amount of the outflow required by an entity. Section 21 sets out different approaches to dealing with these uncertainties in arriving at an estimate of the provision, depending upon whether it arises from a single obligation or from a large population of items.

Where a provision arises from a single obligation, the individual most likely outcome may be the best estimate of the amount required to settle the obligation. However, even in such a case, the other possible outcomes should be considered. When the other possible outcomes are mostly higher than the most likely outcome, the best estimate will be higher than the individual most likely amount. Conversely, when other possible outcomes are mostly lower, the best estimate will be lower than the individual most likely amount. *[FRS 102.21.7(b)]*. In effect, this adjustment builds into the measure of the provision an allowance to reflect the risk that the actual outcome is an amount other than the individual most likely outcome.

When the provision involves a large population of items, the best estimate of the amount required to settle the obligation should reflect the weighting of all possible outcomes by their associated probabilities, i.e. a probability-weighted expected value calculation should be performed. *[FRS 102.21.7(a)].* This method is illustrated by Example 4 in the Appendix to Section 21, which considers the estimation of a provision for product warranties, as set out below.

Example 17.7:   Calculation of expected value: Warranties [FRS 102.21A.4]

A manufacturer gives warranties at the time of sale to purchasers of its product. Under the terms of the contract for sale, the manufacturer undertakes to make good, by repair or replacement, manufacturing defects that become apparent within three years from the date of sale. On the basis of experience, it is probable that there will be some claims under the warranties. Accordingly it is determined that the obligating event is the sale of a product with a warranty and an outflow of resources in settlement is probable for the warranties as a whole (i.e. it is more likely than not that the manufacturer will have to settle some warranties given on past sales). The entity therefore recognises a provision for the best estimate of the costs of making good under the warranty products sold before the reporting date.

In 2015, goods are sold for £1,000,000. Experience indicates that 90 per cent of products sold require no warranty repairs; 6 per cent of products require minor repairs costing 30 per cent of the sale price; and 4 per cent of products require major repairs or replacement costing 70 per cent of sale price. Therefore, estimated warranty costs are:

Possible outcome	Probability weighted cost	Expected value (£)
No repair required	£1,000,000 × 90% × 0	0
Minor repairs	£1,000,000 × 6% × 30%	18,000
Major repairs	£1,000,000 × 4% × 70%	28,000
Expected value		46,000

Where the provision involves a large population of items and there is a continuous range of possible outcomes, and each point in that range is as likely as any other, the mid-point of the range is used as the best estimate of the amount required to settle the obligation. *[FRS 102.21.7(a)].*

3.7.2   Discounting the estimated cash flows to a present value

When the effect of the time value of money is material, the amount of a provision should be the present value of the amount expected to be required to settle the obligation. The discount rate (or rates) should be a pre-tax rate (or rates) that reflect(s) current market assessments of the time value of money and the risks specific to the liability. The risks specific to the liability should be reflected either in the discount rate or in the estimation of the amounts required to settle the obligation, but not both. *[FRS 102.21.7].*

This requirement is illustrated in the following example taken from the Appendix to Section 21.

Chapter 17

Example 17.8:   Discounting the estimated cash flows to a present value [FRS 102.21A.4]

The fact pattern is the same as Example 17.7 above, with the probability-weighted estimate of total warranty costs for goods sold in 2015 expected to be £46,000. In this case, the expenditures for warranty repairs and replacements are expected to be made 60 per cent in 2016, 30 per cent in 2017 and 10 per cent in 2018, in each case at the end of the period. Because the estimated cash flows already reflect the probabilities of the cash outflows, and assuming there are no other risks or uncertainties that must be reflected, to determine the present value of those cash flows the entity uses a 'risk free' discount rate based on government bonds with the same term as the expected cash outflows (6 per cent for one-year bonds and 7 per-cent for two-year and three-year bonds). Calculation of the present value, at the end of 2015, of the estimated cash flows related to the warranties for products sold in 2015 is as follows:

Year		Expected cash payments (£)	Discount rate	Discount factor	Present value (£)
1	60% × £46,000	27,600	6%	0.9434 (at 6% for 1 year)	26,038
2	30% × £46,000	13,800	7%	0.8734 (at 7% for 2 years)	12,053
3	10% × £46,000	4,600	7%	0.8163 (at 7% for 3 years)	3,755
Present value					41,846

The entity will recognise a warranty obligation of £41,846 at the end of 2015 for products sold in 2015.

FRS 102 gives no further guidance on how an entity should determine the appropriate discount rate to use. However, the example above refers to a government bond rate with a similar term as the related obligation. This is consistent with the application of similar requirements in IAS 37 and FRS 12.

The main types of provision where the impact of discounting will be significant are those relating to decommissioning and other environmental restoration liabilities, which are discussed at 4.1 and 4.2 below.

3.7.2.A   Real or nominal rate

Section 21 does not indicate whether the discount rate should be a real discount rate or a nominal discount rate. FRS 12 notes that the discount rate used depends on whether: [FRS 12.50]

- the future cash flows are expressed in current prices, in which case a real discount rate (which excludes the effects of general inflation) should be used; or

- the future cash flows are expressed in expected future prices, in which case a nominal discount rate (which includes a return to cover expected inflation) should be used.

In our view, either alternative would be acceptable, and these methods may produce the same amount for the initial present value of the provision. However, the effect of the unwinding of the discount will be different in each case (see 3.8.1 below).

3.7.2.B Adjusting for risk and using a government bond rate

Section 21 requires that risk is taken into account in the calculation of a provision, but gives little guidance as to how this should be done. It merely states that the risks specific to the liability should be reflected in either the discount rate or in the estimate of the amounts required to settle the obligation, but not in both. *[FRS 102.21.7]*. FRS 12 suggested that using a discount rate that reflects the risk associated with the liability (a risk-adjusted rate) may be easier than trying to adjust the future cash flows for risk. *[FRS 12.49]*. It gave no indication of how to calculate such a risk adjusted rate, but a little more information could be obtained from the ASB's earlier Working Paper *Discounting in Financial Reporting*[1] on which the following example is based.

Example 17.9: Calculation of a risk-adjusted rate

A company has a provision for which the expected value of the cash outflow in three years' time is £150, and the risk-free rate (i.e. the nominal rate unadjusted for risk) is 5%. However, the possible outcomes from which the expected value has been determined lie within a range between £100 and £200. The company is risk averse and would settle instead for a certain payment of, say, £160 in three years' time rather than be exposed to the risk of the actual outcome being as high as £200. The effect of risk in calculating the present value can be expressed as either:

(a) discounting the risk-adjusted cash flow of £160 at the risk-free (unadjusted) rate of 5%, giving a present value of £138; or

(b) discounting the expected cash flow (which is unadjusted for risk) of £150 at a risk-adjusted rate that will give the present value of £138, i.e. a rate of 2.8%.

As can be seen from this example, the risk-adjusted discount rate is a *lower* rate than the unadjusted (risk-free) discount rate. This may seem counter-intuitive initially, because the experience of most borrowers is that banks and other lenders will charge a higher rate of interest on loans that are assessed to be higher risk to the lender. However, in the case of a provision a risk premium is being suffered to eliminate the possibility of the actual cost being higher (thereby capping a liability), whereas in the case of a loan receivable a premium is required to compensate the lender for taking on the risk of not recovering its full value (setting a floor for the value of the lender's financial asset). In both cases the actual cash flows incurred by the paying entity are higher to reflect a premium for risk. In other words, the discount rate for an asset is increased to reflect the risk of recovering less and the discount rate for a liability is reduced to reflect the risk of paying more.

A problem with changing the discount rate to account for risk is that this adjusted rate is a theoretical rate, as it is unlikely that there would be a market assessment of the risks specific to the liability alone. *[FRS 102.21.7]*. However the lower discount rate in the above example is consistent with the premise that a risk-adjusted liability should be higher than a liability without accounting for the risk that the actual settlement amount is different to the estimate. It is also possible for the risk-adjusted rate to be negative, although in practice the maximum amount a liability could increase to is the nominal amount of the expected future cash flow. It is also difficult to see how a risk-adjusted rate could be obtained in practice. In the above example, it was obtained only by reverse-engineering; it was already known that the net present value of a risk-adjusted liability was £138, so the risk-adjusted rate was just the discount rate applied to unadjusted cash flow of £150 to give that result.

Chapter 17

The alternative approach, to adjust the cash flows instead of using a risk-adjusted discount rate, *[FRS 102.21.7]*, is conceptually more straightforward, but still presents the problem of how to adjust the cash flows for risk. It could be inferred from Example 17.7 at 3.7.1 above that estimated cash flows which reflect the probabilities of cash outflows represent risk adjusted cash flows. However, whilst a best estimate based solely on the expected value approach or the mid-point of a range addresses the uncertainties relating to there being a variety of possible outcomes, it does not fully reflect risk, because the actual outcome could still be higher or lower than the estimate. Nevertheless, adjusting estimated cash flows to reflect risk may be easier than attempting to risk-adjust the discount rate.

Where the risks specific to the liability are reflected in the estimated cash flows, they should not also be included in the discount rate. *[FRS 102.21.7]*. The discount rate to be applied in this case should therefore be a risk free rate. As suggested in Example 17.8 at 3.7.2 above, it would be appropriate to apply a government bond rate with a similar currency and remaining term as the provision. It follows that because a risk-adjusted rate is always lower than the risk-free rate, an entity cannot justify the discounting of a provision at a rate higher than a government bond rate with a similar currency and term as the provision.

In recent years, government bond rates have been more volatile as markets have changed rates to reflect (among other factors) heightened perceptions of sovereign debt risk. The question has therefore arisen whether government bond rates, at least in certain jurisdictions, should continue to be regarded as the default measure of a risk-free discount rate. Whilst the current volatility in rates has highlighted the fact that no debt (even government debt) is totally risk free, the challenge is to find a more reliable measure as an alternative. Any adjustment to the government bond rate to 'remove' the estimate of sovereign debt risk is conceptually flawed, as it not possible to isolate one component of risk from all the other variables that influence the setting of an interest rate. Another approach might be to apply some form of average bond rate over a period of 3, 6 or 12 months to mitigate the volatility inherent in applying the spot rate at the period end. However, this is clearly inappropriate given the requirements in Section 21 to determine the best estimate of an obligation by reference to the expenditure required to settle it 'at the reporting date' *[FRS 102.21.7]* and to determine the discount rate on the basis of 'current market assessments' of the time value of money. *[FRS 102.21.7]*.

With 'risk' being a measure of potential variability in returns, it remains the case that in most countries a government bond will be subject to the lowest level of variability in that jurisdiction. As such, it normally remains the most suitable of all the observable measures of the time value of money in a particular country.

3.7.2.C   Own credit risk is not taken into account

In adjusting either the estimated cash flows or discount rate for risk, an entity should not adjust for its own credit risk (i.e. the risk that the entity could be unable to settle the amount finally determined to be payable). This is because Section 21 requires either the discount rate or estimated cash flows to reflect 'the risks specific to the liability'. *[FRS 102.21.7]*. Credit risk is a risk of the entity rather than a risk specific to the liability.

3.7.3   *Anticipating future events that may affect the estimate of cash flows*

The amount that an entity expects will be required to settle an obligation in future may depend upon expectations and assumptions concerning future events, such as changes in legislation or technological advances. Section 21 does not address the extent to which such expectations should be built into an entity's best estimate of the amount required to settle the obligation. IAS 37 and FRS 12 provide guidance in this area. Both Standards state that 'future events that may affect the amount required to settle an obligation shall be reflected in the amount of a provision where there is sufficient objective evidence that they will occur'. *[IAS 37.48, FRS 12.51].*

The requirement for objective evidence means that it is not appropriate to reduce the best estimate of future cash flows simply by assuming that a completely new technology will be developed before the liability is required to be settled. There will need to be sufficient objective evidence that such future developments are likely. For example, an entity may believe that the cost of cleaning up a site at the end of its life will be reduced by future changes in technology. The amount recognised has to reflect a reasonable expectation of technically qualified, objective observers, taking account of all available evidence as to the technology that will be available at the time of the clean-up. It would be appropriate to include, for example, expected cost reductions associated with increased experience in applying existing technology.

Similarly, if new legislation is to be anticipated, both IAS 37 and FRS 12 require that there needs to be evidence both of what the legislation will demand and whether it is virtually certain to be enacted and implemented. In many cases sufficient objective evidence will not exist until the new legislation is enacted. *[IAS 37.50, FRS 12.53].*

3.7.4   *Provisions should exclude gains on expected disposal of assets*

An entity should exclude gains from the expected disposal of assets from the measurement of a provision. *[FRS 102.21.8].* We would instead expect such gains to be recognised at the time specified by the section of FRS 102 dealing with the assets concerned. This is likely to be of particular relevance in relation to restructuring provisions which are discussed at 3.3.5.B above.

3.7.5   *Reimbursement of amounts required to settle a provision*

An entity may sometimes be reimbursed all or part of an amount required to settle a provision, for example through an insurance claim. The reimbursement should be recognised only when it is virtually certain that the entity will receive the reimbursement on settlement of the obligation. *[FRS 102.21.9].* It should be recognised as an asset in the statement of financial position and should not be offset against the provision. *[FRS 102.21.9].* However, the expense relating to a provision can presented net of reimbursement in the income statement. *[FRS 102.21.9].* The amount recognised for the reimbursement should not exceed the amount of the provision. *[FRS 102.21.9].*

Except when an obligation is determined to be joint and several (see 3.7.6 below), any form of net presentation in the balance sheet is prohibited. This is because the entity would remain liable for the whole cost if the third party failed to pay for any reason, for example as a result of the third party's insolvency.

Chapter 17

3.7.6   *Joint and several liability*

When an entity is jointly and severally liable for an obligation, it recognises only its own share of the obligation, based on the amount that it is probable that the entity will pay. The remainder that is expected to be met by other parties is treated as a contingent liability. *[FRS 102.21.12]*.

Arguably, the economic position in the case of joint and several liability is no different than if the entity was liable for the whole obligation but expected to be reimbursed part of the amount required to settle the provision under the terms of an insurance contract. In both cases, the entity is exposed to further loss in the event that the other parties are unable or unwilling to pay. However, in the case of joint and several liability, the entity and the parties with whom it shares liability each have a direct (albeit shared) obligation for the past event. This contrasts with the case where the entity expects to be reimbursed part of the amount required to settle a provision. In this case, the insurance company from whom the reimbursement is expected has a contractual relationship only with the entity and has no direct obligation for the past event itself. Accordingly, any disclosed liability should not be reduced on the basis that the entity holds valid insurance against the obligation.

3.8   Subsequent measurement of provisions

After initial recognition, provisions should be reviewed at each reporting date and adjusted to reflect the current best estimate of the amount required to settle the obligation. *[FRS 102.21.11]*. Any adjustments to the amounts previously recognised should be recognised in profit or loss unless the provision was originally recognised as part of the cost of an asset. *[FRS 102.21.11]*.

An entity should charge against a provision only those expenditures for which the provision was originally recognised. *[FRS 102.21.10]*. Therefore, if a provision is no longer required, the amount of the provision should be reversed. Provisions may not be redesignated or used for expenses for which the provision was not originally recognised.

When a provision is measured at the present value of the amount required to settle the obligation, the unwinding of the discount should be recognised as a finance cost in profit or loss in the period it arises. *[FRS 102.21.11]*. However, the amount of finance cost recognised as an unwinding of the discount depends upon whether the provision has been discounted at a real or a nominal rate, and also whether the entity has used a risk free or risk adjusted discount rate. This is not addressed by Section 21 but is discussed at 3.8.1 and 3.8.2 below. In addition, Section 21 provides no guidance on the effect of changes in interest rates on the discount rates applied. This is discussed at 3.8.3 below.

3.8.1   *Unwinding of the discount: Impact of using real or nominal discount rates*

As discussed at 3.7.2.A above, Section 21 provides no guidance on whether a real or nominal discount rate should be used to discount a provision. Whilst both methods may produce the same figure for the initial present value of the provision, the effect of the unwinding of the discount will be different in each case. This is best illustrated by way of an example.

Example 17.10:   Effect on future profits of choosing a real or nominal discount rate

A provision is required to be set up for an expected cash outflow of £100,000 (estimated at current prices), payable in three years' time. The appropriate nominal discount rate is 7.5%, and inflation is estimated at 5%.

If the provision is discounted using the nominal rate, the expected cash outflow has to reflect future prices. Accordingly, if prices increase at the rate of inflation, the cash outflow will be £115,762 (£100,000 × 1.05³). The net present value of £115,762, discounted at 7.5%, is £93,184 (£115,762 × 1 ÷ (1.075)³). If all assumptions remain valid throughout the three-year period, the movement in the provision would be as follows:

	Undiscounted cash flows	Provision
	£	£
Year 0	115,762	93,184
Unwinding of discount (£93,184 × 0.075)		6,989
Revision to estimate		–
Year 1	115,762	100,173
Unwinding of discount (£100,173 × 0.075)		7,513
Revision to estimate		–
Year 2	115,762	107,686
Unwinding of discount (£107,686 × 0.075)		8,076
Revision to estimate		–
Year 3	115,762	115,762

If the provision is calculated based on the expected cash outflow of £100,000 (estimated at current prices), then it needs to be discounted using a real discount rate. This may be thought to be 2.5%, being the difference between the nominal rate of 7.5% and the inflation rate of 5%. However, it is more accurately calculated using the Fisher relation (an equation used to estimate the relationship between real and nominal interest rates under inflation) or formula as 2.381%, being (1.075 ÷ 1.05) – 1. Accordingly, the net present value of £100,000, discounted at 2.381%, is £93,184 (£100,000 × 1 ÷ (1.02381)³), the same as the calculation using future prices discounted at the nominal rate.

If all assumptions remain valid throughout the three-year period, the movement in the provision would be as follows:

	Undiscounted cash flows	Provision
	£	£
Year 0	100,000	93,184
Unwinding of discount (£93,184 × 0.02381)		2,219
Revision to estimate (£100,000 × 0.05)	5,000	4,770
Year 1	105,000	100,173
Unwinding of discount (£100,173 × 0.02381)		2,385
Revision to estimate (£105,000 × 0.05)	5,250	5,128
Year 2	110,250	107,686
Unwinding of discount (£107,686 × 0.02381)		2,564
Revision to estimate (£110,250 × 0.05)	5,512	5,512
Year 3	115,762	115,762

Chapter 17

Although the total expense in each year is the same under either method, what will be different is the allocation of the change in provision between operating costs (assuming the original provision was treated as an operating expense) and finance charges. It can be seen from the second table in the above example that using the real discount rate will give rise to a much lower finance charge each year. However, this does not lead to a lower provision in the balance sheet at the end of each year. Provisions have to be revised annually to reflect the current best estimate of the amount required to settle the obligation. *[FRS 102.21.11]*. Thus, the provision in the above example at the end of each year needs to be adjusted to reflect current prices at that time (and any other adjustments that arise from changes in the estimate of the provision), as well as being adjusted for the unwinding of the discount. For example, the revised provision at the end of Year 1 is £100,173, being £105,000 discounted for two years at 2.381%. After allowing for the unwinding of the discount, this required an additional provision of £4,770.

3.8.2   Unwinding of the discount: Impact of using risk-free or risk-adjusted discount rates

The decision made by an entity to use a risk free or risk adjusted discount rate impacts on the unwinding of the discount and the amount recognised in finance costs in respect of the unwind. This is illustrated in the following example:

Example 17.11:   Effect on future profits of choosing a risk-free or risk-adjusted discount rate

A company is required to make a provision for which the expected value of the cash outflow in three years' time is £150, when the risk-free rate (i.e. the rate unadjusted for risk) is 5%. However, the possible outcomes from which the expected value has been determined lie within a range between £100 and £200. The reporting entity is risk averse and would settle instead for a certain payment of, say, £160 in three years' time rather than be exposed to the risk of the actual outcome being as high as £200. The measurement options to account for risk can be expressed as either:

(a) discounting the risk-adjusted cash flow of £160 at the risk free (unadjusted) rate of 5%, giving a present value of £138; or

(b) discounting the expected cash flow (which is unadjusted for risk) of £150 at a risk-adjusted rate that will give the present value of £138, i.e. a rate of 2.8%

Assuming that there are no changes in estimate required to be made to the provision during the three-year period, alternative (a) will unwind to give an overall finance charge of £22 and a final provision of £160. Alternative (b) will unwind to give an overall finance charge of £12 and a final provision of £150.

In this example, the unwinding of different discount rates gives rise to different provisions. The difference of £10 (£22 – £12) relates to the risk adjustment that has been made to the provision. As the actual date of settlement comes closer, the estimates of the range of possible outcomes (and accordingly the expected value of the outflow) and the premium the entity would accept for certainty will converge. As such, the effect of any initial difference related to the decision to apply a risk-free or risk-adjusted rate will be lost in the other estimation adjustments that would be made over time.

3.8.3   The effect of changes in interest rates on the discount rate applied

Section 21 requires the discount rate to reflect current market assessments of the time value of money. *[FRS 102.21.7]*. It follows that where interest rates change, the provision should be recalculated on the basis of revised interest rates. This will give rise to an adjustment to the carrying value of the provision, but Section 21 does not address how this should be classified in the income statement. We believe that the adjustment to the provision is a change in accounting estimate, as defined in Section 10 of FRS 102 – *Accounting Policies, Estimates and Errors*. Accordingly, it should be reflected in the line item of the income statement in which the expense establishing the provision was originally recorded. Where the original provision was recorded as part of the cost of an asset such as inventory or property, plant and equipment, the effect of any subsequent adjustment to discount rates should be added to or deducted from the cost of the asset to which the provision relates.

Calculating this adjustment is not straightforward either, because Section 21 gives no guidance on how it should be done. For example, should the new discount rate be applied during the year or just at the year-end and should the rate be applied to the new estimate of the provision or the old estimate? Because Section 21 requires the value of a provision to reflect the best estimate of the expenditure required to settle the obligation to be assessed as at the end of the reporting period, *[FRS 102.21.7]*, it would appear that the effect of a change in the estimated discount rate is accounted for prospectively from the end of the reporting period. This is illustrated in the following example:

Example 17.12: Accounting for the effect of changes in the discount rate

A provision is required to be set up for an expected cash outflow of £100,000 (estimated at current prices), payable in three years' time. The appropriate nominal discount rate is 7.5%, and inflation is estimated at 5%. At future prices the cash outflow will be £115,762 (£100,000 × 1.05^3). The net present value of £115,762, discounted at 7.5%, is £93,184 (£115,762 × 1 ÷ $(1.075)^3$).

At the end of Year 2, all assumptions remain valid, except it is determined that a current market assessment of the time value of money and the risks specific to the liability would require a decrease in the discount rate to 6.5%. Accordingly, at the end of Year 2, the revised net present value of £115,762, discounted at 6.5%, is £108,697 (£115,762 ÷ 1.065).

The movement in the provision would be reflected as follows:

	Undiscounted cash flows	Provision
	£	£
Year 0	115,762	93,184
Unwinding of discount (£93,184 × 0.075)		6,989
Revision to estimate		–
Year 1	115,762	100,173
Unwinding of discount (£100,173 × 0.075)		7,513
	115,762	107,686
Revision to estimate (£108,697 – £107,686)		1,011
Year 2	115,762	108,697
Unwinding of discount (£108,697 × 0.065)		7,065
Revision to estimate		–
Year 3	115,762	115,762

In Year 2, the finance charge is based on the previous estimate of the discount rate and the revision to the estimate of the provision would be charged to the same line item in the income statement that was used to establish the provision of £93,184 at the start of Year 1.

3.9   Funding commitments (other than loan commitments)

The requirements of FRS 102 regarding funding commitments, other than commitments to make a loan, are set out in Section 34 – *Specialised Activities,* rather than in Section 21. Nevertheless, the Standard requires an entity to consider the requirements of both Section 21 and Section 2 when accounting for funding

Chapter 17

commitments. *[FRS 102.34.58]*. Loan commitments fall within the scope of Section 11 and Section 12. *[FRS 102.34.57]*. In our opinion, it would also be appropriate to regard other commitments to provide resources that will result in the recognition of a financial instrument as being within the scope of Sections 11 and 12 (see Chapter 8).

3.9.1   Recognition of a funding commitment as a liability

Section 34 requires that an entity recognises a liability and, usually, a corresponding expense, when it has made a commitment that it will provide resources to another party, if, and only if:

(a)   the definition and recognition criteria for a liability have been satisfied (see 3.3 above);

(b)   the obligation (which may be a constructive obligation) is such that the entity cannot realistically withdraw from it; and

(c)   the entitlement of the other party to the resources does not depend on the satisfaction of performance-related conditions. *[FRS 102.34.59]*.

The definition of a liability requires that there be a present obligation, and not merely an expectation of a future outflow. *[FRS 102.34A.1]*. A general statement that the entity intends to provide resources to certain classes of potential beneficiaries in accordance with its objectives does not in itself give rise to a liability, as the entity may amend or withdraw its policy, and potential beneficiaries do not have the ability to insist on their fulfilment. Similarly, a promise to provide cash conditional on the receipt of future income in itself may not give rise to a liability where the entity cannot be required to fulfil it if the future income is not received and it is probable that the economic benefits will not be transferred. *[FRS 102.34A.2]*.

A liability is recognised only for a commitment that gives the recipient a valid expectation that payment will be made and from which the grantor cannot realistically withdraw. One of the implications of this is that a liability only exists where the commitment has been communicated to the recipient. *[FRS 102.34A.3]*.

Commitments that are performance-related will be recognised when those performance-related conditions are met. *[FRS 102.34.60]*. Performance-related conditions are defined in FRS 102 as conditions that require the performance of a particular level of service or units of output to be delivered, with payment of, or entitlement to, the resources conditional on that performance. *[FRS 102 Appendix I]*. Commitments are not recognised if they are subject to performance-related conditions. In such a case, the entity is required to fulfil its commitment only when the performance-related conditions are met and no liability exists until that time. *[FRS 102.34A.4]*.

A commitment may contain conditions that are not performance-related conditions. For example, a requirement to provide an annual financial report to the grantor may serve mainly as an administrative tool because failure to comply would not release the grantor from its commitment. This may be distinguished from a requirement to submit a detailed report for review and consideration by the grantor of how funds will be utilised in order to secure payment. A mere restriction on the specific purpose for which the funds are to be used does not in itself constitute a performance-related condition. *[FRS 102.34A.5].*

Whether an arrangement gives rise to a funding commitment and when such commitments are recognised is a matter of judgement based on the facts and circumstances of the case, as illustrated in Example 17.13 below.

Example 17.13:   Accounting for donations to non-profit organisations

An entity decides to enter into an arrangement to 'donate' £1m in cash to a university. A number of different options are available for the arrangement and the entity's management want to determine whether the terms of these options make any difference to the timing, measurement or presentation of the £1m expenditure, as follows:

Option 1:
The entity enters into an unenforceable contract to contribute £1m for general purposes. The benefits to the entity are deemed only to relate to its reputation as a 'good corporate citizen'; the entity does not receive any consideration or significant benefit from the university in return for the donation.

Option 2:
As per Option 1 except the entity publishes a press release in relation to the donation and announcing that payment is to be made in equal instalments of £200,000 over 5 years.

Option 3:
As per Option 2, except that the contract is legally enforceable in the event that the entity does not pay all the instalments under the contract.

Option 4:
As per Option 2, except that the entity is only required to make the donation if the university raises £4m from other sources.

Option 5:
As per Option 2, except that the contract is legally enforceable and the funds will be used for research and development activities specified by the entity. The entity will retain proprietary rights over the results of the research.

Applying the requirements in respect of funding commitments discussed above:

- In Option 1, the contract is unenforceable, there is no announcement or conditions preceding payment and there is no exchange of benefits. Accordingly, an expense would be recognised only when the entity transfers cash to the university.

- For Option 2, it may be appropriate for the entity to conclude that the entity's announcement of the donation to be paid by instalments indicates that there is a constructive obligation because the entity has a created a valid expectation that it will make all of the payments promised. Alternatively, it could determine that once the first instalment is paid, the entity has created a valid expectation that it will make the remaining payments. This is a matter of judgement. In this case the entity would recognise an expense and a liability, measured at the net present value of the 5 instalments of £200,000, at the point when it is determined that a constructive obligation exists.

- Option 3 involves an enforceable contract with no exchange of benefits. Therefore a liability and an expense are recognised on signing the enforceable contract, measured at the present value of the 5 instalments of £200,000.

- Under Option 4, the contract is unenforceable and the donation is subject to a performance condition. In these circumstances, no liability exists until the performance condition is met (i.e. when the additional funds have been raised). *[FRS 102.34.60]*. Only then would a liability and expense be recognised, measured at the net present value of the £1m promised.

- Option 5 involves an enforceable contract. Therefore a liability is recognised when the contract is signed. In addition, there is an exchange of benefits relating to the research and development activities performed on behalf of the entity. Whether these benefits have a value close to the present value of the 5 instalments of £200,000 is a matter of judgement. If it is determined that this is an exchange transaction, the entity would apply the criteria in Section 18 – *Intangible Assets other than Goodwill* – to determine whether an asset or expense could be recognised for the related research and development costs (see Chapter 14).

Where the arrangement gives rise to an exchange transaction rather than a donation, the expenditure incurred by the donor is recorded in accordance with the relevant section of FRS 102. An exchange transaction is a reciprocal transfer in which each party receives and sacrifices approximately equal value. Assets and liabilities are not recognised until each party performs their obligations under the arrangement.

3.10   Disclosure requirements

3.10.1   *Presentation of Provisions*

Entities are required by Schedule 1 of the Regulations to present 'Provisions for liabilities' separately on the face of the balance sheetinto the following categories:

- Provisions for pensions and similar obligations;
- Provisions for tax; and
- Other provisions.

3.10.2   *Disclosures about Provisions*

For each class of provision an entity should provide a reconciliation showing:

(a)   the carrying amounts at the beginning and end of each period;

(b)   additions during the period, including adjustments that result from changes in measuring the discounted amount;

(c)   amounts charged against the provision during the period; and

(d)   unused amounts reversed during the period. *[FRS 102.21.14]*.

Disclosure (ii) requires additions in the period and adjustments that result from changes in measuring the discounted amount to be disclosed as one line item in the reconciliation. This differs from the disclosure requirements of IAS 37 and FRS 12, both of which require the disclosure of additions during the period and the increase in the discounted amount of the provision arising from the passage of time and the effect of any changes in discount rates as separate line items within the reconciliation. *[IAS 37.84, FRS 12.89]*.

In addition, for each class of provision, an entity should disclose:

(a)   a brief description of the nature of the obligation and the expected amount and timing of any resulting payments;

(b)   an indication of the uncertainties about the amount or timing of those outflows; and

(c)   the amount of any expected reimbursements, stating the amount of any asset that has been recognised for the expected reimbursement. *[FRS 102.21.14].*

Disclosure (a) requires disclosure of the expected amount and timing of any resulting payments. This differs from IAS 37 and FRS 12 which require disclosure only of the expected timing of outflows. *[IAS 37.85(a), FRS 12.90(a)].* In many cases, the expected amount of the payments will be the same as the carrying amount of the provision at the end of the period. However, where a provision has been discounted to its present value it is unclear from Section 21 whether the disclosure of the expected amount of payments should be expressed based on current prices or expected future prices.

Comparative information is not required for any of the disclosures about provisions. *[FRS 102.21.14].*

UK Company Law (i.e. the Regulations) requires disclosure of the amount of provisions at the beginning and the end of the year and movements during the year. Entities must disclose the source and application of movements other than any movements resulting from the provision being used for the purpose for which it was established. Where the amount within the statutory heading 'other provisions' is material, the Regulations requires the disclosure of the nature of amounts included in that balance. *[1 Sch 59].*

3.10.3   Disclosures about Contingent liabilities

Unless the possibility of any outflow of resources in settlement is remote, an entity should disclose, for each class of contingent liability at the reporting date, a brief description of the nature of the contingent liability and, when practicable:

•   an estimate of its financial effect, measured in accordance with paragraphs 7 to 11 of Section 21 (see 3.7 above);

•   an indication of the uncertainties relating to the amount or timing of any outflow; and

•   the possibility of any reimbursement. *[FRS 102.21.15].*

If it is impracticable to make one or more of these disclosures, that fact should be stated. *[FRS 102.21.15].* Applying a requirement is impracticable when the entity cannot apply it after making every reasonable effort to do so. *[FRS 102 Appendix I].*

Section 21 does not define or put a numerical measure of probability on the term 'remote'. In our view, it is reasonable to interpret 'remote' as meaning a likelihood of an outflow of resources that is not significant (see 3.6 above).

Chapter 17

The Regulations require disclosure of the following for any contingent liability not provided for:

- the amount or estimated amount of that liability;

- its legal nature; and

- whether any valuable security has been provided by the company in connection with that liability and if so, what. *[1 Sch 63(2)].*

3.10.4   Disclosures about Contingent assets

If an inflow of economic benefits is probable (more likely than not) but not virtually certain, an entity should disclose:

- a description of the nature of the contingent assets at the end of the reporting period; and

- when practicable, an estimate of their financial effect, measured using the principles set out in paragraphs 7 to 11 of Section 21 (see 3.7 above).

If it is impracticable to make one or more of these disclosures, that fact should be stated. *[FRS 102.21.16].* Applying a requirement is impracticable when the entity cannot apply it after making every reasonable effort to do so. *[FRS 102 Appendix I].*

Section 21 does not define or put a numerical measure of probability on the term 'virtually certain'. In our view, it is reasonable to interpret 'virtually certain' as being close to 100% as to make the remaining uncertainty insignificant. However, this is not definitive and the facts and circumstances of each case must be considered.

3.10.5   Disclosure when information is seriously prejudicial

Section 21 contains an exemption from disclosure of information in the following circumstances. It says that, 'in extremely rare cases, disclosure of some or all of the information required by [the disclosure requirements at 3.10.2 to 3.10.4 above] can be expected to prejudice seriously the position of the entity in a dispute with other parties on the subject matter of the provision, contingent liability or contingent asset'. *[FRS 102.21.17].*

In such circumstances, the information need not be disclosed. However, the entity must disclose the general nature of the dispute. They must also disclose the fact that, and the reason why, the information has not been disclosed. *[FRS 102.21.17].*

It should be noted, however, that the exemption applies only to the disclosure requirements of Section 21. It does not apply to the disclosures required by the Regulations (see 3.10.2 and 3.10.3 above).

3.10.6   Disclosures about financial guarantee contracts

An entity should disclose the nature and business purpose of any financial guarantee contracts it has issued. *[FRS 102.21.17A].* This appears to be required regardless of whether the financial guarantee contract meets the recognition criteria for provisions or disclosure criteria for contingent liabilities discussed at 3.3 and 3.4 above. In addition, where these criteria are met, the general disclosures required for provisions (set out at 3.10.2 above) or contingent liabilities (set out at 3.10.3 above) should also be provided. *[FRS 102.21.17A].*

The Regulations also require disclosure of the particulars of any financial commitments that have not been provided for and are relevant to assessing the company's state of affairs. *[1 Sch 63(5)]*.

3.10.7   *Disclosures about funding commitments (other than loan commitments)*

An entity that has made a funding commitment (see 3.9 above) is required to disclose the following:

(a)   the commitment made;

(b)   the time-frame of that commitment;

(c)   any performance-related conditions attached to that commitment; and

(c)   details of how that commitment will be funded. *[FRS 102.34.62]*.

Separate disclosure is required for recognised and unrecognised commitments. Within each category, disclosure can be aggregated provided that such aggregation does not obscure significant information. *[FRS 102.34.63]*. Accordingly, material commitments should be disclosed separately.

For funding commitments that are not recognised, it is important that full and informative disclosures are made of their existence and of the sources of funding for these unrecognised commitments. *[FRS 102.34A.6]*.

4   OTHER EXAMPLES OF PROVISIONS

Section 21 provides specific guidance in respect of a limited number of situations, which are discussed at 3.3.4 and 3.3.5 above. This section considers other common provisions not specifically addressed by Section 21. As there is no specific guidance on accounting for these provisions within FRS 102, entities may, under the hierarchy set out in Section 10 of FRS 102, refer to the requirements and guidance of IFRS in formulating an appropriate accounting policy for these obligations. Accordingly, it would be appropriate to refer to Chapter 27 of EY International GAAP 2015.

4.1   Decommissioning provisions

Decommissioning costs arise when an entity is required to dismantle or remove an asset at the end of its useful life and to restore the site on which it has been located, for example, when an oil rig or nuclear power station reaches the end of its economic life.

Examples in the appendices to IAS 37 and FRS 12 illustrate that the decommissioning liability is recognised as soon as the obligation arises (normally at the commencement of operations), rather than being built up as the asset is used over its useful life. This is because the construction of the asset (and the environmental damage caused by it) creates the past obliging event requiring restoration in the future.

Given that Section 21, IAS 37 and FRS 12 apply the same principles to the recognition and measurement of provisions, we believe that this approach is also appropriate for entities reporting under FRS 102. The accounting for

Chapter 17

decommissioning provisions under IFRS is covered in detail in EY International GAAP 2015, Chapter 27, at 6.3. Chapter 27 also discusses:

- IFRIC 1 – *Changes in Existing Decommissioning, Restoration and Similar Liabilities* – which provides guidance on how to account for the effect of changes in measurement of existing provisions for obligations to dismantle, remove or restore items of property, plant and equipment; and

- IFRIC 5 – *Rights to Interests arising from Decommissioning, Restoration and Environmental Rehabilitation Funds* – which addresses the accounting by an entity when it participates in a 'decommissioning fund', with the purpose of segregating assets to fund some or all of the costs of decommissioning or environmental liabilities for which it has to recognise a provision under IAS 37.

Section 21 provides no specific guidance on the matters addressed within IFRIC 1 and IFRIC 5. There is also no equivalent guidance to these Interpretations under previous UK GAAP. However, the approach applied by IFRIC 1 is consistent with the guidance in the UK SORP – *Accounting for Oil and Gas Exploration, Development, Production and Decommissioning Activities*. It is also consistent with the approach commonly applied in practice by entities outside of the oil and gas industry.

4.2   Environmental provisions

IAS 37 and FRS 12 set out two examples of circumstances where environmental provisions would be required, both in relation to contaminated land. The examples illustrate that an entity can have an obligation to clean up contaminated land either as a result of legislation or as a result of a widely publicised environmental policy. The accounting applied in these examples is consistent with the principles of Section 21. These examples and the recognition and measurement of environmental provisions are discussed in EY International GAAP 2015, Chapter 27, at 6.8.

4.3   Liabilities associated with emissions trading schemes

A number of countries around the world either have, or are developing, schemes to encourage reduced emissions of pollutants, in particular of greenhouse gases. These schemes comprise tradable emissions allowances or permits, an example of which is a 'cap and trade' model whereby participants are allocated emission rights or allowances equal to a cap (i.e. a maximum level of allowable emissions) and are permitted to trade those allowances.

Whilst there is currently no guidance under either IFRS or previous UK GAAP on accounting for cap and trade emission rights schemes, a discussion of the methods applied in practice can be found at EY International GAAP 2015, Chapter 27, at 6.5.

4.4   EU Directive on Waste Electrical and Electronic Equipment

This Directive, which came into force in the UK on 2 January 2007, regulates the collection, treatment, recovery and environmentally sound disposal of waste electrical or electronic equipment (WE&EE). It applies to entities involved in the manufacture and resale of electrical or electronic equipment, including entities (both European and Non-European) that import such equipment into the EU.

The Directive states that the cost of waste management for historical household equipment should be borne by producers of that type of equipment that are in the market during a period to be specified in the applicable legislation of each Member State (the measurement period). The Directive states that each Member State shall establish a mechanism to have producers contribute to costs proportionately e.g. in proportion to their respective share of the market by type of equipment.

Both IFRIC 6 – *Liabilities arising from Participating in a Specific Market – Waste Electrical and Electronic Equipment –* and UITF 45 – *Liabilities arising from Participating in a Specific Market – Waste Electrical and Electronic Equipment –* clarify that the obligation under the Directive is linked to participation in the market during the measurement period, with their being no obligation unless and until a market share exists during the measurement period. The obligation is not linked to the production or sale of the items to be disposed of. The application of IFRIC 6 is discussed in EY International GAAP 2015, Chapter 27, at 6.7.

4.5   Levies charged on entities operating in a specific market

When governments or other public authorities impose levies on entities in relation to their activities, it is not always clear when the liability to pay a levy arises and when a provision should be recognised. In May 2013, the IFRS Interpretations Committee issued IFRIC 21 – *Levies* – to address this question. It requires that, for levies within its scope, an entity should recognise a liability only when the activity that triggers payment, as identified by the relevant legislation, occurs. *[IFRIC 21.8]*. Given that Section 21 and IAS 37 apply the same principles to the recognition and measurement of provisions, entities may wish to apply the guidance in IFRIC 21 to the recognition of liabilities for levies under FRS 102. IFRIC 21 is discussed further in EY International GAAP 2015, Chapter 27, at 6.9.

4.6   Repairs and maintenance of owned assets

Both IAS 37 and FRS 12 include an example within their appendices illustrating how the principles for the recognition of a provision are applied strictly in the case of an obligation to incur repairs and maintenance costs in the future on owned assets. This is the case even when this expenditure is substantial, distinct from what may be regarded as routine maintenance and essential to the continuing operations of the entity, such as major refit or refurbishment of the asset. This is discussed at EY International GAAP 2015, Chapter 27, at 5.2.

Repairs and maintenance provisions for owned assets are generally prohibited under IAS 37 and FRS 12. Given that Section 21, IAS 37 and FRS 12 apply the same principles to the recognition and measurement of provisions, we would also not generally expect provisions for repairs and maintenance of owned assets to be recognised under FRS 102.

Chapter 17

4.7   Dilapidations and other provisions relating to leased assets

Whilst it is not generally appropriate to recognise provisions that relate to repairs and maintenance of owned assets (including assets held under finance leases) the position can be different in the case of obligations relating to assets held under operating leases.

Operating leases often contain clauses which specify that the lessee should incur periodic charges for maintenance, make good dilapidations or other damage occurring during the rental period or return the asset to the configuration that existed as at inception of the lease. These contractual provisions may restrict the entity's ability to change its future conduct to avoid the expenditure. The contractual obligations in a lease could therefore create an environment in which a present obligation could exist as at the reporting date from which the entity cannot realistically withdraw.

The recognition of provisions relating to leased assets is discussed in EY International GAAP 2015, Chapter 27, at 6.9.

4.8   Self-insurance

Another situation where entities sometimes make provisions is self insurance which arises when an entity decides not to take out external insurance in respect of a certain category of risk because it would be uneconomic to do so. The same position may arise when a group insures its risks with a captive insurance subsidiary. Self-insurance is not explicitly addressed in FRS 102 or IAS 37 but was dealt with by way of an example within FRS 12. The conclusion reached in the example was that no such provision could be made, as the entity did not have a present obligation for the amount. The same conclusion would be reached by applying the recognition criteria for provisions within Section 21. FRS 103 – *Insurance Contracts* – also clarifies that self insurance is not insurance as there is no insurance contract because there is no agreement with another party. *[FRS 103.A219(c)].*

Therefore, losses are recognised based on their actual incidence and any provisions that appear in the balance sheet should reflect only the amounts expected to be paid in respect of those incidents that have occurred by the end of the reporting period.

In certain circumstances, a provision will often be needed not simply for known incidents, but also for those which insurance companies call IBNR – Incurred But Not Reported – representing an estimate of claims that have occurred at the end of the reporting period but which have not yet been notified to the reporting entity. We believe that it is appropriate that provision for such expected claims is made.

4.9   Parent company guarantees given in connection with audit exemption

For financial years ending on or after 1 October 2012, the Companies Act 2006 exempts some subsidiary companies from the requirement to be audited, subject to a number of conditions. One of the conditions requires that the parent company files with the registrar a statutory guarantee of all of the outstanding financial liabilities of the subsidiary at the end of the financial year for which the subsidiary seeks an exemption from audit. *[s394A, s479A].*In our view, the statutory guarantee is not a contract. It therefore does not meet the definition of a financial guarantee contract within FRS 102 and should be accounted for under Section 21. If it is only a remote possibility that the guarantee will be called upon by the subsidiary's creditors, the parent does not recognise a provision nor disclose the guarantee in their separate financial statement. If it is possible (but not probable) that the guarantee will be called upon, the parent should disclose a contingent liability in their separate financial statements. If it is probable that the guarantee will be called upon, the parent must recognise a provision for the best estimate of the amount required to settle the obligation under the guarantee at the reporting date.

5   SUMMARY OF GAAP DIFFERENCES

	FRS 102	*Previous UK GAAP*	*IFRS*
Scope – Provisions, contingent liabilities and contingent assets covered by another Section / Standard	Section 21 does not apply to provisions, contingent liabilities and contingent assets covered by another section of FRS 102. However, where those other sections contain no specific requirements to deal with contracts that have become onerous, Section 21 applies to those contracts.	In contrast to FRS 102, where a provision, contingent liability or contingent asset was covered by another Standard and that Standard contained no specific requirements to deal with onerous contracts, there was no requirement that FRS 12 be applied to those contracts. However, operating leases that became onerous were explicitly in scope of FRS 12.	In contrast to FRS 102, where a provision, contingent liability or contingent asset was covered by another Standard and that Standard contained no specific requirements to deal with onerous contracts, there is no requirement that IAS 37 be applied to those contracts. However, operating leases that become onerous are explicitly in scope of IAS 37.
Scope – Financial guarantee contracts	Financial guarantee contracts are in scope of Section 21 unless: the entity has chosen to apply IAS 39 or IFRS 9 to its financial instruments; or the entity has elected under FRS 103 to continue the application of insurance contract accounting.	For entities not applying FRS 26, financial guarantee contracts were in scope of FRS 12. For entities applying FRS 26, financial guarantee contracts were out of scope of FRS 12 and were accounted for as financial instruments.	Financial guarantee contracts are out of scope of IAS 37. They are accounted for as financial instruments unless the entity has elected under IFRS 4 to continue the application of insurance contract accounting.

Chapter 17

	FRS 102	Previous UK GAAP	IFRS
Future operating losses	Provisions should not be recognised for future operating losses.	Generally, provisions for future operating losses were not permitted. However, FRS 3 included an exception. Where a decision had been made to sell or terminate an operation, any consequential provisions should reflect the extent to which obligations had been incurred that were not expected to be covered by the future profits of the operation. The provision should cover only the direct costs of the sale or termination and any operating losses up to the date of sale or termination (after taking into account the aggregate profit, if any, from the future profits of the operation). Provisions were only made when the entity was demonstrably committed to the sale or termination of the operation at the balance sheet date, which, for a sale, required a binding sale agreement.	Same as FRS 102
Disclosure – Provisions	Included within the disclosure requirements for provisions is a requirement to disclose the expected amount of payments resulting from an obligation. There is no requirement to disclose: Major assumptions concerning future events that may affect the amount required to settle an obligation; or a separate line item in the reconciliation of opening and closing provision balances showing the increase during the period in the discounted amount arising from the passage of time and the effect of any change in discount rate.	Included within the disclosure requirements for provisions were requirements to disclose: Major assumptions concerning future events that may affect the amount required to settle an obligation where this is necessary to provide adequate information; and a separate line item in the reconciliation of opening and closing provision balances showing the increase during the period in the discounted amount arising from the passage of time and the effect of any change in discount rate.	Included within the disclosure requirements for provisions are requirements to disclose: Major assumptions concerning future events that may affect the amount required to settle an obligation where this is necessary to provide adequate information; and a separate line item in the reconciliation of opening and closing provision balances showing the increase during the period in the discounted amount arising from the passage of time and the effect of any change in discount rate.

	FRS 102	*Previous UK GAAP*	*IFRS*
Disclosure – Provisions *(continued)*		There was no requirement to disclose the expected amount of payments resulting from an obligation.	There is no requirement to disclose the expected amount of payments resulting from an obligation.
Disclosure – Financial guarantee contracts	An entity must disclose the nature and business purpose of any financial guarantee contracts in scope of Section 21, regardless of whether a provision is required. In addition, to the extent a provision is recognised for financial guarantee contracts, or a contingent liability disclosed, the general provision / contingent liability disclosures within Section 21 are also required.	There was no specific requirement for entities to disclose the nature and business purpose of any financial guarantee contracts it has issued, regardless of whether or not they are applying FRS 26. For those entities applying FRS 26, financial guarantee contracts were in scope of the disclosure requirement of FRS 29 – *Financial instruments: disclosures*, not FRS 12.	There is no specific requirement for entities to disclose the nature and business purpose of any financial guarantee contracts it has issued. Financial guarantee contracts are in scope of the disclosure requirement of IFRS 7 – *Financial Instruments: Disclosures*, not IAS 37.

References

1 Discounting in Financial Reporting, ASB, April 1997.

Chapter 17

Chapter 18   Revenue

Chapter 18

List of examples

Chapter 18

Chapter 18   Revenue

1   INTRODUCTION

1.1   Scope

Section 23 – *Revenue* – applies to accounting for revenue arising from the sale of goods, the rendering of services, construction contracts and the use of assets yielding interest, royalties and dividends.

Section 23 does not apply to revenue or other income arising from:

- lease agreements (Section 20 – *Leases*);

- dividends and other income arising from investments that are accounted for using the equity method (Section 14 – *Investments in Associates* – and Section 15 – *Investments in Joint Ventures*);

- changes in the fair value of financial assets and liabilities or their disposal (Section 11 – *Basic Financial Instruments* – and Section 12 – *Other Financial Instruments Issues*);

- changes in the fair value of investment property (Section 16 – *Investment Property*);

- initial recognition and changes in the fair value of biological assets related to agricultural activity and the initial recognition of agricultural produce (Section 34 – *Specialised Activities*); and

- income from insurance contracts (FRS 103 – *Insurance Contracts*).

The accounting for interest, royalties and dividends from the use by others of the entity's assets is within the scope of Section 23, whilst FRS 5 – *Reporting the substance of transactions – Application Note G* (FRS 5 ANG) – addresses only the sale of goods and services and does not deal with interest, royalties and dividends.

Under the previous UK GAAP, for listed entities and unlisted entities using accounting policies that are consistent with the fair value accounting rules of the Companies Act 2006,[1] FRS 26 – *Financial instruments: recognition and measurement* – would be the relevant accounting standard for interest. For entities that do not apply FRS 26, FRS 4 – *Capital instruments* – is the relevant standard.

Section 23 states 'interest shall be recognised using the effective interest method' in line with Section 11 which is discussed in Chapter 8. Under the previous UK GAAP, for entities that apply FRS 4, differences may arise as FRS 4 requires interest to be recognised at a constant rate on the carrying amount.

There is no specific guidance under the previous UK GAAP for the accounting for dividends and royalties. However the general principles under FRS 5 ANG are expected to apply for royalties i.e. 'a seller recognises revenue...to the extent that, it obtains the right to consideration in exchange for its performance.' [FRS 5.ANG.4].

Section 23 excludes the initial recognition and changes in the fair value of biological assets related to agricultural activity and the initial recognition of agricultural produce which are not excluded from FRS 5 ANG.

FRS 102, Section 23 has a narrower scope with regard to construction contracts than previous UK GAAP (SSAP 9 – *Stocks and long-term contracts*) and IFRS (IAS 11 – *Construction Contracts*), dealing primarily with the accounting for revenue from construction contracts, rather than revenue and costs. This part of Section 23 is, however, based on IAS 11 and we would expect users of FRS 102 to turn to IAS 11 for further guidance in this area following the hierarchy in Section 10 – *Accounting policies, estimates and errors*.

Accounting for construction contracts under SSAP 9 was already very similar to IAS 11, and these common elements are features of Section 23. IAS 11 and SSAP 9 both prescribe the percentage of completion method of accounting for contracts when the outcome of a contract can be estimated reliably, although differences exist in the way the method is applied under the two standards. Both require accounting to be performed on a contract-by-contract basis, although in certain circumstances it is necessary to combine or segment contracts in order to reflect their substance.

Also, both standards require that an entity should recognise a loss on a contract when it is probable that losses will be incurred in respect of a construction/long-term contract. Similarly, when the outcome of a contract cannot be estimated reliably, no profit should be recognised.

Contract costs generally comprise all direct and indirect costs that are attributable to, and reimbursable under, the contract. Pre-contract costs incurred before recognition criteria detailed in 3.2 below are met are expensed to profit and loss, and cannot be reinstated.

Entities reporting under IFRS also apply IFRIC 15 – *Agreements for the Construction of Real Estate* – which has no direct equivalent in UK GAAP. The requirements of IFRIC 15 form the basis of Example 12 in the Appendix to Section 23. [FRS 102.23A.14, 23A.15].

2 COMPARISON BETWEEN SECTION 23, PREVIOUS UK GAAP AND IFRS

Excluding revenue from construction contracts, previous UK GAAP refers to FRS 5 – *Reporting the substance of transactions - Application Note G Revenue recognition* (FRS 5 ANG), UITF 26 – *Barter transactions for advertising*, UITF 36 – *Contracts for sales of capacity* – and UITF 40 – *Revenue recognition and service contracts*. Reference to IFRS refers to IAS 18 – *Revenue*, IFRIC 13 – *Customer Loyalty Programmes*, IFRIC 18 – *Transfers of Assets from Customers* – and SIC Interpretation 31 – *Revenue – Barter transactions involving advertising services*.

The principles and guidance between FRS 102, previous UK GAAP and IFRS are very similar, therefore, whilst there are differences (see 5 below) in the written content of the standards, differences in accounting are not necessarily expected to arise in practice hence the differences are not regarded to be key differences.

2.1 Key differences to Previous UK GAAP for construction contracts

2.1.1 Separation of contracts

Whilst SSAP 9 and Section 23 are very similar, SSAP 9 had no guidance on when to separate long term contracts and no guidance on grouping of contracts, although the principles of paragraph G25 of FRS 5 would have provided guidance requiring separation of contractual arrangements where individual components operate independently of each other. As detailed in 3.13 below, FRS 102 allows for contracts to be separated or grouped provided that certain criteria have been met.

2.1.2 Recognition of revenue from contract variations

Section 23 provides no guidance on the elements of contract revenue. SSAP 9 considered the occurrence of contract variations and claims and concluded that these should be accounted for as follows:

- Approved contract variations should be treated as part of the total sales estimate using a conservative estimate of the amount likely to be received; and

- Claims should be accounted for when negotiations had reached an advanced stage and there is sufficient evidence of the acceptability of the claim in principle to the purchaser.

Given that variations and claims occur regularly in long term contracts and that FRS 102 provides no guidance in this area we might expect companies to continue to adopt these policies in determining the amount of contract revenue to be used in the percentage of completion method calculation.

2.1.3 Contract costs

Section 23 deals primarily with revenue from construction contracts and does not consider the composition of costs allocated to the contracts and used in the percentage of completion method calculation. This is an area that SSAP 9 provided significantly more guidance on, stating that costs include the costs of purchase, costs of conversion and production overheads and where they are specific to financing a long term contract, interest costs. General overheads are excluded from the cost of a long term contract.

SSAP 9 did in some instances permit the inclusion of selling costs. Also there was no requirement to capitalise borrowing costs although the capitalisation of interest on borrowings financing the production of the asset is permitted under company law.

Again given the lack of guidance in FRS 102, we would expect companies to continue to adopt policies based on the SSAP 9 guidance.

2.2   Key differences to IFRS for construction contracts

Although the construction contracts section of Section 23 of FRS 102 is based on IAS 11, there are a number of paragraphs of IAS 11 which have been omitted from FRS 102. In general these provide further guidance on specific areas. Given the hierarchy in Section 10 – *Accounting policies, estimates and errors*, we would expect users of the standard to consider the requirements and guidance of EU-IFRS dealing with similar and related issues. *[FRS 102.10.6].*

2.2.1   *Construction of a separate asset*

IAS 11 provides guidance on accounting where either the contract provides for the construction of an additional asset at the option of the customer, or may be amended to include the construction of an additional asset. The standard concludes that this should be treated as a new contract if:

- The asset differs significantly in design, technology or function from the asset or assets covered by the original contract; or
- The price of the asset is negotiated without regard to the original contract price. *[IAS 11.10].*

This guidance has been omitted from FRS 102, however we would expect preparers to follow this guidance given the similarities between FRS 102 and IAS 11. This is discussed further in 4.6 below.

2.2.2   *Contract revenue*

IAS 11 also provides guidance on the composition of contract revenue. This has not been included in FRS 102. See 3.14 for further discussion on this.

2.2.3   *Contract costs*

Again IAS 11 provides further guidance on the composition of contract costs, which has not been included in FRS 102. See 3.15 below for further discussion on this.

2.2.4   *Recognition of contract revenue and expenses*

Although FRS 102 covers the fact that the percentage of completion method must be used when the outcome of the contract can be reliably estimated, and that an entity shall recognise as an expense immediately any costs whose recovery is not probable, it provides no further guidance on the recognition of contract revenue and expenses. Further discussion on this is given in 4.7 below.

2.2.5   *Presentation and disclosure*

IAS 11 provides further guidance on how to calculate the gross amount due from customers for contract work and the gross amount due to customers for contract work, which is not provided in FRS 102. This is discussed further at 4.8 below.

IAS 11 also requires the following disclosures which have not been included in FRS 102.

In the case of contracts in progress at the end of the reporting period, an entity should disclose each of the following:

*   The aggregate amount of costs incurred and recognised profits (less recognised losses) to date;

*   The amount of advances received; and

*   The amount of retentions. *[IAS 11.40]*.

Retentions, progress billings and advances are defined as follows:

'Retentions are amounts of progress billings which are not paid until the satisfaction of conditions specified in the contract for the payment of such amounts or until defects have been rectified. Progress billings are amounts billed for work performed on a contract whether or not they have been paid by the customer. Advances are amounts received by the contractor before the related work is performed.' *[IAS 11.41]*.

Although not specifically required by FRS 102, preparers may wish to make these disclosures if they feel that they would improve understanding for the readers of the financial statements.

3   REQUIREMENTS OF SECTION 23 FOR REVENUE

3.1   Terms used by Section 23

The following are the key terms in Section 23: *[FRS 102 Appendix I]*

Term	Definition
Agent	An entity is acting as an agent when it does not have exposure to the significant risks and rewards associated with the sale of goods or the rendering of services. One feature indicating that an entity is acting as an agent is that the amount the entity earns is predetermined, being either a fixed fee per transaction or a stated percentage of the amount billed to the customer.
Asset	A resource controlled by the entity as a result of past events and from which future economic benefits are expected to flow to the entity.
Construction contract	A contract specifically negotiated for the construction of an asset or a combination of assets that are closely interrelated or independent in terms of their design, technology and function or their ultimate purpose or use.

Chapter 18

Imputed rate of interest	The more clearly determinable of either:
	(a) the prevailing rate for a similar instrument of an issuer with a similar credit rating; or
	(b) a rate of interest that discounts the nominal amount of the instrument to the current cash sales price of the goods or services.
Onerous contract	A contract in which the unavoidable costs of meeting the obligations under the contract exceed the economic benefit expected to be received under it.
Principal	An entity is acting as a principal when it has exposure to the significant risks and rewards associated with the sale of goods or the rendering of services. Features that indicate that an entity is acting as a principal include:
	(a) the entity has the primary responsibility for providing the goods or services to the customer or for fulfilling the order, for example by being responsible for the acceptability of the products or services ordered or purchased by the customer;
	(b) the entity has inventory risk before or after the customer order, during shipping or on return;
	(c) the entity has latitude in establishing prices, either directly or indirectly, for example by providing additional goods or services; and
	(d) the entity bears the customer's credit risk for the amount receivable from the customer.
Revenue	The gross inflow of economic benefits during the period arising in the course of the ordinary activities of an entity when those inflows result in increases in equity, other than increases relating to contributions from equity participants.

This section focuses on the requirements of Section 23 and also refers to the Appendix to Section 23 which provides guidance for applying the requirements in recognising revenue. The Appendix, however, does not form part of Section 23.

3.2   Measurement of revenue

Revenue within the scope of Section 23 shall only be recognised if it meets, at a minimum, the following two criteria: *[FRS 102.23.10(c), (d), FRS 102.23.14(a), (b), FRS 102.23.28]*

- revenue can be measured reliably; and
- it is *probable* that the economic benefits associated with the transaction will flow to the entity.

'Probable' is defined as 'more likely than not'. *[FRS 102 Appendix I]*. The consideration receivable may not be regarded to be probable until the actual consideration is received or when a condition is met that removes any uncertainty.

In addition to the above criteria, there are other conditions that need to be met for the recognition of revenue from the sale of goods *[FRS 102.23.10]* and the rendering of services. *[FRS 102.23.14]*. These are further discussed below at 3.6 and 3.7 respectively.

3.2.1 Discounts, rebates and sales incentives

Revenue shall be measured at the fair value of the consideration received or receivable taking into account trade discounts, prompt settlement discounts and volume rebates allowed by the entity. *[FRS 102.23.3]*. Section 23 also requires an entity to exclude from revenue amounts collected on behalf of third parties such as sales taxes and value added taxes (VAT). *[FRS 102.23.4]*.

Where an entity provides sales incentives to a customer when entering into a contract, these are usually treated as rebates and will be included in the measurement of (i.e. deducted from) revenue when the goods are delivered or services provided.

Where the incentive is in the form of cash, revenue will be recognised at a reduced amount taking into account the rebate factor from the cash incentive.

Prompt settlement discounts (for example, customers are offered a reduction of 5% of the selling price for paying an invoice within 7 days instead of the usual 60 days) should be estimated at the time of sale and deducted from revenues.

Non-cash incentives take a variety of forms. Where the seller provides 'free postage' this would impose an additional cost on the entity but would not impact revenue. However, where the seller provides free delivery and *undertakes this service itself*, this would either be a separate component of a multiple element transaction to which some of the transaction price should be allocated (see 3.5.1 below), or more commonly, where risks and rewards of the goods are not transferred to the customer until delivery, the total revenue will not be recognised until that point.

Non-cash incentives may comprise products or services from third parties. If these are provided as part of a sales transaction they will represent separate components of a multiple element transaction to which revenue must be attributed. The seller will need to determine whether they are acting as an agent or principal for that element of the transaction. If the seller is acting as agent and has no further obligations in respect of that component, then it will immediately recognise the margin on that element as its own revenue. If acting as principal, it will recognise the full transaction price as revenue but it will need to defer any element that relates to the provision of the good or service by the third party if that party still needs to provide that good or service (for example where the incentive is in the form of a voucher that is redeemable by the third party at a later date). Principle versus agent and multiple element arrangements are discussed in further detail below at 3.2.2 and 3.5 respectively.

Some of these non-cash incentives e.g. money off vouchers, air miles or loyalty cards, may fall under the scope of loyalty awards which is discussed at 3.5.2 below.

3.2.2 Principal versus agent

An entity shall include in revenue only the gross inflows of economic benefits received and receivable by the entity on its own account and not the revenue collected on behalf of any third parties. If the entity is an agent, it shall include in revenue only the amount of its commission as any amounts collected on behalf of the principal are not revenue of the entity. *[FRS 102.23.4]*.

Chapter 18

FRS 102 provides the following guidance on identifying whether a relationship is as an agent or principal.

'An entity is acting as an agent when it does not have exposure to the significant risks and rewards associated with the sale of goods or the rendering of services. One feature indicating that an entity is acting as an agent is that the amount the entity earns is predetermined, being either a fixed fee per transaction or a stated percentage of the amount billed to the customer.' *[FRS 102 Appendix I]*.

'An entity is acting as a principal when it has exposure to the significant risks and rewards associated with the sale of goods or the rendering of services. Features that indicate that an entity is acting as a principal include:

- the entity has the primary responsibility for providing the goods or services to the customer or for fulfilling the order, for example by being responsible for the acceptability of the products or services ordered or purchased by the customer;

- the entity has inventory risk before or after the customer order, during shipping or on return;

- the entity has latitude in establishing prices, either directly or indirectly, for example by providing additional goods or services; and

- the entity bears the customer's credit risk for the amount receivable from the customer.' *[FRS 102 Appendix I]*.

Previous UK GAAP provides additional analysis to determine whether a seller is operating as a principal or agent and included the criteria of whether a seller had disclosed it is acting as an agent. The absence of such a disclosure, gave rise to a rebuttable presumption that it was acting as principal. There is no such criterion in FRS 102. However, in practice, we would not generally expect differences under FRS 102 compared to the previous UK GAAP in respect of assessing whether an entity is acting as principal or agent.

The Appendix to Section 23 also provides examples for consignment sales and sales to intermediate parties. When goods are shipped subject to conditions e.g. consignment sales under which the buyer agrees to sell the goods on behalf of the seller, the seller recognises the revenue only when the goods are sold by the buyer to a third party. *[FRS 102.23A.6]*. Another example is when sales are made to intermediate parties such as distributors, dealers or others for resale. The seller generally recognises revenue from such sales when the risks and rewards of ownership have been transferred. However if the buyer is acting, in substance, as an agent, the sale is treated as a consignment sale. *[FRS 102.23A.11]*.

3.3   Deferred payments

If the consideration receivable from the sale of goods or services is deferred, the arrangement is in effect a financing transaction, and the fair value of the consideration is the present value of all the future receipts calculated using an imputed rate of interest. Examples of a financing transaction are when an entity provides interest-free credit to the buyer or the entity accepts a note receivable bearing a below-market interest rate from the buyer as consideration.

FRS 102 provides more guidance on how the imputed rate of interest is calculated compared to the previous UK GAAP. Section 23 sets out two methods (as noted below) to arrive at the appropriate rate of interest compared to FRS 5 ANG which simply states '…the amount of revenue recognised should be the present value of the cash inflows expected to be received…'. *[FRS 5.ANG.8].*

The imputed rate of interest is, depending on which is the more clearly determinable, either:

- the prevailing rate for a similar instrument of an issue with a similar credit rating; or

- a rate of interest that discounts the nominal amount of the instrument to the current cash sales price of the goods or services. *[FRS 102.23.5].*

The difference between the nominal amount of the consideration and the present value of all future receipts is recognised as interest revenue using the effective interest method. *[FRS 102.23A.13].*

3.4   Exchanges of goods and services

Entities may enter transactions which involve exchanging or the swapping of goods or services, also known as barter transactions. Examples of this include exchanges of commodities such as oil or milk where suppliers exchange inventories in different locations to fulfil demand. Other examples include exchanges of capacity in the telecommunications sector and barter of advertising services.

An entity shall not recognise revenue if: *[FRS 102.23.6]*

- the entity exchanges goods or services for goods and services that are of a similar nature and value; or

- if the transaction lacks commercial substance even if the goods or services are dissimilar.

Hence an entity shall recognise revenue from the exchange of goods or services for dissimilar goods or services as long as the transaction has commercial substance. The entity shall then measure the transaction at: *[FRS 102.23.7]*

- the fair value of the goods or services received adjusted by the amount of any cash or cash equivalents transferred; or

- if the above cannot be measured reliably, the fair value of the goods or services given up adjusted by the amount of any cash or cash equivalents transferred; or

- if the fair value of neither the goods or services received or given up can be measured reliably, then revenue is recognised at the carrying amount of the goods or services given up adjusted by the amount of any cash or cash equivalents transferred.

Section 23 addresses the scenario whereby goods or services are exchanged for goods or services of a similar nature and value or exchanged for dissimilar goods or services but the transaction lacks commercial substance. However FRS 5 ANG does not include guidance on exchange transactions hence practice may vary but generally the principles under UITF 36 and UITF 26 may be applied. UITF 36 requires that transactions that are artificial or lacking in substance should not be recognised. *[UITF 36.15].* UITF 26 sets

Chapter 18

out that no turnover should be recognised unless there is persuasive evidence of the value at which the advertising could be sold for cash in a similar transaction. The UITF believed such circumstances would be rare so the expectation is that revenue is unlikely to be recognised when services are exchanged for similar services. *[UITF 26.4]*. In addition, the Companies Act 2006 restriction,[2] in respect of recognition of unrealised profits, discourages the recognition of gains on barter transactions in the profit and loss account. Therefore whilst both GAAPs acknowledge no recognition should be given to transactions that lack commercial substance, the lack of guidance on the treatment of exchanges under the previous UK GAAP may give rise to differences.

3.5   Identification of the revenue transaction

3.5.1   *Separately identifiable components*

The revenue recognition criteria in Section 23 is usually applied separately to each transaction. However, if there are 'separately identifiable components' of a single transaction, the revenue recognition criteria will be applied to each component to reflect the substance of the transaction. Entities should analyse the transactions in accordance with their economic substance to determine whether there are separately identifiable components and whether they should be combined or separated for revenue recognition purposes. In assessing whether there are separately identifiable components, an entity should consider whether it has in the past sold the individual components separately or plans to do so in the future. However, absent such evidence, the components may still be deemed to be separately identifiable if the individual components are sold separately by others in the market.

For example, if the sale of a product included an identifiable amount for subsequent servicing, the entity would apply the recognition criteria to the separately identifiable components i.e. the sale of the product and the sale of the servicing element. *[FRS 102.23.8]*. The Appendix to Section 23 includes an example which sets out that the seller defers the identifiable amount for subsequent servicing and recognises it as revenue over the period the service is performed. The amount that is deferred will cover the expected costs of the services together with a reasonable profit on those services. *[FRS 102.23A.19]*. Section 23 does not explain what constitutes a 'reasonable profit'.

If two or more transactions are linked in such a way that the commercial effect cannot be understood without reference to the series of transactions as whole, then the recognition criteria would be applied to the linked transactions together. For example, if an entity sells goods and at the same time enters into a separate agreement to repurchase the goods at a later date, the entity would apply the recognition criteria to the two transactions together. *[FRS 102.23.8]*.

Section 23 does not provide any further guidance to identify the separate identifiable components. FRS 5 ANG, however, provides more detailed guidance on accounting for multiple element arrangements and focuses on whether the individual components 'operate independently' of each other. 'Operate independently' means that each component represents a separable good or service that can be provided to customers, either on a stand-alone basis or as an optional extra. *[FRS 5.ANG.25]*. FRS 5 ANG also provides further guidance on accounting for contracts depending on whether they are accounted for as a single transaction (bundled) or whether the components operate independently of each other (unbundled). This difference in guidance may lead to differences in the separate components identified.

The basic principle for measurement of revenue under FRS 102 requires that revenue is measured at its fair value. Therefore, the separately identifiable components should be recorded at their fair value. However a contract with multiple elements may have a contract fair value that is lower than the aggregate of the fair values of the separately identifiable components. The difference between these two fair values should be allocated to the separable identifiable components, using an appropriate allocation method.

Example 18.1: Accounting for differences in the contract fair value and the fair values of the separately identifiable components

An entity sells a software product for £10,000 and also provides support and maintenance services for £2,000 per annum. The entity sells these two products and services together to a customer for a contract value of £11,000. In other words, a total discount of £1,000 has been given.

Using the relative fair value approach, the discount allocated to the software product is £833 (£1,000 × (£10,000 / £12,000)) and the discount allocated to the support and maintenance services is £167 (£1,000 × (£2,000 / £12,000)).

FRS 102 does not provide additional guidance in identifying the separate components and how revenue should be allocated to the separate components. An allocation of revenue based on relative fair values would be considered an appropriate basis but this is not an explicit requirement and other bases may be appropriate. As such, an entity must use its judgement to select the most appropriate methodology, taking into consideration all relevant facts and circumstances.

See section 3.7 below for discussion on accounting for revenue from rendering of services and section 4 below considers some of the practical implementation issues in accounting for revenue on the separation (unbundling) and linking (bundling) of contractual arrangements, including accounting for contracts that include the receipt of initial fees.

3.5.2 Loyalty awards

An entity may grant its customers a loyalty award, as part of a sales transaction, that the customer may redeem in the future for free or discounted goods or services. For example, money-off vouchers, air miles offered by airlines and retail stores that provide loyalty cards used to earn points as purchases are made, which can be used against future purchases. The award credit shall be accounted for as a separately identifiable component of the initial sales transaction, as discussed at 3.5.1 above. The fair value of the consideration received, or receivable, shall be allocated between the award credits and the other components of the sale. The consideration of the award credits shall be the fair value which is the amount for which the award credits could be sold separately. [FRS 102.23.9].

The guidance in Section 23 itself is limited compared to FRS 5 ANG, however the accompanying appendix to Section 23 provides an example that illustrates how Section 23 may be applied in practice.

Chapter 18

Example 18.2:   Sale with a customer loyalty award

An entity sells product A for CU100. Purchasers of product A get an award credit enabling them to buy product B for CU10. The normal selling price of product B is CU18. The entity estimates that 40 per cent of the purchasers of product A will use their award to buy product B at CU10. The normal selling price of product A, after taking into account discounts that are usually offered but that are not available during this promotion, is CU95.

The fair value of the award credit is 40 per cent × [CU18 – CU10] = CU3.20. The entity allocates the total revenue of CU100 between product A and the award credit by reference to their relative fair values of CU95 and CU3.20 respectively. Therefore:

(a) Revenue for product A is CU100 × [CU95 ÷ (CU95 + CU3.20)] = CU96.74

(b) Revenue for product B is CU100 × [CU3.20 ÷ (CU95 + CU3.20)] = CU3.26

[FRS 102.23A.16-17].

The example illustrates that a number of factors should be taken into account including:

- the percentage of awards expected to be redeemed;
- the normal selling price of the initial sales goods or service when the loyalty award is not available; and
- the normal selling price for the goods or service for which the voucher is being offered against.

The entity would then allocate the total consideration received or receivable, between the initial sales good or service and the award credit according to their relative fair values.

If the sales incentive is in the form of a voucher that is issued independently of a sales transaction (e.g. one that entitles the customer to money off if they choose to make a purchase) there will be no impact on revenue. They also do not give rise to a liability unless the products or services would be sold at a loss, and therefore a provision for an onerous contract may be required in accordance with Section 21 – *Provisions and Contingencies.*

3.6   Sale of goods

Revenue from the sale of goods is recognised when all of the following conditions are satisfied: *[FRS 102.23.10]*

- the significant risks and rewards of ownership of the goods has been transferred to the buyer;
- the entity no longer has any continuing managerial involvement usually associated with ownership nor effective control over the goods sold;
- the amount of revenue can be measured reliably;
- it is probable that the economic benefits associated with the transaction will flow to the entity; and
- the costs incurred (or to be incurred) in respect of the transaction can be measured reliably.

Assessing when an entity has transferred the significant risks and rewards of ownership to the buyer requires the specific circumstances of the transaction to be assessed. The transfer of risks and rewards usually coincides with the transfer of the legal title or when possession of the goods is passed to the buyer, as is the case for most retail sales. However the transfer of risks and rewards can occur at a different time to the transfer of legal title or taking possession of the goods. *[FRS 102.23.11].*

If an entity retains the significant risks of ownership, it does not, therefore, recognise the revenue. Examples of when an entity may retain the significant risks and rewards of ownership are: *[FRS 102.23.12]*

- when an entity retains an obligation for unsatisfactory performance not covered by normal warranties;
- when the receipt of revenue from a sale is contingent on the buyer selling the goods;
- when the goods are shipped but are subject to installation and the installation is a significant part of the contract and is incomplete; and
- when the buyer has the right to rescind the purchase for a reason specified in the sale contract or at the buyer's sole discretion without any reason and the entity is uncertain about the probability of return.

An entity recognises the revenue on a sale if the entity retains only an insignificant risk of ownership. For example, the seller would recognise the sale if the entity retains the legal title to the goods solely to protect the collectability of the amount due.

3.6.1   Goods with a right of return

Where an entity sells goods with a right of return, as commonly seen for clothing or on-line retailers, the entity recognises the revenue in full, if the entity can estimate the returns reliably. A provision for the returns would then be recognised against revenue, in accordance with Section 21. *[FRS 102.23.13].*

If the entity cannot estimate the returns reliably, the revenue is recognised in accordance with 3.6.3 (b) below.

3.6.2   'Bill and hold' sales

The term 'bill and hold' sale is used to describe a transaction where delivery is delayed at the buyer's request, but the buyer takes title and accepts billing.

Under the guidance provided in the Appendix to Section 23, revenue is recognised when the buyer takes title, provided: *[FRS 102.23A.3]*

(a)   it is probable that delivery will be made;

(b)   the item is on hand, identified and ready for delivery to the buyer at the time the sale is recognised;

(c)   the buyer specifically acknowledges the deferred delivery instructions; and

(d)   the usual payment terms apply.

Revenue is not recognised when there is simply an intention to acquire or manufacture the goods in time for delivery.

Chapter 18

3.6.3   *Goods shipped subject to conditions*

The Appendix to Section 23 identifies scenarios where goods are shipped subject to various conditions: *[FRS 102.23A.4-7]*

(a)   installation and inspection

Revenue is normally recognised when the buyer accepts delivery, and installation and inspection are complete. Revenue is recognised immediately upon the buyer's acceptance of delivery when:

(i)   the installation process is simple in nature, e.g. the installation of a factory-tested television receiver which only requires unpacking and connection of power and antennae; or

(ii)   the inspection is performed only for purposes of final determination of contract prices, for example, shipments of iron ore, sugar or soya beans.

(b)   on approval when the buyer has negotiated a limited right of return

If there is uncertainty about the possibility of return, revenue is recognised when the shipment has been formally accepted by the buyer or the goods have been delivered and the time period for rejection has elapsed.

(c)   consignment sales under which the recipient (buyer) undertakes to sell the goods on behalf of the shipper (seller)

Revenue is recognised by the shipper when the goods are sold by the recipient to a third party.

(d)   cash on delivery sales

Revenue is recognised when delivery is made and cash is received by the seller or its agent.

3.6.4   *Layaway sales (goods delivered when final payment made)*

The term 'layaway sales' applies to transactions where the goods are delivered only when the buyer makes the final payment in a series of instalments. This is fairly common in the retail sector, e.g. mail order clothing and household goods. Revenue from such sales is recognised when the goods are delivered. However, when experience indicates that most sales are completed, revenue may be recognised when a significant deposit is received, provided the goods are on hand, identified and ready for delivery to the buyer. *[FRS 102.23A.8]*.

3.6.5   *Payments in advance*

In certain sectors, for example, furniture and kitchen retail, payment or partial payment is received from the customer when an order is placed for the goods. This is often well in advance of delivery for goods which are not presently held in inventory, if, for example, the goods are still to be manufactured or will be delivered directly to the customer by a third party. In such cases, revenue is recognised when the goods are delivered to the customer. *[FRS 102.23A.9]*.

In other sectors, for example, utilities, companies receive advance payments from customers for services to be provided in the future. In some cases, these advance payments are long term in nature. The issue that arises is whether or not interest should be accrued on these advances and if so, how revenue should be measured in these circumstances.

Section 23 requires entities to measure revenue 'at the fair value of the consideration received or receivable'. *[FRS 102.23.3]*. It also refers to the situations in which an entity either provides interest-free credit to the buyer or accepts a note receivable bearing a below-market interest rate from the buyer as consideration for the sale of goods. If the arrangement effectively constitutes a financing transaction, Section 23 requires that the entity determines the fair value of the consideration by discounting all future receipts using an imputed rate of interest. *[FRS 102.23.5]*. Although Section 23 does not address the reverse situation of the receipt of interest-free advances from customers, a similar rationale may be applied to justify the accruing of interest, i.e. there is a financing element to the transaction and this must be taken into account, if revenue is to be measured at the fair value of the consideration at the time the good or service is provided.

IFRS users also face this same issue and in drafting IFRIC 18, the Interpretations Committee considered the concept of accruing interest on advance payments received from customers but the majority of respondents commenting on the draft disagreed that this was necessary. The Interpretations Committee subsequently agreed with this majority view and noted that 'paragraph 11 of IAS 18 requires taking the time value of money into account only when payments are deferred'. *[IFRIC 18.BC22]*. This is the same as the requirement in Section 23.

Given this lack of clarity we believe it is a policy choice under FRS 102 (and IAS 18) of whether or not to accrue interest on advance payments received from customers. If interest is accrued it will be calculated based upon the incremental borrowing rate of the entity and revenue will ultimately be recognised based upon the nominal value of the advance payments received from customers plus this accrued interest. Whichever accounting policy is adopted, it should be applied consistently.

3.6.6 Sale and repurchase agreements

Sale and repurchase agreements take many forms: the seller concurrently agrees to repurchase the same goods at a later date, or the seller has a call option to repurchase, or the buyer has a put option to require the repurchase, by the seller, of the goods.

In a sale and repurchase agreement for an asset other than a financial asset, the terms of the agreement need to be analysed to determine whether, in substance, the seller has transferred the risks and rewards of ownership to the buyer hence revenue is recognised. When the seller has retained the risks and rewards of ownership, even though legal title has been transferred, the transaction is a financing arrangement and does not give rise to revenue. *[FRS 102.23A.10]*. Sale and leaseback arrangements, repurchase agreements and options are discussed in Chapter 16. For a sale and repurchase agreement on a financial asset, the derecognition provisions of Section 11 applies (see Chapter 8).

Chapter 18

3.6.7   *Subscriptions to publications*

Publication subscriptions are generally paid in advance and are non-refundable. As the publications will still have to be produced and delivered to the subscriber, the subscription revenue cannot be regarded as having been earned until production and full delivery takes place. This is the approach adopted by Section 23, which requires that revenue is recognised on a straight-line basis over the period in which the items are despatched when the items involved are of similar value in each time period. When the items vary in value from period to period, revenue is recognised on the basis of the sales value of the item despatched in relation to the total estimated sales value of all items included in the subscription. *[FRS 102.23A.12]*.

3.7   Rendering of services

Section 23 requires that for transactions involving the rendering of services that are incomplete at the end of the reporting period, revenue shall be recognised based on the stage of completion if the outcome can be estimated reliably. The outcome of a transaction can be estimated reliably when all of the following are satisfied: *[FRS 102.23.14]*

- the amount of revenue can be measured reliably;
- it is probable that the economic benefits associated with the transaction will flow to the entity;
- the stage of completion at the end of the reporting period can be measured reliably; and
- the costs incurred for the transaction and the costs to complete can be measured reliably.

When the outcome of a transaction cannot be estimated reliably, revenue can be recognised only to the extent of the expenses recognised that are recoverable. *[FRS 102.23.16]*.

See 3.8 below for further guidance for applying the percentage of completion method.

When the services are performed by an 'indeterminate number of acts over a specified period of time' an entity shall recognise the revenue on a straight-line basis over the specified period or another method if that method better reflects the stage of completion. *[FRS 102.23.15]*.

3.7.1   *Contingent fee arrangements*

When fees are contingent on the performance of a significant act i.e. a specific act is much more significant than any other act, the entity shall postpone the recognition of revenue until that significant act is met. *[FRS 102.23.15]*.

3.8   Percentage of completion method

Section 23 also provides guidance on the possible methods that are available to entities to determine the stage of completion. The percentage of completion method is used to recognise revenue from rendering services and also from construction contracts which is discussed at 3.16 below.

An entity shall use the most reliable method for measuring the work performed to arrive at the stage of completion. Possible methods include: *[FRS 102.23.22]*

- the proportion of costs incurred for work performed to date (excluding costs related to future activity such as materials and prepayments) compared to the estimated total costs;

- surveys of work performed; and

- completion of a physical proportion of the contract work or completion of a proportion of the service contract.

Payments received in advance including progress payments do not always reflect the work performed. An entity shall also, when necessary, review and revise the estimates of revenue and costs as the work or service progresses. *[FRS 102.23.21-22]*.

If costs are incurred in relation to future activity, such as material or prepayments, and the costs will be recovered, the entity shall recognise those costs as an asset. *[FRS 102.23.23]*. If recovery of the costs is not probable, the entity shall expense those costs immediately. *[FRS 102.23.24]*.

If an amount is recognised as revenue, and at a later date, the collectability of that amount is not probable, the entity shall recognise the uncollectable amount as an expense and not an adjustment to the revenue. *[FRS 102.23.27]*.

The Appendix to Section 23 also provides a number of examples to provide guidance on the application of Section 23 which are noted below.

3.8.1 Installation fees

Installation fees are recognised as revenue by reference to the stage of completion of the installation, unless they are incidental to the sale of a product in which case they are recognised when the goods are sold. *[FRS 102.23A.18]*. However, in certain circumstances where the installation fees are linked to a contract for future services (for example, in the telecommunications industry: see 4.3 below) it may be more appropriate to defer such fees over either the contract period or the average expected life of the customer relationship, depending on the circumstances.

3.8.2 Advertising commissions

The Appendix to Section 23 adopts the performance of the service as the critical event for the recognition of revenue derived from the rendering of advertising services. Consequently, media commissions are recognised when the related advertisement or commercial appears before the public. Production commissions are recognised by reference to the stage of completion of the project. *[FRS 102.23A.20]*. Barter transactions involving advertising services are addressed at 3.4 above.

Chapter 18

3.8.3   *Insurance agency commissions*

The critical event for the recognition of insurance agency commissions is the commencement or renewal date of the policy. Hence, the Appendix to Section 23 sets out that insurance agency commissions received or receivable which do not require the agent to render further service are recognised as revenue on the effective commencement or renewal dates of the related policies. However, when it is probable that the agent will be required to render further services during the life of the policy, the commission, or part of it, is deferred and recognised as revenue over the period of the policy. *[FRS 102.23A.21].*

3.8.4   *Financial services fees*

The recognition of revenue for financial service fees depends on the purpose of the fees and the basis of accounting for any associated financial instrument. The description of the fee may not be indicative of the nature and substance of the services provided therefore entities will need to distinguish the fees that are an integral part of the effective interest rate, fees that are earned over the period the services are provided and fees that are earned on the occurrence of a significant act. *[FRS 102.23A.21A].*

It is common practice in some countries for credit card companies to levy a charge, payable in advance, on its cardholders. Although such charges may be seen as commitment fees for the credit facilities offered by the card, they may also cover the many other services available to cardholders. Accordingly, it may be appropriate for the fees to be deferred and recognised on a straight-line basis over the period the fee entitles the cardholder to use the card.[3]

3.8.5   *Admission fees*

Admission fees to 'artistic performances, banquets and other special events' are recognised when the event takes place. If there is a subscription to a number of events, fees may be allocated on a basis that reflects the extent to which services are performed at each event. *[FRS 102.23A.22].*

3.8.6   *Tuition fees*

The guidance in Section 23 sets out that the revenue is recognised over the period of instruction. *[FRS 102.23A.23].*

3.8.7   *Initiation, entrance and membership fees*

Revenue recognition depends on the nature of the services provided. If the fee permits membership only, and all other services or products are paid for separately, or if there is a separate annual subscription, the fee is recognised as revenue immediately as long as no significant uncertainty as to its collectability exists. If the fee entitles the member to services or publications to be provided during the membership period, or to purchase goods or services at prices lower than those charged to non-members, it is recognised on a basis that reflects the timing, nature and value of the benefits provided. *[FRS 102.23A.24].*

3.9 Franchise fees

Franchise agreements between franchisors and franchisees can vary widely both in complexity and in the extent to which various rights, duties and obligations are explicitly addressed. There is no standard franchise agreement which would dictate standard accounting practice for the recognition of all franchise fee revenue. Therefore, only a full understanding of the franchise agreement will reveal the substance of a particular arrangement so that the most appropriate accounting treatment can be determined. The following are the more common areas which are likely to be addressed in any franchise agreement and which will be relevant to the reporting of franchise fee revenue:

(a) *rights transferred by the franchisor:* the agreement gives the franchisee the right to use the trade name, processes, know-how of the franchisor for a specified period of time or in perpetuity;

(b) *the amount and terms of payment of initial fees:* payment of initial fees (where applicable) may be fully or partially due in cash, and may be payable immediately, over a specified period or on the fulfilment of certain obligations by the franchisor;

(c) *amount and terms of payment of continuing franchise fees:* the franchisee will normally be required to pay a continuing fee to the franchisor – usually on the basis of a percentage of gross revenues; and

(d) *services to be provided by the franchisor, both initially and on a continuing basis:* the franchisor will usually agree to provide a variety of services and advice to the franchisee, such as:

- site selection;
- the procurement of fixed assets and equipment – these may be either purchased by the franchisee, leased from the franchisor or leased from a third party (possibly with the franchisor guaranteeing the lease payments);
- advertising;
- training of franchisee's personnel;
- inspecting, testing and other quality control programmes; and
- book-keeping services.

The Appendix to Section 23 includes a broad discussion of the receipt of franchise fees, stating that they are recognised as revenue on a basis that reflects the purpose for which the fees were charged. *[FRS 102.23A.25].* The following methods of franchise fee recognition are appropriate:

Chapter 18

- *Supplies of equipment and other tangible assets*: the fair value of the assets sold are recognised as revenue when the items are delivered or title passes; *[FRS 102.23A.26]*.

- *Supplies of initial and subsequent services*:

  - Fees for initial services should only be recognised when the services have been 'substantially performed' (it is unlikely that substantial performance will have been completed before the franchisee opens for business);

  - Fees for continuing services, whether part of the initial fee or a separate fee, are recognised as revenue as the services are performed. When the separate fee does not cover the cost of the continuing services together with a reasonable profit, part of the initial fee, to cover the costs of continuing services and to provide a reasonable profit on those services is deferred and recognised as revenue as the services are performed; *[FRS 102.23A.27]*

  - The portion that relates to the franchise rights may be recognised in full immediately unless part of it has to be deferred because the continuing fee does not cover the cost of continuing services to be provided by the franchisor plus a reasonable profit. In this case a portion of the initial fee should be deferred and recognised as services are provided;

  - The franchise agreement may provide for the franchisor to supply tangible assets, such as equipment or inventories, at a price lower than that charged to others or at a price that does not provide a reasonable profit on those sales. In which case, part of the initial fee to cover estimated costs in excess of that price and to provide a reasonable profit on those sales, is deferred and recognised over the period the goods are likely to be sold to the franchisee. The remaining initial fee is recognised as revenue when performance of all the initial services and other obligations (such as assistance with site selection, staff training, financing and advertising) has been substantially performed by the franchisor; *[FRS 102.23A.28]*

  - The initial services and other obligations under an area franchise agreement may depend on the number of individual outlets established in the area. In which case, the fees attributable to the initial services are recognised as revenue in proportion to the number of outlets for which the initial services have been substantially completed; *[FRS 102.23A.29]*

  - If the initial fee is collectible over an extended period and there is significant uncertainty that it will be collected in full, the fee is recognised as the cash is received; *[FRS 102.23A.30]*

- *Continuing Franchise Fees*: fees charged for the use of continuing rights granted by the agreement, or for other services provided during the period of the agreement, are recognised as the services are provided or the rights used; *[FRS 102.23A.31]* and

- *Agency Transactions*: transactions under the franchise agreement may, in substance, involve the franchisor acting as agent for the franchisee. For example, the franchisor may order supplies and arrange for their delivery to the franchisee at no profit. Section 23 guidance states that 'such transactions do not give rise to revenue'. *[FRS 102.23A.32]*.

In summary, it is necessary to break down the initial fee into its various components, e.g. the fee for franchise rights, fee for initial services to be performed by the franchisor, fair value of tangible assets sold etc. The individual components may be recognised at different stages.

3.10   Interest, royalties and dividends

If an entity's assets are used by others, yielding interest, royalties or dividends, an entity shall recognise that revenue when it is probable that the entity will receive the economic benefits associated with the transaction and the amount of the revenue can be measured reliably. *[FRS 102.23.28].*

The following bases shall be used to recognise revenue: *[FRS 102.23.29]*

- Interest shall be recognised using the effective interest method – see Section 11. When calculating the effective interest rate, any related fees, finance charges paid or received, transaction costs and other premiums or discounts shall be included;

- Royalties shall be recognised on an accruals basis in accordance with the substance of the relevant agreement; and

- Dividends shall be recognised when the shareholder's right to receive payment is established.

3.10.1   *Licence fees and royalties*

The Appendix to Section 23 provides guidance for licence fees and royalties. *[FRS 102.23A.34-36].* Previous UK GAAP has no specific guidance. However the general principles under FRS 5 ANG would apply to licence fees and royalties i.e. 'a seller recognises revenue...to the extent that, it obtains the right to consideration in exchange for its performance.', *[FRS 5.ANG.4]*, hence transition to FRS 102 is not expected to give rise to differences.

The guidance in Section 23 states that 'fees and royalties paid for the use of an entity's assets (such as trademarks, patents, software, music copyright, record masters and motion picture films) are normally recognised in accordance with the substance of the agreement. As a practical matter, this may be on a straight-line basis over the life of the agreement, for example, when a licensee has the right to use certain technology for a specified period of time'. *[FRS 102.23A.34].*

Therefore, under normal circumstances, the accounting treatment of advance royalties or licence receipts is straightforward; under the accruals concept the advance should be treated as deferred income when received, and released to the profit and loss account when earned under the terms of the licence or royalty agreement.

Companies in the media sector often enter into arrangements in which one party receives upfront sums of a similar nature, e.g. a music company may receive fees from another party for content that will be accessed via the internet, e.g. digital downloading or streaming of music. If so, the same considerations apply and revenue will be recognised when earned under the terms of the licence or royalty agreement. Often the terms of such arrangements call for the music company to make its current product (past recordings) available and may also require that the

Chapter 18

future product be made available to the other party in exchange for an upfront payment (often called a 'minimum guarantee') that is recouped against future amounts owed to the music company by the other party. This revenue will generally be recognised over the term of the arrangement. However, in cases where there is no expectation or obligation to provide future content (arrangement is for past recordings only), revenue would generally be recognised by the music company once its product has been made available to the other party. In the latter instance, the arrangement would likely be viewed as an in-substance sale, as discussed below.

Advance receipts may comprise a number of components that may require revenue to be recognised on different bases. Advance royalty or licence receipts have to be distinguished from assignments of rights that are, in substance, sales. The Appendix to Section 23 explains the following:

'An assignment of rights for a fixed fee or non-refundable guarantee under a non-cancellable contract which permits the licensee to exploit those rights freely and the licensor has no remaining obligations to perform is, in substance, a sale. An example is a licensing agreement for the use of software when the licensor has no obligations subsequent to delivery. Another example is the granting of rights to exhibit a motion picture film in markets where the licensor has no control over the distributor and expects to receive no further revenues from the box office receipts. In such cases, revenue is recognised at the time of sale.' *[FRS 102.23A.35].*

Software revenue recognition and the granting of rights to exhibit motion pictures are discussed at 4.2 and 4.5 below respectively, but in-substance sales are not restricted to these sectors. Some arrangements in the pharmaceutical sector can also be accounted for as in-substance sales.

Licence fees or royalties may be receivable only on the occurrence of a future event, in which case revenue will be recognised only when it is probable that the fee or royalty will be received. This is normally when the event has occurred. *[FRS 102.23A.36].*

3.10.2   Dividends

Section 23 requires dividends to be 'recognised when the shareholder's right to receive payment is established'. *[FRS 102.23.29(c)].* This is in line with the current practice under the previous UK GAAP thus no differences are expected.

3.11   Disclosures

The following disclosures are required for revenue:

*   the accounting policies adopted for revenue recognition including the methods to determine the stage of completion involving rendering of services;
*   the amount of revenue recognised during the period, showing separately, at a minimum, the amount of each category from:

i.   the sale of goods;
ii. the rendering of services;
iii. interest;
iv. royalties;
v.   dividends;
vi. commissions;
vii. grants; and
ix. any other significant types of revenue.

The disclosures relating to revenue from construction contracts are discussed below.

3.12   Whether an arrangement is a construction contract

Determining whether an arrangement is a construction contract is critical as this determines whether revenue is recognised under the percentage of completion method under Section 23. Otherwise revenue is not recognised until the risks and rewards of ownership and control have passed. The definition of a construction contract is given in 3.1 above.

The underlying principal of FRS 102, Section 23 is that, once the outcome of a construction contract can be estimated reliably, revenue associated with the construction contract should be recognised by reference to the stage of completion of the contract activity at the end of the reporting period. *[FRS 102.23.17].*

3.13   Combination and segmentation of contracts

The requirements in Section 23 should usually be applied separately to each construction contract. However, in order to reflect the substance of the transaction it may be necessary for a contract to be sub-divided and the Section to be applied individually to each component, or for a group of contracts to be treated as one. *[FRS 102.23.18].* FRS 102 provides guidance on two separate cases. The first case is where a single contract covers the construction of a number of separate assets, each of which is in substance a separate asset. This would be treated as a separate contract for each asset provided that the following criteria are met; *[FRS 102.23.19]*

*   Separate proposals have been submitted for each asset;
*   Each asset has been subject to separate negotiation, and the contractor and customer are able to accept or reject that part of the contract relating to each asset; and
*   The costs and revenues of each asset can be identified.

The second case is effectively the reverse of the first and deals with situations where in substance there is only a single contract with a customer, or a group of customers. The group of contracts should be treated as a single contract where: *[FRS 102.23.20]*

*   The group of contracts is negotiated as a single package;
*   The contracts are so closely interrelated that they are, in effect, part of a single project with an overall profit margin; and
*   The contracts are performed concurrently or in a continuous sequence.

Chapter 18

3.14   Contract revenue

FRS 102 does not define what should be included in contract revenue, therefore we would expect users to turn to IAS 11 for further guidance using the hierarchy in Section 10. Under IAS 11 contract revenue comprises the amount of revenue initially agreed by the parties together with any variations, claims and incentive payments as long as it is probable that they will result in revenue and can be measured reliably. *[IAS 11.11]*. It is also worth noting that the overriding principles of Section 23 are that revenue must be able to be reliably measured and that a flow of economic benefits to the entity is probable, and that these are the same principles as noted above in IAS 11. Both Section 23 and IAS state that such revenue is to be measured at the fair value of the consideration received and receivable. *[FRS 102.23.3, IAS 11.12]* In this context, fair value includes the process whereby the consideration is to be revised as events occur and uncertainties are resolved. These may include contractual matters such as increases in revenue in a fixed price contract as a result of cost escalation clauses or, when a contract involves a fixed price per unit of output, contract revenue may increase as the number of units is increased. Penalties for delays may reduce revenue. In addition variations and claims must be taken into account. *[IAS 11.12]*. Variations are instructions by the customer to change the scope of the work to be performed under the contract, including changes to the specification or design of the asset or to the duration of the contract. Variations may only be included in contract revenue when it is probable that the customer will approve the variation and the amount to be charged for it, and the amount can be reliably measured. *[IAS 11.13]*.

Given the extended periods over which contracts are carried out and changes in circumstances prevailing whilst the work is in progress, it is quite normal for a contractor to submit claims for additional sums to a customer. Claims may be made for costs not included in the original contract or arising as an indirect consequence of approved variations, such as customer caused delays, errors in specification or design or disputed variations. Because their settlement is by negotiation (which can in practice be very protracted), they are subject to a high level of uncertainty; consequently, no credit should be taken for these items unless negotiations have reached an advanced stage such that:

- it is probable that the customer will accept the claim; and
- the amount that it is probable will be accepted by the customer can be measured reliably. *[IAS 11.14]*.

This means that, as a minimum, the claims must have been agreed in principle and, in the absence of an agreed sum, the amount to be accrued must have been carefully assessed.

Contracts may provide for incentive payments, for example, for an early completion or superior performance. They may only be included in contract revenue when the contract is at such a stage that it is probable the required performance will be achieved and the amount can be measured reliably. *[IAS 11.15]*.

3.15 Contract costs

Section 23 only covers revenue from service transactions and construction contracts, and does not cover the amounts that should be included in contract costs in the percentage of completion method calculation.

Although Section 13 – *Inventories* – of FRS 102 excludes from its scope work in progress arising under construction contracts, this can be used to determine the costs to be included in the percentage of completion method. This is due to the hierarchy in Section 10 that requires users to consider the requirements of other Sections in FRS 102 in developing and applying an accounting policy for an event or transaction. *[FRS 102.10.5]*. Under Section 13 costs of inventories include all costs of purchase, costs of conversion and other costs incurred in bringing the inventories to their present location and condition. *[FRS 102.13.5]*. Costs of conversion include costs directly related to the units of production, such as direct labour. They also include a systematic allocation of fixed and variable production overheads that are incurred in converting materials into finished goods. *[FRS 102.13.8]*. Although not dealing directly with construction contracts the above guidance can be applied in broad terms to construction contracts.

Again, we would expect users to refer to IAS 11 for further guidance in this area as this deals specifically with construction contract costs. The following details the relevant paragraphs of IAS 11 which have been omitted from FRS 102.

Contract costs are those that relate directly to the specific contract and to those that are attributable to contract activity in general that can be allocated to the contract. In addition, they include costs that are specifically chargeable to the customer under the terms of the contract. *[IAS 11.16]*.

Directly related costs include: *[IAS 11.17]*

- direct labour costs, including site supervision;
- costs of materials used in construction;
- depreciation of plant and equipment used on the contract;
- costs of moving plant, equipment and materials to and from the contract site;
- costs of hiring plant and equipment;
- costs of design and technical assistance that is directly related to the contract;
- the estimated costs of rectification and guarantee work, including expected warranty costs; and
- claims from third parties.

If the contractor generates incidental income from any directly related cost, e.g. by selling surplus materials and disposing of equipment at the end of the contract, this is treated as a reduction on contract costs. *[IAS 11.17]*.

The second category of costs comprises those attributable to contract activity in general that can be allocated to a particular contract. These include design and technical assistance not directly related to an individual contract, insurance, and construction overheads such as the costs or preparing and processing the payroll for the personnel actually working on the contract. These must be allocated using

Chapter 18

a systematic and rational method, consistently applied to all costs having similar characteristics. Allocation must be based on the normal level of construction activity. *[IAS 11.18]*.

There are various costs that, in most circumstances, are specifically precluded by IAS 11 from being attributed to contract activity or allocated to a contract. These are general administration costs, selling costs, research and development costs and the depreciation of idle plant and equipment that is not used on a particular contract. *[IAS 11.20]*. However, the entity is allowed to classify general administration costs and research and development as contract costs if they are specifically reimbursable under the terms of the contract. *[IAS 11.19-20]*.

Costs may be attributed to a contract from the date on which it is secured until its final completion. Additionally, the costs relating directly to the contract, which have been incurred in gaining the business, may be included in contract costs if they have been incurred once it is probable the contract will be obtained. These costs must be separately identified and measured reliably. Costs that have been written off cannot be reinstated if the contract is obtained in a subsequent period. *[IAS 11.21]*.

3.15.1   *Borrowing costs*

Borrowing costs may be specific to individual contracts or attributable to contract activity in general. Section 25 of FRS 102 – *Borrowing costs*, requires capitalisation of borrowing costs that are directly attributable to the acquisition, construction or production of qualifying assets. *[FRS 102.25.2]*. We would expect users to apply this by analogy to construction contracts and to include borrowing costs which are directly attributable to the asset being constructed.

3.15.2   *Inefficiencies*

Section 13 specifically excludes from the cost of inventories 'abnormal amounts of wasted materials, labour and other production costs'. *[FRS 102.13.13(a)]*. There is no such requirement in Section 23 and this is reflected in a degree of uncertainty about how to account for inefficiencies and 'abnormal costs' incurred during the course of a construction contract. If these costs are simply added to the total contract costs, this may affect the stage of completion if contract activity is estimated based on the total costs that have been incurred.

Following the principles of IAS 11, it is clear that abnormal costs and inefficiencies that relate solely to a particular period ought to be expensed in that period as they are not 'costs that relate directly to a specific contract'. *[IAS 11.16(a)]*. The issue is often a practical one on how to distinguish such costs from revisions of estimates that can be more reasonable treated as contract costs.

Usually, inefficiencies that result from an observable event can be identified and expensed. For example, if a major supplier collapses and the materials from another supplier are more expensive, this may be an inefficiency that ought to be expensed, as well as one where costs ought to be identifiable without undue difficulty. By contrast, an unexpected increase in costs of materials unrelated to such an event may be a revision to the estimate of costs. Other situations may be less clear. It is relatively easy to distinguish cases at either extreme but much less so when issues are marginal, where judgement will have to be exercised.

3.16 Percentage of completion method

FRS 102 requires the percentage of completion method to be used in order to recognise revenue from the rendering of services and from construction contracts. Estimates of revenue and costs should be reviewed and, when necessary, revised as the service transaction or construction contract progresses. *[FRS 102.23.21].* This will include any contract inefficiencies which do not relate to a specific period (see 3.15.2 above).

The percentage of completion method is applied on a cumulative basis in each accounting period to the current estimates of revenue and costs. FRS 102 does not specify how to use these revised estimates, however IAS 11 clarifies that revised estimates must be used in determining the amount of revenue and expenses recognised in profit or loss in the period in which the change is made, and in subsequent periods. *[IAS 11.38].*

The standard allows the stage of completion of a transaction or contract to be determined in a number of ways, including:

- the proportion that costs incurred for work performed to date bear to the estimated total costs. Costs incurred for work performed to date do not include costs relating to future activity, such as for materials or prepayments;

- surveys of work performed; and

- completion of a physical proportion of the contract work or completion of a proportion of the service contract. *[FRS 102.23.22].*

These could, of course, give different answers regarding the stage of completion of the contract as demonstrated in the following example:

Example 18.3:   Determination of revenue

A company is engaged in a construction contract with an expected sales value of £10,000. It is the end of the accounting period during which the company commenced work on this contract and it needs to compute the amount of revenue to be reflected in the profit and loss account for this contract.

Scenario (i)   **Stage of completion is measured by the proportion that contract costs incurred for work performed to date bear to the estimated total contract costs**

The company has incurred and applied costs of £4,000. £3,000 is the best estimate of costs to complete. The company should therefore recognise revenue of £5,714, being the appropriate proportion of total contract value, and computed thus:

$$\frac{4,000}{7,000} \times 10,000 = 5,714$$

Chapter 18

Scenario (ii)   Stage of completion is measured by surveys of work performed

An independent surveyor has certified that at the period-end the contract is 55% complete and that the company is entitled to apply for cumulative progress payments of £5,225 (after a 5% retention). In this case the company would record revenue of £5,500 being the sales value of the work done. (If it is anticipated that rectification work will have to be carried out to secure the release of the retention money then this should be taken into account in computing the stage of completion – but the fact that there is retention of an amount does not, in itself, directly impact the amount of revenue to be recorded.)

Scenario (iii)   Stage of completion is measured by completion of a physical proportion of the contract work

The company's best estimate of the physical proportion of the work it has completed is that it is 60% complete. The value of the work done and, therefore, the revenue to be recognised is £6,000.

Note that in each of the above scenarios the computation of the amount of revenue is quite independent of the question of how much profit (if any) should be taken. This is as it should be, because even if a contract is loss making the sales price will be earned and this should be reflected by recording revenue as the contract progresses. In the final analysis, any loss arises because costs are greater than revenue, and costs should be reflected through cost of sales. Different methods of determining revenue will, as disclosed above, produce different results, which highlights the importance of disclosing the method adopted by the entity.

Where an entity uses a method of determining the stage of completion other than by measuring the proportion of costs incurred to date compared to the total estimated contract costs, an entity may find that the profit margin recognised is not in line with expectations due to the timing of the recognition of costs. For example, a survey of work performed may indicate that the work is 70% complete, but significantly more costs have been incurred, resulting in a lower than expected profit margin and costs that cannot be expensed under this method recorded as an asset. It is not clear in FRS 102 how such costs could be treated as work in progress. Likewise, if costs incurred are lower than expected, it would normally be inappropriate for entities to accrue for costs not yet incurred. In this circumstance, entities may need to reassess whether the method selected for determining the stage of completion is the most appropriate. The method chosen should accurately reflect the progress in the contract and should be applied consistently.

There are of course other ways of measuring work done, e.g. labour hours, which depending upon the exact circumstances might lead to a more appropriate basis for computing revenue.

If the stage of completion is determined by reference to the contract costs incurred to date, it is fundamental that this figure includes only those contract costs that reflect work actually performed so far. Any contract costs that relate to future activity on the contract must be excluded from the calculation.

3.17   The determination of contract revenue and expenses

FRS 102 provides no illustrative examples on the determination of contract revenue and expenses. We would therefore expect users to refer to the Illustrative Examples in IAS 11 for further guidance. The following example is based on an illustrative example from IAS 11.

Example 18.4:   Cumulative example – the determination of contract revenue and expenses

The following example illustrates the determination of the stage of completion of a contract and the timing of the recognition of contract revenue and expenses, measured by the proportion that contract costs incurred for work performed to date bear to the estimated total contract costs.

A construction contractor has a fixed price contract to build a bridge. The initial amount of revenue agreed in the contract is £9,000. The contractor's initial estimate of contract costs is £8,000. It will take 3 years to build the bridge.

By the end of year 1, the contractor's estimate of contract costs has increased to £8,050.

In year 2, the customer approves a variation resulting in an increase in contract revenue of £200 and estimated additional contract costs of £150. At the end of year 2, costs incurred include £100 for standard materials stored at the site to be used in year 3 to complete the project.

The contractor determines the stage of completion of the contract by calculating the proportion that contract costs incurred for work performed to date bear to the latest estimated total contract costs. A summary of the financial data during the construction period is as follows:

	Year 1 £	Year 2 £	Year 3 £
Initial amount of revenue agreed in contract	9,000	9,000	9,000
Variation	–	200	200
Total contract revenue	9,000	9,200	9,200
Contract costs incurred to date	2,093	6,168	8,200
Contract costs to complete	5,957	2,023	–
Total estimated contract costs	8,050	8,200	8,200
Estimated profit	950	1,000	1,000
Stage of completion	26%	74%	100%

The constructor uses the percentages calculated as above to calculate the revenue, contract costs and profits over the term of the contract. The stage of completion for year 2 (74%) is determined by excluding from contract costs incurred for work performed to date the £100 of standard materials stored at the site for use in year 3.

The amounts of revenue, expenses and profit recognised in profit or loss in the three years are as follows:

	To date	Recognised in prior years	Recognised in current years
Year 1			
Revenue (9,000 × 26%)	2,340	–	2,340
Expenses	2,093	–	2,093
Profit	247	–	247
Year 2			
Revenue (9,200 × 74%)	6,808	2,340	4,468
Expenses (6,168 incurred less 100 of materials in storage)	6,068	2,093	3,975
Profit	740	247	493

Year 3

Revenue (9,200 × 100%)	9,200	6,808	2,392
Expenses	8,200	6,068	2,132
Profit	1,000	740	260

This does not mean that contract activity is necessarily based on the total costs that have been incurred by the entity. Contract costs that relate to future activity, such as for material or prepayments, should be deferred and recognised as an asset if it is probable that the costs will be recovered. *[FRS 102.23.23].*

FRS 102 requires that where it is not probable that costs will be recovered, these costs should be expensed immediately. *[FRS 102.23.24].* FRS 102 again does not provide any examples of situations in which this may occur, however IAS 11 provides further guidance in this area. There may be deficiencies in the contract, which means that it is not fully enforceable. Other problems may be caused by the operation of law, such as the outcome of pending litigation or legislation or the expropriation of property. The customer or the contractor may be unable for some reason to complete the contract. *[IAS 11.34].*

3.18 Inability to estimate the outcome of a contract reliably

When the outcome of a construction contract cannot be estimated reliably, an entity will first have to determine whether it has incurred costs that it is probable will be recovered under the contract. It can then recognise revenue to the extent of these costs. Contract costs should be recognised as an expense in the period in which they are incurred, *[FRS 102.23.25],* unless, of course, they relate to future contract activity, such as materials purchased for future use on the contract as explained above.

It is often difficult to estimate the outcome of a contract reliably during its early stages. This means that it is not possible to recognise contract profit. However, the entity may be satisfied that some, at least, of the contract costs it has incurred will be recovered and it will be able to recognise revenue to this extent.

3.19 Loss making contracts and uncollectible revenue

As soon as the entity considers that it is probable that the contract costs will exceed contract revenue it must recognise immediately the expected loss as an expense, with a corresponding provision for an onerous contract. *[FRS 102.23.26].*

An entity does not adjust the cumulative revenue it has recognised if it transpires in a subsequent period that there are doubts about the recoverability of an amount it has recognised as revenue and it consequently has to make provision against its debtor. Instead the amount that is no longer considered recoverable is written off as an expense. *[FRS 102.23.27].*

3.20 Disclosures for construction contracts

FRS 102 requires the following disclosures in relation to construction contracts:

- the amount of contract revenue recognised as revenue in the period;
- the methods used to determine the contract revenue recognised in the period; and
- the methods used to determine the stage of completion of contracts in progress; *[FRS 102.23.31]* and
- the gross amount due from customers for contract work, as an asset; and
- the gross amount due to customers for contract work, as a liability. *[FRS 102.23.32]*.

3.21 Examples of construction contract revenue recognition under the principles of Section 23

FRS 102 in its Appendix provides two examples in relation to the construction of real estate to help determine when the percentage of completion method should be used.

An entity that undertakes the construction of real estate, directly or through subcontractors, and enters into an agreement with one or more buyers before construction is complete, shall account for the agreement using the percentage of completion method, only if:

- the buyer is able to specify the major structural elements of the design of the real estate before construction begins and/or specify major structural changes once construction is in progress (whether it exercises that ability or not); or
- the buyer acquires and supplies constriction materials and the entity provides only construction services. *[FRS 102.23A.14]*.

If the entity is required to provide services together with construction materials in order to perform its contractual obligation to deliver real estate to the buyer, the agreement shall be accounted for as the sale of goods. In this case, the buyer does not obtain control or the significant risks and rewards of ownership of the work in progress in its current state as construction progresses. Rather the transfer occurs only on delivery of the completed real estate to the buyer. *[FRS 102.23A.15]*.

4 PRACTICAL IMPLEMENTATION ISSUES

Although Section 23 lays down general principles of revenue recognition, there is a lack of specific guidance in relation to matters, such as multiple-element revenue arrangements and industry specific issues. Section 10 provides additional guidance if an FRS or FRC Abstract does not specifically address a transaction, event or condition, and that management shall use its judgement in developing and applying an accounting policy that results in information that is relevant and reliable. *[FRS 102.10.4]*. In making the judgement, management may also consider the requirements and guidance in *EU-adopted IFRS* dealing with similar and related issues. *[FRS 102.10.6]*.

4.1   Receipt of initial fees

It is common practice in certain industries to charge an initial fee at the inception of a service (or signing of a contract) followed by subsequent service fees that can present revenue allocation problems. It is not always clear what the initial fee represents; it is necessary to determine what proportion, if any, of the initial fee has been earned on receipt, and how much relates to the provision of future services. For example, if an initial fee is paid on signing a contract, before this receipt is recognised as revenue, the entity needs to consider a number of factors including what the customer is receiving in return for the initial fee, whether the entity has delivered a service for which the initial consideration is a fair consideration, and whether a service is yet to be delivered following receipt of the fee. The fact the initial fee is non-refundable does not alone, support revenue recognition. In some cases, large initial fees are paid for the provision of a service, whilst continuing fees are relatively small in relation to future services to be provided. If it is probable that the continuing fees will not cover the cost of the continuing services to be provided plus a reasonable profit, then a portion of the initial fee should be deferred over the period of the service contract such that a reasonable profit is earned throughout the service period. Accounting for initial fees has proved problematic and practice does vary. The actual terms and conditions for each contract would need to be assessed before concluding on the appropriate revenue recognition treatment.

4.2   Software revenue recognition

The software services industry face a number of issues such as when to recognise revenue from contracts to develop software, software licensing fees, customer support services and data services. However, these issues have not been addressed in Section 23 which provides only one sentence of guidance, being 'fees from the development of customised software are recognised as revenue by reference to the stage of completion of the development, including completion of services provided for post-delivery service support.' *[FRS 102.23A.33].* IAS 18 also does not address these issues.

Because of the nature of the products and services involved, applying the general revenue recognition principles to software transactions can sometimes be difficult. As a result, software companies have used a variety of methods to recognise revenue, often producing significantly different financial results from similar transactions.

Software arrangements range from those that simply provide a licence for a single software product, to those that require significant production, modification or customisation of the software. Arrangements may also include multiple products or services.

4.2.1   Accounting for a software licence

If the arrangement is for a simple provision of a licence for a single software product, then the guidance for accounting for licences, as discussed at 3.10.1 above, should be applied.

4.2.2   Accounting for software arrangements with multiple elements

Software arrangements may provide licences for many products or services such as additional software products, upgrades/enhancements, rights to exchange or return software or post-contract customer support (PCS).

We have noted at 3.5 above that in certain circumstances it is necessary to apply the recognition criteria to the separately identifiable components of a single transaction in order to reflect the substance of the transaction. *[FRS 102.23.8]*. Section 3.7 above also notes that when services are performed by an indeterminate number of acts over a specified period of time, an entity shall recognise revenue on a straight-line basis over that period, unless another method better reflects the stage of completion. *[FRS 102.23.15]*.

4.2.3 Accounting for arrangements which require significant production, modification or customisation of software

Where companies are running well-established computer installations with systems and configurations that they do not wish to change, off-the-shelf software packages are generally not suitable for their purposes. For this reason, some software companies will enter into a customer contract whereby they agree to customise a generalised software product to meet the customer's specific requirements. A simple form of customisation is to modify the system's output reports so that they integrate with the customer's existing management reporting system. However, customisation will often entail more involved obligations, e.g. having to translate the software so that it is able to run on the customer's specific hardware configuration, data conversion, system integration, installation and testing.

The question that arises, therefore, is what is the appropriate basis on which a software company recognises revenue when it enters into a contract that involves significant obligations? Section 23 includes guidance on accounting for construction contracts and the guidance, including the percentage of completion method, may also, in some circumstances, be applied to contracts with separately identifiable components. *[FRS 102.23.18]*. The percentage of completion method is discussed at 3.8 and 3.16 above.

Consequently, where an entity is able to make reliable estimates as to the extent of progress towards completion of a contract, the related revenues and the related costs, and where the outcome of the contract can be assessed with reasonable certainty, the percentage of completion method of profit recognition should be applied.

4.3 Revenue recognition issues in the telecommunications sector

There are significant revenue recognition complexities that affect the telecommunications sector, and about which FRS 102, previous UK GAAP and IFRS is effectively silent. The complexities differ depending upon the type of telecommunications services being considered. Recognition issues may differ between fixed line (principally voice and data) services and wireless (principally mobile voice and data) services. In addition customers may purchase elements of both as part of a bundled package.

A number of general factors underlie the accounting issues. For example, local regulatory laws may dictate the way business is done by the operators, there may be restrictions on the discounting of handsets, handsets may be branded in some countries but not in others, both branded and unbranded handsets may co-exist in the same country and there may be varying degrees of price protection.

Connection and up-front fees are an issue for both fixed line and mobile operators.

Chapter 18

4.3.1   *Recording revenue for multiple service elements ('bundled offers')*

Section 23 notes that when necessary to reflect the substance of the transaction, revenue shall be recognised for the separately identifiable components of a single transaction and refers specifically to situations where the selling price of a product includes an identifiable amount for subsequent servicing, in which case that amount is deferred and recognised as revenue over the period during which the service is performed. *[FRS 102.23A.19].* This is directly relevant to some aspects of multiple deliverable arrangements offerings, where customers are offered a 'bundle' of assets and services.

When a consumer enters into a mobile phone contract with a provider, the contract may be a package that includes a handset and various combinations of talktime, text messages and data allowances (internet access). The bundle may also include fixed line products, such as voice, video and broadband services.

Consumers may pay for their bundle of assets and services in a number of different ways: a payment for the handset (which may be discounted); connection charges related to activation of the handset; monthly fixed or usage-based payments; and prepayments by credit card or voucher. None of these payments may relate directly to the cost of the services being provided by the operator, and operators also may offer loyalty programs that entail the provision of future services at substantially reduced prices.

As there is no specific guidance within FRS 102 (nor the previous UK GAAP or IFRS) on the subject of multiple deliverable arrangements beyond the brief references as noted above, companies will need to apply judgement in applying the requirements of Section 23 relevant to the facts and circumstances of each transaction.

4.3.1.A   *Accounting for handsets and monthly service arrangements*

Many of the mobile operators that provide handsets to customers who subscribe to service contracts do so at heavily discounted prices or even free of charge. Most telecommunications operators have an accounting policy under which handsets and airtime are separately identifiable components but they apply a form of 'residual method' to the amount of revenue taken for the sale of the handset, recognising no more than the amount contractually receivable for it.

However, although FRS 102 requires revenue to be measured at its fair value, it is not definitive on the method of allocation. Usually, an allocation of revenue based on relative fair values would be considered an appropriate basis but this is not an explicit requirement. This is discussed at 3.5 above.

4.3.1.B   *'Free' services*

'Free' services are often included in the monthly service arrangement for contract subscribers as an additional incentive to encourage subscribers to sign up for a fixed contract period, typically one or two years.

'Free' services can either be provided up-front as inclusive services for a fixed monthly fee, or as an incentive after a specific threshold has been exceeded, intended to encourage subscribers to spend more than their specified amount.

As a result, one of the challenges for mobile operators is the accounting treatment for the 'free' service period. In our opinion, the total amount that is contractually required to be paid by the customer is recognised as revenue rateably over the entire service period, including the period in which the 'free' services are provided.

The following example illustrates the accounting for free minutes granted at subscription date by a mobile operator to a subscriber:

Example 18.5: Accounting for free minutes

An operator enters into a service contract with a customer for a period of 12 months. Under the contract specifications, the customer is offered for the first 2 months 60 free minutes talktime per month and for the remaining 10 months of the contract the customer will pay a fixed fee of £30 per month for 60 minutes of communication per month. The operator considers the recoverability of the amounts due under the contract from the customer to be probable.

In our view, since the free minutes offer is linked to the non-cancellable contract, the fee receivable for the non-cancellable contract is spread over the entire contract term.

Consequently, the fixed fee of £300 (£30 × 10 months) to be received from the subscriber would be recognised on a straight-line basis over the 12 month contract period, being the stage of completion of the contract. The operator therefore would recognise £25 each month over the twelve month period (£30 × 10 / 12 = £25).

4.3.1.C   Connection and up-front fees

Connection fees can be a feature of both the wireless (mobile) and the fixed line activities.

When the mobile telecoms industry was in its infancy, upfront costs such as connection fees, contract handling fees, registration fees, fees for changing plans etc., were commonly charged by operators. Such charges have been phased out over the years and are no longer a common feature in a number of markets.

Nevertheless, there are still occasions in which a telecommunications operator charges its subscribers a one-time non-refundable fee for connection to its network. The contract for telecommunications services between the operator and the subscriber has either a finite or an indefinite life and includes the provision of the network connection and on-going telecommunications services. The direct/incremental costs incurred by the operator in providing the connection service are primarily the technician's salary and related benefits; this technician provides both connection and physical installation services at the same time.

In such cases, the connection service and the telecommunications services have to be analysed in accordance with their economic substance in order to determine whether they should be combined or segmented for revenue recognition purposes. When the connection transaction is bundled with the service arrangement in such a way that the commercial effect cannot be understood without reference to the two transactions as a whole, the connection fee revenue should be recognised over the expected term of the customer relationship under the arrangement which generated the connection. In our view, the expected term of the customer relationship may not necessarily be the contract period, but may be the estimated average life of the customer relationship, provided that this can be estimated reliably.

Chapter 18

Charging fees remains relatively common for connection to a fixed telephone line. Although connection fees are commonly recognised over the contract period, upfront recognition of the non-refundable fee may be possible if there is a clearly demonstrable separate service and it is provided at the inception of the contract.

4.3.2   *'Gross versus net' issues*

The difficulty of deciding whether to record revenue gross or net is pervasive in the telecommunications sector. The problem occurs because of the difficulty in deciding whether the parties involved in any particular agreement are acting as principal or agent. Section 23 sets out that in an agency relationship, the amounts collected on behalf of the principal are not revenue and instead, revenue is the amount of commission. *[FRS 102.23.4]*.

The principal versus agent assessment is further discussed at 3.2.2 above but does not necessarily help decide the matter in many telecoms scenarios. A frequent arrangement is where there is data content provided by third parties that is subject to a separate provider agreement.

Content, such as music, navigation and other downloads such as 'apps' can either be included in the monthly price plan, or purchased separately on an *ad hoc* basis. Operators can either develop the content in-house, or use third party providers to offer a range of items to their subscribers, with charges based either on duration (news, traffic updates etc.) or on quantity (number of ringtones, games etc.).

The issue is whether the operator should report the content revenue based on the gross amount billed to the subscriber because it has earned revenue from the sale of the services or the net amount retained (that is, the amount billed to the subscriber less the amount paid to a supplier) because it has only earned a commission or fee. Is the substance of the transaction with the supplier one of buying and on-selling goods or selling goods on consignment (i.e. an agency relationship)? The two most important considerations for most of these arrangements are:

- whether the operator has the primary responsibility for providing the services to the customer or for fulfilling the order, for example by being responsible for the acceptability of the services ordered or purchased by the customer; and

- whether it has latitude in establishing prices, either directly or indirectly, for example by providing additional goods or services.

Inventory risk is unlikely to be relevant for a service provision and credit risk may be only a weak indicator as the amounts are individually small and may be paid to access the download.

Therefore, if the content is an own-brand product or service, then the revenue receivable from subscribers should be recorded as revenue by the operator, and the amounts payable to the third party content providers should be recorded as costs.

By contrast, if the content is a non-branded product/service that is merely using the mobile operator's network as a medium to access its subscriber base, then the amounts receivable from subscribers should not be recorded as revenue. The operator's revenue will comprise only the commissions receivable from the content providers for the use of the operator's network.

4.3.3   Accounting for roll-over minutes

Where an operator offers a subscriber a finite number of call minutes for a fixed amount per period with the option of rolling over any unused minutes, the question arises as to how the operator should account for the unused minutes that the subscriber holds. The operator is not obliged to reimburse the subscriber for unused minutes, but is obliged (normally subject to a ceiling) to provide the accumulated unused call minutes to the subscriber until the end of the contract, after which they expire.

In such cases, revenue is recognised at the time the minutes are used. Any minutes unused at the end of each month should be recognised as deferred revenue.

However, in some instances, the operator has relevant and reliable evidence that shows that a portion of those unused minutes will not be used before the expiration of the validity period. In that case, the operator could consider an alternative revenue recognition policy that would take account of the probability of unused minutes at the end of the validity period in the computation of the revenue per minute used by the subscriber. This would result in allocating a higher amount of revenue per minute used.

When the validity period expires, any remaining balance of unused minutes would be recognised as revenue immediately, since the obligation of the operator to provide the contractual call minutes is extinguished.

4.3.4   Accounting for the sale of prepaid calling cards

Prepaid cards are normally sold by an operator either through its own sales outlet or through distributors. The credit sold with the cards may have an expiry date that varies from one operator to another, although, in certain limited jurisdictions, there is no expiry date. For example, prepaid cards may be sold with an initial credit of £10 covering 60 minutes of communication and the credit has a validity period of 90 days from the date of activation. If not used within this period, the credit is lost.

When the cards are sold through distributors, the distributor is usually obliged to sell the cards to the customers at the face value of the card. On sale of the card, the distributor pays the operator the face value less a commission. The distributor has a right to return unsold cards to the operator. Once the distributor has sold the cards, it has no further obligation to the operator.

In our view, when an operator sells calling cards directly, revenue is recognised at the time the minutes are used. Any minutes unused at the end of each month should be recognised as deferred revenue. However, if the operator has relevant and reliable evidence that shows that a portion of those unused minutes will not be used before the expiration of the validity period then it could consider an alternative revenue recognition policy. This would take account of the probability of unused minutes at the end of the validity period in the computation of the revenue per minute recognised as the minutes are used by the customer.

When an operator sells calling cards through a distributor, the revenue is required to be recognised based on the substance of the arrangement with the distributor.

It is usually the case that the distributor is in substance acting as an agent for the operator. The revenue associated with the sale of the calling card is recognised when

Chapter 18

the subscriber uses the minutes. The difference between the card's usage value, which is charged to the subscriber, and the amount paid to the operator is the distributor's commission.

In our view, unless the distributor is also an operator or the calling card could be used on any operator's network (which is rare), it would be difficult to conclude that the distributor is the principal in the arrangement with the subscriber, because the distributor would not have the capacity to act as the principal under the terms of the service provided by the calling card to the subscriber (see 3.2.2 and 4.3.2 above).

4.4   Excise taxes and goods and services taxes: recognition of gross versus net revenues

Many jurisdictions around the world raise taxes that are based on components of sales or production. These include excise taxes and goods and services or value added taxes. In some cases, these taxes are, in effect, collected by the entity from customers on behalf of the taxing authority. In other cases, the taxpayer's role is more in the nature of principal than agent. The regulations (for example, excise taxes in the tobacco and drinks industries) differ significantly from one country to another. The practical accounting issue that arises concerns the interpretation of whether excise taxes and goods and services taxes be deducted from revenue (net presentation) or included in the cost of sales and, therefore, revenue (gross presentation). *[FRS 102.23.4].*

The appropriate accounting treatment will depend on the particular circumstances. In determining whether gross or net presentation is appropriate, the entity needs to consider whether it is acting in a manner similar to that of an agent or principal.

4.5   Film exhibition and television broadcast rights

Revenue received from the licensing of films for exhibition at cinemas and on television should be recognised in accordance with the general recognition principles discussed in this chapter.

Contracts for the television broadcast rights of films normally allow for multiple showings within a specific period; these contracts usually expire either on the date of the last authorised telecast, or on a specified date, whichever occurs first. Rights for the exhibition of films at cinemas are generally sold either on the basis of a percentage of the box office receipts or for a flat fee.

The Appendix to Section 23 states that 'an assignment of rights for a fixed fee or non-refundable guarantee under a non-cancellable contract that permits the licensee to exploit those rights freely and the licensor has no remaining obligations to perform is, in substance, a sale'. When a licensor grants rights to exhibit a motion picture film in markets where it has no control over the distributor and expects to receive no further revenues from the box office receipts, revenue is recognised at the time of sale. *[FRS 102.23A.35].*

Therefore, it is our view that the revenue from the sale of broadcast, film or exhibition rights may be recognised in full upon commencement of the licence period provided the following conditions are met:

(a) a contract has been entered into;

(b) the film is complete and available for delivery;

(c) there are no outstanding performance obligations, other than having to make a copy of the film and deliver it to the licensee; and

(d) collectability is reasonably assured.

This applies even if the rights allow for multiple showings within a specific period for a non-refundable flat fee and the contract expires either on the date of the last authorised telecast, or on a specified date, whichever occurs first. The sale can be recognised even though the rights have not yet been used by the purchaser. We do not believe it is appropriate to recognise revenue prior to the date of commencement of the licence period since it is only from this date that the licensee is able to freely exploit the rights of the licence and hence has the rewards of ownership. *[FRS 102.23.10(a)]*.

When the licensor is obliged to perform any significant acts or provide any significant services subsequent to delivery of the film to the licensee – for example to promote the film – it would be appropriate to recognise revenue as the acts or services are performed (or, as a practical matter, on a straight-line basis over the period of the licence). *[FRS 102.23.15]*.

Rights for the exhibition of a film at cinemas may be granted on the basis of a percentage of the box office receipts, in which case revenue should be recognised as the entitlement to revenue arises based on box office receipts.

If the fees only become payable when the box office receipts have exceeded a minimum level, revenue should not be recognised until the minimum level has been achieved. The Appendix to Section 23 sets out that revenue that is contingent on the occurrence of a future event is recognised only when it is probable that the fee or royalty will be received, which is normally when the event has occurred. *[FRS 102.23A.36]*.

4.6 Construction of a separate asset

An area where it is necessary to consider whether contracts should be combined is in contract options and additions. Combining of contracts is important because of its potential impact the recognition of revenue and profits on transactions. If any optional asset is treated as part of the original contract, contract revenue will be recognised using the percentage of completion method over the combined contract.

FRS 102 does not specifically consider the option of an additional asset, only whether a contract covering a number of assets should be treated as a separate construction contract for each asset. This is discussed further at 3.13 above.

IAS 11 considers the circumstances in which a contract that gives a customer an option for an additional asset (or is amended in this manner) and concludes that this should be treated as a new contract if:

- the asset differs significantly in design, technology of function from the asset or assets covered by the original contract; or
- the price of the asset is negotiated without regard to the original contract price. *[IAS 11.10]*.

Chapter 18

This means, for example, that the contract for an additional, identical asset would be treated as a separate contract if its price was negotiated separately from the original contract price. Costs often decline with additional production, not only because of the effects of initial costs but also because of the 'learning curve' (the time taken by the workforce to perform activities decreases with practice and repetition). This could result in a much higher profit margin on the additional contract. If, for example, a government department takes up its option with a defence contractor for five more aircraft, in addition to the original twenty five that had been contracted for, but the option was unpriced and the new contract is priced afresh, then it cannot be combined with the original contract regardless of the difference in profit margins. The combining of contracts may also have unexpected results. If, for example, an entity has a contract with a government to build two satellites and a priced option to build a third, it may be obliged to combine the contracts at the point at which the option is exercised. This could well be in a different accounting period to the commencement of the contract and there will be a cumulative catch up of revenue and probably profits. In subsequent periods results will be based on the combined contracts.

4.7   The recognition of contract revenue and expenses

IAS 11 identifies two types of construction contract, fixed price and cost plus contracts. This differentiation is not made in FRS 102, with cost plus contracts not being considered. We would however expect users of FRS 102 to turn to IAS 11 for further guidance under the hierarchy in section 10.

In the case of a fixed price contract, the standard states that the outcome of a construction contract can be estimated reliably when all the conditions discussed below are satisfied.

- First, it must be probable that the economic benefits associated with the contract will flow to the entity, which must be able to measure total contract revenue reliably. As discussed further below, these conditions will usually be satisfied when there are adequate contractual arrangements between parties;

- Second, both the contract costs to complete the contract and the stage of contract completion at the end of the reporting period must be able to be measured reliably; and

- Third, the entity must be able to identify and measure reliably the contract costs attributable to the contract so that actual contract costs incurred can be compared with prior estimates. *[IAS 11.23]*. This means that it must have adequate resources and budgeting systems.

Cost plus contracts are not subject to all of the same uncertainties as fixed price contracts. As with any transaction, it must be probable that the economic benefits associated with the contract will flow to the entity in order to recognise income at all. In most contracts this will be evidenced by the contract documentation. The fundamental criterion for a cost plus contract is the proper measurement of contract costs. Therefore, the contract costs attributable to the contract, whether or not specifically reimbursable, must be clearly identified and measured reliably. *[IAS 11.24]*.

There are certain general principles that apply whether the contract is classified as a fixed cost or as a cost plus. Recognition of revenue is by reference to the 'stage of completion method', and contact revenue and costs are recognised as revenue and expenses in profit or loss in the period in which the work is performed.

This does not mean that contract activity is necessarily based on the total costs that have been incurred by the entity. As noted above at 3.17 above contract costs that relate to future contract activity (i.e. that activity for which revenue has not yet been recognised) may be deferred and recognised as an asset as long as it is probable that they will be recovered. These costs are usually called contract work in progress. Otherwise, contract costs are recognised in the profit or loss as they are incurred.

Importantly, neither does it mean that an entity can determine what it considers to be an appropriate profit margin for the whole contract and spread costs over the contract so as to achieve this margin, thereby classifying deferred costs as work in progress. Neither FRS 102 nor IAS 11 seek to achieve a uniform profit margin throughout the contract, unless, of course, it is a cost plus contract.

4.8 Disclosures

IAS 11 provides further guidance on the disclosures which are also required by FRS 102. In respect of the disclosure required by FRS 102.23.32 detailed in 3.20 above, IAS 11 provides the following:

The gross amount due from customers for contract work is the net amount of:

- Costs incurred plus recognised profits; less
- The sum of recognised losses and progress billings

for all contracts in progress for which progress billings exceed costs incurred plus recognised profits (less recognised losses) exceeds progress billings. *[IAS 11.43]*.

5 SUMMARY OF GAAP DIFFERENCES

The differences between FRS 102, previous UK GAAP and IFRS in accounting for revenue are set out below.

	FRS 102	*Previous UK GAAP*	*IFRS*
Scope – interest, royalties and dividends	Section 23 includes accounting for interest, royalties and dividends	Interest accounted for under FRS 4 and FRS 26. No specific accounting standard for royalties and dividends	IAS 18 includes accounting for interest, royalties and dividends
Scope – agricultural activity and product	Excluded from Section 23	Not excluded from FRS 5 ANG	Excluded from IAS 18
Scope – investment property	Excluded from Section 23	Not excluded from FRS 5 ANG	Not excluded from IAS 18.

	FRS 102	*Previous UK GAAP*	*IFRS*
Exchange of goods or services	Includes guidance on the accounting for when the fair value of the goods or services received or given up is not reliably measurable.	Not specifically included within FRS 5 ANG however some guidance within UITF 26 and UITF 36	Does not provide guidance on the accounting for when the fair value of the goods or services received or given up is not available. However IAS 16 – *Property, Plant and Equipment* – includes some guidance which may be applied
Interest	Accounted for using the effective interest rate (EIR) method	Accounted for at a constant rate for those adopting FRS 4 or using EIR method for those adopting FRS 26	Accounted for using the EIR method
Deferred consideration	Present value calculated using the imputed rate of interest calculated as either the prevailing rate for a similar instrument and issuer or the rate of interest that discounts the nominal amount of the consideration to the current sales price of the goods or services	Present value calculated using the imputed rate of interest but no guidance on the appropriate rate	Present value calculated using the imputed rate of interest calculated as either the prevailing rate for a similar instrument and issuer or the rate of interest that discounts the nominal amount of the consideration to the current sales price of the goods or services

Disclosures – Amount of revenue recognised during the period	Amount of revenue for each category from the sale of goods, rendering of services interest, royalties, dividends, commissions, grants and 'other significant types' of revenue	No mandatory disclosures under FRS 5 ANG. Where the seller is an agent, disclosure of gross value of sales throughput is encouraged. In addition a brief description of the relationship of recognised turnover to the gross value of sales throughput should be given	Amount of revenue for each category from the sale of goods, rendering of services interest, royalties and dividends. In addition, disclosure required of the revenue recognised from the exchange of goods or services analysed by the above categories
Segmental disclosures	Entities with publically traded debt or equity instruments[4] shall disclose segmental information in line with IFRS 8 – *Operating Segments* – revenues from external customers, intra-segment revenues, revenue that is 10% or more of the combined revenue of all operating segments and a reconciliation of the reportable segments' revenues to the total entity revenue	Segmental disclosures required per SSAP 25 – *Segmental Reporting* – of sales by origin and destination and inter-company sales by origin	Entities within the scope of IFRS 8 – *Operating Segments* – shall also disclose revenues from external customers, intra-segment revenues, revenue that is 10% or more of the combined revenue of all operating segments and a reconciliation of the reportable segments' revenues to the total entity revenue
Separation of contracts	Allows for contracts to be separated or grouped provided that certain criteria are met.	No guidance under SSAP 9.	Same as FRS 102
Revenue from contract variations	No guidance provided.	Approved contract variations should be treated as part of total sales using a conservative estimate of the amount likely to be received. Claims should be accounted for when negotiations have reached an advanced stage and there is sufficient evidence of the acceptability of the claim in principle to the purchaser.	Variations may only be included in contract revenue when it is probable that the customer will approve the variation and the amount to be charged for it, and the amount can be measured reliably.
Contact cost	No guidance provided.	Provided guidance on the determination of contract costs.	Provides guidance on the determination of contract costs.

Chapter 18

References

1 Section D of both the Large & Med-sized Cos & Groups (Accounts & Reports) Regs 2008, Sch 1, Pt 2 and Small Cos & Groups (Accounts & Directors' Report) Regs 2008, Sch 1, Pt 2.

2 Para 13 of Sch 1 SI 2008/409 and Para 13 Sch 1 SI 2008/410.

3 This is also the view taken under US GAAP; see FASB ASC 310-20-35-5.

4 An entity whose debt or financial instruments are publicly traded, or that files, or is in the process of filing its financial statements with a securities commission or other regulatory organisation for the purpose of issuing instruments in a public market. *[FRS 102.1.15]*.

Chapter 19   Government grants

List of examples

Chapter 19   Government grants

1   INTRODUCTION

Section 24 of FRS 102 – *Government Grants* – covers the accounting and disclosure requirements for government grants. It also covers disclosure requirements for any other forms of government assistance provided to the entity. Government grants typically involve a transfer of resources by a government body to an entity to support specified activities or projects. The transfer of funds is usually dependent on past or future compliance with certain conditions relating to the entity's operating activities. *[FRS 102.24.1]*. Such assistance has been available to businesses for many years, although the exact nature of the support varies over time as governments and their priorities change.

The main accounting issue that arises from government grants is how to deal with the benefit that the grant represents in the profit and loss account. Section 24 gives an accounting policy choice over one of two models for recognising the benefit; the performance model and the accrual model. *[FRS 102.24.4]*. These methods are discussed at 3.4 and 3.5 below.

Section 24 also recognises that an entity may receive other forms of government assistance, such as free technical or marketing advice and the provision of guarantees, including assistance which cannot reasonably have a value placed upon them. Rather than prescribe how these should be accounted for, it requires disclosure about such assistance. *[FRS 102.24.6(d), 7]*.

2   KEY DIFFERENCES TO PREVIOUS UK GAAP AND IFRS

There are some differences between the accounting and disclosure requirements in Section 24 compared to previous UK GAAP (SSAP 4 – *Accounting for Government Grants*) and IFRS (IAS 20 – *Accounting for Government Grants and Disclosure of Government Assistance*). The key differences are discussed at 2.1 and 2.2 below respectively and are summarised at 4 below.

2.1   Key differences to previous UK GAAP

2.1.1   *Scope*

Section 24 specifically excludes from its definition of government grants those forms of government assistance that cannot reasonably be valued and transactions with government that are indistinguishable from the normal trading transaction of the entity. *[FRS 102.24.2]*.

SSAP 4 has no similar exclusions.

2.1.2   *Recognition and measurement*

Section 24 provides an accounting policy choice for recognising grants as income using either a performance model or an accrual model. *[FRS 102.24.4]*. The performance model means the grant is recognised as income as the performance related conditions are met. *[FRS 102.24.5B]*. The accrual model means that the grant is recognised as income when the related expenses are recognised. *[FRS 102.24.5D]*.

SSAP 4 does not offer a choice and requires grant income to be recognised in profit or loss to match with the related expenditure; in essence, the same basis as the accrual model in Section 24. *[SSAP 4.23]*.

2.1.3   *Presentation*

Section 24 prohibits the deferred element of a grant that relates to an asset being deducted from the carrying amount of the asset. *[FRS 102.24.5G]*.

SSAP 4 allows the option for the deduction of the deferred element of grants from the carrying amount of the related asset. However, this option is not permitted to be applied by those entities preparing accounts under the Companies Act 2006. *[SSAP 4.25]*.

2.2   Key differences to IFRS

2.2.1   *Recognition and measurement*

Section 24 provides an accounting policy choice for recognising grants as income using either a performance model or an accrual model. *[FRS 102.24.4]*. The performance model means the grant is recognised as income as the performance related conditions are met. *[FRS 102.24.5B]*. The accrual model means that the grant is recognised as income when the related expenses are recognised. *[FRS 102.24.5D]*.

IAS 20 follows an accruals-based approach requiring grants to be recognised in profit or loss on a systematic basis as the entity recognises the related expense. *[IAS 20.12].* IAS 20 does not permit a performance model approach.

3   REQUIREMENTS OF SECTION 24 FOR GOVERNMENT GRANTS

3.1   Terms used in Section 24

The following terms are used in Section 24 with the meanings specified:

Term	Definition
Government	Government, government agencies and similar bodies whether local, national or international. *[FRS 102 Appendix I].*
Government assistance	Action by government designed to provide an economic benefit specific to an entity or range of entities qualifying under specified criteria. *[FRS 102.24.7].*
Government grant	Assistance by government in the form of a transfer of resources to an entity in return for past or future compliance with specified conditions relating to the operating activities of the entity. *[FRS 102.24.1, FRS 102 Appendix I].*
Fair value	The amount for which an asset could be exchanged, a liability settled, or an equity instrument granted could be exchanged, between knowledgeable, willing parties in an arm's length transaction. *[FRS 102 Appendix I].*
Operating activities	The principal revenue-producing activities of the entity and other activities that are not investing or financing activities. *[FRS 102 Appendix I].*
Performance-related condition	A condition that requires the performance of a particular level of service or units of output to be delivered, with payment of, or entitlement to, the resources conditional on that performance. *[FRS 102 Appendix I].*
Liability	A present obligation of the entity arising from past events, the settlement of which is expected to result in an outflow from the entity of resources embodying economic benefits. *[FRS 102 Appendix I].*

3.2   Scope

The accounting requirements in Section 24 apply to all government grants, defined as assistance by government in the form of a transfer of resources to an entity in return for past or future compliance with specified conditions relating to the operating activities of the entity. *[FRS 102.24.1, FRS 102 Appendix I].* In this context, the term 'government' includes government agencies and similar bodies whether local, national or international. *[FRS 102 Appendix I].*

Section 24 also distinguishes government grants from 'government assistance', defined as action by government designed to provide an economic benefit specific to an entity or range of entities qualifying under specified criteria. Examples include free technical or marketing advice, the provision of guarantees, and loans at nil or low interest rates. *[FRS 102.24.7]*.

The recognition and measurement provisions of Section 24 do not apply to government assistance that does not meet the definition of a grant and to grants in the form of government assistance that:

- cannot reasonably have a value placed on them; *[FRS 102.24.2]*

- comprise transactions with government that cannot be distinguished from the normal trading transactions of the entity; *[FRS 102.24.2]* or

- are provided in the form of benefits that are available in determining taxable profit or loss or are determined or limited on the basis of income tax liability. *[FRS 102.24.3]*.

FRS 102 does not provide examples of assistance that might be incapable of reasonable measurement or examples of transactions that are indistinguishable from the normal trading transactions of the entity; but these might include cases when financial guarantees are provided by government in the absence of any commercial alternative source; or where the entity is being favoured by a government's procurement policy. Examples are offered in the Standard of assistance provided via the tax system, being income tax holidays, investment tax credits, accelerated depreciation allowances and reduced income tax rates. *[FRS 102.24.3]*. The treatment of investment tax credits are discussed further at 3.2.1 below and in Chapter 24 at 3.4.

Whilst the recognition and measurement provisions of Section 24 do not apply to the forms of government assistance noted above, certain disclosures are required, as discussed at 3.8 below.

3.2.1   Investment tax credits

Section 24 excludes from its scope government assistance either provided by way of a reduction in taxable profit; or determined or limited according to an entity's income tax liability, citing investment tax credits as an example. *[FRS 102.24.3]*. The Standard states that taxes based on income are required to be accounted under Section 29 – *Income Tax*. *[FRS 102.24.3]*. This implies that those investment tax credits that are excluded from the scope of Section 24 would be accounted for under Section 29 (see Chapter 24). However, if government assistance is described as an investment tax credit, but it is neither determined nor limited by the entity's income tax liability nor provided in the form of an income tax deduction, such assistance should be accounted for as a government grant under Section 24.

Investment tax credits are not defined in FRS 102 and can take different forms and be subject to different terms. Sometimes a tax credit is given as a deductible expense in computing the entity's tax liability, and sometimes as a deduction from the tax liability, rather than as a deductible expense. In other cases, the assistance is chargeable to corporation tax and in others it is not. Entitlement to assistance can be determined in a variety of ways. Some investment tax credits may relate to direct investment in property, plant and equipment. Other entities may receive investment tax credits relating to research and development or other specific activities. Some credits may be realisable only through a reduction in current or future corporation tax payable, while others may be settled directly in cash if the entity is loss-making or otherwise does not have sufficient corporation tax payable to offset the credit within a certain period. Access to the credit may be limited according to the total of all taxes paid to the government providing the assistance, including employment taxes (such as PAYE and NIC) and VAT, in addition to corporation tax. There may be other conditions associated with receiving the investment tax credit, for example with respect to the conduct and continuing activities of the entity, and the credit may become repayable if ongoing conditions are not met.

This raises the question as to how an entity should assess whether a particular investment tax credit gives rise to assistance in the form of benefits that are available in determining taxable profit or loss or are determined or limited on the basis of income tax liability *[FRS 102.24.3]* and, therefore, whether Section 24 or Section 29 should be applied. In our view, such a judgment would be informed by reference to the specific terms of the arrangement including the following factors:

Feature of credit	Indicator of Section 24 treatment	Indicator of Section 29 treatment
Method of realisation	Directly settled in cash where there are insufficient taxable profits to allow credit to be fully offset, or available for set off against payroll taxes, VAT or amounts owed to government other than income taxes payable	Only available as a reduction in income taxes payable (i.e. benefit is forfeit if there are insufficient income taxes payable). However, the longer the period allowed for carrying forward unused credits, the less relevant this indicator becomes
Number of conditions not related to tax position (e.g. minimum employment, ongoing use of purchased assets)	Many	None or few
Restrictions as to nature of expenditure required to receive the grant	Highly specific	Broad criteria encompassing many different types of qualifying expenditure
Tax status of grant income	Taxable	Not taxable

In group accounts, in which entities from a number of different jurisdictions may be consolidated, it is desirable that each particular investment tax credit should be consistently accounted for, either as a government grant or as an element of income tax. However, the fact that judgement is required in making this determination may mean that predominant practice by FRS 102 reporters relating to a specific type of tax credit differs from predominant practice by FRS 102 reporters for a substantially similar credit in another jurisdiction. We believe that, in determining whether

Section 24 or Section 29 should be applied, an entity should consider the following factors in the order listed below:

- the predominant treatment by FRS 102 reporters for a specific credit in the relevant tax jurisdiction;
- if there is no predominant treatment, the group wide accounting policy for such a credit;
- in the absence of a predominant local treatment or a group wide accounting policy, the indicators listed in the table above should provide guidance.

This may occasionally mean that an entity operating in a number of territories adopts different accounting treatments for apparently similar arrangements in different countries, but it at least ensures a measure of comparability between different FRS 102 reporters operating in the same tax jurisdiction.

The treatment of investment tax credits accounted under Section 29 is discussed in Chapter 24 at 3.4.

Example 19.1:   UK research and development expenditure credit (RDEC)

The UK Finance Act 2013 introduced a new investment tax credit known as the RDEC (sometimes referred to colloquially as the 'above-the-line' tax credit) that applies on an elective basis to qualifying expenditure incurred from 1 April 2013 and is mandatory from 1 April 2016. Features of the tax credit relevant to an accounting analysis are:

- entities are generally entitled to a gross credit of 10% of qualifying R&D expenditure (with some entities entitled to a higher rate);
- the gross credit is treated as taxable income;
- the available credit is first set against the entity's corporation tax liability for the current period;
- the amount of any remaining credit (net of corporation tax) is 'capped' by reference to employment expenditure (measured by reference to the entity's PAYE and NIC liabilities);
- any remaining credit (net of corporation tax and the employment costs cap) can be carried back or carried forward to reduce the entity's corporation tax liability for certain earlier and later periods, or ceded by way of group relief;
- any unrecovered excess can be offset against the entity's other outstanding tax liabilities (e.g. PAYE and NIC); and
- any amount not recovered in any of the ways listed above is recoverable in cash from the tax authority (HMRC).

Should the RDEC credit be treated as a government grant or an element of income tax?

Analysis of these features by reference to the criteria suggested above leads us to the view that the RDEC credit is more appropriately regarded as a government grant, and therefore reflected in profit before tax. In particular, the benefits of the tax credit are capable of being realised in cash where there is insufficient corporation tax capacity; the tax credit relates to specific qualifying expenditure; and the grant income is determined on a pre-tax basis and is itself taxable.

Such an analysis requires a thorough understanding of the rules applying to the particular relief. Other seemingly similar reliefs should be treated as income taxes under Section 29 if, for example, the relief is not itself taxable; the relief could only be recovered by offset against other liabilities to corporation tax; or, where there is a cash payment alternative, the expected cash inflow approximates more closely to the value of the tax benefit rather than to the value of the expenditure incurred.

3.3   Recognition and measurement

3.3.1   *General conditions for recognition*

Section 24 requires that government grants should be recognised only when there is reasonable assurance that:

(a)   the entity will comply with the conditions attaching to them; and

(b)   the grants will be received. *[FRS 102.24.3A]*.

The standard does not define 'reasonable assurance'. However, we would not expect an entity to recognise government grants before it was at least probable (or 'more likely than not' *[FRS 102 Appendix I]*) that the entity would comply with the conditions attached to them (even though these conditions may relate to future performance and other future events) and that the grants would be received.

3.3.2   *Measurement*

All government grants are measured on initial recognition at the fair value of the asset received or receivable. *[FRS 102.24.5]*. The asset will normally be cash but could be a non-monetary asset such as land or other resources.

In this context, fair value is the amount for which an asset could be exchanged, between knowledgeable, willing parties in an arm's length transaction. Where guidance on determining the fair value of a specific asset is not available in the relevant section of FRS 102, the guidance in paragraphs 11.27 to 11.32 of FRS 102 should be used (see Chapter 8). *[FRS 102 Appendix I]*.

3.3.3   *Basis of recognition in income*

Section 24 gives entities an accounting policy choice over the method of recognition of government grants in the income statement:

•   the performance model (see 3.4 below); or

•   the accrual model (see 3.5 below).

The policy choice must be applied on a class-by-class basis. *[FRS 102.24.4]*.

A class of assets is defined in FRS 102 as a grouping of assets of a similar nature and use in an entity's operations. *[FRS 102 Appendix I]*. A class of financial asset is a grouping that is appropriate to the nature of the information disclosed and that takes into account the characteristics of the financial assets. *[FRS 102.11.48(c)]*. Therefore, it would appear that government grants of a similar nature and subject to similar conditions should be recognised in income in a similar way.

Any accounting policy choice should be made according to the requirements of Section 10 – *Accounting Policies, Estimates and Errors,* in particular, that the chosen policy results in information that is relevant to the decision-making needs of users of the financial statements and reflects the economic substance of transactions, other events and conditions, and not merely their legal form. *[FRS 102.10.4]*. In that regard, an understanding of the purpose for which the grant was awarded is a relevant consideration.

3.4   The performance model

Under this model, grant income is recognised by reference to the achievement of performance-related conditions, as follows:

- If there are no imposed, specified future performance-related conditions on the entity, then the grant is recognised in income when the grant proceeds are received or receivable.

- If there are imposed, specified future performance-related conditions on the entity, then the grant is recognised in income only when the performance-related conditions are met.

- Any grant received in advance of being able to be recognised as income under either of the above circumstances is recognised as a liability. *[FRS 102.24.5B].*

FRS 102 defines a performance-related condition as a condition that requires the performance of a particular level of service or units of output to be delivered, with payment of, or entitlement to, the resources conditional on that performance. *[FRS 102 Appendix I].*

Where the performance model is applied, a grant with no performance-related conditions will be recognised in income in full when received or receivable (i.e. when the general recognition requirements at 3.3.1 above are met), irrespective of the nature or timing of the expenditure to which it is contributing.

If a performance-related condition operates over time, the question arises as to how the grant is recognised. In the ASB staff guidance – *Grants* – they use an example (see Example 19.2 below) where a grant contributed to the build cost of a factory but with a performance-related condition of usage and employment. They note that 'the mechanism for recognising the grant during the specified period would depend on the detailed terms and conditions, but it would not generally be based on the expected useful life of the building'.[1]

One of the most relevant terms and conditions to consider will be how any potential obligation to repay the grant varies as the performance period elapses. There are two most likely scenarios:

(a)   If the potential obligation to repay the grant remains equal to the full amount of the grant throughout the performance period and that obligation is only discharged in full at the end of the performance period then, in our view, the full grant should be recognised at the end of the performance period.

(b)   If the potential obligation to repay the grant reduces as the performance period elapses then it may be appropriate to recognise the release of the grant to income over the performance period in line with the corresponding reduction in the amount potentially repayable.

Example 19.2:   Grant towards a fixed asset – the performance model

A manufacturing company secures a UK government grant of £200,000 as an incentive to open a factory in a region of high unemployment. There are no further conditions associated with the grant, other than that it is used to pay for the construction of this factory. A second grant is secured from the European Union of £130,000 in relation to the construction of the same factory. An additional condition relating to this grant is that the company continues to operate the factory for a period of five years, subject to repayment of the grant on a time-apportioned basis. The company constructs the factory for a total cost of £600,000 and begins to use it. In the same year it receives both grants. The company has a policy of depreciating buildings over a useful life of 50 years.

How should the company recognise the grants in the income statement?

Under the performance model, the whole of the UK government grant is recognised in income when the factory is opened, because this is the only condition imposed under the grant. However, the grant from the European Union is subject to an additional condition requiring use of the asset for at least five years. This grant would be recognised in income evenly over that five year period.

3.5   The accrual model

Under this model, the entity is required to classify a grant as relating to either revenue or assets. *[FRS 102.24.5C]*.

3.5.1   *Grants relating to revenue*

Grants relating to revenue should be recognised in the income statement on a systematic basis that matches them with the related costs that they are intended to compensate. *[FRS 102.24.5D]*.

Grants that become receivable as compensation for costs of losses incurred or to give immediate financial support to the entity with no future related costs should be recognised in income when it becomes receivable. *[FRS 102.24.5E]*.

Most problems of accounting for grants relate to implementing the requirement to match the grant against the costs that it is intended to compensate. This apparently simple principle can be difficult to apply in practice, because it is sometimes far from clear what the essence of the grant was and, therefore, what costs are being subsidised. Moreover, grants are sometimes given for a particular kind of expenditure that forms an element of a larger project, making the allocation a highly subjective matter. For example, government assistance that is in the form of a training grant could be recognised in income in any of the following ways:

(a)   matched against direct training costs;

(b)   taken over a period of time against the salary costs of the employees being trained, for example over the estimated duration of the project;

(c)   taken over the estimated period for which the company or the employees are expected to benefit from the training;

(d)   matched against total project costs together with other project grants receivable;

(e)   taken to income systematically over the life of the project, for example the total grant receivable may be allocated to revenue on a straight-line basis;

(f)   allocated against project costs or income over the period over which the grant is paid (instead of over the project life); or

(g)   taken to income when received in cash.

Depending on the circumstances, any of these approaches might produce an acceptable result. However, our observations on these alternative methods are as follows.

Under method (a), the grant could be recognised as income considerably in advance of its receipt, since often the major part of the direct training costs will be incurred at the beginning of a project and payment is usually made retrospectively. As the total grant receivable may be subject to adjustment, this may not be prudent or may lead to a mismatch of costs and revenues.

Methods (b) to (e) all rely on different interpretations of the expenditure to which the grant is expected to contribute, and could all represent an appropriate form of matching.

Method (f) has less to commend it, but the period of payment of the grant might in fact give an indication (in the absence of better evidence) of the duration of the project for which the expenditure is to be subsidised.

Similarly, method (g) is unlikely to be the most appropriate method *per se*, but may approximate to one of the other methods, or may, in the absence of any conclusive indication as to the expenditure intended to be subsidised by the grant, be the only practicable method that can be adopted.

In the face of the problems described above of attributing a grant to related costs, it is difficult to offer definitive guidance; entities will have to make their own judgements as to how the matching principle is to be applied. The only overriding considerations are that the method should be systematically and consistently applied, and that for material grants the policy adopted should be adequately disclosed.

3.5.2   *Grants relating to assets*

Grants relating to assets should be recognised in the income statement on a systematic basis over the expected useful life of the asset. *[FRS 102.24.5F]*.

For grants relating to depreciable assets, this means they are usually recognised as income over the periods, and in the proportions, in which depreciation on those assets is charged. Grants relating to non-depreciable assets may also require the fulfilment of certain obligations, in which case they would be recognised as income over the periods in which the costs of meeting the obligations are incurred. For example, a grant of land may be conditional upon the erection of a building on the site and it may be appropriate to recognise it as income over the life of the building.

3.6   Repayment of government grants

A government grant that becomes repayable should be recognised as a liability when the repayment meets the definition of a liability. *[FRS 102.24.5A]*.

3.7   Presentation

Where part of a grant is deferred to be released over the expected useful life of a related asset it should be recognised as deferred income and not deducted from the carrying amount of the asset. *[FRS 102.24.5G]*.

FRS 102 does not state where grant income should be presented in the income statement. The most appropriate caption will usually be as part of other operating income, possibly separately identified if significant. Wherever presented, the approach taken should be consistently applied from year to year.

3.8 Disclosure requirements

An entity is required to disclose the following in respect of government grants:

(a) the accounting policy adopted for government grants in particular whether the performance or accrual model has been adopted;

(b) the nature and amount of grants recognised in the financial statements;

(c) unfulfilled conditions and other contingencies attaching to grants that have been recognised in income; and

(d) an indication of any other forms of government assistance from which the entity has directly benefitted. *[FRS 102.24.6].*

Hence, through (d) Section 24, requires certain disclosures for all forms of government assistance even though it only includes government grants, as defined, in scope of its accounting requirements. For the purposes of item (d) above, other forms of government assistance include action by government designed to provide an economic benefit specific to an entity or a range of entities qualifying under specified criteria, such as free technical or marketing advice and the provision of guarantees, and loans at nil or low interest rates. *[FRS 102.24.7].*

4   SUMMARY OF GAAP DIFFERENCES

The key differences between FRS 102, previous UK GAAP and IFRS in accounting for government grants are set out below.

	FRS 102	*Previous UK GAAP*	*IFRS*
Scope	Specifically excludes from its definition of government grants those forms of government assistance that cannot reasonably be valued and transactions with government that are indistinguishable from the normal trading transaction of the entity	No such scope exclusions	As for FRS 102
Recognition	Accounting policy choice using either a performance model (grant is recognised as income as the performance related conditions are met) or an accrual model (grant is recognised as income when the related expenses are recognised)	Only allows accrual model	Only allows accrual model

	FRS 102	*Previous UK GAAP*	*IFRS*
Measurement	All government grants are measured on initial recognition at the fair value of the asset received or receivable *[FRS 102.24.5]*	As for FRS 102	Allows non-monetary government grants to be recorded at a nominal amount as an alternative to fair value
Presentation	Prohibits the deferred element of a grant that relates to an asset being deducted from the carrying amount of the asset	Allows the option for the deduction of the deferred element of grants from the carrying amount of the related asset but only in non Companies Act 2006 accounts	Allows two options, deferred income or deduction against the asset

References

1 Accounting and Reporting Policy: FRS 102 – *Staff Education Note 8 Government Grants*, Financial Reporting Council, para 16.

Chapter 20   Borrowing costs

List of examples

Chapter 20   Borrowing costs

1   INTRODUCTION

A common question when determining the initial measurement of an asset is whether or not borrowing (or finance) costs incurred on its acquisition or during the period of its construction should be capitalised as part of the cost of the asset or expensed through profit or loss. Section 25 – *Borrowing Costs* – specifies the accounting for borrowing costs.

2   COMPARISON BETWEEN SECTION 25, PREVIOUS UK GAAP AND IFRS

Overall, Section 25 is similar to previous UK GAAP as, consistent with UK company law, an entity has an accounting policy choice as to whether to capitalise borrowing costs when certain criteria are satisfied. This is different to IFRS since IAS 23 – *Borrowing Costs* – requires capitalisation of borrowing costs when the criteria are satisfied.

The key differences between Section 25, previous UK GAAP and IFRS are also discussed at 2.1 and 2.2 below, respectively. See 4 below for the summary of GAAP differences.

2.1   Key differences between Section 25 and previous UK GAAP

2.1.1   Qualifying assets

Under FRS 102, capitalisation of borrowing costs applies to the acquisition, construction or production of an asset provided it is a 'qualifying asset' which, depending on circumstances, may include inventories, manufacturing plants, power generation facilities, intangible assets and investment properties (see definition at 3.1 below).

Under previous UK GAAP, the concept of a 'qualifying asset' did not exist. FRS 15 – *Tangible fixed assets* – permitted finance costs directly attributable to a tangible fixed asset to be capitalised and provided guidance on the circumstances in which such costs should be capitalised. In addition, The Large and Medium-sized Companies and Groups (Accounts and Reports) Regulations 2008 (The Regulations) permits interest on capital borrowed to finance the production of any fixed or current asset insofar as it arises in the period of production. *[1 Sch 27(3), 2 Sch 35(3), 3 Sch 45(3)].*

Unlike FRS 102, the Regulations do not restrict the assets on which eligible borrowing costs can be capitalised. This means that interest could have been capitalised on 'non-qualifying' assets (e.g. financial assets). However, in practice, we believe few entities previously capitalised finance costs for assets that are not 'qualifying assets' under FRS 102.

2.1.2   Unit of account

Under FRS 102, when an entity adopts a policy of capitalisation of borrowing costs, that policy must be applied consistently to a class of qualifying assets (see 3.5.1 below).

FRS 15 required that, when an entity adopted a policy of capitalisation of finance costs, it should be applied consistently to all tangible fixed assets where finance costs fall to be capitalised. *[FRS 15.20]*.

This means that users have more flexibility under FRS 102 in deciding which assets to capitalise finance costs for than under previous UK GAAP.

2.1.3   Investment income on unspent funds

Under FRS 102, when an entity obtains funds specifically for the purpose of obtaining a qualifying asset, the amount of borrowing costs eligible for capitalisation are the actual borrowing costs incurred, less any investment income on the temporary investment of those funds not yet spent. *[FRS 102.25.2B]*.

FRS 15 was silent on whether investment income on the temporary investment of funds not yet spent should be deducted from the borrowing costs eligible for capitalisation.

2.1.4   Disclosure differences

Disclosure differences between FRS 102 and previous UK GAAP are discussed at 4 below.

2.2   Key differences between Section 25 and IFRS

2.2.1   Capitalisation of borrowing costs

Under FRS 102, capitalisation of borrowing costs directly attributable to the acquisition, construction or production of a qualifying asset is an accounting policy choice applied separately to each class of qualifying assets (see 3.2 below).

Under IFRS, capitalisation of borrowing costs is mandatory for most qualifying assets (i.e. there is no accounting policy choice). However, capitalisation is an accounting policy choice for a qualifying asset measured at fair value or inventories that are manufactured, or otherwise produced, in large quantities on a repetitive basis. *[IAS 23.4]*.

2.2.2   General borrowings

The general borrowings under FRS 102, on which the capitalisation rate is based, exclude the borrowings specifically for the purpose of obtaining either qualifying or non-qualifying assets. Therefore, only the general borrowings are included in the computation of the capitalisation rate (see 3.5.3.A below).

IFRS explicitly excludes only the borrowings that are specifically for the purpose of obtaining qualifying assets, thus together with all the general borrowings, specific borrowings to obtain non-qualifying assets are also included in computing the capitalisation rate.

2.2.3   *Expenditure on qualifying assets*

Under FRS 102, for the purpose of applying the capitalisation rate to the expenditure on the qualifying asset, the expenditure on the asset is the average carrying amount of the asset during the period, including borrowing costs previously capitalised. *[FRS 102.25.2C].*

Under IFRS, the average carrying amount of the asset during a period, including borrowing costs previously capitalised, is regarded as a reasonable approximation of the expenditures to which the capitalisation rate is applied in that period. Expenditures on a qualifying asset are explicitly limited to those expenditures that have resulted in payments of cash, transfers of other assets or the assumption of interest-bearing liabilities and reduced by any progress payments received and grants received in connection with the asset. *[IAS 23.18].*

2.2.4   *Disclosure differences*

Disclosure differences between FRS 102 and IFRS are discussed at 4 below.

3   THE REQUIREMENTS OF SECTION 25 FOR BORROWING COSTS

3.1   Terms used in Section 25

The main terms used throughout Section 25 are as follows: *[FRS 102 Appendix I]*

Term	Definition
Borrowing costs	Interest and other costs incurred by an entity in connection with the borrowing of funds.
Effective interest method	A method of calculating the amortised cost of a financial asset or a financial liability (or a group of financial assets or financial liabilities) and of allocating the interest income or interest expense over the relevant period.
Qualifying asset	An asset that necessarily takes a substantial period of time to get ready for its intended use or sale. Depending on the circumstances any of the following may be qualifying assets: • inventories; • manufacturing plants; • power generation facilities; • intangible assets; and • investment properties. Financial assets and inventories that are produced over a short period of time, are not qualifying assets. Assets that are ready for their intended use or sale when acquired are not qualifying assets.

These definitions are discussed in the relevant sections below.

3.2   Accounting for borrowing costs

For borrowing costs directly attributable to the acquisition, construction or production of a qualifying asset, Section 25 provides an accounting policy choice to either:

- capitalise those borrowing costs; or
- recognise all borrowing costs as an expense in profit or loss in the period in which they are incurred. *[FRS 102.25.2].*

Accordingly, all borrowing costs should be recognised as an expense in profit or loss in the period in which they are incurred unless a policy of capitalising borrowing costs is adopted. In addition, borrowing costs that are not directly attributable to a qualifying asset must be expensed as incurred.

Where an entity adopts a policy of capitalisation of borrowing costs for qualifying assets, it should be applied consistently to a class of qualifying assets. *[FRS 102.25.2].* The definition of class is discussed at 3.5.1 below.

Since an entity has a policy choice, a change in accounting policy (i.e. capitalisation versus expense) would require retrospective restatements in accordance with Section 10 – *Accounting Policies, Estimates and Errors. [FRS 102.10.11(d), 12].*

3.3   Scope of Section 25

Borrowing costs are interest and other costs incurred by an entity in connection with the borrowing of funds. Borrowing costs include:

- interest expense calculated using the effective interest method as described in Section 11 – *Basic Financial Instruments* (see Chapter 8);
- finance charges in respect of finance leases recognised in accordance with Section 20 – *Leases* (see Chapter 16); and
- exchange differences arising from foreign currency borrowings to the extent that they are regarded as an adjustment to interest costs (see 3.5.4 below). *[FRS 102.25.1].*

Section 25 does not deal with the actual or imputed costs of equity used to fund the acquisition or construction of an asset. This would mean that any distributions or other payments made in respect of equity instruments, as defined by Section 22 – *Liabilities and Equity*, are not within the scope of Section 25. Conversely, interest and dividends payable on instruments that are legally equity but classified as financial liabilities under FRS 102 appear to be within the scope of Section 25 (see 3.5.5.D below).

When an entity adopts a policy of capitalising borrowing costs, Section 25 addresses whether or not to capitalise borrowing costs as part of the cost of the asset. The identification and measurement of finance costs are not directly dealt with in Section 25. It does not address many of the ways in which an entity may finance its operations or other finance costs that it may incur. Examples of these other finance costs and their eligibility for capitalisation under Section 25 are discussed in 3.5.5 below.

Section 25 does not preclude the classification of costs, other than those it identifies, as borrowing costs. However, they must meet the basic criterion in the standard, i.e. that they are 'costs that are directly attributable to the acquisition, construction or production of a qualifying asset', which would, therefore, preclude treating the unwinding of discounts on provisions as borrowing costs. Many unwinding discounts are treated as finance costs in profit or loss. These include discounts relating to various provisions such as those for onerous leases and decommissioning costs. These finance costs will not be borrowing costs under Section 25 because they do not arise in respect of funds borrowed by the entity that can be attributed to a qualifying asset. Therefore, they cannot be capitalised. *[FRS 102.25.1, 2].* In addition, as in the case of exchange differences, capitalisation of such costs should be permitted only 'to the extent that they are regarded as an adjustment to interest costs' (see 3.5.4 below). *[FRS 102.25.1].*

3.4   Definition of a qualifying asset

Section 25 defines a qualifying asset as an asset that necessarily takes a substantial period of time to get ready for its intended use or sale. Depending on the circumstances any of the following may be qualifying assets:

* inventories;
* manufacturing plants;
* power generation facilities;
* intangible assets; and
* investment properties. *[FRS 102 Appendix I].*

Financial assets and inventories that are produced over a short period of time, are not qualifying assets. Assets that are ready for their intended use or sale when acquired are also not qualifying assets. *[FRS 102 Appendix I].*

Section 25 is silent as to whether other types of assets not mentioned in the definition (e.g. owner occupied property, biological assets) can be qualifying assets. In our view, there is nothing to prohibit other assets meeting the definition of a qualifying asset.

Section 25 does not define 'substantial period of time' and this will therefore require the exercise of judgement after considering the specific facts and circumstances. However, an asset that normally takes twelve months or more to be ready for its intended use will usually be a qualifying asset.

3.5   Borrowing costs eligible for capitalisation

Borrowing costs are eligible for capitalisation if they are directly attributable to the acquisition, construction or production of a qualifying asset (whether or not the funds have been borrowed specifically). *[FRS 102.25.2].*

Section 25 starts from the premise that directly attributable borrowing costs are those that would have been avoided if the expenditure on the qualifying asset had not been made. *[FRS 102.25.2A].* Recognising that it may not always be easy to identify a direct relationship between particular borrowings and a qualifying asset and to determine the borrowings that could otherwise have been avoided, Section 25 includes separate requirements for specific borrowings and general borrowings.

3.5.1   *Class of qualifying assets*

Where an entity adopts a policy of capitalisation of borrowing costs, it should be applied consistently to a class of qualifying assets. *[FRS 102.25.2]*. There is no specific definition of a 'class of qualifying assets'. However, a 'class of assets' is defined as 'a grouping of assets of a similar nature and use in an entity's operations.' *[FRS 102 Appendix I]*. Therefore, it may be possible to have a capitalisation policy only in relation to plant under construction but not to machinery under construction or inventories that are qualifying assets.

3.5.2   *Specific borrowings*

To the extent that an entity borrows funds specifically for the purpose of obtaining a qualifying asset, the borrowing costs that are directly related to that qualifying asset can be readily identified. The borrowing costs eligible for capitalisation are the actual borrowing costs incurred on those specific borrowings during the period less any investment income on the temporary investment of those borrowings. *[FRS 102.25.2B]*.

Entities frequently borrow funds in advance of expenditure on qualifying assets and may temporarily invest the borrowings. The standard makes it clear that any investment income earned on the temporary investment of those borrowings needs to be deducted from the borrowing costs incurred and only the net amount capitalised (see Example 20.2 below).

There is no restriction in Section 25 on the type of investments in which the funds can be invested but, in our view, to ensure that the funds are specific borrowings, the investment must be of a nature that does not expose the principal amount to the risk of not being recovered. The more risky the investment, the greater is the likelihood that the borrowing is not specific to the qualifying asset. If the investment returns a loss rather than income, such losses are not added to the borrowing costs to be capitalised.

3.5.3   *General borrowings*

To the extent that funds applied to obtain a qualifying asset form part of the entity's general borrowings, Section 25 requires the application of a capitalisation rate to the expenditure on that asset in determining the amount of borrowing costs eligible for capitalisation. However, the amount of borrowing costs an entity capitalises during a period cannot exceed the amount of borrowing costs it incurred during that period. *[FRS 102.25.2C]*.

The capitalisation rate used in an accounting period should be the weighted average of rates applicable to the general borrowings of the entity that are outstanding during the period, other than borrowings made specifically for the purpose of obtaining a qualifying asset. The capitalisation rate is then applied to the expenditure on the qualifying asset. For this purpose, the expenditure on the asset is the average carrying amount of the asset during the period, including borrowing costs previously capitalised. *[FRS 102.25.2C]*.

Section 25 does not provide specific guidance regarding interest income earned from temporarily investing excess general funds. However, any interest income earned is unlikely to be directly attributable to the acquisition or construction of a qualifying asset. In addition, the capitalisation rate required by Section 25 focuses on the borrowings of the entity outstanding during the period of construction or acquisition and does not include temporary investments. As such, borrowing costs capitalised should not be reduced by interest income earned from the investment of general borrowings nor should such income be included in determining the appropriate capitalisation rate.

In some circumstances all borrowings made by the group can be taken into account in determining the weighted average of the borrowing costs. In other circumstances only those borrowings made by individual subsidiaries may be taken into account. It is likely that this will largely be determined by the extent to which borrowings are made centrally (and, perhaps, interest expenses met in the same way) and passed through to individual group companies via intercompany accounts and intra-group loans. The capitalisation rate is discussed further at 3.5.3.D below.

There may be practical difficulties in identifying a direct relationship between particular borrowings and a qualifying asset and in determining the borrowings that could otherwise have been avoided. This could be the case if the financing activity of an entity is co-ordinated centrally, for example, if an entity borrows to meet its funding requirements as a whole and the construction of the qualifying asset is financed out of general borrowings. Other circumstances that may cause difficulties are identified by the standard as follows:

- a group has a treasury function that uses a range of debt instruments to borrow funds at varying rates of interest and lends those funds on various bases to other entities in the group; or

- loans are denominated in or linked to foreign currencies and the group operates in highly inflationary economies or there are fluctuations in exchange rates.

In these circumstances, determining which borrowing costs are attributable to the acquisition of a qualifying asset may be difficult and require the exercise of judgement.

3.5.3.A   Definition of general borrowings

As noted at 3.5.3 above, determining general borrowings will not always be straightforward and, as a result, the determination of the amount of borrowing costs that are directly attributable to the acquisition of a qualifying asset is difficult and the exercise of judgement is required.

Section 25 explicitly states that the capitalisation rate used shall be the weighted average of rates applicable to the entity's 'general borrowings that are outstanding during the period' which means that any specific borrowings related to obtaining either qualifying assets or non-qualifying assets would be excluded. *[FRS 102.25.2C]*. This is similar with the principle used under previous UK GAAP.

The general borrowings under FRS 15 explicitly exclude borrowings that are specifically for the purpose of constructing or acquiring other tangible fixed assets (e.g. lease liabilities) or for other specific purposes, e.g. loans to hedge foreign investments. Therefore, only the general borrowings are included in the computation of capitalisation rate. *[FRS 15.23]*.

Under IFRS, IAS 23 is not explicit on the treatment of borrowings used to purchase a specific non-qualifying asset, however, it is explicit that only specific borrowings used to acquire another qualifying assets would be excluded from the determination of the capitalisation rate. *[IAS 23.14].*

The key objective when dealing with general borrowings is to determine a reasonable measure of the directly attributable finance costs. For this purpose, it would appear that both approaches described above (i.e. whether to include or exclude any specific borrowings related to obtaining non-qualifying assets when computing the capitalisation rate) are acceptable and both are used in practice. Complying with the requirement of Section 8 – *Notes to the Financial Statements* – an entity should therefore include an explanation in its accounting policies the judgement used in determining the measure of the directly attributable finance costs involving general borrowings (see 3.7.2 below) which must be consistently applied.

Another issue that arises is whether a specific borrowing undertaken to obtain a qualifying asset ever changes its nature into a general borrowing. Differing views exist as to whether or not borrowings change their nature throughout the period they are outstanding. Some consider that once the asset for which the borrowing was incurred has been completed, and the entity chooses to use its funds on constructing other assets rather than repaying the loan, this changes the nature of the loan into a general borrowing. However, to the extent that the contract links the repayment of the loan to specific proceeds generated by the entity, its nature as a specific borrowing would be preserved. Others take the view that once the borrowing has been classified as specific, its nature does not change while it remains outstanding. Management will therefore need to exercise judgement in determining its policy and assessing the nature of the loans when construction activity is completed.

3.5.3.B   Expenditure on the asset

Section 25 explicitly states that for purposes of applying the capitalisation rate to the expenditure on the qualifying asset, 'the expenditure on asset is the average carrying amount of the asset during the period, including borrowing costs previously capitalised'. *[FRS 102.25.2C].*

Accordingly, unlike in IFRS, expenditure is not restricted to that resulting in the payment of cash, the transfer of other assets or the assumption of interest-bearing liabilities. Therefore, in principle, costs of a qualifying asset that have only been accrued but have not yet been paid in cash would also be included although by definition, no interest can have been incurred on an accrued payment. The same principle can be applied to non-interest bearing liabilities e.g. non-interest-bearing trade payables or retention money that is not payable until the asset is completed.

3.5.3.C   Assets carried below cost in the statement of financial position

An asset may be recognised in the financial statements during the period of production on a basis other than cost, i.e. it may have been written down below cost as a result of being impaired. An asset may be impaired when its expected ultimate cost, including costs to complete and the estimated capitalised interest thereon, exceed its estimated recoverable amount or net realisable value (see 3.6.2.A below).

The question then arises whether the calculation of interest to be capitalised should be based on the cost or carrying amount of the impaired asset. It could be argued that in this case, cost should be used, as this is the amount that the entity or group has had to finance. However, Section 25 explicitly states that the expenditure on the asset is the average carrying amount (not the cost) of the asset during the period. Nevertheless, in the case of an impaired asset, continued capitalisation based on cost (instead of average carrying value) may well necessitate a further impairment. Accordingly, although the amount capitalised will be different, this should not affect net profit and loss as this is simply a paper allocation of costs between finance costs and impairment.

3.5.3.D   Calculation of capitalisation rate

As noted at 3.5.3 above, determining general borrowings will not always be straightforward, it will be necessary to exercise judgement to meet the main objective – a reasonable measure of the directly attributable finance costs.

The following example illustrates the practical application of the method of calculating the amount of finance costs to be capitalised:

Example 20.1:   Calculation of capitalisation rate (no investment income)

On 1 April 2015 a company engages in the development of a property, which is expected to take five years to complete, at a cost of £6,000,000. The statements of financial position at 31 December 2014 and 31 December 2015, prior to capitalisation of interest, are as follows:

	31 December 2014 £	31 December 2015 £
Development property	–	1,200,000
Other assets	6,000,000	6,000,000
	6,000,000	7,200,000
Loans		
5.5% debenture stock	2,500,000	2,500,000
Bank loan at 6% p.a.	–	1,200,000
Bank loan at 7% p.a.	1,000,000	1,000,000
	3,500,000	4,700,000
Shareholders' equity	2,500,000	2,500,000

The bank loan with an effective interest rate at 6% was drawn down to match the development expenditure on 1 April 2015, 1 July 2015 and 1 October 2015.

Expenditure was incurred on the development as follows:

	£
1 April 2015	600,000
1 July 2015	400,000
1 October 2015	200,000
	1,200,000

If the bank loan at 6% p.a. is a new borrowing specifically to finance the development then the amount of interest to be capitalised for the year ended 31 December 2015 would be the amount of interest charged by the bank of £42,000 ((£600,000 × 6% × 9/12) + (£400,000 × 6% × 6/12) + (£200,000 × 6% × 3/12)).

However, if all the borrowings were general (i.e. the bank loan at 6% was not specific to the development) and would have been avoided but for the development, then the amount of interest to be capitalised would be:

$$\frac{\text{Total interest expense for period}}{\text{Weighted average total borrowings}} \times \text{Development expenditure}$$

Total interest expense for the period

	£
£2,500,000 × 5.5%	137,500
£1,200,000 (as above)	42,000
£1,000,000 × 7%	70,000
	249,500

Therefore the capitalisation rate would be calculated as:

$$\frac{249,500}{3,500,000 + 700,000} = 5.94\%$$

The capitalisation rate would then be applied to the expenditure on the qualifying asset, resulting in an amount to be capitalised of £41,580 as follows:

	£
£600,000 × 5.94% × 9/12	26,730
£400,000 × 5.94% × 6/12	11,880
£200,000 × 5.94% × 3/12	2,970
	41,580

In this example, all borrowings are at fixed rates of interest and the period of construction extends at least until the end of the period, simplifying the calculation. The same principle is applied if borrowings are at floating rates i.e. only the interest costs incurred during that period, and the weighted average borrowings for that period, will be taken into account.

Note that shareholders' equity (i.e. equity instruments – see further discussion in 3.5.5.D below) cannot be taken into account and at least part of the outstanding borrowings is presumed to finance the acquisition or construction of qualifying assets – unless they are specific borrowings (see discussion in 3.5.3.A above).

The above example also assumes that loans are drawn down to match expenditure on the qualifying asset. If, however, a loan is drawn down immediately and investment income is received on the unapplied funds, then the calculation differs from that in Example 20.1. This is illustrated in Example 20.2.

Example 20.2:   Calculation of amount to be capitalised – specific borrowings with investment income

On 1 April 2015 a company engages in the development of a property, which is expected to take five years to complete, at a cost of £6,000,000. In this example, a bank loan of £6,000,000 with an effective interest rate at 6% was taken out on 31 March 2015 and fully drawn. The total interest charge for the year ended 31 December 2015 was consequently £270,000.

However, investment income was also earned at 3% on the unapplied funds during the period as follows:

	£
£5,400,000 × 3% × 3/12	40,500
£5,000,000 × 3% × 3/12	37,500
£4,800,000 × 3% × 3/12	36,000
	114,000

Consequently, the amount of interest to be capitalised for the year ended 31 December 2015 is:

	£
Total interest charge	270,000
Less: investment income	(114,000)
	156,000

3.5.4   Exchange differences as a borrowing cost

An entity may borrow funds in a currency that is not its functional currency e.g. a Sterling loan financing a development in a company which has Euro as its functional currency. This may have been done on the basis that, over the period of the development, the borrowing costs, even after allowing for exchange differences, were expected to be less than the interest cost of an equivalent Euro loan.

Section 25 defines borrowing costs as including exchange differences arising from foreign currency borrowings to the extent that they are regarded as an adjustment to interest costs. *[FRS 102.25.1(c)].* Section 25 does not expand on this point. Therefore, judgement will be required in its application and appropriate disclosure of accounting policies and judgements would provide users with the information they need to understand the financial statements.

In our view, as exchange rate movements are partly a function of differential interest rates, in many circumstances the foreign exchange differences on directly attributable borrowings will be an adjustment to interest costs that can meet the definition of borrowing costs. However, care is needed if there are fluctuations in exchange rates that cannot be attributed to interest rate differentials. In such cases, we believe that a practical approach is to limit exchange losses taken as borrowing costs such that the total borrowing costs capitalised do not exceed the amount of borrowing costs that would be incurred on functional currency equivalent borrowings.

If this approach is used and the construction of the qualifying asset takes more than one accounting period, there could be situations where in one period only a portion of foreign exchange differences could be capitalised. However, in subsequent years, if the borrowings are assessed on a cumulative basis, foreign exchange losses previously expensed may now meet the recognition criteria. The two methods of dealing with this are illustrated in Example 20.3 below.

In our view, whether foreign exchange gains and losses are assessed on a discrete period basis or cumulatively over the construction period is a matter of accounting policy, which must be consistently applied. Section 8 requires clear disclosure of significant accounting policies and judgements that are relevant to an understanding of the financial statements (see 3.7.2 below).

Example 20.3:   Foreign exchange differences in more than one period

Method A – The discrete period approach

The amount of foreign exchange differences eligible for capitalisation is determined for each period separately. Foreign exchange losses that did not meet the criteria for capitalisation in previous years are not capitalised in subsequent years.

Method B – The cumulative approach

The borrowing costs to be capitalised are assessed on a cumulative basis based on the cumulative amount of interest expense that would have been incurred had the entity borrowed in its functional currency. The amount of foreign exchange differences capitalised cannot exceed the amount of foreign exchange losses incurred on a cumulative basis at the end of the reporting period. The cumulative approach looks at the construction project as a whole as the unit of account ignoring the occurrence of reporting dates. Consequently, the amount of the foreign exchange differences eligible for capitalisation as an adjustment to the borrowing cost in the period is an estimate, which can change as the exchange rates vary over the construction period.

An illustrative calculation of the amount of foreign exchange differences that may be capitalised under Method A and Method B is set out below.

	Year 1 £	Year 2 £	Total £
Interest expense in foreign currency (A)	25,000	25,000	50,000
Hypothetical interest expense in functional currency (B)	30,000	30,000	60,000
Foreign exchange loss (C)	6,000	3,000	9,000
Method A – Discrete Approach			
Foreign exchange loss capitalised – lower of C and (B minus A)	5,000	3,000	8,000
Foreign exchange loss expensed	1,000	–	1,000
Method B – Cumulative Approach			
Foreign exchange loss capitalised	5,000 *	4,000 **	9,000
Foreign exchange loss expensed	1,000	(1,000)	–

*   Lower of C and (B minus A) in Year 1

**   Lower of C and (B minus A) in total across the two years. In this example this represents the sum of the foreign exchange loss of £3,000 capitalised using the discrete approach plus the £1,000 not capitalised in year 1.

3.5.5   Other finance costs as a borrowing cost

An entity may incur other finance costs. Section 25 does not specifically address these. Below are examples of other finance costs including discussion on their eligibility for capitalisation under Section 25.

3.5.5.A   Derivative financial instruments

Many derivative financial instruments such as interest rate swaps, floors, caps and collars are commonly used to manage interest rate risk on borrowings. The most straightforward and commonly encountered derivative financial instrument used to manage interest rate risk is a floating to fixed interest rate swap, as in the following example.

Example 20.4: *Floating to fixed interest rate swaps*

Entity A has borrowed £4 million for five years at a floating interest rate to fund the construction of a building. In order to hedge the cash flow interest rate risk arising from these borrowings, A has entered into a matching pay-fixed receive-floating interest rate swap, based on the same underlying nominal sum and duration as the original borrowing, that effectively converts the interest on the borrowings to fixed rate. The net effect of the periodic cash settlements resulting from the hedged and hedging instruments is as if A had borrowed £4 million at a fixed rate of interest.

Section 25 is silent on the use of hedging instruments in determining directly attributable borrowing costs. Section 12 – *Other Financial Instruments Issues* – sets out the basis on which derivatives are recognised and measured. Accounting for hedges is discussed in Chapter 8.

An entity may consider that a specific derivative financial instrument, such as an interest rate swap, is directly attributable to the acquisition, construction or production of a qualifying asset. If the instrument does not meet the conditions for hedge accounting then the effects on income will be different from those if it does, and they will also be dissimilar from year to year. What is the impact of the derivative on borrowing costs eligible for capitalisation? In particular, does the accounting treatment of the derivative financial instrument affect the amount available for capitalisation? If hedge accounting is not adopted, does this affect the amount available for capitalisation?

The following examples illustrate the potential differences.

Example 20.5: *Cash flow hedge of variable-rate debt using an interest rate swap*

Entity A is constructing a building and expects it to take 18 months to complete. To finance the construction, on 1 January 2014, the entity issues an eighteen month, £20,000,000 variable-rate note payable, due on 30 June 2015 at a floating rate of interest plus a margin of 1%. At that date the market rate of interest is 8%. Interest payment dates and interest rate reset dates occur on 1 January and 1 July until maturity. The principal is due at maturity. On 1 January 2014, the entity also enters into an eighteen month interest rate swap with a notional amount of £10,000,000 from which it will receive periodic payments at the floating rate and make periodic payments at a fixed rate of 9%, with settlement and rate reset dates every 30 June and 31 December. The fair value of the swap is zero at inception.

On 1 January 2014, the debt is recorded at £20,000,000. No entry is required for the swap on that date because its fair value was zero at inception.

During the eighteen month period, floating interest rates change as follows:

	Cash payments	
	Floating rate on principal	Rate paid by Entity A
Period to 30 June 2014	8%	9%
Period to 31 Dec 2014	8.5%	9.5%
Period to 30 June 2015	9.75%	10.75%

Under the interest rate swap, Entity A receives interest at the market floating rate as above and pays at 9% on the nominal amount of £10,000,000 throughout the period.

At 31 December 2014, the swap has a fair value of £37,500, reflecting the fact that it is now in the money as Entity A is expected to receive a net cash inflow of this amount in the period until the instrument is terminated. There are no further changes in interest rates prior to the maturity of the swap and the fair value of the swap declines to zero at 30 June 2015. Note that this example excludes the effect of issue costs and discounting. In addition, it is assumed that, if Entity A is entitled to, and applies, hedge accounting, there will be no ineffectiveness.

The cash flows incurred by the entity on its borrowing and interest rate swap are as follows:

| | Cash payments | | |
	Interest on principal	Interest rate swap (net)	Total
	£	£	£
30 June 2014	900,000	50,000	950,000
31 Dec 2014	950,000	25,000	975,000
30 June 2015	1,075,000	(37,500)	1,037,500
Total	2,925,000	37,500	2,962,500

There are a number of different ways in which Entity A could calculate the borrowing costs eligible for capitalisation, including the following.

(i)   The interest rate swap meets the conditions for, and entity A applies, hedge accounting. The finance costs eligible for capitalisation as borrowing costs will be £1,925,000 in the year to 31 December 2014 and £1,037,500 in the period ended 30 June 2015.

(ii) Entity A does not apply hedge accounting. Therefore, it will reflect the fair value of the swap in income in the year ended 31 December 2014, reducing the net finance costs by £37,500 to £1,887,500 and increasing the finance costs by an equivalent amount in 2015 to £1,075,000. However, it considers that it is inappropriate to reflect the fair value of the swap in borrowing costs eligible for capitalisation so it capitalises costs based on the net cash cost on an accruals accounting basis. In this case this will give the same result as in (i) above.

(iii) Entity A does not apply hedge accounting and considers only the costs incurred on the borrowing, not the interest rate swap, as eligible for capitalisation. The borrowing costs eligible for capitalisation would be £1,850,000 in 2014 and £1,075,000 in 2015.

In our view, all these methods are valid interpretations of Section 25; however, the preparer will need to consider the most appropriate method in the particular circumstances after taking into consideration the discussion below.

In particular, if using method (ii), it is necessary to demonstrate that the gains or losses on the derivative financial instrument are directly attributable to the construction of a qualifying asset. In making this assessment it is necessary to consider the term of the derivative and this method may not be appropriate if the derivative has a different term to the underlying directly attributable borrowing.

Based on the facts in this example, method (iii) appears to be inconsistent with the underlying principle of Section 25 – that the costs eligible for capitalisation are those costs that could have been avoided if the expenditure on the qualifying asset had not been made – and is not therefore appropriate. *[FRS 102.25.2A]*. However, it may not be possible to demonstrate that the gains or losses on a specific derivative financial instrument are directly attributable to a particular qualifying asset, rather than being used by the entity to manage its interest rate exposure on a more general basis. In such a case, method (iii) may be an appropriate method to use.

Note that method (i) appeared to be permitted under US GAAP for fair value hedges. IAS 23 makes reference in its basis of conclusion that under US GAAP derivative gains and losses (arising from the effective portion of a derivative instrument that qualifies as a fair value hedge) are considered to be part of the capitalised interest cost. *[IAS 23.BC21]*.

Whichever policy is chosen by an entity, it needs to be consistently applied in similar situations.

3.5.5.B   *Gains and losses on derecognition of borrowings*

If an entity repays borrowings early, in whole or in part, then it may recognise a gain or loss on the early settlement. Such gains or losses include amounts attributable to expected future interest rates; in other words, it includes an estimated prepayment of the future cash flows under the instrument. The gain or loss is a function of relative interest rates and how the interest rate of the instrument differs from current and anticipated future interest rates. There may be circumstances in which a loan is repaid while the qualifying asset is still under construction. Section 25 does not address this issue.

In our view, gains and losses on derecognition of borrowings are generally not eligible for capitalisation. Decisions to repay borrowings early are not usually directly attributable to the qualifying asset but to other circumstances of the entity.

The same approach would be applied to gains and losses arising from a refinancing when there is a substantial modification of the terms of borrowings.

3.5.5.C   *Gains or losses on termination of derivative financial instruments*

If an entity terminates a derivative financial instrument, for example, an interest rate swap, before the end of the term of the instrument, it will usually have to either make or receive a payment, depending on the fair value of the instrument at that time. This fair value is typically based on expected future interest rates; in other words it is an estimated prepayment of the future cash flows under the instrument.

The treatment of the gain or loss for the purposes of capitalisation will depend on the following:

- the basis on which the entity capitalises the gains and losses associated with derivative financial instruments attributable to qualifying assets (see 3.5.5.A above); and

- whether the derivative is associated with a borrowing that has also been terminated.

Entities must adopt a treatment that is consistent with their policy for capitalising the gains and losses from derivative financial instruments that are attributable to qualifying investments (see 3.5.5.A above).

The accounting under Section 12 will differ depending on whether the instrument has been designated as a hedge or not; in the former case, and assuming that the borrowing has not also been repaid, the entity will usually continue to account for the cumulative gain or loss on the instrument as if the hedge were still in place. In such a case, the amounts that are reclassified from other comprehensive income will be eligible for capitalisation for the remainder of the period of construction.

If the entity is not hedge accounting for the derivative financial instrument, but considers it to be directly attributable to the construction of the qualifying asset then it will have to consider whether part of the gain or loss relates to a period after construction is complete.

If the underlying borrowing is also terminated then the gain or loss will not be capitalised and the treatment will mirror that applied on derecognition of the borrowing, as described in 3.5.5.B above.

3.5.5.D   Dividends payable on shares classified as financial liabilities

An entity might finance its operations in whole or in part by the issue of preference shares and in some circumstances these will be classified as financial liabilities (see Chapter 8). In some circumstances the dividends payable on these instruments would meet the definition of borrowing costs. For example, an entity might have funded the development of a qualifying asset by issuing redeemable preference shares that are redeemable at the option of the holder and so are classified as financial liabilities under Section 22. In this case, the 'dividends' would be treated as interest and meet the definition of borrowing costs and so should be capitalised following the principles on specific borrowings discussed at 3.5.2 above.

Companies with outstanding preference shares which are treated as liabilities under Section 22 might subsequently obtain a qualifying asset. In such cases, these preference share liabilities would be considered to be part of the company's general borrowings. The related 'dividends' would meet the definition of borrowing costs and could be capitalised following the principles on general borrowings discussed at 3.5.3 above – i.e. that they are directly attributable to a qualifying asset.

If these shares were irredeemable, but still treated as liabilities under Section 22 (see Chapter 8), and treated as general borrowings, it would generally be difficult to demonstrate that such borrowings would have been avoided if the expenditure on the qualifying asset had not been made. In such a case capitalisation of related 'dividends' would not be appropriate, unless the qualifying asset is demonstrably funded (at least partly) by such borrowing. In cases where such instruments were just a part of a general borrowing 'pool', it would be appropriate to include applicable 'dividends' in determining the borrowing costs eligible for capitalisation (see 3.5.2 above), notwithstanding the fact that these instruments are irredeemable, provided that:

- at least part of any of the general borrowings in the pool was applied to obtain the qualifying asset; or
- it can be demonstrated that at least part of the fund specifically allocated for repaying any of the redeemable part of the pool was used to obtain the qualifying asset.

Capitalisation of dividends or other payments made in respect of any instruments that are classified as equity in accordance with Section 22 is not appropriate as these instruments would not meet the definition of financial liabilities. In addition, as discussed at 3.3 above, Section 25 does not deal with the actual or imputed cost of equity, including preferred capital not classified as a liability.

3.5.6   Capitalisation of borrowing costs in hyperinflationary economies

While Section 31 – *Hyperinflation* – provides guidance in situations where an entity's functional currency is the currency of a hyperinflationary economy, it does not provide specific guidance on the impact of inflation to accounting for borrowing costs. Thus, entities may wish to consider the specific guidance in IFRS. Under IFRS, In situations where IAS 29 – *Financial Reporting in Hyperinflationary Economies* – applies, an entity needs to distinguish between borrowing costs that compensate for inflation and those incurred in order to acquire or construct a qualifying a qualifying asset.

IAS 29 states that '[t]he impact of inflation is usually recognised in borrowing costs. It is not appropriate both to restate the capital expenditure financed by borrowing and to capitalise that part of the borrowing costs that compensates for the inflation during the same period. This part of the borrowing costs is recognised as an expense in the period in which the costs are incurred.' *[IAS 29.21]*.

Accordingly, the borrowing costs that can be capitalised should be restricted and the entity must expense the part of borrowing costs that compensate for inflation during the same period.

3.5.7 Group considerations

3.5.7.A Borrowings in one company and development in another

A question that can arise in practice is whether it is appropriate to capitalise interest in the group financial statements on borrowings that appear in the financial statements of a different group entity from that carrying out the development. Based on the underlying principle of Section 25, capitalisation in such circumstances would only be appropriate if the amount capitalised fairly reflected the interest cost of the group on borrowings from third parties that could have been avoided if the expenditure on the qualifying asset were not made.

Although it may be appropriate to capitalise interest in the group financial statements, the entity carrying out the development should not capitalise any interest in its own financial statements as it has no borrowings. If, however, the entity has intra-group borrowings then interest on such borrowings may be capitalised in its own financial statements.

3.5.7.B Qualifying assets held by joint ventures

A number of sectors carry out developments through the medium of joint ventures (see Chapter 11) – this is particularly common with property developments. In such cases, the joint venture may be financed principally by equity and the joint venturers may have financed their participation in this equity through borrowings.

In situations where the joint venture is classified as a jointly controlled entity (JCE) in accordance with Section 15 – *Investments in Joint Ventures*, it is not appropriate to capitalise interest in the JCE on the borrowings of the venturers as the interest charge is not a cost of the JCE. Neither would it be appropriate to capitalise interest in the financial statements of the venturers, whether separate or consolidated financial statements, because the qualifying asset does not belong to them. The investing entities have an investment in a financial asset (i.e. an equity instrument of another entity) which is excluded by Section 25 from being a qualifying asset (see 3.4 above).

In situations where the joint venture is classified as a jointly controlled operation (JCO) or jointly controlled assets (JCA) in accordance with Section 15 and the venturers are accounting for their own and their share of the assets, liabilities, revenue and expenses, then the venturers should capitalise borrowing costs incurred that relate to their own and their share of any qualifying asset. Borrowing costs eligible for capitalisation would be based on the venturer's obligation for the loans of such JCO or JCA and any direct borrowings of the venturer itself if the venturer funds part of the acquisition of such joint venture's qualifying asset.

3.6   Commencement, suspension and cessation of capitalisation

3.6.1   *Commencement of capitalisation*

Section 25 requires that an entity capitalise borrowing costs as part of the cost of a qualifying asset from the point when:

- it first incurs both expenditure on the asset and borrowing costs; and
- undertakes activities necessary to prepare the asset for its intended use or sale. *[FRS 102.25.2D(a)]*.

Section 25 has no further guidance on 'activities necessary to prepare an asset for its intended use or sale'. However, some guidance is provided by IAS 23 which states that the activities necessary to prepare an asset for its intended use or sale can include more than the physical construction of the asset. Necessary activities can start before the commencement of physical construction and include, for example, technical and administrative work such as obtaining permits. This does not mean that borrowing costs can be capitalised if it is not expected that permits that are necessary for the construction will be obtained. Following the general principle in capitalisation and recognition of an asset, borrowing costs are capitalised as part of the cost of the asset when it is probable that they will result in future economic benefits to the entity and the costs can be measured reliably. *[FRS 102.2.27]*. Therefore, in assessing whether borrowing costs can be capitalised in advance of obtaining permits – assuming the borrowing costs otherwise meet the criteria – a judgement must be made, at the date the expenditures are incurred, as to whether it is sufficiently probable that the relevant permits will be granted. Conversely, if the granting of necessary permits is no longer expected, capitalisation of borrowing costs should cease and the asset should be tested for impairment.

Borrowing costs may not be capitalised during a period in which there are no activities that change the condition of the asset. For example a house-builder or property developer may not capitalise borrowing costs on its 'land bank' i.e. that land which is held for future development. Borrowing costs incurred while land is under development are capitalised during the period in which activities related to the development are being undertaken. However, borrowing costs incurred while land acquired for building purposes is held without any associated development activity represent a holding cost of the land and hence would be considered a period cost (i.e. expensed as incurred). *[IAS 23.19]*.

An entity may make a payment to a third party contractor before that contractor commences construction activities. It is unlikely to be appropriate to capitalise borrowing costs in such situation until the contractor commences activities that are necessary to prepare the asset for its intended use or sale.

3.6.2   *Suspension of capitalisation*

Section 25 states that capitalisation should be suspended during extended periods in which active development of the asset has paused. *[FRS 102.25.2D(b)]*. No further guidance is provided. For example, Section 25 does not distinguish between extended periods of interruption (when capitalisation would be suspended) and periods of temporary delay that are a necessary part of preparing the asset for its intended purpose (when capitalisation is not normally suspended).

Applying guidance provided by IAS 23, capitalisation continues during periods when inventory is undergoing slow transformation – for example, inventories taking an extended time to mature such as Scotch whisky or Cognac. Similarly, capitalisation would continue in the case of a bridge construction delayed by temporary adverse weather conditions, where such conditions are common in the region. *[IAS 23.21]*. Borrowing costs incurred during extended periods of interruption caused, for example, by a lack of funding or a strategic decision to hold back project developments during a period of economic downturn are not considered a necessary part of preparing the asset for its intended purpose and should not be capitalised.

3.6.2.A   *Impairment considerations*

When it is determined that capitalisation is appropriate, an entity continues to capitalise borrowing costs that are directly attributable to the acquisition, construction or production of a qualifying asset as part of the cost of the asset even if the capitalisation causes the expected ultimate cost of the asset to exceed its recoverable amount exceeds its net realisable value (inventories) or recoverable amount (all other qualifying assets.

If the carrying amount of the qualifying asset exceeds its recoverable amount or net realisable value (depending on the type of asset), the asset must be written down in accordance with the Section 27 – *Impairment of Assets* (see Chapter 22).

3.6.3   **Cessation of capitalisation**

Section 25 requires capitalisation to cease when substantially all the activities necessary to prepare the qualifying asset for its intended use or sale are complete. *[FRS 102.25.2D(c)]*.

IAS 23 provides additional guidance that may be useful in assisting preparers of financial statements as to when a qualifying asset is considered as complete, including when such assets are completed in parts. IAS 23 states that an asset is normally ready for its intended use or sale when the physical construction of the asset is complete, even though routine administrative work might still continue. If minor modifications, such as the decoration of a property to the purchaser's or user's specification, are all that are outstanding, this indicates that substantially all the activities are complete. *[IAS 23.23]*. In some cases there may be a requirement for inspection (e.g. to ensure that the asset meets safety requirements) before the asset can be used. Usually 'substantially all the activities' would have been completed before this point in order to be ready for inspection. In such a situation, capitalisation would cease prior to the inspection.

When the construction of a qualifying asset is completed in parts and each part is capable of being used while construction continues on other parts, capitalisation should cease for the borrowing costs on the portion of borrowings attributable to that part when substantially all the activities necessary to prepare that part for its intended use or sale are completed. *[IAS 23.24]*. An example of this might be a business park comprising several buildings, each of which is capable of being fully utilised while construction continues on other parts. *[IAS 23.25]*. This principle also applies to single buildings where one part is capable of being fully utilised even if the building as a whole is incomplete.

For a qualifying asset that needs to be complete in its entirety before any part can be used as intended, it would be appropriate to capitalise related borrowing costs until all the activities necessary to prepare the entire asset for its intended use or sale are substantially complete. An example of this is an industrial plant, such as a steel mill, involving processes which are carried out in sequence at different parts of the plant within the same site. *[IAS 23.25]*.

3.7   Disclosures

The disclosure requirements of Section 25 are set out at 3.7.1 below. Disclosures in respect of borrowing costs required by other sections of FRS 102 and the Regulations in respect of borrowing costs are set out in 3.7.2 and 3.7.3 below.

3.7.1   *Disclosures required by Section 25*

When a policy of capitalising borrowing costs is not adopted, Section 25 does not require any additional disclosure. *[FRS 102.25.3]*.

Where a policy of capitalisation is adopted, an entity shall disclose:

* the amount of borrowing costs capitalised in the period; and
* the capitalisation rate used. *[FRS 102.25.3A]*.

3.7.2   *Disclosures required by other sections of FRS 102 in respect of borrowing costs*

In addition to the disclosure requirements in Section 25, an entity may need to disclose additional information in relation to its borrowing costs in order to comply with requirements in other sections of FRS 102. These include:

* presentation requirements for items of profit or loss including interest payable, is required by Section 5 – *Statement of Comprehensive Income and Income Statement* (see Chapter 4); *[FRS 102.5.5]*
* disclosure of total interest expense (using effective interest method for financial liabilities that are not at fair value through profit or loss is required by Section 11 (see Chapter 8); *[FRS 102.11.48(b)]*
* Section 8 – *Notes to the Financial Statements* (see Chapter 4) requires the following:
    * the measurement bases used in preparing the financial statements and other accounting policies used that are relevant to an understanding of the financial statements (e.g. clear policy to adopt capitalisation of borrowing costs); *[FRS 102.8.5]*; and
    * the significant judgements made in the process of applying an entity's accounting policies that have the most significant effect on the recognised amounts (e.g. criteria in determining a qualifying asset, including definition of 'substantial period of time'; determination of capitalisation rate and treatment of foreign exchange gains and losses as

part of borrowing costs, including any derivatives used to hedge such foreign exchange exposures). *[FRS 102.8.6].*

3.7.3 Additional disclosures required by the Regulations

Where a policy of capitalisation is adopted, the Regulations require an entity to disclose in the notes:

- the fact that interest is included in determining the production cost of the qualifying asset (usually achieved by a clear accounting policy – see 3.7.2 above); and

- the aggregate amount of interest so included in the cost of qualifying assets. *[1 Sch 27(3), 2 Sch 35(3), 3 Sch 45(3)].*

4 SUMMARY OF GAAP DIFFERENCES

The key differences between FRS 102, previous UK GAAP and IFRS in accounting for PP&E are set out below.

	FRS 102	*Previous UK GAAP*	*IFRS*
Scope	Section 25 applies to all qualifying assets (same definition of qualifying asset as IAS 23).	The scope of FRS 15 only applies to tangible fixed assets although The Regulations permit interest on capital borrowed to finance the production of any fixed or current asset insofar as it arises in the period of production to be capitalised.	IAS 23 applies to all qualifying assets (same definition of qualifying asset as FRS 102).
	Borrowing costs include exchange differences arising from foreign currency borrowings to the extent that they are regarded as an adjustment to interest costs.	Silent as to whether exchange differences arising from foreign currency borrowings to the extent regarded as an adjustment to interest costs can be regarded as finance costs.	Borrowing costs include exchange differences arising from foreign currency borrowings to the extent that they are regarded as an adjustment to interest costs.

Chapter 20

	FRS 102	*Previous UK GAAP*	*IFRS*
Capitalisation of borrowing costs	Capitalisation of eligible borrowing costs in respect of qualifying assets is a policy choice (i.e. optional).	Capitalisation of finance costs is a policy choice as permitted under The Regulations.	Capitalisation of eligible borrowing costs is mandatory. However, the standard need not be applied to a qualifying asset measured at fair value or inventories that are manufactured or otherwise produced, in large quantities on a repetitive basis.
	Where an entity adopts a policy of capitalisation of borrowing costs, it shall be applied consistently to a class of qualifying assets.	The same accounting policy must apply to all tangible fixed assets (i.e. capitalise or expense). A policy of capitalisation is optional for all other assets (The Regulations are silent on consistent application by class).	An accounting policy choice exists only for a qualifying asset measured at fair value or inventories that are manufactured or otherwise produced, in large quantities on a repetitive basis. Capitalisation of eligible borrowing costs is mandatory for all other qualifying assets.
	Where specific borrowings are used, actual borrowing costs incurred, less any investment income on temporary investment of those funds not yet spent, are capitalised.	While investment income is not explicitly deducted in determining finance costs to be capitalised, FRS 15 requires that finance costs to be capitalised are the actual costs incurred in respect of the expenditure on the asset. In practice, investment income is deducted.	Where specific borrowings are used, actual borrowing costs incurred, less any investment income on temporary investment of those funds not yet spent, are capitalised.
	There is no guidance concerning the impact of inflation to the treatment of borrowing costs when an entity's functional currency is the currency of a hyperinflationary economy	When an entity applies FRS 24 – *Financial reporting in hyperinflationary economies*, it recognises as an expense the part of borrowing costs that compensates for inflation during the same period.	When an entity applies IAS 29 – *Financial Reporting in Hyperinflationary Economies*, it recognises as an expense the part of borrowing costs that compensates for inflation during the same period.

	FRS 102	*Previous UK GAAP*	*IFRS*
Capitalisation rate	The capitalisation rate is the weighted average of rates applicable to general borrowings outstanding in the period. This excludes borrowings made specifically for the purpose of obtaining other qualifying asset and non-qualifying assets.	The capitalisation rate is based on the weighted average rates applicable to general borrowings outstanding in the period. General borrowings under FRS 15, however, explicitly exclude borrowings for other specific purposes, e.g. acquiring other tangible assets, finance leases or loans to hedge foreign investments.	The capitalisation rate is the weighted average of the borrowing costs applicable to borrowings outstanding in the period other than borrowings made specifically for the purpose of obtaining a qualifying asset. This means that specific borrowings to acquire non-qualifying assets may be included in the computation.
	For purposes of applying the capitalisation rate to the expenditure on the qualifying asset, the expenditure on asset is the average carrying amount of the asset during the period, including borrowing costs previously capitalised. However, we expect entities will follow the guidance under IFRS.	No explicit guidance in defining 'expenditures' for purposes of applying capitalisation rate. In practice, many entities followed guidance in IFRS.	Expenditures on a qualifying asset are explicitly limited to those expenditures that have resulted in payments of cash, transfers of other assets or the assumption of interest-bearing liabilities and reduced by any progress payments received and grants received in connection with the asset.

	FRS 102	*Previous UK GAAP*	*IFRS*
Commencement suspension and cessation of capitalisation	No further guidance on 'activities that are necessary to prepare the asset for its intended use or sale'.	Additional guidance is provided on 'activities that are necessary to prepare the asset for its intended use or sale'.	Additional guidance is provided e.g. borrowing costs incurred are expensed if the asset is held without any associated development activities i.e. activities that change the physical condition of the asset.
	No further guidance about treatment of borrowing costs in periods of temporary delay.	No further guidance in relation to treatment of borrowing costs during a period of temporary delay. In practice, IFRS guidance is being followed.	Capitalisation is not normally suspended when substantial technical and administrative work are being carried out or when a temporary delay is a necessary part of the process of getting an asset ready for its intended use or sale.
	No further guidance about cessation of capitalisation of borrowing costs for qualifying assets being constructed in parts.	Explicit guidance is provided for construction of assets in parts although this is in the context of tangible fixed assets, therefore no reference as to when the asset is ready for sale (e.g. for inventories).	Explicit guidance is provided for construction of a qualifying asset in parts and each part is capable of being used or sold while construction continues on other parts.
Disclosures	If the company adopts a policy of capitalising borrowing costs, disclosure is required of the amount of borrowing costs capitalised during the period and the capitalisation rate used. It also needs to disclose the aggregate amount of interest so included in the cost of qualifying assets. No additional disclosures are required if a policy of capitalising borrowing costs is not adopted.	Those applicable to current assets will need to comply only with the Companies Act which requires the inclusion of the interest in determining the cost of the asset (i.e. accounting policy) and the amount of the interest so included is disclosed in a note to the accounts. For fixed assets, FRS 15 requires the above plus the amount of finance costs capitalised during the period; amount of finance costs recognised in the profit and loss account during the period; and the capitalisation rate used.	An entity shall disclose the amount of borrowing costs capitalised during the period and the capitalisation rate used.

Chapter 21   Share-based payment

Chapter 21

Chapter 21

Chapter 21

List of examples

Chapter 21   Share-based payment

1   INTRODUCTION

1.1   Background

Most share-based payment transactions undertaken by entities are awards of shares and options as remuneration to employees, in particular senior management and directors. One advantage of shares and options as remuneration is that they need not entail any cash cost to the entity. If an executive is entitled under a bonus scheme to a free share, the entity can satisfy this award simply by printing another share certificate, which the executive can sell, so that the cash cost of the award is effectively borne by shareholders rather than by the entity itself. However, this very advantage was the source of controversy surrounding share-based remuneration.

Investors became increasingly concerned that share-based remuneration was resulting in a significant cost to them, through dilution of their existing shareholdings. As a result, there emerged an increasing consensus among investors that awards of shares and share options should be recognised as a cost in the financial statements.

Accounting for share-based payment transactions is addressed in Section 26 of FRS 102. However, many of the requirements of Section 26 are virtually impossible to interpret without recourse to IFRS 2 – *Share-based Payment* – from which many of the requirements of Section 26 are ultimately derived.

The IASB published IFRS 2 in February 2004. There have been two subsequent amendments to IFRS 2 as well as a number of clarifications through the IASB's Annual Improvements process.

A UK version of IFRS 2 (FRS 20 – *(IFRS 2) Share-based payment*) – was issued by the ASB in April 2004. The amendments to IFRS 2 referred to above were also applied to FRS 20. The requirements, scope and effective date of FRS 20 were identical to those of IFRS 2 with two exceptions:

- an exemption for entities applying the FRSSE; and
- a later application date for unlisted entities.

FRS 20 is superseded by the requirements of FRSs 100 to 102 (see 1.3 below).

1.2   Overview of accounting approach

The overall approach to accounting for share-based payment transactions is complex, in part because it is something of a hybrid. Essentially the total cost (i.e. measurement) of an award is calculated by determining whether the award is a liability or an equity instrument, using criteria somewhat different from those used in accounting for financial instruments but then applying measurement principles based on those generally applicable to financial liabilities or equity instruments. However the periodic allocation (i.e. recognition) of the cost[1] is determined using something closer to a straight-line accruals methodology, which would not generally be used for financial instruments.

This inevitably has the result that, depending on its legal form, a transaction of equal value to the recipient can result in several different potential charges in profit or loss. Moreover, many of the requirements are rules derived from the 'anti-avoidance' approach of IFRS 2. This means that an expense often has to be recorded for transactions that either have no ultimate value to the counterparty or to which, in some cases, the counterparty actually has no entitlement at all.

1.2.1   *Classification differences between share-based payments and financial instruments*

As noted above, not only are there differences between the accounting treatment of liabilities or equity in a share-based payment transaction as compared with that of other transactions involving liabilities or equity instruments (Section 22 – *Liabilities and Equity* of FRS 102), but the classification of a transaction as a liability or equity transaction may differ.

The most important difference is that a share-based payment transaction involving the delivery of equity instruments is always accounted for as an equity transaction, whereas a similar transaction outside the scope of the share-based payment accounting requirements might well be classified as a liability if the number of shares to be delivered varies.

1.3   Scope of Chapter 21

As noted at 1.1 above, the requirements of FRS 20 have been superseded by those in Section 26 but this has meant that much of the application and implementation guidance that was in FRS 20 no longer forms part of, or accompanies, the requirements. Without this guidance, the practical application of the requirements of Section 26 is difficult and we therefore draw on the guidance in IFRS 2 as part of the explanation in this Chapter.

We refer throughout the Chapter to IFRS 2 rather than to FRS 20 as IFRS 2 remains in issue.

Accounting for share-based payment transactions is complex and the application of Section 26 – and IFRS 2 – to a variety of practical situations is unclear. Whilst this Chapter addresses some of the complexities, other areas of discussion are beyond the scope of this Chapter. EY International GAAP 2015 includes a more detailed analysis in certain areas, as indicated later in this Chapter.

2 COMPARISON BETWEEN SECTION 26, PREVIOUS UK GAAP AND IFRS

This section summarises the principal differences between Section 26 of FRS 102 and the requirements of IFRS 2 and FRS 20 (hereafter just referred to in terms of IFRS 2 – see 1.3 above). In some of the areas referred to below, the difference between the standards is explicit but there are others where the lack of guidance or explanation in Section 26 means that it is unclear whether or not a different accounting treatment is intended.

All of the areas below are addressed in more detail in the remainder of this Chapter, as indicated.

2.1 Scope

2.1.1 Definitions and transactions within scope

Unlike IFRS 2, Section 26 does not provide guidance or examples in areas such as:

- the meaning of 'goods' in 'goods and services' when used in the definition of a share-based payment transaction;
- vested transactions;
- transactions with shareholders as a whole;
- business combinations; or
- the interaction with the requirements of FRS 102 relating to financial instruments.

The differences are discussed in more detail at 3.2 and 3.3 below and, in the case of replacement awards in a business combination, at 12 below.

2.2 Recognition

2.2.1 Accounting after vesting date

FRS 102 includes no guidance on accounting for awards after vesting whereas IFRS 2 specifically prohibits a reversal of expense (see 7.1.3 below).

2.3 Measurement of equity-settled share-based payment transactions

2.3.1 Vesting conditions and non-vesting conditions

FRS 102 does not include a definition of 'vesting conditions' which is a defined term in IFRS 2. As the term is included in italics in Section 26, implying that it should be defined in the glossary to FRS 102, it seems that the omission is simply a drafting error and we make the assumption that the definition of such conditions is intended to be the same as under IFRS 2.

Neither Section 26 nor IFRS 2 includes a definition of a 'non-vesting condition' but IFRS 2 includes examples of such conditions as part of its implementation guidance (see 4 and 7 below).

2.3.2   *Treatment of service and non-market performance conditions in measurement of fair value*

Unlike IFRS 2, Section 26 does not make it explicitly clear that service conditions and non-market performance vesting conditions should not be taken into account in determining the fair value of equity-settled share-based payment transactions but should be taken into account in estimating the number of awards expected to vest. In our view, an approach consistent with the explicit requirements of IFRS 2 should be adopted and we believe that this may be inferred from the final sentence of paragraph 9 of Section 26 (see 7 below).

2.3.3   *Employees and others providing similar services*

Both Section 26 and IFRS 2 distinguish between awards to employees (and others providing similar services) and those to other parties providing goods or services. The recognition and measurement of equity-settled share-based payment transactions differ according to whether the counterparty is treated as an employee.

Section 26 provides no additional guidance on the meaning of 'others providing similar services' whereas IFRS 2 defines/explains this term in Appendix A (see 6.2.1 below).

In dealing with the recognition and measurement of share-based payments, FRS 102 sometimes refers only to employees without specifying the treatment for non-employee awards. In such cases, we assume that a similar accounting treatment is intended for non-employee awards.

2.3.4   *Valuation methodology*

IFRS 2 requires the use of a market price or an option pricing model for the valuation of equity-settled share-based payment transactions. FRS 102 draws a more explicit distinction than IFRS 2 between the valuation of shares and the valuation of options and appreciation rights. Section 26 specifies the following valuation hierarchy:

- observable market price,
- entity-specific observable market data,
- directors' valuation using a generally accepted methodology

and gives limited examples for both shares and options/appreciation rights of the type of approach that might be taken. As part of this guidance, Section 26 does not mandate the use of an option pricing model for the valuation of share options when market prices are unavailable; instead it allows use of a valuation methodology 'such as an option pricing model'.

This approach to valuation is included by the FRC in Appendix II to FRS 102 as a significant difference between FRS 102 and the IFRS for SMEs (and therefore IFRS 2). In practical terms, it is not entirely clear what alternatives to an option pricing model are likely to provide a reliable indication of the fair value (see 9.2 and 9.3 below).

IFRS 2 includes guidance in Appendix B about the selection and application of option pricing models, none of which is reproduced in FRS 102 (see 9 below).

2.3.5 Awards where fair value cannot be measured reliably

Section 26 assumes as part of its requirements relating to the measurement of equity-settled share-based payment transactions that it will always be possible to derive a fair value for the award (see 9.2 and 9.3 below). IFRS 2 includes an approach based on the intrinsic value of the equity instruments for the 'rare cases' in which an entity is unable to measure reliably the fair value of those instruments. *[IFRS 2.24]*. The intrinsic value approach is not addressed in this Chapter.

2.3.6 Cancellation of awards

IFRS 2 makes clear that an award may be cancelled either by the entity or by the counterparty and also that a failure to meet non-vesting conditions should, in certain situations, be considered to amount to the cancellation of an award. Section 26 includes no explicit requirements to mirror those in IFRS 2. (See 7.4.3 and 8.4 below.)

2.3.7 Settlement of awards

Section 26 states that a settlement of an unvested equity-settled share-based payment should be treated as an acceleration of vesting. It does not specify the treatment where the fair value of the settlement exceeds the fair value of the award being cancelled. Under IFRS 2, any incremental fair value is expensed at the date of settlement but any settlement value up to the fair value of the cancelled award is debited to equity.

Similarly, Section 26 contains no guidance on the repurchase of vested equity instruments whereas IFRS 2 requires any incremental fair value to be expensed as at the date of repurchase. (See 8.4 below.)

2.3.8 Replacement awards following a cancellation or settlement

Section 26 includes no guidance on the accounting treatment of equity-settled awards to replace an award cancelled during the vesting period and whether, as under IFRS 2, they may be accounted for on the basis of their incremental fair value rather than being treated as a completely new award (see 8.4.4 below).

2.4 Cash-settled share-based payment transactions

There are no significant differences between Section 26 and IFRS 2 in the recognition and measurement of cash-settled share-based payment transactions.

2.5 Share-based payment transactions with cash alternatives

2.5.1 Entity or counterparty has choice of equity- or cash-settlement

Section 26 includes a presumption of cash-settlement unless there is a past practice of settlement in equity or the cash settlement option has no commercial substance.

IFRS 2 includes separate requirements depending on whether it is the entity or the counterparty with the choice of settlement method. Broadly, the requirement under IFRS 2 is to apply a split accounting approach (between a liability and equity) to an award with counterparty choice and to determine whether there is a present obligation to settle in cash in cases where the entity has the choice (see 11 below).

2.5.2   *Settlement in cash of award accounted for as equity-settled (or vice versa)*

Section 26 contains no guidance on how to account for the settlement in cash of an award accounted for as equity-settled (or *vice versa*). This is specifically addressed in IFRS 2 and discussed at 11.1.3 below.

2.6   Group plans

2.6.1   *Accounting by group entity with obligation to settle an award when another group entity receives goods or services*

Section 26 makes clear that a group entity receiving goods or services, but with no obligation to settle the transaction with the provider of those goods or services, accounts for a share-based payment transaction as equity-settled. However, the accounting treatment in the entity settling the transaction is not specified. In a specific section on group schemes, IFRS 2 makes clear when the settling entity should treat an award as equity-settled and when it should account on a cash-settled basis. This is discussed at 3.2.1 and 13.2 below.

2.6.2   *Alternative accounting treatment for group plans*

Where a share-based payment award is granted by an entity to the employees of one or more members of a group, those members are permitted – as an alternative to the general recognition and measurement requirements of Section 26 – to recognise and measure the share-based payment expense on the basis of a reasonable allocation of the group expense (see 3.2.1 and 13.2.3.A below). There is no corresponding alternative treatment in IFRS 2.

2.7   Government-mandated plans

2.7.1   *Unidentifiable goods/services*

For certain government-mandated plans where the goods/services received or receivable in exchange for equity instruments are not identifiable, Section 26 requires the award to be valued on the basis of the equity instruments rather than the goods or services. Under IFRS 2, the scope is not restricted to government-mandated plans and it is unclear whether entities applying Section 26 should apply the principle more widely (see 3.2.3 below).

2.8   Disclosures

The disclosure requirements of Section 26 are generally derived from, but less extensive than, those of IFRS 2. However, Section 26 has three specific requirements that are not found in IFRS 2:

- if a valuation methodology is used to determine the fair value of equity-settled awards, the entity is required to disclose both the method and reason for choosing it;
- for cash-settled share-based payment transactions, an entity is required to disclose how the liability was measured; and
- where the alternative accounting treatment is adopted for group plans, disclosure of this fact is required together with the basis of allocation.

More generally, unlike IFRS, FRS 102 includes exemptions from disclosure for certain entities.

The disclosure requirements are discussed at 14 below.

2.9 First-time adoption

The first-time adoption provisions of FRS 102 are set out in Section 35 – *Transition to this FRS* of the standard. The specific requirements relating to share-based payments are discussed at 17 below. Unlike IFRS 1 – *First-time Adoption of International Financial Reporting Standards*, Section 35 does not specify the accounting treatment of an award that was granted prior to transition but subsequently modified.

3 SCOPE OF SECTION 26 OF FRS 102

This section covers the scope of the share-based payment accounting requirements of Section 26 as follows:

- definitions from the Glossary to FRS 102 that are relevant to determining whether transactions are within the scope of Section 26 (see 3.1 below);

- a discussion of transactions that fall within the scope of Section 26 (see 3.2 below) including group arrangements (see 3.2.1 below), transactions with employee benefit trusts (EBTs) and similar vehicles (see 3.2.2 below) and transactions where the consideration received might not be clearly identifiable (see 3.2.3 below);

- a discussion of transactions that fall outside the scope of Section 26 (see 3.3 below); and

- some examples of situations commonly encountered in practice and a discussion of whether they are within scope of Section 26 (see 3.4 below).

3.1 Definitions

The following definitions from the Glossary to FRS 102 are relevant to the scope of Section 26.

A *share-based payment transaction* is 'a transaction in which the entity:

(a) receives goods or services (including employee services) as consideration for its own equity instruments (including shares or share options); or

(b) receives goods or services but has no obligation to settle the transaction with [the] supplier; or

(c) acquires goods or services by incurring liabilities to the supplier of those goods or services for amounts that are based on the price (or value) of the entity's shares or other equity instruments of the entity or another group entity.'

The drafting of this definition is not as precise as it might be. Part (b) does not specify that the goods or services are received in return either for equity instruments of the entity (or another group entity) or for cash (or other assets) based on the price (or value) of such equity instruments. Part (c) does not specify that it is a liability to transfer cash or other assets (see the definition of 'cash-settled share-based payment transaction' below). We have assumed throughout this Chapter that these are the intended readings of the definitions in line with the wider scope of Section 26 and the corresponding requirements in IFRS 2.

An *equity-settled share-based payment transaction* is 'a share-based payment transaction in which the entity:

(a)   receives goods or services as consideration for its own equity instruments (including shares or share options); or

(b)   receives goods or services but has no obligation to settle the transaction with the supplier.'

A *cash-settled share-based payment transaction* is 'a share-based payment transaction in which the entity acquires goods or services by incurring a liability to transfer cash or other assets to the supplier of those goods or services for amounts that are based on the price (or value) of the entity's shares or other equity instruments of the entity or another group entity'.

Group entity is not defined but *group* is defined as 'a parent and all its subsidiaries'.

Equity instrument is not defined but *equity* is defined as 'the residual interest in the assets of the entity after deducting all its liabilities'.

A *share option* is 'a contract that gives the holder the right, but not the obligation, to subscribe to the entity's shares at a fixed or determinable price for a specific period of time'.

It will be seen from these definitions that FRS 102 applies not only to awards of shares and share options but also to awards of cash (or other assets) of a value equivalent to the value, or a movement in the value, of a particular number of shares.

3.2   Transactions within the scope of Section 26

Subject to the exceptions noted in 3.3 below, Section 26 of FRS 102 must be applied to all share-based payment transactions, including:

(a)   equity-settled share-based payment transactions (discussed at 5 to 9 below);

(b)   cash-settled share-based payment transactions (discussed at 10 below); and

(c)   transactions where either the entity or the supplier of goods or services can choose whether the transaction is to be equity-settled or cash-settled (discussed at 11 below). *[FRS 102.26.1].*

Whilst the boundaries between these types of transaction are reasonably self-explanatory, there may – as discussed in more detail at 10 and 11 below – be transactions that an entity may intuitively regard as equity-settled which are in fact required to be treated as cash-settled.

Although the majority of share-based payment transactions are with employees, the scope of Section 26 is not restricted to employee transactions. For example, if an external supplier of goods or services, including another group entity, is paid in shares or share options, or cash of equivalent value, Section 26 must be applied.

A share-based payment transaction as defined in FRS 102 (see 3.1 above) requires goods or services to be received or acquired, but FRS 102 does not define 'goods' or give any additional guidance as to what might be included within such a term. IFRS 2 includes the following within its scope and it seems appropriate to use this guidance for the purposes of Section 26:

- inventories,

- consumables,

- property, plant and equipment (PP&E),

- intangibles, and

- other non-financial assets. *[IFRS 2.5].*

It will be seen that 'goods' do not include financial assets, which raises some further issues (see 3.3.6 below).

Although not always explicitly stated, the scope of Section 26 extends to:

- certain transactions by other group entities and by shareholders of group entities (see 3.2.1 below);

- transactions with EBT's and similar vehicles (see 3.2.2 below);

- certain transactions where the identifiable consideration received appears to be less than the consideration given (see 3.2.3 below); and

- 'all employee' share plans (see 3.2.4 below).

Section 26 is silent on certain other transactions or arrangements, including vested transactions (see 3.2.5 below), where it is unclear whether the transactions or arrangements fall within the scope of the share-based payment accounting requirements.

In the absence of specific guidance in FRS 102 we suggest that entities follow the requirements of IFRS 2, or general practice that has evolved through the application of IFRS 2, as set out in the sections below.

3.2.1   Transactions by other group entities and shareholders

The definition of 'share-based payment transaction' (see 3.1 above) and additional requirements in paragraph 1A of Section 26 have the effect that the scope of Section 26 is not restricted to transactions where the reporting entity acquires goods or services in exchange for providing its own equity instruments (or cash or other assets based on the cost or value of those equity instruments). Within a group of companies it is common for one member of the group (typically the parent) to have the obligation to settle a share-based payment transaction in which services are provided to another member of the group (typically a subsidiary). This transaction is within the scope of Section 26 for the entity receiving the services (even though it is not a direct party to the arrangement between its parent and its employee), the entity settling the transaction and the group as a whole.

Accordingly, Section 26 requires an entity to account for a transaction in which it either:

- receives goods or services when another entity in the same group (or shareholder of any group entity) has the obligation to settle the share-based payment transaction; or

- has an obligation to settle a share-based payment transaction when another entity in the same group receives the goods or services

unless the transaction is clearly for a purpose other than payment for goods or services supplied to the entity receiving them. *[FRS 102.26.1A].*

Moreover, the definition of 'equity-settled share-based payment transaction' (see 3.1 above) has the effect that the analysis of the transaction as equity-settled or cash-settled (and its accounting treatment) may differ when viewed from the perspective of the entity receiving the goods or services, the entity settling the transaction and the group as a whole depending on whether or not an entity is required to settle the award and whether that settlement is in its own equity instruments.

IFRS 2 explicitly requires the entity settling a share-based payment transaction to account for the transaction as a cash-settled share-based payment transaction when:

- another group entity is receiving the goods and services; and

- the award is not settled with the equity instruments of the settling entity. *[IFRS 2.43C].*

We assume that the wording of paragraph 1A of Section 26, when read with paragraph 1, requires a similar accounting approach.

3.2.1.A   *Scenarios illustrating scope requirements for group entities*

In this section we consider seven scenarios, all based on the simple structure in Figure 21.1. These scenarios are by no means exhaustive, but cover the situations most commonly seen in practice.

It should be noted that the scenarios below are based on the scope requirements of Section 26 as set out at 3.2.1 above and do not reflect the additional exemption for members of group schemes. This exemption allows the group expense to be allocated between members of the group on a reasonable basis rather than requiring each group entity to recognise and measure its expense in accordance with the general requirements of Section 26. *[FRS 102.26.16].* The exemption and the accounting treatment of group share schemes generally are discussed in more detail at 13 below.

Figure 21.1:   Scope of IFRS 2

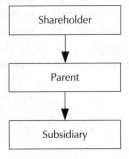

The scenarios assume that:

- the shareholder is not a group entity; and
- the subsidiary is directly owned by the parent company (see also 13.2.1 below in relation to intermediate parent companies).

Scenario	Who grants the award?	Who receives the goods or services?	Who settles the award?	On whose shares is award based?	Settled in shares or cash?
1	Parent	Subsidiary	Parent	Parent	Shares
2	Shareholder	Subsidiary	Shareholder	Parent	Shares
3	Subsidiary	Subsidiary	Subsidiary	Parent	Shares
4	Subsidiary	Subsidiary	Subsidiary	Subsidiary	Shares
5	Parent	Subsidiary	Parent	Subsidiary	Shares
6	Parent	Subsidiary	Parent	Parent	Cash
7	Shareholder	Subsidiary	Shareholder	Parent	Cash

Scenario 1

Parent awards equity shares in Parent to employees of Subsidiary in exchange for services to Subsidiary. Parent settles the award with the employees of Subsidiary.

Consolidated financial statements of Parent

Under the definition of 'share-based payment transaction', 'the entity [i.e. the Parent group] ... receives goods or services ... as consideration for its own equity instruments ...'.

The transaction is classified as an equity-settled transaction because it is settled in an equity instrument of the group.

Separate financial statements of Parent

Parent does not receive the goods or services but it does have the obligation to settle. This is within the scope of paragraph 1A(b) of Section 26 as Parent 'has an obligation to settle a share-based payment transaction when another entity in the same group receives the goods or services'. As noted at 3.2.1 above, Section 26 does not explicitly cover the accounting by the settling entity in this situation.

Based on the requirements of IFRS 2 for a comparable situation, Parent should account for the transaction as equity-settled because it is settled in an equity instrument of Parent.

Subsidiary

Under the definitions of 'share-based payment transaction' and 'equity-settled share-based payment transaction', 'the entity [i.e. Subsidiary] ... receives goods or services but has no obligation to settle the transaction with [the] supplier ...' and so accounts for the award as equity-settled.

Even if Subsidiary is not a party to the agreement with its employees, it nevertheless records a cost for this transaction. In effect, the accounting treatment is representing that Subsidiary has received a capital contribution from Parent, which Subsidiary has then 'spent' on employee remuneration. This treatment is often referred to as 'push-down' accounting – the idea being that a transaction undertaken by one group entity (in this case, Parent) for the benefit of another group entity (in this case, Subsidiary) is 'pushed down' into the financial statements of the beneficiary entity.

Scenario 2

Shareholder awards equity shares in Parent to employees of Subsidiary in exchange for services to Subsidiary. Shareholder settles the award with the employees of Subsidiary.

Consolidated financial statements of Parent

Paragraph 1A of Section 26 refers to awards settled by a shareholder of a group entity on behalf of the entity receiving the goods or services.

The transaction is classified as an equity-settled transaction, because the Parent group 'receives goods or services but has no obligation to settle the transaction with [the] supplier'.

Separate financial statements of Parent

Scenario 2 is not within the scope of Section 26 for the separate financial statements of Parent because Parent (as a separate entity) receives no goods or services, nor does it settle the transaction.

Subsidiary

The transaction is classified as an equity-settled transaction. Under the definitions of 'share-based payment transaction' and 'equity-settled share-based payment transaction', 'the entity [i.e. Subsidiary] ... receives goods or services but has no obligation to settle the transaction with [the] supplier.'

Scenario 3

Subsidiary awards equity shares in Parent to employees of Subsidiary in exchange for services to Subsidiary. Subsidiary settles the award with the employees of Subsidiary.

Consolidated financial statements of Parent

The transaction is classified as an equity-settled transaction. Under the definitions of 'share-based payment transaction' and 'equity-settled share-based payment transaction', 'the entity [i.e. the Parent group] ... receives goods or services ... as consideration for its own equity instruments'.

Separate financial statements of Parent

Scenario 3 is not within the scope of Section 26 for the separate financial statements of Parent because Parent (as a separate entity) receives no goods or services, nor does it settle the transaction.

Subsidiary

Under the definition of 'share-based payment transaction', 'the entity [i.e. Subsidiary] ... acquires goods or services by incurring liabilities to the supplier of those goods or services for amounts that are based on the price (or value) of the entity's shares or other equity instruments of the entity or another group entity'.

The transaction is classified as a cash-settled transaction because Subsidiary has the obligation to settle the award with equity instruments issued by Parent – i.e. a financial asset in Subsidiary's separate financial statements – rather than with Subsidiary's own equity instruments.

However, for the approach in this Scenario to apply, it must be the case that Subsidiary grants the award as a principal rather than as agent for Parent. If Subsidiary appears to be granting an award but is really doing so only on the instructions of Parent, as will generally be the case for UK companies, then the approach in Scenario 1 above is more likely to apply. This is discussed in more detail at 13.2.5.B below.

Scenario 4

Subsidiary awards equity shares in Subsidiary to employees of Subsidiary in exchange for services to Subsidiary. Subsidiary settles the award with the employees of Subsidiary.

Consolidated financial statements of Parent

The transaction is classified as an equity-settled transaction because it is settled in an equity instrument of the group. Under the definitions of 'share-based payment transaction' and 'equity-settled share-based payment transaction', 'the entity [i.e. the Parent group] ... receives goods or services ... as consideration for its own equity instruments'.

In the consolidated financial statements of Parent, shares of Subsidiary not held by Parent are a non-controlling interest.

Subsidiary

The transaction is classified as an equity-settled transaction because it is settled in an equity instrument of Subsidiary. Under the definitions of 'share-based payment transaction' and 'equity-settled share-based payment transaction', 'the entity [i.e. Subsidiary] ... receives goods or services (including employee services) as consideration for its own equity instruments (including shares or share options)'.

Scenario 5

Parent awards equity shares in Subsidiary to employees of Subsidiary in exchange for services to Subsidiary. Parent settles the award with the employees of Subsidiary.

Consolidated financial statements of Parent

Under the definition of 'share-based payment transaction', 'the entity [i.e. the Parent group] ... receives goods or services ... as consideration for its own equity instruments ...'. The transaction is classified as an equity-settled transaction because it is settled in an equity instrument of the group. In the consolidated financial statements of Parent, shares of Subsidiary not held by Parent are a non-controlling interest.

Separate financial statements of Parent

Parent does not receive the goods or services but it does have the obligation to settle. This is within the scope of paragraph 1A(b) of Section 26 as Parent 'has an obligation to settle a share-based payment transaction when another entity in the same group receives the goods or services'. As noted at 3.2.1 above, Section 26 does not explicitly cover the accounting by the settling entity in this situation.

Based on the requirements of IFRS 2 for a comparable situation, the transaction is classified as a cash-settled transaction, because it is settled not in an equity instrument issued by Parent, but in an equity instrument issued by a subsidiary held by Parent – i.e. a financial asset in Parent's separate financial statements.

Subsidiary

The transaction is classified as an equity-settled transaction. Under the definitions of 'share-based payment transaction' and 'equity-settled share-based payment transaction', 'the entity [i.e. Subsidiary] ... receives goods or services but has no obligation to settle the transaction with [the] supplier'.

Scenario 6

Parent awards cash based on the value of shares in Parent to employees of Subsidiary in exchange for services to Subsidiary. Parent settles the award with the employees of Subsidiary.

Consolidated financial statements of Parent

Under the definitions of 'share-based payment transaction' and 'cash-settled share-based payment transaction', 'the entity [i.e. the Parent group] ... acquires goods or services by incurring liabilities to the supplier of those goods or services for amounts that are based on the price (or value) of the entity's shares or other equity instruments of the entity or another group entity.'

The transaction is classified as a cash-settled transaction, because it is settled in cash of the group.

Separate financial statements of Parent

Parent does not receive the goods or services but it does have the obligation to settle. This is within the scope of paragraph 1A(b) of Section 26 as Parent 'has an obligation to settle a share-based payment transaction when another entity in the same group receives the goods or services'. As noted at 3.2.1 above, Section 26 does not explicitly cover the accounting by the settling entity in this situation.

Based on the requirements of IFRS 2 for a comparable situation, the transaction is classified as a cash-settled transaction, because it is settled not in an equity instrument issued by Parent, but in cash based on the value of shares in Parent.

Subsidiary

When the drafting of the definition of a 'share-based payment transaction' is examined closely, it is not absolutely clear that this arrangement is within the scope of Section 26 for Subsidiary. Part (c) of the definition of a 'share-based payment transaction' appears to deal only with a situation where the entity's own cash (or other assets) is used in settlement, and not when another group entity settles the transaction. Part (b) of the definition refers to 'a transaction in which the entity ... receives goods or services but has no obligation to settle the transaction with [the] supplier' which might be broad enough to include this arrangement when taken with the general scope requirements in paragraphs 1 and 1A.

We believe that the exclusion of such transactions from the definition of 'share-based payment transaction' should be disregarded as an unfortunate drafting slip and that the transaction should be classified as an equity-settled transaction by Subsidiary, because Subsidiary 'receives goods or services but has no obligation to settle the transaction with the supplier'.

Scenario 7

Shareholder awards cash based on the value of shares in Parent to employees of Subsidiary in exchange for services to Subsidiary. Shareholder settles the award with the employees of Subsidiary.

For the reasons set out in Scenario 6 above, this transaction is not strictly in the scope of Section 26 as drafted either for the consolidated financial statements of Parent or for the separate financial statements of Parent or Subsidiary. As noted in Scenario 6 above, the definitions of 'share-based payment transaction' and 'cash-settled share-based payment transaction' as drafted exclude any arrangement that is settled in cash by a party other than the reporting entity.

Nevertheless, we believe that the transaction should be treated as being within the scope of Section 26 for the consolidated financial statements of Parent and the separate financial statements of Subsidiary and the transaction accounted for as equity-settled.

Chapter 21

3.2.2   *Transactions with employee benefit trusts and similar vehicles*

It is common for an entity to establish a trust to hold shares in the entity for the purpose of satisfying share-based awards to employees. In such cases, it is often the trust, rather than any entity within the legal group, that actually makes share-based awards to employees. Awards by EBT's and similar vehicles are within the scope of Section 26 and are discussed at 13.3 below.

3.2.3   *Transactions where the identifiable consideration received appears to be less than the consideration given*

3.2.3.A   *Government-mandated plans*

A share-based payment transaction as defined (see 3.1 above) involves the receipt of goods or services. Nevertheless, Section 26 also applies to government-mandated plans 'established under law by which equity investors (such as employees) are able to acquire equity without providing goods or services that can be specifically identified (or by providing goods or services that are clearly less than the fair value of the equity instruments granted). This indicates that other consideration has been or will be received (such as past or future employee services) ...'. *[FRS 102.26.17]*.

Such arrangements are treated as equity-settled share-based payment transactions under FRS 102 and the unidentifiable goods or services are measured as the difference between the fair value of the share-based payment and the fair value of any identifiable goods or services received (or to be received) measured at the grant date. *[FRS 102.26.17]*. The determination of the grant date is addressed at 6.3 below.

Section 26 offers no further explanation or guidance as to the type of arrangement that is expected to fall within the scope of this paragraph. The reference to employees and employee services is somewhat puzzling since share-based payment transactions with employees are always measured at the fair value of the share-based payment rather than the fair value of the employee services, identifiable or otherwise.

What is also not made explicitly clear in paragraph 17 is that, in this situation, the fair value of a share-based payment with a non-employee would need to be that of the equity instruments rather than that of the goods or services (as would normally be the case for an award to a non-employee – see 6.1 and 6.4 below).

As Section 26 refers only to 'programmes mandated under law' beneath the heading 'Government-mandated' plans, it appears that an entity is not required to apply the requirements of paragraph 17 to other transactions with non-employees in which the value of goods or services received or receivable falls short of the fair value of the equity instruments or cash transferred.

IFRS 2 includes a similar requirement for transactions with non-employees where no specifically identifiable goods or services have been (or will be) received but does not restrict the scope to government-mandated plans. *[IFRS 2.2]*.

IFRS 2 asserts that, if the identifiable consideration received (if any) appears to be less than the fair value of consideration given in any share-based payment arrangement, the implication is that, in addition to the identifiable goods and services acquired, the entity must also have received some unidentifiable consideration equal to the difference between the fair value of the share-based payment and the fair value of any identifiable consideration received. Accordingly, the cost of the unidentified consideration must be accounted for in accordance with IFRS 2. *[IFRS 2.13A]*.

For example, if an entity agrees to pay a supplier of services with a clearly identifiable market value of £1,000 by issuing shares with a value of £1,500, IFRS 2 requires the entity to recognise an expense of £1,500. This is notwithstanding the normal requirement of IFRS 2 that an equity-settled share-based payment transaction with a non-employee be recognised at the fair value of the goods or services received (see 6.1 and 6.4 below).

3.2.3.B   Other transactions

In rare circumstances a transaction may occur in which no goods or services are received by the entity. For example, a principal shareholder of an entity, for reasons of estate planning, may transfer shares to a relative. In the absence of indications that the relative has provided, or is expected to provide, goods or services to the entity in exchange for the shares, such a transfer would be outside the scope of Section 26. *[FRS 102.26.1A]*.

3.2.4   'All employee' share plans

Many countries, including the UK, encourage wider share-ownership by allowing companies to award a limited number of free or discounted shares to employees without either the employee or the employer incurring tax liabilities which would apply if other benefits in kind to an equivalent value were given to employees.

There is no exemption from the scope of Section 26 for such plans (unless they are immaterial).

3.2.5   Vested transactions

Section 26 does not specifically address the accounting treatment of awards once they have vested. Drawing on the requirements of IFRS 2, a transaction accounted for as a share-based payment does not necessarily cease to be within the scope of Section 26 once it has vested in the counterparty (see 4 below). This is made clear by the numerous provisions of IFRS 2 referring to the accounting treatment of vested awards.

Once shares have been delivered or beneficially transferred to the counterparty (e.g. as the result of the vesting of an award of shares, or the exercise of a vested option over shares), those shares should generally be accounted for under Section 22 of FRS 102. If, however, the holder of a share or vested option enjoys rights not applicable to all holders of that class of share, such as a right to put the share to the entity for cash, the share or option might remain in the scope of Section 26 as long as any such rights continue to apply. The same is true of modifications made after vesting which add such rights to a vested share or option.

Chapter 21

3.3   Transactions not within the scope of Section 26

Section 26 does not include any examples of transactions that are outside the scope of its requirements. IFRS 2 includes some specific scope exemptions and we imagine that similar exemptions are intended to apply in the application of Section 26. The following transactions are outside the scope of IFRS 2:

- transactions with shareholders as a whole and with shareholders in their capacity as such (see 3.3.1 below);
- transfers of assets in certain group restructuring arrangements (see 3.3.2 below);
- business combinations (see 3.3.3 below);
- combinations of businesses under common control and the contribution of a business to form a joint venture (see 3.3.4 below); and
- transactions in the scope of IAS 32 – *Financial Instruments: Presentation* – and IAS 39 – *Financial Instruments: Recognition and Measurement* (see 3.3.5 below). The scope exemptions in IFRS 2 combined with those in IAS 32 and IAS 39 appear to have the effect that there is no specific guidance in IFRS for accounting for certain types of investments when acquired in return for shares (see 3.3.6 below).

However, as noted at 3.2.4 above, there is no exemption for share schemes aimed mainly at lower- and middle-ranking employees, referred to in different jurisdictions by terms such as 'all-employee share schemes', 'employee share purchase plans' and 'broad-based plans'.

3.3.1   *Transactions with shareholders in their capacity as such*

IFRS 2 does not apply to transactions with employees (and others) purely in their capacity as shareholders. For example, an employee may already hold shares in the entity as a result of previous share-based payment transactions. If the entity then raises funds through a rights issue, whereby all shareholders (including the employee) can acquire additional shares for less than the current fair value of the shares, such a transaction is not a 'share-based payment transaction' for the purposes of IFRS 2. *[IFRS 2.4]*.

3.3.2   *Transfer of assets in group restructuring arrangements*

In some group restructuring arrangements, one entity will transfer a group of net assets, which does not meet the definition of a business, to another entity in return for shares. Careful consideration of the precise facts and circumstances is needed in order to determine whether, for the separate or individual financial statements of any entity affected by the transfer, such a transfer meets the definition of a share-based payment transaction. If the transfer is considered primarily to be a transfer of goods by their owner in return for shares then, in our view, this should be accounted for as a share-based payment transaction. However, if the transaction is for another purpose and is driven by the group shareholder in its capacity as such, the transaction may be outside the scope of IFRS 2 (see 3.3.1 above).

3.3.3 Business combinations

IFRS 2 does not apply to share-based payments to acquire goods (such as inventories or property, plant and equipment) in the context of a business combination to which IFRS 3 – *Business Combinations* – applies. We assume that shares issued as consideration for business combinations under Section 19 – *Business Combinations and Goodwill* of FRS 102 are similarly outside the scope of Section 26.

Equity instruments granted to the employees of the acquiree in their capacity as employees (e.g. in return for continued service) are within the scope of IFRS 2, as are the cancellation, replacement or modification of a share-based payment transaction as the result of a business combination or other equity restructuring. *[IFRS 2.5].*

Thus, if a vendor of an acquired business remains as an employee of that business following the business combination and receives a share-based payment for transferring control of the entity and for remaining in continuing employment, it is necessary to determine how much of the share-based payment relates to the acquisition of control (which forms part of the cost of the combination) and how much relates to the provision of future services (which is a post-combination operating expense under IFRS 2). Detailed guidance on this issue is beyond the scope of this publication.

3.3.4 Common control transactions and formation of joint arrangements

IFRS 2 also does not apply to a combination of entities or businesses under common control or the contribution of a business on the formation of a joint venture as defined by IFRS 11 – *Joint Arrangements. [IFRS 2.5].*

It should be noted that the contribution of assets (which do not constitute a business) to a joint venture in return for shares is within the scope of IFRS 2.

IFRS 2 does not directly address other types of transactions involving joint ventures or transactions involving associates.

3.3.5 Transactions in the scope of IAS 32 and IAS 39 or Section 22 of FRS 102 (financial instruments)

IFRS 2 does not apply to transactions within the scope of IAS 32 or IAS 39. Therefore, if an entity enters into a transaction to purchase, in return for shares, a commodity surplus to its production requirements or with a view to short-term profit taking, the contract is treated as a financial instrument under IAS 32 and IAS 39 rather than a share-based payment transaction under IFRS 2. *[IFRS 2.6].*

Some practical examples of scope issues involving IFRS 2 and IAS 32 / IAS 39 are discussed at 3.4 below.

Whilst Section 26 of FRS 102 has no specific corresponding reference to financial assets or liabilities, Section 22 – *Liabilities and Equity* – states that that Section applies to all types of financial instrument except '... Financial instruments, contracts and obligations under share-based payment transactions to which Section 26 applies...'.

Chapter 21

3.3.6   *Transactions relating to investments in subsidiaries, associates and joint ventures*

As noted in 3.2 above, IFRS 2 applies to share-based payment transactions involving goods or services, with 'goods' defined so as to exclude financial assets. This means that, when (as is commonly the case) an entity acquires an investment in a subsidiary, associate or joint venture for the issue of equity instruments, there is no explicit guidance as to the required accounting in the separate financial statements of the investor when it chooses to apply a policy of 'cost' under paragraph 24 of Section 9 – *Consolidated and Separate Financial Statements* (see separate chapter on the requirements of Section 9).

3.4   Some practical applications of the scope requirements

This section addresses the application of the scope requirements of Section 26 to a number of situations frequently encountered in practice. The situations are not specifically addressed in Section 26 but the following sections draw on the requirements of Section 26 together with related guidance in IFRS 2 and our experience of the practical application of IFRS 2:

- remuneration in non-equity shares and put rights over equity shares (see 3.4.1 below);
- an increase in the counterparty's ownership interest with no change in the number of shares held (see 3.4.2 below);
- awards for which the counterparty has paid 'fair value' (see 3.4.3 below);
- a cash bonus which depends on share price performance (see 3.4.4 below);
- cash-settled awards based on an entity's 'enterprise value' or other formula (see 3.4.5 below); and
- holding own shares to satisfy or 'hedge' awards (see 3.4.6 below).

The following aspects of the scope requirements are covered elsewhere in this Chapter:

- employment taxes on share-based payment transactions (see 15 below); and
- instruments such as limited recourse loans that sometimes fall within the scope of the share-based payment, rather than financial instruments, requirements because of the link both to the entity's equity instruments and to goods or services received in exchange (see 16.2 below).

3.4.1   *Remuneration in non-equity shares and put rights over equity shares*

A transaction is within the scope of Section 26 only where it involves the delivery of an equity instrument, or cash or other assets based on the price or value of 'an entity's shares or other equity instruments of the entity or another group entity' (see 3.1 above).

There can sometimes be advantages to giving an employee, in lieu of a cash payment, a share that carries a right to a 'one-off' dividend, or is mandatorily redeemable, at an amount equivalent to the intended cash payment. Such a share would almost certainly be classified as a liability (based on Section 22 of FRS 102). Payment in such a share would not fall in the scope of Section 26 since the consideration paid by the entity for services received is a financial liability rather than an equity instrument (see the definitions at 3.1 above).

If, however, the amount of remuneration delivered in this way were equivalent to the value of a particular number of equity instruments issued by the entity, then the transaction would be in scope of Section 26 as a cash-settled share-based payment transaction, since the entity would have incurred a liability (i.e. by issuing the redeemable shares) for an amount based on the price of its equity instruments.

Similarly, if an entity grants an award of equity instruments to an employee together with a put right whereby the employee can require the entity to purchase those shares, both elements of that transaction are in the scope of Section 26 as a single cash-settled transaction (see 10 below). This is notwithstanding the fact that, in other circumstances, the share and the put right might well be analysed as a single synthetic instrument and classified as a liability with no equity component.

3.4.2   Increase in ownership interest with no change in number of shares held

An increasingly common arrangement, typically found in entities with venture capital investors, is one where an employee (often part of the key management) subscribes initially for, say, 1% of the entity's equity with the venture capitalist holding the other 99%. The employee's equity interest will subsequently increase by a variable amount depending on the extent to which certain targets are met. This is achieved not by issuing new shares but by cancelling some of the venture capitalist's shares. In our view, such an arrangement falls within the scope of Section 26 as the employee is rewarded with an increased equity stake in the entity if certain targets are achieved. The increased equity stake is consistent with the definition of equity as 'a residual interest' notwithstanding the fact that no additional shares are issued.

In such arrangements, it is often asserted that the employee has subscribed for a share of the equity at fair value. However, the subscription price paid must represent a fair value using a Section 26 valuation basis in order for there to be no additional Section 26 expense to recognise (see 3.4.3 below).

3.4.3   Awards for which the counterparty has paid 'fair value'

In certain situations, such as where a special class of share is issued, the counterparty might be asked to subscribe a certain amount for the share which is agreed as being its 'fair value' for taxation or other purposes. This does not mean that such arrangements fall outside the scope of Section 26, either for measurement or disclosure purposes, if the arrangement meets the definition of a share-based payment transaction. In many cases, the agreed 'fair value' will be lower than a fair value measured in accordance with Section 26 because it will reflect the impact of service and non-market performance vesting conditions which are excluded from a Section 26 fair value (see 7 and 9 below). This is addressed in more detail at 16.4.5 below.

3.4.4   Cash bonus dependent on share price performance

An entity might agree to pay its employees a £100 cash bonus if its share price remains at £10 or more over a given period. Intuitively, this does not appear to be in the scope of Section 26, since the employee is not being given cash of equivalent value to a particular number of shares. However, it could be argued that it does fall within the scope of Section 26 on the basis that the entity has incurred a liability, and the amount of that liability is 'based on' the share price (in accordance with the definition of a cash-settled share-based payment transaction) – it is nil if the share price is below £10 and £100 if the share price is £10 or more. In our view, either interpretation is acceptable.

3.4.5   Cash-settled awards based on an entity's 'enterprise value' or other formula

As noted at 3.1 above, Section 26 includes within its scope transactions in which the entity acquires goods or services by incurring a liability 'based on the price (or value) of the entity's shares or other equity instruments of the entity or another group entity'. Employees of an unquoted entity may receive a cash award based on the value of the equity of that entity. Such awards are typically, but not exclusively, made by venture capital investors to the management of entities in which they have invested and which they aim to sell in the medium term. Further discussion of the accounting implications of awards made in connection with an exit event may be found at 16.4 below.

More generally, where employees of an unquoted entity receive a cash award based on the value of the equity, there is no quoted share price and an 'enterprise value' has therefore to be calculated as a surrogate for it. This begs the question of whether such awards are within the scope of Section 26 (because they are based on the value of the entity's equity) or that of Section 28 – *Employee Benefits*.

In order for an award to be within the scope of Section 26, any calculated 'enterprise value' must represent the fair value of the entity's equity. Where the calculation uses techniques recognised by Section 26 as yielding a fair value for equity instruments (as discussed at 9 below), we believe that the award should be regarded as within the scope of Section 26.

An unquoted entity may have calculated the value of its equity based on net assets or earnings (see 9.3 below). In our view, this may be appropriate in some cases.

Where, however, the enterprise value is based on a constant formula, such as a fixed multiple of earnings before interest, tax, depreciation and amortisation (EBITDA), in our view it is unlikely that this will represent a good surrogate for the fair value of the equity on an ongoing basis, even if it did so at the inception of the transaction. It is not difficult to imagine scenarios in which the fair value of the equity of an entity could be affected with no significant change in EBITDA, for example as a result of changes in interest rates and effective tax rates, or a significant impairment of assets. Alternatively, there might be a significant shift in the multiple of EBITDA equivalent to fair value, for example if the entity were to create or acquire a significant item of intellectual property.

The treatment of equity-settled awards based on the 'market price' of an unquoted entity raises similar issues, as discussed more fully at 7.3.7 below.

3.4.6 *Holding own shares to satisfy awards*

Entities often seek to 'hedge' the cost of share-based payment transactions by buying their own equity instruments in transactions with existing shareholders. For example, an entity could grant an employee options over 10,000 shares and buy 10,000 of its own shares into treasury, or into its employee benefit trust, at the date that the award is made. If the award is share-settled, the entity will deliver the shares to the counterparty. If it is cash-settled, it may be in a position to sell the shares to raise the cash it is required to deliver to the counterparty. In either case, the cash cost of the award is capped at the amount paid for the shares at the date the award is made, less any amount paid by the employee on exercise. It could of course be argued that such an arrangement only 'hedges' an increase in the price of the shares. If the share price goes down so that the option is never exercised, the entity is left holding 10,000 of its own shares that cost more than they are now worth.

Whilst these strategies may limit the cash cost of share-based payment transactions that are eventually exercised, they will not have any effect on the charge to profit or loss required by Section 26 for such transactions. This is because purchases and sales of own shares are accounted for as movements in equity and are therefore never included in profit or loss, i.e. the recognition of an expense under Section 26 for the share-based payment transaction and accounting for movements in own shares are two completely distinct areas which should be treated separately for accounting purposes (see 5.1 below).

4 GENERAL RECOGNITION PRINCIPLES

The recognition rules in Section 26 of FRS 102 are based on a so-called 'service date model'. In other words, the standard requires an entity to recognise the goods or services received or acquired in a share-based payment transaction when it obtains the goods or as the services are received. *[FRS 102.26.3]*. For awards to employees (or others providing similar services), this contrasts with the measurement rules, which normally require a share-based payment transaction to be measured as at the date on which the transaction was entered into, which may be some time before or after the related services are received – see 5 to 8 below.

Where the goods or services received or acquired in exchange for a share-based payment transaction do not qualify for recognition as assets they should be expensed. *[FRS 102.26.4]*. Typically, services will not qualify as assets and should therefore be expensed immediately, whereas goods will generally be initially recognised as assets and expensed later as they are consumed. However, some payments for services may be capitalised (e.g. as part of the cost of PP&E or inventories) and some payments for goods may be expensed immediately (e.g. where they are for items included within development costs written off as incurred).

The corresponding credit entry is, in the case of an equity-settled transaction, an increase in equity and, in the case of a cash-settled transaction, a liability (or decrease in cash or other assets). *[FRS 102.26.3]*.

The primary focus of the discussion in the remainder of this Chapter is the application of these rules to transactions with employees, with the accounting treatment of transactions with non-employees addressed at 3.2.3 above and 6.1 and 6.4 below.

4.1   Vesting and vesting conditions

Under Section 26 of FRS 102, the point at which a cost is recognised for goods or services depends on the concept of 'vesting'.

A share-based payment to a counterparty is said to *vest* when it becomes an entitlement of the counterparty. The term is further defined as follows:

'Under a share-based payment arrangement, a counterparty's right to receive cash, other assets or equity instruments of the entity vests when the counterparty's entitlement is no longer conditional on the satisfaction of any vesting conditions.' *[FRS 102 Appendix I].*

This definition refers only to equity instruments of the entity and omits any reference to equity instruments of other group entities. This appears to be a drafting oversight given that the scope of Section 26 and the definitions of equity- and cash-settled share-based payment transactions in the glossary to FRS 102 all refer to the equity instruments of the entity and other group entities.

Although the definition above refers to 'vesting conditions', this term is not defined in FRS 102. IFRS 2 defines a vesting condition as 'a condition that determines whether the entity receives the services that entitle the counterparty to receive cash, other assets or equity instruments of the entity, under a share-based payment arrangement. A vesting condition is either a service condition or a performance condition.' *[IFRS 2 Appendix A].* This is echoed in paragraph 9 of Section 26 which states that 'a grant of equity instruments might be conditional on employees satisfying specified vesting conditions related to service or performance' and goes on to provide examples of such conditions. *[FRS 102.26.9].* These are discussed later in this section.

The IFRS 2 definition of a vesting condition emphasises the receipt of services by the entity. The recognition principles in FRS 102 are consistent with this approach and underpin the differing accounting treatments, discussed further below, depending on whether the share-based payment transaction includes a service condition.

The absence of a service requirement means that an award will vest, or be deemed to vest, immediately as there is no service to be rendered before the counterparty becomes unconditionally entitled to the award. This concept of immediate vesting is reinforced by the fact that FRS 102 requires an entity to presume, in the absence of evidence to the contrary, that services rendered by an employee as consideration for the share-based payments have already been received. Where there is immediate vesting, the entity is required to recognise the services received, i.e. the cost of the award, in full on the grant date of the award with a corresponding credit to equity or liabilities. *[FRS 102.26.5].*

If, as will generally be the case for employee awards, the share-based payments do not vest until the employee completes a specified period of service, the entity should presume that the services to be rendered by the counterparty as consideration for those share-based payments will be received in the future, during the vesting period, i.e. the period over which the services are being rendered in order for the award to vest. The entity is required to account for those services as they are rendered by the employee during the vesting period, with a corresponding increase in equity or liabilities. *[FRS 102.26.6].* For example, if an employee is granted a share option with a service condition of remaining in employment with an entity for three years, the award vests three years after the date of grant. Accordingly, if the employee is still employed by the entity the cost of the award will be recognised over that three-year period.

As mentioned above, the vesting of awards might also be conditional on performance conditions which require both the counterparty to complete a specified period of service and specified performance targets to be met. FRS 102 includes the following general definition of a 'performance-related condition':

'A condition that requires the performance of a particular level of service or units of output to be delivered, with payment of, or entitlement to, the resources conditional on that performance.' *[FRS 102 Appendix I].*

Examples of performance conditions are a specified increase in the entity's profit over a specified period of time (a non-market condition – see 7.2 below) or a specified increase in the entity's share price (a market condition – see 7.3 below). *[FRS 102.26.9].* As discussed more fully at 4.2 below, performance conditions refer to performance by an employee (such as a personal sales target) or performance by the entity (or part of the entity), rather than an external performance indicator, such as a general stock market index.

Thus a condition that an award vests if, in three years' time, earnings per share have increased by 10% and the employee is still in employment, is a performance condition. If, however, the award vests in three years' time if earnings per share have increased by 10%, irrespective of whether the employee is still in employment, that condition is not a performance condition, but a 'non-vesting' condition (see 4.2 below).

In addition to the general discussion above and in the remainder this section, specific considerations relating to awards that vest on a flotation or change of control (or similar exit event) are addressed at 16.4 below.

4.2   Non-vesting conditions (conditions that are neither service conditions nor performance conditions)

Some share-based payment transactions are dependent on the satisfaction of conditions that are neither service conditions nor performance conditions. For example, an employee might be given the right to 100 shares in three years' time, subject only to the employee not working in competition with the reporting entity during that time. An undertaking not to work for another entity does not include a requirement for the counterparty to complete a specified period of service with the entity – the employee could sit on a beach for three years and still be entitled to collect the award. Accordingly, such a condition is not regarded as a vesting condition for the purposes of IFRS 2, but is instead referred to as a 'non-vesting condition'.

Section 26 of FRS 102 introduces the term 'non-vesting condition' when discussing the measurement of equity-settled awards but does not otherwise explain or define the term. *[FRS 102.26.9].* Given the similarities of approach to recognition and measurement in IFRS 2 and Section 26, we presume that the concept of a non-vesting condition under FRS 102 is intended to be the same as that under IFRS 2 and this is the approach adopted in this Chapter. The accounting impact of non-vesting conditions is discussed in detail at 7.4 below.

Although IFRS 2 contains a little more explanation about non-vesting conditions than is found in FRS 102, it does not explicitly define 'non-vesting condition' but uses the term to describe a condition that is neither a service condition nor a performance condition. However, the concept of the 'non-vesting' condition is not entirely clear and the identification of such conditions is not always straightforward. This has sometimes resulted in differing views on the appropriate classification of certain types of condition depending on whether or not they were considered to be measures of the entity's performance or its activities and hence performance vesting conditions.

As noted at 4.1 above, IFRS 2 defines a *vesting* condition as a condition that determines whether the entity receives the services that entitle the counterparty to receive payment in equity or cash. Performance conditions are those that require the counterparty to complete a specified period of service and specified performance targets to be met (such as a specified increase in the entity's profit over a specified period of time).

The Basis for Conclusions to IFRS 2 adds that the feature that distinguishes a performance condition from a non-vesting condition is that the former has an explicit or implicit service requirement and the latter does not. *[IFRS 2.BC171A]*.

In issuing its *Annual Improvements to IFRSs 2010-2012 Cycle* in December 2013 the IASB considered whether a definition of 'non-vesting condition' is needed. It decided that 'the creation of a stand-alone definition ... would not be the best alternative for providing clarity on this issue'. *[IFRS 2.BC364]*. Instead, it sought to provide further clarification in the Basis for Conclusions to IFRS 2, as follows:

'...the Board observed that the concept of a non-vesting condition can be inferred from paragraphs BC170-BC184 of IFRS 2, which clarify the definition of vesting conditions. In accordance with this guidance it can be inferred that a non-vesting condition is any condition that does not determine whether the entity receives the services that entitle the counterparty to receive cash, other assets or equity instruments of the entity under a share-based payment arrangement. In other words, a non-vesting condition is any condition that is not a vesting condition.' *[IFRS 2.BC364]*.

For a condition to be a performance vesting condition, it is not sufficient for the condition to be specific to the performance of the entity. There must also be an explicit or implied service condition. For example, a condition that requires the entity's profit before tax or its share price to reach a minimum level, but without any requirement for the employee to remain in employment throughout the performance period, is not a performance condition, but a non-vesting condition.

Specific examples of non-vesting conditions given by IFRS 2 include:

- a requirement to make monthly savings during the vesting period;
- a requirement for a commodity index to reach a minimum level;
- restrictions on the transfer of vested equity instruments; or
- an agreement not to work for a competitor after the award has vested – a 'non-compete' agreement. *[IFRS 2.BC171B, IG24]*.

The IASB has also clarified in the Basis for Conclusions to IFRS 2 that a condition related to a share market index target (rather than to the specific performance of the entity's own shares) is a non-vesting condition because a share market index reflects not only the performance of an entity but also that of other entities outside the group. Even where an entity's share price makes up a substantial part of the share market index, the IASB confirmed that this would still be a non-vesting condition because it reflects the performance of other, non-group, entities. *[IFRS 2.BC354-BC358].*

Thus, whilst conditions that are not related to the performance of the entity are always, by their nature, non-vesting conditions, conditions that relate to the performance of the entity may or may not be non-vesting conditions depending on whether there is also a requirement for the counterparty to render service.

As noted at 4.1 above, FRS 102 has a general definition of a performance-related condition. The more detailed definition in IFRS 2 clarifies the extent to which the period of achieving the performance target(s) needs to coincide with the service period and states that this performance period:

(a)   shall not extend beyond the end of the service period; and

(b)   may start before the service period on the condition that the commencement date of the performance target is not substantially before the commencement of the service period.

In the absence of specific guidance in FRS 102, we suggest that a similar approach is adopted. Notwithstanding the amended definition, however, there clearly remains an element of judgement in the interpretation of 'substantially' as used in the definition.

There is further discussion of the accounting treatment of non-vesting conditions at 7.4 below.

4.3   Vesting period

As noted at 4.1 above, the vesting period is the period during which all the specified vesting conditions of a share-based payment arrangement are to be satisfied. This is not the same as the exercise period or the life of the option, as illustrated by Example 21.1 below.

Example 21.1:   Meaning of 'vesting period' – award with vesting conditions only

An employee is awarded options that can be exercised, if the employee remains in service for at least three years from the date of the award, at any time between three and ten years from the date of the award. For this award, the vesting period is three years; the exercise period is seven years; and the life of the option is ten years. However, as discussed further in 9 below, for the purposes of calculating the cost of the award, the life of the award is taken as the period ending with the date on which the counterparty is most likely actually to exercise the option, which may be some time before the full ten year life expires.

It is also important to distinguish between vesting conditions and other restrictions on the exercise of options and/or trading in shares, as illustrated by Example 21.2 below.

Example 21.2:   Meaning of 'vesting period' – award with vesting conditions and other restrictions

An employee is awarded options that can be exercised, if the employee remains in service for at least three years from the date of the award, at any time between five and ten years from the date of the award. In this case, the vesting period remains three years as in Example 21.1 above, provided that the employee's entitlement to the award becomes absolute at the end of three years – in other words, the employee does not have to provide services to the entity in years 4 and 5. The restriction on exercise of the award in the period after vesting is a non-vesting condition, which would be reflected in the original valuation of the award at the date of grant (see 5, 6 and 9 below).

The implications of vesting conditions, non-vesting conditions and vesting periods for equity-settled transactions are discussed in 5 to 8 below and for cash-settled transactions in 10 below.

5   EQUITY-SETTLED TRANSACTIONS – OVERVIEW

5.1   Summary of accounting treatment

The provisions relating to accounting for equity-settled transactions are complex, even when supplemented by additional guidance as is found in the appendices and implementation guidance to IFRS 2. As noted at 1.3 above, FRS 102 does not replicate this guidance and so we have referred to IFRS 2 to supplement the requirements of FRS 102.

The key points can be summarised as follows.

(a)   All equity-settled transactions are measured at fair value. However, transactions with employees are measured using a 'grant date model' (i.e. the transaction is recorded at the fair value of the equity instrument at the date when it is originally granted), whereas transactions with non-employees are normally measured using a 'service date model' (i.e. the transaction is recorded at the fair value of the goods or services received at the date they are received). As noted in 4 above, all transactions, however *measured*, are *recognised* using a 'service date model' (see 6 below).

(b)   Where an award is made subject to future fulfilment of conditions, a 'market condition' (i.e. one related to the market price of the entity's equity instruments) or a 'non-vesting condition' (i.e. one that is neither a service condition nor a performance condition) is taken into account in determining the fair value of the award. However, the effect of conditions other than market or non-vesting conditions is ignored in determining the fair value of the award (see 4 above and 7 below).

(c)   Where an award is made subject to future fulfilment of service or performance vesting conditions, its cost is recognised over the period during which the conditions are fulfilled (see 4 above and 7 below). The corresponding credit entry is recorded within equity (see 5.2 below).

(d)   Until an equity instrument has vested (i.e. the entitlement to it is no longer conditional on future service) any amounts recorded are in effect contingent and will be adjusted if more or fewer awards vest than were originally anticipated to do so. However, an equity instrument awarded subject to a market condition or a non-vesting condition is considered to vest irrespective of whether or not that market or non-vesting condition is fulfilled, provided that all other vesting conditions (if any) are satisfied (see 7 below).

(e)   No adjustments are made, either before or after vesting, to reflect the fact that an award has no value to the person entitled to it e.g. in the case of a share option, because the option exercise price is above the current market price of the share (see 7.1.1 and 7.1.3 below).

(f)   If an equity instrument is cancelled, whether by the entity or the counterparty (see (g) below) before vesting, any amount remaining to be expensed is charged in full at that point (see 8.4 below). If an equity instrument is modified before vesting (e.g. in the case of a share option, by changing the performance conditions or the exercise price), the financial statements must continue to show a cost for at least the fair value of the original instrument, as measured at the original grant date, together with any excess of the fair value of the modified instrument over that of the original instrument, as measured at the date of modification (see 8.3 below).

(g)   Where an award lapses during the vesting period due to a failure by the counterparty to satisfy a non-vesting condition within the counterparty's control, or a failure by the entity to satisfy a non-vesting condition within the entity's control, the lapse of the award is accounted for as if it were a cancellation (see (f) above and 7.4.3 below).

(h)   In determining the cost of an equity-settled transaction, whether the entity satisfies its obligations under the transaction with a fresh issue of shares or by purchasing its own shares in the financial markets or from private company shareholders is completely irrelevant to the charge in profit or loss, although there is clearly a difference in the cash flows. Where own shares are purchased, they are accounted for as treasury shares (see 3.4.6 above).

The requirements summarised in (d) to (g) above can have the effect that an entity is required to record a cost for an award that is deemed to vest for accounting purposes but ultimately has no value to the counterparty because the award either does not vest or vests but is not exercised. These rather counter-intuitive requirements are in part 'anti-abuse' provisions to prevent entities from applying a 'selective' grant date model, whereby awards that increase in value after grant date remain measured at grant date while awards that decrease in value are remeasured. This is discussed further in the detailed analysis at 6 to 8 below.

5.2   The credit entry

As noted at (c) in the summary in 5.1 above, the basic accounting entry for an equity-settled share-based payment transaction is:

   Dr   Profit or loss for the period (employee costs)

      Cr   Equity. *[FRS 102.26.3]*.

FRS 102 does not prescribe whether the credit should be to a separate reserve or, if the entity chooses to treat it as such, how it should be described. Under the Companies Act 2006, an entity is permitted to credit a separate 'other reserve' rather than the credit being allocated initially to the profit and loss reserve. The 'other reserve' is generally labelled as 'shares to be issued' or 'share-based payment reserve' with the share-based payment credit held within this reserve until the award vests (if an award of free shares), is exercised or lapses (an award of options). When such trigger events occur, it will be appropriate for the entity to make a transfer between reserves.

The FRS 102 credit is not taken to share capital and share premium as these are used to record the legal proceeds of a share issue.

Overall, there will be a net nil impact on equity and on distributable profits arising from the FRS 102 accounting as the profit and loss expense is ultimately reflected in the profit and loss reserve and offset by the credit taken directly to equity.

Occasionally there will be a credit to profit or loss (see for instance Example 21.12 at 7.2.4 below) and a corresponding reduction in equity.

6   EQUITY-SETTLED TRANSACTIONS – COST OF AWARDS

6.1   Cost of awards – overview

The general measurement rule in FRS 102 is that an entity must measure the goods or services received, and the corresponding increase in equity, directly, at the fair value of the goods or services received, unless that fair value cannot be estimated reliably. If the fair value of the goods or services received cannot be estimated reliably, the entity must measure their value, and the corresponding increase in equity, indirectly, by reference to the fair value of the equity instruments granted. *[FRS 102.26.7]*.

'Fair value' is defined in the glossary to FRS 102 as 'the amount for which an asset could be exchanged, a liability settled, or an equity instrument granted could be exchanged, between knowledgeable, willing parties in an arm's length transaction'. The definition goes on to make clear that, in the absence of more specific guidance within individual sections of FRS 102, paragraphs 27 to 32 of Section *11 – Basic Financial Instruments* should be used for determining fair value. Therefore, where the fair value of a share-based payment is based on the fair value of the goods or services, the Section 11 guidance should be used. Where the share-based payment is measured on the basis of the fair value of the equity instruments rather than the goods or services, Section 26 of FRS 102 has its own specific rules in relation to determining the fair value which differ from the more general fair value measurement requirements of FRS 102 (see 6.5 below).

On their own, the general measurement principles of paragraph 7 of Section 26 might suggest that the reporting entity must determine in each case whether the fair value of the equity instruments granted or that of the goods or services received is more reliably determinable. However, paragraph 7 goes on to clarify that, in the case of transactions with employees and others providing similar services, the fair value of the equity instruments must always be used 'because typically it is not possible to estimate reliably the fair value of the services received' (see 6.2 below). *[FRS 102.26.7]*.

Moreover, transactions with employees and others providing similar services are measured at the date of grant (see 6.2 below), whereas those with non-employees are measured at the date when the entity obtains the goods or the counterparty renders service (see 6.4 below). *[FRS 102.26.8]*.

The overall position can be summarised by the following matrix.

Counterparty	Measurement basis	Measurement date	Recognition date
Employee	Fair value of equity instruments awarded	Grant date	Service date
Non-employee	Fair value of goods or services received or, if goods or services not reliably measurable, fair value of equity instruments awarded	Service date	Service date

One effect of a grant date measurement model is that, applied to a grant of share options that is eventually exercised, it 'freezes' the accounting cost at the (typically) lower fair value at the date of grant. This excludes from the post-grant financial statements the increased cost and volatility that would be associated with a model that constantly remeasured the award to fair value until exercise date.

The price to be paid in accounting terms for the grant date model is that, when an award falls in value after grant date, it continues to be recognised at its higher grant date value. It is therefore quite possible that, during a period of general economic downturn, financial statements will show significant costs for options granted in previous years, but which are currently worthless.

6.2   Transactions with employees and others providing similar services

These will comprise the great majority of transactions accounted for as equity-settled share-based payments under Section 26 and include all remuneration in the form of shares, share options and any other form of reward settled in equity instruments of the entity or a member of its group.

6.2.1   Who is an 'employee'?

Given the difference between the accounting treatment of equity-settled transactions with employees and with non-employees, it is obviously important to understand what is meant by 'employees and others providing similar services'. *[FRS 102.26.7].* FRS 102 does not provide a definition but IFRS 2 defines 'employees and others providing similar services' as individuals who render personal services to the entity and either:

(a)   the individuals are regarded as employees for legal or tax purposes;

(b)   the individuals work for the entity under its direction in the same way as individuals who are regarded as employees for legal or tax purposes; or

(c)   the services rendered are similar to those rendered by employees.

The term encompasses all management personnel, i.e. those persons having authority and responsibility for planning, directing and controlling the activities of the entity, including non-executive directors. *[IFRS 2 Appendix A].*

Chapter 21

The implication of (a) and (b) above is that it is not open to an entity to argue that an individual who is not an employee as a matter of law is therefore automatically a non-employee for the purposes of IFRS 2 and FRS 102.

The implication of (b) and (c) above is that, where a third party provides services pursuant to a share-based payment transaction that could be provided by an employee (e.g. where an external IT consultant works alongside an in-house IT team), that third party is treated as an employee rather than a non-employee for the purposes of IFRS 2 and FRS 102.

Conversely, however, where an entity engages a consultant to undertake work for which there is not an existing in-house function, the implication is that such an individual is not regarded as an employee. In other words, in our view, the reference in (c) to 'services ... similar to those rendered by employees' is to services rendered by employees that the entity actually has, rather than to employees that the entity might have if it were to recruit them. Otherwise, the distinction in IFRS 2 and FRS 102 between employees and non-employees would have no effect, since it would always be open to an entity to argue that it could employ someone to undertake any task instead of engaging a contractor.

Exceptionally there might be cases where the same individual is engaged in both capacities. For example, a director of the entity might also be a partner in a firm of lawyers and be engaged in that latter capacity to advise the entity on a particular issue. It might be more appropriate to regard payment for the legal services as made to a non-employee rather than to an employee.

6.2.2   Basis of measurement

As noted above, equity-settled transactions with employees must be measured by reference to the fair value of the equity instruments granted at 'grant date' (see 6.3 below). *[FRS 102.26.8]*. FRS 102 offers no explanation as to why this should be the case, but IFRS 2 asserts that this approach is necessary because shares, share options and other equity instruments are typically only part of a larger remuneration package, such that it would not be practicable to determine the value of the work performed in consideration for the cash element of the total package, the benefit-in-kind element, the share option element and so on. *[IFRS 2.12]*.

In essence, this is really an anti-avoidance provision. The underlying concern is that, if an entity were able to value options by reference to the services provided for them, it might assert that the value of those services was zero, on the argument that its personnel are already so handsomely rewarded by the non-equity elements of their remuneration package (such as cash and health benefits), that no additional services are (or indeed could be) obtained by granting options.

6.3   Grant date

The determination of grant date is critical to the measurement of equity-settled share-based transactions with employees, since grant date is the date at which such transactions must be measured (see 6.2 above). Grant date is defined as:

'The date at which the entity and another party (including an employee) agree to a share-based payment arrangement, being when the entity and the counterparty have a shared understanding of the terms and conditions of the arrangement. At grant date the entity confers on the counterparty the right to cash, other assets or equity instruments of the entity, provided the specified vesting conditions, if any, are met. If that agreement is subject to an approval process (for example, by shareholders), grant date is the date when that approval is obtained.' *[FRS 102 Appendix I].*

In practice, it is not always clear when a shared understanding of the award (and, therefore, grant date) has occurred. Issues of interpretation can arise as to:

- how precise the shared understanding of the terms of the award must be; and
- exactly what level of communication between the reporting entity and the counterparty is sufficient to ensure the appropriate degree of 'shared understanding'.

The determination of the grant date is often difficult. We discuss the following issues in more detail in the sections below:

- basic determination of grant date (see 6.3.1 below);
- the communication of awards to employees and cases where services are rendered in advance of grant date (see 6.3.2 below);
- awards where the exercise price depends on the share price (see 6.3.3 below);
- awards where the exercise price is paid in shares (see 6.3.4 below);
- an award of equity instruments to a fixed monetary value (see 6.3.5 below);
- awards with multiple service periods (see 6.3.6 below);
- awards subject to modification or discretionary re-assessment by the entity after the original grant date (see 6.3.7 below); and
- mandatory or discretionary awards to 'good leavers' (see 6.3.8 below).

Some arrangements give rise to significant issues of interpretation in relation to the determination of grant date and the appropriate accounting treatment. For example:

- automatic full or *pro rata* entitlement to awards on cessation of employment (se 6.3.8.C below); and
- awards over a fixed pool of shares (including 'last man standing' arrangements) (see 6.3.9 below).

An outline of the nature of these arrangements is given in this Chapter but a detailed discussion is beyond the scope of this publication.

6.3.1 Determination of grant date

The definition of 'grant date' in the glossary to FRS 102 (see 6.3 above) emphasises that a grant occurs only when all the conditions are known and agreed. This is reinforced by the implementation guidance accompanying the same definition in IFRS 2 which, in our view, should also be considered by an entity applying FRS 102.

For example, if an entity makes an award 'in principle' to an employee of options whose terms are subject to review or approval by a remuneration committee or the shareholders, 'grant date' is the later date when the necessary formalities have been completed. *[FRS 102 Appendix I, IFRS 2.IG1-3].*

The implementation guidance to IFRS 2 notes that employees may begin rendering services in consideration for an award before it has been formally ratified. For example, a new employee might join an entity on 1 January 2015 and be granted options relating to performance for a period beginning on that date, but subject to formal approval by the remuneration committee at its quarterly meeting on 15 March 2015. In that case, the entity would typically begin expensing the award from 1 January 2015 based on a best estimate of its fair value, but would subsequently adjust that estimate so that the ultimate cost of the award was its actual fair value at 15 March 2015 (see 6.3.2 below). *[IFRS 2.IG4].* This reference to formal approval could be construed as indicating that, in fact, FRS 102 and IFRS 2 require not merely that there is a mutual understanding of the award (which might well have been in existence since 1 January 2015), but also that the entity has completed all processes necessary to make the award a legally binding agreement.

6.3.2   Communication of awards to employees and services in advance of grant date

As discussed at 6.3.1 above, the definition of grant date in FRS 102 together with the implementation guidance to IFRS 2 indicate that, in order for a grant to have been made, there must not merely be a mutual understanding of the terms – including the conditions attached to the award – but there must also be a legally enforceable arrangement. Thus, if an award requires board or shareholder approval for it to be legally binding on the reporting entity, it has not been granted until such approval has been given, even if the terms of the award are fully understood at an earlier date. However, if services are effectively being rendered for an award from a date earlier than the grant date as defined in IFRS 2, the cost of the award should be recognised over a period starting with that earlier date. *[IFRS 2.IG4].* In our view, this approach applies in situations where the precise terms and conditions of an award have yet to be confirmed as well as to situations where formal approval does not take place until a later date. Whilst not a requirement of Section 26, we believe that a similar approach would be appropriate where the effect is significant.

The implications of this approach are illustrated in Example 21.3 below for a situation where formal approval of an award is delayed. It is important, however, to retain a sense of proportion. In cases where the share price or value is not particularly volatile, whether the grant date is, say, 1 January or 1 April may not make a great difference to the valuation of the award, particularly when set beside the range of acceptable valuations resulting from the use of estimates in the valuation process.

Example 21.3:   Determination of grant date

Scenario 1

On 1 January 2015 an entity advises employees of the terms of a share award designed to reward performance over the three years ended 31 December 2017. The award is subject to board approval, which is given on 1 March 2015. Grant date is 1 March 2015. However, the cost of the award would be recognised over the three year period beginning 1 January 2015, since the employees would have effectively been rendering service for the award from that date.

Scenario 2

On 1 January 2015 an entity's board resolves to implement a share scheme designed to reward performance over the three years ended 31 December 2017. The award is notified to employees on 1 March 2015. Grant date is again 1 March 2015. *Prima facie*, in this case, the cost of the award would be recognised over the two years and ten months period beginning 1 March 2015, since the employees could not be regarded as rendering service in January and February for an award of which they were not aware at that time.

However, if a similar award is made each year, and according to a similar timescale, there might be an argument that, during January and February 2015, employees are rendering service for an award of which there is high expectation, and that the cost should therefore, as in Scenario 1, be recognised over the full three year period.

Scenario 3

On 1 January 2015 an entity advises employees of the terms of a share award designed to reward performance over the three years ended 31 December 2017. The award is subject to board approval, which is given on 1 March 2015. However, in giving such approval, the Board makes some changes to the performance conditions as originally communicated to employees on 1 January. The revised terms of the award are communicated to employees on 1 April 2015. Grant date is 1 April 2015. However, the cost of the award would be recognised over the three year period beginning 1 January 2015, since the employees would have effectively been rendering service for the award from that date.

Examples of situations where an employee might render service in advance of the formal grant date because the precise conditions of an award are outstanding are considered at 6.3.3 to 6.3.6 and at 16.4.1 below.

6.3.3 Exercise price or performance target dependent on a formula or future share price

Some share plans define the exercise price not in absolute terms, but as a factor of the share price. For example, the price might be expressed as:

- a percentage of the share price at exercise date; or
- a percentage of the lower of the share price at grant date and at exercise date.

The effect of this is that, although the actual exercise price is not known until the date of exercise, both the entity and the counterparty already have a shared understanding of how the price will be calculated.

A similar approach might be applied in the setting of performance targets, i.e. they are set by reference to a formula rather than in absolute terms.

In order for there to be a shared understanding, the formula or method of determining the outcome needs to be sufficiently clear and objective to allow both the entity and the counterparty to make an estimate of the outcome of the award during the vesting period. Accordingly, in our view, grant date is the date on which the terms and conditions (including the formula for calculating the exercise price or performance target) are determined sufficiently clearly and agreed by the entity and the counterparty, subject to the matters discussed at 6.3.2 above.

Chapter 21

6.3.4   *Exercise price paid in shares (net settlement of award)*

Some share awards allow the exercise price to be paid in shares. In practical terms, this means that the number of shares delivered to the counterparty will be the total 'gross' number of shares awarded less as many shares as have, at the date of exercise, a fair value equal to the strike price.

In our view, this situation is analogous to that in 6.3.3 above in that, whilst the absolute 'net' number of shares awarded will not be known until the date of exercise, the basis on which that 'net' number will be determined is established in advance. Accordingly, in our view, grant date is the date on which the terms and conditions (including the ability to surrender shares to a fair value equal to the exercise price) are determined and agreed by the entity and the counterparty, subject to the matters discussed at 6.3.2 above.

Such a scheme could also be analysed as a share-settled share appreciation right (whereby the employee receives shares to the value of the excess of the value of the shares given over the exercise price), which is accounted for as an equity-settled award.

6.3.5   *Award of equity instruments to a fixed monetary value*

Some entities may grant awards to employees of shares to a fixed value. For example, an entity might award as many shares as are worth £10,000, with the number of shares being calculated by reference to the share price as at the vesting date. The number of shares ultimately received will not be known until the vesting date. This begs the question of whether such an award can be regarded as having been granted until that date, on the argument that it is only then that the number of shares to be delivered – a key term of the award – is known, and therefore there cannot be a 'shared understanding' of the terms of the award until that later date.

In our view, this situation is analogous to those in 6.3.3 and 6.3.4 above in that, whilst the absolute number of shares awarded will not be known until the vesting date, the basis on which that number will be determined is established in advance in a manner sufficiently clear and objective as to allow an ongoing estimate by the entity and by the counterparty of the number of awards expected to vest. Accordingly, in our view, grant date is the date on which the terms and conditions are determined sufficiently clearly and agreed by the entity and the counterparty, subject to the matters discussed at 6.3.2 above.

FRS 102 does not address the valuation of such awards and IFRS 2 does not address it directly. Intuitively, it might seem obvious that an award which promises (subject to vesting conditions) shares to the value of £10,000 must have a grant date fair value of £10,000, adjusted for the time value of money, together with market conditions and non-vesting conditions. However, matters are not so clear-cut, as Example 21.4 illustrates:

Example 21.4: Award of shares to a fixed monetary value

On 1 January 2015, the reporting entity grants:

- to Employee A an award of 1,000 shares subject to remaining in employment until 31 December 2017; and

- to Employee B £10,000 subject to remaining in employment until 31 December 2017, to be paid in as many shares as are (on 31 December 2017) worth £10,000.

Both awards vest, and the share price on 31 December 2017 is £10, so that both employees receive 1,000 shares.

The charge for A's award is clearly 1000 × the fair value as at 1 January 2015 of a share deliverable in three years' time. What is the charge for B's award – the same as for A's or £10,000, adjusted for the time value of money?

Whilst there are hints in the Basis for Conclusions to IFRS 2 that the IASB thought that the two awards should be similarly valued, this treatment is not made explicitly clear.

Some argue that an award of shares to a given monetary amount contains a market condition, since the number of shares ultimately delivered (and therefore vesting) depends on the market price of the shares on the date of delivery. This allows the award to be valued at a fixed amount at grant date. We acknowledge that a literal reading of the definition of 'market condition' in FRS 102 and IFRS 2 supports this view, but question whether this can really have been intended. In our view, the essential feature of a share-based payment transaction subject to a market condition must be that the employee's ultimate entitlement to the award depends on the share price.

In our view, in the absence of clear guidance, entities may take a number of views on how to value awards of shares to a given value, but should adopt a consistent approach for all such awards.

6.3.6 Awards with multiple service periods

Entities frequently make awards that cover more than one reporting period, but with different performance conditions for each period, rather than a single cumulative target for the whole vesting period. In such cases, the grant date may depend on the precision with which the terms of the award are communicated to employees, as illustrated by Example 21.5 below.

Example 21.5: Awards with multiple service periods

Scenario 1

On 1 January 2015, the entity enters into a share-based payment arrangement with an employee. The employee is informed that the maximum potential award is 40,000 shares, 10,000 of which will vest on 31 December 2015, and 10,000 more on each of 31 December 2016, 31 December 2017 and 31 December 2018. Vesting of each tranche of 10,000 shares is conditional on:

(a) the employee having been in continuous service until 31 December of the relevant year;

(b) revenue targets for each of those four years, as communicated to the employee on 1 January 2015, having been attained.

In this case, the terms of the award are clearly understood by both parties at 1 January 2015, and this is therefore the grant date under FRS 102 (subject to issues such as any requirement for later formal approval – see 6.3 above). The cost of the award would be recognised using a 'graded' vesting approach – see 7.2.2 below.

Scenario 2

On 1 January 2015, the entity enters into a share-based payment arrangement with an employee. The employee is informed that the maximum potential award is 40,000 shares, 10,000 of which will vest on 31 December 2015, and 10,000 more on each of 31 December 2016, 31 December 2017 and 31 December 2018. Vesting of each tranche of 10,000 shares is conditional on:

(a) the employee having been in continuous service until 31 December of the relevant year;

(b) revenue targets for each of those four years, to be communicated to the employee on 1 January of each year in respect of that year only, having been attained.

In this case, in our view, as at 1 January 2015, there is a clear shared understanding only of the terms of the first tranche of 10,000 shares that will potentially vest on 31 December 2015. There is no clear understanding of the terms of the tranches potentially vesting in 2016 to 2018 because their vesting depends on revenue targets for those years which have not yet been set.

Accordingly, each of the four tranches of 10,000 shares has a separate grant date (and, therefore, a separate measurement date) – i.e. 1 January 2015, 1 January 2016, 1 January 2017 and 1 January 2018 – and a vesting period of one year from the relevant grant date.

6.3.7   *Awards subject to modification by entity after original grant date*

Some employee share awards are drafted in terms that give the entity discretion to modify the detailed terms of the scheme after grant date. Some have questioned whether this effectively means that the date originally determined as the 'grant date' is not in fact the grant date as defined in FRS 102, on the grounds that the entity's right to modify means that the terms are not in fact understood by both parties in advance.

In our view, this is very often not an appropriate analysis. If it were, it could mean that significant numbers of share-based awards to employees (including most in the UK) would be required to be measured at vesting date, which clearly was not the IASB's intention when it developed the grant date model in IFRS 2 which forms the basis of the approach adopted in Section 26.

However, assessment of whether or not an intervention by the entity after grant date constitutes a modification is often difficult. Some situations commonly encountered in practice are considered in the sections below.

6.3.7.A   *Significant equity restructuring or transactions*

Many schemes contain provisions designed to ensure that the value of awards is maintained following a major capital restructuring (such as a share split or share consolidation – see 8.7 below) or a major transaction with shareholders as a whole (such as a major share buyback or the payment of a special dividend). These provisions will either specify the adjustments to be made in a particular situation or, alternatively, may allow the entity to make such discretionary adjustments as it sees fit in order to maintain the value of awards. In some cases the exercise of such discretionary powers may be relatively mechanistic (e.g. the adjustment of the number of shares subject to options following a share split). In other cases, more subjectivity will be involved (e.g. in determining whether a particular dividend is a 'special' dividend for the purposes of the scheme).

In our view, where the scheme rules specify the adjustments to be made or where there is a legal requirement to make adjustments in order to remedy any dilution that would otherwise arise, the implementation of such adjustments would not result in the recognition of any incremental fair value. This assumes that the adjustment would simply operate on an automatic basis to put the holders of awards back to the position that they would have been in had there not been a restructuring and hence there would be no difference in the fair value of the awards before and after the restructuring (or other specified event).

However, where there is no such explicit requirement in the scheme rules or under relevant legislation, we believe that there should be a presumption that the exercise of the entity's discretionary right to modify is a 'modification' as outlined in FRS 102. In such a situation, the fair values before and after the modification may differ and any incremental fair value should be expensed over the remaining vesting period (see 8.3 below).

6.3.7.B   Interpretation of general terms

More problematic might be the exercise of any discretion by the entity to interpret the more general terms of a scheme. In this case, there might be more of an argument that the entity's intervention constitutes a modification.

If such an intervention were not regarded as a modification, then the results might be different depending on the nature of the award and the conditions attached to it. Where an award is subject to a market condition, or to a non-vesting condition, an expense might well have to be recognised in any event, if all the non-market vesting conditions (e.g. service) were satisfied – see 7.3 and 7.4 below.

However, suppose that an award had been based on a non-market performance condition, such as a profit target, which was met, but only due to a gain of an unusual, non-recurring nature. The Board of Directors concludes that this should be ignored, with the effect that the award does not vest. If this is regarded as the exercise of a pre-existing right to ensure that the award vests only if 'normal' profit reaches a given level, then there has been no modification. On this analysis, the award has not vested, and any expense previously recognised would be reversed. If, however, the Board's intervention is regarded as a modification, it would have no impact on the accounting treatment in this case, as the effect would be to reduce the fair value of the award and this would be ignored under the general requirements of FRS 102 relating to modifications (see 8.3.2 below).

6.3.7.C   Discretion to make further awards

Some schemes may contain terms that give the entity the power to increase an award in circumstances where the recipient is considered to have delivered exceptional performance, or some such similar wording. In our view, unless the criteria for judging such exceptional performance are so clear as to be, in effect, performance conditions, the presumption should be that any award made pursuant to such a clause is granted, and therefore measured, when it is made. There may be circumstances where an award described as 'discretionary' may not truly be so, since the entity has created an expectation amounting to a constructive obligation to make the award. However, we believe that it would be somewhat contradictory to argue that such expectations had been created in the case of an award stated to be for (undefined) exceptional performance only.

6.3.8   *'Good leaver' arrangements*

It is common for awards to contain a so-called 'good leaver' clause. A 'good leaver' clause is one which makes provision for an employee who leaves before the end of the full vesting period of an award nevertheless to receive some or all of the award on leaving (see 6.3.8.A below).

In other cases, the original terms of an award will either make no reference to 'good leavers' or will not be sufficiently specific to allow the accounting treatment on cessation of employment to be an automatic outcome of the original terms of the scheme. In such cases, and where awards are made to leavers on a fully discretionary basis, the accounting approach differs from that required where the original terms are clear about 'good leaver' classification and entitlement (see 6.3.8.B below).

6.3.8.A   *Provision for 'good leavers' made in original terms of award*

In some cases the types of person who are 'good leavers' may be explicitly defined in the original terms of the arrangement (common examples being persons who die or reach normal retirement age before the end of the full vesting period, or who work for a business unit that is sold or closed during the vesting period). In other cases, the entity may have the discretion to determine on a case-by-case basis whether a person should be treated as a 'good leaver'.

In addition, some schemes may specify the entitlement of a 'good leaver' on leaving (e.g. that the leaver receive a portion of the award pro-rata to the extent that the performance conditions have been met as at the date of leaving), whereas others leave the determination of the award to the entity at the time that the employee leaves.

Whichever situation applies, any expense relating to an award to a good leaver must be fully recognised by the leaving date (or date of unconditional entitlement, if earlier than the usual vesting date) because, at that point, the good leaver ceases to provide any services to the entity for the award and any remaining conditions attached to the award will be treated as non-vesting rather than vesting conditions (see 4.2 above).

In our view, an award which vests before the end of the original vesting period due to the operation of a 'good leaver' clause is measured at the original grant date only where – under the rules of the scheme as understood by both parties at the original grant date – the award is made:

- to a person clearly identified as a 'good leaver'; and
- in an amount clearly quantified or quantifiable.

Where, as outlined above, the rules of the scheme make clear the categories of 'good leaver' and their entitlement, the entity should assess at grant date how many good leavers there are likely to be and to what extent the service period for these particular individuals is expected to be shorter than the full vesting period. The grant date fair value of the estimated awards to good leavers should be separately determined, where significant, and the expense relating to good leavers recognised over the expected period between grant date and leaving employment (or date of unconditional entitlement). In this situation the entity would re-estimate the number of good leavers and adjust the cumulative expense at each reporting date.

This would be a change of estimate rather than a modification of the award as it would all be in accordance with the original terms and would require no discretionary decisions on the part of the entity. We would generally expect an entity not to have significant numbers of good leavers under such an arrangement.

6.3.8.B   Discretionary awards to 'good leavers'

Awards where the arrangements for leavers are clear as at the original grant date of the award are discussed at 6.3.8.A above. However, where – as is more usually the case – the entity determines only at the time that the employee leaves either that the employee is a 'good leaver' or the amount of the award, grant date should be taken as the later of the date on which such determination is made, or the date on which the award is notified to the employee. This is because the employee had no clear understanding at the original grant date of an automatic entitlement to equity instruments other than through full vesting of the award. The award at the time of leaving is therefore considered, depending on the precise circumstances, to be either a modification of an original award or the forfeiture or cancellation of the original award and the granting of a completely new award on a discretionary basis (see 8.3 and 8.5 below).

In some cases, a good leaver will be allowed, on a discretionary basis, to keep existing awards that remain subject to the fulfilment of the conditions established at the original grant date. In this situation, any conditions that were previously treated as vesting conditions will become non-vesting conditions following the removal of the service requirement (see 4.1 and 4.2 above). This will be the case whether the discretionary arrangement is accounted for as the forfeiture or cancellation of the old award plus a new grant or as a modification of the original award.

The non-vesting conditions will need to be reflected in the measurement of the fair value of the award as at the date of modification or new grant (although the non-vesting conditions alone will not result in any incremental fair value). Any fair value that is unrecognised as at the date of the good leaver ceasing employment will need to be expensed immediately as there is no further service period over which to recognise the expense.

There is further discussion of modifications at 8.3 below and of replacement awards granted on termination of employment at 8.5 below.

6.3.8.C   Automatic full or pro rata entitlement on cessation of employment

In some cases, entities establish schemes where a significant number of the participants will potentially leave employment before the end of the full vesting period and will be allowed to keep a *pro rata* share of the award.

Such arrangements are encountered relatively infrequently and mostly outside the UK. Accordingly, a detailed discussion of the accounting treatment is beyond the scope of this publication. There is further detail available in EY International GAAP 2015.

6.3.9   Awards over a fixed pool of shares (including 'last man standing' arrangements)

An award over a fixed pool of shares is sometimes granted to a small group of, typically senior, employees. Such awards might involve an initial allocation of shares to each individual but also provide for the redistribution of each employee's shares to the other participants should any individual leave employment before the end of the vesting period. This is often referred to as a 'last man standing' arrangement.

The accounting requirements for such an arrangement are unclear and beyond the scope of this publication. In the absence of specific guidance, several interpretations are possible and these are discussed in EY International GAAP 2015.

6.4   Transactions with non-employees

In accounting for equity-settled transactions with non-employees, the starting point is that the value of the goods or services received provides the more reliable indication of the fair value of the transaction. The fair value to be used is that at the date on which the goods are obtained or the services rendered. *[FRS 102.26.3, 7-8]*. This implies that, where the goods or services are received on a number of dates over a period, the fair value at each date should be used, although in the case of a relatively short period there may be no great fluctuation in fair value.

If the entity rebuts the presumption that the goods or services provide the more reliable indication of fair value, it may use as a surrogate measure the fair value of the equity instruments granted, but as at the date when the goods or services are received, not the original grant date. However, where the goods or services are received over a relatively short period and the share price does not change significantly, an average share price can be used in calculating the fair value of equity instruments granted.

6.4.1   Effect of change of status from employee to non-employee (or vice versa)

Neither FRS 102 nor IFRS 2 gives specific guidance on how to account for an award when the status of the counterparty changes from employee to non-employee (or *vice versa*) but, in all other respects, the award remains unchanged. In our view, the accounting following the change of status will depend on the entity's assessment of whether or not the counterparty is performing the same or similar services before and after the change of status.

If it is concluded that the counterparty is providing the same or similar services before and after the change of status, the measurement approach remains unchanged. However, if the services provided are substantially different, the accounting following the change of status will be determined by the counterparty's new status.

A change of status is rare in practice. A detailed discussion is beyond the scope of this publication but addressed in EY International GAAP 2015.

6.5 Determining the fair value of equity instruments

As discussed in 6.2 to 6.4 above, FRS 102 requires the following equity-settled transactions to be measured by reference to the fair value of the equity instruments issued rather than that of the goods or services received:

- all transactions with employees; and

- transactions with non-employees where, exceptionally, the presumption that the fair value of goods or services provided is more reliably measurable is rebutted.

There will also be situations where the identifiable consideration received (if any) from non-employees appears to be less than the fair value of consideration given. In such cases, an entity will need to determine the fair value of the equity instruments (see 3.2.3 above).

For all transactions measured by reference to the fair value of the equity instruments granted, fair value should be measured at the 'measurement date' – i.e. grant date in the case of transactions with employees and service date in the case of transactions with non-employees. *[FRS 102.26.8].* Fair value should be based on market prices if available. *[FRS 102.26.10-11].* In the absence of market prices or other entity-specific market data, a valuation method should be used to estimate what the market price would have been on the measurement date in an arm's length transaction between knowledgeable and willing parties. The technique used should be a generally recognised valuation methodology for valuing equity instruments that is appropriate to the circumstances of the entity and uses market data to the greatest extent possible. *[FRS 102.26.10-11].*

Paragraphs 10 to 11 of Section 26 of FRS 102 contain outline requirements on valuation and are discussed at 9 below, supplemented by guidance from the appendices and implementation guidance to IFRS 2. As noted elsewhere in this Chapter, the 'fair value' of equity instruments under Section 26 takes account of some, but not all, conditions attached to an award rather than being a 'true' fair value (see 7.3 and 7.4 below on the treatment of market and non-vesting conditions).

7 EQUITY-SETTLED TRANSACTIONS – ALLOCATION OF EXPENSE

7.1 Overview

Equity-settled transactions, particularly those with employees, raise particular accounting problems since they are often subject to vesting conditions (see 4.1 above) that can be satisfied only over an extended vesting period.

An award of equity instruments that vests immediately is presumed, in the absence of evidence to the contrary, to relate to services that have already been rendered, and is therefore expensed in full at grant date. *[FRS 102.26.5].* This may lead to the immediate recognition of an expense for an award to which the employee may not be legally entitled for some time, as illustrated in Example 21.6.

Chapter 21

Example 21.6:   Award with non-vesting condition only

An entity grants a director share options on condition that the director does not compete with the reporting entity for a period of at least three years. The 'non-compete' clause is considered to be a non-vesting condition (see 4.2 above and 7.4 below). As this is the only condition to which the award is subject, the award has no vesting conditions and therefore vests immediately. The fair value of the award at the date of grant, including the effect of the 'non-compete' clause, is determined to be £150,000. Accordingly, the entity immediately recognises a cost of £150,000.

This cost can never be reversed, even if the director goes to work for a competitor and loses the award. This is discussed more fully at 7.4 below.

Where equity instruments are granted subject to vesting conditions (as in many cases they will be, particularly where payments to employees are concerned), FRS 102 creates a presumption that they are a payment for services to be received in the future, during the 'vesting period', with the transaction being recognised during that period, as illustrated in Example 21.7. *[FRS 102.26.6, 9].*

Example 21.7:   Award with service condition only

An entity grants a director share options on condition that the director remain in employment for three years. The requirement to remain in employment is a service condition, and therefore a vesting condition, which will take three years to fulfil. The fair value of the award at the date of grant, ignoring the effect of the vesting condition, is determined to be £300,000. The entity will record a cost of £100,000 a year in profit or loss for three years, with a corresponding increase in equity.

In practice, the calculations required by FRS 102 are unlikely to be as simple as that in Example 21.7. In particular:

- the final number of awards that vest cannot be known until the vesting date (because employees may leave before the vesting date, or because relevant performance conditions may not be met); and/or

- the length of the vesting period may not be known in advance (since vesting may depend on satisfaction of a performance condition with no, or a variable, time-limit on its attainment).

In order to deal with such issues, FRS 102 requires a continuous re-estimation process as summarised in 7.1.1 below.

7.1.1   The continuous estimation process of Section 26 of FRS 102

The overall objective is that, at the end of the vesting period, the cumulative cost recognised in profit or loss (or, where applicable, included in the carrying amount of an asset), should represent the product of:

- the number of equity instruments that have vested, or would have vested, but for the failure to satisfy a market condition (see 7.3 below) or a non-vesting condition (see 7.4 below); and

- the fair value (excluding the effect of any non-market vesting conditions, but including the effect of any market conditions or non-vesting conditions) of those equity instruments at the date of grant.

It is essential to appreciate that the 'grant date' measurement model in FRS 102 seeks to capture the value of the contingent right to shares promised at grant date, to the extent that that promise becomes (or is deemed to become – see 7.1.2 below) an entitlement of the counterparty, rather than the value of any shares finally delivered. Therefore, if an option vests, but is not exercised because it would not be in the counterparty's economic interest to do so, FRS 102 still recognises a cost for the award.

In order to achieve this outcome, FRS 102 requires the following process to be applied:

(a)   at grant date, the fair value of the award (excluding the effect of any service and non-market performance vesting conditions, but including the effect of any market conditions or non-vesting conditions) is determined;

(b)   at each subsequent reporting date until vesting, the entity calculates a best estimate of the cumulative charge to profit or loss at that date, being the product of:

    (i)   the grant date fair value of the award determined in (a) above;

    (ii)   the current best estimate of the number of awards that will vest (see 7.1.2 below); and

    (iii)   the expired portion of the vesting period;

(c)   the charge (or credit) to profit or loss for the period is the cumulative amount calculated in (b) above less the amounts already charged in previous periods. There is a corresponding credit (or debit) to equity *[FRS 102.26.3-9]*;

(d)   once the awards have vested, no further accounting adjustments are made to the cost of the award, except in respect of certain modifications to the award – see 8 below; and

(e)   if a vested award is not exercised, an entity may (but need not) make a transfer between reserves – see 7.1.3 below.

The overall effect of this process is that a cost is recognised for every award that is granted, except when it is forfeited for failure to meet a vesting condition (see 7.1.2 below). *[FRS 102.26.9]*.

It is stated above, and assumed throughout this Chapter, that service conditions and non-market performance vesting conditions are not taken into account in determining the fair value of an equity-settled share-based payment transaction. This approach is explicit in paragraph 19 of IFRS 2 and may be inferred from paragraph 9 of Section 26 of FRS 102 which refers to market conditions and non-vesting conditions being reflected in the fair value of awards and to other vesting conditions being taken into account in estimating the number of awards expected finally to vest.

7.1.2   Vesting and forfeiture

In normal English usage, and in many share scheme documents, an award is described as 'vested' when all the conditions needed to earn it have been met, and as 'forfeited' where it lapses before vesting because one or more of the conditions has not been met.

IFRS 2 uses the term 'forfeiture' in a much more restricted sense to refer to an award that does not vest in IFRS 2 terms. FRS 102 takes a similar approach although it does not specifically refer to 'forfeiture' of an award. Essentially the approach is as follows:

- where an award is subject only to vesting conditions other than market conditions, failure to satisfy any one of the conditions is treated as a forfeiture (and any cumulative expense recognised to date is reversed);

- where an award is subject to both

  - vesting conditions other than market conditions, and

  - market conditions and/or non-vesting conditions,

  failure to satisfy any one of the vesting conditions other than market conditions is treated as a forfeiture. Otherwise (i.e. where all the vesting conditions other than market conditions are satisfied), the award is deemed to vest even if the market conditions and/or non-vesting conditions have not been satisfied; and

- where an award is subject only to non-vesting conditions, it is always deemed to vest.

As a result of the interaction of the various types of condition, the reference in the summary at 7.1.1 above to the 'best estimate of the number of awards that will vest' really means the best estimate of the number of awards for which it is expected that all non-market vesting conditions will be met.

In practice, however, it is not always clear how that best estimate is to be determined, and in particular what future events may and may not be factored into the estimate. This is discussed further at 7.2 to 7.4 and 8.6 below.

7.1.3   *Accounting after vesting*

FRS 102 does not address specifically the treatment of share-based payment transactions once they have vested but it seems appropriate to adopt the approach required by IFRS 2.

Once an equity-settled transaction has vested (or, in the case of a transaction subject to one or more market or non-vesting conditions, has been treated as vested – see 7.1.2 above), no further accounting entries are made to reverse the cost already charged, even if the instruments that are the subject of the transaction are subsequently forfeited or, in the case of options, are not exercised. However, the entity may make a transfer between different components of equity. *[IFRS 2.23]*. For example, an entity's accounting policy might be to credit all amounts recorded for share-based transactions to a separate reserve such as 'Shares to be issued'. Where an award lapses after vesting, it would then be appropriate to transfer an amount equivalent to the cumulative cost for the lapsed award from 'Shares to be issued' to another component of equity, usually the profit and loss reserve.

This prohibition against 'truing up' (i.e. reversing the cost of vested awards that lapse) is controversial, since it has the effect that a cost is still recognised for options that are never exercised, typically because they are 'underwater' (i.e. the current share price is lower than the option exercise price), so that it is not in the holder's interest to exercise the option.

7.2 Vesting conditions other than market conditions

7.2.1 Awards with service conditions

Most share-based payment transactions with employees are subject to explicit or implied service conditions. The application of the general periodic allocation principles discussed in 7.1 above to awards subject only to service conditions is illustrated by Examples 21.8 and 21.9 below which are based on the implementation guidance to IFRS 2. *[IFRS 2.IG11].*

Example 21.8: Award with no re-estimation of number of awards vesting

An entity grants 100 share options to each of its 500 employees. Vesting is conditional upon the employees working for the entity over the next three years. The entity estimates that the fair value of each share option is £15. The entity estimates that 20% of the original 500 employees will leave during the three year period and therefore forfeit their rights to the share options.

If everything turns out exactly as expected, the entity will recognise the following amounts during the vesting period for services received as consideration for the share options.

Year	Calculation of cumulative expense	Cumulative expense (£)	Expense for period‡ (£)
1	50,000 options × 80%* × £15 × 1/3†	200,000	200,000
2	50,000 options × 80% × £15 × 2/3	400,000	200,000
3	50,000 options × 80% × £15 × 3/3	600,000	200,000

* The entity expects 20% of employees to leave and therefore only 80% of the options to vest.

† The vesting period is 3 years, and 1 year of it has expired.

‡ In each case the expense for the period is the difference between the calculated cumulative expense at the beginning and end of the period.

Example 21.9: Award with re-estimation of number of awards vesting due to staff turnover

As in Example 21.8 above, an entity grants 100 share options to each of its 500 employees. Vesting is conditional upon the employee working for the entity over the next three years. The entity estimates that the fair value of each share option is £15.

In this case, however, 20 employees leave during the first year, and the entity's best estimate at the end of year 1 is that 15% of the original 500 employees will have left before the end of the vesting period. During the second year, a further 22 employees leave, and the entity revises its estimate of total employee departures over the vesting period from 15% to 12% of the original 500 employees. During the third year, a further 15 employees leave. Hence, a total of 57 employees (20 + 22 + 15) forfeit their rights to the share options during the three year period, and a total of 44,300 share options (443 employees × 100 options per employee) finally vest.

The entity will recognise the following amounts during the vesting period for services received as consideration for the share options.

Year	Calculation of cumulative expense	Cumulative expense (£)	Expense for period (£)
1	50,000 options × 85% × £15 × 1/3	212,500	212,500
2	50,000 options × 88% × £15 × 2/3	440,000	227,500
3	44,300 options × £15 × 3/3	664,500	224,500

Note that in Example 21.9 above, the number of employees that leave during year 1 and year 2 is not directly relevant to the calculation of cumulative expense in those years, but would naturally be a factor taken into account by the entity in estimating the likely number of awards finally vesting.

7.2.2   *Equity instruments vesting in instalments ('graded' vesting)*

An entity may make share-based payments that vest in instalments (sometimes referred to as 'graded' vesting). For example, an entity might grant an employee 600 options, 100 of which vest if the employee remains in service for one year, a further 200 after two years and the final 300 after three years. In today's more mobile labour markets, such awards are increasingly favoured over awards which vest only on an 'all or nothing' basis after an extended period.

It is consistent with the overall recognition approach of Section 26 (and with the implementation guidance to IFRS 2) to treat such an award as three separate awards, of 100, 200 and 300 options, on the grounds that the three different vesting periods will mean that the three tranches of the award have different fair values. This may well have the effect that, compared to the expense for an award with a single 'cliff' vesting, the expense for an award vesting in instalments will be for a different amount in total and require accelerated recognition of the expense in earlier periods, as illustrated in Example 21.10 below.

Example 21.10:   Award vesting in instalments ('graded' vesting)

An entity is considering the implementation of a scheme that awards 600 free shares to each of its employees, with no conditions other than continuous service. Two alternatives are being considered:

- All 600 shares vest in full only at the end of three years.
- 100 shares vest after one year, 200 shares after two years and 300 shares after three years. Any shares received at the end of years 1 and 2 would have vested unconditionally.

The fair value of a share delivered in one year's time is £3; in two years' time £2.80; and in three years' time £2.50.

For an employee that remains with the entity for the full three year period, the first alternative would be accounted for as follows:

Year	Calculation of cumulative expense	Cumulative expense (£)	Expense for period (£)
1	600 shares × £2.50 × 1/3	500	500
2	600 shares × £2.50 × 2/3	1,000	500
3	600 shares × £2.50 × 3/3	1,500	500

For the second alternative, the analysis is that the employee has simultaneously received an award of 100 shares vesting over one year, an award of 200 shares vesting over two years and an award of 300 shares vesting over 3 years. This would be accounted for as follows:

Year	Calculation of cumulative expense	Cumulative expense (£)	Expense for period (£)
1	[100 shares × £3.00] + [200 shares × £2.80 × 1/2] + [300 shares × £2.50 × 1/3]	830	830
2	[100 shares × £3.00] + [200 shares × £2.80 × 2/2] + [300 shares × £2.50 × 2/3]	1,360	530
3	[100 shares × £3.00] + [200 shares × £2.80 × 2/2] + [300 shares × £2.50 × 3/3]	1,610	250

At first sight, such an approach seems to be taking account of non-market vesting conditions in determining the fair value of an award, contrary to the basic principle of paragraph 9 of Section 26 (see 7.1.1 above). However, it is not the vesting conditions that are being taken into account *per se*, but the fact that the varying vesting periods will give rise to different lives for the award (which are generally required to be taken into account – see 8.2 and 9 below).

Provided all conditions are clearly understood at the outset, the accounting treatment illustrated in Example 21.10 would apply even if the vesting of shares in each year also depended on a performance condition unique to that year (e.g. that profit in that year must reach a given minimum level), as opposed to a cumulative performance condition (e.g. that profit must have grown by a minimum amount by the end of year 1, 2 or 3). This is because there is a service condition covering a longer period. In other words, an award that vests at the end of year 3 conditional on profitability in year 3 is also conditional on the employee providing service for three years from the date of grant in order to be eligible to receive the award. This is discussed further at 6.3.6 above.

7.2.3 Transactions with variable vesting periods due to non-market performance vesting conditions

An award may have a vesting period which is subject to variation. For example, the award might be contingent upon the achievement of a particular performance target (such as achieving a given level of cumulative earnings) within a given maximum period, but vesting immediately the target has been reached. Alternatively, an award might be contingent on levels of earnings growth over a period, but with vesting occurring more quickly if growth is achieved more quickly. Also some plans provide for 're-testing', whereby an original target is set for achievement within a given vesting period, but if that target is not met, a new target and/or a different vesting period are substituted.

FRS 102 has no specific requirements in respect of variable vesting periods – it simply refers to revising the number of awards expected to vest if new information becomes available about vesting conditions. *[FRS 102.26.9]*. However, it seems appropriate to follow the requirements of IFRS 2 in this area. Therefore, in such cases, the entity needs to estimate the length of the vesting period at grant date, based on the most likely outcome of the performance condition. Subsequently, it is necessary continuously to re-estimate not only the number of awards that will finally vest, but also the date of vesting, as shown by Example 21.11. *[IFRS 2.15(b), IG12]*. This contrasts with the IFRS 2 treatment of awards with market conditions and variable vesting periods, where the initial estimate of the vesting period may not be revised (see 7.3.4 below).

Example 21.11: Award with non-market vesting condition and variable vesting period

At the beginning of year 1, the entity grants 100 shares each to 500 employees, conditional upon the employees remaining in the entity's employment during the vesting period. The shares will vest:

- at the end of year 1 if the entity's earnings increase by more than 18%;
- at the end of year 2 if the entity's earnings increase by more than an average of 13% per year over the two year period; or
- at the end of year 3 if the entity's earnings increase by more than an average of 10% per year over the three year period.

The award is estimated to have a fair value of £30 per share at grant date. It is expected that no dividends will be paid during the whole three year period.

By the end of the first year, the entity's earnings have increased by 14%, and 30 employees have left. The entity expects that earnings will continue to increase at a similar rate in year 2, and therefore expects that the shares will vest at the end of year 2. The entity expects, on the basis of a weighted average probability, that a further 30 employees will leave during year 2, and therefore expects that an award of 100 shares each will vest for 440 (500 – 30 – 30) employees at the end of year 2.

By the end of the second year, the entity's earnings have increased by only 10% and therefore the shares do not vest at the end of that year. 28 employees have left during the year. The entity expects that a further 25 employees will leave during year 3, and that the entity's earnings will increase by at least 6%, thereby achieving the average growth of 10% per year necessary for an award after 3 years, so that an award of 100 shares each will vest for 417 (500 – 30 – 28 – 25) employees at the end of year 3.

By the end of the third year, a further 23 employees have left and the entity's earnings have increased by 8%, resulting in an average increase of 10.67% per year. Therefore, 419 (500 – 30 – 28 – 23) employees receive 100 shares at the end of year 3.

The entity will recognise the following amounts during the vesting period for services received as consideration for the shares.

Year	Calculation of cumulative expense	Cumulative expense (£)	Expense for period (£)
1	440 employees × 100 shares × £30 × 1/2*	660,000	660,000
2	417 employees × 100 shares × £30 × 2/3*	834,000	174,000
3	419 employees × 100 shares × £30	1,257,000	423,000

*   The entity's best estimate at the end of year 1 is that it is one year through a two year vesting period and at the end of year 2 that it is two years through a three year vesting period.

It will be noted that in Example 21.11, which is based on IG Example 2 in the implementation guidance to IFRS 2, it is assumed that the entity will pay no dividends (to any shareholders) throughout the maximum possible three year vesting period. This has the effect that the fair value of the shares to be awarded is equivalent to their market value at the date of grant.

If dividends were expected to be paid during the vesting period, this would no longer be the case. Employees would be better off if they received shares after two years rather than three, since they would have a right to receive dividends from the end of year two.

One solution might be to use the approach in IG Example 4 in the implementation guidance to IFRS 2 (the substance of which is reproduced as Example 21.13 at 7.2.5 below). That Example deals with an award whose exercise price is either £12 or £16, dependent upon various performance conditions. Because vesting conditions other than market conditions are ignored in determining the value of an award, the approach is in effect to treat the award as the simultaneous grant of two awards, whose value, in that case, varies by reference to the different exercise prices.

The same principle could be applied to an award of shares that vests at different times according to the performance conditions, by determining different fair values for the shares (in this case depending on whether they vest after one, two or three years). The charge during the vesting period would be based on a best estimate of which outcome will occur, and the final cumulative charge would be based on the actual outcome.

Such an approach appears at first sight to be taking account of non-market vesting conditions in determining the fair value of an award, contrary to the basic principle of paragraph 9 of Section 26 of FRS 102 (see 7.1.1 above). However, it is not the vesting conditions that are being taken into account *per se*, but the fact that the varying vesting periods will give rise to different lives for the award (which are generally required to be taken into account – see 8.2 and 9 below).

Economically speaking, the entity in Example 21.11 has made a single award, the true fair value of which must be a function of the weighted probabilities of the various outcomes occurring. However, under the accounting model for share-settled awards, the probability of achieving non-market performance conditions is not taken into account in valuing an award. If this is required to be ignored, the only approach open is to proceed as in Example 21.11 above.

Some might object that this methodology is not relevant to the award in Example 21.11 above, since it is an award of shares rather than, in the case of Example 21.13 below, an award of options. However, an award of shares is no more than an award of options with an exercise price of zero. Moreover, the treatment in the previous paragraph is broadly consistent with the IFRS 2 treatment of an award vesting in instalments (see 7.2.2 above).

In Example 21.11 above, the vesting period, although not known, is at least one of a finite number of known possibilities. The vesting period for some awards, however, may be more open-ended, such as an award that vests on a trade sale or flotation of the business. Such awards are discussed further at 16.4 below.

7.2.4   Transactions with variable number of equity instruments awarded depending on non-market performance vesting conditions

More common than awards with a variable vesting period are those where the number of equity instruments awarded varies, typically increasing to reflect the margin by which a particular minimum target is exceeded. In accounting for such awards, the entity must continuously revise its estimate of the number of shares to be awarded in line with the requirement to revise the estimate of the number of equity instruments expected to vest if new information indicates that this number differs from previous estimates. *[IFRS 102.26.9].* This is illustrated in Example 21.12 below (which is based on IG Example 3 in the implementation guidance to IFRS 2).

Example 21.12:   Award with non-market performance vesting condition and variable number of equity instruments

At the beginning of year 1, an entity grants an option over a variable number of shares (see below), estimated to have a fair value at grant date of £20 per share under option, to each of its 100 employees working in the sales department on the following terms. The share options will vest at the end of year 3, provided that the employees remain in the entity's employment, and provided that the volume of sales of a particular product increases by at least an average of 5% per year. If the volume of sales of the product increases by an average of between 5% and 10% per year, each employee will be entitled to exercise 100 share options. If the volume of sales increases by an average of between 10% and 15% each year, each employee will be entitled to exercise 200 share options. If the volume of sales increases by an average of 15% or more, each employee will be entitled to exercise 300 share options.

By the end of the first year, seven employees have left and the entity expects that a total of 20 employees will leave by the end of year 3. Product sales have increased by 12% and the entity expects this rate of increase to continue over the next two years, so that 80 employees will be entitled to exercise 200 options each.

By the end of the second year, a further five employees have left. The entity now expects only three more employees to leave during year 3, and therefore expects a total of 15 employees to have left during the three year period. Product sales have increased by 18%, resulting in an average of 15%

over the two years to date. The entity now expects that sales will average 15% or more over the three year period, so that 85 employees will be entitled to exercise 300 options each.

By the end of year 3, a further seven employees have left. Hence, 19 employees have left during the three year period, and 81 employees remain. However, due to trading conditions significantly poorer than expected, sales have increased by a 3 year average of only 12%, so that the 81 remaining employees are entitled to exercise only 200 share options.

The entity will recognise the following amounts during the vesting period for services received as consideration for the options.

Year	Calculation of cumulative expense	Cumulative expense (£)	Expense for period (£)
1	80 employees × 200 options × £20 × 1/3	106,667	106,667
2	85 employees × 300 options × £20 × 2/3	340,000	233,333
3	81 employees × 200 options × £20	324,000	(16,000)

This Example reinforces the point that it is quite possible for an equity-settled transaction to give rise to a credit to profit or loss for a particular period during the period to vesting.

7.2.5   Transactions with variable exercise price due to non-market performance vesting conditions

Another mechanism for delivering higher value to the recipient of a share award so as to reflect the margin by which a particular target is exceeded might be to vary the exercise price depending on performance. IFRS 2 requires such an award to be dealt with, in effect, as more than one award and we believe that it is appropriate to adopt a similar approach under FRS 102. The fair value of each award is determined, and the cost during the vesting period based on the best estimate of which award will actually vest, with the final cumulative charge being based on the actual outcome. *[IFRS 2.IG12, IG Example 4].*

This is illustrated in Example 21.13 below.

Example 21.13:   Award with non-market performance vesting condition and variable exercise price

An entity grants to a senior executive 10,000 share options, conditional upon the executive remaining in the entity's employment for three years. The exercise price is £40. However, the exercise price drops to £30 if the entity's earnings increase by at least an average of 10% per year over the three year period.

On grant date, the entity estimates that the fair value of the share options, with an exercise price of £30, is £16 per option. If the exercise price is £40, the entity estimates that the share options have a fair value of £12 per option. During year 1, the entity's earnings increased by 12%, and the entity expects that earnings will continue to increase at this rate over the next two years. The entity therefore expects that the earnings target will be achieved, and hence the share options will have an exercise price of £30.

During year 2, the entity's earnings increased by 13%, and the entity continues to expect that the earnings target will be achieved. During year 3, the entity's earnings increased by only 3%, and therefore the earnings target was not achieved. The executive completes three years' service, and therefore satisfies the service condition. Because the earnings target was not achieved, the 10,000 vested share options have an exercise price of £40.

The entity will recognise the following amounts during the vesting period for services received as consideration for the options.

Year	Calculation of cumulative expense	Cumulative expense (£)	Expense for period (£)
1	10,000 options × £16 × 1/3	53,333	53,333
2	10,000 options × £16 × 2/3	106,667	53,334
3	10,000 options × £12	120,000	13,333

At first sight this may seem a rather surprising approach. In reality, has not the entity in Example 21.13 made a single award, the fair value of which must lie between £12 and £16, as a function of the weighted probabilities of either outcome occurring? Economically speaking, this is the case. However, under the accounting model for share-settled awards in IFRS 2 and FRS 102, the probability of achieving non-market performance conditions is not taken into account in valuing an award. If this is required to be ignored, the only approach open is to proceed with the 'two award' analysis as above.

7.3   Market conditions

7.3.1   What is a 'market condition'?

A market condition is defined as 'a condition upon which the exercise price, vesting or exercisability of an equity instrument depends that is related to the market price of the entity's equity instruments, such as attaining a specified share price or a specified amount of intrinsic value of a share option, or achieving a specified target that is based on the market price of the entity's equity instruments relative to an index of market prices of equity instruments of other entities'. *[FRS 102 Appendix I]*. In order for a market condition to be treated as a performance vesting condition rather than as a non-vesting condition, there must also be an implicit or explicit service condition (see 4.2 above).

The 'intrinsic value' of a share option is defined as 'the difference between the fair value of the shares to which the counterparty has the (conditional or unconditional) right to subscribe or which it has the right to receive, and the price (if any) the counterparty is (or will be) required to pay for those shares'. *[FRS 102 Appendix I]*. In other words, an option to acquire for £8 a share with a fair value of £10 has an intrinsic value of £2. A performance condition based on the share price and one based on the intrinsic value of the option are effectively the same, since the values of each will obviously move in parallel.

Section 26 includes a specified increase in the entity's share price as an example of a market condition. *[FRS 102.26.9]*. A market condition often seen in practice, although more common in a listed entity and not specifically mentioned in FRS 102, is a condition based on total shareholder return (TSR). TSR is a measure of the increase or decrease in a given sum invested in an entity over a period on the assumption that all dividends received in the period had been used to purchase further shares in the entity. The market price of the entity's shares is an input to the calculation.

However, a condition linked to a purely internal financial performance measure such as profit or earnings per share is not a market condition. Such measures will affect the share price or value, but are not directly linked to it, and hence are not market conditions.

A condition linked solely to a general market index is not a market condition, but a non-vesting condition (see 4.2 above and 7.4 below), because the reporting entity's own share price is not relevant to the satisfaction of the condition.

However, if the condition were that the entity's own share price had to outperform a general index of shares of entities listed in Hong Kong, that condition would be a market condition because the reporting entity's own share price is then relevant to the satisfaction of the condition.

7.3.2   *Summary of accounting treatment*

The key feature of the accounting treatment of an equity-settled transaction subject to a market condition is that the market condition is taken into account in valuing the award at the date of grant, 'with no subsequent adjustment irrespective of the outcome of the market or non-vesting condition, provided that all other vesting conditions are satisfied'. *[FRS 102.26.9]*. In other words, an award is treated as vesting irrespective of whether the market condition is satisfied, provided that all other service and non-market performance vesting conditions are satisfied. The requirements relating to market conditions can have rather controversial consequences, as illustrated by Example 21.14.

Example 21.14:   Award with market condition

An entity grants an employee an option to buy a share on condition of remaining in employment for three years and the share price at the end of that period being at least £7. At the end of the vesting period, the share price is £6.80. The share price condition is factored into the initial valuation of the option, and the option is considered to vest provided that the employee remains for three years, irrespective of whether the share price does in fact reach £7. Thus, an award is sometimes treated as vesting (and a cost is recognised for that award) when it does not actually vest in the natural sense of the word. See also Example 21.16 at 7.3.4 below.

This treatment is clearly significantly different from that for transactions involving a non-market vesting condition, where no cost would be recognised where the conditions were not met. As discussed in 7.2 above, the methodology prescribed for transactions with a vesting condition other than a market condition is to determine the fair value of the option ignoring the condition and then to multiply that fair value by the estimated (and ultimately the actual) number of awards expected to vest based on the likelihood of that non-market vesting condition being met.

In any event, it appears that it may be possible to soften the impact of the rules for market conditions relatively easily by introducing a non-market vesting condition closely correlated to the market condition. For instance, the option in Example 21.14 above could be modified so that exercise was dependent not only upon the £7 target share price and continuous employment, but also on a target growth in earnings per share. Whilst there would not be a perfect correlation between earnings per share and the share price, it would be expected that they would move roughly in parallel, particularly if the entity has historically had a fairly consistent price/earnings ratio. Thus, if the share price target were not met, it would be highly likely that the earnings per share target would not be met either. This would allow the entity to show no cumulative cost for the option, since only one (i.e. not *all*) of the non-market related vesting conditions would have been met.

Similarly, entities in sectors where the share price is closely related to net asset value (e.g. property companies and investment trusts) could incorporate a net asset value target as a non-market performance condition that would be highly likely to be satisfied only if the market condition was satisfied.

The matrices below illustrate the interaction of market conditions and vesting conditions other than market conditions. Matrix 1 summarises the possible outcomes for an award with the following two vesting conditions:

- the employee remaining in service for three years (service condition); and
- the entity's share price increasing by 10% over the vesting period (share price target).

Matrix 1

	Service condition met?	Share price target met?	Section 26 expense?
1	Yes	Yes	Yes
2	Yes	No	Yes
3	No	Yes	No
4	No	No	No

It will be seen that, to all intents and purposes, the 'Share price target met?' column is redundant, as this is not relevant to whether or not the award is treated as vesting for accounting purposes. The effect of this is that the entity would recognise an expense for outcome 2, even though no awards truly vest.

Matrix 2 summarises the possible outcomes for an award with the same conditions as in Matrix 1, plus a requirement for earnings per share to grow by a general inflation index plus 10% over the period ('EPS target').

Matrix 2

	Service condition met?	Share price target met?	EPS target met?	Section 26 expense?
1	Yes	Yes	Yes	Yes
2	Yes	No	Yes	Yes
3	Yes	Yes	No	No
4	Yes	No	No	No
5	No	Yes	Yes	No
6	No	No	Yes	No
7	No	Yes	No	No
8	No	No	No	No

Again it will be seen that, to all intents and purposes, the 'Share price target met?' column is redundant, as this is not relevant to whether or not the award is treated as vesting. The effect of this is that the entity would recognise an expense for outcome 2, even though no awards truly vest. However, no expense would be recognised for outcome 4, which is, except for the introduction of the EPS target, equivalent to outcome 2 in Matrix 1, for which an expense is recognised. This illustrates that the introduction of a non-market vesting condition closely related to a market condition may mitigate the impact of the accounting requirements.

Examples of the application of the accounting treatment for transactions involving market conditions are given in 7.3.3 and 7.3.4 below.

Chapter 21

7.3.3   *Transactions with market conditions and known vesting periods*

Following on from the discussion at 7.3.2 above, the accounting for these transactions is essentially the same as that for transactions without market conditions but with a known vesting period, except that adjustments are made to reflect the changing probability of the achievement of the non-market vesting conditions only, as illustrated by Example 21.15 below (based partly on Example 5 in the implementation guidance to IFRS 2). *[FRS 102.26.9].*

Example 21.15:   Award with market condition and fixed vesting period

At the beginning of year 1, an entity grants to 100 employees 1,000 share options each, conditional upon the employees remaining in the entity's employment until the end of year 3. However, the share options cannot be exercised unless the share price has increased from £50 at the beginning of year 1 to more than £65 at the end of year 3.

If the share price is above £65 at the end of year 3, the share options can be exercised at any time during the next seven years, i.e. by the end of year 10. The entity applies an option pricing model which takes into account the possibility that the share price will exceed £65 at the end of year 3 (and hence the share options become exercisable) and the possibility that the share price will not exceed £65 at the end of year 3 (and hence the options will be forfeited). It estimates the fair value of the share options with this market condition to be £24 per option.

FRS 102 requires the entity to recognise the services received from a counterparty who satisfies all other vesting conditions (e.g. services received from an employee who remains in service for the specified service period), irrespective of whether that market condition is satisfied. It makes no difference whether the share price target is achieved, since the possibility that the share price target might not be achieved has already been taken into account when estimating the fair value of the share options at grant date. However, the options are subject to another condition (i.e. continuous employment) and the cost recognised should be adjusted to reflect the ongoing best estimate of employee retention.

By the end of the first year, seven employees have left and the entity expects that a total of 20 employees will leave by the end of year 3, so that 80 employees will have satisfied all conditions other than the market condition (i.e. continuous employment).

By the end of the second year, a further five employees have left. The entity now expects only three more employees will leave during year 3, and therefore expects that a total of 15 employees will have left during the three year period, so that 85 employees will have satisfied all conditions other than the market condition.

By the end of year 3, a further seven employees have left. Hence, 19 employees have left during the three year period, and 81 employees remain. However, the share price is only £60, so that the options cannot be exercised. Nevertheless, as all conditions other than the market condition have been satisfied, a cumulative cost is recorded as if the options had fully vested in 81 employees.

The entity will recognise the following amounts during the vesting period for services received as consideration for the options (which in economic reality do not vest).

Year	Calculation of cumulative expense	Cumulative expense (£)	Expense for period (£)
1	80 employees × 1,000 options × £24 × 1/3	640,000	640,000
2	85 employees × 1,000 options × £24 × 2/3	1,360,000	720,000
3	81 employees × 1,000 options × £24	1,944,000	584,000

7.3.4 *Transactions with variable vesting periods due to market conditions*

Where a transaction has a variable vesting period due to a market condition, a best estimate of the most likely vesting period will have been used in determining the fair value of the transaction at the date of grant. IFRS 2 requires the expense for that transaction to be recognised over an estimated expected vesting period consistent with the assumptions used in the valuation, without any subsequent revision. *[IFRS 2.15(b), IG14]*. FRS 102 does not specify the accounting treatment in this situation but it seems consistent with the general requirement in paragraph 9 of Section 26 that there should be 'no subsequent adjustment irrespective of the outcome of the market ... condition' to adopt a similar approach to that required by IFRS 2.

This may mean, for example, that if the actual vesting period for an employee share option award turns out to be longer than that anticipated for the purposes of the initial valuation, a cost is nevertheless recorded in respect of all employees who reach the end of the *anticipated* vesting period, even if they do not reach the end of the *actual* vesting period, as shown by Example 21.16 below, which is based on Example 6 in the implementation guidance in IFRS 2.

Example 21.16: Award with market condition and variable vesting period

At the beginning of year 1, an entity grants 10,000 share options with a ten year life to each of ten senior executives. The share options will vest and become exercisable immediately if and when the entity's share price increases from £50 to £70, provided that the executive remains in service until the share price target is achieved.

The entity applies an option pricing model which takes into account the possibility that the share price target will be achieved during the ten year life of the options, and the possibility that the target will not be achieved. The entity estimates that the fair value of the share options at grant date is £25 per option. From the option pricing model, the entity determines that the most likely vesting period is five years. The entity also estimates that two executives will have left by the end of year 5, and therefore expects that 80,000 share options (10,000 share options × 8 executives) will vest at the end of year 5.

Throughout years 1 to 4, the entity continues to estimate that a total of two executives will leave by the end of year 5. However, in total three executives leave, one in each of years 3, 4 and 5. The share price target is achieved at the end of year 6. Another executive leaves during year 6, before the share price target is achieved.

IFRS 2 and FRS 102 require the entity to recognise the services received over the expected vesting period, as estimated at grant date, and also require the entity not to revise that estimate. Therefore, the entity recognises the services received from the executives over years 1-5. Hence, the transaction amount is ultimately based on 70,000 share options (10,000 share options × 7 executives who remain in service at the end of year 5). Although another executive left during year 6, no adjustment is made, because the executive had already completed the expected vesting period of 5 years.

The entity will recognise the following amounts during the initial expected five year vesting period for services received as consideration for the options.

Year	Calculation of cumulative expense	Cumulative expense (£)	Expense for period (£)
1	8 employees × 10,000 options × £25 × 1/5	400,000	400,000
2	8 employees × 10,000 options × £25 × 2/5	800,000	400,000
3	8 employees × 10,000 options × £25 × 3/5	1,200,000	400,000
4	8 employees × 10,000 options × £25 × 4/5	1,600,000	400,000
5	7 employees × 10,000 options × £25	1,750,000	150,000

IFRS 2 does not specifically address the converse situation, namely where the award actually vests before the end of the anticipated vesting period. In our view, where this occurs, any expense not yet recognised at the point of vesting should be immediately accelerated. We consider that this treatment is most consistent with the overall requirement of IFRS 2 – and FRS 102 – to recognise an expense for share-based payment transactions 'as the services are received'. *[IFRS 2.7, FRS 102.26.3]*. It is difficult to regard any services being received for an award after it has vested.

Moreover, the prohibition in paragraph 15 of IFRS 2 on adjusting the vesting period as originally determined refers to 'the estimate of the expected vesting period'. In our view, the acceleration of vesting that we propose is not the revision of an estimated period, but the substitution of a known vesting period for an estimate.

Suppose in Example 21.16 above, the award had in fact vested at the end of year 4. We believe that the expense for such an award should be allocated as follows:

Year	Calculation of cumulative expense	Cumulative expense (£)	Expense for period (£)
1	8 employees × 10,000 options × £25 × 1/5	400,000	400,000
2	8 employees × 10,000 options × £25 × 2/5	800,000	400,000
3	8 employees × 10,000 options × £25 × 3/5	1,200,000	400,000
4	8 employees × 10,000 options × £25 × 4/4	2,000,000	800,000

7.3.5   Transactions with multiple outcomes depending on market conditions

In practice, it is very common for an award subject to market conditions to give varying levels of reward that increase depending on the extent to which a 'base line' market performance target has been exceeded. Such an award is illustrated in Example 21.17 below.

Example 21.17:   Award with market conditions and multiple outcomes

On 1 January 2015, the reporting entity grants an employee an award of shares that will vest on the third anniversary of grant if the employee is still in employment on the third anniversary of grant. The number of shares depends on the share price achieved at the end of the three-year period. The employee will receive:

- no shares if the share price is below £10.00;
- 100 shares if the share price is in the range £10.00 – £14.99;
- 150 shares if the share price is in the range £15.00 – £19.99; or
- 180 shares if the share price is £20.00 or above.

In effect the entity has made three awards, which need to be valued as follows:

(a)   100 shares if the employee remains in service for three years and the share price is in the range £10.00 – £14.99;

(b)   50 (150 – 100) shares if the employee remains in service for three years and the share price is in the range £15.00 – £19.99; and

(c)   30 (180 – 150) shares if the employee remains in service for three years and the share price is £20.00 or more.

Each award would be valued, ignoring the impact of the three-year service condition but taking account of the share price target. This would result in each tranche of the award being subject to an increasing level of discount to reflect the relative probability of the share price target for each tranche of the award being met. All three awards would then be expensed over the three-year service period, and forfeited only if the awards lapsed as a result of the employee leaving during that period.

It can be seen that the (perhaps somewhat counterintuitive) impact of this is that an equity-settled award that increases in line with increases in the entity's share price may nevertheless have a fixed grant date value irrespective of the number of shares finally awarded.

7.3.6 Transactions with independent market conditions and non-market vesting conditions

The discussion at 7.3.2 above addressed the accounting treatment of awards with multiple conditions that must all be satisfied, i.e. a market condition *and* a non-market vesting condition. However, it is increasingly common for entities to make awards with multiple conditions, only one of which need be satisfied, i.e. the awards vest on satisfaction of either a market condition *or* a non-market vesting condition. Neither FRS 102 nor IFRS 2 provides any explicit guidance on the treatment of such awards and the requirements are far from clear, as illustrated by Example 21.18 below.

Example 21.18: Award with independent market conditions and non-market vesting conditions

An entity grants an employee 100 share options that vest after three years if the employee is still in employment and the entity achieves either:

- an increase in its share price over three years of at least 15%, or
- cumulative profits over three years of at least £200 million.

The fair value of the award, ignoring vesting conditions, is £300,000. The fair value of the award, taking account of the share price condition, but not the other conditions, is £210,000.

In our view, the entity has, in effect, simultaneously issued two awards – call them 'A' and 'B' – which vest as follows:

A   on achievement of three years' service plus minimum share price increase,

B   on achievement of three years' service plus minimum earnings growth.

If the conditions for both awards are simultaneously satisfied, one or other effectively lapses.

It is clear that award A, if issued separately, would require the entity to recognise an expense of £210,000 if the employee were still in service at the end of the three year period. It therefore seems clear that, if the employee does remain in service, there should be a charge of £210,000 irrespective of whether the award actually vests. It would be anomalous for the entity to avoid recording a charge that would have been recognised if the entity had made award A in isolation simply by packaging it with award B.

If in fact the award vested because the earnings condition, but not the market condition, had been satisfied, it would then be appropriate to recognise a total expense of £300,000. This begs the question of whether the award should be accounted for:

(i)   On the assumption in years 1 and 2 that it will vest because of the earnings condition, with an adjustment in the final year if the award vests by virtue of the share price condition (or the award does not vest, but the employee remains in service). This would give rise to annual expense as follows:

Year	Calculation of cumulative expense	Cumulative expense (£)	Expense for period (£)
1	300,000 × 1/3	100,000	100,000
2	300,000 × 2/3	200,000	100,000
3	210,000 × 3/3	210,000	10,000

(ii) On the assumption in years 1 and 2 that it will vest by virtue of the share price condition being met (or the employee remaining in service), with a 'catch-up' adjustment in the final period, if the award vests by virtue of the earnings condition, but not the share price condition, being satisfied. This would give rise to annual expense as follows:

Year	Calculation of cumulative expense	Cumulative expense ($£$)	Expense for period ($£$)
1	$210,000 \times 1/3$	70,000	70,000
2	$210,000 \times 2/3$	140,000	70,000
3	$300,000 \times 3/3$	300,000	160,000

(iii) At each reporting date, on the basis of the probability, as assessed at that date, of the award vesting by virtue of the earnings condition, but not the share price condition, being satisfied. Assume (for example) that the entity assesses at the end of year 1 that the award is likely to vest by virtue of the share price condition, and at the end of year 2 that it is likely to vest by virtue of the earnings condition, and that the award actually does not vest, but the employee remains in service. This would give rise to annual expense as follows:

Year	Calculation of cumulative expense	Cumulative expense ($£$)	Expense for period ($£$)
1	$210,000 \times 1/3$	70,000	70,000
2	$300,000 \times 2/3$	200,000	130,000
3	$210,000 \times 3/3$	210,000	10,000

We believe that treatment (iii) should generally be followed as ongoing reassessment during the vesting period is most consistent with the general accounting approach to awards with a number of possible outcomes.

Of course, as for other awards, the accounting treatment would also require an assessment of whether the employee was actually going to remain in service or not.

A further question that arises is how the award should be accounted for if both conditions are satisfied. It would clearly be inappropriate to recognise an expense of $£510,000$ (the sum of the separate fair values of the award) – this would be double-counting, because the employee receives only one package of 100 options. However, should the total expense be taken as $£210,000$ or $£300,000$? In our view, it is more appropriate to recognise a cost of $£300,000$ since the non-market vesting condition has been satisfied.

7.3.7   Awards based on the market value of a subsidiary or business unit

Awards with a market condition are frequently based on the market value of the (typically quoted) equity of the parent entity. However, entities are increasingly implementing share-based remuneration schemes which aim to reward employees by reference to the market value of the equity of the business unit for which they work. The detail of such schemes varies, but the general effect is typically as follows:

- at grant date, the employee is allocated a (real or notional) holding in the equity of the employing subsidiary, the market value of which is measured at grant date; and

- the employee is granted an award of as many shares of the listed parent as have a value, at a specified future date (generally at or shortly after the end of the vesting period), equal to the increase in the market value of the holding in the equity of the employing subsidiary over the vesting period.

Some take the view that such a scheme contains a market condition, since it is based on the fair value of the subsidiary's shares, with the result that the grant date fair value per share:

- reflects this market condition (see 7.3.2 above); and

- is fixed, irrespective of how many parent company shares are finally issued, since the entity has effectively issued a market-based award with multiple outcomes based on the market value of the equity of a subsidiary (see 7.3.5 above).

In our view, however, the required accounting treatment of such schemes is not as straightforward as suggested by this analysis. A fundamental issue is whether any award dependent on the change in value of the equity of an unquoted entity contains a market condition at all. A market condition is defined (see 7.3.1 above) as one dependent on the 'market price' of the entity's equity. *Prima facie*, if there is no market, there is no market price.

Notwithstanding the absence of a market, some would argue that there are generally accepted valuation techniques for unquoted equities which can yield a fair value as a surrogate for market value. The difficulty with that argument, in our view, is that the definition of 'market condition' refers to 'market price' and not to 'fair value'. The latter term is, of course, used extensively elsewhere in Section 26 (and in IFRS 2), which suggests that the two terms were not considered to be interchangeable. This concern is reinforced by that fact that, in the 'valuation hierarchy' for the measurement of share awards in paragraph 10 of Section 26, a quoted market price is given as the preferred (but not the only) method of arriving at fair value (see 9 below).

An entity implementing such an award must therefore make an assessment, in any particular situation, of whether the basis on which the subsidiary equity is valued truly yields a market price (or value) or merely a fair value according to a hypothetical valuation model.

Furthermore, in order for there to be a market condition there needs to be a specified performance target. It is not always clear in such situations that there is such a target if the various outcomes depend on an exchange of shares regardless of the level of market price or value achieved by the subsidiary.

If it is considered that there is no market condition within the arrangement and there is simply an exchange of shares – in effect, using one entity's shares as the currency for the other – then the arrangement might be viewed as containing a non-vesting condition (similar to when an arrangement depends on the performance of an index for example (see 4.2 above and 7.4 below)). Like a market condition, a non-vesting condition would be taken into account in determining the fair value of the award and would result in a fixed grant date fair value irrespective of the number of shares finally delivered.

Awards based on the 'enterprise value' of an unquoted entity raise similar issues in terms of determining whether there is a market price or value, as discussed more fully at 3.4.5 above.

Chapter 21

7.3.7.A   *Awards with a condition linked to flotation price*

The situations discussed above and at 3.4.5 relate to ongoing conditions linked to the calculated value of an unlisted entity and therefore differ from those where the condition is linked to the market price at which a previously unlisted entity floats. On flotation there is clearly a market and a market price for the entity's equity instruments and the achievement of a specific price on flotation would, in our view, be a market condition when accompanied by a corresponding service requirement (see 16.4 below).

7.4   Non-vesting conditions

As noted at 4.2 above, FRS 102 does not define 'non-vesting condition' or specify the accounting treatment of such conditions other than to state that '... non-vesting conditions shall be taken into account when estimating the fair value of the shares or share options at the measurement date, with no subsequent adjustment irrespective of the outcome of the ... non-vesting condition, provided that all other vesting conditions are satisfied'. *[FRS 102.26.9]*.

The accounting treatment for awards with non-vesting conditions has some similarities to that for awards with market conditions in that:

- the fair value of the award at grant date is reduced to reflect the impact of the condition; and
- an expense is recognised for the award irrespective of whether the non-vesting condition is met, provided that all vesting conditions (other than market conditions) are met.

However, under IFRS 2 – and, in the absence of specific guidance, FRS 102 – the accounting for non-vesting conditions differs from that for market conditions as regards the timing of the recognition of expense if the non-vesting condition is not satisfied (see 7.4.3 below).

7.4.1   *Awards with no conditions other than non-vesting conditions*

Any award that has only non-vesting conditions (e.g. an option award to an employee that may be exercised on a trade sale or IPO of the entity, irrespective of whether the employee is still in employment at that time) must be expensed in full at grant date. This is discussed further at 4.2 above and at 16.4 below, and illustrated in Example 21.6 at 7.1 above.

7.4.2   *Awards with non-vesting conditions and variable vesting periods*

Neither FRS 102 nor IFRS 2 explicitly addresses the determination of the vesting period for an award with a non-vesting condition but a variable vesting period (e.g. an award which delivers 100 shares when the price of gold reaches a given level, but without limit as to when that level must be achieved, so long as the employee is still in employment when the target is reached). However, given the close similarity between the required treatment for awards with non-vesting conditions and that for awards with market conditions, we believe that entities should follow the guidance for awards with market conditions and variable vesting periods (see 7.3.4 above).

7.4.3   *Failure to meet non-vesting conditions*

As noted above, the accounting under IFRS 2 – and, in the absence of specific guidance, FRS 102 – for non-vesting conditions differs from that for market conditions in the timing of the recognition of expense if the non-vesting condition is not satisfied. The treatment depends on the nature of the non-vesting condition, as follows:

* if a non-vesting condition within the control of the counterparty (e.g. making monthly savings) is not satisfied during the vesting period, the failure to satisfy the condition is treated as a cancellation (see 8.4 below), with immediate recognition of any expense for the award not previously recognised *[IFRS 2.28A, IG24]*;

* if a non-vesting condition within the control of the entity (e.g. continuing to operate the scheme) is not satisfied during the vesting period, the failure to satisfy the condition is treated as a cancellation (see 8.4 below), with immediate recognition of any expense for the award not previously recognised *[IFRS 2.28A, IG24]*; but

* if a non-vesting condition within the control of neither the counterparty nor the entity (e.g. a financial market index reaching a minimum level) is not satisfied, there is no change to the accounting and the expense continues to be recognised over the vesting period, unless the award is otherwise treated as forfeited by IFRS 2. *[IFRS 2.BC237A, IG24]*. In our view, the reference to the vesting period would include any deemed vesting period calculated as described in 7.4.2 above.

If there is a failure to satisfy a non-vesting condition after the end of the vesting period (e.g. a requirement for an employee not to work for a competitor for a two year period after vesting), no adjustment is made to the expense previously recognised, consistent with the general provisions for accounting for awards in the post-vesting period (see 7.1.3 above). This would be the case even if shares previously issued to the employee were required to be returned to the entity.

8   EQUITY-SETTLED TRANSACTIONS – MODIFICATION, CANCELLATION AND SETTLEMENT

8.1   Background

It is quite common for equity instruments to be modified or cancelled before or after vesting. Typically this is done where the conditions for an award have become so onerous as to be virtually unachievable, or (in the case of an option) where the share price has fallen so far below the exercise price of an option that it is unlikely that the option will ever be 'in the money' to the holder during its life. An entity may take the view that such equity awards are so unattainable as to have little or no motivational effect, and accordingly replace them with less onerous alternatives. Conversely, and more rarely, an entity may make the terms of a share award more onerous (possibly because of shareholder concern that targets are insufficiently demanding). In addition an entity may 'settle' an award, i.e. cancel it in return for cash or other consideration.

The provisions in FRS 102 relating to modification, cancellation and settlement are derived from those in IFRS 2 and, where necessary, we have drawn on the guidance in IFRS 2 to supplement and explain the FRS 102 requirements. The provisions in both standards (like the summary of them below) are framed in terms of share-based payment transactions with employees. IFRS 2 indicates that the provisions are equally applicable to transactions with parties other than employees that are measured by reference to the fair value of the equity instruments granted (see 6.4 above) and it seems appropriate to adopt a similar approach in the application of FRS 102. For transactions with parties other than employees, however, all references to 'grant date' should be taken as references to the date on which the third party supplied goods or rendered service.

In the discussion below, any reference to a 'cancellation' is to any cancellation, whether instigated by the entity or the counterparty. Cancellations include:

• a failure by the entity to satisfy a non-vesting condition within the control of the entity; and

• a failure by the counterparty to satisfy a non-vesting condition within the control of the counterparty (see 7.4.3 above).

The basic principles of the rules for modification, cancellation and settlement, which are discussed in more detail at 8.3 and 8.4 below, can be summarised as follows.

• The entity must recognise the amount that would have been recognised for the award if it remained in place on its original terms.

• If the value of an award to an employee is reduced (e.g. by reducing the number of equity instruments subject to the award or, in the case of an option, by increasing the exercise price), there is no reduction in the cost recognised in profit or loss.

• However, if the value of an award to an employee is increased (e.g. by increasing the number of equity instruments subject to the award or, in the case of an option, by reducing the exercise price), the incremental fair value must be recognised as a cost. The incremental fair value is the difference between the fair value of the original award and that of the modified award, both measured at the date of modification. [FRS 102.26.12].

8.2 Valuation requirements when an award is modified, cancelled or settled

These provisions have the important practical consequence that, when an award is modified, cancelled or settled, the entity must obtain a fair value not only for the modified award, but also for the original award, updated to the date of modification. If the award had not been modified, there would have been no need to obtain a valuation for the original award after the date of grant.

Any modification of a performance condition clearly has an impact on the 'real' value of an award but it may have no direct effect on the value of the award for accounting purposes. As discussed at 7.2 to 7.4 above, this is because market vesting conditions and non-vesting conditions are taken into account in valuing an award whereas non-market vesting conditions are not. Accordingly, by implication, a change to a non-market performance condition will not necessarily affect the expense recognised for the award.

For example, if an award is contingent upon sales of a given number of units and the number of units required to be sold is decreased, the 'real' value of the award is clearly increased. However, as the performance condition is a non-market condition, and therefore not relevant to the original determination of the value of the award, there is no incremental fair value required to be accounted for. However, if the change in the condition results in an increase in the estimated number of awards expected to vest, the change of estimate will give rise to an accounting charge (see 7.1 to 7.4 above).

If an award is modified by changing the service period, the situation is somewhat more complex. A service condition does not of itself change the fair value of the award for the purposes of FRS 102 and IFRS 2, but a change in service period may well indirectly change the life of the award, which is relevant to its value (see 9 below). Similar considerations apply where performance conditions are modified in such a way as to alter the anticipated vesting date.

The valuation requirements relating to cancelled and settled awards are considered further at 8.4 below.

8.3   Modification

When an award is modified, the entity must as a minimum recognise the cost of the original award as if it had not been modified (i.e. based on the original grant date fair value, spread over the original vesting period, and subject to the original vesting conditions). *[FRS 102.26.12(b)]*.

In addition, a further cost must be recognised for any modifications that increase the fair value of the award. If the modification occurs during the vesting period, this additional cost is spread over the period from the date of modification until the vesting date of the modified award, which might not be the same as that of the original award. *[FRS 102.26.12(a)]*. Although not explicitly stated in Section 26, but nevertheless consistent with its requirements, where a modification is made after the original vesting period has expired, and is subject to no further vesting conditions, any incremental fair value should be recognised immediately. *[IFRS 2 B43]*.

Whether a modification increases or decreases the fair value of an award is determined as at the date of modification, as illustrated by Example 21.19. *[FRS 102.26.12]*.

Example 21.19:   Does a modification increase or decrease the value of an award?

On 1 January 2015 an entity granted two executives, A and B, a number of options worth £100 each.

On 1 January 2016, A's options are modified such that they have a fair value of £85, their current fair value being £80. This is treated as an increase in fair value of £5 (even though the modified award is worth less than the original award when first granted). Therefore an additional £5 of expense would be recognised in respect of A's options.

On 1 January 2017, B's options are modified such that they have a fair value of £120, their current fair value being £125. This is treated as a reduction in fair value of £5 (even though the modified award is worth more than the original award when first granted). There is no change to the expense recognised for B's options.

This treatment ensures that movements in the fair value of the original award are not reflected in the entity's profit or loss, consistent with the accounting treatment of other equity instruments.

Appendix B and the implementation guidance to IFRS 2 provide further detailed guidance on these requirements as set out in the following sections.

8.3.1   Modifications that increase the value of an award

8.3.1.A   Increase in fair value of equity instruments granted

If the modification increases the fair value of the equity instruments granted, (e.g. by reducing the exercise price or changing the exercise period), the incremental fair value, measured at the date of modification, must be recognised over the period from the date of modification to the date of vesting for the modified instruments, as illustrated in Example 21.20 below (which is based on Example 7 in the implementation guidance to IFRS 2). *[FRS 102.26.12(a), IFRS 2.B43(a)]*.

Example 21.20:   Award modified by repricing

At the beginning of year 1, an entity grants 100 share options to each of its 500 employees. Each grant is conditional upon the employee remaining in service over the next three years. The entity estimates that the fair value of each option is £15.

By the end of year 1, the entity's share price has dropped, and the entity reprices its share options. The repriced share options vest at the end of year 3. The entity estimates that, at the date of repricing, the fair value of each of the original share options granted (i.e. before taking into account the repricing) is £5 and that the fair value of each repriced share option is £8.

40 employees leave during year 1. The entity estimates that a further 70 employees will leave during years 2 and 3, so that there will be 390 employees at the end of year 3 (500 – 40 – 70).

During year 2, a further 35 employees leave, and the entity estimates that a further 30 employees will leave during year 3, so that there will be 395 employees at the end of year 3 (500 – 40 – 35 – 30).

During year 3, 28 employees leave, and hence a total of 103 employees ceased employment during the original three year vesting period, so that, for the remaining 397 employees, the original share options vest at the end of year 3.

IFRS 2 (and FRS 102) requires the entity to recognise:

- the cost of the original award at grant date (£15 per option) over a three year vesting period beginning at the start of year 1, plus

- the incremental fair value of the repriced options at repricing date (£3 per option, being the £8 fair value of each repriced option less the £5 fair value of the original option) over a two year vesting period beginning at the date of repricing (end of year one).

This would be calculated as follows.

Year	Calculation of cumulative expense Original award (a)	Modified award (b)	Cumulative expense (£) (a+b)	Expense for period (£)
1	390 employees × 100 options × £15 × 1/3		195,000	195,000
2	395 employees × 100 options × £15 × 2/3	395 employees × 100 options × £3 × 1/2	454,250	259,250
3	397 employees × 100 options × £15	397 employees × 100 options × £3	714,600	260,350

In effect, the original award and the incremental value of the modified award are treated as if they were two separate awards.

A similar treatment to that in Example 21.20 above is adopted where the fair value of an award subject to a market condition has its value increased by the removal or mitigation of the market condition. *[IFRS 2.B43(c)]*. Where a vesting condition other than a market condition is changed, the treatment set out in 8.3.1.C below is adopted. The standards do not specifically address the situation where the fair value of an award is increased by the removal or mitigation of a non-vesting condition. It seems appropriate, however, to account for this increase in the same way as for a modification caused by the removal or mitigation of a market condition – i.e. as in Example 21.20 above.

8.3.1.B   *Increase in number of equity instruments granted*

Paragraph 12 of Section 26 on modification of awards begins by referring solely to modifications to the conditions on which equity instruments were granted rather than the number of equity instruments granted. However, in discussing the related accounting treatment, paragraph 12 goes on to refer both to the fair value of an award and to the number of equity instruments granted. If the modification increases the number of equity instruments granted, the fair value of the additional instruments, measured at the date of modification, must be recognised over the period from the date of modification to the date of vesting for the modified instruments. *[FRS 102.26.12(a)]*. Although not explicitly stated, it follows that if there is no further vesting period for the modified instruments, the incremental cost should be recognised immediately.

It is often the case, however, that a change in the number of equity instruments granted is combined with other modifications to the award – such situations are considered further at 8.3.2 and 8.3.4 below.

8.3.1.C   *Removal or mitigation of non-market related vesting conditions*

Where a vesting condition, other than a market condition, is modified, the modified vesting condition should be taken into account when applying the general requirements of FRS 102 as discussed in 7.1 to 7.4 above – in other words, the entity would continuously estimate the number of awards likely to vest and/or the vesting period. This is consistent with the general principle that vesting conditions, other than market conditions, are not taken into account in the valuation of awards, but are reflected by recognising a cost for those instruments that ultimately vest on achievement of those conditions. See also the discussion at 8.2 above.

The standards do not provide an example that addresses this point specifically, but we assume that the intended approach is as in Example 21.21 below.

Example 21.21:   Modification of non-market performance condition in employee's favour

At the beginning of year 1, the entity grants 1,000 share options to each member of its sales team, with exercise conditional upon the employee remaining in the entity's employment for three years, and the team selling more than 50,000 units of a particular product over the three year period. The fair value of the share options is £15 per option at the date of grant.

At the end of year 1, the entity estimates that a total of 48,000 units will be sold, and accordingly records no cost for the award in year one.

During year 2, there is so severe a downturn in trading conditions that the entity believes that the sales target is too demanding to have any motivational effect, and reduces the target to 30,000 units, which it believes is achievable. It also expects 14 members of the sales team to remain in employment throughout the three year performance period. It therefore records an expense in year 2 of £140,000 (£15 × 14 employees × 1,000 options × 2/3). This cost is based on the originally assessed value of the award (i.e. £15) since the performance condition was never factored into the original valuation, such that any change in performance condition likewise has no effect on the valuation.

By the end of year 3, the entity has sold 35,000 units, and the share options vest. Twelve members of the sales team have remained in service for the three year period. The entity would therefore recognise a total cost of £180,000 (12 employees × 1,000 options × £15), giving an additional cost in year 3 of £40,000 (total charge £180,000, less £140,000 charged in year 2).

The difference between the accounting consequences for different methods of enhancing an award could cause confusion in some cases. For example, it may sometimes not be clear whether an award has been modified by increasing the number of equity instruments or by lowering the performance targets, as illustrated in Example 21.22.

Example 21.22:   Increase in number of equity instruments or modification of vesting conditions?

An entity grants a performance-related award which provides for different numbers of options to vest after 3 years, depending on different performance targets as follows.

Profit growth	Number of options
5%-10%	100
10%-15%	200
over 15%	300

During the vesting period, the entity concludes that the criteria are too demanding and modifies them as follows.

Profit growth	Number of options
5%-10%	200
over 10%	300

This raises the issue of whether the entity has changed:

(a)   the performance conditions for the vesting of 200 or 300 options; or

(b)   the number of equity instruments awarded for achieving 5%-10% or over 10% growth.

In our view, the reality is that the change is to the performance conditions for the vesting of 200 or 300 options, and should therefore be dealt with as in 8.3.1.C, rather than 8.3.1.B above. Suppose, however, that the conditions had been modified as follows.

Profit growth	Number of options
5%-10%	200
10%-15%	300
over 15%	400

In that case, there has clearly been an increase in the number of equity instruments subject to an award for an increase of over 15% growth, which would have to be accounted for as such (i.e. under 8.3.1.B, rather than 8.3.1.C above). In such a case, it might seem more appropriate to deal with the changes to the lower bands as changes to the number of shares awarded rather than changes to the performance conditions.

8.3.2   Modifications that decrease the value of an award

Modifications that decrease the value of an award to the counterparty do not occur very often as their effect would be somewhat demotivating and, in some cases, contrary to local labour regulations. However, there have been occasional examples of an award being made more onerous – usually in response to criticism by shareholders that the original terms were insufficiently demanding. The general requirement of FRS 102 and of IFRS 2 is that, where an award is made more onerous (and therefore less valuable), the financial statements must still recognise the cost of the original award. This rule is in part an anti-avoidance measure since, without it, an entity could reverse the cost of an out-of-the-money award by modifying it so that it was unlikely to vest (for example, by adding unattainable performance conditions) rather than cancelling the award and triggering an acceleration of expense as in 8.4 below.

8.3.2.A   Decrease in fair value of equity instruments granted

If the modification decreases the fair value of the equity instruments (e.g. by increasing the exercise price or reducing the exercise period), the decrease in value is effectively ignored and the entity continues to recognise a cost for services as if the awards had not been modified. *[IFRS 2.B44(a)]*. This approach applies to reductions in the fair value of an award by the addition of a market condition or by making an existing market condition more onerous *[IFRS 2.B44(c)]*, Although the standards have no specific guidance on this point, we assume that reductions in the fair value resulting from the addition or amendment of a non-vesting condition are similarly ignored.

8.3.2.B   Decrease in number of equity instruments granted

If the modification reduces the number of equity instruments granted, IFRS 2 requires the reduction to be treated as a cancellation of that portion of the award (see 8.4 below). *[IFRS 2.B44(b)]*. Essentially this has the effect that any previously unrecognised cost of the cancelled instruments is immediately recognised in full, whereas the cost of an award whose value is reduced by other means continues to be spread in full over the remaining vesting period.

However, in situations where a decrease in the number of equity instruments is combined with other modifications so that the total fair value of the award remains the same or increases, it is unclear whether the approach required is one based on the value of the award as a whole or, as in the previous paragraph, one based on each equity instrument as the unit of account. This is considered further at 8.3.4 below.

8.3.2.C   Additional or more onerous non-market related vesting conditions

Where a non-market vesting condition is modified in a manner that is not beneficial to the employee, the modification is ignored and a cost recognised as if the original award had not been modified, as shown by Example 21.23. *[IFRS 2.B44(c), IG15, IG Example 8]*.

Example 21.23: Award modified by changing non-market performance conditions

At the beginning of year 1, the entity grants 1,000 share options to each member of its sales team, conditional upon the employee remaining in the entity's employment for three years, and the team selling more than 50,000 units of a particular product over the three year period. The fair value of the share options is £15 per option at the date of grant. During year 2, the entity believes that the sales target is insufficiently demanding and increases it to 100,000 units. By the end of year 3, the entity has sold 55,000 units, and the share options are forfeited. Twelve members of the sales team have remained in service for the three year period.

On the basis that the original target would have been met, and twelve employees would have been eligible for awards, the entity would recognise a total cost of £180,000 (12 employees × 1,000 options × £15). The cumulative cost in years 1 and 2 would, as in the Examples above, reflect the entity's best estimate of the *original* 50,000 unit sales target being achieved at the end of year 3. If, conversely, sales of only 49,000 units had been achieved, any cost booked for the award in years 1 and 2 would have been reversed in year 3, since the original target of 50,000 units would not have been met.

8.3.3   *Modifications with altered vesting period*

Where an award is modified so that its value increases, FRS 102 and IFRS 2 require the entity to continue to recognise an expense for the grant date fair value of the unmodified award over its *original* vesting period, even where the vesting period of the modified award is longer (see 8.3.1 above). This appears to have the effect that an expense may be recognised for awards that do not actually vest, as illustrated by Example 21.24 (which is based on Example 21.20 above).

Example 21.24:   Award modified by reducing the exercise price and extending the vesting period

At the beginning of year 1, an entity grants 100 share options to each of its 500 employees, with vesting conditional upon the employee remaining in service over the next three years. The entity estimates that the fair value of each option is £15.

By the end of year 1, the entity's share price has dropped, and the entity reprices its share options. The repriced share options vest at the end of year 4. The entity estimates that, at the date of repricing, the fair value of each of the original share options granted (i.e. before taking into account the repricing) is £5 and that the fair value of each repriced share option is £7.

40 employees leave during year 1. The entity estimates that a further 70 employees will leave during years 2 and 3, and a further 25 employees during year 4, such that there will be 390 employees at the end of year 3 (500 – 40 – 70) and 365 (500 – 40 – 70 – 25) at the end of year 4.

During year 2, a further 35 employees leave, and the entity estimates that a further 30 employees will leave during year 3 and 30 more in year 4, such that there will be 395 employees at the end of year 3 (500 – 40 – 35 – 30) and 365 (500 – 40 – 35 – 30 – 30) at the end of year 4.

During year 3, 28 employees leave, and hence a total of 103 employees ceased employment during the original three year vesting period, so that, for the remaining 397 employees, the original share options would have vested at the end of year 3. The entity now estimates that only a further 20 employees will leave during year 4, leaving 377 at the end of year 4. In fact 25 employees leave, so that 372 satisfy the criteria for the modified options at the end of year 4.

In our view the entity is required to recognise:

- the cost of the original award at grant date (£15 per option) over a three year vesting period beginning at the start of year 1, based on the ongoing best estimate of, and ultimately the actual, number of employees at the end of the *original three year* vesting period;

- the incremental fair value of the repriced options at repricing date (£2 per option, being the £7 fair value of each repriced option less the £5 fair value of the original option) over a three year vesting period beginning at the date of repricing (*end* of year one), but based on the ongoing best estimate of, and ultimately the actual, number of employees at the end of the *modified four year* vesting period.

This would be calculated as follows.

Year	Calculation of cumulative expense		Cumulative expense (£)	Expense for period (£)
	Original award	Modified award		
1	390 employees × 100 options × £15 × 1/3		195,000	195,000
2	395 employees × 100 options × £15 × 2/3	365 employees × 100 options × £2 × 1/3	419,333	224,333
3	397 employees × 100 options × £15	377 employees × 100 options × £2 × 2/3	645,767	226,434
4	397 employees × 100 options × £15	372 employees × 100 options × £2	669,900	24,133

It may seem strange that a cost is being recognised for the original award in respect of the 25 employees who leave during year 4, who are never entitled to anything. However, in our view, this is consistent with:

* the overall requirement of FRS 102 and IFRS 2 that the minimum cost of a modified award should be the cost that would have been recognised if the award had not been modified; and

* IG Example 8 in IFRS 2 (the substance of which is reproduced in Example 21.23 above) where an expense is clearly required to be recognised to the extent that the original performance conditions would have been met if the award had not been modified.

Moreover, as Examples 21.23 and 21.24 illustrate, the rule in FRS 102 and IFRS 2 requiring recognition of a minimum expense for a modified award (i.e. as if the original award had remained in place) applies irrespective of whether the effect of the modification is that an award becomes less valuable to the employee (as in Example 21.23) or more valuable to the employee (as in Example 21.24).

8.3.4 Modifications that reduce the number of equity instruments granted but maintain or increase the value of an award ('value for value' exchanges and 'give and take' modifications)

As discussed at 8.3.2.B above, IFRS 2 requires cancellation accounting to be applied to a reduction in the number of equity instruments when a modification reduces both the number of equity instruments granted and the total fair value of the award. *[IFRS 2.B44(b)]*. FRS 102 is silent on the accounting treatment of such arrangements and we therefore suggest that entities follow the IFRS 2 requirements. The IFRS 2 approach is consistent with the fact that part of the award has been removed without compensation to the employee. However, a modification of this kind is rarely seen in practice because of the demotivating effect and, in some jurisdictions, a requirement to pay compensation to the counterparty. An entity is more likely to modify an award so that the overall fair value remains the same, or increases, even if the number of equity instruments is reduced. These types of modification, sometimes known as 'value for value' exchanges or 'give and take' modifications, are considered below.

Where an entity reduces the number of equity instruments but also makes other changes so that the total fair value of the modified award either remains the same as that of the original award as at the modification date or exceeds it, it is unclear whether the unit of account for accounting purposes should be an individual equity instrument or the award as a whole. Examples 21.25 and 21.26 below illustrate the two situations and the two approaches.

Chapter 21

Example 21.25:   Modification where number of equity instruments is reduced but total fair value is unchanged

An entity granted an employee 200 share options on 1 January 2015. On 31 December 2016 the exercise price of the options is significantly higher than the market price and the options have a fair value of £5 per option. On this date, the entity modifies the award and exchanges the 200 underwater options for 100 'at the money' options with a fair value of £10 each. The fair value of the new awards of £1,000 (100 × £10) equals the fair value of the awards exchanged (200 × £5) so there is no incremental fair value.

View 1 is that the unit of account is an individual option. Taking this approach, the decrease in the number of options from 200 to 100 will be accounted for as a cancellation with an acceleration at the modification date of any unexpensed element of the grant date fair value of 100 options. The grant date fair value of the remaining 100 options continues to be recognised over the remainder of the vesting period so that, in total, £1,000 will have been expensed.

View 2 is that the total number of options exchanged is the more appropriate unit of account. In this case, the cancellation of the original options and the grant of replacement options are accounted for as a modification. There would therefore be no acceleration of expense in respect of the reduction in the number of options from 200 to 100 and the grant date fair value of the original award would continue to be recognised over the vesting period.

Example 21.26:   Modification where number of equity instruments is reduced but total fair value is increased

An entity has previously granted to its employees 1,000 share options with an exercise price equal to the market price of the shares at grant date. The grant date fair value is £10 per option. The entity's share price has declined significantly so that the share price is currently significantly less than the exercise price. The entity decides to reduce the exercise price of the options and, as part of the modification, it also reduces the number of options from 1,000 to 800. At the date of modification, the fair value of the original options is £7 per option and that of the modified options £11 per option.

View 1 is that the unit of account is an individual option. Taking this approach, the decrease in the number of options from 1,000 to 800 will be accounted for as a cancellation with an acceleration at the modification date of any remaining grant date fair value relating to those 200 options. The grant date fair value of the remaining 800 options continues to be recognised over the remainder of the vesting period together with the incremental fair value of those awards as measured at the modification date. In total the entity will recognise an expense of £13,200 (original grant date fair value of £10,000 (1,000 × £10) plus incremental fair value of £3,200 (800 × £(11 − 7)).

View 2 is that the unit of account is the total number of options as there are linked modifications forming one package. In this case, the incremental fair value is calculated as the difference between the total fair value before and after the modification. In total the entity will recognise an expense of £11,800 (original grant date fair value of £10,000 (1,000 × £10) plus incremental fair value on modification of £1,800 ((800 × £11) − (1,000 × £7)).

Given the lack of clarity, we believe that an entity may make an accounting policy choice as to whether it considers the unit of account to be an individual equity instrument or an award as a whole. Further detail on the arguments underpinning each of the two approaches is given in EY International GAAP 2015 but is beyond the scope of this publication.

Once made, the accounting policy choice should be applied consistently to all modifications that reduce the number of equity instruments but maintain or increase the overall fair value of an award. Whatever the policy choice, the entity will still need to determine whether or not the amendments to the arrangement are such that it is appropriate to treat the changes as a modification rather than as a completely new award (see 8.4.2 and 8.4.4 below).

8.3.5   Modification of award from equity-settled to cash-settled (and vice versa)

Occasionally an award that was equity-settled when originally granted is modified so as to become cash-settled, or an originally cash-settled award is modified so as to become equity-settled. FRS 102 and IFRS 2 provide no explicit guidance on such modifications but we believe that it is possible to arrive at a reasonable approach by analogy to the provisions of IFRS 2 in respect of:

- the modification of equity-settled awards during the vesting period (see 8.3 above);

- the addition of a cash-settlement alternative to an equity-settled award after grant date (as illustrated in Example 9 in the implementation guidance to IFRS 2);

- the settlement of equity-settled awards in cash (see 8.4 below); and

- the settlement in equity of awards where the entity has a choice of settlement, but which have been accounted for as cash-settled during the vesting period (see 11.1.3 below).

A detailed discussion of this topic is beyond the scope of this publication but the subject is addressed more fully in EY International GAAP 2015.

8.4   Cancellation and settlement

Paragraph 13 of Section 26 is headed 'cancellations and settlements' but, whilst its treatment of cancellations is consistent with the basic requirement of IFRS 2 (as set out in (a) below), it does not specify the accounting treatment of a settlement (i.e. an award cancelled with some form of compensation). Section 26 also does not address the treatment of replacement awards following a cancellation.

In the absence of specific guidance in FRS 102, we consider it appropriate to follow the full guidance in IFRS 2, as outlined below, for the cancellation, replacement or settlement of an award other than by forfeiture for failure to satisfy the vesting conditions.

When an award accounted for under FRS 102 is settled, it is perhaps debatable whether any incremental amount paid in settlement is required to be expensed, as for IFRS 2 (see (b) below) or whether any difference could be accounted for in equity as would be the case with the repurchase of equity instruments outside a share-based payment transaction. In our view, an approach consistent with that of IFRS 2 is appropriate given the extent to which the requirements of Section 26 generally are derived from those of IFRS 2.

IFRS 2 requires the following approach:

(a)   if the cancellation or settlement occurs during the vesting period, it is treated as an acceleration of vesting, and the entity recognises immediately the amount that would otherwise have been recognised for services received over the remainder of the vesting period; *[FRS 102.26.13, IFRS 2.28, 29]*

(b)   where the entity pays compensation for a cancelled award:

    (i)   any compensation paid up to the fair value of the award at cancellation or settlement date (whether before or after vesting) is accounted for as a deduction from equity, as being equivalent to the redemption of an equity instrument;

    (ii)   any compensation paid in excess of the fair value of the award at cancellation or settlement date (whether before or after vesting) is accounted for as an expense in profit or loss; and

    (iii)   if the share-based payment arrangement includes liability components, the fair value of the liability is remeasured at the date of cancellation or settlement. Any payment made to settle the liability component is accounted for as an extinguishment of the liability; and

(c)   if the entity grants new equity instruments during the vesting period and, on the date that they are granted, identifies them as replacing the cancelled or settled instruments, the entity is required to account for the new equity instruments as if they were a modification of the cancelled or settled award. Otherwise it accounts for the new instruments as an entirely new award. *[IFRS 2.28, 29]*.

It should be noted that the calculation of any additional expense in (b) above depends on the fair value of the award at the date of cancellation or settlement, not on the cumulative expense already charged. This has the important practical consequence that, when an entity pays compensation on cancellation or settlement of an award, it must obtain a fair value for the original award, updated to the date of cancellation or settlement. If the award had not been cancelled or settled, there would have been no need to obtain a valuation for the original award after the date of grant.

These requirements raise some further detailed issues of interpretation on a number of areas, as follows:

- the distinction between 'cancellation' and 'forfeiture' (see 8.4.1 below);
- the distinction between 'cancellation' and 'modification' (see 8.4.2 below);
- the calculation of the expense on cancellation (see 8.4.3 below); and
- replacement awards (see 8.4.4 and 8.5 below).

8.4.1   Distinction between cancellation and forfeiture

The above provisions of IFRS 2 apply when an award of equity instruments is cancelled or settled 'other than a grant cancelled by forfeiture when the vesting conditions are not satisfied'. *[IFRS 2.28]*. The significance of this is that the terms of many share-based awards provide that they are, or can be, 'cancelled' on forfeiture. IFRS 2 is clarifying that, where an award is forfeited (within the meaning of that term in IFRS 2 – see 7.1.2 above), the entity should apply the accounting treatment for a forfeiture (i.e. reversal of expense previously recognised), even if the award is legally cancelled as a consequence of the forfeiture. FRS 102 does not have such an explicit distinction but we presume that a similar treatment is intended.

8.4.1.A   Termination of employment by entity

In some cases, it is not clear whether cancellation or forfeiture has occurred, particularly where options lapse as the result of a termination of employment by the entity. For example, an entity might grant options to an employee on 1 January 2015 on condition of his remaining in employment until at least 31 December 2017. During 2016, however, economic conditions require the entity to make a number of its personnel, including that employee, redundant, as a result of which his options lapse. Is this lapse a forfeiture or a cancellation for accounting purposes?

The uncertainty arises because it could be argued either that the employee will be unable to render the service required in order for the options to vest (suggesting a forfeiture) or that the options lapse as a direct result of the employer's actions (suggesting a cancellation). Following clarification by the IASB in its *Annual Improvements to IFRSs 2010-2012 Cycle*, any failure to meet a service condition, including a situation where the entity terminates the employment contract, is a forfeiture rather than a cancellation and we suggest this approach is followed by entities applying FRS 102.[2]

8.4.1.B   Surrender of award by employee

It is sometimes the case that an employee, often a member of senior management, will decide – or be encouraged by the entity – to surrender awards during the vesting period. The question arises as to whether this should be treated as a cancellation or forfeiture for accounting purposes. FRS 102 and IFRS 2 allow forfeiture accounting, and the consequent reversal of any cumulative expense, only in situations where vesting conditions are not satisfied. A situation where the counterparty voluntarily surrenders an award and therefore 'fails' to meet the service condition does not, in our view, meet the criteria for treatment as a forfeiture and should be treated as a cancellation of the award by the employee.

8.4.2   Distinction between cancellation and modification

One general issue raised by the approach to modification and cancellation in FRS 102 and IFRS 2 is where the boundary lies between 'modification' of an award in the entity's favour and outright cancellation of the award. As a matter of legal form, the difference is obvious. However, if an entity were to modify an award in such a way that there was no realistic chance of it ever vesting (for example, by introducing a requirement that the share price increase 1,000,000 times by vesting date), some might argue that this amounts to a *de facto* cancellation of the award. The significance of the distinction is that, whereas the cost of a 'modified' award continues to be recognised on a periodic basis (see 8.3 above), the remaining cost of a cancelled award is recognised immediately.

8.4.3   *Calculation of the expense on cancellation*

The basic accounting treatment for a cancellation and settlement is illustrated in Example 21.27 below.

Example 21.27: Cancellation and settlement – basic accounting treatment

At the start of year 1 an entity grants an executive 30,000 options on condition that she remain in employment for three years. Each option is determined to have a fair value of £10.

At the end of year 1, the executive is still in employment and the entity charges an expense of £100,000 (30,000 × £10 × 1/3). At the end of year 2, the executive is still in employment. However, the entity's share price has suffered a decline which the entity does not expect to have reversed by the end of year 3, such that the options, while still 'in the money' now have a fair value of only £6.

The entity cancels the options and in compensation pays the executive £6.50 per option cancelled, a total payment of £195,000 (30,000 options × £6.50).

FRS 102 and IFRS 2 first require the entity to record a cost as if the options had vested immediately. The total cumulative cost for the award must be £300,000 (300 options × £10). £100,000 was recognised in year 1, so that an additional cost of £200,000 is recognised.

As regards the compensation payment, the fair value of the awards cancelled is £180,000 (30,000 options × £6.00). Accordingly, £180,000 of the payment is accounted for as a deduction from equity, with the remaining payment in excess of fair value, £15,000, charged to profit or loss (as required by IFRS 2 – and, in our view, a reasonable approach to apply under FRS 102).

The net effect of this is that an award that ultimately results in a cash payment to the executive of only £195,000 (i.e. £6.50 per option) has resulted in a total charge to profit or loss of £315,000 (i.e. £10.50 per option, representing £10 grant date fair value + £6.50 compensation payment – £6.00 cancellation date fair value).

Example 21.27 illustrates the basic calculation of the required cancellation 'charge'. In more complex situations, however, the amount of the 'charge' may not be so clear-cut, due to an ambiguity in the drafting of paragraph 28(a) of IFRS 2 and paragraph 13 of Section 26, which state that an entity:

> 'shall account for the cancellation or settlement as an acceleration of vesting, and therefore shall recognise immediately the amount that otherwise would have been recognised for services received over the remainder of the vesting period.' *[FRS 102.26.13, IFRS 2.28(a)]*.

There is something of a contradiction within this requirement as illustrated by Example 21.28.

Example 21.28: Cancellation and settlement – best estimate of cancellation expense

On 1 January 2015, an entity (A) granted 150 employees an award of free shares, with a grant date fair value of £5, conditional upon continuous service and performance targets over the 3-year period ending 31 December 2017. The number of shares awarded varies according to the extent to which targets (all non-market vesting conditions) have been met, and could result in each employee still in service at 31 December 2017 receiving a minimum of 600, and a maximum of 1,000 shares.

On 1 July 2016, A is acquired by B, following which all of A's share awards are cancelled. At the time of the cancellation, 130 of the original 150 employees were still in employment. At that time, it was A's best estimate that, had the award run to its full term, 120 employees would have received 900 shares each. Accordingly, the cumulative expense recognised by A for the award as at the date of takeover would, under the normal estimation processes discussed at 7.1 to 7.4 above, be £270,000 (900 shares × 120 employees × £5 × 18/36).

How should A account for the cancellation of this award?

The opening phrase of paragraph 28(a) of IFRS 2 (echoed in paragraph 13 of FRS 102) – 'the entity shall account for the cancellation ...as an acceleration of vesting' – suggests that A should recognise a cost for all 130 employees in service at the date of cancellation. However, the following phrase – '[the entity] shall therefore recognise immediately the amount that would otherwise have been recognised for services received over the remainder of the vesting period' – suggests that the charge should be based on only 120 employees, the best estimate, as at the date of cancellation of the number of employees in whom shares will finally vest. In our view, either reading is possible.

There is then the issue of the number of shares per employee that should be taken into account in the cancellation charge. Should this be 1,000 shares per employee (the maximum amount that could vest) or 900 shares per employee (the amount expected by the entity at the date of cancellation actually to vest)?

In our view, the intention was probably that the cancellation charge should be based on the number of shares considered likely, at the date of cancellation, to vest for each employee (900 shares in this example). However, given the lack of clarity in the wording – as discussed above – an entity could also choose an accounting policy based on the maximum number of shares (1000 shares in this example).

In extreme cases, the entity might conclude as at the date of cancellation that no awards are likely to vest. In this situation, no cancellation expense would be recognised. However, there would need to be evidence that this was not just a rather convenient assessment made as at the date of cancellation. Typically, the previous accounting periods would also have reflected a cumulative expense of zero on the assumption that the awards would not vest.

An effect of these requirements is that they create an accounting arbitrage between an award that is 'out of the money' but not cancelled (which continues to be spread over the remaining period to vesting) and one which is formally cancelled (the cost of which is recognised immediately). Entities might well prefer to opt for cancellation so as to create a 'one-off' charge to earnings rather than continue to show, particularly during difficult trading periods, significant periodic costs for options that no longer have any real value. However, such early cancellation of an award precludes any chance of the cost of the award being reversed through forfeiture during, or at the end of, the vesting period.

8.4.4   Replacement awards

FRS 102 contains no specific requirements or guidance in relation to replacement awards and so we consider it appropriate to draw on those in IFRS 2. The remainder of this section therefore reflects the IFRS 2 requirements. Whilst the requirements relating to accounting for replacement awards are generally clear under IFRS 2, there are nevertheless some issues of interpretation.

8.4.4.A   Designation of award as replacement award

Whether or not an award is a 'replacement' award (and therefore recognised at only its incremental, rather than its full, fair value) is determined by whether or not the entity designates it as such on the date that it is granted.

Entities need to ensure that designation occurs on grant date as defined by IFRS 2 (and FRS 102) (see 6.3 above). For example, if an entity cancels an award on 15 March 2015 and notifies an employee in writing on the same day of its intention to ask the remuneration committee to grant replacement options at its meeting on 15 May 2015, such notification (although formal and in writing) may not strictly meet the requirement for designation on grant date (i.e. 15 May 2015).

As drafted, IFRS 2 gives entities an apparently free choice to designate any newly granted awards as replacement awards. In our view, however, such designation cannot credibly be made unless there is evidence of some connection between the cancelled and replacement awards. This might be that the cancelled and replacement awards involve the same counterparties, or that the cancellation and replacement are part of the same arrangement.

8.4.4.B   *Incremental fair value of replacement award*

Where an award is designated as a replacement award, it must be recognised, over its vesting period, at its incremental fair value. This is the difference between the fair value of the replacement award and the 'net fair value' of the cancelled or settled award, both measured at the date on which the replacement awards are granted. The net fair value of the cancelled or settled award is the fair value of the award, immediately before cancellation, less any compensation payment that is accounted for as a deduction from equity. *[IFRS 2.28(c)].* Thus the 'net fair value' of the original award can never be less than zero (since any compensation payment in excess of the fair value of the cancelled award would be accounted for in profit or loss, not in equity – see Example 21.27 at 8.4.3 above).

There is some confusion within IFRS 2 as to whether a different accounting treatment is intended to result from, on the one hand, modifying an award and, on the other hand, cancelling it and replacing it with a new award on the same terms as the modified award. This is explored in the discussion of Example 21.29 below, which is based on the same fact pattern as Example 21.20 at 8.3.1.A above.

Example 21.29:   Is there an accounting arbitrage between modification and cancellation of an award?

At the beginning of year 1, an entity grants 100 share options to each of its 500 employees. Each grant is conditional upon the employee remaining in service over the next three years. The entity estimates that the fair value of each option is £15.

By the end of year 1, the entity's share price has dropped. The entity cancels the existing options and issues options which it identifies as replacement options, which also vest at the end of year 3. The entity estimates that, at the date of cancellation, the fair value of each of the original share options granted is £5 and that the fair value of each replacement share option is £8.

40 employees leave during year 1. The entity estimates that a further 70 employees will leave during years 2 and 3, so that there will be 390 employees at the end of year 3 (500 – 40 – 70).

During year 2, a further 35 employees leave, and the entity estimates that a further 30 employees will leave during year 3, so that there will be 395 employees at the end of year 3 (500 – 40 – 35 – 30).

During year 3, 28 employees leave, and hence a total of 103 employees ceased employment during the original three year vesting period, so that, for the remaining 397 employees, the replacement share options vest at the end of year 3.

Paragraph BC233 of IFRS 2 suggests that the intention of the IASB was that the arrangement should be accounted for in exactly the same way as the modification in Example 21.20 above.

However, it is not clear that this intention is actually reflected in the drafting of paragraph 28 of IFRS 2 which seems to require the cancellation of the existing award to be treated as an acceleration of vesting – explicitly and without qualification and any 'new equity instruments' granted to be accounted for in the same way as a modification of the original grant of equity instruments.

The application of, firstly, the main text of IFRS 2 and, secondly, the Basis for Conclusions to IFRS 2 to the entity in Example 21.29 is set out below.

The main text in IFRS 2 appears to require the entity to recognise:

- The entire cost of the original options at the end of year 1 (since cancellation has the effect that they are treated as vesting at that date), based on the 390 employees expected at that date to be in employment at the end of the vesting period. This is not the only possible interpretation of the requirement of paragraph 28(a) – see the broader discussion in Example 21.28 at 8.4.3 above.

- For the options replacing the 390 cancelled awards, the incremental fair value of the replacement options at repricing date (£3 per option, being the £8 fair value of each replacement option less the £5 fair value of the cancelled option) over a two year vesting period beginning at the date of cancellation (end of year 1), based on the (at first estimated and then actual) number of employees at the end of year 3 (i.e. the final number could be less than the estimate of 390).

- For any additional replacement options (i.e. replacement options awarded in excess of the 390 × 100 options that were expected to vest at cancellation date), the full incremental fair value at repricing date (being the £8 fair value of each replacement option) over a two year vesting period beginning at the repricing date (end of year 1). The expense is based on the (at first estimated and then actual) number of employees in excess of 390 at the end of year 3.

This would be calculated as follows:

Year	Calculation of cumulative expense Original award	Replacement award	Cumulative expense (£)	Expense for period (£)
1	390 employees × 100 options × £15	–	585,000	585,000
2	390 employees × 100 options × £15	390 employees × 100 options × £3 × 1/2 5 employees × 100 options × £8 × 1/2	645,500	60,500
3	390 employees × 100 options × £15	390 employees × 100 options × £3 7 employees × 100 options × £8	707,600	62,100

By contrast, the accounting treatment implied by the Basis for Conclusions is as follows (see Example 21.20 above):

Year	Calculation of cumulative expense Original award (a)	Modified award (b)	Cumulative expense (£) (a+b)	Expense for period (£)
1	390 employees × 100 options × £15 × 1/3	–	195,000	195,000
2	395 employees × 100 options × £15 × 2/3	395 employees × 100 options × £3 × 1/2	454,250	259,250
3	397 employees × 100 options × £15	397 employees × 100 options × £3	714,600	260,350

It will be seen that both the periodic allocation of expense and the total expense differ under each interpretation. This is because, under the first interpretation, the cost of the original award is accelerated at the end of year 1 for all 390 employees expected at that date to be in employment at the end of the vesting period, whereas under the second interpretation a cost is recognised for the 397 employees whose awards finally vest. The difference between the two total charges of £7,000 (£714,600 – £707,600) represents 397 – 390 = 7 employees @ £1,000 [100 options × £10[£18-£8]] each = £7,000.

In practice, the second (modification accounting) approach tends to be seen more frequently. However, we believe that either interpretation is valid, and an entity should adopt one or other consistently as a matter of accounting policy.

Chapter 21

In Example 21.29 above, we base the cancellation calculations on 390 employees (the number expected to be employed at the end of the vesting period as estimated at the cancellation date) rather than on 460 employees (the number in employment at the cancellation date). As discussed in Example 21.28 at 8.4.3 above, either approach may be adopted but the selected approach should be applied consistently.

8.4.4.C   Replacement of vested awards

The rules for replacement awards summarised in paragraph (c) at 8.4 above apply 'if a grant of equity instruments is cancelled or settled during the vesting period ...'. *[IFRS 2.28]*. FRS 102 does not explicitly state that its requirements relate solely to awards cancelled or settled during the vesting period but this seems to be implied by the references to 'an acceleration of vesting' and 'the remainder of the vesting period'. *[FRS 102.26.13]*. However, if the original award has already vested when a replacement award is granted, there is no question of accelerating the cost of the cancelled award, as it has already been recognised during the vesting period. The issue is rather the treatment of the new award itself. Whilst neither IFRS 2 nor FRS 102 explicitly addresses this point, it appears that such a replacement award should be treated as if it were a completely new award. In other words, its full fair value should be recognised immediately or, if there are any vesting conditions for the replacement award, over its vesting period.

By contrast, the rules in IFRS 2 for modification of awards (discussed in 8.3 above) apply whether the award has vested or not. Paragraphs 26 and 27 of IFRS 2 (modifications) are not restricted to events 'during the vesting period' in contrast to paragraph 28 (cancellation and settlement, including replacement awards), which is restricted to events 'during the vesting period'. *[IFRS 2.26-28]*. In FRS 102, any such distinction is less clear because the paragraph on modifications is written in the context of a modification of vesting conditions and, whilst it refers explicitly to the accounting treatment of modifications during the vesting period, it is silent on the modification of vested awards. *[FRS 102.26.12]*. In the absence of explicit guidance, we believe that it is appropriate to follow the accounting approach of IFRS 2.

The treatment outlined above has the effect that the accounting cost of modifying an already vested award (i.e. the incremental fair value of the modified award) may, at first sight, appear to be lower than the cost of cancelling and replacing it, which requires the full fair value of the new award to be expensed. However, the fair value of the new replacement award will be reduced by the fair value of the cancelled award that the employee has surrendered as part of the consideration for the new award. This analysis will, in many cases, produce an accounting outcome similar to that of the modification of an unvested award.

8.5   Replacement award on termination of employment

When an employee's employment is terminated during the vesting period of an award of shares or options, the award will typically lapse in consequence. It is common in such situations, particularly where the employee was part of the senior management, for the entity to make an alternative award, or to allow the employee to retain existing awards, as part of the package of benefits agreed with the employee on termination of employment.

Generally, such an award is an *ex gratia* award – in other words, it is a voluntary award to which the outgoing employee had no legal entitlement. However, a number of plan rules set out, in a 'good leaver' clause (see 6.3.8 above), the terms on which any *ex gratia* award may be made, usually by applying a formula to determine, or limit, how much of the original award can be considered to have vested. In many cases the award will be made on a fully vested basis, i.e. the employee has full entitlement without further conditions needing to be fulfilled. In other cases, however, an employee will be allowed to retain awards that remain subject to the fulfilment of the original conditions (other than future service). Whichever form the award takes, in accounting terms it will be treated as vesting at the date of termination of employment because any remaining conditions will be accounted for as non-vesting conditions in the absence of an explicit or implied service condition (see 4.2 above).

It has not always been clear whether the termination of employment should be accounted for as a forfeiture or as a cancellation. However, as discussed at 8.4.1.A above, the IASB's *Annual Improvements to IFRSs 2010-2012 Cycle* included a clarification that if an employee is unable to satisfy a service condition for any reason, including termination of employment, this should be accounted for as a forfeiture rather than as a cancellation. It appears appropriate for entities accounting under FRS 102 also to apply forfeiture accounting.

The IASB's amendments did not specifically address the accounting for any replacement awards granted on termination of employment. It would be consistent with the treatment of the termination of employment as a forfeiture to:

- reverse any expense relating to the forfeited award; and
- recognise the ex gratia award as a completely new award granted at the date of termination of employment.

8.6   Entity's plans for future modification or replacement of award – impact on estimation process at reporting date

As discussed at 7.1.1 and 7.1.2 above, FRS 102 requires an entity to determine a cumulative charge at each reporting date by reference to an estimate of the number of awards that will vest (within the special meaning of that term in FRS 102). The process of estimation at each reporting date should take into account any new information that indicates a change to previous estimates.

In addition to the normal difficulties inherent in any estimation process, this brings the further complication that it is not entirely clear which anticipated future events should be taken into account in the estimation process and which should not, as illustrated by Example 21.30 below.

Example 21.30:   Estimation of number of awards expected to vest – treatment of anticipated future events

On 1 January 2015, an entity granted an award of 1,000 shares to each of its 600 employees at a particular manufacturing unit. The award vests on completion of three years' service at 31 December 2017. As at 31 December 2015, the entity firmly intends to close the unit, and terminate the employment of employees, as part of a rationalisation programme. This closure would occur on or around 1 July 2016. The entity has not, however, announced its intentions or taken any other steps so as to allow provision for the closure.

Under the original terms of the award, the award would lapse on termination of employment. However, the entity intends to compensate employees made redundant by changing the terms of their award so as to allow full vesting on termination of employment.

What is the 'best estimate', as at 31 December 2015, of the number of awards expected to vest? Specifically, should the entity:

(a) ignore the intended closure altogether, on the grounds that there is no other recognition of it in the financial statements;

(b) take account of the impact of the intended closure on vesting of the current award, but ignore the intended modification to the terms of the award to allow vesting; or

(c) take account of both the intended closure and the intended modification of the award?

In our view, there is no basis in FRS 102 for anticipating the modification of an award. The entity must account for awards in issue at the reporting date, not those that might be in issue in the future. Accordingly we do not consider approach (c) above to be appropriate.

Equally, we struggle to support approach (a) above. FRS 102 requires the entity to use an estimate of the number of awards expected to vest and its best available estimate must be that the unit will be closed, and the employees' employment terminated, in 2016. This view is supported by the fact that, unlike other areas of accounting such as impairment and provisions, accounting for share-based payment transactions does not explicitly prohibit an entity from taking account of the consequences of reorganisations and similar transactions to which it is not yet committed.

Accordingly, we believe that approach (b) should be followed. Taking the view that such a termination is a forfeiture (see 8.4.1.A above), the entity's best estimate, at 31 December 2015, must be that the award currently in place will vest in no employees (because they will be made redundant before the end of the vesting period). It therefore reverses any cost previously recorded for the award. When the award is modified at the time of the redundancy in 2016 to allow full vesting, the entity will recognise the full cost of the modified award. This will have what many may see as the less than ideal result that the entity will recognise a credit in profit or loss in 2015 and a loss in 2016, even though there has been no change in management's best estimate of the overall outcome. This follows from the analysis, discussed above, that we do not believe that the entity can, in 2015, account for the award on the basis of what its terms may be in 2016.

The best estimate of the number of awards expected to vest is made as at each reporting date. A change in estimate made in a later period in response to subsequent events affects the accounting expense for that later period (i.e. there is no restatement of earlier periods presented).

8.7   Share splits and consolidations

It is relatively common for an entity to divide its existing equity share capital into a larger number of shares (share splits) or to consolidate its existing share capital into a smaller number of shares (share consolidations). The impact of such splits and consolidations is not specifically addressed in either FRS 102 or IFRS 2.

Suppose that an employee has options over 100 shares in the reporting entity, with an exercise price of £1. The entity undertakes a '1 for 2' share consolidation – i.e. the number of shares in issue is halved such that, all other things being equal, the value of one share in the entity after the consolidation is twice that of one share before the consolidation.

IFRS 2 is required to be applied to modifications to an award arising from equity restructurings (FRS 102 is silent on this). *[IFRS 2.BC24].* However, in most cases, a share scheme will provide that, following the consolidation, the employee holds options over only 50 shares with an exercise price of £2. As discussed at 6.3.7.A above, all things being equal, it would be expected that the modified award would have the same fair value as the original award and, therefore, there would be no incremental expense to be accounted for.

It may be that the scheme has no such provision for automatic adjustment, such that the employee still holds options over 100 shares. The clear economic effect is that the award has been modified, since its value has been doubled. It could be argued that, on a literal reading of IFRS 2, no modification has occurred, since the employee holds options over 100 shares at the same exercise price before and after the consolidation. In our view, whilst it would seem appropriate to have regard to the substance of the transaction, and treat it as giving rise to a modification, it must be admitted that such a treatment can be argued not to be required by FRS 102 or IFRS 2 as drafted.

Sometimes, the terms of an award give the entity discretion to make modifications at a future date in response to more complex changes to the share structure, such as those arising from bonus issues, share buybacks and rights issues where the effect on existing options may not be so clear-cut. These are discussed further at 6.3.7.A above.

9 EQUITY-SETTLED TRANSACTIONS – VALUATION

9.1 Introduction

As noted at 6.1 above, an equity-settled share-based payment transaction is valued either at the fair value of the goods or services received – using the general requirements of FRS 102 for the determination of fair value – or at the fair value of the equity instruments granted – using the specific requirements set out in Section 26. The timing of the fair value measurement, and whether it is based on the goods or services or on the equity instruments, is driven by a number of factors including the relative reliability of measurement and the identity of the counterparty (see 6 above).

In this section we consider the specific requirements in Section 26 for the valuation of shares, share options and equity-settled share appreciation rights. No distinction is drawn between awards to employees and to non-employees and the requirements should therefore be applied to the measurement of employee awards at grant date and non-employee awards at service date.

Chapter 21

9.2   Shares

Section 26 requires the fair value of shares (and the related goods or services received) to be determined using the following three-tier measurement hierarchy:

(a)   if an observable market price is available for the equity instruments granted, use that price;

(b)   if an observable market price is not available, measure the fair value of equity instruments granted using entity-specific observable market date such as:

    (i)   a recent transaction in the entity's shares; or

    (ii)   a recent independent fair valuation of the entity or its principal assets;

(c)   if an observable market price is not available and obtaining a reliable measurement of fair value under (b) is impracticable, indirectly measure the fair value of the shares using a valuation method that uses market data to the greatest extent practicable to estimate what the price of those equity instruments would be on the grant date in an arm's length transaction between knowledgeable, willing parties. The entity's directors should use their judgement to apply a generally accepted valuation methodology for valuing equity instruments that is appropriate to the circumstances of the entity. *[FRS 102.26.10]*.

It seems unlikely that the market price referred to in (a), or the entity-specific observable market data referred to in (b), will be available for the measurement of the vast majority of share-based awards granted by unlisted entities. Most entities will therefore be required to apply the approach required by (c) and use an appropriate valuation methodology.

The selection of an appropriate methodology for valuing the equity of an unlisted entity is beyond the scope of this publication but, in many cases of awards of free shares (which are akin to options with a zero strike price), it is likely that an approach similar to that used for valuing share options will be adopted (see 9.3 below).

FRS 102 makes no mention of adjusting the market price, or estimated market price, of an entity's shares to take into account the terms and conditions on which they were granted (which would, typically, reduce the value). IFRS 2 specifies that the fair value should take into account the terms and conditions on which the shares were granted, other than those vesting conditions that are required to be excluded in determining the grant date fair value (see 7.2 above). *[IFRS 2.B2]*.

For example, under the requirements of IFRS 2, the valuation should take account of restrictions on the counterparty's right:

•   to receive dividends in the vesting period (see below); or

•   to transfer shares after vesting, but only to the extent that such restrictions would affect the price that a knowledgeable and willing market participant would pay for the shares. Where the shares are traded in a deep and liquid market, the effect may be negligible.

The valuation should not, however, take account of restrictions that arise directly from the existence of the vesting conditions (such as the right to transfer shares during the vesting period). *[IFRS 2.B3]*.

When the grant date fair value of shares granted to employees is estimated, no adjustment is required if the employees are entitled to receive dividends, or dividend equivalents paid in cash, during the vesting period (as they are in no different a position in this respect than if they already held shares). However, where employees are not entitled to receive dividends during the vesting period, IFRS 2 requires the valuation to be reduced by the present value of dividends expected to be paid during the vesting period. *[IFRS 2.B31, B33-34]*.

The accounting treatment of awards which give the right to receive dividends during the vesting period is discussed further at 16.3 below.

If an entity is taking approach (c) above in determining a fair value for the equity instruments then it seems appropriate to adjust for the terms and conditions on which the shares have been awarded in line with the guidance in IFRS 2. Where an entity is using approaches (a) or (b), it appears that it is required to use an unadjusted market price or other observable price without adjusting for the specific terms and conditions of the share-based payment.

9.3   Share options and equity-settled share appreciation rights

A share option is defined in FRS 102 as 'a contract that gives the holder the right, but not the obligation, to subscribe to the entity's shares at a fixed or determinable price for a specific period of time'. *[FRS 102 Appendix I]*.

A share appreciation right (SAR) is not specifically defined in FRS 102 but is a grant where the counterparty will become entitled either to shares (or, more commonly, to a future cash payment) based on the increase in the entity's share price or value from a specified level over a period of time (see further discussion at 10 below on cash-settled awards).

Section 26 requires the fair value of share options and equity-settled share appreciation rights (and the related goods or services received) to be determined using the following three-tier measurement hierarchy:

(a)   if an observable market price is available for the equity instruments granted, use that price;

(b)   if an observable market price is not available, measure the fair value of share options and share appreciation rights granted using entity-specific observable market date such as for a recent transaction in the share options;

(c)   if an observable market price is not available and obtaining a reliable measurement of fair value under (b) is impracticable, indirectly measure the fair value of share options or share appreciation rights using an alternative valuation methodology such as an option pricing model. The inputs for an option pricing model (such as the weighted average share price, exercise price, expected volatility, option life, expected dividends and the risk-free interest rate) shall use market data to the greatest extent possible. Paragraph 26.10 provides guidance on determining the fair value of the shares used in determining the weighted average share price. The entity shall derive an estimate of expected volatility consistent with the valuation methodology used to determine the fair value of the shares. *[FRS 102.26.11]*.

The fact that Section 26 does not mandate the use of an option pricing model is cited as a key change from the requirements of the IFRS for SMEs on which FRS 102 is based (and is also a change from IFRS 2). However, in practice, it is likely that use of a pricing model will often be a practical basis for determining the fair value of options and appreciation rights.

A discussion of valuation methodology is beyond the scope of this publication.[3] Whilst not addressing the subject of valuation in detail, EY International GAAP 2015 draws on the guidance in Appendix B to IFRS 2 relating to the valuation of share-based payments and addresses some aspects of the pricing of options, particularly with respect to employee awards.

10   CASH-SETTLED TRANSACTIONS

Throughout the discussion in this section, 'cash' should be read as including 'other assets' in accordance with the definition of a cash-settled share-based payment transaction (see 3.1 above).

10.1   Scope of requirements

Section 26 notes that cash-settled share-based payment transactions include:

- share appreciation rights (SARs), where employees are entitled to a future cash payment (rather than an equity instrument) based on the increase in an entity's share price from a specified level over a specified period of time; and

- a right to a future cash payment through a grant of shares (including shares to be issued upon the exercise of share options) that are redeemable, either mandatorily (e.g. upon cessation of employment) or at the employee's option. *[FRS 102.26.2].*

Another type of cash-settled arrangement frequently encountered in practice is a grant of phantom options, where employees are entitled to a cash payment equivalent to the gain that would have been made by exercising options at a notional price over a notional number of shares and then selling the shares at the date of exercise.

As is clear from the inclusion of certain types of redeemable share as a specific example of a cash-settled share-based payment arrangement, FRS 102 looks beyond the simple issue of whether an award entitles an employee to receive instruments that are in form shares or options to the terms of those instruments. The fact that certain redeemable shares would be treated as a cash-settled, not an equity-settled, award is consistent with the fact that a share with these terms would be regarded as a financial liability rather than an equity instrument of the issuer (based on Section 22 of FRS 102).

In some cases the boundary between equity-settled and cash-settled schemes may appear somewhat blurred, so that further analysis may be required to determine whether a particular arrangement is equity-settled or cash-settled. Some examples of such arrangements are discussed at 10.2 below.

10.2   What constitutes a cash-settled award?

There are a number of possible circumstances in which, on, or shortly after, settlement of an equity-settled award either:

- the entity incurs a cash outflow equivalent to that that would arise on cash-settlement (e.g. because it purchases its own shares to deliver to counterparties); or

- the counterparty receives a cash inflow equivalent to that that would arise on cash-settlement (e.g. because the shares are sold for cash on behalf of the counterparty).

Such situations raise the question of whether such schemes are in fact truly equity-settled or cash-settled.

Examples of relatively common mechanisms for delivering the cash-equivalent of an equity-settled award to employees are discussed below. It emerges from the analysis below that, in reality, the accounting for share-based payment transactions is driven by questions of form rather than substance. To put it rather crudely, what matters is often not so much whether the entity has written a cheque for the fair value of the award, but rather the name of the payee on the cheque.

The significance of this is that the analysis affects the profit or loss charge for the award, as illustrated by Example 21.31 below.

Example 21.31: Equity-settled award satisfied by purchase of own shares

An entity awards an employee a free share with a fair value at grant date of £5 which has a fair value of £8 at vesting. At vesting the entity acquires one of its own shares from an existing shareholder for £8 for delivery to the employee. If the scheme were treated as cash-settled, there would be a charge to profit or loss of £8 (the fair value at vesting date – see 10.3 below). If it were treated as equity-settled (as required in this case by FRS 102), profit or loss would show a charge of only £5 (the fair value at grant date), with a further net charge of £3 in equity, comprising the £8 paid for the share accounted for as a treasury share or own share less the £5 credit to equity (being the credit entry corresponding to the £5 charge to profit or loss – see 5.2 above).

The analyses below all rely on a precise construction of the definition of a cash-settled share-based payment transaction, i.e. one 'in which the entity acquires goods or services *by incurring a liability to transfer cash or other assets to the supplier of those goods or services* for amounts that are based on the price (or value) of the entity's shares or other equity instruments of the entity or another group entity' (emphasis added). *[FRS 102 Appendix I]*. Thus, if the entity is not actually required – legally or constructively – to pay cash to the *counterparty*, there is no cash-settled transaction under FRS 102, even though the arrangement may give rise to an external cash flow and, possibly, another form of recognised liability.

Some have raised the question of whether the entity should recognise some form of liability to repurchase own equity in situations where the entity has a stated policy of settling equity-settled transactions using previously purchased treasury or own shares. In our view, the normal provisions of accounting for financial instruments apply and there would be no question of recognising a liability to repurchase own equity on the basis merely of a declared intention. It is only when the entity enters into a forward contract or a call option with a third party that some accounting recognition of a future share purchase may be required.

It sometimes happens that an entity, having issued shares in settlement of an equity-settled transaction, will shortly thereafter purchase a similar number of its own shares. This raises the question of whether such a scheme would be considered as in substance cash-settled. In our view, further enquiry into the detailed circumstances of the purchase is required in order to determine the appropriate analysis.

Broadly speaking, so long as there is no obligation (explicit or implicit) for the entity to settle in cash with the counterparty, such arrangements will not require a scheme to be treated as cash-settled under Section 26. However, in our view, there might be situations in which post-settlement share purchases are indicative of an obligation to the counterparty, such that treatment as a cash-settled scheme would be appropriate.

For example, if the entity were to create an expectation by employees that any shares awarded can always be liquidated immediately, because the entity will ensure that there is a market for the shares, it could well be appropriate to account for such a scheme as cash-settled. This will often be the case with awards granted to the employees of an unlisted company. The treatment of schemes in which the entity has a choice of settlement, but has created an expectation of cash-settlement, provides a relevant analogy (see 11.1 below).

A more extreme example of such a situation would be where the entity has arranged for the shares delivered to the counterparty to be sold on the counterparty's behalf, but has at the same time entered into a contract to purchase those shares. In that situation, in our view, the substance is that:

- the entity has created an expectation by the counterparty of a right to receive cash; and

- the intermediate purchaser or broker is no more than an agent paying that cash to the counterparty on behalf of the entity.

Accordingly, it would be appropriate to account for such an arrangement as a cash-settled award.

Similar issues arise in the application of 'drag along' and 'tag along' rights in the context of an exit event and these are discussed at 16.4.6 below.

10.3   Required accounting for cash-settled share-based payment transactions

10.3.1   Basic accounting treatment

For a cash-settled share-based payment transaction, Section 26 requires an entity to measure the goods or services acquired and the corresponding liability incurred at the fair value of the liability. Until that liability is settled, the entity should remeasure the fair value at each reporting date and at the date of settlement. Any changes in fair value arising from this process of remeasurement should be recognised in profit or loss for the period. *[FRS 102.26.14]*.

It is clear that the ultimate cost of a cash-settled transaction must be the actual cash paid to the counterparty, which will be the fair value at settlement date but the periodic determination of the liability is as follows:

- at each reporting date between grant and settlement the fair value of the award is determined in accordance with the requirements of Section 26;

- during the vesting period, the liability recognised at each reporting date is the Section 26 fair value of the award at that date multiplied by the expired portion of the vesting period;

- from the end of the vesting period until settlement, the liability recognised is the full fair value of the liability at the reporting date.

Where the cost of services received in a cash-settled transaction is recognised in the carrying amount of an asset (e.g. inventory) in the entity's statement of financial position, the carrying amount of the asset should not be adjusted for changes in the fair value of the liability.

Although paragraph 14 of Section 26 refers to 'fair value' it provides no further guidance about how the fair value of a cash-settled share-based payment liability should be determined. The glossary to FRS 102 includes a definition of 'fair value' as:

'the amount for which ... a liability [could be] settled ... between knowledgeable, willing parties in an arm's length transaction. In the absence of any specific guidance provided in the relevant section of this FRS, the guidance in paragraphs 11.27 to 11.32 shall be used in determining fair value.'

The reference to 'fair value' in paragraph 14 is not highlighted as a defined term and so it is not clear whether the defined term in the FRS 102 glossary is intended to apply to liabilities for cash-settled share-based payments. Section 26 specifies how fair value should be determined for equity-settled share-based payment transactions (see 9.2 and 9.3 above) but contains no specific guidance for cash-settled share-based payment transactions. In our view, an acceptable approach would be to use the guidance in Section 11 of FRS 102 but also to draw on IFRS 2 to provide some more practical guidance on the approach to be taken in fair valuing a cash-settled share-based payment transaction.

Section 11 indicates that an appropriate valuation technique should be used and that this might include an option pricing model. The use of a pricing model is consistent with the requirement in IFRS 2 that fair value be determined by applying an option pricing model, taking into account the terms and conditions on which the cash-settled transaction was granted, and the extent to which the employees have rendered service to date.

10.3.2 Application of the accounting treatment

The treatment required by Section 26 for cash-settled transactions is illustrated by Example 21.32 which is based on Example 12 in the implementation guidance to IFRS 2.

Example 21.32: Cash-settled transaction

An entity grants 100 cash share appreciation rights (SARs) to each of its 500 employees, on condition that the employees remain in employment with the entity for the next three years. The SARs can be exercised on the third, fourth and fifth anniversary of the grant date.

During year 1, 35 employees leave. The entity estimates that a further 60 will leave during years 2 and 3 (i.e. the award will vest in 405 employees).

During year 2, 40 employees leave and the entity estimates that a further 25 will leave during year 3 (i.e. the award will vest in 400 employees).

During year 3, 22 employees leave, so that the award vests in 403 employees. At the end of year 3, 150 employees exercise their SARs (leaving 253 employees still to exercise).

Another 140 employees exercise their SARs at the end of year 4, leaving 113 employees still to exercise, who do so at the end of year 5.

The entity estimates the fair value of the SARs at the end of each year in which a liability exists as shown below. The intrinsic values of the SARs at the date of exercise (which equal the cash paid out) at the end of years 3, 4 and 5 are also shown below.

Year	Fair value £	Intrinsic value £
1	14.40	
2	15.50	
3	18.20	15.00
4	21.40	20.00
5		25.00

The entity will recognise the cost of this award as follows.

Year	Calculation of liability	Calculation of cash paid	Liability (£)	Cash paid (£)	Expense for period (£)*
1	405 employees × 100 SARs × £14.40 × 1/3		194,400	–	194,400
2	400 employees × 100 SARs × £15.50 × 2/3		413,333	–	218,933
3	253 employees × 100 SARs × £18.20	150 employees × 100 SARs × £15.00	460,460	225,000	272,127
4	113 employees × 100 SARs × £21.40	140 employees × 100 SARs × £20.00	241,820	280,000	61,360
5	–	113 employees × 100 SARs × £25.00	–	282,500	40,680

*   Liability at end of period + cash paid in period – liability at start of period

The accounting treatment for cash-settled transactions is therefore (despite some similarities in the methodology) significantly different from that for equity-settled transactions. An important practical issue is that, for a cash-settled transaction, the entity must determine the fair value at each reporting date rather than at grant date (and at the date of any subsequent modification or settlement) as would be the case for equity-settled transactions. As Example 21.32 shows, it is not necessary to determine the fair value of a cash-settled transaction at grant date in order to determine the share-based payment expense.

The requirements of FRS 102 and IFRS 2 and the illustrative example in IFRS 2 raise some issues of interpretation on detailed aspects of the methodology such as:

- determining the vesting period (see 10.3.2.A below);
- periodic allocation of cost (see 10.3.2.B below);
- treatment of non-market vesting conditions (see 10.3.2.C below);
- treatment of market conditions and non-vesting conditions (see 10.3.2.D below); and
- treatment of modification, cancellation and settlement (see 10.3.2.E below).

10.3.2.A   Determining the vesting period

Under FRS 102, the rules for determining vesting periods are the same as those applicable to equity-settled transactions, as discussed in 7.1 to 7.4 above. Where an award vests immediately, there is a presumption that, in the absence of evidence to the contrary, the award is in respect of services that have already been rendered, and should therefore be expensed in full at grant date. *[FRS 102.26.5]*.

Where cash-settled awards are made subject to vesting conditions (as in many cases they will be, particularly where payments to employees are concerned), there is a presumption that the awards are a payment for services to be received in the future, during the 'vesting period', with the transaction being recognised during that period, as illustrated in Example 21.32 above.

10.3.2.B   Periodic allocation of cost

The required treatment for cash-settled transactions under Section 26 is simply to measure the fair value of the liability at each reporting date *[FRS 102.26.14]*, which might suggest that the *full* fair value, and not just a time-apportioned part of it, should be recognised at each reporting date – as would be the case for any liability that is a financial instrument measured at fair value.

However, paragraph 14 needs to be read with paragraph 6 which states that if the counterparty is required to complete a specified period of service, the entity 'shall account for those services as they are rendered during the vesting period, with a corresponding increase in ... liabilities'. This indicates that a spreading approach is to be adopted. *[FRS 102.26.6]*.

10.3.2.C   Non-market vesting conditions

As currently drafted, neither FRS 102 nor IFRS 2 specifically addresses the impact of vesting conditions (other than service conditions) in the context of cash-settled transactions – the provisions relating to vesting conditions are to be found under headings relating to equity-settled share-based payment transactions.

Where a vesting condition is a minimum service period, the liability should be estimated on the basis of the current best estimate of the number of awards that will vest, this estimate being made exactly as for an equity-settled transaction.

As regards other non-market performance conditions, the treatment is unclear. However, in February 2014,[4] the IASB decided to amend IFRS 2 to clarify that accounting for such conditions relating to a cash-settled share-based payment should follow the approach used for equity-settled share-based payments (i.e. in line with the treatment of service periods in IG Example 12 in IFRS 2). Until such time as the resulting amendments to IFRS 2 are clarified, we believe that the fair value of the liability until vesting date, as measured under IFRS 2, may either fully take account of the probability of the conditions being achieved or exclude the conditions and be adjusted to reflect the current best estimate of the outcome of those conditions by analogy to the treatment of service conditions. We believe that entities applying FRS 102 have a similar choice in determining the fair value of the liability.

10.3.2.D   Market conditions and non-vesting conditions

There is no specific guidance in FRS 102 and IFRS 2 (as currently drafted) as to whether, in the case of a cash-settled transaction, a distinction is to be drawn between non-vesting conditions or vesting conditions that are market conditions and other non-market vesting conditions, as would be the case for an equity-settled transaction (see 7.2 to 7.4 above).

As discussed at 10.3.2.C above, this is a matter that has recently been discussed in the context of IFRS 2 and there is a proposed amendment to IFRS 2 to clarify the position and to draw a distinction between the different types of condition during the vesting period.

Under both the current and proposed versions of IFRS 2, market performance conditions and non-vesting conditions should be taken into account in measuring the fair value of the cash-settled share-based payment. However, there will be no ultimate cost for an award subject to a market condition or non-vesting condition that is not satisfied as any liability would be reversed.

This differs from the accounting model for equity-settled transactions with market conditions or non-vesting conditions, which can result in a cost being recognised for awards subject to a market or non-vesting condition that is not satisfied (see 7.3 and 7.4 above).

10.3.2.E   Modification, cancellation and settlement

FRS 102 provides no specific guidance on modification, cancellation and settlement of cash-settled awards. However, as cash-settled awards are accounted for using a full fair value model no such guidance is needed. It is clear that:

- where an award is modified, the liability recognised at and after the point of modification will be based on its new fair value, with the effect of any movement in the liability recognised immediately;
- where an award is cancelled the liability will be derecognised, with a credit immediately recognised in profit or loss; and
- where an award is settled, the liability will be derecognised, and any gain or loss on settlement immediately recognised in profit or loss.

10.4   Modification of award from equity-settled to cash-settled or from cash-settled to equity-settled

As noted at 8.3.5 above, a detailed discussion of this topic is beyond the scope of this publication but is addressed more fully in EY International GAAP 2015.

11   TRANSACTIONS WITH EQUITY AND CASH ALTERNATIVES

11.1   Awards giving the counterparty or entity a choice of settlement method

Some share-based payment transactions (particularly those with employees) provide either the entity or the counterparty with the choice of settling the transaction either in shares (or other equity instruments) or in cash (or other assets). Section 26 requires such transactions to be accounted for as cash-settled share-based payment transactions unless either:

(a) the entity has a past practice of settling by issuing equity instruments; or

(b) the option has no commercial substance because the cash settlement amount bears no relationship to, and is likely to be lower in value than, the fair value of the equity instrument. *[FRS 102.26.15].*

If (a) or (b) applies, paragraph 15 requires the transaction to be treated as equity-settled.

Where the counterparty has a choice of settlement in either shares or cash, it will generally be the case that the arrangement will be accounted for as a cash-settled share-based payment transaction (see 10 above). In cases where the fair values of the cash and equity alternatives are similar, this is broadly consistent with the outcome of the approach required by IFRS 2. IFRS 2 requires a split accounting approach, between liabilities and equity, which mainly has an impact where the fair value of the equity alternative exceeds that of the cash alternative.

Paragraph 15 of Section 26 contains a stronger presumption of cash-settlement where the entity has a choice of settlement method than is the case under IFRS 2, particularly when an entity grants an award for the first time and has no history of settling in equity. The general principle of IFRS 2 is that a transaction with a cash alternative, or the components of that transaction, should be accounted for:

(a) as a cash-settled transaction if, and to the extent that, the entity has incurred a liability to settle in cash or other assets; or

(b) as an equity-settled transaction if, and to the extent that, no such liability has been incurred. *[IFRS 2.34].*

11.1.1 'Backstop' cash settlement rights

Some schemes may provide cash settlement rights to the holder so as to cover more or less remote contingencies.

If the terms of the award provide the employee with a general right of cash-settlement, FRS 102 requires the award to be treated as cash-settled. This is the case even if the right of cash settlement is unlikely to be exercised except in the most extreme circumstances (e.g. because it would give rise to adverse tax consequences for the employee as compared with equity settlement). If, however, the right to cash-settlement is exercisable only in specific circumstances, a more detailed analysis may be required (see 11.2 below).

11.1.2 Transactions with settlement alternatives of different value

In many share-based payment transactions with a choice of settlement, the value of the share and cash alternatives is equal. The counterparty will have the choice between (say) 1,000 shares or the cash value of 1,000 shares. Under FRS 102, this transaction would be accounted for as a cash-settled transaction.

However, it is not uncommon, particularly in transactions with employees, for the equity-settlement alternative to have more value. For example, an employee might be able to choose at vesting between the cash value of 1,000 shares immediately or 2,000 shares (often subject to further conditions such as a minimum holding period, or a further service period). In such a situation, it will need to be decided whether the arrangement falls within part (b) of paragraph 15 of Section 26 (see 11.1 above) leading to the entire arrangement being accounted for as an equity-settled transaction.

11.1.3   *Accounting at date of settlement for awards where there is a choice of equity- or cash-settlement*

FRS 102 contains no guidance about how to account as at the date of settlement for an award that has been accounted for as cash-settled but which is settled in equity, or *vice versa*. We suggest the following approach based on the requirements of IFRS 2 or practice that has evolved in the application of that standard.

11.1.3.A   *Settlement of an award treated as cash-settled during vesting period*

IFRS 2 gives no specific guidance as to the accounting treatment on settlement where an entity has accounted for an award as cash-settled but it is settled in equity. However, it is clear from other provisions of IFRS 2, including the general rules on settlement and the provisions relating to settlement of an award where the counterparty has the choice of settlement method, that:

- the liability should be remeasured to fair value through the income statement at settlement date;
- if cash settlement occurs, the cash paid is applied to reduce the liability; and
- if equity settlement occurs, the liability is transferred into equity.

11.1.3.B   *Settlement of an award treated as equity-settled during vesting period*

When a transaction that has been accounted for as equity-settled is settled, IFRS 2 specifies the following approach:

(a)   subject to (b) below:

    (i)   if the transaction is cash-settled, the cash is accounted for as a deduction from equity; or

    (ii)   if the transaction is equity-settled, there is a transfer from one component of equity to another (if necessary); and

(b)   if the two methods of settlement are of different fair value at the date of settlement, and the entity chooses the method with the higher fair value, the entity recognises an additional expense for the excess fair value of the chosen method. *[IFRS 2.43]*.

This is illustrated in Examples 21.33 and 21.34 below.

Example 21.33:   *Settlement of transaction treated as equity-settled where fair value of cash settlement exceeds fair value of equity settlement*

An entity has accounted for a share-based payment transaction where there is a choice of settlement as an equity-settled transaction, and has recognised a cumulative expense of £1,000 based on the fair value at grant date.

At settlement date the fair value of the equity-settlement option is £1,700 and that of the cash-settlement option £2,000. If the entity settles in equity, no further accounting entry is required by IFRS 2. However, there may be a transfer within equity of the £1,000 credited to equity during the vesting period.

If the entity settles in cash, the entity must recognise an additional expense of £300, being the difference between the fair value of the equity-settlement option (£1,700) and that of the cash-settlement option (£2,000). The accounting entry is:

	£	£
Profit or loss (employee costs)	300	
Equity	1,700	
Cash		2,000

Example 21.34:   Settlement of transaction treated as equity-settled where fair value of equity settlement exceeds fair value of cash settlement

As in Example 21.33, an entity has accounted for a share-based payment transaction where there is a choice of settlement as an equity-settled transaction, and has recognised a cumulative expense of £1,000 based on the fair value at grant date.

In this case, however, at settlement date the fair value of the equity-settlement option is £2,000 and that of the cash-settlement option £1,700. If the transaction is settled in equity, the entity must recognise an additional expense of £300, being the difference between fair value of the equity-settlement option (£2,000) and that of the cash-settlement option (£1,700). The accounting entry is:

	£	£
Profit or loss (employee costs)	300	
Equity		300

No further accounting entry is required by IFRS 2. However, there may be a transfer within equity of the £1,300 credited during the vesting period and on settlement.

If the entity settles in cash, no extra expense is recognised, and the accounting entry is:

	£	£
Equity	1,700	
Cash		1,700

It can be seen in this case that, if the transaction is settled in equity, an additional expense is recognised. If, however, the transaction had simply been an equity-settled transaction (i.e. with no cash alternative), there would have been no additional expense on settlement and the cumulative expense would have been only £1,000 based on the fair value at grant date.

As FRS 102 does not specify the accounting for a settlement – either generally (see 8.4 above) or where there is a settlement choice – it is debatable whether the recognition of an additional expense on remeasurement is required, or whether any difference could be accounted for in equity as would be the case with the repurchase of equity instruments outside a share-based payment transaction. However, in our view, it is appropriate to adopt an approach consistent with that of IFRS 2 given the extent to which the requirements of Section 26 generally, including those relating to modification and cancellation, are derived from those of IFRS 2.

11.1.4   Change in classification of award after grant date

Neither FRS 102 nor IFRS 2 specifies whether a transaction where the entity has a choice of settlement in equity or cash should be assessed as equity-settled or cash-settled only at the inception of the transaction or whether this should also be assessed at each reporting date until the transaction is settled.

FRS 102 states that a transaction should be treated as cash-settled unless either criterion (a) or criterion (b) in paragraph 15 of Section 26 applies (see 11.1 above). As it is not specified that this assessment takes place only at inception of the award, in our view FRS 102 requires an ongoing assessment of the relevance of these criteria.

However, given the restrictive criteria for an award to be treated as anything other than cash-settled, it is likely that changes of classification will be rare in practice.

FRS 102 does not specify the accounting treatment to be followed if a change in classification is considered appropriate. In our view, the most appropriate treatment is to account for such a change as if it were a modification of the manner of settlement of the award (see 10.4 above). In the case of an award with a settlement choice, the entity is in effect able to choose the manner of settlement which, in substance, is the same as choosing to modify the manner of settlement of an award which does not already give the entity a choice. These situations are distinct from those where the manner of settlement depends on the outcome of a contingent event outside the entity's control (see 11.2 below).

11.2   Awards requiring cash settlement in specific circumstances (awards with contingent cash settlement)

Rather than giving a general right to cash settlement to either the entity or the counterparty, some awards require cash settlement in certain specific and limited circumstances – sometimes referred to as contingent settlement provisions. In the absence of specific guidance, questions arise as to whether such an award should be accounted for as equity-settled or cash-settled and whether this should be re-assessed on an ongoing basis during the vesting period. This is a subject that has recently been discussed in the context of IFRS 2 although no changes have yet been made, or indeed proposed, to the published guidance (see 11.2.3).

11.2.1   *Analysis 1 – Treat as cash-settled if contingency is outside entity's control*

One approach might be to consider whether the reporting entity can unilaterally avoid cash-settlement. Under this approach, it is first necessary to consider whether the event that requires cash-settlement is one over which the entity has control. If the event, however improbable, is outside the entity's control, then under this analysis the award should be treated as cash-settled. However, if the event is within the entity's control, the award should be treated as cash-settled only if the entity has a liability by reference to the criteria summarised in 11.1 above.

This analysis does not seem entirely satisfactory. For example, it is common for an equity-settled share-based payment award to contain a provision to the effect that, if the employee dies in service, the entity will pay to the employee's estate the fair value of the award in cash. The analysis above would lead to the conclusion that the award must be classified as cash-settled, on the basis that it is beyond the entity's control whether or not an employee dies in service. This seems a somewhat far-fetched conclusion, and is moreover inconsistent with the accounting treatment that the entity would apply to any other death-in-service benefit.

11.2.2   *Analysis 2 – Treat as cash-settled if contingency is outside entity's control and probable*

In the US, an interpretation[5] of FASB ASC 718 – *Compensation – Stock Compensation* states that a cash settlement feature that can be exercised only upon the occurrence of a contingent event that is outside the employee's control (such as an initial public offering) does not give rise to a liability until it becomes probable that that event will occur.

In our view, this approach based on the probability of a contingent event that is outside the control of both the counterparty and the entity is also acceptable in the absence of specific guidance in FRS 102 (and IFRS 2) and has frequently been used in practice by entities applying IFRS 2.

The impact of Analysis 1 and Analysis 2 can be illustrated by reference to an award that requires cash-settlement in the event of a change of control of the entity (see 11.2.3 below).

11.2.3 Awards requiring cash settlement on a change of control

It is not uncommon for an award to be compulsorily cash-settled if there is a change of control of the reporting entity. Such a provision ensures that there is no need for any separate negotiations to buy out all employee options, so as to avoid non-controlling (minority) interests arising in the acquired entity as equity-settled awards are settled after the change of control.

The determination of whether or not a change of control is within the control of the entity is beyond the scope of this publication.

If the facts and circumstances of a particular case indicate that a change of control is within the entity's control, the conclusion under either Analysis 1 or Analysis 2 above would be that the award should be treated as cash-settled only if the entity has a liability by reference to the criteria summarised in 11.1 above.

If, however, the change of control is not considered to be within the control of the reporting entity, the conclusion will vary depending on whether Analysis 1 or Analysis 2 is followed. Under Analysis 1, an award requiring settlement in cash on a change of control outside the control of the entity would be treated as cash-settled, however unlikely the change of control may be. Under Analysis 2 however, an award requiring settlement in cash on a change of control outside the control of the entity would be treated as cash-settled only if a change of control were probable.

A difficulty with Analysis 2 is that it introduces rather bizarre inconsistencies in the accounting treatment for awards when the relative probability of their outcome is considered. As noted at 11.1 above, an award that gives the counterparty an absolute right to cash-settlement is accounted for as a liability, however unlikely it is that the counterparty will exercise that right (unless the cash settlement option is considered to have no commercial substance). Thus, under this approach, the entity could find itself in the situation where it treats:

- as a liability: an award with a unrestricted right to cash-settlement for the counterparty, where the probability of the counterparty exercising that right is less than 1%; but

- as equity: an award that requires cash settlement in the event of a change of control which is assessed as having a 49% probability of occurring.

In our view, an entity may adopt either of these accounting treatments, but should do so consistently and state its policy for accounting for such transactions if material.

It should be noted in the selection of an accounting policy that the IASB has had recent discussions – but has not concluded – on whether an approach based on the 'probable' outcome, as set out here, should be applied under IFRS 2 or whether an approach based on the accounting treatment for a compound financial instrument should be used. Any further developments in this area could affect the availability of the two alternative treatments in future. The detailed discussions are beyond the scope of this publication but are addressed in EY International GAAP 2015.

There is further discussion at 16.4 below of awards that vest or are exercisable on a flotation or change of control.

11.2.4   Accounting for change in manner of settlement where award is contingent on future events outside the control of the entity and the counterparty

When, under Analysis 2 above, the manner of settlement of an award changes solely as a consequence of a re-assessment of the probability of a contingent event, there is no settlement of the award or modification of its original terms. The award is such that there have been two potential outcomes, one equity-settled and one cash-settled, running in parallel since grant date. At each reporting date the entity should assess which outcome is more likely and account for the award on an equity- or cash-settled basis accordingly. In our view, any adjustments to switch between the cumulative cash-settled award and the cumulative equity-settled award should be taken to profit or loss in the current period. This is similar to the approach for an award with multiple independent vesting conditions (see 7.3.6 above).

Taking the approach that the two outcomes have both been part of the arrangement from grant date rather than being a matter of choice, the fair value of the equity-settled award would be measured only at the original grant date and would not be remeasured at the date of change in settlement method. As the cash-settled award would be remeasured on an ongoing basis, a switch in the manner of settlement during the period until the shares vest or the award is settled in cash could give rise to significant volatility in the cumulative expense. At the date of vesting or settlement, however, the cumulative expense will equate to either the grant date fair value of the equity-settled approach or the settlement value of the cash-settled approach depending on whether or not the contingent event has happened.

The situation discussed above (i.e. an arrangement with two potential outcomes from grant date) contrasts with an award where the manner of settlement is entirely within the entity's control. Where such a choice of settlement exists, a change in the manner of settlement would be treated as a modification with a potential catch-up through equity as at the date of modification (see 10.4 above).

11.3   Cash settlement alternative not based on share price

Some awards may provide a cash-settlement alternative that is not based on the share price. For example, an employee might be offered a choice between 500 shares or £1,000,000 on the vesting of an award. Whilst an award of £1,000,000, if considered in isolation, would obviously not be a share-based payment transaction, in our view it falls within the scope of Section 26 if it is offered as an alternative to a transaction that is within the scope of that Section. FRS 102 has no specific guidance in this area but we draw on the Basis for Conclusions to IFRS 2 which states that the cash alternative may be fixed or variable and, if variable, may be determinable in a manner that is related, or unrelated, to the price of the entity's shares. *[IFRS 2.BC256].*

Under the requirements of paragraph 15 of Section 26, the award will be treated as cash-settled unless the option arrangements do not have commercial substance (see 11.1 above).

12 REPLACEMENT SHARE-BASED PAYMENT AWARDS ISSUED IN A BUSINESS COMBINATION

12.1 Background

It is relatively common for an entity (A) to acquire another (B) which, at the time of the business combination, has outstanding employee share options or other share-based awards. If no action were taken by A, employees of B would be entitled, once any vesting conditions had been satisfied, to shares in B. This is not a very satisfactory outcome for either party: A now has non-controlling (minority) shareholders in its hitherto wholly-owned subsidiary B, and the employees of B are the owners of unmarketable shares in an effectively wholly-owned subsidiary.

The obvious solution, adopted in the majority of cases, is for some mechanism to be put in place such that the employees of B end up holding shares in the new parent A. This can be achieved, for example, by:

- A granting the employees of B options over the shares of A in exchange for the surrender of their options over the shares of B; or

- changing the terms of the options so that they are over a special class of shares in B which are mandatorily convertible into shares of A.

FRS 102 contains no guidance about how such a substitution transaction should be accounted for in the consolidated financial statements of A and this area is considered to be beyond the scope of this publication. Under IFRS, the relevant guidance is included in IFRS 3 – *Business Combinations* – and the requirements, which are based on accounting for the modification of share-based payments, are addressed in EY International GAAP 2015.

The treatment in the single entity financial statements of B is discussed at 12.2 below.

12.2 Financial statements of the acquired entity

For the acquired entity, the replacement of an award based on the acquiree's equity with one based on the acquirer's equity appears to be a cancellation and replacement. In our view, this should to be accounted for in accordance with the general principles for such transactions (see 8.4 above) but taking into account the specific provisions of Section 26 in respect of group share schemes (see 13 below). Therefore, in addition to considerations about whether this is accounted for as a separate cancellation and new grant or as a modification of the original terms, the acquiree needs to take into account its new status as a subsidiary of the acquirer. If the acquiree's employees are now receiving awards granted by the new parent, the new subsidiary might choose to apply the provisions for groups in paragraph 16 of Section 26 (see 13.2.3.A below) rather than the general approach for an entity receiving goods or services but not obliged to settle the award.

13　　GROUP SHARE SCHEMES

In this section we consider various aspects of share-based payment arrangements operated within a group of companies and involving several legal entities. The main areas covered are as follows:

- typical features of a group share scheme (see 13.1 below);

- a summary of the accounting treatment of group share schemes (see 13.2 below);

- EBT's and similar vehicles (see 13.3 below);

- an example of a group share scheme (based on an equity-settled award satisfied by a purchase of shares) illustrating the accounting by the different entities involved (see 13.4 below);

- an example of a group share scheme (based on an equity-settled award satisfied by a fresh issue of shares) illustrating the accounting by the different entities involved (see 13.5 below);

- an example of a group cash-settled transaction where the award is settled by an entity other than the one receiving goods or services (see 13.6 below); and

- the accounting treatment when an employee transfers between group entities (see 13.7 below).

Associates and joint arrangements do not meet the definition of group entities but there will sometimes be share-based payment arrangements that involve the investor or venturer and the employees of its associate or joint venture. Such arrangements are beyond the scope of this publication but are addressed in EY International GAAP 2015.

13.1　　Typical features of a group share scheme

In this section we use the term 'share scheme' to encompass any transaction falling within the scope of Section 26, whether accounted for as equity-settled or cash-settled.

It is common practice for a group to operate a single share scheme covering the employees of the parent and/or several subsidiaries but the precise terms and structures of group share schemes are so varied that it is rare to find two completely identical arrangements. From an accounting perspective, however, group share schemes can generally be reduced to a basic prototype, as described below, which will serve as the basis of the discussion.

A group scheme typically involves transactions by several legal entities:

- the parent, over whose shares awards are granted and which is often responsible for settling the award (either directly or through a trust);

- the subsidiary employing an employee who has been granted an award ('the employing subsidiary'); and

in some cases, an employee benefit trust ('EBT') that administers the scheme. The accounting treatment of transactions with EBTs is discussed at 13.3 below. In some cases the scheme may be directed by a group employee services entity. Where an employee services company is involved it will be necessary to evaluate the precise group arrangements in order to determine which entity is receiving an employee's services and which entity is responsible for settling the award. It will often be the case that the services company is simply administering the arrangements on behalf of the parent entity.

A share-based award is often granted to an employee by the parent, or a group employee services entity, which will in turn have an option exercisable against the EBT for the shares that it may be required to deliver to the employee. Less commonly, the trustees of the EBT make awards to the employees and enter into reciprocal arrangements with the parent.

If the parent takes the view that it will satisfy any awards using existing shares it will often seek to fix the cash cost of the award by arranging for the EBT to purchase, on the day that the award is made, sufficient shares from existing shareholders to satisfy all or part of the award. This will be funded by external borrowings, a loan from the parent, a contribution from the employing subsidiary, or some combination. The cash received from the employee on exercise of the option can be used by the EBT to repay any borrowings.

If the parent takes the view that it will satisfy the options with a fresh issue of shares, these will be issued to the EBT, either:

(a) at the date on which the employee exercises his option (in which case the EBT will subscribe for the new shares using the cash received from the employee together with any non-refundable contribution made by the employing subsidiary – see below). Such arrangements are generally referred to as 'simultaneous funding';

(b) at some earlier date (in which case the EBT will subscribe for the new shares using external borrowings, a loan from the parent or a contribution from the employing subsidiary, or some combination. The cash received from the employee on exercise of the option may then be used by the EBT to repay any borrowings). Such arrangements are generally referred to as 'pre-funding'; or

(c) some shares will be issued before the exercise date as in (b) above, and the balance on the exercise date as in (a) above.

As noted in (a) above, the employing subsidiary often makes a non-refundable contribution to the EBT in connection with the scheme, so as to ensure that employing subsidiaries bear an appropriate share of the overall cost of a group-wide share scheme.

13.2 Accounting treatment of group share schemes – summary

13.2.1 Background

From a financial reporting perspective, it is generally necessary to consider the accounting treatment in:

• the group's consolidated financial statements;

• the parent's separate financial statements; and

• the employing subsidiary's financial statements.

We make the assumption throughout this section on group share schemes that the subsidiary is directly owned by the parent company. In practice, there will often be one or more intermediate holding companies between the ultimate parent and the subsidiary. The intermediate parent company generally will not be the entity granting the award, receiving the goods or services or responsible for settling the award. Therefore, under Section 26, we believe that there is no requirement for the intermediate company to account for the award in its separate financial statements.

The accounting entries to be made in the various financial statements will broadly vary according to:

- whether the award is satisfied using shares already held or a fresh issue of shares;
- whether any charge is made to the employing subsidiary for the cost of awards to its employees;
- whether an EBT is involved. The accounting treatment of transactions undertaken with and by EBTs is discussed in more detail at 13.3 below; and
- the tax consequences of the award. For the purposes of the discussion below, tax effects are ignored. A more general discussion of the tax effects of share-based payment transactions may be found at 15 below.

The sections below largely discuss the application of the basic requirements of Section 26 to share-based payment transactions within a group of entities. However, in addition to the application of those requirements, Section 26 allows an alternative treatment based on the allocation of a group share-based payment expense to group entities on a reasonable basis (see 13.2.3.A below).

13.2.2   Scope of Section 26 for group share schemes

By virtue of the definition of 'share-based payment transaction' (see 3.1 and 3.2.1 above), a group share-based payment transaction is in the scope of Section 26 of FRS 102 for:

- the consolidated financial statements of the group (the accounting for which follows the general principles set out in 4 to 11 above);
- the separate or individual financial statements of the entity in the group that receives goods or services (see 13.2.3 below); and
- the separate or individual financial statements of the entity in the group (if different from that receiving the goods or services) that settles the transaction with the counterparty. This entity will typically, but not necessarily, be the parent (see 13.2.4 below).

As discussed at 3 above, the scope paragraphs of Section 26, together with the definitions in the glossary to FRS 102, indicate whether transactions are to be accounted for as equity-settled or as cash-settled in most group situations including:

- transactions settled in the equity of the entity, or in the equity of its parent (see 13.2.5 below); and
- cash-settled transactions settled by a group entity other than the entity receiving the goods or services (see 13.2.6 below).

At 3.2.1 above, we consider seven scenarios commonly found in practice and outline the approach required by Section 26 in the consolidated and separate or individual financial statements of group entities depending on whether the award is settled in cash or shares and which entity grants the award, settles the award and receives the goods or services. These scenarios do not reflect the alternative treatment for group plans in Section 26 (see 13.2.3.A below).

It is common practice in a group share scheme to require each participating entity in the group to pay a charge, either to the parent or to an EBT, in respect of the cost of awards made under the scheme to employees of that entity. This is generally done either as part of the group's cash-management strategy, or in order to obtain tax relief under applicable local legislation. The amount charged could in principle be at the discretion of the group, but is often based on either the fair value of the award at grant date or the fair value at vesting, in the case of an award of free shares, or exercise, in the case of an award of options.

Neither FRS 102 nor IFRS 2 directly addresses the accounting treatment of such intragroup management charges and other recharge arrangements, which is discussed further at 13.2.7 below. *[IFRS 2.B46]*.

Worked examples illustrating how these various principles translate into accounting entries are given at 13.4 to 13.6 below.

13.2.3   *Entity receiving goods or services*

The entity in a group receiving goods or services in a share-based payment transaction determines whether the transaction should be accounted for as equity-settled or cash-settled in its separate or individual financial statements. It does this by assessing the nature of the awards granted and its own rights and obligations.

The entity accounts for the transaction as equity-settled when either the awards granted are the entity's own equity instruments, or the entity has no obligation to settle the share-based payment transaction. Otherwise, the entity accounts for the transaction as cash-settled. Where the transaction is accounted for as equity-settled it is remeasured after grant date only to the extent permitted or required by Section 26 for equity transactions generally, as discussed at 4 to 7 above.

A possible consequence of these requirements is that the amount recognised by the entity may differ from the amount recognised by the consolidated group or by another group entity settling the share-based payment transaction. This is discussed further at 13.6 below.

The cost recognised by the entity receiving goods or services is calculated according to the principles set out above unless the group applies the alternative treatment for group plans in Section 26 (see 13.2.3.A below). The cost under Section 26 is not adjusted for any intragroup recharging arrangements, the accounting for which is discussed at 13.2.7 below.

13.2.3.A   *Alternative treatment for group plans*

As an alternative to the accounting treatment in paragraphs 3 to 15 of Section 26 (discussed in sections 4 to 11 and 13 of this Chapter), in an arrangement where an award is granted by the entity to the employees of one or more members of the group, those group members are permitted to recognise and measure the share-based payment expense on the basis of a reasonable allocation of the group expense. *[FRS 102.26.16].*

It is not made clear in Section 26 whether this alternative treatment is intended only to apply in situations where the group expense is calculated on a basis consistent with the requirements of FRS 102. A similar, but not identical, requirement in the IFRS for SMEs specifies that the group expense should be calculated in accordance with the IFRS for SMEs or IFRS 2. In the absence of explicit guidance, we would generally expect the group expense being allocated to be based on the requirements of FRS 102, IFRS 2 or an equivalent framework under the FRS 102 hierarchy.

13.2.4   *Entity settling the transaction*

As noted at 3.2.1 above, Section 26 does not separately specify the accounting treatment when the entity settling the transaction does not receive the goods or services although the obligation to settle a transaction is explicitly within scope. In this situation, we suggest that the requirements of paragraphs 1 and 1A of Section 26 are read in line with the provisions of IFRS 2 in to order make the requirements clear. Under IFRS 2, a group entity which settles a share-based payment transaction in which another group entity receives goods or services accounts for the transaction as an equity-settled share-based payment transaction only if it is settled in the settling entity's own equity instruments. Otherwise, the transaction is accounted for as cash-settled. *[IFRS 2.43C].*

The above requirements relate only to the credit entry – the classification of the transaction as equity- or cash-settled, and its measurement. They do not specify the debit entry, which is therefore subject to the general requirement of IFRS 2 (and Section 26 of FRS 102) that a share-based payment transaction should normally be treated as an expense, unless there is the basis for another treatment (see 4 above).

In our view, the settling entity should not normally treat the transaction as an expense. Instead:

- Where the settling entity is a parent (direct or indirect) of the entity receiving the goods or services, it accounts for the settlement of the award as an addition to the cost of its investment in the employing subsidiary (or of that holding company of the employing subsidiary which is the settling entity's directly-held subsidiary). It may then be necessary to review the carrying value of that investment to ensure that it is not impaired.

- In other cases (i.e. where the settling entity is a subsidiary (direct or indirect) or fellow subsidiary of the entity receiving the goods or services), it should treat the settlement as a distribution, and charge it directly to equity. Whether or not such a settlement is a legal distribution is a matter of law in the jurisdiction concerned.

We adopt this approach in the worked examples set out in 13.4 to 13.6 below.

13.2.5 Transactions settled in equity of the entity or its parent

13.2.5.A   Awards settled in equity of subsidiary

Where a subsidiary grants an award to its employees and settles it in its own equity, the subsidiary accounts for the award as equity-settled. *[FRS 102.26.1].*

The parent accounts for the award as equity-settled in its consolidated financial statements. In its separate financial statements, the parent does not account for the award under FRS 102 (see 3.2.1 above). In both cases, the transaction may have implications for other aspects of the financial statements, since its settlement results in the partial disposal of the subsidiary.

Where the parent settles the award, it accounts for the transaction as equity-settled in its consolidated financial statements. In its separate financial statements, however, it accounts for the award as cash-settled, since it is settled not in its own equity, but in the equity of the subsidiary (see 3.2.1 above). From the perspective of the parent's separate financial statements, the equity of a subsidiary is a financial asset.

13.2.5.B   Awards settled in equity of the parent

Where the parent grants an award directly to the employees of a subsidiary and settles it in its own equity, the subsidiary accounts for the award as equity-settled, with a corresponding increase in equity as a contribution from the parent. *[FRS 102.26.1, 1A].*

The parent accounts for the award as equity-settled in both its consolidated and separate financial statements (see 3.2.1 above).

Where a subsidiary grants an award of equity in its parent to its employees and settles the award itself, it accounts for the award as cash-settled, since it is settled not in its own equity, but in the equity of its parent. From the perspective of the subsidiary's separate or individual financial statements, the equity of the parent is a financial asset. *[FRS 102.26.1].*

This requirement potentially represents something of a compliance burden. For the purposes of the parent's consolidated financial statements the fair value of the award needs to be calculated once, at grant date. For the purposes of the subsidiary's financial statements, however, the basic requirements of Section 26 require the award to be accounted for as cash-settled, with the fair value recalculated at each reporting date. In some cases, the rather unclear wording of paragraph 16 of Section 26 might mean that the arrangements are considered to meet the criteria for the alternative accounting treatment for group schemes. If this were the case, the subsidiary could, in effect, account on an equity-settled basis until the point of settlement (see 13.2.3.A above).

It is, however, important to note that the approach that results in equity-settled accounting in the consolidated financial statements and cash-settled accounting in the subsidiary financial statements applies only when a subsidiary 'grants', and is therefore obliged to settle, such an award. In some jurisdictions, including the UK, it is normal for grants of share awards to be made by the parent, or an employee service company or EBT, rather than by the subsidiary, although the subsidiary may well make recommendations to the grantor of the award as to which of its employees should benefit.

In those cases, the fact that the subsidiary may communicate the award to the employee does not necessarily mean that the subsidiary itself has granted the award. It may simply be notifying the employee of an award granted by another group entity. In that case the subsidiary should apply the normal requirement of Section 26 to account for the award as equity-settled.

13.2.6   *Cash-settled transactions not settled by the entity receiving goods or services*

The scope section of Section 26 (see 3 above) considers arrangements in which the parent has an obligation to make cash payments to the employees of a subsidiary linked to the price of:

- the subsidiary's equity instruments, or
- the parent's equity instruments.

In both cases, the subsidiary has no obligation to settle the transaction. Therefore, unless the alternative accounting rules are applied (see below), the subsidiary accounts for the transaction as equity-settled, recognising a corresponding credit in equity as a contribution from its parent. *[FRS 102.26.1-1A].*

The subsidiary subsequently remeasures the cost of the transaction only for any changes resulting from non-market vesting conditions not being met in accordance with the normal provisions of Section 26 discussed at 4 to 7 above. Section 26 does not make the point – made in IFRS 2 – that this will differ from the measurement of the transaction as cash-settled in the consolidated financial statements of the group. *[IFRS 2.B56-57].*

As noted at 3 above, Section 26 does not specify the accounting treatment required by the settling entity in these situations. In both cases, the parent has an obligation to settle the transaction in cash. Accordingly, and following the more detailed guidance in IFRS 2, the parent should account for the transaction as cash-settled in both its consolidated and separate financial statements. *[IFRS 2.B58].*

The requirement for the subsidiary to measure the transaction as equity-settled is somewhat controversial. The essential rationale for requiring the subsidiary to record the cost of a share-based payment transaction settled by its parent is to reflect that the subsidiary is effectively receiving a capital contribution from its parent. Many commentators consider that it would be more appropriate to measure that contribution by reference to the cash actually paid by the parent, rather than to use a notional accounting cost derived from a valuation model.

Using the alternative accounting treatment for group plans set out in Section 26 (see 13.2.3.A above), it appears that the subsidiary in this situation could in fact base its expense either on an equity-settled calculation or on an allocation of the group cash-settled expense.

13.2.7 *Intragroup recharges and management charges*

As noted at 13.2.2 above, neither FRS 102 nor IFRS 2 deals specifically with the accounting treatment of intragroup recharges and management charges that may be levied on the subsidiary that receives goods or services, the consideration for which is equity or cash of another group entity.

The accounting requirements of FRS 102 for group share schemes derive from requirements in IFRS 2 which evolved, via an Interpretation, from an exposure draft (D17) published in 2005.[6] In the absence of more specific guidance, we suggest that the treatment outlined below is applied to recharge arrangements in place between entities applying FRS 102. For entities applying the Companies Act 2006, the accounting treatment under D17 is also addressed in Section 7 of TECH 02/10: *Guidance on the determination of realised profits and losses in the context of distributions under the Companies Act 2006.*[7]

D17 proposed that any such payment made by a subsidiary should be charged directly to equity, on the basis that it represents a return of the capital contribution recorded as the credit to equity required by IFRS 2 (see 13.2.3 and 13.2.6 above) up to the amount of that contribution, and a distribution thereafter.

In our view, whilst IFRS 2 and FRS 102 as currently drafted clearly do not explicitly require this treatment, this is the more appropriate analysis for most subsidiaries. Indeed, the only alternative, 'mechanically' speaking, would be to charge the relevant amount to profit or loss. This would result in a double charge (once for the FRS 102 or IFRS 2 charge, and again for the management charge or recharge) which we consider less appropriate in cases where the amount of the recharge is directly related to the value of the share-based payment transaction.

Many intragroup recharge arrangements are based directly on the value of the underlying share-based payment – typically at grant date, vesting date or exercise date. In other cases, a more general management charge might be levied that reflects not just share-based payments but also a number of other arrangements or services provided to the subsidiary by the parent. Where there is a more general management charge of this kind, we believe that it is more appropriate for the subsidiary to recognise a double charge to profit or loss rather than debiting the management charge to equity as would be the case for a direct recharge.

IFRS 2 and FRS 102 also do not address how the parent should account for a recharge or management charge received. In our view, to the extent that the receipt represents a return of a capital contribution made to the subsidiary, the parent may choose whether to credit:

- the carrying amount of its investment in the subsidiary; or

- profit or loss (with a corresponding impairment review of the investment).

Even if part of the recharge received is credited to the carrying amount of the investment, any amount received in excess of the capital contribution previously debited to the investment in subsidiary should be accounted for as a distribution from the subsidiary and credited to the income statement of the parent. Where applicable, the illustrative examples at 13.4 to 13.6 below show the entire amount as a credit to the income statement of the parent rather than part of the recharge being treated as a credit to the parent's investment in its subsidiary.

A further issue that arises in practice is the timing of recognition of the recharge by the parties to the arrangement. In the absence of a contractual agreement, the treatment adopted might depend on the precise terms and whether there are contractual arrangements in place, but two approaches generally result in practice:

- to account for the recharge when it is actually levied or paid (which is consistent with accounting for a distribution); or

- to accrue the recharge over the life of the award or the recharge agreement even if, as is commonly the case, the actual recharge is only made at vesting or exercise date.

An entity should choose the more appropriate treatment for its particular circumstances. The first approach is often the more appropriate in a group context where recharge arrangements might not be binding until such time as payment is required to be made. It is also consistent with the overall recognition of the arrangement through equity and with a situation where there are likely to be uncertainties during the vesting period about the existence of a present obligation (it will depend on whether the awards are expected to vest) and about the estimated cash outflow. The second approach treats the recharge more like a provision or financial liability but would reflect changes in the liability through equity rather than profit or loss and would build up the liability over the life of the award rather than recognising it in full when a present obligation has been identified.

Where applicable, the examples at 13.4 to 13.6 below illustrate the first of the two treatments outlined above and recognise the recharge only when it becomes payable at the date of exercise.

Whichever accounting treatment is adopted, any adjustments to the amount to be recognised as a recharge, whether arising from a change in the Section 26 expense or other changes, should be recognised in the current period and previous periods should not be restated.

13.3   Employee benefit trusts ('EBTs') and similar entities

13.3.1   *Background*

For some time entities have established trusts and similar arrangements for the benefit of employees. These are known by various names but, for the sake of convenience, in this section we will use the term 'EBT' ('employee benefit trust') to cover all such vehicles by whatever name they are actually known.

The commercial purposes of using such vehicles vary from employer to employer but may include the following:

- An EBT, in order to achieve its purpose, needs to hold shares that have either been issued to it by the entity or been bought by the EBT on the open market.

- In the case of longer-term benefits the use of an EBT may 'ring fence' the assets set aside for the benefit of employees in case of the insolvency of the entity.

- The use of an EBT may be necessary in order to achieve a favourable tax treatment for the entity or the employees, or both.

The detailed features of an EBT will again vary from entity to entity but typical features often include the following:

- The EBT provides a warehouse for the sponsoring entity's shares, for example by acquiring and holding shares that are to be sold or transferred to employees in the future. The trustees may purchase the shares with finance provided by the sponsoring entity (by way of cash contributions or loans), or by a third-party bank loan, or by a combination of the two. Loans from the entity are usually interest-free. In other cases, the EBT may subscribe directly for shares issued by the sponsoring entity or acquire shares in the market.

- Where the EBT borrows from a third party, the sponsoring entity will usually guarantee the loan, i.e. it will be responsible for any shortfall if the EBT's assets are insufficient to meet its debt repayment obligations. The entity will also generally make regular contributions to the EBT to enable the EBT to meet its interest payments, i.e. to make good any shortfall between the dividend income of the EBT (if any) and the interest payable. As part of this arrangement the trustees may waive their right to dividends on the shares held by the EBT.

- Shares held by the EBT are distributed to employees through an employee share scheme. There are many different arrangements – these may include:

  - the purchase of shares by employees when exercising their share options under a share option scheme;

  - the purchase of shares by the trustees of an approved profit-sharing scheme for allocation to employees under the rules of the scheme; or

  - the transfer of shares to employees under some other incentive scheme.

- The trustees of an EBT may have a legal duty to act at all times in accordance with the interests of the beneficiaries under the EBT. However, most EBTs (particularly those established as a means of remunerating employees) are specifically designed so as to serve the purposes of the sponsoring entity, and to ensure that there will be minimal risk of any conflict arising between the duties of the trustees and the interest of the entity.

13.3.2   Accounting for EBTs

Historically, transactions involving EBTs were accounted for according to their legal form. In other words, any cash gifted or lent to the EBT was simply treated as, respectively, an expense or a loan in the financial statements of the employing entity.

However, this treatment gradually came to be challenged, not least by some tax authorities who began to question whether it was appropriate to allow a corporate tax deduction for the 'expense' of putting money into an EBT which in some cases might remain in the EBT for some considerable time (or even be lent back to the entity) before being actually passed on to employees. Thus, the issue came onto the agenda of the national standard setters.

The accounting solution proposed by some standard setters, including the UK Accounting Standards Board, was to require a reporting entity to account for an EBT as an extension of the entity. The basis for this treatment was essentially that, as noted at 13.3.1 above, EBTs are specifically designed to serve the purposes of the sponsoring entity, and to ensure that there will be minimal risk of any conflict arising between the duties of the trustees and the interest of the entity, suggesting that they are under the *de facto* control of the entity.

The requirement to treat an EBT as an extension of the entity continues under Section 9 of FRS 102. *[FRS 102.9.35-37]*. This treatment has the following broad consequences for the consolidated and separate financial statements of the reporting entity:

- Until such time as the entity's own shares held by the EBT vest unconditionally in employees any consideration paid for the shares should be deducted in arriving at shareholders' equity.

- Other assets and liabilities (including borrowings) of the EBT should be recognised as assets and liabilities in the financial statements of the sponsoring entity.

- No gain or loss should be recognised in profit or loss or other comprehensive income on the purchase, sale, issue or cancellation of the entity's own shares. Consideration paid or received for the purchase or sale of the entity's own shares in an EBT should be shown separately from other purchases and sales of the entity's own shares ('true' treasury shares held by the reporting entity) in the statement of changes in equity.

- Any dividend income arising on own shares should be excluded from profit or loss and deducted from the aggregate of dividends paid. In our view, the deduction should be disclosed if material.

- Finance costs and any administration expenses should be charged as they accrue and not as funding payments are made to the EBT.

13.3.3   *Illustrative Examples – awards satisfied by shares purchased by, or issued to, an EBT*

The following Examples show the interaction of accounting for the EBT with the requirements of Section 26. Example 21.35 illustrates the treatment where an award is satisfied using shares previously purchased by the EBT. Example 21.36 illustrates the treatment where freshly issued shares are used.

Example 21.35:   Interaction of accounting for share purchase by EBT and accounting for share-based payment transactions

On 1 January 2015, the EBT of company ABC made a market purchase of 100,000 shares of ABC plc at £2.50 per share. These were the only ABC shares held by the EBT at that date.

On 1 May 2015, ABC granted executives options over between 300,000 and 500,000 shares at £2.70 per share, which will vest on 31 December 2015, the number vesting depending on various performance criteria. It is determined that the cost to be recognised in respect of this award under FRS 102 is 15p per share.

On 1 September 2015, the EBT made a further market purchase of 300,000 shares at £2.65 per share.

On 31 December 2015, options vested over 350,000 shares and were exercised immediately.

The accounting entries for the above transactions in the consolidated financial statements of ABC would be as follows.

	£	£
1 January 2015		
Own shares (equity)	250,000	
Cash		250,000
To record purchase of 100,000 £1 shares at £2.50/share		
1 May 2015 – 31 December 2015		
Profit or loss	52,500	
Equity†		52,500
To record cost of vested 350,000 options at 15p/option		
1 September 2015		
Own shares (equity)	795,000	
Cash		795,000
To record purchase of 300,000 £1 shares at £2.65/share		
31 December 2015		
Cash	945,000	
Equity†1		945,000
Receipt of proceeds on exercise of 350,000 options at £2.70/share		
Equity†	914,375	
Own shares (equity)2		914,375
Release of shares from EBT to employees		

1   This reflects the fact that the entity has had an increase in resources as a result of a transaction with an owner, which gives rise to no gain or loss and is therefore credited direct to equity.

2   It is necessary to transfer the cost of the shares 'reissued' by the EBT out of own shares, as the deduction for own shares would otherwise be overstated. The total cost of the pool of 400,000 shares immediately before vesting was £1,045,000 (£250,000 purchased on 1 January 2015 and £795,000 purchased on 1 September 2015), representing an average cost per share of £2.6125. £2.6125 × 350,000 shares = £914,375.

†   These amounts should all be accounted for in the profit and loss reserve or, until the awards are exercised, a separate reserve for share-based payments.

Example 21.35 illustrates the importance of keeping the accounting for the cost of the shares completely separate from that for the cost of the share-based payment award. In cash terms, ABC has made a 'profit' of £30,625, since it purchased 350,000 shares with a weighted average cost of £914,375 and issued them to the executives for £945,000. However, this 'profit' is accounted for entirely within equity, whereas a calculated expense of £52,500 is recognised in profit or loss.

Example 21.36:   Interaction of accounting for fresh issue of shares to EBT and accounting for share-based payment transactions

On 1 January 2015, the EBT of company ABC subscribed for 100,000 £1 shares of ABC at £2.50 per share, paid for in cash provided by ABC by way of loan to the EBT. In accordance with the Companies Act, these proceeds must be credited to the share capital account up to the par value of the shares issued, with any excess taken to a share premium account. These were the only ABC shares held by the EBT at that date.

On 1 May 2015, ABC granted executives options over between 300,000 and 500,000 shares at £2.70 per share, which will vest on 31 December 2015, the number vesting depending on various performance criteria. It is determined that the cost to be recognised in respect of this award is 15p per share.

On 1 September 2015, the EBT subscribed for a further 300,000 shares at £2.65 per share, again paid for in cash provided by ABC by way of loan to the EBT.

On 31 December 2015, options vested over 350,000 shares and were exercised immediately.

The accounting entries for the above transactions in the consolidated financial statements of ABC would be as follows.

	£	£
1 January 2015		
Equity[†1]	250,000	
Share capital		100,000
Share premium		150,000
To record issue of 100,000 £1 shares to EBT at £2.50/share		
1 May 2015 – 31 December 2015		
Profit or loss	52,500	
Equity[†]		52,500
To record cost of vested 350,000 options at 15p/option		
1 September 2015		
Equity[†1]	795,000	
Share capital		300,000
Share premium		495,000
To record issue of 300,000 £1 shares at £2.65/share		
31 December 2015		
Cash	945,000	
Equity[2†]		945,000
Receipt of proceeds on exercise of 350,000 options at £2.70/share		

1   This entry is required to reconcile the legal requirement to record an issue of shares with the fact that, in reality, there has been no increase in the resources of the reporting entity. All that has happened is that one member of the reporting group (the EBT) has transferred cash to another (the parent entity). In our view, this amount should not strictly be accounted for within any 'Own shares reserve' in equity, which should be restricted to shares acquired from third parties, although it is increasingly common in practice to see an entry in 'own shares' to reflect such a holding of shares by an EBT.

2   This reflects the fact that the entity has had an increase in resources as a result of a transaction with an owner, which gives rise to no gain or loss and is therefore credited direct to equity.

†   These amounts should all be accounted for in the profit and loss reserve (subject to note 1 above) or, until the awards are exercised, a separate reserve for share-based payments.

13.3.4 Financial statements of the EBT

The EBT may be required to prepare financial statements in accordance with requirements imposed by local law or by its own trust deed. The form and content of such financial statements are beyond the scope of this publication.

13.4 Illustrative example of group share scheme – equity-settled award satisfied by purchase of shares

The discussion in 13.4.1 to 13.4.3 below is based on Example 21.37 and addresses the accounting treatment for three distinct aspects of a group share scheme – a share-based payment arrangement involving group entities (see 13.2 above), the use of an EBT (see 13.3 above) and a group recharge arrangement (see 13.2.7 above).

Example 21.37: Group share scheme (purchase of shares)

On 1 July 2015 an employee of S Limited, a subsidiary of the H plc group, is awarded options under the H group share scheme over 3,000 shares in H plc at £1.50 each, exercisable between 1 July 2020 and 1 July 2021, subject to a service condition and certain performance criteria being met in the three years ending 30 June 2018.

H plc is the grantor of the award, and has the obligation to settle it. On 1 January 2016, in connection with the award, the H plc group EBT purchases 3,000 shares from existing shareholders at the then prevailing price of £2.00 per share, funded by a loan from H plc. On exercise of the option, S Limited is required to pay the differential between the purchase price of the shares and the exercise price of the option (50p per share) to the EBT.

For the purposes of FRS 102, the options are considered to have a fair value at grant date of £1 per option. Throughout the vesting period of the option, H takes the view that the award will vest in full.

The option is exercised on 1 September 2020, at which point the EBT uses the option proceeds, together with the payment by S Limited, to repay the loan from H plc.

H plc and its subsidiaries have a 31 December year end.

13.4.1 Consolidated financial statements

So far as the consolidated financial statements are concerned, the transactions to be accounted for are:

- the purchase of the shares by the EBT and their eventual transfer to the employee; and

- the cost of the award.

Transactions between H plc or S Limited and the EBT are ignored since the EBT is treated as an extension of H plc (see 13.3 above). The accounting entries required are set out below. As in other examples in this Chapter, an entry to equity is not allocated to a specific reserve as this will vary between entities (although the most common for an entity complying with the Companies Act 2006 will be the profit and loss reserve or a separate 'other reserve' for share-based payments).

		£	£
y/e 31.12.2015	Profit or loss (employee costs)*	500	
	Equity		500
1.1.2016	Own shares (equity)	6,000	
	Cash		6,000
y/e 31.12.2016	Profit or loss (employee costs)*	1,000	
	Equity		1,000
y/e 31.12.2017	Profit or loss (employee costs)*	1,000	
	Equity		1,000
y/e 31.12.2018	Profit or loss (employee costs)*	500	
	Equity		500
1.9.2020	Cash (option proceeds)†	4,500	
	Equity‡	1,500	
	Own shares (equity)**		6,000

*   Total cost £3,000 (3000 options × £1) spread over 36 months. Charge for period to December 2015 is 6/36 × £3,000 = £500, and so on. In practice, where options are granted to a group of individuals, or with variable performance criteria, the annual charge will be based on a continually revised cumulative charge (see further discussion at 7.1 to 7.4 above).

†   3,000 options at £1.50 each.

‡   This reflects the fact that the overall effect of the transaction for the group *in cash terms* has been a 'loss' of £1,500 (£6,000 original cost of shares less £4,500 option proceeds received). However, under FRS 102 this is an equity transaction, not an expense.

**   £6,000 cost of own shares purchased on 1 January 2016 now transferred to the employee. In practice, it is more likely that the appropriate amount to be transferred would be based on the weighted average price of shares held by the EBT at the date of exercise, as in Example 21.35 at 13.3.3 above. In such a case there would be a corresponding adjustment to the debit to equity marked with ‡ above.

13.4.2   Parent

13.4.2.A   Subsidiary company as employing company

The parent accounts for the share-based payment transaction under FRS 102 as an equity-settled transaction since the parent settles the award by delivering its own equity instruments to the employees of the subsidiary (see 13.2.4 above). However, as discussed at 13.2.4 above, instead of recording an expense, as in its consolidated financial statements, the parent records an increase in the carrying value of its subsidiary. It might then be necessary to consider whether the ever-increasing investment in subsidiary is supportable or is in fact impaired. As this is a matter to be determined in the light of specific facts and circumstances, it is not considered in this example. Any impairment charge would be recorded in profit or loss.

In addition to accounting for the share-based payment transaction, the parent records the transactions of the EBT and the purchase of shares.

This gives rise to the following entries:

			£	£
y/e 31.12.2015	Investment in subsidiary*		500	
	Equity			500
1.1.2016	Own shares (equity)		6,000	
	Cash			6,000
y/e 31.12.2016	Investment in subsidiary*		1,000	
	Equity			1,000
y/e 31.12.2017	Investment in subsidiary*		1,000	
	Equity			1,000
y/e 31.12.2018	Investment in subsidiary*		500	
	Equity			500
1.9.2020	Cash†		6,000	
	Equity‡		1,500	
	Profit or loss§			1,500
	Own shares** (equity)			6,000

*   Total increase in investment £3,000 (3000 shares × £1 fair value of each option) spread over 36 months. Increase during period to December 2015 is 6/36 × £3,000 = £500, and so on. In practice, where options were granted to a group of individuals, or with variable performance criteria, the annual adjustment would be based on a continually revised cumulative adjustment (see further discussion at 7.1 to 7.4 above).

†   £4,500 option exercise proceeds from employee plus £1,500 contribution from S Limited.

‡   This is essentially a balancing figure representing the fact that the entity is distributing own shares with an original cost of £6,000, but has treated £1,500 of the £6,000 of the cash it has received as income (see § below) rather than as payment for the shares.

§   The £1,500 contribution by the subsidiary to the EBT has been treated as a distribution from the subsidiary (see 13.2.7 above) and recorded in profit or loss. It might then be necessary to consider whether, as a result of this payment, the investment in the subsidiary had become impaired. As this is a matter to be determined in the light of specific facts and circumstances, it is not considered in this example. Any impairment charge would be recorded in profit or loss.

** £6,000 cost of own shares purchased on 1 January 2016 now transferred to employee. In practice, it is more likely that the appropriate amount to be transferred would be based on the weighted average price of shares held by the EBT at the date of exercise, as in Example 21.35 at 13.3.3 above.

13.4.2.B   Parent company as employing company

If, in Example 21.37, the parent rather than the subsidiary were the employing entity, the parent would record an expense under FRS 102. It would also normally waive £1,500 of its £6,000 loan to the EBT (i.e. the shortfall between the original loan and the £4,500 option proceeds received from the employee).

As the EBT is treated as an extension of the parent, the accounting entries for the parent would be the same as those for the group, as set out in 13.4.1 above.

13.4.3   Employing subsidiary

The employing subsidiary is required to account for the FRS 102 expense and the contribution to the EBT on exercise of the award. This gives rise to the accounting entries set out below. The entries to reflect the expense are required by FRS 102 (see 13.2.3 above). The treatment of the contribution to the EBT as a distribution is discussed at 13.2.7 above.

		£	£
y/e 31.12.2015	Profit or loss*	500	
	Equity		500
y/e 31.12.2016	Profit or loss*	1,000	
	Equity		1,000
y/e 31.12.2017	Profit or loss*	1,000	
	Equity		1,000
y/e 31.12.2018	Profit or loss*	500	
	Equity		500
1.9.2020	Equity†	1,500	
	Cash		1,500

*   Total cost £3,000 (3000 options × £1) spread over 36 months. Charge for period to December 2015 is 6/36 × £3,000 = £500, and so on. In practice, where options were granted to a group of individuals, or with variable performance criteria, the annual charge would be based on a continually revised cumulative charge (see further discussion at 7.1 to 7.4 above).

†   This should be treated as a reduction of whatever component of equity was credited with the £3,000 quasi-contribution from the parent in the accounting entries above.

13.5   Illustrative example of group share scheme – equity-settled award satisfied by fresh issue of shares

The discussion in 13.5.1 to 13.5.3 below is based on Example 21.38 and addresses the accounting treatment for three distinct aspects of a group share scheme – a share-based payment arrangement involving group entities (see 13.2 above), the use of an EBT (see 13.3 above) and a group recharge arrangement (see 13.2.7 above).The Example assumes that the share-based payment arrangement is settled by a fresh issue of shares. Where an award is settled by shares purchased in the market, or from other existing shareholders, the consolidated accounts and, where applicable, the single entity accounts of the parent company, will also need to account for the purchased shares as treasury shares.

Example 21.38:   Group share scheme (fresh issue of shares)

On 1 July 2015 an employee of S Limited, a subsidiary of the H plc group, is awarded options under the H group share scheme over 3,000 shares in H plc at £1.50 each, exercisable between 1 July 2020 and 1 July 2021, subject to a service condition and certain performance criteria being met in the three years ending 30 June 2018. The fair value of the options on 1 July 2015 is £1 each.

H plc grants the award and has the obligation to settle it.

When preparing accounts during the vesting period H plc and its subsidiaries assume that the award will vest in full. The options are finally exercised on 1 September 2020, at which point H plc issues 3,000 new shares to the EBT at the then current market price of £3.50 for £10,500. The EBT funds the purchase using the £4,500 option proceeds received from the employee together with £6,000 contributed by S Limited, effectively representing the fair value of the options at exercise date (3,000 × [£3.50 – £1.50]). H plc and its subsidiaries have a 31 December year end.

13.5.1   Consolidated financial statements

The consolidated financial statements need to deal with:

- the charge required by FRS 102 in respect of the award; and
- the issue of shares.

Transactions between H plc or S Limited and the EBT are ignored since the EBT is treated as an extension of H plc (see 13.3 above). The accounting entries required are set out below. As in other examples in this Chapter, an entry to equity is not allocated to a specific reserve as this will vary between entities (although the most common for an entity complying with the Companies Act 2006 will be the profit and loss reserve or a separate 'other reserve' for share-based payments).

		£	£
y/e 31.12.2015	Profit or loss*	500	
	Equity		500
y/e 31.12.2016	Profit or loss*	1,000	
	Equity		1,000
y/e 31.12.2017	Profit or loss*	1,000	
	Equity		1,000
y/e 31.12.2018	Profit or loss*	500	
	Equity		500
1.9.2020	Cash	4,500	
	Other equity†	6,000	
	Share capital / premium†		10,500

*   Total cost £3,000 (3000 options × £1) spread over 36 months. Charge for period to December 2015 is 6/36 × £3,000 = £500, and so on. In practice, where options were granted to a group of individuals, or with variable performance criteria, the annual charge would be based on a continually revised cumulative charge (see further discussion at 7.1 to 7.4 above).

†   From the point of view of the consolidated group, the issue of shares results in an increase in net assets of only £4,500 (i.e. the exercise price received from the employee), since the £6,000 contribution from the employing subsidiary to the EBT is an intragroup transaction. However, an entity applying the Companies Act 2006 is required to increase its share capital and share premium accounts by the £10,500 legal consideration for the issue of shares. The £6,000 consideration provided from within the group is effectively treated as a bonus issue.

13.5.2   Parent

13.5.2.A   Subsidiary as employing company

The parent accounts for the share-based payment transaction under FRS 102 as an equity-settled transaction since the parent settles the award by delivering its own equity instruments to the employees of the subsidiary (see 13.2.4 above). However, as discussed at 13.2.4 above, instead of recording an expense, as in its consolidated financial statements, the parent records an increase in the carrying value of its subsidiary. It might then be necessary to consider whether the ever-increasing investment in subsidiary is supportable or is in fact impaired. As this is a matter to be determined in the light of specific facts and circumstances, it is not considered in this example. Any impairment charge would be recorded in profit or loss.

In addition to accounting for the share-based payment transaction, the parent records the transactions of the EBT and the issue of shares.

		£	£
y/e 31.12.2015	Investment in subsidiary*	500	
	Equity		500
y/e 31.12.2016	Investment in subsidiary*	1,000	
	Equity		1,000
y/e 31.12.2017	Investment in subsidiary*	1,000	
	Equity		1,000
y/e 31.12.2018	Investment in subsidiary*	500	
	Equity†		500
1.9.2020	Cash†	10,500	
	Equity‡	6,000	
	Profit or loss**		6,000
	Share capital/premium‡		10,500

* Total increase in investment £3,000 (3000 shares × £1 fair value of each option) spread over 36 months. Increase during period to December 2015 is 6/36 × £3,000 = £500, and so on. In practice, where options were granted to a group of individuals, or with variable performance criteria, the annual adjustment would be based on a continually revised cumulative adjustment (see further discussion at 7.1 to 7.4 above).

† £4,500 option exercise proceeds from employee plus £6,000 contribution from the subsidiary.

‡ This assumes that local law requires the entity to record share capital and share premium of £10,500, as in 13.5.1 above. However, FRS 102 *prima facie* requires the £6,000 cash received by the EBT from the subsidiary to be treated as income (see ** below) rather than as part of the proceeds of the issue of shares. In order, in effect, to reconcile these conflicting analyses, £6,000 of the £10,500 required by law to be capitalised as share capital and share premium has been treated as an appropriation out of other equity.

** The £6,000 contribution by the subsidiary to the EBT has been treated as a distribution from the subsidiary (see 13.2.7 above) and recorded in profit or loss. It might then be necessary to consider whether, as a result of this payment, the investment in the subsidiary had become impaired. As this is a matter to be determined in the light of specific facts and circumstances, it is not considered in this Example. Any impairment charge would be recorded in profit or loss.

13.5.2.B   *Parent company as employing company*

If, in Example 21.38, the employing entity were the parent rather than the subsidiary, it would clearly have to record an expense under FRS 102. It would also have to fund the £6,000 shortfall between the option exercise proceeds of £4,500 and the £10,500 issue proceeds of the shares.

As the EBT is treated as an extension of the parent, the accounting entries for the parent would be the same as those for the group, as set out in 13.5.1 above.

13.5.3   *Employing subsidiary*

The employing subsidiary is required to account for the FRS 102 expense and the contribution to the EBT on exercise of the award. This gives rise to the accounting entries set out below. The entries to reflect the expense are required by FRS 102 (see 13.2.3 above). The treatment of the contribution to the EBT as a distribution is discussed at 13.2.7 above.

y/e 31.12.2015		£	£
y/e 31.12.2015	Profit or loss*	500	
	Equity		500
y/e 31.12.2016	Profit or loss*	1,000	
	Equity		1,000
y/e 31.12.2017	Profit or loss*	1,000	
	Equity		1,000
y/e 31.12.2018	Profit or loss*	500	
	Equity		500
1.9.2020	Equity†	6,000	
	Cash		6,000

* Total cost £3,000 (3000 options × £1) spread over 36 months. Charge for period to December 2015 6/36 × £3,000 = £500, and so on. In practice, where options were granted to a group of individuals, or with variable performance criteria, the annual charge would be based on a continually revised cumulative charge (see further discussion at 7.1 to 7.4 above).

† £3,000 of this payment should be treated as a reduction of whatever component of equity was credited with the £3,000 quasi-contribution from the parent in the accounting entries above. The remaining £3,000 would be treated as a distribution and deducted from any appropriate component of equity.

13.6 Illustrative example – cash-settled transaction not settled by the entity receiving goods or services

The discussion in 13.6.1 to 13.6.3 below is based on Example 21.39.

Example 21.39: Cash-settled scheme not settled by receiving entity

On 1 July 2015 an employee of S Limited, a subsidiary of the H plc group, is awarded a right, exercisable between 1 July 2020 and 1 July 2021, to receive cash equivalent to the value of 3,000 shares in H plc at the date on which the right is exercised. Exercise of the right is subject to a service condition and certain performance criteria being met in the three years ending 30 June 2018. The cash will be paid to the employee not by S, but by H. Throughout the vesting period of the award, H and S take the view that it will vest in full.

The award does in fact vest, and the right is exercised on 1 September 2020.

The fair value of the award (per share-equivalent) at various relevant dates is as follows:

Date	Fair value
	£
1.7.2015	1.50
31.12.2015	1.80
31.12.2016	2.70
31.12.2017	2.40
31.12.2018	2.90
31.12.2019	3.30
1.9.2020	3.50

If the award had been equity-settled (i.e. the employee had instead been granted a right to 3,000 free shares), the grant date fair value of the award would have been £1.50 per share.

H plc and its subsidiaries have a 31 December year end.

13.6.1   Consolidated financial statements

The group has entered into a cash-settled transaction which is accounted for using the methodology discussed at 10.3 above. This gives rise to the following accounting entries:

		£	£
y/e 31.12.2015	Profit or loss*	900	
	Liability		900
y/e 31.12.2016	Profit or loss*	3,150	
	Liability		3,150
y/e 31.12.2017	Profit or loss*	1,950	
	Liability		1,950
y/e 31.12.2018	Profit or loss*	2,700	
	Liability		2,700
y/e 31.12.2019	Profit or loss*	1,200	
	Liability		1,200
y/e 31.12.2020	Profit or loss*	600	
	Liability		600
1.9.2020	Liability	10,500	
	Cash		10,500

*   Charge for period to 31 December 2015 is 6/36 × 3000 × £1.80 [reporting date fair value] = £900. Charge for year ended 31 December 2016 is 18/36 × 3000 × £2.70 = £4,050 less £900 charged in 2015 = £3,150 and so on (refer to Example 21.32 at 10.3.2 above). In practice, where options were granted to a group of individuals, or with variable performance criteria, the annual charge would be based on a continually revised cumulative charge (see further discussion at 10 above).

13.6.2   Parent company

The parent accounts for the share-based payment transaction under FRS 102 as a cash-settled transaction, since the parent settles the award by delivering cash to the employees of the subsidiary (see 13.2.4 above). However, as discussed at 13.2.4 above, instead of recording a cost, as in its consolidated financial statements, the parent records an increase in the carrying value of its subsidiary. It might then be necessary to consider whether the ever-increasing investment in subsidiary is supportable or is in fact impaired. As this is a matter to be determined in the light of specific facts and circumstances, it is not considered in this example.

This would result in the following accounting entries:

		£	£
y/e 31.12.2015	Investment in subsidiary*	900	
	Liability		900
y/e 31.12.2016	Investment in subsidiary*	3,150	
	Liability		3,150
y/e 31.12.2017	Investment in subsidiary*	1,950	
	Liability		1,950
y/e 31.12.2018	Investment in subsidiary*	2,700	
	Liability		2,700
y/e 31.12.2019	Investment in subsidiary*	1,200	
	Liability		1,200

		£	£
y/e 31.12.2020	Investment in subsidiary*	600	
	Liability		600
1.9.2020	Liability	10,500	
	Cash		10,500

* Increase in investment to 31 December 2015 is $6/36 \times 3000 \times £1.80$ [reporting date fair value] $= £900$. Increase for year ended 31 December 2016 is $18/36 \times 3000 \times £2.70 = £4,050$ less $£900$ charged in 2015 $= £3,150$ and so on (refer to Example 21.32 at 10.3.2 above). In practice, where options were granted to a group of individuals, or with variable performance criteria, the annual charge would be based on a continually revised cumulative charge (see further discussion at 10 above).

Where the parent entity was also the employing entity (and therefore receiving goods or services), it would apply the same accounting treatment in its separate financial statements as in its consolidated financial statements (see 13.6.1 above).

13.6.3 Employing subsidiary

The employing subsidiary accounts for the transaction as equity-settled, since it receives services, but incurs no obligation to its employees (see 13.2.3 and 13.2.6 above). This gives rise to the following accounting entries:

		£	£
y/e 31.12.2015	Profit or loss*	750	
	Equity		750
y/e 31.12.2016	Profit or loss*	1,500	
	Equity		1,500
y/e 31.12.2017	Profit or loss*	1,500	
	Equity		1,500
y/e 31.12.2018	Profit or loss*	750	
	Equity		750

* Charge for period to 31 December 2015 is $6/36 \times 3000 \times £1.50$ [grant date fair value] $= £750$, and so on. In practice, where options were granted to a group of individuals, or with variable performance criteria, the annual charge would be based on a continually revised cumulative charge (see further discussion at 7.1 to 7.4 above).

The effect of this treatment is that, while the group ultimately records a cost of £10,500, the subsidiary records a cost of only £4,500.

However, there may be cases where the subsidiary records a higher cost than the group. This would happen if, for example:

- the award vests, but the share price has fallen since grant date, so that the value of the award at vesting (as reflected in the consolidated financial statements) is lower than the value at grant (as reflected in the subsidiary's financial statements); or

- the award does not actually vest because of a failure to meet a market condition and/or a non-vesting condition (so that the cost is nil in the consolidated financial statements) but is treated by FRS 102 as vesting in the subsidiary's financial statements, because it is accounted for as equity-settled (see 7.3 and 7.4 above).

13.7   Employee transferring between group entities

It is not uncommon for an employee to be granted an equity-settled share-based payment award while in the employment of one subsidiary in the group, to transfer to another subsidiary in the group before the award is vested, but with the entitlement to the award remaining unchanged.

Section 26 does not specifically address the accounting in such cases. For entities applying the special rules for group plans in paragraph 16 of Section 26, that paragraph appears to support an appropriate allocation of any Section 26 expense between the employing entities (see 13.2.3.A above). In other cases, we suggest that group entities adopt an approach based on that in IFRS 2. Under IFRS 2, each subsidiary measures the services received from the employee by reference to the fair value of the equity instruments at the date those rights to equity instruments were originally granted, and the proportion of the vesting period served by the employee with each subsidiary. *[IFRS 2.B59]*. In other words, for an award with a three-year vesting period granted to an employee of subsidiary A, who transfers to subsidiary B at the end of year 2, subsidiary A will (cumulatively) record an expense of 2/3, and subsidiary B 1/3, of the fair value at grant date. However, any subsidiary required to account for the transaction as cash-settled in accordance with the general principles discussed at 13.2 above accounts for its portion of the grant date fair value and also for any changes in the fair value of the award during the period of employment with that subsidiary. *[IFRS 2.B60]*.

After transferring between group entities, an employee may fail to satisfy the vesting conditions, for example by leaving the employment of the group. In this situation each subsidiary adjusts the amount previously recognised in respect of the services received from the employee in accordance with the general principles of FRS 102 and IFRS 2 (see 7.1 to 7.4 above). *[IFRS 2.B61]*.

14   DISCLOSURES

The disclosure requirements of Section 26 fall into three main categories:

- the nature and extent of share-based payment arrangements (see 14.1 below);
- the measurement of share-based payment arrangements (see 14.2 below); and
- the effect on the financial statements of share-based payment transactions (see 14.3 below).

The requirements apply to all entities applying FRS 102 although a 'qualifying entity', as defined in Section 1 – *Scope* of FRS 102, may take advantage in its individual financial statements of an exemption from the requirements of paragraphs 18(b), 19 and 21 to 23 of Section 26 provided the following criteria are met:

- if the qualifying entity is a subsidiary, the share-based payment arrangement concerns equity instruments of another group entity;
- if the qualifying entity is an ultimate parent, the share-based payment arrangement relates to its own equity instruments and its separate financial statements are presented alongside the consolidated financial statements of the group;

and, in both cases:

- provided that the equivalent disclosures required by FRS 102 are included in the consolidated financial statements of the group in which the entity is consolidated. *[FRS 102.1.8-12].*

14.1 Nature and extent of share-based payment arrangements

IFRS 2 contains a general requirement that an entity should 'disclose information that enables users of the financial statements to understand the nature and extent of share-based payment arrangements that existed during the period' *[IFRS 2.44]* and then lists the minimum disclosures required to meet the overall requirement.

FRS 102 does not include the overall requirement from IFRS 2 but picks up some of the detailed disclosures and requires an entity to 'disclose the following information about the nature and extent of share-based payment arrangements that existed during the period:

(a) A description of each type of share-based payment arrangement that existed at any time during the period, including the general terms and conditions of each arrangement, such as vesting requirements, the maximum term of options granted, and the method of settlement (e.g. whether in cash or equity). An entity with substantially similar types of share-based payment arrangements may aggregate this information.

(b) The number and weighted average exercise prices of share options for each of the following groups of options:

    (i)   outstanding at the beginning of the period;

    (ii) granted during the period;

    (iii) forfeited during the period;

    (iv) exercised during the period;

    (v) expired during the period;

    (vi) outstanding at the end of the period; and

    (vii) exercisable at the end of the period.' *[FRS 102.26.18].*

The reconciliation in (b) above should, in our view, reflect all changes in the number of equity instruments outstanding. Therefore, in addition to awards with a grant date during the period, the reconciliation should include subsequent additions to earlier grants, e.g. options or shares added to the award in recognition of dividends declared during the period (where this is part of the original terms of the award), and changes to the number of equity instruments as a result of share splits or consolidations and other similar changes.

As drafted, the requirements in (b) above appear to apply only to share options. However, since there is little distinction between the treatment of an option with a zero exercise price and the award of a free share, in our view the disclosures should not be restricted to awards of options.

14.2   Measurement of share-based payment arrangements

IFRS 2 contains a general requirement that an entity should 'disclose information that enables users of the financial statements to understand how the fair value of the goods or services received, or the fair value of the equity instruments granted, during the period was determined' *[IFRS 2.46]* and then lists the minimum disclosures required to meet the overall requirement.

FRS 102 contains its own general disclosure requirements for equity-settled, cash-settled, modified and group share-based payment arrangements but does not mandate the disclosure of specific details other than as set out at 14.2.1 to 14.2.4 below.

14.2.1   *Equity-settled arrangements*

For equity-settled share-based payment arrangements, FRS 102 requires an entity to 'disclose information about how it measured the fair value of goods or services received or the value of the equity instruments granted. If a valuation methodology was used, the entity shall disclose the method and the reason for choosing it'. *[FRS 102.26.19].*

Unlike IFRS 2, FRS 102 has no specific requirement to disclose the inputs to an option pricing model and other assumptions made in the determination of fair value.

The requirement in FRS 102 to disclose the reason for choosing the valuation methodology used is not found in IFRS 2 but is consistent with the fact that FRS 102 allows directors to select an appropriate method of valuation rather than requiring the use of an option-pricing model (as is the case in IFRS 2 when market price information is not available).

14.2.2   *Cash-settled arrangements*

FRS 102 includes a requirement to disclose information about how the liability for a cash-settled arrangement was measured but does not expand on this general requirement. *[FRS 102.26.20].* There is no direct correlation between this requirement and the disclosure requirements of IFRS 2 as the latter do not specifically address the measurement of cash-settled arrangements. The FRS 102 requirement is therefore potentially more onerous.

14.2.3   *Modification of share-based payment arrangements*

Where share-based payment arrangements have been modified during the accounting period, FRS 102 requires an explanation of those modifications *[FRS 102.26.21]* although, unlike IFRS 2, there is no specific requirement to disclose the incremental fair value or information about how that incremental value was measured.

14.2.4   *Group share-based payment arrangements*

If the reporting entity is part of a group share-based payment arrangement and it recognises and measures its share-based payment expense on the basis of a reasonable allocation of the expense recognised for the group (in accordance with paragraph 16 of Section 26 – see 13.2.3.A above), then disclosure is required of that fact and of the basis for the allocation. *[FRS 102.26.22].*

14.3 Effect of share-based payment transactions on financial statements

IFRS 2 contains a general requirement that an entity should 'disclose information that enables users of the financial statements to understand the effect of share-based payment transactions on the entity's profit or loss for the period and on its financial position' *[IFRS 2.50]* and then lists the minimum disclosures required to meet the overall requirement.

FRS 102 does not include such a general requirement but picks up some of the detailed disclosures and requires an entity to 'disclose the following information about the effect of share-based payment transactions on the entity's profit or loss for the period and on its financial position:

(a) the total expense recognised in profit or loss for the period.

(b) the total carrying amount at the end of the period for liabilities arising from share-based payment transactions'. *[FRS 102.26.23].*

15 TAXES RELATED TO SHARE-BASED PAYMENT TRANSACTIONS

15.1 Income tax deductions for the entity

The particular issues raised by the accounting treatment for income taxes on share-based payment transactions are discussed in Chapter 24 at 7.7.

15.2 Employment taxes of the employer

An employing entity is required to pay National Insurance on share options and other share-based payment transactions with employees, just as if the employees had received cash remuneration. This raises the question of how such taxes should be accounted for as FRS 102 contains no specific guidance in this area.

The previous version of UK GAAP included UITF Abstract 25: *National Insurance contributions on share option gains* and, in our view, entities should continue to apply this interpretation in the absence of more specific guidance. UITF 25 required a provision to be made for National Insurance ('NI') contributions on outstanding share options (and similar awards) that are expected to be exercised. Under UITF 25, the provision should be:

- calculated at the latest enacted NI rate applied to the difference between the market value of the underlying shares at the reporting date and the option exercise price;

- allocated over the period from grant date to the end of the vesting period, after which it should be updated using the current market value of the shares; and

- expensed through profit or loss unless the options form part of capitalised staff costs.

In some situations the entity may require employees to reimburse the amount of NI paid. In line with the requirements of UITF 25, this should be treated in accordance with the general rules in Section 21 – *Provisions and Contingencies* of FRS 102 for the reimbursement of the expenditure required to settle a provision.

15.3   Sale of shares by employee to meet employee's tax liability ('sell to cover')

An award of shares or options to an employee generally gives rise to a personal tax liability for the employee, often related to the fair value of the award when it vests or, in the case of an option, is exercised. In order to meet this tax liability, employees may wish to sell as many shares as are needed to raise proceeds equal to the tax liability (sometimes described as 'sell to cover').

This *in itself* does not, in our view, require the scheme to be considered as cash-settled, any more than if the employee wished to liquidate the shares in order to buy a car or undertake home improvements. However, if the manner in which the cash is passed to the employee gives rise to a legal or constructive obligation for the employer, then the scheme might well be cash-settled (see 10.2 above), to the extent of any such obligation.

Where employees must pay income tax on share awards, the tax is initially collected from the employer, but with eventual recourse by the tax authorities to the employee for tax not collected from the employer. Such tax collection arrangements mean that even an equity-settled award results in a cash cost for the employer for the income tax.

In such a situation, the employer may require the employee, as a condition of taking delivery of any shares earned, to indemnify the entity against the tax liability, for example by:

- direct payment to the entity;
- authorising the entity to deduct the relevant amount from the employee's salary; or
- surrendering as many shares to the entity as have a fair value equal to the tax liability.

If the entity requires the employee to surrender the relevant number of shares, in our view the scheme must be treated as cash-settled to the extent of the indemnified amount, as explained in Example 21.40 below.

Example 21.40:   Surrendering of vested shares by employee to indemnify liability of entity to pay employee's tax liability

An individual has a personal tax rate of 40% and free shares are taxed at their fair value on vesting. The individual is granted an award of 100 free shares with a grant date fair value of £3 each. The fair value at vesting date is £5, so that the employee's tax liability (required to be discharged in the first instance by the employer via PAYE) is £200 (40% of £500). If the employee were required to surrender the 40 shares needed to settle the tax liability, in our view the substance of the transaction is that, at grant date, the entity is making an award of only 60 shares (with a grant date fair value of £3 each) and is bearing the cost of the employment tax itself. On this analysis, the entity will have recorded the following entries by the end of the vesting period:

	£	£
Employee costs	180	
Equity		180
Employee costs	200	
Employment tax liability		200

The award is then satisfied by the delivery of 60 shares by the entity to the employee. If, however, the employee has a free choice as to how to indemnify the employer, the employer will have recorded the following entries by the end of the vesting period:

	£	£
Employee costs	300	
Equity		300
Receivable from employee	200	
Employment tax liability		200

The award is then satisfied by the delivery of 100 shares to the employee and the employee indicates that he wishes to surrender 40 shares to discharge his obligation to the employer under the indemnity arrangement. The entity therefore receives 40 shares from the employee in settlement of the £200 receivable from him.

In practice, this would almost certainly be effected as a net delivery of 60 shares, but in principle there are two transactions:

- a release of 100 shares to the employee; and
- the re-acquisition of 40 of those shares at £5 each from the employee.

The entity then settles the tax liability:

	£	£
Employment tax liability	200	
Cash		200

Even in this case, however, some might take the view that the substance of the arrangement is that the employee has the right to put 40 shares to the employer, and accordingly 40% of the award should be accounted for as cash-settled, resulting in essentially the same accounting as when the employee is required to surrender 40 shares, as set out above.

16 OTHER PRACTICAL ISSUES

We consider below the application of Section 26 to the following types of arrangement that do not fit easily into any one of the sections above:

- matching share awards (see 16.1 below);
- limited recourse and full recourse loans (see 16.2 below);
- awards entitled to dividends during the vesting period (see 16.3 below); and
- awards vesting or exercisable on a flotation (or change of control, trade sale etc.) (see 16.4 below).

16.1 Matching share awards

As noted in the discussion at 11.1.2 above, in our view the rules in Section 26 for awards where there is a choice of equity- or cash-settlement do not fully address awards where the equity and cash alternatives may have significantly different fair values and vesting periods. A matching share award is an example of the type of scheme giving rise to such issues.

Under a matching share award, the starting point is usually that an employee is awarded a bonus for a one year performance period. At the end of that period, the employee may then be either required or permitted to take all or part of that bonus in shares rather than cash. To the extent that the employee takes shares rather than cash, the employing entity may then be required or permitted to make a 'matching' award of an equal number of shares (or a multiple or fraction of that number). The matching award will typically vest over a longer period.

Whilst such schemes can appear superficially similar, the accounting analysis may vary significantly, according to whether:

- the employee has a choice, or is required, to take some of the 'base' bonus in shares; and/or

- the employer has a choice, or is required, to match any shares taken by the employee.

The detailed accounting for such arrangements is beyond the scope of this publication but is addressed in EY International GAAP 2015. It should be noted that the requirements of FRS 102 and IFRS 2 are not identical for awards where there is a choice of settlement. However, it is expected that most companies with a matching share scheme will be part of a larger group arrangement and will potentially be able to push down an expense based on the group expense in accordance with paragraph 16 of Section 26 of FRS 102 (see 13.2.3.A above).

16.2   Limited recourse and full recourse loans

Share awards to employees are sometimes made by means of so-called 'limited recourse loan' schemes. The detailed terms of such schemes vary, but typical features include the following:

- the entity makes an interest-free loan to the employee which is immediately used to acquire shares to the value of the loan on behalf of the employee;

- the shares may be held by the entity, or a trust controlled by it (see 13.3 above), until the loan is repaid;

- the employee is entitled to dividends, except that these are treated as paying off some of the outstanding loan;

- within a given period (say, five years) the employee must either have paid off the outstanding balance of the loan, at which point the shares are delivered to the employee, or surrendered the shares. Surrender of the shares by the employee is treated as discharging any outstanding amount on the loan, irrespective of the value of the shares.

The effect of such an arrangement is equivalent to an option exercisable within five years with a strike price per share equal to the share price at grant date less total dividends since grant date. There is no real loan at the initial stage. The entity has no right to receive cash or another financial asset, since the loan can be settled by the employee returning the (fixed) amount of equity 'purchased' at grant date.

Indeed, the only true cash flow in the entire transaction is any amount paid at the final stage if the employee chooses to acquire the shares at that point. The fact that the strike price is a factor of the share price at grant date and dividends paid between grant date and the date of repayment of the 'loan' is simply an issue for the valuation of the option.

It is consistent with the general requirements of FRS 102 for the share-based payment expense relating to the option to be recognised in full at grant date as the award is subject to no future service or performance condition (see 7.1 above).

Under more complex arrangements, the loan to the employee to acquire the shares is a full recourse loan (i.e. it cannot be discharged simply by surrendering the shares). However, the amount repayable on the loan is reduced not only by dividends paid on the shares, but also by the achievement of performance targets, such as the achievement of a given level of earnings.

The appropriate analysis of such awards is more difficult, as they could be viewed in two ways. The first is that the employer has made a loan (which the employee has chosen to use to buy a share), accounted for as a financial asset, and has then entered into a performance-related cash bonus arrangement with the employee, accounted for as an employee benefit. The second analysis is that the transaction is a share option where the strike price varies according to the satisfaction of performance conditions and the amount of dividends on the shares, accounted for under Section 26. The different analyses give rise to potentially significantly different expenses. This will particularly be the case where one of the conditions for mitigation of the amount repayable on the loan is linked to the price of the employer's equity. As this is a market condition, the effect of accounting for the arrangement under Section 26 may be that an expense is recognised in circumstances where no expense would be recognised if the arrangement were treated as an employee benefit under Section 28.

Such awards need to be carefully analysed, in the light of their particular facts and circumstances, in order to determine the appropriate treatment. Factors that could suggest that Section 26 is the more relevant would, in our view, include:

- the employee can use the loan only to acquire shares;
- the employee cannot trade the shares until the loan is discharged; or
- the entity has a practice of accepting (e.g. from leavers) surrender of the shares as full discharge for the amount outstanding on the loan and does not pursue any shortfall between the fair value of the shares and the amount owed by the employee. This would tend to indicate that, in substance, the loan is not truly full recourse.

16.3 Awards entitled to dividends during the vesting period

Some awards entitle the holder to receive dividends on unvested shares (or dividend equivalents on options) during the vesting period.

For example, an entity might award shares that are regarded as fully vested for the purposes of tax legislation (typically because the employee enjoys the full voting and dividend rights of the shares), but not for accounting purposes (typically because the shares are subject to forfeiture if a certain minimum service period is not achieved). In practice, the shares concerned are often held by an EBT until the potential forfeiture period has expired.

Another variant of such an award that is sometimes seen is where an entity grants an employee an option to acquire shares in the entity which can be exercised immediately. However, if the employee exercises the option but leaves within a certain minimum period from the grant date, he is required to sell back the share to the entity (typically either at the original exercise price, or the lower of that price or the market value of the share at the time of the buy-back).

Such awards do not fully vest for the purposes of Section 26 until the potential forfeiture or buy-back period has expired. The cost of such awards should therefore be recognised over this period.

This raises the question of the accounting treatment of any dividends paid to employees during the vesting period. Conceptually, it could be argued that such dividends cannot be dividends for financial reporting purposes since the equity instruments to which they relate are not yet regarded as issued for financial reporting purposes. This would lead to the conclusion that dividends paid in the vesting period should be charged to profit or loss as an employment cost.

However, the charge to be made for the award under Section 26 will already have been increased to take account of the fact that the recipient is entitled to receive dividends during the vesting period. Thus, it could be argued that also to charge profit or loss with the dividends paid is a form of double counting. Moreover, whilst the relevant shares may not have been fully issued for financial reporting purposes, the basic Section 26 accounting does build up an amount in equity over the vesting period. It could therefore be argued that – conceptually, if not legally – any dividend paid relates not to an issued share, but rather to the equity instrument represented by the cumulative amount that has been recorded for the award as a credit to equity, and can therefore appropriately be shown as a deduction from equity.

However, this argument is valid only to the extent that the credit to equity represents awards that are expected to vest. It cannot apply to dividends paid to employees whose awards are either known not to have vested or treated as expected not to vest when applying Section 26 (since there is no credit to equity for these awards). Accordingly, we believe that the most appropriate approach is to analyse the dividends paid so that, by the date of vesting, cumulative dividends paid on awards treated by Section 26 as vested are deducted from equity and those paid on awards treated by Section 26 as unvested are charged to profit or loss. The allocation for periods before that in which vesting occurs should be based on a best estimate of the final outcome, as illustrated by Example 21.41 below.

Example 21.41:   Award with rights to receive (and retain) dividends during vesting period

An entity grants 100 free shares to each of its 500 employees. The shares are treated as fully vested for legal and tax purposes, so that the employees are eligible to receive any dividends paid. However, the shares will be forfeited if the employee leaves within three years of the award being made. Accordingly, for the purposes of Section 26, vesting is conditional upon the employee working for the entity over the next three years. The entity estimates that the fair value of each share (including the right to receive dividends during the Section 26 vesting period) is £15. Employees are entitled to retain any dividend received even if the award does not vest.

20 employees leave during the first year, and the entity's best estimate at the end of year 1 is that 75 employees will have left before the end of the vesting period. During the second year, a further 22 employees leave, and the entity revises its estimate of total employee departures over the vesting period from 75 to 60. During the third year, a further 15 employees leave. Hence, a total of 57

employees (20 + 22 + 15) forfeit their rights to the shares during the three year period, and a total of 44,300 shares (443 employees × 100 shares per employee) finally vest.

The entity pays dividends of £1 per share in year 1, £1.20 per share in year 2, and £1.50 in year 3.

Under FRS 102, the entity will recognise the following amounts during the vesting period for services received as consideration for the shares.

Year	Calculation of cumulative expense	Cumulative expense (£)	Expense for period (£)
1	100 shares × 425 employees × £15 × 1/3	212,500	212,500
2	100 shares × 440 employees × £15 × 2/3	440,000	227,500
3	100 shares × 443 × £15 × 3/3	664,500	224,500

On the assumption that all employees who leave during a period do so on the last day of that period (and thus receive dividends paid in that period), in our view the dividends paid on the shares should be accounted for as follows:

		£	£
Year 1	Profit or loss (employee costs)[1]	7,500	
	Equity[1]	42,500	
	Cash[2]		50,000
Year 2	Profit or loss (employee costs)[3]	3,300	
	Equity[3]	54,300	
	Cash[4]		57,600
Year 3	Profit or loss (employee costs)[5]	1,590	
	Equity[5]	67,110	
	Cash[6]		68,700

1 20 employees have left and a further 55 are anticipated to leave. Dividends paid to those employees (100 shares × 75 employees × £1 = £7,500) are therefore recognised as an expense. Dividends paid to other employees are recognised as a reduction in equity.

2 100 shares × 500 employees × £1.

3 22 further employees have left and a further 18 are anticipated to leave. The cumulative expense for dividends paid to leavers and anticipated leavers should therefore be £10,800 (100 shares × 20 employees × £1 = £2,000 for leavers in year 1 + 100 shares × 40 employees × [£1 + £1.20] for leavers and anticipated leavers in year 2 = £8,800). £7,500 was charged in year 1, so the charge for year 2 should be £10,800 − £7,500 = £3,300. This could also have been calculated as charge for leavers and expected leavers in current year £4,800 (100 shares × 40 [22 + 18] employees × £1.20) less reversal of expense in year 1 for reduction in anticipated final number of leavers £1,500 (100 shares × 15 [75 − 60] employees × £1.00). Dividends paid to other employees are recognised as a reduction in equity.

4 100 shares × 480 employees in employment at start of year × £1.20.

5 15 further employees have left. The cumulative expense for dividends paid to leavers should therefore be £12,390 (£2,000 for leavers in year 1 (see 4 above) + 100 shares × 22 employees × [£1 + £1.20] = £4,840 for leavers in year 2 + 100 shares × 15 employees × [£1 + £1.20 + £1.50] = £5,550 for leavers in year 3). A cumulative expense of £10,800 (see 4 above) was recognised by the end of year 2, so the charge for year 3 should be £12,390 − £10,800 = £1,590. This could also have been calculated as charge for leavers in current year £2,250 (100 shares × 15 employees × £1.50) less reversal of expense in years 1 and 2 for reduction in final number of leavers as against estimate at end of year 2 £660 (100 shares × 3 [60 − 57] employees × [£1.00 + £1.20]). Dividends paid to other employees are recognised as a reduction in equity.

6 100 shares × 458 employees in employment at start of year × £1.50.

Chapter 21

16.4   Awards vesting or exercisable on flotation (or change of control, trade sale etc.)

Entities frequently issue awards connected to a significant event such as a flotation, change of control or a trade sale of the business. It may be the case, as discussed at 11.2 above, that an award that would normally be only equity-settled becomes cash-settled on such an event.

However, it may also be the case that an award vests only on such an event, which raises various issues of interpretation, as discussed below.

The sections below should be read together with the more general discussions elsewhere in this Chapter on grant date, vesting period and vesting and non-vesting conditions and referred to in the narrative below. References to flotation should be read as also including other exit events.

16.4.1   Grant date

Sometimes awards are structured so that they will vest on flotation, or so that they will vest on flotation subject to further approval at that time. For awards in the first category, grant date as defined in FRS 102 will be the date on which the award is first communicated to employees. For awards in the second category, grant date will be at or around the date of flotation, when the required further approval is given.

This means that the cost of awards subject to final approval at flotation will generally be significantly higher than that of awards that do not require such approval. Moreover, as discussed further at 6.3 above, it may well be the case that employees begin rendering service for such awards before grant date (e.g. from the date on which the entity communicates its intention to make the award in principle). In that case, the entity would need to consider making an initial estimate of the value of the award for the purpose of recognising an expense from the date services have been provided, and continually re-assessing that value up until the actual grant date. As with any award dependent on a non-market vesting condition (see 16.4.3 below for further discussion on this classification), an expense would be recognised only to the extent that the award is considered likely to vest.

16.4.2   Vesting period

Many awards that vest on flotation have a time limit – in other words, the award lapses if flotation (or another similar event) has not occurred on or before a given future date. In principle, as discussed at 7.2.3 above, when an award has a variable vesting period due to a non-market performance condition, the reporting entity should make a best estimate of the likely vesting period at each reporting date and calculate the Section 26 charge on the basis of that best estimate.

In practice, the likely timing of a future flotation is notoriously difficult to assess months, let alone years, in advance. In such cases, it would generally be acceptable simply to recognise the cost over the full potential vesting period until there is real clarity that a shorter period may be more appropriate. However, in making the assessment of the likelihood of vesting, it is important to take the company's circumstances into account. The likelihood of an exit event in the short- to medium-term is perhaps greater for a company owned by private equity investors seeking a return on their investment than for a long-established family-owned company considering a flotation.

It is worth noting that once an exit event becomes likely, the Section 26 expense will in some cases need to be recognised over a shorter vesting period than was originally envisaged as the probability of the exit event occurring will form the basis at the reporting date of the estimate of the number of awards expected to vest (see also the discussion at 8.6 above).

16.4.3   *Is flotation or sale a vesting condition or a non-vesting condition?*

There was debate in the past about whether a requirement for a flotation or sale to occur in order for an award to vest was a vesting condition or a non-vesting condition. The argument for it being a non-vesting condition was that flotation or sale may occur irrespective of the performance of the entity. The counter-argument was essentially that the price achieved on flotation or sale, which typically affects the ultimate value of the award (see 16.4.4 below), reflects the performance of the entity and is therefore a non-market performance condition (provided there is an associated service condition).

On the basis of discussions on the interpretation of IFRS 2 by the IASB and the IFRS Interpretations Committee, it appears appropriate to treat a requirement to float or be sold as a performance vesting condition rather than as a non-vesting condition, provided there is also a service condition for the duration of the performance condition (see 4.2 above). If the service period is not at least as long as the duration of the flotation or sale condition, the condition will need to be accounted for as a non-vesting condition.

16.4.4   *Awards requiring achievement of a minimum price on flotation or sale*

Some awards contingent on flotation (or another similar event) vest only if a minimum price per share is achieved. For example, an entity might grant all its employees share options, the vesting of which is contingent upon a flotation or sale of the shares at a price of at least £5 per share within five years, and the employee still being in employment at the time of the flotation or sale.

Assuming that the requirement for a flotation or sale to occur is treated as a vesting condition (see 16.4.3 above), the question arises as to whether, in addition to the service requirement, such an award comprises:

- a single market performance condition (i.e. float or sell within five years at a share price of at least £5); or
- two conditions:
    - a market performance condition (share price at time of flotation or sale at least £5); and
    - a non-market performance conditions (flotation or sale achieved within five years).

The significance of this is the issue discussed at 7.3 above, namely that an expense must always be recognised for all awards with a market condition, if *all* the non-market vesting conditions are satisfied, even if the market condition is not. In either case, however, there is a market condition which needs to be factored into the valuation of the award.

If the view is that 'flotation or sale at £5 within five years' is a single condition, the entity will recognise an expense for the award for all employees still in service at the end of the five year period, since the sole non-market vesting condition (i.e. service) will have been met. Note that this assumes that the full five-year period is considered the most likely vesting period at grant date (see 16.4.2 above).

If, on the other hand, the view is that 'flotation or sale within five years' and 'flotation or sale share price £5' are two separate conditions, and no flotation or sale occurs, no expense will be recognised since the performance element of the non-market vesting condition (i.e. 'flotation or sale within five years') has not been satisfied. However, even on this second analysis, if a sale or flotation is achieved at a price less than £5, an expense must be recognised, even though the award does not truly vest, since the non-market condition (i.e. 'flotation or sale within five years' with its associated service requirement) will have been met.

In our view, the appropriate analysis is to regard 'flotation or sale within five years' and 'flotation/sale share price £5' as two separate conditions.

The example above assumes that there is a service condition equal in duration to the other condition attached to the award and hence the analysis above only considers vesting conditions. If the fact pattern were such that there was no service condition, or a service condition that was of a shorter duration than the other conditions, then those conditions would need to be treated as non-vesting conditions rather than as performance vesting conditions.

16.4.5 Awards 'purchased for fair value'

As noted at 3.4.3 above, entities that are contemplating a flotation or trade sale may invite employees to subscribe for shares (often a special class of share) for a relatively nominal amount. In the event of a flotation or trade sale occurring, these shares may be sold or will be redeemable at a substantial premium. It is often argued that the initial subscription price paid represents the fair value of the share at the time, given the inherent high uncertainty as to whether a flotation or trade sale will in fact occur.

The premium paid on a flotation or trade sale will typically be calculated in part by reference to the price achieved. The question therefore arises as to whether such awards fall within the scope of Section 26. It might be argued for example that, as the employee paid full fair value for the award at issue, there has been no share-based payment and, accordingly, the award is not within the scope of Section 26.

In our view, in order to determine whether the arrangement falls within the scope of FRS 26 – *(IAS 39) Financial Instruments: recognition and measurement*, it is necessary to consider whether the award has features that would not be expected in 'normal' equity – specifically a requirement for the holder of the shares to remain in employment until flotation or sale. If this is the case, regardless of the amount subscribed, the terms suggest that the shares are being awarded in return for employee services and hence that the award is within the scope of Section 26. This may mean that, even if the award has no material fair value once the subscription price has been taken into account (and therefore gives rise to no FRS 102 expense), it may be necessary to make the disclosures required by Section 26.

Moreover, even if the amount paid by the employees can be demonstrated to be fair value for tax or other purposes, that amount would not necessarily meet the valuation requirements of Section 26. Specifically, a 'true' fair value would take into account non-market vesting conditions (such as a requirement for the employee to remain in employment until flotation or a trade sale occurs). However, a valuation for Section 26 purposes would not take such conditions into account (see 6.5 and 7.2.1 above) and would therefore typically be higher than the 'true' fair value.

A special class of share such as that described above might well be classified as a liability rather than as equity. However, if the redemption amount is linked to the flotation price of the 'real' equity, the arrangement will be a cash-settled share-based payment transaction under Section 26 (see 3.4.1 above).

It is common in such situations for the cost of satisfying any obligations to the special shareholders to be borne by shareholders rather than by the entity itself. This raises a number of further issues, which are discussed at 3.2.1 above and 16.4.6 below.

16.4.6   'Drag along' and 'tag along' rights

An increasingly common form of award is for the management of an entity to be allowed to acquire a special class of equity at fair value (as in 16.4.5 above), but (in contrast to 16.4.5 above) with no redemption right on an exit event. However, rights are given:

- to any buyer of the 'normal' equity also to buy the special shares (sometimes called a 'drag along' right);

- to a holder of the special shares to require any buyer of the 'normal' equity also to buy the special shares (sometimes called a 'tag along' right).

Such schemes are particularly found in entities where the 'normal' equity is held by a provider of venture capital, which will generally be looking for an exit in the medium term.

It may well be that, under the scheme, the entity itself is required to facilitate the operation of the drag along or tag along rights, which may involve the entity collecting the proceeds from the buyer and passing them on to the holder of the special shares.

This raises the issue of whether such an arrangement is equity-settled or cash-settled. The fact that, in certain circumstances, the entity is required to deliver cash to the holder of a share suggests that the arrangement is an award requiring cash settlement in specific circumstances, the treatment of which is discussed at 11.2 above.

However, if the terms of the award are such that the entity is obliged to pass on cash to the holder of the share only if, and to the extent that, proceeds are received from an external buyer, in our view the arrangement may be economically no different to the so-called 'broker settlement' arrangements typically entered into by listed entities.

Under such broker settlement arrangements, the entity may either sell employees' shares in the market on the employees' behalf or, more likely, arrange for a third party broker to do so. A sale of shares on behalf of an employee is undertaken by the entity as agent and does not give rise to an increase in equity and an expense, although a share-based payment expense will be recognised for the award of shares. Such an arrangement does not of itself create a cash-settled award, provided that the entity has not created any obligation to the employees. If, however, the entity has either created an expectation among employees that it will step in to make good any lack of depth in the market, or has indeed itself contracted to repurchase the shares in question, that may well mean that analysis as a cash-settled scheme is more appropriate. However, as the entity may enter into much the same transaction with a broker whether it is selling shares on its own behalf or on behalf of its employees the challenge is for the entity to be able to demonstrate the true economic nature of the transaction.

Following on from the approach to broker settlement arrangements outlined above, an arrangement where the employees' shares are being sold to an external buyer could be regarded as equity-settled because the entity's only involvement as a principal is in the initial delivery of shares to employees. However, consideration must be given to all the factors that could suggest that the scheme is more appropriately regarded as cash-settled.

In making such an assessment, care needs to be taken to ensure that the precise facts of an arrangement are considered. For example, a transaction where the entity has some discretion over the amount of proceeds attributable to each class of shareholder might indicate that it is inappropriate to treat the entity simply as an agent in the cash payment arrangement. It might also be relevant to consider the extent to which, under relevant local law, the proceeds received can be 'ring fenced' so as not to be available to settle other liabilities of the entity.

It is also the case that arrangements that result in employees obtaining similar amounts of cash can be interpreted very differently under Section 26 depending on how the arrangement is structured and whether, for example:

- the entity is required to pay its employees cash on an exit (having perhaps held shares itself via a trust and those shares having been subject to 'drag along' rights); or

- the employees themselves have held the right to equity shares on a restricted basis with vesting – and 'drag along' rights – taking effect on a change of control and the employees receiving cash for their shares.

The appropriate accounting treatment in such cases requires a significant amount of judgement based on the precise facts and circumstances.

17　FIRST-TIME ADOPTION AND TRANSITIONAL PROVISIONS

17.1　Transitional provisions on first-time adoption of FRS 102

Section 35 sets out the transitional provisions for first-time adoption of FRS 102. Issues arising from the specific requirements of Section 35 in relation to share-based payment transactions are discussed below.

Subject to the special provisions outlined below, a first-time adopter is not required to apply Section 26:

- to equity instruments that were granted before the date of transition to FRS 102; or

- to liabilities arising from share-based payment transactions that were settled before the date of transition to FRS 102. *[FRS 102.35.10(b)].*

There are special provisions for first-time adopters of FRS 102 that have previously applied FRS 20 or IFRS 2 to grants of equity instruments. For equity instruments granted before the date of transition to FRS 102, such entities should 'apply either FRS 20 / IFRS 2 (as applicable) or Section 26 of this FRS at the date of transition'. Therefore, unlike the full exemption from accounting for pre-transition grants given to those first-time adopters that have not previously accounted for share-based payments, those who have previously applied FRS 20 or IFRS 2 are required to continue accounting for ongoing awards either under the previous standard or under Section 26 of FRS 102. *[FRS 102.35.10(b)]*. In our view, the intention is simply that an entity may complete the accounting for a pre-transition grant using the original grant date fair value and it is not intended that the application of Section 26 of FRS 102 to such grants should necessarily result in a remeasurement. However, there is nothing in paragraph 10(b) of Section 35 to prohibit such a remeasurement (for example, as a result of applying the group allocation arrangements of paragraph 16 of Section 26).

As noted in 11 above, the classification of a share-based payment transaction as equity-settled or cash-settled might differ depending on whether an entity is applying FRS 102 or IFRS 2 (FRS 20). Under the requirements of Section 35, it appears that an entity could continue with the IFRS 2 (FRS 20) classification previously adopted, even if new grants would be classified differently under FRS 102.

There is also a lack of clarity in relation to other aspects of the requirements for those entities with share-based payments to which FRS 20 or IFRS 2 has previously been applied but where the accounting treatment of such arrangements differs, or could differ, under Section 26. For example, it is unclear whether a company which has recognised an expense for a transaction for which no apparent consideration has been received has a choice as to whether it carries on doing so (given that there is no general equivalent of paragraph 13A of IFRS 2/FRS 20 (see 3.2.3 above)).

17.2 Modification of awards following transition

Section 35 does not address the treatment of equity-settled awards granted before the date of transition but modified at a later date. Therefore a first-time adopter (other than one who has previously applied FRS 20 or IFRS 2) could potentially avoid a charge for a new award by modifying (or cancelling or settling) an out of scope old award instead. However, in practice, the potential to do this is likely to be limited to those entities previously applying the FRSSE which, in most cases, are unlikely to have had extensive equity-settled share-based payment arrangements in place prior to transition to FRS 102.

18　SUMMARY OF GAAP DIFFERENCES

	FRS 102	FRS 20 (previous UK GAAP) / IFRS 2
Scope: Definitions and transactions within scope (see 2.1 above)	FRS 102 does not provide guidance or examples in areas such as: 1.　the meaning of 'goods' in 'goods and services' when used in the definition of a share-based payment transaction; 2.　vested transactions; 3.　transactions with shareholders as a whole; 4.　business combinations; or 5.　interaction with accounting for financial instruments.	IFRS 2 and FRS 20 have specific guidance or examples in these areas.
Recognition: Accounting after the vesting date (see 2.2.1 above)	FRS 102 includes no guidance on accounting for awards after vesting.	IFRS 2 and FRS 20 specifically prohibit a reversal of the expense once awards have vested.
Measurement of equity-settled transactions: Vesting conditions and non-vesting conditions (see 2.3.1 above)	FRS 102 does not include a definition of 'vesting conditions'. It is assumed that this is a drafting error and that it is intended that the definition be the same as that in IFRS 2. FRS 102 contains no definition of, or guidance on, non-vesting conditions.	'Vesting conditions' are defined in IFRS 2 and FRS 20. IFRS 2 and FRS 20 do not include a definition of a 'non-vesting condition' but include examples of such conditions as part of the Implementation Guidance.
Treatment of service and non-market performance conditions in measurement of fair value (see 2.3.2 above)	FRS 102 does not make it explicitly clear that service and non-market performance conditions should not be incorporated into the determination of fair value but should be taken into accounting in estimating the number of awards expected to vest. This treatment may be inferred from FRS 102.	IFRS 2 and FRS 20 have explicit requirements in this area.
Employees and others providing similar services (see 2.3.3 above)	FRS 102 offers no additional guidance on the meaning of 'others providing similar services'.	This term is explained/defined in Appendix A to IFRS 2 and FRS 20.

Valuation methodology (see 2.3.4 above)	FRS 102 draws a more explicit distinction than IFRS 2 between the valuation of shares and the valuation of options and appreciation rights. It does not mandate use of an option pricing model in the absence of market price information.	IFRS 2 and FRS 20 require the use of a market price or an option pricing model for the valuation of equity-settled transactions. The standards include guidance in Appendix B about the selection and application of option pricing models that is not reproduced in FRS 102.
Cancellation of awards (see 2.3.6 above)	FRS 102 contains no specific requirements to mirror those in IFRS 2.	IFRS 2 and FRS 20 make clear that an award may be cancelled either by the entity or the counterparty and also that a failure to meet non-vesting conditions should, in certain situations, be considered cancellation of an award.
Settlement of awards (see 2.3.7 above)	FRS 102 states that settlement of an unvested award should be treated as an acceleration of vesting but does not specify the treatment when the settlement value exceeds the fair value of the award being cancelled. Similarly, there is no specific guidance on the repurchase of vested equity instruments.	Under IFRS 2 and FRS 20, any incremental fair value is expensed at the date of settlement but any settlement value up to the fair value of the cancelled award is debited to equity. When vested equity instruments are repurchased, IFRS 2 and FRS 20 require any incremental fair value to be expensed at the date of repurchase.
Replacement awards following a cancellation or settlement (see 2.3.8 above)	FRS 102 includes no guidance on the accounting treatment of equity-settled awards to replace a cancelled award.	Under IFRS 2 and FRS 20 replacement awards may be accounted for on the basis of their incremental fair value rather than being treated as a completely new award.
Share-based payment transactions with cash alternatives: Entity or counterparty has choice of settlement in equity or cash (see 2.5.1 above)	FRS 102 has a presumption of cash-settlement unless there is a past practice of settlement in equity or the cash settlement option has no commercial substance.	IFRS 2 and FRS 20 have separate requirements depending on whether it is the entity or the counterparty with the choice of settlement method.
Settlement in cash of award accounted for as equity-settled (or *vice versa*) (see 2.5.2 above)	There is no guidance in FRS 102 on how to account for the settlement in cash of an award accounted for as equity-settled or *vice versa*.	IFRS 2 and FRS 20 specifically address the accounting for a basis of settlement that differs from the accounting basis.

Chapter 21

	FRS 102	FRS 20 (previous UK GAAP) / IFRS 2
Group plans: Accounting by group entity with obligation to settle an award when another group entity receives goods or services (see 2.6.1 above)	FRS 102 makes clear that an entity receiving goods or services, but with no obligation to settle the transaction, accounts for the transaction as equity-settled. However, although explicitly within scope, the accounting in the entity settling the transaction is not specified.	IFRS 2 and FRS 20 make clear when the settling entity should treat an award as equity-settled and when as cash-settled.
Alternative accounting treatment for group plans (see 2.6.2 above)	Where a share-based payment award is granted by an entity to the employees of one or more members of a group, those members are permitted – as an alternative to the general recognition and measurement requirements of FRS 102 – to recognise the share-based payment expense on the basis of a reasonable allocation of the group expense.	IFRS 2 and FRS 20 have no corresponding alternative treatment.
Unidentifiable goods or services (see 2.7.1 above)	For certain government-mandated plans where the goods or services received or receivable are not identifiable, FRS 102 requires the award to be valued on the basis of the equity instruments rather than the goods or services.	Under IFRS 2 and FRS 20, the scope is not restricted to government-mandated plans.
Disclosures (see 2.8 above)	The disclosure requirements of FRS 102 are generally derived from, but less extensive than, those of IFRS 2. However, there are certain specific requirements that are not found in IFRS 2. There are disclosure exemptions for certain entities.	There are no exemptions from disclosure under IFRS 2 and FRS 20.

References

1 For convenience, throughout this Chapter we refer to the recognition of a cost for share-based payments. In some cases, however, a share-based payment transaction may initially give rise to an asset (e.g. where employee costs are capitalised as part of the cost of PP&E or inventories).

2 *Annual Improvements to IFRSs 2010-2012 Cycle*, IASB, December 2013.
3 More detailed guidance on this may be found in a publication such as Options, Futures, and Other Derivatives, John C. Hull.
4 *IASB Update*, IASB, February 2014.

5 FASB Staff Position 123(R)-4, *Classification of Options and Similar Instruments Issued as Employee Compensation That Allow for Cash Settlement upon the Occurrence of a Contingent Event.*

6 D17 – *IFRS 2 – Group and Treasury Share Transactions*, IASB, 2005, para. IE5.

7 TECH 02/10: Guidance on the determination of realised profits and losses in the context of distributions under the Companies Act 2006, ICAEW Technical Release, October 2010, paragraphs 7.53-7.56.

Chapter 21

Chapter 22   Impairment of assets

List of examples

Chapter 22

Chapter 22   Impairment of assets

1   INTRODUCTION

In principle an asset is impaired when an entity will not be able to recover that asset's balance sheet carrying value, either through use or sale. If circumstances arise which indicate assets might be impaired, a review should be undertaken of their cash generating abilities either through use (value in use) or sale (fair value less costs to sell). This review will produce an amount which should be compared with the asset's carrying value. If the carrying value is higher, the difference must be written off as an impairment loss.

These principles are consistent with those under both IAS 36 – *Impairment of Assets* – and the previous UK standard FRS 11 – *Impairment of fixed assets and goodwill*, although there are some differences in application as discussed at 2 below. The relevant provisions are set out within Section 27 – *Impairment of Assets* – of FRS 102 and are discussed at 3 to 8 below.

Section 27 requires less specific disclosures than were required by either FRS 11 or IAS 36. The specific disclosure requirements under Section 27 are discussed at 8 below.

2   COMPARISON BETWEEN SECTION 27, PREVIOUS UK GAAP AND IFRS

2.1   Key differences between Section 27 and previous UK GAAP

2.1.1   Scope

The scope of Section 27 includes inventories. This differs from FRS 11 which applied only to goodwill and tangible fixed assets (with a limited number of exceptions). The requirements for impairment of inventories under previous UK GAAP were dealt with in SSAP 9 – *Stocks and long-term contracts*. Differences between SSAP 9 and Section 27 are discussed in Chapter 9.

The scope of Section 27 is discussed at 3.1 below.

2.1.2   Timing of impairment tests

On an annual basis, entities must consider whether there are indicators of impairment in respect of all assets within scope of Section 27. Entities need only undertake a full impairment test when such indicators are found.

This differs to the process under FRS 10 – *Goodwill and intangible assets*, which required annual impairment tests for goodwill and intangible assets with estimated useful lives of more than 20 years; and for goodwill and intangibles amortised over less than 20 years, an impairment test at the end of the first full financial year following the acquisition and in other periods where events or changes in circumstance indicated that the carrying value may not be recoverable. *[FRS 10.37, 34].* Additionally, under FRS 15 – *Tangible fixed assets*, entities were required to undertake annual impairment tests on tangible fixed assets (other than non-depreciable land and heritage assets) for which either no depreciation was charged on grounds that it would be immaterial or where the estimated remaining useful life of the asset exceeded 50 years. *[FRS 15.89].*

The timing of impairment tests under Section 27 is discussed at 4.1 below.

2.1.3   Allocation of goodwill

Under FRS 11, goodwill was allocated to income generating units (IGUs) in the same way as were the assets and liabilities of the acquired entity. *[FRS 11.35].* However under Section 27, goodwill acquired in a business combination is allocated to each of the acquirer's cash-generating units (CGUs) that are expected to benefit from the synergies of the combination, irrespective of whether other assets or liabilities of the acquire are assigned to those units. *[FRS 102.27.25].*

If it is not possible to allocate goodwill to a CGU (or group of CGUs) non-arbitrarily, Section 27 also allows entities to test for impairment by determining the recoverable amount of either the acquired entity as a whole (if goodwill relates to a non-integrated acquired entity) or the entire group of entities, excluding non-integrated entities (if goodwill relates to an integrated entity). This approach did not exist under previous UK GAAP.

The allocation of goodwill under Section 27 is discussed at 5 below.

2.1.4   Merging of newly acquired businesses

Under FRS 11, when an acquired business was merged with an existing business, a notional gross-up was applied to the carrying amount of the existing business to take account of any unrecognised internally generated goodwill. Any impairment loss arising on merging the businesses was applied to the acquired business only and any subsequent impairment loss was allocated pro-rata between the existing and acquired business with only the latter being recognised. *[FRS11.50].* No such gross up is required under Section 27.

2.1.5   Allocation of impairment losses

FRS 11 required impairment losses on IGUs to be allocated first against associated goodwill, thereafter to any intangible assets and finally to the tangible assets in the unit on a pro-rata (or more appropriate) basis. *[FRS 11.48].*

Section 27 omits the intermediate step, such that impairment losses are allocated first to reduce any goodwill allocated to the unit and then to the other assets on a pro-rata basis based on the carrying amount of each asset in the CGU. *[FRS 102.27.21]*.

The allocation of impairment losses under Section 27 is discussed at 6 below.

2.1.6 Subsequent monitoring of cash flows

Under FRS 11 entities were required to monitor actual cash flows against forecast for the five years following each impairment review where recoverable amount had been based on VIU. If the actual cash flows were so much less than those forecast that use of the actual cash flows could have required recognition of an impairment in previous periods, then entities were required to re-perform the original impairment calculations using the actual cash flows, with recognition of any impairment recognised in the current period (unless the impairment had subsequently reversed and the reversal was permitted to be recognised under the standard). *[FRS 11.54]*. No such requirement exists under Section 27.

2.2 Key differences between Section 27 and IFRS

2.2.1 Scope

The scope of Section 27 includes inventories unlike IAS 36. The requirements for impairment of inventories under IFRS are dealt with in IAS 2– *Inventories*. Differences between IAS 2 and Section 27 are discussed in Chapter 9.

The scope of Section 27 is discussed at 3.1 below.

2.2.2 Timing of impairment tests

On an annual basis, entities must consider whether there are indicators of impairment in respect of all assets within the scope of Section 27. Entities need only undertake a full impairment test when such indicators are found.

This differs to the process under IAS 36, which requires annual impairment tests for goodwill, indefinite-lived intangibles and intangibles not yet available for use. *[IAS 36.10]*.

The timing of impairment tests under Section 27 is discussed at 4.1 below.

2.2.3 Allocation of goodwill

Under both IAS 36 and Section 27, goodwill acquired in a business combination is allocated to each of the acquirer's CGUs that are expected to benefit from the acquisition, whether or not the acquiree's other assets or liabilities are assigned to those units. *[IAS 36.80, FRS 102.27.25]*.

However, if it is not possible to allocate goodwill to a CGU (or group of CGUs) non-arbitrarily, Section 27 contains provisions that allow entities to test for impairment by determining the recoverable amount of either the acquired entity as a whole (if goodwill relates to a non-integrated acquired entity) or the entire group of entities, excluding non-integrated entities (if goodwill relates to an integrated entity). *[FRS 102.27.27]*.

The allocation of impairment losses under Section 27 is discussed at 6 below.

Chapter 22

2.2.4   Reversal of goodwill impairment

Under IAS 36, impairment reversals on goodwill are prohibited. This prohibition does not exist under Section 27, although any impairment reversals are restricted to cases where the reasons for the original impairment loss have ceased to apply. Situations where the impairment loss has reversed purely over the passage of time (due to the effects of discount unwind) would not meet this criterion.

The requirements for impairment reversals under Section 27 are discussed at 7 below.

3   REQUIREMENTS OF SECTION 27 FOR IMPAIRMENT

3.1   Objective and scope

Section 27 explains that an impairment loss occurs when the carrying amount of an asset exceeds its recoverable amount, whether that is its value in use or its fair value less costs to sell. If, and only if, the recoverable amount of an asset is less than its carrying amount, the entity shall reduce the carrying amount of the asset to its recoverable amount. That reduction is an impairment loss. *[FRS 102.27.1, 5]*. Section 27 has a general application to all assets, but the following are outside its scope:

- assets arising from construction contracts (see Section 23 – *Revenue*);

- deferred tax assets (see Section 29 – *Income Tax*);

- assets arising from employee benefits (see Section 28 – *Employee Benefits*);

- financial assets within the scope of Section 11 – *Basic Financial Instruments* or Section 12 – *Other Financial Instruments Issues*;

- investment property measured at fair value (see Section 16 – *Investment Property*);

- biological assets related to agricultural activity measured at fair value less estimated costs to sell (see Section 34 – *Specialised Activities*); and

- deferred acquisition costs and intangible assets arising from contracts within the scope of FRS 103 – *Insurance Contracts*. *[FRS 102.27.1-1A]*.

This means that the scope of Section 27 includes investments in

- subsidiaries (as defined in Section 9 – *Consolidated and Separate Financial Statements*);

- associates (as defined in Section 14 – *Investments in Associates*); and

- joint ventures whether in the form of jointly controlled entities, operations or assets (as defined in Section 15 – *Investments in Joint Ventures*).

in the separate financial statements of the parent as well as investments in joint ventures and associates in the individual financial statements of an investor that is not a parent. It also includes within its scope investments in associates and joint ventures accounted for using the equity method in the consolidated accounts of a group.

3.2   Terms used in Section 27

The key definitions used in FRS 102 are similar in effect to the previous UK standard FRS 11, but not identical. The key definitions used are set out in the Glossary in Appendix I to FRS 102 and are given below. *[FRS 102 Appendix I].*

Term	Definition
Carrying amount	The amount at which an asset or liability is recognised in the statement of financial position.
Cash-generating unit	The smallest identifiable group of assets that generates cash inflows that are largely independent of the cash inflows from other assets or groups of assets.
Depreciated replacement cost	The most economic cost required for the entity to replace the service potential of an asset (including the amount that the entity will receive from its disposal at the end of its useful life) at the reporting date.
Fair value less costs to sell	The amount obtainable from the sale of an asset or cash-generating unit in an arm's length transaction between knowledgeable willing parties, less the costs of disposal.
Impairment loss	The amount by which the carrying amount of an asset exceeds: • in the case of inventories, its selling price less costs to complete and sell; or • in the case of other assets, its recoverable amount.
Recoverable amount	The higher of an asset's (or cash-generating unit's) fair value less costs to sell and its value in use.
Service potential	The economic utility of an asset, based on the total benefit expected to be derived by the entity from use (and/or through sale) of the asset.
Value in use	The present value of the future cash flows expected to be derived from an asset or cash-generating unit.
Value in use (in respect of assets held for their service potential)	The present value to the entity of the asset's remaining service potential if it continues to be used, plus the net amount that the entity will receive from its disposal at the end of its useful life.

3.3   Impairment of inventories

While Section 27 includes specific requirements relating to the impairment of inventories, readers should refer to Chapter 9 where we have chosen to discuss those requirements together with the other principles on the recognition and measurement of inventories.

4   IMPAIRMENT OF ASSETS OTHER THAN INVENTORIES

4.1   General principles

Section 27 requires an impairment test to be carried out if there is an indication of impairment. An entity is not required to perform an impairment test if there is no indication of impairment. *[FRS 102.27.7].*

As it might be unduly onerous for all assets in scope to be tested for impairment every year, Section 27 requires assets to be tested only if there is an indication that impairment may have occurred. If there are indications that the carrying amount of an asset may not be fully recoverable, an entity shall estimate the recoverable amount. The 'indications' of impairment may relate to either the assets themselves or to the economic environment in which they are operated. Possible indicators of impairment are discussed further at 4.3 below.

The purpose of the impairment test is to ensure that tangible and intangible assets, including goodwill, are not carried at a figure greater than their recoverable amount. This recoverable amount is compared with the carrying value of the asset to determine if the asset is impaired.

Recoverable amount is defined as the higher of fair value less costs to sell (FVLCS) and value in use (VIU); the general principle being that an asset should not be carried at more than the amount it will raise, either from selling it now or from using it.

Fair value less costs to sell essentially means what the asset could be sold for, having deducted costs of disposal (incrementally incurred direct selling costs). Value in use is defined in terms of discounted future cash flows, as the present value of the cash flows expected from the future use and eventual sale of the asset at the end of its useful life. As the recoverable amount is to be expressed as a present value, not in nominal terms, discounting is a central feature of the impairment test. Diagrammatically, this comparison between carrying value and recoverable amount, and the definition of recoverable amount, can be shown as follows:

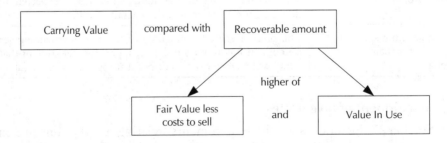

It may not always be necessary to identify both VIU and FVLCS, as if either of VIU or FVLCS is higher than the carrying amount then there is no impairment and no write-down is necessary. Thus, if FVLCS is greater than the carrying amount then no further consideration need be given to VIU, or to the need for an impairment write down. The more complex issues arise when the FVLCS is not greater than the carrying value, and so a VIU calculation is necessary.

If, and only if, the recoverable amount of an asset is less than its carrying amount, the entity shall reduce the carrying amount of the asset to its recoverable amount. That reduction is an impairment loss. *[FRS 102.27.5].*

4.2 Testing individual assets or cash generating units

If it is not possible to estimate the recoverable amount of the individual asset, an entity shall estimate the recoverable amount of the cash generating unit to which the asset belongs. This may be the case because measuring recoverable amount requires forecasting cash flows, and sometimes individual assets do not generate cash inflows by themselves. An asset's cash generating unit is the smallest identifiable group of assets that includes the asset and generates cash inflows that are largely independent of the cash inflows from other assets or groups of assets. *[FRS 102.27.8].*

The group of assets that is considered together should be as small as is reasonably practicable, i.e. the entity should be divided into as many CGUs as possible – an entity must identify the lowest aggregation of assets that generate largely independent cash inflows. It should be emphasised that the focus is on the asset group's ability to generate cash *inflows*, not cash outflows or indeed any basis on which costs might be allocated. The division should not go beyond the level at which each income stream is *capable* of being separately monitored. For example, it may be difficult to identify a level below an individual factory as a CGU but of course an individual factory may or may not be a CGU.

A practical approach to identifying CGUs involves two stages, the first being to work down to the smallest group of assets for which a stream of cash inflows can be identified. These groups of assets will be CGUs unless the performance of their cash inflow-generating assets is dependent on those generated by other assets, or *vice versa* their cash inflows are affected by those of other assets. If the cash inflows generated by the group of assets are not largely independent of those generated by other assets, the second stage is to add other assets to the group to form the smallest collection of assets that generates largely independent cash inflows. The existence of a degree of flexibility over what constitutes a CGU is obvious.

The identification of cash generating units will require judgement and Section 27 itself does not give any further guidance on this area. However, under the hierarchy in Section 10 – *Accounting Policies, Estimates and Errors* – of the Standard, users may wish to refer to the associated guidance in IAS 36.

Under IAS 36, in identifying whether cash inflows from an asset are largely independent of the cash inflows from other assets, entities are advised to consider various factors including:

- how management monitors the entity's operations (such as by product lines, businesses, individual locations, districts or regional areas); or

- how management makes decisions about continuing or disposing of the entity's assets and operations. *[IAS 36.69].*

While monitoring by management may help identify CGUs, it does not override the requirement that the identification of CGUs is based on largely independent cash *inflows*.

Chapter 22

Example 22.1:   Identification of CGUs – Independent cash flows

A bus company provides services under contract with a municipality that requires minimum service on each of five separate routes. Assets devoted to each route and the cash flows from each route can be identified separately. One of the routes operates at a significant loss.

Because the entity does not have the option to curtail any one bus route, the lowest level of identifiable cash inflows that are largely independent of the cash inflows of other assets or groups of assets are the cash inflows generated by the five routes together. The cash generating unit for each route is the bus company as a whole.

Example 22.2:   Identification of CGUs – Management monitoring and decision making

A publisher owns 150 magazine titles of which 70 were purchased and 80 were self-created. The price paid for a purchased magazine title is recognised as an intangible asset. The costs of creating magazine titles and maintaining the existing titles are recognised as an expense when incurred. Cash inflows from direct sales and advertising are identifiable for each magazine title. Titles are managed by customer segments. The level of advertising income for a magazine title depends on the range of titles in the customer segment to which the magazine title relates. Management has a policy to abandon old titles before the end of their economic lives and replace them immediately with new titles for the same customer segment.

It is likely that the recoverable amount of an individual magazine title can be assessed. Even though the level of advertising income for a title is influenced, to a certain extent, by the other titles in the customer segment, cash inflows from direct sales and advertising are identifiable for each title. In addition, although titles are managed by customer segments, decisions to abandon titles are made on an individual title basis.

Therefore, it is likely that individual magazine titles generate cash inflows that are largely independent of each other and that each magazine title is a separate cash-generating unit.

In addition to monitoring by management, IAS 36 stresses the significance of an active market for the output of an asset in identifying a CGU. If an active market exists for the output produced by an asset or group of assets, that asset or group of assets shall be identified as a cash generating unit, even if some or all of the output is used internally. *[IAS 36.70]*. The existence of an active market means that the assets or CGU could generate cash inflows independently from the rest of the business by selling on the active market. There are active markets for many metals, energy products (various grades of oil product, natural gas) and other commodities that are freely traded.

An active market is defined in FRS 102 as one in which all of the items traded are homogeneous, where willing buyers and sellers can normally be found at any time and which has prices that are available to the public.

Example 22.3:   Identification of CGUs – Active market

Entity M produces a single product and owns plants A, B and C. Each plant is located in a different continent. A produces a component that is assembled in either B or C. The combined capacity of B and C is not fully utilised. M's products are sold worldwide from either B or C. For example, B's production can be sold in C's continent if the products can be delivered faster from B than from C. Utilisation levels of B and C depend on the allocation of sales between the two sites. There is also an active market for A's product.

As there is an active market for its products, it is likely that A is a separate cash-generating unit. Although there is an active market for the products assembled by B and C, cash inflows for B and C depend on the allocation of production across the two sites. It is unlikely that the future cash inflows for B and C can be determined individually. Therefore, it is likely that B and C together are the smallest identifiable group of assets that generates cash inflows that are largely independent.

In determining the value in use of A and B plus C, M adjusts financial budgets/forecasts to reflect its best estimate of future prices that could be achieved in arm's length transactions for A's products.

In practice, different entities will have varying approaches to determining their CGUs. While a CGU as defined in Section 27 is the smallest identifiable group of assets that generates cash inflows that are largely independent, the level of judgement involved means that there is still likely to be a reasonable degree of flexibility in most organisations. In practice, most entities may tend towards larger rather than smaller CGUs to keep the complexity of the process within reasonable bounds, but this leads to the risk that lower level impairments are avoided because poor cash flows from some assets may be offset by better ones from other assets in the CGU.

4.3 Indicators of impairment

An entity shall assess at each reporting date whether there is any indication that an asset may be impaired. If any such indication exists, the entity shall estimate the recoverable amount of the asset. If there is no indication of impairment, it is not necessary to estimate the recoverable amount. *[FRS 102.27.7].*

The 'indications' of impairment may relate to either the assets themselves or to the economic environment in which they are operated. Section 27 gives examples of indications of impairment, but makes it clear this is not an exhaustive list. An entity may identify other indications that an asset is impaired that would equally trigger an impairment review.

The indicators given in Section 27 are divided into external and internal indications.

External sources of information:

(a) During the period, an asset's market value has declined significantly more than would be expected as a result of the passage of time or normal use.

(b) Significant changes with an adverse effect on the entity have taken place during the period, or will take place in the near future, in the technological, market, economic or legal environment in which the entity operates or in the market to which an asset is dedicated.

(c) Market interest rates or other market rates of return on investments have increased during the period, and those increases are likely to affect materially the discount rate used in calculating an asset's value in use and decrease the asset's fair value less costs to sell.

(d) The carrying amount of the net assets of the entity is more than the estimated fair value of the entity as a whole (such an estimate may have been made, for example, in relation to the potential sale of part or all of the entity).

Internal sources of information:

(e) Evidence is available of obsolescence or physical damage of an asset.

(f) Significant changes with an adverse effect on the entity have taken place during the period, or are expected to take place in the near future, in the extent to which, or manner in which, an asset is used or is expected to be used. These changes include the asset becoming idle, plans to discontinue or restructure the operation to which an asset belongs, plans to dispose of an asset before the previously expected date, and reassessing the useful life of an asset as finite rather than indefinite.

Chapter 22

(g) Evidence is available from internal reporting that indicates that the economic performance of an asset is, or will be, worse than expected. In this context economic performance includes operating results and cash flows. *[FRS 102.27.9].*

While it is not specifically set out in Section 27, the presence of indicators of impairment will not necessarily mean that the entity has to calculate the recoverable amount of the asset. A previous calculation may have shown that an asset's recoverable amount was significantly greater than its carrying amount and it may be clear that subsequent events have been insufficient to eliminate this headroom. Similarly, previous analysis may show that an asset's recoverable amount is not sensitive to one or more of these indicators.

Clearly there is an important judgement to be made in deciding whether an impairment review is needed. As discussed below, once triggered, an impairment review can become a complicated process with serious implications for the financial statements of an entity. Many will therefore wish to avoid performing such a process and thus may wish to argue that there has not been an indication of impairment of significant consequence. Much might turn on the judgement of matters such as whether there has been a *significant* adverse change in the market or just an adverse change.

Section 27 also explains that if there is an indication that an asset may be impaired, this may indicate that the entity should review the remaining useful life, the depreciation (amortisation) method or the residual value for the asset and adjust it in accordance with the section of FRS 102 applicable to the asset (e.g. Section 17 – *Property, Plant and Equipment* – and Section 18 – *Intangible Assets other than Goodwill*), even if no impairment loss is recognised for the asset. *[FRS 102.27.10].*

4.3.1   Future performance

The specific wording in (g) above makes clear that FRS 102 requires an impairment review to be undertaken if performance is or will be worse than expected. In particular, there may be indicators of impairment even if the asset is profitable in the current period if budgeted results for the future indicate that there will be losses or net cash outflows when these are aggregated with the current period results.

4.3.2   Individual assets or part of CGU?

Some of the indicators are aimed at individual fixed assets rather than the CGU of which they are a part, for example a decline in the market value of an asset or evidence that it is obsolete or damaged. However, they may also imply that a wider review of the business or CGU is required. For example, if there is a property slump and the market value of the entity's new head office falls below its carrying value this would constitute an indicator of impairment and trigger a review. At the level of the individual asset, as FVLCS is below carrying amount, this might indicate that a write-down is necessary. However, the building's recoverable amount may have to be considered in the context of a CGU of which it is a part. This is an example of a situation where it may not be necessary to re-estimate an asset's recoverable amount because it may be obvious that the CGU has suffered no impairment. In short, it may be irrelevant to the recoverable amount of the CGU that it contains a head office whose market value has fallen.

4.3.3   *Interest rates*

Including interest rates as indicators of impairment could imply that assets are judged to be impaired if they are no longer expected to earn a market rate of return, even though they may generate the same cash flows as before. However, it may well be that an upward movement in general interest rates will not give rise to a write-down in assets because they may not materially affect the rate of return expected from the asset or CGU itself.

An entity would not be required to make a formal estimate of an asset's recoverable amount if the discount rate used in calculating the asset's VIU is unlikely to be affected by the increase in market rates. The discount rate used in a VIU calculation should be based on the rate specific for the asset, and if the asset has a long remaining useful life this may not be materially affected by increases in short-term rates. Previous sensitivity analyses of the recoverable amount may also show that it is unlikely that there will be a material decrease because future cash flows are also likely to increase to compensate. Consequently, the potential decrease in recoverable amount may simply be unlikely to be material.

4.4   Measuring recoverable amount

Section 27 requires the carrying amount to be compared with the recoverable amount when there is an indicator of impairment. The recoverable amount of an asset or a CGU is the higher of its fair value less costs to sell and its value in use. *[FRS 102.27.11]*. If either the FVLCS or the VIU is higher than the carrying amount, the asset is not impaired and it is not necessary to estimate the other amount. *[FRS 102.27.12]*.

Recoverable amount is calculated for an individual asset, unless that asset does not generate cash inflows that are largely independent of those from other assets or groups of assets, in which case the recoverable amount should be estimated for the CGU to which the asset belongs. *[FRS 102.27.8]*.

FRS 102 defines VIU as the present value of the future cash flows expected to be derived from an asset or CGU. FVLCS is defined as the amount obtainable from the sale of an asset or CGU in an arm's length transaction between knowledgeable, willing parties, less the costs of disposal.

Estimating the VIU of an asset involves estimating the future cash inflows and outflows that will be derived from the continuing use of the asset and from its ultimate disposal, and discounting them at an appropriate rate. *[FRS 102.27.15]*. There can be complex issues involved in determining the relevant cash flows and choosing a discount rate and these are discussed in 4.6 below.

When estimating FVLCS, the best evidence is a price in a binding sale agreement in an arm's length transaction or a market price in an active market. Where such evidence is not available, management should base their estimate of FVLCS on the best information available. This can be a complex process as discussed at 4.5 below.

Section 27 mentions circumstances in which it may be appropriate to use an asset or CGU's FVLCS without calculating its VIU, as the measure of its recoverable amount. There may be no reason to believe that an asset's VIU materially exceeds its FVLCS,

Chapter 22

in which case the asset's FVLCS may be used as its recoverable amount. *[FRS 102.27.13]*. This is the case, for example, if management is intending to dispose of the asset or CGU, as apart from its disposal proceeds there will be few if any cash flows from further use.

It is not uncommon for the FVLCS of an asset to be readily obtainable while the asset itself does not generate largely independent cash inflows, as is the case with many property assets held by entities. If the FVLCS of the asset is lower than its carrying value then the recoverable amount (which means both FVLCS and VIU) will have to be calculated by reference to the CGU of which the asset is a part.

4.5   Fair value less costs to sell (FVLCS)

FVLCS is defined as the amount obtainable from the sale of an asset (or CGU) in an arm's length transaction between knowledgeable willing parties, less the costs of disposal. The best evidence of an asset's FVLCS is a price in a binding sale agreement in an arm's length transaction or a market price in an active market. If there is no binding sale agreement or active market for an asset, FVLCS is based on the best information available to reflect the amount that an entity could obtain, at the reporting date, from the disposal of the asset in an arm's length transaction between knowledgeable, willing parties, after deducting the costs of disposal. In determining this amount, an entity considers the outcome of recent transactions for similar assets within the same industry. *[FRS 102.27.14]*.

Section 27 therefore makes clear that if there is a binding sales agreement in an arm's length transaction or an active market then that price *must* be used. In reality, however, there are few active markets for most tangible and intangible assets, given that the Glossary in Appendix I to FRS 102 defines an active market as one in which all of the items traded are homogeneous, where willing buyers and sellers can normally be found at any time and which has prices that are available to the public. Consequently, most estimates of fair value will be based on estimates of the market price of the asset in an arm's length transaction. This will involve consideration of the outcome of recent transactions for similar assets in the same industry. The entity will use the best information it has available at the balance sheet date to construct the price payable in an arm's length transaction between knowledgeable, willing parties.

While Section 27 does not mention any other valuation techniques, it may be that the use of such techniques is the only way to obtain the best estimate of fair value. This may be the case where there is no binding sales agreement, where no active market for the asset exists and transactions for similar assets do not happen often enough to provide a reliable measure of fair value. In such cases entities need to rely on other valuation techniques in considering the best information available at the balance sheet date. This is discussed further at 4.5.1 below.

In all cases, FVLCS should take account of estimated disposal costs. These include legal costs, stamp duty and other transaction taxes, costs of moving the asset and other direct incremental costs.

The following simple example illustrates how an entity might determine FVLCS for an asset.

Example 22.4: Estimating FVLCS

An entity owns a fleet of vehicles that it uses to deliver its products. At the end of 2015 a particular truck has a carrying amount of £9,000 (original cost of £19,000; accumulated depreciation of £10,000). The original estimate of the useful life of the truck was seven years (measured from the date the truck was first recognised by the entity) and it has an estimated residual value of £5,000.

Because of the low fuel efficiency of this truck, the entity has dramatically decreased usage of the truck. The market price for similar trucks in an active resale market is £6,000. Licence and title fees associated with selling the truck are £200.

The change in use is an internal indicator that the truck is impaired. The decline in the market price of the truck is an external indicator of impairment.

The price in an active market provides an estimate of fair value. The entity has no reason to believe that the truck's VIU is higher than its FVLCS. Consequently, the recoverable amount of the truck is £5,800 (£6,000 fair value less £200 costs to sell). The entity makes the following entries to record the impairment of the truck.

	Dr	Cr
Dr Profit or loss		
(impairment of vehicles)	£3,200	
Cr Accumulated impairment		
(property, plant and equipment)		£3,200
To recognise the impairment loss on property, plant and equipment.		

4.5.1 Estimating fair value less costs to sell without an active market

Few assets are traded on an active market and there are no obvious examples of traded CGUs. However, it may be possible to determine fair value provided there is a basis for making a reliable estimate of the amount obtainable from the sale of the asset in an arm's length transaction between knowledgeable and willing parties.

Section 27 requires entities to consider 'the outcome of recent transactions for similar assets within the same industry'. *[FRS 102.27.14]*. If the entity has only recently acquired the asset or CGU in question then it may be able to demonstrate that its purchase price remains an appropriate measure of FVLCS, although it would have to make adjustments for material costs to sell.

To rely on the outcome of a recent transaction for a similar asset by a third party, the following conditions should be considered:

- the transaction should be in the same industry, unless the asset is generic and its fair value would not be affected by the industry in which the purchaser operates;

- the assets should be shown to be substantially the same as to their nature and condition; and

- the economic environment of the entity should be similar to the environment in which the previous sale occurred (e.g. no material circumstances have arisen since the earlier transaction that affect the value of the asset). This means that previous transactions are particularly unreliable if markets are falling.

It would be unusual to be able to estimate FVLCS reliably from a single market transaction. As discussed below, if reliable market assumptions are known, it is much more likely that a recent market transaction would be one of the factors taken into account in the calculation of FVLCS. For example, if the economic environment is slightly different, or if the asset sold is not exactly the same as the one for which a FVLCS is being estimated, then it may still be possible to use the transaction as a starting point from which adjustments could be made for differing characteristics in the asset or the economic environment. Judgement will be required and consideration will have to be given to all relevant facts and circumstances.

Similarly, if the entity cannot demonstrate that a recent transaction alone provides a reliable estimate of FVLCS, the transaction may be one of the sources of evidence used to validate an estimate of FVLCS using other valuation techniques. This is particularly likely to be the case if the impairment review is of a CGU or CGU group rather than an individual asset, as market transactions for CGUs may be less relevant.

Section 27 itself provides no specific guidance on other valuation techniques, which could be used. However, within the definition for fair value in the Glossary in Appendix I to FRS 102, it is stated that in the absence of any specific guidance provided in the relevant section of this FRS, the guidance in paragraphs FRS 102.11.27 to FRS 102.11.32 shall be used in determining fair value. In terms of valuation technique, FRS 102.11.28-29 are the relevant paragraphs. They contain the following guidance.

Valuation techniques include using recent arm's length market transactions for an identical asset between knowledgeable, willing parties, if available, reference to the current fair value of another asset that is substantially the same as the asset being measured, discounted cash flow analysis and option pricing models. If there is a valuation technique commonly used by market participants to price the asset and that technique has been demonstrated to provide reliable estimates of prices obtained in actual market transactions, the entity uses that technique. *[FRS 102.11.28].*

The objective of using a valuation technique is to establish what the transaction price would have been on the measurement date in an arm's length exchange motivated by normal business considerations. Fair value is estimated on the basis of the results of a valuation technique that makes maximum use of market inputs, and relies as little as possible on entity-determined inputs. A valuation technique would be expected to arrive at a reliable estimate of the fair value if:

- it reasonably reflects how the market could be expected to price the asset; and
- the inputs to the valuation technique reasonably represent market expectations and measures of the risk return factors inherent in the asset. *[FRS 102.11.29].*

The first of these paragraphs makes clear that in calculating FVLCS it may be appropriate to use cash flow valuation techniques such as discounted cash flows or other valuation techniques such as earnings multiples, if it can be demonstrated that they would be used by the relevant 'market participants' i.e. other businesses in the same industry; while the second paragraph emphasises the need to prioritise market inputs i.e. those which are visible to all, over inputs determined by the entity itself.

When selecting and using a valuation technique to estimate FVLCS, an entity would consider all of the following:

- relevance of the available valuation models – this may include consideration of industry practice, for example, a multiple of EBITDA is often used in the hotel industry to estimate fair value, while discounted cash flows are used by many manufacturing entities;

- assumptions used in the model – these should only be those that other market participants would use. They should not be based on management's uncorroborated views or information that would not be known or considered by other market participants; and

- whether there is reliable evidence showing that these assumptions would be taken into account by market participants. For this purpose, it may be necessary for the entity to obtain external advice.

Additionally, when markets are unstable entities should ensure that multiples remain valid. They should not assume that the basis underlying the multiples remains unchanged.

A discounted cash flow technique may be used if this is commonly used in that industry to estimate fair value. Cash flows used when applying the model may only reflect cash flows that market participants would take into account when assessing fair value. This includes the type of cash flows, for example future capital expenditure, as well as the estimated amount of cash flows. For example, an entity may wish to take into account cash flows relating to future capital expenditure, which would not be permitted for a VIU calculation (see 4.6.3 below). These cash flows can be included if, but only if, other market participants would consider them when evaluating the asset. It is not permissible to include assumptions about cash flows or benefits from the asset that would not be available to or considered by a typical market participant. Obtaining reliable evidence of market assumptions is not straightforward, and may not be available to many entities wishing to apply valuation techniques. However, if the information is available then entities ought to take it into account in calculating FVLCS.

It is also important to ensure that the cash flows included in the discounted cash flow model are consistent with the asset or CGU being tested. For example if working capital balances such as trade debtors and creditors are included in the carrying value of the CGU, the cash inflows and outflows from those assets and liabilities should be included in the related cash flow projections.

4.5.2   Effect of restrictions on fair value

When determining an asset's fair value less costs to sell, consideration shall be given to any restrictions imposed on that asset. Costs to sell shall also include the cost of obtaining relaxation of a restriction where necessary in order to enable the asset to be sold. If a restriction would also apply to any potential purchaser of an asset, the fair value of the asset may be lower than that of an asset whose use is not restricted. *[FRS 102.27.14A].*

Where a restriction on the sale or use of an asset would apply to any potential purchaser of the asset, the effect of that restriction should be taken into account in pricing the fair value of the asset. Where the restriction is specific to the entity holding the asset and so would not transfer to a potential purchaser, then that restriction would not reduce the fair value of the asset.

The following example illustrates a situation where a certain restriction would apply to any potential purchaser of the asset concerned while a further restriction applies to the specific entity holding the asset, but not to other market participants. Only the first of these restrictions will reduce fair value when compared with an equivalent unrestricted asset.

Example 22.5:   Restrictions on assets

A donor of land specifies that the land must be used by a sporting association as a playground in perpetuity. Upon review of relevant documentation, the association determines that the donor's restriction would not transfer to potential purchasers if the association sold the asset (i.e. the restriction on the use of the land is specific to the association). Furthermore, the association is not restricted from selling the land. Without the restriction on the use of the land, the land could be used as a site for residential development. In addition, the land is subject to an easement (a legal right that enables a utility to run power lines across the land).

Under these circumstances, the effect of the restriction and the easement on the fair value measurement of the land is as follows:

(a) Donor restriction on use of land – The donor restriction on the use of the land is specific to the association and thus would not apply to potential purchasers. Therefore, regardless of the restriction on the use of the land by the association, the fair value of the land would be measured based on the higher of its indicated value:

   (i) As a playground (i.e. the maximum value of the land is through its use in combination with other assets or with other assets and liabilities); or

   (ii) As a residential development (i.e. the fair value of the asset would be maximized through its use by market participants on a standalone basis).

(b) Easement for utility lines – Because the easement for utility lines would apply to any potential purchaser, the fair value of the land would include the effect of the easement, regardless of whether the land's valuation premise is as a playground or as a site for residential development.

4.6   Value in use (VIU)

Value in use (VIU) is defined as the present value of the future cash flows expected to be derived from an asset or cash-generating unit. *[FRS 102 Appendix I]*.

The calculation of VIU involves the following steps:

• estimating the future cash inflows and outflows to be derived from continuing use of the asset and from its ultimate disposal; and

• applying the appropriate discount rate to those future cash flows. *[FRS 102.27.15]*.

Section 27 requires the following elements to be reflected in the VIU calculation:

(a) an estimate of the future cash flows the entity expects to derive from the asset;

(b) expectations about possible variations in the amount or timing of those future cash flows;

(c) the time value of money, represented by the current market risk-free rate of interest;

(d) the price for bearing the uncertainty inherent in the asset; and

(e) other factors, such as illiquidity, that market participants would reflect in pricing the future cash flows the entity expects to derive from the asset. *[FRS 102.27.16]*.

Section 27 requires uncertainty as to the timing of cash flows or the market's assessment of risk in the assets ((d) and (e) above) to be taken into account *either* by adjusting the cash flows or the discount rate. The intention is that the VIU should be the expected present value of those future cash flows. *[FRS 102.27.20]*.

If it is not possible to estimate the recoverable amount of an individual asset, the entity shall estimate the recoverable amount of the CGU to which the asset belongs. *[FRS 102.27.8]*. This will frequently be necessary because:

- the single asset may not generate sufficiently independent cash inflows, as is often the case; and

- in the case of the possible impairment of a single asset, FVLCS will frequently be lower than the carrying amount.

Where a CGU is being reviewed for impairment, this will involve calculation of the VIU of the CGU as a whole unless a reliable estimate of the CGU's FVLCS can be made and the resulting FVLCS is above the total of the CGU's net assets.

VIU calculations at the level of the CGU will thus be required when no satisfactory FVLCS is available or FVLCS is below the CGU's carrying amount and:

- goodwill is suspected of being impaired;

- a CGU itself is suspected of being impaired; or

- individual assets are suspected of being impaired and individual future cash flows cannot be identified for them.

In order to calculate VIU there are a series of steps to follow, as set out below. Within each step, we shall discuss the practicalities and difficulties in determining the VIU of an asset. The steps in the process are:

Step 1: Dividing the entity into CGUs (4.2 above);

Step 2: Estimating the future pre-tax cash flows of the CGU under review (4.6.1-4.6.4 below);

Step 3: Identifying an appropriate discount rate and discounting the future cash flows (4.6.5 below);

Step 4: Comparing carrying value with VIU and recognising impairment losses (6 below).

Although this process describes the determination of the VIU of a CGU, steps 2 to 4 are the same as those that would be applied to an individual asset if it generated cash inflows independently of other assets.

Example 22.6 illustrates a simple example of how an entity would calculate the VIU of an individual asset following the principles set out in 4.6.1-4.6.5 below.

Example 22.6:   Estimating value in use

Entity A manufactures an electrical component using a specialised machine. During 20X0, one of Entity A's competitors starts producing an alternative component using a less expensive material. The competitor is able to market their product at a lower cost than Entity A and so sales of Entity A's product fall sharply.

Entity A's specialised machine cannot be modified to work with this cheaper material and so at the end of 20X0 they test the machine for impairment. The machine was bought five years ago for

£300,000 when its useful life was estimated to be 15 years and the estimated residual value was nil. At 31 December 20X0, after recognising the depreciation change for 20X0, the machine's carrying amount is £200,000 and the remaining useful life is 10 years.

The machine's VIU is calculated using a pre-tax discount rate of 14 per cent per year. Budgets approved by management reflect estimated costs necessary to maintain the level of economic benefit expected to arise from the machine in its current condition.

Assume for simplicity, expected future cash flows occur at the end of the reporting period. An estimation of the VIU of the machine at the end of 20X0 is shown below:

Year	Probability-weighted future cash flow	Present value factor 14%[1]	Discounted cash flow
	£		£
20X1	19,949	0.877193	17,499
20X2	19,305	0.769468	14,855
20X3	18,084	0.674972	12,206
20X4	21,016	0.592080	12,443
20X5	20,767	0.519369	10,786
20X6	19,115	0.455587	8,709
20X7	17,369	0.399637	6,941
20X8	16,596	0.350559	5,818
20X9	14,540	0.307508	4,471
20Y0[2]	12,568	0.269744	3,390
Value in use			97,118

[1] The present value factor is calculated as $k+1/(1+i)^n$ where i is the discount rate and n is the number of periods of discount e.g. for 20Y0 the present value factor is calculated as follows: $1/(1.14)^{10} = 1/3.707221 = 0.269744$.

[2] The expected future cash flow for year 20Y0 includes £2,500 expected to be paid for the disposal of the asset at the end of its useful life. Note that the residual value is nil because it is expected that the machine will be scrapped at the end of 20Y0.

Assuming that the FVLCS is lower than VIU (and thus VIU is the recoverable amount), the calculation of the impairment loss at the end of 20X0 is as follows:

Carrying amount before impairment loss	£200,000
Less recoverable amount	(£97,118)
Impairment loss	£102,882
Carrying amount after impairment loss	£97,118

As a consequence of the impairment loss recognised at 31 December 20X0, the carrying amount of the machine immediately after the impairment recognition is equal to the recoverable amount of the machine i.e. £97,118. In this case, in subsequent periods, assuming all variables remain the same as at the end of 20X0, the depreciable amount will be £97,118, so the depreciation charge will be £9,712 per year.

4.6.1   Estimating the future pre-tax cash flows of the CGU under review

In measuring value in use, estimates of future cash flows shall include:

- projections of cash inflows from the continuing use of the asset;

- projections of cash outflows that are necessarily incurred to generate the cash inflows from continuing use of the asset (including cash outflows to prepare the asset for use) and can be directly attributed, or allocated on a reasonable and consistent basis, to the asset; and

- net cash flows, if any, expected to be received (or paid) for the disposal of the asset at the end of its useful life in an arm's length transaction between knowledgeable, willing parties.

The entity may wish to use any recent financial budgets or forecasts to estimate the cash flows, if available. To estimate cash flow projections beyond the period covered by the most recent budgets or forecasts an entity may wish to extrapolate the projections based on the budgets or forecasts using a steady or declining growth rate for subsequent years, unless an increasing rate can be justified. *[FRS 102.27.17]*.

As noted at 4.6 above, uncertainties as to the timing of cash flows or the market's assessment of risk in the assets should be taken into account *either* by adjusting the cash flows or the discount rate. Entities must take care to avoid double counting.

Although not specified in Section 27, our normal expectation would be for entities to apply a similar rule of thumb to that under IAS 36 and previous UK GAAP, being the application of a five year maximum, for the period before which a steady or declining growth rate could be assumed. This five year rule is based on general economic theory that postulates above-average growth rates will only be achievable in the short-term, because such above-average growth will lead to competitors entering the market. This increased competition will, over a period of time, lead to a reduction of the growth rate, towards the average for the economy as a whole.

Cash flows can be estimated by taking into account general price changes caused by inflation, or on the basis of stable prices. If inflation is excluded from the cash flow then the discount rate selected should also be adjusted to remove the inflationary effect. Generally entities will use whichever method is most convenient to them and that is consistent with the method they use in their budgets and forecasts. It is, of course, fundamental that cash flows and discount rate are both estimated on a consistent basis.

If the cash inflows generated by an asset or CGU are based on internal transfer pricing, management should use their best estimate of an external arm's length transaction price in estimating the future cash flows to determine the asset's or CGU's VIU.

The cash inflows attributable to an asset or CGU may be generated in a foreign currency. Section 27 does not provide any guidance on this issue, but under the hierarchy in Section 10 of the Standard, companies may wish to consider the guidance in IAS 36. IAS 36 states that foreign currency cash flows should first be estimated in the currency in which they will be generated and then discounted using a discount rate appropriate for that currency. The entity can then translate the present value calculated in the foreign currency using the spot exchange rate at the date of the VIU calculation.

This is to avoid the problems inherent in using forward exchange rates, which would result in double-counting the time value of money, first in the discount rate and then in the forward rate. Arriving at a suitable discount rate could be an extremely difficult exercise as many different factors need to be taken into account including relative inflation rates and relative interest rates as well as appropriate discount rates for the currencies in question. Entities may wish to engage valuers to assist them in this situation.

Chapter 22

4.6.2   *Financing and taxation*

Estimates of future cash flows shall not include:

*   cash inflows or outflows from financing activities; or

*   income tax receipts or payments. *[FRS 102.27.18].*

The first of these exclusions is required because the discount rate applied to the cash flow projections represents the associated financing costs (so to include financing cash flows would be double counting this effect). Similarly, income tax receipts and payments must also be excluded on consistency grounds as Section 27 requires the use of a pre-tax discount rate to be used in the VIU calculation. *[FRS 102.27.20].*

4.6.3   *Restructuring and improvements*

While cash flow projections should include costs of day-to-day servicing, future cash flows shall be estimated for the asset in its current condition. Estimates of future cash flows shall not include estimated future cash inflows or outflows that are expected to arise from:

*   a future restructuring to which an entity is not yet committed; or

*   improving or enhancing the asset's performance. *[FRS 102.27.19].*

While the restriction on enhanced performance may be understandable, it adds an element of unreality that is hard to reconcile with other assumptions made in the VIU calculation process. For example, the underlying forecast cash flows an entity uses in its VIU calculation are likely to be based on the business as it is actually expected to develop in the future, growth, improvements and all. Producing a special forecast based on unrealistic assumptions, even for this limited purpose, may be difficult.

Nevertheless, paragraph 19 explicitly states that projected cash flows shall not include expenditure to improve or enhance performance of an asset. The implication of this requirement is that if an asset is impaired, and even if the entity is going to make the future expenditure to reverse that impairment, the asset will still have to be written down. Subsequently, the asset's impairment can be reversed, to the degree appropriate, after the expenditure has taken place. Reversal of asset impairment is discussed at 7 below.

An assumption of new capital investment is in practice intrinsic to the VIU test. What has to be assessed are the future cash flows of a productive unit such as a factory or hotel. The cash flows, out into the far future, will include the sales of product, cost of sales, administrative expenses, etc. They must necessarily include capital expenditure as well, at least to the extent required to keep the CGU functioning as forecast.

Accordingly, *some* capital expenditure cash flows must be built into the forecast cash flows. Whilst improving capital expenditure may not be recognised, routine or replacement capital expenditure necessary to maintain the function of the asset or assets in the CGU has to be included. Entities must therefore distinguish between maintenance, replacement and enhancement expenditure. This distinction may not be easy to draw in practice, as shown in the following example.

Example 22.7:   Distinguishing enhancement and maintenance expenditure

A telecommunications company provides fixed line, telephone, television and internet services. It must develop its basic transmission infrastructure (by overhead wires or cables along streets or railway lines etc.) and in order to service a new customer it will have to connect the customer's home via cable and other equipment. It will extend its network to adjoining areas and perhaps acquire an entity with its own network. It will also reflect changes in technology, e.g. fibre optic cables replacing copper ones.

Obviously, when preparing the budgets which form the basis for testing the network for impairment, it will make assumptions regarding future revenue growth and will include the costs of connecting those customers. However, its infrastructure maintenance spend will inevitably include replacing equipment with the current technology. There is no option of continuing to replace equipment with something that has been technologically superseded. Once this technology exists it will be reflected in the entity's budgets and taken into account in its cash flows when carrying out impairment tests, even though this new equipment will enhance the performance of the transmission infrastructure.

Further examples indicate another problem area – the effects of future expenditure that the entity has identified but which the entity has not yet incurred. An entity may have acquired an asset with the intention of enhancing it in future and may, therefore, have paid for future synergies which will be reflected in the calculation of goodwill. Another entity may have plans for an asset that involve expenditure that will enhance its future performance and without which the asset may be impaired.

Examples could include:

- a TV transmission company that, in acquiring another, would expect to pay for the future right to migrate customers from analogue to digital services; or

- an aircraft manufacturer that expects to be able to use one of the acquired plants for a new model at a future point, a process that will involve replacing much of the current equipment.

In both cases the long-term plans reflect both the capital spent and the cash flows that will flow from it. There is no obvious alternative to recognising an impairment when calculating the CGU or CGU group's VIU as Section 27 states that the impairment test has to be performed for the asset in its current condition. This means that it is not permitted to include the benefit of improving or enhancing the asset's performance in calculating its VIU.

An entity in this situation may attempt to avoid an impairment write down by calculating the appropriate FVLCS, as this is not constrained by rules regarding future capital expenditure. As discussed above, these cash flows can be included only to the extent that other market participants would consider them when evaluating the asset. It is not permissible to include assumptions about cash flows or benefits from the asset that would not be available to or considered by a typical market participant.

Section 27 contains similar rules with regard to any future restructuring that may affect the VIU of the asset or CGU. The prohibition on including the results of restructuring applies only to those plans to which the entity is not committed. Again, this is because of the general rule that the cash flows must be based on the asset in its current condition so future events that may change that condition should not be taken into account. When an entity becomes committed to a restructuring

Section 27 then allows an entity's estimates of future cash inflows and outflows to reflect the cost savings and other benefits from the restructuring, based on the most recent financial budgets/forecasts approved by management.

As is the case for improvement expenditure above, entities will sometimes be required to recognise impairment losses on assets or CGUs that will be reversed once the expenditure has been incurred and the restructuring completed.

4.6.4   *Terminal values*

In the case of non-current assets, a large component of value attributable to an asset or CGU arises from its terminal value, which is the net present value of all of the forecast free cash flows that are expected to be generated by the asset or CGU after the explicit forecast period.

Where an asset is to be sold at the end of its useful life the disposal proceeds and costs should be based on current prices and costs for similar assets, adjusted if necessary for price level changes if the entity has chosen to include this factor in its forecasts and selection of a discount rate. The entity should ensure that its estimate is based on a proper assessment of the amount that would be received in an arm's length transaction.

However, CGUs usually have indefinite lives, as have some assets, and the terminal value is calculated by having regard to the forecast maintainable cash flows that are expected to be generated by the asset or CGU in the final year of the explicit forecast period ('the terminal year').

It is essential that the terminal year cash flows reflect maintainable cash flows as otherwise any material one-off or abnormal cash flows that are forecast for the terminal year will inappropriately increase or decrease the valuation.

The maintainable cash flow expected to be generated by the asset or CGU is then capitalised by a perpetuity factor based on either:

- the discount rate if cash flows are forecast to remain relatively constant; or
- the discount rate less the long term growth rate if cash flows are forecast to grow.

Care is required in assessing the growth rate to ensure consistency between the long term growth rate used and the assumptions used by the entity generally in its business planning.

4.6.5   *Discount rate*

After identifying the relevant cash flows for the asset or CGU, the next step is to identify an appropriate discount rate to use in deriving the present value of those cash flows.

Section 27 states that the discount rate (rates) used in the present value calculation shall be a pre-tax rate (rates) that reflect(s) current market assessments of:

- the time value of money; and
- the risks specific to the asset for which the future cash flow estimates have not been adjusted.

The discount rate (rates) used to measure an asset's value in use shall not reflect risks for which the future cash flow estimates have been adjusted, to avoid double-counting. *[FRS 102.27.20]*.

This means the discount rate to be applied should be an estimate of the rate that the market would expect on an equally risky investment. The discount rate specific for the asset or CGU will take account of the period over which the asset or CGU is expected to generate cash inflows and it may not be sensitive to changes in short-term rates.

If at all possible, the rate should be obtained from market transactions or market rates. It should be the rate implicit in current market transactions for similar assets or the weighted average cost of capital (WACC) of a listed entity that has a single asset (or a portfolio of assets) with similar service potential and risks to the asset under review.

In most cases an asset-specific rate will not be available from the market and therefore estimates will be required. Determining the discount rate that investors would require if they were to choose an investment that would generate cash flows of amounts, timing and risk profile equivalent to those that the entity expects to derive from the asset will not be easy.

As a starting point, the entity may take into account the following rates:

- the entity's weighted average cost of capital determined using techniques such as the Capital Asset Pricing Model;
- the entity's incremental borrowing rate; and
- other market borrowing rates.

From that starting point the rate should be adjusted to:

- reflect the specific risks associated with the projected cash flows (such as country, currency, price and cash flow risks);
- exclude risks that are not relevant to the asset or CGU concerned;
- avoid double counting, by ensuring that the discount rate does not reflect risks for which future cash flow estimates have already been adjusted; and
- reflect a pre-tax rate if the basis for the starting rate is post-tax (such as WACC).

As the rate required is one which is specific to the asset (or CGU) and not to the entity, the discount rate should be independent of the entity's capital structure and the way it financed the purchase of the asset.

In practice many entities will use the WACC as a starting point to estimate the appropriate discount rate, just as they did under previous UK GAAP or IAS 36. WACC is an accepted methodology based on a well-known formula and widely available information and in addition, many entities already know their own WACC. However, it can only be used as a starting point for determining an appropriate discount rate. Some of the issues that must be taken into account are as follows:

Chapter 22

a)   the WACC is a post-tax rate and Section 27 requires VIU to be calculated using pre-tax cash flows and a pre-tax rate. Converting the former into the latter is not simply a question of grossing up the post-tax rate by the effective tax rate;

b)   other tax factors may need to be considered, whether or not these will result in tax cash flows in the period covered by budgets and cash flows;

c)   an entity's own WACC may not be suitable as a discount rate if there is anything atypical about the entity's capital structure compared with 'typical' market participants;

d)   the WACC must reflect the risks specific to the asset and not the risks relating to the entity as a whole, such as default risk; and

e)   the entity's WACC is an average rate derived from its existing business, yet entities frequently operate in more than one sector. Within a sector, different types of projects may have different levels of risk (e.g. a start-up as against an established product).

The selection of the discount rate is obviously a crucial part of the impairment testing process and in practice it will probably not be possible to obtain a theoretically perfect rate. The objective, therefore, must be to obtain a rate which is sensible and justifiable and in order to do so, specialist advice may be needed. For further discussion on calculation of an appropriate discount rate and on how entities can derive the appropriate pre-tax equivalent rate from a starting point of WACC, readers may wish to refer to section 4.5 of Chapter 20 of EY International GAAP 2015. Ultimately the selection of discount rates leaves considerable room for judgement and it is likely that many very different approaches will be applied in practice, even though this may not always be evident from the financial statements. Once the discount rate has been chosen, the future cash flows are discounted in order to produce a present value figure representing the VIU of the CGU or individual asset that is the subject of the impairment test.

4.6.6   Assets held for their service potential

While in a for-profit entity, it is appropriate to determine VIU by measuring the present value of the cash flows derived from an asset or CGU, this may be less relevant in the context of Public Benefit Entities (PBEs). A PBE is defined in FRS 102 as an entity whose primary objective is to provide goods or services for the general public, community or social benefit and where any equity is provided with a view to supporting the entity's primary objectives rather than with a view to providing a financial return to equity providers, shareholders or members.

In a PBE assets may be held not for cash generating purposes but for their service potential i.e. where the benefits are expected to be derived through use of the asset along with proceeds from sale. To acknowledge this, Section 27 includes the following alternative approach for such assets.

For assets held for their service potential a cash flow driven valuation (such as value in use) may not be appropriate. In these circumstances value in use (in respect of assets held for their service potential) is determined by the present value of the asset's remaining service potential plus the net amount the entity will receive from its disposal. In some cases this may be taken to be costs avoided by possession of the asset. Therefore, depreciated replacement cost, may be a suitable measurement model but other approaches may be used where more appropriate. *[FRS 102.27.20A].*

4.6.7 Corporate assets

An entity may have assets that are inherently incapable of generating cash inflows independently, such as headquarters buildings or central IT facilities that contribute to more than one CGU. The characteristics that distinguish these corporate assets are that they do not generate cash inflows independently of other assets or groups of assets and their carrying amount cannot be fully attributed to one CGU. Section 27 provides no specific guidance on how to deal with such assets, although they would certainly fall within its scope. Under the hierarchy in Section 10 of the Standard, users may consider guidance which is provided under IAS 36.

Corporate assets present a problem in the event of those assets showing indications of impairment. It also raises a question of what those indications might actually be, in the absence of cash inflows directly relating to this type of asset. Some, but not all, of these assets may have relatively easily determinable fair values but while this is usually true of a headquarters building, it could not be for a central IT facility. We have already noted at 4.3.2 above that a decline in value of the asset itself may not trigger a need for an impairment review and it may be obvious that the CGUs of which corporate assets are a part are not showing any indications of impairment – unless, of course, management has decided to dispose of the asset. It is most likely that a corporate asset will show indications of impairment if the CGU or group of CGUs to which it relates are showing indications and this is reflected in the methodology in IAS 36 by which corporate assets are tested.

The corporate asset's carrying value should be tested for impairment along with CGUs. This allocation allows the recoverable amount of all of the assets involved, both CGU and corporate ones, to be considered.

If possible, the corporate assets should be allocated to individual CGUs on a reasonable and consistent basis. If the carrying value of a corporate asset can be allocated on a reasonable and consistent basis between individual CGUs, each CGU should have its impairment test done separately and its carrying value includes its share of the corporate asset.

If the corporate asset's carrying value cannot be allocated to an individual CGU, IAS 36 suggests three steps as noted below. As noted above, indicators of impairment for corporate assets that cannot be allocated to individual CGUs are likely to relate to the CGUs that use the corporate asset as well. First the CGU is tested for impairment and any impairment written off. Then a group of CGUs is identified to which, as a group, all or part of the carrying value of the corporate asset can be allocated. This group should include the CGU that was the subject of the first test. Finally, all CGUs in this group should be tested to determine if the group's carrying value (including the allocation of the corporate asset's carrying value) is in excess of the group's VIU. If it is not in excess the impairment loss should be allocated pro-rata to all assets in the group of CGUs as the allocated portion of the corporate asset.

In the illustrative examples accompanying IAS 36, Example 8 has a fully worked example of the allocation and calculation of a VIU involving corporate assets. The Example below is included, and serves to illustrate the allocation of the corporate asset to CGUs:

Example 22.8:   Allocation of corporate assets

An entity comprises three CGUs and a headquarters building. The carrying amount of the headquarters building of 150 is allocated to the carrying amount of each individual cash-generating unit. A weighted allocation basis is used because the estimated remaining useful life of A's cash-generating unit is 10 years, whereas the estimated remaining useful lives of B and C's cash-generating units are 20 years.

Schedule 1. Calculation of a weighted allocation of the carrying amount of the headquarters building

End of 20X0	**A**	**B**	**C**	**Total**
Carrying amount	100	150	200	450
Remaining useful life	10 years	20 years	20 years	
Weighting based on useful life	1	2	2	
Carrying amount after weighting	100	300	400	800
Pro-rata allocation of the building	(100/800)= 12%	(300/800)= 38%	(400/800)= 50%	100%
Allocation of the carrying amount of the building (based on pro-rata above)	18	57	75	150
Carrying amount (after allocation of the building)	118	207	275	600

The allocation need not be made on carrying value or financial measures such as turnover – employee numbers or a time basis might be a valid basis in certain circumstances.

One effect of this pro-rata process is that the amount of the head office allocated to each CGU will change as the useful lives and carrying values change. In the above example, the allocation of the head office to CGU A will be redistributed to CGUs B and C as A's remaining life shortens. The entity will have to ensure that B and C can support an increased head office allocation. Similar effects will be observed if the sizes of any other factor on which the allocation to the CGUs is made change relative to one another.

5   GOODWILL AND ITS ALLOCATION TO CGUS

Goodwill, by itself, cannot be sold. Nor does it generate cash flows to an entity that are independent of other assets. As a consequence, the fair value of goodwill cannot be measured directly. Therefore, the fair value of goodwill must be derived from measurement of the fair value of the CGU(s) of which the goodwill is a part. *[FRS 102.27.24]*.

For the purpose of impairment testing, goodwill acquired in a business combination shall, from the acquisition date, be allocated to each of the acquirer's CGUs that are expected to benefit from the synergies of the combination, irrespective of whether other assets or liabilities of the acquiree are assigned to those units. *[FRS 102.27.25]*.

Example 22.9: Allocating goodwill to CGUs – a simple example

On 1 January 20X1 Entity A acquired Entity B. As a consequence of the business combination, Entity B became a wholly owned subsidiary of entity A. Entities A and B each have one CGU. Goodwill of £1,000 arose from the business combination, all of which is attributable to synergies of the combination which are expected to arise in Entity B's CGU only.

For the purposes of impairment testing, £1,000 goodwill is allocated to Entity B's CGU. No goodwill is allocated to Entity A's CGU.

Example 22.10: Allocating goodwill to more than one CGU

The facts are the same as Example 22.9. However, in this example, 60 per cent of the goodwill is attributable to synergies of the combination that are expected to occur in Entity A's CGU. The rest of the goodwill is attributable to synergies in Entity B's CGU.

For the purposes of impairment testing, £600 goodwill is allocated to Entity A's CGU and £400 goodwill is allocated to Entity B's CGU.

The examples above are fairly simple, but the allocation of goodwill to individual CGUs or groups of CGUs at the date of acquisition is likely to require significant judgement by management. In some cases management may conclude that it is not possible to allocate goodwill on anything but an arbitrary basis. Section 27 addresses this issue by allowing management to test the associated goodwill for impairment by splitting the entity into two parts. The requirement is set out as follows.

If goodwill cannot be allocated to individual CGUs (or groups of CGUs) on a non-arbitrary basis, then for the purposes of testing goodwill the entity shall test the impairment of goodwill by determining the recoverable amount of either:

- the acquired entity in its entirety, if the goodwill relates to an acquired entity that has not been integrated. Integrated means the acquired business has been restructured or dissolved into the reporting entity or other subsidiaries; or

- the entire group of entities, excluding any entities that have not been integrated, if the goodwill relates to an entity that has been integrated.

In applying this paragraph, an entity will need to separate goodwill into goodwill relating to entities that have been integrated and goodwill relating to entities that have not been integrated. Also the entity shall follow the requirements for CGUs in this section when calculating the recoverable amount of, and allocating impairment losses and reversals to, assets belonging to, the acquired entity or group of entities. *[FRS102.27.27].*

It is not clear how often this method will be applied in practice as we would generally expect management to have a reasonable basis of allocating goodwill to individual CGUs or group of CGUs. The application of paragraph 27 is shown in the following example.

Example 22.11: Non-allocated goodwill and integrated/non-integrated subsidiaries

Group A comprises a parent company and several subsidiaries. Management of Group A considers that goodwill cannot be allocated to individual CGUs or groups of CGUs on a non-arbitrary basis.

On 1 January 20X2 Group A acquired 100 per cent of the ordinary share capital of Entity Z for £10,000. Goodwill of £1,000 arose in accounting for that business combination. That goodwill is amortised using the straight line basis over 10 years.

At 31 December 20X2 the total carrying amount of goodwill after amortisation, and any impairment made in prior years, in Group A's consolidated financial statements is £3,900 (note: the £3,900 includes goodwill from a number of business combinations including the acquisition of Entity Z).

On 31 December 20X2, as impairment indicators are present, Group A performs an impairment test on all of its goodwill.

Assume that, at 31 December 20X2, the recoverable amount of Group A (excluding Entity Z) is £34,000, the recoverable amount of Entity Z is £10,500 and the recoverable amount of Group A (including Entity Z) is £44,500.

Scenario 1 – Non-integrated subsidiary – Entity Z is engaged in dissimilar activities from the rest of Group A. Entity Z has therefore not been integrated into Group A.

At 31 December 20X2 the carrying amount of the net assets of Group A and Entity Z were as follows:

	Goodwill	Carrying amount (excluding Goodwill) at 31/12/20X2[(1)]
	£	£
Group A (excluding Z)	[(2)]3,000	30,000
Entity Z	[(3)]900	10,000
Group A	3,900	40,000

[(1)] After depreciation and amortisation

[(2)] Goodwill relating to the acquisition of subsidiaries other than Entity Z.

[(3)] Goodwill relating to the acquisition of Entity Z.

Because Entity Z's activities are not integrated into Group A, in accordance with FRS 102.27.27(a), the goodwill arising on Entity Z is tested separately from the goodwill relating to Group A's other business combinations. The impairment loss is calculated as follows:

Entity Z (non-integrated entity): impairment = £400 (carrying amount £10,900 less recoverable amount £10,500). The impairment loss reduces goodwill by £400.

Group A (excluding Entity Z): no impairment as the recoverable amount of Group A (excluding Entity Z) of £34,000 exceeds the carrying amount of Group A (excluding Entity Z) of £33,000.

Total impairment loss for Group A = £400.

Scenario 2 – Subsidiary is integrated – Entity Z has been integrated into Group A.

At 31 December 20X2 the carrying amount of the net assets of Group A are:

	Goodwill	Carrying amount at 31/12/20X2[(1)]
	£	£
Group A	[(2)]3,900	40,000

[(1)] After depreciation and amortisation

[(2)] Goodwill relating to the acquisition of subsidiaries including the acquisition of Entity Z.

The goodwill arising on the acquisition of Entity Z is combined with the rest of the goodwill relating to Group A from the date of acquisition of Entity Z. The impairment loss is calculated as follows:

Group A: no impairment because the recoverable amount £44,500 exceeds the carrying amount of £43,900 (£3,900 goodwill plus £40,000 other assets at group carrying amounts).

As can be seen from the example above, an incidental effect of this approach may be to reduce the incidence of write-downs, as the higher the level at which the goodwill is tested for impairment, the more likely that an impairment loss can be avoided. Judgement will be required in order to assess whether an arbitrary allocation of goodwill is genuinely all that is possible.

5.1 Goodwill on non-controlling interests

As required by Section 19 of FRS 102 – *Business Combinations and Goodwill,* an acquirer shall, at the acquisition date:

- recognise goodwill acquired in a business combination as an asset; and
- initially measure that goodwill at its cost, being the excess of the cost of the business combination over the acquirer's interest in the net amount of the identifiable assets, liabilities and contingent liabilities recognised and measured in accordance with paragraphs FRS 102.19.15-15B. *[FRS 102.19.22].*

Non-controlling interests (NCI) are measured at the acquisition date at their proportionate share of the acquiree's identifiable net assets, which excludes goodwill i.e. goodwill attributable to NCI is not recognised in the parent's consolidated financial statements. However the recoverable amount would be calculated for the whole CGU, i.e. part of the recoverable amount of the CGU determined in accordance with Section 27 that is attributable to the non-controlling interest in goodwill.

Therefore, for the purposes of impairment testing of a non-wholly owned CGU with goodwill, the carrying amount of that unit is notionally adjusted, before being compared with its recoverable amount, by grossing up the carrying amount of goodwill allocated to the unit to include the goodwill attributable to the NCI. This notionally adjusted carrying amount is then compared with the recoverable amount of the unit to determine whether the CGU is impaired. *[FRS 102.27.26].*

FRS 102 provides no specific guidance on how the gross up should be performed, but we expect the default method will be a simple mechanical gross up based on ownership percentages. This is shown in Example 22.12 below. However, in the absence of specific guidance we consider that an entity is not precluded from grossing up goodwill on a basis other than ownership percentages if to do so is reasonable.

Example 22.12: Notionally adjusting the carrying amount of goodwill for non-controlling interests

On 30 December 20X5 Entity A acquired 75% of Entity Z. As a consequence of the business combination, Entity Z become a subsidiary of Entity A. Entities A and Z each have one CGU. Goodwill of £750 arose from the business combination, all of which is attributable to synergies of the combination that are expected to occur only in Entity Z's CGU.

In the group's consolidated statement of financial position NCI is measured at their proportionate interest (25%) of the group carrying amount of Entity Z's net assets excluding goodwill.

If Entity Z's CGU was tested for impairment on 31 December 20X5, the £750 goodwill asset allocated to entity Z's CGU would, solely for the purpose of the impairment test at group level, be grossed up by £250 to £1,000 (i.e. it would be notionally increased to include goodwill attributable to the NCI's 25% interest in the CGU).

In the event of an impairment, the entity allocates the impairment loss as usual, first reducing the carrying amount of goodwill allocated to the CGU. However, because only the parent's goodwill is recognised, the impairment loss is apportioned between that attributable to the parent and that attributable to the NCI, with only the former being recognised.

Example 22.15 in section 6.4 below shows an impairment calculation where goodwill has been notionally adjusted to take account of NCI.

6   RECOGNISING AND MEASURING IMPAIRMENT LOSSES

An impairment loss occurs when the carrying amount of an asset or CGU exceeds its recoverable amount. The following sections set out how such impairment losses should be recognised.

6.1   Recognising an impairment loss on an individual asset

In the case of individual assets, Section 27 requires that an entity shall recognise an impairment loss immediately in profit or loss, unless the asset is carried at a revalued amount in accordance with another section of FRS 102 (for example in accordance with the revaluation model in Section 17). Any impairment loss of a revalued asset shall be treated as a revaluation decrease in accordance with that other section. *[FRS 102.27.6].*

If there is an impairment loss on an asset that has not been revalued, it is recognised in profit or loss. An impairment loss on a revalued asset is first used to reduce the revaluation surplus for that asset. Only when the impairment loss exceeds the amount in the revaluation surplus for that same asset is any further impairment loss recognised in profit or loss. *[FRS 102.17.15F].*

An impairment loss will reduce the depreciable amount of an asset and the revised amount will be depreciated or amortised prospectively over the remaining life. However, an entity ought also to review the useful life and residual value of its impaired asset as both of these may need to be revised. The circumstances that give rise to impairments frequently affect these as well. *[FRS 102.27.10].*

6.2   Recognising an impairment loss on a CGU

An impairment loss shall be recognised for a CGU if, and only if, the recoverable amount of the unit is less than the carrying amount of the unit. The impairment loss shall be allocated to reduce the carrying amount of the assets of the unit in the following order:

- first, to reduce the carrying amount of any goodwill allocated to the CGU;
- then to the other assets of the unit *pro rata* on the basis of the carrying amount of each asset in the CGU. *[FRS 102.27.21].*

This principle is illustrated in Example 22.13 below.

Example 22.13:   Impairment loss for a CGU with goodwill – a simple example

On 31 December 20X1, Entity T acquires 100% of voting rights in Entity M for £10,000. Entity M has manufacturing plants in three countries, A, B and C, each of which is considered a CGU.

The fair value of identifiable assets in Entity M is £7,000 and goodwill of £3,000 arising on the acquisition has been allocated across the three CGUs A, B and C.

During 20X2, a new government is elected in Country A. It passed legislation that significantly restricts exports of the main product produced by Entity T and its subsidiaries (i.e. Group T). As a result, and for the foreseeable future, Group T's production in Country A will be cut by 40 percent. The significant export restriction and the resulting production decrease require Group T to estimate the recoverable amount of Country A's CGU at the end of 20X2.

Management estimates cash flow forecasts for Country A's operations and determines the CGU's recoverable amount to be £1,360. The carrying amounts of goodwill and identifiable assets of

Country A are £800 and £1,833 respectively. The calculation and allocation of the impairment loss for Country A's CGU at the end of 20X2 is as follows:

	Carrying amount	Impairment (1)	Carrying amount after impairment
	£		£
Goodwill	800	(800)	–
Asset A	500	(129)	371
Asset B	457	(118)	339
Asset C	876	(226)	650
Total identifiable assets	1,833	(473)	1,360
Total assets	2,633	(1,273)	1,360

(1) Impairment allocated pro-rata to identifiable assets e.g. for Asset A this is (500 ÷ 1,833) × 473 = 129.

The impairment loss is recorded first against the carrying amount of goodwill (£800) and next, pro-rata against the carrying amount of Country A's identifiable assets (£473).

However, an entity shall not reduce the carrying amount of any asset in the CGU below the highest of:

- its fair value less costs to sell (if determinable);

- its value in use (if determinable); and

- zero. *[FRS 102.27.22].*

Any excess amount of the impairment loss that cannot be allocated to an asset because of the restriction in paragraph 27.22 shall be allocated to the other assets of the unit *pro rata* on the basis of the carrying amount of those other assets. *[FRS 102.27.23].*

The Example below illustrates how this approach would be applied in practice.

Example 22.14: Impairment loss for a CGU with goodwill

An entity's CGU produces a product in a continuous process using three machines i.e. the output of Machine A is the input (raw material) for Machine B, the output of which is the input for Machine C. The output from Machine C is the entity's only marketable product.

After recognising depreciation and amortisation for the year ended 20X1 the carrying amount of the CGU containing Machines A, B and C including Goodwill is £72,220. This can be broken down as £13,000 for Machine A, £29,250 for Machine B, £22,750 for Machine C and £7,220 for goodwill.

As there has been a significant downturn in the market for its products, the entity must conduct an impairment test on the associated CGU. The value in use of the CGU is calculated to be £55,000.

With a carrying value of £72,220 and a value in use of £55,000, this gives rise to an impairment loss of £17,220. The impairment loss is first allocated to the goodwill (£7,220) and then to the other assets of the CGU on a *pro rata* basis reflecting the carrying amount of each asset in the CGU.

Management have been able to determine the FVLCS of Machine A at £12,500. They have not been able to determine the FVLCS or VIU of any other individual asset within the CGU.

Absent the information about the FVLCS of Machine A, the remaining impairment loss of £10,000 (total impairment of £17,220 less £7,220 allocated to goodwill) would be allocated to Machines A, B and C on a pro-rata basis as follows:

	Carrying amount before impairment	Carrying amount in relation to CGU's carrying amount	Notional impairment allocation	Notional carrying amount after impairment
	£	%	£	£
Machine A	13,000	20	2,000	11,000
Machine B	29,250	45	4,500	24,750
Machine C	22,750	35	3,500	19,250
Total	65,000		10,000	55,000

However, this allocation would reduce the carrying amount of Machine A to £11,000, which is lower than its FVLCS of £12,500. Consequently, in accordance with FRS 102.27.22(a), the impairment loss allocated to Machine A is limited to £500 (i.e. £13,000 carrying amount less £12,500 FVLCS). The remaining impairment loss of £1,500 (i.e. £2,000 less £500 allocated to Machine A) is allocated to Machines B and C on the basis of each machine's carrying amount in relation to the total carrying amount of the two machines as follows:

	Carrying amount after first impairment	Carrying amount in relation to CGU's carrying amount	Second impairment allocation
	£	%	£
Machine B	24,750	56.25	844
Machine C	19,250	43.75	656
Total	44,000		1,500

The total impairment loss allocated to each machine is shown below, together with the carrying amounts of Machines A, B and C immediately after recognising the impairment loss.

	Carrying amount before impairment	First impairment allocation	Second impairment allocation	Total impairment	Carrying amount after impairment
	£	£	£	£	£
Machine A	13,000	500	–	500	12,500
Machine B	29,250	4,500	844	5,344	23,906
Machine C	22,750	3,500	656	4,156	18,594
Goodwill	7,220	7,220	–	7,220	–
Total	72,220	15,720	1,500	17,220	55,000

In the above example, the impairment loss is fully allocated across the assets of the CGU. However, as individual assets cannot be written down below the higher of their FVLCS and their VIU, this may not always be the case, thus an element of the impairment charge may not be recognised.

6.3   Recognising an impairment loss on a group of CGUs

It is important when applying the requirements above, that impairment testing is conducted in the right order. If there are indicators of impairment in connection with a CGU with which goodwill is associated, i.e. the CGU is part of a CGU group to which goodwill is allocated, the individual CGU should be tested and any necessary impairment loss taken, before the 'CGU group' goodwill is tested for impairment. These impairment losses and consequent reductions in carrying values are treated in exactly the same way as those for individual assets as explained at 6.1 above.

6.4 Recognising an impairment loss on a CGU with goodwill and non-controlling interests

As noted at 5.1 above, when impairment testing a non-wholly owned CGU with goodwill, the carrying amount of that unit must be notionally adjusted, before being compared with its recoverable amount, by grossing up the carrying amount of goodwill allocated to the unit to include the goodwill attributable to the NCI. *[FRS 102.27.26].*

If there is an impairment, the entity allocates the impairment loss as usual, first reducing the carrying amount of goodwill allocated to the CGU. However, because only the parent's goodwill is recognised, the impairment loss is apportioned between that attributable to the parent and that attributable to the NCI, with only the former being recognised.

If any impairment loss remains, it is allocated in the usual way to the other assets of the CGU *pro rata* on the basis of the carrying amount of each asset in the CGU.

These requirements are illustrated in the following example.

Example 22.15:   A CGU with goodwill and non-controlling interest

Entity X acquires an 80 per cent ownership interest in Entity Y for £1,600 on 1 January 20X3. At that date, Entity Y's identifiable net assets have a fair value of £1,500. Entity X recognises in its consolidated financial statements:

(a)   goodwill of £400, being the difference between the cost of the business combination of £1,600 and acquirer's interest in the identifiable net assets of Entity Y of £1,200 (being 80% of £1,500);

(b)   Entity Y's identifiable net assets at their fair value of £1,500; and

(c)   a non-controlling interest of £300, being the remaining 20% of Entity Y's identifiable net assets.

The group considers Entity Y to be a CGU and the full £400 of goodwill is allocated to that CGU. For simplicity, we shall ignore the amortisation of goodwill in this example.

At the end of 20X3, the carrying amount of Entity Y's identifiable assets (excluding goodwill) has reduced to £1,350 and Entity X determines that the recoverable amount of Entity Y is £1,000.

The carrying amount of Entity Y must be notionally adjusted to include goodwill attributable to the non-controlling interest, before being compared with the recoverable amount of £1,000. Goodwill attributable to Entity X's 80% interest in Entity Y at 31 December 20X3 is £400. Therefore, goodwill notionally attributable to the 20% non-controlling interest in Entity Y at the acquisition date is £100, being £400 × 20 ÷ 80. Testing Entity Y for impairment at the end of 20X3 gives rise to an impairment loss of £850 calculated as follows:

	Goodwill £	Identifiable net assets £	Total £
Carrying amount	400	1,350	1,750
Unrecognised non-controlling interest	100	–	100
Notionally adjusted carrying amount	500	1,350	1,850
Recoverable amount			1,000
Impairment loss			850

The impairment loss of £850 is allocated to the assets in the CGU by first reducing the carrying amount of goodwill to zero. Therefore, £500 of the £850 impairment loss for Entity Y is allocated to the goodwill. However, because Entity X only holds a 80% ownership interest in Entity Y, it recognises only 80 per cent of that goodwill impairment loss (i.e. £400). The remaining impairment loss of £350 is recognised by reducing the carrying amounts of Entity Y's identifiable assets, as follows:

	Goodwill £	Identifiable net assets £	Total £
Carrying amount	400	1,350	1,750
Impairment loss	(400)	(350)	(750)
Carrying amount after impairment loss	–	1,000	1,000

Of the impairment loss of £350 relating to Entity Y's identifiable assets, £70 (i.e. 20% thereof) would be attributed to the non-controlling interest.

In this example the same result would have been achieved by just comparing the recoverable amount of £1,000 with the carrying amount of £1,750. However, what if the recoverable amount of the CGU had been greater than the carrying amount of the identifiable net assets prior to recognising the impairment loss?

Assume the same facts as above, except that at the end of 20X3, Entity X determines that the recoverable amount of Entity Y is £1,400. In this case, testing Entity Y for impairment at the end of 20X3 gives rise to an impairment loss of £450 calculated as follows:

	Goodwill £	Identifiable net assets £	Total £
Carrying amount	400	1,350	1,750
Unrecognised non-controlling interest	100	–	100
Notionally adjusted carrying amount	500	1,350	1,850
Recoverable amount			1,400
Impairment loss			450

All of the impairment loss of £450 is allocated to the goodwill. However, Entity X recognises only 80 per cent of that goodwill impairment loss (i.e. £360). This allocation of the impairment loss results in the following carrying amounts for Entity Y in the financial statements of Entity X at the end of 20X3:

	Goodwill £	Identifiable net assets £	Total £
Carrying amount	400	1,350	1,750
Impairment loss	(360)	–	(360)
Carrying amount after impairment loss	40	1,350	1,390

Of the impairment loss of £360, none of it is attributable to the non-controlling interest since it all relates to the majority shareholder's goodwill.

In this case the total carrying amount of the identifiable net assets and the goodwill has not been reduced to the recoverable amount of £1,400, but is actually less than the recoverable amount. This is because the recoverable amount of goodwill relating to the non-controlling interest (20% of [£500 – £450]) is not recognised in the consolidated financial statements.

7   REVERSAL OF AN IMPAIRMENT LOSS

Section 27 states that an impairment loss recognised for all assets, including goodwill, shall be reversed in a subsequent period if and only if the reasons for the impairment loss have ceased to apply. *[FRS 102.27.28]*.

It goes on to say that an entity shall assess at each reporting date whether there is any indication that an impairment loss recognised in prior periods may no longer exist or may have decreased. Indications that an impairment loss may have decreased or may no longer exist are generally the opposite of those set out in paragraph 27.9 (as discussed at 4.3 above). If any such indication exists, the entity shall determine whether all or part of the prior impairment loss should be reversed. The procedure for making that determination will depend on whether the prior impairment loss on the asset was based on:

- the recoverable amount of that individual asset; or
- the recoverable amount of the cash-generating unit to which the asset belongs. *[FRS 102.27.29]*.

The indicators of impairment set out in FRS 102.27.9 are discussed at 4.3 above. The process to be followed for the reversal of an impairment on an individual asset is at 7.1 and for a CGU at 7.2 below.

7.1   Reversal where recoverable amount was estimated for an individual impaired asset

Section 27 states that when the prior impairment loss was based on the recoverable amount of the individual impaired asset, the following requirements apply:

(a)   The entity shall estimate the recoverable amount of the asset at the current reporting date.

(b)   If the estimated recoverable amount of the asset exceeds its carrying amount, the entity shall increase the carrying amount to recoverable amount, subject to the limitation described in (c) below. That increase is a reversal of an impairment loss. The entity shall recognise the reversal immediately in profit or loss unless the asset is carried at revalued amount in accordance with another section of this FRS (for example, the revaluation model in Section 17). Any reversal of an impairment loss of a revalued asset shall be treated as a revaluation increase in accordance with the relevant section of this FRS.

(c)   The reversal of an impairment loss shall not increase the carrying amount of the asset above the carrying amount that would have been determined (net of amortisation or depreciation) had no impairment loss been recognised for the asset in prior years.

(d)   After a reversal of an impairment loss is recognised, the entity shall adjust the depreciation (amortisation) charge for the asset in future periods to allocate the asset's revised carrying amount, less its residual value (if any), on a systematic basis over its remaining useful life. *[FRS 102.27.30]*.

Therefore if there are indications that a previously recognised impairment loss has disappeared or reduced, it is necessary to determine the recoverable amount (i.e. the higher of FVLCS or VIU) so that the reversal can be quantified.

In the event of an individual asset's impairment being reversed, Section 27 makes it clear that the reversal may not raise the carrying value above the figure it would have been (after taking into account the depreciation charge which would have applied) had no impairment originally been recognised. This requirement is illustrated in the example below.

Example 22.16:   Impairment reversal for an individually impaired asset

The facts are the same as in Example 22.6. During 20X4, it becomes apparent that the cheaper material used by Entity A's competitor was not fit for purpose and their components need replacement after a year. Sales of Entity A's product start to return to their previous levels. At 31 December 20X4 the machine has a carrying amount of £58,271. Management has reassessed the future cash flows based on changed circumstances since the end of 20X0 and determined VIU at the end of 20X4 to be £122,072. Management believes FVLCS is less than VIU.

At the end of 20X4, the machine's recoverable amount i.e. its VIU (£122,072) is higher than the machine's carrying amount before the recognition of any reversal of the impairment loss recognised in 20X0 (£58,271). It is an indication that the impairment loss recognised in 20X0 no longer exists or may have decreased.

End of 20X4	Machine
	£
Recoverable amount	122,072
Carrying amount before the reversal of the impairment loss recognised in 20X0	58,271
Difference	63,801

The difference is only an indication of the amount of the reversal because the reversal cannot increase the carrying amount of the asset above the carrying amount that would have been determined had no impairment loss been recognised for the asset in prior years. At 31 December 20X4, the carrying amount that would have been determined, had no impairment loss been recognised for the asset in prior years, is £120,000 (cost £300,000 less accumulated depreciation £180,000). Thus £120,000 is the maximum carrying amount for the asset after the reversal of impairment.

The entity compares the carrying amount at 20X4 if no impairment loss had been recognised, with the carrying amount at 20X4 and determines that the maximum impairment reversal is £61,729.

End of 20X4	Machine
	£
Cost	300,000
Less notional depreciation since acquisition until 20X4	(180,000)
Notional carrying amount at 31/12/20X4 if no impairment loss had been recognised for the asset in 20X0	120,000
Less carrying amount at the year ended 31/12/20X4, before the reversal of the impairment loss recognised in prior reporting periods	(58,271)
Reversal of prior year's impairment loss	61,729

As a consequence of the reversal of part of the impairment loss recognised at 31 December 20X0, the carrying amount of the machine is £120,000 i.e. equal to the carrying amount that would have been determined had no impairment loss been recognised for the asset in prior years. In subsequent periods, assuming that all variables remain the same as at the end of 20X4, the depreciable amount will be £120,000, so the depreciation charge will be £20,000 (£120,000 depreciable amount depreciated over remaining 6 year remaining useful life).

7.2 Reversal when recoverable amount was estimated for a cash-generating unit

When the original impairment loss was based on the recoverable amount of the cash-generating unit to which the asset, including goodwill belongs, the following requirements apply:

(a) The entity shall estimate the recoverable amount of that cash-generating unit at the current reporting date.

(b) If the estimated recoverable amount of the cash-generating unit exceeds its carrying amount, that excess is a reversal of an impairment loss. The entity shall allocate the amount of that reversal to the assets of the unit, pro rata with the carrying amounts of those assets and goodwill in the order set out below, subject to the limitation described in (c) below. Those increases in carrying amounts shall be treated as reversals of impairment losses and recognised immediately in profit or loss unless the asset is carried at revalued amount in accordance with another section of this FRS (for example, the revaluation model in Section 17). Any reversal of an impairment loss of a revalued asset shall be treated as a revaluation increase in accordance with the relevant section of this FRS.

    (i) First the assets (other than goodwill) of the unit *pro rata* on the basis of the carrying amount of each asset in the cash-generating unit, and

    (ii) then to any goodwill allocated to the cash-generating unit.

(c) In allocating a reversal of an impairment loss for a cash-generating unit, the reversal shall not increase the carrying amount of any asset above the lower of:

    (i) its recoverable amount; and

    (ii) the carrying amount that would have been determined (net of amortisation or depreciation) had no impairment loss been recognised for the asset in prior periods.

(d) Any excess amount of the reversal of the impairment loss that cannot be allocated to an asset because of the restriction in (c) above shall be allocated *pro rata* to the other assets of the cash-generating unit.

(e) After a reversal of an impairment loss is recognised, if applicable, the entity shall adjust the depreciation (amortisation) charge for each asset in the cash-generating unit in future periods to allocate the asset's revised carrying amount, less its residual value (if any), on a systematic basis over its remaining useful life. *[FRS 102.27.31]*.

The above requirements are illustrated in the example below.

Example 22.17: Impairment reversal for a cash generating unit

The facts are the same as those in Example 22.13. In 20X4 the government is still in office in Country A but the business situation is improving. The effects of the export laws on Entity T's production are proving to be less drastic than initially expected by management. As a result, management estimates that production will increase. This favourable change requires Entity T to re-estimate the recoverable amount of the CGU for the net assets of the Country A operations. Management estimates that the recoverable amount of the Country A CGU is now £2,010. Management are unable to estimate the FVLCS or VIU of any individual asset within the CGU. To calculate the reversal of the impairment loss, Entity T compares the recoverable amount and the net carrying amount of Country A's CGU.

	Goodwill	Identifiable assets	Total
	£	£	£
Historical cost	1,000	2,000	3,000
Accumulated amortisation/depreciation	(200)	(167)	(367)
Accumulated impairment loss	(800)	(473)	(1,273)
Carrying amount after impairment loss at 31/12/20X2	–	1,360	1,360
20X3 and 20X4			
Depreciation (2 years)[1]	–	(247)	(247)
Carrying amount before impairment reversal	–	1,113	1,113

[1] Two years of depreciation based on carrying amount of £1,360 at 1/1/20X3 and revised useful life of 11 years ((£1,360 ÷ 11 years = £123.6 per year) × 2 years = £247).

Comparing this with the recoverable amount of the CGU:

End of 20X4	CGU A
	£
Recoverable amount	2,010
Carrying amount before the reversal of the impairment loss recognised in 20X2	1,113
Difference	897

The difference is only an indication of the amount of the possible reversal because of the restriction in FRS 102.27.31(b)(i), which requires that any impairment reversal must first be applied to assets of the unit other than goodwill (subject to the limitation that the reversal cannot increase the carrying amount of any asset above the lower of its recoverable amount and the carrying amount that would have been determined (net of amortisation or depreciation) had no impairment loss been recognised for the asset in prior periods). As can be seen below, this results in the impairment reversal being restricted to £787.

	Goodwill	Identifiable assets	Total
	£	£	£
Carrying amount before impairment reversal	–	1,113	1,113
Carrying amount assuming no prior period impairment)[2]	400	1,500	1,900
Impairment reversal applied to identifiable assets	–	387	
Impairment reversal applied to goodwill	400	–	
Total impairment reversal recognised			787

[2] Goodwill continues to be amortised over 5 years at £200 per year and identifiable assets continue to be depreciated over 12 years @£166.70 per year.

Note: if management were able to estimate the recoverable amount for any of the individual identifiable assets then these amounts (if lower) would be used in restricting the impairment reversal.

8   DISCLOSURES

An entity shall disclose the following for each class of assets indicated in the paragraph below:

- the amount of impairment losses recognised in profit or loss during the period and the line item(s) in the statement of comprehensive income (or in the income statement, if presented) in which those impairment losses are included; and

- the amount of reversals of impairment losses recognised in profit or loss during the period and the line item(s) in the statement of comprehensive income (or in the income statement, if presented) in which those impairment losses are reversed. *[FRS 102.27.32]*.

The information above is required for each of the following classes of asset:

- inventories;
- property, plant and equipment (including investment property accounted for by the cost method);
- goodwill;
- intangible assets other than goodwill;
- investments in associates; and
- investments in joint ventures. *[FRS 102.27.33]*.

An entity shall disclose a description of the events and circumstances that led to the recognition or reversal of the impairment loss. *[FRS 102.27.33A]*.

8.1   Companies Act disclosure requirements

Schedule 1 of the Large- and Medium-sized Companies and Groups (Accounts and Reports) Regulations 2008, (the Regulations), requires provisions for diminution in value to be made in respect of any fixed asset if the reduction in value is expected to be permanent. Where the reasons for the provision have ceased to apply, the provision must be written back to the extent that it is no longer necessary. In either case, amounts not shown in the profit and loss account must be disclosed in the notes to the accounts. *[1 Sch 19-20]*.

As accounts prepared under FRS 102 are Companies Act accounts, they must follow one of the four profit and loss account formats set out in the Regulations. Under Formats 2 and 4 in Schedule 1 of the Regulations, where expenses are classified by type, there are specific line items, 7(a) and 4(a) respectively, headed 'Depreciation and other amounts written off tangible and intangible fixed assets' where impairment losses should be shown. Under Formats 1 and 3, where expenses are classified by function, impairment losses should generally be shown in the same category of expense as depreciation of the relevant asset.

Chapter 22

The Regulations also require certain information to supplement the balance sheet. In respect of fixed assets, this includes:

- the cumulative amount of provisions for depreciation or diminution in value as at the beginning of the financial year and at the balance sheet date;

- the amount of any such provisions made in respect of the financial year;

- the amount of any adjustments made in respect of any such provisions during that year in consequence of the disposal of any assets; and

- the amount of any other adjustments made in respect of any such provisions during that year. *[1 Sch 51(3)]*.

9   SUMMARY OF GAAP DIFFERENCES

The key differences between FRS 102, previous UK GAAP and IFRS in accounting for impairments are set out below.

	FRS 102	*Previous UK GAAP*	*IFRS*
Timing of impairment tests	Impairment testing required only when indicators of impairment exist.	Mandatory annual testing for goodwill, intangible assets with an estimated useful life of more than 20 years, tangible assets with an estimated life of more than 50 years or on which no depreciation is charged on grounds of materiality.	Mandatory annual testing for goodwill and indefinite lived intangibles.
Assets held for service potential	Possible to use depreciated replacement cost as a measurement model.	Silent.	Silent.
Guidance on inputs to VIU calculations	No guidance	Guidance provided on identification of IGUs, treatment of central assets, basis for cash flow estimates and discount rate.	Guidance provided on identifying CGUs, allocating goodwill to those CGUs, estimating cash flows and discount rates and treatment of corporate assets.

When an acquired business is merged with an existing business	Silent	Carrying value of combined business is grossed up to reflect notional pre-existing internally generated goodwill and any impairment losses are allocated pro-rata between the purchased goodwill and the notional internally generated goodwill (with only the former recognised).	Silent
Allocation of goodwill to CGUs for purposes of impairment testing	Allocated to each of the acquirer's CGUs that are expected to benefit from the acquisition, whether or not the acquiree's other assets or liabilities are allocated to those units. If unable to allocate to CGUs non-arbitrarily, can test based on simplified split between integrated and non-integrated entities.	Allocated to individual IGUs or groups of IGUs in line with assets and liabilities of acquired entity.	Allocated to each of the acquirer's CGUs that are expected to benefit from the acquisition, whether or not the acquiree's other assets or liabilities are allocated to those units. Each CGU or group of CGUs to which goodwill is allocated shall represent the lowest level at which goodwill is monitored and cannot be larger than an IFRS 8 – *Operating Segments* – operating segment before aggregation.
Allocation of impairment losses	Impairment losses allocated first against goodwill, then against remaining assets on a pro-rata basis.	Impairment losses allocated first against goodwill, then against intangible assets and then against tangible assets on a pro-rata basis.	Impairment losses allocated first against goodwill, then against remaining assets on a pro-rata basis
Post impairment monitoring	No requirement.	Subsequent monitoring of cash flows explicitly required for 5 years after recoverable amount based on VIU, with re-performance of original impairment calculation if actual cash flows are significantly less than forecast.	No requirement.
Reversal of goodwill impairment	Permitted in certain circumstances.	Permitted in certain circumstances.	Not permitted.

Chapter 22

	FRS 102	*Previous UK GAAP*	*IFRS*
Disclosures	Limited to amount of impairment losses recognised/reversed and circumstances leading to it.	Additional requirements where an impairment loss has been recognised, including details of discount rates, periods over which cash flows projected and growth rates used in VIU calculations.	Extensive additional disclosures required in respect of goodwill/indefinite lived intangibles even where no impairment recognised – includes amounts of goodwill/indefinite lived intangibles allocated to particular CGUs, key assumptions, period over which cash flows projected, growth rates and discount rates applied and further detail where a reasonably possible change in a key assumption could give rise to an impairment.

Chapter 23   Employee benefits

Chapter 23

List of examples

Chapter 23

Chapter 23   Employee benefits

1   INTRODUCTION

Employee benefits typically form a very significant part of any entity's costs, and can take many varied forms. These are covered in two separate sections of FRS 102, Section 28 – *Employee Benefits* – which is dealt with in this chapter, and Section 26 – *Share-based Payment* (which is dealt with in Chapter 21).

Many issues in accounting for employee benefits can be straight forward, such as the allocation of wages paid to an accounting period. In contrast accounting for the costs of retirement benefits in the financial statements of employers presents one of the most difficult challenges within the field of financial reporting. The amounts involved are large, the timescale is long, the estimation process is complex and involves many areas of uncertainty for which assumptions must be made.

2   COMPARISON BETWEEN SECTIONS 28, PREVIOUS UK GAAP AND IFRS

2.1   Key differences from previous UK GAAP

2.1.1   Scope

Section 28 of FRS 102 has a much broader scope than previous UK GAAP (FRS 17 – *Retirement benefits*) which only dealt with retirement benefits. Section 28 also includes in its scope the accounting for short-term and long-term employee benefits, and termination benefits. Although the accounting for many of these would have been picked up by FRS 12 – *Provisions, contingent liabilities and assets*, there will be a requirement to account for short-term compensated absences (see 3.3 below) which may not have been accounted for under FRS 12. The occurrence of compensated absences may lead to a transition adjustment. In addition under previous UK GAAP, discounting was only required where it was material. Under FRS 102, long-term employee benefits and termination benefits are required to be discounted where they are due after more than 12 months from the reporting date. It is therefore unlikely that this requirement to discount will lead to a material transition adjustment.

2.1.2   *Defined benefit pension schemes*

2.1.2.A   *Net interest*

Under FRS 17 an entity would have recognised in its profit and loss account the interest cost and the expected return on assets as a net item in other finance costs (or income) adjacent to interest. *[FRS 17.56].* The calculation of the interest cost was based on the discount rate and the expected return on assets based on long term expectations for these assets. *[FRS 17.53-54].* Section 28 follows the accounting in IAS 19 Revised – *Employee Benefits*, with the net interest recognised in the income statement being calculated based on the discount rate. *[FRS 102.28.24].* Therefore, there are differences between the two standards in the calculation of interest being recognised in the income statement and remeasurements/actuarial gains and losses (the other side of this difference) being recognised in other comprehensive income. The calculation of net interest under Section 28 is detailed in 3.6.8.A below, and remeasurements in 3.6.8.B below.

2.1.2.B   *Past service costs*

FRS 17 defined past service costs as 'the increase in the present value of the scheme liabilities related to employee service in prior periods arising in the current period as a result of the introduction of, or improvement to, retirement benefits'. *[FRS 17.3].* The standard required that past service costs were recognised in the profit and loss account on a straight line basis over the period in which the increases in benefit vest. *[FRS 17.60].* Although not specifically referred to as 'past service costs' in FRS 102, the standard requires that changes in the net defined benefit liability arising as a result of plan introductions or changes are recognised in profit and loss immediately. *[FRS 102.28.21].* This means that any unrecognised past service costs under previous UK GAAP will need to be recognised on transition to FRS 102.

2.1.2.C   *Group schemes*

Where it was not possible for a group defined benefit pension scheme to separately identify the share of underlying assets and liabilities for each individual company which participates in the scheme because the scheme was not run on this basis, FRS 17 allowed the individual companies to account for the scheme as a defined contribution scheme, with additional disclosures required. *[FRS 17.12].* FRS 102 does not offer this option, instead it requires a full actuarial valuation of the scheme as a whole to be obtained and for the scheme to be recognised on the balance sheet of at least one group entity. Where there is a stated policy for charging the net defined benefit cost to individual group entities, each entity recognises in its individual financial statements that cost. If there is no such agreement or policy, then the net defined benefit cost of a defined benefit plan shall be recognised in the individual financial statements of the group entity which is legally responsible for the plan. In this instance other group entities will recognise a cost equal to their contribution for the period to the plan in their individual financial statements. *[FRS 102.28.38].* This will lead to more pension deficits or surpluses being recognised on the balance sheets of individual entities than under previous UK GAAP, and may have a significant impact on the distributable reserves of any entity recognising a deficit. This is discussed further at 3.10 below.

2.1.2.D   Multi-employer schemes

FRS 17 required defined benefit multi-employer schemes to be accounted for as a defined benefit scheme, unless:

*   The employers' contributions were set in relation to the current service period only; or

*   The employers' contributions are affected by a surplus or deficit in the scheme, but the employer is unable to identify its share of the underlying assets and liabilities of the scheme on a consistent and reasonable basis.

In both cases the individual company is able to account for the scheme as a defined contribution scheme, but with additional disclosures being required in the second case. *[FRS 17.9]*.

FRS 102 also allows a defined benefit multi-employer scheme to be accounted for as a defined contribution scheme if sufficient information is not available to use defined benefit accounting, and also requires additional disclosures. *[FRS 102.28.11]*. This is discussed further at 3.4.2 below.

An additional requirement under FRS 102 is that where a defined benefit multi-employer plan is accounted for as a defined contribution scheme (as detailed above), and the entity has entered into an agreement with the plan that determines how an entity will fund a deficit, then the entity is required to a recognise a liability for the contributions payable arising from the agreement (to the extent that they relate to the deficit) and record the resulting expense in the profit and loss account. *[FRS 102.28.11A]*. This will lead to additional liabilities being recognised under FRS 102 than under previous UK GAAP.

2.1.2.E   Pension surpluses

Both FRS 17 and FRS 102 allow an entity to recognise a surplus 'only to the extent that it is able to recover the surplus either through reduced contributions in the future or through refunds from the plan'. *[FRS 17.37, FRS 102.28.22]*. Although both standards use the above words, FRS 102 does not elaborate any further. FRS 17 provided further guidance on how to determine the amount that can be recovered through future contributions adding that a pension surplus could only be recognised if the amount to be recovered from refunds to the scheme had been agreed by the pension trustees at the balance sheet date. *[FRS 17.42]*. In practice this meant that very few surpluses were recorded on the balance sheets of entities reporting under previous UK GAAP.

As a result it is possible that a surplus that had not previously been recognised under previous UK GAAP may be recognised under FRS 102. The amount of the surplus that can be recognised under FRS 102 requires judgement and is discussed further at 3.6.6 below.

Chapter 23

2.1.2.F   Presentation

As discussed at 2.2.4 below, presentation of a defined benefit deficit or surplus under FRS 102 will differ from previous UK GAAP as these will be presented gross of deferred tax under FRS 102. Under previous UK GAAP pension deficits or surpluses were presented net of deferred tax. *[FRS 17.49]*.

2.2   Key differences from IFRS

2.2.1   Past service costs

IAS 19 Revised defines past service costs as the change in the present value of the defined benefit obligation for employee service in prior periods, resulting from a plan amendment (the introduction or withdrawal of, or changes to, a defined benefit plan) or curtailment (a significant reduction by the entity in the number of employees covered by a plan). *[IAS 19.8]*. FRS 102 does not use the term past service costs, but still requires the cost of plan introductions, benefit changes, curtailments and settlements to be recorded in profit or loss. *[FRS 102.28.23(c)]*. As both standards require a charge to the profit and loss account the only difference is concerned with disclosure.

2.2.2   Asset ceilings and IFRIC 14 guidance

In practice, defined benefit pension plans tend to be funded on a more prudent basis than would be the case if a surplus or deficit measured in accordance with IAS 19 or FRS 102. This is usually due to the discount rate being used for funding purposes typically being lower than that specified in the standards. For this reason IAS 19 and FRS 102 valuations may result in a pension surplus, when for funding purposes there is a deficit.

As noted in 2.1.2.E above, FRS 102 requires that entity should recognise a plan surplus as a defined benefit asset only to the extent that it is able to recover the surplus either through reduced contributions in the future or through refunds from the plan. *[FRS 102.28.22]*. This is identical to the method used in IAS 19 which refers to the present value of the reduction in future contributions as the asset ceiling. FRS 102 does not elaborate on how this restriction is quantified, however IFRIC 14 – *IAS 19 – The Limit on a Defined Benefit Asset, Minimum Funding Requirements and their Interaction* – provides guidance on this issue.

The lack of guidance provided by FRS 102 will lead to management being required to make a judgement on the amount of a defined benefit pension surplus to be recognised under the standard. In making judgements the standard states that management may consider the requirements and guidance in EU-adopted IFRS dealing with similar or related issues, as discussed in Chapter 7 at 3.2. *[FRS 102.10.6]*. Given that the treatment of pension surpluses is dealt with under previous UK GAAP and EU-adopted IFRS, but with potentially different outcomes as a result of the strict requirements under previous UK GAAP that the amount to be recovered from refunds of the scheme should only reflect those that have been agreed by the pension scheme trustees at the balance sheet date *[FRS 17.42]*, as discussed at 2.1.2.E above, this may lead to a diversity in practice under FRS 102.

Due to the problems encountered in practice in applying the asset ceiling test in IAS 19, the issue was considered by the Interpretations Committee, and IFRIC 14 was issued. At present the guidance from IFRIC 14 has not been included within FRS 102. The interpretation set out to address the issues of:

- When refunds or reductions in future contributions should be regarded as available in accordance with the definition of the asset ceiling in IAS 19.8.

- How a minimum funding requirement might affect the availability of reductions in future contributions.

- When a minimum funding requirement might give rise to a liability.

The issue arising from the absence of this guidance within FRS 102 has been the subject of much discussion by the UK GAAP Technical Advisory Group (TAG). In August 2014, FRED 55 was issued which proposes to amend FRS 102 to confirm that an entity is not required to recognise additional liabilities to reflect an agreement with a defined benefit plan to fund a deficit.

The requirements of IFRIC 14 are discussed in full in EY International GAAP in Chapter 32.

2.2.3   *Attributing benefit to years of service*

IAS 19 requires benefits to be attributed to the periods in which the obligation to provide post-employment benefits arises. In applying the projected unit credit method, IAS 19 normally requires benefits to be attributed to periods of service under the plan's benefit formula, however if an employee's service in later years will lead to a materially higher level of benefit the benefit should be attributed on a straight line basis from:

- The date when service by the employee first leads to benefits under the plan; until

- The date when further service by the employee will lead to no material amount of further benefits under the plan, other than from further salary increases. *[IAS 19.70]*.

FRS 102 also notes that the present value of an entity's obligations under defined benefit plans should include the effects of benefit formulas that give employees greater benefits for later years of service, *[FRS 102.28.16]*, but does not state that this should be attributed on a straight line basis. Given the GAAP hierarchy in Section 10 – *Accounting Policies, Estimates and Errors* – we would expect users of the standard to follow the principles in IAS 19, but they are not required to.

2.2.4   *Presentation*

As FRS 102 requires the primary statements to follow the formats of the Large and Medium-sized companies and Groups (Accounts and Reports) Regulations 2008 Regulations ('The Regulations'), presentation under FRS 102 will differ from that required by IAS 1 – *Presentation of Financial Statements*. The Regulations show pension deficits as the first line item within provisions, and pension surpluses are presented in the same place as pension deficits (i.e. after accruals and deferred income) under format 1 of the Regulations, but after prepayments and accrued income under format 2 of the Regulations. FRS 17 required defined benefit pension assets or liabilities to be presented after accruals and deferred income, but before capital and reserves. *[FRS 17.47]*. This presentation was based on an interpretation of law. *[FRS 17 Appendix II.6]*. As a result there is likely to be divergence in practice in the presentation of defined benefit pension surpluses and deficits under FRS 102. This is further discussed at 3.12.4 below.

3   THE REQUIREMENTS OF SECTION 28 FOR EMPLOYEE BENEFITS

3.1   Terms used in Section 28

The following definitions are included within the FRS 102 Glossary.

Term	Definition
Accumulating compensated absences	Compensated absences that are carried forward and can be used in future periods if the current period's entitlement is not used in full.
Actuarial assumptions	An entity's unbiased and mutually compatible best estimates of the demographic and financial variables that will determine the ultimate cost of providing post-employment benefits.
Actuarial gains and losses	Changes in the present value of the defined benefit obligation resulting from: • experience adjustments (the effects of differences between the previous actuarial assumptions and what has actually occurred); and • the effects of changes in actuarial assumptions.
Assets held by a long term employee benefit fund	An asset (other than non-transferable financial instruments issued by the reporting entity) that: • is held by an entity (a fund) that is legally separate from the reporting entity and exists solely to pay or fund employee benefits; and • is available to be used only to pay or fund employee benefits, is not available to the reporting entity's own creditors (even in bankruptcy), and cannot be returned to the reporting entity, unless either: • the remaining assets of the fund are sufficient to meet all the related employee benefit obligations of the plan or the reporting entity; or the assets are returned to the reporting entity to reimburse it for employee benefits already paid.
Constructive obligation	An obligation that derives from an entity's actions where: • by an established pattern of past practice, published policies or a sufficiently specific current statement, the entity has indicated to other parties that it will accept certain responsibilities; and • as a result, the entity has created a valid expectation on the part of those other parties that it will discharge those responsibilities.

Defined benefit obligation (present value of)	The present value, without deducting any plan assets, of expected future payments required to settle the obligation resulting from employee service in the current and prior periods.
Defined benefit plans	Post-employment benefit plans other than defined contribution plans.
Defined contribution plans	Post-employment benefit plans under which an entity pays fixed contributions into a separate entity (a fund) and has no legal or constructive obligation to pay further contributions or to make direct benefit payments to employees if the fund does not hold sufficient assets to pay all employee benefits relating to employee service in the current and prior periods.
Employee benefits	All forms of consideration given by an entity in exchange for service rendered by employees.
Funding (of post-employment benefits)	Contributions by an entity, and sometimes its employees, into an entity, or fund, that is legally separate from the reporting entity and from which the employee benefits are paid.
Multi-employer (benefit) plans	Defined contribution plans (other than state plans) or defined benefit plans (other than state plans) that: • pool the assets contributed by various entities that are not under common control, and • use those assets to provide benefits to employees of more than one entity, on the basis that contribution and benefit levels are determined without regard to the identity of the entity that employs the employees concerned.
Net defined benefit liability	The present value of the defined benefit obligation at the reporting date minus the fair value at the reporting date of plan assets (if any) out of which the obligations are to be settled.
Plan assets (of employee benefit plan)	(a) assets held by a long-term employee benefit fund; and (b) qualifying insurance policies.
Post-employment benefits	Employee benefits (other than termination benefits and short-term employee benefits) that are payable after the completion of employment.
Post-employment benefit plans	Formal or informal arrangements under which an entity provides post-employment benefits for one or more employees.
Projected unit credit method	An actuarial valuation method that sees each period of service as giving rise to an additional unit of benefit entitlement and measures each unit separately to build up the final obligation (sometimes known as the accrued benefit method pro-rated on service or as the benefit/years of service method).

Chapter 23

Qualifying insurance policies	An insurance policy issued by an insurer that is not a related party of the reporting entity, if the proceeds of the policy: • can be used only to pay or fund employee benefits under a defined benefit plan; and • are not available to the reporting entity's own creditors (even in bankruptcy) and cannot be paid to the reporting entity, unless either: • the proceeds represent surplus assets that are not needed for the policy to meet all the related employee benefit obligations; or • the proceeds are returned to the reporting entity to reimburse it for employee benefits already paid. A qualifying insurance policy is not necessarily an insurance contract.
Retirement benefit plan	Arrangements whereby an entity provides benefits for employees on or after termination of service (either in the form of an annual income or as a lump sum) when such benefits, or the contributions towards them, can be determined or estimated in advance of retirement from the provisions of a document or from the entity's practice.
State (employee benefit) plan	Employee benefit plans established by legislation to cover all entities (or all entities in a particular category, for example a specific industry) and operated by national or local government or by another body (for example an autonomous agency created specifically for this purpose) which is not subject to control or influence by the reporting entity.
Termination benefits	Employee benefits provided in exchange for the termination of an employee's employment as a result of either: • an entity's decision to terminate an employee's employment before the normal retirement date; or • an employee's decision to accept voluntary redundancy in exchange for those benefits.

3.2   Scope and general recognition principles

FRS 102 Section 28 is not restricted to pensions and other post-retirement benefits, but addresses all forms of consideration (except for share based payment transactions which are dealt with by Section 26 of the standard and in Chapter 21 of this publication) given by an employer in exchange for services rendered by employees or for the termination of employment. *[FRS 102.28.1]*. In particular it covers employee benefits of the following four types:

- Short-term employee benefits, which are employee benefits (other than termination benefits) that are expected to be settled wholly before twelve months after the end of the reporting period in which the employees render the related service. The accounting for these is discussed at 3.3 below.

- Post-employment benefits, which are employee benefits (other than termination benefits and short-term employee benefits) that are payable after the completion of employment. The accounting for these is discussed at 3.4 to 3.6 below.

- Other long-term employee benefits, which are all employee benefits other than short-term employee benefits, post-employment benefits and termination benefits. The accounting for these is discussed at 3.8 below.

- Termination benefits, which are employee benefits provided in exchange for the termination of an employee's employment as a result of either:

  - the entity's decision to terminate an employee's employment before the normal retirement date, or

  - an employee's decision to accept voluntary redundancy in exchange for those benefits. The accounting for these is discussed at 3.9 below.

In this section the term employees includes management and directors. *[FRS 102.28.1].*

The general recognition principle for all employee benefits is that an entity must recognise the cost of employee benefits to which its employees have become entitled as a result of service rendered to the entity during the period:

- As a liability, after deducting amounts that have been paid either directly to the employees or as a contribution to an employee benefit fund. If the amount paid exceeds the obligation arising from service before the reporting date, an entity shall recognise that excess as an asset to the extent that the prepayment will lead to a reduction in future payments or a cash refund.

- An expense, unless another section of the FRS requires the cost to be recognised as part of the cost of an asset such as inventories or property, plant and equipment. *[FRS 102.28.3].*

An employee benefit fund may have been set up as an intermediary payment arrangement. Contributions made to the fund need to be accounted for in accordance with paragraphs 9.33 to 9.38 of the standard. This means that when the employer is a sponsoring employer of the fund, the assets and liabilities of the fund will be accounted for by the sponsoring employer as an extension of its own business. As a consequence the payments to the employee benefit fund do not extinguish the liability of the employer. *[FRS 102.28.3(a)].* The accounting for Employee Benefit funds is covered in Chapter 21 at 13.3. A pension plan is independent of the employer and is therefore not accounted for as an extension of the employers business.

3.3 Short-term employee benefits

Short-term employee benefits are employee benefits (other than termination benefits) that are expected to be settled wholly before twelve months after the end of the annual reporting period in which the employees render the related service. *[FRS 102.28.4].*

The standard provides the following examples of short-term employee benefits:

- wages, salaries and social security contributions;

- paid annual leave and paid sick leave;

- profit-sharing and bonuses; and

- non-monetary benefits (such as medical care, housing, cars and free or subsidised goods or services) for current employees.

Chapter 23

Accounting for short-term employee benefits is relatively straight forward as no discounting is required due to their short term nature. An entity should recognise the undiscounted amount expected to be paid in respect of short-term benefits attributable to services that have been rendered in the period as an expense or as part of the cost of an asset where required by another section of FRS 102. *[FRS 102.28.5]*. As detailed in the general recognition principles details in 3.2 above, any amount of the expense which has not been paid at the reporting date should be recognised as a liability.

Short-term compensated absences, where the employee does not provide services to the employer but benefits continue to accrue, may be made for various reasons including absences for annual leave and sick leave. These can either be accumulating or non-accumulating absences. Accumulating absences are those that can be carried forward and used in future periods if the entitlement in the current period is not used in full. An entity should recognise the expected cost of accumulating compensated absences when the employees render service that increases their entitlement to future compensated absences. The amount recognised will be the undiscounted additional amount that the entity expects to pay as a result of the unused entitlement that has accumulated at the end of reporting period. This liability shall be presented on the balance sheet as falling due within one year at the reporting date. *[FRS 102.28.6]*.

An example of an accumulating compensated absence is holiday not taken in the current year which can be carried forward.

Example 23.1:   *Accumulating compensated absences*

An entity has 100 employees, who are each entitled to twenty five working days of paid holiday for each year. Unused holiday may be carried forward for one calendar year. Holiday is taken first out of the current year's entitlement and then out of any balance brought forward from the previous year (a LIFO basis). At 31 December 2014, the average unused entitlement is two days per employee. The entity expects, based on past experience which is expected to continue, that 92 employees will take no more than twenty five days of paid holiday in 2015 and that the remaining eight employees will take an average of twenty six and a half days each.

The entity expects that it will pay an additional 12 days of holiday pay as a result of the unused entitlement that has accumulated at 31 December 2014 (one and a half days each, for eight employees). Therefore, the entity recognises a liability equal to 12 days of holiday pay.

Non-accumulating absences are those where there is no entitlement to carry forward unused amounts/days. An entity shall record the cost of these absences when they occur at the undiscounted amount of salaries and wages paid or payable for the period of absence. *[FRS 102.28.7]*. Examples of non-accumulating compensating absences include sick leave, maternity leave and jury service.

In applying the general recognition criteria to profit sharing and bonus payments, an entity should recognise the expected cost of profit-sharing and bonus payments when, and only when:

- the entity has a present legal or constructive obligation to make such payments as a result of past events (this means that the entity has no realistic alternative but to make the payments); and

- a reliable estimate of the obligation can be made. *[FRS 102.28.8]*.

A legal obligation may not always be present, however an entity's past practice in paying profit sharing or bonuses may have established a constructive obligation, requiring the cost to be recognised.

A constructive obligation is defined at 3.1 above.

FRS 102 provides no guidance on how to determine whether an estimate may be reliable. In looking for guidance over what this standard means by a 'reliable estimate' users may turn to IAS 19. This standard states that a reliable estimate of a constructive or legal obligation under a profit sharing or bonus plan can usually be made when, and only when:

- the formal terms of the plan contain a formula for determining the amount of the benefit;

- the entity determines the amounts to be paid before the financial statements are authorised for issue; or

- past practice gives clear evidence of the amount of the entity's constructive obligation. *[IAS 19.22]*.

Profit sharing and bonus plans should only be accounted as short term benefits when they are expected to be wholly settled within twelve months from the end of the reporting period, plans which are expected to be settled over a longer period should be accounted for as other long term benefits, which are discuss at 3.8 below.

3.4 Post-employment benefits: Distinction between defined contribution plans and defined benefit plans

Post-employment benefits are defined as employee benefits (other than termination benefits and short term employee benefits) that are payable after the completion of employment. *[FRS 102 Appendix I]*. They include, for example:

a) retirement benefits, such as pensions; and

b) other post-employment benefits, such as post-employment life insurance and post-employment medical care. *[FRS 102.28.9]*.

The standard confirms that arrangements whereby an entity provides post-employment benefits are post-employment benefit plans as defined. Section 28 applies to all post-employment benefit plans, whether or not they involve the establishment of a separate legal entity to receive contributions or pay benefits. In some cases, these arrangements are imposed by law rather than by the action of the entity. In some cases these arrangements arise from actions of the entity even in the absence of a formal documented plan. *[FRS 102.28.9]*.

3.4.1 Distinction between defined contribution plans and defined benefit plans

The standard draws the natural, but important, distinction between defined contribution plans and defined benefit plans. The determination is made based on the economic substance of the plan as derived from its principal terms and conditions. The approach it takes is to define defined contribution plans, with the defined benefit plans being the default category. These definitions are stated in 3.1

above. The standard also provides guidance on how to apply the requirements to insured benefits, multi-employer plans (including state plans) and group plans.

Defined contribution plans are post-employment benefit plans under which an entity pays fixed contributions into a separate entity (a fund) and has no legal or constructive obligation to pay further contributions or to make direct benefit payments to employees if the fund does not hold sufficient assets to pay all the employee benefits relating to employee service in the current or prior periods. Thus, the amount of the post-employment benefits received by the employee is determined by the amount of contributions paid by an entity (and perhaps also the employee) to a post-employment benefit plan or to an insurer, together with investment returns arising from the contributions. *[FRS 102.28.10(a)]*.

Defined benefit plans are post-employment benefit plans other than defined contribution plans. Under defined benefit plans, the entity's obligation is to provide the agreed benefits to current and former employees, and actuarial risk (that benefits will cost more or less than expected) and investment risk (that returns on assets set aside to fund the benefits will differ from expectations) are borne, in substance, by the entity. If actuarial or investment experience is worse than expected, the entity's obligation may be increased, and *vice versa* if actuarial or investment experience is better than expected. *[FRS 102.28.10(b)]*.

The most significant difference between defined contribution and defined benefit plans is that, under a defined benefit plans some actuarial risk or investment risk falls on the employer. Consequently because the employer is in substance underwriting the actuarial and investment risks associated with the plan, the expense recognised for a defined benefit plan is not necessarily the amount of the contribution due for the period. In contrast the benefits received by the employee from a defined contribution plan are determined by contributions paid (both by the employer and employee) to the benefit plan or insurance company, together with investment returns, and therefore actuarial and investment risk fall in substance on the employee. Hence the expense of a defined contribution plan is the contributions due for the period from the employer.

Under defined benefit plans the employer's obligation is not limited to the amount that it agrees to contribute to the fund. Rather, the employer is obliged (legally or constructively) to provide the agreed benefits to current and former employees.

An example of a constructive obligation could be a historical practice of discretionary pension increases going beyond the formal terms of the plan or statutory minimum increases.

3.4.2   *Multi-employer and state plans*

Multi-employer plans, other than state plans, under Section 28 are defined contribution plans or defined benefit plans that:

(a)   pool assets contributed by various entities that are not under common control; and

(b)   use those assets to provide benefits to employees of more than one entity, on the basis that contribution and benefit levels are determined without regard to the identity of the entity that employs the employees. *[FRS 102 Appendix I]*.

In the UK these are typically industry wide schemes. They exclude group administration plans, which simply pool the assets of more than one employer under common control, for investment purposes and the reduction of administrative and investment costs, but keep the claims of different employers segregated for the sole benefit of their own employees. The accounting for these plans is dealt with at 3.10 below.

A multi-employer plan should be classified as either a defined contribution plan or a defined benefit plan in accordance with its terms, including any constructive obligation that goes beyond the formal terms of the plan, in the normal way (see 3.4.1 above). However, if sufficient information is not available to use defined benefit accounting for a multi-employer plan that is a defined benefit plan, the entity shall account for the plan as if it were a defined contribution plan and make relevant disclosures (see 3.11.3 below). *[FRS 102.28.11]*.

Where an entity participates in a defined benefit plan, which is a multi-employer plan and this plan is accounted for as a defined contribution plan under the Standard, if the entity has entered into an agreement with the multi-employer plan that determines how an entity will fund a deficit, the entity shall recognise a liability for the contributions payable that arise from the agreement (to the extent they are related to the deficit). The resulting expense is recognised in the profit and loss account. *[FRS 102.28.11A]*.

In the UK the Pensions Act 2004 has required that where a defined benefit plan is underfunded (i.e. it does not have sufficient assets to cover its obligations), the trustees must establish a recovery plan which confirms how the Statutory Funding Objective must be met and the period over which this is to be met. This recovery plan will detail the contributions to be made by each participating company. From this agreement it may be possible to establish sufficient information to allow defined benefit accounting as the schedule of deficit funding contributions provides information on how the deficit will be funded by each of the participating employers, and hence the share of assets and liabilities.

A state plan is an employee benefit plan established by legislation to cover all entities (or all other entities in a particular category, for example a specific industry) and operated by national or local government or by another body (for example an autonomous agency created specifically for this purpose) which is not subject to control or influence by the reporting entity. *[FRS 102 Appendix I]*. A state plan should be accounted for in the same way as a multi-employer plan. *[FRS 102.28.11]*.

Neither FRS 102 nor IAS 19 address the accounting treatment required if sufficient information becomes available for a multi-employer plan which has previously been accounted for as a defined contribution scheme. There are two possible approaches to this:

- record an immediate charge/credit to profit or loss equal to the deficit/surplus; or
- record an actuarial gain or loss.

It can be argued that the first approach is correct as starting defined benefit accounting is akin to introducing a new scheme and, as discussed in 3.6.5 below, plan introductions result in the corresponding amount of any increase or decrease in a liability being taken to profit and loss.

Chapter 23

On the other hand it could be argued that defined contribution accounting was the best estimate for what the defined benefit accounting should have been given the information available, and the emergence of new information is a change in estimate and therefore recorded as a remeasurement.

Given the lack of guidance in the standards we believe that either approach would be acceptable as long as it is applied consistently.

3.4.3   *Insured benefits*

One factor that can complicate making the distinction between defined benefit and defined contribution plans is the use of external insurers.

Section 28 helps users to make this distinction by stating that where insurance premiums are paid to fund post-employment benefits, the employer should treat the plan as a defined contribution plan unless it has (either directly or indirectly through the plan) a legal or constructive obligation to:

(a)   pay the employee benefits directly when they fall due; or

(b)   pay further amounts if the insurer does not pay all future employee benefits relating to employee service in the current and prior periods.

If a plan involving insurance is determined to be a defined benefit plan, the insurance policies will represent plan assets which are discussed at 3.6.3 below.

If the employer has retained such a legal or constructive obligation it should treat the plan as a defined benefit plan. The standard states that a constructive obligation could arise indirectly through the plan, through the mechanism for setting future premiums, or through a related party relationship with the insurer. *[FRS 102.28.12]*.

FRS 102 provides limited guidance on how to account for the insurance policy, other than requiring that if a plan asset is an insurance policy which exactly matches the timing and amount of some of the benefits payable under the plan, the fair value of the asset is deemed to be the present value of the related obligation (see 3.6.3 below).

Qualifying insurance policies are defined as an insurance policy issued by an insurer that is not a related party of the reporting entity, if the proceeds of the policy:

- can be used only to pay or fund employee benefits under a defined benefit plan; and

- are not available to the reporting entity's own creditors (even in bankruptcy) and cannot be paid to the reporting entity unless either;

  - the proceeds represent surplus assets that are not needed for the policy to meet all the related employee benefit obligations; or

  - the proceeds are returned to the reporting entity to reimburse it for employee benefits already paid. *[FRS 102 Appendix I]*.

Under the standard qualifying insurance policies are accounted for as plan assets, however it provides no guidance on accounting for other insurance policies which do not meet the definition of a qualifying insurance policy. Under IAS 19 these are accounted for as reimbursement rights (providing the criteria for recognition as reimbursement rights are met). See 3.6.4 below.

3.5　Defined contribution plans

3.5.1　General

Accounting for defined contribution plans is straightforward under Section 28 because, as the section observes, the reporting entity's obligation for each period is determined by the amounts to be contributed for that period. Consequently, no actuarial assumptions are required to be made in order to measure the obligation or the expense and there is no possibility of any actuarial gain or loss to the reporting entity. Moreover, the obligations are measured on an undiscounted basis, except where they are not expected to be settled wholly before twelve months after the end of the period in which the employees render the related service. Where discounting is required, the discount rate should be determined in the same way as for defined benefit plans, which is discussed at 3.6.2.B below. *[FRS 102.28.13A]*. In general, though, it would seem unlikely for a defined contribution scheme to be structured with such a long delay between the employee service and the employer contribution.

Section 28 requires that, when an employee has rendered service during a period, the employer should recognise the contribution payable to a defined contribution plan in exchange for that service:

(a)　as a liability, after deducting any contribution already paid. If the contribution already paid exceeds the contribution due for service before the end of the reporting period, the excess should be recognised as an asset (prepaid expense) to the extent that the prepayment will lead to, for example, a reduction in future payments or a cash refund; and

(b)　as an expense, unless another section of the FRS requires the cost to be recognised as part of the cost of an asset such as inventories or property, plant and equipment – see Chapters 9 and 13 respectively. *[FRS 102.28.13]*.

As discussed at 3.4.2 above, Section 28 requires multi-employer defined benefit plans to be accounted for as defined contribution plans in certain circumstances. The standard makes clear that contractual arrangements to make contributions to fund a deficit should be fully provided for (on a discounted basis) even if they are to be paid over an extended period. The unwinding of any discount is recognised as a finance cost in profit or loss. *[FRS 102.18.13A]*.

3.6　Defined benefit plans

Accounting for defined benefit plans is complex because actuarial assumptions are required to measure both the obligation and the expense, and there is a possibility of actuarial gains and losses. Moreover, because the obligations are settled many years after the employees render the related service, the obligations are measured on a discounted basis.

3.6.1   Recognition

The Section requires users to apply the general recognition principal (see 3.2 above) to defined benefit plans, and requires an entity to recognise: *[FRS 102.28.14]*

- a liability for its obligations under the defied benefit plans net of plan assets – it's 'net defined benefit liability'; and

- the change in that liability during the period as the cost of its defined benefit plans during the period.

Guidance on how to account for these is covered below.

3.6.2   Measurement of plan liabilities

The Section requires the entity to measure the net defined benefit liability for its obligations under defined benefit plans at the net total of the following amounts: *[FRS 102.28.15]*

- the present value of its obligations under defined benefit plans (its defined benefit obligation) at the reporting date; minus

- the fair value at the reporting date of the plan assets (if any) out of which the obligations are to be settled. If the asset is an insurance policy that exactly matches the amount and timing of some or all of the benefits payable under the plan, the fair value of the asset is deemed to be the present value of the related obligation. (See 3.6.3 below).

3.6.2.A   Legal and constructive obligations

The present value of an entity's obligations under defined benefit plans at the reporting date should reflect the estimated amount of benefit that employees have earned in return for their service in the current and prior periods, including benefits that are not yet vested (see below) and including the effects of benefit formulas that give employees greater benefits for later years of service. This requires the entity to determine how much benefit is attributable to the current and prior periods on the basis of the plans benefit formula and to make estimates (actuarial assumptions) about demographic variables (such as employee turnover and mortality) and financial variables (such as future increases in salaries and medical costs) that influence the cost of the benefit. The actuarial assumptions should be unbiased (neither imprudent nor excessively conservative), mutually compatible, and selected to lead to the best estimate of the future cash flows that will arise under the plan. *[FRS 102.28.16]*.

Although the standard does not use the term 'attribution of benefit to years of service', the fact that it states that defined benefit obligations should reflect the estimated amount of benefit that employees have earned in return for their service, including benefits that are not year vested, and it requires the effects of benefit formulas that give employees greater benefits for later years of service to be taken into account essentially has the same meaning. In doing this FRS 102 requires the projected unit credit method to be used (see 3.6.2.C below). FRS 102, however, does not provide detail on how greater benefits for later years of service should be taken into account. IAS 19 requires that when an employee's service in later years will lead to a materially higher level of benefit, the benefit should be attributed on a straight line basis from:

- the date when service by the employee first leads to benefits under the plan; until

- the date when further service by the employee will lead to no material amount of further benefits under the plan, other than from further salary increases. *[IAS 19.70].*

This requirement is considered necessary because the employee's service throughout the entire period will ultimately lead to benefit at that higher level.

FRS 102 explains that the employee service gives rise to an obligation under a defined benefit plan even if the benefits are conditional on future employment (in other words they have not vested). Employee service before the vesting date gives rise to a constructive obligation because, at each successive reporting date, the amount of future service that an employee will have to render before being entitled to the benefit is reduced. When calculating its defined obligation (attributing benefits to years of service) an entity must consider the probability that some employees may not satisfy the vesting requirements (i.e. leave before retirement age). Similarly, although some post-employment benefits (such as post-employment medical benefits) become payable only if a specified event occurs when an employee is no longer employed (such as illness), the obligation is created when the employee renders the service that provides entitlement to the benefit if the specified event occurs. The probability that the specified event will occur affects the measurement of the obligation, but does not determine whether the obligation exists. *[FRS 102.28.26].*

3.6.2.B   Discount rate

Due to the long timescales involved, post-employment benefit obligations are required to be discounted. The rate used should be determined 'by reference to' the market yield (at the end of the reporting period) on high quality corporate bonds of currency and term consistent with liabilities. In countries where there is no deep market in such bonds, the entity shall use the market yields on government bonds instead. *[FRS 102.28.17].*

FRS 102 does not explain what is meant by 'high quality'. In practice it is considered to mean bonds rated AA or higher by Standard and Poor's, or an equivalent rating from another rating agency.

3.6.2.C   Actuarial methodology

The standard requires an entity to use the projected unit credit method to measure its defined benefit obligation and the related expense. It is defined as an actuarial valuation method that sees each period of service as giving rise to an additional unit of benefit entitlement and measures each unit separately to build up the final obligation. *[FRS 102 Appendix I].* The standard observes that if defined benefits are based on future salaries, the projected unit method requires an entity to measure its defined benefit obligations on a basis that reflects estimated future salary increases. In addition, the projected unit credit method requires an entity to make various actuarial assumptions in measuring the defined benefit obligation, including

Chapter 23

discount rates, employee turnover, mortality and (for defined benefit medical plans) medical cost trend rates. *[FRS 102.28.18]*.

As above this method uses both the vested and non-vested benefits.

IAS 19 provides a simple example of the projected unit credit method *[IAS 19.68]*:

Example 23.2:   The projected unit credit method

A lump sum benefit is payable on termination of service and equal to 1% of final salary for each year of service. The salary in year 1 is 10,000 and is assumed to increase at 7% (compound) each year. The discount rate used is 10% per year. The following table shows how the obligation builds up for an employee who is expected to leave at the end of year 5, assuming that there are no changes in actuarial assumptions. For simplicity, this example ignores the additional adjustment needed to reflect the probability that the employee may leave the entity at an earlier or later date.

Year	*1*	*2*	*3*	*4*	*5*
Benefit attributed to:					
– prior years	0	131	262	393	524
– current year (1% of final salary)	131	131	131	131	131
– current and prior years	131	262	393	524	655
Opening Obligation	–	89	196	324	476
Interest at 10%	–	9	20	33	48
Service Cost	89	98	108	119	131
Closing Obligation	89	196	324	476	655

Note:
– The Opening Obligation is the present value of benefit attributed to prior years.
– The Current Service Cost is the present value of benefit attributed to the current year.
– The Closing Obligation is the present value of benefit attributed to current and prior years.

As can be seen in this simple example, the projected unit credit method also produces a figure for service cost and interest cost. These cost components are discussed at 3.6.8 below.

The underlying workings relevant to the above are as follows:

Final salary at year 5 (10,000 compounded at 7%)	$10,000 \times (1 + 0.07)^4 = 13,100$
1% of final salary attributed to each year	131
Expected final benefit	5 years $\times$ 1% $\times$ 131,000 = 655

Service cost, being present value of 131 discounted at 10%: e.g.

Year 1	$131 \times (1 + 0.1)^{-4} = 89$
Year 2	$131 \times (1 + 0.1)^{-3} = 98$

Closing obligation, being years served multiplied by present value of 131: e.g.

Year 3	3 years $\times$ 131 $\times$ $(1 + 0.1)^{-2} = 324$

3.6.2.D   Actuarial assumptions

As noted above, the projected unit credit method requires an entity to make various actuarial assumptions in measuring the defined benefit obligation. These are defined as an entity's unbiased and mutually compatible best estimates of the demographic and financial variables that will determine the ultimate cost of providing post-employment benefits. *[FRS 102 Appendix I].*

Demographic assumptions concern the future characteristics of current and former employees (and their dependents) who are eligible for benefits and deal with matters such as:

- mortality, both during and after employment;
- rates of employee turnover, disability and early retirement;
- the proportion of plan members with dependents who will be eligible for benefits; and
- claim rates under medical plans.

Financial assumptions deal with items such as:

- the discount rate (see 3.6.2.B);
- future salary and benefit levels, excluding the cost of benefits that will be met by the employees;
- in the case of medical benefits, future medical costs, including claim handling costs; and
- price inflation.

The actuarial assumptions must be unbiased (neither imprudent nor excessively conservative), mutually compatible, and selected to lead to the best estimate of the future cash flows that will arise under the plan. *[FRS 102.28.16].*

The actuarial assumptions used in the calculation are the responsibility of the directors, although they may use the advice of an independent actuary (although they are not required to under FRS 102). *[FRS 102.28.20].*

The standard also deals with the situation where the level of defined benefits payable by a scheme are reduced for the amounts that will be paid to employees under government-sponsored benefits. When this is the case an entity shall measure its defined benefit obligations on a basis that reflects the benefits payable under the plans, but only if:

- those plans were enacted before the reporting date; or
- past history, or other reliable evidence, indicates that those state benefits will change in some predictable manner, for example, in line with future changes in general price levels or general salary levels. *[FRS 102.28.27].*

3.6.2.E   Frequency of valuations and use of an independent actuary

An entity must measure its defined benefit obligation and plan assets at the reporting date. *[FRS 102.28.15].* The standard does not require an entity to engage an independent actuary to perform the comprehensive actuarial valuation needed to

Chapter 23

calculate the defined benefit obligation, nor does it require that a comprehensive valuation to be performed annually. If the principal actuarial assumptions have not changed significantly in periods between the comprehensive actuarial valuations, the defined benefit obligation can be measured by adjusting the prior period measurement for changes in employee demographics such as employee numbers or salary levels. *[FRS 102.28.20]*.

In practice we expect that most entities will engage an independent actuary to perform the comprehensive actuarial valuation given its complexity.

3.6.3   *Measurement of plan assets*

The Section requires plan assets to be measured at fair value at the reporting date in accordance with the provisions of FRS 102 dealing with Fair Value (see Chapter 8), except that if an asset is an insurance policy that exactly matches the amount and timing of some or all of the benefits payable under the plan, the fair value of the asset is deemed to be the present value of the related obligation. *[FRS 102.28.15(b)]*.

Plan assets are defined as comprising: *[FRS 102 Appendix I]*

- assets held by a long-term employee benefit fund; and
- qualifying insurance policies.

Assets held by a long-term employee benefit fund are an asset (other than non-transferable financial instruments issued by the reporting entity) that: *[FRS 102 Appendix I]*

- is held by an entity (a fund) that is legally separate from the reporting entity and exists solely to pay or fund employee benefits; and
- is available to be used only to pay or fund employee benefits, is not available to the reporting entity's own creditors (even in bankruptcy) and cannot be returned to the reporting entity, unless either:
  - the remaining assets of the fund are sufficient to meet all the related employee benefit obligations of the plan or the reporting entity; or
  - the assets are returned to the reporting entity to reimburse it for employee benefits already paid.

A qualifying insurance policy is defined at 3.4.3. A footnote to the definition clarifies that an insurance policy is not necessarily an insurance contract.

3.6.4   *Reimbursement rights*

Some employers may have in place arrangements to fund defined benefit obligations which do not meet the definition of qualifying insurance policies, but which do provide for another party to reimburse some or all of the expenditure required to settle a defined benefit obligation. In such cases, the expected receipts under the arrangement are not classified as plan assets.

The standard provides that when an entity is virtually certain that another party will reimburse some or all of the expenditure required to settle a defined benefit obligation, the entity should recognise its right to the reimbursement as a separate asset, which should be treated the same way as other plan assets. *[FRS 102.28.28]*.

3.6.5 Plan introductions, changes, curtailments and settlements

The standard requires that when a defined benefit plan has been introduced or the benefits have changed in the current period, the entity should increase its net defined benefit liability to reflect the change and recognise the increase/(decrease) as an expense/(income) in the profit and loss account in the current period. *[FRS 102.28.21].*

Where a defined benefit plan has been curtailed (i.e. the benefits or group of covered employees are reduced) or settled (the relevant part of the employer's obligation is completely discharged) in the current period, the defined benefit obligation should be decreased or eliminated and the resulting gain or loss recognised in profit and loss in the current period. *[FRS 102.28.21A].* This gain or loss should be disclosed separately as part of the reconciliation of the defined benefit obligation along with the expense/(income) arising from plan introductions and changes. *[FRS 102.28.41(f)(iv)].* This expense/(income) should be disclosed separately as part of the required reconciliation of the defined benefit obligation. *[FRS 102.28.41(f)(iv)].* See 3.4.12 for further details on disclosure requirements.

An employer may acquire an insurance policy to fund all or some of the employee benefits relating to employee service in the current and prior periods. The acquisition of such a policy is not a settlement if the employer retains a legal or constructive obligation to pay further amounts if the insurer does not pay the employee benefits specified in the insurance policy. However, the acquisition of an insurance policy will mean that the entity has an asset which it needs measure at fair value. As discussed at 3.6.3 above, certain insurance policies are valued at an amount equal to the present value of the defined benefit obligation they match. The cost of buying such a policy will typically greatly exceed its subsequent carrying amount. That raises the question of how to treat the resultant loss. One view might be that the loss in substance is very similar to a settlement loss and should be recognised in profit or loss. Another view is that because the loss results from exchanging one plan asset for another it is an actuarial loss and therefore should be recognised in other comprehensive income. In our view, either approach is acceptable if applied consistently and, where material, disclosed.

3.6.6 Restriction on plan assets

In practice, defined benefit pension plans tend to be funded on a more prudent basis than would be the case if the surplus or deficit was measured in accordance with FRS 102. This is due to the discount rate used for funding purposes typically being lower than that specified in the standard. For this reason an FRS 102 valuation may result in a pension asset (surplus), when for funding purposes there is a deficit. FRS 102 states that if the present value of the defined benefit obligation at the reporting date is less than the fair value of plan assets at that date, the plan has a surplus. It goes on to observe that an entity should recognise a plan surplus as a defined benefit asset only to the extent that it is able to recover the surplus either through reduced contributions in the future or through refunds from the plan. *[FRS 102.28.22].*

Chapter 23

No further explanation is given of the meaning of 'reduced contributions in the future or through refunds from the plan.' This lack of guidance will require judgement as to the amount of a defined benefit pension surplus to be recognised under the standard. In making judgements the standard states that management may consider the requirements and guidance in EU-adopted IFRS dealing with similar or related issues (see Chapter 7 at X). Given that the treatment of pension surpluses is dealt with under previous UK GAAP and EU-adopted IFRS, but with potentially different outcomes (as discussed at 2.1.2.E above), this may lead to diversity in practice under FRS 102.

Due to the problems encountered in practice in applying the asset ceiling test the issue was considered by the Interpretations Committee, and IFRIC 14 was issued. At present the IFRIC 14 requirements have not been included within FRS 102. The interpretation set out to address the issues of:

- When refunds or reductions in future contributions should be regarded as available in accordance with the definition of the asset ceiling in IAS 19.8.

- How a minimum funding requirement might affect the availability of reductions in future contributions.

- When a minimum funding requirement might give rise to a liability.

Although FRS 102 does not include the requirements from IFRIC 14, FRED 55 – *Pension Obligations* – proposes an amendment to Section 28 paragraph 18A which will state: 'Where an entity has measured its defined benefit obligation using the projected unit credit method (including the use of appropriate actuarial assumptions), as set out in paragraph 28.18, it is not required to recognise any additional liabilities to reflect differences from the assumptions used for the most recent actuarial valuation of the plan for funding purposes. For the avoidance of doubt, it is not required to recognise any additional liabilities to reflect an agreement with the defined benefit plan to fund a deficit, even if such an agreement would otherwise be considered onerous.' This means that entities turning to IFRIC 14 under the hierarchy will not be required to recognise a liability for a minimum funding requirement. For this reason we have not included a discussion on minimum funding requirements within this publication, but further details can be found within EY International GAAP 2015.

3.6.6.A   IFRIC 14 – General requirements concerning the limit on a defined benefit asset

IFRIC 14 clarifies that economic benefits, in the form of refunds or reduced future contributions, are available if they can be realised at some point during the life of the plan or when plan liabilities are settled. In particular, such an economic benefit may be available even if it is not realisable immediately at the end of the reporting period. *[IFRIC 14.8].* Furthermore, the benefit available does not depend on how the entity intends to use the surplus. The entity should determine the maximum economic benefit available from refunds and reductions in future contributions that are mutually exclusive. *[IFRIC 14.9].*

3.6.6.B   Economic benefit available through a refund

The interpretation observes that an unconditional right to a refund can exist whatever the funding level of a plan at the end of the reporting period. However, if the right to a refund of a surplus depends on the occurrence or non-occurrence of one or more uncertain future events not wholly within an entity's control, the entity does not have an unconditional right and should recognise the asset. *[IFRIC14.12]*. Furthermore, the interpretation states that benefits are available as a refund only if the entity has an unconditional right to the refund: *[IFRIC 14.11-12]*.

- During the life of the plan, without assuming that the plan liabilities must be settled in order to obtain the refund; or

- Assuming the gradual settlement of the plan liabilities over time until all members have left the plan; or

- Assuming the full settlement of the plan liabilities in a single event (i.e. as a plan wind up).

The economic benefit available as a refund should be measured as the amount of the surplus at the end of the reporting period (being the fair value of the plan assets less the present value of the defined benefit obligation) that the entity has a right to receive as a refund, less any associated costs. For example if a refund would be subject to a tax other than income tax of the reporting entity it should be measured net of tax. *[IFRIC 14.13]*.

In measuring the amount of a refund available when the plan is wound up (point (c) above), the costs to the plan of settling the plan liabilities and making the refund should be included. For example, a deduction should be made for professional fees if these are paid by the plan rather than the entity, and the costs of any insurance premiums that may be required to secure the liability on wind up. *[IFRIC 14.14]*.

There is currently diversity in practice under IFRS in relation to accounting for costs associated with a pension plan. When a UK pension scheme makes a refund (known in tax law as 'an authorised surplus payment') to an employer, the refund gives rise to a liability for the pension scheme to pay a tax of 35% of the amount refunded (a 'refund tax'). As above, IFRIC 14.13 requires that taxes other than income taxes should be deducted from the measurement of the refund.

If a refund tax is not considered to be an income tax, this has the following consequences for UK pension schemes:

- Where an entity has a surplus on a scheme (measured under FRS 102 or IAS 19) that is recognised on the basis of a potential refund, IFRIC 14 requires the surplus to be restricted to the net of tax amount, and where the refund tax is believed to not be an income tax then this will be deducted (i.e. 65% of the gross surplus is recognised). The argument that a refund tax is not an income tax of the sponsoring employer is based on the fact that it is not charged to the employer and does not appear in the employer's tax calculation.

- Others in the UK have deemed the refund tax to be an income tax, and therefore this has not been deducted in measuring the refund. This argument is based on the refund tax being economically an income tax of the employer in the sense that it has the effect of claiming back tax relief given to the employer on contributions to the scheme.

In our view either approach is acceptable.

Another relatively common situation in the UK is for pension schemes to have a defined benefit section and a defined contribution section. Trustees may be empowered under the trust deed to use any surplus arising on the defined benefit section in paying up contributions to the defined contribution section. Whilst this is equivalent to obtaining a refund for accounting purposes, it may not be regarded as an 'authorised payment' for tax purposes. Therefore, where an entity is recognising a surplus on a defined benefit section on the basis that it could be refunded through a transfer to a defined contribution section of the same plan, there may be no need to provide for the effect of a refund tax.

Commonly, the trustees of a pension fund will be independent and have absolute discretion to set the investment strategy, asset allocation and also the ability to buy annuities to settle pension liabilities.

These powers would allow the trustees to 'spend' any current or future surplus. Investing plan assets in ultra-cautious investments (yielding less that the unwinding discount on the obligation) could unwind any surplus over time. Settlements by way of buying annuities would absorb surpluses because the cost of settlement typically exceeds the FRS 102/IAS 19 measure of the obligation.

These trustee powers raise the following questions:

- whether the exercise of such powers by the trustees are 'uncertain future events not wholly within [the entity's] control'; and

- if so, whether 'the entity's right to a refund of a surplus depends on the occurrence or non-occurrence of' them and accordingly no surplus could be recognised in any scenario where trustees have such powers.

Our view is that such a trustee powers should not, of themselves, preclude the recognition of a surplus under IFRIC 14. However this issue is currently being discussed by the IFRIC (see 3.6.6.D below).

3.6.6.C   Economic benefit available through reduced future contributions where there is no minimum funding requirement

IFRIC 14 addresses separately cases where there are minimum funding requirements for contributions relating to future service, and cases where there are no such funding requirements.

This section deals with the situation where there are no such funding requirements. The implications of future service minimum funding requirements are discussed at 3.6.6.D below.

IFRIC 14 requires that the economic benefit available by way of reduced future contributions be determined as the future service cost to the entity for each period over the shorter of the expected life of the plan and the expected life of the entity. The future service cost to the entity excludes amounts that will be borne by employees. *[IFRIC 14.16]*.

Future service costs should be determined using assumptions consistent with those used to determine the defined benefit obligation and with the situation that exists at the end of the reporting period as determined by FRS 102/IAS 19. Accordingly, no future changes to the benefits to be provided by a plan should be assumed until the plan is amended, and a stable workforce in the future should be assumed unless the entity makes a reduction in the number of employees covered by the plan. In the latter case, the assumption about the future workforce should include the reduction. The present value of the future service cost should be determined using the same discount rate as that used in the calculation of the defined benefit obligation (discount rates are discussed at 3.6.2.B above). *[IFRIC 14.17]*.

3.6.6.D   *Recent IFRIC discussions in IFRIC 14*

Under IFRIC 14 our view is that trustee powers should not, of themselves, preclude the recognition of a surplus. However this matter is currently being discussed by the Interpretations Committee, who discussed a question about whether an employer has an unconditional right to a refund of the surplus in the following circumstances:

- The trustee acts on behalf of the plan's members and is independent from the employer; and

- The trustee has discretion in the event of a surplus arising in the plan to make alternative use of that surplus by augmenting the benefits payable to members or by winding up the plan through purchase of annuities, or both.

The question discussed related to plan that is closed to future accrual of future benefits, such that there will be no future service costs, and so no economic benefit is available through reductions in future contributions. The Committee also noted that:

- The fact that an existing surplus at the balance sheet date could be decreased or extinguished by uncertain future events that are beyond the control of the entity is not relevant to the existence of the right to a refund;

- If the trustee can use a surplus by augmenting the benefits in the future, pursuant to the formal terms of a plan (or a constructive obligation that goes beyond those terms), this fact should be considered when the entity measures its defined benefit obligation; and

- The amount of surplus to be recognised could be zero, as a consequence of the measurement of the defined benefit obligation.

The committee discussed the matter again at its meeting in July 2014 and considered the informal feedback received from IASB members. The Committee noted the difficulty associated with assessing the consequences of the trustee's future actions and its effect on the entity's ability to estimate reliably the amount to be received. Consequently a majority of Committee members observed that no asset should be recognised in this circumstance.

However, some Committee members were concerned about the consequences that this conclusion could have on the accounting for a minimum funding requirement and the consistency of this conclusion with the recognition and measurement requirements of IAS 19.

Consequently, the Interpretations Committee requested the staff to perform further analyses on the interaction of this tentative decision with the requirement to recognise an additional liability when a minimum funding requirement applies and the relationship with the general requirements of IAS 19.

Chapter 23

Although FRED 55 should lead to minimum funding requirements not being recognised as a liability, the ability of preparers of FRS 102 financial statements to be able to turn to the relevant IFRS standard will mean that developments in IAS 19 and IFRIC 14 will be relevant to FRS 102 (as if under the hierarchy in section 10 the accounting under these standards is followed any amendments will also need to be followed) and in the case of the discussion above the requirement to recognise a pension surplus.

3.6.7   Presentation of the net defined benefit liability/asset

FRS 102 requires that an entity present a statement of financial position in accordance with one of the formats prescribed by Schedules 1, 2 or 3 of the Large and Medium sized companies Regulations to the Companies Act (see Chapter 4). The Regulations show pension deficits as the first line item in provisions and pension surpluses either in the same place as a pension deficit under format 1 of the Regulations, or after prepayments and accrued income under format 2 of the Regulations. The presentation under FRS 17, which was based on an interpretation of company law, could also be used under FRS 102 as it does not conflict with the Companies Act. FRS 17 required defined benefit pension assets or liabilities to be presented after accruals and deferred income, but before capital and reserves (see 2.2.4 above). As a result there is likely to be divergence in practice in the presentation of defined benefit pension surpluses and deficits under FRS 102.

The cost of a defined benefit plan would be included within administration expenses in the income statement, and net interest either within interest receivable and similar income or interest payable and similar charges dependent on whether net interest was an income or expense.

Where an entity has more than one defined benefit pension plan it is possible that it may have a plan with a surplus and another with a deficit. As Section 28 does not deal directly with the presentation of pension plans in the statement of financial position, users are required to look to other sections of the standard which deal with the issue. Paragraph 2.52 of the standard states that an entity shall not offset assets and liabilities unless required or permitted by an FRS. We would therefore expect defined benefit pension surpluses and deficits to be presented separately on the face of the statement of financial position.

3.6.8   Treatment of defined benefit plans in profit and loss, and other comprehensive income.

Section 28 requires the cost of a defined benefit plan to be recognised as follows:

* the change in the net defined benefit liability arising from employee service rendered during the reporting period in profit or loss;

* net interest on the defined benefit liability during the reporting period in profit of loss (see 3.6.8.A below);

* the cost of plan introductions, benefit changes, curtailments and settlements in profit or loss (see 3.6.5 above); and

* remeasurement of the net defined benefit liability in other comprehensive income (see 3.6.8.B below).

Except to the extent that another Section of FRS 102 requires part or all of the cost to be recognised as part of the cost of an asset such as inventories or plant, property and equipment. See Chapters 9 and 13 respectively. *[FRS 102.28.3(b)]*.

Some defined benefit plans require employees or third parties to contribute to the cost of the plan. Contributions by employees reduce the cost of benefits to the entity. *[FRS 102.28.23]*.

3.6.8.A   Net interest

The net interest on the net defined benefit liability is determined by multiplying the net defined benefit liability by the discount rate (see 3.6.2.B above), both as determined at the start of the reporting period, taking into account any changes in the net defined liability during the period as a result of contributions and benefit payments. *[FRS 102.28.24]*.

In our view, the requirement to take account of payments to and from the fund implies that an entity should also take account of other significant changes in the net defined benefit liability, for example settlements and curtailments.

As the net item in the statement of financial position is comprised of two or three separate components (the defined benefit obligation, plan assets and the asset restriction, if any), the net interest is made up of interest unwinding on each of these components in the manner described above. *[FRS 102.28.24A]*. Although, for the purposes of presentation in profit or loss, net interest is a single net amount.

Interest on plan assets calculated as described above will not, other than by coincidence, be the same as the actual return on plan assets. The difference is a remeasurement which is recognised in other comprehensive income. *[FRS 102.28.24B]*.

3.6.8.B   Remeasurements

Remeasurements of the net defined benefit liability (asset) comprise:

- actuarial gains and losses; and
- the return on plan assets, excluding amounts included in net interest on the net defined benefit liability. *[FRS 102.28.25]*.

Remeasurements of the net defined benefit liability are recognised in other comprehensive income, and are not reclassified to profit or loss in a subsequent period. *[FRS 102.28.25A]*.

Actuarial gains and losses are changes in the present value of defined benefit obligation resulting from: experience adjustments (the effects of differences between the previous actuarial assumptions and what has actually occurred); and the effects of changes in actuarial assumptions. *[FRS 102 Appendix I]*.

3.7   Costs of administering employee benefit plans

Some employee benefit plans incur costs as part of delivering employee benefits. The costs are generally more significant for post-retirement benefits such as pensions. Examples of costs would include actuarial valuations, audits and the costs of managing any plan assets.

Chapter 23

FRS 102 does not include any guidance on accounting for these costs. As noted above at 2.2.2 entities may refer to IAS 19 using the GAAP hierarchy in Section 10 of FRS 102.

IAS 19 deals with some costs, but is silent on others.

The following costs are required to be factored into the measurement of the defined benefit obligation:

- in the case of medical benefits, future medical costs, including claim handling costs (i.e. the costs that will be incurred in processing and resolving claims, including legal and adjuster's fees); and
- taxes payable by the plan on contributions relating to service before the reporting date or on benefits resulting from that service. *[IAS 19.76(b)]*.

The following costs (and no others) are deducted from the return on plan assets:

- the costs of managing the plan assets; and
- any tax payable by the plan itself, other than tax included in the actuarial assumptions used to measure the defined benefit obligation. *[IAS 19.130]*.

As discussed at 3.6.8.B above, net interest on the net liability or asset is reported in the income statement. This is a wholly computed amount which is uninfluenced by actual asset returns; the difference between actual asset returns and the credit element of the net interest amount forms part of remeasurements reported in other comprehensive income.

So, although not expressed in these terms, costs of administering plan assets and the tax mentioned above are under IAS 19, reported in other comprehensive income.

Both standards are silent on the treatment of any other costs of administering employee benefit plans. However, the Basis for Conclusions on IAS 19 contains the following: 'the Board decided that an entity should recognise administration costs when the administration services are provided. This practical expedient avoids the need to attribute costs between current and past service and future service.' *[IAS 19.BC127]*. The Board may well have taken that decision, however it did not include such a requirement in the standard.

In our view, such an approach is certainly an acceptable way to account for costs not dealt with in the standard; however other approaches could be acceptable, for example, that in relation to closed schemes discussed below. In addition FRS 102 allows only those items permitted or required by the standard to be presented in other comprehensive income. *[FRS 102.5.5A]*. Costs of administering employee benefit plans are not required or permitted to be recognised in other comprehensive income and therefore should be presented within profit or loss.

One alternative to simple accruals-accounting as costs are incurred could be relevant to closed plans, where employees are no longer exchanging services for defined benefits. In this situation, it is clear that any and all future costs of administering the plan relate to past periods and no attribution is necessary. An entity with such an arrangement may select a policy of full provision of all costs of 'running-off' the plan.

3.8 Other long-term employee benefits

3.8.1 Meaning of other long term benefits

Other long term employee benefits include items such as the following, if they are not expected to be wholly settled within 12 months after the end of the annual reporting period in which the employees have rendered the related service:

- long-term paid absences such as long-service or sabbatical leave;

- other long-service benefits;

- long-term disability benefits;

- profit sharing and bonuses; and

- deferred remuneration. *[FRS 102.28.29]*.

3.8.2 Recognition and measurement

For such benefits FRS 102 requires a simplified version of the accounting treatment required in respect of defined benefit plans (which is discussed in detail in 3.6 above). The amount recognised as a liability for other long term employee benefits should be the net total, at the end of the reporting period, of the present value of the defined benefit obligation and the fair value of plan assets (if any) out of which the obligations are to be settled directly. The change in the liability should be recognised in profit or loss, except to the extent that FRS 102 requires or permits their inclusion in the cost of an asset. *[FRS 102.28.30]*.

In other words, all assets, liabilities, income and expenditure relating to such benefits should be accounted for in the same way, as those relating to a defined benefit plan (see 3.6 above), except that remeasurements are recognised in profit or loss.

A simple example of a long term employee benefit would be where an employee receives a bonus of £100,000 in 5 years' time provided he/she continues to stay employed by the entity for this period. This cost will be spread over the 5 year period using the attribution of benefit period method described in 3.6.2.C above.

3.9 Termination benefits

Termination benefits occur when an entity is committed, by legislation, by contractual or other agreements with employees or their representatives or by a constructive obligation based on business practice, custom or desire to act equitably, to make payments (or to provide other benefits) to employees when it terminates their employment. *[FRS 102.28.31]*. Rather than being earned through providing services to an entity, termination benefits arise as a result of an event such as a decision to reduce the size of the workforce.

The standard requires that termination benefits are recognised by an entity as an expense in profit and loss immediately, as they do not provide an entity with future economic benefits. *[FRS 102.28.32]*.

Chapter 23

Termination benefits shall be recognised as a liability and expense only when the entity is demonstrably committed either:

- to terminate the employment of an employee or group of employees before the normal retirement age; or

- to provide termination benefits as a result of an offer made in order to encourage voluntary redundancy. *[FRS 102.28.34].*

An entity becomes demonstrably committed to a termination only when it has a detailed formal plan for the termination and is without realistic possibility of withdrawal from the plan. *[FRS 102.28.35].* The standard notes an example of the features of a detailed formal plan for restructuring, which may include termination benefits, is given when it identifies at least:

- the business or part of a business concerned;

- the principal locations affected;

- the location, function, and approximate number of employees who will be compensated for terminating their services;

- the expenditures that will be undertaken; and

- when the plan will be implemented; and

- It has raised a valid expectation in those affected that it will carry out the restructuring by starting to implement that plan or announcing its main features to those affected by it. *[FRS 102.21.11C].*

The standard notes that when an entity recognises termination benefits, it may also have to account for a plan amendment or a curtailment of other employee benefits. *[FRS 102.28.33].*

An entity is required to measure termination benefits at the best estimate of the amount that would be required to settle the obligation at the reporting date. If an offer was made to encourage voluntary redundancy, the measurement of termination benefits shall be based on the number of employees expected to accept the offer. *[FRS 102.28.36].*

Where termination benefits are not due to be settled wholly within 12 months after the end of the reporting period, they should be discounted to their present value using the methodology and discount rate specified as for defined benefit pension schemes (see 3.6.2.B above). *[FRS 102.28.37].*

Some employers will pay 'stay bonuses' to encourage employees who have been told that they will be made redundant to continue to work for the employer for a further period of time (for example to complete a project). These bonuses are not termination benefits as the individuals are still employed by the entity and therefore the expense does not meet the definition of a termination benefit (see above), and therefore the cost of the stay bonus should be recognised over the period over which the employee is working to earn this bonus.

3.10   Group plans

Where an entity participates in a defined benefit plan that shares risks between entities under common control (a group plan), it is required to obtain information about the plan as a whole measured in accordance with FRS 102, on the basis of assumptions that apply to the plan as a whole. If there is a contractual agreement or stated policy for charging the net defined benefit cost of a defined benefit plan as a whole to individual group entities, then the entity is required to recognise the net defined benefit costs based on this allocation in its individual financial statements. *[FRS 102.28.38].*

If there is no contractual agreement or stated policy for charging the net defined benefit cost to individual group entities, the net defined benefit cost of a defined benefit plan shall be recognised in the individual financial statements of the group entity which is legally responsible for the plan. The other group entities shall recognise a cost equal to their contribution payable for the period in their individual financial statements. *[FRS 102.28.38].*

The Accounting Council's Advice to the FRC confirms that although paragraph 38 of section 28 only explicitly refers to the cost of the pension plan, the net defined benefit cost is calculated by reference to both the defined benefit obligation and the fair value of the plan assets. Therefore this paragraph does require the recognition of the relevant net defined benefit liability in the individual financial statements of any group entities recognising a net defined benefit cost. *[AC Advice].*

3.11 Death-in service benefits

The provision of death-in service benefits is a common part of employment packages (either as part of as a defined benefit plan or on a stand-alone basis). Unfortunately no guidance is provided by FRS 102 or IAS 19 on how to account for such benefits. Guidance had been proposed under E54 – *Employee Benefits October 1996* (the exposure draft preceding earlier versions of IAS 19). We suggest that an appropriate approach could be that:

- death in service benefits provided as part of a defined benefit post-employment plan are factored into the actuarial valuation. In this case any insurance cover should be accounted for in accordance with the normal rules of IAS 19. An important point here is that insurance policies for death in service benefits typically cover only one year, and hence will have a low or negligible value. As a result, it will not be the case that the insurance asset is equal and opposite to the defined benefit obligation;

- other death in service benefits which are externally insured are accounted for by expensing the premiums as they become payable; and

- other death in service benefits which are not externally insured are provided for as deaths in service occur.

An alternative approach could be to view death in service benefits as being similar to disability benefits. The accounting for disability benefits under IAS 19 is as follows:

- Where a long-term disability benefit depends on the length of service of the employee, an obligation arises as the employee renders service, which is to be measured according to the probability that payment will be required and the length of time for which payment is expected to be made.

- If however the level of benefit is the same for all disabled employees regardless of years of service, the expected cost is recognised only when an event causing a disability occurs. *[IAS 19.157].*

Chapter 23

Given the lack of explicit guidance on death in service benefits in IAS 19 itself, practice will be mixed in accounting for these benefits.

Under previous UK GAAP, UITF 35 – *Death in service and incapacity benefits*, reached a consensus that the cost of providing death in service benefits and incapacity benefits where these benefits are not insured and are provided through a defined benefit pension scheme, the scheme liability and cost should be measured using the projected unit credit method in accordance with FRS 17.

Given the lack of any guidance in FRS 102 and IAS 19, we would expect practice to be mixed in accounting for death in service benefits under FRS 102.

3.12   Disclosures

3.12.1   *Disclosures about short-term employee benefits*

Section 28 does not require any specific disclosures about short-term employee benefits *[FRS 102.28.39]*, but preparers of financial statements should also consider the requirements of Section 33 – *Related Party Disclosures* – discussed in Chapter 28 at 3.2.

3.12.2   *Disclosures about other long-term benefits*

The standard requires the disclosure for each category of other long-term benefits that it provides to its employees, the nature of the benefit, the amount of its obligation and the extent of funding at the reporting date. *[FRS 102.28.42].*

3.12.3   *Disclosures about defined contribution plans*

The section requires the disclosure of the profit and loss expense for defined contribution plans. *[FRS 102.28.40].*

When a multi-employer plan is treated as a defined contribution plan because sufficient information is not available to use defined contribution accounting (see 3.4.2 above) entities should:

- disclose the fact that it is a defined benefit plan and the reason why it is being accounted for as a defined contribution plan, along with any available information about the plan's surplus or deficit and the implications, if any, for the entity;

- include a description of the extent to which the entity can be liable to the plan for other entities' obligations under the terms and conditions of the multi-employer plan; and

- disclose how any liability recognised as a result of the entity entering into an agreement to fund a deficit (see 3.4.2 above) has been determined. *[FRS 102.28.40A].*

3.12.4   *Disclosures about defined benefit plans*

As described in 2.1.2.F above, FRS 102 requires that the statement of financial performance and income statement should be presented in accordance with The Large and Medium sized companies and Groups (Accounts and Reports) Regulations 2008.

3.12.4.A   General disclosures

An entity is required to disclose the following information about defined benefit plans (except for defined benefit multi-employer plans that as treated as defined contribution plans – see 3.4.2 above). If an entity has more than one defined benefit plan, these disclosures may be made in aggregate, separately for each plan, or in such groupings as considered to be the most useful:

- A general description of the type of plan, including funding policy.
- The date of the most recent comprehensive actuarial valuation and, if it was not as of the reporting date, a description of the adjustments that were made to measure the defined benefit obligation at the reporting date.
- A reconciliation of opening and closing balances for each of the following:
  - The net defined benefit obligation;
  - The fair value of the plan assets; and
  - Any reimbursement right recognised as an asset.
- Each of the reconciliations above shall show each of the following, if applicable:
  - The change in the net defined benefit liability arising from employee service rendered during the period;
  - Interest income or expense;
  - Remeasurements of the defined benefit liability, showing separately actuarial gains and losses and the return on plan assets less amounts included in interest income/expense above; and
  - Plan introductions, changes, curtailments and settlements.
- The cost relating to defined benefit plans for the period, disclosing separately the amounts:
  - Recognised in profit or loss as an expense; and
  - Included in the cost of an asset.
- For each major class of plan assets, which shall include but is not limited to, equity instruments, debt instruments, property, and all other assets, the percentage or amount that each major class constitutes of the fair value of the total plan assets at the reporting date.
- The amounts included in the fair value of plan assets for:
  - Each class of the entity's own financial instruments; and
  - Any property occupied by, or other assets used by, the entity.
- The return on plan assets
- The principal actuarial assumptions used, including when applicable:
  - The discount rates;
  - The expected rates of salary increases;
  - Medical cost trend rates; and
  - Any other material actuarial assumptions used.

The reconciliations above need not be presented for prior periods. *[FRS 102.28.41].*

Chapter 23

3.12.4.B   Disclosures for plans which share risks between entities under common control

If an entity participates in a defined benefit plan that shares risks between entities under common control (see 3.9 above) it is required to disclose the following information:

- The contractual agreement or stated policy for charging the cost of a defined benefit plan or the fact that there is no policy.

- The policy for determining the contribution to be paid by the entity.

- If the entity accounts for an allocation of the net defined benefit cost, all the information required in section 3.12.4.A above.

If the entity accounts for the contributions payable for the period, the following information is also required:

- A general description of the type of plan, including funding policy.

- The date of the most recent comprehensive actuarial valuation and, if it was not as of the reporting date, a description of the adjustments that were made to measure the defined benefit obligation at the reporting date.

- For each major class of plan assets, which shall include but is not limited to, equity instruments, debt instruments, property, and all other assets, the percentage or amount that each major class constitutes of the fair value of the total plan assets at the reporting date.

- The amounts included in the fair value of plan assets for:

  - Each class of the entity's own financial instruments; and

  - Any property occupied by, or other assets used by, the entity.

This information can be disclosed by cross-reference to disclosures in another group entity's financial statements if: the group entity's financial statements separately identify and disclose the information required about the plan; and that group entity's financial statements are available to users of the financial statements on the same terms as the financial statements of the entity and at the same time as, or earlier than, the financial statements of the entity. *[FRS 102.28.41A]*.

3.12.5   Disclosures about termination benefits

For each category of termination benefits provided to employees the following should be disclosed:

- the nature of the benefit;

- its accounting policy; and

- the amount of its obligation and the extent of funding at the reporting date. *[FRS 102.28.43]*.

When there is uncertainty about the number of employees who will accept an offer of termination benefits, a contingent liability exists. Section 21 – *Provisions and Contingencies* – requires the disclosure of contingent liabilities unless the possibility of an outflow in settlement is remote (this is discussed in Chapter 17 at 3.10). *[FRS 102.28.44]*.

4 COMPANIES ACT REQUIREMENTS

4.1 Disclosures

The Companies Act does not require any specific disclosure requirements for employee benefits, however there are numerous disclosure requirements for salaries, pensions and other benefits payable to directors. These requirements are within Schedule 5 to the Large and Medium sized Companies and Groups (Accounts and Reports) Regulations 2008. In addition s411 of the Companies Act requires the disclosure of other pension costs as part of the disclosure of staff costs.

5 SUMMARY OF GAAP DIFFERENCES

The following table shows the key differences between previous UK GAAP, IFRS and FRS 102.

	FRS 102	*Previous UK GAAP*	*IFRS*
Scope	FRS 102 also covers short-term and long-term employee benefits and termination benefits.	FRS 17 only covered retirement benefits	IAS 19 also covers short-term and long-term employee benefits and termination benefits.
Defined benefit schemes	Net interest is calculated with reference to the discount rate	Expected return on assets is calculated with reference to the expected rate of return, interest cost is calculated with reference to the discount rate	Net interest is calculated with reference to the discount rate
Group schemes	FRS 102 requires the net defined benefit deficit/asset of schemes under common control to be allocated to group companies either based on a contractual agreement or stated policy for charging the cost, or recognising the net defined benefit deficit/asset in the financial statements of the entity which is legally responsible for the plan.	Where the underlying assets and liabilities of defined benefit schemes under common control could not be identified on a reasonable and consistent basis, FRS 17 allowed group entities to account for these schemes as defined contribution schemes	IAS 19 requires the net defined benefit deficit/asset of schemes under common control to be allocated to group companies either on based on a contractual agreement or stated policy for charging the cost, or recognising the net defined benefit deficit/asset in the financial statements of the entity which is legally responsible for the plan.
Multi-employer schemes	FRS 102 requires a liability to be recorded for deficit funding commitments where a multi-employer scheme has been accounted for as a defined contribution scheme.	FRS 17 did not require any additional liabilities to be recorded for multi-employer schemes accounted for as defined contribution schemes.	IAS 19 requires a liability to be recorded for deficit funding commitments where a multi-employer scheme has been accounted for as a defined contribution scheme.

Chapter 23

	FRS 102	Previous UK GAAP	IFRS
Pension surpluses/ asset ceilings	FRS 102 provides little guidance on recognition of plan surpluses, other than it can be recognised to the extent it can be recovered through reductions in future contributions or refunds	FRS 17 only allowed the recognition of pension surpluses if the amount to be recovered through refunds to the scheme had been agreed by the trustees at the balance sheet date.	IAS 19 allows the recognition of defined benefit surpluses provided that the refund is available, but restricts it to the lower of the refund and the asset ceiling. IFRIC 14 provides guidance on the asset ceiling.
Presentation	FRS 102 requires primary statements to be presented in accordance with the Regulations, although the presentation under FRS 17 may be applied as it was based on an interpretation of company law.	FRS 17 required pension deficits to be presented on the balance sheet below accruals and deferred income, but before capital and reserves.	Follow the general requirements of IAS 1 for the presentation on the statement of financial position.

Chapter 24   Income tax

Chapter 24

List of examples

Chapter 24   Income tax

1   INTRODUCTION

Section 29 – *Income Tax* – covers not only accounting for income tax, but also includes specific provisions in relation to withholding tax on dividend income (see 3.3 below) and on accounting for Value Added Tax (VAT) and other sales taxes (discussed at 4 below).

Income tax is defined in Section 29 to include:

- all domestic and foreign taxes that are based on taxable profit; and

- taxes, such as withholding taxes, that are payable by a subsidiary, associate or joint arrangement on distributions to the reporting entity. *[FRS 102.29.1].*

The Standard requires an entity to recognise the current and future tax consequences of transactions and other events that have been recognised in the financial statements. These recognised tax amounts comprise current tax and deferred tax. Current tax is tax payable (refundable) in respect of the taxable profit (tax loss) for the current period or past reporting periods. Deferred tax represents the future tax consequences of transactions and events recognised in the financial statements of the current and previous periods. *[FRS 102.29.2].*

1.1   Allocation of tax income and expense between periods

The most significant accounting question which arises in relation to taxation is how to allocate tax expense (income) between accounting periods. The particular period in which transactions are recognised in the financial statements is determined by FRS 102. However, the timing of the recognition of transactions for the purposes of measuring the taxable profit is governed by tax law, which sometimes prescribes an accounting treatment different from that used in the financial statements. The generally accepted view is that it is necessary for the financial statements to seek some reconciliation between these different treatments.

Broadly speaking, those tax consequences that are legal assets or liabilities at the reporting date are referred to as current tax. The other tax consequences, which are expected to give rise to legal assets or liabilities in a future period, are referred to as deferred tax.

This is illustrated by Example 24.1, and the further discussion in 1.1.1 to 1.12 below.

Example 24.1:   PP&E attracting tax deductions in advance of accounting depreciation

An item of equipment is purchased on 1 January 2015 for £50,000 and is estimated to have a useful life of five years, at the end of which it will be scrapped. There is no change to the estimated residual amount of zero over the life of the equipment. The depreciation charge will therefore be £10,000 per year for five years.

The applicable corporate tax rate is 30%. No tax deductions are given for depreciation charged in the financial statements. Instead, the cost may be deducted from taxes payable in the year that the asset is purchased. The entity's profit before tax, including the depreciation charge, for each of the five years ended 31 December 2015 to 31 December 2019 is £100,000. All components of pre-tax profit, other than the accounting depreciation, are taxable or tax-deductible.

The entity's tax computations for each year would show the following:[1]

£s	2015	2016	2017	2018	2019
Accounting profit	100,000	100,000	100,000	100,000	100,000
Accounting depreciation	10,000	10,000	10,000	10,000	10,000
Tax depreciation	(50,000)	–	–	–	–
Taxable profit	60,000	110,000	110,000	110,000	110,000
Tax payable @ 30%	18,000	33,000	33,000	33,000	33,000

1.1.1   No provision for deferred tax ('flow through')

If the entity in Example 24.1 above were to account only for the tax legally due in respect of each year ('current tax'), it would report the amounts in the table below in profit or loss. Accounting for current tax only is generally known as the 'flow through' method.

£s	2015	2016	2017	2018	2019	Total
Profit before tax	100,000	100,000	100,000	100,000	100,000	500,000
Current tax (at 1.1 above)	18,000	33,000	33,000	33,000	33,000	150,000
Profit after tax	82,000	67,000	67,000	67,000	67,000	350,000
Effective tax rate (%)	18	33	33	33	33	30

The 'effective tax rate' in the last row of the table above is the ratio, expressed as a percentage, of the profit before tax to the charge for tax in the financial statements, and is regarded a key performance indicator by many preparers and users of financial statements. As can be seen from the table above, over the full five-year life of the asset, the entity pays tax at the statutory rate of 30% on its total profits of £500,000, but with considerable variation in the effective rate in individual accounting periods.

The generally held view is that simply to account for the tax legally payable as above is distortive, and that the tax should therefore be allocated between periods. Under FRS 102 this allocation is achieved by means of deferred taxation (see 1.1.2 below).

1.1.2   Provision for deferred tax (the timing difference approach)

Over the last eighty years or so, numerous methods for accounting for deferred tax have evolved and been superseded. The approach required by Section 29 is known as the 'timing difference liability' approach, which seeks to measure the impact on future tax payments of the cumulative difference, as at the reporting date, between income or expenditure (in the case of Example 24.1 above, depreciation) in the financial statements and the amounts recognised for the same income or expense in the tax computation. Such differences are known as 'timing differences'. Timing differences are said to 'originate' in those periods in which the cumulative difference between book and tax income (expense) increases and to 'reverse' in those periods in which that cumulative difference decreases. In Example 24.1 above the differences originate and reverse as follows:

£s	2015	2016	2017	2018	2019
Accounting depreciation	10,000	10,000	10,000	10,000	10,000
Tax depreciation	(50,000)	–	–	–	–
(Origination)/reversal	(40,000)	10,000	10,000	10,000	10,000
Cumulative[1]	(40,000)	(30,000)	(20,000)	(10,000)	–

As discussed in more detail at 7 below, Section 29 requires an entity to recognise a liability for deferred tax on the timing difference arising between book and tax depreciation, as follows.

£s	2015	2016	2017	2018	2019
Cumulative difference (per table above)	(40,000)	(30,000)	(20,000)	(10,000)	–
Deferred tax[1]	(12,000)	(9,000)	(6,000)	(3,000)	–
Movement in deferred tax in period	12,000	(3,000)	(3,000)	(3,000)	(3,000)

[1]   Cumulative timing difference multiplied by the tax rate of 30%. As discussed at 7 below, Section 29 requires deferred tax to be measured by reference to the tax rates and laws expected to apply when the timing differences will reverse (referred to as the 'liability method').

The deferred tax liability is recognised in the statement of financial position and any movement in the deferred tax liability during the period is recognised as deferred tax income or expense in profit or loss, with the following impact:

£s	2015	2016	2017	2018	2019	Total
Profit before tax	100,000	100,000	100,000	100,000	100,000	500,000
Current tax (at 1.1 above)	18,000	33,000	33,000	33,000	33,000	150,000
Deferred tax	12,000	(3,000)	(3,000)	(3,000)	(3,000)	–
Total tax	30,000	30,000	30,000	30,000	30,000	150,000
Profit after tax	70,000	70,000	70,000	70,000	70,000	350,000
Effective tax rate (%)	30	30	30	30	30	30

It can be seen that the effect of accounting for deferred tax is to present an effective tax rate of 30% in profit or loss for each period.

Chapter 24

In the example above, the deferred tax could also have been calculated by comparing to the net carrying amount of the asset in the financial statements to its carrying amount for tax purposes (i.e. the amount of future tax deductions available for the asset). For example, at the end of 2015, the carrying amount of the asset would be £40,000 (cost of £50,000 less one year's depreciation of £10,000), and its carrying amount for tax purposes would be nil. The difference between £40,000 and nil is £40,000, the same as the difference between the tax depreciation of £50,000 and the book depreciation of £10,000.

In practice, therefore, deferred tax is often calculated by comparing the carrying amount of an asset and its tax value, since balance sheet carrying amounts are usually easier to 'track' than cumulative income or expenditure. However, such 'short-cut' methods must be applied with great care, since some differences between the book and tax carrying amounts of an asset arise not from timing differences, but from permanent differences (see 1.2 below).

1.2   Permanent differences

Some differences between an entity's taxable profit and accounting profit arise not because the same items are recognised in taxable profit and accounting profit but in different periods (i.e. timing differences), but because an item recognised in accounting profit is never recognised in taxable profit and vice-versa. For example:

- An item of PP&E is depreciated but its cost is not deductible for tax purposes other than on sale. An example in the UK would be an industrial building. Any depreciation of such an asset recognised for accounting purposes is a permanent difference.

- In the UK a company may obtain a tax deduction for a share-based payment transaction based on its value at vesting or exercise, which is typically higher than its value at grant, on which the expense in the financial statements is based. Any excess of the tax deduction over the expense recognised in the financial statements is a permanent difference.

As discussed further at 6.5 below, Section 29 requires that deferred tax is not recognised on permanent differences, except for differences arising on first accounting for a business combination. *[FRS 102.29.10]*.

2   KEY DIFFERENCES TO IFRS AND PREVIOUS UK GAAP

2.1   Withholding taxes on dividends and VAT and other sales taxes

The requirements of Section 29 in relation to withholding taxes on dividends (see 3.4 below) and on VAT and other sales taxes (see 4 below) are essentially the same as previous UK GAAP, as set out in FRS 16 – *Current tax [FRS 16.8, 9]* and in SSAP 5 – *Accounting for value added tax*, respectively.

Unlike Section 29, IAS 12 – *Income Taxes* – does not include in its scope withholding taxes on income from entities other than a subsidiary, associate or joint venture. Accordingly, entities moving from IFRS to FRS 102 may find themselves grossing up withholding taxes on income from such investments for the first time.[2]

IAS 12 does not include VAT and similar sales taxes in its scope. Taxes outside the scope of IAS 12 fall under the general requirements of IAS 37 – *Provisions, Contingent Liabilities and Contingent Assets. [IFRIC 21.BC4]*. Specific provisions of other standards, notably in IAS 18 – *Revenue,* IAS 2 – *Inventories,* and IAS 16 – *Property, Plant and Equipment,* result in an accounting treatment for VAT and other sales taxes that is essentially the same as that required in FRS 102.[3]

2.2   Current tax and deferred tax

The requirements of Section 29, FRS 16 and IAS 12 in respect of the recognition and measurement of current tax are essentially the same. However, there are some subtle differences between FRS 102 and FRS 16 which require an approach that is similar to IFRS in certain circumstances. For example, where different tax rates apply to distributed and undistributed earnings, the undistributed rate applies until a liability to pay a dividend is recognised. *[FRS 102.29.14]*. This provision was not part of FRS 16, presumably because such differential rates have not been a feature of the UK tax system. However, it is relevant in relation to profits arising in other jurisdictions.

As regards deferred tax, Section 29 adopts the same 'timing differences' approach as FRS 19 – *Deferred tax,* with the following significant differences:

- unlike FRS 19, there is no exception in FRS 102 to the recognition of deferred tax in relation to the revaluation of non-monetary assets (where the revaluation is recognised outside profit or loss) or in relation to gains on sale of non-monetary assets when it is more likely than not that rollover relief will be obtained; *[FRS 19.14.15]*

- when accounting for a business combination, and as an exception to the general 'timing differences' approach in FRS 102, entities are required to recognise deferred tax for all differences between the value at which acquired assets (other than goodwill) and liabilities are recorded and the amount that will be assessed for tax purposes (see 6.6 below); *[FRS 102.29.11]* and

- discounting of deferred tax liabilities is not permitted. *[FRS 102.29.17]*.

IAS 12 requires income taxes to be accounted for using a temporary difference approach, whereby deferred tax is recognised on the difference between the carrying amount of an asset or liability and the amount at which that asset or liability is assessed for tax purposes (referred to as its 'tax base'). However, there are some exceptions to this, most notably the initial recognition exception, whereby no deferred tax is recorded on a difference between the carrying amount of an asset or liability and its tax base where that difference arose on the initial recognition of the asset or liability in a transaction which gave rise to no accounting profit or loss and no tax effect and was not a business combination.

This means that Section 29 accounts for deferred tax differently to both previous UK GAAP and IFRS, even though the underlying 'timing differences' approach of Section 29 (other than when accounting for a business combination) is closer to previous UK GAAP. The main difference between Section 29 and IFRS is that IAS 12 requires deferred tax to be recognised on any difference between the carrying amount of an asset or liability and its tax base that arises after the initial recognition of the asset or liability. Section 29 would prohibit the recognition of such differences that are not the result of timing differences, such as changes to the tax-deductible amount of an asset arising from legislative change after the asset has been acquired (see 6.5 below). In practical terms, entities applying FRS 102 should expect to recognise deferred tax in more cases that than under FRS 19, but in fewer cases than under IAS 12.

3   SCOPE OF SECTION 29

Section 29 covers not only accounting for income tax, but also includes specific provisions in relation to withholding taxes on dividend income (see 3.3 below) and on accounting for Value Added Tax (VAT) and other similar sales taxes that are not income taxes (see 4 below). *[FRS 102.29.1, 2A].*

3.1   Terms used in Section 29 of FRS 102

The following terms are used in Section 29 with the meanings specified. *[FRS 102 Appendix I].*

Term	Definition
Current tax	The amount of income tax payable (refundable) in respect of the taxable profit (tax loss) for the current period or past reporting periods.
Deferred tax	Income tax payable (recoverable) in respect of the taxable profit (tax loss) for future reporting periods as a result of past transactions or events.
Deferred tax assets	Income tax recoverable in future reporting periods in respect of: (a) future tax consequences of transactions and events recognised in the financial statements of the current and previous periods; (b) the carry forward of unused tax losses; and (c) the carry forward of unused tax credits.
Deferred tax liabilities	Income tax payable in future reporting periods in respect of future tax consequences of transactions and events recognised in the financial statements of the current and previous periods.
Income tax	All domestic and foreign taxes that are based on taxable profits. Income tax also includes taxes, such as withholding taxes, that are payable by a subsidiary, associate or joint venture on distributions to the reporting entity.
Permanent differences	Differences between an entity's taxable profits and its total comprehensive income as stated in the financial statements, other than timing differences.
Probable	More likely than not.

Substantively enacted	Tax rates shall be regarded as substantively enacted when the remaining stages of the enactment process historically have not affected the outcome and are unlikely to do so.
	A UK tax rate shall be regarded as having been substantively enacted if it is included in either:
	(a) a Bill that has been passed by the House of Commons and is awaiting only passage through the House of Lords and Royal Assent; or
	(b) a resolution having statutory effect that has been passed under the Provisional Collection of Taxes Act 1968. (Such a resolution could be used to collect taxes at a new rate before that rate has been enacted. In practice, corporation tax rates are now set a year ahead to avoid having to invoke the Provisional Collection of Taxes Act for the quarterly payment system).
	A Republic of Ireland tax rate can be regarded as having been substantively enacted if it is included in a Bill that has been passed by the Dail.
Tax expense	The aggregate amount included in total comprehensive income or equity for the reporting period in respect of current tax and deferred tax.
Taxable profit (tax loss)	The profit (loss) for a reporting period upon which income taxes are payable or recoverable, determined in accordance with the rules established by the taxation authorities. Taxable profit equals taxable income less amounts deductible from taxable income.
Timing differences	Differences between taxable profits and total comprehensive income as stated in the financial statements that arise from the inclusion of income and expenses in tax assessments in periods different from those in which they are recognised in financial statements.

3.2 What is an 'income tax'?

Income tax as defined in Section 29 includes:

- all domestic and foreign taxes that are based on taxable profit; and
- taxes, such as withholding taxes, that are payable by a subsidiary, associate or joint arrangement on distributions to the reporting entity. *[FRS 102.29.1].*

This definition is somewhat circular, since 'taxable profit' is, in turn, defined in terms of profits 'upon which income taxes are payable'. *[FRS 102 Appendix I].*

UK corporation tax is an 'income tax' as defined, since it takes as its starting point the totality of a reporting entity's accounting profits. However, both the UK and overseas jurisdictions raise 'taxes' on sub-components of net profit. These include:

- sales taxes;
- goods and services taxes;
- value added taxes;
- levies on the sale or extraction of minerals and other natural resources;
- taxes on certain goods as they reach a given state of production or are moved from one location to another; or
- taxes on gross production margins.

Chapter 24

Taxes that are simply collected by the entity from one third party (generally a customer or employee) on behalf of another third party (generally local or national government) are not 'income taxes' for the purposes of Section 29. This view is supported by the requirement of Section 23 – *Revenue* – that taxes which are collected from customers by the entity on behalf of third parties do not form part of the entity's revenue *[FRS 102.23.4]* (and therefore, by implication, are not an expense of the entity either).

In cases where such taxes are a liability of the entity, they may often have some characteristics both of production or sales taxes (in that they are payable at a particular stage in the production or extraction process and may well be allowed as an expense in arriving at the tax on net profits) and of income taxes (in that they may be determined after deduction of certain allowable expenditure). This can make the classification of such taxes (as income taxes or not) difficult.

Further discussion of factors that are considered in determining whether a particular tax meets the definition of an income tax under IFRS may be found in EY International GAAP 2015, Chapter 30 at 4.1.

3.2.1   Levies

A number of jurisdictions, including the UK, charge levies in relation to certain activities or on certain types of entity, particularly those in the financial services sector. In many cases the levies are expressed as a percentage of a measure of revenue or net assets, or some component(s) of revenue or net assets, at a particular date. Such levies are not income taxes and should be accounted for in accordance with Section 21 – *Provisions and Contingencies* (see Chapter 17).

3.2.2   Tonnage tax

In the UK, entities that operate qualifying vessels that are 'strategically and commercially managed in the UK', can take advantage of the tonnage tax regime. The tonnage tax regime differs from the main corporation tax system in a number of key respects, the most significant from an accounting point of view being that an entity in the tonnage tax regime is not assessed to tax on the basis of its reported profits from qualifying activities. Instead, its corporate tax liability is determined by reference to the qualifying tonnage of qualifying vessels. For this reason, it is not an income tax as defined in Section 21. Another feature of the tonnage tax regime is that a qualifying entity does not receive capital allowances for the cost of its ships.

The accounting implications for vessels taken into the tonnage tax regime are discussed at 6.3.1 below.

3.3   Withholding and similar taxes

Section 29 includes in its scope those taxes, such as withholding taxes, which are payable by a subsidiary, associate or joint arrangement on distributions to the reporting entity. *[FRS 102.29.1]*. As noted at 3.2 above, FRS 102 also sets specific requirements in relation to withholding taxes on income from entities other than a subsidiary, associate or joint venture. This gives rise to further questions of interpretation which are not addressed by the standard.

When an entity pays dividends to its shareholders, it may be required to pay a portion of the dividends to taxation authorities on behalf of shareholders. Outgoing dividends and similar amounts payable shall be recognised at an amount that includes any withholding tax but excludes other taxes, such as attributable tax credits. *[FRS 102.29.18]*.

Incoming dividends and similar income receivable shall be recognised at an amount that includes any withholding tax but excludes other taxes, such as attributable tax credits. Any withholding tax suffered shall be shown as part of the tax charge. *[FRS 102.29.19]*.

The rationale for the treatment as income taxes of taxes payable by a subsidiary, associate or joint arrangement on distributions to the investor is discussed further at 6.4 below. Essentially, however, the reason for considering withholding taxes within the scope of income tax accounting derives from the accounting treatment of the investments themselves. The accounting treatment for such investments – whether by consolidation or the equity method – results in the investor recognising profit that may be taxed twice: once as it is earned by the investee entity concerned, and again as that entity distributes the profit as dividends to the investor. Section 29 ensures that the financial statements reflect both tax consequences.

3.4 Investment tax credits

Investment tax credits are not defined in FRS 102 and can take different forms and be subject to different terms. Sometimes a tax credit is given as a deductible expense in computing the entity's tax liability, and sometimes as a deduction from the tax liability, rather than as a deductible expense. In other cases, the value of the credit is chargeable to corporation tax and in others it is not. Entitlement to investment tax credits can be determined in a variety of ways. Some investment tax credits may relate to direct investment in property, plant and equipment. Other entities may receive investment tax credits relating to research and development or other specific activities. Some credits may be realisable only through a reduction in current or future corporation tax payable, while others may be settled directly in cash if the entity is loss-making or otherwise does not have sufficient corporation tax payable to offset the credit within a certain period. Access to the credit may be limited according to total of all taxes paid, including employment taxes (such as PAYE and NIC) and VAT, in addition to corporation tax. There may be other conditions associated with receiving the investment tax credit, for example with respect to the conduct and continuing activities of the entity, and the credit may become repayable if ongoing conditions are not met.

Section 24 of FRS 102 – *Government Grants* – excludes from its scope government assistance that is either provided by way of a reduction in taxable income, or determined or limited according to an entity's income tax liability, citing investment tax credits as an example and then stating that taxes based on income are required to be accounted under Section 29. *[FRS 102.24.3]*. This implies that those investment tax credits that are excluded from the scope of Section 24 should be accounted for as income tax. However, if government assistance is described as an investment tax credit, but it is neither determined or limited by the entity's income tax liability nor provided in the form of an income tax deduction, such assistance should be accounted for as a government grant under Section 24 (see Chapter 19 at 3.2.1).

This raises the question as to how an entity should assess whether a particular investment tax credit gives rise to assistance in the form of benefits that are available in determining taxable profit or loss or are determined or limited on the basis of income tax liability *[FRS 102.24.3]* and, therefore, whether Section 24 or Section 29 should be applied. In our view, such a judgment would be informed by reference to the specific terms of the arrangement including the following factors:

Feature of credit	Indicator of Section 29 treatment (income tax)	Indicator of Section 24 treatment (grant)
Method of realisation	Only available as a reduction in income taxes payable (i.e. benefit is forfeit if there are insufficient income taxes payable). However, the longer the period allowed for carrying forward unused credits, the less relevant this indicator becomes.	Directly settled in cash where there are insufficient taxable profits to allow credit to be fully offset, or available for set off against payroll taxes, VAT or amounts owed to government other than income taxes payable.
Number of conditions not related to tax position (e.g. minimum employment, ongoing use of purchased assets)	None or few	Many
Restrictions as to nature of expenditure required to receive the grant.	Broad criteria encompassing many different types of qualifying expenditure	Highly specific
Tax status of grant income	Not taxable	Taxable

In group accounts, in which entities from a number of different jurisdictions may be consolidated, it is desirable that each particular investment tax credit should be consistently accounted for, either as a government grant or as an element of income tax. However, the fact that judgment is required in making this determination may mean that predominant practice by FRS 102 reporters relating to a specific type of tax credit differs from predominant practice by FRS 102 reporters for a substantially similar credit in another jurisdiction. We believe that, in determining whether Section 24 or Section 29 should be applied, an entity should consider the following factors in the order listed below:

- the predominant treatment by FRS 102 reporters for a specific credit in the relevant tax jurisdiction;
- if there is no predominant treatment, the group wide accounting policy for such a credit;
- in the absence of a predominant local treatment or a group wide accounting policy, the indicators listed in the table above should provide guidance.

This may occasionally mean that an entity operating in a number of territories adopts different accounting treatments for apparently similar arrangements in different countries, but it at least ensures a measure of comparability between different FRS 102 reporters operating in the same tax jurisdiction.

Where a tax credit is accounted for as income tax, an entity will need to determine whether the related benefit is more appropriately accounted for as a discrete tax asset akin to a tax loss, or as a deduction in respect of a specific asset and therefore akin to accelerated capital allowances. In most cases, we believe that it will generally be more appropriate to treat a tax credit that is accounted for as income tax as a discrete tax asset akin to a tax loss. As a result, the recoverability of any amounts that are unused and available for carry forward to future years would be assessed in accordance with the criteria discussed at 6.2 below.

Example 24.2:   UK research and development expenditure credit (RDEC)

The UK Finance Act 2013 introduced a new investment tax credit known as the RDEC (sometimes referred to colloquially as the 'above-the-line' tax credit) that applies on an elective basis to qualifying expenditure incurred from 1 April 2013 and is mandatory from 1 April 2016. Features of the tax credit relevant to an accounting analysis are:

- entities are generally entitled to a gross credit of 10% of qualifying R&D expenditure (with some entities entitled to a higher rate);
- the gross credit is treated as taxable income;
- the available credit is first set against the entity's corporation tax liability for the current period;
- the amount of any remaining credit (net of corporation tax) is 'capped' by reference to employment expenditure (measured by reference to the entity's PAYE and NIC liabilities)
- any remaining credit (net of corporation tax and the employment costs cap) can be carried back or carried forward to reduce the entity's corporation tax liability for certain earlier and later periods, or ceded by way of group relief;
- any unrecovered excess can be offset against the entity's other outstanding tax liabilities (e.g. PAYE and NIC); and
- any amount not recovered in any of the ways listed above is recoverable in cash from the tax authority (HMRC).

Should the RDEC credit be treated as a government grant or an element of income tax?

Analysis of these features by reference to the criteria set out above leads us to conclude that the RDEC credit is more appropriately regarded as a government grant. In particular, the benefits of the tax credit are capable of being realised in cash where there is insufficient corporation tax capacity; the tax credit relates to specific qualifying expenditure; and the grant income is determined on a pre-tax basis and is itself taxable.

Such an analysis requires a thorough understanding of the rules applying to the particular relief. Other seemingly similar reliefs should be treated as income taxes under Section 29 if, for example, the relief is not itself taxable; the relief could only be recovered by offset against other liabilities to corporation tax; or, where there is a cash payment alternative, the expected cash inflow approximates more closely to the value of the tax benefit rather than to the value of the expenditure incurred.

3.5   Interest and penalties

UK tax law (and that of other jurisdictions) provide for interest and/or penalties to be paid on late payments of tax. This raises the question of whether or not such penalties fall within the scope of Section 29. The issue is primarily one of presentation in the income statement. If such penalties and interest fall within the scope of Section 29, they are presented as part of tax expense. If they do not fall within the scope of Section 29, they should be included within profit before tax.

In our view:

- Where interest and penalties are not deductible in determining taxable income, there are reasonable grounds for treating them as either part of the tax charge or as an expense in arriving at profit before tax. Entities should determine their accounting policy for such items and apply it consistently.

- Where interest and penalties are tax-deductible, we believe that it is more generally appropriate to treat them as an expense in arriving at profit before tax.

3.6   Effectively tax-free entities

Certain classes of entity (for example, in the UK, pension funds and certain partnerships) are exempt from income tax, and accordingly are not within the scope of Section 29.

However, a more typical, and more complex, situation is that tax legislation has the effect that certain classes of entities, whilst not formally designated as 'tax-free' in law, are nevertheless exempt from tax provided that they meet certain conditions that, in practice, they are almost certain to meet. Examples in the UK are certain investment vehicles that pay no tax, provided that they distribute all, or a minimum percentage, of their earnings to investors.

Accounting for the tax affairs of such entities raises a number of challenges, as discussed further at 7.6 below.

3.7   Discontinued operations – interaction with Section 5

Section 5 – *Statement of Comprehensive Income and Income Statement* – requires the post-tax results of discontinued operations to be shown separately on the face of the statement of comprehensive income (and any separate income statement presenting the components of profit or loss). This is discussed further in Chapter 4.

The definitions of income tax, tax expense and taxable profit in Section 29 (see 3.1 above) do not distinguish between the results of continuing and discontinued operations, or the tax on those results. Thus, Section 29 applies not only to the tax income or expense on continuing operations, but also to any tax income or expense relating to the results of discontinued operations.

4.   VALUE ADDED TAX ('VAT') AND OTHER SIMILAR SALES TAXES

FRS 102 requires turnover shown in profit or loss to exclude VAT and other similar taxes on taxable outputs, and VAT imputed under the flat rate[4] VAT scheme. Similarly, recoverable VAT and other similar recoverable sales taxes should be excluded from expenses. Irrecoverable VAT that can be allocated to fixed assets and to other items disclosed separately in the financial statements should be included in the cost of those items where it is practical to do so, and the effect is material. *[FRS 102.29.20]*.

5   CURRENT TAX

Current tax is the amount of income taxes payable (refundable) in respect of the taxable profit (tax loss) for the current period or a past reporting period. *[FRS 102 Appendix I]*.

An entity recognises a current tax liability for tax payable on taxable profits for the current and past periods. If the amount already paid for the current and past periods exceeds the tax payable for those periods, the excess should be recognised as a current tax asset. *[FRS 102.29.3]*. An entity should recognise a current tax asset relating to a tax loss that can be carried back to recover tax paid in a previous period. *[FRS 102.29.4]*. Tax losses that can be carried *forward* to future periods are reflected in deferred tax.

Current tax should be measured at the amount expected to be paid to or recovered from the tax authorities by reference to tax rates and laws that have been enacted or substantively enacted by the end of the reporting period (see 5.1 below). *[FRS 102.29.5]*. Current tax assets or liabilities should not be discounted. *[FRS 102.29.17]*.

5.1   Enacted or substantively enacted tax legislation

5.1.1   UK

In the UK, legislation is enacted when it receives Royal Assent. For the purposes of FRS 102, tax rates are regarded as substantively enacted when the remaining stages of the enactment process historically have not affected the outcome and are unlikely to do so.

A UK tax rate is regarded as having been substantively enacted if it is included in either:

- a Bill that has been passed by the House of Commons and is awaiting only passage through the House of Lords and Royal Assent; or

- a resolution having statutory effect that has been passed under the Provisional Collection of Taxes Act 1968. Such a resolution is used to collect taxes at a new rate before that rate has been enacted. FRS 102 notes that, in practice, corporation tax rates are now set a year ahead to avoid having to invoke the Provisional Collection of Taxes Act for the quarterly payment system. *[FRS 102 Appendix I]*.

The main body of Section 29 refers to 'tax rates *and laws*' [emphasis added] that have been enacted or substantively enacted, whereas the definition of 'substantively enacted' in the Glossary in Appendix 1 to FRS 102 refers only to 'tax rates'. In our view, there is no intentional distinction, and the guidance in the glossary should be applied equally to determining whether tax laws or tax rates have been substantively enacted.

This test of 'substantive enactment' is applied very strictly. Section 32 – *Events after the End of the Reporting Period* – identifies the enactment or announcement of a change in tax rates and laws after the end of the reporting period as an example of a non-adjusting event. *[FRS 102.32.11(h)]*. For example, an entity with a reporting period ending on 31 December issuing its financial statements on 20 April the following year would measure its tax assets and liabilities by reference to tax rates and laws enacted or substantively enacted as at 31 December even if these had changed significantly before 20 April. However, the entity would have to disclose the impact of those changes if the effect is expected to be significant (see 11.2 below).

5.1.2   *Republic of Ireland*

FRS 102 provides that a Republic of Ireland tax rate can be regarded as having been substantively enacted if it is included in a Bill that has been passed by the Dail. *[FRS 102 Appendix I]*.

5.1.3   *Other jurisdictions*

FRS 102 gives no guidance as to how this requirement is to be interpreted in other jurisdictions. For the purposes of IAS 12, however, a consensus has emerged in most jurisdictions as to the meaning of 'substantive enactment' for that jurisdiction. This is discussed more fully in EY International GAAP 2015 Chapter 30 at 5.1.

5.2   Uncertain tax positions

In recording the amounts of current tax expected to be paid or recovered, *[FRS 102.29.5]*, the entity will sometimes have to deal with uncertainty. For example, tax legislation may allow the deduction of research and development expenditure, but there may be uncertainty as to whether a specific item of expenditure falls within the definition of eligible research and development costs in the legislation. In some cases, it may not be clear how tax law applies to a particular transaction, if at all. In other situations, a tax return might have been submitted to the tax authorities, who are yet to opine on the treatment of certain transactions, or even have indicated that they disagree with the entity's interpretation of tax law.

These situations are commonly referred to as 'uncertain tax positions' and estimating the outcome of an uncertain tax position is often one of the most complex and subjective areas in accounting for tax. However, like FRS 19 and IAS 12, FRS 102 does not specifically address the measurement of uncertain tax positions, beyond the general requirement of the standard to measure current tax at the amount expected to be paid or recovered. *[FRS 102.29.5]*.

In these situations, FRS 102 requires an entity's management to use its judgment in developing and applying an appropriate accounting policy. *[FRS 102.10.4]*. It would be appropriate to refer to other sections of FRS 102, *[FRS 102.10.5]*, for example to the guidance in Section 21 on the determination of a 'best estimate of the amount required to settle an obligation at the reporting date' *[FRS 102.21.7]* (see Chapter 17 at 3.7.1). An entity could equally look to the approaches applied by IFRS reporters dealing with uncertain tax positions under IAS 12. *[FRS 102.10.6]*. These approaches are discussed in EY International GAAP 2015 Chapter 30 at 9.

One of the judgments required to be made by management is to determine the unit of account. This might be an entire tax computation, individual uncertain positions, or a group of related uncertain positions (e.g. all positions in a particular tax jurisdiction, or all positions of a similar nature or relating to the same interpretation of tax legislation). The estimated outcome could be different depending on whether the probability of outcomes is considered on an item by item basis or across the population of uncertainties as a whole.

Another consideration required in estimating an uncertain tax position is the question of 'detection risk', which refers to the likelihood that the tax authority examines every single amount reported to it by the entity and the extent to which the tax authority has full knowledge of all relevant information. In our view, it is normally not appropriate to factor detection risk into the recognition and measurement of uncertain tax positions.

In many jurisdictions, including the UK, the tax law imposes a legal obligation on an entity operating in that jurisdiction to disclose its full liability to tax, or to assess its own liability to tax, and to make all relevant information available to the tax authorities. In such a tax jurisdiction it would be difficult, as a matter of corporate governance, for an entity to record a tax provision calculated on the basis that the tax authority will not become aware of a particular position which the entity has a legal obligation to disclose to that authority.

5.2.1 Classification of uncertain tax positions

Uncertain tax positions generally relate to the estimate of current tax payable or receivable. Any amount recognised for an uncertain current tax position should normally be classified as current tax, and presented (or disclosed) as current or non-current in accordance with the general requirements of Section 4 – *Statement of Financial Position* – and companies' legislation.

However, there are circumstances where an uncertain tax position affects the measurement of timing differences as at the reporting date, or to the tax base of an asset or liability acquired in a business combination and therefore relates to deferred tax. For example, there might be doubt as to the amount of tax depreciation that can be deducted in respect of a particular asset, which in turn would lead to doubt as to the tax base of the asset, or to the cumulative difference between depreciation charged to date and amounts recognised in the tax returns. There may sometimes be an equal and opposite uncertainty relating to current and deferred tax. For example, there might be uncertainty as to whether a particular item of income is taxable, but – if it is – any tax payable will be reduced to zero by a loss carried forward from a prior period. As discussed at 10.1.1.C below, it is not appropriate to offset current and deferred tax items.

5.3 'Prior year adjustments' of previously presented tax balances and expense (income)

The determination of the tax liability for all but the most straightforward entities is a complex process. It may be several years after the end of a reporting period before the tax liability for that period is finally agreed with the tax authorities and settled. Therefore, the tax liability initially recorded at the end of the reporting period to which it relates is no more than a best estimate at that time, which will typically require revision in subsequent periods until the liability is finally settled.

Tax practitioners often refer to such revisions as 'prior year adjustments' and regard them as part of the overall tax charge or credit for the current reporting period whatever their nature. However, for financial reporting purposes, the normal provisions of Section 10 – *Accounting Policies, Estimates and Errors* (see Chapter 7) apply to tax balances and the related expense (income). Therefore, the nature of any revision to a previously stated tax balance should be considered to determine whether the revision represents:

- a correction of a material prior period error (in which case it should be accounted for retrospectively, with a restatement of comparative amounts and, where applicable, the opening balance of assets, liabilities and equity at the start of the earliest period presented); *[FRS 102.10.21]* or

- a refinement in the current period of an estimate made in a previous period (in which case it should be accounted for in the current period). *[FRS 102.10.17]*.

In some cases the distinction is clear. If, for example, the entity used an incorrect substantively enacted tax rate (see 5.1 above) to calculate the liability in a previous period, the correction of that rate would – subject to materiality – be a prior year adjustment. A more difficult area is the treatment of accounting changes to reflect the resolution of uncertain tax positions (see 5.2 above). These are in practice almost always treated as measurement adjustments in the current period. However, a view could be taken that the eventual denial, or acceptance, by the tax authorities of a position taken by the taxpayer indicates that one or other party (or both of them) were previously taking an erroneous view of the tax law. As with other aspects of accounting for uncertain tax positions, this is an area where considerable judgment may be required.

5.4   Intra-period allocation, presentation and disclosure

The allocation of current tax income and expense to components of total comprehensive income and equity is discussed at 8 below. The presentation and disclosure of current tax income expense and assets and liabilities are discussed at 10 and 11 below.

6   DEFERRED TAX – RECOGNITION

Deferred tax is defined as the amount of income tax payable (recoverable) in respect of the taxable profit (tax loss) for future reporting periods as a result of past transactions or events. *[FRS 102 Appendix I]*. Section 29 requires deferred tax to be recognised in respect of all timing differences at the reporting date (see 6.1 below), subject to further considerations relating to: *[FRS 102.29.6]*

- unrelieved losses and other deferred tax assets (see 6.2 below);

- tax allowances for the cost of a fixed asset when all the conditions for retaining the tax allowances have been met (see 6.3 below);

- certain timing differences relating to the recognition in the financial statements of income and expenses from a subsidiary, associate, branch or an interest in a joint venture (see 6.4 below).

Deferred tax is usually not recognised in respect of permanent differences (see 6.5 below). *[FRS 102.29.10]*. However, the general 'timing differences approach' of Section 29 does not apply when an entity accounts for the acquisition of assets and liabilities in a business combination. In this situation, deferred tax is recognised in respect of the differences between the values recognised in the financial statements for the acquired assets (other than goodwill) and liabilities in the business combination and the respective amounts that can be deducted or otherwise assessed for tax purposes. *[FRS 102.29.11]*. Accounting for deferred tax in a business combination is discussed at 6.6 below.

6.1   Recognition of deferred tax on timing differences

Timing differences are differences between taxable profits and total comprehensive income as stated in the financial statements that arise from the inclusion of income and expenses in tax assessments in periods different from those in which they are recognised in financial statements. *[FRS 102.29.6]*. Timing differences are said to originate in the accounting period in which they first arise or increase and to reverse in subsequent periods when they decrease, eventually to zero.

6.1.1   Examples of timing differences

A deferred tax liability arises when:

- expenditure is recognised for tax purposes before it is recognised in the financial statements; or
- income is recognised in the financial statements before it is recognised for tax purposes.

A deferred tax asset arises when:

- expenditure is recognised for tax purposes after it is recognised in the financial statements; or
- income is recognised in the financial statements after it is recognised for tax purposes.

Examples of timing differences include:

- tax deductions for the cost of property, plant and equipment are recorded before (deferred tax liability) or after (deferred tax asset) the related depreciation is charged to the income statement;
- tax deductions are available in respect of provisions (for example in respect of decommissioning costs) only when payments are made to settle the obligation. In this case, a deferred tax asset will arise when the entity recognises a provision for that obligation in the financial statements;
- expenditure is capitalised in the financial statements, whereas tax deductions are obtained as the expenditure is incurred. Examples include capitalised borrowing costs and capitalised development costs. Another example arises when an entity accounts for tax-deductible loan issue costs (as a reduction in the recorded net proceeds as required by Section 11 and Section 12), whereas tax relief is given when the issue costs are incurred. In these cases a deferred tax liability will be recognised, because the tax deduction is received before the related cost is depreciated or amortised through the income statement;
- pensions liabilities are recognised in the financial statements but are allowed for tax purposes only when contributions are paid at a later date. This will give

rise to a deferred tax asset when a pension liability is recorded and a deferred tax liability to the extent that a pension asset is recognised;

- revaluations of property, plant and equipment give rise to a gain or loss recorded through other comprehensive income, but do not attract a tax charge until the asset is sold. In this example, a deferred tax liability would be recognised. A similar situation arises when an asset is sold and the related taxable gain is rolled over into the cost of a replacement asset;

- in consolidated financial statements, the elimination of intra-group profits in inventory will give rise to a timing difference (deferred tax asset) because tax is payable on the inter-company transfer before the sale of the related inventory (by the transferee subsidiary) is recognised in the consolidated income statement;

- where a tax loss or tax credit is not relieved against past or current taxable profits but can be carried forward to reduce future taxable profits, a timing difference arises. Subject to the additional criteria set out at 6.2 below, this may give rise to a deferred tax asset being recognised; and

- where an entity holds an investment in a subsidiary, associate or joint venture and additional tax is payable when dividends are remitted to the investor, a timing difference will arise (deferred tax liability) to the extent that profits are recognised in the consolidated income statement before the related earnings are distributed by the investee. In certain circumstances the related timing difference is not required to be recognised, as explained at 6.4 below.

6.1.2   *Deferred taxable gains*

The UK (and some overseas) tax regime mitigates the tax impact of some asset disposals by allowing some or all of the tax liability on such transactions to be deferred, typically subject to conditions, such as a requirement to reinvest the proceeds from the sale of the asset disposed of in a similar 'replacement' asset. The postponement of tax payments achieved in this way may either be for a fixed period (holdover relief) or for an indefinite period until the new asset is disposed of without the sale proceeds being again reinvested in another replacement asset (rollover relief).

The ability to postpone tax payments in this way does not affect the recognition of deferred tax. The original disposal transaction gives rise to a timing difference on which deferred tax must be recognised.

6.2   Restrictions on the recognition of deferred tax assets

Embodied in the definition of an asset in FRS 102 is the expectation of an inflow of future economic benefits. *[FRS 102 Appendix I]*. Accordingly, Section 29 restricts the recognition of unrelieved tax losses and other deferred tax assets to the extent that it is probable that they will be recovered against the reversal of deferred tax liabilities or other future taxable profits. Section 29 observes that the very existence of unrelieved tax losses is strong evidence that there may not be other future table profits against which the losses will be relieved. *[FRS 102.29.7]*.

By contrast to FRS 19 or IAS 12, FRS 102 provides no additional guidance on the interpretation of this general requirement. However, we believe that the guidance in those standards are relevant in forming a view as to whether to recognise a deferred tax asset under Section 29. Accordingly, in our opinion, the entity needs to consider:

- recovery against the reversal of recognised deferred tax liabilities; and
- the availability of future taxable profits.

6.2.1   Recovery against the reversal of recognised deferred tax liabilities

IAS 12 states that it is 'probable' that there will be sufficient taxable profit if a deferred tax asset can be offset against a deferred tax liability relating to the same tax authority which will reverse in the same period as the asset, or in a period into which a loss arising from the asset may be carried back or forward. *[IAS 12.28]*. Any deferred tax liability used as the basis for recognising a deferred tax asset must represent a future tax liability against which the future tax deduction represented by the deferred tax asset can actually be offset. For example, in a tax jurisdiction where revenue and capital items are treated separately for tax purposes, a deferred tax asset representing a capital loss cannot be recognised by reference to a deferred tax liability relating to PP&E against which the capital loss could never be offset in a tax return.

Where there are insufficient deferred tax liabilities relating to the same tax authority to offset a deferred tax asset, the entity should then look to the availability of future taxable profits.

6.2.2   The availability of future taxable profits

A deferred tax asset can be recovered only out of future *taxable* profit. Evidence of future accounting profit is not necessarily evidence of future taxable profit (for example, if significant tax deductions or credits not reflected in the accounting profit are likely to be claimed by the entity in the relevant future periods). Whilst FRS 102 notes that the 'very existence of unrelieved tax losses is strong evidence that there may not be other future table profits against which the losses will be relieved', *[FRS 102.29.7]*, we do not believe this represents a prohibition on their recognition in the absence of recognised deferred tax liabilities; just that more convincing evidence of the existence of profits is required.

IAS 12 suggests that a deferred tax asset should be recognised to the extent that:

- it is probable that in future periods there will be sufficient taxable profits:
  - relating to the same tax authority;
  - relating to the same taxable entity; and
  - arising in the same period as the reversal of the difference or in a period into which a loss arising from the deferred tax asset may be carried back or forward; or
- tax planning opportunities are available that will create taxable profit in appropriate periods. *[IAS 12.29]*.

In our view, any deferred tax liability or future taxable profit used as the basis for recognising a deferred tax asset must also represent a future tax liability against which the future tax deduction can actually be realised. For example, where revenue and capital items are treated separately for tax purposes, a deferred tax asset representing a capital loss cannot be recognised by reference to an expected taxable profit from revenue items, against which the capital loss could never be offset in a tax return.

Where a deferred tax asset is recognised on the basis of expected future taxable profits from trading activities, the 'quality' of those profits must be considered. For example, it might be appropriate to give more weight to (say) revenues from existing orders and contracts than to those from merely anticipated future trading. Where an entity expects to recover from a recent loss-making position, greater scepticism as to the speed of a recovery in profits would also be appropriate.

We do not believe that it will generally be appropriate to restrict the assumed availability of future taxable profit to an arbitrary future timeframe (e.g. 3 years, 5 years etc.) unless such a restriction is imposed because losses expire under tax law. For example, it may well be the case that a deferred tax asset recoverable in twenty years from profits from a currently existing long-term supply contract with a creditworthy customer may be more robust than one recoverable in one year from expected future trading by a start-up company. In the UK, it is also relevant that tax losses can normally be carried forward indefinitely.

To the extent that it is not probable that taxable profit will be available against which the unused tax losses, unused tax credits or other timing differences can be utilised, a deferred tax asset is not recognised. *[FRS 102.29.7].*

6.2.2.A   Tax planning strategies

Where an entity recognises a deferred tax asset on the basis that it will be recovered through profits generated as a result of a tax planning strategy, in our view the entity must:

- be able to demonstrate that the strategy is one that it will undertake, not merely one that it could theoretically undertake;

- measure any deferred tax asset recognised on the basis of a tax planning strategy net of any cost of implementing that strategy (measured, where applicable, on an after-tax basis); and

- expect to be in a net taxable profit position at the relevant time. Where the entity is expected to remain tax loss-making (such that the strategy effectively will simply reduce future tax losses), we believe that the strategy does not generally form the basis for recognising a deferred tax asset, except to the extent that it will create *net* future taxable profits.

6.3   Capital allowances – when all conditions for their retention have been met

Section 29 requires deferred tax to be recognised on timing differences arising when the tax allowances for the cost of a fixed asset are accelerated (i.e. received before the depreciation of the asset is recognised in profit or loss) or decelerated (i.e. received after the depreciation of the asset is recognised in profit or loss). However, any recorded deferred tax should be reversed if and when all conditions for retaining the allowances have been met. *[FRS 102.29.8].*

A past example of a situation giving rise to such a reversal in the UK related to entities that had previously claimed industrial buildings allowances (IBAs) which ceased to be subject to clawback (or a balancing charge) if the asset had been held for 25 years. However, IBAs were phased out in the UK by 2012.

6.3.1   Treatment of assets brought into the UK tonnage tax regime

Companies subject to UK corporation tax, which operate qualifying vessels that are 'strategically and commercially managed in the UK', can take advantage of the tonnage tax regime. The tonnage tax regime differs from the main corporation tax system in a number of key respects, the most significant from an accounting point of view being that an entity in the tonnage tax regime is not assessed to tax on the basis of its reported profits from qualifying activities and does not receive capital allowances for the cost of its ships. Therefore, an entity's operations within the tonnage tax regime are outside the scope of Section 29, because tonnage tax does not meet the definition of an income tax discussed at 3.2 above.

When an entity first enters the tonnage tax regime, not only does it cease to qualify for further capital allowances in relation to the vessels it held at the time of the change, but it is also exempt from any balancing charges on disposals of those vessels made while it is still in the tonnage tax regime. However, if the entity returns to the corporation tax system at a later date, there are rules which may cause this exposure to be reinstated. Membership of the tonnage tax regime is determined for a fixed period, albeit with a renewal option at the entity's discretion; but HMRC also has the power in limited circumstances to withdraw an entity from the tonnage tax regime.

The question therefore arises as to whether an entity entering the tonnage tax regime should derecognise the deferred tax balances related to its vessels on the basis that, 'all conditions for retaining the tax allowances have been met'. *[FRS 102.29.8].* In our view it is appropriate for entities reporting under FRS 102 to continue the practice applied under previous UK GAAP and IFRS of derecognising the deferred tax balances related to assets brought into the tonnage tax regime unless there is evidence of a real possibility that the entity will become subject to the main corporation tax regime at a later date. Consideration should be given to the need to disclose (as a contingent liability) the financial consequences of a return to the main corporation tax system. An entity should not anticipate the effect of entering the tonnage tax regime before it is evident that the necessary clearances have been granted by the tax authorities.

6.4   Income or expenses from a subsidiary, associate, branch or joint venture

Entities are required to recognise deferred tax on timing differences that arise when income or expenses from a subsidiary, branch, associate or joint venture have been recognised in the financial statements and will be assessed to or allowed for tax in a future period, except where: *[FRS 102.29.9]*

*   the reporting entity is able to control the reversal of the timing difference; and

*   it is probable that the timing difference will not reverse in the foreseeable future.

Section 29 notes that such timing differences may arise where there are undistributed profits in a subsidiary, branch, associate or joint venture. *[FRS 102.29.9].* For example, an entity may have recognised in its consolidated financial statements the profits of its subsidiaries or recognised in its consolidated income statement an amount in respect of its share of the earnings of its equity-accounted associates and joint ventures. In cases where the investee is required to deduct withholding tax on any distribution of those profits to its parent, there will be future tax consequences relating to those earnings that have been recognised in the entity's financial statements. Subject to the exception above, deferred tax should be recognised for such timing differences.

6.4.1   'Control' over reversal of timing differences

For this exception to apply, the investor must be able to control the reversal of the timing difference and not expect there to be a reversal in the foreseeable future. *[FRS 102.29.9].* Section 29 does not discuss what is meant by 'control' in this context. However, IAS 12, in discussing the similar requirements of IAS 12, takes the following position:

- in respect of a subsidiary or a branch, the parent is able to control when and whether retained earnings are distributed. Therefore, no provision need be made for the tax consequences of distributing profits if the parent has determined that those profits will not be distributed in the foreseeable future; *[IAS 12.40]*

- in the case of a joint venture, no amount is recorded for the tax consequences of distributing the share of profits recognised by the entity in its statement of comprehensive income to the extent that the joint venture agreement requires the consent of the entity before a dividend can be paid and the entity expects that it will not give such consent in the foreseeable future; *[IAS 12.43]* and

- in the case of an associate, however, the investor cannot usually control distribution policy. Therefore provision should be made for the tax consequences of the distribution of the share of profits recognised by the entity from its associate, except to the extent that there is a shareholders' agreement to the effect that those earnings will not be distributed in the foreseeable future. *[IAS 12.42].*

We believe that an entity should consider these criteria in determining whether it controls the reversal of such timing differences. Of course, if control is deemed to exist, but the entity expects its investee to make a distribution in the foreseeable future, any related tax consequences will have to be recognised at the reporting date.

6.5   Permanent differences

Permanent differences are differences between an entity's taxable profits and its total comprehensive income as stated in the financial statements, other than timing differences. *[FRS 102 Appendix I].* Permanent differences arise because certain types of income or expenses are non-taxable or disallowable, or because certain tax charges or allowances are greater than or smaller than the corresponding income or expense in the financial statements. *[FRS 102.29.10]*. These latter items are sometimes referred to as 'super-deductible' or 'partially-deductible' assets and liabilities. Under Section 29, deferred tax is not recognised on permanent differences, except when an entity is accounting for assets and liabilities acquired in a business combination (see 6.6 below). *[FRS 102.29.10]*.

A permanent difference generally arises from the tax status of an asset (or liability) at the time of its initial recognition. For example, in the UK certain categories of building attract no tax deduction in respect of their use within the business, but only on a subsequent sale. Conversely, the tax deductions made available may exceed the actual expenditure incurred, such as in the case of certain companies engaged in North Sea exploration activities. Another example of a permanent difference arises where an asset is transferred at book value from one member of a group to another, together with its tax history. In this case, the selling subsidiary derecognises the asset and any related deferred tax; but the buying subsidiary recognises only the asset, despite the fact that the cost may only be partially deductible for tax purposes.

In other cases, a permanent difference can be created as a result of changes in tax law subsequent to the original recognition of the asset, for example when the cost of an asset becomes deductible for tax purposes having previously been disallowed. Such changes can give rise to the recognition of deferred tax assets or liabilities under IFRS, but do not under Section 29, where the effect is recognised prospectively as timing differences arise.

In most cases, the application of this requirement for permanent differences is straightforward – either an item is deductible or assessable for tax, or it is not. However, certain items give rise to accounting income and expenditure of which some is assessable or deductible for tax, and some is not. Accounting for the deferred tax effects of such items can raise some issues of interpretation which particularly affect:

- non-deductible assets subject to revaluation (see 6.5.1 below); and
- partially deductible and super-deductible assets (see 6.5.2.below).

6.5.1   *Non-deductible assets subject to revaluation*

Where a non-deductible asset is acquired separately (i.e. not as part of a larger business combination), the difference between the original cost of the asset and the amount deductible for tax (i.e. zero) is a permanent difference on which no deferred tax is recognised.

If gains on disposal of such an asset are taxable and the asset is subsequently revalued, however, the revaluation would give rise to a timing difference as it results in the recognition of income which is expected to be taxed at a later date. This is illustrated in Examples 24.3 and 24.4 below.

Example 24.3:   Revaluation of non-depreciated, non-deductible asset

On 1 January 2015 an entity paying tax at 20% acquires a non tax-deductible office building for £2,000,000. Application of Section 17 – *Property, Plant and Equipment* – results in no depreciation being charged on the building.

On 1 January 2016 the entity revalues the building to £2,400,000. The revaluation of £400,000 is a timing difference giving rise to a deferred tax expense at 20% of £80,000. This tax expense would be recognised in other comprehensive income with the related revaluation gain (see 8 below).

Example 24.4:   Revaluation of depreciated, non-deductible asset

On 1 January 2015 an entity paying tax at 20% acquires a non-tax-deductible office building for £2,000,000. The building is depreciated over 20 years at £100,000 per year to a residual value of zero. The entity's financial year ends on 31 December.

At 31 December 2016, the carrying amount of the building is £1,800,000, and it is revalued upwards by £900,000 to its current market value of £2,700,000. As there is no change to the estimated residual value of zero, or to the expected life of the building, this will be depreciated over the next 18 years at £150,000 per year.

As the building is depreciated in future periods the £900,000 timing difference relating to the revaluation will reverse. However, £1,800,000 of the depreciation charged in each period relates to the original cost which is not taxable. Accordingly, in our view, for the purposes of applying Section 29, 9/27 of the depreciation charged in future periods should be considered as giving rise to a reversal of the timing difference created by the revaluation, and 18/27 should be considered as giving rise to a permanent difference. For example, in 2017:

	Total depreciation £	Permanent difference £	Timing difference £
	150,000	100,000	50,000

The revaluation in 2016 gives rise to a timing difference of £900,000 giving rise to a deferred tax charge against OCI at 20% of £180,000 in the year ended 31 December 2016. As the difference reverses in 2017 the entity recognises deferred tax income of £10,000, representing the tax effect at 20% of the £50,000 depreciation relating to the revalued element of the building (see table above).

6.5.2   Partially deductible and super-deductible assets

The tax deductions for an asset are generally based on the cost of that asset to the legal entity that owns it. However, in some jurisdictions, certain categories of asset are deductible for tax but for an amount either less than the cost of the asset ('partially deductible') or more than the cost of the asset ('super-deductible').

In such cases the difference between the cost and the tax-deductible amount (whether lower or higher) is a permanent difference as defined in Section 29. Section 29 provides no specific guidance on the treatment of partially deductible and super-deductible assets. The issues raised by such assets are illustrated in Examples 24.5 and 24.6 below.

Example 24.5:   Partially deductible asset

An entity acquires an asset with a cost of £100,000, for which tax deductions of only £60,000 are available, in a transaction which is not a business combination. The asset is depreciated to a residual value of zero over 10 years, and qualifies for tax deductions of 20% per year over 5 years. In our view, in applying Section 29, the entity could analyse the annual depreciation of £10,000 per annum into a tax-deductible element of £6,000 and a non-deductible element of £4,000, reflecting the fact that only 60% of the cost of the asset is tax-deductible. Timing differences are then calculated by reference to the interaction of tax deductions claimed with the tax-deductible 'element' of the depreciation as set out below.

Year	Depreciation	40% non-deductible element	60% deductible element	Tax deductions	Cumulative timing difference
	a	b (40% of a)	c (60% of a)	d	c – d
1	10,000	4,000	6,000	12,000	6,000
2	10,000	4,000	6,000	12,000	12,000
3	10,000	4,000	6,000	12,000	18,000
4	10,000	4,000	6,000	12,000	24,000
5	10,000	4,000	6,000	12,000	30,000
6	10,000	4,000	6,000	–	24,000
7	10,000	4,000	6,000	–	18,000
8	10,000	4,000	6,000	–	12,000
9	10,000	4,000	6,000	–	6,000
10	10,000	4,000	6,000	–	–

If the entity pays tax at 30%, the amounts recorded for this transaction during year 1 (assuming that there are sufficient other taxable profits to absorb the tax loss created) would be as follows:

	€
Depreciation of asset	(10,000)
Current tax income[1]	3,600
Deferred tax charge[2]	(1,800)
Net tax credit	1,800
Post tax depreciation	(8,200)

1   £100,000 [cost of asset] × 60% [deductible element] × 20% [tax depreciation rate] × 30% [tax rate]

2   £6,000 [timing difference] × 30% [tax rate] = £1,800 – brought forward deferred tax balance [nil] = £1,800

If this calculation is repeated for all 10 years, the following would be reported in the financial statements.

Year	Depreciation	Current tax credit	Deferred tax (charge)/credit	Total tax credit	Effective tax rate
	a	b	c	d (=b+c)	e (=d/a)
1	(10,000)	3,600	(1,800)	1,800	18%
2	(10,000)	3,600	(1,800)	1,800	18%
3	(10,000)	3,600	(1,800)	1,800	18%
4	(10,000)	3,600	(1,800)	1,800	18%
5	(10,000)	3,600	(1,800)	1,800	18%
6	(10,000)	–	1,800	1,800	18%
7	(10,000)	–	1,800	1,800	18%
8	(10,000)	–	1,800	1,800	18%
9	(10,000)	–	1,800	1,800	18%
10	(10,000)	–	1,800	1,800	18%

This methodology has the result that, throughout the life of the asset, a consistent tax credit is reported in each period. The effective tax rate in each period corresponds to the effective tax rate for the transaction as a whole – i.e. cost of £100,000 attracting total tax deductions of £18,000 (£60,000 at 30%), an overall rate of 18%.

However, this approach cannot be said to be required by Section 29 and other methodologies could well be appropriate, provided that they are applied consistently in similar circumstances.

Example 24.6:   *Super-deductible asset*

The converse situation to that in Example 24.5 arises where tax authorities seek to encourage certain types of investment by giving tax allowances for an amount in excess of the expenditure actually incurred. Suppose that an entity invests £1 million in PP&E, for which tax deductions of £1.2 million are available, in a transaction which is not a business combination. The asset is depreciated to a residual value of zero over 10 years, and qualifies for five annual tax deductions of 20% of its deemed tax cost of £1,200,000.

The methodology we propose in Example 24.5 could be applied 'in reverse' – i.e. with the tax deductions, rather than the depreciation, of the asset being apportioned in the ratio 10:2 into a 'cost' element and a 'super deduction' element, and the timing difference calculated by reference to the 'cost' element as follows.

Year	Depreciation a	Tax deduction b	'Super deduction' element c (=2/12 of b)	Cost element d (=10/12 of b)	Cumulative timing difference a − d
1	100,000	240,000	40,000	200,000	100,000
2	100,000	240,000	40,000	200,000	200,000
3	100,000	240,000	40,000	200,000	300,000
4	100,000	240,000	40,000	200,000	400,000
5	100,000	240,000	40,000	200,000	500,000
6	100,000	–	–	–	400,000
7	100,000	–	–	–	300,000
8	100,000	–	–	–	200,000
9	100,000	–	–	–	100,000
10	100,000	–	–	–	–

If the entity pays tax at 30%, the amounts recorded for this transaction during year 1 (assuming that there are sufficient other taxable profits to absorb the tax loss created) would be as follows:

	£
Depreciation of asset	(100,000)
Current tax income[1]	72,000
Deferred tax charge[2]	(30,000)
Net tax credit	42,000
Profit after tax	(58,000)

1   £1,200,000 [deemed tax cost of asset] × 20% [tax depreciation rate] × 30% [tax rate]

2   £100,000 [timing difference] × 30% [tax rate] = £30,000 – brought forward balance [nil] = £30,000.

If this calculation is repeated for all 10 years, the following would be reported in the financial statements.

Year	Depreciation a	Current tax credit b	Deferred tax (charge)/credit c	Total tax credit d (=b+c)	Effective tax rate e (=d/a)
1	(100,000)	72,000	(30,000)	42,000	42%
2	(100,000)	72,000	(30,000)	42,000	42%
3	(100,000)	72,000	(30,000)	42,000	42%
4	(100,000)	72,000	(30,000)	42,000	42%
5	(100,000)	72,000	(30,000)	42,000	42%
6	(100,000)	–	30,000	30,000	30%
7	(100,000)	–	30,000	30,000	30%
8	(100,000)	–	30,000	30,000	30%
9	(100,000)	–	30,000	30,000	30%
10	(100,000)	–	30,000	30,000	30%

This results in an effective 42% tax rate for this transaction being reported in years 1 to 5, and a rate of 30% in years 6 to 10, in contrast to the average effective rate of 36% for the transaction as a whole – i.e. cost of £1,000,000 attracting total tax deductions of £360,000 (£1,200,000 at 30%). This is because, in the case of a partially deductible asset as in Example 24.5 above, there is an accounting mechanism (i.e. depreciation) for allocating the non-deductible cost on a straight-line basis. However, in the present case of a super deductible asset there is no basis for spreading the £60,000 tax super-deductions, and these are therefore reflected as current tax income in the years in which they are claimed.

Again, as in Example 24.5 above, no single approach can be said to be required by FRS 102 and other methodologies could well be appropriate, provided that they are applied consistently in similar circumstances.

6.5.3 UK indexation allowance

UK tax legislation provides that when certain types of asset are disposed of the cost of the asset deducted in calculating any taxable gain on disposal may be increased by an 'indexation allowance' that is broadly intended to exclude from taxation any gains arising simply as a result of general price inflation.

On a strict interpretation of the definition of 'permanent difference', an indexation allowance is a permanent difference since it is effectively an item of expenditure that appears in taxable profit, but not in total comprehensive income. However, in our view – supported by long-standing practice under FRS 19 under which the same issue of interpretation would have arisen – it is more appropriate to deal with indexation allowance in the measurement of the related deferred tax liabilities (see 7.5 below).

6.6 Business combinations

As an exception to the general 'timing differences' approach to the recognition of deferred tax in Section 29, an entity is required to recognise deferred tax on the differences between the values recognised for assets (other than goodwill) and liabilities acquired in a business combination and the amounts at which those assets and liabilities will be assessed for tax. *[FRS 102.29.11].* Any such differences are permanent differences to the acquiring entity as defined in FRS 102, because they arise from:

- gains or losses recognised by (and/or tax charged to or credited by) the acquiree before its acquisition;

- fair value adjustments made by the reporting entity on acquisition (which are effectively recognised in goodwill, not in total comprehensive income); and

- the effect of permanent differences that were not recognised in the financial statements of the acquired entity.

Accordingly, the amount of deferred tax required to be recognised in a business combination may be greater than just the differences between the fair values of assets and liabilities acquired and their previous carrying amounts in the financial statements of the acquired entity.

Deferred tax recognised in a business combination is reflected in the measurement of goodwill, and not taken to total comprehensive income or equity. *[FRS 102.29.11]*. This requirement may lead to the creation of goodwill which, on a literal reading of Section 27 – *Impairment of Assets*, would be required to be immediately impaired, as illustrated by Example 24.7 below.

Example 24.7:   Apparent 'day one' impairment arising from recognition of deferred tax in a business combination

Entity A, which is taxed at 20%, acquires Entity B for £100m in a transaction that is a business combination. The fair values of the identifiable net assets of Entity B, and the amounts deductible for those net assets for tax purposes are as follows:

	Fair value (£m)	*Tax deduction* (£m)
Brand name	60	–
Other net assets	20	15

This will give rise to the following consolidation journal:

	£m	£m
Goodwill (balance)	33	
Brand name	60	
Other net assets	20	
Deferred tax[1]		13
Cost of investment		100

[1] 20% of (£[60m + 20m] – £15m)

The fair value of the consolidated assets of the subsidiary (excluding deferred tax) and goodwill as presented in the financial statements is now £115m, but the cost of the subsidiary is only £100m. Clearly £15m of the goodwill arises solely from the recognition of deferred tax. However, Section 27, paragraph 18(b), explicitly requires tax to be excluded from the estimate of future cash flows used to calculate any impairment. This raises the question of whether there should not be an immediate impairment write-down of the assets to £100m. In our view, this cannot have been the intention of Section 27, as discussed in Chapter 22.

6.6.1 *Acquisition of subsidiary not accounted for as a business combination*

Occasionally, an entity may acquire a subsidiary which is accounted for as the acquisition of an asset rather than as a business combination. This will most often be the case where the subsidiary concerned is a 'single asset entity' holding a single item of property, plant and equipment which is not considered to comprise a business as defined in FRS 102 (see Chapter 15). Where an asset is acquired in such circumstances, the normal provisions of Section 29 apply. Accordingly, any difference between the cost of the asset and the amount (if any) that will be deductible for tax in respect of that asset is a permanent difference, and deferred tax should not be recognised.

7 DEFERRED TAX – MEASUREMENT

Like current tax, deferred tax should not be discounted *[FRS 102.27.17]* and should be measured by reference to the tax rates and laws that have been enacted or substantively enacted by the reporting date. *[FRS 102.29.12]*. 'Enacted or substantively enacted' for the purposes of deferred tax has the same meaning as for the purposes of calculating current tax, as discussed at 5.1 above.

In measuring deferred tax assets and deferred tax liabilities, an entity is required to apply those enacted rates that are expected to apply to the reversal of the timing difference, except in the case of timing differences arising from the revaluation of non-depreciable assets and deferred tax relating to investment property measured at fair value (see 7.1 below). *[FRS 102.29.12]*.

When different tax rates apply to different levels of taxable profit, deferred tax assets and liabilities are measured using the average enacted or substantively enacted rates that are expected to apply to the taxable profit (tax loss) of the periods in which the entity expects the deferred tax asset to be realised or the deferred tax liability to be settled. *[FRS 102.29.13]*.

7.1 Revalued non-depreciable assets and investment property measured at fair value

Section 29 provides two exceptions to the general measurement requirement summarised above as follows:

*   deferred tax relating to a non-depreciable asset that is measured using the revaluation model in Section 17 – *Property, Plant and Equipment* – should be measured using the tax rates and allowances that apply to the sale of the asset; *[FRS 102.29.15]* and

*   deferred tax relating to investment property that is measured at fair value in accordance with Section 16 – *Investment Property* – should be measured using the tax rates and allowances that apply to the sale of the asset, except for investment property that has a limited useful life and is held within a business model whose objective is to consume substantially all of the economic benefits embodied in the property over time. *[FRS 102.29.16]*.

These provisions of Section 29 are derived from IAS 12, where they appear as an exception to a more general principle that measurement of deferred tax should have regard to the manner in which an entity expects to recover the asset, or settle the liability, to which the deferred tax relates. *[IAS 12.51, 51B, 51C].* However, there is no such equivalent general principle expressed in Section 29, although it could be implied from the requirement that deferred tax is measured using the tax rates 'that are expected to apply to the reversal of the timing difference'. *[FRS 102.29.12].* In an 'editorial clarification' issued on 12 November 2013, the FRC clarified that, in measuring deferred tax arising on a business combination, an entity should consider the manner in which it expects, at the end of the reporting period, to recover or settle the carrying amount of its assets and liabilities. Whilst this clarification strictly applies only to the measurement of deferred tax arising on a business combination, we believe that its underlying principle should be applied more generally. The concept of the 'manner of recovery' is discussed in more detail at 7.4 below.

7.2   Uncertain tax positions

'Uncertain tax position' is not discussed in FRS 102, but is generally understood to refer to an item the tax treatment of which is unclear or is a matter subject to an unresolved dispute between the reporting entity and the relevant tax authority. An uncertain tax position generally occurs where there is an uncertainty as to the meaning of the tax law, or to the applicability of the law to a particular transaction, or both.

As discussed at 5.2 above, uncertain tax positions generally relate to the estimate of current tax payable or receivable. However, in some situations an uncertain tax position affects the measurement of timing differences as at the reporting date, or to the tax base of an asset or liability acquired in a business combination. For example, there might be doubt as to the amount of tax depreciation that can be deducted in respect of a particular asset, which in turn would lead to doubt as to any related deferred tax arising in a business combination, or to the cumulative difference between depreciation charged to date and amounts recognised in the tax returns. In these circumstances the discussion at 5.2 above will also be relevant to the measurement of deferred tax assets and liabilities.

7.3   'Prior year adjustments' of previously presented tax balances and expense (income)

The requirement to revise estimates of amounts recognised as deferred tax assets and liabilities at successive reporting dates is an inevitable consequence of the Standard and, in that respect, the normal requirements of Section 10 apply (see Chapter 7). As discussed in the context of current tax at 5.3 above, the nature of any revision to a previously stated deferred tax balance should be considered to determine whether the revision represents:

- a correction of a material prior period error (in which case it should be accounted for retrospectively, with a restatement of comparative amounts and, where applicable, the opening balance of assets, liabilities and equity at the start of the earliest period presented); *[FRS 102.10.21]* or

- a refinement in the current period of an estimate made in a previous period (in which case it should be accounted for in the current period). *[FRS 102.10.17].*

7.4   Expected manner of recovery of assets or settlement of liabilities

As noted at 6.6 above, the FRC has clarified that, in measuring deferred tax arising on a business combination for the purposes of Section 29, an entity should consider the manner in which it expects to recover or settle the carrying amount of its assets and liabilities. We believe that this principle should be applied in measuring all deferred tax, in order to meet the requirement of Section 29 to measure deferred tax using the tax rates and laws that are 'expected' to apply to the reversal of the timing difference. [*FRS 102.29.12*]. If a different rate or law would apply to the reversal of the difference depending on the manner of reversal (e.g. depreciation or sale), the expected manner of reversal is an essential input to the assessment of the expected applicable tax rate or law.

7.4.1   Tax planning strategies

As discussed at 6.2.2.A above, we believe that it may be appropriate for an entity to have regard to tax planning strategies in determining whether a deferred tax asset may be recognised.

Some believe that this principle should be extended and argue that, where an entity has the ability and intention to undertake transactions that will lead to its being taxed at a lower rate, it may take this into account in measuring deferred tax liabilities relating to timing differences that will reverse in future periods when the lower rate is expected to apply.

In our view, this is not appropriate. While tax planning opportunities may be relevant in assessing whether a deferred tax asset should be *recognised*, they do not impact on the *measurement* of deferred tax until the entity has undertaken them, or is at least irrevocably committed to doing so.

7.4.2   Assets and liabilities with more than one tax base ('dual-based' assets)

In the UK, and some jurisdictions, the manner in which an entity recovers (settles) the carrying amount of an asset (liability) may affect either or both of:

- the tax rate applicable when the entity recovers (settles) the carrying amount of the asset (or liability); and
- the amount at which the asset or liability is recognised for tax purposes.

For example, in the UK, many types of building are not eligible for capital allowances while they are in use, but are deductible on sale for an amount equal to cost plus indexation allowance. Assets which are treated differently for tax purposes depending on whether their value is recovered through use or sale are commonly referred to as 'dual-based' assets.

In practice, however, many such assets are not realised wholly through use or wholly through sale, but are routinely acquired, used for part of their life and then sold before the end of that life. This is particularly the case with long-lived assets such as property. We set out below the approach which we believe should be adopted in assessing the manner of recovery of:

- depreciable PP&E and intangible assets (see 7.4.2.A below);
- non-depreciable PP&E, investment properties and intangible assets (see 7.4.2.B below); and
- other assets and liabilities (see 7.4.2.C below).

7.4.2.A   Depreciable PP&E and intangible assets

Depreciable PP&E and investment properties are accounted for in accordance with Section 17. Amortised intangibles are accounted for in accordance with Section 18 – *Intangible Assets other than Goodwill* – Section 17 and Section 18, which are discussed in detail in Chapters 13 and 14, require the carrying amount of a depreciable asset to be separated into a 'residual value' and a 'depreciable amount'.

'Residual value' is defined as:

> '... the estimated amount that an entity would currently obtain from disposal of an asset, after deducting the estimated costs of disposal, if the asset were already of the age and condition expected at the end of its useful life'

and 'depreciable amount' as:

> '... the cost of an asset, or other amount substituted for cost ... , less its residual value'. *[FRS 102 Appendix I].*

It is inherent in the definitions of 'residual value' and 'depreciable amount' that, in determining residual value, an entity is effectively asserting that it expects to recover the depreciable amount of an asset through use and its residual value through sale. If the entity does not expect to sell an asset, but to use and scrap it, then the residual value (i.e. the amount that would be obtained from sale) must be nil.

Accordingly, we believe that, in determining the expected manner of recovery of an asset for the purposes of Section 29, an entity should assume that, in the case of an asset accounted for under Section 17 or Section 18, it will recover the residual value of the asset through sale and the depreciable amount through use. Such an analysis is also consistent with the requirement of Section 10 to account for similar transactions consistently (see Chapter 7). This suggests that consistent assumptions should be used in determining both the residual value of an asset for the purposes of Section 17 or Section 18 and the expected manner of its recovery for the purposes of Section 29.

The effect of this treatment is as follows.

Example 24.8:   Dual-based asset

As part of a business combination an entity purchases an opencast mine to which there is assigned a fair value of £10 million. The tax system of the jurisdiction where the mine is located provides that, if the site is sold (with or without the minerals *in situ*), £9 million will be allowed as a deduction in calculating the taxable profit on sale. The profit on sale of the land is taxed as a capital item. If the mine is exploited through excavation and sale of the minerals, no tax deduction is available.

The entity intends fully to exploit the mine and then to sell the site for retail development. Given the costs that any developer will need to incur in preparing the excavated site for development, the ultimate sales proceeds are likely to be nominal. Thus, for the purposes of Section 17, the mine is treated as having a depreciable amount of £10 million and a residual value of nil.

On the analysis above:

- as the asset is used, the amount that can be deducted for tax (nil) is £10 million less than the amount at which it is recognised in the financial statements (£10 million)

- when the asset is finally sold, the amount that can be deducted for tax (£9 million) is £9 million more than the amount at which the residual value is carried (nil).

On this analysis, the entity would provide a deferred tax liability on the excess of the carrying value of depreciable amount of the mine over the amount deductible for tax. Whether or not a deferred tax asset can be recognised in respect of the excess of amount deductible on sale over the carrying amount of the residual value will be determined in accordance with the criteria discussed in 7.2 above. In some tax regimes, capital profits and losses are treated more or less separately from revenue profits and losses to a greater or lesser degree, so that it may be difficult to recognise such an asset due to a lack of suitable taxable profits.

However, we acknowledge that this is not the only possible interpretation of Section 29, and some might persuade themselves that there is a single net deferred tax liability based on the net book-tax difference of £1 million.

7.4.2.B   Non-depreciable PP&E and investment properties at fair value

As noted at 7.1 above, Section 29 requires that where a non-depreciable asset is accounted for using the revaluation model, any deferred tax on the revaluation should be calculated by reference to the tax consequences that would arise on sale of the asset. *[FRS 102.29.15]*. Section 29 also requires any deferred tax asset or liability associated with an investment property that is measured at fair value in accordance with Section 16 is measured by reference to the tax consequences that would arise on sale of the asset, except when the investment property is has a limited useful life and the entity's business model is to consume substantially all the economic benefits embodied in the investment property over time. *[FRS 102.29.16]*.

7.4.2.C   Other assets and liabilities

In a number of areas of accounting FRS 102 effectively requires a transaction to be accounted for in accordance with an assumption as to the ultimate settlement of that transaction that may not reflect the entity's expectation of the actual outcome.

For example, if the entity enters into a share-based payment transaction with an employee that gives the employee the right to require settlement in either shares or cash, Section 26 – *Share-based Payment* – requires the transaction to be accounted for on the assumption that it will be settled in cash, however unlikely this may be. Section 28 – *Employee Benefits* – may assert that an entity has a surplus on a defined benefit pension scheme on an accounting basis, when in reality it has a deficit on a funding basis. Similarly, if an entity issues a convertible bond that can also be settled in cash at the holder's option, Section 11 – *Basic Financial Instruments* – requires the bond to be accounted for on the assumption that it will be repaid, however probable it is that the holders will actually elect for conversion. It may well be that such transactions have different tax consequences depending on the expected manner of settlement, as illustrated in Example 24.9 below.

One view would be that deferred tax should be recognised and measured based on management's actual expectation of the manner of recovery of the asset (or settlement of the liability) to which the deferred tax relates, even where this differs from the expectation inherent in the accounting treatment. The contrary view would be that

Chapter 24

should be recognised and measured based on the expectation inherent in the accounting treatment of the manner of recovery of the asset (or settlement of the liability) to which the deferred tax relates, even where this differs from management's actual expectation.

In our view, the treatment should be based on management's actual expectation. We see a difference between the analysis here and that relating to depreciable PP&E and intangible assets discussed at 7.4.2.A above. In the case of depreciable PP&E and intangibles, Sections 17 and 18 effectively require management to assess whether such assets will be realised through use or sale, and it therefore seems reasonable to use that same assessment for the purpose of measuring deferred tax under Section 29. In the case of the items discussed immediately above, however, FRS 102 may require management to make assumptions that are directly contrary to its expectations, which therefore need not be used for the purposes of Section 29.

7.4.3   Timing differences relating to subsidiaries, branches, associates and joint ventures

Such differences, and the special recognition criteria applied to them in Section 29, are discussed in more detail at 6.4 above.

Where deferred tax is recognised on such a timing difference, the question arises as to how it should be measured. Broadly speaking, investors can realise an investment in one of two ways – either indirectly (by remittance of retained earnings or capital) or directly (through sale of the investment). In many jurisdictions, the two means of realisation have very different tax consequences.

In our view, the entity should apply the general principle (discussed above) that, where there is more than one method of recovering an investment, the entity should measure any associated deferred tax asset or liability by reference to the expected manner of recovery of the investment. In other words, to the extent that the investment is expected to be realised through sale, the deferred tax is measured according to the tax rules applicable on sale, but to the extent that the temporary difference is expected to be realised through a distribution of earnings or capital, the deferred tax is measured according to the tax rules applicable on distribution.

Where the expected manner of recovery is through distribution, there may be tax consequences for more than one entity in the group. For example, the paying company may be required to deduct a withholding tax on the dividend paid and the receiving company may suffer income tax on the dividend received. In such cases, provision should be made for the cumulative effect of all tax consequences. A withholding tax on an intragroup dividend is not accounted for in the consolidated financial statements as a withholding tax (i.e. within equity), but as a tax expense in profit or loss, since the group is not making a distribution but transferring assets from a group entity to a parent of that entity.

7.4.4   Change in expected manner of recovery of an asset or settlement of a liability

A change in the expected manner recovery of an asset or settlement of a liability should be dealt with as an item of deferred tax income or expense for the period in which the change of expectation occurs, and recognised in profit or loss or in other comprehensive income or movements in equity for that period as appropriate (see 9 below).

This may have the effect, in certain situations, that some tax consequences of a disposal transaction are recognised before the transaction itself. For example, an entity might own an item of PP&E which has previously been held for use but which the entity now expects to sell. In our view, any deferred tax relating to that item of PP&E should be measured on a 'sale' rather than a 'use' basis from that point, even though the disposal itself, and any related current tax, may not be accounted for until the disposal occurs.

7.5   UK indexation allowance

A UK company, in computing the taxable gain on the sale of an asset, is allowed to increase the cost of the asset by an indexation allowance, the broad intention of which is to exclude purely inflationary gains from taxation. As noted at 6.5.3 above, the indexation allowance could be construed as a permanent difference. However, practice under FRS 19 has been to take account of the indexation allowance in measuring any deferred tax that would be expected to arise on the sale of an asset.

In our view, deferred tax at the reporting date should be computed based on the indexation that would be available if disposal were to occur at the balance sheet date. Possible increases in the allowance due to future inflation should not be assumed.

The benefit of an indexation allowance can be taken only to the extent that it reduces a tax liability. It cannot be used to create or increase a tax loss. Therefore, a deferred tax asset should not be recognised in respect of an asset whose indexed cost for tax purposes is greater than its carrying amount.

7.6   Effectively tax-free entities

In the UK, and elsewhere, certain types of entity, typically investment vehicles, are exempt from corporate income tax provided that they fulfil certain criteria, which generally include a requirement to distribute all, or a minimum percentage, of their annual income as a dividend to investors. Examples in the UK include investment trusts and real estate investment trusts 'REITs'. This raises the question of how such entities should measure income taxes.

One view would be that such an entity has a liability to tax at the normal rate until the dividend for a year becomes a liability. The liability for a dividend for an accounting period typically arises after the end of that period. Under this analysis, therefore, such an entity would be required, at each period end, to record a liability for current tax at the standard corporate rate. That liability would be released in full when the dividend is recognised as a liability in the following period. This would mean that, on an ongoing basis, the income statement would show a current tax charge or credit comprising:

- a charge for a full liability for the current period, and
- a credit for the reversal of the corresponding liability for the prior period.

In addition, deferred tax would be recognised at the standard tax rate on all timing differences.

A second view – which we prefer – would be that the provisions of Section 29 regarding different tax rates for distributed and undistributed tax rates are intended to apply where the only significant factor determining the differential tax rate is the retention or distribution of profit. By contrast, the tax status of an investment fund typically depends on many more factors than whether or not profits are distributed, such as restrictions on its activities, the nature of its investments and so forth. On this view, the analysis would be that such an entity can choose to operate within one of two tax regimes (a 'full tax' regime or a 'no tax' regime), rather than that it operates in a single tax regime with a dual tax rate depending on whether profits are retained or distributed.

7.7   Share-based payment transactions

The accounting treatment of share-based payment transactions, some knowledge of which is required to understand the discussion below, is dealt with in Chapter 21.

In the UK, and many other jurisdictions, an entity receives a tax deduction in respect of remuneration paid in shares, share options or other equity instruments of the entity. The amount of any tax deduction may differ from the related remuneration expense, and may arise in a later accounting period. For example, in the UK, an entity recognises an expense for employee services in accordance with Section 26 (based on the fair value of the award at the date of grant), but does not receive a tax deduction until the award is exercised (in the case of options) or vests (in the case of free shares). The tax deduction is for the fair value of the award at the date of vesting or exercise (as the case may be), which will be equal to the intrinsic value at that date.

Under Section 29, any tax deduction received in excess of the amount recognised as an expense under Section 26 gives rise to a permanent difference which is recognised as current tax when it is received. However, recognition of the Section 26 expense in advance of the tax deduction being received to the extent of that expense gives rise to timing differences, on which a deferred tax asset should be recognised (subject to the general restrictions discussed at 6.2 above).

Section 29 does not prescribe how these timing differences should be calculated. As the tax relief will ultimately be given for the intrinsic value of the award, this forms a reasonable basis for computing the timing difference, which has generally been followed in practice under UK GAAP. However, practice varies as to whether the timing difference is computed as:

- the lower of (a) the total expected tax deduction based on the intrinsic value at the reporting date and (b) the cumulative share-based payment expense (Approach 1); or

- the lower of (a) the cumulative share-based payment expense and (b) the total expected tax deduction based on the intrinsic value at the reporting date, multiplied by the expired portion of the vesting period at that date (Approach 2).

Where the intrinsic value of the award is equal to, or more than, the grant date fair value used in applying Section 26, the two approaches have the same effect. However, where the intrinsic value falls below the grant date fair value, the two approaches give rise to a different result, as illustrated by Example 24.9 below.

Example 24.9: *Timing differences on share-based payment transactions*

On 1 January 2015, an entity with a reporting date of 31 December makes an award of free shares to an employee with a grant date fair value of £300,000. The vesting period is three years. In applying Section 26, it is assumed throughout the vesting period that the award will vest in full. The award actually vests, and is fully deducted for tax in the year of vesting at its intrinsic value on vesting date.

The expense recognised under Section 26 would therefore be as follows:

Year ending	Expense for period £	Cumulative expense £
31 December 2015	100,000	100,000
31 December 2016	100,000	200,000
31 December 2017	100,000	300,000

The intrinsic value of the award at each reporting date is as follows:

	£
31 December 2015	270,000
31 December 2016	290,400
31 December 2017	320,000

Under Approach 1 above, the timing difference would be calculated as the lower of (a) the total intrinsic value at the reporting date and (b) the cumulative share-based payment expense.

Year ending	Total intrinsic value a £	Cumulative expense b £	Timing difference Lower of a and b £
31 December 2015	270,000	100,000	100,000
31 December 2016	290,400	200,000	200,000
31 December 2017	320,000	300,000	N/A[1]

1   The award vests at this point so that any tax relief is recognised as current tax.

Under Approach 2 above, the timing difference would be calculated as the lower of (a) the cumulative share-based payment expense and (b) the total intrinsic value, multiplied by the expired portion of the vesting period at that date.

Year ending	Total intrinsic value a £	Pro-rated intrinsic value b £	Cumulative expense c £	Lower of b and c £
31 December 2015	270,000	90,000	100,000	90,000
31 December 2016	290,400	193,600	200,000	193,600
31 December 2017	320,000	320,000	300,000	N/A[1]

1   The award vests at this point so that any tax relief is recognised as current tax.

In our view, either approach is acceptable, but should be adopted consistently.

Under Section 29 all tax on share-based payment transactions is accounted for in profit or loss (in contrast to the allocation between profit or loss and equity required under IFRS).

Chapter 24

8   ALLOCATION OF TAX CHARGE OR CREDIT

Section 29 requires an entity to present changes in current tax and deferred tax as tax income or tax expense, except for those changes that arise on a business combination which enter into the determination of goodwill or negative goodwill (see 6.6 above). *[FRS 102.29.21].*

Section 29 also requires an entity to present tax expense (or tax income) in the same component of comprehensive income (i.e. continuing or discontinued operations, and in profit or loss or in other comprehensive income) or equity as the transaction or other event that resulted in the transaction or other event that resulted in the tax expense (or tax income). *[FRS 102.29.22].*

This requirement to have regard to the previous history of a transaction in accounting for its tax effects is commonly referred to as 'backward tracing'.

Unlike previous UK GAAP or IFRS, Section 29 does not explicitly require tax that does not directly relate to any particular component of total comprehensive income or equity to be accounted for in profit or loss. In our view, where – under Section 5 – total comprehensive income is reported in two statements (an income statement and a statement of comprehensive income), any tax expense or tax income that cannot be directly allocated to a particular component of total comprehensive income or equity should be accounted for in the income statement. This approach is consistent with the requirement of Section 5 that all items are presented in the income statement except those that are permitted or required by FRS 102 to be recognised outside profit or loss *[FRS 102.5.2(b)]* – see Chapter 4.

Section 29 does not address the question of the allocation of income tax expense or income arising from the remeasurement of deferred tax asset or liability subsequent to its initial recognition. In our view such remeasurements should be allocated to the same component of total comprehensive income or equity to which the remeasured item was originally allocated. This approach is consistent with IAS 12.

8.1   Dividends and transaction costs of equity instruments

8.1.1   *Dividend subject to differential tax rate*

In some jurisdictions, the rate at which tax is paid depends on whether profits are distributed or retained. In other jurisdictions, distribution may lead to an additional liability to tax, or a refund of tax already paid. Section 29 requires current and deferred taxes to be measured using the rate applicable to undistributed profits until a liability to pay a dividend is recognised, at which point the tax consequences of that dividend should also be recognised. *[FRS 102.29.14].* This is discussed further at 7 above.

Where taxes are remeasured on recognition of a liability to pay a dividend, the difference should normally be recognised in profit or loss rather than directly in equity, even though the dividend itself is recognised directly in equity under FRS 102. Section 29 implicitly takes the view that any additional (or lower) tax liability relates to the original profit now being distributed rather than to the distribution itself. Where, however, the dividend is paid out of profit arising from a transaction that was originally recognised in other comprehensive income or equity, the adjustment to the tax liability should also be recognised in other comprehensive income or equity.

8.1.2 Dividend subject to withholding tax

Where dividends are paid by the reporting entity subject to withholding tax that is required to be paid to the tax authorities on behalf of shareholders, the withholding tax should be included as part of the dividend deducted from equity. Other taxes, such as attributable tax credits, should be excluded from the amount recorded as a dividend. *[FRS 102.29.18]*.

Section 29 requires incoming dividends and similar income to be recognised at an amount that includes any withholding taxes, but excludes other taxes, such as attributable tax credits. Any withholding tax suffered is shown as part of the tax charge. *[FRS 102.29.19]*.

'Attributable tax credits' in this context would include any double tax relief for underlying tax on dividends received by a UK entity.

8.1.2.A Distinction between a withholding tax and a differential rate for distributed profits

These provisions of Section 29 may prove somewhat problematic in practice. There may be little economic difference, from the paying entity's perspective, between a requirement to pay a 5% 'withholding tax' on all dividends and a requirement to pay an additional 5% 'income tax' on distributed profit. Yet, the accounting treatment varies significantly depending on the analysis. If the tax is considered a withholding tax, it is treated as a deduction from equity in all circumstances. If, however, it is considered as an additional income tax, it will generally be treated as a charge to profit or loss (see 8.1.1 above).

8.1.2.B Intragroup dividend subject to withholding tax

Where irrecoverable withholding tax is suffered on intragroup dividends, the withholding tax does not relate to an item recognised in equity in the consolidated financial statements (since the intragroup dividend to which it relates has been eliminated in those financial statements). The tax should therefore be accounted for in profit or loss for the period.

8.1.3 Tax benefits of distributions and transaction costs of equity instruments

It is not entirely clear how FRS 102 requires the tax effects of certain equity transactions to be dealt with, as illustrated by Example 24.10 below.

Example 24.10: Tax deductible distribution on equity instrument

An entity paying tax at 25% has issued a capital instrument that is treated as equity for accounting purposes (because distributions are discretionary), but as debt for tax purposes (i.e. all distributions are tax deductible). The entity makes a distribution of £1 million and is able to claim a tax deduction of £250,000. There are no restrictions on the recoverability of that deduction for tax purposes.

Some could take the view that the tax deduction clearly relates to the distribution, which was accounted for in equity, and that the deduction should therefore be credited to equity. Others could take the view that the provisions of Section 29 regarding differential tax rates for retained and distributed profits (see 7 above) apply. We believe that either view is acceptable, provided that it is applied consistently.

Chapter 24

8.2   Gain/loss in profit or loss and loss/gain outside profit or loss offset for tax purposes

It often happens that a gain or loss accounted for in profit or loss can be offset for tax purposes against a gain or loss accounted for in other comprehensive income (or an increase or decrease in equity). This raises the question of how the tax effects of such transactions should be accounted for, as illustrated by Example 24.11 below.

Example 24.11: Loss in other comprehensive income and gain in profit or loss offset for tax purposes

During the year ended 31 December 2015, an entity that pays tax at 20% makes a taxable profit of £50,000 comprising:

- £80,000 trading profit less finance costs accounted for in profit or loss; and
- £30,000 foreign exchange losses accounted for in other comprehensive income ('OCI').

Should the total tax liability of £10,000 (20% of £50,000) be presented as either:

(a)   a charge of £10,000 in profit or loss; or

(b)   a charge of £16,000 (20% of £80,000) in profit or loss and a credit of £6,000 (20% of £30,000) in other comprehensive income?

In our view, (b) is the appropriate treatment, since the amount accounted for in other comprehensive income represents the difference between the tax that would have been paid absent the exchange loss accounted for in other comprehensive income and the amount actually payable. This indicates that this is the amount of tax that, in the words of paragraph 22 of Section 29, 'resulted' from items that are recognised in equity.

Similar issues may arise where a transaction accounted for outside profit or loss generates a suitable taxable profit that allows recognition of a previously unrecognised tax asset relating to a transaction previously accounted for in profit or loss, as illustrated by Example 24.12 below.

Example 24.12: Recognition of deferred tax asset in profit or loss on the basis of tax liability accounted for outside profit or loss

An entity that pays tax at 20% has brought forward unrecognised deferred tax assets (with an indefinite life) totalling £1 million, relating to trading losses accounted for in profit or loss in prior periods. On 1 January 2015 it invests £100,000 in government bonds, which it holds until they are redeemed for the same amount on maturity on 31 December 2018. For tax purposes, any taxable income arising from revaluation of the bonds can be offset against the brought forward tax losses.

The entity elects to account for the bonds as available-for-sale and therefore carries them at fair value (see Chapter 8). Over the period to maturity the fair value of the bonds at the end of each reporting period (31 December) is as follows:

	£000
2015	110
2016	115
2017	120
2018	100

Movements in value would be accounted for in other comprehensive income ('OCI'). Taken in isolation, the valuation gains in 2015 to 2018 would give rise to current tax liabilities (at 20%) of £2,000 (2015), £1,000 (2016) and £1,000 (2017). However, these liabilities can be offset against the losses brought forward. This raises the question as to whether there should be either:

(a) no tax charge or credit in either profit or loss or other comprehensive income in any of the periods affected; or

(b) in each period, a current tax charge in other comprehensive income (in respect of the taxable income arising from valuation gains on the bonds) and current tax income in profit or loss (representing the recognition of the previously unrecognised deferred tax asset).

In our view, the treatment in (b) should be followed. Although the previously unrecognised deferred tax asset can only be recovered as the result of the recognition of a current tax liability arising from a transaction accounted for in other comprehensive income, the previously unrecognised asset relates to a trading loss previously recorded in profit or loss. Accordingly, the current tax credit arising from the recognition of the asset is properly accounted for in profit or loss.

8.3 Discontinued operations

As noted above, Section 29 requires tax income and tax expense to be allocated between continuing and discontinued operations. Some of the practical issues raised by this requirement are illustrated by Examples 24.13 to 24.15 below.

Example 24.13: Profit in continuing operations and loss in discontinued operations offset for tax purposes

Entity A, which pays tax at 25%, has identified an operation as discontinued for the purposes of Section 5. During the period the discontinued operation incurred a loss of £2 million and the continuing operations made a profit of £10 million. The net £8 million profit is fully taxable in the period, and there is no deferred tax income or expense. In our view, the tax expense should be allocated as follows:

	£m	£m
Current tax expense (continuing operations)[1]	2.5	
Current tax income (discontinued operation)[2]		0.5
Current tax liability[3]		2.0

1   Continuing operations profit £10m @ 25% = £2.5m
2   Discontinued operations loss £2m @ 25% = £0.5m.
3   Net taxable profit £8m @ 25% = £2.0m

The tax allocated to the discontinued operation represents the difference between the tax that would have been paid absent the loss accounted for in discontinued operations and the amount actually payable.

Example 24.14: Taxable profit on disposal of discontinued operation reduced by previously unrecognised tax losses

Entity B disposes of a discontinued operation during the current accounting period. The disposal gives rise to a charge to tax of £4 million. However, this is reduced to zero by offset against brought forward tax losses, which relate to the continuing operations of the entity, and for which no deferred tax asset has previously been recognised.

In our view, even though there is no overall tax expense, this should be reflected for financial reporting purposes as follows:

	£m	£m
Current tax expense (discontinued operation)	4.0	
Current tax income (continuing operations)		4.0

Chapter 24

This allocation reflects that fact that, although the transaction that allows recognition of the brought forward tax losses is accounted for as a discontinued operation, the losses themselves arose from continuing operations. This is essentially the same analysis as is used in Example 24.12 above (where a deferred tax liability recognised in other comprehensive income gives rise to an equal deferred tax asset recognised in profit or loss).

Example 24.15:   Taxable profit on disposal of discontinued operation reduced by previously recognised tax losses

Entity B disposes of a discontinued operation during the current accounting period. The disposal gives rise to a charge to tax of £4 million. However, this is reduced to zero by offset against brought forward tax losses, which relate to the entities continuing operations, and for which a deferred tax asset has previously been recognised.

In our view, even though there is no overall tax expense, this should be reflected for financial reporting purposes as follows:

	£m	£m
Current tax expense (discontinued operation)	4.0	
Deferred tax expense (continuing operations)	4.0	
Current tax income (continuing operations)		4.0
Deferred tax asset (statement of financial position)		4.0

This allocation reflects that fact that, although the transaction that allows recognition of the brought forward tax losses is accounted for as a discontinued operation, the losses themselves arose from continuing operations. This is essentially the same analysis as is used in Example 24.13 above.

8.4   Defined benefit pension plans

Section 28 requires an entity, in accounting for a defined benefit post-employment benefit plan, to recognise actuarial gains and losses relating to the plan in full in other comprehensive income ('OCI'). At the same time, a calculated current (and, where applicable, past) service cost and finance income and expense relating to the plan assets and liabilities are recognised in profit or loss – see Chapter 23.

In the UK, and many other jurisdictions, tax deductions for post-employment benefits are given on the basis of cash contributions paid to the plan fund (or benefits paid when a plan is unfunded).

This significant difference between the way in which defined plans are treated for tax and financial reporting purposes can make the allocation of tax deductions for them between profit or loss and OCI somewhat arbitrary, as illustrated by Example 24.16 below.

Example 24.16:   Tax deductions for defined benefit pension plans

At 1 January 2015 an entity that pays tax at 20% has a fully-funded defined benefit pension scheme. During the year ended 31 December 2015 it records a total cost of £1 million, of which £800,000 is allocated to profit or loss and £200,000 to other comprehensive income ('OCI'). In January 2016 it makes a funding payment of £400,000, a tax deduction for which is received through the current tax charge for the year ended 31 December 2015.

Assuming that the entity is able to recognise a deferred tax asset for the entire £1 million charged in 2014, it will record the following entry for income taxes in 2014.

	£	£
Deferred tax asset [£1,000,000 @ 20%]	200,000	
Deferred tax income (profit or loss) [£800,000 @ 20%]		160,000
Deferred tax income (OCI) [£200,000 @ 20%]		40,000

When the funding payment is made in January 2016, the accounting deficit on the fund is reduced by £400,000. This gives rise to a current tax deduction of £80,000 (£400,000 @ 20%), in relation to the contribution paid to the pension scheme, and a deferred tax expense of £80,000 in respect of the reversal of the temporary difference arising as some of the deferred tax asset as at 31 December 2014 is released. The difficulty is how to allocate this movement in the deferred tax asset between profit or loss and OCI, as it is ultimately a matter of arbitrary allocation as to whether the funding payment is regarded as making good (for example):

- £400,000 of the £800,000 deficit previously accounted for in profit or loss;

- the whole of the £200,000 of the deficit previously accounted for in OCI and £200,000 of the £800,000 deficit previously accounted for in profit or loss; or

- a pro-rata share of those parts of the total deficit accounted for in profit or loss and OCI.

In the example above, the split is of relatively minor significance, since the entity was able to recognise 100% of the potential deferred tax asset associated with the pension liability. This means that, as the scheme is funded, there will be an equal and opposite amount of current tax income and deferred tax expense. The only real issue is therefore one of presentation, namely whether the gross items comprising this net nil charge are disclosed within the tax charge in profit or loss or in OCI.

In other cases, however, there might be an amount of net tax income or expense that needs to be allocated. Suppose that, as above, the entity recorded a pension cost of £1 million in 2015 but determined that the related deferred tax asset did not meet the criteria for recognition under Section 29. In 2016, the entity determines that an asset of £50,000 can be recognised in view of the funding payments and taxable profits anticipated in 2016 and later years. This results in a total tax credit of £130,000 (£80,000 current tax, £50,000 deferred tax) in 2016, raising the question of whether it should be allocated to profit or loss, to OCI, or allocated on a pro-rata basis. This question might also arise if, as the result of newly enacted tax rates, the existing deferred tax balance were required to be remeasured. In our view, any reasonable method of allocation may be used, provided that it is applied on a consistent basis.

One approach might be to compare the funding payments made to the scheme in the previous few years with the charges made to profit or loss under Section 28 in those periods. If, for example, it is found that the payments were equal to or greater than the charges to profit or loss, it might reasonably be concluded that the funding payments have 'covered' the charge recognised in profit or loss, so that any surplus or deficit on the statement of financial position is broadly represented by items that have been accounted for in OCI.

However, a surplus may also arise from funding the scheme to an amount greater than the liability recognised under Section 28 (for example under a minimum

Chapter 24

funding requirement imposed by local legislation or agreed with the pension fund trustees). In this case, the asset does not result from previously recognised income but from a reduction in another asset (i.e. cash). The entity should assess the expected manner of recovery of any asset implied by the accounting treatment of the surplus – i.e. whether it has been recognised on the basis that it will be 'consumed' (resulting in an accounting expense) or refunded to the entity in due course.

Where it is concluded that the asset will be 'consumed' (resulting in accounting expense), the entity will need to determine whether such an expense is likely to be recognised in profit or loss or in OCI in a future period.

The previous UK standard FRS 17 – *Retirement benefits* – prescribed a methodology for allocating the tax effects of pension transactions between profit or loss and OCI. This methodology may provide useful guidance in applying Section 29 to defined benefit pension costs, but should be used with caution as its somewhat mechanistic allocation of tax income or expense may not always be the most appropriate reflection of the underlying economic reality, particularly where there is a significant funding programme.

9   CONSOLIDATED TAX RETURNS AND OFFSET OF TAXABLE PROFITS AND LOSSES WITHIN GROUPS

In some jurisdictions one member of a group of companies may file a single tax return on behalf of all, or some, members of the group. In other jurisdictions, such as the UK, it is possible for one member of a group to transfer tax losses to one or more other members of the group in order to reduce their tax liabilities. In some groups a company whose tax liability is reduced by such an arrangement may be required, as a matter of group policy, to make a payment to the member of the group that pays tax on its behalf, or transfers losses to it, as the case may be. In other groups no such charge is made.

Such transactions raise the question of the appropriate accounting treatment in the separate financial statements of the group entities involved – in particular, whether the company benefiting from such an arrangement should reflect income (or, more likely, a capital contribution) from another member of the group equal to the tax expense mitigated as a result of the arrangement.

Some argue that the effects of such transactions should be reflected in the separate financial statements of the entities involved. Others argue that, except to the extent that a management charge is actually made (see 9.1 below), there is no need to reflect such transactions in the separate financial statements of the entities involved. This has historically been the normal approach adopted in the UK. In our view, either approach may be adopted on a consistent basis.

9.1   Payments for intragroup transfer of tax losses

Where one member of a group transfers tax losses to another member of the group, the entity whose tax liability is reduced may be required, as matter of group policy, to pay an amount of compensation to the member of the group that transfers the losses to it. Such payments are known by different terms in different jurisdictions, but are referred to in the discussion below as 'group relief payments'.

Group relief payments are generally made in an amount equal to the tax saved by the paying company. In some cases, however, payment may be made in an amount equal to the nominal amount of the tax loss, which will be greater than the amount of tax saved. This raises the question of how such payments should be accounted for.

The first issue is whether such payments should be recognised:

- in total comprehensive income, or
- as a distribution (in the case of a payment from a subsidiary to a parent) or a capital contribution (in the case of a payment from a parent to a subsidiary).

The second issue is, to the extent that the payments are accounted for in total comprehensive income, whether they should be classified as:

- income tax, allocated between profit or loss, other comprehensive income or equity (see 9 above). The argument for this treatment is that the payments made or received are amounts that would otherwise be paid to or received from (or offset against an amount paid to) a tax authority, or
- operating income or expense in profit or loss (on the grounds that, as a matter of fact, the payments are not made to or received from any tax authority).

There is a long-standing practice in the UK that such payments are treated as if they were income taxes. We believe that this practice is appropriate to the extent that the intragroup payment is for an amount up to the amount of tax that would otherwise have been paid by the paying company. Where a tax loss payment is made in excess of this amount, we consider that it is more appropriate to account for the excess not as an income tax but as either:

- a distribution or capital contribution (as applicable), or
- operating income or expense (as applicable).

The chosen treatment should be applied consistently.

10 PRESENTATION

10.1 Statement of financial position

The statutory balance sheet formats require the liability for current taxation and social creditor to be included within the balance sheet caption 'Other creditors including tax and social security' and be separately disclosed. Section 29 requires deferred tax liabilities to be included within provisions for liabilities and deferred tax assets to be included within debtors. *[FRS 102.29.23].*

10.1.1 *Offset*

10.1.1.A *Current tax*

Current tax assets and liabilities should be offset if, and only if, the entity:

- has a legally enforceable right to set off the amounts; and
- intends either to settle them net or simultaneously. *[FRS 102.29.24].*

10.1.1.B   Deferred tax

Deferred tax assets and liabilities should be offset if, and only if:

- the entity has a legally enforceable right to set off current tax assets and liabilities; and

- the deferred tax assets and liabilities concerned relate to income taxes raised by the same taxation authority on either:

    - the same taxable entity; or

    - different taxable entities which intend to settle their current tax assets and liabilities either on a net basis or simultaneously, in each future period in which significant amounts of deferred tax are expected to be settled or recovered. *[FRS 102.24A]*.

The offset criteria for deferred tax are less clear than those for current tax. The position is broadly that, where in a particular jurisdiction current tax assets and liabilities relating to future periods will be offset, deferred tax assets and liabilities relating to that jurisdiction and those periods must be offset (even if the deferred tax balances actually recognised in the statement of financial position would not satisfy the criteria for the offset of current tax).

IAS 12 (from which these requirements are derived) suggests that this slightly more pragmatic approach was adopted in order to avoid the detailed scheduling of the reversal of temporary differences that would be necessary to apply the same criteria as for current tax. However, IAS 12 notes that, in rare circumstances, an entity may have a legally enforceable right of set-off, and an intention to settle net, for some periods but not for others. In such circumstances, detailed scheduling may be required to determine the extent of permitted offset.

10.1.1.C   Offset of current and deferred tax

Section 29 contains no provisions allowing or requiring the offset of current tax and deferred tax. Accordingly, in our view, given the general restrictions on offset in Section 2 – *Concepts and Pervasive Principles* (see Chapter 3) current and deferred tax may not be offset against each other and should always be presented gross.

10.2   Statement of comprehensive income

As discussed at 8 above, the tax expense (or income) should be accounted in the same component of comprehensive income to which it relates.

The results of discontinued operations should be presented on a post-tax basis. *[FRS 102.5.7D]*.

The results of equity-accounted entities should be presented on a post-tax basis. *[FRS 102.14.8]*.

10.3   Statement of cash flows

Cash flows arising from taxes on income are separately disclosed and classified as cash flows from operating activities, unless they can be specifically identified with financing and investing activities. Where tax cash flows are allocated over more than one class of equity, the total amount of taxes paid should be disclosed. *[FRS 102.7.17].*

11 DISCLOSURE

Section 29 imposes extensive disclosure requirements as summarised below.

11.1 Components of tax expense

The major components of tax expense (or income) should be disclosed separately. These may include: *[FRS 102.29.26]*

(a) current tax expense (or income);

(b) any adjustments recognised in the period for current tax of prior periods;

(c) the amount of deferred tax expense (or income) relating to the origination and reversal of timing differences;

(d) the amount of deferred tax expense (or income) relating to changes in tax rates or the imposition of new taxes;

(e) adjustments to deferred tax expense (or income) arising from a change in the tax status of the entity or its shareholders; and

(f) the amount of tax expense (or income) relating to changes in accounting policies and errors (see the discussion of Section 10 in Chapter 7).

11.2 Other disclosures required by FRS 102

The following should also be disclosed separately: *[FRS 102.29.27]*

(a) the aggregate current and deferred tax relating to items that are recognised as items of other comprehensive income or equity; and

(b) a reconciliation between the tax expense (income) included in profit or loss and the profit or loss on ordinary activities multiplied by the applicable tax rate;

(c) the amount of the net reversal of deferred tax assets and deferred tax liabilities expected to occur during the year beginning after the reporting period together with a brief explanation for the expected reversal;

(d) an explanation of changes in the applicable tax rate(s) compared with the previous reporting period;

(e) the amount of deferred tax liabilities and deferred tax assets at the end of the reporting period for each type of timing difference;

(f) the amount of unused tax losses and tax credits;

(g) the expiry date, if any, of timing differences, unused tax losses and unused tax credits; and

(h) where different tax rates apply to retained and distributed profits (see 7 above), an explanation of the nature of the potential income tax consequences that would result from the payment of dividends to shareholders.

Chapter 24

The requirement at (c) above is noteworthy in that it was previously required neither by FRS 19 nor IAS 12, nor even in the IFRS for SMEs. It is not clear what benefit is intended to be derived from this disclosure.

In addition, Section 32 requires entities to provide information about the nature of any changes in tax rates or tax laws enacted or announced after the reporting period that have a significant effect on current and deferred tax assets and liabilities. *[FRS 102.32.11(h)]*. An estimate of the financial effect of these changes should also be disclosed, or a statement given that such an estimate cannot be made. *[FRS 102.32.10]*. The requirements of Section 32 are discussed in Chapter 27.

11.3   Disclosures required by entities subject to UK and Irish legislation

Under previous UK and Irish GAAP, accounting standards in many cases included the disclosure requirements for entities established under UK and Irish legislation. This is not the case in FRS 102. Entities should therefore consider any additional requirements arising from legal and regulatory requirements. For example, UK incorporated entities must also comply with the requirements of the Large and Medium-sized Companies and Groups (Accounts and Reports) Regulations 2008, which are discussed further in Chapter 4.

12   SUMMARY OF SIGNIFICANT GAAP DIFFERENCES

	FRS 102	*Previous UK GAAP*	*IFRS*
Deferred tax on revaluations of PP&E	Recognise.	Only if there is a binding agreement at the reporting date that will give rise to tax.	Recognise.
Deferred tax on rolled over gains	Recognise.	Not until the assets are sold.	Recognise.
Deferred tax on acquisition fair value adjustments	Recognise.	Only if they would be recognised in the accounts of the acquire (e.g. asset write downs).	Recognise.
Deferred tax on unremitted earnings of subsidiaries etc.	Recognise in relation to timing differences only, and subject to a control test.	Only if accrued or binding agreement to distribute.	Control test.
Deferred tax on ACAs where conditions for retaining allowances are met.	Derecognise.	Derecognise.	Continue to recognise.
Deferred tax relating to effect of changes in tax base (e.g. grant of North Sea Field Allowance)	Not recognised (only changes measurement of previously recognised deferred tax).	Not recognised (only changes measurement of previously recognised deferred tax).	Recognised.

Deferred tax on excess tax relief on share-based payments.	Permanent difference, no deferred tax.	Permanent difference, no deferred tax	Recognise deferred tax in equity
Allocation of tax related to items recognised in equity (e.g. tax on share issue costs)	Equity.	P+L.	Equity.
Balance sheet classification of current tax	Not prescribed.	Not prescribed.	Separate line items on face of balance sheet.
Disclose split of current tax charge between domestic and foreign tax	Not specified in Section 29. Only disclose if UK or Irish law requires it.	Required.	Not required.
Disclose effect of double tax relief	Not specified in Section 29. Only disclose if UK or Irish law requires it.	Required.	Not required.
Tax reconciliation – profit at a standard rate to tax charge	Total tax in profit or loss.	Current tax in profit or loss.	Total tax in profit or loss..
Disclose effect of previously unrealised losses being utilised	Not specified in Section 29. Only disclose if UK or Irish law requires it.	Required.	Not required.
Disclose nature of evidence to support recognition of deferred tax assets	Not required.	Required.	Required.
Disclose expected net reversal of timing differences in the following reporting period	Required.	Not required.	Not required.
Disclosure of total tax expense relating to discontinued operations	Required.	Not required.	Required.

Chapter 24

References

1 The tax treatment in this example is purely illustrative, and does not reflect current UK tax law on capital allowances.

2 Practice in this area is diverse under IFRS. In some cases such income is measured gross and in other cases net of withholding taxes. See International GAAP 2015, Chapter 30 at 4.2.

3 *IAS 18 – Revenue,* para. 8, *IAS 2 – Inventories,* para. 11, *and IAS 16 – Property, Plant and Equipment,* para. 16.

4 The flat rate scheme provides for a simplified calculation of VAT for entities with turnover less than £150,000. Input VAT is not reclaimed and output VAT is levied at a fixed percentage according to category of business. For example eligible lawyers charge 14.5%; post offices 5%; and Agriculture 6.5%.

Chapter 25   Foreign currency translation

List of examples

Chapter 25

Chapter 25   Foreign currency translation

1   INTRODUCTION

1.1   Background

An entity can conduct foreign activities in two ways. It may enter directly into transactions which are denominated in foreign currencies, the results of which need to be translated into the currency in which the company measures its results and financial position. Alternatively, it may conduct foreign operations through a foreign entity, such as a subsidiary, associate, joint venture or branch which keeps its accounting records in terms of its own currency. In this case it will need to translate the financial statements of the foreign entity for the purposes of inclusion in the consolidated financial statements.

This chapter discusses the requirements of Section 30 – *Foreign Currency Translation* – for including foreign currency transactions and foreign operations in the financial statements of an entity and how to translate financial statements into a presentation currency.

Section 30 of FRS 102 is similar to IAS 21 – *The Effects of Changes in Foreign Exchange Rates* (and FRS 23 – *The effects of changes in foreign exchange rates*), with the key differences discussed below. These differences mainly relate to issues addressed by IAS 21 and FRS 23 that are not discussed in FRS 102.

We expect most adopters of FRS 102 will currently be applying SSAP 20 – *Foreign currency translation* – rather than FRS 23 or IAS 21, and whilst the basic principles of FRS 102 are similar to those in SSAP 20, there are several significant differences.

2   COMPARISON BETWEEN SECTION 30, PREVIOUS UK GAAP AND IFRS

2.1   Key differences between Section 30 and previous UK GAAP

As we expect most adopters of FRS 102 will currently be applying SSAP 20 rather than FRS 23 or IAS 21, this section compares Section 30 of FRS 102 with SSAP 20. Differences between FRS 23 (which is virtually identical to IAS 21) and FRS 102 are discussed in 2.2 below.

The key differences between section 30 and SSAP 20 are as follows:

(i)   The term 'functional currency' is used in FRS 102, whereas SSAP 20 uses the term 'local currency'. *[SSAP 20.39]*. Although the definitions of each are identical, the guidance for determining an entity's functional or local currency is much more prescriptive in FRS 102 than in SSAP 20. In some situations this may result in an entity having a different functional currency under FRS 102 than the entity's local currency under SSAP 20.

(ii)   There is no concept of presentation currency under SSAP 20, with a presumption that financial statements are prepared in the entity's local currency. FRS 102 allows an entity to select its presentation currency, which may be different from its functional currency.

(iii)   FRS 102 does not allow the use of a contracted or forward rate instead of the closing rate to retranslate foreign currency balances, whereas SSAP 20 does in certain situations. *[SSAP 20.48]*.

(iv)   FRS 102 requires that exchange differences arising on monetary items that form part of an entity's net investment in a foreign operation should be recognised in profit or loss in the separate financial statements of the reporting entity (see 3.7.6 below). SSAP 20 does not explicitly address the treatment of such exchange differences in the individual financial statements of an entity and therefore some entities may have recognised the difference in equity rather than in profit or loss as required by Section 30, or not at all, e.g. on the grounds that in substance such a receivable was a non-monetary item.

(v)   SSAP 20 allows the closing or average rate to be used when translating the profit and loss account of a foreign operation. *[SSAP 20.17]*. Section 30 requires that an average rate is used. *[FRS 102.30.18-19]*.

(vi)   SSAP 20 includes special provisions relating to foreign equity investments that are financed by foreign currency borrowings. Where certain conditions apply, an entity may denominate its foreign equity investments in the appropriate foreign currencies and translate the carrying amounts at the end of each accounting period at the closing rates of exchange. Where investments are treated in this way, any resulting exchange differences should be taken directly to reserves, against which the exchange rate gains or losses on the associated borrowings would be offset, as a reserve movement. *[SSAP 20.51]*. There are no equivalent provisions in Section 30, which would indicate that (unless the entity was treating the associated borrowings as a fair value hedge of the investment) as a non-monetary asset the foreign investment would be translated at the exchange rate at the date of the transaction (or the exchange rate at the date the fair value of the investment was determined if the investment is carried at fair value), and the exchange gains or losses on the retranslation of the associated foreign currency borrowings at each period end would be recorded in profit or loss.

2.2   Key difference between Section 30 and IFRS

There is only one significant difference between IAS 21 (FRS 23) and Section 30. Under IAS 21 all exchange differences arising on translation of a foreign operation that have been accumulated in equity are reclassified to profit and loss on disposal of the net investment. *[IAS 21.48]*. Section 30 of FRS 102 prohibits such reclassifications on disposal. *[FRS 102.30.13]*.

3   REQUIREMENTS OF SECTION 30 FOR FOREIGN CURRENCY TRANSLATION

3.1   Definitions

The definitions of terms used in Section 30 are as follows: *[FRS 102 Appendix I]*

Term	Definition
Closing rate	The spot exchange rate at the end of the reporting period.
Fair Value	The amount for which an asset could be exchanged, a liability settled, or an equity instrument granted could be exchanged, between knowledgeable, willing parties in an arm's length transaction. In the absence of any specific guidance provided in the relevant section of FRS 102, the guidance in paragraphs 11.27 to 11.32 shall be used in determining fair value.
Financing activities	Activities that result in changes in the size and composition of the contributed equity and borrowings of the entity.
Foreign operation	An entity that is a subsidiary, associate, joint venture or branch of a reporting entity, the activities of which are based or conducted in a country or currency other than those of the reporting entity.
Functional currency	The currency of the primary economic environment in which the entity operates.
Group	A parent and all its subsidiaries.
Monetary items	Units of currency held and assets and liabilities to be received or paid in a fixed or determinable number of units of currency.
Net investment in a foreign operation	The amount of the reporting entity's interest in the net assets of that operation.
Operating activities	The principal revenue-producing activities of the entity and other activities that are not investing or financing activities.
Presentation currency	The currency in which the financial statements are presented.

Chapter 25

3.2   Scope

An entity can conduct foreign activities in two ways. It may have transactions in foreign currencies or it may have foreign operations. In addition, an entity may present its financial statements in a foreign currency. Section 30 prescribes how to include foreign currency transactions and foreign operations in the financial statements of an entity and how to translate financial statements into a presentation currency. *[FRS 102.30.1].*

Section 30 does not apply to hedge accounting of foreign currency items. This is dealt with in Section 12 – *Other Financial Instruments Issues* (see Chapter 8). *[FRS 102.30.1].*

3.3   Summary of the approach required by Section 30

In preparing financial statements, the following approach should be followed:

- Each entity – whether a stand-alone entity, an entity with foreign operations (such as a parent) or a foreign operation (such as a subsidiary or branch) – determines its functional currency. *[FRS 102.30.2].* This is discussed at 3.4 below.

  In the case of group financial statements, there is not a 'group' functional currency; each entity included within the group financial statements, be it the parent, a subsidiary, associate, joint venture or branch, has its own functional currency.

- Where an entity enters into a transaction denominated in a currency other than its functional currency, it translates those foreign currency items into its functional currency and reports the effects of such translation in accordance with those provisions of Section 30 discussed at 3.5 below.

- The results and financial position of any individual entity within the reporting entity whose functional currency differs from the presentation currency are translated in accordance with the provisions of Section 30 discussed at 3.7 below.

Many reporting entities comprise a number of individual entities (e.g. a group is made up of a parent and one or more subsidiaries). Entities may also have investments in associates or joint ventures or have branches (see 3.4.2 below). It is necessary for the results and financial position of each individual entity included in the reporting entity to be translated into the currency in which the reporting entity presents its financial statements (if this presentation currency is different from the individual entity's functional currency). *[FRS 102.30.17].*

3.4   Determination of an entity's functional currency

Functional currency is defined as the currency of 'the primary economic environment in which the entity operates'. This will normally be the one in which it primarily generates and expends cash. *[FRS 102.30.3].*

Section 30 sets out a number of factors or indicators that an entity should or may need to consider in determining its functional currency. When the factors or indicators are mixed and the functional currency is not obvious, management should use its judgement to determine the functional currency that most faithfully represents the economic effects of the underlying transactions, events and conditions. We believe that as part of this approach, management should give priority to the most important indicators before considering the other indicators, which are designed to provide additional supporting evidence to determine an entity's functional currency.

The following are the most important factors an entity considers in determining its functional currency: *[FRS 102.30.3]*

(a)   the currency:

  (i)   that mainly influences sales prices for goods and services. This will often be the currency in which sales prices for its goods and services are denominated and settled; and

  (ii)   of the country whose competitive forces and regulations mainly determine the sales prices of its goods and services; and

(b)   the currency that mainly influences labour, material and other costs of providing goods or services. This will often be the currency in which such costs are denominated and settled.

Where the functional currency of the entity is not obvious from the above, the following factors may also provide evidence of an entity's functional currency: *[FRS 102.30.4]*

(a)   the currency in which funds from financing activities (issuing debt and equity instruments) are generated; and

(b)   the currency in which receipts from operating activities are usually retained.

An operation that carries on business as if it were an extension of the parent's operations, will have the same functional currency as the parent. In this context, the term parent is drawn broadly and is the entity that has the foreign operation as its subsidiary, branch, associate or joint venture. Therefore the following additional factors are also considered in determining the functional currency of a foreign operation, particularly whether its functional currency is the same as that of the reporting entity: *[FRS 102.30.5]*

(a)   Whether the activities of the foreign operation are carried out as an extension of the reporting entity, rather than being carried out with a significant degree of autonomy. An example of the former is when the foreign operation only sells goods imported from the reporting entity and remits the proceeds to it. An example of the latter is when the operation accumulates cash and other monetary items, incurs expenses, generates income and arranges borrowings, all substantially in its local currency.

(b)   Whether transactions with the reporting entity are a high or a low proportion of the foreign operation's activities.

(c)   Whether cash flows from the activities of the foreign operation directly affect the cash flows of the reporting entity and are readily available for remittance to it.

(d)   Whether cash flows from the activities of the foreign operation are sufficient to service existing and normally expected debt obligations without funds being made available by the reporting entity.

Since an entity's functional currency reflects the underlying transactions, events and conditions that are relevant to it, once it is determined, Section 30 requires that the

Chapter 25

functional currency is not changed unless there is a change in those underlying transactions, events and conditions. *[FRS 102.30.15]*. The implication of this is that management of an entity cannot decree what the functional currency is – it is a matter of fact, albeit subjectively determined fact based on management's judgement of all the circumstances.

3.4.1   Intermediate holding companies or finance subsidiaries

For many entities the determination of functional currency will be relatively straightforward. However, for some entities, particularly entities within a group, this may not be the case. One particular difficulty is the determination of the functional currency of an intermediate holding company or finance subsidiary within an international group.

Example 25.1:   Functional currency of intermediate holding companies or finance subsidiaries

An international group is headquartered in the UK. The UK parent entity has a functional currency of pound sterling, which is also the group's presentation currency. The group has three international sub-operations, structured as follows:

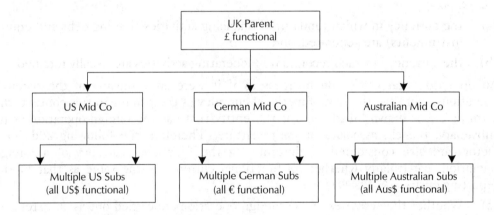

What is the functional currency of the three Mid Cos?

There are a variety of factors to be considered for intermediate holding companies or finance subsidiaries when deciding on the appropriate functional currency. Therefore, there will not be a single analysis applicable to all such entities.

FRS 102 defines a 'foreign operation' as 'an entity that is a subsidiary...the activities of which are based or conducted in a country or currency other than those of the reporting entity' (see 3.1 above). This definition would seem to suggest that a foreign operation must have its own 'activities'.

Also, paragraph 3 of the Section 30 states that the functional currency is 'the currency of the primary economic environment in which the entity operates'. However, under paragraph 3 this is determined by reference to the currency that mainly influences sales prices and the operation's costs (see 3.4 above), and is therefore not directly relevant to intermediate holding companies or finance subsidiaries. Paragraphs 4 and 5 set out a number of factors to consider in determining the functional currency of a foreign operation. The theme running through these factors is the extent to which the activities and cash flows of the foreign operation are independent of those of the reporting entity.

In the case of an intermediate holding company or finance subsidiary, the acid-test question to consider is whether it is an extension of the parent and performing the functions of the parent – i.e. whether its role is simply to hold the investment in, or provide finance to, the foreign operation on behalf of the parent company or whether its functions are essentially an extension of a local operation (e.g. performing selling, payroll or similar activities for that operation) or indeed it is undertaking activities on its own account.

This means that subsidiaries that do nothing but hold investments or borrow money on behalf of the parent will normally have the functional currency of the parent. The borrowings of such companies are frequently guaranteed by the parent, which is itself likely to be a relevant factor. In other words, on whose credit is the lender relying? If the lender is looking to the ultimate parent, then the functional currency is likely to be that of the ultimate parent. However, if the lender is looking to the sub-group, then the functional currency of the companies in the sub-group will be relevant. Accordingly, any analysis that such a company has a functional currency other than that of the parent will require careful consideration of the features of the entity which give rise to that conclusion. Complex situations are likely to require the application of careful management judgement.

As for other entities within a group, the circumstances of each entity should be reviewed against the indicators and factors set out in the standard. This review requires management to use its judgement in determining the functional currency that most faithfully represents the economic effects of the underlying transactions, events and conditions applicable to that entity.

3.4.2 Branches and divisions

Section 30 uses the term 'branch' to describe an operation within a legal entity that may have a different functional currency from the entity itself. However, it contains no definition of that term, nor any further guidance on what arrangements should be regarded as a branch.

Many countries' governments have established legal and regulatory regimes that apply when a foreign entity establishes a place of business (often called a branch) in that country. Where an entity has operations that are subject to such a regime, it will normally be appropriate to regard them as a branch and evaluate whether those operations have their own functional currency. In this context, the indicators in paragraph 5 used to assess whether an entity has a functional currency that is different from its parent (see 3.4 above) will be particularly relevant.

An entity may also have an operation, e.g. a division, that operates in a different currency environment to the rest of the entity but which is not subject to an overseas branch regime. If that operation represents a sufficiently autonomous business unit it may be appropriate to view it as a branch and evaluate whether it has a functional currency that is different to the rest of the legal entity. However, in our experience, this situation will not be a common occurrence.

3.5 Reporting foreign currency transactions in the functional currency of an entity

Where an entity enters into a transaction denominated in a currency other than its functional currency then it will have to translate those foreign currency items into its functional currency and report the effects of such translation. The general requirements of Section 30 are as follows.

3.5.1   *Initial recognition*

A foreign currency transaction is a transaction that is denominated or requires settlement in a foreign currency, including transactions arising when an entity: *[FRS 102.30.6]*

(a)   buys or sells goods or services whose price is denominated in a foreign currency;

(b)   borrows or lends funds when the amounts payable or receivable are denominated in a foreign currency; or

(c)   otherwise acquires or disposes of assets, or incurs or settles liabilities, denominated in a foreign currency.

On initial recognition, foreign currency transactions should be translated into the functional currency using the spot exchange rate between the foreign currency and the functional currency on the date of the transaction. *[FRS 102.30.7]*.

The date of a transaction is the date on which the transaction first qualifies for recognition in accordance with FRS 102. For practical reasons, a rate that approximates the actual rate at the date of the transaction is often used, for example, an average rate for a week or a month might be used for all transactions in each foreign currency occurring during that period. However, if exchange rates fluctuate significantly, the use of the average rate for a period is inappropriate. *[FRS 102.30.8]*.

3.5.2   *Identifying the date of transaction*

The date of a transaction is the date on which it first qualifies for recognition in accordance with FRS 102. Although this sounds relatively straightforward, the following example illustrates the difficulty that can sometimes arise in determining the transaction date:

Example 25.2:   Establishing the transaction date (1)

A UK entity buys an item of inventory from a Canadian supplier. The dates relating to the transaction, and the relevant exchange rates, are as follows:

Date	Event	£1=C$
14 April 2015	Goods are ordered	1.50
5 May 2015	Goods are shipped from Canada and invoice dated that day	1.53
7 May 2015	Invoice is received	1.51
10 May 2015	Goods are received	1.54
14 May 2015	Invoice is recorded	1.56
7 June 2015	Invoice is paid	1.60

Section 13 – *Inventories* – does not make any reference to the date of initial recognition of inventory and Section 11 – *Basic Financial Instruments* – deals with the initial recognition of financial liabilities only in general terms. Generally an entity does not recognise a liability at the time of the commitment but delays recognition until the ordered goods have been shipped or delivered, i.e. the date that the risks and rewards of ownership have passed. Accordingly, it is unlikely that the date the goods are ordered should be used as the date of the transaction.

If the goods are shipped free on board (f.o.b.) then as the risks and rewards of ownership pass on shipment (5 May) then this date should be used.

If, however, the goods are not shipped f.o.b. then the risks and rewards of ownership will often pass on delivery (10 May) and therefore the date the goods are received should be treated as the date of the transaction. In practice, the transaction date will depend on the precise terms of the agreement (which are often based on standardised agreements such as the Incoterms rules).

The dates on which the invoice is received and is recorded are irrelevant to when the risks and rewards of ownership pass and therefore should not in principle be considered to be the date of the transaction. In practice, it may be acceptable that as a matter of administrative convenience that the exchange rate at the date the invoice is recorded is used, particularly if there is no undue delay in processing the invoice. If this is done then care should be taken to ensure that the exchange rate used is not significantly different from that ruling on the 'true' date of the transaction.

It is clear from Section 30 that the date the invoice is paid is not the date of the transaction because if it were then no exchange differences would arise on unsettled transactions.

The above example illustrated that the date that a transaction is recorded in an entity's books and records is not necessarily the same as the date at which it qualifies for recognition under FRS 102. Other situations where this is likely to arise is where an entity is recording a transaction that relates to a period, rather than one being recognised at a single point in time, as illustrated below:

Example 25.3:   Establishing the transaction date (2)

On 30 September 2015 Company A, whose functional currency is the pound sterling, acquires a US dollar bond for US$8,000. The bond carries fixed interest of 5% per annum paid quarterly, i.e. US$100 per quarter. The exchange rate on acquisition is US$1 to £1.50.

On 31 December 2015, the US dollar has appreciated and the exchange rate is US$1 to £2.00. Interest received on the bond on 31 December 2015 is US$100 (= £200).

Although the interest might only be recorded on 31 December 2015, the rate on that date is not the spot rate ruling at the date of the transaction. Since the interest has accrued over the 3 month period, it should be translated at the spot rates applicable to the accrual of interest during the 3 month period. Accordingly, a weighted average rate for the 3 month period should be used. Assuming that the appropriate average rate is US$1 to £1.75 the interest income is £175 (= US$100 × 1.75).

Accordingly, there is also an exchange gain on the interest receivable of £25 (= US$100 × [2.00 − 1.75]) to be reflected in profit or loss. The journal entry for recording the receipt of the interest on 31 December 2015 is therefore as follows:

	£	£
Cash	200	
Interest income (profit or loss)		175
Exchange gain (profit or loss)		25

3.5.3   Using average rates

Rather than using the actual rate ruling at the date of the transaction 'an average rate for a week or month may be used for all foreign currency transactions occurring during that period', if the exchange rate does not fluctuate significantly (see 3.5.1 above). *[FRS 102.30.8].* For entities which engage in a large number of foreign currency transactions it will be more convenient for them to use an average rate rather than using the exact rate for each transaction.

3.5.4   Dual rates or suspension of rates

One practical difficulty in translating foreign currency amounts is where there is more than one exchange rate for that particular currency depending on the nature of the transaction. In some cases the difference between the exchange rates can be small and therefore it probably does not matter which rate is actually used. However, in other situations the difference can be quite significant. So what rate should be used?

Chapter 25

There is no specific guidance on this matter in FRS 102. So in accordance with the hierarchy set out in Section 10 – *Accounting Policies, Estimates and Errors*, an entity could look to the requirements in IFRS for guidance. IAS 21 states that 'when several exchange rates are available, the rate used is that at which the future cash flows represented by the transaction or balance could have been settled if those cash flows had occurred at the measurement date'. *[IAS 21.26]*. Companies would therefore normally look at the nature of the transaction and apply the appropriate exchange rate.

Another practical difficulty which could arise is where for some reason exchangeability between two currencies is temporarily lacking at the transaction date or subsequently at the end of the reporting period. Again FRS 102 provides no specific guidance but IAS 21 requires that the rate to be used is 'the first subsequent rate at which exchanges could be made'. *[IAS 21.26]*.

3.5.5   *Reporting at the ends of the subsequent reporting periods*

At the end of each reporting period, an entity shall: *[FRS 102.30.9]*

(a)   translate foreign currency monetary items using the closing rate;

(b)   translate non-monetary items that are measured in terms of historical cost in a foreign currency using the exchange rate at the date of the transaction; and

(c)   translate non-monetary items that are measured at fair value in a foreign currency using the exchange rates at the date when the fair value was determined.

The treatment of exchange differences arising from this is set out at 3.5.6 and 3.5.7 for monetary and non-monetary items respectively.

3.5.6   *Treatment of exchange differences – monetary items*

The general rule in Section 30 is that exchange differences on the settlement or retranslation of monetary items should be recognised in profit or loss in the period in which they arise. *[FRS 102.30.10]*.

These requirements can be illustrated in the following examples:

Example 25.4:   Reporting an unsettled foreign currency transaction in the functional currency

A UK entity purchases plant and equipment on credit from a Canadian supplier for C$328,000 in January 2015 when the exchange rate is £1=C$1.64. The entity records the asset at a cost of £200,000. At the UK entity's year end at 31 March 2015 the account has not yet been settled. The closing rate is £1=C$1.61. The amount payable would be retranslated at £203,727 in the balance sheet and an exchange loss of £3,727 would be reported as part of the profit or loss for the period. The cost of the asset would remain as £200,000.

Example 25.5:   Reporting a settled foreign currency transaction in the functional currency

A UK entity sells goods to a German entity for €87,000 on 28 February 2015 when the exchange rate is £1=€1.45. It receives payment on 31 March 2015 when the exchange rate is £1=€1.50. On 28 February the UK entity will record a sale and corresponding receivable of £60,000. When payment is received on 31 March the actual amount received is only £58,000. The loss on exchange of £2,000 would be reported as part of the profit or loss for the period.

There are situations where the general rule above will not be applied. The first exception relates to exchange differences arising on a monetary item that, in substance, forms part of an entity's net investment in a foreign operation (see 3.7.4 below). In this situation the exchange differences should be recognised in other comprehensive income and accumulated in equity. However, this treatment only applies in the financial statements that include the foreign operation and the reporting entity (e.g. consolidated financial statements when the foreign operation is a subsidiary). It does not apply to the reporting entity's separate financial statements or the financial statements of the foreign operation. Rather, the exchange differences will be recognised in profit or loss in the period in which they arise in the financial statements of the entity that has the foreign currency exposure. *[FRS 102.30.12-13].* This is discussed further at 3.7.6 below.

The next exception relates to hedge accounting for foreign currency items, to which Section 12 applies. The application of hedge accounting requires an entity to account for some exchange differences differently from the treatment required by Section 30. For example, Section 12 requires that exchange differences on monetary items that qualify as hedging instruments in a cash flow hedge are recognised initially in other comprehensive income to the extent the hedge is effective. Hedge accounting is discussed in more detail in Chapter 8.

Another situation where exchange differences on monetary items are not recognised in profit or loss in the period they arise would be where an entity capitalises borrowing costs under Section 25 – *Borrowing Costs* – since that section of FRS 102 requires exchange differences arising from foreign currency borrowings to be capitalised to the extent that they are regarded as an adjustment to interest costs (see Chapter 20 at 3.5.4). *[FRS 102.25.1].*

3.5.7 Treatment of exchange differences – non-monetary items

When non-monetary items are measured at fair value in a foreign currency they should be translated using the exchange rate as at the date when the fair value was determined. *[FRS 102.30.9(c)].* Therefore, any re-measurement gain or loss will include an element relating to the change in exchange rates. In this situation, the exchange differences are recognised as part of the gain or loss arising on the fair value re-measurement.

When a gain or loss on a non-monetary item is recognised in other comprehensive income, any exchange component of that gain or loss should also be recognised in other comprehensive income. *[FRS 102.30.11].* For example, Section 17 – *Property, Plant and Equipment* – requires some gains and losses arising on a revaluation of property, plant and equipment to be recognised in other comprehensive income (see Chapter 13 at 3.6.3). When such an asset is measured in a foreign currency, the revalued amount should be translated using the rate at the date the value is determined, resulting in an exchange difference that is also recognised in other comprehensive income.

Conversely, when a gain or loss on a non-monetary item is recognised in profit or loss, e.g. financial instruments that are measured at fair value through profit or loss in accordance with Section 12 (see Chapter 8 at 4.4.2) or an investment property accounted for using the fair value model (see Chapter 12 at 3.3), any exchange component of that gain or loss should be recognised in profit or loss. *[FRS 102.30.11].*

3.5.8   *Determining whether an item is monetary or non-monetary*

Section 30 generally requires that monetary items denominated in foreign currencies be retranslated using closing rates at the end of the reporting period and non-monetary items should not be retranslated (see 3.5.6 and 3.5.7 above). Monetary items are defined as 'units of currency held and assets and liabilities to be received or paid in a fixed or determinable number of units of currency'. *[FRS 102 Appendix I].* The standard does not elaborate further on this, however IAS 21 states that 'the essential feature of a monetary item is a right to receive (or an obligation to deliver) a fixed or determinable number of units of currency'. Some examples given by IAS 21 (and which would also apply under FRS 102) are pensions and other employee benefits to be paid in cash; provisions that are to be settled in cash; and cash dividends that are recognised as a liability. More obvious examples are cash and bank balances; trade receivables and payables; and loan receivables and payables.

Conversely, the essential feature of a non-monetary item is the absence of a right to receive (or an obligation to deliver) a fixed or determinable number of units of currency. Examples are amounts prepaid for goods and services (e.g. prepaid rent); goodwill; intangible assets; inventories; property, plant and equipment; and provisions that are to be settled by the delivery of a non-monetary asset. Investments in equity instruments are generally non-monetary items. However there are a number of situations where the distinction may not be altogether clear.

3.5.9   *Deposits or progress payments*

Entities may be required to pay deposits or progress payments when acquiring certain assets, such as property, plant and equipment or inventories, from foreign suppliers. The question then arises as to whether such payments should be retranslated as monetary items or not.

Example 25.6:   Deposits or progress payments

A UK entity contracts to purchase an item of plant and machinery for €10,000 on the following terms:

Payable on signing contract (1 August 2015)	–10%
Payable on delivery (19 December 2015)	–40%
Payable on installation (7 January 2016)	–50%

At 31 December 2015 the entity has paid the first two amounts on the due dates when the respective exchange rates were £1=€1.25 and £1=€1.20. The closing rate at the end of its reporting period, 31 December 2015, is £1=€1.15.

		(i) £	(ii) £
First payment	–€1,000	800	870
Second payment	–€4,000	3,333	3,478
		4,133	4,348

(i)   If the payments made are regarded as prepayments or as progress payments then the amounts should be treated as non-monetary items and included in the balance sheet at £4,133. This would appear to be consistent with US GAAP which in defining 'transaction date' states: 'A long-term commitment may have more than one transaction date (for example, the due date of each progress payment under a construction contract is an anticipated transaction date).'

(ii) If the payments made are regarded as deposits, and are refundable, then the amounts could possibly be treated as monetary items and included in the balance sheet at £4,348 and an exchange gain of £215 recognised in profit or loss. A variant of this would be to only treat the first payment as a deposit until the second payment is made, since once delivery is made it is less likely that the asset will be returned and a refund sought from the supplier.

In practice, it will often be necessary to consider the terms of the contract to ascertain the nature of the payments made in order to determine the appropriate accounting treatment.

3.5.10   Investments in preference shares

Entities may invest in preference shares of other entities. Whether such shares are monetary items or not will depend on the rights attaching to the shares. As discussed in 3.5.8 above investments in equity instruments are generally considered to be non-monetary items. Thus, if the terms of the preference shares are such that they are classified by the issuer as equity, rather than as a financial liability, then they are non-monetary items. However, if the terms of the preference shares are such that they are classified by the issuer as a financial liability (e.g. a preference share that provides for mandatory redemption by the issuer for a fixed or determinable amount at a fixed or determinable future date), then it would appear that they should be treated as monetary items.

3.5.11   Assets and liabilities arising from insurance contracts

FRS 103 – *Insurance Contracts* – states that for the purposes of applying the requirements of Section 30 an entity shall treat all assets and liabilities arising from an insurance contract as monetary items. *[FRS 103.2.26]*. This means that items such as deferred acquisition costs and unearned premiums that arose in a foreign currency will be retranslated in to the entity's functional currency at the closing exchange rate at each reporting date even though they have characteristics that are more akin to a non-monetary item.

3.6   Change in functional currency

Section 30 requires management to use its judgement to determine the entity's functional currency such that it most faithfully represents the economic effects of the underlying transactions, events and conditions that are relevant to the entity (see 3.4 above). Accordingly, once the functional currency is determined, it may be changed only if there is a change to those underlying transactions, events and conditions. For example, a change in the currency that mainly influences the sales prices of goods and services may lead to a change in an entity's functional currency. *[FRS 102.30.15]*.

When there is a change in an entity's functional currency, the entity should apply the translation procedures applicable to the new functional currency prospectively from the date of the change. In other words, an entity translates all items into the new functional currency using the exchange rate at the date of the change. The resulting translated amounts for non-monetary items are treated as their historical cost. *[FRS 102.30.14, 16]*.

Chapter 25

Example 25.7:   *Change in functional currency*

The management of Entity A has considered the functional currency of the entity to be the euro. However, as a result of change in circumstances affecting the operations of the entity, management determines that on 1 January 2015 the functional currency of the entity is now the US dollar. The exchange rate at that date is €1=US$1.20. The balance sheet of Entity A at 1 January 2015 in its old functional currency is as follows:

	€
Property, plant and equipment	200,000
Current assets	
Inventories	10,000
Receivables	20,000
Cash	5,000
	35,000
Current liabilities	
Payables	15,000
Taxation	3,000
	18,000
Net current assets	17,000
	217,000
Long-term loans	120,000
	97,000

Included within the balance sheet at 1 January 2015 are the following items:

- Equipment with a cost of €33,000 and a net book value of €16,500. This equipment was originally purchased for £20,000 in 2009 and has been translated at the rate ruling at the date of purchase of £1=€1.65.

- Inventories with a cost of €6,000. These were purchased for US$6,000 and have been translated at the rate ruling at the date of purchase of €1=US$1.00.

- Payables of €5,000 representing the US$6,000 due in respect of the above inventories, translated at the rate ruling at 1 January 2015.

- Long-term loans of €15,000 representing the outstanding balance of £10,000 on a loan originally taken out to finance the acquisition of the above equipment, translated at £1=€1.50, the rate ruling at 1 January 2015.

Entity A applies the translational procedures applicable to its new functional currency prospectively from the date of change. Accordingly, all items in its balance sheet at 1 January 2015 are translated at the rate of €1=US$1.20 giving rise to the following amounts:

	$
Property, plant and equipment	240,000
Current assets	
Inventories	12,000
Receivables	24,000
Cash	6,000
	42,000
Current liabilities	
Payables	18,000
Taxation	3,600
	21,600
Net current assets	20,400
	260,400
Long-term loans	144,000
	116,400

As far as the equipment that was originally purchased for £20,000 is concerned, the cost and net book value in terms of Entity A's new functional currency are US$39,600 and US$19,800 respectively, being €33,000 and €16,500 translated at €1=US$1.20. Entity A does not go back and translate the £20,000 cost at whatever the £ sterling/US dollar exchange rate was at the date of purchase and calculate a revised net book value on that basis.

Similarly, the inventories purchased in US dollars are included at $7,200, being €6,000 translated at €1=US$1.20. This is despite the fact that Entity A knows that the original cost was $6,000.

As far as the payables in respect of the inventories are concerned, these are included at $6,000, being €5,000 translated at €1=US$1.20. This represents the original amount payable in US dollars. However, this is as it should be since the original payable had been translated into euros at the rate ruling at 1 January 2015 and has just been translated back into US dollars at the same rate. The impact of the change in functional currency is that whereas Entity A had recognised an exchange gain of €1,000 while the functional currency was the euro, no further exchange difference will be recognised in respect of this amount payable. Exchange differences will now arise from 1 January 2015 on those payables denominated in euros, whereas no such differences would have arisen on such items prior to that date.

Similarly, the £10,000 amount outstanding on the loan will be included at $18,000, being €15,000 translated at €1=US$1.20. This is equivalent to the translation of the £10,000 at a rate of £1=US$1.80, being the direct exchange rate between the two currencies at 1 January 2015. In this case, whereas previously exchange gains and losses would have been recognised on this loan balance based on movements of the £/€ exchange rate, as from 1 January 2015 the exchange gains and losses will be recognised based on the £/$ exchange rate.

Often an entity's circumstances change gradually over time and it may not be possible to determine a precise date on which the functional currency changes. In these circumstances an entity will need to apply judgement to determine an appropriate date from which to apply the change, which might coincide with the beginning or end of an interim or annual accounting period.

3.7   Use of a presentation currency other than the functional currency

An entity may present its financial statements in any currency (or currencies) (see 3.3 above). If the presentation currency differs from the entity's functional currency, it needs to translate its results and financial position into the presentation currency. For example, when a group contains individual entities with different functional currencies, the results and financial position of each entity are expressed in a common currency so that consolidated financial statements may be presented. *[FRS 102.30.17]*. There is no concept of a 'group' functional currency. Each entity within the group has its own functional currency, and the results and financial position of each entity have to be translated into the presentation currency that is used for the consolidated financial statements.

The requirements of Section 30 in respect of this translation process are discussed below. The procedures to be adopted apply not only to the inclusion of foreign subsidiaries in consolidated financial statements but also to the incorporation of the results of associates and joint ventures. They also apply when the results of a foreign branch are to be incorporated into the financial statements of an individual entity and to a stand-alone entity presenting financial statements in a currency other than its functional currency.

In addition to these procedures, Section 30 has additional provisions that apply when the results and financial position of a foreign operation are translated into a presentation currency so that the foreign operation can be included in the financial statements of the reporting entity by consolidation or the equity method. These additional provisions are covered at 3.7.3 to 3.7.12 below.

Chapter 25

3.7.1   *Translation to the presentation currency*

The method of translation depends on whether the entity's functional currency is that of a hyperinflationary economy or not, and if it is, whether it is being translated into a presentation currency which is that of a hyperinflationary economy or not. A hyperinflationary economy is defined in Section 31 – *Hyperinflation* (see Chapter 26 at 3.2). This chapter only covers the requirements for translating an operation into a presentation currency of a non-hyperinflationary economy. For information on translation to the presentation currency which is that of a hyperinflationary economy refer to Chapter 26.

The results and financial position of an entity whose functional currency is not the currency of a hyperinflationary economy should be translated into a different presentation currency using the following procedures: *[FRS 102.30.18]*

(a)   assets and liabilities for each balance sheet presented (i.e. including comparatives) are translated at the closing rate at the date of that balance sheet;

(b)   income and expenses for each statement of comprehensive income (i.e. including comparatives) are translated at exchange rates at the dates of the transactions; and

(c)   all resulting exchange differences are recognised in other comprehensive income.

For practical reasons, the reporting entity may use a rate that approximates the actual exchange rate, e.g. an average rate for the period, to translate income and expense items. However, if exchange rates fluctuate significantly, the use of the average rate for a period is inappropriate. *[FRS 102.30.19]*.

Section 30 indicates that the exchange differences referred to in item (c) above result from: *[FRS 102.30.20]*

•   translating income and expenses at the exchange rates at the dates of the transactions and assets and liabilities at the closing rate; and

•   translating the opening net assets at a closing rate that differs from the previous closing rate.

This is not in fact completely accurate since if the entity has had any transactions with equity holders that have resulted in a change in the net assets during the period there are likely to be further exchange differences that need to be recognised to the extent that the closing rate differs from the rate used to translate the transaction. This will particularly be the case where a parent has subscribed for further equity shares in a subsidiary.

The application of these procedures is illustrated in the following example.

Example 25.8:   Translation of a non-hyperinflationary functional currency to a non-hyperinflationary presentation currency

An UK entity owns 100% of the share capital of a foreign entity which was set up a number of years ago when the exchange rate was £1=FC2. It is consolidating the financial statements of the subsidiary in its consolidated financial statements for the year ended 31 December 2015. The exchange rate at the year-end is £1=FC4 (2013: £1=FC3). For the purposes of illustration, it is assumed that exchange rates have not fluctuated significantly and the appropriate weighted average rate for the year was £1=FC3.5, and that the currency of the foreign entity is not that of a hyperinflationary economy. The income statement of the subsidiary for that year and its balance sheet at the beginning and end of the year in its functional currency and translated into £ are as follows:

Income statement

	FC	£
Sales	35,000	10,000
Cost of sales	(33,190)	(9,483)
Depreciation	(500)	(143)
Interest	(350)	(100)
Profit before taxation	960	274
Taxation	(460)	(131)
Profit after taxation	500	143

Balance sheets	2014	2015	2014	2015
	FC	FC	£	£
Property, plant and equipment	6,000	5,500	2,000	1,375
Current assets				
Inventories	2,700	3,000	900	750
Receivables	4,800	4,000	1,600	1,000
Cash	200	600	67	150
	7,700	7,600	2,567	1,900
Current liabilities				
Payables	4,530	3,840	1,510	960
Taxation	870	460	290	115
	5,400	4,300	1,800	1,075
Net current assets	2,300	3,300	767	825
	8,300	8,800	2,767	2,200
Long-term loans	3,600	3,600	1,200	900
	4,700	5,200	1,567	1,300
Share capital	1,000	1,000	500	500
Retained profits*	3,700	4,200	1,500	1,643
Exchange reserve*			(433)	(843)
	4,700	5,200	1,567	1,300

* The opening balances for 2014 in £ have been assumed and represent cumulative amounts since the foreign entity was set up.

The movement of £(410) in the exchange reserve included as a separate component of equity is made up as follows:

(i) the exchange loss of £392 on the opening net investment in the subsidiary, calculated as follows:

Opening net assets at opening rate	– FC4,700 at FC3 = A$1 =	£1,567
Opening net assets at closing rate	– FC4,700 at FC4 = A$1 =	£1,175
Exchange loss on net assets		£392

(ii) the exchange loss of £18, being the difference between the income account translated at an average rate, i.e. £143, and at the closing rate, i.e. £125.

When the exchange differences relate to a foreign operation that is consolidated but not wholly-owned, accumulated exchange differences arising from translation and attributable to non-controlling interests are allocated to, and recognised as part of, non-controlling interests in the consolidated balance sheet. *[FRS 102.30.20].*

Chapter 25

3.7.2   *Functional currency is that of a hyperinflationary economy*

A UK based group preparing consolidated financial statements under FRS 102 might have a subsidiary that operates in, and has a functional currency of, a country subject to hyperinflation. In this case, FRS 102 requires the subsidiary's results and financial position to be adjusted using the procedures specified in Section 31 (see Chapter 26) before applying the procedures in Section 30 to translate them into the group's presentation currency for the consolidated financial statements. *[FRS 102.30.21].*

However, *prima facie*, the procedures used to translate entities' financial statements into the group's presentation currency for the consolidated financial statements set out at 3.7.1 above apply only to entities with a non-hyperinflationary functional currency.

In the absence of clear requirements in Section 30 it may be appropriate, using the hierarchy on Section 10, to follow the requirements in IAS 21. In these circumstances, IAS 21 requires assets, liabilities, equity items, income and expenses of the foreign operation to be translated into the group's presentation currency at the closing rate at the date of the most recent statement of financial position. However, comparative amounts should be those that were presented as current year amounts in the relevant prior year financial statements (i.e. not adjusted for subsequent changes in the price level or subsequent changes in exchange rates as they would be in the operation's own financial statements – see Chapter 26 at 3.3). *[IAS 21.42].*

3.7.3   *Exchange differences on intragroup balances*

The incorporation of the results and financial position of a foreign operation with those of the reporting entity should follow normal consolidation procedures, such as the elimination of intragroup balances and intragroup transactions of a subsidiary. *[FRS 102.30.22].* On this basis, there is a tendency sometimes to assume that exchange differences on intragroup balances should not impact on the reported profit or loss for the group in the consolidated financial statements. However, an intragroup monetary asset (or liability), whether short-term or long-term, cannot be eliminated against the corresponding intragroup liability (or asset) without the entity with the currency exposure recognising an exchange difference on the intragroup balance.

This exchange difference will be reflected in that entity's profit or loss for the period (see 3.5.6 above) and, except as indicated at 3.7.4 below, Section 30 requires this exchange difference to continue to be included in profit or loss in the consolidated financial statements. This is because the monetary item represents a commitment to convert one currency into another and exposes the reporting entity to a gain or loss through currency fluctuations. *[FRS 102.30.22].*

3.7.4   *Monetary items included as part of the net investment in a foreign operation – general*

As an exception to the general rule at 3.7.3 above, where an exchange difference arises on an intragroup balance that, in substance, forms part of an entity's net investment in a foreign operation, the exchange difference is not recognised in profit or loss in the consolidated financial statements, but is recognised in other comprehensive income and accumulated in a separate component of equity. *[FRS 102.30.13, 22].*

The 'net investment in a foreign operation' is defined as being 'the amount of the reporting entity's interest in the net assets of that operation'. *[FRS 102 Appendix I].* This will include a monetary item that is receivable from or payable to a foreign operation for which settlement is neither planned nor likely to occur in the foreseeable future (often referred to as a 'permanent as equity' loan) because it is, in substance, a part of the entity's net investment in that foreign operation. Such monetary items may include long-term receivables or loans. They do not include trade receivables or trade payables. *[FRS 102.30.12].*

In our view, trade receivables and payables can be included as part of the net investment in the foreign operation, but only if cash settlement is not made or planned to be made in the foreseeable future. However, if a subsidiary makes payment for purchases from its parent, but is continually indebted to the parent as a result of new purchases, then in these circumstances, since individual transactions are settled, no part of the inter-company balance should be regarded as part of the net investment in the subsidiary. Accordingly, exchange differences on such balances should be recognised in profit or loss.

These requirements are illustrated in the following example.

Example 25.9:   Receivables/payables included as part of net investment in a foreign operation

A UK entity, A, has a Belgian subsidiary, B. A has a receivable due from B amounting to £1,000,000.

In each of the following scenarios, could the receivable be included as part of A's net investment in B?

Scenario 1

The receivable arises from the sale of goods, together with interest payments and dividend payments which have not been paid in cash but have been accumulated in the inter-company account. A and B agree that A can claim at any time the repayment of this receivable. It is likely that there will be a settlement of the receivable in the foreseeable future.

Although the standard states that trade receivables and payables are not included, we do not believe that it necessarily precludes deferred trading balances from being included. In our view, such balances can be included as part of the net investment in the foreign operation, but only if cash settlement is not made or planned to be made in the foreseeable future.

In this scenario, the settlement of A's receivable due from B is not planned; however, it is likely that a settlement will occur in the foreseeable future. Accordingly, the receivable does not qualify to be treated as part of A's net investment in B. The term 'foreseeable future' is not defined and no specific time period is implied. It could be argued that the receivable should only be considered as part of the net investment if it will be repaid only when the reporting entity disinvests from the foreign operation. However, it is recognised that in most circumstances this would be unrealistic and therefore a shorter time span should be considered in determining the foreseeable future.

Scenario 2

The receivable represents a loan made by A to B and it is agreed that the receivable will be repaid in 20 years.

In this scenario, A's receivable due from B has a specified term for repayment. This suggests that settlement is planned. Accordingly, the receivable does not qualify to be treated as part of A's investment in B.

Chapter 25

Scenario 3

A and B have previously agreed that the receivable under scenario 2 will be repaid in 20 years but A now decides that it will replace the loan on maturity either with a further inter-company loan or with an injection of equity. This approach is consistent with A's intention to maintain the strategic long-term investment in B.

In this scenario, the words from paragraph 12 of Section 30 '... settlement is neither planned nor likely to occur in the foreseeable future ...' are potentially problematic, since a loan with a fixed maturity must, *prima facie*, have a planned settlement. However, from the date A decides that it will re-finance the inter-company debt upon maturity with a further long-term instrument, or replace it with equity, the substance of the inter-company loan is that it is part of the entity's net investment in the foreign operation, and there is no actual 'intent' to settle the investment without replacement. On this basis, loans with a stated maturity may qualify to be treated in accordance with paragraph 13 of Section 30, with foreign currency gains and losses recognised in other comprehensive income and accumulated in a separate component of equity in the consolidated financial statements. However, in our view, management's intention to refinance the loan must be documented appropriately, for example in the form of a minute of a meeting of the management board or board of directors. In addition, there should not be any established historical pattern of the entity demanding repayment of such inter-company debt without replacement.

Consequently, when the purpose of the loan is to fund a long-term strategic investment then it is the entity's overall intention with regard to the investment and ultimate funding thereof, rather than the specific terms of the inter-company loan funding the investment, that should be considered.

Scenario 4

The receivable arises from the sale of goods, together with interest payments and dividend payments which have not been paid in cash but have been accumulated in the inter-company account. However, in this scenario, A and B agree that A can claim the repayment of this receivable only in the event that the subsidiary is disposed of. A has no plans to dispose of entity B.

In this scenario, the settlement of A's receivable due from B is not planned nor is it likely to occur in the foreseeable future. Although the term 'foreseeable future' is not defined, it will not go beyond a point of time after the disposal of a foreign operation. Accordingly, the receivable does qualify for being treated as part of a net investment in a foreign operation.

The question of whether or not a monetary item is as permanent as equity can, in certain circumstances, require the application of significant judgement.

3.7.5   Monetary items included as part of the net investment in a foreign operation – currency of the monetary item

When a monetary item is considered to form part of a reporting entity's net investment in a foreign operation and is denominated in the functional currency of the reporting entity, an exchange difference will be recognised in profit or loss in the foreign operation's individual financial statements. If the item is denominated in the functional currency of the foreign operation, an exchange difference will be recognised in profit or loss in the reporting entity's separate financial statements. Such exchange differences are recognised in other comprehensive income and accumulated in a separate component of equity in the financial statements that include the foreign operation and the reporting entity (i.e. financial statements in which the foreign operation is consolidated or accounted for using the equity method). *[FRS 102.30.12-13].*

Example 25.10: *Monetary item in functional currency of either the reporting entity or the foreign operation*

A UK entity has a Belgian subsidiary. On the last day of its financial year, 31 March 2015, the UK entity lends the subsidiary £1,000,000. Settlement of the loan is neither planned nor likely to occur in the foreseeable future, so the UK entity regards the loan as part of its net investment in the Belgian subsidiary. The exchange rate at 31 March 2015 was £1=€1.40. Since the loan was made on the last day of the year there are no exchange differences to recognise for that year. At 31 March 2016, the loan has not been repaid and is still regarded as part of the net investment in the Belgian subsidiary. The relevant exchange rate at that date was £1=€1.50. The average exchange rate for the year ended 31 March 2016 was £1=€1.45.

In the UK entity's separate financial statements no exchange difference is recognised since the loan is denominated in its functional currency of pound sterling. In the Belgian subsidiary's financial statements, the liability to the parent is translated into the subsidiary's functional currency of euros at the closing rate at €1,500,000, giving rise to an exchange loss of €100,000, i.e. €1,500,000 less €1,400,000 (£1,000,000 @ £1=€1.40). This exchange loss is reflected in the Belgian subsidiary's profit or loss for that year. In the UK entity's consolidated financial statements, this exchange loss included in the subsidiary's profit or loss for the year will be translated at the average rate for the year, giving rise a loss of £68,966 (€100,000@ £1=€1.45). This will be recognised in other comprehensive income and accumulated in the separate component of equity together with an exchange gain of £2,299, being the difference between the amount included in the Belgian subsidiary's income statement translated at average rate, i.e. £68,966, and at the closing rate, i.e. £66,667 (€100,000@ £1=€1.50). The overall exchange loss recognised in other comprehensive income is £66,667. This represents the exchange loss on the increased net investment of €1,400,000 in the subsidiary made at 31 March 2015, i.e. £1,000,000 (€1,400,000 @ £1=€1.40) less £933,333 (€1,400,000 @ £1=€1.50).

If, on the other hand, the loan made to the Belgian subsidiary had been denominated in the equivalent amount of euros at 31 March 2015, i.e. €1,400,000, the treatment would have been as follows:

In the UK entity's separate financial statements, the amount receivable from the Belgian subsidiary would be translated at the closing rate at £933,333 (€1,400,000 @ £1=€1.50), giving rise to an exchange loss of £66,667, i.e. £1,000,000 (€1,400,000 @ £1=€1.40) less £933,333, which is included in its profit or loss for the year. In the Belgian subsidiary's financial statements, no exchange difference is recognised since the loan is denominated in its functional currency of euros. In the UK entity's consolidated financial statements, the exchange loss included in its profit or loss for the year in its separate financial statements will be recognised in other comprehensive income and accumulated in the separate component of equity. As before, this represents the exchange loss on the increased net investment of €1,400,000 in the subsidiary made at 31 March 2015, i.e. £1,000,000 (€1,400,000 @ £1=€1.40) less £933,333 (€1,400,000 @ £1=€1.40).

In most situations, intragroup balances for which settlement is neither planned nor likely to occur in the foreseeable future will be denominated in the functional currency of either the reporting entity or the foreign operation. However, this will not always be the case. If a monetary item is denominated in a currency other than the functional currency of either the reporting entity or the foreign operation, the exchange difference arising in the reporting entity's separate financial statements and in the foreign operation's individual financial statements is also recognised in other comprehensive income, and accumulated in the separate component of equity, in the financial statements that include the foreign operation and the reporting entity (i.e. financial statements in which the foreign operation is consolidated or accounted for using the equity method).

Chapter 25

3.7.6   *Monetary items included as part of the net investment in a foreign operation – treatment in individual financial statements*

The exception for exchange differences on monetary items forming part of the net investment in a foreign operation applies only in the consolidated financial statements. In the individual financial statements of the entity (or entities) with the currency exposure the exchange differences should be reflected in that entity's profit or loss for the period.

SSAP 20 does not explicitly address the treatment of such exchange difference in the individual financial statements of an entity and therefore some entities may have recognised the difference in equity rather than in profit or loss as required by Section 30, or not at all, e.g. on the grounds that in substance such a receivable was a non-monetary item.

3.7.7   *Monetary items becoming part of the net investment in a foreign operation*

An entity's plans and expectations in respect of an intragroup monetary item may change over time and the status of such items should be assessed each period. For example, a parent may decide that its subsidiary requires refinancing and instead of investing more equity capital in the subsidiary decides that an existing inter-company account, which has previously been regarded as a normal monetary item, should become a long-term deferred trading balance and no repayment of such amount will be requested within the foreseeable future. In our view, such a 'capital injection' should be regarded as having occurred at the time it is decided to redesignate the inter-company account. Consequently, the exchange differences arising on the account up to that date should be recognised in profit or loss and the exchange differences arising thereafter would be recognised in other comprehensive income on consolidation. This is discussed further in the following example.

Example 25.11:   Monetary item becoming part of the net investment in a foreign operation

A UK entity has a wholly owned Canadian subsidiary whose net assets at 31 December 2014 were C$2,000,000. These net assets were arrived at after taking account of a liability to the UK parent of £250,000. Using the closing exchange rate of £1=C$2.35 this liability was included in the Canadian company's balance sheet at that date at C$587,500. On 30 June 2015, when the exchange rate was £1=C$2.45, the parent decided that in order to refinance the Canadian subsidiary it would regard the liability of £250,000 as a long-term liability which would not be called for repayment in the foreseeable future. Consequently, the parent thereafter regarded the loan as being part of its net investment in the subsidiary. In the year ended 31 December 2015 the Canadian company made no profit or loss other than any exchange difference to be recognised on its liability to its parent. The relevant exchange rate at that date was £1=C$2.56. The average exchange rate for the year ended 31 December 2015 was £1=C$2.50.

The financial statements of the subsidiary in C$ and translated using the closing rate are as follows:

Balance sheet	31 December 2015		31 December 2014	
	C$	£	C$	£
Assets	2,587,500	1,010,742	2,587,500	1,101,064
Amount due to parent	640,000	250,000	587,500	250,000
Net assets	1,947,500	760,742	2,000,000	851,064
Income statement				
Exchange difference		(52,500)		

If the amount due to the parent is not part of the parent's net investment in the foreign operation, this exchange loss would be translated at the average rate and included in the consolidated profit and loss account as £21,000. As the net investment was C$2,000,000 then there would have been an exchange loss recognised in other comprehensive income of £69,814, i.e. £851,064 less £781,250 (C$2,000,000 @ £1=C$2.56), together with an exchange gain of £492, being the difference between profit or loss translated at average rate, i.e. £21,000, and at the closing rate, i.e. £20,508.

However, the parent now regards the amount due as being part of the net investment in the subsidiary. The question then arises as to when this should be regarded as having happened and how the exchange difference on it should be calculated. No guidance is given in Section 30.

In our view, the 'capital injection' should be regarded as having occurred at the time it is decided to redesignate the inter-company account. The exchange differences arising on the account up to that date should be recognised in profit or loss. Only the exchange difference arising thereafter would be recognised in other comprehensive income on consolidation. The inter-company account that was converted into a long-term loan becomes part of the entity's (UK parent's) net investment in the foreign operation (Canadian subsidiary) at the moment in time when the entity decides that settlement is neither planned nor likely to occur in the foreseeable future, i.e. 30 June 2015. Accordingly, exchange differences arising on the long-term loan are recognised in other comprehensive income and accumulated in a separate component of equity from that date. The same accounting treatment would have been applied if a capital injection had taken place at the date of redesignation.

At 30 June 2015 the subsidiary would have translated the inter-company account as C$612,500 (£250,000 @ £1=C$2.45) and therefore the exchange loss up to that date was C$25,000. Translated at the average rate this amount would be included in consolidated profit or loss as £10,000, with only an exchange gain of £234 recognised in other comprehensive income, being the difference between profit or loss translated at average rate, i.e. £10,000, and at the closing rate, i.e. £9,766. Accordingly, £11,000 (£21,000 less £10,000) offset by a reduction in the exchange gain on the translation of profit or loss of £258 (£492 less £234) would be recognised in other comprehensive income. This amount represents the exchange loss on the 'capital injection' of C$612,500. Translated at the closing rate this amounts to £239,258 which is £10,742 less than the original £250,000.

Some might argue that an approach of regarding the 'capital injection' as having occurred at the beginning of the accounting period would have the merit of treating all of the exchange differences for this year in the same way. However, for the reasons provided above we do not regard such an approach as being acceptable.

Suppose, instead of the inter-company account being £250,000, it was denominated in dollars at C$587,500. In this case the parent would be exposed to the exchange risk; what would be the position?

The subsidiary's net assets at both 31 December 2014 and 2015 would be:

Assets	C$2,587,500
Amount due to parent	587,500
Net assets	C$2,000,000

As the inter-company account is expressed in Canadian dollars, there will be no exchange difference thereon in the subsidiary's profit or loss.

There will, however, be an exchange loss in the parent as follows:

C$587,500	@ 2.35 =	£250,000
	@ 2.56 =	£229,492
		£20,508

Again, in the consolidated financial statements as the inter-company account is now regarded as part of the equity investment some of this amount should be recognised in other comprehensive income. For the reasons stated above, in our view it is only the exchange differences that have arisen after the date of redesignation, i.e. 30 June 2015, that should be recognised in other comprehensive income.

Chapter 25

On this basis, the exchange loss would be split as follows:

C$587,500	@ 2.35 =	£250,000	
	@ 2.45 =	£239,796	
			£10,204
	@ 2.45 =	£239,796	
	@ 2.56 =	£229,492	
			£10,304

The exchange loss up to 30 June 2015 of £10,204 would be recognised in consolidated profit or loss and the exchange loss thereafter of £10,304 would be recognised in other comprehensive income. This is different from when the account was expressed in sterling because the 'capital injection' in this case is C$587,500 whereas before it was effectively C$612,500.

3.7.8   *Monetary items ceasing to be part of the net investment in a foreign operation*

The previous section dealt with the situation where a pre-existing monetary item was subsequently considered to form part of the net investment in a foreign operation. However, what happens where a monetary item ceases to be considered part of the net investment in a foreign operation, either because the circumstances have changed such that it is now planned or is likely to be settled in the foreseeable future or indeed that the monetary item is in fact settled?

Where the circumstances have changed such that the monetary item is now planned or is likely to be settled in the foreseeable future, then similar issues to those discussed at 3.7.4 above apply; i.e. are the exchange differences on the intragroup balance to be recognised in profit or loss only from the date of change or from the beginning of the financial year? For the same reasons set out in Example 25.11 above, in our view, the monetary item ceases to form part of the net investment in the foreign operation at the moment in time when the entity decides that settlement is planned or is likely to occur in the foreseeable future. Accordingly, exchange differences arising on the monetary item up to that date are recognised in other comprehensive income and accumulated in a separate component of equity. The exchange differences that arise after that date are recognised in profit or loss.

Consideration also needs to be given as to the treatment of the cumulative exchange differences on the monetary item that have been recognised in other comprehensive income, including those that had been recognised in other comprehensive income in prior years. The treatment of these exchange differences is to recognise them in other comprehensive income and accumulate them in a separate component of equity. *[FRS 102.30.22]*. The principle question is whether the change in circumstances or actual settlement in cash of the intragroup balance represents a disposal or partial disposal of the foreign operation and this is considered in more detail at 3.8 below.

3.7.9   *Dividends*

If a subsidiary pays a dividend to the parent during the year the parent should record the dividend at the rate ruling when the dividend was declared. An exchange difference will arise in the parent's own financial statements if the exchange rate moves between the declaration date and the date the dividend is actually received.

This exchange difference is required to be recognised in profit or loss and will remain there on consolidation.

The same will apply if the subsidiary declares a dividend to its parent on the last day of its financial year and this is recorded at the year-end in both entities' financial statements. There is no problem in that year as both the intragroup balances and the dividends will eliminate on consolidation with no exchange differences arising. However, as the dividend will not be received until the following year an exchange difference will arise in the parent's financial statements in that year if exchange rates have moved in the meantime. Again, this exchange difference should remain in consolidated profit or loss as it is no different from any other exchange difference arising on intragroup balances resulting from other types of intragroup transactions. It should not be recognised in other comprehensive income.

It may seem odd that the consolidated results can be affected by exchange differences on inter-company dividends. However, once the dividend has been declared, the parent now effectively has a functional currency exposure to assets that were previously regarded as part of the net investment. In order to minimise the effect of exchange rate movements entities should, therefore, arrange for inter-company dividends to be paid on the same day the dividend is declared, or as soon after the dividend is declared as possible.

3.7.10   Unrealised profits on intragroup transactions

The other problem area is the elimination of unrealised profits resulting from intragroup transactions when one of the parties to the transaction is a foreign subsidiary.

Example 25.12:   Unrealised profits on intragroup transaction

A UK parent has a wholly owned Swiss subsidiary. On 30 November 2015 the subsidiary sold goods to the parent for CHF1,000. The cost of the goods to the subsidiary was CHF700. The goods were recorded by the parent at £685 based on the exchange rate ruling on 30 November 2015 of £1=CHF1.46. All of the goods are unsold by the year-end, 31 December 2015. The exchange rate at that date was £1=CHF1.52. How should the intragroup profit be eliminated?

Section 30 contains no specific guidance on this matter. However, US GAAP requires the rate ruling at the date of the transaction to be used.

The profit shown by the subsidiary is CHF300 which translated at the rate ruling on the transaction of £1=CHF1.46 equals £205. Consequently, the goods will be included in the balance sheet at:

Per parent company balance sheet	£685
Less unrealised profit eliminated	205
	£480

It can be seen that the resulting figure for inventory is equivalent to the original euro cost translated at the rate ruling on the date of the transaction. Whereas if the subsidiary still held the inventory it would be included at £461 (CHF700 @ £1=CHF1.52).

If in the above example the goods had been sold by the Italian parent to the Swiss subsidiary then the approach in US GAAP would say the amount to be eliminated is the amount of profit shown in the Italian entity's financial statements. Again, this will not necessarily result in the goods being carried in the consolidated financial statements at their original cost to the group.

Chapter 25

3.7.11   *Non-coterminous period ends*

Unlike IAS 21, Section 30 does not deal with situations where a foreign operation is consolidated on the basis of financial statements made up to a different date from that of the reporting entity. However, in accordance with the hierarchy set out in Section 10 an entity could apply the guidance in IAS 21. In such a case, IAS 21 initially states that the assets and liabilities of the foreign operation are to be translated at the exchange rate at the end of the reporting period of the foreign operation rather than at the date of the consolidated financial statements. However, it then goes on to say that adjustments are made for significant changes in exchange rates up to the end of the reporting period of the reporting entity in accordance with IFRS 10 – *Consolidated Financial Statements*. This approach is consistent with the requirements in paragraph 16(a) of Section 9 – *Consolidated and Separate Financial Statements* – which requires adjustments be made for the effects of significant transactions that occur between the date of subsidiary financial statements and the date of the consolidated financial statements. The same approach is used in applying the equity method to associates and joint ventures in accordance with IAS 28 – *Investments in Associates and Joint Ventures*.

The rationale for this approach is not explained in IAS 21. The initial treatment is that required by US GAAP and the reason given in that standard is that this presents the functional currency performance of the subsidiary during the subsidiary's financial year and its position at the end of that period in terms of the parent company's reporting (presentation) currency. The subsidiary may have entered into transactions in other currencies, including the functional currency of the parent, and monetary items in these currencies will have been translated using rates ruling at the end of the subsidiary's reporting period. The income statement of the subsidiary will reflect the economic consequences of carrying out these transactions during the period ended on that date. In order that the effects of these transactions in the subsidiary's financial statements are not distorted, the financial statements should be translated using the closing rate at the end of the subsidiary's reporting period.

However, an alternative argument could have been advanced for using the closing rate ruling at the end of the parent's reporting period. All subsidiaries within a group should normally prepare financial statements up to the same date as the parent entity so that the parent can prepare consolidated financial statements that present fairly the financial performance and financial position about the group as that of a single entity. The use of financial statements of a subsidiary made up to a date earlier than that of the parent is only an administrative convenience and a surrogate for financial statements made up to the proper date. Arguably, therefore the closing rate that should have been used is that which would have been used if the financial statements were made up to the proper date, i.e. that ruling at the end of the reporting period of the parent. Another reason for using this rate is that there may be subsidiaries that have the same functional currency as the subsidiary with the non-coterminous year end that do make up their financial statements to the same date as the parent company and therefore in order to be consistent with them the same rate should be used.

3.7.12 Goodwill and fair value adjustments

Any goodwill arising on the acquisition of a foreign operation and any fair value adjustments to the carrying amounts of assets and liabilities arising on the acquisition of that foreign operation shall be treated as assets and liabilities of the foreign operation. Thus, they shall be expressed in the functional currency of the foreign operation and shall be translated at the closing rate in accordance with paragraph 30.18. *[FRS 102.30.23]*.

3.8 Disposal of a foreign operation

Exchange differences resulting from the translation of a foreign operation to a different presentation currency are to be recognised in other comprehensive income and accumulated within a separate component of equity (see 3.7.4 above).

On the disposal of a foreign operation, the exchange differences relating to that foreign operation that have been recognised in other comprehensive income and accumulated in the separate component of equity are not recognised in profit or loss. *[FRS 102.30.13]*. Instead, the cumulative exchange differences relating to the foreign operation that have accumulated in the separate component of equity should be transferred directly to retained earnings on disposal. *[FRS 102.9.18B]*.

This is a clear difference to IAS 21 which requires reclassification of the exchange differences from equity to profit or loss on disposal of the foreign operation.

Example 25.13: Disposal of a foreign operation

A UK entity has a Swiss subsidiary which was set up on 1 January 2013 with a share capital of CHF200,000 when the exchange rate was £1=CHF1.55. The subsidiary is included in the parent's separate financial statements at its original cost of £129,032. The profits of the subsidiary, all of which it has retained, for each of the three years ended 31 December 2015 were CHF40,000, CHF50,000 and CHF60,000 respectively, so that the net assets at 31 December 2015 are CHF350,000. In the consolidated financial statements the results of the subsidiary have been translated at the respective average rates of £1=CHF1.60, £1=CHF1.68 and £1=CHF1.70 and the net assets at the respective closing rates of £1=CHF1.71, £1=CHF1.65 and £1=CHF1.66. All exchange differences have been recognised in other comprehensive income and accumulated in a separate exchange reserve. The consolidated reserves have therefore included the following amounts in respect of the subsidiary:

	Retained profit £	Exchange reserve £
1 January 2013	–	–
Movement during 2013	25,000	(13,681)
31 December 2013	25,000	(13,681)
Movement during 2014	29,762	5,645
31 December 2014	54,762	(8,036)
Movement during 2015	35,294	(209)
31 December 2015	90,056	(8,245)

The net assets at 31 December 2015 of CHF350,000 are included in the consolidated financial statements at £210,843.

On 1 January 2016 the subsidiary is sold for CHF400,000 (£240,964), thus resulting in a gain on disposal in the parent entity's books of £111,932, i.e. £240,964 less £129,032.

In the consolidated financial statements for 2016, Section 9 and Section 30 requires the cumulative exchange losses of £8,245 to be transferred directly to retained earnings without being recognised in profit or loss. The gain recognised in the consolidated financial statements would be £30,121 (the difference between the proceeds of £240,964 and net asset value of £210,843 at the date of disposal).

3.9   Tax effects of all exchange differences

Gains and losses on foreign currency transactions and exchange differences arising on translating the results and financial position of an entity (including a foreign operation) into a different currency may have tax effects to which Section 29 – *Income Tax* – applies. The requirements of Section 29 are discussed in Chapter 24. In broad terms the tax effects of exchange differences will follow the reporting of the exchange differences, i.e. they will be recognised in profit or loss except to the extent they relate to exchange differences recognised in other comprehensive income, in which case they will also be recognised in other comprehensive income. *[FRS 102.29.22]*.

3.10   Disclosure requirements

Section 30 requires an entity to disclose:

(a)   the amount of exchange differences recognised in profit or loss during the period, except for those arising on financial instruments measured at fair value through profit or loss in accordance with Section 11 and Section 12;

(b)   the amount of exchange differences arising during the period and classified in equity at the end of the period; *[FRS 102.30.25]*

(c)   the currency in which the financial statements are presented. When the presentation currency is different from the functional currency, the entity should state that fact and should disclose the functional currency and the reason for using a different presentation currency. *[FRS 102.30.26]*. For this purpose, in the case of a group, the references to 'functional currency' are to that of the parent; and *[FRS 102.30.24]*

(d)   when there is a change in the functional currency of either the reporting entity or a significant foreign operation, that fact and the reason for the change in functional currency. *[FRS 102.30.27]*.

4   UK COMPANY LAW MATTERS

The Companies Act contains a general prohibition against recognising unrealised profits in profit and loss, although there is an exception to this rule when the fair value provisions of the Act are applied.

TECH 02/10 – *Guidance on the determination of realised profits and losses* – provides guidance on realised and distributable profits under the Companies Act 2006. The main aspects of TECH 02/10 that deal with foreign exchange are:

- Unless there are doubts as to the convertibility or marketability of the currency in question, foreign exchange profits arising on the retranslation of monetary items are realised, irrespective of the maturity date of the monetary item. However, a profit on retranslation of a monetary asset will not be a realised profit where the underlying balance on which the exchange difference arises does not itself meet the definition of 'qualifying consideration' – e.g. some long term intercompany balances. *[TECH 02/10 3.21, 3.21A, 3.21B]*.

- Realised profits and losses are measured by reference to the functional currency of the company. Therefore an accounting gain or loss arising from the retranslation of an entity's accounts from its functional currency to a presentation currency is not a profit or loss as a matter of law. It cannot therefore be a realised profit or loss. *[TECH 02/10 11.11]*.

- The profit or loss arising on the necessary retranslation of an autonomous branch, from its functional currency into the functional currency of the company, is a realised profit or loss to the extent that the branch net assets were qualifying consideration when the profit or loss arose. *[TECH 02/10 11.13, 11.14]*.

- Where a company's shares, irrespective of whether those shares are classified as equity or debt, are denominated in a currency other than the company's functional currency, the adjustment arising upon any translation for accounting purposes of the share capital is not a profit or loss at law. Therefore it is not a realised profit or loss. *[TECH 02/10 11.20]*.

- Where share capital is denominated in a currency other than the functional currency, it is fixed at that other currency amount. A distribution cannot be made if it would reduce the company's net assets below the level of the company's share capital. *[TECH0 2/10 11.21]*. This needs to be considered when assessing the distribution that can be made.

5   SUMMARY OF GAAP DIFFERENCES

	FRS 102	*Previous UK GAAP*	*IFRS*
Determining functional currency	'Functional currency' is defined as the currency of the primary economic environment in which the entity operates. More guidance is provided in FRS 102 on determining an entity's 'functional currency' compared to the equivalent guidance in determining 'local currency' under SSAP 20.	Under SSAP 20 an entity is required to determine its 'local currency' rather than 'functional currency'. However, the definition of 'local currency' is similar to 'functional currency' under IFRS and FRS 102. 'Local currency' defined as the primary economic environment in which the entity operates and generates net cash flows.	'Functional currency' is defined as the currency of the primary economic environment in which the entity operates. More guidance is provided in IAS 21 on determining an entity's 'functional currency' compared to the equivalent guidance in FRS 102.

Chapter 25

	FRS 102	*Previous UK GAAP*	*IFRS*
Initial recognition of foreign currency transactions – use of forward/ contracted rates	Section 30 does not permit the use of contracted or forward rates instead of the closing rate to retranslate foreign currency balances.	SSAP 20 requires that where a transaction is to be settled at a contracted rate, that rate should be used. Where a trading transaction is covered by a related or matching forward contract, the rate of exchange specified in that contract may be used.	IAS 21 does not permit the use of contracted or forward rates instead of the closing rate to retranslate foreign currency balances.
Translation to a presentation currency – general	FRS 102 allows an entity to select its presentation currency. Its results and financial position will then be translated into that presentation currency.	There is no concept of a presentation currency under SSAP 20. Financial statements are generally prepared in the entity's 'local currency', which is the equivalent of 'functional' currency under IFRS and FRS 102.	IAS 21 allows an entity to select its presentation currency. Its results and financial position will then be translated into that presentation currency.
Translation to a presentation currency – use of a closing rate	Section 30 requires that an average rate is used when translating amounts in the profit and loss account of a foreign operation.	SSAP 20 allows the closing rate or average rate to be used when translating amounts in the profit and loss account of a foreign operation.	IAS 21 (and FRS 23) requires that an average rate is used when translating amounts in the profit and loss account of a foreign operation.
Net investment in a foreign operation – monetary items [Separate financial statements]	In the separate financial statements of the investing company, the exchange differences are recognised in profit or loss.	SSAP 20 does not explicitly address the treatment of exchange differences arising on monetary items that form part of an entity's net investment in a foreign operation in the individual financial statements of an entity. Some entities therefore may have recognised the difference in equity rather than in profit or loss as required by Section 30, or not at all, e.g. on the grounds that in substance such a receivable was a non-monetary item.	In the separate financial statements of the investing company, the exchange differences are recognised in profit or loss.

Foreign equity investments financed by foreign currency borrowings	There are no equivalent special provisions in Section 30. This would indicate that (unless the entity was treating the associated borrowings as a fair value hedge of the investment) as a non-monetary asset the foreign investment would be translated at the exchange rate at the date of the transaction (or the exchange rate at the date the fair value of the investment was determined if the investment is carried at fair value), and the exchange gains or losses on the retranslation of the associated foreign currency borrowings at each period end would be recorded in profit or loss.	SSAP 20 includes special provisions relating to foreign equity investments that are financed by foreign currency borrowings. Where certain conditions apply, an entity may denominate its foreign equity investments in the appropriate foreign currencies and translate the carrying amounts at the end of each accounting period at the closing rates of exchange. Where investments are treated in this way, any resulting exchange differences should be taken directly to reserves, against which the exchange rate gains or losses on the associated borrowings would be offset, as a reserve movement.	There are no equivalent special provisions in IAS 21 (or FRS 23). This would indicate that (unless the entity was treating the associated borrowings as a fair value hedge of the investment) as a non-monetary asset the foreign investment would be translated at the exchange rate at the date of the transaction (or the exchange rate at the date the fair value of the investment was determined if the investment is carried at fair value), and the exchange gains or losses on the retranslation of the associated foreign currency borrowings at each period end would be recorded in profit or loss.
Disposal of a foreign operation	On disposal of a foreign operation, the exchange differences relating to that foreign operation that have been accumulated in the separate component of equity are not recognised in profit and loss. The cumulative exchange differences are transferred directly to retained earnings on disposal.	On disposal of a foreign operation, the exchange differences relating to that foreign operation that have been accumulated in the separate component of equity are not recognised in profit and loss.	Exchange differences arising on translation of a foreign operation that have been accumulated in equity are reclassified to profit and loss on disposal of the net investment.

Chapter 26   Hyperinflation

Chapter 26

Chapter 26   Hyperinflation

1   INTRODUCTION

1.1   The concept of hyperinflation

Accounting standards are applied on the assumption that the value of money (the unit of measurement) is constant over time, which normally is an acceptable practical assumption. However, when the effect of inflation on the value of money is no longer negligible, the usefulness of historical cost based financial reporting is often significantly reduced. High rates of inflation give rise to a number of problems for entities that prepare their financial statements on a historical cost basis, for example:

- historical cost figures expressed in terms of monetary units do not show the value to the business of assets;

- holding gains on non-monetary assets that are reported as operating profits do not represent real economic gains;

- financial information presented for the current period is not comparable with that presented for the prior periods; and

- real capital can be reduced because profits reported do not take account of the higher replacement costs of resources used in the period. Therefore, if calculating a nominal return on capital based on profit, and not distinguishing this properly from a real return of capital, the erosion of capital may go unnoticed in the financial statements. This is the underlying point in the concept of capital maintenance.

For entities used to working in economies with low inflation it is easy to overlook that there are countries where inflation is still a major economic concern. In some of these countries, inflation has reached such levels that (1) the local currency is no longer a useful measure of value in the economy and (2) the general population may prefer not to hold its wealth in the local currency. Instead, they hold their wealth in a stable foreign currency or non-monetary assets. Such a condition is often referred to as hyperinflation.

1.2   Relevance in the UK

FRS 102 Section 31 – *Hyperinflation* – sets out the accounting requirements for an entity that has a functional currency which is the currency of a hyperinflationary economy. It requires such an entity to prepare financial statements that have been adjusted for the effects of hyperinflation. *[FRS 102.31.1].*

The UK clearly does not suffer from hyperinflation, but it would be theoretically possible, although extremely unlikely, for a UK company to have the functional currency of a hyperinflationary economy. In that case, the requirements of Section 31 would apply in full to the accounting and disclosures in that company's own financial statements.

A more likely scenario would be that of a UK based group preparing consolidated financial statements under FRS 102 with a subsidiary that operates in, and has a functional currency of, a country subject to hyperinflation.

In this case, FRS 102 Section 30 – *Foreign Currency Translation* – requires the subsidiary's results and financial position to be adjusted using the procedures specified in Section 31 before applying the procedures in Section 30 to translate them into the group's presentation currency for the consolidated financial statements. *[FRS 102.30.21].*

However, *prima facie*, Section 30 explicitly excludes hyperinflationary operations from the scope of the procedures used to translate entities' financial statements into the group's presentation currency for the consolidated financial statements. *[FRS 102.30.18].*

In the absence of clear requirements in Section 30 it may be appropriate, using the hierarchy in Section 10 – *Accounting Policies, Estimates and Errors*, to follow the requirements in IAS 21 – *The Effects of Changes in Foreign Exchange Rates*. In these circumstances, IAS 21 requires assets, liabilities, equity items, income and expenses of the foreign operation to be translated into the group's presentation currency at the closing rate at the date of the most recent statement of financial position. However, comparative amounts should be those that were presented as current year amounts in the relevant prior year financial statements (i.e. not adjusted for subsequent changes in the price level or subsequent changes in exchange rates as they would be in the operation's own financial statements – see 3.3 below). *[IAS 21.42].*

2   COMPARISON BETWEEN SECTION 31, PREVIOUS UK GAAP AND IFRS

There are differences between the accounting and disclosure requirements in Section 31 compared to previous UK GAAP (either FRS 24 – *Financial reporting in hyperinflationary economies* – or UITF 9 – *Accounting for Operations in hyper-inflationary Economies*) and IFRS (IAS 29 – *Financial Reporting in Hyperinflationary Economies*). The key ones are discussed below.

2.1 Key differences to previous UK GAAP

If an entity applied FRS 26 – *Financial instruments: recognition and measurement* (e.g. because it was listed on an EU regulated market) then FRS 24 would have been applied which is identical to IAS 29 (see 2.2 below).

If an entity did not apply FRS 26 then UITF 9 would have applied (along with SSAP 20 – *Foreign currency translation*). UITF 9 explains that adjustments are required where the effects of hyperinflation would affect the true and fair view of the financial statements. Adjustments would always be necessary where the cumulative inflation rate over three years is approaching, or exceeds, 100 per cent and the operation in the hyperinflationary economy is material. In contrast, Section 31 suggests that a cumulative inflation rate over three years approaching, or exceeding, 100 per cent is merely an indicator of hyperinflation that needs considering with other factors to determine whether adjustment is necessary (see 3.2 below). UITF 9 normally allows the effects of hyperinflation in a given subsidiary to be adjusted by one of two methods: either using current price levels before consolidation (in essence the same approach as Section 31) or by using a relatively stable currency as the deemed functional currency for the relevant subsidiary.

An entity that has previously applied the second option under UITF 9 (relatively stable currency) may experience some adjustments on transition to FRS 102.

2.2 Key differences to IFRS

There is little substantive difference between the principles in IAS 29 and Section 31, although IAS 29 contains more application guidance.

3 REQUIREMENTS OF SECTION 31 FOR HYPERINFLATION

3.1 Terms used in Section 31

The key terms used within Section 31 have the meanings specified in the following table: *[FRS 102 Appendix I]*

Term	Definition
Functional currency	The currency of the primary economic environment in which the entity operates
Monetary items	Units of currency held and assets and liabilities to be received or paid in a fixed or determinable number of units of currency
Presentation currency	The currency in which the financial statements are presented.

3.2   A hyperinflationary economy

Section 31 does not establish an absolute level at which an economy is deemed hyperinflationary. An entity should make that judgement by considering all available information including, but not limited to, the following possible indicators of hyperinflation: *[FRS 102.31.2]*

(a)   The general population prefers to keep its wealth in non-monetary assets or in a relatively stable foreign currency. Amounts of local currency held are immediately invested to maintain purchasing power.

(b)   The general population regards monetary amounts not in terms of the local currency but in terms of a relatively stable foreign currency. Prices may be quoted in that currency.

(c)   Sales and purchases on credit take place at prices that compensate for the expected loss of purchasing power during the credit period, even if the period is short.

(d)   Interest rates, wages and prices are linked to a price index.

(e)   The cumulative inflation rate over three years is approaching, or exceeds, 100 per cent.

3.3   Measuring unit in the financial statements

Section 31 requires that amounts in the financial statements of an entity whose functional currency is the currency of a hyperinflationary economy should be stated in terms of the measuring unit current at the end of the reporting period. The comparative information in those financial statements for the previous period required by Section 3 – *Financial Statement Presentation*, paragraph 14, and any information presented in respect of earlier periods, should also be stated in terms of the measuring unit current at the reporting date. *[FRS 102.31.3]*.

The restatement of financial statements in accordance with Section 31 requires the use of a general price index that reflects changes in general purchasing power. Section 31 says that in most economies there is a recognised general price index, normally produced by the government, which entities will follow. *[FRS 102.31.4]*.

However, as noted below, in more extreme cases of hyperinflation such indices may not be available, especially if the prevailing circumstances that led to hyperinflation significantly impact the operation of governmental and/or social systems.

Section 31 provides no further guidance on what is meant by a general price index. It is generally accepted practice to use a Consumer Price Index (CPI) for this purpose, unless that index is clearly flawed. National statistical offices in most countries issue several price indices that potentially could be used for the purposes of Section 31. Important characteristics of a good general price index include the following:

- a wide range of goods and services has been included in the price index;
- continuity and consistency of measurement techniques and underlying assumptions;
- free from bias;
- frequently updated; and
- available for a long period.

The entity should assess the above characteristics and select the most reliable and most readily available general price index and use that index consistently. It is important that the index selected is representative of the real position of the hyperinflationary currency concerned.

If the general price index is not available for all periods for which the restatement of long-lived assets is required, guidance is provided in IAS 29 which requires an entity to make an estimate of the price index. The entity could base the estimate, for example, on the movements in the exchange rate between the functional currency and a relatively stable foreign currency. *[IAS 29.17]*.

It should be noted that this method is only acceptable if the currency of the hyperinflationary economy is freely exchangeable, i.e. not subject to currency controls and 'official' exchange rates. Entities should be mindful that, especially in the short term, the exchange rate may fluctuate significantly in response to factors other than changes in the domestic price level.

Entities could use a similar approach when they cannot find a general price index that is sufficiently reliable (e.g. if the national statistical office in the hyperinflationary economy is subject to significant political bias). However, this would only be acceptable if all available general price indices are fatally flawed.

3.4 Procedures for restating historical cost financial statements

3.4.1 Statement of financial position

Amounts in the statement of financial position that are not expressed in terms of the measuring unit current at the end of the reporting period are restated by applying a general price index. *[FRS 102.31.5]*.

Monetary items (money held and items to be received or paid in money) are not restated because they are expressed in terms of the measuring unit current at the end of the reporting period. *[FRS 102.31.6]*.

Assets and liabilities linked by agreement to changes in prices, such as index-linked bonds and loans, are adjusted in accordance with the agreement and presented at this adjusted amount in the restated statement of financial position. *[FRS 102.31.7]*.

All other assets and liabilities are non-monetary: *[FRS 102.31.8]*

(a) Some non-monetary items are carried at amounts current at the end of the reporting period, such as net realisable value and fair value, so they are not restated. All other non-monetary assets and liabilities are restated.

(b) Most non-monetary items are carried at cost or cost less depreciation; hence they are expressed at amounts current at their date of acquisition. The restated cost, or cost less depreciation, of each item is determined by applying to its historical cost and accumulated depreciation the change in a general price index from the date of acquisition to the end of the reporting period.

(c) The restated amount of a non-monetary item is reduced, in accordance with Section 27 – *Impairment of Assets* (see Chapter 22), when it exceeds its recoverable amount.

Chapter 26

At the beginning of the first period of application of Section 31, the components of equity, except retained earnings, are restated by applying a general price index from the dates the components were contributed or otherwise arose. Restated retained earnings are derived from all the other amounts in the restated statement of financial position. *[FRS 102.31.9].*

At the end of the first period and in subsequent periods, all components of owners' equity are restated by applying a general price index from the beginning of the period or the date of contribution, if later. The changes for the period in owners' equity are disclosed in accordance with Section 6 – *Statement of Changes in Equity and Statement of Income and Retained Earnings.*(see Chapter 4). *[FRS 102.31.10].*

3.4.2   Statement of comprehensive income and income statement

All items in the statement of comprehensive income (and in the income statement, if presented) should be expressed in terms of the measuring unit current at the end of the reporting period. Therefore, all amounts need to be restated by applying the change in the general price index from the dates when the items of income and expenses were initially recognised in the financial statements. If general inflation is approximately even throughout the period, and the items of income and expense arose approximately evenly throughout the period, an average rate of inflation may be appropriate. *[FRS 102.31.11].*

3.4.3   Statement of cash flows

An entity should express all items in the statement of cash flows in terms of the measuring unit current at the end of the reporting period. *[FRS 102.31.12].*

3.4.4   Gain or loss on net monetary position

In a period of inflation, an entity holding an excess of monetary assets over monetary liabilities loses purchasing power, and an entity with an excess of monetary liabilities over monetary assets gains purchasing power, to the extent the assets and liabilities are not linked to a price level. An entity should therefore include in profit or loss the gain or loss on the net monetary position. An entity should offset the adjustment to those assets and liabilities linked by agreement to changes in prices (see 3.4.1 above) against the gain or loss on net monetary position. *[FRS 102.31.13].*

3.4.5   Economies ceasing to be hyperinflationary

When an economy ceases to be hyperinflationary and an entity discontinues the application of Section 31, it should treat the amounts expressed in the presentation currency at the end of the previous reporting period as the basis for the carrying amounts in its subsequent financial statements. *[FRS 102.31.14].*

3.5   Disclosures

An entity which applies Section 31 in its own financial statements should disclose the following: *[FRS 102.31.15]*

(a)   the fact that financial statements and other prior period data have been restated for changes in the general purchasing power of the functional currency;

(b)   the identity and level of the price index at the reporting date and changes during the current reporting period and the previous reporting period; and

(c)   the amount of gain or loss on monetary items.

Chapter 27   Events after the end of the reporting period

List of examples

Chapter 27   Events after the end of the reporting period

1   INTRODUCTION

Section 32 – *Events after the End of the Reporting Period* – defines events after the end of the reporting period and sets out principles for recognising, measuring and disclosing those events that occur between the end of the reporting period and the date when the financial statements are authorised for issue. *[FRS 102.32.1, 2].* The definition includes all events occurring between those dates irrespective of whether they relate to conditions that existed at the end of the reporting period. The principal issue is determining which events after the reporting date to reflect in the financial statements.

2   COMPARISON BETWEEN SECTION 32, PREVIOUS UK GAAP AND IFRS

There are no key differences between Section 32 and the comparable previous UK GAAP standard, FRS 21 – *Events after the balance sheet date* – and the comparable IFRS standard, IAS 10 – *Events after the Reporting Period.*

3   REQUIREMENTS OF SECTION 32 FOR EVENTS AFTER THE END OF THE REPORTING PERIOD

The following key term in Section 32 is defined in the Glossary: *[FRS 102 Appendix I]*

Reporting period is the period covered by financial statements or by an interim financial report.

The following timeline of an entity with a 31 December reporting date illustrates events after the end of the reporting period that are within the scope of Section 32:

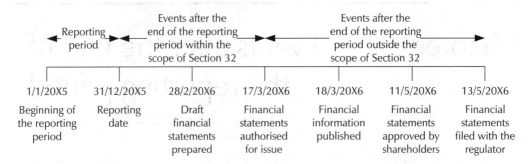

The financial statements of an entity present, among other things, an entity's financial position at the end of the reporting period. Therefore, it is appropriate to adjust the financial statements for all events that offer greater clarity concerning the conditions that existed at the end of the reporting period, that occur prior to the date the financial statements are authorised for issue. Section 32 requires entities to adjust the amounts recognised in the financial statements for 'adjusting events' that provide evidence of conditions that existed at the end of the reporting period. *[FRS 102.32.4].* An entity does not recognise in the financial statements those events that relate to conditions that arose after the reporting period, 'non-adjusting events'. However, if non-adjusting events are material, Section 32 requires certain disclosures about them. *[FRS 102.32.6, 10].*

Section 32 deals with the accounting for and the disclosure of events after the reporting period, which are defined as 'those events, favourable and unfavourable, that occur between the end of the reporting period and the date when the financial statements are authorised for issue'. *[FRS 102.32.2].* The definition includes all events that provide evidence of conditions that existed at the end of the reporting period (adjusting events) and those events that are indicative of conditions that arose after the end of the reporting period (non-adjusting events).

Events after the end of the reporting period include all events that occur up to the date the financial statements are authorised for issue, even if those events occur after the public announcement of profit or loss or other financial information. *[FRS 102.32.3].*

One exception to the general rule of Section 32 for non-adjusting events is when the going concern basis becomes inappropriate. This is treated as an adjusting event (see 3.3 below0. *[FRS 102.32.7A].*

The requirements of Section 32 and practical issues resulting from these requirements are dealt with below.

3.1   Date when financial statements are authorised for issue

Given the definition above, the meaning of 'the date when the financial statements are authorised for issue' is clearly important. Section 32 states that events after the end of the reporting period including all events up to the date that the financial statements are authorised for issue, even if those events occur after the public announcement of profit or loss or other selected financial information. *[FRS 102.32.3]*.

The example below illustrates a situation when an entity releases preliminary information, but not a complete set financial statements, before the date of the authorisation for issue.

Example 27.1:   Release of financial information before date of authorisation for issue

The management of an entity completes the primary financial statements (e.g. statement of financial position, statement of comprehensive income, statement of cash flows and statement of changes in equity) for the year to 31 December 20X5 on 21 January 20X6, but has not yet completed the explanatory notes. On 26 January 20X6, the board of directors (which includes management and non-executives) reviews the primary financial statements and authorises them for public media release. The entity announces its profit and certain other financial information on 28 January 20X6. On 1 February 20X6 an error is discovered in the year-end stock valuation of £1m. On 11 February 20X6, management issues the financial statements (with full explanatory notes) to the board of directors, which approves the financial statements for filing on 18 February 20X6. The entity files the financial statements with a regulatory body on 21 February 20X6.

The financial statements are authorised for issue on 18 February 20X6 (date the board of directors, approves the financial statements for filing). Therefore, the error discovered in the year-end stock valuation on 1 February 20X6, before the financial statements have been authorised for issue, is an adjusting event after the end of the reporting period which must be reflected, if material, in the 31 December 20X5 financial statements (see 3.2.1 below).

Accordingly, as illustrated above in Example 27.1, the information in the financial statements might differ from the equivalent information in a preliminary announcement.

3.2   Recognition and measurement of events occurring after the end of the reporting period

3.2.1   Adjusting events

Adjusting events are 'those that provide evidence of conditions that existed at the end of the reporting period.' *[FRS 102.32.2(a)]*. An entity shall adjust the amounts recognised in its financial statements, including any related disclosures, to reflect adjusting events. *[FRS 102.32.4]*.

The following are examples of adjusting events after the end of the reporting period that require amounts in the financial statements to be adjusted or to recognise items that were not previously recognised: *[FRS 102.32.5(a)-(e)]*

- The settlement after the end of a reporting period of a court case that confirms that the entity had a present obligation at the end of the reporting period. In this situation, an entity adjusts any previously recognised provision related to this court case under Section 21 – *Provisions and Contingencies* – or recognises a new provision. Mere disclosure of a contingent liability is not sufficient because the settlement provides additional evidence of conditions that existed at the end of the reporting period that would give rise to a provision in accordance with Section 21 (see Chapter 17).

- The receipt of information after the end of the reporting period indicating that an asset was impaired at the end of the reporting period, or that the amount of a previously recognised impairment loss for that asset needs to be adjusted. For example:

    - the bankruptcy of a customer that occurs after the end of the reporting period usually confirms that a loss existed at the end of the reporting period on a trade receivable and that the entity needs to adjust the carrying amount of the trade receivable; and

    - the sale of inventories after the end of the reporting period may give evidence about their selling price at the end of the reporting period for the purpose of assessing impairment at that date.

- The determination after the end of the reporting period of the cost of assets purchased, or the proceeds from assets sold, before the end of the reporting period.

- The determination after the end of the reporting period of the amount of profit-sharing or bonus payments, if the entity had a legal or constructive obligation at the end of the reporting period to make such payments as a result of events before that date.

- The discovery of fraud or errors that show that the financial statements are incorrect (see 4.5 below).

In addition, those entities that apply IAS 33 – *Earnings per Share* – as permitted by Section 1 – *Scope* – are required to make adjustments to earnings per share for certain share transactions after the reporting period (such as bonus issues, share splits or share consolidations), even though the transactions themselves are non-adjusting events (see 3.2.2 below).

3.2.2   *Non-adjusting events*

Non-adjusting events are 'those that are indicative of conditions that arose after the end of the reporting period'. *[FRS 102.32.2(b)]*. An entity shall not adjust the amounts recognised in its financial statements to reflect non-adjusting events. *[FRS 102.32.6]*.

Examples of non-adjusting events are as follows: *[FRS 102.32.7]*

- a decline in market value of investments between the end of the reporting period and the date when the financial statements are authorised for issue. A decline in market value does not normally relate to the condition of the investments at the end of the reporting period but reflects circumstances that have arisen subsequent to the end of the reporting period; or

- an amount that becomes receivable as a result of a settlement of a court case after the reporting date but before the financial statements are authorised for issue. This would be a contingent asset at the reporting date (see Section 21 – *Provisions and Contingencies* and Chapter 17) and disclosure may be required. However, if an agreement is reached before the reporting date, on the amount of damages that was not previously recognised on the basis it could not be measured reliably, this may constitute an adjusting event.

The following are further examples of non-adjusting events after the end of the reporting period that would generally result in disclosure. The disclosures will reflect information that becomes known after the end of the reporting period but before the financial statements are authorised for issue: *[FRS 102.32.11]*

- a major business combination or disposal of a major subsidiary (Section 19 – *Business Combinations and Goodwill* – does not require any specific disclosures in respect of business combinations occurring after the reporting date);
- announcing a plan to discontinue an operation;
- major purchases of assets, disposal or plans to dispose of assets, or expropriation of major assets by governments;
- the destruction of a major production plant by a fire;
- announcing, or commencing the implementation of a major restructuring;
- the issue or repurchase of an entity's debt or equity instruments;
- abnormally large changes in asset prices or foreign exchange rates;
- changes in tax rates or the enactment or announcement of tax laws that significantly affect current and deferred tax assets and liabilities;
- entering into significant commitments or contingent liabilities, for example, by issuing significant guarantees; and
- commencing major litigation arising solely out of events that occurred after the end of the reporting period.

3.3   Going concern

If management determines after the reporting period either that it intends to liquidate the entity or to cease trading, or that it has no realistic alternative but to do so, the financial statements should not be prepared on the going concern basis. *[FRS 102.32.7A].*

Deterioration in operating results and financial position after the reporting period may indicate a need to consider whether the going concern assumption is still appropriate. If the going concern assumption is no longer appropriate, Section 32 states that the effect is so pervasive that it results in a fundamental change in the basis of accounting, rather than an adjustment to the amounts recognised within the original basis of accounting. *[FRS 102.32.7B].*

Section 3 – *Financial Statement Presentation* – contains guidance and specific disclosure requirements when the financial statements are not prepared on a going concern basis or when there are uncertainties that cast significant doubt upon an entity's ability to continue as a going concern – see Chapter 4.

3.4   Dividends

Dividends declared by an entity to holders of its equity instruments after the end of the reporting period are not adjusting events as no obligation exists at the end of the reporting period. However, although dividends declared after the reporting date are not liabilities, entities may present the amount of dividends declared after the end of the reporting period, as a segregated component of retained earnings. *[FRS 102.32.8].*

Chapter 27

This allows entities to show the amount of retained earnings that are set aside for future dividends, as at the date the financial statements are authorised for issue.

The accounting for dividends in FRS 102 reflects the legal status of dividends under the Companies Act 2006. ICAEW/ICAS Technical Release 02/10 – *Guidance on the Determination of Realised Profits and Losses in the Context of Distributions under the Companies Act 2006* (TECH 02/10) states that a distribution is made when it becomes a legally binding liability of the company, regardless of the date on which it is to be settled. In the case of a final dividend, this is when it is declared by the company in a general meeting or, for private companies, by the members passing a general resolution. In the case of interim dividends authorised under common articles of association, normally no legally binding liability is established prior to payment being made. In such cases, dividends are normally recognised when they are paid although Tech 02/10 also provides guidance in determining whether an interim dividend is a legally binding liability at a date earlier than when payment is made. *[TECH 02/10.2.10].*

The examples of non-adjusting events illustrated at 3.2.2 above do not include declared dividends. However, the Companies Act requires disclosure of any dividends proposed before the date of approval of the financial statements (see 3.5.4 below).

3.5   Disclosures

Section 32 does not require any disclosures in respect of adjusting events as disclosures of such transactions follow the applicable sections in FRS 102 since the financial statements reflect such transactions.

3.5.1   Date when financial statements are authorised for issue

An entity shall disclose the date when the financial statements were authorised for issue and who authorised the financial statements for issue. If the owners of the entity, or others, have the power to amend the financial statements after issue, disclosure of that fact is required. *[FRS 102.32.9].*

3.5.2   Non-adjusting events

An entity shall disclose the following for each category of non-adjusting events after the end of the reporting period: *[FRS 102.32.10]*

- the nature of the event; and
- an estimate of its financial effect, or a statement that such an estimate cannot be made.

Examples of non-adjusting events after the end of the reporting period that would generally result in disclosures are provided at 3.2.2 above.

3.5.3   Breach of a long-term loan covenant and its subsequent rectification

The subsequent rectification of the breach or default of a loan payable, or the renegotiation of the terms of the loan is not an adjusting event and therefore does not change the classification of the liability in the statement of financial position from current to non-current.

When a breach or default of a loan payable exists at the reporting date, an entity shall disclose, whether the breach or default was remedied, or the terms of the loan payable was renegotiated, before the financial statements were authorised for issue. *[FRS 102.11.47(c)]*. These disclosures are not required for qualifying entities that are non-financial institutions.

3.5.4 Additional Companies Act 2006 disclosure requirements in respect of reserves and dividends

The Large and Medium-sized Companies and Groups (Accounts and Reports) Regulations 2008 (SI 2008/410) (the Regulations) requires the following disclosures in respect of reserves and dividends intended to be distributed after the reporting period:

- any amount set aside or proposed to be set aside to, or withdrawn, or proposed to be withdrawn from, reserves; and

- the aggregate amount of dividends that are proposed before the date of approval of the financial statements. *[1 Sch 43, 2 Sch 56, 3 Sch 64]*.

4. PRACTICAL IMPLEMENTATION ISSUES

Section 32 alludes to practical issues such as those discussed below. It states that a decline in fair value of investments after the reporting period does not *normally* relate to conditions at the end of the reporting period (see 3.2.2 above). At the same time, Section 32 asserts that the bankruptcy of a customer that occurs after the reporting period *usually* confirms that a loss on a trade receivable existed at the end of the reporting period (see 3.2.1 above). Judgement of the facts and circumstances is required to determine whether an event that occurs after the reporting period provides evidence about a condition that existed at the end of the reporting period, or whether the condition arose subsequent to the reporting period.

4.1 Valuation of inventory

The sale of inventories after the reporting period is normally a good indicator of their selling price at that date. Section 32 states that such sales 'may give evidence about their selling price at the end of the reporting period' (see 3.2.1 above). However, in some cases, selling prices decrease because of conditions that did not exist at the end of the reporting period.

Therefore, the problem is determining why a selling price decreased. Did it decrease because of circumstances that existed at the end of the reporting period, which subsequently became known, or did it decrease because of circumstances that arose subsequently? A decrease in price is merely a response to changing conditions so it is important to assess the reasons for these changes.

Chapter 27

Some examples of changing conditions are as follows:

- Price reductions caused by a sudden increase in cheap imports:

  Whilst it is arguable that the 'dumping' of cheap imports after the reporting period is a condition that arises subsequent to that date, it is more likely that this is a reaction to a condition that already existed such as overproduction in other parts of the world. Thus, it might be more appropriate in such a situation to adjust the value of inventories based on its subsequent selling price.

- Price reductions caused by increased competition:

  The reasons for price reductions and increased competition do not generally arise overnight but normally occur over a period. For example, a competitor may have built up a competitive advantage by investing in machinery that is more efficient. In these circumstances, it is appropriate for an entity to adjust the valuation of its inventories because its own investment in production machinery is inferior to its competitor's and this situation existed at the end of the reporting period.

- Price reductions caused by the introduction of an improved competitive product:

  It is unlikely that a competitor developed and introduced an improved product overnight. Therefore, it is correct to adjust the valuation of inventories to their selling price after that introduction because the entity's failure to maintain its competitive position in relation to product improvements that existed at the end of the reporting period.

Competitive pressures that cause a decrease in selling price after the reporting period are generally additional evidence of conditions that developed over a period and existed at the end of the reporting period. Consequently, their effects normally require adjustment in the financial statements.

However, for certain types of inventory, there is clear evidence of a price at the end of the reporting period and it is inappropriate to adjust the price of that inventory to reflect a subsequent decline. An example is inventories for which there is a price on an appropriate commodities market. In addition, inventory may be physically damaged or destroyed after the reporting period (e.g. by fire, flood, or other disaster). In these cases, the entity does not adjust the financial statements. However, the entity may be required to disclose the subsequent decline in selling price of the inventories if the impact is material (see 3.2.2 above).

4.2   Percentage of completion estimates

Events after the reporting period frequently give evidence about the profitability of construction contracts (or other contracts for which revenue is recognised using a percentage of completion method) that are in progress at the end of the reporting period.

Section 23 – *Revenue* – requires an assessment to be made as of the end of the reporting period, of the outcome of a construction contract to recognise revenue and expenses under the percentage of completion method (see Chapter 18). *[FRS 102.23.17]*. In such an assessment, consideration should be given to events that occur after the reporting period and a determination should be made as to whether they are adjusting or non-adjusting events for which the financial effect is included in the percentage of completion calculation.

4.3 Insolvency of a debtor

The insolvency of a debtor or inability to pay debts usually builds up over a period. Consequently, if a debtor has an amount outstanding at the end of the reporting period and this amount is written off because of information received after the reporting period, the event is normally adjusting. Section 32 states that the 'bankruptcy of a customer that occurs after the end of the reporting period usually confirms that a loss existed at the end of the reporting period' (see 3.2.1 above). If, however, there is evidence to show that the insolvency of the debtor resulted solely from an event occurring after the reporting period, then the event is a non-adjusting event. However if the impact is material, the entity may be required to disclose the impact of the debtor's default.

4.4 Valuation of investment property at fair value and tenant insolvency

The fair value of investment property reflects, among other things, the quality of tenants' covenants and the future rental income from the property. If a tenant ceases to be able to meet its lease obligations due to insolvency after the reporting period, an entity considers how this event is reflected in the valuation at the end of the reporting period.

In addition, professional valuations generally reference the state of the market at the date of valuation without the use of hindsight. Consequently, the insolvency of a tenant is not normally an adjusting event to the fair value of the investment property because the investment property still holds value in the market. However, it would generally be indicative of an adjusting event for any amounts due from the tenant at the end of the reporting period.

Section 32 states that 'a decline in market value of investments between the end of the reporting period and the date when the financial statements are authorised for issue' is a non-adjusting event, as the decline does not normally relate to a condition at the end of the reporting period (see 3.2.2 above). This decline in fair value, however, may be required to be disclosed if material.

4.5 Discovery of fraud after the end of the reporting period

When fraud is discovered after the reporting date the implications on the financial statements should be considered. In particular it should be determined whether the fraud is indicative of a prior period error, and that financial information should be requested, or merely a change of estimate requiring prospective adjustment. Application of the definitions of a prior period error and a change in accounting policy included in Section 10 – *Accounting Policies, Estimates and Errors* – requires judgement in the case of a fraud. The facts and circumstances should be evaluated to determine if the discovery of fraud resulted from previous failure to use, or misuse of, reliable information; or from new information. If the fraud meets the definition of a prior period error, the fraud would be an adjusting event as it relates to conditions that existed at the end of the reporting period. However, if the fraud meets the definition of a change in estimate, the application of Section 32 is required to determine whether financial information is required to be adjusted, or whether disclosure is sufficient. The facts and circumstances are

Chapter 27

evaluated to determine if the fraud provides evidence of circumstances that existed at the end of the reporting period or circumstances that arose after that date. Determining this is a complex task and requires judgement and careful consideration of the specifics to each case.

Chapter 28

Related party disclosures

List of examples

Chapter 28 — Related party disclosures

1 INTRODUCTION

Section 33 – *Related Party Disclosures* – requires an entity to include in its financial statements the disclosures necessary to draw attention to the possibility that its financial position and profit or loss have been affected by the existence of related parties and by transactions and outstanding balances with such entities. *[FRS 102.33.1]*.

Section 33 requires disclosures only. It does not establish any recognition or measurement requirements. Related party transactions are accounted for in accordance with the requirements of the section of FRS 102 applicable to the transaction. The disclosures required by Section 33 are in addition to those required by other sections. For example, a loan to a related party will also be subject to the disclosure requirements of Section 11 – *Basic Financial Instruments*.

1.1 Scope of Section 33

Section 33 applies to all financial statements that are required by FRS 102 including both group and individual financial statements. However, disclosure is not required:

- in consolidated financial statements, of any transactions or balances between group entities that have been eliminated on consolidation (see 1.1.1 below); and

- of *transactions* entered into between two members of a group, provided that any subsidiary which is a party to the transaction is wholly owned by such a member (see 1.1.2 below). *[FRS 102.33.1A]*.

1.1.1 Transactions eliminated on consolidation

Although Section 33 does not specifically include a paragraph stating that intra-group transactions eliminated on consolidation are not required to be disclosed in the consolidated financial statements of an entity, this is not so much an exemption as a statement of the obvious since, so far as the group accounts are concerned, such items do not exist. The effect is that no related party disclosures relating to subsidiary undertakings are required in group accounts. However, disclosure is still required in respect of transactions or balances with associates or joint ventures since these are not 'eliminated' on consolidation, although they may be subject to consolidation adjustments.

1.1.2   *Transactions between wholly-owned subsidiaries*

The wording of this exemption (which is not entirely clear) is identical to that contained previously in FRS 8 – *Related party disclosures. [FRS 8.3(c)].* However, Section 33 does not carry over the guidance contained in paragraph 38 of Appendix IV of FRS 8 which interprets this to mean that all subsidiary undertakings which are a party to the transaction must be wholly owned, directly or indirectly, by the ultimate controlling entity of the group (rather than interpreting the 'wholly owned' criterion to apply only to the sub-group which includes the entities (members) involved in the transaction).

The application of the exemption as interpreted in the guidance contained in paragraph 38 of Appendix IV of FRS 8 is illustrated in the following example.

Example 28.1:   Application of the exemption from disclosure of transactions between wholly-owned subsidiary undertakings

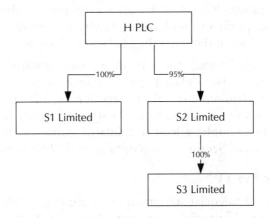

Because H PLC only owns 95% of S2 Limited, the wholly owned subsidiaries exemption cannot be used in (a) the individual company financial statements of H PLC in respect of transactions with S2 Limited and S3 Limited, (b) the consolidated and/or individual financial statements of S2 Limited in respect of any transactions with H PLC, S1 Limited or S3 Limited, (c) the financial statements of S3 Limited in respect of any transactions with H PLC, S1 Limited or S2 Limited, and (d) the financial statements of S1 Limited in respect of transactions with S2 Limited and S3 Limited. The exemption is available for transactions between S1 Limited and H PLC in the individual financial statements of these companies.

The exemption has no other conditions. Therefore, it can be applied, for example, even if the group does not prepare consolidated financial statements.

The Accounting Council's advice to the Financial Reporting Council clarifies that this exemption applies only to transactions between wholly owned subsidiary undertakings and not to outstanding balances between those entities. This is because the exemption derives from Company Law which does not provide an exemption from the disclosure of balances with group undertakings. *[FRS 102.AC.93].*

2 COMPARISON BETWEEN SECTION 33, PREVIOUS UK GAAP AND IFRS

Section 33 has the same definition of a 'related party' as FRS 8 and the same definition as IAS 24 – *Related Party Disclosures* – prior to the amendment issued in December 2013 as part of the *Annual Improvements to IFRSs 2010-2012 Cycle*. However, there are differences between Section 33 and both standards in respect of the disclosures that are required.

2.1 Principal differences between Section 33 and previous UK GAAP

The principal differences between Section 33 and FRS 8 are in respect of:

- disclosure of pension contributions (see 2.1.1 below);
- disclosure of key management personnel compensation (see 2.1.2 below);
- the use of a 'confidentiality' exemption (see 2.1.3 below);
- State-related parties (see 2.1.4 below); and
- aggregation of disclosures (see 2.1.5 below).

In summary, unless a reporting entity is controlled, jointly controlled or significantly influenced by a State, the disclosure requirements of Section 33 are likely to be slightly more onerous than those of FRS 8.

2.1.1 Disclosure of pension contributions

Section 33 does not have an exemption from disclosure of pensions contributions paid into a pension fund as a related party transaction.

FRS 8 did have such an exemption, *[FRS 8.3(d)]*, presumably because the information was already required to be disclosed for both defined contribution and defined benefit plans under FRS 17 – *Retirement benefits*. However, disclosure of amounts 'paid' to either a defined contribution or defined benefit plan is not required specifically by Section 28 – *Employee Benefits*.

2.1.2 Disclosure of key management personnel compensation

Section 33 requires an entity to disclose key management personnel compensation in total. *[FRS 101.33.7]*. This disclosure is in addition to any Company Law disclosures required in respect of directors' remuneration (see section 3.2.4 below).

FRS 8 did not require disclosure of key management personnel compensation. *[FRS 8.3(e)]*.

2.1.3 The use of a 'confidentiality' exemption

Section 33 gives no exemption from disclosure on the grounds of confidentiality.

FRS 8 did not require any related party transaction to be disclosed where this conflicted with the reporting entity's duties of confidentiality arising by operation of law. However, this concession was aimed principally at banks and similar institutions and covered only those obligations imposed by a generally applicable statute or common law. *[FRS 8.16, Appendix 4.17]*.

2.1.4   *State-related parties*

Section 33 exempts an entity from disclosing information about related party transactions with a related party that is a state or another entity related because that same state has control, joint control or significant influence over it (see 3.2.3.C below).

FRS 8 had no similar exemption.

2.1.5   *Aggregation of disclosures*

Section 33 requires related party transactions to be disclosed separately for each of the following categories:

- entities with control, joint control or significant influence over the reporting entity;
- entities over which the entity has control, joint control or significant influence;
- key management personnel of the entity or its parent (in aggregate); and
- other related parties. *[FRS 102.33.10].*

FRS 8 did not require separate disclosures to be made for these categories. Instead, it stated that disclosures may be made on an aggregated basis (aggregated by similar transactions by type of related party) unless disclosure of an individual transaction, or connected transactions, is necessary for an understanding of the impact on the financial statements of the reporting entity or as required by law. *[FRS 8.6].*

2.2   Principal differences between Section 33 and IFRS

The principal differences between Section 33 and IAS 24 are in respect of:

- the provision of key management personnel services by an entity (see 2.2.1 below);
- the scope exemption for wholly-owned subsidiaries (see 2.2.2 below);
- the state-related exemption (see 2.2.3 below);
- disclosure of key management compensation (see 2.2.4 below);
- aggregation of disclosures (see 2.2.5 below); and
- disclosure of commitments (see 2.2.6 below).

In summary, the disclosure requirements of Section 33 are less onerous to a reporting entity than those of IAS 24.

2.2.1   *The provision of key management personnel services by an entity*

Section 33 is silent as to whether an entity that provides key management personnel services to a reporting entity is a related party. It also does not state whether employees of a management entity that provides key management personnel services should be regarded as key management personnel (see 3.1.1.B below).

IAS 24 was amended in December 2013 to clarify that if an entity receives key management personnel services from another entity (described as a 'management entity') the reporting entity is not required to apply the disclosure requirements for key management personnel compensation to the compensation paid or payable by the management entity to the management entity's employees or directors. *[IAS 24.17A]*. Instead, overall amounts incurred by the entity for provision of key management personnel services by the separate management entity are disclosed. *[IAS 24.18A]*.

2.2.2 Scope exemption for wholly-owned subsidiaries

Section 33 has an exemption from disclosure of transactions entered into between two members of a group, provided that any subsidiary which is a party to the transaction is wholly-owned by such a member (see 1.1.2 above). IAS 24 does not have such an exemption.

2.2.3 State-related exemption

Section 33 exempts an entity from disclosing information about related party transactions with a related party that is a state or another entity related because that same state has control, joint control or significant influence over it. See 3.2.3.C below.

IAS 24 has a similar but not identical exemption for government-related entities. However, the IAS 24 exemption is conditional on disclosure of (i) the nature and amount of each individually significant transaction; and (ii) for other transactions that are collectively, but not individually, significant, a qualitative or quantitative indication of their type. *[IAS 24.25-26]*. The exemption in Section 33 is not conditional on these additional disclosures.

2.2.4 Disclosure of key management compensation

Section 33 requires key management compensation to be disclosed only in total. *[FRS 102.33.7]*. However, directors' remuneration is subject to additional Company Law requirements (see 4.1 and 4.3 below).

IAS 24 requires key management compensation to be disclosed in total and also split between short-term employee benefits, post-employment benefits, other long-term benefits, termination benefits and share-based payment. *[IAS 24.17]*.

2.2.5 Aggregation of disclosures

Section 33 requires related party transactions to be made separately for the following categories in aggregate (a) entities with control, joint control or significant influence over the reporting entity; (b) entities over which the entity has control, joint control or significant influence (c) key management personnel of the entity or its parent (in aggregate); and (d) other related parties. *[FRS 102.33.10]*.

IAS 24 has a similar requirement but requires the disclosures to be made separately for seven categories instead of four. *[IAS 24.19]*.

2.2.6 Disclosure of commitments

Section 33 states that information about 'commitments' should be disclosed if necessary for an understanding of the potential effect of the related party relationship on the financial statements. *[FRS 102.33.9]*.

IAS 24 states explicitly that 'a commitment to do something if a particular event occurs or does not occur in the future, including executory contracts (recognised and unrecognised)' is a transaction requiring disclosure if it is with a related party. In addition, a commitment is listed as an example of a related party transaction requiring disclosure. *[IAS 24.21(i)].*

3   REQUIREMENTS OF SECTION 33 FOR RELATED PARTY DISCLOSURES

Section 33 defines a related party and then requires various disclosures of related party transactions, balances and relationships.

3.1   Definition of a related party

A related party is defined as 'a person or entity that is related to the entity that is preparing its financial statements (the reporting entity)'. *[FRS 102.33.2].*

Preparers should use this definition of 'related party' when applying concepts elsewhere in FRS 102 where this term or similar terms are used and not otherwise defined.

In considering each possible related party relationship, attention is directed to the substance of the relationship and not merely the legal form. *[FRS 102.33.3].*

A related party transaction is defined as 'a transfer of resources, services or obligations between a reporting entity and a related party regardless of whether a price is charged'. *[FRS 102.33.8].*

The following are considered to be related parties of the reporting entity:

- certain persons or a close member of that person's family (see 3.1.1 below);
- entities that are members of the same group (see 3.1.2 below);
- entities that are associates or joint ventures (see 3.1.3 below);
- entities that are joint ventures of the same third party (see 3.1.4 below);
- entities that are joint ventures and associates of the same third entity (see 3.1.5 below);
- post-employment benefit plans (see 3.1.6 below);
- entities under control or joint control of certain categories of persons or close members of such a person's family (see 3.1.7 below); and
- entities under significant influence of certain categories of persons or close members of such a person's family (see 3.1.8 below).

3.1.1   *Persons or close members of a person's family that are related parties*

A person or close member of that person's family is related to a reporting entity if that person: *[FRS 102.33.2(a)]*

(i)   has control or joint control over the reporting entity;

(ii)   has significant influence over the reporting entity; or

(iii)   is a member of the key management personnel of the reporting entity or of a parent of the reporting entity.

'Control', 'joint control' and 'significant influence' have the same meanings here as in Section 9 – *Consolidated and Separate Financial Statements*, Section 14 – *Investments in Associates* – and Section 15 – *Investments in Joint Ventures*.

3.1.1.A   Close members of a family

Close members of a family of a person are defined as 'those family members who may be expected to influence, or be influenced by, that person in their dealings with the entity' including *[FRS 102 Appendix I]*

(a)   that person's children and spouse or domestic partner;

(b)   children of that person's spouse or domestic partner; and

(c)   dependants of that person or that person's spouse or domestic partner.

The definition appears to provide no scope to argue that there are circumstances in which the specific family members described in (a) to (c) above are not related parties. Dependants are not limited to children and may include elderly or infirm parents. As well as those specific family members described in (a) to (c) above, the definition also applies to any other family members who may be expected to influence or be influenced by that person in their dealings with the reporting entity. For example, this may include parents, siblings or relatives that are even more distant.

3.1.1.B   Key management personnel

Key management personnel are those persons with authority and responsibility for planning, directing and controlling the activities of an entity, directly or indirectly, including any director (whether executive or otherwise) of that entity. *[FRS 102.33.6]*.

A related party includes all key management personnel of a reporting entity and of a parent of the reporting entity. This means that all key management personnel of all parents (i.e. the immediate parent, any intermediate parent and the ultimate parent) of a reporting entity are related parties of the reporting entity.

Some entities may have more than one level of key management. For example, some entities may have a supervisory board, whose members have responsibilities similar to those of non-executive directors, as well as a board of directors that sets the overall operating strategy. All members of either board will be considered to be key management personnel.

The definition of key management personnel is not restricted to directors. It also includes other individuals with authority and responsibility for planning, directing and controlling the activities of an entity. For example, a chief financial officer or a chief operating officer may not be directors but could meet the definition of key management personnel. Other examples of the type of persons who are not directors but may meet the definition of key management personnel include a divisional chief executive or a director of a major trading subsidiary of the entity, but not of the entity itself, who nevertheless participates in the management of the reporting entity. A reference to individuals who are not directors in a reporting entity's strategic review might indicate that those persons are considered to be key management personnel.

Key management personnel are normally employees of the reporting entity (or of another entity in the same group). However, the definition does not restrict itself to employees. Therefore, seconded staff and persons engaged under management or outsourcing contracts may also have a level of authority or responsibility such that they are key management personnel.

The definition of key management personnel refers to 'persons'. The term 'person' can include both a 'corporate person' and a 'natural person'. Additionally, in some situations, the responsible entity of funds or trusts (i.e. the body acting as key management personnel) must be a corporate entity and, by law, has the authority and responsibility for planning, directing and controlling the activities of the fund for the benefit of the fund's investors in accordance with the fund's constitution and relevant statutes. We therefore believe that the definition can include a corporate entity.

A further issue is whether staff acting for the corporate 'director' could be considered to be key management personnel of the reporting entity. Section 33 is silent on this matter. However, IAS 24, which otherwise has the same definition of a related party as Section 33, was amended in December 2013 to state that if a reporting entity obtains key management personnel services from another entity (described as a 'management entity') the reporting entity is not required to apply the disclosure requirements for key management personnel compensation (see 3.2.2 below) to the compensation paid or payable by the management entity to the management entity's employees or directors. Instead, overall amounts incurred by the entity for the provision of key management personnel services that are provided by the separate management entity are disclosed. Under the hierarchy for the selection and application of accounting policies in FRS 102 (see Chapter 7), management may consider the requirements and guidance in EU-adopted IFRS dealing with similar and related issues when FRS 102 does not specifically address the matter.

3.1.2   Entities that are members of the same group

'An entity is related to a reporting entity if:

> (i)   the entity and the reporting entity are members of the same group (which means that each parent, subsidiary and fellow subsidiary is related to the others).' *[FRS 102.33.2(b)(i)].*

'Parent' and 'subsidiary' have the same meanings as in Section 9. Therefore, all entities that are controlled by the same ultimate parent are related parties. This would include entities where the reporting entity holds less than a majority of the voting rights but which are still considered to be subsidiaries. There are no exceptions to this rule although transactions between wholly-owned subsidiaries are not required to be disclosed (see 1.1.2 above).

3.1.3   Entities that are associates or joint ventures

'An entity is related to a reporting entity if:

...

> (ii)   one entity is an associate or joint venture of the other entity (or an associate or joint venture of a member of a group of which the other entity is a member)'. *[FRS 102.33.2(b)(ii)].*

'Associate' and 'joint venture' have the same meanings as in Sections 14 and 15 respectively.

In the definition of a related party, an associate includes subsidiaries of the associate and a joint venture includes subsidiaries of the joint venture. Therefore, for example, an associate's subsidiary and the investor that has significant influence over the associate are related to each another. *[FRS 102.33.4A].*

The definition also means that an associate of a reporting entity's parent is also a related party of the reporting entity.

However, the definition does not cause investors in a joint venture to be related to each other (see 3.1.9 below).

3.1.4   Entities that are joint ventures of the same third party

'An entity is related to a reporting entity if:

...

> (iii)   both entities are joint ventures of the same third party'. *[FRS 102.33.2(b)(iii)].*

As discussed at 3.1.3 above, a joint venture includes subsidiaries of the joint venture. *[FRS 102.33.4A].*

3.1.5   Entities that are joint ventures and associates of the same third entity

'An entity is related to a reporting entity if:

...

> (iv)   one entity is a joint venture of a third entity and the other entity is an associate of the third entity'. *[FRS 102.33.2(b)(iv)].*

This definition treats joint ventures in a similar manner to subsidiaries.

3.1.6   Post-employment benefit plans

'An entity is related to a reporting entity if:

...

> (v)   the entity is a post-employment benefit plan for the benefit of employees of either the reporting entity or an entity related to the reporting entity. If the reporting entity is itself such a plan, the sponsoring employers are also related to the reporting entity'. *[FRS 102.33.2(b)(v)].*

The definition is quite wide-ranging and includes post-employment benefit plans of any entity related to the reporting entity. This includes, for example, post-employment benefit plans of an associate or joint venture of the reporting entity or a post-employment benefit plan of an associate of the reporting entity's parent.

Sponsoring employers are also related parties of a post-employment benefit plan.

3.1.7   Entities under control or joint control of certain persons or close members of their family

'An entity is related to a reporting entity if:

...

> (vi)   the entity is controlled or jointly controlled by a person or close member of that person's family who has control or joint control over the reporting entity; has significant influence over the reporting entity; or is a member

of key management personnel of the reporting entity or of a parent of the reporting entity.' *[FRS 102.33.2(b)(vi)]*.

This is intended to cover situations in which an entity is controlled or jointly controlled by a person or close family member of that person and that person or close family member also controls, jointly controls, has significant influence or is a member of key management personnel of the reporting entity.

3.1.8   Entities under significant influence of certain persons or close members of their family

An entity is related to a reporting entity if:

...

> (vii)   a person or a close family member of that person who has control or joint control or significant influence over the reporting entity or is a member of the key management personnel of the reporting entity (or of a parent of the entity) has significant influence over the entity or is a member of the key management personnel of the entity (or of a parent of the entity). *[FRS 102.33.2(b)(vii)]*.

This is the reciprocal of 3.1.7 above.

Entities that are significantly influenced by the same person or close member of that person's family or who simply share the same key management personnel are not related parties in the absence of any control or joint control by those persons (see 3.1.9 below).

3.1.9   Parties that are not related parties

Having included such a detailed definition of related parties, Section 33 clarifies that the following are not related parties: *[FRS 102.33.4]*

- two entities simply because they have a director or other member of key management personnel in common or because a member of key management personnel of one entity has significant influence over the other entity;

- two venturers simply because they share joint control over a joint venture;

- providers of finance, trade unions, public utilities, and departments and agencies of a government that do not control, jointly control or significantly influence the reporting entity, simply by virtue of their normal dealings with the entity (even though they may affect the freedom of action of an entity or participate in its decision-making process); and

- a customer, supplier, franchisor, distributor or general agent with whom an entity transacts a significant volume of business, simply by virtue of the resulting economic dependence.

The reason for these exclusions is that, without them, many entities that are not normally regarded as related parties could fall within the definition of related party. For example, a small clothing manufacturer selling 90% of its output to a single customer could be under the effective economic control of that customer.

These exclusions are effective only where these parties are 'related' to the reporting entity simply because of the relationship noted above. If there are other reasons why a party is a related party, the exclusions do not apply.

3.1.10 Illustrative examples of related party relationships

The following examples, based on examples in IAS 24 which has the same definition of a related party as Section 33, illustrate the related party relationships discussed at Sections 3.1.1 to 3.1.8 above.

Example 28.2: Related party relationships between entities

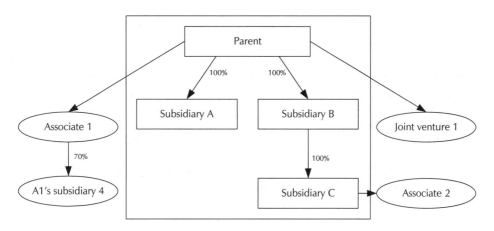

In Parent's consolidated financial statements, Subsidiaries A, B and C, Joint Venture 1 and Associates 1, 2 and 4 are related parties to the group.

In Parent's individual financial statements, Subsidiaries A, B and C, Joint Venture 1 and Associates 1, 2 and 4 are related parties. However, Parent need not disclose transactions entered into with Subsidiaries A, B and C as they are 100% owned by Parent.

For Subsidiary B's consolidated financial statements, Parent, Subsidiary A, Subsidiary C, Joint Venture 1 and Associates 1, 2 and 4 are related parties. However, Subsidiary B need not disclose transactions with Parent or Subsidiaries A and C as both Subsidiary B and Subsidiaries A and C are 100% owned by Parent.

For Subsidiary A, Subsidiary B and Subsidiary C's individual financial statements, Parent, all fellow subsidiaries, Joint Venture 1 and Associates 1, 2 and 4 are related parties. However, the subsidiaries need not disclose transactions entered into with Parent or the other subsidiaries as all entities party to the any transaction are 100% owned by a member of the group.

For Joint Venture 1's individual financial statements, Parent, Subsidiaries A, B and C and Associates 1, 2 and 4 are related parties.

For Associate 1's consolidated financial statements, Parent, Subsidiaries A, B and C and Joint Venture 1 are related parties. Associate 2 is not a related party.

For Associate 1's individual financial statements, Parent, Subsidiaries A, B and C, Joint Venture 1 and Associate 4 (Associate 1's subsidiary) are related parties. Associate 2 is not a related party. Associate 1 must disclose transactions with Associate 4 as Associate 4 is not 100% owned by Associate 1.

For Associate 2's individual financial statements, Parent, Subsidiaries A, B and C and Joint Venture 1 are related parties. Associates 1 and 4 are not related to Associate 2.

For Associate 4's individual financial statements, Associate 1, Parent, Subsidiaries A, B and C and Joint Venture 1 are related parties. Associate 2 is not a related party. Associate 4 must disclose transactions with Associate 1 as Associate 4 is not 100% owned by Associate 1.

Example 28.3:   Close members of the family holding investments

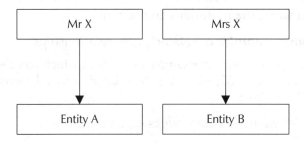

Mr X is the spouse of Mrs X. Mr X has an investment in Entity A and Mrs X has an investment in Entity B.

For Entity A's financial statements, if Mr X controls or jointly controls Entity A, Entity B is related to Entity A when Mrs X has control, joint control or significant influence over Entity B.

For Entity B's financial statements, if Mrs X controls or jointly controls Entity B, Entity A is related to Entity B when Mr X has control, joint control or significant influence over Entity A.

If Mr X has significant influence (but not control or joint control) over Entity A and Mrs X has significant influence (but not control or joint control) over Entity B, Entities A and B are not related to each other.

If Mr X is a member of the key management personnel of Entity A but does not have control or joint control over Entity A and Mrs X is a member of the key management personnel of Entity B, but does not have control or joint control over Entity B then Entities A and B are not related to each other.

3.2   Disclosures of related party transactions, balances and relationships

The following disclosures are required:

- parent-subsidiary relationships (see 3.2.1 below);
- key management personnel compensation (see 3.2.2 below); and
- related party transactions and balances (see 3.2.3 below).

There is no requirement to disclose information about related party transactions in one comprehensive note. However, it may be more useful to users of the financial statements to present information this way.

Section 3 – *Financial Statement Presentation* – requires that, except when FRS 102 permits otherwise (which Section 33 does not), comparative information in respect of the previous period must be disclosed for all amounts reported in the current period's financial statements. *[FRS 102.3.14].*

3.2.1   *Disclosure of parent-subsidiary relationships*

An entity shall disclose:

- the name of its parent; and, if different,
- the name of its ultimate controlling party.

If neither the entity's parent nor the ultimate controlling party produces financial statements available for public use, the name of the next most senior parent that does so (if any) shall also be disclosed. *[FRS 102.33.5].*

The use of the word 'party' means that the disclosure applies to both individuals and to entities. Disclosure must be made even if the parent or ultimate controlling party does not prepare financial statements.

The ultimate controlling party could be a group of individuals or entities acting together. Section 33 is silent on the issue of individuals or entities acting together to exercise joint control as a result of contractual relationships. Two venturers are not are not related parties simply because they share joint control over a joint venture *[FRS 102.33.4(b)]*. Section 33 is also silent on whether a group of individuals acting in an informal way could be considered to be the ultimate controlling party of an entity. However, is likely that such an informal arrangement would at least give such individuals acting collectively significant influence over the reporting entity and as such those individuals collectively would be related parties to the reporting entity.

It is stressed that these relationships between a parent and its subsidiary must be disclosed irrespective of whether there have been related party transactions. *[FRS 102.33.5]*.

3.2.2   Disclosure of key management personnel compensation

Compensation includes all employee benefits (as defined in Section 28 – *Employee Benefits*) including those in the form of share-based payments. Employee benefits includes all forms of consideration paid, payable or provided by the entity, or on behalf of the entity (e.g. by its parent or shareholder), in exchange for services rendered to the entity. It also includes such consideration paid on behalf of a parent of the entity in respect of goods and services provided to the entity. *[FRS 102.33.6]*.

Disclosure is required only of key management compensation in total. There is no need to split the amount into its constituent parts. There is also no requirement to disclose individual key management compensation or to name those individuals considered to be key management.

One practical difficulty for an entity in a group is that the disclosure of its key management personnel compensation is for the services rendered to the reporting entity. Accordingly, where key management personnel of the reporting entity also provide services to other entities within the group, an apportionment of the compensation is necessary. Likewise, where the reporting entity receives services from key management personnel that are also key management personnel of other entities within the group, the reporting entity may have to impute the compensation received. Such apportionments and allocations required judgment and an assessment of the time commitment involved.

Company Law requires disclosures in respect of directors' remuneration which are in addition to the requirement to disclose key management personnel compensation (see 3.2.4 below).

3.2.3   Disclosure of related party transactions and balances

3.2.3.A   Definition of and examples of related party transactions

A related party transaction 'is a transfer of resources, services or obligations between a reporting entity and a related party, regardless of whether a price is charged'.

Examples of related party transactions include but are not limited to:

(a)   transactions between an entity and its principal owner(s);

(b)   transactions between an entity and another entity when both entities are under the common control of a single entity or person; and

(c)   transactions in which an entity or person that controls the reporting entity incurs expenses directly that would have been borne by the reporting entity. *[FRS 102.33.8]*.

Section 33 provides the following examples of transactions that shall be disclosed if they are with a related party:

- purchases or sales of goods (finished or unfinished);
- purchases or sales of property and other assets;
- rendering or receiving of services;
- leases;
- transfers of research and development;
- transfers under licence agreements;
- transfers under finance agreements (including loans and equity contributions in cash or in kind);
- provisions of guarantees or collateral;
- settlement of liabilities on behalf of the entity or by the entity on behalf of another party; and
- participation by a parent or a subsidiary in a defined benefit plan that shares risks between group entities. *[FRS 102.33.12]*.

This list is not intended to be exhaustive. Information about commitments should be disclosed if necessary for an understanding of the potential effect of the related party relationship on the financial statements. *[FRS 102.33.9]*.

Items of a similar nature may be disclosed in aggregate except where separate disclosure is necessary for an understanding of the effects of related party transactions on the financial statements of an entity. *[FRS 102.33.14]*.

3.2.3.B   *Disclosures required in respect of related party transactions*

If an entity has related party transactions of the type described at 3.2.3.A above, it shall disclose the nature of the related party relationship as well as information about the transactions, outstanding balances and commitments necessary for an understanding of the potential effect of the relationship on the financial statements. These disclosure requirements are in addition to the requirements to disclose key management personnel compensation (see 3.2.2 above). At a minimum, disclosures shall include:

(a)   the amount of the transactions;

(b)   the amount of the outstanding balances and:

    (i)   their terms and conditions, including whether they are secured, and the nature of the consideration to be provided in settlement; and

    (ii)   details of any guarantees given or received;

(c)   provisions for uncollectible receivables related to the amount of outstanding balances; and

(d)   the expense recognised during the period in respect of bad or doubtful debts due from related parties. *[FRS 102.33.9].*

The disclosures required above shall be made separately for each of the following categories in aggregate:

*   entities with control, joint control or significant influence over the entity;
*   entities over which the entity has control, joint control or significant influence;
*   key management personnel of the entity or its parent (in the aggregate); and
*   other related parties. *[FRS 102.33.10].*

Section 33 stresses that an entity shall not state that related party transactions were made on terms equivalent to those that prevail in arm's length transactions unless such terms can be substantiated. *[FRS 102.33.13].* However, there is no requirement to state that transactions have not been made on an arm's length basis.

There is no exemption from disclosure on the grounds of confidentiality. However, since there is no requirement to disclose the name of a related party (apart from the name of the parent, or if different, the ultimate controlling entity), this lack of exemption is likely to be less of a concern.

In determining whether an entity discloses related party transactions in financial statements, the general concept of materiality is applied. Section 33 does not refer specifically to materiality since this qualitative characteristic is described in Section 2 – *Concepts and Pervasive Principles.* Omissions or misstatements of items are material 'if they could, individually or collectively, influence the economic decisions of users taken on the basis of the financial statements. Materiality depends on the size and nature of the omission or misstatement, judged in the surrounding circumstances. The size or nature of the item, or a combination of both, could be the determining factor.' *[FRS 102.2.6].*

This may have the effect that any related party transaction whose disclosure is considered sensitive (for tax reasons perhaps) is by definition material because it is expected by the reporting entity to influence a user of the financial statements. Therefore, it may not be possible to avoid disclosing such items on the grounds that they are financially immaterial. In addition, a transaction conducted at advantageous terms to either the related party or the reporting entity is more likely to be material than one conducted at arm's length. Since Section 33 requires disclosure of related party transactions irrespective of whether consideration is received, disclosure cannot be avoided on the argument that, since there is no consideration, the transaction must be immaterial.

3.2.3.C   Disclosure exemption for state-related entities

An entity is exempt from the disclosure requirements discussed at 3.2.3.B above in relation to:

*   a state (a national, regional or local government) that has control, joint control or significant influence over the reporting entity; and
*   another entity that is a related party because the same state has control, joint control or significant influence over both the reporting entity and the other entity.

This is a generous exemption as there is no requirement to give even an indication of the type of transactions with the state or other state-related entity that is a related party.

However, the entity must still disclose a parent-subsidiary relationship as discussed at 3.2.1 above. *[FRS 102.33.11]*.

3.2.4   Additional company law disclosures

Company law requires disclosure in respect of transactions with directors including disclosure of directors' remuneration and disclosure of directors' advances, credits and guarantees.

These disclosures are in addition to the disclosure of key management personnel compensation discussed at 3.2.2 above.

3.2.4.A   Disclosure of directors' remuneration

Disclosure of directors' remuneration is required for all entities.

Quoted companies are required to prepare a directors' remuneration report. A quoted company is a company whose equity share capital is included in the official list of the UK Listing Authority, officially listed in an EEA state or admitted to dealing on either the New York Stock Exchange or NASDAQ. *[s385(2)]*. AIM and OFEX companies are not quoted. The contents of a directors' remuneration report are specified by Schedule 8 of The Large and Medium-sized Companies and Groups (Accounts and Report) Regulations 2008 (SI 2008/410) (The Regulations).

All other companies must make the directors' remuneration disclosures required by Schedule 5 of The Regulations.

3.2.4.B   Disclosure of directors' advances credits and guarantees

Disclosure of directors' advances, credits and guarantees is required by Section 413 of the Companies Act 2006 for all entities. These disclosures are required for each credit, advance or guarantee.

Disclosure is required in respect of all transactions during the reporting period as well as balances outstanding at the reporting date. Disclosure is required of transactions with any person who was a director of the company at any time during the period, irrespective of whether that person was a director at such time that the transaction or arrangement was made.

3.2.5   Stock exchange requirements

In addition to the requirements of the Companies Act, there are explicit statutory, London Stock Exchange (LSE) and Disclosure and Transparency Rules (DTR) requirements and reliefs regarding disclosure of certain related party transactions and relationships. These disclosure requirements are not addressed in detail in this chapter and reference should be made to the original regulatory requirements. The disclosure requirements go beyond those required by FRS 102.

Both the LSE and AIM have definitions of a related party which differ from the definition in FRS 102. For related party transactions meeting certain thresholds, the Listing Rules *[LR 19]* require the company to make notification of the related party transaction, and to send a circular containing specified details to shareholders, and to obtain shareholder approval. There are modified rules for smaller related party transactions. AIM Rules 13 and 16 also require notification of related party transactions meeting certain thresholds. Disclosure of certain related party transactions can be required in the financial statements. *[LR 9.8.4R (3) and AIM Rule 19].*

4. SUMMARY OF GAAP DIFFERENCES

	FRS 102	*Previous UK GAAP*	*IFRS*
Definition of related party	No reference to a management entity that provides key management personnel services.	No reference to a management entity that provides key management personnel services.	A management entity that provides key management personnel services is a related party.
Transactions between wholly owned subsidiaries	Exemption	Exemption	No exemption
Disclosure of pension contributions	No exemption	Exemption	No exemption
Disclosure of key management personnel compensation	Disclose in total only	No disclosure	Disclose in total and by five categories
Confidentiality exemption	None	Yes (aimed at financial institutions)	None
State-related parties	Exemption	No exemption	Exemption conditional on certain disclosures
Aggregation of disclosures by category	Disclosure by four categories	No specific categories but aggregation by type of transaction	Disclosure by seven categories
Disclosure of commitments	Disclose if necessary for understanding of relationship	Not mentioned	Explicit statement that commitment is a type of related party transaction.

Chapter 29   Specialised activities

Chapter 29

List of examples

Chapter 29 Specialised activities

1 INTRODUCTION

This chapter covers (unless stated otherwise below) the financial reporting requirements for entities applying FRS 102 involved in the following types of specialised activities:

- Agriculture (see 2 below);

- Extractive Activities (see 3 below);

- Service Concession Arrangements (see 4 below);

- Heritage Assets (see 5 below);

- Incoming Resources from Non-Exchange Transactions and Public Benefit Entities (see 6 below);

- Financial Institutions (see Chapter 8 at 8.4); and

- Funding Commitments (see Chapter 17 at 3.9).

These are all dealt with in Section 34 – *Specialised Activities.*

2 AGRICULTURE

2.1 Introduction

Section 34 – sets out the recognition, measurement and disclosure requirements for agricultural activities. While these requirements are based on the IFRS for SMEs, the FRC included in FRS 102 an additional accounting policy choice to apply either a fair value model or a cost model.

Originally, the proposed requirements for agriculture were predominantly based on a fair value model in line with IAS 41 – *Agriculture.* As noted in the Accounting Council's advice to the FRC 'respondents questioned the proposed requirements noting that current FRSs do not set out accounting requirements and although the proposals included an exemption from applying fair value where there is undue cost or effort, the fair value information is inconsistent with the way most agricultural businesses are managed and would not benefit the users of financial statements.' The Accounting Council therefore advised that that entities engaged in agricultural activities should be permitted an accounting policy choice. *[FRS 102.AC.94-97].*

2.2   Definitions and scope

2.2.1   *Definitions*

Agricultural activity is defined as 'the management by an entity of the biological transformation of biological assets for sale, into agricultural produce or into additional biological assets.' *[FRS 102 Appendix I]*. Agricultural activity covers a wide range of activities, such as 'raising livestock, forestry, annual or perennial cropping, cultivating orchards and plantations, floriculture, and aquaculture (including fish farming). *[IAS 41.6]*.

FRS 102 includes the following terms that are relevant to agriculture: *[FRS 102 Appendix I]*

*   *Biological asset* – 'A living animal or plant'; and
*   *Agricultural produce* – 'The harvested product of the entity's biological assets.'

These definitions can be illustrated as follows: *[IAS 41.4]*

Biological assets	Agricultural produce	Products that are the result of processing after harvest
Sheep	Wool	Yarn, carpet
Trees in a plantation forest	Felled trees	Logs, lumber
Plants	Cotton	Thread, clothing
	Harvested cane	Sugar
Dairy cattle	Milk	Cheese
Pigs	Carcass	Sausages, cured hams
Bushes	Leaf	Tea, cured tobacco
Vines	Grapes	Wine
Fruit trees	Picked fruit	Processed fruit

2.2.2   *Scope*

An entity using FRS 102 that is engaged in agricultural activity should determine an accounting policy for each class of biological asset and its related agricultural produce. *[FRS 102.34.2]*. In addition, biological assets held by lessees under finance leases and biological assets provided by lessors under operating leases should be measured in accordance with Section 34. *[FRS 102.20.1(d)]*.

Biological assets may be outside the scope of Section 34 when they are not used in agricultural activity. For example, animals in a zoo (or game park) that does not have an active breeding programme and rarely sells any animals or animal products would be outside the scope of the standard. Another example is activities in the pharmaceutical industry that involve the culture of bacteria. Such activity would not fall within the scope of Section 34. While the bacteria may be considered a biological asset, the development of a culture by a pharmaceutical company would not constitute agricultural activity.

Section 34 also does not apply to:

*   Agricultural produce after the point of harvest, which is accounted for under Section 13 – *Inventories*; *[FRS 102.13.2(c)]*.
*   Land and property, plant and equipment related to agricultural activity, which falls within the scope of Section 17 – *Property, Plant and Equipment*. *[FRS 102.17.3(a)]*.

2.3   Recognition

An entity should only recognise a biological asset or an item of agricultural produce when:

(a)   the entity controls the asset as a result of past events;

(b)   it is probable that future economic benefits associated with the asset will flow to the entity; and

(c)   the fair value or cost of the asset can be measured reliably. *[FRS 102.34.3]*.

Section 34 only applies to agricultural produce (i.e. harvested crops) at the point of harvest and not prior or subsequent to harvest. Unharvested agricultural produce is considered to be part of the biological asset from which it will be harvested. Therefore, before harvest, agricultural produce should not be recognised separately from the biological asset from which it comes. For example, grapes on the vine are accounted for as part of the vines themselves right up to the point of harvest.

2.4   Measurement

For each class of biological asset and its related agricultural produce, Section 34 provides an entity an accounting policy choice to use either: *[FRS 102.34.3A]*

(a)   the fair value model set out at 2.5 below; or

(b)   the cost model set out at 2.6 below.

However, once an entity has elected to use the fair value model for a class of biological asset and its related agricultural produce, it is not subsequently permitted change its accounting policy to the cost model. *[FRS 102.34.3B]*.

2.5   Fair value model

2.5.1   Measurement

If an entity applies the fair value model, it should measure a biological asset on initial recognition and at each reporting date at its fair value less costs to sell. Changes in fair value less costs to sell should be recognised in profit or loss. *[FRS 102.34.4]*. Agricultural produce harvested from an entity's biological assets should be measured at the point of harvest at its fair value less costs to sell, which is the cost at that date when applying Section 13 – *Inventories* or another applicable section of FRS 102. *[FRS 102.34.5]*.

Fair value less costs to sell is 'the amount obtainable from the sale of an asset or cash-generating unit in an arm's length transaction between knowledgeable, willing parties, less the costs of disposal.' *[FRS 102 Appendix I]*. The costs of disposal would include costs that are necessary for a sale to occur but that would not otherwise arise, such as commissions to brokers and dealers, levies by regulatory agencies and commodity exchanges, and transfer taxes and duties. *[IAS 41.BC3]*.

Chapter 29

2.5.2   *Fair value hierarchy*

Section 34 provides guidance on determining fair value and establishes a hierarchy that can be summarised as follows:

(a)   the price for the asset in an active market (see 2.5.2.A below);

(b)   absent an active market, one or more of the following types of market data (see 2.5.2.B below):

    (i)   the most recent market transaction price;

    (ii)   adjusted market prices for similar assets; or

    (iii)   sector benchmarks;

(c)   the present value of expected net cash flows from the asset (see 2.5.2.C below).

2.5.2.A   *Active market*

Where an active market exists for a biological asset or agricultural produce in its present location and condition, the quoted price in that market is the appropriate basis for determining the fair value of that asset. *[FRS 102.34.6(a)]*. Under FRS 102, an active market is one in which all the following conditions exist: *[FRS 102 Appendix I]*

(a)   the items traded in the market are homogeneous;

(b)   willing buyers and sellers can normally be found at any time; and

(c)   prices are available to the public.

If an entity has access to different active markets then it should use the price in the market that it expects to use. *[FRS 102.34.6(a)]*.

2.5.2.B   *Market-based data*

If there is no active market then an entity should consider the following types of market-based data in determining fair value: *[FRS 102.34.6(b)]*

(a)   the most recent market transaction price, provided that there has not been a significant change in economic circumstances between the date of that transaction and the end of the reporting period;

(b)   market prices for similar assets with adjustment to reflect differences; and

(c)   sector benchmarks such as the value of an orchard expressed per export tray, bushel, or hectare, and the value of cattle expressed per kilogram of meat.

The above market-based data may suggest different conclusions as to the fair value of a biological asset or an item of agricultural produce. In those cases, an entity considers the reasons for those differences, to arrive at the most reliable estimate of fair value within a relatively narrow range of reasonable estimates. *[FRS 102.34.6(c)]*.

2.5.2.C   *Present value*

Fair value may sometimes be readily determinable even though market determined prices or values are not available for a biological asset in its present condition. Therefore, an entity should consider whether the present value of expected net cash flows from the asset discounted at a current market determined rate results in a reliable measure of fair value. *[FRS 102.34.6(d)]*.

The purpose of a calculation of the present value of expected net cash flows is to determine the fair value of a biological asset in its present location and condition. Therefore, in determining the present value of expected net cash flows, an entity includes the net cash flows that market participants would expect the asset to generate in its most relevant market. An entity should ensure that it uses assumptions for determining a discount rate that are consistent with those used in estimating the expected cash flows; this is to avoid double-counting or overlooking risks. In any case, the entity should exclude the cash flows for financing the assets, taxation or re-establishing biological assets after harvest, for example, the cost of replanting trees in a plantation forest after harvest.

2.5.2.D   *Fair value not reliably measurable*

If an entity cannot measure the fair value of a biological asset reliably then it should apply the cost model (see 2.6 below) to that biological asset in accordance with paragraphs 34.8 and 34.10A of FRS 102 until such time that the fair value can be reliably measured. *[FRS 102.34.6A]*.

2.5.3   **Disclosures**

An entity should disclose the following information for each class of biological asset that is measured using the fair value model: *[FRS 102.34.7]*

(a)   A description of each class of biological asset;

(b)   The methods and significant assumptions applied in determining the fair value of each class of biological asset; and

(c)   A reconciliation of changes in the carrying amount of each class of biological asset between the beginning and the end of the current period. The reconciliation should include:

(i)   the gain or loss arising from changes in fair value less costs to sell;

(ii)   increases resulting from purchases;

(iii)   decreases attributable to sales;

(iv)   decreases resulting from harvest;

(v)   increases resulting from business combinations; and

(vi)   other changes.

This reconciliation need not be presented for prior periods.

In grouping biological assets, an entity may consider distinguishing between different types of assets, such as consumable biological assets, bearer biological assets or mature and immature assets. In particular, it should be noted that for the purposes of the reconciliation at (c) above, it would be unhelpful to combine information about annual crops (which are akin to inventory) with that on bearer plant or long-lived biological assets (which are more like property, plant and equipment).

If an entity measures any individual biological assets at cost in accordance with paragraph 34.6A (see 2.5.2.D above), it should explain why fair value cannot be reliably measured. If the fair value of such a biological asset becomes reliably measurable during the current period an entity shall explain why fair value has become reliably measurable and the effect of the change. *[FRS 102.34.7A]*.

Finally, an entity should disclose the methods and significant assumptions applied in determining the fair value at the point of harvest of each class of agricultural produce. *[FRS 102.34.7B]*.

2.6   Cost model

2.6.1   *Measurement*

2.6.1.A   *Biological assets*

An entity that applies the cost model should measure biological assets at cost less any accumulated depreciation and any accumulated impairment losses. *[FRS 102.34.8]*.

'Historical cost' is the amount of cash or cash equivalents paid or the fair value of the consideration given to acquire the asset at the time of its acquisition. Amortised historical cost is the historical cost of an asset or liability plus or minus that portion of its historical cost previously recognised as an expense or income. *[FRS 102.2.34(a)]*. In determining cost and depreciated cost an entity should consider the guidance in Section 17 on Property, Plant and Equipment.

Impairment losses on biological asset measured under the cost model should be determined in accordance with Section 27 – *Impairment of Assets* (see Chapter 22). *[FRS 102.27.1(f)]*.

2.6.1.B   *Agricultural produce*

Section 34 requires that in applying the cost model, agricultural produce harvested from an entity's biological assets should be measured at the point of harvest at either:

(a)   the lower of cost and estimated selling price less costs to complete and sell; or

(b)   its fair value less costs to sell. Any gain or loss arising on initial recognition of agricultural produce at fair value less costs to sell should be included in profit or loss for the period in which it arises.

That amount is then the cost at that date when applying Section 13 or another applicable section of this FRS. *[FRS 102.34.9]*.

In other words, if an entity elects to measure its biological assets under the cost model, it will still be allowed to measure agricultural produce under the fair value model. However, the converse would not be true, if an entity measures its biological assets under the fair value model then it must measure the resulting agricultural produce under the fair value model as well.

2.6.2   *Disclosures*

For each class of biological asset measured under the cost model, an entity should disclose the following: *[FRS 102.34.10]*

(a)   a description of each class of biological asset;

(b)   the depreciation method used;

(c)   the useful lives or the depreciation rates used; and

(d) a reconciliation of changes in the carrying amount of each class of biological asset between the beginning and the end of the current period. The reconciliation shall include:

(i) increases resulting from purchases;

(ii) decreases attributable to sales;

(iii) decreases resulting from harvest;

(iv) increases resulting from business combinations;

(v) impairment losses recognised or reversed in profit or loss in accordance with Section 27 Impairment of Assets; and

(vi) other changes.

This reconciliation need not be presented for prior periods.

In addition, an entity should disclose, for any agricultural produce measured at fair value less costs to sell, the methods and significant assumptions applied in determining the fair value at the point of harvest of each class of agricultural produce. *[FRS 102.34.10A]*.

In grouping biological assets, an entity may consider distinguishing between different types of assets, such as consumable biological assets, bearer biological assets or mature and immature assets. In particular, it should be noted that for the purposes of the reconciliation at (c) above, it would be unhelpful to combine information about annual crops (which are akin to inventory) with that on bearer plant or long-lived biological assets (which are more like property, plant and equipment).

3 EXTRACTIVE INDUSTRIES

3.1 Introduction

An entity applying FRS 102 which is engaged in the exploration for and/or evaluation of mineral resources (extractive industries) must apply the requirements of IFRS 6 – *Exploration for and Evaluation of Mineral Resources*. This Standard covers the accounting for exploration and evaluation (E&E) expenditures which are 'expenditures incurred by an entity in connection with the exploration for and evaluation of mineral resources before the technical feasibility and commercial viability of extracting mineral resources are demonstrable', while E&E assets are 'exploration and evaluation expenditures recognised as assets in accordance with the entity's accounting policy'. *[IFRS 6 Appendix A]*. IFRS 6 is limited to accounting for E&E expenditures and does not address the other aspects of accounting for entities engaged in these activities. This section will therefore not apply to expenditures incurred before the exploration for and evaluation of mineral resources (e.g. expenditures incurred before the entity has obtained legal rights to explore in a specific area) or after the technical feasibility and commercial viability of extracting a mineral resource are demonstrable. *[IFRS 6.5]*. Equipment used in the E&E phase, e.g. property, plant and equipment and any other intangibles such as software, are not in the scope of IFRS 6, instead they are in the scope of sections 17 – *Property, Plant and Equipment*, and 18 – *Intangible Assets other than Goodwill*.

The scope and objectives of IFRS 6 are covered in further detail in section 3.1 of Chapter 40 of EY International GAAP 2015.

Activities outside the E&E phase which are not covered by IFRS 6, may be covered by the following sections of FRS 102:

- Section 13 – *Inventories*
- Section 17 – *Property, Plant and Equipment*
- Section 18 – *Intangible Assets other than Goodwill*
- Section 20 – *Leases*

In many of these sections 'minerals and mineral reserves' are excluded from their scope, although the exact wording of the scope exclusions differs between standards.

3.2   Key differences to IFRS and previous UK GAAP

As noted below, FRS 102 requires an entity engaged in extractive industries to apply the requirements of IFRS 6 – *Exploration for and Evaluation of Mineral Resources* – to account for E&E expenditures.

Under previous UK GAAP, entities involved in oil and gas exploration, development and/or production activities would have followed the recommendations of the Statement of Recommended Practice (SORP) for *Accounting for Oil and Gas Exploration, Development, Production and Decommissioning Activities* (7th June 2001). Under this SORP two methods of accounting for pre-production activities were allowed. These were full cost accounting and successful efforts accounting.

The full cost method under most national GAAPs requires all costs incurred in prospecting, acquiring mineral interests, exploration, appraisal, development, and construction to be accumulated in large cost centres, e.g. individual countries, groups of countries, or the entire world. However, although an entity is permitted by IFRS 6 to develop an accounting policy without reference to other IFRSs or to the hierarchy in Section 10 – *Accounting Policies, Estimates and Errors*, IFRS 6 cannot be extrapolated or applied by analogy to permit application of the full cost method outside the E&E phase. In January 2006, the Interpretations Committee confirmed that IFRS 6 gives relief to E&E activities only and there is no basis for interpreting IFRS 6 as granting any additional relief in areas outside its scope.[1]

There are several other areas in which application of the full cost method under IFRS is restricted because:

- while the full cost method under most national GAAPs requires application of some form of 'ceiling test', IFRS 6 requires – when impairment indicators are present – an impairment test is to be performed in accordance with IAS 36 – *Impairment of Assets*;
- IFRS 6 requires E&E assets to be classified as tangible or intangible assets according to the nature of the assets. *[IFRS 6.15]*. In other words, even when an entity accounts for E&E costs in relatively large pools, it will still need to distinguish between tangible and intangible assets; and
- once the technical feasibility and commercial viability of extracting mineral resources are demonstrable, IFRS 6 requires E&E assets to be tested for impairment under IAS 36 (although in accordance with IFRS 6 E&E assets can be allocated to Cash Generating Units (CGUs) or groups of CGUs which may include

producing CGUs, provided certain criteria are met – refer to 3.5.2 of EY International GAAP 2015 for further information), reclassified in the statement of financial position and accounted for under IAS 16 – *Property, Plant and Equipment* (or Section 17 of FRS 102) or IAS 38 – *Intangible Assets* (or Section 18 of FRS 102). *[IFRS 6.17, FRS 102.34.11A]*. That means that it is not possible to account for successful and unsuccessful projects within one cost centre or pool.

For these reasons, it is not possible to apply the full cost method of accounting under IFRS/FRS 102, without making very significant modifications in the application of the method. An entity might want to use the full cost method as its starting point in developing its accounting policy for E&E assets under IFRS/ FRS 102. However, it will rarely be appropriate to describe the resulting accounting policy as a 'full cost method' because key elements of the full cost method are not permitted under IFRS/FRS 102.

Under the successful efforts method an entity will generally consider each individual mineral lease, concession or production sharing contract as a cost centre.

When an entity applies the successful efforts method under IFRS, it will need to account for prospecting costs incurred before the E&E phase under IAS 16 or IAS 38. As economic benefits are highly uncertain at this stage of a project, prospecting costs will typically be expensed as incurred. Costs incurred to acquire undeveloped mineral rights, however, should be capitalised under IFRS if an entity expects an inflow of future economic benefits.

To the extent that costs are incurred within the E&E phase of a project, IFRS 6 does not prescribe any recognition and measurement rules. Therefore, it would be acceptable for such costs to be recorded as assets and written off when it is determined that the costs will not lead to economic benefits or to be expensed as incurred if the outcome is uncertain. Deferred costs of an undeveloped mineral right may be depreciated over some determinable period, subject to an impairment test each period with the amount of impairment charged to expense, or an entity may choose to carry forward the deferred costs of the undeveloped mineral right until the entity determines whether the property contains mineral reserves.[2] However, E&E assets should no longer be classified as such when the technical feasibility and commercial viability of extracting mineral resources are demonstrable. *[IFRS 6.17]*. At that time the asset should be tested for impairment under Section 27/IAS 36, reclassified in the statement of financial position and accounted for under Section 17/IAS 16 or Section 18/IAS 38. If it is determined that no commercial reserves are present, then the costs capitalised should be expensed. Costs incurred after the E&E phase should be accounted for in accordance with the applicable FRS 102 Sections/IFRSs (i.e. Section 17/IAS 16 and Section 18/IAS 38).

There is further discussion on the successful efforts method in section 5.2.1 of Chapter 40 of EY International GAAP 2015.

Under FRS 102/IFRS 6 the impairment loss is measured and disclosed in accordance with Section 27/IAS 36, except that FRS 102/IFRS 6 makes two important modifications:

- it defines separate impairment testing 'triggers' for E&E assets; and
- it allows groups of cash generating units to be used for impairment testing.

This is further discussed in section 3.5 of Chapter 40 of International GAAP 2015.

Under previous UK GAAP, impairment testing was carried out in accordance with FRS 11 – *Impairment of fixed assets and goodwill.* For full cost companies the test was carried out if events or changes in circumstances indicated that the net book amount of expenditure within each cost pool, less any provisions for decommissioning costs and deferred production or revenue related taxes, may not be recoverable from the anticipated future net revenue for oil and gas reserves attributable to the company's interest in that pool. For successful efforts companies the impairment test triggers are identical, but are measured at a cost centre level. Therefore post transition to FRS 102, companies will need to test E&E assets for impairment first, and if they had previously used the full cost approach may not be able to combine both successful and unsuccessful E&E projects for the purpose of impairment testing.

3.3   Requirements of Section 34 for Extractive Industries

An entity engaged in extractive activities which is applying FRS 102 should apply the requirements of IFRS 6 – *Exploration for and Evaluation of Mineral Resources.* [FRS 102.34.11].

We have not discussed IFRS 6 in detail in this book, but refer readers to section 3 of Chapter 40 of International GAAP 2015 which covers this standard in detail.

IFRS 6 contains within it a number of references to other standards. In applying FRS 102, the references within IFRS 6 should be taken to mean the relevant section or paragraph of FRS 102. [FRS 102.34.11A]. For example, paragraph 6 of IFRS 6 refers to IAS 8 – *Accounting Policies, Changes in Accounting Estimates and Errors.* The relevant section of FRS 102 in this case would be Section 10.

However, when applying paragraph 21 of IFRS 6, which deals with the allocation of E&E assets to CGUs and requires that a CGU or group of CGU's cannot be larger than an operating segment as defined by IFRS 8 – *Operating Segments*, the reference to IFRS 8 shall be ignored and a CGU or group of CGUs shall be no larger than an operating segment. [FRS 102.34.11B]. The allocation of E&E assets to CGU or groups of CGUs is performed for the purpose of impairment testing under FRS 102/ IFRS 6.

If on first-time adoption, the entity determines that it is impractical to apply any of the requirements of paragraph 18 of IFRS 6, which relates to the measurement and recognition of impairment losses in respect of Exploration and Evaluation Assets, to comparative information the entity will need to disclose this fact. [FRS 102.34.11C].

On transition to FRS 102, an entity which previously accounted for exploration and development costs for oil and gas properties in the development or production phases under the full cost accounting method may elect to measure these assets on the following basis:

- Exploration and evaluation assets at the amount determined under the entity's previous GAAP.

- Assets in the development or production phases at the amount determined for the cost centre under the entity's previous GAAP. The entity shall allocate this amount to the cost centre's underlying assets *pro rata* using reserve volumes or reserve values as of that date.

Both E&E assets and assets in the production and development phases should be tested for impairment in accordance with Section 34 (IFRS 6) or Section 27 respectively. *[FRS 102.35.10(j)].*

This transitional provision should eliminate the requirement for a restatement for companies which had previously adopted the full cost method and make the process of allocating E&E assets into CGUs required under FRS 102 easier.

3.4 Practical implementation issues

Practical issues in the oil and gas industry are covered in section 5 of Chapter 40 of EY International GAAP 2015. In particular, E&E costs are covered in section 5.2 of this chapter.

4 SERVICE CONCESSION ARRANGEMENTS

4.1 Introduction

Service concession arrangements have been developed in many countries as a mechanism for procuring public services using private sector finance and management expertise. Under a service concession arrangement (SCA), private capital is used to provide major economic and social facilities for public use. The concept is that, rather than having bodies in the public sector taking on the entire responsibility and risk of funding and building infrastructure assets such as roads, bridges, railways, hospitals, prisons and schools, some of these should be contracted out to private sector entities from which the public sector bodies would rent the assets and buy services. In the UK, such arrangements are referred to as Public Private Partnerships and formerly as arrangements under the Private Finance Initiative.

Service concession arrangements are of great complexity and are often devised to meet political as well as purely commercial ends. SCAs are contractual arrangements between the public sector body and the private section operator which set out in great detail the rights of each party, the related performance obligations and measures and the mechanisms for payment. The transactions involved in a typical service concession are wide-ranging and include the construction or refurbishment of infrastructure assets, the delivery of operating and maintenance services, collection of revenues from the public, and the receipt of payments from the public sector body (some of which may have been deferred). As a result, the accounting issues raised by service concessions range across a number of areas, including accounting for construction contracts, property, plant and equipment, leasing, intangible assets, financial instruments, revenue and borrowing costs (as these arrangements are often financed by borrowings of the operator).

Paragraphs 12 to 16A in Section 34 require an entity to determine whether an arrangement meets the definition of a service concession and then directs that entity to the other sections of FRS 102 that should be applied to each component of the transaction. Central to the definition of an SCA is whether the public sector body (or grantor) has control over the infrastructure, by virtue of both its rights under the contract to direct how the assets are used during the concession and thereafter by controlling any significant residual interest in the assets. *[FRS 102.34.12A].*

An operator first applying FRS 102 can elect to retain the same asset classification (property, plant and equipment or financial asset) as it applied under previous UK GAAP and apply Section 34 to SCAs entered into after its date of transition. *[FRS 102.35.10(i)].* However, no such relief is available to grantors.

4.2   Key differences to IFRS and previous UK GAAP

4.2.1   *Key differences compared to previous UK GAAP*

The guidance under previous UK GAAP was more detailed than Paragraphs 12 to 16A in Section 34 of FRS 102. FRS 5 Application Note F – *Private Finance Initiative and Similar Contracts* (FRS 5 ANF) adopted an approach based on an analysis of risks and rewards, rather than control, and determined an accounting treatment on the basis of the nature of the benefits to which each party in the arrangement have access. *[FRS 5.ANF.F4, F5].* Under this approach, either the public sector body or the operator could be determined to have rights requiring the recognition of the infrastructure as an asset; or the arrangement could give rise to the operator recognising a financial asset. *[FRS 5.ANF.F51, F52, F59, F60].* An operator in an arrangement falling within the scope of Section 34 will never show the infrastructure as an asset on its balance sheet. *[FRS 102.34.12I].*

The scope of Section 34 is narrower than FRS 5 ANF, which applies to all contracts for the provision of services under the Private Finance Initiative, including arrangements where the operator retains legal title to the assets, or the grantor acquires legal title to the assets at market value at the end of the contract term. *[FRS 5.ANF.F2].* Section 34 only applies to contracts that confer to the grantor control over any significant residual interest in the assets at the end of the term of the arrangement. *[FRS 102.34.12A].*

4.2.2   *Key differences compared to IFRS*

Under IFRS, two Interpretations apply to the treatment of service concessions: IFRIC 12 – *Service Concession Arrangements* – and SIC-29 – *Service Concession Arrangements: Disclosures.*

Unlike IFRIC 12, FRS 102 sets out requirements for accounting by the public sector body in an SCA, requiring it to recognise a finance lease liability and related asset, to the extent that it has a contractual obligation to make payments to the operator in respect of the infrastructure assets. *[FRS 102.34.12F].* IFRIC 12 does not specify the accounting by grantors. *[IFRIC 12.9].*

For operators in a service concession, Section 34 applies the same control criteria as IFRIC 12 (see 4.3.2 below). However, whilst the resulting accounting principles are very similar to those established in IFRIC 12, what is set out in FRS 102 is very much a simplification of the Interpretation and there is no guidance on how the control criteria might be interpreted in different situations; exactly what is meant by services 'for the benefit of the public'; and how to classify arrangements where only part of the infrastructure is controlled by the grantor (see 4.3.2.A below). In addition, Section 34 does not consider situations where the following features exist in a service concession arrangement:

- assets of the operator are used in the service concession;
- payments are made by the operator to the grantor (for example rentals payable for assets retained by the grantor or for other services provided by the public sector body);
- payments under the service concession contract are variable;
- where both an intangible asset and a financial asset exists; and
- major upgrade, replacement or maintenance works are required at intervals during the concession term.

IFRIC 12 also provides a number of examples, tables and flow charts to assist entities in implementing its requirements. None of these are included in Section 34.

As discussed at 4.3.4.F below, Section 10 implies that entities may also consider the requirements and guidance in IFRIC 12 in these circumstances, *[FRS 102.10.6]*, which are discussed in Chapter 26 of EY International GAAP 2015.

Section 34 does not set out any disclosure requirements for SCAs. Having referred a grantor or an operator to the relevant sections of FRS 102 for the recognition and measurement of the various transactions within an SCA, grantors and operators are required to provide the related disclosures according to each section respectively.

4.3 Requirements of FRS 102 for Service Concession Arrangements

4.3.1 Terms used in Section 34 on Service Concession Arrangements

The following terms are used in paragraphs 34.12 to 34.16A of Section 34 with the meanings specified. *[FRS 102 Appendix I].*

Term	Definition
Borrowing costs	Interest and other costs incurred by an entity in connection with the borrowing of funds.

Financial asset [extract]	An asset that is:
	(a) cash;
	(c) a contractual right:
	    (i) to receive cash or another financial asset from another entity; or
	    (ii) to exchange financial assets or financial liabilities with another entity under conditions that are potentially favourable to the entity; ...

Infrastructure assets	Infrastructure for public services, such as roads, bridges, tunnels, prisons, hospitals, airports, water distribution facilities, energy supply and telecommunications networks.

Term	*Definition*
Intangible asset	An identifiable non-monetary asset without physical substance. Such an asset is identifiable when: (a) it is separable, i.e. capable of being separated or divided from the entity and sold, transferred, licensed, rented or exchanged, either individually or together with a related contract, asset or liability; or (b) it arises from contractual or other legal rights, regardless of whether those rights are transferable or separable from the entity or from other rights and obligations..
Public benefit entity	An entity whose primary objective is to provide goods or services for the general public, community or social benefit and where any equity is provided with a view to supporting the entity's primary objectives rather than with a view to providing a financial return to equity providers, shareholders or members.
Residual value (of an asset)	The estimated amount that an entity would currently obtain from disposal of an asset, after deducting the estimated costs of disposal, if the asset were already of the age and in the condition expected at the end of its useful life.
Revenue	The gross inflow of economic benefits during the period arising in the course of the ordinary activities of an entity when those inflows result in increases in equity, other than increases relating to contributions from equity participants.
Service concession arrangement	An arrangement whereby a public sector body or public benefit entity (the grantor) contracts with a private sector entity (the operator) to construct (or upgrade), operate and maintain infrastructure assets for a specified period of time (the concession period).
Useful life	The period over which an asset is expected to be available for use by an entity or the number of production or similar units expected to be obtained from the asset by an entity.

4.3.2   Scope

A service concession arrangement arises from a contractual agreement between a public sector body or public benefit entity (the grantor) and a private sector entity (the operator) to construct or upgrade, operate and maintain infrastructure assets for a specified period of time (the concession period). The operator is paid for its services over the period of the arrangement. *[FRS 102.34.12]*. Such payments are often referred to as 'unitary charges' because the amounts to be paid under the contract compensate the operator for both services in constructing or upgrading the infrastructure assets and for their maintenance and operation over a longer period.

A common feature of a SCA is the public service nature of the obligation undertaken by the operator, whereby the arrangement contractually obliges the operator to provide services to, or on behalf of, the grantor for the benefit of the public. *[FRS 102.34.12]*. This feature, that the operator is providing services to the public or for public benefit, is often applied to distinguish a service concession from the provision by a private sector entity of outsourcing, leasing or other services to a public sector body or public benefit entity (see 4.3.2.A below).

Specifically an arrangement is an SCA when the following conditions apply:

(a)   the grantor controls or regulates what services the operator must provide using the infrastructure assets, to whom, and at what price; and

(b)   the grantor controls, through ownership, beneficial entitlement or otherwise, any significant residual interest in the assets at the end of the term of the arrangement. *[FRS 102.34.12A]*.

Where the infrastructure assets have no significant residual value at the end of the term of the arrangement (i.e. the concession is for the entire useful life of the related infrastructure), then the arrangement is accounted for as a service concession if the grantor controls or regulates the services provided using the infrastructure as described at (a) above. *[FRS 102.34.12A]*.

For the purpose of condition (b) above, the grantor's control over any significant residual interest should both restrict the operator's practical ability to sell or pledge the infrastructure assets and give the grantor a continuing right of use throughout the concession period. *[FRS 102.34.12A]*. Control over the residual interest does not require that the infrastructure is returned to the grantor at the end of the concession. It is sufficient that the deployment of the infrastructure is controlled by the grantor, as illustrated in the example below.

Example 29.1:   Residual arrangements

A gas transmission system is being operated under a concession arrangement with the State Gas Authority. At the end of the term, the grantor will either acquire the infrastructure assets at their net book value, determined on the basis of the contract, or it may decide to grant a new SCA on the basis of a competitive tender, which will exclude the current operator. If the grantor elects to do the latter, the operator will be entitled to the lower of the following two amounts:

(a)   the net book value of the infrastructure, determined on the basis of the contract; and

(b)   the proceeds of a new competitive bidding process to acquire a new contract.

Although the operator cannot enter the competitive tender, it also has the right to enter into a new concession term but, in order to do so, it must match the best tender offer made. It has to pay to the grantor the excess of the best offer (b) above the amount in (a); should the tender offer be lower than (a), it will receive an equivalent refund.

In this arrangement, the grantor will control the residual. It can choose to take over the activities of the concession itself or it can allow potential operators, including the incumbent, to bid for a second term. The price that might be received by the operator, or paid by the grantor, is not relevant.

FRS 102 states that a concession may contain a group of contracts and sub-arrangements as elements of the SCA as a whole. Such an arrangement is treated as a whole when the group of contracts and sub-arrangements are linked in such a way that the commercial effect cannot be understood without reference to them as a whole. Accordingly, the contractual terms of certain contracts or arrangements may meet both the scope requirements of and SCA under Section 34, as noted above, and paragraphs 34.12 and 34.12A, and as a leasing contract under Section 20 – *Leases*. Where this is the case, the requirements of Section 34 shall prevail. *[FRS 102.34.12C]*.

4.3.2.A   *Judgements required in determining whether an arrangement is an SCA*

Arrangements within scope will be those that meet the following criteria:

- the arrangement is a contract between a public sector grantor and a private sector operator *[FRS 102.34.12]* ;

- the grantor controls or regulates the services *[FRS 102.34.12A(a)]*;

- the grantor controls any significant residual interest *[FRS 102.34.12A(b)]*;

- the infrastructure is constructed or upgraded in order to provide services to, or on behalf of, the public *[[FRS 102.34.12]*; and

- the operator has either a contractual right to receive cash from or at the direction of the grantor; or a contractual right to charge users of the service. *[FRS 102.34.13]*.

If an arrangement meets all of these criteria then the concession is in scope of Section 34. The last question also determines which accounting model, financial asset or intangible asset, described at 4.3.4 below, should be applied by the operator.

Because of the commercial and contractual complexities of SCAs and seemingly similar arrangements, the determination of whether or to what extent these criteria are met are always likely to be a matter of judgement and there will be different views in practice. Section 34 acknowledges that some arrangements might more appropriately be classified as leases *[FRS 102.34.12C]* and, as noted at 4.3.2 above, where the contract does not involve the provision of services to the public, depiction of a lease could be more appropriate. For example, where a government department has outsourced its information technology function to a private sector operator, it would be more usual to account for this arrangement as an IT services contract rather than a service concession.

This, and a number of other judgements familiar to IFRS reporters trying to assess whether an arrangement falls within the scope of IFRIC 12, are not addressed in Section 34. These include:

- determining what constitutes services to the public. Do members of the public have to consume the services being provided (for example by using a road or bridge) or does a wider concept of public benefit apply (for example in the provision of services by private contractors to the Ministry of Defence)?

- deciding how to classify arrangements where the use of only part of the infrastructure is controlled under the terms of the contract, or for part of the time. For example, a private contractor might be given the contract to build and operate an airport. The services to be provided for passengers, for airport security and to airlines might be regulated under the contract; but the operator might have total freedom over the design, operation and pricing of the parking, retail and other space in the airport complex.

Section 10 of FRS 102 suggests that entities may also consider the requirements and guidance in IFRIC 12 in these circumstances. *[FRS 102.10.6]*. The scope of IFRIC 12 is discussed in Section 2 of Chapter 26 of EY International GAAP 2015.

4.3.2.B   Accounting for arrangements determined not to be SCAs under FRS 102

Where an arrangement does not meet both the definition of an SCA and the control criteria noted at 4.3.2 above, Section 34 does not apply and the arrangement should be accounted for in accordance with Section 17 – *Property, Plant and Equipment*, Section 18 – *Intangible Assets other than Goodwill*, Section 20 – *Leases* – or Section 23 – *Revenue*, as appropriate, based on the nature of the arrangement. *[FRS 102.34.12D]*.

4.3.3   Accounting by grantors – finance lease liability model

Section 34 requires a grantor to account for its interest in a service concession contract as a finance lease. This is because the grantor in an SCA controls both the use to which the infrastructure is put during the contract term as well as any significant residual interest in the infrastructure at the end of the concession. *[FRS 102.34.12A]*. The contract also requires the grantor to pay the operator for the construction and operation of the assets, or to establish arrangements for the users of the infrastructure pay the operator themselves.

Therefore, the infrastructure assets are recognised as assets of the grantor together with a liability for its obligation under the concession. *[FRS 102.34.12E]*. The grantor should initially recognise the infrastructure assets and associated liability in accordance with paragraphs 9 and 10 of Section 20. *[FRS 102.34.12F]*. The liability is recognised as a finance lease liability and subsequently accounted for in accordance with paragraph 11 of Section 20. *[FRS 102.34.12G]*. Accounting for finance leases is discussed in Chapter 16.

The infrastructure assets are recognised as property, plant and equipment or as intangible assets, as appropriate, and subsequently accounted for in accordance with Section 17 or Section 18. *[FRS 102.34.12H]*. This includes the determination of useful lives and amortisation methods for the assets; the estimation of residual values; and accounting for impairment, as discussed in Chapters 13 and 14 for property, plant and equipment and for intangible assets respectively.

If the grantor is not required to recognised a liability to make payments to the operator, for example because the operator is expected to charge the users of the infrastructure directly, the grantor does shall not recognise the infrastructure assets. *[FRS 102.34.12F]*. In other words, the grantor recognises an asset only to the extent of its obligation to make payments to the operator for the construction of the infrastructure, its upgrade or its residual value at the end of the concession.

4.3.4   Accounting by operators

Accounting by the operator is more complicated, because its involvement in the concession comprises transactions relating to the construction of the infrastructure or its upgrade; the provision of scrvices to the public using the infrastructure; and the collection of payments from either the grantor, users of the service or a combination of both.

Looking first at the infrastructure, because control over the use of the assets during the concession term and any significant residual interest in them after the contract has ended lie with the grantor, *[FRS 102.34.12A]*, an operator in an arrangement determined to be a service concession does not recognise the infrastructure assets as property, plant and equipment. The operator only has a right of access to the assets in order to provide the public service on behalf of the grantor in accordance with the terms specified in the concession. *[FRS 102.34.12I]*.

A service concession contract gives the operator the right to receive payment in return for meeting its obligations to construct, upgrade, operate and maintain the infrastructure assets controlled by the grantor. Accordingly, Section 34 set out two principal categories of concession:

In one, the operator receives a financial asset – an unconditional contractual right to receive a specified or determinable amount of cash or another financial asset from, or at the direction of, the grantor in return for constructing (or upgrading) the infrastructure assets and then operating and maintaining the asset for a specified period of time. This category includes guarantees by the grantor to pay for any shortfall between amounts received from users of the public service and specified or determinable amounts. *[FRS 102.34.13(a)]*.

In the other, the operator receives an intangible asset – a right to charge for the use of the infrastructure assets that it constructs (or upgrades) and then operates and maintains for a specified period of time. A right to charge users is not an unconditional right to receive cash because the amounts are contingent on the extent to which the public uses the service. *[FRS 102.34.13(b)]*.

As noted above, sometimes an SCA may entitle the operator to receive payment from both the grantor and the users of the infrastructure. To the extent that the grantor has given an unconditional guarantee of payment for the construction (or upgrade) of the infrastructure assets, the operator has a financial asset; to the extent that the operator receives a right to charge the public for using the service the operator has an intangible asset. *[FRS 102.34.13]*.

No guidance is provided in Section 34 on the determination of whether the financial asset model or the intangible asset model is applied. The application of similar requirements under IFRIC 12 is discussed in Chapter 26 of EY International GAAP 2015 at 4.1.2. A comparison between the different models can be illustrated in the following table:

	Arrangement	*Applicable model*
1	Grantor pays – fixed payments	Financial asset
2	Grantor pays – payments vary with demand	Intangible asset
3	Grantor retains demand risk – users pay but grantor guarantees amounts	Financial asset or bifurcated (part financial, part intangible)
4	Grantor retains demand risk – operator collects revenues from users until it achieves specified return	Intangible asset
5	Users pay – no grantor guarantees	Intangible asset

4.3.4.A   Financial asset model

The operator shall recognise a financial asset to the extent it has an unconditional contractual right to receive cash or another financial asset from, or at the direction of, the grantor for the construction (or upgrade) services. The operator shall initially recognise the financial asset at the fair value of the consideration received or receivable, based on the fair value of the construction (or upgrade) services provided. Thereafter, it shall account for the financial asset in accordance with Section 11 – *Basic Financial Instruments* – and Section 12 – *Other Financial Instruments Issues.* *[FRS 102.34.14].*

Whether the financial asset represents a basic financial instrument within the scope of Section 11 or Section 12 will depend on the terms of the Concession and judgement is required (see Chapter 8). The following example is based on Illustrative Example 1 in IFRIC 12.

Example 29.2:   The Financial Asset Model – recording the construction asset

Table 1 Concession terms

The terms of the arrangement require an operator to construct a road – completing construction within two years – and maintain and operate the road to a specified standard for eight years (i.e. years 3-10). The terms of the concession also require the operator to resurface the road at the end of year 8. At the end of year 10, the arrangement will end. The operator estimates that the costs it will incur to fulfil its obligations will be:

	Year	£
Construction services (per year)	1-2	500
Operation services (per year)	3-10	10
Road resurfacing	8	100

The terms of the concession require the grantor to pay the operator £200 per year in years 3-10 for making the road available to the public.

For the purpose of this illustration, it is assumed that all cash flows take place at the end of the year.

Table 2 Contract revenue

The operator recognises contract revenue and costs in accordance with Section 23 – *Revenue.* The costs of each activity – construction, operation, maintenance and resurfacing – are recognised as expenses by reference to the stage of completion of that activity. Contract revenue – the fair value of the amount due from the grantor for the activity undertaken – is recognised at the same time.

The total consideration (£200 in each of years 3-8) reflects the fair values for each of the services, which are:

	Fair value		
Construction	Forecast cost	+	5%
Operation and maintenance	" "	+	20%
Road resurfacing	" "	+	10%
Lending rate to grantor	**6.18% per year**		

In year 1, for example, construction costs of £500, construction revenue of £525 (cost plus 5 per cent), and hence construction profit of £25 are recognised in the income statement.

Financial asset

The amount due from the grantor meets the definition of a receivable in Section 11. The receivable is measured initially at fair value. It is subsequently measured at amortised cost, i.e. the amount initially recognised plus the cumulative interest on that amount calculated using the effective interest method minus repayments.

Table 3 Measurement of receivable

	£
Amount due for construction in year 1	525
Receivable at end of year 1*	525
Effective interest in year 2 on receivable at the end of year 1 (6.18% × £525)	32
Amount due for construction in year 2	525
Receivable at end of year 2	1,082
Effective interest in year 3 on receivable at the end of year 2 (6.18% × £1,082)	67
Amount due for operation in year 3 (£10 × (1 + 20%))	12
Cash receipts in year 3	(200)
Receivable at end of year 3	961

* No effective interest arises in year 1 because the cash flows are assumed to take place at the end of the year.

4.3.4.B   Intangible asset model

Under this accounting model, the operator recognises an intangible asset to the extent that it receives a right (a licence) to charge users of the public service. The operator shall initially recognise the intangible asset at the fair value of the consideration received or receivable, based on the fair value of the construction (or upgrade) services provided. Thereafter, it shall account for the intangible asset in accordance with Section 18. *[FRS 102.34.15]*. The following example is based on Example 2 in IFRIC 12.

Example 29.3:   The Intangible Asset Model – recording the construction asset

Arrangement terms

The terms of a service arrangement require an operator to construct a road – completing construction within two years – and maintain and operate the road to a specified standard for eight years (i.e. years 3-10). The terms of the arrangement also require the operator to resurface the road when the original surface has deteriorated below a specified condition. The operator estimates that it will have to undertake the resurfacing at the end of the year 8. At the end of year 10, the service arrangement will end. The operator estimates that the costs it will incur to fulfil its obligations will be:

Table 1 Contract costs

	Year	£
Construction services (per year)	1-2	500
Operation services (per year)	3-10	10
Road resurfacing	8	100

The terms of the arrangement allow the operator to collect tolls from drivers using the road. The operator forecasts that vehicle numbers will remain constant over the duration of the contract and that it will receive tolls of £200 in each of years 3-10.

For the purpose of this illustration, it is assumed that all cash flows take place at the end of the year.

Intangible asset

The operator provides construction services to the grantor in exchange for an intangible asset, i.e. a right to collect tolls from road users in years 3-10. In accordance with Section 18, the operator recognises the intangible asset at cost, i.e. the fair value of consideration received or receivable.

During the construction phase of the arrangement the operator's asset (representing its accumulating right to be paid for providing construction services) is classified as an intangible asset (licence to charge users of the infrastructure). The operator estimates the fair value of its consideration received to be equal to the forecast construction costs plus 5 per cent margin. It is also assumed that the operator adopts the allowed alternative treatment in Section 25 – *Borrowing Costs* – and therefore capitalises the borrowing costs, estimated at 6.7 per cent, during the construction phase:

Table 2 Initial measurement of intangible asset

	£
Construction services in year 1 (£500 × (1 + 5%))	525
Capitalisation of borrowing costs	34
Construction services in year 2 (£500 × (1 + 5%))	525
Intangible asset at end of year 2	1,084

The intangible asset is amortised over the period in which it is expected to be available for use by the operator, i.e. years 3-10. In this case, the directors determine that it is appropriate to amortise using a straight-line method. The annual amortisation charge is therefore £1,084 divided by 8 years, i.e. £135 per year.

Construction costs and revenue

The operator recognises the revenue and costs in accordance with Section 23, i.e. by reference to the stage of completion of the construction. It measures contract revenue at the fair value of the consideration received or receivable. Thus in each of years 1 and 2 it recognises in its income statement construction costs of £500, construction revenue of £525 (cost plus 5 per cent) and, hence, construction profit of £25.

Toll revenue

The road users pay for the public services at the same time as they receive them, i.e. when they use the road. The operator therefore recognises toll revenue when it collects the tolls.

4.3.4.C   Measuring the fair value of construction services

Under both the financial asset model and the intangible asset model, the asset that is the operator initially recognises is measured at the fair value of the consideration received or receivable, based on the fair value of the construction (or upgrade) services provided. *[FRS 102.34.14, 15]*. The operator only recognises an asset in respect of the contractual obligations that have been satisfied at this stage, namely the provision of construction or upgrade services. Under Section 34, there is no suggestion that an operator would recognise an asset for the present value of all the contractual payments to be received under the contract (including for operating services).

Section 34 provides no guidance on the calculation of the fair value of the construction (or upgrade) services provided, and no guidance on the allocation of consideration between construction (or upgrade) services and operating services where the operator is paid under a single payment mechanism throughout the term of the concession.

Under IFRIC 12, the value of the construction services is determined in accordance with IAS 11 – *Construction Contracts*. *[IFRIC 12.14]*. Applying a similar approach under FRS 102 would result in the fair value of the construction (or upgrade) services provided being calculated, and revenue recognised, in accordance with Section 23 (see Chapter 18). This approach has been applied in Examples 29.2 and 29.3 above, where an appropriate profit margin (5%) was added to the construction costs incurred. Under Section 23, revenue would be recognised by reference to the stage of completion of the construction (or upgrade) services.

4.3.4.C   Operating services

Section 34 requires the operator to account for revenue relating to the operating services it performs in accordance with Section 23. *[FRS 102.34.16]*. Accordingly, revenue may be recognised on a straight-line basis over the contract period; or as the infrastructure is used; or as other performance obligations are determined to have been satisfied (see Chapter 18).

4.3.4.D   Borrowing costs incurred during the construction or upgrade phase

Many operators will borrow funds to finance the up-front construction or upgrade costs associated with the SCA. Only under the intangible asset model will an operator have the option to capitalise any borrowing costs. Otherwise, borrowing costs attributable to the concession should be recognised as an expense. Entities should account for its borrowing costs in accordance with Section 25 – *Borrowing Costs*. *[FRS 102.34.16A]*. Accounting for borrowing costs is discussed in Chapter 20.

4.3.4.E   Relief from retrospective application by operators of SCAs

An operator adopting FRS 102 for the first time is not required to apply Section 34 to SCAs that were entered into before the date of transition. Such concessions would continue to be classified as property, plant and equipment or as financial assets in accordance with FRS 5 ANF and Section 34 would be applied only to concessions entered into after the date of transition. *[FRS 102.35.10(i)]*. This relief relates only to the classification of the concession asset recognised by the operator. All other assets and liabilities of the operator at the transition date should be accounted for in accordance to the requirements of Section 35 – *Transition to this FRS* (see Chapter 30).

There are no transitional reliefs available to grantors.

4.3.4.F   Aspects of SCA accounting not addressed in Section 34

As noted at 4.2.2 above, a number of features often seen in SCAs and familiar to IFRS reporters are not addressed in Section 34. These include accounting for the following features:

- assets of the operator used in the service concession;
- payments made by the operator to the grantor (for example rentals payable for assets retained by the grantor or for other services provided by the public sector body);
- the existence of variable payment terms under the service concession contract;
- where both an intangible asset and a financial asset exists; and
- where a major upgrade, replacement or maintenance works are required at intervals during the concession term.

Section 10 of FRS 102 suggests that entities may also consider the requirements and guidance in IFRIC 12 in these circumstances. *[FRS 102.10.6]*. These features of service concession arrangements under IFRIC 12 are discussed in Sections 4 and 5 of Chapter 26 of EY International GAAP 2015.

4.3.5   *Disclosures relating to service concession arrangements*

Section 34 does not set out any required disclosures for SCAs. Having referred a grantor or an operator to the relevant sections of FRS 102, be that Leases (Section 20); Property, Plant and Equipment (Section 17); Basic Financial Instruments (Section 11); Financial Instruments Issues (Section 12); Intangible Assets (Section 18); or Borrowing Costs (Section 25), grantors and operators should provide the related disclosures according to each section respectively.

In addition, there is the requirement in Section 8 – *Notes to the Financial Statements* – to provide 'information that is not presented elsewhere in the financial statements but is relevant to an understanding of them'. *[FRS 102.8.2(c)]*.   In that context, an entity might consider making the following disclosures, set out in SIC-29 for IFRS reporters:

(a)   a description of the arrangement;

(b)   significant terms of the arrangement that may affect the amount, timing and certainty of future cash flows (e.g. the period of the concession, re-pricing dates and the basis upon which re-pricing or re-negotiation is determined);

(c)   the nature and extent (e.g. quantity, time period or amount as appropriate) of:

   (i)   rights to use specified assets;

   (ii)   obligations to provide or rights to expect provision of services;

   (iii)   obligations to acquire or build items of property, plant and equipment;

   (iv)   obligations to deliver or rights to receive specified assets at the end of the concession period;

   (v)   renewal and termination options; and

   (vi)   other rights and obligations (e.g. major overhauls);

(d)   changes in the arrangement occurring during the period; and

(e)   how the service arrangement has been classified. *[SIC-29.6]*.

IFRS reporters are also required to disclose 'the amount of revenue and profits or losses recognised in the period on exchanging construction services for a financial asset and an intangible asset'. *[SIC-29.6A]*.

4.4   Summary of GAAP differences

	FRS 102	*Previous UK GAAP*	*IFRS*
Scope	Contracts between a public sector grantor and private sector operator where the grantor controls or regulates the use of the infrastructure and any significant residual interest.	Arrangements under the Private Finance Initiative, including those where the operator retains title to the asset at the end of the contract or the grantor has the option to purchase the asset for market value.	Same as FRS 102.
Accounting model	Control model – grantor controls use of infrastructure and any significant residual interest.	Risks and rewards model – assessment made on the basis of which party has rights to benefits from the asset and exposure to related risks.	Same as FRS 102.
Accounting by Grantor	Recognise a finance lease liability and related asset to the extent that there is a contractual obligation to pay for the infrastructure assets.	Two alternative outcomes: (a) recognise the property as an asset and a related liability. Measured at fair value of the property; or (b) Operating expense (contract for services).	Not specified in IFRIC 12.
Accounting by operator	Recognise revenue for construction or upgrade services and either a financial asset (right to payment) or an intangible asset (right to charge users) or both.	Two alternative outcomes: (a) recognise the property as an asset and record revenue over the concession term; or (b) record the construction and disposal of the property at fair value and recognise a financial asset. Any receipts above the amounts applied against the financial asset are recorded in operating profit.	Same as FRS 102.
Disclosures	None specified – refer to other applicable sections of FRS 102.	Disclosures specified.	Disclosures specified.

5   HERITAGE ASSETS

Section 34 – *Specialised Activities* – includes guidance on the accounting for heritage assets, defined as 'Tangible and intangible assets with historic, artistic, scientific, technological, geophysical, or environmental qualities that are held and maintained principally for their contribution to knowledge and culture'. *[FRS 102 Appendix I]*.

In summary, the recognition and measurement accounting requirements for heritage assets are the same as for property, plant and equipment. However, the disclosure requirements are different.

5.1 Comparison between Section 34 (Heritage assets), previous UK GAAP and IFRS

Overall, the requirements of the paragraphs in Section 34 that deal with heritage assets are very similar to those contained previously in FRS 30 – *Heritage assets*. There is no specific guidance on heritage assets in IFRS.

5.1.1 Key differences between Section 34 (Heritage assets) and previous UK GAAP

5.1.1.A Scope

Heritage assets within the scope of the requirements of Section 34 do not include investment property, property, plant and equipment or intangible assets which fall within the scope of Section 16 – *Investment Property*, Section 17 – *Property, Plant and Equipment* – and Section 18 – *Intangible Assets other than Goodwill*. *[FRS 102.34.49]*.

All tangible assets that meet the description of a heritage asset were within the scope of FRS 30. *[FRS 30.3]*. This would therefore include property, plant and equipment and investment property normally falling within the scope of FRS 15 – *Tangible fixed assets* – and SSAP 19 – *Accounting for Investment Properties*.

The scope of Section 34 is therefore more restrictive in its definition of a heritage asset than previous UK GAAP. As a result, some assets that were heritage assets under previous UK GAAP may not qualify as heritage assets under Section 34.

5.1.1.B Depreciation of heritage assets with indefinite lives

Heritage assets within the scope of Section 34 are recognised and measured in accordance with Section 17. *[FRS 102.34.51]*. Section 17 does not refer to assets with indefinite lives other than to state that there are some exceptions to the principle of depreciation such as land which generally has an unlimited useful life and is not depreciated. *[FRS 102.17.16]*.

FRS 30 did not require depreciation of heritage assets with indefinite lives. *[FRS 30.23]*.

5.1.1.C Donations of heritage assets

Section 34 has no specific guidance on the initial measurement of donated assets. However, donations received by public benefit entities or entities within a public benefit entity group are dealt with separately in Section 34 and are discussed at 6 below.

FRS 30 required that donations of heritage assets be reported in the profit and loss account at valuation. *[FRS 30.25]*.

5.1.2 Key differences between Section 34 and IFRS

IFRS has no specific requirements for heritage assets. Therefore, heritage assets would be accounted for according to their nature under either IAS 16 – *Property, Plant and Equipment*, IAS 38 – *Intangible Assets* – or IAS 40 – *Investment Property*.

5.2   Requirements of section 34 for heritage assets

5.2.1   *Scope of the requirements dealing with heritage assets*

Heritage assets are 'tangible and intangible assets with historic, artistic, scientific, technological, geophysical, or environmental qualities that are held and maintained principally for their contribution to knowledge and culture'. *[FRS 102 Appendix I].*

Having defined a heritage asset as a tangible and intangible asset, Section 34 goes on to state that its paragraphs relating to heritage assets do not apply to investment property, property, plant and equipment or intangible assets that fall within the scope of Section 16, Section 17, and Section 18. *[FRS 102.34.49].* This is a somewhat circular reference since the scope of both Sections 17 and 18 (but not Section 16) state that they do not apply to heritage assets. *[FRS 102.17.3, FRS 102.18.3].* However, the intent of this wording appears to be to clarify that property, plant and equipment and intangible assets with historic, artistic, scientific, technological, geographical or environmental qualities that are not held principally for their contribution to knowledge and culture cannot be heritage assets. Investment property is property held to earn rentals or for capital appreciation or both *[FRS 102.16.2]* and not property held and maintained for its contribution to knowledge and culture.

Section 34 further explains that works of art and similar objects held by commercial companies are not heritage assets as they are not maintained principally for their contribution to knowledge and culture. Instead, such assets shall be accounted for in accordance with Section 17. Similarly, heritage assets used by the entity itself, for example historic buildings used by teaching establishments, shall also be accounted for under Section 17. The reason for this is that an operational perspective is likely to be most relevant for users of the financial statements. Section 34 goes on to state that entities that use historic buildings or similar assets for their own use may wish to provide the disclosures required for heritage assets although it does not require these disclosures. *[FRS 102.34.50].* Given that heritage assets are recognised and measured in accordance with Section 17, this distinction drawn by the FRC between heritage assets maintained for their contribution to knowledge and culture and heritage assets used for some other purpose affects only disclosure and not recognition and measurement.

5.2.2   *Recognition and measurement of heritage assets*

The general requirement of Section 34 is that heritage assets should be recognised and measured in accordance with Section 17, as if property plant and equipment, using either the cost or revaluation model. *[FRS 102.34.51].* Accounting for property plant and equipment is discussed in Chapter 13.

Heritage assets must be recognised in the statement of financial position separately from other assets. *[FRS 102.34.52].*

It is assumed that when heritage assets have previously been capitalised or are recently purchased that information on the cost or value of the asset will be available. However, when this information is not available, and cannot be obtained at a cost which is commensurate with the benefit to the users of the financial statements, the assets shall not be recognised. However, in those circumstances, additional disclosures are required explaining why the assets are not recognised, the significance and nature of those assets and information helpful in assessing the value of the assets (see 5.2.3 below). *[FRS 102.34.53].*

At each reporting date, an entity shall apply the requirements of Section 27 – *Impairment of Assets* – to determine whether a heritage asset is impaired and, if so, how to recognise and measure the impairment loss. Section 34 states that physical deterioration, breakage or doubts arising as to an asset's authenticity are examples of impairment indicators for heritage assets. *[FRS 102.34.54].* The requirements of Section 27 are discussed in Chapter 22.

5.2.3　Disclosures required for heritage assets

An entity should disclose the following for all heritage assets it holds: *[FRS 102.34.55]*

- an indication of the nature and scale of heritage assets held;
- the policy for the acquisition, preservation, management and disposal of heritage assets (including a description of the records maintained by the entity of its cost model or revaluation model and information on the extent to which access to the assets is permitted);
- the accounting policies adopted for heritage assets, including details of the measurement bases used;
- the amount of the adjustment relating to periods before those presented, to the extent practicable; and
- an explanation if it is impracticable to determine the amounts to be disclosed above.
- for heritage assets that have not been recognised in the statement of financial position (see 5.2.2 above), the notes to the financial statements shall:
  - explain the reasons why;
  - describe the significance and nature of those assets;
  - disclose information that is helpful in assessing the value of those heritage assets.
- when heritage assets are recognised in the statement of financial position the following disclosure is required;
  - the carrying amount of heritage assets at the beginning of the reporting period and the reporting date, including an analysis between classes or groups of heritage assets recognised at cost and those recognised at valuation; and
  - when assets are recognised at valuation, sufficient information to assist in understand the valuation being recognised (date of valuation, method used, whether carried out by external valuer and if so their qualification and any significant limitations on the valuation).
- a summary of transactions relating to heritage assets for the reporting period and each of the previous four reporting periods disclosing;
  - the cost of acquisitions or heritage assets;
  - the value of heritage assets acquired by donations;
  - the carrying amount of heritage assets disposed of in the period and proceeds received; and

- any impairment recognised in the period.

The summary shall show separately those transactions included in the statement of financial position and those that are not.

- in exceptional circumstances when it is impracticable to obtain a valuation of heritage assets acquired by donation the reason shall be stated.

Disclosures can be aggregated for groups or classes of heritage assets, provided this does not obscure significant information.

Where it is impracticable to do so, the disclosure of the summary of heritage asset transactions for the reporting period and each of the previous four reporting periods (see above) need not be given for any accounting period earlier than the previous comparable period. If impracticability applies, then a statement shall be made to that effect. *[FRS 102.34.56]*.

There are no additional company law matters particular to heritage assets.

FRS 30 contained several detailed examples to illustrate the disclosure requirements, which are not included in FRS 102.

5.3   Summary of GAAP differences

	FRS 102	*Previous UK GAAP*	*IFRS*
Scope	Applies to heritage assets which do not meet the definition of investment property, property, plant and equipment or intangible assets.	Applies to all tangible assets that meet the definition of a heritage asset.	No specific requirements for heritage assets. Accounting will follow the nature of the asset (e.g.: property, plant and equipment, intangible or investment property).
Recognition and measurement	In accordance with Section 17 – *Property, Plant and Equipment* (which requires depreciated cost or fair value with valuation gains/losses through OCI).	In accordance with FRS 15 – *Tangible fixed assets* (which required depreciated cost or valuation with valuation gains/losses through STRGL).	Not applicable.
Depreciation of indefinite life heritage assets.	Not mentioned.	Depreciation not required.	Not applicable.
Donations of heritage assets	Not mentioned (donations to public benefit entities addressed separately within Section 34 of FRS 102).	Donations of heritage assets are reported in the profit and loss account at valuation.	Not applicable.
Disclosures	Separate disclosures are required for heritage assets.	Separate disclosures required for heritage assets (same disclosures as FRS 102).	No specific disclosures for heritage assets.

6   PUBLIC BENEFIT ENTITIES

6.1   Background

This section deals with the paragraphs in Section 34 proceeded with 'PBE' which relate to Public Benefit Entities.

6.2   Terms used in Section 34

The following terms are used in Section 34 with the meanings specified. *[FRS 102 Appendix I].*

Term	*Definition*
Non-exchange transaction	A transaction whereby an entity receives value from another entity without directly giving approximately equal value in exchange, or gives value to another entity without directly receiving approximately equal value in exchange.
Performance-related condition	A condition that requires the performance of a particular level of service or units of output to be delivered, with payment of, or entitlement to, the resources conditional on that performance.
Public benefit entity	An entity whose primary objective is to provide goods or services for the general public, community or social benefit and where any equity is provided with a view to supporting the entity's primary objectives rather than with a view to providing a financial return to equity providers, shareholders or members[3]
Public benefit entity group	A public benefit entity parent and all of its wholly-owned subsidiaries.
Public benefit entity concessionary loan	A loan made or received between a public benefit entity or an entity within a public benefit entity group and another party: (a) at below the prevailing market rate of interest; (b) that is not repayable on demand; and (c) is for the purposes of furthering the objectives of the public benefit entity or public benefit entity parent.
Restriction	A requirement that limits or directs the purposes for which a resource may be used that does not meet the definition of a performance-related condition.

6.3   Incoming resources from non-exchange transactions

6.3.1   Introduction

FRS 102 defines a non-exchange transaction as one where an entity receives value from another entity without directly giving approximately equal value in exchange, or gives value to another entity without directly receiving approximately equal value in exchange. *[FRS 102 Appendix I, FRS 102.PBE34.65].*

Chapter 29

A non-exchange transaction that meets the definition of a government grant should be accounted for in accordance with the requirements of Section 24 – *Government Grants*, and these are covered in Chapter 19. *[FRS 102.PBE34.64]*.

Where public benefit entities, or entities within a public benefit entity group, receive other resources by way of non-exchange transactions then Section 34 (and the additional guidance in its Appendix B) are applied to determine the appropriate accounting. *[FRS 102.PBE34.65]*.

The Section adds that, in this context, non-exchange transactions can include, but are not limited to, donations (of cash, goods, and services) and legacies (see 6.3.2.C below). *[FRS 102.PBE34.66]*.

6.3.2   Recognition

Overview of the requirements

An entity should recognise receipts of resources from non-exchange transactions as follows: *[FRS 102.PBE34.67]*

(a)   on transactions that do not impose specified future performance-related conditions on the entity are recognised in income when the resources are received or receivable;

(b)   on transactions that do impose specified future performance-related conditions on the entity are recognised in income only when the performance-related conditions are met;

(c)   where resources are received before the revenue recognition criteria are satisfied, the entity recognises a liability.

The Standard defines a 'restriction' as 'a requirement that limits or directs the purposes for which a resource may be used that does not meet the definition of a performance related condition'. *[FRS 102 Appendix I]*. The existence of such a restriction does not prohibit a resource from being recognised in income when receivable. *[FRS 102.PBE34.68]*. An example of a restriction would be a where a donor requires that a donation must be used to fund a specific activity but the donor does not set any requirements making the donation conditional on the performance or service levels of the activity.

The receipt of resources will usually result in an entity recognising an asset and corresponding income for the fair value of resources when those resources become received or receivable. Instances when this may not be the case include where: *[FRS 102.PBE34B.1]*

(a)   an entity received the resources in the form of services (see 6.3.2.A below); or

(b)   there are performance-related conditions attached to the resources, which have yet to be fulfilled (see 6.3.2.B below).

When applying the above recognition requirements, an entity must take into consideration whether the resource being received can be measured reliably and whether the benefits of recognising the resource outweigh the costs. *[FRS 102.PBE34.69]*.

Incoming resources should only be recognised when their fair value can be measured reliably. Hence, where it is impracticable to make a sufficiently reliable estimate of the value of the incoming resource, the related income should be recognised in the financial period when the resource is sold or distributed. A common example would be that of high volume, low value second-hand goods which have been donated for resale. *[FRS 102.PBE34.70, PBE34B.2, 4].*

The guidance to Section 34 notes that the concepts of materiality, and the balance between cost and benefit (see Chapter 3) should be considered when deciding which resources received should be recognised in the financial statements. *[FRS 102.PBE34B.3].*

An entity should recognise a liability for any resource, previously received and recognised in income, when a subsequent failure to meet restrictions or performance-related conditions attached to it causes repayment to become probable. *[FRS 102.PBE34.71].*

6.3.2.A   Services

The Standard notes that donations of services that can be reasonably quantified will usually result in the recognition of income and an expense rather than an asset because the service is consumed immediately. An asset will be recognised only when those services are used to produce an asset, in which case the services received will be capitalised as part of the cost of that asset in accordance with the relevant Section of the standard. *[FRS 102.PBE34.72].*

An example would be in the construction of a building where the plumbing and electrical services have been donated. Such donated services would be recognised as a part of the cost of that building provided they meet the recognition criteria in Section 17 – *Property, Plant and Equipment. [FRS 102.PBE34B.9].*

Donated services that can be reasonably quantified should be recognised in the financial statements when they are received. The Standard notes that examples of such services that can be reasonably quantified include donated facilities, such as office accommodation, are services that would otherwise have been purchased and services usually provided by an individual or an entity as part of their trade or profession for a fee. The guidance to the Section adds it is expected that contributions made by volunteers cannot be reasonably quantified and therefore such services should not be recognised. *[FRS 102.PBE34B.8, PBE34B.10, PBE34B.11].*

6.3.2.B   Performance-related conditions

Some resources come with performance-related conditions attached requiring the recipient to use the resources to provide a specified level of service to be entitled to retain the resources. An entity should not recognise income from those resources until these performance-related conditions have been met. *[FRS 102.PBE34B.13].*

However, some requirements are stated so broadly that they do not actually impose a performance-related condition on the recipient. In these cases the recipient should recognise income on receipt of the transfer of resources. *[FRS 102.PBE34B.14].*

Chapter 29

6.3.2.C   *Legacies*

Donations in the form of legacies should be recognised when it is probable that the legacy will be received and its value can be measured reliably. These criteria will normally be met following probate once the executors of the estate have established that there are sufficient assets in the estate, after settling liabilities, to pay the legacy. *[FRS 102.PBE34B.5]*.

Evidence that the executors have determined that a payment can be made may arise on the agreement of the estate's accounts or notification that payment will be made. Where notification is received after the year-end but it is clear that the executors have agreed prior to the year-end that the legacy can be paid, the legacy is accrued in the financial statements. The certainty and measurability of the receipt may be affected by subsequent events such as valuations and disputes. *[FRS 102.PBE34.B.6]*.

The Standard permits entities that are in receipt of numerous immaterial legacies for which individual identification would be burdensome to take a portfolio approach. *[FRS 102.PBE34B.7]*.

6.3.3   *Measurement*

An entity should measure incoming resources from non-exchange transactions as follows: *[FRS 102.PBE34.73]*

(a)   Donated services and facilities that would otherwise have been purchased should be measured at the value to the entity.

(b)   All other incoming resources from non-exchange transactions should be measured at the fair value of the resources received or receivable.

The value placed on the donated services and facilities in (a) should be the estimated value to the entity of the service or facility received. This will be the price the entity estimates it would pay in the open market for an equivalent service or facility. *[FRS 102.PBE34B.15]*.

In (b) the fair values are usually the price that the entity would have to pay on the open market for an equivalent resource. *[FRS 102.PBE34B.16]*.

When there is no direct evidence of an open market value for an equivalent item the Standard notes suggests that a value may be derived from sources such as: *[FRS 102.PBE34B.17]*.

(a)   the cost of the item to the donor; or

(b)   in the case of goods that are expected to be sold, the estimated resale value (which may reflect the amount actually realised) after deducting the cost to sell the goods.

As noted earlier, donated services are recognised as income with an equivalent amount recognised as an expense in income and expenditure, unless the expense can be capitalised as part of the cost of an asset. *[FRS 102.PBE34B.18]*.

6.3.4 Disclosure

An entity should disclose the following relating to non-exchange transactions: *[FRS 102.PBE34.74].*

(a) the nature and amounts of resources receivable from non-exchange transactions recognised in the financial statements;

(b) any unfulfilled conditions or other contingencies attaching to resources from non-exchange transactions that have not been recognised in income; and

(c) an indication of other forms of resources from non-exchange transactions from which the entity has benefited.

The disclosure required by (c) would include the disclosure of unrecognised volunteer services. *[FRS 102.PBE34B.12].*

6.4 Public benefit entity combinations

These requirements apply only to public benefit entities for the following categories of entity combinations which involve a whole entity or parts of an entity combining with another entity: *[FRS 102.PBE34.75].*

- combinations at nil or nominal consideration which are in substance a gift; and

- combinations which meet the definition and criteria of a merger.

Combinations which are determined to be acquisitions should be accounted for in accordance with Section 19 – *Business Combinations and Goodwill. [FRS 102.PBE34.76].*

6.4.1 Combinations that are in substance a gift

The Standard requires that a combination that is in substance a gift should be accounted for in accordance with Section 19 except for following matters: *[FRS 102.PBE34.77].*

(a) Any excess of the fair value of the assets received over the fair value of the liabilities assumed is recognised as a gain in income and expenditure. This gain represents the gift of the value of one entity to another and should be recognised as income. *[FRS 102.PBE34.78].*

(b) Any excess of the fair value of the liabilities assumed over the fair value of the assets received is recognised as a loss in income and expenditure. This loss represents the net obligations assumed, for which the receiving entity has not received a financial reward and should be recognised as an expense. *[FRS 102.PBE34.79].*

6.4.2 Combinations that are a merger

An entity combination that is a merger should apply merger accounting as set out below: *[FRS 102.PBE34.80]*

Any entity combination which is neither a combination that is in substance a gift nor a merger should be accounted for as an acquisition in accordance with Section 19. *[FRS 102.PBE34.81].*

Under merger accounting the following procedures are applied:

- the carrying value of the assets and liabilities of the parties to the combination are not adjusted to fair value, although adjustments should be made to achieve uniformity of accounting policies across the combining entities;

- the results and cash flows of all the combining entities should be brought into the financial statements of the newly formed entity from the beginning of the financial period in which the merger occurs;

- the comparative amounts (marked as 'combined figures') should be restated by including the results for all the combining entities for the previous accounting period and their statement of financial positions for the previous reporting date; and

- all costs associated with the merger should be charged as an expense in the period incurred. *[FRS 102.PBE34.82-85].*

For each entity combination accounted for as a merger in the reporting period the following disclosure is required in the newly formed entity's financial statements: *[FRS 102.PBE34.86]*

- the names and descriptions of the combining entities or businesses;

- the date of the merger;

- an analysis of the principal components of the current year's total comprehensive income to indicate:

  - the amounts relating to the newly formed merged entity for the period after the date of the merger; and

  - the amounts relating to each party to the merger up to the date of the merger.

- an analysis of the previous year's total comprehensive income between each party to the merger;

- the aggregate carrying value of the net assets of each party to the merger at the date of the merger; and

- the nature and amount of any significant adjustments required to align accounting policies and an explanation of any further adjustments made to net assets as a result of the merger.

6.5   Public benefit entity concessionary loans

These requirements address the recognition, measurement and disclosure of public benefit entity concessionary loan arrangements within the financial statements of public benefit entities or entities within a public benefit entity group making or receiving public benefit entity concessionary loans. The requirements apply to public benefit entity concessionary loan arrangements only and are not applicable to loans which are at a market rate or to other commercial arrangements. *[FRS 102.PBE34.87].*

Public benefit entity concessionary loans are defined in the Standard as loans made or received between a public benefit entity, or an entity within the public benefit entity group, and another party at below the prevailing market rate of interest that are not repayable on demand and are for the purposes of furthering the objectives of the public benefit entity or public benefit entity parent. *[FRS 102.PBE34.88].*

The prevailing market rate of interest is defined in the Standard as the rate of interest that would apply to the entity in an open market for a similar financial instrument. *[FRS 102 Appendix I].*

6.5.2   Accounting policy choice

Entities making or receiving public benefit entity concessionary loans have a policy choice and should use either:

(a)   the recognition, measurement and disclosure requirements in Section 11 – *Basic Financial Instruments* – or Section 12 – *Other Financial Instruments Issues*, or

(b)   the accounting treatment set out in 6.5.2 below.

A public benefit entity or an entity within a public benefit entity group should apply the same accounting policy to concessionary loans both made and received. *[FRS 102.PBE34.89].*

6.5.2   Accounting requirements

6.5.2.A   Initial measurement

A public benefit entity or an entity within a public benefit entity group making or receiving concessionary loans should initially measure these arrangements at the amount received or paid and recognise them in the statement of financial position. *[FRS 102.PBE34.90].*

6.5.2.B   Subsequent measurement

In subsequent years, the carrying amount of concessionary loans in the financial statements should be adjusted to reflect any accrued interest payable or receivable. *[FRS 102.PBE34.91].*

To the extent that a loan that has been made is irrecoverable, any impairment loss should be recognised as an expense. *[FRS 102.PBE34.92].*

6.5.2.C   Presentation and disclosure

Concessionary loans made and concessionary loans received should be presented by the entity either as separate line items on the face of the statement of financial position or in the notes to the financial statements. *[FRS 102.PBE34.93].*

Concessionary loans should be presented separately between amounts repayable or receivable within one year and amounts repayable or receivable after more than one year. *[FRS 102.PBE34.94].*

The entity should disclose in the summary of significant accounting policies the measurement basis used for concessionary loans and any other accounting policies which are relevant to the understanding of these transactions within the financial statements. *[FRS 102.PBE34.95].*

The entity should also disclose: *[FRS 102.PBE34.96]*

(a)   the terms and conditions of concessionary loan arrangements, for example the interest rate, any security provided and the terms of the repayment; and

(b)   the value of concessionary loans which have been committed but not taken up at the year end.

Chapter 29

Concessionary loans made or received should be disclosed separately. However multiple loans made or received may be disclosed in aggregate, providing that such aggregation does not obscure significant information. *[FRS 102.PBE34.97].*

References

1 IFRIC update, IASB, January 2006, pp 2-3.
2 IASC Issues Paper 4.20.
3 FRS 102, Appendix 1, footnote 29 to the definition of Public Benefit Entity provides additional Guidance.

Chapter 30   Transition to FRS 102

Chapter 30

List of examples

Chapter 30   Transition to FRS 102

1   INTRODUCTION

Section 35 – *Transition to this FRS* – addresses the first-time adoption of FRS 102. The guidance in Section 35 is a simplified version of IFRS 1 – *First-time Adoption of International Financial Reporting Standards* – that contains significant modifications compared to Section 35 of the IFRS for SMEs.

The underlying principle in Section 35 is that a first-time adopter should prepare financial statements applying FRS 102 retrospectively. However, there are a number of exemptions that allow and exceptions that require a first-time adopter to deviate from this principle in preparing its opening statement of financial position at the date of transition (i.e. at the beginning of the earliest period presented).

1.1   Summary of Section 35

Section 35 applies to the first set of financial statements prepared in conformity with FRS 102 – with a full, unreserved statement of compliance with FRS 102. *[FRS 102.35.3]*.

In preparing its opening statement of financial position, an entity must follow the requirements of FRS 102, subject to application of the mandatory exceptions and optional exemptions provided in Section 35. *[FRS 102.35.7]*. Adjustments are recognised directly in retained earnings (or, if appropriate, another category of equity). *[FRS 102.35.8]*. Under the mandatory exceptions, an entity cannot retrospectively change the accounting followed under its previous financial reporting framework for: derecognition of financial assets and liabilities, accounting estimates, discontinued operations and measuring non-controlling interests. From the date of transition, FRS 102 must be applied in full (except where otherwise provided in Section 35). *[FRS 102.35.7]*.

Section 35 sets out the disclosures required to explain the transition to FRS 102. These include reconciliations from previous GAAP to FRS 102 of equity at the date of transition and the comparative period end, and of the comparative profit or loss. *[FRS 102.35.13-15]*.

1.2   References to IFRS 1

IFRS 1 as referred to throughout this chapter is the version of IFRS 1 as issued at September 2014. However, as described below, IFRS 1 continues to be amended as changes are made to other IFRSs. Hence, to understand the differences between IFRS 1 and Section 35 on transition, it is important to make reference to the latest version of IFRS 1.

2   KEY DIFFERENCES TO IFRS

The transition exceptions and exemptions included in Section 35 are similar to those included in IFRS 1. However, Section 35 omits certain exceptions and exemptions that are included in IFRS 1, but adds certain others and modifies the wording in places. Finally, Section 35 contains significantly less guidance and examples on the application of the transition exceptions and exemptions than IFRS 1. The main differences are listed below:

- Section 35 contains relief where it is impracticable for an entity to restate the opening statement of financial position or make the required disclosures. *[FRS 102.35.11].*

- Section 35 does not address the presentation of interim financial reports. Hence, there are no requirements to apply Section 35 in interim financial statements. *[FRS 102.3.25].*

    However, in November 2014, the FRC published FRED 56 – Draft FRS 104 – *Interim Financial Reporting* – which may be applied to interim financial reports prepared by a FRS 102 reporter. Draft FRS 104 sets out disclosures concerning transition to be included in interim financial reports that cover part of the first financial reporting period applying FRS 102 (see 6.5 below).

- The disclosure requirements regarding transition are less extensive in Section 35, for example, there are no requirements:

    - to present an opening statement of financial position and related notes;

    - to explain how the transition affects the reported cash flows or to disclose the adjustments made for impairment or reversal of impairment in preparing the opening statement of financial position. *[FRS 102.35.12];* or

    - to reconcile total comprehensive income from previous GAAP to FRS 102. *[FRS 102.35.13(c)].*

- In addition, Section 35 includes the following exemptions not in IFRS 1:

    - discontinued operations (see 4.3 below); *[FRS 102.35.9d]*

    - dormant companies (see 5.13 below);

    - pre-transition lease incentives (operating leases) (see 5.12 below);

    - public benefit entity combinations effected pre-transition (see 5.3 below); and

    - deferred development costs as deemed cost (see 5.6 below).

Where FRS 102 does not specifically address a transaction, Section 10 – *Accounting Policies, Estimates and Errors* – requires management to use judgement in developing and applying a relevant and reliable accounting policy. In making that judgement, management *must* refer to and consider the sources listed in Section 10, and *may* consider the requirements and guidance in EU-adopted IFRS dealing with similar and related issues. *[FRS 102.10.4-10.6]*. Consequently, management may refer to the IFRS 1 requirements and guidance relating to the same exception or exemption. However, care should be taken in doing so where the first-time adoption or underlying accounting for the item differs.

3   DEFINITIONS, SCOPE, AND PREPARATION OF THE OPENING FRS 102 STATEMENT OF FINANCIAL POSITION

3.1   Key definitions

The following terms in Section 35 are defined in the Glossary to FRS 102. Other terms used in Section 35 will be explained in the sections in this Chapter addressing the related issue. *[FRS 102 Appendix I]*.

Term	Definition
Carrying amount	The amount at which an asset or liability is recognised in the statement of financial position.
Date of transition	The beginning of the earliest period for which an entity presents full comparative information in a given standard in its first financial statements that comply with that standard.
Deemed cost	An amount used as a surrogate for cost or depreciated cost at a given date. Subsequent depreciation or amortisation assumes that the entity had initially recognised the asset or liability at the given date and that its cost was equal to the deemed cost.
Fair value	The amount for which an asset could be exchanged, a liability settled, or an equity instrument granted could be exchanged, between knowledgeable, willing parties in an arm's length transaction.
First FRS 102 financial statements	The first financial statements (excluding interim financial statements) in which the entity makes an explicit and unreserved statement of compliance with FRS 102.
First-time adopter	An entity that presents its first annual financial statements that conform to FRS 102, regardless of whether its previous accounting framework was EU-adopted IFRS or another accounting framework.
Opening statement of financial position	The statement of financial position as of its date of transition to FRS 102 (i.e. the beginning of the earliest period presented). *[FRS 102.35.7]*.
Reporting date	The end of the latest period covered by financial statements or by an interim financial report.
Reporting period	The period covered by financial statements or by an interim financial report.

Throughout this Chapter, the *Large and Medium-sized Companies and Groups (Accounts and Reports) Regulations 2008* (SI 2008/410) is referred to as the 'Regulations'.

3.2   Scope of Section 35

Section 35 applies to a first-time adopter of FRS 102, regardless of whether its previous accounting framework was EU-adopted IFRS or another set of generally accepted accounting principles (GAAP) such as its national accounting standards, or another framework such as the local income tax basis. *[FRS 102.35.1].*

Most FRS 102 reporters will be UK and Irish companies preparing statutory financial statements under the Companies Act 2006 or Companies Act 1963 respectively. In such cases, the previous accounting framework will be previous UK GAAP, FRS 101, the FRSSE or EU-adopted IFRS.

A first-time adopter must apply the requirements of Section 35 in its first financial statements that conform to FRS 102. *[FRS 102.35.3].* These are the first financial statements (excluding interim financial statements) in which the entity makes an explicit and unreserved statement of compliance with FRS 102. *[FRS 102.35.4].* These financial statements are referred to as the 'first FRS 102 financial statements' below.

3.2.1   *Who is a first-time adopter?*

Normally it will be clear whether an entity is a first-time adopter of FRS 102 as defined at 3.1 above. However, Section 35 clarifies that financial statements prepared in accordance with FRS 102 are an entity's first FRS 102 financial statements if, for example, the entity:

- did not present financial statements for previous periods;
- presented its most recent previous financial statements under previous UK and Republic of Ireland requirements that are therefore not consistent with FRS 102 in all respects; or
- presented its most recent previous financial statements in conformity with EU-adopted IFRS. *[FRS 102.35.4].*

The first FRS 102 financial statements must be a complete set of financial statements, as defined in paragraph 3.17 of FRS 102 (see Chapter 4 at 3.5). This means that the financial statements must include a full set of primary statements and notes (together with comparatives). *[FRS 102.35.4-35.6].*

The first FRS 102 financial statements of a UK company will usually be the statutory financial statements, but this may not always be the case (e.g. first-time adoption in an offering document). In practice, most companies publishing offering documents are likely to be applying IFRSs or EU-adopted IFRS rather than FRS 102.

An entity is not a first-time adopter if it presented financial statements in the previous year that contained an explicit and unreserved statement of compliance with FRS 102 but its auditors qualified the audit report on those financial statements.

3.2.2 Repeat application of FRS 102

An entity that has applied FRS 102 in a previous reporting period, but whose most recent previous annual financial statements did not contain an explicit and unreserved statement of compliance with FRS 102, has a choice *either* to apply Section 35 *or* else to apply Section 10 retrospectively as if the entity had never stopped applying FRS 102. *[FRS 102.35.2].*

In practice, such changes in financial reporting framework often occur if an entity becomes or ceases to be admitted to trading on a regulated market or following a change in ownership (in order to align with the accounting framework adopted by the rest of the group to which the entity belongs).

Where the entity chooses to re-apply Section 35, it must apply the transition exceptions and exemptions without regard to the elections made when it applied Section 35 previously. The entity will, therefore, apply the exceptions and exemptions set out in paragraphs 35.9 to 35.11B, based on its new date of transition to FRS 102.

Where an entity chooses to apply Section 10 retrospectively, it does so as if the entity had never stopped applying FRS 102. *[FRS 102.35.2].* Therefore, the entity must retain the transition exceptions and exemptions applied in its first FRS 102 financial statements.

3.3 First-time adoption timeline

An entity's first FRS 102 financial statements must include at least two statements of financial position, two statements of comprehensive income, two separate income statements (if presented), two statements of cash flows and two statements of changes in equity and related notes. *[FRS 102.35.5, 3.17, 3.20].* Where permitted by the standard, two statements of income and retained earnings may be included in place of the statements of comprehensive income and statements of changes in equity. *[FRS 102.3.18, 6.4].*

The beginning of the earliest comparative period for which the entity presents full comparative information under FRS 102 will be treated as its date of transition. *[FRS 102.35.6].*

The diagram below shows how the above terms are related for an entity with a December year-end:

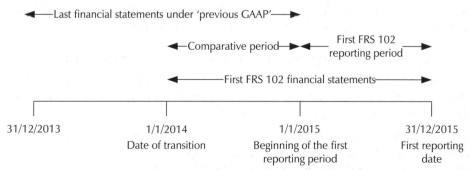

The diagram above illustrates that there is a period of overlap, for the financial year 2014, which is reported first under the entity's previous GAAP and then as a comparative period under FRS 102. The following example illustrates how an entity should determine its date of transition to FRS 102.

Example 30.1:   Determining the date of transition to FRS 102

(i)   *Entity A's year-end is 31 December and it presents financial statements that include one comparative period. Entity A is required to prepare financial statements in conformity with FRS 102 for the first accounting period starting on or after 1 January 2015.*

Entity A's first financial statements in conformity with FRS 102 are for the period ending on 31 December 2015. Its date of transition to FRS 102 is 1 January 2014, which is the beginning of the comparative period included in its first financial statements in conformity with FRS 102.

(ii)   *Entity B's year-end is 31 July and it presents financial statements that include two comparative periods. Entity B is required to prepare financial statements in conformity with FRS 102 for the first accounting period starting on or after 1 January 2015.*

Entity B's first financial statements in conformity with FRS 102 are for the period ending on 31 July 2016. Its date of transition to FRS 102 is 1 August 2013, which is the beginning of the earliest period for which full comparative information is included in its first financial statements in conformity with FRS 102.

(iii)   *Entity C's most recent financial statements under its previous GAAP are for the period from 1 July 2012 to 31 December 2013. Entity C presents its first financial statements (with one comparative period) in conformity with FRS 102 for the period ending 31 December 2014.*

Entity C's date of transition is 1 July 2012. While paragraphs 35.5 and 35.6 of FRS 102 require presentation of at least one comparative period, neither FRS 102 (nor the Companies Act 2006, for a UK company) require the comparative period to be a 12-month period. Thus, the entity's date of transition will be the beginning of the earliest comparative period, irrespective of the length of that period. However, the financial statements must disclose that the comparative period is not a 12-month period, the reason why the comparative period is not 12 months and that the periods presented are not entirely comparable. *[FRS 102.3.10].*

3.4   Determining the previous GAAP

Although FRS 102 does not define 'previous GAAP', it is generally taken to mean the same as under IFRS 1, i.e. 'the basis of accounting that a first-time adopter used immediately before adopting IFRSs'. *[IFRS 1.Appendix A].*

All UK companies are required to prepare and file statutory accounts (with the exception of certain dormant subsidiary companies and certain unlimited companies that are not required to file statutory accounts). *[s394-394C, s448, s448A, s480-481].* Consequently, for a UK company, it will generally be appropriate to regard the GAAP used in the latest set of statutory accounts prior to implementation of FRS 102 as the previous GAAP. While there may be scope for judgement in certain situations over what is the previous GAAP, such situations are likely to be rare.

3.5   Preparation of the opening FRS 102 statement of financial position

The fundamental principle in Section 35 is to require full retrospective application of FRS 102, subject to certain mandatory exceptions and optional exemptions that can be applied at the date of transition. *[FRS 102.35.7].*

Except as provided in paragraphs 35.9 to 35.11B (which set out certain mandatory exceptions, and optional exemptions to full retrospective application of FRS 102), an entity must, in the opening statement of financial position:

(a)   recognise all assets and liabilities whose recognition is required by FRS 102;

(b)   not recognise items as assets and liabilities if FRS 102 does not permit such recognition;

(c)   reclassify items that it recognised under its previous financial reporting framework as one type of asset, liability or component of equity, but are a different type of asset, liability or component of equity under FRS 102; and

(d)   apply FRS 102 in measuring all recognised assets and liabilities. *[FRS 102.35.7].*

An entity may identify previous GAAP errors in transitioning to FRS 102. The standard requires material prior period errors to be adjusted retrospectively, to the extent practicable. *[FRS 102.10.21].* Such errors should be adjusted at the date of transition. If a first-time adopter becomes aware of errors made under its previous financial reporting framework, the reconciliations required by paragraphs 35.13(b) and (c) should, to the extent practicable, distinguish the correction of those errors from changes in accounting policies (see 6.3 below).

Where the accounting policies applied in the opening statement of financial position under FRS 102 differ from those applied under previous GAAP, the resulting adjustments arise from transactions, other events or conditions before the date of transition. Therefore, an entity must recognise those adjustments directly in retained earnings (or, if appropriate, another category of equity – see Examples 30.2 and 30.3 below) at the date of transition to FRS 102. *[FRS 102.35.8].*

Example 30.2:   Revaluation of property

On transition to FRS 102, Entity A adopts a policy of revaluation for its freehold property. *[FRS 102.17.15E-F].* The freehold property, with a net book value of £500,000 under previous UK GAAP (where the cost model had been applied), is revalued to £1.1m, being its fair value at the date of transition. A revaluation reserve of £600,000 is recognised at the date of transition.

If Entity A is a UK company preparing statutory accounts, the freehold property is revalued through other comprehensive income. In accordance with the alternative accounting rules in the Regulations, a statutory revaluation reserve is required to be established in the above case. The related deferred taxation charge through other comprehensive income arising on the revaluation under FRS 102 may be offset against the statutory revaluation reserve in accordance with the alternative accounting rules rather than taken to retained earnings. See 5.5 below.

Example 30.3:   Financial instruments

Other examples of transition adjustments that are recognised in a category of equity other than retained earnings principally relate to financial instruments. This example ignores tax effects.

Entity B has an interest rate swap, which has a carrying amount of £nil (i.e. it is 'off balance sheet') under previous UK GAAP, that hedges a floating rate loan liability. Entity B applies IAS 39 – *Financial Instruments: Recognition and Measurement* – to the recognition and measurement of financial instruments and, as required by IFRS 1 paragraphs B4 to B6, establishes the hedging relationship in its opening statement of financial position. The swap, as a derivative, is measured at its fair value of £50,000 (liability) at the date of transition and the £50,000 adjustment made to its previous carrying amount is recognised in a cash flow hedge reserve (see 5.16 below for discussion of the transition exception for hedge accounting). Where Entity B is a UK company preparing statutory accounts, the adjustment is recognised in the statutory 'fair value reserve'. See 3.5.3 below.

Entity C has a 5% trade investment in a quoted company carried at cost of £100,000 (but with a fair value of £160,000). Under FRS 102, Entity C applies IAS 39 to the recognition and measurement of financial instruments and the trade investment qualifies as an available-for-sale financial asset. On transition, Entity C remeasures the investment to its fair value of £160,000 and recognises the £60,000 uplift in its value in equity. Where Entity C is a UK company preparing statutory accounts, the adjustment is recognised in the statutory 'fair value reserve'. See 3.5.3 below.

Chapter 30

IFRS 1 includes additional requirements and guidance in respect of the transition compared to FRS 102 that can provide further insight into the requirements of Section 35. The application of specific exceptions and exemptions (including any relevant additional guidance in IFRS 1) are addressed at 4 and 5 below, respectively. However, some general issues are discussed below, namely:

- changes of accounting policy made on transition to FRS 102 (see 3.5.1 below);
- impairment testing of assets (see 3.5.2 below);
- use of the fair value accounting rules or alternative accounting rules (by UK companies and other entities preparing Companies Act accounts) (see 3.5.3 below); and
- impracticability exemption and subsequent application (see 3.5.4).

3.5.1   *Changes of accounting policy made on transition to FRS 102*

The fundamental principle in Section 35 is to require full retrospective application of FRS 102, and means that consistent accounting policies should be used in the opening statement of financial position and for all periods presented in its first FRS 102 financial statements. *[FRS 102.10.7, 35.8]*.

A first-time adopter is not under a general obligation to ensure that its FRS 102 accounting policies are as similar as possible to its previous GAAP accounting policies. Therefore, a first-time adopter could adopt a revaluation model for property, plant and equipment even if it had applied a cost model under previous GAAP (or *vice versa*).

A first-time adopter would, however, need to take into account the requirements of Section 10 to ensure that its choice of accounting policy results in information that is relevant and reliable. *[FRS 102.10.3-6]*. In doing so, in situations where an FRS or FRC Abstract does not specifically address the issue, management must refer to the hierarchy set out in paragraph 10.5 and may consider the requirements and guidance in EU-adopted IFRS dealing with similar and related issues. *[FRS 102.10.3-6]*.

In our view, transitional provisions in FRS 102, other FRC standards such as FRS 103 – *Insurance Contracts*, FRC Abstracts, IAS 39 (where applied), and other IFRSs that are required to be applied by certain FRS 102 reporters are ignored for the purposes of the transition. This is the case unless the transitional provisions are stated to apply to a first-time adopter (as is the case for FRS 103) *[FRS 103.6.1-6.4]* or are provided for as a specific transition exception or exemption in Section 35.

3.5.2   *Impairment testing at the date of transition*

FRS 102 permits first-time adopters to make use of deemed cost for certain assets as the initial carrying amount on transition. The standard only requires that the carrying amount of oil and gas assets be tested for impairment where the exemption in paragraph 35.10(j) is taken (see 5.7 below). However, while FRS 102 does not specifically call for an impairment test of other assets, a first-time adopter should be mindful that there are no exemptions from full retrospective application of the requirements set out in Section 27 – *Impairment of Assets*. Therefore, an entity should consider whether there is an indicator of impairment (or reversal of previous impairment) of assets at the date of transition that might require an impairment test to be performed.

An impairment test might also be appropriate if an entity uses fair value as deemed cost for assets whose fair value is above cost, as it should not ignore indications that the recoverable amount of other assets may have fallen below their carrying amount.

Impairment losses are reversed under Section 27 if, and only if, the reasons for the impairment loss have ceased to apply. Hence, there should be no practical differences between applying Section 27 fully retrospectively or applying it at the date of transition. *[FRS 102.27.28]*. Performing the test at the date of transition should result in recognition of any required impairment as of that date, remeasuring any previous GAAP impairment to comply with the approach in Section 27, or recognition of any additional impairment or reversing any previous GAAP impairment that is no longer necessary.

The estimates used to determine whether a first-time adopter recognises an impairment loss or provision at the date of transition to FRS 102 should normally be consistent with estimates made for the same date under previous UK GAAP (after adjustments to reflect any difference in accounting policies), unless there is objective evidence that those estimates were in error. If a first-time adopter needs to make estimates for that date that were not necessary under its previous UK GAAP, such estimates and assumptions should not reflect conditions that arose after the date of transition to FRS 102.

If a first-time adopter's opening FRS 102 statement of financial position reflects impairment losses (e.g. recognised under previous GAAP or upon transition to FRS 102), any later reversal of those impairment losses should be recognised in profit or loss provided that Section 27 does not require such reversal to be treated as a revaluation. *[FRS 102.27.30(b)]*.

Where an entity makes use of deemed cost exemptions at transition, deemed cost is used as a surrogate for cost at the date the deemed cost is established. Therefore, if the carrying amount at the date the deemed cost is established reflects previous impairment, these impairment losses cannot be later reversed and also any later impairment losses are reflected in profit or loss. Certain transition exemptions permit use of a deemed cost equal to the carrying amount of the asset as determined under previous GAAP – an example includes investments in subsidiaries, associates or jointly controlled entities in individual or separate financial statements. *[FRS 102.35.10(f)]*. Where this is the case, we consider that application of Section 27 could lead to a further impairment on transition, but should not lead to a reversal of a previous GAAP impairment (as reflecting a reversal of impairment is not consistent with the deemed cost being equal to the previous GAAP carrying amount). See 5.5 below.

Section 35 does not require specific disclosures regarding any impairment losses recognised or reversed on transition to FRS 102; however, where material, disclosure of such adjustments is likely to be relevant to an explanation of the transition. *[FRS 102.35.12]*. See 6.3 below.

3.5.3 *Use of the fair value accounting and alternative accounting rules*

A UK company's statutory accounts prepared in accordance with FRS 102 are Companies Act accounts. Therefore, the company, in preparing its FRS 102 opening statement of financial position, should consider whether it makes use of the historical cost, alternative accounting rules or fair value accounting rules set out in Part 2 (sections C and D) of Schedule 1 to the Regulations (and the equivalents in Schedules 2 and 3 to the

Regulations). This is relevant both to whether any adjustments made at the date of transition should be reported in retained earnings or another component of equity, and to subsequent accounting and disclosure requirements. For example, where the revaluation model is applied to property, plant and equipment, a statutory revaluation reserve should be established under the alternative accounting rules. Chapter 4 at 9.2 and 9.3 explains the alternative accounting rules and fair value accounting rules in more detail.

3.5.3.A   Deemed cost

A number of the transition exemptions permit an entity to establish a deemed cost that may differ from the historical cost carrying amount under previous UK GAAP. The implications of deemed cost are discussed at 5.5 below. For a UK company's statutory accounts, the deemed cost will need to comply with either the alternative accounting rules or the fair value accounting rules, as applicable. For example, if a UK company records an item of property, plant and equipment at fair value at the date of transition or treats a previous GAAP revaluation as a deemed cost at the date of the revaluation *[FRS 102.35.10(c)-(d)]*, application of the alternative accounting rules may require the company to establish (or maintain an existing) statutory revaluation reserve.

3.5.3.B   Investment property – transitional adjustments

Under FRS 102, investment property must be carried at fair value through profit and loss (unless its fair value cannot be measured reliably without undue cost or effort on an ongoing basis). *[FRS 102.16.1]*. In a UK company's statutory accounts, this accounting makes use of the fair value accounting rules.

Under previous UK GAAP, investment property in the scope of SSAP 19 – *Accounting for investment properties* – is accounted for at open market value with revaluations reflected in revaluation reserve (except to the extent that a deficit or its reversal on an individual investment property is expected to be permanent, in which case it would be reflected in profit and loss). *[SSAP 19.13]*. In a UK company's statutory accounts, the SSAP 19 accounting treatment makes use of the alternative accounting rules. FRS 102 does not address this issue, but one view is that an FRS 102 first-time adopter should reclassify any existing revaluation reserve relating to the investment property to retained earnings (as this is no longer a revaluation under the alternative accounting rules). However, this does not preclude a transfer of the revaluation reserve to a separate non-distributable reserve. *[FRS 102.A4.28]*.

It is possible that a first-time adopter previously accounted for investment property using the cost model because, for example, the property was rented to other group companies and thereby outside the scope of SSAP 19. Where the fair value model is applied to the investment property under FRS 102, the adjustment of the carrying amount to fair value at the date of transition should be included in retained earnings (or transferred to a separate non-distributable reserve) as the revaluation applies the fair value accounting rules.

It may not be possible to apply the fair value model going forward under FRS 102 because fair value cannot be measured reliably without undue cost or effort. In that case, the investment property would either need to be restated to original historical cost, or if a deemed cost were used at transition, a revaluation reserve would need to be established as required under the alternative accounting rules.

Under FRS 19 – *Deferred tax*, deferred tax was rarely provided on revaluations of investment properties. However, on transition, deferred tax should be provided on the revaluation, in accordance with Section 29 – *Income Tax*, as this is generally a timing difference recognised on or prior to transition. Deferred tax relating to investment property measured at fair value shall be measured using the tax rates and allowances that apply to sale of the asset, except for investment property that has a limited useful life and is held within a business model whose objective is to consume substantially all of the economic benefits embodied in the property over time. *[FRS 102.29.6, 29.16].*

Example 30.4:   Investment property

Entity A (which is a UK company) has an investment property carried at open market value of £2.1m at 31 December 2013 and £1.5m at 31 December 2014 under SSAP 19. The historical cost of the property and its tax base (indexation is ignored in this example) is £1m. The tax rate in all periods, including those in which the investment property is expected to be sold is 20%.

Under previous UK GAAP, a revaluation reserve of £1.1m at 31 December 2013 was recognised and no depreciation was charged. *[SSAP 19.10-11, 13].* No deferred tax was recognised on the revaluation movements as Entity A had not entered into a binding agreement to sell the property. *[FRS 19.14].*

FRS 102 requires investment property to be carried at fair value through profit and loss (unless the fair value cannot be measured reliably without undue cost or effort on an ongoing basis). *[FRS 102.16.1].* No depreciation is charged. While non-depreciation of investment property generally requires use of the true and fair override under the Companies Act 2006 under previous UK GAAP *[SSAP 19.17]*, this is not the case under FRS 102 since the fair value accounting rules are applied. On transition, the statutory revaluation reserve previously recognised under SSAP 19 (under the alternative accounting rules) is transferred to retained earnings (or can be transferred to a non-distributable reserve).

On transition to FRS 102, there is no adjustment to the carrying amount of the investment property, being at fair value. However, FRS 102 requires recognition of a deferred tax liability of £220,000 and £100,000 on the revaluation above historical cost (tax base) at 1 January 2014 and at 31 December 2014 respectively. *[FRS 102.29.6].*

The downward revaluation in the comparative period, recognised in the statement of total recognised gains and losses under previous UK GAAP, is reversed. The downward valuation is instead recognised in profit or loss (with the related deferred tax credit of £120,000) for the financial year ended 31 December 2014.

3.5.4   Impracticability exemption and subsequent application

If it is impracticable to restate the opening statement of financial position at the date of transition for one or more of the adjustments required by paragraph 35.7(a) to (d), an entity must:

- apply paragraphs 35.7 to 35.10 (i.e. retrospective application of FRS 102, subject to the transition exceptions and exemptions) for such adjustments in the earliest period for which it is practicable to do so; and

- identify the data presented for prior periods that are not comparable with data for the period in which it prepares its first FRS 102 financial statements. If it is impracticable for an entity to provide any disclosures required by FRS 102 for any period before the period in which it prepares its first FRS 102 financial statements, it must disclose the omission. *[FRS 102.35.11].*

Applying a requirement is impracticable when an entity cannot apply it, after making every reasonable effort to do so. *[FRS 102 Appendix I].*

If it is not practical on first-time adoption to apply a particular requirement of paragraph 18 of IFRS 6 – *Exploration for and Evaluation of mineral Resources* - to previous comparative amounts an entity shall disclose that fact. *[FRS 102.34.11C]*.

Section 35 states that, where applicable to the transactions, events or arrangements affected by applying the exemptions, an entity may continue to use the exemptions that are applied at the date of transition to FRS 102 when preparing subsequent financial statements, until such time when the assets and liabilities associated with those transactions, events or arrangements are derecognised. *[FRS 102.35.11A]*. This simply confirms that in preparing FRS 102 financial statements after first-time adoption, the exemptions and exceptions taken at the date of transition continue to be applied as opposed to Section 35 *only* applying to the first FRS 102 financial statements. Once the associated assets and liabilities are derecognised, those transition exemptions cease, in any event, to have any accounting effect.

However, where there is subsequently a significant change in the circumstances or conditions associated with transactions, events or arrangements that existed at the date of transition, to which an exemption has been applied, an entity shall reassess the appropriateness of applying that exemption in preparing subsequent financial statements in order to maintain fair presentation in accordance with Section 3 – *Financial Statement Presentation. [FRS 102.35.11B]*. It is not clear what circumstances are envisaged by paragraph 35.11B (there is no equivalent text in the IFRS for SMEs), but this paragraph appears to permit the possibility of an entity later ceasing to use transition exemptions taken.

4   MANDATORY EXCEPTIONS TO RETROSPECTIVE APPLICATION

Section 35 prohibits retrospective application of its requirements in some areas, many of which correspond to similar mandatory *exceptions* in IFRS 1. The mandatory exceptions in FRS 102 cover areas where full retrospective application could be costly or onerous, or may involve use of hindsight.

The mandatory exceptions in Section 35 cover the following areas:

- derecognition of financial assets and financial liabilities (see 4.1 below);
- accounting estimates (see 4.2 below);
- discontinued operations (see 4.3 below); and
- non-controlling interests (see 4.4 below).

Each of the exceptions is explained further below.

In FRS 102 (March 2013), the first-time adoption provisions regarding hedge accounting were presented as an exception. In July 2014, the FRC published an amendment to FRS 102 that considers the transitional guidance on hedge accounting to be an exemption (see 5 below). We note, though, that the exemptions regarding hedge accounting (see 5.16 below), a parent becoming a first-time adopter later than its subsidiary (see 5.15.2 below), and a parent adopting FRS 102 in its separate financial statements earlier or later than in its consolidated financial statements (see 5.15.4 below) contain certain mandatory requirements.

4.1 Derecognition of financial assets and financial liabilities.

Financial assets and liabilities derecognised under an entity's previous accounting framework before the date of transition shall not be recognised upon adoption of FRS 102. Conversely, for financial assets and liabilities that would have been derecognised under FRS 102 in a transaction that took place before the date of transition, but that were not derecognised under an entity's previous accounting framework, an entity may choose to either derecognise them on adoption of FRS 102, or to continue to recognise them until disposed of, or settled. *[FRS 102.35.9(a)]*. Derecognition is defined as the removal of a previously recognised asset or liability from an entity's statement of financial position. *[FRS 102 Appendix I]*.

4.1.1 Implementation issues

There is no further implementation guidance on this transition exception. The main first-time adoption implementation issues are:

- what comprises derecognition of financial assets and financial liabilities under previous GAAP (see 4.1.1.A, 4.1.2 and 4.1.3 below); and

- whether there are financial assets and financial liabilities that would have been derecognised under FRS 102 in a pre-transition transaction, but were not derecognised under previous GAAP (see 4.1.1.B below).

Comparatives need to be restated in accordance with the standard applied to the recognition and measurement of financial instruments.

An FRS 102 reporter has a choice of applying Section 11 – *Basic Financial Instruments* – and Section 12 – *Other Financial Instruments Issues*, IAS 39 (as adopted by the European Union), or IFRS 9 – *Financial Instruments* – and/or IAS 39 (as amended by IFRS 9) to the recognition and measurement of financial instruments. *[FRS 102.11.2, 12.2]*.

The derecognition requirements in FRS 26 – *Financial instruments: recognition and measurement* – are the same as those of IAS 39 and IFRS 9. However, the derecognition requirements in FRS 5 – *Reporting the substance of transactions* – differ significantly from those in IAS 39, IFRS 9 and Sections 11 and 12. There are also differences between the requirements of IAS 39, IFRS 9 and Sections 11 and 12 (see Chapter 8 at 6).

4.1.1.A Financial assets and liabilities previously derecognised

Financial assets and liabilities derecognised under previous GAAP before the date of transition (and consequently not recognised on transition to FRS 102) would be re-recognised if they qualify for recognition as a result of a later transaction or event (i.e. subsequent to the date of transition) using the standard applied to the recognition and measurement of financial instruments under FRS 102.

FRS 102's requirements on consolidation of special purpose entities (SPEs) are based on a simplified version of SIC-12 – *Consolidation – Special Purpose Entities*. *[FRS 102.9.10-9.12]*. Since there are no specific transitional or first-time adoption provisions, these requirements must be applied fully retrospectively by first-time adopters. Therefore, financial assets and liabilities derecognised on transfer to an

SPE that was not consolidated under previous UK GAAP (but would be required to be consolidated under FRS 102) will be re-recognised on transition to FRS 102 by way of consolidation of the SPE. In practice, however, many SPEs consolidated under FRS 102 may have qualified as subsidiary undertakings or quasi-subsidiary undertakings consolidated under previous UK GAAP. Some arrangements for the transfer of assets, particularly securitisations, may last for some time, with the result that transfers might be made both before and on or after the date of transition under the same arrangement. Under FRS 102, transfers on or after the date of transition would be subject to the full requirements of whichever standard is followed for the recognition and measurement of financial instruments.

4.1.1.B   *Financial assets and liabilities previously not derecognised*

The requirements of the standard applied to the recognition and measurement of financial instruments are followed where an entity, on adoption of FRS 102, chooses to derecognise financial assets or financial liabilities that would have been derecognised under FRS 102 in a pre-transition transaction (using the standard applied to the recognition and measurement of financial instruments) but which were not derecognised under previous UK GAAP.

4.1.2   Transition from previous UK GAAP (not FRS 26)

Previous UK GAAP reporters (not applying FRS 26) applied FRS 5 to the recognition and derecognition of financial assets and financial liabilities. FRS 5 provides for a number of different treatments, such as continued recognition of an asset in its entirety (with linked presentation for transactions meeting specified criteria), ceasing to recognise an asset in its entirety and partial derecognition. *[FRS 5.21, 23-24, 26-27].*

4.1.2.A   *Derecognition of financial assets*

Financial assets derecognised under previous UK GAAP are not re-recognised on transition. *[FRS 102.35.9(a)].* The question therefore arises as to whether linked presentation (which is not permitted under any of the recognition and measurement policy choices available under FRS 102) and partial derecognition under FRS 5 constitute derecognition.

Under FRS 5, linked presentation is used where the transaction is in substance a financing – and therefore meets the criteria for continued recognition – but the financing 'ring fences' the item. *[FRS 5.26-28].* Consequently, linked presentation does not represent derecognition under previous UK GAAP and will need to be adjusted retrospectively on transition to FRS 102.

Section 35 does not state whether partial derecognition under FRS 5 is regarded as derecognition for the purposes of paragraph 35.9(a). Moreover, Section 11, unlike IAS 39 and IFRS 9, does not refer to derecognition of *parts* of a financial asset (although it does so in respect of parts of a financial liability). *[FRS 102.11.33, 36, 12.14].*

Examples of partial derecognition under FRS 5 include an interest rate strip or the novation of a proportionate share of all of the cash flows from a loan receivable. Part of the original financial asset, the loan receivable, has been removed from the balance sheet under FRS 5. In our view, both of these examples would meet FRS 102's definition of a financial asset and, therefore, partial derecognition under FRS 5 should be regarded as derecognition of a financial asset for the purposes of the exception in paragraph 35.9(a). Consequently, the part of the original financial asset derecognised under FRS 5 would not be reinstated on transition to FRS 102.

Other examples discussed in FRS 5 include a sale and repurchase agreement such as the sale of an equity investment with a call option to repurchase, but with a real possibility the option fails to be exercised and a sale of an equity investment for deferred contingent consideration. Where the criteria for partial derecognition are met, FRS 5 requires that the description and monetary amount of the asset previously recognised is changed. *[FRS 5.72-73].* In our view, it would be appropriate to regard this accounting as derecognition of the equity investment under previous GAAP and not to reinstate the original financial asset on transition to FRS 102.

The measurement requirements of FRS 102 should be applied to the asset (and any related liability) reported under previous GAAP as at transition and that the first-time adopter continues to recognise under FRS 102.

4.1.2.B   *Derecognition of financial liabilities*

Financial liabilities derecognised under previous UK GAAP are not re-recognised on transition. *[FRS 102.35.9(a)].* Since derecognition is the removal of a previously recognised liability from an entity's statement of financial position, it will generally be clear whether a financial liability was derecognised under previous UK GAAP.

FRS 5 only addresses derecognition of financial assets and does not directly address derecognition of financial liabilities. FRS 4 – *Capital instruments* (which applies only to entities not applying FRS 26) states that gains and losses arising on the repurchase or early settlement of debt should be recognised in the profit and loss account in the period during which the repurchase or early settlement is made. *[FRS 4.32].* FRS 4 does not, however, address exchanges or modifications of the terms of debt instruments or debt for equity swaps. Consequently, it is possible that such transactions may have been accounted for differently compared to Sections 11 and 12 (or IAS 39 or IFRS 9), which do address such transactions.

There may be cases where a financial liability was not derecognised under previous UK GAAP but would have been derecognised under IAS 39, IFRS 9 or Sections 11 and 12. For example, an exchange or modification of a loan that would be considered a 'substantial modification' and treated as an extinguishment under these standards might not have been derecognised under FRS 4. A first-time adopter is permitted to either continue to recognise the loan or to derecognise it on transition (and account for the new modified loan as at the date of the modification in accordance with the requirements of the standard applied for recognition and measurement of financial instruments). Where the entity continues to recognise a financial liability, it must retrospectively apply the standard applied for the recognition and measurement of financial instruments. Therefore, in the above example, where the loan is carried at amortised cost under the standard applied, its measurement will include the effects of the modifications in cash flows under the effective interest method.

IAS 39, IFRS 9 and Sections 11 and 12 require an entity to derecognise a financial liability (or part of a financial liability) only when it is extinguished (i.e. when the obligation specified in the contract is discharged, is cancelled or expires). *[FRS 102.11.36,12.14, IAS 39.39, IFRS 9.3.3.1]*. Sections 11 and 12 contain the same basic requirements on accounting for exchanges of financial instruments between an existing borrower and lender and the modification of terms of an existing financial liability as IFRSs but do not contain the application guidance in IFRSs *[IAS 39.AG57-63, IFRS 9.B3.3.1-3.3.7]*. The implications are discussed further at 4.1.3.B below. Further guidance on derecognition of financial liabilities under IAS 39 and IFRS 9 is included in EY International GAAP 2015, Chapter 49 at 6 and on derecognition of financial liabilities under Sections 11 and 12 in Chapter 8 at 6.

4.1.3   *Transition from FRS 26*

FRS 102 first-time adopters that previously applied FRS 26 are likely to apply IAS 39. As the derecognition requirements for financial assets and financial liabilities in FRS 26 and IAS 39 are identical, no differences in respect of derecognition of financial assets and financial liabilities should arise on transition to FRS 102, where IFRSs are applied to the recognition and measurement of financial instruments.

Where an entity derecognised non-derivative financial assets or non-derivative financial liabilities under its previous accounting policies as a result of a transaction that occurred before the beginning of the comparative period for which FRS 26 was first applied, the financial assets and financial liabilities were not re-recognised under FRS 26 (unless they qualified for recognition as a result of a later transaction or event). *[FRS 26.108E-F]*. Any such financial assets or financial liabilities still existing at the date of transition remain derecognised on transition to FRS 102 because of the derecognition exception in paragraph 35.9(a).

The discussion at 4.1.3.A and 4.1.3.B below only applies if a previous FRS 26 reporter wishes to apply Sections 11 and 12 to the recognition and measurement of financial instruments.

4.1.3.A   *Financial assets*

Generally, it will be clear whether a financial asset has been derecognised under FRS 26 and therefore must not be re-recognised on transition to FRS 102. However, Section 35 does not specifically address whether derecognition of a part of a financial asset or continued recognition of an asset to the extent of its continuing involvement are regarded as derecognition for the purposes of paragraph 35.9(a).

FRS 26 requires an entity to determine whether the derecognition requirements are to be applied to a part of a financial asset (or a part of a group of financial assets) or a financial asset (or a group of similar financial assets) in its entirety.

For the reasons noted at 4.1.2.A above, derecognition of a part of a financial asset under FRS 26 should be regarded as derecognition for the purposes of the exception in paragraph 35.9(a).

FRS 26 states that if the entity neither transfers nor retains substantially all the risks and rewards of ownership of the financial asset but has retained control, it shall continue to recognise the financial asset to the extent of its continuing involvement.

It sets out how the continuing involvement in the asset (or part of the asset) and the associated liability should be measured. *[FRS 26.20(c)(ii), 30-35]*. It is not clear whether recognising an asset (or part of an asset) to the extent of its continuing involvement could be regarded as derecognition for the purposes of paragraph 35.9(a). However, it would seem unlikely that an entity with assets (or parts of assets) recognised to the extent of continuing involvement would be applying Sections 11 and 12 since these sections do not set out rules for accounting for such arrangements.

4.1.3.B   Financial liabilities

FRS 26 addresses derecognition of financial liabilities, and modifications and exchanges of loans. Hence, it will be clear whether a financial liability has been derecognised under FRS 26 and therefore must not be re-recognised on transition.

Sections 11 and 12's requirements on derecognition of financial liabilities (including parts of financial liabilities) are the same as those of FRS 26, but do not include its additional application guidance (see Chapter 8 at 6). In particular, the application guidance covers the evaluation of whether an exchange or modification of debt has substantially different terms, and accounting for an exchange or modification.

An FRS 26 reporter may not have accounted for an exchange or modification of a loan as an extinguishment of the original financial liability. There is no exemption from measuring the loan in accordance with the requirements of Sections 11 and 12. FRS 26's application guidance addresses the treatment of costs associated with the modification, requiring that these are amortised over the remaining term of the modified liability *[FRS 26.AG62]* but does not explicitly state whether an adjustment is made to the carrying amount of the financial liability (or whether the effective interest rate must be changed) (see EY International GAAP 2015, Chapter 49 at 6).

Sections 11 and 12 do not include FRS 26's application guidance. Therefore, until more definitive guidance is issued or a consensus approach emerges, entities need to develop an accounting policy based on one of the following approaches:

- since Sections 11 and 12 are silent, the general requirements of the effective interest method apply to the modification (i.e. that the carrying amount of the financial liability is adjusted to reflect the actual and revised estimated cash flows discounted at the original effective interest rate); or *[FRS 102.11.20]*.

- as the basic derecognition requirements of IFRSs and Sections 11 and 12 are the same, an entity may look to the requirements of IFRSs under the hierarchy set out in Section 10 of the standard.

4.2   Accounting estimates

4.2.1   Exception

On first-time adoption of FRS 102, an entity must not retrospectively change the accounting that it followed under its previous financial reporting framework for accounting estimates. *[FRS 102.35.9(c)]*. However, FRS 102 offers no further guidance in respect of this exception. Since paragraph 35.9(c) does not refer to accounting estimates *at the date of transition*, as other exceptions do, it seems that the exception relates to accounting estimates made under previous GAAP in *both* the opening statement of financial position at transition and in the comparative period(s) presented. As this is consistent with the corresponding exception in IFRS 1, entities may want to consider the guidance in that standard.

IFRS 1 requires an entity to use estimates under IFRSs that are consistent with the estimates made for the same date under its previous GAAP – after adjusting for any difference in accounting policy – unless there is objective evidence that those estimates were in error. *[IFRS 1.14]*. Under IFRS 1 an entity cannot apply hindsight and make 'better' estimates when it prepares its first IFRS financial statements. Therefore, an entity is not allowed to consider subsequent events that provide evidence of conditions that existed at that date, but that came to light after the date its previous GAAP financial statements were finalised. If an estimate made under previous GAAP requires adjustment because of new information after the relevant date, an entity treats this information in the same way as a non-adjusting event after the reporting period. In addition, the exception also ensures that a first-time adopter need not conduct a search for, and change the accounting for, events that might have otherwise qualified as adjusting events, e.g. the resolution of a court case relating to an obligation as at the date of transition or end of the comparative period.

Where FRS 102 requires a first-time adopter to make estimates that were not required under its previous GAAP, the general approach should be to base those estimates on conditions that existed at the date of transition.

4.2.2   *Post-balance sheet events and correction of errors*

FRS 102 requires changes in accounting estimates to be reflected prospectively. *[FRS 102.10.15-10.17]*. Adjustments for post-balance sheet events are only made where these provide evidence of conditions existing at the end of the reporting period. *[FRS 102.32.2(a)]*. Section 10 further explains that 'changes in accounting estimates result from new information or new developments and, accordingly, are not corrections of errors. When it is difficult to distinguish a change in an accounting policy from a change in an accounting estimate, the change is treated as a change in an accounting estimate'. *[FRS 102.10.15]*. See Chapter 7 at 3.5.

That distinction may be relevant, for example, when reporting derivatives or other financial assets at fair value under FRS 102 that were off balance sheet or carried at cost under previous UK GAAP. A UK company is required by the Regulations to disclose the fair values of derivatives (even if not accounted for at fair value) in its statutory accounts. The effect of the transition exception is that these previous fair value estimates should be used, unless objectively in error. *[1 Sch 67]*.

Material errors identified at transition and in the comparatives must be retrospectively corrected (even if these would not have been fundamental errors under previous UK GAAP). *[FRS 102.10.21]*.

4.3   Discontinued operations

An entity shall not retrospectively change the accounting that it followed under its previous financial reporting framework for discontinued operations. *[FRS 102.35.9(d)]*. However, no guidance in respect of this exception is included in FRS 102 or the IFRS for SMEs, which contains the same exception.

There are two ways in which the exception is commonly understood:

(a)   an entity should not retrospectively change the accounting that it applied in the *comparative periods* to discontinued operations under its previous GAAP; and

(b)   an entity should not retrospectively change the accounting that it applied *before its date of transition* to discontinued operations under its previous GAAP.

An entity applying either of these interpretation should be aware of the issues that exist regarding the scope and presentation requirements, as explained at 4.3.1 and 4.3.2 below.

4.3.1   Scope of the exception

The definition of discontinued operations, the presentational requirements for discontinued operations and the accounting treatment for loss of control of a subsidiary under FRS 102 differ significantly from previous UK GAAP and indeed IFRSs. FRS 102 defines a 'discontinued operation' as:

'A component of an entity that has been disposed of and:

(a)   represented a separate major line of business or geographical area of operations;

(b)   was part of a single co-ordinated plan to dispose of a separate major line of business or geographical area of operations; or

(c)   was a subsidiary acquired exclusively with a view to resale.' *[FRS 102 Appendix I]*.

A 'component of an entity' is defined as 'operations and cash flows that can be clearly distinguished, operationally and for financial reporting purposes, from the rest of the entity.' *[FRS 102 Appendix I]*.

This definition differs significantly from the definition of a discontinued operation in FRS 3 – *Reporting financial performance*. It also differs from the definition used in IFRS 5 – *Non-current Assets Held for Sale and Discontinued Operations*, which includes 'a component of an entity that has been disposed of *or held for sale*' and contains more guidance on its definition of discontinued operations.

The exception does not explicitly refer to operations that became discontinued *before the date of transition* (in which case, given that the operations have to be disposed of to qualify as discontinued, it is unlikely there is much accounting effect of the exception). Therefore, the exception could be read as applying to operations that became discontinued in the comparative period too.

4.3.2   Accounting followed under previous financial reporting framework

Previous UK GAAP, IFRSs and FRS 102 have presentation but *no* recognition and measurement requirements *specific* to discontinued operations. IFRS 5 addresses the recognition, measurement and presentational requirements for assets and disposal groups that are held for sale or held for distribution and FRS 3 addresses the accounting for provisions on a sale or termination of an operation *[FRS 3.18, 45]*. However, these requirements apply both to continuing and discontinued operations.

FRS 102 only has presentational requirements for discontinued operations and does not address the accounting for held for sale assets and disposal groups (the concept 'held for sale' does not exist in FRS 102). Moreover, FRS 102 reporters are required to follow the formats for the profit and loss account and balance sheet included in the Regulations (or where applicable, the LLP Regulations). This requirement applies to all entities (including those that do not report under the Companies Act 2006, except to the extent that this would not be permitted by any statutory framework under which such entities report). *[FRS 102.4.1-4.2, 5.1, 5.5].*

Applying the transition exception to presentational requirements may not be possible where this would result in conflicts with the statutory formats. In addition, it would often not be helpful for a previous UK GAAP reporter to present comparatives for its discontinued operations (as defined in FRS 102) using the presentation under FRS 3, while applying FRS 102 to all other operations in the comparative period and to the current period. We note further that maintaining the same accounting for a discontinued operation that was followed under the previous financial reporting framework has potential to conflict with the mandatory exception relating to accounting for the loss of control over a subsidiary in paragraph 35.9(e) (see 4.4 below).

Consequently, there are situations where applying the exception to discontinued operations occurring before the date of transition and adjusting the comparative period(s) in accordance with FRS 102 would result in the more appropriate accounting treatment.

4.4　Non-controlling interests

FRS 2 – *Accounting for subsidiary undertakings* (and the Regulations) refer to 'minority interest' whereas FRS 102 refers to 'non-controlling interest' – these concepts are not identical. The definition of non-controlling interest and accounting for non-controlling interest is discussed in Chapter 6 at 3.6.

In measuring non-controlling interests, the requirements (in Section 9 of FRS 102 – *Consolidated and Separate Financial Statements*):

- to allocate profit or loss and total comprehensive income between non-controlling interest and owners of the parent (see Chapter 6 at 2.2.8);

- for accounting for changes in the parent's ownership interest in a subsidiary that do not result in a loss of control (see Chapter 6 at 3.6.2 and 3.6.4); and

- for accounting for a loss of control over a subsidiary (see Chapter 6 at 3.6.3)

must be applied prospectively from the date of transition to FRS 102 (or from such earlier date as FRS 102 is applied to restate business combinations – see paragraph 35.10(a)). *[FRS 102.35.9(e)].*

The application of the exception is straightforward. It simply states that the accounting in FRS 102 is applied prospectively from the date of transition (or where pre-transition business combinations are restated in accordance with Section 19 – *Business Combinations and Goodwill*, from the earlier date from which business combinations are restated – see 5.2 below). Retrospective changes for previous allocations of profit or loss and total comprehensive income are otherwise prohibited. *[FRS 102.35.9(e)].*

Consequently, where a provision has been made under UK GAAP against a minority debit balance prior to the date of transition (or that earlier date from which Section 19 is applied), this should not be reversed on transition to FRS 102.

FRS 102's requirements regarding non-controlling interest differ significantly from those in previous UK GAAP (see Chapter 6 at 2.1.6 and 2.1.7); a first-time adopter may, therefore, need to restate the non-controlling interest in its comparative period. In addition, changes to assets and liabilities of a subsidiary with a non-controlling interest made at the date of transition will have a consequential effect on non-controlling interest at that date.

5   OPTIONAL EXEMPTIONS TO RETROSPECTIVE APPLICATION

5.1   Introduction

Section 35 sets out optional *exemptions* from the general requirement of full retrospective application of the requirements of FRS 102. *[FRS 102.35.10].* While many of these correspond to exemptions in IFRS 1 – but worded differently – other exemptions are specific to FRS 102. The optional exemptions in Section 35 cover the following areas:

- Business combinations, including group reconstructions (see 5.2 below);
- Public benefit entity combinations (see 5.3 below);
- Share-based payment transactions (see 5.4 below);
- Fair value as deemed cost (see 5.5 below);
- Previous revaluation as deemed cost (see 5.5 below);
- Deferred development costs as a deemed cost (see 5.6 below);
- Deemed cost for oil and gas assets (see 5.7 below);
- Decommissioning liabilities included in the cost of property, plant and equipment (see 5.8 below);
- Individual and separate financial statements (see 5.9 below);
- Service concession arrangements – accounting by operators (see 5.10 below);
- Arrangements containing a lease (see 5.11 below);
- Lease incentives (see 5.12 below);
- Dormant companies (see 5.13 below);
- Borrowing costs (see 5.14 below);
- Assets and liabilities of subsidiaries, associates and joint ventures (see 5.15 below);
- Hedge accounting (see 5.16 below);
- Designation of previously recognised financial instruments (see 5.17 below); and
- Compound financial instruments (see 5.18 below).

Each of the exemptions is explained further below.

Chapter 30

5.2   Business combinations, including group reconstructions

A first-time adopter may elect not to apply Section 19 to business combinations that were effected before the date of transition to FRS 102. However, if a first-time adopter restates any business combination to comply with Section 19, it shall restate all later business combinations.

If a first-time adopter does not apply Section 19 retrospectively, the first-time adopter shall recognise and measure all its assets and liabilities acquired or assumed in a past business combination at the date of transition in accordance with paragraphs 35.7 to 35.9 or if applicable, with paragraphs 35.10(b) to (c) except for:

- intangible assets other than goodwill – intangible assets subsumed within goodwill shall not be separately recognised; and

- goodwill – no adjustment shall be made to the carrying value of goodwill. *[FRS 102.35.10(a)].*

The business combinations exemption permits a first-time adopter not to restate business combinations that occurred prior to its date of transition in accordance with Section 19. Whether or not a first-time adopter elects to restate pre-transition business combinations, it may still need to restate the carrying amounts of the acquired assets and assumed liabilities (see 5.2.3 below).

The requirements to allocate profit or loss and total comprehensive income between non-controlling interest and owners of the parent; for accounting for changes in the parent's ownership interest in a subsidiary that do not result in a loss of control; and for accounting for a loss of control over a subsidiary must be applied prospectively from the date of transition (or from such earlier date as FRS 102 is applied to restate business combinations). *[FRS 102.35.9(e)].*

Paragraphs PBE 34.75 to 34.86 of FRS 102 contain specific requirements on accounting for public benefit entity combinations, which are discussed at 5.3 below.

Unlike IFRS 1, Section 35 provides no guidance beyond the wording of the transition exemption itself. While there may be other approaches, we consider that Appendix C of IFRS 1 can be helpful in interpreting the transition exemption and will refer to that guidance where appropriate. There are some GAAP differences between IFRS 1 and FRS 102 regarding the business combinations exemption; therefore some aspects of the guidance in Appendix C are not relevant. This commentary is organised as follows:

- option to restate business combinations retrospectively (see 5.2.1 below);

- scope of the transition exemption (see 5.2.2 below);

- application of the transition exemption – general (see 5.2.3 below);

- restatement of goodwill (see 5.2.4 below);

- changes in scope of consolidation (see 5.2.5 below); and

- business combinations transition example (see 5.2.6 below).

5.2.1 *Option to restate business combinations retrospectively*

A first-time adopter must account for business combinations occurring *after* its date of transition under Section 19. Therefore, any business combination during the comparative period(s) needs to be restated in accordance with FRS 102.

An entity may elect to apply Section 19 to business combinations occurring before the date of transition, but must then restate any subsequent business combinations under Section 19. In other words, a first-time adopter can choose any date in the past from which it wants to account for all business combinations under Section 19 without restating business combinations that occurred before that date. Although there is no prohibition from applying Section 19 to all past business combinations, this would generally not be appropriate if it involved undue use of hindsight.

If any pre-transition business combinations are restated, the first-time adopter must also apply FRS 102's requirements on the measurement of non-controlling interests from the date of the earliest business combination that is restated (see 4.4 above).

5.2.1.A *Considerations on restatement of business combinations*

If the exemption from restating pre-transition business combinations is not applied, the requirements of Section 19 (see Chapter 15) would need to be applied retrospectively. This might be an onerous exercise that might require undue use of hindsight. For example, restatement would require:

- reassessment as to whether the previous GAAP classification of the business combination (as an acquisition by the legal acquirer, reverse acquisition by the legal acquiree, merger accounting) was appropriate;

- a fair value exercise to be performed, at the date of the business combination, if the purchase method is required;

- the amounts recognised in the business combination to be restated under Section 19 and, subsequently, to be accounted for under FRS 102; and

- any adjustments to assets and liabilities may also impact deferred tax and non-controlling interests.

If a business combination were restated under Section 19, the adjustments to the fair values of the assets and liabilities at the date of the business combination (including any changes to deferred tax and non-controlling interest) would be reflected as an adjustment to goodwill. Therefore, applying Section 19 to the pre-transition business combination would allow restatement of goodwill arising on the acquisition adjusted for any subsequent amortisation and impairment.

In particular, Section 29 may require additional deferred tax to be recognised on a business combination *[FRS 102.29.11]*, compared to say, FRS 19 under previous UK GAAP (see 5.2.3.C below). Where the exemption not to restate business combinations is taken, any adjustments to the assets and liabilities acquired or assumed will be reflected in retained earnings (or if appropriate, another category of equity). *[FRS 102.35.9]*. Where the business combination involves a purchase of trade and assets reflected in the individual financial statements of a UK company, recognising additional deferred tax liabilities on fair value adjustments, but not adjusting goodwill would have an adverse effect on the company's distributable reserves.

Chapter 30

5.2.2   Scope of the transition exemption

A transaction must be a business combination or a group reconstruction (as defined in FRS 102 – see Chapter 15 at 2.2 and 5.1 respectively) to qualify for the transition exemption; otherwise, it will need to be retrospectively restated subject to the mandatory exceptions and optional exemptions included in Section 35. FRS 6 – *Acquisitions and mergers* – does not define a business; consequently, some transactions may have been accounted for as a business combination under FRS 6 that would not fall within the scope of Section 19.

The application of the purchase method in Section 19 differs in certain respects from acquisition accounting under FRS 6. See Chapter 15 at 3.3 for details of application of the purchase method under Section 19.

Section 35 does not, like IFRS 1, extend the exemption from applying the principles in Section 19 to acquisitions of associates and interests in joint ventures before the date of transition. *[IFRS 1.C5]*. These are not business combinations, as defined and would therefore appear to require retrospective adjustment.

5.2.3   Application of the transition exemption – general

Although there are GAAP differences between IFRS 1 Appendix C and Section 35 in respect of the treatment of intangible assets previously subsumed within goodwill (which must not be reinstated as intangible assets under Section 35), the guidance in Appendix C can be helpful in interpreting the transition exemption. The commentary below, therefore, draws on IFRS 1 in suggesting approaches that preparers may want to consider.

5.2.3.A   Classification of business combination

If a first-time adopter does not restate a business combination then it would keep the same classification of the business combination (as an acquisition by the legal acquirer, reverse acquisition by the legal acquiree, merger accounting or pooling of interests) as in its previous GAAP financial statements. However, if a transaction is restated in accordance with Section 19 of FRS 102, the classification of the business combination may change.

5.2.3.B   Recognition and derecognition of assets and liabilities

A first-time adopter that applies the exemption should recognise all assets and liabilities at the date of transition that were acquired or assumed in a past business combination, other than:

- financial assets and financial liabilities that were derecognised in accordance with previous GAAP that fall under the derecognition exception in paragraph 35.9(a) (see 4.1 above);
- assets (including goodwill) and liabilities that were not recognised in the acquirer's consolidated statement of financial position in accordance with previous GAAP that also would not qualify for recognition as an asset or liability under FRS 102 in the separate (or individual) statement of financial position of the acquiree; and
- intangible assets previously subsumed within goodwill.

The entity must exclude items it recognised under previous GAAP that do not qualify for recognition as an asset or liability under FRS 102 (subject to the derecognition exception for financial assets and financial liabilities).

Any resulting change is recognised by adjusting retained earnings (or another component of equity). *[FRS 102.35.8]*. No adjustment is made to the carrying amount of goodwill. *[FRS 102.35.10(a)]*.

5.2.3.C   *Measurement of assets and liabilities*

In essence, the approach to recognising and measuring assets and liabilities is to apply FRS 102 retrospectively (subject to the exceptions and exemptions taken at the date of transition), but without revisiting the fair value exercise. This means that where assets and liabilities acquired or assumed in a past business combination were not recognised under previous GAAP, these should normally be reflected at the amounts that would be recognised in the separate or individual financial statements of the acquiree and no adjustments are made to goodwill. The previous GAAP carrying amounts as at the date of the acquisition are treated as a deemed cost for the purposes of cost-based depreciation and amortisation. Note that this does not preclude the deemed cost exemptions available on transition from being subsequently applied to assets acquired in the business combination that are still held at the date of transition (see 5.5 below).

FRS 102 requires that, where the paragraph 35.10(a) exemption is used, no adjustments are made to the carrying amount of goodwill at the date of transition. *[FRS 102.35.10(a)]*. However, 5.2.4 below sets out situations where it may be necessary to adjust the carrying amount of goodwill, notwithstanding this prohibition.

A first-time adopter should also consider the following implementation issues on measuring assets acquired and liabilities assumed in business combinations:

(a)   *Subsequent measurement of assets and liabilities under FRS 102 not based on cost* – Where FRS 102 requires subsequent measurement of some assets and liabilities on a basis that is not based on original cost, such as fair value (e.g. certain financial instruments) or on specific measurement bases (e.g. share-based payment or employee benefits), a first-time adopter should measure these assets and liabilities on that basis in its opening FRS 102 statement of financial position, even if they were acquired or assumed in a past business combination. Any resulting change is recognised by adjusting retained earnings (or another component of equity).

(b)   *Previous GAAP carrying amount as deemed cost* – The carrying amount in accordance with previous GAAP of assets acquired and liabilities assumed in the business combination, immediately after the business combination, is their deemed cost in accordance with FRS 102 at that date. If FRS 102 requires a cost-based measurement of those assets and liabilities at a later date that deemed cost should be the basis for cost-based depreciation or amortisation from the date of the business combination (i.e. the carrying values under previous GAAP *at the date of the business combination* are 'grandfathered' under the business combination transition exemption).

In our view, a first-time adopter would not use provisionally determined fair values of assets acquired and liabilities assumed in applying the business combinations exemption. Since the final fair value adjustments made under previous GAAP effectively result in a restatement of the balances at the date of transition in a manner that is consistent with the approach permitted by FRS 102, it is appropriate to reflect these adjustments in the opening FRS 102 statement of financial position. Since the adjustments are effectively made at the date of transition, it is also appropriate to use the window period permitted by previous GAAP provided that this does not extend into the first FRS 102 reporting period. For previous UK GAAP reporters, this would mean that goodwill is adjusted retrospectively at the date of transition for the changes to the provisional fair values. While neither Section 35 nor IFRS 1 explicitly addresses this issue, this is consistent with practice under IFRSs.

By contrast, under previous GAAP, the entity may have amortised intangible assets or depreciated property, plant and equipment from the date of the business combination. If this amortisation or depreciation is not in compliance with FRS 102 (or indeed the asset was not amortised or depreciated under previous GAAP, but this is required under FRS 102), this is not 'grandfathered' under the business combination exemption. If the amortisation or depreciation methods and rates are not acceptable and the difference has a material impact on the financial statements, a first-time adopter must adjust the accumulated amortisation or depreciation on transition (see 5.5.2 below).

(c) *Measurement of items not recognised under previous UK GAAP* – If an asset acquired or liability assumed in a past business combination was not recognised under previous GAAP, this does not mean that such items have a deemed cost of zero in the opening FRS 102 statement of financial position. Instead, the acquirer normally recognises and measures those items in its opening statement of financial position on the basis that FRS 102 would require in the statement of financial position of the acquiree. Conversely, if an asset or liability was subsumed in goodwill in accordance with previous GAAP but would have been recognised separately under Section 19, that asset or liability remains in goodwill unless FRS 102 would require its recognition in the financial statements of the acquiree. However, intangible assets previously subsumed within goodwill under previous UK GAAP are not separately recognised. *[FRS 102.35.10(a)].* Financial assets and financial liabilities derecognised under previous UK GAAP in a pre-transition transaction are not re-recognised. *[FRS 102.35.9(a)].*

(d) *Measurement of non-controlling interests and deferred tax* – The measurement of non-controlling interests (see also 4.4 above) and deferred tax follows from the measurement of other assets and liabilities. Consequently, deferred tax and non-controlling interests should be recalculated after all assets acquired and liabilities assumed have been adjusted under Section 35. Any resulting change in the carrying amount of deferred taxes and non-controlling interest is recognised by adjusting retained earnings or another component of equity.

The recognition and measurement of deferred tax is addressed in Section 29 of the standard. Section 29 must be applied retrospectively as no transition exemptions or exceptions apply. In particular, first-time adopters will need to consider what deferred tax would have been recognised at the date of the business combination, as adjusted by subsequent movements in timing differences recognised under Section 29.

5.2.4   Restatement of goodwill

Notwithstanding the prohibition in paragraph 35.10(a) from making adjustments to goodwill where past business combinations are not restated, there may be certain situations where an adjustment to goodwill is appropriate. These could include:

- where there is an indicator that the goodwill may be impaired at the date of transition (see 5.2.4.A below);

- the interaction with FRS 102's requirements to restate goodwill for adjustments to contingent consideration (see 5.2.4.B below);

- a potential conflict with FRS 102's requirements to retranslate goodwill and fair value adjustments relating to a foreign operation. (see 5.2.4.C below); and

- changes in the scope of consolidation (see 5.2.5 below).

Negative goodwill and goodwill previously deducted from equity (see 5.2.4.D below) are not explicitly addressed in FRS 102, although IFRS 1 Appendix C addresses the latter.

FRS 102's accounting requirements for negative goodwill (see Chapter 15 at 3.8) are very similar to those of FRS 10 – *Goodwill and intangible assets* – under previous UK GAAP. Consequently, for previous UK GAAP reporters, no restatement would be expected to the carrying amount of negative goodwill. *[FRS 10.49-50].*

5.2.4.A   Impairment of goodwill

Section 35 does not require an impairment review of goodwill to be performed as at the date of transition. However, Section 27 requires that an entity must assess at each reporting date whether there is any indication of impairment (or its reversal). *[FRS 102.35.7, 27.29].* For example, where an entity uplifts the carrying amount of property, plant and equipment to fair value at the date of transition, the total carrying amount of the acquired net assets including goodwill may not exceed the recoverable amount of the relevant cash-generating unit.

Section 35 states that no adjustments shall be made to the carrying amount of goodwill. *[FRS 102.35.10(a)].* However, it would be inappropriate to recognise an impairment loss on the first day of the comparative period of the FRS 102 financial statements when that impairment already existed at the date of transition itself. Therefore, if there is an indicator of impairment at transition then the goodwill should be reviewed for impairment at the date of transition.

Any impairment losses identified at the date of transition would be reflected in retained earnings in accordance with paragraph 35.8, unless Section 27 permits it to be recognised in revaluation surplus (e.g. an associated impairment of property, plant and equipment carried at valuation under FRS 102).

Chapter 30

5.2.4.B   Transition accounting for contingent consideration

Contingent consideration should be remeasured under the general principles in FRS 102 as there are no exemptions under Section 35. *[FRS 102.19.12-13].*

Normally, there should not be any adjustments to contingent consideration when entities transition to FRS 102 from previous UK GAAP. The amount reported as contingent consideration (and goodwill) is likely to be the same under both GAAPs because the requirements in FRS 7 – *Fair values in acquisition accounting* – and Section 19 are similar (albeit not identical). See Chapter 15 at 2.1.5.B.

The interaction between the requirements on contingent consideration and those on financial instruments is rather complicated. Where Sections 11 and 12 of the standard are applied to the recognition and measurement of financial instruments, they scope out the accounting by the acquirer for contracts for contingent consideration in a business combination – and instead refer to Section 19. *[FRS 102.12.3(g)].* Consequently, goodwill must be adjusted (prospectively) for subsequent changes to the measurement of contingent consideration.

Where an entity chooses to apply IAS 39 or IFRS 9 to the recognition and measurement of financial instruments, it applies the scope of the relevant standard to its financial instruments. *[FRS 102.11.2,12.2].* IAS 39 and IFRS 9 do not scope out contingent consideration that is a financial asset or liability from its requirements. The requirements on contingent consideration in IFRS 3 – *Business Combinations* – do not apply to companies reporting under FRS 102. Therefore, such an entity should normally apply the requirement in paragraph 19.12 that contingent consideration is recognised where the adjustments to consideration are probable and can be measured reliably, with subsequent adjustments to goodwill.

5.2.4.C   Goodwill on pre-transition business combination that is a foreign operation (where not restated under Section 19)

Section 35 is not explicit on how to treat goodwill relating to an acquisition of a foreign operation in a business combination that is not restated under Section 19.

While paragraph 35.10(a) specifies that no adjustments should be made to goodwill, Section 30 – *Foreign Currency Translation* – requires goodwill arising on the acquisition of a foreign operation to be translated. Where a conflict between paragraph 35.10(a) and Section 30 arises, management will need to use judgement to determine an appropriate policy.

5.2.4.D   Goodwill previously deducted from equity

Prior to the implementation of FRS 10 (which was mandatory, effective for periods ending on or after 23 December 1998), UK GAAP permitted goodwill to be eliminated against reserves. On transition to FRS 10, entities were not required to restate such goodwill (but could choose to restate all or certain elements of such goodwill as an asset). *[FRS 10.68-71].* However, such goodwill eliminated against reserves would be charged or credited in the profit and loss account on subsequent disposal or closure of the business to which it related. *[FRS 2.52, FRS 9.40, FRS 10.71].*

In our view, where the exemption not to restate pre-transition business combinations in accordance with Section 19 is taken, the requirement that no adjustment shall be made to the carrying value of goodwill means that there is no change to the amount of goodwill recognised as an asset (i.e. the goodwill remains eliminated against equity). *[FRS 102.35.9(a)].*

FRS 102 does not permit or require recycling of goodwill previously deducted from equity to profit or loss when the related operation is disposed of or closed. However, because FRS 102 financial statements are Companies Act accounts, a UK company preparing statutory accounts will need to give the disclosures in the notes to the group accounts of the cumulative amount of goodwill resulting from acquisitions in that and earlier financial years (net of any goodwill attributable to subsidiary undertakings or businesses disposed of prior to the balance sheet date) which has been written off otherwise than in the consolidated profit and loss account for that or any earlier financial year. *[6 Sch 14].*

5.2.4.E   Goodwill and intangible asset amortisation

FRS 102 requires that goodwill and intangible assets be amortised on a systematic basis over a finite useful life using an amortisation method that reflects the expected pattern of consumption of economic benefits. A straight-line basis is used if the entity cannot determine that pattern reliably. If an entity is unable to make a reliable estimate of the useful life of goodwill or an intangible asset, the life shall not exceed five years. *[FRS 102.18.19-22, 19.23, Appendix I].* See Chapter 15 at 3.8 and Chapter 18 at [x] for a fuller discussion.

The question arises as to whether an entity should adjust the life of goodwill and how any such adjustment is treated. Under FRS 10, many entities used a twenty-year life as the standard contained a rebuttable presumption that the useful lives of purchased goodwill and intangible assets are limited to periods of twenty years or less. *[FRS 10.19].* We would expect previous UK GAAP reporters to continue to use a twenty-year life, provided that the goodwill's remaining life at transition can be reliably estimated. Any change to the previous life would need to be justified and reflect changes in circumstances (unless the previous life was objectively in error).

In *Staff Education Note 13: Transition to FRS 102*, the FRC staff state:

> 'If a first-time adopter elects not to apply Section 19 retrospectively, it will still need to apply Section 19 prospectively to any goodwill recognised in its balance sheet at the date of transition. As noted above, the carrying amount of the goodwill would not be adjusted on transition, however it would be amortised over a finite useful life going forward. For an entity that has previously determined a finite useful life for goodwill, the entity can continue to amortise that goodwill over this period so long as it can reliably estimate that useful life. For an entity that has previously determined an indefinite useful life for goodwill, the entity will need to reassess the remaining useful life going forward. If an entity is unable to reliably estimate the useful life of goodwill, then the useful life shall not exceed five years.'

Where goodwill was previously determined to have an indefinite life under FRS 10, it is logical that, absent a change in circumstances (or the previous life was objectively in error), the remaining useful life should be at least twenty years from the date of transition. This is because otherwise the presumption that the goodwill life was twenty years or less would have been rebutted (FRS 10 required entities to reassess the useful life of goodwill annually). *[FRS 10.19, 33]*.

A first-time adopter may also need to consider the following implementation issues:

(a) *Adjustments to goodwill lives where no restatement of business combinations under Section 19* – Where an entity is not restating the business combination in accordance with Section 19, paragraph 35.10(a) requires that no adjustment is made to the carrying amount of goodwill. Consequently, any adjustment to goodwill lives is prospective (unless the previous life was objectively in error). This is the case, whether or not the goodwill was amortised over a finite life or was regarded as having an indefinite life.

The Accounting Council's advice to the FRC states that 'The Accounting Council noted that FRS 102 does not permit goodwill to have an indefinite useful life, unlike current FRS. On transition to FRS 102, entities that previously determined that goodwill had an indefinite useful life will need to reassess goodwill to determine its remaining useful life, and subsequently amortise the goodwill over that period.' *[FRS 102.AC.161]*.

The Accounting Council Advice does not appear to distinguish between goodwill relating to past business combinations restated in accordance with Section 19 and goodwill that is not restated, but we believe it is intended to apply only where the exemption in paragraph 35.10(a) not to restate business combinations is taken.

(b) *Restatement of business combinations* – Where a first-time adopter restates a business combination in accordance with Section 19 and has previously ascribed a finite life to goodwill, any adjustment to that life is accounted for prospectively over the remaining revised life determined under FRS 102 as a change in estimate.

Where, however, an indefinite life was used under previous GAAP, amortisation should be adjusted for retrospectively from the date of the business combination. This is because this is a change in accounting policy (not a change in estimate) and the requirement in paragraph 35.10(a) that no adjustment shall be made to the carrying amount of goodwill does not apply. On transition to FRS 102, however, goodwill and intangible assets *must* be amortised over a finite life. Therefore, in our view, a move from an indefinite life to a finite life for goodwill is required to be retrospectively effected – such that the goodwill at transition represents the carrying amounts after adjusting for amortisation on the basis of the finite life determined under FRS 102.

(c) *Intangible assets* – There are no special transition requirements for intangible assets (other than goodwill) and therefore FRS 102's requirements are applied retrospectively. *[FRS 102.35.7]*.

Where an entity amortised an intangible asset over a longer finite life than five years under previous UK GAAP, it can continue to use that life, providing that the remaining useful life can be reliably estimated. In particular, it would be difficult to argue that the life should simply default to a five-year life. Any changes to the useful life of an intangible asset would need to be justified by reference to a change in circumstances (unless the previous life was objectively in error) and be recognised prospectively as a change in estimate. However, if an entity ascribed an indefinite life to an intangible asset under FRS 10, in our view, the intangible asset must be amortised retrospectively over its new finite useful life since this is a change in accounting policy (FRS 102 does not permit use of an indefinite life).

The above conclusions apply to all intangible assets, whether acquired separately or in a business combination (and do not depend on whether the business combination is restated in accordance with Section 19 or not).

5.2.5   Changes in scope of consolidation

The scope of consolidation under previous UK GAAP may differ from the scope of consolidation under FRS 102. Therefore, a first-time adopter may not have consolidated a subsidiary acquired in a past business combination under previous UK GAAP or a subsidiary previously consolidated qualifies to be excluded from consolidation under FRS 102.

5.2.5.A   Changes in consolidation compared to previous UK GAAP

The definition of a subsidiary in Section 9 of FRS 102 is generally consistent with (although not identical to) the definition of a subsidiary undertaking included in FRS 2 *[FRS 2.14]* and section 1162 of the Companies Act 2006. However, entities should consider Section 9's requirements on control (in particular, in relation to currently exercisable options or convertible instruments; where control is exercised through an agent; and Special Purpose Entities) and the extended definition of subsidiaries held exclusively for resale (which are excluded from consolidation). *[FRS 102.9.6, 9.9B, 10-12]*. These are discussed further in Chapter 6 at 3.3 and 3.4.2.

5.2.5.B   Previously unconsolidated subsidiaries

If, under previous GAAP, an FRS 102 first-time adopter did not consolidate a subsidiary that it is required to consolidate under FRS 102, it must retrospectively apply FRS 102 to the carrying amounts of the assets and liabilities of that subsidiary, subject to the transition exceptions and transition exemptions set out in Section 35. *[FRS 102.35.7]*. FRS 102 does not explain how a first-time adopter should consolidate a subsidiary for the first time (whether because the reporting entity did not consider the entity to be a subsidiary under previous GAAP or did not prepare consolidated financial statements). However, as set out below, management should apply the requirements of paragraph 35.10(r) (see 5.15.2 below) and may want to consider paragraphs IG26 to IG31 of IFRS 1 to the extent that these do not conflict with FRS 102:

(a)   *Subsidiary acquired in a business combination: entity uses the transition exemption not to restate past business combinations* – If an entity becomes a first-time adopter later than its subsidiary, associate or joint venture the entity shall in its consolidated financial statements, measure the assets and liabilities of the subsidiary (or associate or joint venture) at the same carrying amounts as in the FRS 102 financial statements of the subsidiary (or associate or joint venture), after adjusting for consolidation and equity accounting adjustments and for the effects of the business combination in which the entity acquired the subsidiary (or transaction in which it acquired the associate or joint venture). Where the subsidiary (or associate or joint venture) has not previously adopted FRS 102, the reference above to the 'same carrying amounts' is to the amounts FRS 102 would require in the statement of financial position of the subsidiary (or associate or joint venture). *[FRS 102.35.10(r), IFRS 1.IG27].*

In our view, the transition adjustments to derecognise the cost of investment (and recognise the assets and liabilities of the subsidiary would be reflected in retained earnings (or other component of equity), following the general requirements in Section 35. This differs from the requirement in Appendix C4(j) in IFRS 1 to establish a deemed cost of goodwill, which appears to conflict with paragraph 35.10(a) that no adjustment is made to goodwill at the date of transition.

(b) *Subsidiary acquired in a business combination restated under Section 19* – Where the previously unconsolidated subsidiary was acquired in a business combination restated under Section 19, the goodwill and fair values of the identifiable net assets recognised at the date of the business combination would be retrospectively restated. The first-time adopter would need to restate either all pre-transition business combinations or all later business combinations. Other assets acquired and liabilities assumed *since* the business combination and still held at the acquirer's date of transition are reported at:

- the carrying amounts that FRS 102 would require in the subsidiary's own statement of financial position; or

- where the subsidiary has already adopted FRS 102 before its parent, the amounts included in the latter's statement of financial position in its FRS 102 financial statements,

after adjusting for consolidation procedures. *[FRS 102.35.10(r)].*

(c) *Subsidiary not acquired in a business combination* – The first-time adopter would adjust the carrying amounts of the subsidiary's assets and liabilities to the amounts that FRS 102 would require in the subsidiary's own statement of financial position (or where the subsidiary has already adopted FRS 102 before its parent, the amounts included in its statement of financial position in its FRS 102 financial statements), after adjusting for consolidation procedures. *[FRS 102.35.10(r)].*

Where the subsidiary was not acquired in a business combination, no goodwill is recognised. Instead, any difference between the carrying amounts and the net identifiable assets determined above is treated as an adjustment to retained earnings at the date of transition, representing the accumulated profits or losses that would have been recognised as if the subsidiary has always been consolidated. *[IFRS 1.IG27(c)].*

5.2.5.C   *Previously consolidated entities that are not subsidiaries*

A first-time adopter may have consolidated an investment under previous UK GAAP that does not meet the definition of a consolidated subsidiary under FRS 102. In such a case, the entity should first determine the appropriate classification under FRS 102 and then apply Section 35's requirements.

In general, such previously consolidated investments should be accounted for as:

* an associate or jointly controlled entity;
* a financial asset;
* an executory contract; or
* a service concession arrangement.

The requirements of FRS 102 should be applied retrospectively subject to any transition exceptions and exemptions available and, where applicable, the use of the impracticability exemption available in paragraph 35.11A (see 3.5.4 above). *[FRS 102.35.7,11A].*

Unlike IFRS 1, the exemption from restating business combinations in paragraph 35.9(a) is not extended to transactions in which interests in associates and jointly controlled entities are acquired. *[FRS 102.35.9(a), IFRS 1.Appendix C5].*

5.2.6   *Business combination – transition example*

The following example illustrates a number of the considerations relevant to the treatment of business combinations on transition.

Example 30.5:   Business combination example

On 31 December 2013, Entity A purchased Entity B for £1m. Entity A intends to use paragraph 35.10(a) not to restate the business combination in accordance with Section 19.

The assets and liabilities acquired were as follows:

	Book value (and tax base) in B's financial statements £000	Fair value (previous UK GAAP) £000	Fair value (Section 19) £000
Intangible asset (customer contract – 5 year life)	–	–	300
Property (5 year life – nil residual value)	100	500	500
Investment in listed equity shares	100	200	200
Inventory	50	50	70
Deferred tax (at 20%)	(40)	(40)	(204)
Net assets acquired	–	710	866
Consideration (including acquisition costs)	–	1,010	1,010
Goodwill	–	300	144

Under previous UK GAAP, no deferred tax was recognised on the fair value adjustments to the investment in listed equity shares and property.

The property was accounted for using the cost model under previous UK GAAP. The investment in listed equity shares was accounted for at cost under previous UK GAAP. Goodwill was amortised over a period of 20 years under previous UK GAAP and its remaining useful life at the date of transition can be reliably estimated.

Chapter 30

Under previous UK GAAP, no contingent consideration was recognised at the date of the business combination as no amounts were expected to be paid, but an adjustment to goodwill of £100,000 was recognised at 31 December 2014 in relation to a reassessment of the amount of contingent consideration that was subsequently considered to be probable.

Under FRS 102, Entity A continues to account for the property using the cost model (and does not make use of any deemed cost exemptions – see 5.5 below). Entity A elects to apply Sections 11 and 12 and is required to account for the investment in listed equity shares at fair value through profit and loss. *[FRS 102.11.14(d)].* At 31 December 2014, the investment in listed equity shares has a fair value of £350,000.

An income tax rate of 20% applies in all periods and indexation is ignored.

At the date of transition, Entity A:

- does not restate the carrying amounts of the property or inventory, even though the fair value of the inventory at the date of the business combination would have differed had Section 19 been applied (this is because Section 19 requires fair value whereas FRS 7 specifies that inventory – that is not traded on a market in which the acquirer participates as both a buyer and a seller – is valued at the lower of replacement cost and net realisable value). The values ascribed under previous UK GAAP are treated as deemed cost at the date of the business combination.

- does not record an adjustment for the customer contract intangible assets previously subsumed within goodwill. *[FRS 102.35.10(a)].*

- records a deferred tax liability of £80,000 relating to the fair value adjustment to property and £20,000 relating to the fair value adjustment of the investment in listed equity shares at the date of transition. *[FRS 102.29.11].*

There is no adjustment to the carrying amount of goodwill of £300,000 at the date of transition, and therefore the additional deferred tax liability of £100,000 arising on the difference between the fair values and tax values of the property and investment in listed equity shares at the date of the business combination is recognised in retained earnings. *[FRS 102.35.10(a)].*

In the comparative period, there is no adjustment to the uplift of goodwill for the reassessment of contingent consideration. *[FRS 102.19.12-19.13].* There is also no adjustment to the goodwill amortisation charged under previous UK GAAP, since the remaining useful life can be reliably estimated. *[FRS 102.19.23].*

However, a deferred tax credit of £16,000 arises in comparative profit or loss relating to reversal of timing differences on the property (relating to depreciation) and the carrying amount of the listed investment is remeasured to its fair value of £350,000, recording a fair value gain of £150,000 (and a related deferred tax charge of £30,000) in comparative profit or loss. *[FRS 102.11.14(d), 29.6].*

If the business combinations exemption had not been taken, the business combination would be restated in accordance with Section 19 (see the final column in the table above). Goodwill of £144,000 would be amortised over 20 years from the date of the business combination. Therefore, there would be an adjustment to decrease the carrying amount of goodwill by £156,000 at the date of transition with £7,800 lower goodwill amortisation recognised in the comparative period. In the comparative period, there is no adjustment to the uplift of goodwill for the reassessment of contingent consideration made under previous UK GAAP.

As when the paragraph 35.10(a) exemption is taken, a deferred tax credit of £16,000 arises in comparative profit or loss relating to reversal of timing differences on the property and the carrying amount of the listed investment is remeasured to its fair value of £350,000, recording a fair value gain of £150,000 (and deferred tax charge of £30,000) in the comparative period. Amortisation of the acquired intangible asset of £60,000 (and deferred tax credit of £12,000) will also be recognised in the comparative period. If the inventory is sold in 2014, the cost of sales will be £20,000 higher than under previous UK GAAP, with a tax credit arising from reversal of the deferred tax liability recognised on the business combination of £4,000.

5.3 Public-benefit entity combinations

A public benefit entity is 'an entity whose primary objective is to provide goods or services for the general public, community or social benefit and where any equity is provided with a view to supporting the entity's primary objective rather than with a view to providing a financial return to equity providers, shareholders or members.' *[FRS 102 Appendix I].*

FRS 102 specifies the accounting for different types of public benefit entity combinations (see Chapter 29 at 6). *[FRS 102.PBE34.75-86].*

A first-time adopter may elect not to apply paragraphs PBE 34.75 to PBE 34.86 relating to public benefit entity combinations to combinations that were effected before the date of transition to FRS 102. However, if on first-time adoption, a public benefit entity restates any entity combination to comply with this section, it shall restate all later entity combinations. *[FRS 102.35(q)].*

Section 35 does not add further guidance. However, entities may want to interpret paragraph 35.10(q) in the same way as the exemption for pre-transition business combinations (including group reconstructions) in paragraph 35.10(a). See 5.2 above.

5.4 Share-based payment transactions

A first-time adopter is not required to apply Section 26 – *Share-based Payment* – to equity instruments that were granted before the date of transition to FRS 102, or to liabilities arising from share-based payment transactions that were settled before the date of transition to FRS 102.

However, a first-time adopter previously applying FRS 20 – *Share-based payment* (IFRS 2) or IFRS 2 – *Share-based Payment* – shall, in relation to equity instruments that were granted before the date of transition to FRS 102, apply either FRS 20 / IFRS 2 (as applicable) or Section 26 at the date of transition. *[FRS 102.35.10(b)].*

Entities applying the FRSSE were not required to account for share-based payments and are, therefore, permitted not to apply Section 26 to equity-settled share based payments granted before the date of transition (or to liabilities arising from share-based transactions settled prior to transition).

Unlike the full exemption from accounting for pre-transition grants given to those first-time adopters that have not previously accounted for share-based payments, those who have previously applied FRS 20 or IFRS 2 are required to continue accounting for ongoing awards either under the previous standard or under Section 26. *[FRS 102.35.10(b)].* However, there are differences between the requirements of FRS 20 / IFRS 2 and Section 26 (see Chapter 21 at 2) and some areas where Section 26 is silent or has less guidance.

The exemption allows an entity to complete the accounting for a pre-transition grant using the original grant date fair value and it is not expected that the application of Section 26 to such grants would often result in a remeasurement. Paragraph 35.10(b) does not prohibit such a remeasurement (e.g. as a result of applying the group allocation arrangements of paragraph 16 of Section 26, where the entity chooses to apply Section 26 to pre-transition grants of equity instruments).

Chapter 30

As noted in Chapter 21 at 11, the classification of a share-based payment transaction as equity-settled or cash-settled might differ depending on whether an entity is applying FRS 102 or FRS 20 / IFRS 2. Under the requirements of Section 35, it appears that an entity could continue with the FRS 20 / IFRS 2 classification previously adopted, even if new grants would be classified differently under FRS 102.

Section 35 does not address the treatment of equity-settled awards granted before the date of transition but modified (or cancelled or settled) at a later date. Therefore, a first-time adopter (other than one who has previously applied FRS 20 or IFRS 2) would need to develop an appropriate accounting policy for such transactions.

5.5   Fair value or previous revaluation as deemed cost

A first-time adopter may elect to measure an:

- item of property, plant and equipment;
- an investment property; or
- an intangible asset which meets the recognition criteria and the criteria for revaluation as set out in Section 18 – *Intangible Assets other than Goodwill*

on the date of transition to FRS 102 at its fair value (see definitions at 3.1 above) and use that fair value as its deemed cost at that date. *[FRS 102.35.10(c)].* Fair value at the date of transition should reflect the conditions that existed at transition date. FRS 102 requires that, in the absence of specific guidance in the relevant section of the standard dealing with an item, the guidance in paragraphs 11.27 to 11.32 should be used in determining fair value. *[FRS 102 Appendix I].*

A first-time adopter may elect to use a previous GAAP revaluation of an item of property, plant and equipment, an investment property, or an intangible asset at, or before, the date of transition to FRS 102 as its deemed cost at the revaluation date. *[FRS 102.35.10(d)].*

Establishing the original cost may be onerous where the requirements differ from previous GAAP. In particular, many previous UK GAAP reporters have frozen past revaluations of tangible fixed assets on implementation of FRS 15 – *Tangible fixed assets. [FRS 15.104].* Use of the deemed cost exemption would allow a first-time adopter that revalued the property, plant and equipment under previous UK GAAP to retain the revalued amount at the date of transition, when moving to the cost model on adoption of FRS 102; it would also allow first-time adopters to reflect a one-off revaluation at the date of transition. Section 35 includes further deemed cost exemptions for:

- deferred development costs (see 5.6 below);
- oil and gas properties (see 5.7 below); and
- cost of investments in subsidiaries, associates and joint ventures in separate or individual financial statements (see 5.9 below).

5.5.1 Scope of the deemed cost exemption

The exemptions in paragraphs 35.10(c) and (d) are available on an item-by-item basis (so need not be applied consistently to a class of assets).

In practice, this exemption is likely to be most useful for items of property, plant and equipment, where there are few restrictions to its application.

Investment property is required to be measured at fair value through profit and loss unless it cannot be measured reliably without undue cost or effort on an ongoing basis. *[FRS 102.16.1]*. It would be hard to argue that investment property previously revalued under SSAP 19 cannot be measured reliably without undue cost or effort on an ongoing basis, so use of the deemed cost exemption is likely to be limited.

The deemed cost exemption can only be applied to intangible assets that meet the recognition criteria and criteria for revaluation in Section 18, including the existence of an active market. Therefore, the exemption is of limited practical relevance to intangible assets.

5.5.2 Establishing deemed cost at a date other than transition

If the deemed cost of an asset is determined before the date of transition, then an FRS 102-compliant accounting policy needs to be applied to that deemed cost in the intervening period to determine what the carrying amount of the asset is in the opening FRS 102 statement of financial position. This means that a first-time adopter that uses a previous GAAP revaluation prior to the date of transition will need to start depreciating the item from the date for which the entity established the revaluation (i.e. deemed cost) not from the date of transition to FRS 102.

This requirement is unlikely to give rise to a GAAP difference where an entity previously adopted UK GAAP provided the depreciation methods, lives and residual values previously applied remain acceptable under FRS 102. It should be noted that there are subtle differences between previous UK GAAP and FRS 102, for example, regarding the definition of residual value and the non-depreciation of tangible fixed assets (See Chapter 13 at 2.1). Where it is difficult to apply FRS 102's requirements on depreciation retrospectively, an entity can always use a deemed cost equal to fair value at the date of transition.

5.5.3 Impairment

As deemed cost is a surrogate for cost from the date of the measurement, any later impairment must be recognised in profit or loss. Moreover, any previous impairment recognised prior to the date that the deemed cost is established cannot be reversed. Section 27 does not permit reversal of impairment of an asset above the carrying amount that would have been determined (net of amortisation or depreciation) had no impairment loss been recognised in prior years (i.e. depreciated cost based on the deemed cost at the date of measurement). *[FRS 102.27.30(b), 27.31(c)(ii)]*.

5.5.4 Deferred tax

Where a deemed cost is established based on a previous GAAP valuation, or fair value at transition, the past revaluation on or prior to transition generally represents a timing difference for which deferred tax will need to be recognised in accordance with the requirements of Section 29. Under the alternative accounting rules, any deferred tax relating to amounts credited or debited to the revaluation reserve (relating to the same asset) may also be recognised in the revaluation reserve as an alternative to retained earnings. *[1 Sch 35(3)(b)].*

If after transition, the deferred tax is remeasured (e.g. because of a change in tax rate) and the asset concerned was revalued outside profit or loss under previous UK GAAP, an entity needs to determine whether the resulting deferred tax income or expense should be recognised in, or outside, profit or loss. FRS 102 requires that an entity shall present tax expense (income) in the same component of total comprehensive income (i.e. continuing or discontinued operations, and profit or loss or other comprehensive income) or equity as the transaction or other event that resulted in the tax expense (income). *[FRS 102.19.22].*

5.5.5   *Revaluation reserve*

UK companies preparing statutory accounts are required by the Regulations to establish or maintain a statutory revaluation reserve under the alternative accounting rules on transition (see 3.5.3.A above) where property, plant and equipment or intangible assets are included at a deemed cost measurement at the date of transition. While a subsequent impairment of an asset carried at deemed cost should be reflected in profit or loss, this does not preclude a transfer between revaluation reserves and retained earnings in respect of the impairment loss (where it is less than the amount of revaluation reserve related to that asset). Similarly, any excess depreciation (based on revalued amount compared to the historical cost amount) can also be transferred from the revaluation reserve to retained earnings. *[1 Sch 35(3)(a)].*

FRS 102 requires investment property normally to be carried at fair value through profit and loss. This makes use of the fair value accounting rules under the Regulations whereas the accounting under SSAP 19 made use of the alternative accounting rules. Adjustments on transition (including the treatment of the revaluation reserve established under previous UK GAAP) to investment properties are addressed in 3.5.3.B above.

Chapter 4 at 9.2 and 9.3 addresses the alternative accounting rules and fair value accounting rules, including related disclosure requirements, in detail.

5.6   Deferred development costs as a deemed cost

A first-time adopter may elect to measure the carrying amount at the date of transition to FRS 102 for development costs deferred in accordance with SSAP 13 – *Accounting for research and development* – as its deemed cost at that date. *[FRS 102.35.10(n)].*

Section 18 provides a choice of policy as to whether to capitalise or expense development costs, which must be applied consistently to all expenditure meeting the capitalisation criteria in paragraph 18.8H. *[FRS 102.18.8K].* Therefore, first-time adopters have the opportunity to change the policy applied to development costs from that applied under SSAP 13.

The transition exemption only applies where a previous UK GAAP reporter has capitalised development costs under SSAP 13 and intends to continue a policy of capitalisation under FRS 102. As Section 18 has recognition criteria (based on the requirements in IAS 38 – *Intangible Assets*) that differ from SSAP 13, the transition exemption allows an entity to avoid assessing whether the costs capitalised under previous UK GAAP would qualify under Section 18 and to grandfather the development costs deferred under SSAP 13.

Section 18 must be applied retrospectively if the transition exemption is not taken or if an entity that previously expensed development costs adopts a policy of capitalisation under FRS 102 (see Chapter 14 at 3.3.3). A first-time adopter, in applying Section 18 retrospectively as at the date of transition, must not capitalise costs incurred before the recognition criteria in Section 18 were met and avoid the use of hindsight in general.

Where business combinations are restated in accordance with Section 19, intangible assets (including development costs) should be recognised at their fair values where the recognition criteria in Section 19 are met, even if a policy of expensing development costs is followed under Section 18.

5.7 Deemed cost for oil and gas assets

A first-time adopter that under a previous GAAP accounted for exploration and development costs for oil and gas properties in the development or production phases, in cost centres that included all properties in a large geographical area may elect to measure oil and gas assets at the date of transition to FRS 102 on the following basis:

(i) Exploration and evaluation assets at the amount determined under the entity's previous GAAP.

(ii) Assets in the development or production phases at the amount determined for the cost centre under the entity's previous GAAP. The entity shall allocate this amount to the cost centre's underlying assets *pro rata* using reserve volumes or reserve values as of that date.

The entity shall test exploration and evaluation assets and assets in the development and production phases for impairment at the date of transition to FRS 102 in accordance with Section 34 – *Specialised Activities* – or Section 27 respectively and, if necessary, reduce the amount determined in accordance with (i) or (ii) above. For the purposes of this paragraph, oil and gas assets comprise only those assets used in the exploration, evaluation, development or production of oil and gas. *[FRS 102.35.10(j)].*

Oil and gas entities may account for exploration and development costs for properties in development or production in cost centres that include all properties in a large geographical area, e.g. under the 'full cost accounting method' (as permitted under the OIAC SORP for previous UK GAAP reporters). However, this method of accounting allows the use of a unit of account that is larger than is acceptable under FRS 102, which does not allow cash-generating units to be larger than an operating segment. Applying FRS 102 fully retrospectively would pose significant problems for first-time adopters because – as the IASB noted in paragraph BC47A of IFRS 1 – it would require amortisation 'to be calculated (on a unit of production basis) for each year, using a reserves base that has changed over time because of changes in factors such as geological understanding and prices for oil and gas. In many cases, particularly for older assets, this information may not be available.' Even when such information is available, the effort and cost to determine the opening balances at the date of transition would usually be very high.

To avoid the use of deemed cost resulting in an oil and gas asset being measured at more than its recoverable amount, oil and gas assets are required to be tested for impairment at the date of transition. The deemed cost amounts should be reduced to take account of any impairment charge in accordance with Section 34 (for exploration and evaluation assets) and Section 27 (for assets in the development and production phases). The requirements of Section 34 are based on those in IFRS 6 (with certain adaptations) Section 34 would, therefore, require an entity to determine an accounting policy for allocating exploration and evaluation assets to cash-generating units for impairment purposes. A cash-generating unit or group of cash-generating units (used for exploration and evaluation assets) shall be no larger than an operating segment. *[FRS 102.34.11C]*.

5.8   Decommissioning liabilities included in the cost of property, plant and equipment

Paragraph 17.10(c) states that the cost of an item of property, plant and equipment includes the initial estimate of the costs, recognised and measured in accordance with Section 21 – *Provisions and Contingencies*, of dismantling and removing the item and restoring the site on which it is located, the obligation for which an entity incurs either when the item is acquired or as a consequence of having used the item during a particular period for purposes other than to produce inventories during that period. A first-time adopter may elect to measure this component of the cost of an item of property, plant and equipment at the date of transition to FRS 102, rather than on the date(s) when the obligation initially arose. *[FRS 102.35.10(l)]*.

IFRIC 1 – *Changes in Existing Decommissioning, Restoration and Similar Liabilities* – contains more detailed requirements than Section 21 or in previous UK GAAP. Therefore, an entity may want to consider IFRIC 1 in accounting for changes in existing decommissioning, restoration and similar liabilities and the guidance on the related first-time adoption exemption in IFRS 1.

The transition exemption, which is based on a comparable exemption in IFRS 1, provides a pragmatic approach to determining the decommissioning component of the carrying amount of an item of property, plant and equipment. Depreciation and impairment losses on the asset can cause differences between the carrying amount of the liability and the amounts included in the carrying amount of the asset. The transition exemption provides an exemption from determining the changes to the carrying amount of the asset that occurred before the date of transition.

Most previous UK GAAP reporters should already be following an accounting treatment for decommissioning provisions (and adjustments to the related assets) consistent with FRS 102 and are unlikely to apply the transition exemption.

5.9   Individual and separate financial statements

When an entity prepares individual or separate financial statements, paragraphs 9.26, 14.4 and 15.9 require the entity to account for its investments in subsidiaries, associates, and jointly controlled entities either at cost less impairment, or at fair value.

If a first-time adopter measures such an investment at cost, it shall measure that investment at one of the following amounts in its individual or separate opening statement of financial position, as appropriate, prepared in accordance with FRS 102:

- cost determined in accordance with Section 9; or

- deemed cost, which shall be the carrying amount at the date of transition as determined under the entity's previous GAAP. *[FRS 102.35.10(f)].*

An entity must apply the same model (cost or fair value) to all investments in a single class (subsidiaries, associates or jointly controlled entities) but can elect different policies for different classes. *[FRS 102.9.26, 14.4, 15.9].* See Chapter 6 at 4.1 and 4.2.

Where the cost model is applied, the transition exemption would permit the choice of cost or deemed cost to be applied on an investment-by-investment basis. See 5.9.1 below for specific considerations where deemed cost is used for investments.

The transition exemption allows a first-time adopter to 'grandfather' the previous UK GAAP carrying amount at the date of transition as a deemed cost at that date. Unlike the comparable exemption in IFRS 1, however, Section 35 does not permit use of deemed cost equal to the fair value at the date of transition (unless that happens to be the previous carrying amount).

Previous UK GAAP reporters that have revalued investments in the past or retranslated investments in foreign operations in the individual accounts (where hedging a net investment in a foreign operation with foreign borrowings) *[SSAP 20.51]* may wish to use the deemed cost exemption, if they intend to apply the cost model in FRS 102. See also 5.16.5 below.

Previous IFRS reporters that applied the cost model under IFRSs may also wish to use the deemed cost exemption where the carrying amount of the investment under IFRSs does not represent cost under FRS 102 (e.g. where deemed cost was used on transition to IFRSs, where the cost of the investment has been reduced by the amount of pre-acquisition dividends or where IAS 27 – *Separate Financial Statements* – specifies the cost of investment in certain group reorganisations).

5.9.1   Use of deemed cost for investments – implementation issues

Under previous UK GAAP, where a UK company acquired an investment accounted for at cost in a share-for-share exchange, the initial carrying amount of the investment was reported either at its fair value at the date of the transaction or at an amount excluding any reliefs that would have been required to be reflected in share premium but for the existence of merger relief or group reconstruction relief. Paragraph A4.24 in FRS 102 implies that this approach remains available where the cost model is applied. Hence, it is not necessary to establish a 'deemed cost' on transition where the previous carrying amount was net of such reliefs.

Where a UK company preparing statutory accounts uses a deemed cost at the date of transition that reflects a previous GAAP revaluation, this would generally mean that the investment is carried at a revalued amount that makes use of the alternative accounting rules or the fair value accounting rules (which apply to Companies Act accounts). This is the case whether or not the first-time adopter previously applied IFRSs or previous UK GAAP. See 3.5.3 above and Chapter 4 at 9.2 and 9.3.

Investments in subsidiaries, associates and jointly controlled entities in the individual or separate financial statements are subject to the impairment requirements of Section 27.

5.10   Service concession arrangements – Accounting by operators

A first-time adopter is not required to apply paragraphs 34.12I to 34.16A to service concession arrangements that were entered into before the date of transition to FRS 102. Such service concession arrangements shall continue to be accounted for using the same accounting policies being applied at the date of transition to FRS 102. *[FRS 102.35.10(i)].*

Previous UK GAAP reporters applying FRS 5 – *Application Note F Private Finance Initiative and Similar Contracts* – adopt accounting for service concession arrangements (as a financial asset or tangible fixed asset) which differs significantly from the requirements of FRS 102.

Service concession arrangements can be in place for several years and the accounting can be important to the economics of such arrangements. Where the transition exemption is not used, operators must account retrospectively in accordance with the requirements of paragraphs 34.12I to 16A. These set out two principal categories of service concession arrangements – a financial asset model and an intangible asset model for accounting for service concession arrangements – based on a simplified version of IFRIC 12 – *Service Concession Arrangements* (see Chapter 29 at 4).

The FRS 102 transition exemption differs from the comparable exemption for service concession arrangements included in IFRS 1, paragraph D22 which allows first-time adopters to apply the transitional provisions of IFRIC 12. *[IFRS 1.D22].* Therefore, operators that are previous IFRS reporters (or have reported under IFRSs for the purposes of group reporting) may have applied transitional arrangements on adopting IFRIC 12 that would need to be revisited if the transition exemption is not taken and FRS 102's requirements on service concession arrangements were applied fully retrospectively.

The exemption relates only to the accounting policies for the service concession arrangement itself, not to all the accounting policies applied by the operator.

Grantors of service concession arrangements are required to follow the finance lease model requirements of paragraphs 34.12E to 12H retrospectively.

5.11   Arrangements containing a lease

A first-time adopter may elect to determine whether an arrangement existing at the date of transition to FRS 102 contains a lease (see paragraph 20.3A) on the basis of facts and circumstances existing at the date of transition, rather than when the arrangement was entered into. *[FRS 102.35.10(k)].*

Section 35 does not include any specific exemptions from retrospective application of Section 20 – *Leases* (other than in relation to operating lease incentives, described at 5.12 below). Therefore, a first-time adopter is required to classify leases as operating or finance leases under Section 20, based on the circumstances existing at the inception of the lease or subsequent modification. *[FRS 102.20.8].*

FRS 102 sets out criteria for determining whether an arrangement contains a lease (see Chapter 16 at 3.2). Previous UK GAAP reporters may not have applied the same criteria in determining whether an arrangement contains a lease. The transition exemption allows an entity to avoid the practical difficulties of going back many years by allowing this assessment to be made at the date of transition.

The transition exemption is similar to the exemption in IFRS 1. However, IFRS 1 allows a first-time adopter not to reassess its previous GAAP determination of whether the arrangement contains a lease on transition, where it would give the same outcome as applying IAS 17 – *Leases* – and IFRIC 4 – *Determining whether an Arrangement contains a Lease*, but was made at a date other than that required by IFRIC 4. FRS 102 would not permit such previous GAAP assessments to be 'grandfathered' on transition and requires a first-time adopter to apply Section 20 either fully retrospectively or reassess the determination at the date of transition.

5.12   Lease incentives (operating leases)

A first-time adopter is not required to apply paragraphs 20.15A and 20.25A to lease incentives provided the term of the lease commenced before the date of transition to FRS 102. The first-time adopter shall continue to recognise any residual benefit or cost associated with these lease incentives on the same basis as that applied at the date of transition to FRS 102. *[FRS 102.35.10(p)].*

FRS 102 requires that a lessee in an operating lease recognises the aggregate benefit of lease incentives as a reduction to the lease expense recognised over the lease term on a straight-line basis unless another systematic basis is representative of the time pattern of the lessee's benefit from the use of the leased asset. Similarly, a lessor in an operating lease recognises the aggregate cost of lease incentives as a reduction to the lease income recognised over the lease term, on a straight-line basis unless another systematic basis is representative of the time pattern over which the lessor's benefit from the leased asset is diminished. *[FRS 102.20.15A, 25A].*

Since FRS 102's requirements on lease incentives differ from those in previous UK GAAP, the FRC has introduced a transition exemption that would allow first-time adopters to choose to continue the previous accounting treatment for lease incentives (which may have a faster recognition profile) provided the lease term commenced before the date of transition. Where the transition exemption is not taken, the requirements of FRS 102 are applied retrospectively.

5.13   Dormant companies

A company within the Companies Act definition of a dormant company (section 1169 of the Companies Act 2006) may elect to retain its accounting policies for reported assets, liabilities and equity at the date of transition to FRS 102 until there is any change to those balances or the company undertakes any new transactions. *[FRS 102.35.10(m)]*. Hence, as long as a company remains dormant, it can retain its previous GAAP accounting policies.

Without this transition exemption, dormant companies would be required to assess whether there are changes to the existing accounting under FRS 102 compared to previous UK GAAP. A change in accounting could lead to the company ceasing to be dormant. For UK companies, this could impact on the requirements to prepare and file statutory accounts (as exemptions are available to qualifying subsidiary companies that are dormant companies supported by a statutory guarantee from an EEA parent) and on the availability of audit exemptions. *[s394-s394C, s448A, s480-s481]*.

An example of a situation that could lead to a change in accounting might be changes to the carrying amounts of intercompany loans (that do not pay a market rate of interest, or are not repayable at par on demand) when measured under the requirements of Sections 11 and 12 of the standard, or IFRSs depending on the policy choice selected under FRS 102.

Dormant companies must, like all FRS 102 reporters, give a complete and unreserved statement of compliance with FRS 102. *[FRS 102.3.3]*. We consider that dormant companies using the transition exemption should disclose this fact as this is important to explaining the transition *[FRS 102.35.12]* and the accounting policies applied. *[FRS 102.8.5]*.

Where there is potential to become non-dormant in the future, a dormant company may consider whether it is beneficial to take (and accordingly state use of) other exemptions such as deemed cost on transition in relation to the cost of investments in subsidiaries, associates and jointly controlled entities – see 5.9 above *[FRS 102.35.10(f)]*. This is because, if the company becomes non-dormant in the future and can no longer retain its existing accounting policies, it will no longer be a first-time adopter (and so cannot make use of new exemptions at that time). However, in many cases, dormant companies may have simple affairs and other transition exemptions may not be relevant.

While the exemption does not explicitly state this, we consider that the wording of the exemption, in particular its references to accounting policies at the date of transition, more closely supports the view that the exemption is only available to companies that are dormant at the date of transition (until such time as they cease to be dormant) rather than being available to companies that become dormant during the period prior to the first reporting period in which FRS 102 is applied.

In our view, the reference to 'dormant company' is intentional given that the purpose of the exemption was to enable UK dormant companies not to change their status, and lose entitlement to various accounting and audit exemptions under the Companies Act 2006. However, the reference in section 1169(4) that 'Any reference in the Companies Acts to a body corporate other than a company being dormant has a corresponding meaning' could support an extension to an entity like a dormant LLP that has a comparable status to a dormant company under UK law.

5.14   Borrowing costs

An entity electing to adopt an accounting policy of capitalising borrowing costs as part of the cost of a qualifying asset may elect to treat the date of transition to FRS 102 as the date on which capitalisation commences. *[FRS 102.35.10(o)]*.

FRS 102 offers a policy choice of expensing borrowing costs as incurred or of capitalising borrowing costs that are directly attributable to the acquisition, construction or production of a qualifying asset as part of the cost of that asset. Where a capitalisation policy is adopted, this must be applied consistently to a class of qualifying assets (see Chapter 20 at 3.5.1). *[FRS 102.25.2]*.

First-time adopters, that want to adopt a capitalisation policy for borrowing costs under Section 25 – *Borrowing Costs*, can use the transition exemption which offers relief by allowing an entity to commence capitalising borrowing costs arising on qualifying assets from the date of transition. That way these entities can avoid difficult restatement issues, such as determining which assets would have qualified for capitalisation of borrowing costs in past periods, which costs met the definition of borrowing costs and determining the amount of borrowing costs that qualified for capitalisation in past periods.

A first-time adopter of IFRS that establishes a deemed cost for an asset (see 5.5 to 5.7 above) cannot capitalise borrowing costs incurred before the measurement date of the deemed cost. *[IFRS 1.IG23]*. While FRS 102 does not include an explicit statement to this effect, it would generally be appropriate to follow the same treatment under FRS 102. This would avoid an entity that has recognised an asset at a deemed cost equal to its fair value at a particular date increasing its carrying value to recognise interest capitalised before that date. However, the entity could make use of the transition exemption to commence capitalising borrowing costs from the date of transition in accordance with Section 25.

5.15 Assets and liabilities of subsidiaries, associates and joint ventures

Within groups, some subsidiaries, associates and joint ventures may have a different date of transition to FRS 102 from the parent/investor. As this could result in permanent differences between the FRS 102 figures in a subsidiary's own financial statements and those it reports to its parent, FRS 102 includes a special exemption regarding the assets and liabilities of subsidiaries, associates and joint ventures.

Paragraph 35.10(r) contains detailed guidance on the approach to be adopted when a parent adopts FRS 102 before its subsidiary (see 5.15.1 below) and also on when a subsidiary adopts FRS 102 before its parent (see 5.15.2 below).

These provisions also apply when FRS 102 is adopted at different dates by:

- an associate and the entity that has significant influence over it (i.e. the investor in the associate); or

- a joint venture and the entity that has joint control over it (i.e. a venturer in the joint venture).

In the discussion that follows at 5.15.1 to 5.15.3 below, 'parent' should be read as including an investor that has significant influence in an associate or a venturer in a joint venture, and 'subsidiary' as including an associate or a joint venture. References to consolidation adjustments should be read as including similar adjustments made when applying equity accounting.

Chapter 30

FRS 102 does not elaborate on exactly what constitutes 'consolidation adjustments' but in our view it would encompass adjustments required in order to harmonise accounting policies as well as purely 'mechanical' consolidation adjustments such as the elimination of intragroup balances, profits and losses.

Paragraph 35.10(r) also addresses the requirements for a parent that adopts FRS 102 at different dates for the purposes of its consolidated and its separate financial statements (see 5.15.4 below).

5.15.1   Subsidiary becomes a first-time adopter later than its parent

If a subsidiary becomes a first-time adopter later than its parent, it should in its financial statements measure its assets and liabilities at either:

(i)   the carrying amounts that would be included in the parent's consolidated financial statements, based on the parent's date of transition to FRS 102, if no adjustments were made for consolidation procedures and for the effects of the business combination in which the parent acquired the subsidiary; or

(ii) the carrying amounts required by the rest of FRS 102, based on the subsidiary's date of transition to FRS 102. These carrying amounts could differ from those described in (i) when:

(a)   the exemptions in FRS 102 result in measurements that depend on the date of transition to FRS 102;

(b)   the accounting policies used in the subsidiary's financial statements differ from those in the consolidated financial statements. For example, the subsidiary may use as its accounting policy the cost model in Section 17 – *Property, Plant and Equipment*, whereas the group may use the revaluation model.

A similar election is available to an associate or joint venture that becomes a first-time adopter later than an entity that has significant influence or joint control over it. *[FRS 102.35.10(r)].*

The following example, which is based on IFRS 1, illustrates how an entity should apply these requirements. *[IFRS 1, IG Example 8].*

Example 30.6:   Parent adopts FRS 102 before subsidiary

Background

Entity A presents its first FRS 102 consolidated financial statements in 2013. Subsidiary B, wholly owned by Entity A (its parent) since formation, prepares information under FRS 102 for internal consolidation purposes from that date, but Subsidiary B will not present its first FRS 102 financial statements until 2015.

Application of requirements

If Subsidiary B applies option (i) in paragraph 35.10(r), the carrying amounts of its assets and liabilities are the same in both its opening FRS 102 statement of financial position at 1 January 2014 and Entity A's consolidated balance sheet (except for adjustments for consolidation procedures) and are based on Entity A's date of transition to FRS 102.

Alternatively, Subsidiary B may apply option (ii) in paragraph 35.10(r), and measure all its assets or liabilities based on its own date of transition to FRS 102 (1 January 2014). However, the fact that Subsidiary B becomes a first-time adopter in 2015 does not change the carrying amounts of its assets and liabilities in Entity A's consolidated financial statements.

Under option (ii), a subsidiary would prepare its own FRS 102 financial statements, completely ignoring the FRS 102 elections that its parent used when it adopted FRS 102 for its consolidated financial statements. Under option (i), the numbers in a subsidiary's FRS 102 financial statements would be as close as possible to those used by its parent. However, differences other than those arising from business combinations (and consolidation adjustments) will still exist in many cases, for example:

- a subsidiary may have hedged an exposure by entering into a transaction with a fellow subsidiary. Such transaction could qualify for hedge accounting in the subsidiary's own financial statements but not in the parent's consolidated financial statements; or

- a pension plan may have to be classified as a defined contribution plan from the subsidiary's point of view, but is accounted for as a defined benefit plan in the parent's consolidated financial statements.

The transition exemption will rarely succeed in achieving more than a moderate reduction of the number of reconciling differences between a subsidiary's own reporting and the numbers used by its parent.

Most importantly, the choice of option (i) prevents the subsidiary from electing to apply all the other voluntary exemptions offered by Section 35, since the parent had already made the choices for the group at its date of adoption. Therefore, option (i) may not be appropriate for a subsidiary that prefers to use a different exemption. Application of option (i) would be difficult if a parent and its subsidiary had different financial years. In that case, Section 35 would seem to require the FRS 102 information for the subsidiary to be based on the parent's date of transition, which may not even coincide with an interim reporting date of the subsidiary.

A subsidiary may become a first-time adopter later than its parent, because it previously prepared a reporting package under FRS 102 for consolidation purposes, but did not present a full set of financial statements under FRS 102. Adjustments made centrally to an unpublished reporting package are not considered to be corrections of errors for the purposes of the disclosure requirements in FRS 102. However, a subsidiary is not permitted to ignore misstatements that are immaterial to the consolidated financial statements of its parent but material to its own financial statements.

If a subsidiary was acquired after the parent's date of transition to FRS 102, then it cannot apply option (i) because there are no carrying amounts included in the parent's consolidated financial statements, based on the parent's date of transition. Therefore, the subsidiary is unable to use the carrying amounts recognised in the group accounts when it was acquired, since push-down of the group's purchase accounting values are not allowed in the subsidiary's financial statements.

The exemption is also available to associates and joint ventures and the same considerations as above apply. This means that in many cases an associate or joint venture that wants to apply option (i) will need to choose which shareholder it considers its investor or venturer for FRS 102 purposes and determine the FRS 102 carrying amount of its assets and liabilities by reference to that investor's or venturer's date of transition to FRS 102.

Chapter 30

5.15.2   Parent becomes a first-time adopter later than its subsidiary

If an entity becomes a first-time adopter later than its subsidiary, associate or joint venture the entity shall in its consolidated financial statements, measure the assets and liabilities of the subsidiary (or associate or joint venture) at the same carrying amounts as in the financial statements of the subsidiary (or associate or joint venture), after adjusting for consolidation and equity accounting adjustments and for the effects of the business combination in which the entity acquired the subsidiary (or transaction in which it acquired the associate or joint venture. *[FRS 102.35.10(r)].*

While located within the transition exemptions, paragraph 35.10(r) does not offer a choice between different accounting alternatives. In fact, while a subsidiary that adopts FRS 102 later than its parent can choose to prepare its first FRS 102 financial statements by reference to its own date of transition to FRS 102 or that of its parent, the parent itself *must* use the FRS 102 measurements already used in the subsidiary's financial statements, adjusted as appropriate for consolidation procedures and the effects of the business combination in which the parent acquired the subsidiary.

This requirement does not preclude the parent from adjusting the subsidiary's assets and liabilities for a different accounting policy (e.g. cost or revaluation for accounting for property, plant and equipment). It, however, limits the choice of exemptions (e.g. the deemed cost exemption) available to a first-time adopter with respect to the financial statements of the subsidiary in the transition date consolidated financial statements.

The following example, which is based on IFRS 1, illustrates how an entity should apply these requirements. *[IFRS 1, IG Example 9].*

Example 30.7:   Subsidiary adopts FRS 102 before parent

Entity C presents its first consolidated FRS 102 financial statements in 2015. Its subsidiary D, wholly owned by Entity C since formation, presented its first FRS 102 financial statements in 2013 (as it had been incorporated that year and chose to adopt FRS 102 early). Until 2015, Subsidiary D prepared information for internal consolidation purposes under Entity C's previous GAAP.

The carrying amounts of Subsidiary D's assets and liabilities at 1 January 2014 are the same in both Entity C's opening FRS 102 consolidated statement of financial position and Subsidiary D's own financial statements (except for adjustments for consolidation procedures) and are based on Subsidiary D's date of transition to FRS 102.

When a subsidiary adopts FRS 102 before its parent, this will limit the parent's ability to choose first-time adoption exemptions in Section 35 freely as related to that subsidiary, as illustrated in the example below.

Example 30.8:   Limited ability to choose first-time adoption exemptions

Entity E will adopt FRS 102 for the first time in 2015 and its date of transition is 1 January 2014. Subsidiary F adopted FRS 102 in 2013 and its date of transition was 1 January 2011:

(a)   *Subsidiary F and Entity E both account for their property, plant and equipment at historical cost under Section 17.*

Upon first-time adoption, Entity E may only adjust the carrying amounts of Subsidiary F's assets and liabilities for the effects of consolidation, equity accounting and business combinations. Entity E can therefore not apply the exemption to use fair value as deemed cost of Subsidiary F's property, plant and equipment as at its own date of transition (1 January 2014).

(b) *Subsidiary F accounts for its property, plant and equipment at revalued amounts under Section 17, while Entity E accounts for its property, plant and equipment at historical cost under Section 17.*

In this case, Entity E would not be allowed to apply the exemption to use fair value as deemed cost of Subsidiary F's property, plant and equipment at its own date of transition because paragraph 35.10(r) would only permit adjustments for the effects of consolidation, equity accounting and business combinations. Although a consolidation adjustment would be necessary, this would only be to adjust Subsidiary F's revalued amounts to figures based on historical cost.

5.15.3 Implementation guidance

The Implementation Guidance in IFRS 1 notes the following issues that are also relevant to FRS 102 reporters that apply the requirements discussed at 5.15.1 and 5.15.2 above, as these do not override the following requirements of Section 35:

- the parent's election to use the business combinations exemption in paragraph 35.10(a) (see 5.2 above) which applies to assets and liabilities of a subsidiary acquired in a business combination that occurred *before* the parent's date of transition to FRS 102. The rules summarised at 5.15.2 above (parent adopting FRS 102 after subsidiary) apply only to assets and liabilities acquired and assumed by the subsidiary after the business combination and still held and owned by it at the parent's date of transition to FRS 102;

- to apply the requirements in Section 35 in measuring assets and liabilities for which the provisions summarised in paragraph 35.10(r) regarding different parent and subsidiary adoption dates are not relevant (e.g. use of the exemption to measure assets and liabilities at the carrying amounts in the parent's consolidated financial statements does not affect the restrictions in paragraph 35.9(c) (see 4.2 above) concerning changing valuation assumptions or estimates made at the same dates under previous GAAP); and

- a first-time adopter must give all the disclosures required by Section 35 as of its own date of transition. See 6 below. *[IFRS 1.IG30].*

5.15.4 Adoption of IFRSs on different dates in separate and consolidated financial statements

If a parent becomes a first-time adopter for its separate financial statements earlier or later than for its consolidated financial statements, it must measure its assets and liabilities at the same amounts in both financial statements, except for consolidation adjustments. *[FRS 102.35.10(r)].*

An entity may sometimes become an FRS 102 first-time adopter for its separate financial statements earlier or later than for its consolidated financial statements. Such a situation may arise for example where the parent takes advantage of an exemption from preparing consolidated financial statements. Subsequently, the parent may cease to be entitled to the exemption or may choose not to use it and, may therefore choose to apply FRS 102 in its consolidated financial statements.

As drafted, the requirement is merely that the 'same amounts', except for consolidation adjustments, be used for the measurement of the assets and liabilities in both sets of financial statements, without being explicit as to which set of financial statements should be used as the benchmark. However, it seems clear from the context that the intention is that the measurement basis used in whichever set of financial statements first comply with FRS 102 must also be used when FRS 102 is subsequently adopted in the other set.

For a UK company preparing statutory accounts, the Regulations require that any differences in accounting rules between the parent company's individual accounts and its group accounts for the financial year be disclosed in a note, with reasons for the difference given. *[6 Sch 5].* However, application of paragraph 35.10(r) should mean that, in most cases, no differences should arise.

5.16   Hedge accounting

Following the July 2014 amendments to FRS 102 (which have the same effective date as the original standard), the transition requirements regarding hedge accounting were moved from the exceptions to paragraph 35.10(t) of the exemptions, although some aspects are mandatory.

An FRS 102 reporter is permitted to apply Sections 11 and 12, IFRS 9 (and/or IAS 39) or IAS 39 (as adopted by the EU) to the recognition and measurement of financial instruments as an accounting policy choice. Section 12, IAS 39 and IFRS 9 require derivatives to be recognised at fair value and all distinguish three types of hedging relationship between a hedging instrument and hedged item – cash flow hedges, fair value hedges, and hedges of a net investment in a foreign operation. The hedge accounting requirements of Section 12 are discussed in Chapter 8 at 7 while IAS 39 and IFRS 9 are discussed in EY International GAAP 2015 in Chapters 50 and 51, respectively.

Each of these standards has requirements for designation and documentation of hedging relationships. However, the detailed requirements for hedge accounting differ. For example, the ongoing eligibility criteria for hedge accounting in Section 12 are more relaxed compared to both IAS 39 and IFRS 9. However, under each standard ineffectiveness must still be measured and recognised in profit and loss where appropriate, and the basic criteria for hedge accounting need to be assessed and continue to be met.

Given its simpler accounting than IFRSs, it may be easier to apply hedge accounting under Section 12. Where Section 12 is applied, the transition requirements set out in paragraph 35.10(t) can mean that even where a hedging relationship between a hedging instrument and hedged item was not hedge accounted under previous GAAP or fails the detailed conditions in FRS 26 for hedge accounting, a first-time adopter may be able to reflect hedge accounting in the opening statement of financial position on transition to FRS 102. The number of adjustments required on transition will vary depending on the UK GAAP currently applied.

5.16.1   *Reporter previously applied UK GAAP including FRS 26*

The hedge accounting requirements of FRS 26 are the same as those in IAS 39 and it is not expected that transition adjustments will arise, where an accounting policy choice is taken to apply IAS 39 for the recognition and measurement of financial instruments. However, it is possible that transition adjustments may arise where Section 12 or IFRS 9 is applied. In particular, more hedge relationships may be eligible under Section 12 and IFRS 9. Also, IFRS 9 may require an entity to rebalance the hedge ratio on transition.

5.16.2   *Reporter previously applied UK GAAP not including FRS 26*

Previous UK GAAP (not applying FRS 26) did not address hedge accounting and therefore a variety of approaches may have been adopted to account for hedging relationships. For example, accounting policies might have included those where the derivative was:

- not explicitly recognised as an asset or liability (e.g. in the case of a forward contract used to hedge an expected but uncontracted future transaction);

- recognised as an asset or liability but at an amount different from its fair value (e.g. a purchased option recognised at its original cost less amortisation; or an interest rate swap accounted for by accruing the periodic interest payments and receipts); or

- subsumed within the accounting for another asset or liability (e.g. a foreign currency denominated monetary item and a matching forward contract or swap accounted for as a 'synthetic' functional currency denominated monetary item).

Hedge accounting policies under previous UK GAAP (not applying FRS 26) might also have included one or all of the following accounting treatments:

- derivatives were measured at fair value but, to the extent they were regarded as hedging future transactions, the gain (or loss) arising was reported as a liability (or asset) such as deferred (or accrued) income;

- realised gains or losses arising on the termination of a previously unrecognised derivative used in a hedging relationship (such as an interest rate swap hedging a borrowing) were included in the balance sheet as deferred or accrued income and amortised over the remaining term of the hedged exposure; or

- on the application of SSAP 20, hedge accounting for a net investment in a foreign operation may be included in the individual accounts.

Accordingly, a previous UK GAAP reporter (not applying FRS 26) may hold derivatives and other financial instruments that were regarded as hedging items off balance sheet, recognise deferred gains and losses that do not meet the definition of an asset or liability, or apply synthetic accounting for hedged exposures. None of the above approaches are permitted under FRS 102, regardless which standard is applied to the recognition and measurement of financial instruments. The only exception is net investment hedge accounting in individual accounts for a foreign operation that is a branch with a different functional currency. See 5.16.5 below.

It was uncommon for previous UK GAAP reporters (not applying FRS 26) to formally document and designate a hedging relationship or to assess, test and measure effectiveness of the hedge. Therefore, the hedging relationships that were hedge accounted under previous UK GAAP (not applying FRS 26) often would not meet the detailed conditions in order to apply hedge accounting under FRS 102.

Paragraph 35.10(t) sets out different transitional provisions regarding hedge accounting depending on whether the FRS 102 reporter applies Section 12 (see 5.16.3 below) or IFRSs (see 5.16.4 below). Section 35 has the same transitional provisions for all first-time adopters (even if an entity previously applied FRS 26).

Chapter 30

Section 35 sets out various hedge accounting exemptions for entities applying Section 12, but its requirements for entities applying IAS 39 or IFRS 9 are mandatory. There is a relief available in respect of the timing of documentation and designation of a hedging relationship available for the first FRS 102 financial statements where Section 12, IFRS 9 or IAS 39 are followed. Once an entity ceases to be a first-time adopter (i.e. in its next financial statements under FRS 102), the usual requirements on designation and documentation of the hedging relationship at the inception of hedges apply, regardless what standard is followed for the recognition and measurement of financial instruments.

An FRS 102 first time adopter will need to:

- recognise derivatives at fair value and eliminate any deferred gains and losses arising or synthetic accounting from previous GAAP hedge accounting (except where permitted by the transitional provisions);

- reflect hedging relationships in the opening statement of financial position (where required or permitted by the transitional provisions);

- designate and document hedging relationships (required where hedge accounting is to be applied under all the standards). Paragraph 35.10(t) however, includes a concession on the timing of when such designation and documentation is completed; and

- consider the subsequent accounting for hedging relationships reflected in the opening statement of financial position.

5.16.3   Transition exemptions – FRS 102 reporter applying Section 12

5.16.3.A   Optional exemption – hedge accounting

An entity may use one or more of the following exemptions in preparing its first financial statements that conform to FRS 102: *[FRS 102.35.10(t)(i)-(iii)].*

(i)   *A hedging relationship existing on the date of transition*

A first-time adopter may choose to apply hedge accounting to a hedging relationship of a type described in paragraph 12.19 which exists on the date of transition between a hedging instrument and a hedged item, provided the conditions of paragraphs 12.18(a) to (c) are met on the date of transition to FRS 102 and the conditions of paragraphs 12.18(d) and (e) are met no later than the date the first financial statements that comply with FRS 102 are authorised for issue. This choice applies to each hedging relationship existing on the date of transition.

Hedge accounting as set out in Section 12 of FRS 102 may commence from a date no earlier than the conditions of paragraphs 12.18(a) to (c) are met:

- In a fair value hedge the cumulative hedging gain or loss on the hedged item from the date hedge accounting commenced to the date of transition, shall be recorded in retained earnings (or if appropriate, another category of equity).

- In a cash flow hedge and net investment hedge, the lower of the following (in absolute amounts) shall be recorded in equity (in respect of cash flow hedges in the cash flow hedge reserve):

  (a) the cumulative gain or loss on the hedging instrument from the date hedge accounting commenced to the date of transition; and

  (b) the cumulative change in fair value (i.e. the present value of the cumulative change of expected future cash flows) on the hedged item from the date hedge accounting commenced to the date of transition.

(ii) *A hedging relationship that ceased to exist before the date of transition because the hedging instrument has expired, was sold, terminated or exercised prior to the date of transition*

A first-time adopter may elect not to adjust the carrying amount of an asset or liability for previous GAAP accounting effects of a hedging relationship that has ceased to exist.

A first-time adopter may elect to account for amounts deferred in equity in a cash flow hedge under a previous GAAP, as described in paragraph 12.23(d) from the date of transition. Any amounts deferred in equity in relation to a hedge of a net investment in a foreign operation under a previous GAAP shall not be reclassified to profit or loss on disposal or partial disposal of the foreign operation.

(iii) *A hedging relationship that commenced after the date of transition*

A first-time adopter may elect to apply hedge accounting to a hedging relationship of a type described in paragraph 12.19 that commenced after the date of transition between a hedging instrument and a hedged item, starting from the date the conditions of paragraphs 12.18(a) to (c) are met, provided that the documentation conditions in paragraphs 12.18(d) and (e) are met no later than the date the first financial statements that comply with FRS 102 are authorised for issue. The choice applies to each hedging relationship that commenced after the date of transition.

5.16.3.B   General comments

The elections available in paragraphs 35.10(t)(i)-(ii) provide considerable flexibility for an entity applying Section 12 to begin, cease or continue hedge accounting on transition. These allow entities to apply a degree of hindsight in deciding whether or not to apply hedge accounting, since they provide a concession on the timing of completing hedge documentation for both hedging relationships at the date of transition (see 5.16.3.D below) and those entered into after the date of transition (see 5.16.3.E below). The Accounting Council is mindful of this but, on balance, considered that flexibility should take precedence over restrictions aimed at preventing abuse. However, it is worth noting that without this relaxation, for December year ends, no hedge accounting could be applied in the opening FRS 102 balance sheet unless all the documentation requirements were met by 1 January 2014, which would not be feasible given the hedge accounting amendments were only issued in July 2014.

Paragraph 35.10(t) distinguishes between the situation where a hedging relationship *exists* or *does not exist* on the date of transition. The hedging relationship exists where there is a cash flow hedge, fair value hedge or hedge of a net investment of a foreign operation, and the hedging instrument and hedged item both exist at the date of transition. A hedging relationship therefore does not exist where the hedging instrument is terminated (even if there is still a hedged item).

Paragraph 35.10(t)(i) permits a hedge accounting relationship meeting its specified conditions to be reflected for an existing hedging relationship between a hedging instrument and hedged item (see 5.16.3.D below). An entity can choose whether to reflect existing hedge relationships in the opening balance sheet on a hedge-by-hedge basis.

Paragraph 35.10(t)(ii) sets out optional exemptions that apply to a hedging relationship that ceased to exist before the date of transition because the hedging instrument was sold, terminated or exercised prior to the date of transition (see 5.16.3.C below). We consider that an entity can choose whether or not to apply the exemptions for each past hedging relationship.

Where the elections are not taken, FRS 102's requirements are retrospectively applied and the hedge accounting adjustments made under previous UK GAAP would therefore need to be eliminated to retained earnings (or other component of equity) on transition.

5.16.3.C   Reporting derivatives and eliminating deferred adjustments

All derivatives need to be recorded at fair value, as required by FRS 102. *[FRS 102.12.3, 7-8]*. In addition, the general requirements on transition set out in paragraph 35.8 would require elimination of deferred gains and losses since these do not meet the definition of an asset and liability under FRS 102. *[FRS 102.35.8]*.

Paragraph 35.10(t)(ii) clarifies that amounts deferred in equity in relation to a hedge of a net investment in a foreign operation under previous GAAP are not reclassified to profit or loss on disposal or partial disposal of the foreign operation (consistent with the requirements of paragraph 12.24 of FRS 102). *[FRS 102.12.24]*. It also sets out optional exemptions that apply to a hedging relationship that ceased to exist before the date of transition because the hedging instrument was sold, terminated or exercised prior to the date of transition:

(a)   A first-time adopter may elect not to adjust the carrying amount of an asset or liability for previous GAAP accounting effects of a hedging instrument that has ceased to exist. So where hedging gains (losses) from a hedge of a forecast purchase or committed purchase of inventory or property, plant and equipment have been included in the carrying amount of the asset before the date of transition, there is no requirement to adjust the carrying amount of the asset to eliminate the effects of hedging gains (losses) as at the date of transition.

Also, if a previous FRS 26 reporter had applied fair value hedge accounting for a fixed to floating interest rate swap (now terminated) hedging a fixed rate loan (that still exists), no change is needed to the hedge accounting adjustments made to the loan, as at the date of transition.

So if the first time adopter chose not to apply these exemptions, the old hedge accounting would be reversed and the previously hedged items would need to be held in the opening balance sheet at the appropriate carrying amount on application of FRS 102 without regard for any previous hedge accounting.

(b) A first-time adopter may elect to account for amounts deferred in equity in a cash flow hedge under previous GAAP, as described in paragraph 12.23(d) from the date of transition (see Chapter 8 at 7.8). This situation is only likely to arise where the first-time adopter previously applied FRS 26, for example:

- Where a floating to fixed interest rate swap (now terminated) hedged a floating rate loan (that still exists), the amounts deferred in equity in the cash flow hedge would not change as at the date of transition, but are subsequently reclassified to profit or loss as required by paragraph 12.23(d). This in effect allows the existing treatment on discontinuation previously followed under FRS 26 to endure.

- In addition, FRS 26 permits the deferral of gains and losses in equity in relation to a cash flow hedge of a forecast transaction that subsequently resulted in the recognition of a non-financial asset or a non-financial liability (e.g. a purchase of a non-financial asset such as property, plant and equipment or inventory).

  The guidance in paragraph 35.10(t)(iii) refers to paragraph 12.23(d)(i), which requires inclusion of the associated gains and losses previously recognised through other comprehensive income in the initial cost or other carrying amount of the asset or liability (this treatment is also available by choice in FRS 26). Therefore, it appears that first-time adopters would need to retrospectively adjust the carrying amount of non-financial assets (or liabilities) on transition to reflect the equivalent of a basis adjustment in order to comply with paragraph 12.23(d).

Paragraph 35.10(t)(ii) does not spell out the accounting treatment where an entity does not take up the elections to reverse the previous accounting treatment for now ceased hedging relationships. However, the FRC allows a choice to continue to apply hedge accounting for hedging relationships between a hedged item and hedging instrument existing at the date of transition. In our view, the FRC intended that entities would have a choice to post adjustments to eliminate deferred gains and losses (including amounts included in the carrying amount of an asset or liability) to retained earnings or another component of equity. Therefore, a previous UK GAAP reporter not taking the election would restate the carrying amount of the asset or liability to eliminate the effects of previous hedge accounting, with an adjustment to retained earnings (or other component of equity). Similarly, where the election is not taken, amounts relating to a cash flow hedge that were previously deferred in a cash flow hedge reserve can be reclassified to retained earnings.

Paragraph 35.10(t)(ii) focuses on the hedging relationships that have now ceased, and gives an option to keep (or reverse) the previous GAAP accounting effect of that hedging relationship. The guidance does not address situations where the hedging relationship still existed on transition, but for which hedge accounting had ceased prior to transition (e.g. the designation of the hedge was revoked, the hedge ceased to be effective, or the forecasted transaction in a cash flow hedge ceased to be highly probable but was still expected to occur). Paragraph 35.10(t)(i) applies where there remains an existing hedging relationship at the date of transition (even if not hedge accounted) (see 5.16.3.D below). Therefore, a first-time adopter could choose to apply hedge accounting provided the eligibility and documentation conditions in paragraph 35.10(t)(i) are met. For example, if hedge accounting under FRS 26 ceased because the hedge relationship failed the effectiveness test (but the entity continued with the hedge economically), if the hedge meets the criteria in paragraph 12.18(a)-(c) of FRS 102, then arguably hedge accounting could be reinstated in the opening balance sheet. However, if hedge accounting ceased because a forecasted transaction in a cash flow hedge was no longer highly probable, the hedging relationship would not meet the criteria in paragraph 12.18(a) and hedge accounting could not be reinstated.

Where the entity does not re-establish hedge accounting in accordance with paragraph 35.10(t)(i), or the conditions to apply hedge accounting on transition are not met, the question arises as to whether the entity can continue to reflect the previous GAAP hedge accounting for the discontinued hedge in the statement of financial position and apply Section 12's requirements for discontinuance of hedge accounting prospectively from the date of transition (which would generally result in similar accounting to that already applied under FRS 26). However, as the elections in paragraph 35.10(t)(i) and (ii) do not apply, the FRC presumably intended that such hedge accounting adjustments be eliminated to retained earnings.

Under previous UK GAAP (not applying FRS 26), it was common to defer the gain or loss arising on the termination of a hedging instrument in the statement of financial position, to be recognised as the hedged item affected profit or loss. Application of the general requirements of Section 35 would lead to elimination of such deferred gains or losses (to retained earnings) since these do not represent an asset or liability (and consequently paragraph 35.10(t)(ii) does not provide transitional relief).

5.16.3.D   *Hedging relationships existing at the date of transition*

Paragraph 35.10(t)(i) addresses the situation where, at the date of transition, a hedging relationship exists. It is clear from the context that a hedging relationship can only exist at the date of transition if there is both a hedged item and hedging instrument at that date. If the hedging instrument has ceased to exist before the date of transition, the hedging relationship does not exist on the date of transition, although paragraph 35.10(t)(ii) may apply (see 5.16.3.C above).

Not all hedging relationships established under previous UK GAAP are of a type covered in Section 12 (e.g. a hedge of the net investment in a foreign operation other than a branch, effected in the individual financial statements under SSAP 20 is not a permitted hedging relationship under any of these standards) (see 5.16.5 below for discussion of the treatment on transition). In addition, not all hedging relationships established under previous UK GAAP will meet the conditions for hedge accounting (e.g. restrictions over eligible hedging instruments) in Section 12.

The exemption in paragraph 35.10(t)(i) is only relevant for those hedging relationships of a type described in paragraph 12.19 existing at the date of transition, meeting the eligibility and documentation conditions for hedge accounting required by the transitional provisions. A first-time adopter has two choices for relevant hedging relationships:

(a) *choose not to hedge account*, in which case, FRS 102 is applied retrospectively to the measurement of the hedged item and hedging instrument; or

(b) *choose to apply hedge accounting* – Where a hedging relationship of a type described in paragraph 12.19 exists on the date of transition between a hedging instrument and a hedged item, the first-time adopter may choose to apply hedge accounting provided:

- the conditions in paragraphs 12.18(a) to (c) are met on the date of transition (see Chapter 8 at 7.4); and

- the conditions of paragraphs 12.18(d) and (e) (i.e. documentation of the hedging relationship and determining and documenting causes of ineffectiveness, see Chapter 8 at 67.4.4) are met not later than the date the first FRS 102 financial statements are authorised for issue.

This choice applies to each hedging relationship existing on the date of transition. *[FRS 102.35.10(t)(i)].*

Hedge accounting as set out in Section 12 may commence from a date no earlier than the conditions of paragraphs 12.18(a) to (c) are met. *[FRS 102.35.10(t)(i)].* These requirements would appear to allow first-time adopters some flexibility over when hedge accounting commences from. If hedge accounting commences at the date of transition, there will be no amounts deferred in equity for a cash flow hedge or hedge of net investment in a foreign operation, and no adjustments made to the carrying amount of the hedged item for a fair value hedge. If hedge accounting commences from the date of inception of the hedging relationship, this is likely to avoid the ineffectiveness that might result where the hedging instrument has a non-zero fair value at the commencement of hedge accounting.

The ability to hedge account for existing hedging relationships meeting the above conditions is available regardless of the standard followed under previous GAAP and also whether or not the entity previously applied hedge accounting to that existing relationship. The nature of the adjustments required, however, may well depend on what previous accounting was followed – for example, where a previous FRS 26 reporter chooses to continue to hedge account for a hedging relationship under Section 12, there may often be no adjustment required on transition.

Where an entity chooses to apply hedge accounting to a hedging relationship existing at the date of transition, paragraph 35.10(t)(i) (see 5.16.3.A above) describes how a fair value hedge, cash flow hedge or net investment hedge should be reflected at the date of transition.

For a UK company preparing statutory accounts in accordance with FRS 102, the Regulations require that the cash flow hedge reserve is included in the statutory fair value reserve, as the fair value accounting rules are used. *[1 Sch 40-41].* For a UK company preparing statutory accounts, the Regulations require that exchange differences on monetary items that form part of the net investment in a foreign operation (and the effective portion of the gain or loss on the hedging instrument) are included in the statutory fair value reserve, as the fair value accounting rules are used. *[1 Sch 40-41].*

Chapter 30

5.16.3.E   *Hedging relationship starting after the date of transition*

A first-time adopter may elect to apply hedge accounting to a hedging relationship of a type described in paragraph 12.19 (i.e. a cash flow hedge, fair value hedge, hedge of a net investment in a foreign operation) that commenced after the date of transition between a hedging instrument and a hedged item, starting no earlier than the date the conditions of paragraphs 12.18(a) to (c) are met, provided that the conditions of paragraphs 12.18(d) and (e) are met no later than the date the first financial statements that comply with FRS 102 are authorised for issue. The choice applies to each hedging relationship that commenced after the date of transition. *[FRS 102.35.10(t)(i)-(iii)].*

This relief allows a degree of hindsight to be applied by entities in documenting a hedging relationship (and for entities to cherry pick which hedging relationships to hedge account). However, once a hedge accounting relationship has been documented in line with paragraph 12.18(d) and (e), any election to discontinue the hedge accounting must be documented and takes effect prospectively.

Once an entity ceases to be a first-time adopter (i.e. in subsequent financial statements prepared under FRS 102) the usual requirements on designation and documentation of the hedging relationship at the inception of the hedge will apply.

5.16.3.F   *Subsequent accounting for hedging relationships*

Where an existing hedging relationship is reflected in the opening FRS 102 statement of financial position, as permitted by paragraph 35.10(t)(i), an entity may:

- *Continue hedge accounting* – where the hedging relationship continues to comply with the conditions for hedge accounting in the applicable standard (and meets the documentation requirements set out in the transitional provisions); or

- *Discontinue hedge accounting* (see Chapter 8 at 6.10) – This would be required if an entity chooses to discontinue hedge accounting for a relationship or the conditions cease to be met. Discontinuance is applied prospectively from the date an entity documents its election to discontinue hedge accounting (under Section 12) or from the date that the conditions for hedge accounting cease to be met. *[FRS 102.12.25-25A].*

The entity accounts for the continuance or discontinuance of hedge accounting in accordance with the Section 12 (see Chapter 8 at 6.7 to 6.10).

Where Section 12 is applied, and the hedging relationship ceased to exist at the date of transition because the hedging instrument has expired, was sold, terminated or exercised prior to the date of transition, an entity may elect to account for amounts deferred in equity in a cash flow hedge under previous UK GAAP as described in paragraph 12.23(d) (i.e. as a discontinuance) (see Chapter 8 at 6.10).

The guidance in paragraph 35.10(t)(ii) permits an entity to elect not to adjust the previous GAAP carrying amount of an asset or liability that reflected hedging accounting adjustments for hedging relationships that had ceased to exist by the date of transition because the hedging instrument has expired, was sold, terminated or exercised, However, section 35 does not spell out the subsequent accounting. In our view, this establishes a deemed carrying amount for the item and no further adjustments to the carrying amount for ongoing hedging gains and losses are made from the date of transition. Still, as for a discontinuance, we consider that any adjustment to the carrying amount (arising from fair value hedge accounting) of a hedged financial instrument carried at amortised cost using the effective interest method shall be amortised to profit and loss. *[FRS 102.12.22]*. This requirement is similar to the corresponding requirements in IAS 39 *[IAS 39.91-92]*.

5.16.3.G   Examples of hedge accounting

The following examples illustrate the guidance considered above. For simplicity, the tax implications of the situations considered are not addressed.

Example 30.9:   *Pre-transition cash flow hedges*

Case 1: All hedge accounting conditions met from date of transition and thereafter (and hedge accounting applied)

In 2005 Entity A borrowed £10m from a bank. The terms of the loan provide that a coupon of 3-month LIBOR plus 2% is payable quarterly in arrears and the principal is repayable in 2020. In 2008, Entity A decided to 'fix' its coupon payments for the remainder of the term of the loan by entering into a twelve-year pay-fixed, receive-floating interest rate swap. The swap has a notional amount of £10m and the floating leg resets quarterly based on 3-month LIBOR.

In Entity A's final financial statements prepared under previous UK GAAP (not applying FRS 26), the swap was clearly identified as a hedging instrument in a hedge of the loan and was accounted for as such. The fair value of the swap was not recognised in Entity A's statement of financial position and the periodic interest settlements were accrued and recognised as an adjustment to the loan interest expense. On 1 January 2014, Entity A's date of transition to FRS 102, the loan and the swap were still in place and the swap had a positive fair value of £1m and a £nil carrying amount. Entity A met all the conditions in Section 12 to permit the use of hedge accounting for this arrangement throughout 2014 and 2015 (in accordance with the transition provisions in Section 35).

If Entity A elected to apply hedge accounting in its opening FRS 102 statement of financial position, it should:

- recognise the interest rate swap as an asset at its fair value of £1m; and
- credit the lower of the cumulative gain or loss on the swap (£1m) and the cumulative change in the fair value (present value) of the expected future cash flows on the hedged item from the date hedge accounting commences

The hedge accounting could commence at inception (e.g. 2008, if the specified conditions were met at the time). If Entity A chose to commence hedge accounting from the date of transition, there would be no cash flow hedge reserve reflected at the date of transition. However, there will likely be ineffectiveness arising in the future as a result of the non-zero starting value of the swap. Hedge accounting would be applied throughout 2014 and 2015.

Case 2: Hedge terminated prior to date of transition

The facts are as in Case 1, except that in April 2013 Entity A decided to terminate the hedge and the interest rate swap was settled for its then fair value of £1.5m. Under previous UK GAAP (not applying FRS 26), Entity A's stated accounting policy in respect of terminated hedges was to defer any realised gain or loss on terminated hedging instruments where the hedged exposure remained. These gains or losses would be recognised in profit or loss at the same time as gains or losses on the hedged exposure. At the end of December 2013, Entity A's statement of financial position included a liability (unamortised gain) of £1.4m.

Where Section 12 is applied, in our view, Entity A must derecognise the deferred gain of £1.4m with an adjustment to retained earnings. Paragraph 35.10(t)(ii) sets out transitional provisions where there is no existing hedging relationship at the date of transition because the hedging instrument has expired, was sold, terminated or exercised prior to the date of transition that allow an entity not to adjust the previous GAAP carrying amount where this reflects hedging accounting adjustments under previous GAAP. This does not apply in this case, as the deferred gain is not a liability.

Example 30.10:   Pre-transition fair value hedges

Case 1: All hedge accounting conditions met from date of transition and thereafter (and hedge accounting applied) (1)

On 15 November 2013, Entity B entered into a one-year forward contract to sell 50,000 barrels of crude oil to hedge all changes in the fair value of certain inventory. The historical cost of the forward contract is £nil and at the date of transition the forward had a negative fair value of £50.

In Entity B's final financial statements prepared under previous UK GAAP (not applying FRS 26), the forward was clearly identified as a hedging instrument in a hedge of the inventory and was accounted for as such. The contract was recognised as a liability at its fair value and the resulting loss was deferred in the statement of financial position as an asset. In the period between 15 November 2013 and 1 January 2014 the fair value of the inventory increased by £47. In addition, Entity B met all the conditions in Section 12 to permit the use of hedge accounting for this arrangement (in accordance with the transition provisions in Section 35) until the forward expired.

If Entity B elected to apply hedge accounting in its opening FRS 102 statement of financial position it should:

- continue to recognise the forward contract as a liability at its fair value of £50;
- derecognise the £50 deferred loss on the forward contract;
- recognise the crude oil inventory at its carrying value adjusted by the cumulative hedging gain from the date hedge accounting commences; and
- record the net adjustment in retained earnings.

The hedge accounting could commence at inception (i.e. 15 November 2013 if the specified conditions were met at that time). If so, the carrying amount of the crude oil inventory is adjusted by £47, being the change in fair value of the hedged item attributable to the hedged risk, whereas the deferred loss of £50 on the forward is eliminated, with a net adjustment of £3 in retained earnings. If Entity B chose to commence hedge accounting from the date of transition, there would be no adjustments to the crude oil inventory carrying value at the date of transition. However, there would likely be ineffectiveness arising in the future as a result of the non-zero starting value of the swap on designation as at the date of transition. Hedge accounting would be applied throughout 2014 until the forward expired.

Case 2: All hedge accounting conditions met from date of transition and thereafter (and hedge accounting applied) (2)

In 2005, Entity C borrowed £10m from a bank. The terms of the loan provide that a coupon of 8% is payable quarterly in arrears and the principal is repayable in 2020. In 2008, Entity C decided to alter its coupon payments for the remainder of the term of the loan by entering into a twelve-year pay-floating, receive-fixed interest rate swap. The swap has a notional amount of £10m and the floating leg resets quarterly based on 3-month LIBOR.

In Entity C's final financial statements prepared under previous UK GAAP (not applying FRS 26), the swap was clearly identified as a hedging the loan and accounted for as such. The fair value of the swap was not recognised in Entity C's statement of financial position and the periodic interest settlements on the swap were accrued and recognised as an adjustment to the loan interest expense.

On 1 January 2014, Entity C's date of transition to FRS 102, the loan and the swap were still in place and the swap had a negative fair value of £1m and a £nil carrying amount. The cumulative change in the fair value of the loan attributable to changes in 3-month LIBOR was £1.1m, although this change was not recognised in Entity C's statement of financial position because the loan was accounted for at cost. Entity C met all the conditions in Section 12 to permit the use of hedge accounting for this arrangement throughout 2014 and 2015 (in accordance with the Section 35).

If Entity C elected to apply hedge accounting in its opening FRS 102 statement of financial position, it should:

- recognise the interest rate swap as a liability at its fair value of £1m; and
- adjust the carrying amount of the loan by the cumulative hedging gain from the date hedge accounting commences.

The hedge accounting could commence at inception (if the specified conditions are met). Where hedge accounting commences at inception of the hedge the carrying amount of the interest rate swap would be recognised as a liability of £1m and there would be a £1.1m adjustment to the carrying amount of the loan, with a net adjustment of £0.1m to retained earnings. If Entity C chose to commence hedge accounting from the date of transition, there would be no adjustments to the loan carrying value at the date of transition. However, there would likely be ineffectiveness arising in the future as a result of the non-zero starting value of the swap. Hedge accounting would be applied throughout 2014 and 2015.

Case 3: Hedge terminated prior to date of transition

The facts are as in Case 2 above, except that in April 2013 Entity C decided to terminate the fair value hedge and the interest rate swap was settled for its then negative fair value of £1.5m. Under previous UK GAAP (not FRS 26), Entity C's stated accounting policy in respect of terminated hedges was to defer any gain or loss on the hedging instrument as a liability or an asset where the hedged exposure remained and this gain or loss was recognised in profit or loss at the same time as the hedged exposure. At 31 December 2013, the unamortised loss recognised as an asset by Entity C's was £1.4m. The cumulative change through April 2013 in the fair value of the loan attributable to changes in 3-month LIBOR that had not been recognised was £1.6m.

Where Section 12 is applied, in our view, in the opening FRS 102 statement of financial position, Entity C must derecognise the deferred loss of £1.4m with an adjustment to retained earnings. Paragraph 35.10(t)(ii) sets out transitional provisions where there is no existing hedging relationship at the date of transition because the hedging instrument has expired, was sold, terminated or exercised prior to the date of transition that allow an entity not to adjust the previous GAAP carrying amount where this reflects hedging accounting adjustments under previous GAAP. This does not apply in this situation as the deferred loss does not qualify as an asset.

5.16.4   Transition requirements – FRS 102 reporter applying IAS 39 or IFRS 9

5.16.4.A   Mandatory requirement – hedge accounting

Paragraph 35.10(t)(iv), which applies to entities taking the accounting policy choice under paragraphs 11.2(b) or (c) or paragraphs 12.2(b) or (c) to apply IAS 39 or IFRS 9, requires the following: *[FRS 102.35.10(t)(iv)]*

- A first-time adopter adopting an accounting policy set out in paragraphs 11.2(b) or (c) or paragraphs 12.2(b) or (c) shall not apply the transitional provisions of paragraphs 35(t)(i) to (iii). Such a first-time adopter shall apply the transitional requirements applicable to hedge accounting in IFRS 1, paragraphs B4 to B6, except that the designation and documentation of a hedging relationship may be completed after the date of transition, and no later than the date the first financial statements that comply with FRS 102 are authorised for issue, if the hedging relationship is to qualify for hedge accounting from the date of transition.

- A first-time adopter adopting an accounting policy set out in paragraphs 11.2(b) or (c) or paragraphs 12.2(b) or (c) that has entered into a hedging relationship as described in IAS 39 or IFRS 9 in the period between the date of transition and the reporting date for the first financial statements that comply with FRS 102 may elect to apply hedge accounting prospectively from the date all qualifying conditions for hedge accounting in IAS 39 or IFRS 9 are met, except that an entity shall complete the formal designation and documentation of a hedging relationship no later than the date the first financial statements that comply with FRS 102 are authorised for issue.

As required by IAS 39 or IFRS 9, at the date of transition, an entity shall: *[IFRS 1.B4]*

- measure all derivatives at fair value;

- eliminate all deferred losses and gains arising on derivatives that were reported in accordance with previous GAAP as if they were assets and liabilities.

An entity shall not reflect in its opening statement of financial position a hedging relationship of a type that does not qualify for hedge accounting (under the relevant IFRS that is followed). Not all economic hedge relationships will meet this requirement. Some examples of ineligible types of hedge relationships are provided below: *[IFRS 1.B5]*

- if applying IAS 39, hedging relationships where the hedging instrument is a cash instrument or written option; where the hedged item is a net position; or where the hedge covers interest risk in a held-to-maturity investment; or

- if applying IFRS 9, hedging relationships where the hedging instrument is a stand-alone written option or a net written option; or where the hedged item is a net position in a cash flow hedge for another risk than foreign currency risk.

    However, if an entity designated a net position as a hedged item in accordance with previous GAAP, it may designate an individual item within that net position as a hedged item in accordance with IFRSs (or where IFRS 9 is applied, a net position if that meets the requirements in paragraph 6.6.1 of IFRS 9), provided that it does so no later than the date of transition to FRS 102.

If before the date of transition to FRS 102, an entity had designated a hedging relationship that was of an eligible type for hedge accounting, but the hedging relationship does not meet all the conditions for hedge accounting in paragraph 88 of IAS 39 (or paragraph 6.4.1 of IFRS 9), the entity shall apply paragraphs 91 and 101 of IAS 39 (or paragraphs 6.5.6 and 6.5.7 of IFRS 9) to discontinue hedge accounting prospectively immediately after transition. Transactions entered into before the date of transition to IFRSs shall not be retrospectively designated as hedges. *[IFRS 1.B6]*.

5.16.4.B   General comments

An FRS 102 reporter applying IAS 39 or IFRS 9 to the recognition and measurement of financial instruments must apply paragraphs B4 to B6 of IFRS 1 on transition (see EY International GAAP 2015 Chapter 5 at 4.5). However, there is a concession over the timing of completing hedge documentation for both hedging relationships at the date of transition and those entered into after the date of transition (see 5.16.4.C below).

The implementation guidance in IFRS 1 on accounting for cash flow hedges, fair value hedges and net investment hedges is not referred to by paragraph 35.10(t)(iv). However, we consider that an FRS 102 reporter applying IAS 39 or IFRS 9 may follow IG60A and IG60B (although we note that IG60 is not relevant due to the different documentation requirements in paragraph 35.10(t)(iv) compared to IFRS 1) under the hierarchy set out in Section 10 of the standard. *[FRS 102.10.3-6]*. Note that application of IFRS 1.IG60A and IFRS 1.IG60B will mean that the transitional adjustments for a fair value and cash flow hedge differ to the transitional adjustments specified by paragraph 35.10(t) where Sections 11 and 12 are applied.

While IFRS 1 is not explicit on this point, in our view a first time adopter must reflect in the opening statement of financial position hedging relationships of a type that qualifies for hedge accounting under IFRS 9 or IAS 39 (as applicable) that were hedge accounted under previous GAAP (even if hedge accounting must be discontinued prospectively if all the hedging conditions are not met at the date of transition). This also applies where the hedging instrument had terminated prior to the date of transition but the hedged item remains in existence at that date or where a cash flow hedge of a forecast purchase of non-financial asset or non-financial liability, is still expected to occur, or a firm commitment in a fair value hedge is still expected to occur. Hedge accounting adjustments made at the date of transition impact the results in later periods even if the hedge is immediately discontinued (e.g. a cash flow hedge reserve established at transition date is reclassified to profit or loss as the hedged item affects profit or loss).

This is a key difference to the transition provisions for an FRS 102 first-time adopter applying Section 12, which allows considerable flexibility as to whether or not to establish hedging relationships in the opening statement of financial position.

Unlike IFRS 1, Section 35 is not explicit that transitional requirements in accounting standards do not apply on first-time adoption. However, our view is that this is the case (see 3.5.1 above). Therefore, an FRS 102 first-time adopter previously applying FRS 26 should be aware that the transitional provisions in IFRS 9 (for ongoing IFRS reporters) do not apply.

5.16.4.C   Relief on documentation

An IFRS 1 first-time adopter is unable to hedge account for eligible types of hedge relationships from the date of transition unless it has documented and designated the hedge prior to that date, in accordance with the requirements of IAS 39 or IFRS 9 (as applicable). The relevant IFRS requirements under IAS 39 and IFRS 9 are discussed in EY International GAAP 2015, Chapter 50 at 5.1 and Chapter 51 at 5.1, respectively.

In their first FRS 102 financial statements, entities applying either IFRS 9 or IAS 39 for the recognition and measurement of financial instruments are permitted to complete the documentation and designation for: *[FRS 102.35.10(t)(iv)]*

- hedging relationships existing at the date of transition; and/or
- hedging relationships which commenced after the date of transition but prior to the reporting date for the first FRS 102 financial statements,

at the latest, by the date of authorisation of the first FRS 102 financial statements.

This relief would not appear to allow transactions entered into before the date of transition to be retrospectively designated as hedges where IAS 39 or IFRS 9 (and/or IAS 39) are applied, as this is explicitly prohibited by paragraph B6 of IFRS 1.

Once an entity ceases to be a first-time adopter (i.e. in its next financial statements under FRS 102), the usual requirements on designation and documentation of the hedging relationship at the inception of the hedge will apply.

Chapter 30

5.16.5   Hedges of net investment in a foreign operation in individual accounts under SSAP 20 – treatment on transition.

Under SSAP 20, an entity may have accounted for investments in foreign enterprises in its individual accounts in ways that are not permitted under FRS 102:

- an entity may have regarded an investment made by means of long-term loans or intercompany deferred trading balances that are intended to be, for all practical purposes, as permanent as equity, as part of the net investment in the foreign enterprise. In such circumstances, the entity may have recognised exchange differences arising on such loans and intercompany balances as adjustments to reserves; *[SSAP 20.20]* or, more commonly, regarded the monetary item as in substance a 'non-monetary item' and not retranslated the item.

- where a company has used foreign currency borrowings to finance or provide a hedge against its foreign equity investments (and specified conditions were met), an entity may have denominated its equity investments in the appropriate foreign currencies and retranslated the carrying amounts at closing rates at the end of each accounting period. Any exchange differences arising on the equity investments were taken to reserves and the exchange differences arising on the foreign currency borrowings were then offset (to the extent of exchange differences arising on the equity investments), as a reserve movement, against these exchange differences. *[SSAP 20.51]*.

Under FRS 102, exchange differences arising on a monetary item that forms part of the net investment in a foreign operation shall be recognised in profit or loss in the separate financial statements of the reporting entity or the individual financial statements of the foreign operation, as appropriate. *[FRS 102.30.13]*. Accordingly, where a monetary item was viewed 'as permanent as equity' and had not been retranslated under SSAP 20, the item will need to be retranslated on the date of transition, with adjustments to equity.

Where a previous UK GAAP reporter has taken exchange differences on foreign currency borrowings hedging an investment in a foreign enterprise (other than a branch) to reserves under SSAP 20 in the separate or individual financial statements of the reporting entity, this is a hedging relationship of a type not permitted in the separate or individual financial statements by Section 12, IAS 39 or IFRS 9. Example 30.11 sets out relevant considerations on transition.

Example 30.11:   Exchange risk of a net investment of a foreign operation in individual financial statements under SSAP 20

A hedge of exchange risk in a foreign operation (other than a branch) in individual financial statements in accordance with SSAP 20 is not a type of hedging relationship permitted by IAS 39 or IFRS 9 or Section 12. Consequently, paragraph 35.10(t)(i) does not apply to this hedging relationship.

The hedging instrument, if still in existence at the date of transition, would be measured under IAS 39 or IFRS 9 or Sections 11 and 12, as applicable (which for a loan, may be the same as the previous GAAP carrying amount, but for a derivative, would require measurement at fair value).

The investment should be restated to cost, or fair value (depending on the policy followed for carrying investments in subsidiaries under FRS 102). However, where the cost model is used, an entity may take advantage of the transition exemption to retain the previous GAAP carrying amount for an investment in a subsidiary, associate or jointly controlled entity as a deemed cost at the date of transition. *[FRS 102.35.10(f)]*. See 5.5 above.

In addition, where Section 12 is applied to the recognition and measurement of financial instruments and the hedging instrument is no longer in existence at the date of transition, paragraph 35.10(t)(ii) would also allow an entity to elect not to adjust the previous GAAP carrying amount for the effects of hedge accounting under previous GAAP. It expressly states that amounts deferred in equity under a previous GAAP in relation to a hedge of a net investment in a foreign operation are not reclassified on disposal or partial disposal of the foreign operation.

Entities that wish to obtain the effects of hedge accounting in individual financial statements might wish to use the deemed cost exemption as at the date of transition. The investment in the foreign operation would reflect exchange retranslations made under SSAP 20 prior to the date of transition. Thereafter, under the transitional provisions in paragraph 35.10(t), an entity could document a fair value hedge of the exchange risk in the investment as at the date of transition (provided the conditions for hedge accounting under the transitional provisions are met from that date, and documentation and designation of the hedging relationship is completed at the latest by the date of approval of the first FRS 102 financial statements). *[FRS 102.35.10(t)(i)].*

5.17   Designation of previously recognised financial instruments

FRS 102 permits a financial instrument (provided it meets certain criteria) to be designated on initial recognition as a financial asset or financial liability at fair value through profit or loss. In addition, an entity is permitted to designate, as at the date of transition to FRS 102, any financial asset or financial liability at fair value through profit or loss provided the asset or liability meets the criteria in paragraph 11.14(b) at that date. *[FRS 102.35.10(s)].*

Debt instruments that meet the conditions in paragraph 11.8(b) and commitments to receive a loan and to make a loan to another entity that meet the conditions in paragraph 11.8(c) may upon their initial recognition be designated by the entity as at fair value through profit and loss if the conditions in paragraph 14(b) of FRS 102 are met (see Chapter 8 at 9.7.2). The exemption allows a first-time adopter to make this election as of its date of transition to FRS 102.

It should be noted, though, that Section 12 requires most financial instruments that do not qualify as basic financial instruments to be carried at fair value through profit and loss in any case. *[FRS 102.12.8].*

5.18   Compound financial instruments

Paragraph 22.13 requires an entity to split a compound financial instrument into its liability and equity components at the date of issue (see Chapter 8 at 4). If the liability component of a compound financial instrument is no longer outstanding, a full retrospective application of Section 22 – *Liabilities and Equity* – would involve identifying the original equity component and another component representing the cumulative interest on the liability component, both of which are accounted for in equity.

A first-time adopter need not separate those two components if the liability component is not outstanding at the date of transition to FRS 102. *[FRS 102.35.10(g)].* This transition exemption is of limited practical effect as Section 22 merely requires that the proceeds be allocated between the liability and equity component, and that the allocation between the liability and equity component must not be revised in later periods *[FRS 102.22.13-14].* In addition, Section 22 does not prohibit a subsequent transfer within equity.

The increase in equity arising on an issue of shares is presented in the statement of financial position as determined by relevant law. *[FRS 102.22.10].* Indeed, by final conversion or settlement, the entity would generally have transferred any separately recognised component of equity to another component of equity, so that no further adjustment would be required on transition to FRS 102.

Finally, given that Section 22 includes similar requirements for split accounting of convertible debt and similar compound instruments to previous UK GAAP, it is unlikely that adjustments will be required as at the date of transition in respect of convertible bonds.

6   PRESENTATION AND DISCLOSURE

Section 35 does not exempt a first-time adopter from any of the presentation and disclosure requirements in other standards.

6.1   Comparative information

The entity's first FRS 102 financial statements are required to be a complete set of financial statements and therefore must include at least two statements of financial position, two statements of comprehensive income, two separate income statements (if presented), two statements of cash flows and two statements of changes in equity and related notes, including comparative information. *[FRS 102.35.5, 3.17]*. Where permitted by the standard, two statements of income and retained earnings may be included in place of the statements of comprehensive income and statements of changes in equity. *[FRS 102.3.18, 6.4]*. An opening statement of financial position at the date of transition is not required. *[FRS 102.35.7]*.

Except where FRS 102 permits or requires otherwise, comparative information in respect of the preceding period is required for all amounts presented in the financial statements, as well as narrative and descriptive information when it is relevant to an understanding of the current period's financial statements. *[FRS 102.35.6, 3.14]*. An entity may present comparative information for more than one preceding period.

6.2   Explanation of transition to FRS 102

A first-time adopter is required to explain how the transition from its previous financial reporting framework to FRS 102 affected its reported financial position, and financial performance. *[FRS 102.35.12]*. FRS 102 does not require an explanation of how the transition affected cash flows.

FRS 102 offers a wide range of transition exemptions that a first-time adopter may elect to apply. However, the standard does not explicitly require an entity to disclose which exemptions it has applied and how it applied them, although it does require a description of the nature of each change in accounting policy. *[FRS 102.35.13]*.

For some exemptions, it will be obvious from the reconciliations whether or not an entity has chosen to apply the exemption. For others, users will have to rely on a first-time adopter disclosing in its summary of significant policies, those transitional accounting policies that are 'relevant to an understanding of the financial statements.' *[FRS 102.8.5]*. However, first-time adopters are expected to disclose voluntarily which transition exemptions they applied and which exceptions applied to them, as was the case for first-time adopters transitioning to IFRSs.

If a first-time adopter did not present financial statements for previous periods this fact should be disclosed in its first financial statements that conform to FRS 102. *[FRS 102.35.15]*. For example, entities may not have prepared consolidated financial statements under their previous financial reporting framework and newly incorporated entities may never have prepared financial statements at all.

If it is impracticable to restate the opening statement of financial position at the date of transition for one or more of the adjustments required (see 3.5.4 above), the entity must identify the data presented for prior periods that are not comparable with data for the period in which it prepares its first FRS 102 financial statements. If it is impracticable for an entity to provide any disclosures required by FRS 102 for any period before the period in which it prepares its first FRS 102 financial statements, it must disclose the omission. *[FRS 102.35.11]*.

If it is not practical on first-time adoption to apply a particular requirement of paragraph 18 of IFRS 6 (impairment of exploration and evaluation assets) to previous comparative amounts an entity shall disclose that fact. *[FRS 102.34.11C]*.

6.3 Disclosure of reconciliations

A first-time adopter is required to present in its first financial statements prepared using FRS 102:

- reconciliations of its equity determined in accordance with its previous financial reporting framework to its equity determined in accordance with FRS 102 at:
  - the date of transition to FRS 102; and
  - the end of the latest period presented in the entity's most recent annual financial statements determined in accordance with its previous financial reporting framework *[FRS 102.35.13(b)]*; and
- a reconciliation of the profit or loss determined in accordance with its previous financial reporting framework for the latest period in the entity's most recent annual financial statements to its profit or loss determined in accordance with FRS 102 for the same period. *[FRS 102.35.13(c)]*.

First-time adopters must also describe the nature of each change in accounting policy. *[FRS 102.35.13(a)]*.

If the entity becomes aware of errors made under its previous financial reporting framework, the reconciliations must, to the extent practicable, distinguish the correction of errors from changes in accounting policies. *[FRS 102.35.14]*.

FRS 102 does not specify the format of the reconciliations of equity or profit or loss. In *Staff Education Note 13: Transition to FRS 102*, the FRC staff give two example layouts (in both cases, with supporting notes explaining the adjustments):

- a line-by-line reconciliation of the statement of financial position at the date of transition and at the end of the comparative period, and profit or loss account for the comparative period; and
- a reconciliation of total equity at the date of transition and at the end of the comparative period, and of the total profit or loss for the comparative period.

Chapter 30

A line-by-line reconciliation may be particularly appropriate when a first-time adopter needs to make transitional adjustments that affect a significant number of line items in the primary financial statements. If the adjustments are less pervasive a straightforward reconciliation of equity and profit or loss may be able to provide an equally effective explanation.

In our view, a first-time adopter should include all disclosures required by Section 35 within its first FRS 102 financial statements and not cross-refer to any previously reported information. Any additional voluntary information regarding the conversion to FRS 102 that was previously published but that is not specifically required by Section 35 (or under the general disclosure requirements of Section 8 – *Notes to the Financial Statements*) is not part of the first FRS 102 financial statements.

6.4   Voluntary disclosure of FRS 102 information before adoption

There is no requirement in FRS 102 (or indeed in previous UK GAAP or IFRSs) for an entity to disclose the effects of transition to FRS 102 (i.e. a different financial reporting framework) in its final set of financial statements prepared under previous GAAP; however, an entity may present such information voluntarily.

If an entity wants to quantify the impact of the adoption of FRS 102 before its date of transition in its last financial statements under previous UK GAAP, it would not be able to do this in accordance with Section 35 as it is not a first-time adopter in those financial statements. While an entity would be able to select a date and apply by analogy the requirements of Section 35 to its previous GAAP financial information as of that date, it would not be able to claim that such additional information complied with FRS 102.

6.5   Interim financial statements

FRS 102 does not address the presentation of interim financial reports, it merely requires that an entity that prepares such reports shall describe the basis for preparing and presenting the information. *[FRS 102.3.25]*.

In November 2014, the FRC published FRED 56 – Draft FRS 104 – *Interim Financial Reporting* – which may be applied to interim financial reports prepared by an FRS 102 reporter. Draft FRS 104 sets out disclosures concerning transition to be included in interim financial reports that cover part of the first financial reporting period applying FRS 102.

Draft FRS 104, if finalised, would require an interim financial report that covers part of an annual financial reporting period during which an entity transitions to FRS 102 to disclose the following:

- a description of the nature of each change in accounting policy;
- a reconciliation of its equity determined in accordance with its previous financial reporting framework to its equity determined in accordance with FRS 102 at the date of transition and at the end of the comparable year-to-date period of the immediately preceding financial year; and
- a reconciliation of profit or loss determined in accordance with its previous financial reporting framework for the comparable interim period (current and, if different, year-to-date) of the immediately preceding financial year.

The requirements of paragraph 35.14, i.e. to distinguish the correction of errors from changes in accounting policies, apply to the above reconciliations (see 6.3 above).

6.6   Non-FRS 102 comparative information and historical summaries

FRS 102 requires comparative information that is prepared on the same basis as information relating to the current reporting period. However, it does not address the presentation of historical summaries of selected data for periods before the first period for which an entity presents full comparative information under FRS 102.

Although IFRS 1 is not directly applicable, it provides guidance that could be helpful when an entity needs to present such summaries but cannot comply with the recognition and measurement requirements of IFRSs. In those cases, IFRS 1 requires an entity to:

'(a)   label the previous GAAP information prominently as not being prepared in accordance with IFRSs; and

(b)   disclose the nature of the main adjustments that would make it comply with IFRSs. An entity need not quantify those adjustments.' *[IFRS 1.22].*

Such an approach may also be appropriate for first-time adopters of FRS 102.

Chapter 30

Chapter 31   FRS 101 – Reduced Disclosure Framework

Chapter 31   FRS 101 – Reduced Disclosure Framework

1   INTRODUCTION

In 2012, 2013 and 2014 the Financial Reporting Council (FRC) changed financial reporting standards in the United Kingdom and the Republic of Ireland. These changes replace almost all extant UK GAAP with the following Financial Reporting Standards:

- FRS 100 – *Application of Financial Reporting Requirements* ;
- FRS 101 – *Reduced Disclosure Framework: Disclosure exemptions from EU-adopted IFRS for qualifying entities*;
- FRS 102 – *The Financial Reporting Standard Applicable in the UK and Republic of Ireland*; and
- FRS 103 – *Insurance Contracts.*

This chapter deals only with the application of FRS 101. This is a voluntary framework which can be applied by 'qualifying' entities that previously used either EU-adopted IFRS or UK GAAP (including the FRSSE and FRS 102). FRS 101 may also be adopted by non-UK entities currently applying IFRS as issued by the IASB or another GAAP although application would depend on local legislation. However, this chapter discusses FRS 101 only as it applies to UK companies, LLPs and other entities preparing financial statements under Part 15 of the Companies Act 2006 (the Companies Act).

FRS 101 sets out a framework which addresses the financial reporting requirements and disclosure exemptions for the financial statements of subsidiaries and parents that otherwise apply the recognition, measurement and disclosure requirements of standards and interpretations issued (or adopted) by the International Accounting Standards Board (IASB) that have been adopted in the European Union (EU-adopted IFRS). To use the framework, an entity needs to be a 'qualifying entity' (see section 2.1 below) which is included in publicly available consolidated financial statements of its parent which are intended to give a true and fair view. The shareholders of the qualifying entity must be notified and not object.

An entity reporting under FRS 101 complies with EU-adopted IFRS except as modified in accordance with this FRS. This chapter does not discuss EU-adopted IFRS, which is covered in the EY International GAAP 2015. The FRC's overriding objective is to enable users of accounts to receive high-quality understandable financial reporting proportionate to the size and complexity of the entity and the users' information needs. In other words, the objective of FRS 101 is to enable subsidiary and parent company financial statements to be prepared under the recognition and measurement rules of IFRS without the need for some of the copious disclosures which are perceived to act as a barrier to those entities preparing those financial statements under IFRS.

An entity using the reduced disclosure framework of FRS 101 is unable to make the explicit and unreserved statement that its financial statements comply with EU-adopted IFRS. This is because an accounting framework that allows such reduced disclosures cannot be described as EU-adopted IFRS. Therefore, entities that prepare financial statements under FRS 101 prepare Companies Act individual accounts as defined in s395(1)(a) of the Companies Act. This means that financial statements prepared under FRS 101 are subject to different Companies Act requirements than financial statements prepared under EU-adopted IFRS which are IAS accounts prepared under s395(1)(b) of the Companies Act. These differences are discussed at sections 4, 5 and 7 below.

1.1   Summary of FRS 101

- Adoption of FRS 101 is voluntary;

- FRS 101 can only be applied in individual financial statements (see section 2 below);

- FRS 101 can only be applied by a 'qualifying entity' (see section 2.1 below);

- Approval of shareholders must be obtained to use FRS 101 (see section 2.2 below);

- Entities can transition to FRS 101 from either UK GAAP or IFRS (see section 3 below);

- Entities using FRS 101 apply the recognition and measurement principles of EU-adopted IFRS except as amended by this standard (see section 4 below);

- Entities using FRS 101 must prepare a balance sheet and profit and loss account section of the statement of comprehensive income in accordance with *The Large and Medium-sized Companies and Groups (Accounts and Reports) Regulations 2008* (the Regulations) (see section 5 below);

- Entities using FRS 101 can take advantage of various disclosure exemptions from EU-adopted IFRS. Entities defined as 'financial institutions' have fewer exemptions than entities that are not financial institutions. Some of these disclosure exemptions are conditional on equivalent disclosures being included in the publicly available consolidated financial statements of a parent of the entity which are intended to give a true and fair view and in which the entity is consolidated (see section 6 below); and

- In addition to IFRS disclosures, entities using FRS 101 must comply with disclosures required by Company law and the Regulations (see section 7 below).

1.2   Effective date of FRS 101

FRS 101 was issued on 22 November 2012. A qualifying entity (see section 2.1 below) may apply FRS 101 for accounting periods beginning on or after 1 January 2015. FRS 101 can also be applied early. If an entity applies FRS 101 before 1 January 2015 it shall disclose that fact. *[FRS 101.11]*.

UK entities that wish to transition to FRS 101 from IFRS can only do so for accounting periods ending on or after 1 October 2012 unless there is a relevant change in circumstance (see section 3.1 below). Entities that wish to transition to FRS 101 from UK GAAP or any other GAAP can do so in respect of any financial statements not issued as at 22 November 2012.

Transitional rules and eligibility to adopt FRS 101 are discussed at section 3 below.

1.3   Amendments to FRS 101

The FRC intends to review FRS 101 annually to ensure that the reduced disclosure framework remains effective as EU-adopted IFRS develops. The first such amendments to FRS 101 were issued in July 2014. *Amendments to FRS 101 Reduced Disclosure Framework (2013/14 Cycle)* sets out changes to FRS 101 and its appendices for amendments made to:

- IFRS 10 – *Consolidated Financial Statements* – and IAS 27 – *Separate Financial Statements* – as a result of the IASB's project *Investment Entities (Amendments to IFRS 10 IFRS 12 and IAS 27)*; and

- IAS 36 – *Impairment of Assets* – as a result of the IASB's project *Recoverable Amount Disclosures for Non-Financial Assets (Amendment to IAS 36)*.

In addition, the amendments include a number of editorial changes to clarify the legal requirements applicable to Companies applying FRS 101 that hold financial instruments at fair value subject to paragraph 36(4) of Schedule 1 to the Regulations.

The amendments have the same effective date as FRS 101 (i.e. accounting periods beginning on or after 1 January 2015) and early adoption is permitted to the extent that a qualifying entity can apply the underlying IFRSs (i.e. IFRS 10 and IAS 36). If a qualifying entity has adopted FRS 101 early, then the amendments in respect of IFRS 10 and IAS 36 must be applied for accounting periods beginning on or after 1 January 2014.

1.4   Statement of compliance with FRS 101

A set of financial statements prepared in accordance with FRS 101 must contain a statement in the notes to the financial statements that '*These financial statements were prepared in accordance with Financial Reporting Standard 101 "Reduced Disclosure Framework"*'. FRS 101 also clarifies that because FRS 101 does not comply with all of the requirements of IFRS it should not contain the unreserved statement of compliance with IFRS set out in paragraph 3 of IFRS 1 – *First-time*

Adoption of International Financial Reporting Standards – and paragraph 16 of IAS 1 – *Presentation of Financial Statements.* *[FRS 101.10].*

2   SCOPE OF FRS 101

FRS 101 may be applied to the individual financial statements of a 'qualifying entity' (see section 2.1 below), that are intended to give a true and fair view of the assets, liabilities, financial position and profit or loss for a period. *[FRS 101.2].* FRS 101 cannot be applied to consolidated financial statements.

Individual financial statements to which FRS 101 applies are individual accounts as set out in s394 of the Companies Act or as set out in s72A of the Building Societies Act 1986. Separate financial statements, as defined by IAS 27 or IAS 27 (2012) are included in the meaning of the term individual financial statements. *[FRS 101 Appendix I].*

This means that FRS 101 can be used in:

- individual financial statements of subsidiaries;

- separate financial statements of an intermediate parent which does not prepare consolidated financial statements; and

- separate financial statements of a parent which does prepare consolidated financial statements.

However, the entity applying FRS 101 must be included in a set of consolidated financial statements intended to give a true and fair view (see section 2.1.6 below).

A parent that prepares consolidated financial statements but applies FRS 101 in its separate financial statements can also use the exemption in s408 of the Companies Act from presenting a profit and loss account and related notes in the individual financial statements as well as taking advantage of the reduced disclosures from IFRS.

FRS 101 cannot be applied in consolidated financial statements even if the entity preparing consolidated financial statements is a qualifying entity. *[FRS 101.3].*

Financial statements prepared by qualifying entities in accordance with FRS 101 are not accounts prepared in accordance with EU-adopted IFRS. A qualifying entity must ensure it complies with any relevant legal requirements applicable to it. Therefore, individual financial statements prepared by UK companies in accordance with FRS 101 are Companies Act accounts rather than IAS accounts as set out in section 395(1) of the Companies Act. Therefore, entities that apply FRS 101 must comply with *The Large and Medium-sized Companies and Groups (Accounts and Reports) Regulations 2008* ('the Regulations') including the rules on recognition and measurement, the Companies Act accounts formats and note disclosures. *[FRS 101.4A].*

In order to ensure that financial statements prepared in accordance with FRS 101 to comply with the Companies Act and the Regulations, some limited recognition, measurement and presentational changes have been made by FRS 101 to EU-adopted IFRS. FRS 101 iterates that, for the avoidance of doubt, the amendments necessary to remove conflicts between EU-adopted IFRS and the Companies Act and the Regulations is an integral part of the standard and are applicable to any qualifying entity applying FRS 101 including those that are not companies. *[FRS 101.5(b)]*. These differences are discussed at sections 4 and 5 below.

FRS 101 does not permit the company law formats included in Part 1 'General Rules and Formats' of the Regulations applicable to small companies to be applied. However, our view is that companies subject to the Small Companies Regime can still apply FRS 101, and, in doing so, are not prevented from taking advantage of other Companies Act exemptions applicable to companies subject to the Small Companies Regime. Likewise, medium-sized entities applying FRS 101 can still take advantage of applicable Companies Act disclosure exemptions for medium-sized entities.

A charity cannot be a qualifying entity and therefore cannot apply FRS 101. *[FRS 101 Appendix I]*.

2.1 Definition of a qualifying entity

FRS 101 defines a qualifying entity as 'A member of a group where the parent of that group prepares publicly available consolidated financial statements, which are intended to give a true and fair view (of the assets, liabilities, financial position and profit or loss) and that member is included in the consolidation'. *[FRS 101 Appendix I]*.

The phrase 'included in the consolidation' is referenced to s474(1) of the Companies Act which states that this means that 'the undertaking is included in the accounts by the method of full (and not proportional) consolidation and references to an undertaking excluded from consolidation shall be construed accordingly'. Therefore, entities that are not fully consolidated in the group financial statements, such as subsidiaries of investment entities, which are accounted for at fair value through profit and loss under IFRS 10, cannot use FRS 101. Associates and joint ventures are not qualifying entities.

2.1.1 Reporting date of the consolidated financial statements of the parent

The requirement for the qualifying entity to be included in the consolidation implies that the consolidated financial statements of the parent must be prepared before the FRS 101 individual financial statements of the qualifying entity. FRS 101 is silent on whether the reporting date and period of those consolidated financial statements has to be identical to that of the qualifying entity. In contrast, both s400 and s401 of the Companies Act require that the exemption from preparing group accounts for a parent that is a subsidiary is conditional on the inclusion of the subsidiary in the consolidated financial statements of the parent drawn up to the same date or an earlier date in the same financial year. It would seem logical that the reporting date criteria in s400 and s401 can also be used for FRS 101.

However, when the consolidated financial statements are prepared as at an earlier date than the date of the qualifying entity's financial statements, some of the disclosure exemptions may not be available to the qualifying entity because the consolidated financial statements may not contain the 'equivalent' disclosures (see section 6.2 below).

Chapter 31

2.1.2   *Definition of group and subsidiary*

The definition of a qualifying entity contains a footnote that refers to s474(1) of the Companies Act which defines a 'group' as a parent undertaking and its subsidiary undertakings. EU-adopted IFRS defines a group as 'a parent and its subsidiaries'. *[IFRS 10.A, s474(1)].*

IFRS defines a parent as 'an entity that controls one or more entities' and a subsidiary as 'an entity that is controlled by another entity'. *[IFRS 10.A].*

The Companies Act states that an undertaking is a parent undertaking in relation to another undertaking, a subsidiary undertaking, if:

(a)   it holds a majority of the voting rights in the undertaking; or

(b)   it is a member of the undertaking and has the right to appoint or remove a majority of its board of directors; or

(c)   it has the right to exercise a dominant influence over the undertaking by virtue of provisions in the undertaking's articles or by virtue of a control contract; or

(d)   it is a member of the undertaking and controls alone, pursuant to an agreement with other shareholders or members, a majority of the voting rights in the undertaking.

An undertaking is also a parent undertaking in relation to another undertaking if it has the power to exercise, or actually exercises, dominant control or influence over it, or it and the subsidiary undertaking are managed on a unified basis.

A parent undertaking shall be treated as the parent undertaking of undertakings in relation to which any of its subsidiary undertakings are, or are to be treated as, parent undertakings; and references to its subsidiary undertakings shall be construed accordingly. *[s1162].*

These differences in definition make it possible for an entity to be a subsidiary undertaking under the Companies Act but not under EU-adopted IFRS, for example an entity in which a parent owns a majority of the voting rights but does not control. However, the key issue for the application of FRS 101 is whether the subsidiary is included in the consolidation of the parent's consolidated financial statements. A company that meets the definition of a subsidiary undertaking under the Companies Act but is not included in the consolidation of the consolidated financial statements of its parent cannot apply FRS 101.

2.1.3   *Publicly available consolidated financial statements*

By 'publicly available', we believe that FRS 101 requires that the consolidated financial statements can be accessed by the public as the use of the EU-adopted IFRS disclosure exemptions is conditional on a disclosure by the qualifying entity indicating from where those consolidated financial statements can be obtained (see section 2.2 below). This does not mandate that the consolidated financial statements must be filed with a regulator. However, it does mean that UK consolidated financial statements not yet filed with the Registrar of Companies, at the date that the subsidiary's financial statements prepared in accordance with FRS 101 are approved, must be publicly available via some other medium.

2.1.4 Non UK qualifying entities

There is no requirement that a qualifying entity is a UK entity. Therefore, overseas entities can apply FRS 101 in their individual or separate financial statements subject to meeting the criteria and subject to FRS 101 being allowed in their own jurisdiction.

There is also no requirement that the parent that prepares publicly available consolidated financial statements, in which the qualifying entity is included, is a UK parent (see section 2.1.6 below).

2.1.5 Non-controlling interests

There is no ownership threshold for a subsidiary to apply FRS 101. Therefore, a qualifying entity can apply FRS 101 even if its parent holds less than a majority of the voting rights. However, other shareholders are permitted to object to the use of FRS 101 (see section 2.2 below).

2.1.6 Intended to give a true and fair view

The consolidated financial statements are not required to give an explicit true and fair view of the assets, liabilities, financial position and profit or loss. Rather, they are '*intended* to give a true and fair view' (our emphasis). This means that the consolidated financial statements in which the qualifying entity is consolidated need not contain an explicit opinion that they give a 'true and fair view' (for example, US GAAP financial statements do not have such an opinion) but, in substance, they should be intended to give such a view. The FRC obtained a QC's opinion in 2008 which stated that 'the requirement set out in international accounting standards to present fairly is not a different requirement to that of showing a true and fair view but is a different articulation of the same concept'[1].

In our view, a set of consolidated financial statements drawn up in a manner equivalent to consolidated financial statements that are in accordance with the EU Seventh Directive (i.e. a set of consolidated financial statements that meets the 'equivalence' test of s401 of the Companies Act) is intended to give a true and fair view. The Application Guidance to FRS 100 states that consolidated financial statements of a higher parent will meet the test of equivalence in the Seventh Directive if they:

- give a true and fair view and comply with FRS 102;
- are prepared in accordance with EU-adopted IFRS;
- are prepared in accordance with IFRS, subject to the consideration of the reasons for any failure by the European Commission to adopt a standard or interpretation; or
- are prepared using other GAAPs which are closely related to IFRS, subject to the consideration of the effect of any differences from EU-adopted IFRS. *[FRS 100.AG6].*

The IFRS for SMEs shall be assessed for equivalence with the Seventh Directive considering a number of factors including the disclosure requirements for extraordinary items, additional disclosures for financial liabilities held at fair value, shortening the presumed life of goodwill from 10 to not exceeding 5 years, recognising 'negative goodwill' in the income statement only when it meets the definition of a realised profit, replacing the prohibition on reversal of impairment losses with a requirement to reverse the loss if, and only if, the reasons for the impairment cease to apply and removing the requirement for unpaid called up share capital to be recognised as an offset to equity. *[FRS 100.AG6(f)].*

Other GAAPs should be assessed for equivalence with the Seventh Directive based on the particular facts, including the similarities to and differences from the Seventh Directive. *[FRS 100.AG6(e)].*

The EU has a mechanism to determine the equivalence to IFRS of GAAP from other countries. As of April 2012, via a Commission Implementing Decision amending Decision 2008/961/EC, the EU had determined that the following standards were considered as equivalent to EU-adopted IFRS (for the purposes of the Transparency and Prospectus Directive):

- US GAAP;
- Japanese GAAP;
- GAAP of the People's Republic of China;
- GAAP of Canada;
- GAAP of the Republic of Korea; and
- GAAP of the Republic of India (treated as equivalent for financial years starting before 1 January 2015). *[FRS 100.AG7].*

In theory, there is no reason why consolidated financial statements of a parent prepared under a GAAP that is not 'equivalent' to the Seventh Directive cannot be used provided those consolidated financial statements in which the entity is included are publicly available and are intended to give a true and fair view.

However, a parent company that wishes to claim an exemption from preparing consolidated accounts under either s400 or s401 of the Companies Act must be a subsidiary of a parent that prepares consolidated accounts in accordance with the provisions of the EU Seventh Directive or in a manner so equivalent *[s400(2)(b), s401(2)(b)].*

In addition, a number of the disclosure exemptions from EU-adopted IFRS in FRS 101 are conditional on 'equivalent' disclosures being made in those consolidated financial statements. Where the equivalent disclosure is not made, the relevant disclosure exemptions cannot be applied in the qualifying entity's financial statements prepared under FRS 101 (see section 6.2 below). A GAAP that is not 'equivalent' to the Seventh Directive is less likely to have those 'equivalent' disclosures.

One issue not addressed by FRS 101 is the impact of a qualified audit opinion on the consolidated financial statements. The QC's opinion obtained by the FRC in 2008 stated that 'the scope for arguing that financial statements which do not comply with relevant accounting standards nevertheless give a true and fair view is very limited'.[2]

2.2 Use of the disclosure exemptions

The use of the disclosure exemptions in FRS 101 (see section 6 below) is conditional on all of the following criteria being met:

- the shareholders have been notified in writing about the use of the disclosure exemptions;

- the shareholders have not objected to the disclosure exemptions;

- the reporting entity applies the recognition, measurement and disclosure requirements of EU-adopted IFRS but makes amendments to those requirements where necessary in order to comply with the Companies Act and the Regulations because the financial statements it prepares are Companies Act individual accounts as defined in s395(1) of the Companies Act (see section 4 below);

- the reporting entity provides in the notes to its financial statements;

  - a brief narrative summary of the disclosure exemptions adopted; and

  - the name of the parent of the group in whose consolidated financial statements its financial statements are consolidated and from where those financial statements may be obtained. *[FRS 101.5].*

FRS 101 does not state whether the requirement of the reporting entity to notify its shareholders about the use of the disclosure exemptions is an annual requirement or whether a more open-ended notification can be provided. In addition, no timescale is mentioned. Therefore, there is no requirement that notification occurs in the period covered by the financial statements; it could be earlier or later. In the absence of clear guidance, we would recommend that entities obtain legal advice as to the form in which they should notify shareholders of their intention to use FRS 101.

Objections to the use of FRS 101 may be served on the qualifying entity in accordance with reasonable timeframes and format requirements by a shareholder that is the immediate parent of the entity, or by a shareholder or shareholders holding in aggregate 5% or more of the allotted shares in the entity or more than half of the allotted shares in the entity that are not held by the immediate parent. *[FRS 101.5(a)].* FRS 101 does not explain what is meant by 'reasonable timeframes and format requirements' in respect of any shareholder objection. Entities may wish to obtain legal advice as to what 'reasonable timeframes and format requirements' should be specified in any notice provided to shareholders.

An objection by a shareholder or shareholders holding in aggregate 5% or more of the total allotted shares or more than half of the allotted shares that are not held by the immediate parent (which could be less than 5% of the total allotted shares) automatically means that FRS 101 cannot be applied by the entity. A shareholder is not required to supply a reason for any objection.

2.3 The impact of s400 and s401 of the Companies Act on FRS 101

FRS 101 does not override either s400 or s401 of the Companies Act. S400 exempts a UK parent company from preparing consolidated accounts if it is a subsidiary undertaking of an immediate parent undertaking established under the law of an EEA

State and is included in the consolidated accounts for a larger group drawn up to the same date, or to an earlier date in the same financial year, by a parent undertaking established under the law of an EEA State. S401 exempts a UK parent company from preparing consolidated accounts if it is a subsidiary undertaking of a parent undertaking *not* established under the law of an EEA State and is included in the consolidated accounts for a larger group drawn up to the same date, or to an earlier date in the same financial year, by a parent undertaking. The exemptions from preparing consolidated accounts in both s400 and s401 are subject to various conditions including 'equivalence' (in respect of s401) as discussed at section 2.1.6 above.

If a UK parent company does not meet all of the conditions set out in either s400 or s401 (and is not otherwise exempt under the Companies Act) then it must prepare consolidated financial statements. Such consolidated financial statements cannot be prepared under FRS 101. However, the parent entity could still prepare its individual financial statements under FRS 101.

3   TRANSITION TO FRS 101

An entity can transition to FRS 101 from either EU-adopted IFRS or another form of UK GAAP. In this context, another form of UK GAAP means either FRS 102, the FRSSE or previous UK GAAP.

FRS 101 is adopted in the first accounting period for which a reporting entity has notified its shareholders in writing about the use of the disclosure exemptions (see 2.2 above). When this occurs, the date of transition to FRS 101 is the beginning of the earliest period for which an entity presents full comparative information under a given standard in its first financial statements that comply with that standard, e.g. 1 January 2014 for an entity with a 31 December year-end adopting in its 2015 financial statements. *[FRS 100 Appendix I].*

3.1   Companies Act restrictions on changes to FRS 101

Under the Companies Act, a company which wishes to change from preparing IAS individual accounts to preparing individual accounts under FRS 101 may do so either:

- if there is a 'relevant change of circumstance' as defined in s395(4) of the Companies Act; or
- for financial years ending on or after 1 October 2012, for a reason other than a relevant change of circumstance, once in a five year period. *[FRS 100.A2.14].*

There is no restriction on the number of times an entity can move from Companies Act accounts to IAS accounts or *vice versa* so theoretically an entity could 'flip' from IAS accounts to FRS 101 and back again several times without a 'relevant change in circumstance' provided it reverted back to Companies Act accounts no more than once every five years.

There are no Companies Act restrictions on a change from previous UK GAAP, the FRSSE or FRS 102 to FRS 101 and back again since these are all Companies Act accounts.

3.2   Consistency of financial statements within the group

The Companies Act requires that the directors of a parent company secure that the individual accounts of a parent company and of each of its subsidiary undertakings are prepared under the same financial reporting framework, be it IAS accounts or Companies Act accounts, except to the extent that in the directors' opinion there are good reasons for not doing so. *[s407(1)]*. However, this rule does not apply:

- if the parent company does not prepare group accounts; *[s407(2)]*

- if the accounts of the subsidiary undertaking are not required to be prepared under Part 15 of the Companies Act (for example foreign subsidiary undertakings); *[s407(3)]* or

- to any subsidiary undertakings that are charities (so charities and non-charities within a group are not required to use the same accounting framework). *[s407(4)]*. This is because charities are not permitted to prepare either IAS group or individual accounts. *[s395(2), s403(3)]*.

Additionally, a parent company that prepares both consolidated and separate financial statements under EU-adopted IFRS (i.e. IAS group accounts and IAS individual accounts) is not required to ensure that its subsidiary undertakings all prepare IAS individual accounts. However, it must ensure that its subsidiary undertakings use the same accounting framework in their individual accounts unless there are good reasons for not doing so. *[s407(5)]*.

Therefore, a group that decides to use FRS 101 for any of its qualifying subsidiaries, must ensure, unless there are good reasons, that all UK subsidiaries prepare Companies Act individual accounts (i.e. the same financial reporting framework). Although not explicitly stated by FRS 100, there appears to be no requirement that all subsidiaries in a group must use FRS 101 for their Companies Act individual accounts; some could also use FRS 102, the FRSSE or previous UK GAAP (prior to 2015) since all are Companies Act individual accounts and therefore part of the same financial reporting framework.

Examples of 'good reasons' for not preparing all individual accounts within a group using the same reporting framework are contained in the June 2008 BERR document *Guidance for UK Companies On Accounting and Reporting: Requirements under the Companies Act 2006 and the application of the IAS regulation.*

3.3   Transition from EU-adopted IFRS to FRS 101

In substance, the transition requirements for entities that have been applying EU-adopted IFRS prior to conversion to FRS 101 treat the qualifying entity as not having changed its financial reporting framework. Disclosure is required only where changes are made on transition, because FRS 101 modifies EU-adopted IFRS in certain respects, in order to comply with the Companies Act and the Regulations.

A qualifying entity that is applying EU-adopted IFRS at the date of transition to FRS 101 must consider whether amendments are required to comply with paragraph 5(b) of FRS 101 – see sections 4 and 5 below – but it does not reapply the provisions of IFRS 1. Where amendments in accordance with paragraph 5(b) of FRS 101 are required, the entity shall determine whether the amendments have a

Chapter 31

material effect on the first FRS 101 financial statements presented. *[FRS 100.12]*. Details of measurement differences between EU-adopted IFRS and FRS 101 which might result in a material effect on the financial statements are discussed at section 4 below.

Where there is no material effect of such changes, the qualifying entity shall disclose that it has undergone transition to FRS 101 and give a brief narrative of the disclosure exemptions taken for all periods presented in the financial statements. *[FRS 100.12(a)]*.

Where there is a material effect caused by such changes, the qualifying entity's first FRS 101 financial statements shall include:

- a description of the nature of each material change in accounting policy;

- reconciliations of its equity determined in accordance with EU-adopted IFRS to its equity determined in accordance with FRS 101 for both the date of transition to FRS 101 and for the end of the latest period presented in the entity's most recent annual financial statements prepared in accordance with EU-adopted IFRS; and

- a reconciliation of the profit or loss determined in accordance with EU-adopted IFRS to the profit or loss determined in accordance with FRS 101 for the latest period presented in the entity's most recent annual financial statements prepared in accordance with EU-adopted IFRS. *[FRS 100.12(b)]*.

This means that, for an entity adopting FRS 101 for the first time in its annual financial statements ending on 31 December 2015 (and presenting one comparative period), reconciliations will be required of:

- equity as at 1 January 2014 and 31 December 2014; and

- profit or loss for the year ended 31 December 2014.

There is no requirement for a transition balance sheet to be prepared presumably on the grounds that IFRS 1 is not being reapplied.

Material amendments must be applied retrospectively on transition unless impracticable. Where a retrospective amendment is impracticable, the qualifying entity shall apply the amendment to the earliest period for which it is practicable to do so and shall identify the data presented for prior periods that are not comparable with the data for the period for which it prepares its first financial statements that conform with FRS 101. *[FRS 100.13]*. 'Impracticable' will be as defined in IAS 8 – *Accounting Policies, Changes in Accounting Estimates and Errors*.

Paragraph 5(b) of FRS 101 cross-refers to application guidance that includes presentational changes to the financial statements as well as recognition and measurement differences. The transitional rules contain no explicit requirement to disclose material presentational changes such as the use of balance sheet and profit and loss formats as per the Regulations. However, we recommend that entities explain any material presentational changes compared to EU-adopted IFRS arising from adoption of FRS 101 in order to assist readers of the financial statements.

3.4 Transition from another version of UK GAAP or another GAAP to FRS 101

In substance, the transition requirements treat conversion to FRS 101 from another version of UK GAAP (FRS 102, the FRSSE or previous UK GAAP) or another GAAP as a full first time conversion to EU-adopted IFRS (as modified by FRS 101).

A qualifying entity that transitions to FRS 101 shall, unless it is applying EU-adopted IFRS prior to the date of transition, apply the requirements of paragraphs 6 to 33 of IFRS 1 including the relevant appendices. *[FRS 100.11(b)]*. This means that all of the recognition, measurement and disclosure rules for an IFRS first-time adopter apply to the extent they do not conflict with IFRS as amended by paragraph 5(b) of FRS 101. First-time adoption of IFRS is discussed in Chapter 5 of EY International GAAP 2015.

IFRS 1 sets out requirements for where a subsidiary becomes a first time adopter later than its parent or where a parent becomes a first time adopter later than its subsidiary (or becomes a first-time adopter in its separate financial statements earlier or later than in its consolidated financial statements).

IFRS 1 permits a subsidiary that becomes a first-time adopter later than its parent to measure its assets and liabilities at either the carrying amounts required by IFRS 1, based on the subsidiary's date of transition, or the carrying amounts that would be included in the parent's consolidated financial statements, based on the parent's date of transition if no adjustments were to be made for the effects of consolidation procedures or the business combination in which the parent acquired the subsidiary (the D16 election). There is a similar election available for an associate or joint venture that becomes a first-time adopter later than an entity that has significant influence or joint control over it. *[IFRS 1.D16]*.

Where an entity becomes a first-time adopter later than its subsidiary it shall, in the consolidated financial statements, measure the assets and liabilities of the subsidiary after adjusting for consolidation and equity accounting adjustments and for the effects of the business combination in which the entity acquired the subsidiary. Similarly, if a parent becomes a first time adopter for its separate financial statements earlier or later than for its consolidated financial statements, it shall measure its assets and liabilities at the same amounts in both financial statements, except for consolidation adjustments. *[IFRS 1.D17]*.

Although FRS 101 retains the D16 election and the D17 requirements, the qualifying entity must ensure it measures its assets and liabilities in accordance with FRS 101 (where application of these paragraphs conflicts with EU-adopted IFRS). *[FRS 101.AG1(a)-(b)]*.

3.5 The impact of transition on realised profits

There may be circumstances where a conversion to FRS 101 eliminates a qualifying entity's realised profits or turns those realised profits into a realised loss. TECH 02/10 – *Guidance on the determination of realised profits and losses in the context of distributions under the Companies Act 2006 (TECH 02/10)*, issued by the ICAEW and ICAS, states that the change in the treatment of a retained profit or loss as a result of a change in the law or in accounting standards or interpretations would not render unlawful a distribution already made out of realised profits determined by reference to 'relevant accounts' which had been prepared in accordance with generally acceptable accounting principles applicable to those accounts. This is because the Companies Act defines realised profits or losses for determining the lawfulness of a distribution as 'such profits and loss of the company as fall to be treated as realised in accordance with principles generally accepted at the time when the accounts are prepared'.[3]

The effects of the introduction of a new accounting standard or on the adoption of IFRSs become relevant to the application of the common law capital maintenance rule only in relation to distributions accounted for in periods in which the change will first be recognised in the accounts. This means that a change in accounting policy known to be adopted in a financial year needs to be taken into account in determining the dividend to be approved by shareholders in that year. Therefore, for example, an entity converting to FRS 101 in 2015 must have regard to the effect of adoption of FRS 101 in respect of all dividends payable in 2015 (including any final dividends in respect of 2014) even though the 'relevant accounts' may still be those for 2014 prepared under another GAAP.[4]

4   MEASUREMENT DIFFERENCES BETWEEN FRS 101 AND IFRS

As noted at section 2 above, entities applying FRS 101 use EU-adopted IFRS as amended by the Standard in order to comply with the Regulations. This is because financial statements prepared under FRS 101 are Companies Act individual accounts and not IAS individual accounts. There are several conflicts between the recognition and measurement rules of EU-adopted IFRS and those required by the Regulations. Consequently, entities applying FRS 101 apply a modified version of EU-adopted IFRS designed to eliminate these differences.

FRS 101 changes EU-adopted IFRS in respect of the following matters:

- negative goodwill (see 4.1 below);
- contingent consideration payable by an acquirer in a business combination (see 4.2 below);
- reversal of goodwill impairments (see 4.3 below);
- government grants deducted from the cost of fixed assets (see 4.4 below);
- realised profits (see 4.5 below); and
- equalisation reserves (see 4.6 below)

No changes have been made to EU-adopted IFRS in respect of positive goodwill that is not amortised. Instead, FRS 101 states that paragraph B63(a) of IFRS 3 – *Business Combinations*, which requires that goodwill is measured at cost less impairment, should be read in accordance with paragraph A2.8 of FRS 101. *[FRS 101.AG1(f)]*. The non-amortisation of goodwill required by IFRS 3 conflicts with paragraph 22 of Schedule 1 to the Regulations (and its equivalents in Schedules 2 and 3) which require that acquired goodwill is reduced by provisions for depreciation calculated to write-off the amount systematically over a period chosen by the directors, not exceeding its useful economic life.

Paragraph A2.8 of FRS 101 notes that the non-amortisation of goodwill will usually be a departure, for the overriding purpose of giving a true and fair view, from the requirements of the Regulations. FRS 101 goes on to state that this is not a new instance of the use of the 'true and fair override' and it would have been required for companies reporting under previous UK GAAP which used an indefinite life for goodwill as permitted by FRS 10 – *Goodwill and intangible assets*. *[FRS 101.A2.8]*. This means that the FRC expects that entities with positive goodwill should continue not to amortise that goodwill. Those entities should invoke a true and fair override as permitted by paragraph 10(2) of Schedule 1 of the Regulations (or the equivalents in Schedules 2 and 3) to overcome the prohibition on amortisation of goodwill contained in paragraph 22 of Schedule 1 of the Regulations. The use of the true and fair override would require disclosure of the particulars of the departure from the Regulations, the reasons for it and its effect. *[1 Sch 10(2)]*. Continuation of goodwill amortisation, if permitted under previous GAAP, is not allowed by FRS 101.

It is anticipated that the use of a true and fair override in respect of goodwill amortisation will be limited in application since, in individual financial statements, there will only be goodwill where a business that is not an entity has been acquired.

As FRS 101 specifically amends EU-adopted IFRS to alter the accounting for the matters discussed at sections 4.1 to 4.6 below, to remove conflicts identified between EU-adopted IFRS and the Regulations, the issue of a 'true and fair override' does not arise in respect of these matters.

4.1 Negative goodwill

FRS 101 changes paragraph 34 of IFRS 3 so that any gain arising from a bargain purchase (i.e. negative goodwill) is not recognised immediately in profit and loss. Instead, any amount of the negative goodwill up to the fair values of the non-monetary assets acquired should be recognised in profit and loss in the periods in which the non-monetary assets are recovered, whether through depreciation or sale. Any amount of the negative goodwill in excess of the fair values of the non-monetary assets acquired should be recognised in profit or loss in the periods expected to be benefited. *[FRS 101.AG1(c)]*.

This change to EU-adopted IFRS was necessary because the Seventh Directive (on which the requirements in the Regulations are based) may be inconsistent with the recognition requirements for negative goodwill under EU-adopted IFRS. *[FRS 101.A2 Table 1]*.

Monetary assets are defined in EU-adopted IFRS as 'money held and assets to be received in fixed or determinable amounts of money'. *[IAS 38.8]*. Conversely, an essential feature of a non-monetary asset is the absence of a right to receive a fixed or determinable number of units of currency. IAS 21 – *The Effects of Changes in Foreign Exchange Rates* – gives examples of non-monetary assets as amounts prepaid for goods and services, goodwill, intangible assets, inventories and property, plant and equipment. *[IAS 21.16]*. IAS 39 – *Financial Instruments: Recognition and Measurement* – indicates (and IFRS 9 – *Financial Instruments* – states) that investments in equity instruments are non-monetary items. *[IAS 39.AG83, IFRS 9.B5.7.3]*.

Chapter 31

This suggests that equity investments in subsidiaries, associates or joint ventures are also non-monetary items.

Negative goodwill must be shown on the statement of financial position immediately below goodwill and followed by a subtotal showing the net amount of the goodwill assets and the excess. The excess shall be attributed to the acquirer. *[FRS 101.AG1(c)]*.

4.2 Contingent consideration payable by an acquirer in a business combination

FRS 101 changes paragraphs 39 to 40 and deletes paragraph 58 of IFRS 3 so that an adjustment to the cost of a business combination contingent on future events is recognised only if the estimated amount of the adjustment is probable and can be measured reliably. If the potential adjustment is not recognised at the acquisition date but subsequently becomes probable and can be measured reliably, the additional consideration is treated as an adjustment to the cost of the combination (i.e. goodwill). *[FRS 101.AG1(d)-(e)]*. 'Probable' is defined in IAS 37 – *Provisions, Contingent Liabilities and Contingent Assets* – as 'more likely than not' (i.e. there is a greater than 50% chance of the event occurring).

The EU-adopted version of IFRS 3 requires contingent consideration in a business acquisition to be measured at fair value upon date of acquisition with subsequent adjustments taken to profit or loss. This change to EU-adopted IFRS was necessary because the Regulations do not permit contingent consideration that is a financial liability to be measured at fair value unless it is a derivative. *[FRS 101 Appendix II Table 1]*.

IFRS 3, as modified by FRS 101, is silent as to whether a subsequent re-measurement of probable contingent consideration is an adjustment to goodwill or to profit or loss. The legal requirements appendix to FRS 101 states that the intention was to align the accounting in FRS 101 with paragraphs 19.12 and 19.13 of FRS 102. Although paragraphs 19.12 and 19.13 of FRS 102 are also silent on this matter, the Accounting Council's advice to the FRC which accompanies FRS 102 states that the requirements of FRS 102 in respect of business combinations are based on IFRS 3 (issued 2004). The implication of this is that subsequent re-measurements of contingent consideration once it becomes probable should be treated as adjustments to the cost of consideration, i.e. adjusted against goodwill. *[FRS 101 Appendix II Table 1]*.

FRS 101 is silent on accounting for contingent consideration on the acquisition of a subsidiary, associate or joint venture which is accounted for as an investment under either IAS 27 or IAS 27 (2012). However, we believe the guidance on contingent consideration in a business combination discussed above should be applied.

4.3 Reversal of goodwill impairments

FRS 101 changes paragraph 124 of IAS 36 to permit a goodwill impairment loss to be reversed in a subsequent period if, and only if, the reasons for the impairment loss have ceased to apply. *[FRS 101.AG1(s)]*. EU-adopted IFRS does not permit the reversal of a goodwill impairment.

This change to EU-adopted IFRS was necessary because the Regulations require the reversal of a provision for diminution in value of a fixed asset, if the reason for the provision has ceased to exist. *[FRS 101 Appendix II Table 1].*

However, paragraph 125 of IAS 36, which states that 'any increase in the recoverable amount of goodwill in the periods following the recognition of an impairment loss for that goodwill is likely to be an increase in internally generated goodwill, rather than a reversal of the impairment loss recognised for the acquired goodwill', has not been changed. This suggests that the FRC believes that there is a high hurdle for entities to overcome in order to reverse a goodwill impairment loss. Indeed, the legal requirements appendix to FRS 11 – *Impairment of fixed assets and goodwill* – stated that legal advice had been received that 'a reversal of an impairment loss on goodwill should be recognised only where an external event caused the recognition of the impairment loss in previous periods and subsequent external events clearly and demonstrably reverse the effects of that event in a way that was not foreseen in the original impairment calculations'. *[FRS 11.AII.10].*

4.4 Government grants deducted from the cost of fixed assets

FRS 101 changes paragraph 28 of IAS 16 – *Property, Plant and Equipment* – and paragraphs 24 to 29 of IAS 20 – *Accounting for Government Grants and Disclosure of Government Assistance* – in order to eliminate the option in IFRS that permits a government grant relating to an asset to be deducted in arriving at the carrying amount of the asset. Consequently, all government grants related to assets must be presented in the financial statements by setting up the grant as deferred income and recognising the grant as deferred income in profit or loss on a systematic basis over the useful life of the asset. In addition, the option in paragraph 29 of IAS 20 that permits grants related to income to be deducted in reporting the related expense has been deleted. *[FRS 101.AG1(l)-(r)].*

These changes to EU-adopted IFRS have been necessary because the Regulations prohibit off-setting of items that represent assets against items that represent liabilities unless specifically permitted or required. *[FRS 101 Appendix II Table 1].*

SSAP 4 – *Accounting for Government Grants* – permits entities to deduct a government grant from the purchase price or production cost of an asset where the grant was made as a contribution towards expenditure on that asset. This is despite the fact that this accounting is not permitted by the Regulations. *[SSAP 4.25].* Consequently, under SSAP 4, some entities deduct government grants from the cost of assets and use a 'true and fair override' to overcome the prohibition in the Regulations. As FRS 101 has specifically amended EU-adopted IFRS to remove the option to credit assets with the value of government grants, we do not consider that entities are permitted to use this accounting with a true and fair override under FRS 101 since the accounting standard does not permit this treatment.

4.5 Realised profits under FRS 101

FRS 101 has changed paragraph 88 of IAS 1 to clarify the precedence of the Regulations over IFRS in this matter by adding the words 'or unless prohibited by the Act' after 'an entity shall recognise all items of income and expense arising in a period in profit or loss unless an IFRS requires or permits otherwise'. *[FRS 101.AG1(k)].*

Paragraph 13(a) of Schedule 1 to the Regulations (and its equivalents in Schedules 2 and 3) require that only profits realised at the balance sheet date are included in the profit or loss account. *[FRS 101.A2.12]*. Paragraph 39 of Schedule 1 to the Regulations allows that investment property and living animals and plants that may, under EU-adopted IFRS, be held at fair value may also be held at fair value in Companies Act accounts. *[FRS 101.A2.13]*. Paragraph 40(2) of Schedule 1 to the Regulations (and its equivalents in Schedules 2 and 3) require that, in general, movements in the fair value of financial instruments, investment properties or living animals and plants are recognised in the profit and loss account notwithstanding the usual restrictions allowing only realised profits and losses to be included in the profit and loss account. Therefore, in the opinion of the FRC, paragraph 40 of Schedule 1 overrides paragraph 13(a) of Schedule 1 and such fair value gains can be recognised in profit and loss under FRS 101. *[FRS 101.A2.14]*.

The legal appendix to FRS 101 states that entities measuring investment properties, living animals or plants, or financial instruments at fair value may transfer such amounts to a separate non-distributable reserve instead of carrying them forward in retained earnings but are not required to do so. The FRC suggests that presenting fair value movements that are not distributable profits in a separate reserve may assist with the identification of profits available for that purpose. *[FRS 101.A2.15]*.

Whether profits are available for distribution must be determined in accordance with applicable law. Entities may also refer to TECH 02/10 to determine the profits available for distribution. *[FRS 101.A2.16]*.

4.6   Equalisation provisions

FRS 101 has changed paragraph 14(a) of IFRS 4 – *Insurance Contracts* – to insert the words 'unless otherwise required by the regulatory framework that applies to the entity' at the beginning of the sentence which prohibits the recognition or catastrophe provisions and equalisation provisions and to add the sentence. In addition, the following sentence has been added to the end of the paragraph, 'The presentation of any such liabilities shall follow the requirements of the Regulations (or other legal framework that applies to the entity).' *[FRS 101.AG1.f(A)]*.

These amendments remove a conflict between IFRS 4 (which does not permit the recognition of equalisation and catastrophe provisions for claims that have not been incurred) and Schedule 3 of the Regulations (which requires the recognition of equalisation provisions as a liability). Consequently, equalisation reserves are recognised as a liability under FRS 101 when the Regulations also permit their recognition.

4.7   Investments in associates and joint ventures

The Regulations are clear that, in individual accounts, investments in associates and joint ventures can be measured only at cost or fair value. Neither the equity method of accounting nor proportional consolidation (which for EU-IFRS reporters was allowed in accounting for jointly controlled entities under IAS 31 for annual reporting periods commencing prior to 1 January 2014) are permitted.

There may be some entities that are not parents but have used the equity method or proportional consolidation for associates, joint ventures or jointly controlled entities under EU-adopted IFRS on the grounds that they are not preparing separate financial statements as defined by IAS 27 or IAS 27 (2012).

FRS 101 does not identify this as a potential measurement difference with EU-adopted IFRS.

4.8   Investment entities

As FRS 101 does not apply to consolidated financial statements, the Group Accounts Regulations, 1992, or other legislative provisions pertaining to group accounts should not apply. However, where a parent meets the definition of an investment entity under IFRS 10, and is therefore required to measure its investment in a subsidiary at fair value through profit or loss, it must measure that investment in the same way in its separate financial statements (i.e. at fair value through profit or loss) as required by paragraph 11A of IAS 27. In other words, a qualifying entity that meets the definition of an investment entity must measure its investment in subsidiaries at fair value through profit or loss in its individual financial statements *[FRS 101.A2.17]*.

An investment entity which measures its investments in subsidiaries at fair value through profit or loss will be required to make the additional disclosures required by paragraph 36(4) of Schedule 1 to the Regulations (see 6.3 below). *[FRS 101.A2.20]*.

5   PRESENTATIONAL DIFFERENCES BETWEEN FRS 101 AND IFRS

As noted at section 2 above, entities applying FRS 101 must prepare their financial statements in accordance with the Companies Act and the Regulations. This is because financial statements prepared under FRS 101 are Companies Act individual accounts and not IAS individual accounts as set out in section 395 of the Companies Act. *[FRS 101.A2.3]*. There are several conflicts between the presentational requirements of EU-adopted IFRS and those required by the Regulations. The FRC has therefore changed EU-adopted IFRS to ensure that the financial statements prepared under FRS 101 comply with the Regulations.

Changes to EU-adopted IFRS have been made by FRS 101 to:

- require the balance sheet (or statement of financial position) and profit and loss account to be presented in the formats required by the Regulations rather than the presentation required by IAS 1 (see section 5.1 below);

- require a columnar presentation of discontinued operations on the face of the profit and loss account (see section 5.2 below); and

- permit the presentation of extraordinary activities although these are expected to be extremely rare (see section 5.3 below);

Chapter 31

5.1   Balance sheet and profit and loss formats required by FRS 101

FRS 101 amends IAS 1 by inserting a new paragraph, 53A, which states that 'a qualifying entity shall comply with the balance sheet format requirements of the Act instead of paragraphs 54 to 76 of IAS 1 unless the entity elects to apply those paragraphs and the resulting statement of financial position complies with the balance sheet format requirements of the Act'. *[FRS 101.AG1(h)].*

FRS 101 also amends IAS 1 by inserting a new paragraph, 81C, which states that 'a qualifying entity shall present the components of profit or loss in the statement of comprehensive income (in either the single statement or two statement approach) in accordance with the profit and loss format requirements of the Act instead of paragraphs 82 and 84 to 86 of IAS 1. The entity may elect to apply the requirements of those paragraphs so long as the resulting statement of comprehensive income complies with the profit and loss format requirements of the Act'. *[FRS 101.AG1(i)].*

Footnote text further clarifies that an entity shall apply, as required by company law, either Part 1 'General Rules and Formats' of Schedule 1 to the Regulations; Part 1 'General Rules and Formats' of Schedule 2 to the Regulations; Part 1 'General Rules and Formats' of Schedule 3 to the Regulations; or Part 1 'General Rules and Formats' of Schedule 1 to the LLP Regulations. *[FRS101.AG1(h)-(i)].*

This means that, for balance sheet and profit or loss presentation, a reporting entity under FRS 101 must apply the Regulations where they are different from IAS 1. An insurance entity reporting under Schedule 3, for example, would therefore continue to show separate technical and non-technical accounts rather than a single performance statement as its profit and loss account since technical and non-technical accounts are the profit and loss format required by the Act.

The FRS 101 legal appendix confirms that the requirements of paragraphs 54 to 76, 82 and 84 to 86 of IAS 1 disapply unless their application complies with the Regulations. *[FRS 101 Appendix II Table1].* However, even if these requirements do comply with the Regulations, their application is voluntary.

A UK parent company presenting both consolidated financial statements (either IAS group accounts or Companies Act group accounts) and Companies Act individual financial statements under FRS 101 can take advantage of the exemption in s408 of the Companies Act from presenting a profit and loss account and related notes in respect of its individual profit and loss account.

FRS 101 makes no amendments to the requirement in IAS 1 to present a statement of changes in equity for the reporting period.

There is no requirement to present a statement of cash flows where the reduced disclosure exemption is taken (see section 6.1.8 below).

5.1.1 Practical issues relating to balance sheet and profit and loss presentation

5.1.1.A Debtors due after more than one year

The Regulations require presentation of debtors falling due after more than one year within current assets. Under IAS 1, these would generally be presented as non-current assets. The legal appendix to FRS 101 reproduces the consensus of UITF 4 – *Presentation of long-term debtors in current assets* – that 'in most cases it will be satisfactory to disclose the size of debtors due after more than one year in the notes to the accounts. There will be some instances, however, where the amount is so material in the context of the total net current assets that in the absence of disclosure of debtors due after more than one year on the face of the balance sheet readers may misinterpret the accounts. In such circumstances, the amount should be disclosed on the face of the balance sheet within current assets'. *[FRS 101.A2.10].*

5.1.1.B Non-current assets or disposal groups held for sale

Paragraph 38 of IFRS 5 – *Non-current Assets Held for Sale and Discontinued Operations* – requires an entity to present a non-current asset classified as held for sale and the assets of a disposal group held for sale separately from other assets in the statement of financial position and the liabilities of a disposal group separately from other liabilities in the statement of financial position. Paragraph 54 of IAS 1 requires a single line approach in the balance sheet for both assets and liabilities held for sale. Detailed analysis of the components of the assets and liabilities held for sale is required in the notes to the financial statements.

A one-line presentation approach in the balance sheet is not allowed by FRS 101 because the Regulations do not permit the aggregation of different types of assets or liabilities in this way and paragraph 54 of IAS 1 cannot be applied if it conflicts with the Regulations (see section 5.1 above). One practical solution to this matter could be to present aggregate assets and aggregate liabilities held for sale as a memorandum on the statement of financial position cross-referenced to the detailed analysis in the notes.

5.2 Presentation of discontinued operations

FRS 101 changes IFRS 5 to:

- remove the option to present the analysis of discontinued operations into its component parts (e.g. revenue, expenses, tax) in the notes to the accounts. This analysis must be presented on the face of the statement of comprehensive income; and

- require the analysis above to be shown on the face of the statement of comprehensive income in a column identified as related to discontinued operations (i.e. separately from continuing operations); and

- require a total column (i.e. the sum of continuing and discontinuing operations) to be presented on the face of the statement of comprehensive income; and

- remove the option to present income from continuing operations and from discontinued operations attributable to owners of the parent in the notes to the accounts. *[FRS 101.AG1(g)].*

In substance, this means that the single line presentation of discontinued operations is replaced by a three-column approach with the detailed analysis of the results from the discontinued operation shown on the face of the statement of comprehensive income. This is illustrated in the following example:

Example 1:   Presentation of discontinued operations

Statement of comprehensive income

For the year ended 31 December 20X5

	Continuing operations	Dis-continued operations	Total	Continuing operations	Dis-continued operations	Total
	20X5	20X5	20X5	20X4	20X4	20X4
	£000	£000	£000	£000	£000	£000
Turnover	4,200	1,232	5,432	3,201	1,500	4,701
Cost of Sales	(2,591)	(1,104)	(3,695)	(2,281)	(1,430)	(3,711)
Gross profit	1,609	128	1,737	920	70	990
Administrative expenses	(452)	(110)	(562)	(418)	(120)	(538)
Other operating income	212	–	212	198	–	198
Profit on disposal of operations	–	301	301	–	–	–
Operating profit	1,369	319	1,688	700	(50)	650
Interest receivable and similar income	14	–	14	16	–	16
Interest payable and similar charges	(208)	–	(208)	(208)	–	(208)
Profit on ordinary activities before tax	1,175	319	1,494	508	(50)	458
Taxation	(390)	(4)	(394)	(261)	3	(258)
Profit on ordinary activities after taxation and profit for the financial year	785	315	1,100	247	(47)	200

Other comprehensive income

	Total 20X5	Total 20X4
Actuarial losses on defined benefit pension plans	(108)	(68)
Deferred tax movement relating to actuarial losses	28	18
Total Comprehensive income for the year	**1,020**	**150**

5.3   Presentation of extraordinary items

FRS 101 changes paragraph 87 of IAS 1, and introduces a new paragraph 87A, to distinguish between ordinary activities and extraordinary items. Extraordinary activities are 'material items possessing a high degree of abnormality which arise from events or transactions that fall outside the ordinary activities of the reporting entity and which are not expected to recur. They do not include items occurring within the entity's ordinary activities that are required to be disclosed by paragraph 97 of IAS nor do they include prior period items merely because they relate to a prior period'. *[FRS 101.AG1(j)]*.

Ordinary activities are defined as 'any activities which are undertaken by a reporting entity as part of its business and such related activities in which the reporting entity engages in furtherance of, or incidental to, or arising from, these activities. Ordinary activities include any effects on the reporting entity of any event in the various environments in which it operates, including the political, regulatory, economic and geographical environments, irrespective of the frequency or unusual nature of the events'. *[FRS 101.AG1(j)]*.

These changes have been made to comply with the profit and loss account format of the Regulations which includes an 'extraordinary activities' line item. However, the definitions of both 'ordinary' and 'extraordinary' activities are identical to the definitions of these activities previously contained within FRS 3 – *Reporting financial performance* (except that reference to 'exceptional items' has been replaced by a reference to paragraph 97 of IAS 1 which requires an entity to disclose separately material items of income and expense).

The definition of 'ordinary activities' in FRS 3 was deliberately designed to be so wide such as to render it extremely difficult for an entity to present an event as 'extraordinary'. The explanatory guidance to FRS 3 stated that 'extraordinary items are extremely rare' and 'in view of the extreme rarity of such items no examples are provided'. This view is confirmed in the legal appendix of FRS 101 which states that 'entities should note that extraordinary items are extremely rare as they relate to highly abnormal events or transactions'. *[FRS 101.A2.11]*.

We would anticipate therefore that this change has no practical impact and we would not expect to see disclosure of extraordinary items under FRS 101.

6 IFRS DISCLOSURE EXEMPTIONS FOR QUALIFYING ENTITIES

Qualifying entities may take advantage in their financial statements of a number of disclosure exemptions from EU-adopted IFRS (see section 6.1 below).

Some, but not all, of these exemptions are conditional on 'equivalent' disclosures in the consolidated financial statements of the group in which the entity is consolidated (see section 6.2 below).

In addition, some disclosures required by the Regulations for certain financial instruments that are held at fair value must be made even if the qualifying entity takes advantage of the disclosure exemptions from the disclosure requirements of IFRS 7 – *Financial Instruments: Disclosures* – and IFRS 13 – *Fair Value Measurement* (see section 6.3 below). *[FRS 101.A2.5A]*.

Financial institutions as defined by FRS 101 are not entitled to some disclosure exemptions (see section 6.4 below).

6.1   Disclosure exemptions

Qualifying entities are permitted the following disclosure exemptions from EU-adopted IFRS: *[FRS 101.6-8].*

- the requirements of paragraphs 45(b) and 46 to 52 of IFRS 2 – *Share-based Payment* – provided that for a qualifying entity that is:
    - a subsidiary, the share-based payment arrangement concerns equity instruments of another group entity;
    - an ultimate parent, the share-based payment arrangement concerns its own equity instruments and its separate financial statements are presented alongside the consolidated financial statements of the group;

    and, in both cases, provided that equivalent disclosures are included in the consolidated financial statements of the group in which the entity is consolidated (see section 6.1.1 below);

- the requirements of paragraphs 62, B64(d) to (e), (g) to (h), (j) to (m), n(ii), (o)(ii), (p), (q)(ii), B66 and B67 of IFRS 3 provided that equivalent disclosures are included in the consolidated financial statements of the group in which the entity is consolidated (see section 6.1.2 below);

- the requirements of paragraph 33(c) of IFRS 5 provided that equivalent disclosures are included in the consolidated financial statements of the group in which the entity is consolidated (see section 6.1.3 below);

- the requirements of IFRS 7 provided that equivalent disclosures are included in the financial statements of the group in which the entity is consolidated (see section 6.1.4 below). However, some disclosures are required for certain financial instruments held at fair value such as liabilities which are not held for trading or derivatives, and investments in subsidiary undertakings, joint ventures and associates (see section 6.3 below). Qualifying entities that are financial institutions do not receive this exemption and must apply the disclosure requirements of IFRS 7 in full (see section 6.4 below);

- the requirements of paragraphs 91 to 99 of IFRS 13 provided that equivalent disclosures are included in the consolidated financial statements of the group in which the entity is consolidated. However, qualifying entities that are financial institutions can only take advantage of the exemptions to the extent that they apply to assets and liabilities other than financial instruments (see section 6.1.5 below);

- the requirement in paragraph 38 of IAS 1 to present comparative information in respect of:
    - paragraph 79(a)(iv) of IAS 1;
    - paragraph 73(e) of IAS 16;
    - paragraph 118(e) of IAS 38 – *Intangible Assets*;
    - paragraphs 76 and 79(d) of IAS 40 – *Investment Property*; and
    - paragraph 50 of IAS 41 – *Agriculture* (see section 6.1.6 below);

- the requirements of paragraphs 10(d), 10(f), 16, 38A to 38D, 40A to 40D, 111 and 134 to 136 of IAS 1 (for accounting periods beginning before 1 January 2013 paragraphs 38A to 38D and 40A to 40D of IAS 1 are replaced with paragraphs 39 to 40 of IAS 1). However, qualifying entities that are financial institutions are not permitted to take advantage of the exemptions in paragraphs 134 to 136 of IAS 1 (see section 6.1.7 below);

- the requirements of IAS 7 – *Statement of Cash Flows* (see section 6.1.8 below);

- the requirements of paragraphs 30 and 31 of IAS 8 (see section 6.1.9 below);

- the requirements of paragraph 17 of IAS 24 – *Related Party Disclosures* – and the requirements in IAS 24 to disclose related party transactions entered into between two or more members of a group, provided that any subsidiary which is a party to the transaction is wholly owned by such a member (see section 6.1.10 below); and

- the requirements of paragraphs 130(f)(ii), 130(f)(iii), 134(d) to 134(f) and 135(c) to 135(e) of IAS 36 provided that equivalent disclosures are included in the consolidated financial statements of the group in which the entity is consolidated (see section 6.1.11 below).

Use of the disclosure exemptions is conditional on the following disclosures in the notes to the financial statements:

(a)   a brief narrative summary of the exemptions adopted; and

(b)   the name of the parent of the group in whose consolidated financial statements the reporting entity is consolidated and from where those financial statements may be obtained. *[FRS 101.5(c)].*

There is no requirement to list all of the disclosure exemptions in detail. Reporting entities can also choose to apply the disclosure exemptions on a selective basis. This may be necessary, for example, where not all of the relevant 'equivalent' disclosures are made in the consolidated financial statements of the parent on the grounds of materiality (see section 6.2 below).

Each of the disclosure exemptions listed above is discussed below.

6.1.1   Share-based payment (IFRS 2)

The disclosure exemption eliminates all IFRS 2 disclosures apart from those required by paragraphs 44 and 45(a), (c) and (d) of IFRS 2. In substance, this reduces the disclosure requirements of IFRS 2 to:

- a description of the type of share-based payment arrangements that existed during the reporting period, including general terms and conditions, maximum terms of options granted, and the method of entitlement (e.g. whether in cash or equity);

- weighted average share price information in respect of options exercised during the reporting period; and

- the range of exercise prices and weighted average remaining contractual life of share options outstanding at the end of the reporting period.

Chapter 31

6.1.2   Business combinations (IFRS 3)

In substance, this disclosure exemption eliminates the qualitative disclosures required on a business combination. However, a number of factual or quantitative disclosures are still required for each business combination including:

- the name and description of the acquiree, acquisition date and percentage of voting equity interests acquired;
- the acquisition date fair value of total consideration transferred split by major class;
- the amount recognised at the acquisition date for each major class of assets acquired and liabilities assumed;
- the amount of any negative goodwill recognised and the line item in the statement of comprehensive income in which it is recognised;
- the amount of any non-controlling interest recognised and the measurement basis for the amount (although there should be no non-controlling interests for acquisitions in individual financial statements);
- revenue and profit or loss of the acquiree since acquisition date included in comprehensive income for the period; and
- the information above (except for the details of the acquirees) in aggregate for individually immaterial business combinations that are collectively material.

In addition, an acquirer is still subject to the general requirements of paragraphs 59 to 61 of IFRS 3. These require disclosure of information that enables users of the financial statements to evaluate the nature and effect of a business combination that occurs either during the current reporting period or at the end of the financial reporting period but before the financial statements are authorised for issue and the financial effects of adjustments recognised in the current reporting period relating to business combinations that occurred in the current or previous periods.

6.1.3   Discontinued operations (IFRS 5)

This exemption eliminates the requirement to disclose cash flows attributable to discontinued operations. This cash flow disclosure exemption is contingent on equivalent disclosures in the consolidated financial statements of the parent although equivalent disclosures in the parent are not necessary to make use of the exemption not to prepare a cash flow statement.

6.1.4   Financial instruments (IFRS 7)

This exemption removes all of the disclosure requirements of IFRS 7. However, notwithstanding this exemption, some IFRS 7 disclosures are still required for certain financial instruments held at fair value (see section 6.3 below). In addition, some specific disclosures are required by the Regulations (see section 7.2 below).

Financial institutions are not permitted to use this exemption (see section 6.4 below).

6.1.5   Fair values (IFRS 13)

This exemption removes all of the disclosure requirements of IFRS 13. However, notwithstanding this exemption, some IFRS 13 disclosures are still required for certain financial instruments held at fair value (see section 6.3 below). In addition, specific disclosures in respect of fair values of financial instruments, investment property and living animals and plants carried at fair value are required by the Regulations (see section 7.2 below).

Financial institutions are not permitted to use this IFRS 13 disclosure exemption in respect of financial instruments. However, they can use this exemption in respect of disclosures of non-financial instruments (see section 6.4 below).

6.1.6 Comparatives (IAS 1, IAS 16, IAS 38, IAS 40, IAS 41)

This exemption eliminates the requirement for comparatives to be presented for reconciliations of:

- outstanding shares at the beginning and end of the current period (IAS 1);

- the carrying amount of property plant and equipment at the beginning and end of the current period (IAS 16);

- the carrying amount of intangible assets at the beginning and end of the current period (IAS 38);

- the carrying amount of investment property held at either fair value or cost at the beginning and end of the current period (IAS 40); and

- the carrying amount of biological assets at the beginning and end of the current period (IAS 41).

These comparative disclosures were also not required under previous UK GAAP.

6.1.7 Presentation (IAS 1)

This exemption removes:

- the requirement to present a cash flow statement (see section 6.1.8 below);

- the requirement to present a statement of financial position and related notes at the beginning of the earliest comparative period whenever an entity applies an accounting policy retrospectively, makes a retrospective restatement, or when it reclassifies items in its financial statements;

- the requirement to make an explicit statement of compliance with IFRS. Indeed, FRS 101 prohibits such a statement of compliance and an FRS 101 statement of compliance is required instead – see section 1.4 above; and

- the requirement to disclose information about capital and how it is managed.

Financial institutions are not permitted to use the exemption in respect of the disclosure of information about capital and how it is managed. This is because financial institutions are usually subject to externally imposed capital requirements.

6.1.8 Cash flows (IAS 7)

The exemption removes the requirement for a cash flow statement for any qualifying entity. This exemption therefore goes beyond the exemption in FRS 1 – *Cash flow statements* – which does not require a cash flow statement for only those subsidiary undertakings where 90% or more of the voting rights are controlled within the group, provided the consolidated financial statements in which the subsidiary undertakings are included are publicly available.

Chapter 31

6.1.9 Standards issued but not effective (IAS 8)

This exemption removes the requirement to provide information about the impact of IFRSs that have been issued but are not yet effective.

6.1.10 Related party transactions (IAS 24)

The exemptions in respect of IAS 24 remove:

- the requirement to disclose information about key management personnel compensation; and

- the requirements to disclose related party transactions between two or more members of a group, provided that any subsidiary which is a party to the transaction is wholly owned by such a member.

Although the requirement to disclose key management personnel compensation is eliminated, UK companies are required separately by the Companies Act to disclose information in respect of directors' remuneration and quoted companies must prepare a directors' remuneration report (see section 7.1 below). There is no exemption from other IAS 24 disclosure requirements, so disclosure of other transactions with key management personnel (e.g. loans) is still required.

In this context of FRS 101, we believe that the 'group' being referred to in respect of the exemption from transactions with other wholly owned subsidiaries should be interpreted as being the group headed by the ultimate controlling entity. This interpretation follows paragraph 38 of Appendix IV of FRS 8 – *Related party disclosures* – which clarifies the meaning of the identical disclosure exemption in FRS 8. Oddly, this explanatory wording has not been carried into FRS 101. The ultimate controlling entity may not necessarily be the same entity as the entity that is preparing the publicly available consolidated accounts intended to give a true and fair view in which the qualifying entity is included.

6.1.11 Impairment of assets (IAS 36)

This exemption eliminates all requirements to disclose information about estimates used to measure recoverable amounts of cash-generating units containing goodwill or intangible assets with indefinite useful lives including details of fair value measurements where the recoverable amount is fair value less costs of disposal other than:

- the carrying amounts of goodwill and indefinite life intangibles allocated to cash generating units; and

- the basis on which the recoverable amount of those units has been determined (i.e. value in use or fair value less costs to sell).

Qualifying entities are also still required to make the disclosures required by paragraphs 126 to 133 of IAS 36 in respect of impairment losses (and reversal of impairment losses) recognised in the period.

6.2 'Equivalent' disclosures

Certain of the disclosure exemptions in FRS 101 are dependent on the provision of 'equivalent' disclosures in the publicly available consolidated financial statements of the parent in which the entity is included.

The following table summarises which disclosure exemptions need 'equivalent' disclosures in the consolidated financial statements of the parent and which do not.

Disclosure exemption	*Equivalent disclosures required in parent*
Share-based payment (see section 6.1.1 above)	Yes
Business combinations (see section 6.1.2 above)	Yes
Discontinued operations (see section 6.1.3 above)	Yes
Financial instruments (see section 6.1.4 above)	Yes
Fair values (see section 6.1.5 above)	Yes
Comparatives (see section 6.1.6 above)	No
Presentation (see 6.1.7 above)	No
Cash flows (see 6.1.8 above)	No
Standards issued but not effective (see 6.1.9 above)	No
Related party transactions (see 6.1.10 above)	No
Impairment of assets (see 6.1.11 above)	Yes

FRS 101 refers to the Application Guidance in FRS 100 in deciding whether the consolidated financial statements of the group in which the reporting entity is included provides disclosures that are 'equivalent' to the requirements of IFRS from which relief is provided. *[FRS 101.9]*.

The Application Guidance in FRS 100 states that:

- it is necessary to consider whether the publicly available consolidated financial statements of the parent provide disclosures that meet the basic disclosure requirements of the relevant standard or interpretation without regarding strict conformity with each and every disclosure. This assessment should be based on the particular facts, including the similarities to and differences from the requirements of the relevant standard from which relief is provided. 'Equivalence' is intended to be aligned to that described in s401 of the Act; *[FRS 100.AG8-9]* and

- disclosure exemptions for subsidiaries are permitted where the relevant disclosure requirements are met in the consolidated financial statements, even where the disclosures are made in aggregate or abbreviated form. If, however, no disclosure is made in the consolidated financial statements on the grounds of materiality, the relevant disclosures should be made at the subsidiary level if material in those financial statements. *[FRS 100.AG10]*.

This means that a qualifying entity must review the consolidated financial statements of its parent to ensure that 'equivalent' disclosures have been made for each of the above exemptions that it intends to use. Where a particular 'equivalent' disclosure has not been made then the qualifying subsidiary cannot use the exemption in respect of that disclosure.

Chapter 31

6.3 Disclosures required by the Regulations in the financial statements of non-financial institutions for certain financial instruments held at fair value

Paragraph 36(4) of Schedule 1 of the Regulations (and its equivalents in Schedules 2 and 3) allow certain financial instruments, that are permitted to be held at fair value under IFRS adopted by the EU before 5 September 2006, to be held at fair value only if 'the disclosures required by such accounting standards are made'.

The financial instruments referred to are those in paragraphs 36(2)(c) and 36(3) of Schedule 1 to the Regulations. These are:

- any financial liability which is not held for trading or a derivative (i.e. a financial liability designated at fair value through profit or loss (FVPL) under paragraph 9 of IAS 39);

- loans and receivables originated by the reporting entity, not held for trading purposes, and designated at either available-for-sale (AFS) or FVPL under paragraph 9 of IAS 39;

- interests in subsidiary undertakings, associated undertakings and joint ventures designated at either AFS or FVPL under paragraph 10 of IAS 27 or paragraph 38 of IAS 27 (2012); or

- other financial instruments with such special characteristics that the instruments according to generally accepted accounting principles or practice, should be accounted for differently from other financial instruments. [1 Sch 36].

The Application Guidance to FRS 101 confirms that a qualifying entity that has financial instruments measured at fair value in accordance with the requirements of paragraph 36(4) of Schedule 1 to the Regulations (or equivalent) is legally required to provide the relevant disclosures set out in international accounting standards adopted by the European Commission on or before 5 September 2006. [FRS 100.A2.7].

IAS 32 – *Financial Instruments: Presentation* – was the extant international accounting standard, as adopted in the EU on 5 September 2006, which set out the disclosure requirements around financial instruments measured at fair value. However, the IASB issued IFRS 7, in August 2005, which sought to incorporate and improve the existing disclosure requirements around financial instruments from IAS 32. IFRS 7 was adopted in the EU, in January 2006, and was effective for accounting periods beginning on or after 1 January 2007, however early adoption was permitted. [FRS 100.A2.7A].

In order for a company to meet the requirements set out in paragraph 36(4) of Schedule 1 to the Regulations (should it have any financial instruments that fall within that paragraph), it must make the relevant disclosures required by either IAS 32 or IFRS 7 as adopted in the EU on or before 5 September 2006. For example, if an entity measures a financial instrument (which is subject to the requirements of paragraph 36(4) of Schedule 1 to the Regulations) at fair value through profit or loss, then it must provide the disclosures in relation to instruments measured at fair value through profit or loss as required by either IAS 32 or IFRS 7in order to comply with the Regulations. The same would be applicable to any financial instruments measured at fair value through other comprehensive income. [FRS 100.A2.7B].

In the opinion of the Accounting Council, IFRS 7 is seen as an improvement on the disclosure requirements of IAS 32 and a company would meet the requirements of paragraph 36(4) of Schedule 1 to the Regulations by providing the disclosures required by IFRS 7 as originally adopted in the EU in January 2006. It should be noted that a number of amendments have been made to IFRS 7 since the original version was adopted in 2006, however, if an entity was to provide the relevant disclosures from the current version of IFRS 7, it would, in the opinion of the Accounting Council, still be meeting the requirements of the Regulations. *[FRS 100.A2.7C]*. In practice, we believe that most entities are likely to take this latter approach (i.e. use the current version of IFRS 7).

In addition, qualifying entities that are preparing Companies Act accounts must provide the disclosures required by paragraph 55 of Schedule 1 to the Regulations which sets out requirements relating to financial instruments at fair value. *[FRS 100.A2.7D]*. These disclosures relate to financial instruments held at fair value generally and not just to those financial instruments measured at fair value in accordance with paragraph 36(4) discussed above. Disclosures are required of: *[1 Sch 55]*

- significant assumptions underlying the valuation models and techniques used when determining fair value where fair value of a financial instrument is not determined by reference to its market value or by reference to the market value of its components or of a similar instrument;

- fair value of each category of financial instrument and changes in fair value included in profit or loss or the fair value reserve for those instruments;

- for each class of derivatives, the extent and nature of the instruments, including significant terms and conditions that may affect the timing and uncertainty of future cash flows; and

- a tabular disclosure of amounts transferred to the fair value reserve reconciling the opening and closing balance of the reserve, showing the amount transferred to or from the reserve during the year and the source and application of the amounts so transferred.

6.4 Disclosure exemptions for financial institutions

Financial institutions are permitted to apply FRS 101 but receive fewer disclosure exemptions. A qualifying entity which is a financial institution may take advantage in its individual financial statements of the disclosure exemptions set out in section 6.1 above except for:

- the disclosure exemptions of IFRS 7;

- the disclosure exemptions from paragraphs 91 to 99 of IFRS 13 to the extent that they apply to financial instruments. Therefore, a financial institution can take advantage of the disclosure exemptions from paragraphs 91 to 99 of IFRS 13 for assets and liabilities other than financial instruments (e.g. property plant and equipment, intangible assets, investment property); and

- the capital disclosures of paragraphs 134 to 136 of IAS 1. *[FRS 101.7]*.

The FRC has opted not to provide a generic definition of a financial institution. Instead, it has provided a list of entities that are stated to be financial institutions. A 'financial institution' is stated to be any of the following: *[FRS 101 Appendix I]*

(a)   a bank which is:

    (i)   a firm with a Part IV permission (as defined in s40(4) of the Financial Services and Markets Act 2000) which includes accepting deposits and:

        (a)   which is a credit institution; or

        (b)   whose Part IV permission includes a requirement that it complies with the rules in the General Prudential sourcebook and the Prudential sourcebook for Banks, Building Societies and Investment Firms relating to banks, but which is not a building society, a friendly society or a credit union;

    (ii)   an EEA bank which is a full credit institution;

(b)   a building society which is defined in s119(1) of the Building Societies Act 1986 as a building society incorporated (or deemed to be incorporated) under that Act;

(c)   a credit union, being a body corporate registered under the Industrial and Provident Societies Act 1965 as a credit union in accordance with the Credit Unions Act 1979, which is an authorised person;

(d)   custodian bank, broker-dealer or stockbroker;

(e)   an entity that undertakes the business of effecting or carrying out insurance contracts, including general and life assurance entities;

(f)   an incorporated friendly society incorporated under the Friendly Societies Act 1992 or a registered friendly society registered under section 7(1)(a) of the Friendly Societies Act 1974 or any enactment which it replaced, including any registered branches;

(g)   an investment trust, Irish investment company, venture capital trust, mutual fund, exchange traded fund, unit trust, open-ended investment company (OEIC);

(h)   a retirement benefit plan; or

(i)   any other entity whose principal activity is to generate wealth or manage risk through financial instruments. This is intended to cover entities that have business activities similar to those listed above but are not specifically included in the list above.

    A parent entity whose sole activity is to hold investments in other group entities is not a financial institution.

Category (i) is potentially wide-ranging and, despite the reference to 'similar' business activities, appears to have a different emphasis from (a) to (h) which focus on entities that hold assets in a fiduciary capacity on behalf of others rather than wealth generation or risk management through the use of financial instruments.

The Accounting Council has advised that 'a parent entity whose sole activity is to hold investments in other group entities is not a financial institution, but notes that a subsidiary entity engaged solely in treasury activities for the group as a whole is likely to meet the definition of a financial institution'. *[FRS 102.AC.37]*.

In many groups, there will be entities falling between these two extremes and judgement will need to be applied in assessing whether the principal activities of the entity are to generate wealth or manage risk through financial instruments.

7   ADDITIONAL COMPANIES ACT DISCLOSURES

FRS 101 individual financial statements are subject to disclosures required by the Regulations as well as other disclosures required by the Companies Act or other related regulations. These disclosures are in addition to those required by EU-adopted IFRS.

There are two types of Companies Act disclosures required for a UK entity applying FRS 101:

(a)   those required already for IAS accounts prepared under EU-adopted IFRS and Companies Act accounts prepared under UK GAAP (see section 7.1 below); and

(b)   those required by the Regulations which would have been applied by an entity preparing Companies Act accounts under previous UK GAAP (or the FRSSE or FRS 102) but not by an entity preparing IAS accounts under EU-adopted IFRS (see section 7.2 below).

This means that, in certain scenarios, a move from EU-adopted IFRS to FRS 101 would result in increased disclosures for an entity despite the use of the disclosure exemptions described at section 6 above.

There may also be additional statutory disclosures for types of entities other than companies.

7.1   Existing Companies Act disclosures in the financial statements for IFRS and UK GAAP reporters which also apply under FRS 101

FRS100 identifies the following disclosures: *[FRS 100.A2.19]*

- s410A – off-balance sheet arrangements (unless subject to the Small Companies Regime);

- s411 – employee numbers and costs (unless subject to the Small Companies Regime);

- s412 – directors' benefits: remuneration;

- s413 – directors' benefits: advances, credit and guarantees;

- s415 to 419 – directors' report;

- s420 to 421 – directors remuneration report; and

- s494 – services provided by auditor and associates and related remuneration (disclosures of non-audit services are not required for companies subject to the Small Companies Regime or medium-sized companies).

Chapter 31

The list of disclosures identified by FRS 100 is not complete and omits, for example, the information about related undertakings required by s409. In addition, other Companies Act or related disclosures may apply depending on individual circumstances such as the disclosures required for a parent taking advantage of the exemption from preparing consolidated accounts under either s400 or s401 of the Companies Act.

7.2   Disclosures required by the Regulations in the financial statements under FRS 101 but not previously required under IFRS

The Regulations require various disclosures in the financial statements. In particular, Part 3 of Schedules 1 to 3 require certain disclosures to be made in the notes to the financial statements if not given in the primary statements. The relevant paragraphs are as follows:

- Schedule 1 paragraphs 42 to 72; or
- Schedule 2 paragraphs 52 to 92; or
- Schedule 3 paragraphs 60 to 90.

Although some of these disclosure requirements are replicated in EU-adopted IFRS others are not. Entities that move to FRS 101 from UK GAAP will have made these disclosures previously and therefore these requirements will not increase their reporting burden. Entities that move to FRS 101 from EU-adopted IFRS will not have made these disclosures previously or any other disclosures required by the applicable Schedule above and should consider carefully the impact of these new requirements against the benefits of the reduced disclosures discussed at section 6 above.

Some examples of disclosures not required under EU-adopted IFRS in individual or separate financial statements are:

(a)   Schedule 1 companies (i.e. companies other than banking and insurance companies)

- a statement required by large companies that the accounts have been prepared in accordance with applicable accounting policies; *[1 Sch 45]*
- disclosures in respect of share capital and debentures; *[1 Sch 47-50]*
- disclosure of the split of land between freehold and leasehold and the leasehold land between that held on a long lease and that held on a short lease; *[1 Sch 53]*
- disclosure of information about listed investments; *[1 Sch 54]*
- disclosure of information about the fair value of financial assets and liabilities which, in substance, 'reinstates' some parts of IFRS 7 and IFRS 13. In particular, there are requirements to disclose information about significant assumptions where the fair value of a financial instrument results from generally accepted valuation models and techniques, details of the fair value of financial instruments by category and details concerning significant terms and conditions of derivatives (see 6.3 above); *[1 Sch 55-57]*

- disclosure of information about creditors due after five years; *[1 Sch 61]*

- disclosure of information about loans made in connection with the purchase of own shares; *[1 Sch 64]*

- disclosure of particulars of taxation; *[1 Sch 67]* and

- disclosure of information about turnover by class of business and geographical markets. IFRS 8 – *Operating Segments* – does not require segmental information if an entity's debt or equity instruments are not traded in a public market or the entity is not in the process of filing financial statements for that purpose. *[1 Sch 68]*.

The profit and loss account of a company that falls within s408 of the Act (individual profit and loss account where group accounts prepared) need not contain the information specified in paragraphs 65 to 69 of Schedule 1. *[Regulations 3(2)]*.

(b)   Schedule 2 companies (i.e. banking companies)

- a statement that the accounts have been prepared in accordance with applicable accounting policies; *[2 Sch 54]*

- disclosures in respect of share capital and debentures; *[2 Sch 58-61]*

- disclosure of the split of land between freehold and leasehold and the leasehold land between that held on a long lease and that held on a short lease; *[2 Sch 64]*

- disclosure of a specific maturity analysis for loans and advances and liabilities; *[2 Sch 72]*

- disclosure of arrears of fixed cumulative dividends; *[2 Sch 75]*

- disclosure of details of transferable securities; *[2 Sch 79]*

- disclosure of leasing transactions; *[2 Sch 80]*

- disclosure of assets and liabilities denominated in a currency other than the presentational currency; *[2 Sch 81]*

- disclosure of details of unmatured forward transactions; *[2 Sch 83]*

- disclosure of loans made in connection with the purchase of own shares; *[2 Sch 84]*

- disclosure of particulars of taxation; *[2 Sch 86]* and

- disclosure of certain profit and loss account information by geographical markets. IFRS 8 does not require segmental information if an entity's debt or equity instruments are not traded in a public market or the entity is not in the process of filing financial statements for that purpose. *[2 Sch 87]*.

The profit and loss account of a banking company that falls within s408 of the Act (individual profit and loss account where group accounts prepared) need not contain the information specified in paragraphs 85 to 91 of Schedule 2. *[Regulations 5(2)]*.

(c)   Schedule 3 companies (i.e. insurance companies)

- a statement that the accounts have been prepared in accordance with applicable accounting policies; *[3 Sch 62]*

- disclosures in respect of share capital and debentures; *[3 Sch 65-68]*

- disclosure of the split of land between freehold and leasehold and the leasehold land between that held on a long lease and that held on a short lease; *[3 Sch 71]*

- disclosure of information about listed investments; *[3 Sch 72]*

- disclosure of creditors due after five years; *[3 Sch 79]*

- disclosure of loans made in connection with the purchase of own shares; *[3 Sch 82]*

- disclosure of particulars of taxation; *[3 Sch 84]*

- disclosure of certain profit and loss account information by type of business and by geographical area. IFRS 8 does not require segmental information if an entity's debt or equity instruments are not traded in a public market or the entity is not in the process of filing financial statements for that purpose; *[3 Sch 85-87]* and

- disclosure of total commissions for direct insurance business. *[3 Sch 88]*.

The profit and loss account of an insurance company that falls within s408 of the Act (individual profit and loss account where group accounts prepared) need not contain the information specified in paragraphs 83 to 89 of Schedule 3. *[Regulations 6(2)]*.

Banking and insurance companies are financial institutions (see section 6.4 above) and therefore must comply with IFRS 7 disclosures in full and IFRS 13 disclosures in respect of financial instruments, including disclosures about the fair value of financial assets and liabilities.

The disclosures illustrated above are not intended to be an exhaustive list of additional disclosures required by the Regulations for entities applying FRS 101 that have previously reported under IFRS.

8.   FUTURE CHANGES TO IFRS AND THEIR IMPACT ON FRS 101

Although not specifically addressed by FRS 101, future changes to EU-adopted IFRS would appear to be automatically incorporated into FRS 101 unless they are modified by the FRC.

The Accounting Council has advised the FRC to update FRS 101 at regular intervals, to ensure that the disclosure framework maintains consistency with EU-adopted IFRS. *[FRS 101.AC.20]*.

As a result, the FRC has stated that it intends to review FRS 101 annually to ensure that the reduced disclosure framework remains effective as EU-adopted IFRS develops. In July 2014, the first annual amendments to FRS 101 were issued (see 1.3 above) and these changes have the same effective date as the original version of FRS 101.

Whenever a new IFRS is issued or an amendment is made to an existing IFRS, the FRC has to:

- consider whether any proposed requirements are prohibited by the Companies Act or the Regulations; and

- consider whether exemptions should be provided in respect of any disclosures required by the change.

The principles established are that UK financial reporting standards should:

- have consistency with global accounting standards through the application of an IFRS-based solution unless an alternative clearly better meets the overriding objective;

- reflect up-to-date thinking and developments in the way businesses operate and the transactions they undertake;

- balance consistent principles for accounting by all UK and Republic of Ireland entities with practical solutions, based on size, complexity, public interest and users information needs;

- promote efficiency within groups; and

- be cost-effective to apply. *[FRS 100.AC.8].*

References

1 *The True and Fair Requirement Revised – Opinion*, FRC, May 2008, para. 4(C).

2 *The True and Fair Requirement Revised – Opinion*, FRC, May 2008, para. 4(F).

3 TECH 02/10 – *Guidance on the determination of realised profits and losses in the context of distributions under the Companies Act 2006*, ICAEW/ICAS, February 2010, paras. 3.28 and 3.29.

4 TECH 02/10 – *Guidance on the determination of realised profits and losses in the context of distributions under the Companies Act 2006*, ICAEW/ICAS, February 2010, paras. 3.30 to 3.32.

Chapter 31

Index of standards

FRS 101

FRS 102

FRS 103

SSAP 4

SSAP 9

SSAP 13

SSAP 19

SSAP 20

SSAP 21

TECH 02/10

TECH 14/13

Large and Medium-sized Companies and Groups (Accounts and Reports) Regulations 2008

Regulations

LLP Regulations

FRSSE

Listing and AIM Rules

Small Regulations

FRC Statement of Principles

Foreword to Accounting Standards

Index

Compiled by Indexing Specialists (UK) Ltd